Psychology Today

An Introduction

Third Edition

Chief Adviser

Kurt W. Fischer

Associate Adviser

Phillip Shaver

Contributors

Catherine Brown, M.A., *Tucson, Arizona*
Joseph J. Campos, Ph.D., *University of Denver*
Eric Fischer (doctoral candidate)
Kurt W. Fischer, Ph.D., *University of Denver*
Dennis L. Krebs, Ph.D., *Simon Fraser University*
Joseph Lipinski, M.D., *Harvard Medical School*
Darlene R. Miller, Ph.D., *Fort Logan Mental Health Center*
Carole Wade Offir, Ph.D., *Psychology Today*
L. Anne Peplau, Ph.D., *University of California, Los Angeles*
Jeanne S. Phillips, Ph.D., *University of Denver*
Bruce B. Platt, Ph.D., *University of Denver*
N. Dickon Reppucci, Ph.D., *Yale University*
Zick Rubin, Ph.D., *Harvard University*
Brian Sarata, Ph.D., *University of Nebraska*
Sandra Scarr-Salapatek, Ph.D., *University of Minnesota*
Phillip Shaver, Ph.D., *Columbia University*
Leonore Tiefer, Ph.D., *Colorado State University*

Contributors to Previous Editions

Donald W. Fiske, Ph.D., *University of Chicago*
Daniel X. Freedman, Ph.D., *University of Chicago*
Calvin S. Hall, Ph.D., *University of California, Santa Cruz*
Douglas N. Jackson, Ph.D., *University of Western Ontario*
Neal E. Miller, Ph.D., *Rockefeller University*
Donald A. Norman, Ph.D., *University of California, San Diego*

Chapter Introductions,
written by Isaac Asimov

Editor/Rewriter
Arlyne Lazerson

Psychology Today
An Introduction

Third Edition

CRM/RANDOM HOUSE

CRM Staff

Publisher/Editor, Arlyne Lazerson
Production Editor, Susan Orlofsky
Associate Editor, Patricia Campbell
Publishing Coordinator, Jacqueline Roberge
Graphics Conceptualization, Alastair McLeod, Ph.D.
Senior Designer, Dale Phillips
Associate Designer, Linda Higgins
Photo Editor and Permissions, Linda Rill
Production Manager, Sheridan Hughes
Marketing Development Manager, Psychology, John Ochse

Third Edition

5 6 7 8 9

Library of Congress Catalog Card Number: 74-21784
ISBN: 0-394-31066-7
Manufactured in the United States of America

Preface

A book has a life of its own. Once an author or editor has let go of the last proofs and the presses start to run, the book becomes like a person in some ways. Readers get acquainted with it; some like it, some don't. It may receive a measure of notoriety, good or bad. Like a person, if it is interesting and lively and has energy, it is enjoyed. If it is a bore, it is dropped as swiftly as possible.

And books can grow and develop. When a book goes through a number of editions, it changes. Rough edges get smoothed off, new evidence is added, arguments are refined. Sometimes, youthful frivolities drop out, and there is a kind of maturing process.

That is what has happened to *Psychology Today: An Introduction.* Its first edition appeared in 1969, a bright, dynamic, innovative introductory text. It gained many readers and admirers—and made a few enemies, who didn't like its youthful brashness. In its second edition, note was taken of what readers had liked or disliked in the earlier edition, and some substantial changes were made in content and style. The second edition was better integrated than the first; it was more mature, thoughtful, and responsible. Still, it retained most of the verve of its earlier form. Its success has been reflected not only by the number of readers it has had but also by other publishers' imitation of many of its features.

In this third edition of *Psychology Today: An Introduction,* the book has reached the prime of its life. It is as energetic and spirited as ever—and all the energy is used constructively.

The unmatched CRM graphics are present, and all are used to clarify or augment concepts in the text.

The captions clearly explain all graphs, charts, and illustrations and tie the data or artwork to the text's discussion.

Chapter introductions by Isaac Asimov, one of the world's best writers of science fiction and of books about science for laymen, provide a worldly framework for the chapter's academic content, relating it to historical events, personal experiences, or fictional happenings.

The text is very easy to read—as free of jargon as possible, and full of analogies and examples that make the concepts easy to understand.

A number of new features assure that the book is both easy to teach and learn from: There are outlines at the start of each chapter; each chapter (except Chapter 1) has a complete summary of its content in outline form; key terms and concepts are in boldface type in both the text and the summaries.

A number of books and articles are suggested as further reading for each chapter.

There is a complete glossary of psychological terms and a chapter-by-chapter bibliography citing sources for all theories, studies, or conclusions mentioned in the text or captions.

A basic tenet of developmental psychology is that an individual's development proceeds toward greater differentiation and integration. That is, as each of an organism's parts becomes more specialized, the parts work better together—and this is true of both structure and function. According to this definition, then, the third edition of *Psychology Today: An Introduction* has developed like an organism. Its characteristics—readability, graphic excellence, conceptual organization, teachability—have become both better differentiated and better integrated. It is a unique creation—and now it is on its own.

Arlyne Lazerson
Publisher/Editor

Contents

UNIT I
About Psychology

1
Understanding Psychology: Introduction

When CRM Books, publisher of this textbook, decided it was time to prepare a new edition of *Psychology Today: An Introduction,* they invited a number of psychology professors to come to Del Mar for a few days to participate in a panel that would give advice on the direction the revision should take. To start things off, they presented the panel with two questions: (1) What aspect of psychology are students most curious about when they start the introductory course? and (2) If you could see to it that students would learn *just one thing* from your course, what would it be?

The panel members did not find the first question very hard. At the beginning of the course, they said, the first thing students want to know is how (and whether) psychology relates to everyday life, particularly their own. Next, they want to know what the profession of psychology is like—what sort of work a student who majors in psychology can expect to do whether he or she goes on to graduate school or not. Accordingly, the first part of this chapter discusses psychology and everyday life, pointing out certain sections of *Psychology Today: An Introduction* that you may find especially interesting from a practical standpoint; the second part describes the specialties available to psychologists and the jobs available to psychology majors.

The second question seemed to be more difficult, because it received a number of different answers. The panel members at first seemed to agree that they wanted each of their students to understand his or her own psychological make-up better, to be familiar with the basic principles of psychology, and to know what characterizes the psychological approach to behavior and human experience. So far so good. But, when pressed for details, no two professors seemed to have quite the same opinion about which aspects of one's own psychological functioning it is most important to understand, which principles of psychology are the basic ones, or how

Figure 1.1 A typical psychology department's bulletin board. On the right are advertisements for subjects needed in experiments being done by the department's faculty members. For the undergraduate, participation in these experiments is a good way to learn what psychologists do, even though the pay is low. Next to the white rat, the freshman psychology student is the most studied organism in psychology. On the left side of the board are brochures describing graduate programs in some of the many areas of psychology discussed in this chapter.

Figure 1.2 (opposite) This figure and the two that follow it show episodes in the commonplace sequence of behavioral events described in the text as they might be seen through the eyes of various specialists in psychology. (left) A number of psychologists are interested in making comparisons between complex human behaviors and the simpler behavior patterns of animals. An ethologist might thus see the behavior of the young woman hastening toward a college cafeteria as a food-getting pattern characteristic of the species *Homo sapiens*. A behaviorist might be tempted to compare her behavior to the conditioned responses of such laboratory animals as rats. (middle) A developmental psychologist, seeing the woman paying for her food at the cash register, might think of the genetic heritage, stages of growth, and environmental effects that produced her present behavior. (right) A social psychologist would look at the groups of people in the cafeteria and consider the myriad interactions that are occurring among them.

Figure 1.3 (opposite) A continuation of the various interpretations that different types of psychologists might give to the episodes in the story presented in the text. (left) The young man's arrival at the young woman's table is seen through the eyes of a psychologist interested in motivation and emotion; he interprets the man's behavior in terms of an arousal state (anxiety) and goal-directedness (desire for the notes). (middle) As the couple begin to talk, they are seen from the perspective of an information-processing specialist, who views them as computerlike machines that are taking in, sorting, storing, retrieving, recombining, and putting out large amounts of information even in the most trivial of conversations. (right) As the conversation continues, the pair is viewed by a psychologist specializing in physiology. He is fascinated by the ways in which such physical phenomena as sound waves and molecules are transduced into impulses in each person's nervous system. He also speculates about the parts played by various portions of their brains and nervous systems in regulating the activities of all parts of their bodies.

the "psychological approach" should be defined. Finally, an instructor who had so far taken little part in the discussion spoke up. "What I want my students to learn," he said, "is just what we're demonstrating here. *Psychologists do not agree.*" He sat back and waited. As if to prove his point, several panelists began to explain why they weren't sure *that* was true.

They were right, but so was he. It seems that an introductory textbook should demonstrate areas of disagreement as well as areas of agreement, if only because newcomers to a science often overestimate the extent to which it will lay absolute truth before them. So the final section of this chapter illustrates two common types of disagreement among psychologists: disagreements stemming from differences in psychologists' overall theoretical orientations, which lead them to explain the same phenomenon in different ways; and differences of opinion about what the results of a particular study mean. As you can imagine, disagreements in the latter category tend to be much easier for psychologists to resolve than those in the former. Even on a small scale, though, demonstrating psychological truths can be a formidable task.

PSYCHOLOGY AND EVERYDAY LIFE

How psychology relates to your everyday life depends, not surprisingly, on what your particular everyday life is like: on your activities and, even more, on your interests and values. Most of you are students (at least some of the time), and most of you are interested in some of the topics psychology deals with. Each of you, however, is a unique individual. So, the only way to discuss how psychology relates to all your lives is to describe psychological processes engaged in by everyone, and that is how this section begins. Next, it describes some material in later chapters that you may find useful in a practical way. Finally, it discusses the distinction between psychology as a basic science and as an applied science, partly in an effort to convince you that basic science, although not always immediately relevant to daily life, is still worth studying.

Everyone Behaves

A good way to demonstrate to yourself the general relation between psychology and life is to turn to the contents in the front of this book and read the unit and chapter titles, which describe areas of behavior common to all of us. Everyone learns, remembers, and solves problems; everyone develops, intellectually and socially, from infancy to adulthood; everyone perceives environmental stimuli and interprets the information from his sense organs; everyone's behavior depends on physiological functions—on signals darting to and from the central nervous system; everyone feels emotions and engages in motivated behavior; everyone has a personality, and most of us are curious about where it came from and where it is going; and everyone's behavior is affected by the many social groups, formal and informal, to which he belongs. Not everyone has a behavior disorder or needs therapy, but many people have a relative or friend who does; according to one estimate, about one American in four at some time in his life develops a problem serious enough to warrant treatment. Just about any everyday event involves all or most of these processes and areas of behavior. The following incident can serve as an example.

A young woman, a college student, decides to have lunch at the college cafeteria. She enters the cafeteria, proceeds to the food line, selects her meal, and pays for it. She looks around for someone to sit with but sees no one she knows well, so she chooses an empty table and begins to eat. As she is finishing her coleslaw, a shadow falls across her plate. It is a young man from her English class. She is not happy to see him, mainly because although she finds him quite attractive, he never speaks to her except when he has missed

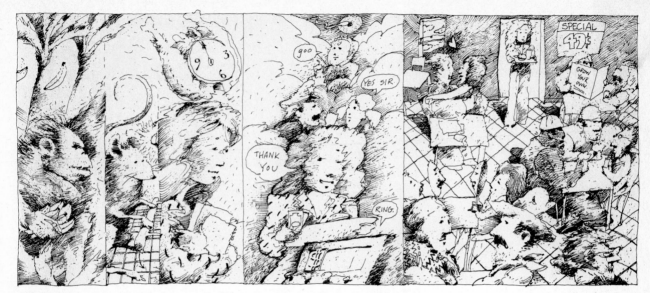

class and wants to borrow her notes. She greets him coolly but he sits down anyway, launching into a rambling tale of last evening's party, which lasted all night, and the hangover he is now enduring. The young woman recalls that he missed their ten o'clock English class and notices that he is eyeing her notebook as he talks. Annoyed, she hurriedly finishes eating and begins to gather her things together. Attempting a casual smile, the young man asks for her notes. Now she is more than annoyed. Although the notes are on top of her pile of books, in plain sight, she says curtly that she's sorry, she left them at the library—to which, as a matter of fact, she must return right away. As she leaves the building, she glances back and sees the young man still sitting at the table, nervously smoking a cigarette. He looks depressed. Suddenly, the young woman feels a bit depressed herself.

Although this is a simple story, the behavior it involves is complex enough to include each of the psychological processes referred to earlier. First of all, the young woman decided to have lunch because of her **physiological state** (she was hungry); in addition, her **motivation** may have included **cognitive** elements (she knew it was noon, her habitual lunchtime). When she entered the cafeteria, she **perceived** different kinds of sensory stimulation than she

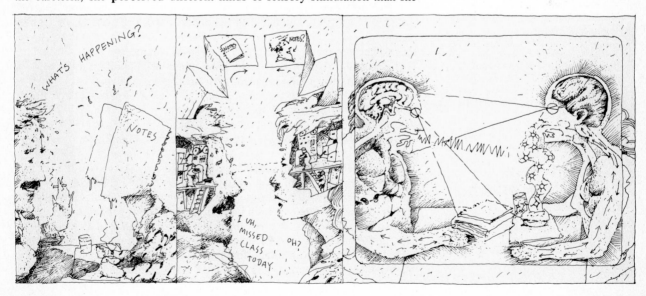

Figure 1.4 In the final episodes of the story described in the text, a personality theorist takes a look at the situation. He perceives the man and the woman as unique individuals. Depending on his training and inclinations, this psychologist may take a highly subjective view and try to comprehend how each person understands and experiences his world from moment to moment; he may try to conceptualize the determinants of their behavior as intrapsychic agencies in conflict; or he may ignore their inner dynamics and think of each as a unique bundle of habits learned over a lifetime.   (right) The closing scene reveals the perspective of the clinical psychologist. It is the abnormalities, the deviances, and the maladaptive behavior patterns that he is especially sensitive to. He might see the young man as about to collapse into a severe depression and the young woman as unnaturally rigid. In his view, other people in the cafeteria are also hurting themselves needlessly or gratifying themselves in very immature ways. Instead of being fully in touch with the present, the people are seen as being haunted by ghosts and demons from the past.

had outside but paid little attention to the new sights, sounds, and smells, except perhaps to note that the food smelled good and that the line of students waiting to get their meals was mercifully short. She went through the line and paid for her food—**learned behavior** not too different from that of a hungry rat that runs a maze for a food reward.

The young woman looked around for a **social group** to join and, seeing none she belonged to, chose an empty table. Soon, the young man joined her. He felt free to do so partly because, on many campuses, there is an implicit rule, or **norm,** that students who have a class together may approach each other socially; this rule usually does not hold for members of looser social groups, such as commuters who ride the same bus. The young woman **remembered** how the young man had behaved toward her in the past and noticed that he seemed to be embarking on the same note-borrowing course, which triggered the **emotional** reaction of anger. However, the young woman did not throw a tantrum, as a two-year-old might, but responded in a way that was more appropriate to her stage of **development** and was, probably, characteristic of her **personality:** She told the young man she did not have the notes (even though he had seen them) and left.

Either student's mode of behavior, if chronic or extreme or always followed by depression, could indicate **disorder.** For example, if the young man commonly relies on others for substantial amounts of help, which he always tries to get in a manipulative way, his behavior might indicate disorder. The young woman might be overly rigid and inhibited. She might interpret even ordinary requests for aid as demands but find herself unable either to meet or to reject the demands in a matter-of-fact way—another possible indicator of disorder. In the context of the story, however, neither student's behavior seems abnormal. As this interpretation of the story suggests, one advantage of knowing some psychology is that it offers a new framework for viewing daily events.

Besides being interesting, the new perspective that a knowledge of psychology offers can permit valuable insights into one's own behavior. For example, a person may be convinced that he is terribly shy, mainly because he is often uncomfortable in certain types of groups. If this person studies even a little social psychology, he will learn that different kinds of groups tend to have different effects on their members, and he may reexamine his shyness with that information in mind. Perhaps he will notice that his discomfort is much milder in structured, task-oriented groups than in unstructured, social ones. That is, he may feel fine at meetings of the school-newspaper staff but miserable at parties. At first glance, this may seem a minor insight, but realizations like "It's not that I'm paralyzingly shy—it's just that I can't stand unstructured groups!" can be powerful enough to change a person's whole conception of himself.

Practical Information

Most introductory psychology courses and textbooks include some material that can be directly applied to certain problems in daily life—not a great deal of such material, for reasons that will be explained shortly, but some. Most of this material falls into two categories: instructions on how to do something and information about the truth or falsity of certain common beliefs.

How to Do It   There are several places in this book where you will be told, in concrete and detailed terms, how to carry out some procedure that you may find useful. For example, Chapter 5 includes a description of several **mnemonic devices,** or memory aids, that can be used to remember information that must be learned by rote. The rhyme beginning "Thirty days hath September" is a mnemonic device that virtually everyone uses to remember the number of days in each month. There are many other mnemonic devices that apply to particular pieces of information, such as FACE and Every Good Boy Deserves Fudge (which indicate the order of musical notes in the spaces and lines of the treble clef) and the name ROY G. BIV, which specifies the order of the colors in the spectrum (red, orange, yellow, green, blue, indigo, violet). Other devices, as explained in Chapter 5, have more general applications and can be used to remember any list of words or numbers—the Presidents of the United States, authors and titles of books, historical dates, shopping lists, telephone numbers, and so on. These devices usually require one to associate each item on the list with some sort of mental picture. Although that in itself is quite a job, memory experts and others are convinced that it is far easier, more reliable, and faster (except perhaps the first time) than memorizing the list without using the mnemonic device.

A second example of a concrete procedure you may want to use sometime occurs in Chapter 27. Toward the end of that chapter there is a detailed description of a **token economy** that a mother and father used to induce their two daughters to perform certain household chores. The design and operation of the system are simple, and the results were spectacular. Each girl was supposed to perform nine tasks a day (brush teeth in the morning, brush teeth in the evening, put dirty clothes in hamper, and so on). Before the token economy was instituted, each girl completed an average of 1.3 tasks per day; under its regimen, each girl completed all nine with only an occasional slip. Unless you have children, you may not be able to use the system right now, but it could be quite a help to you in a few years.

Other parts of the book, although they do not offer detailed instructions, will help you make informed decisions or reach certain goals. For instance, the unit on mental disorder should help a person decide whether he actually does need any type of therapy. Chapters 26, 27, and 28 in that unit describe the various kinds of therapy available to a person who needs help and may assist him in choosing the type best suited for him and his problem. In addition to providing useful information on psychiatric drugs and drug therapy, Chapter 28 also discusses the use of other drugs, such as alcohol and marijuana.

In Chapter 4, the training procedure called **shaping** is described in enough detail for you to use it the next time you have a puppy to train; if you wish, you can also try to figure out what effect the reinforcements you dispense have on the behavior of people around you, and what effect their rewards and punishments have on you. If you have a small child, or know one, you can learn something about the level of understanding he or she has reached by trying out a few of the conservation tasks described in Chapter 8 (though in doing so you should be careful: Your informal test will not give you reliable information about whether the child is "fast" or "slow"). Finally, you will learn in Chapter 20 that geographical proximity has a lot to do with love, which could influence your decision to move into (or out of) a certain city, neighborhood, or apartment.

What to Believe Besides guiding your actions in the ways just described, a knowledge of psychology offers you an objective check on some of your opinions and beliefs. Although one purpose of this chapter is to demonstrate that psychologists do not always agree, another aim of this chapter is to show that psychologists do agree very well on some things—things that have been shown, through definitive and repeated studies, to be true or false. In many cases, the informed and substantiated view of psychologists is in conflict with the "common sense" opinion of most laymen. To see how well your own opinions agree with what psychological studies have demonstrated, look at the list of statements in the adjacent margin. How many of them do you think are true?

Some of you may wonder how much it really matters if a person believes to be true some things that psychologists have shown are false (for all the statements listed in the margin are false). How much can holding such opinions affect the conduct of one's life? It is true that holding a correct opinion sometimes has no practical value and that holding an incorrect one sometimes harms no one. But in some cases, an incorrect belief can have major consequences for you or someone else. For instance, if you believe that mentally retarded people are mentally ill (Item 13) and that many disturbed people are dangerous (Item 14), you may treat someone who merely has the mind of a four-year-old as if he were a homicidal maniac—which will be particularly unfortunate if the person is one you encounter often, such as a member of your own family. If you believe highly intelligent people tend to be socially isolated (Item 6), you may try to suppress signs of unusual intelligence in yourself or your children in the mistaken belief that you can't both have friends and be a "genius."

Psychology, Basic and Applied

When some students who have been in their first psychology course a few weeks ask about the relation of psychology to everyday life, they do so in a challenging tone of voice. Psychology is not, they imply, telling them what they want to know; it is not doing what it ought to be doing. One student objects because psychology is too slow, too painstaking, too plodding. All those intricate studies, many of them conducted with animals by men and women who are rigorously, infuriatingly objective, are *boring*. "Where," this student asks, "is the insight into the nature of humanity that I enrolled in the course for?" Another student objects because psychology is too abstract, too remote—grandiose theories, animal studies (again), experiments on such arcane matters as the smallest change in the brightness of a light that a person can perceive. "What," this student says, "is the *use* of it all? What good will it do me to learn all this?"

The first student may simply not be interested in science. He might prefer literature or philosophy to psychology. Although he may enjoy the writings of some theorists, particularly those who are great writers as well as great psychologists (Sigmund Freud is the best example), and the work of humanistic psychologists who are interested in philosophical questions (such as Rollo May and R. D. Laing), most of contemporary psychology will not give him

1. The behavior of most lower animals—insects, reptiles and amphibians, most rodents, and birds—is instinctive and unaffected by learning.

2. For the first week of life, a baby sees nothing but a gray blur regardless of what he or she "looks at."

3. A child learns to talk more quickly if the adults around him habitually repeat the word he is trying to say, using proper pronunciation.

4. The best way to get a chronically noisy schoolchild to settle down and pay attention is to punish him.

5. Slow learners remember more of what they learn than fast learners.

6. Highly intelligent people—"geniuses"—tend to be physically frail and socially isolated.

7. On the average, you cannot predict from a person's grades at school and college whether he or she will do well in a career.

8. Most national and ethnic stereotypes are completely false.

9. In small amounts, alcohol is a stimulant.

10. LSD causes chromosome damage.

11. The largest drug problem in the United States, in terms of the number of people affected, is marijuana.

12. Psychiatry is a subdivision of psychology.

13. Most mentally retarded people are also mentally ill.

14. A third or more of the people suffering from severe mental disorder are potentially dangerous.

15. Electroshock therapy is an outmoded technique rarely used in today's mental hospitals.

16. The more severe the disorder, the more intensive the therapy required to cure it; for example, schizophrenics usually respond best to psychoanalysis.

17. Quite a few psychological characteristics of men and women appear to be inborn; in all cultures, for example, women are more emotional and sexually less aggressive than men.

18. No reputable psychologist "believes in" such irrational phenomena as ESP, hypnosis, or the bizarre mental and physical achievements of Eastern yogis.

the intuitive insight into human problems that he is seeking. As the eminent psychologist D. O. Hebb pointed out recently,

It is to the literary world, not to psychological science, that you go to learn how to live with people, how to make love, how not to make enemies; to find out what grief does to people, or the stoicism that is possible in the endurance of pain, or how if you're lucky you may die with dignity; to see how corrosive the effects of jealousy can be, or how power corrupts or does not corrupt. For such knowledge and such understanding of the human species, don't look in my *Textbook of Psychology* (or anyone else's), try *Lear* and *Othello* and *Hamlet*. As a supplement to William James [the psychologist], read *Henry* James [his brother, the novelist], and Jane Austen, and Mark Twain.

To the person who finds the scientific approach basically incompatible with his own way of looking at things, we can suggest that psychology might be worth looking into, not as a substitute for literature and philosophy but as a complement to them. To the second student, the one more interested in the applications of psychological knowledge, we can also issue an invitation. Without too much effort, he or she may be able to develop an interest in psychology as a basic science as well. For example, students who find mnemonic devices useful may begin to wonder why they work; if so, they will probably be interested in what psychologists know about the way memories are organized in the human brain. A person who uses a token economy with his or her children may become curious, sooner or later, about the principles of learning on which such economies are based. A person who thinks he needs therapy may want to know not only what type would be best for him but why any therapy is effective and how psychologists think personality disorders develop.

In case the distinction between psychology as a basic science and as an applied science is not already clear, it should be stated. In basic science, knowledge is acquired for its own sake, in order to satisfy a curiosity about the nature of things; the "usefulness" of the knowledge is not an issue. In applied science, certain findings of basic science are used to accomplish practical goals. To illustrate, biologists and physicists usually practice basic science; physicians and engineers practice applied science. Psychologists may practice either. For instance, a developmental psychologist who studies the ability of young infants to perceive patterns is doing basic research. He is not concerned with the implications his findings may have for the design of crib toys, but a psychologist who does applied science (perhaps a psychological consultant to a toy manufacturer) would be. Similarly, a social psychologist studying the friendships among a group of office workers—who likes whom, how much, and why—is doing basic science. If she discovers that one member of the group has no friends at all and another has so many friends he hardly has time to work, the psychologist might try to understand and explain the situation, but she would not try to correct it. She would leave the correction to a practitioner of applied psychology, such as a clinical or industrial psychologist.

One reason it is important to understand the difference between basic and applied psychology is that this book, like virtually all introductory textbooks (and courses), presents psychology chiefly as a basic science. Although the text is liberally sprinkled with examples of how psychological principles operate in everyday life, the student who is *exclusively* interested in applications is almost certain to be disappointed, and he may as well know it early as late.

Students are by no means the only ones who tend to be impatient for applications of psychological principles in daily life. So are newspaper reporters, television newscasters, and people who write books for laymen on such psychological subjects as child care, education, social problems, and mental disorder. In their impatience, they sometimes jump to conclusions about the potential applications of some finding of basic science, stating that the data *prove* a certain pragmatic point when in fact they merely relate to it.

For example, a number of psychologists who do basic research on infant development (such as Wayne Dennis) have found that babies raised in the extremely impoverished environments of some orphanages (where an infant may see nothing at all but a white ceiling and the white cushions on the sides of his crib and have no human contact except when he is being fed or changed) are seriously retarded in their physical, intellectual, and emotional development. Some child-care books for parents describe these studies and then imply that the same fate awaits a child whose parents do not provide him with all sorts of sensory stimulation during his early months—mobiles, construction paper cutouts in different colors and shapes pasted on his crib, a miniature patchwork quilt made from materials of different textures, perhaps a mirror on the ceiling over the changing table.

An understanding of the difference between basic and applied psychology will help you regard such recommendations with skepticism. Take a moment to reflect on the tremendous difference between the bleak institutional environment of an underfunded, understaffed orphanage and the average home environment. Even a baby whose family is very poor almost surely has much more to look at, listen to, and touch than does an infant in such an orphanage. In fact, some psychologists have speculated that infants in crowded homes (five children and two parents in a two-room apartment, say) may get too much stimulation for optimum development. Also, there are studies showing that young animals learn most quickly when their cages are neither totally bare nor visually very "busy" but decorated with just a few enrichment devices. Other studies, done with human infants (such as Burton White's work done in 1969), generally confirm the value of a moderate amount of enrichment but show that some very young babies, confronted with a great deal to look at, ignore it all and cry a lot (see Figure 1.5). All this does not mean that you should *not* decorate your infant's crib; it only means that you should take with a grain of salt someone's insistence that the findings of orphanage studies obligate you to do so.

A final reason for discussing the distinction between applied and basic science is that it may help you understand why psychologists sometimes seem to offer conflicting advice, or none at all, on subjects of pressing concern. Take the question of whether television and movie violence is bad for children. Some people say yes, because psychological studies show that children

Figure 1.5   In an experiment by White, infants in institutions were reared under three conditions of environmental enrichment.   (A) The normal institutional environment; little opportunity for visual or tactual exploration is provided.   (B) A massive enrichment of the environment.   (C) A slightly enriched environment; there is a single toy that can be looked at and grasped. To the surprise of many, White found that infants reared in environment (C) developed reaching behavior sooner than infants reared under either of the other conditions. By systematically exploring the full range of possible levels of stimulation, White discovered that there could be too much stimulation as well as too little.

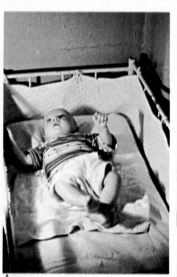

A

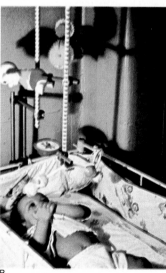

B

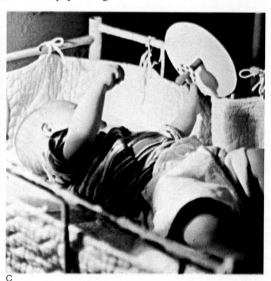

C

imitate what they see. Others say no, that watching crime shows and westerns and war movies actually lowers a child's tendency to behave violently by offering him a vicarious outlet for his aggressive feelings. The reason for this conflicting advice is that there are psychological studies—basic science—supporting both sides of the question. The studies' findings differ because something about the experimental conditions probably differed: For example, the type of violence shown to the children and the way it was portrayed was perhaps substantially different in each of the studies, or the psychologists measured the effects on the children in different ways. As basic science, these studies are a good beginning; as guides for parents and social reformers, they leave a lot to be desired. At this point, there are good arguments for reducing the amount of filmed violence that children (and adults) are exposed to; there are also good arguments for letting a child watch (and read) what he chooses. This matter, like a good many others involving applied psychology, concerns not only psychological questions not yet resolved but other kinds of questions, such as the political ones of censorship and freedom of choice.

PSYCHOLOGY AS A PROFESSION

From what you have just read, you may have gathered that the person who chooses to become a psychologist does well to confine himself to basic research, thus avoiding the thorny problems that confront those who deal in applications. Don't be too hasty. Before you make a firm decision, you should be given a more comprehensive picture of the various specialities and kinds of jobs available to psychologists.

Fields of Specialization

The national professional organization for psychologists is the American Psychological Association (APA), located in Washington, D.C. In 1973, the APA had more than 35,000 members, each of whom belonged to one or more of thirty-three specialized divisions. Figure 1.6 lists the thirteen divisions of the APA that have more than a thousand members. The list includes some overlap, because a psychologist may belong to several divisions if he wishes, but it will give you some idea of the variety of psychological specialties and the range of psychologists' interests.

Another overview of psychological specialties is provided in Table 1.1. It shows how some 19,000 psychologists classified themselves in response to a recent questionnaire from the National Science Foundation.

As you can see from the two figures, **clinical** and **counseling psychology** is perhaps the most popular area of specialization. A clinical psychologist usually has a Ph.D. in clinical psychology; a counseling psychologist usually holds an M.A. or Ph.D. in counseling psychology. Many clinical psychologists practice psychotherapy, either privately or through some agency or institution, such as a mental health hospital, mental health clinic, or juvenile home. Other clinical psychologists specialize in administering and interpreting personality tests of the sort described in Chapter 17; if a person's scores indicate that he or she needs treatment, the psychologist may offer it himself or refer the client elsewhere. Counseling psychologists usually advise people who would be classified as normal rather than as disturbed; if the counseling psychologist finds that his client seems to have a serious problem, he refers the person to a clinical psychologist or a psychiatrist for treatment.

Personality and **social psychology** is another large area of specialization; **developmental psychologists** (APA division: 985 members) are sometimes classified with this group. Personality psychologists study personality development and traits; they also devise personality tests. Social psychologists study groups and their influence on individual behavior; some of them conduct surveys and polls on matters of public interest. Most developmental

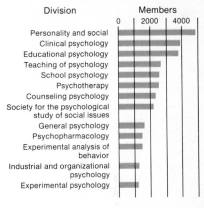

Figure 1.6 Membership in the thirteen most populous divisions of the American Psychological Association in 1972. Note that a psychologist might be a member of more than one division. Psychotherapists and clinicians, for example, are likely also to be members of the Personality and Social Division.

Table 1.1 **Psychologists' Areas of Specialization***

Area of Specialization	Percent
Clinical	37
Experimental	12
Counseling/Guidance	11
Educational	9
Industrial/Personnel	8
School	6
Social	5
Developmental	3
Personality	3
Psychometrics	2
Engineering	2
General and Other	2

*According to replies to a questionnaire from the National Science Foundation.
Source: Jones, D. R. *Psychologists in Mental Health: 1966* (Washington, D.C.: National Institute of Mental Health, Public Service Publications, No. 1984, 1969).

A The Three Laws of Experimental Psychology

The First Law.	If anything can go wrong in an experiment, it will.
The Second Law.	Training takes time, whether or not anything is learned.
The Third Law.	Any well-trained experimental animal, in a controlled environment and subject to controlled stimulation, will do as he damned well pleases.

Figure 1.7 (A) Three principles of basic research that every experimental psychologist learns the hard way. (B) A demonstration of these principles by a rat in an experimental study of punishment. This photograph was captioned "Breakfast in Bed" by the researcher, Nathan Azrin, who took it. Azrin was delivering shocks through the grid floor of the chamber to the rat's feet while it pressed a bar for food. When Azrin's recording equipment showed that the rat, undaunted by the shock, was continuing to press the bar, he looked into the experimental chamber and discovered that the rat was lying on its back while it pressed the bar, using its fur to insulate itself from the shock.

Figure 1.8 Judith Cates' data on the employment settings and median salaries of 1970 B.A.s in psychology who had full-time jobs. Seventy-five percent of the people represented by this data reported that their work was at least somewhat related to their training in psychology.

psychologists study child development (birth to age fifteen), although an increasing number are now devoting themselves to later periods of life or to the total developmental process, sometimes described as cradle-to-grave.

Educational and **school psychologists** study problems related to the education of children and young adults, such as learning, problem solving, and motivation. An educational psychologist is likely to be a college teacher, often in the education department. A school psychologist is usually employed by a public school system or private school, where he advises teachers and principals and counsels children and their parents.

Industrial and **organizational psychologists** may serve as consultants to businesses and industrial firms on such matters as personnel policy, efficiency and productivity, and employee morale. Or they may study more general problems, such as the dehumanizing aspects of work in an industrial society.

Experimental psychologists do basic research in a variety of fields: learning, perception, physiological psychology, psychopharmacology (drugs), comparative psychology, ethology (the study of animals with a view toward comparing the behavior of different species), and others. Usually, an experimental psychologist is employed by a college or university as a teacher; his research is supported by the college or university or by a grant from an outside agency—a private foundation or governmental body such as the National Science Foundation or the National Institute for Mental Health.

The three laws shown in Figure 1.7A were written by experimental psychologists and are quoted from a recent article by D. O. Hebb, one of the outstanding experimental psychologists working today. We present them here in order to temper any overenthusiasm for basic research that may have been generated by the preceding discussion of basic versus applied psychology.

About half the psychologists with graduate degrees, whatever their specialty, work in colleges and universities, teaching and doing research (and sometimes writing textbooks). Most of the rest, including most clinical psychologists, are employed by some agency, institution, or business firm. The number of psychotherapists who support themselves through private practice is relatively small.

Jobs for Psychology Majors

What of the student who does not want or cannot afford graduate training? In the last ten years or so, psychology has become one of the most popular majors in the entire college curriculum. According to Judith Cates of the

Employment Setting and Median Salary for Psychology B.A.s Holding Full-time Jobs in 1970

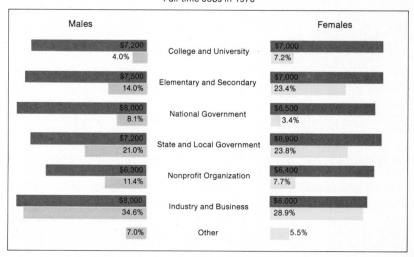

Males		Females
$7,200 — 4.0%	College and University	$7,000 — 7.2%
$7,500 — 14.0%	Elementary and Secondary	$7,000 — 23.4%
$8,000 — 8.1%	National Government	$6,500 — 3.4%
$7,200 — 21.0%	State and Local Government	$6,900 — 23.8%
$6,300 — 11.4%	Nonprofit Organization	$6,400 — 7.7%
$8,000 — 34.6%	Industry and Business	$6,000 — 28.9%
7.0%	Other	5.5%

Table 1.2 Jobs Held by Recent B.A.s in Psychology*

A. *Type of Job Obtained*

Teaching (elementary and secondary schools, day-care centers, preschools, special-education classes)	35%
Business (sales, management, and administration; clerical and secretarial)	27%
Counseling (see B, below)	14%
Psychology-Related Jobs (see C, below)	11%
Labor (house cleaner, commercial fisherman, waitress, nurse's aide)	5%
Technical (dental technician, draftsman)	4%
Professional (attorney, nurse, civil engineer)	4%

B. *Job Titles of Those Holding Counseling Jobs* (29 Graduates)
Caseworker (2); Rehabilitation Counselor (2); Welfare Eligibility Examiner (2); Adult Probation Officer (2); Child-care Worker, Residential Treatment Center (2); Group Counselor (2); Admissions Officer, County Youth Service Center (2); County Probation Counselor (2); Guidance Counselor; Senior Recreation Supervisor; Social Worker; Counselor; Youth Activities Coordinator; House Parent, Drug Treatment Center; Community Representative; Police Officer; Recreation Director; Teacher-Counselor; Placement Counselor; Youth Camp Counselor; Counselor for Juvenile Offenders

C. *Job Titles of Those Holding Psychology-Related Jobs* (22 Graduates)
Research Assistant, Psychology-Related (4); Psychology Instructor, Community College (3); Psychometrist (2); School Psychologist; Parent Educator; Statistician; Instructional Assistant, Institution for Retarded; Mental Health Program Director; Therapist; Occupational Test Development Analyst; Director of Planning, Research, and Evaluation, Opportunities Center; Psychology Teacher; Psychiatric Aide; Interviewer; Monitor/Evaluator; Associate Researcher, Psychology-Related

D. *Most Common Problems Encountered by Graduates Seeking Work*

No Jobs Available	21%
B.A. Too Low a Degree	10%
Lack of Experience	8%
Miscellaneous (personal indecision, poor salary, sex discrimination, etc.)	12%

*From a survey done by the University of Washington of its graduates.
Source: Patricia W. Lunneborg and Vicki M. Wilson, "Evaluation of an Interdepartmental Program to Train BA Psychologists" (unpublished report, University of Washington, 1973).

American Psychological Association, 37,000 B.A.s in psychology were awarded in 1970–71, and the number is supposed to double by 1980–81. The few surveys that are available report that between one-third and two-thirds of psychology majors do not go on to graduate school. For example, an APA survey of 1969 and 1970 B.A.s reported by Cates showed that 29 percent expected to do graduate work in psychology; 24 percent planned to do graduate work in other fields (most often, law or medicine); and 47 percent had no immediate plans for further education. The same survey yielded the information shown in Figure 1.8, which gives the employment settings and median salaries of 1970 psychology B.A.s holding full-time jobs.

The University of Washington, a state university located in Seattle, has conducted a survey of the 60 to 70 percent of their recent graduates in psychology who got jobs (or tried to) rather than entering graduate school. Table 1.2 shows some of the survey results. Although 64 percent of the students queried said they had majored in psychology for vocational reasons (rather than for personal reasons such as "to help me understand myself and others"), many of them were unable to find work that related very directly to their majors. Those who did find psychology-related jobs tended to have taken courses in other departments, such as education and communication, which they found helpful when seeking jobs. This information suggests that psychology majors would do well to look for courses in other departments that will complement their major and help prepare them for the jobs they want.

To a considerable extent, psychology has become a "general major," like English or history—fascinating, informative, worthwhile, but not as directly related to a career as many students wish. If you are considering majoring in psychology but doubt that you want an advanced degree, your best source of information on possible jobs is the Bureau of Appointments at your school. Probably, that office will be able to show you a list of the jobs held by recent graduates who majored in psychology; they may also be able to tell you how those jobs were obtained and what courses, not only in psychology but in other areas, the people who hold them completed. If this line of investigation does not prove fruitful, visit the office of your psychology department and ask your instructor or his secretary for the names of some of last year's graduates, preferably people with interests and abilities roughly comparable to your own. Then get their addresses from the Alumni Association and write to them.

"PSYCHOLOGISTS DO NOT AGREE"

Some pages back, in connection with the distinction between basic and applied psychology, it was mentioned that there are studies supporting both sides of the question: "Is television and movie violence bad for children?" On this and many other questions, psychologists seem to disagree—which strikes many people as strange, since psychology proclaims itself a science, and a science is supposed to offer proofs, not opinions. But no science, not even physics or chemistry, consists solely of demonstrated facts. In each science there are unanswered questions; theories that seem in the main to be accurate but, for one reason or another, have not been validated in every detail; findings that seemed reliable at one time but later turn out to be not quite right (or completely wrong). Probably the people most inclined to believe that science has all the answers are ones who have never studied any of the sciences.

This section will describe—and suggest some reasons for—two different kinds of disagreement among psychologists: disagreements concerning theories and disagreements on the meaning of the results of particular studies. To illustrate theoretical differences, we will examine three approaches to a topic that has generated a good deal of interest in the last few years, the development of sex roles.

The Development of Sex Roles

Turn back several pages and reread the story about the two college students and the class notes but reverse the sexes of the two characters. Does their behavior seem as natural to you as it did in the original version? Is it likely, for instance, that a young woman, even one no more socially skilled than the young man in the story seems to be, would choose to brag to a male acquaintance about her all-night parties and hangovers? Or that a man who has been asked several times for his notes by an attractive female classmate would become annoyed at her? Possibly, but probably not.

How do children learn to behave in the ways that their society deems appropriate for members of their sex? How does a boy learn to act like a boy, and a girl, like a girl? Babies are not born knowing this. Until children are between two and three years old, most of them cannot tell you for sure whether they are boys or girls, and for several more years they may think people can change their sex if they really try. By the time they start school, however, children have begun to acquire some firm beliefs about what males and females are like. For example, most children of five believe that men have more power and prestige than women. Many children, by the age of five, also firmly believe that fathers are supposed to work outside the home while mothers are supposed to stay home.

The following accounts of the ways psychologists think children develop these behaviors and beliefs are merely brief summaries of three approaches aimed at introducing you to theoretical differences. You will understand the theories themselves more fully after you have read Chapter 10, which describes their application to moral development, and Chapter 21, which describes sex-role development in detail.

The Social-Learning Approach   According to social-learning theorists, children behave in ways that the society considers appropriate for their sex because they are taught to do so by other people—parents, teachers, other children. The teaching is carried out in two ways: through **conditioning** and through **modeling.** Conditioning involves rewards (reinforcements) and punishments; it occurs, for example, when a parent praises a little girl for taking good care of her dolls or acts impressed with a boy's prowess on the football field. Modeling is the imitation of someone else's behavior; children are particularly likely to imitate someone else's behavior if they have seen it reinforced. For example, a little girl may see her older sister making cookies, note that her mother approves, and try to do likewise; a little boy may watch his father paint the living room, see that the family likes the results, and decide to decorate the walls of his room with crayons.

Social-learning theory is an outgrowth of behaviorism, the approach to learning described in Chapter 4. Because behaviorists usually study learning in animals, they emphasize conditioning as the basic learning process. Social-learning theory is an attempt to apply behaviorist principles to human learning, particularly personality and social development; thus, it emphasizes not only conditioning but modeling.

Social-learning theorists believe that a child adds behaviors to his repertoire in much the same way that beads are added to a string. The behavioral "beads" may have different sizes and shapes—that is, a child may learn first that he is a boy, then that boys are supposed to be strong, then that strong boys can climb trees, and finally how to climb a tree—but each is learned in the same way, through conditioning or modeling, regardless of how old or how mature the child is when he learns it. For this reason, social-learning theory is called an **incremental theory.**

The two other approaches to sex-role development, in contrast, are **stage theories.** They state that children learn things in qualitatively different ways during different developmental periods—that is, that a two-year-old's learning process is basically different from that of a twelve-year-old.

The Psychoanalytic Approach   The psychoanalytic approach to sex-role development is based on Sigmund Freud's theory of personality development, described in Chapter 18. Freud said that every child in every culture goes through five stages of psychosexual development (oral, anal, phallic, latency, and genital) and that his or her sex-role identity becomes established at the end of the phallic period, around age six. At that time, the child resolves the Oedipus or Electra complex with which he or she has been grappling for several years. At about age three, the child unconsciously falls in love with the opposite-sex parent; wants to get rid of the same-sex parent, who is viewed as a rival; and fears that the same-sex parent will punish him or her for both these feelings. Eventually (and still unconsciously) the child finds a way to cope with these strong emotions: He or she identifies with the parent of his or her own sex. **Identification** with the same-sex parent resolves the Oedipus or Electra conflict because it offers the child a way both to possess the opposite-sex parent vicariously and to avoid the anger of the same-sex parent.

In order to understand the other effects of identification, which include the establishment of a sexual identity, one must know that in Freudian theory identification is a very dramatic phenomenon—a kind of psychological re-shuffling of pieces of the personality. It is not merely that a boy, observing that he and his father are both males, imitates the father's behavior and attitudes; rather, the boy senses a strong and basic sameness between himself and his father. Through identification, the boy *internalizes,* as a unit and so to speak in a single large gulp, his father's standards of behavior. In this way, he acquires his understanding of what it means to be male and also his sense of right and wrong and a variety of other cultural values.

Clearly, this is a very different approach to development than that of social-learning theorists. According to social-learning theorists, a child learns the behavior appropriate to his sex gradually, over a period of years. Although children of different ages may learn different sorts of things, and at different rates, each behavior is learned in the same way, through conditioning or modeling or a combination of the two. Psychoanalytic theory does not assert that all the specifics of sex-typed behavior are mastered at age six, suddenly and without conscious effort. But it does say that the child's basic sexual orientation is established by that time, through an identification process that cannot occur in the same way at any other time of life. In addition, Freud emphasized the role of anatomical differences between the sexes in psycho-logical development. He therefore postulated that boys and girls acquire their sexual identities in somewhat different ways; social-learning theorists (and cognitive developmentalists) believe that the process of acquiring a sexual identity is the same for boys and girls.

The Cognitive Approach   The third approach is based on the work of Jean Piaget in cognitive development, described in Chapter 8. Like psychoanalytic theory, cognitive theory is a stage theory rather than an incremental one: It claims that children develop differently during different age-linked periods. Freud's stages, however, are named for the erotic zones that dominate a child's emotional life during different periods; Piaget's stages relate to intel-lectual orientation—to the child's ways of knowing the world.

Piaget has observed that young children do not see the physical world as constant the way adults do: They do not understand what Piaget calls **conser-vation.** A young baby, for example, does not know that objects continue to exist when he cannot see them, hear them, or touch them; from the infant's point of view, ''mother'' is an object that exists when the infant is being fed, changed, or played with but does not exist when the child is alone. A pre-school child, although he has learned that objects exist when he cannot see them, does not understand that their size and weight can stay the same even if their shape changes. For instance, if you show a four-year-old two balls of clay of the same size and ask him which ''has more clay,'' he will say they are the same. Then, while the child watches, you roll one ball of clay into a long, thin shape and ask your question again. Even though the child has seen that you added no clay to the ball you rolled into the new shape, he will usually say that the long, thin piece of clay ''has more clay'' than the remaining ball.

According to Lawrence Kohlberg, who has elaborated Piaget's theory in the areas of sex-role development and moral development, young children's imperfect understanding of conservation accounts for their belief that one can change one's sex if one wants to. Just as children think that a change in the appearance of a ball of clay results in a change in the amount of clay it contains, they think that a change in external appearance results in a change of gender—that a girl can become a boy if she changes her clothes and hair.

Not until about age six does a child understand that a person's gender stays the same regardless of changes in appearance. Understanding that, Kohlberg says, the child decides that he should behave in ways that are appropriate for his sex.

Cognitive theory, then, relates the development of sex-typed behavior to the child's mental picture of what the world is like. It emphasizes the way the child selects and organizes his perceptions and his knowledge and understanding of what it means to be a boy or girl. The child's thinking, Kohlberg says, goes like this: "I am a boy, so I want to do boy things. Therefore, the chance to do boy things is rewarding to me." A different sequence is suggested by social-learning theorists: "I want to act in ways that will be rewarded. I am rewarded, and see others like me rewarded, for doing boy things. Therefore I will do boy things." (To complete the comparison, the psychoanalytic sequence would be roughly as follows: "I'm afraid my father will punish me for loving my mother so much, but maybe if I act like him he won't hurt me. In fact, I *am* like him—I'm a boy!")

As these sequences suggest, one major difference between the three explanations of how sex-typed behavior develops is that each emphasizes a different aspect of the person. Social-learning theory stresses behavior; psychoanalytic theory stresses feelings; cognitive theory stresses mental operations or thoughts. Although each approach takes some account of all three aspects, it is only a slight exaggeration to state that social-learning theory suggests that a person is what he does; psychoanalytic theory, that he is what he feels; and cognitive theory, that he is what he thinks.

Another important contrast between the three approaches is that each implies a different answer to the question: What (or who) controls a person's behavior? According to social-learning theory, human behavior is shaped and controlled primarily by outside agents, such as the parents who administer rewards and punishments to a child and provide him with models to imitate. According to psychoanalytic theory, behavior is determined chiefly by an interplay of unconscious psychological forces. That is, the crucial processes go on inside the person, but they are not, for the most part, under his conscious control. Cognitive theory postulates an interaction between the environment and the person. It falls between the other two approaches on the matter of external versus internal control, and it awards the person a more active role in his development than does either of the other two approaches.

These three approaches tend to dominate the areas of psychology concerned with development, personality, social psychology, and disorder. But there is a fourth approach that should also be mentioned: **humanistic psychology,** which was not described earlier because it applies chiefly to adult personality functioning rather than to childhood development.

Humanistic psychologists have something in common with cognitive psychologists, because they are interested mainly in psychological characteristics that set humans apart from other animals rather than in the behavior that humans share with the rest of the animal kingdom. Humanists emphasize the human being's self-concept, his capacity for constructive and creative behavior, and his desire for personal fulfillment and a meaningful life. They object to the social-learning approach on the grounds that it is too deterministic: That is, according to the social-learning approach, humans are acted upon by forces in their environment; such environmental factors determine what a person is and does. Humanists object to the psychoanalytic approach because it, too, is deterministic (although the forces in this case are processes of the unconscious rather than environmental ones) and because it emphasizes people's destructive capacities and irrational impulses. In other areas of psychology, there are other approaches.

The four chapters in Unit II describe four fairly distinct approaches to the topic of learning: those based on ethology, on behaviorism, on information processing, and on cognitive theory. When you read the four chapters, you

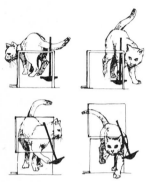

Figure 1.9   Illustrations of the two classic studies of animal learning that probably prompted Bertrand Russell's satirical remarks.   (top) Wolfgang Köhler, a German, studied learning by requiring apes to use objects lying around their cages to reach food that was in sight but out of reach. Observing that they first looked at the situation for a while and then quite suddenly went into action, he concluded that learning takes place by "insight" and consists in a reorganization of existing perceptions.   (bottom) At about the same time, Edward Thorndike, an American, was placing cats in puzzle boxes from which they could escape only by tripping certain levers. He observed that they typically made a large number of random attempts to escape before they accidentally made the right movements. He concluded that learning is a trial-and-error process that does not involve thinking. Obviously, the behavior of the animals in these experiments was determined more by the situations in which they were placed than by the essential nature of the learning process. Each experimenter was a careful observer but placed severe limits on what he could possibly observe by setting up a situation that fitted his own preconceptions.

will probably notice that the approaches to some extent compete with and to some extent complement each other. It has been suggested, for instance, that behaviorists see learning as a trial-and-error process, whereas cognitive psychologists emphasize organized perception and insight. Some people consider these two views incompatible and want to know which one is right; others consider the two views complementary and want to know which process operates when, and why. Bertrand Russell has suggested an amusing answer to the question about which view is right:

One may say broadly that all animals that have been carefully observed have behaved so as to confirm the philosophy in which the observer believed before his observation began. Nay, more, they have all displayed the national characteristics of the observer. Animals studied by Americans rush about frantically with an incredible display of bustle and pep, and at last achieve the desired result by chance. Animals observed by Germans sit still and think, and at last evolve solutions out of their own inner consciousness.

Figure 1.9 illustrates the difference between the views of cognitive psychologists and those of behaviorists.

Why Don't They Agree

You have probably heard the old story about the blind men and the elephant. Each man groped his way toward the elephant and encountered a different part of the animal. The one who found the tail announced the elephant was like a rope. The one who touched its side pronounced it wall-like. The one who found its trunk thought the animal was obviously a snake, and the one who had grasped a tusk shouted, "A spear!" The world looks different, depending on which part of it we choose to examine.

Figure-Ground Problems   Look at the scene framed in Figure 1.10. The woodcut depicts a forest scene, doesn't it? If you do see only a forest scene, the reason may be that you were directed to look at the "framed" area. If the directions had said, "Look at the muddy road," you would probably have seen that the forest was simply a reflection in a puddle. Referring to a "framed scene" seems a neutral thing to do, but its effect is to narrow your vision.

The same thing happens in psychology. There are various ways of viewing such psychological processes as sex-role development, motivation, and learning, each of them supported to some extent by research findings; attending to one view tends to crowd out an appreciation of the others. A psychologist (or student) who finds the psychoanalytic approach to sex-role development truly convincing may have trouble seeing the roles that social learning and cognitive organization play in the process; a psychologist who studies motivation from the standpoint of physiological need or learning from a behaviorist viewpoint may find it hard to see much validity in the cognitive approach to either topic.

It is not necessary for you, as an introductory student, to decide which of these pictures is valid or how they might be combined or redrawn (though it may interest you to consider these matters). But it is important for you to realize that there are at least two approaches to just about every major psychological question, and that the approaches are often incompatible in small or large ways. Psychologists, like other people, have different interests; they have different ideas about which psychological processes are basic and which are peripheral; they have different convictions about the nature of psychology, of science, and of human beings. All these differences are reflected in the ways they formulate and answer psychological questions.

A final controversy, which cuts across many subject areas within psychology, should be mentioned. In psychology today there tends to be a conflict

Figure 1.10 The division of the visual field into figure and ground is one of the most basic of perceptual processes, and, by analogy, it illustrates one reason for the diversity among psychological points of view. When the text directed you to "look at the scene framed," you most likely saw the forest scene as figure and ignored the rest as being ground. But if you had been directed to "look at the pool of water in the muddy track," your perception of what is depicted would probably have been very different. In the same way, if a psychologist, or a psychology student, looks at an individual primarily in terms of, say, his cognitive processes (figure), he may not notice that person's emotional reactions (ground). ("Puddles," by M. C. Escher, Escher Foundation, Haags Gemeentemuseum, The Hague.)

between the ambition to be a science, largely championed by learning theorists and experimentalists, and the ambition to be relevant, championed by some (by no means all) humanistic, social, and clinical psychologists. The practitioners of "hard" science defend their approach by pointing to their precision, thoroughness, and technique; they claim that little is wrong with psychology that time and progress will not fix. The proponents of a "softer" science counterattack by emphasizing their humanism, their respect for humanity's greatest endowments, and their concern with human and social values. They claim that psychology, by overemphasizing the need to be scientific, has failed to respond to immediate human needs and social crises. The challenge, of course, is to construct a body of thought that is both scientifically valid and personally and socially relevant.

Psychology as a Preparadigmatic Science Thomas Kuhn, a historian of science, has offered a different kind of explanation for the fact that psychologists explain and interpret behavior in such different ways. In a book called *The Structure of Scientific Revolutions,* Kuhn says that a mature science (such as physics) is dominated by what he calls a **paradigm:** an approach so comprehensive and so powerful that it determines the field of that science—both what subjects scientists in the field will study and what methods they will use. For instance, Einstein's theory of relativity provides the paradigm for contemporary physics, and Darwin's theory provides the paradigm for evolutionary biology.

Psychology and the other social sciences, Kuhn says, appear to be in a **preparadigmatic** stage of development. Instead of a single approach that dominates psychology as Einstein's dominates physics, there are a number of competing approaches, each of which aspires to become the paradigm. According to Kuhn, one of them may win out (that is, it may come to seem better than its competitors to most of the men and women in the field), or some other approach may be developed and adopted as a paradigm.

Although psychology as a whole is still waiting for its first true paradigm, some approaches have for a time served as what might be called mini-paradigms in certain areas. The best example is the psychoanalytic approach to personality development and disorder, which Sigmund Freud introduced in 1900 and which was generally accepted until, about twenty years ago, it began to come under serious attack, chiefly on the grounds that many of

Freud's assertions did not stand up under experimental scrutiny. The demise of psychoanalytic theory as a mini-paradigm is discussed in Chapter 26. Another example of a mini-paradigm is the behaviorist approach which dominated American experimental psychology from about 1920 to about 1955, when cognitive psychology began to challenge it in a serious way. At present, the cognitive approach to learning has weakened the domination of behaviorism but has not replaced it as a mini-paradigm. In child development, with the rallying point provided by Piaget's theory, cognitive psychologists have a stronger influence and are closer to establishing a mini-paradigm.

Psychoanalytic theory seems unlikely ever to attain paradigmatic status for the field of psychology as a whole. What about the other three approaches? Humanistic psychology must be regarded as a dark horse; the humanists are, at present, a disparate and relatively small group. Although their movement includes some well-known and highly respected psychologists, such as Carl Rogers and the late Abraham Maslow, it has yet to acquire a leader of the stature of Freud, Piaget, Pavlov, or Skinner.

Behaviorism (which, you will recall, has been extended by social-learning theorists into human development and other areas) and cognitive psychology are stronger contenders, but neither approach seems comprehensive enough to pull together the field of psychology as it exists today. Strict behaviorists have little interest in or respect for the subjective aspects of thoughts, feelings, memory, or states of consciousness, although they are willing to study the objective manifestations of these processes, for example, by examining changes in brain waves recorded by an EEG machine. Cognitive psychologists, since they are most interested in higher mental processes, give little attention to the behavior of animals near the bottom of the evolutionary scale—small loss, you may think, but such organisms as fruit flies and flatworms have, from time to time, made substantial contributions to our understanding of such matters as genetics and learning. In addition, cognitive psychologists have done little work so far in the important area of disorder, although George Kelly (whose work is discussed in Chapter 19) and others have made a beginning.

REINTERPRETATIONS OF PARTICULAR STUDIES

Some of the most heated debates among psychologists center not on broad theoretical issues but on specific questions about particular studies. Was the study properly designed and conducted, so that one may have confidence in its results, or were methodological errors made that cast doubt on its validity? Did the investigator who conducted the study interpret his findings and their implications correctly, or did he go too far, not far enough, or perhaps wander off in the wrong direction? Psychologists consider such questions with particular care when a study seems to break new ground—for example, as in the following instance — by identifying a hitherto unrecognized psychological phenomenon.

In 1962, a pediatrician named Lee Salk reported a study on the relation between an infant's prenatal experience and his behavior after birth. Salk's hypothesis was that an unborn child, in the uterus, hears its mother's heart beating and, by the learning process called **imprinting** (described in Chapter 3), comes to associate that sound with the security and comfort that unborn infants are assumed to experience in the womb. If his hypothesis was correct, Salk reasoned, then newborn infants should find heartbeat sounds soothing: They should cry less, sleep more, and gain weight faster than infants who have no opportunity to hear heartbeat sounds.

Salk placed two groups of newborn infants in separate nurseries and played an amplified heartbeat sound in one nursery. He found that the babies in the nursery with the heartbeat sound did cry less, sleep more, and gain weight faster than the babies in the other nursery. He concluded that his hypothesis was confirmed.

Other researchers, however, were not satisfied. Just what characteristics of a heartbeat, they wanted to know, do newborns find so soothing? Is it the *quality* of the sound—the particular thud-thump that a beating heart emits— as Salk believed, or is it perhaps the *rhythmicity* of the sound? Yvonne Brackbill and several colleagues tested the latter possibility by presenting groups of newborn infants with three different rhythmic sounds: a beating heart, a metronome, and a lullaby. As it turned out, all three sounds were equally effective in quieting the babies. This finding cast a certain amount of doubt on Salk's conclusions. Associations that are learned through imprinting are very specific, and although imprinting might account for an association between the sound of a heartbeat and a feeling of comfort, it would be unlikely to account for a more general association between rhythmic sounds and comfort.

Furthermore, Brackbill thought, the crucial factor might not be the rhythmicity of the sound at all. Beating hearts, metronomes, and lullabies are not only rhythmic but constant and monotonous. Brackbill decided to find out what effect other kinds of monotonous stimulation would have on newborns: not only heartbeats but constant light, increased heat, and snug swaddling, which has been used on babies in a number of different cultures, including the Navajo. Using different groups of infants, she assessed the effects of these stimuli singly and in various combinations. Her results were clear: The more types of constant stimulation the infants received, the quieter and more contented they seemed. A comparison of the behavior of the four infant groups that received only one kind of stimulation showed that the single most effective procedure in the study was not the heartbeat sound but swaddling.

This finding has different practical implications from Salk's, as well as different implications for psychologists interested in the effects of prenatal experience. The practical question of how best to soothe a young baby is by no means trivial, as anyone who has spent a few days with a restless infant knows. Salk's study suggested that hospital nurseries and the homes of newborn babies should be equipped with recordings of heartbeat sounds. Brackbill's second study indicates that snug swaddling, perhaps supplemented by other kinds of monotonous stimulation, will do the job better. One result of this series of studies is that many hospital nurses have stopped telling new mothers to wrap their babies loosely so that they can exercise and have started teaching mothers how to wrap their babies tightly.

The sequence of events just described is a very common one. A researcher conducts a study and obtains findings that are widely recognized as interesting, significant, and provocative. Other researchers study the study and find something about it questionable—in this instance, Salk's interpretation of his results as confirming his imprinting hypothesis. They therefore formulate and test hypotheses of their own, which differ in some way from those of the original experimenter. Ideally, these later investigations clarify, correct, and extend the findings of the first study, so that some point about behavior (in this case, that newborn infants find constant, monotonous stimulation soothing) can be regarded as having been conclusively demonstrated.

Psychologists disagree on relatively small issues as well as on large theoretical questions of the sort described earlier. Such disagreements are resolved not through verbal debate, no matter how much of that there may be, but through the accumulation of additional data from carefully designed studies. Psychology today is, after all, a science, and what scientists seek is empirical proof. In the next chapter, you will learn more about how that proof can be obtained—that is, about how to gather and analyze data in ways that provide definitive answers to some psychological questions.

2
Doing Psychology: Methodology

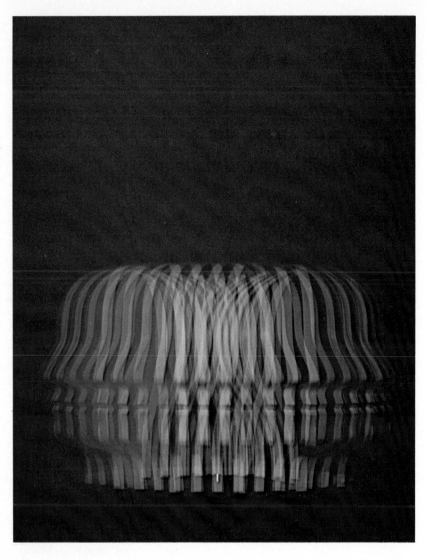

Figure 2.1 Psychology, like other sciences, uses a variety of methods to establish its body of knowledge. You cannot truly understand the knowledge in a science unless you also understand the methods used to establish it. Imagine, for example, how difficult you would find it to understand the biological concept of a cell if you had never looked through a microscope or a magnifying glass. Similarly, in psychology it is not easy to understand how such concepts as learning, intelligence, or pain are used unless you understand how psychologists measure them.

This chapter is about methodology. Are you looking forward to reading it? Not very much, probably. Most people are considerably more interested in what psychologists know than in how they find it out—or in the larger question of what it means, among psychologists, to "know" something. People would rather watch a basketball game than read the rules of the game. They prefer reading a sonnet to studying the poetic conventions that govern the writing of sonnets. They also would rather be told *what* a study demonstrates than learn *how* it was conducted.

This propensity, although understandable, is regrettable. The methods and statistical techniques available to psychologists to a large extent determine both the questions that can and cannot be answered and the kind of answers that are obtained—definitive or suggestive, precise or not so precise, comprehensive or limited. The more a person knows about those methods and techniques, the better able he or she is to understand and evaluate what psychologists say. Possibly you suspect that the details of psychological studies, like the intricacies of American economic policy, are too complicated for anyone but a specialist to hope to follow; but in psychology, as in politics, "leaving it to the experts" is not a very good idea. For one thing, as you have seen in the last chapter, the experts sometimes disagree. For another, the matters they deal with often have social and political as well as scientific significance. Child care, education, race relations, mental health, sex differences, poverty, behavioral engineering—these are only a few of the many topics with social and political implications that psychologists study and, sometimes, express themselves on publicly. You will be much better able to assess both the meaning and the validity of what they say about these matters if you know something about the methods used in the studies they cite to support their assertions.

It may help you develop an interest in methodology if you think of a question you hope this course will answer. Perhaps you are wondering whether mental disorder is inherited. Perhaps you are curious about why some people do so well in competitive situations, like exams, while others do so poorly. Maybe you want to know why people fall in love. Now, suppose you had some money at your disposal and could design and run a psychological study to help answer your question. You probably cannot yet design such a study, but keep your question in mind as you read this chapter, and perhaps after you have finished it, you will be able to do so.

The general procedure psychologists use when conducting studies can be simply described. First, *data are gathered* by means of one or more methods; then, *data are analyzed*, usually by means of statistical techniques.

GATHERING THE DATA: METHODS

Which method a psychologist chooses to use in a particular study depends, not surprisingly, on the nature of the question he or she wants to answer. For example, a social psychologist studying attitudes is likely to conduct a survey; a psychotherapist interested in formulating a new theory of personality may begin with case studies; a developmental psychologist, who wants to assess continuities in behavior from childhood to adulthood may design a longitudinal study; a physiological psychologist studying brain-behavior relationships will probably run a laboratory experiment.

As you read about the various methods, give some thought to the kind of information each of them yields. The basic goal of psychology, broadly stated, is to understand behavior and subjective experience. Specifically, the goals of psychology are to describe, explain, predict, and control behavior and subjective experience. The method used in a particular study in part determines which (if any) goal is attained. For example, naturalistic observation usually allows description but not control; test scores may permit prediction but not explanation; an experiment often makes it possible to control behavior under laboratory conditions but may not provide much understanding of the behavior as it occurs under natural conditions.

No matter what method a researcher uses in gathering his data, it is almost certain that he will have to collect only a **sample** of the data pertaining to his hypothesis. Almost no questions permit the gathering of *all* the relevant data, but the sample must be of adequate size to reflect the universe of information it is meant to represent. For example, an opinion poll meant to reflect the opinions of all Democrats in the United States could not have as its sample only six people. Such a small sample is too likely to produce bias: If the six Democrats happened to come from Mississippi and Alabama, the findings of this poll would probably be **biased** toward the view of southern Democrats (whose views often are opposed to those of northern Democrats).

A sample can be of adequate size and still be biased if the sample is not representative of its universe. A researcher can do one of two things to eliminate such bias. Either he can deliberately go about making sure that he has a **representative sample;** for example, if he is trying to find out about the effects of reinforcement on schoolchildren, he can ensure that his sample includes children of both sexes, of all social classes, of all geographic areas, of both urban and suburban areas, and of various ages. Or he can attempt to eliminate the bias by taking a **random sample,** that is, a sample in which every piece of data in the universe of relevant information has an equal chance of being collected. For example, for the schoolchildren study, he could get a list of names of all the children and choose names at random from the list.

Case Studies

A case study is an intensive investigation of one or a few individuals, usually with reference to a single psychological phenomenon. Case studies provide a

Pride want of Money wordly gane who we are God help us to make the right move With God help we can over come the sin of the world. God help us to do our best. curcomseion [circumcision] *5,000 cases per day* Dear God help me to forget some things. I am sorry I done some thing and will try to do better The part of the brain is much bigger than a dime. And is oppsite from which hand you write with The part is smaller yet that has to do with vision The nerves like telegraph wires to all parts of our body called cranial nerves A baby get it personality from its envirment. How long has it been sence you talked with the lord. And told him your hearts hiden secrets. Why don't our Churches Practice the brotherhood they preach. Billy Graham We need more prayer life. A few min. in prayer help's us so much.   We ate like a bunch of cattle going thourugh a shoot prepairing for market.

My sin cause Christ to be hurt   My sin is also a perfume

We can sin by Using our eye's. We should watch what we see with our eye's.

3 nerves control 1. muscles 2. skin 3. organs inside of us God sure knew what he wasdoing when he made mankind My love for women has been turned from women to men be caus I couldn't make over them. The devil know our week points better than we do. Freind ship How to wind friend

Figure 2.2   This passage is a small part of a diary written by a young man while he was in a deeply disturbed mental state. A document like this is not an easy piece of data to categorize or treat statistically, and one cannot be sure how representative it is of the behavior of all schizophrenics. But it is an accurate record of one person's behavior and probably gives the observer the most direct contact with schizophrenia that he could have without becoming schizophrenic himself.
(From Bert Kaplan, ed., *The Inner World of Mental Illness,* 1964.)

wealth of descriptive information about the phenomenon as it is demonstrated by the person or persons being studied. They allow for considerable depth of analysis and may imply the existence of certain behavioral laws; however, they do not *prove* that any law is operating.

In the hands of a brilliant psychologist, the case-study method can be powerful indeed. Sigmund Freud's theory of personality development, described in Chapter 18, is based on case studies of the patients who came to him for treatment. Jean Piaget's theory of intellectual development, described in Chapter 8, began with intensive observations of the behavior of his own three children as they were growing up.

From the point of view of the reader, an advantage of case studies is that they make people "come alive" in a way that general descriptions of behavioral principles usually do not. For example, the discussion of schizophrenia presented in Chapter 24 of this text describes the behaviors and attitudes characteristic of people diagnosed as suffering from various types of schizophrenia. You might wish to turn to that chapter now and read two or three of those descriptions.

Here is a case study of a woman diagnosed as a schizophrenic: Bertha is a forty-four-year-old woman who was taken into custody by security guards at the White House after demanding to see the President. She later told hospital authorities that she had been "invited to see the President many times" and that prior to her trip she had written to inform him that she was finally coming to Washington. She said that she "hoped the President would stop the 'gum chewing' in her head and would stop the police persecution that had caused her ears to flop and her body to go out of shape." Bertha also complained of "policemen in her ears and riding up and down her nose." Her speech was barely intelligible and her thoughts were incoherent. She claimed that she had first visited the governor of her home state and the Pentagon before coming to the White House. She refused to discuss her previous hospitalization.

Although the case study, and the example of schizophrenic language reproduced in Figure 2.2, do not tell you in general what schizophrenia is like, they do convey the quality of a person's behavior and experience better than a general description can.

Naturalistic Observation

The cardinal rule of naturalistic observation is that the investigator should stay out of the way—for example, he may observe animals from inside an en-

Figure 2.3   An allegory for the sampling problem.   (reading from left to right) A universe of unknowns confronts the researcher. He can collect only a small amount of the data in this universe, and in order to make conclusions about the whole, he must assume that his sample is representative. His first sampling technique produces a biased sample, although he has no way of knowing this at first. If he generalizes from this data, he will conclude incorrectly that the head is filled with pyramids. He now uses a different sampling technique and obtains a random sample. The data he obtains this time suggest correctly that there are cubes, spheres, and pyramids in the head in equal proportions. See Figure 2.13 on page 33 for a continuation of this allegory.

closure or children from behind a one-way window—because the purpose of the method is to find out how behavior occurs under natural conditions, without interference from an outsider.

Naturalistic observation is commonly used by ethologists as a first step in studying the behavior of an animal species. For example, Niko Tinbergen spent a great deal of time observing the behavior of the stickleback fish before he experimented with it in any way. His observations allowed him to outline the sequential stages of courtship and mating shown in Figure 2.4. Later, as described in Chapter 3, Tinbergen exposed males of the species to various models in order to find out what caused them to attack a rival.

A social psychologist might use naturalistic observation to study leadership roles within a commune or a therapy group; a developmental psychologist might use it to study the way four-year-olds interact at a preschool; a cognitive psychologist might use it to study the organization of a species' behavior before, say, designing an experiment meant to find out what kinds of problems members of that species can solve and how they go about it.

Surveys

Probably the most famous survey of recent years is the one that resulted in the Kinsey reports, published in 1948 and 1953. Alfred Kinsey and his staff interviewed more than ten thousand men and women about their sexual behavior and attitudes—as radical a thing to do at the time as the Masters and Johnson studies were about fifteen years later. Kinsey found, among other things, that what had been considered "abnormal" behaviors such as mas-

Figure 2.4 Naturalistic observation is a method comparable to making large numbers of case studies. By observing the behavior of many individual pairs of sticklebacks, ethologist Niko Tinbergen was able to give the general description of stickleback mating behavior illustrated here. (reading from top left to bottom right) In apparent response to the zig-zag dance of a red-bellied male, the female swims directly toward him. He then turns to lead her to the nest he has previously built. She follows, and when he points his head into the nest, she enters it. Then, touching her abdomen, the male trembles, and the female spawns. Finally the male ejaculates to fertilize the new eggs. After observing this sequence of events, Tinbergen went on to prove with experimental methods that the sequence of behaviors was in fact a closely linked causal chain. (After Tinbergen, 1951.)

Table 2.1 Survey Data About Masturbation

	In Females	In Males
Relation to Age and Marital Status		
Accumulative incidence		
Total: experience	62%	93%
Total: with orgasm	58%	92%
By age 12	12%	21%
By age 15	20%	82%
By age 20	33%	92%
Active incidence to orgasm	Increases to middle age	Decreases after teens
Frequency (active median) to orgasm	Uniform to mid-fifties	Steady decrease after teens
Average, unmarried groups	0.3–0.4 per wk.	0.4–1.8 per wk.
Average, married groups	0.2 per wk.	0.1–0.2 per wk.
Individual variation	Very great	Less
Percentage of total outlet		
In unmarried groups	37–85%	31–70%
In married groups	About 10%	4–6%
In previously married groups	13–44%	8–18%
Relation to Educational Level		
Accumulative incidence to orgasm		
Grade school group	34%	89%
High school group	59%	95%
College group	57%	96%

Source: Adapted from Alfred C. Kinsey *et al., Sexual Behavior in the Human Female* (Philadelphia: Saunders, 1953), pp. 173–175.

turbation, homosexuality, and oral-genital sex were much more common than most people had supposed. Some of his findings on masturbation appear in Table 2.1.

Surveys can be oral (interviews) or written (questionnaires). Interviews have the advantage of letting the investigator see his subjects; they also allow him to modify his questions if it seems advisable. Questionnaires take less time to administer and so are particularly useful in gathering information from a large number of people.

In conducting a survey of either sort, the investigator must try to ensure that his sample is representative of the group he is trying to study. In 1936, a telephone poll by *Literary Digest* magazine predicted a massive victory for Alf Landon over Franklin Roosevelt, but Roosevelt won by a landslide. The problem was that the magazine had polled its own subscribers and had collected its information by phone. In those Depression days, people who had telephones and subscribed to literary journals tended to be not only Republicans but also quite affluent.

Social psychologists often use surveys to gather data on people's attitudes and beliefs. One problem they encounter is that people sometimes give misleading answers, either deliberately or accidentally. Some people answer "yes" whenever they can, just to be agreeable; others seem to have a built-in tendency to say "no." If a survey concerns a touchy area, such as sex, money, or race relations, people are especially likely to claim they believe what they think they ought to believe. The psychologist conducting a survey can often control for this problem by including several differently worded questions on the same topic. Thus, a person might say in answer to one question that he has no objection whatever to a certain sexual practice and then, in answer to another, that he has never engaged in the practice and certainly never plans to. In such a case, the psychologist would suspect that his subject's attitude toward the practice was somewhat less positive than the first answer suggested.

Cross-Cultural Comparisons

Cross-cultural comparisons, as the name implies, are used to compare the behavior of people in different countries or cultures. Sometimes they reveal interesting differences. For example, W. Hudson found that Bantus and other native Africans, shown the pictures reproduced in Figure 2.5, were unable to identify the objects' locations in depth, whereas people in Western cultures have no difficulty doing so. Hudson concluded that it is necessary to have undergone specific educational processes in order to be able to interpret the depth cues drawn, such as the converging lines. Other cross-cultural studies demonstrate apparently universal behavior patterns; for example, Lawrence Kohlberg has found that children in several different cultures seem to go through the same stages of moral development in the same order, as described in Chapter 10.

Longitudinal Studies

In a longitudinal study, the same group of people is studied intermittently over a period of years. Longitudinal studies, although time-consuming to conduct, are the best method available to assess consistencies and inconsistencies in behavior over time. To illustrate, suppose that you wanted to know whether children who are characteristically dependent turn out to be dependent adults. One way to find out would be to select a group of adults, assess their dependency, and then try to discover, by reconstructing their biographies, how dependent they were as children. A more reliable way would be to do a longitudinal study: to select a group of children, assess their dependency, and then assess it again every few years as the children grow up and become

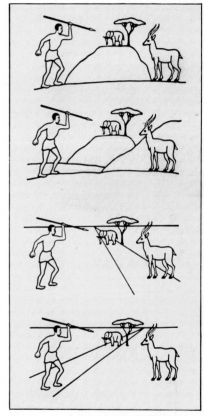

Figure 2.5 Individuals of the Bantu, a people of central and southern Africa, were asked by Hudson to identify the spatial relationships of the objects in this series of pictures. They were asked, for example, whether the man was trying to spear the elephant or the antelope. Western adults make no errors in tasks of this kind. The Bantus' performance, however, depended considerably on whether they had been to school or not. This cross-cultural comparison suggested to Hudson that the perception of depth in pictures is a learned skill quite separate from ordinary depth perception.
(After Hudson, 1960)

Figure 2.6 The results of a longitudinal study. Kagan and Moss wanted to find out how much continuity there is between individuals' behavior in childhood and their behavior as adults. They found the correlations, or degrees of relatedness, between patterns of behavior in the child and the adult that are shown here. Traditional sex roles had a strong influence on whether a childhood behavior pattern died out or survived into adulthood. Passive, dependent girls were more likely to become passive, withdrawn adults than passive, dependent boys were to become passive, withdrawn men. Boys with strong sexual interests in their early teens were more likely to be sexually active as young adults than were girls with such interests.

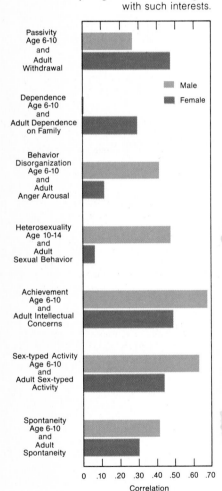

adults. Jerome Kagan and Howard Moss have performed such a study: Following their subjects from birth through early adulthood, they assessed the continuity not only of dependency but of various other behaviors. Some of their findings are shown in Figure 2.6.

The Experiment

Many psychologists regard the experiment as "the method of choice"; that is, they consider the experiment to be more definitive and more scientific than any other method, and they use it in their research whenever the question they are investigating allows them to. The main advantage of the experiment over other methods is that it permits the experimenter to control the conditions of the study and thus to rule out all influences on his subjects' behavior except the one he is examining. Its main disadvantage is that ruling out extraneous influences occasionally creates such an unnatural situation that one is forced to wonder how much the behavior exhibited during the experiment resembles its real-life counterpart.

The essential characteristics of an experiment can be illustrated by citing a relatively simple one conducted by Kenneth Gergen, Mary Gergen, and William Barton, social psychologists. The researchers wondered how a group of people would interact under conditions of perfect anonymity. They formulated a hypothesis that people under such conditions would act in ways different from those dictated by social norms. Norms are the expectations of one's society, family, and friends about how one *should* act in various situations.

The condition they set up to achieve anonymity was a perfectly dark room. The volunteer **subjects** (university students between eighteen and twenty-five years of age) were told only that they would be in the room for an hour with other people and that there were no rules about what to do or what not to do. The subjects were told that each would be escorted from the room alone after the hour and that there would be no chance of subsequently meeting the other subjects. This group of subjects is the **experimental group.**

The researchers also arranged to have a **control group.** These are subjects who have the same characteristics as the experimental subjects except that the independent variable (to be defined in the following paragraphs) is not applied to them. The control group was given instructions identical to the first group's but was ushered into a normally lighted room.

The researchers tape-recorded conversations during the hour the subjects remained in the room; took photographs to record seating arrangements and the like (using infrared cameras for the unlighted room); and, directly after the experiment, asked subjects to write down their impressions of the experience.

In an experiment, the word **variable** is used to refer to any factor that is capable of change. In this experiment the variables were amount of light and amount of talking and touching. The variable that the experimenter deliberately manipulates is called the **independent variable;** in this case, the researchers manipulated the amount of light. The variable that the researcher thinks will change when the independent variable changes is called the **dependent variable**—in this experiment, the amount of talking and touching.

It may help you keep these terms straight if you try to remember that the words "independent" and "dependent" refer to the relationship between the variables. Changes in the independent variable (amount of light, in this case) do *not* depend on changes in the dependent variable (amount of talking and touching); they occur independently of such changes. Changes in the dependent variable (according to the hypothesis being tested) *do* depend on changes in the independent variable. It is also helpful to know that the hypothesis tested in an experiment can always be rephrased into an if/then statement: If a perfectly dark room produces a feeling of anonymity, then under these conditions social interaction—touching and talking—will differ from interactions

A

Theoretical interest: The behavior of the de-individuated person, the person who is anonymous or not likely to be identified by others.

Experimental hypothesis: A group of strangers will interact differently in total darkness than they will in ordinary lighting.

Participants: 46 college students between the ages of eighteen and twenty-five, solicited by advertisement, telephone, or personal contact, gathered in groups of between seven and nine with approximately equal numbers of males and females in each group.

Experimental chamber: A soundproof, doubled-doored room measuring 10 by 12 by 18½ feet, with a carpeted floor and padded walls, and equipped with ventilating fan, microphone, one-way glass, infrared lighting, and ordinary lighting.

Procedure: 1. All participants upon arrival at the laboratory taken to a small room alone where given time-consuming task to do until arrival of other participants. 2. All participants given written instructions informing them of freedom to relate in any manner wished during experimental session and asking them to remove shoes, watches, earrings, rings, glasses, and contents of pockets until after the session. 3. All participants led one by one to experimental chamber. 4. Participants in Black Room Condition (experimental group) left for one hour with no visible illumination except pinpoint of blue light over door. Confederate of experimenter present in case of emergency. Participants in White Room Condition (control group) left for one hour with illumination from normal overhead lighting. 5. All participants led one at a time from the experimental chamber back to original small room and given lengthy questionnaire to fill out.

B

Results: Observations of behavior in the experimental chamber:

	Black Room	White Room
Movement	50% change of position every five minutes.	10% change of position during whole session.
Verbal communication	High during first half-hour, then low.	High throughout session.

Percent of subjects reporting selected behaviors and experiences in questionnaire:

	Black Room	White Room
Talked small talk	96	100
Introduced self by first name	92	100
Laughed or giggled	80	100
Felt close to other person	92	75
Felt suspended—beyond normal time and space	80	65
Touched accidentally	100	5
Felt sexually aroused	75	30
Lay on floor	64	50
Found self in middle of room	84	10
Touched purposefully	88	0
Hugged	48	0
Prevented self from being touched	16	0

that are governed by social norms. The variable that follows the word ''if'' is the independent variable (note that both ''if'' and ''independent'' begin with the letter ''i''); the variable that follows the word ''then'' is the dependent variable.

Figure 2.7A sets out the components of the experiment. Figure 2.7B gives some of the **data,** or results, the researchers obtained. As you can see, their hypothesis was supported. In the lighted room, people kept a conversation going for the entire hour; kept seated (usually three feet away from any other subject) during the hour; and no one touched anyone else. In the dark room, conversation slacked off after the first half hour; subjects moved about a great deal; and touched each other both accidentally and on purpose. In fact, 50 percent of these subjects hugged another person.

The researchers concluded that ''. . . the state of anonymity seems to encourage whatever potentials are most prominent at the moment—whether for good or ill. When we are anonymous we are free to be aggressive or to give affection, whichever expresses most fully our feelings at the time. . . . It appears that people share strong yearnings to be close to each other. However, our social norms make it too costly to express these feelings.''

Experimental Versus Correlational Research

In an experiment, the hypothesis postulates the existence of a **cause-effect relationship** between the variables. When some other method is used, the hypothesis postulates an **association,** or **correlation,** between the variables.

If a psychologist's aim is to establish the validity of a cause-effect relationship, he will, if possible, conduct an experiment rather than some other kind of study. The experiment is the only method that enables him to control all possible influences on the behavior he is interested in and to manipulate just the influence he believes to be the cause of a change in that behavior.

Figure 2.7 The components of the experiment conducted by Gergen, Gergen, and Barton. Note that a complete account of the experiment includes the theoretical thinking that led up to the formation of a specific experimental hypothesis, a description of all the conditions to which the subjects were exposed from beginning to end, and an explanation of how the different variables were controlled and measured. Note also that the results given here are summaries of the data, not a list of every behavior of every subject observed and recorded by the experimenters.

But sometimes, for practical or ethical reasons, a cause-effect question cannot be studied experimentally. For example, a psychologist might suspect that normal visual development in human beings depends not only on physical maturation but on visual experience. An ideal way to test that possibility would be to raise an experimental group of newborn babies in total darkness for six months or a year, preventing them from acquiring any visual experience, and then compare their visual abilities with those of a control group of infants treated exactly the same as those in the experimental group except that they were raised under normal light conditions. Obviously, such an experiment cannot be performed. What the psychologist would probably do instead is perform his experiment on newborn animals rather than on newborn human infants. The alternative to an experiment with animals would be a study of natural instances of visual deprivation in human beings—people who were born blind and later became able to see through surgery, for example—but this sort of study presents serious practical and interpretative difficulties (some studies of this kind are described in Chapter 7).

Often, however, performing an experiment with animal instead of human subjects is not a viable alternative because the behavior to be studied occurs only in human beings. Suppose, for instance, that a psychologist thinks that the ability to hear spoken language is necessary for normal language development—that is, that deafness will cause deficits in the way a child uses language, even if the child is given special training in an effort to compensate for his deafness. In such a case, an animal experiment would be of no use. Instead, the psychologist can conduct a **correlational study** to assess the strength of the relationship between deafness and certain language deficits. Although such a study cannot establish that deafness causes the deficits, it can establish that deafness and certain deficits have a strong tendency to occur in the same people.

A correlation indicates the degree of relatedness between two things. In some instances, the relationship between the two things turns out to be close and positive, meaning that a high rank on one measure is usually accompanied by a high rank on another measure. For example, there is a strong **positive correlation** between IQ scores and academic performance: People who score high on IQ tests tend to get high grades; people who score low on IQ tests tend to get low grades. In other instances, the relationship between the two things is close and negative, meaning that a high rank on one measure is usually accompanied by a low rank on another measure. For example, there is a **negative correlation** between ability to play or compose music and tone deafness (inability to distinguish the pitch of musical notes); the more tone deaf a person is, the less likely it is that he will be able to play an instrument well or compose listenable music. In still other instances, there is little or no relationship between the two things; there is no relationship between eye color and academic success or between hair color and tone deafness. Quantitative descriptions of correlation are discussed in a later section of this chapter.

A problem with correlations is that people often misinterpret them. Instead of seeing a correlation as indicating merely that two things tend to occur together, they see it as indicating cause and effect. Suppose you were told that there is a positive correlation between the number of Popsicles sold by ice-cream vendors at swimming pools and the number of people admitted to hospitals for heat stroke. Would you conclude that Popsicles cause heat stroke?

Correlations do not indicate cause and effect; what they do instead is allow you to make *predictions* about events. If you know that a person has a high IQ, you can predict that he is likely to get good grades; if you know that a person is very tone deaf, you can predict that he is not likely to compose a

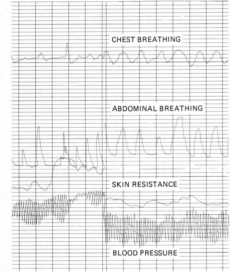

Figure 2.8   Polygraph, or "lie detector," recordings. Note that there are four pen tracings: Abdominal and chest breathing is recorded from rubber tubes fastened around the subject's middle; blood pressure is recorded from a rubber cuff fastened tightly around his upper arm; and galvanic skin response is recorded from a pair of electrodes pasted to his fingertips. The record at the left shows the subject's reaction when he was suddenly asked "What is nine times seven?" He seemed to regard this as a threatening challenge: All physiological measures show marked changes. The record at the right was made previously while the subject was being asked routine questions about his age, occupation, and so forth.

piece of music you would care to hear. Note that, in either case, your prediction could be wrong. Very few events are perfectly correlated.

Tests, Psychophysiological Measures, and Ratings

Tests, psychophysiological measures, and ratings have been grouped together because they are primarily measures of individual behavior. One use of intelligence tests, for example, is to predict how well a given child is likely to do at school; personality tests are used to assess an individual's emotional maturity, his interests and values, and so on. (Intelligence and personality tests are discussed in detail in Chapter 17.)

Psychophysiological measures are used to study psychological events, such as emotional arousal and sleep, which are known to be associated with measurable physiological change. The great value of such measures is that they provide objective, quantitative data on phenomena that are hard to assess precisely in other ways. An electroencephalogram (EEG) of the electrical activity of the brain, for example, makes it possible for a psychologist doing sleep research to tell for certain which of the four stages of sleep his subject is in (see Chapter 13). Similarly, a psychologist studying emotional arousal can learn more about the strength of an emotion if he measures changes in a subject's heart rate, respiration rate, and galvanic skin response, or GSR (a measure of the electrical conductivity of the skin that increases when a person perspires), than he can if he relies only on his subject's outward behavior (such as weeping) or subjective impressions. (See Figure 2.8.)

Subjective impressions are valuable too; one way a psychologist can collect them is in the form of ratings. In an interesting study of fear in sky-divers, Walter Fenz and Seymour Epstein asked novice and experienced sports parachutists to rate the intensity of their subjective fear at various points in the jump sequence and then compared these self-ratings with physiological measures of emotional arousal. The results are shown in Figure 2.9.

Two other types of ratings (in addition to self-ratings) should be mentioned. First, a psychologist may ask his subjects to rate not themselves but something else, in order to see how well their ratings agree. Chapter 15 describes several studies of this sort. In some studies people were asked to rate the similarity of various emotion words. In other studies, people rated which facial expressions (as portrayed in photographs) depicted different emotions. Second, a psychologist may rate his subjects on some quality. As part of a study of interactions between mothers and their children, for example, a researcher might rate the emotional warmth each mother showed toward her child on a scale from one to ten.

ANALYZING THE DATA: STATISTICAL TOOLS

After a psychologist has collected his data (whether in an experiment or other type of study), how does he find out what the data mean? Usually researchers collect their data in a form that can be analyzed by statistics—mathematical methods for analyzing, interpreting, and presenting these separate elements in summary form. There are two main kinds of statistics: descriptive and inferential.

Descriptive Statistics

Descriptive statistics are used to reduce a mass of data to a form that is more manageable and understandable. Using descriptive statistics, an investigator is able to say something meaningful about his findings in a small amount of space, even though there may be a large amount of data and even though the data may vary a great deal. In summarizing test scores, for example, descriptive statistics are used to calculate the average, or most representative, score; the difference between other scores and the average score; and the

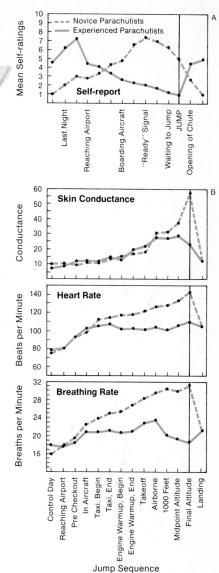

Figure 2.9 (A) When asked to assign numbers to their feelings of fear (with 1 meaning the time of least fear and 10 meaning the time of most fear), novice parachutists reported most fear at the "ready" signal just before the jump. Experienced parachutists said their fear was nearly at its lowest at this time. (B) Physiological measures indicated that both groups became more aroused right up to the time of the jump. Fenz and Epstein suggest that the experienced parachutists' had learned to inhibit their experience of fear in response to the first signs of physiological arousal.
(After Fenz and Epstein, 1967.)

relationship between the average score on one test and the average score on another test. Comparing average scores tells a good deal about the level of performance of the two groups.

Distributions and Averages Suppose a psychologist is studying anxiety in various occupational groups. He has made up a questionnaire containing forty-seven questions that can be answered "Yes" (I am anxious about this at times) or "No" (I never worry about this). He gives the questionnaire to a group of fifty gas-station attendants, then adds up each of their scores. He finds that some of the attendants worry about many things; some worry about fewer things. But no one worries about more than 36 things, and no one worries about fewer than 11. The **range** of the scores is therefore 25 (that is, 36 − 11 = 25). The researcher can now plot a **frequency distribution** of the scores, as shown in Figure 2.10A.

Next, the researcher gives the questionnaire to a group of fifty dentists, and he wants to compare anxiety in the two groups. After he has added up the dentists' scores and plotted a frequency distribution for them (Figure 2.10B), he can find out what the average performance of each group is and compare their averages. When we seek an average of some kind, we are looking for what psychologists call a **measure of central tendency.** There are several measures of central tendency, and which one is used depends on how the scores whose central tendency you want to find are distributed.

One measure of central tendency is the **arithmetic mean:** to find it, you merely add up all the scores and then divide by the number of people who took the test. The mean score for the gas-station attendants was about 21; for the dentists, it was about 32 (Figure 2.10). However, if the distribution of your scores is not a **normal distribution,** as it is in Figure 2.10A and 2.10B, the mean may give you extremely misleading information. (Compare the shape of the distributions in Figures 2.10A and 2.10B with the shape of the curve in Figure 17.7.) Consider the distribution shown in Figure 2.10C: This represents the distribution of salaries at a plastics company. Suppose someone told you that the average income of the fifty people employed there was $9,200 a year, what would that mean to you? Look at the distribution: The president of the company earns $40,000 a year; he pays three executives $30,000 and four executives $20,000. There are six managers who earn $15,000 and six salesmen who earn $10,000. It turns out that the thirty people who run the machines all earn $5,000 a year or less. The mean of all these

Figure 2.10   Three frequency distributions. In each figure, the vertical scale shows the frequency with which a score on the horizontal scale was observed. Note that in (A) and (B) the three measures of central tendency all coincide. Note that these two distributions are very similar except for the locations of their central tendencies. They have similar ranges of variability and both have the "bell" shape characteristic of normal distributions. The distribution in (C) is different in shape from the first two. Here the various measures of central tendency do not coincide. Frequency distributions of this kind—and many others—occur in psychology, but normal distributions are the most common.

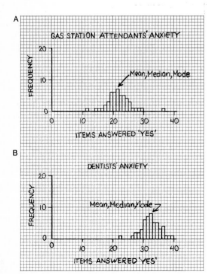

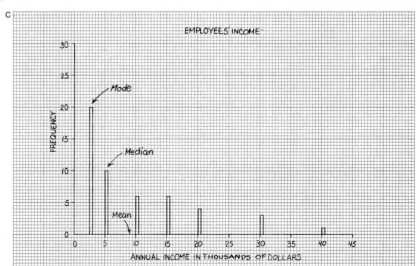

salaries is $9,200, but this measure of central tendency, or average, is not a fair representation of the actual distribution of salaries.

In this case, a better measure of central tendency would be the **median,** which is the score that falls exactly in the middle of the distribution, that is, the score that has the same number of individuals scoring above and below it. In the plastics company, the median income is $5,000.

There is a third measure of central tendency, the **mode,** which is the score made most frequently in any distribution. Note that the mode in the plastics company is $2,500 a year: More people make that than make any other salary.

You can see that it is extremely important for a researcher to know and take account of how his scores are distributed. Even when, in normal distributions, as in Figures 2.10A and 2.10B, the mean, median and mode are all the same, the range of scores in these distributions could be different. For this reason, psychologists need an additional descriptive statistic that tells them how the scores vary about the mean.

Variability and Standard Deviation The measures that tell a researcher how closely clustered or widely spread out his distribution of scores is are called measures of variability. Frequency and range, discussed earlier, are also measures of variability, but variability is usually expressed in terms of the **standard deviation**—a number that indicates the extent to which figures in a given set of data vary from the mean.

Look at the two distributions of history quiz scores shown in Figures 2.11A and 2.11B. The mean for both sets of scores is 58, but the standard deviation for the scores in 2.11A is about 10; that for 2.11B is about 2. By knowing the standard deviation, you know whether the actual scores in the set of scores varied from the mean a lot or a little.

Calculating the standard deviation is not difficult, although it is tedious unless one has the assistance of a computer or mechanical calculator. Here are the steps: (1) Calculate the mean of all the scores you have obtained; (2) subtract the mean from each score and, in each case, square the difference; (3) add all the squares together; (4) divide the sum by the total number of scores you are dealing with; and (5) take the square root of that value. Figures 2.11A and 2.11B also illustrate this procedure as it was used to calculate the standard deviations for the distributions shown.

If you were to measure almost any trait in a large group of people—height, weight, IQ, friendliness—you would find that the largest number of people fall near the mean, while fewer and fewer people would fall at each level on either side of the mean. You would find, in other words, that most traits form a normal distribution. Because of the way the standard deviation is calculated, its value for any normal distribution is such that 68 percent of the scores in the distribution fall between +1 and −1 standard deviations of the mean, 95 percent of the scores fall between +2 and −2 standard deviations of the mean, and 99.75 percent of the scores fall between +3 and −3 standard

Step 1			Step 2		Step 3
x	f	fx	(x−58)	(x−58)²	f(x−58)²
36	1	36	−22	484	484
37	1	37	−21	441	441
38	1	38	−20	400	400
43	1	43	−15	225	225
44	1	44	−14	196	196
46	1	46	−12	144	144
47	1	47	−11	121	121
48	1	48	−10	100	100
49	1	49	−9	81	81
50	2	100	−8	64	128
51	2	102	−7	49	98
52	2	104	−6	36	72
53	2	106	−5	25	50
54	1	54	−4	16	16
55	2	110	−3	9	18
56	2	112	−2	4	8
57	2	114	−1	1	2
58	2	116	0	0	0
59	2	118	1	1	2
60	2	120	2	4	8
61	2	122	3	9	18
62	2	124	4	16	32
63	2	126	5	25	50
64	2	128	6	36	72
65	1	65	7	49	49
66	1	66	8	64	64
67	1	67	9	81	81
68	1	68	10	100	100
69	1	69	11	121	121
70	1	70	12	144	144
71	1	71	13	169	169
73	1	73	15	225	225
75	1	75	17	289	289
76	1	76	18	324	324
77	1	77	19	361	361
79	1	79	21	441	441
	50	2900			5134

Mean $= 2900/50$
$= 58$

Steps 4 and 5
Standard Deviation $= \sqrt{5134/50} = \sqrt{102.68} = 10.13$

Figure 2.11A A frequency distribution with high variability, and the calculation of its mean and standard deviation. Compare this distribution with the distribution in Figure 2.11B, on the next page. Note that the means of these distributions are exactly the same and that both distributions have the "bell" shape (indicated by the colored curves) of the theoretical normal distribution. In the calculations, the letter x stands for the values of various scores. The letter f stands for the frequency with which a score occurred. Note that the total of all the scores is computed in Step 1 by multiplying each score, x, by the number of times it occurred, f, and adding up the resulting products. Note that the sum of the squares in Step 3 is computed similarly.

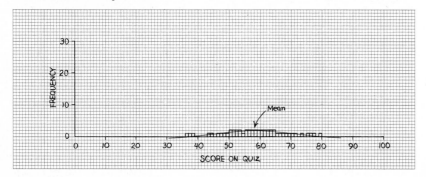

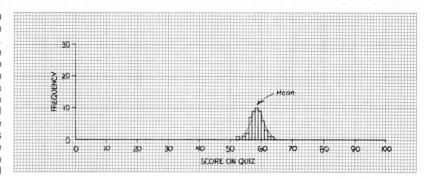

Figure 2.11B A frequency distribution with low variability, and the computation of its mean and standard deviation. Compare this distribution with the one in Figure 2.11A on the previous page. Also compare the computations in each figure. The standard deviation is a measure of the degree to which individual scores differ from the central tendency of all the scores. In Step 1 the central tendency, the mean, is computed. In Steps 2 and 3 the difference between the mean and each individual score is computed and squared, so that positive and negative differences are both given positive weight in the measurement of variability. Finally, the average of these squared differences is computed and the square root is taken in order to bring the result back to the scale of the original scores.

Step 1			Step 2		Step 3
x	f	fx	(x-58)	(x-58)²	f(x-58)²
52	1	52	-6	36	36
54	1	54	-4	16	16
55	2	110	-3	9	18
56	7	392	-2	4	28
57	9	513	-1	1	9
58	10	580	0	0	0
59	9	531	1	1	9
60	6	360	2	4	24
61	3	183	3	9	27
62	1	62	4	16	16
63	1	63	5	25	25
	50	2900			208

Mean = 2900/50
= 58

Steps 4 and 5
Standard Deviation = $\sqrt{208/50}$ = $\sqrt{4.16}$ = 2.04

deviations of the mean, as shown in Figure 17.7. Thus, a psychologist who knows the mean and standard deviation for any set of measurements that forms a normal distribution can construct the exact shape of the bell-shaped curve that represents it.

Measures of central tendency and variability are used to describe a set of observations (such as test scores) for a single variable (the history quiz) or to compare two sets of observations on the same variable (the test scores of one history class compared to those of another). In order to determine the relationship between two variables (the heights of a team of football players and their test scores on a quiz), you would calculate the mathematical correlation between the two sets of scores.

Correlation Coefficients You recall that earlier in this chapter, correlational research was discussed. Psychologists who wish to assess the strength of a correlation (the degree of relatedness between measures of two things) make use of a statistical tool called the correlation coefficient. The number ranges from −1, which indicates a perfect negative correlation, through 0, which indicates no correlation, to +1, which indicates a perfect positive correlation. Thus, the closer a correlation coefficient is to +1 or −1, the stronger the relationship between the correlated events.

The formula for calculating correlation coefficients is rather complicated and need not be described here. It should be mentioned, however, that the formula does *not* yield percents; therefore it is incorrect to interpret a correlation coefficient of .70 as being twice as high as one of .35. Actually, a correlation coefficient of .70 indicates a relationship about twice as strong as does one of .50, and a correlation coefficient of .50 indicates a relationship about twenty-five times as strong as does one of .10. In most psychological studies, the correlations identified are relatively weak. For example, the correlation between the height of a parent and the height of his or her same-sex child is about .50; the correlation between IQ scores and school grades is

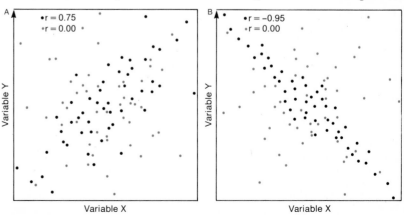

Figure 2.12 Data that are being examined for the existence of correlations are often plotted in the manner shown here. These "scatter plots" reveal visually the degree to which two variables are related. In both of these plots the set of lighter points shows a zero correlation. The darker-colored set of points in (A) represents a moderate positive correlation. The darker points in (B) represent a high negative correlation.

about .45; the correlation between physical punishment by a mother and physical aggression by her child is about .20.

Inferential Statistics

Descriptive statistics are important, but inferential statistics are even more so, for they provide a researcher with ground rules or conventions for determining what conclusion can be drawn from his data. Remember that the researcher begins his study with a hypothesis—a conjecture that, under certain circumstances, people (or animals) will behave in a certain way. He collects data about how a number of people do behave under those specific circumstances, —data that are in a form that can be treated statistically (scores, ratings, and so on). He then summarizes his data using descriptive statistics. Now he must make use of inferential statistics so that he can infer whether his original hypothesis was correct or incorrect. Were his experimental results due primarily to chance or do the data indeed seem to show a significant pattern or relationship? The nature of this problem is illustrated in Figure 2.13. The influence of chance on research results is studied with **probability theory.**

Probability Consider a man tossing a coin 100 times. If it lands heads up 53 times, is the coin biased? What if it lands heads up 79 times? Statisticians have worked out methods for determining the probability of obtaining any given result with any given number of tosses of an unbiased coin. More exactly, if the probability of heads is .50, there are tables to indicate how often in, say, 100 tosses one can expect to obtain 28, 53, 79, or any other number of heads from 0 to 100.

Probability is a complex area of mathematics; our intuitions about ''what the chances are'' are not always correct. For example, assume that a coin has been tossed ten times and that it has landed heads up each time. It is about to be tossed again. Reflect for a moment on what you would predict will occur on this next toss. There are three possible predictions: (1) another head will turn up; (2) a tail will turn up; or (3) the odds are still 50/50 (or .50), so it's impossible to tell. If you predicted that a tail would turn up, you committed a common error known as the ''gambler's fallacy.'' The reason it is a fallacy is that there is no reason to expect that the probability of a tail turning up is any higher than .50 at this point. Indeed, the judgment that has the most merit at this point is probably that another head will turn up, for it appears by this time that the coin you have been dealing with is, for some reason, a biased one.

Figure 2.13 The researcher makes an inference. (reading from left to right) Trekking across a landscape strewn with pyramids, the researcher recalls a similar observation he made previously in Figure 2.3 on page 23. He wonders whether he is about to come upon another huge head. He does not regard the preponderance of pyramids as sufficient evidence to reject this hypothesis. He is, however, mistaken: He should have rejected his hypothesis.

Figure 2.14 A frequency distribution of the outcomes of two hundred tosses of ten pennies at a time. Each tally represents the occurrence of a particular number of heads and tails among the ten pennies on one toss. (Note that if this distribution is looked at sideways, it has a "normal" shape. The most common outcome in this demonstration was five heads and five tails, but an eight-to-two ratio also occurred a number of times. Suppose you had tossed the coins just once and had obtained nine tails and one head. Would you have been justified in judging the coins to be biased?

The odds of getting a head on any given toss of an unbiased coin are 50/50; that is, a head will turn up half the time. To find the odds of getting two heads in a row, you multiply the odds for getting one event (one head) by the odds for getting the second (another head): $1/2 \times 1/2$ is $1/4$. For four heads in a row, the odds would be $1/16$ that such an event would occur by chance alone ($1/2 \times 1/2 \times 1/2 \times 1/2$). The probability that a coin will come up heads ten times in a row is $1/2$ raised to the tenth power, which is $1/1024$; that is, the odds against this event's occurring by chance with a fair coin are more than 1000 to 1, which is why you might begin to suspect in such a case that the coin is biased and that your coin tossing results are not a matter of chance. You can experiment with this yourself by making 200 tosses of ten pennies at a time. You will probably end up with a distribution like that shown in Figure 2.14 (whose shape, you can see, is that of a normal distribution). This is exactly the kind of logic used in inferential statistics. That is, when a psychologist conducts a study, what he wants to know is whether his results did or did not occur by chance. He wants to know how significant his results are.

Statistical Significance Suppose that an experimental group of rats has been given an injection of caffeine, the stimulant in coffee. On the average, these rats learn to run a maze in thirty trials. A control group of animals injected with a placebo (a substance that has no physiological effect), which is given to the control group to ensure that the two groups will not perform differently merely because one has received an injection and the other has not, learns to run the same maze in an average of thirty-eight trials. Is the difference between thirty and thirty-eight trials large enough for the experimenter to conclude that the caffeine increased the speed with which the experimental animals learned the maze, or might it have been obtained merely by chance?

Psychologists have adopted an arbitrary convention for making such decisions. If the odds against a given event's occurring by chance are 20 to 1 (that is, if the event could be expected to occur by chance only 5 percent of the time), then there is a significant likelihood that the results cannot be explained merely in terms of chance variation. If the odds against the event's occurring by chance are 100 to 1 (that is, if the event could be expected to occur by chance alone only 1 percent of the time), then something other than chance very probably accounts for the results.

To test his hypothesis that the caffeine injection enabled the experimental animals to learn faster, the experimenter could make use of an inferential statistic called the **t-test.** The t-test allows him to use the means and standard deviation to calculate the odds that the difference between the means of his experimental and control groups is due to chance alone. If the odds turn out to be 1 in 20, the researcher knows that he would obtain such a difference by chance only 5 percent of the time. He can therefore accept his hypothesis that caffeine increases speed of learning a maze at what psychologists call the **.05 level of significance.** If the odds are 1 in 100, he can accept the hypothesis at what is called the **.01 level of significance.** In this case the researcher knows that he has the chance of being wrong 1 in 100 times. In both cases, what the researcher has ascertained is that he can be reasonably confident his results have some real meaning. If the results (using the t-test or perhaps some other inferential statistic) do not reach the .05 level of significance, then by convention the experimenter assumes that his hypothesis was not accurate, because the odds are too great that his results could have occurred by chance.

SELECTED METHODOLOGICAL PROBLEMS

In describing the methods and statistical techniques that psychologists commonly use, we have made the process of conducting a research study sound considerably simpler and more straightforward than it actually is. To round

Setting:
A psychologist is seated at his desk. There is a knock on his office door.
 	
Psychologist:
Come in.
(A male student enters)
Sit down, please.
 	
I am going to read you a set of instructions. I am not permitted to say anything which is not in the instructions nor can I answer any questions about this experiment. OK? We are developing a test of...
	After the student has completed the experiment, he leaves.
	   There is another knock at the door.
	
	Psychologist:
	Come in.
	(A female student enters)
	Sit down, please.
	(The psychologist smiles)
	I am going to read you a set of instructions. I am not permitted to say anything which is not in the instructions nor can I answer any questions about this experiment. OK? We are developing a test of...
		The only difference between the two episodes is the smile!
		  Can a smile affect the results of an experiment?

out the picture, it is necessary to survey a few of the problems and pitfalls that can invalidate the findings of a psychological study unless they are coped with successfully.

Figure 2.15   This researcher will probably find that females are more sociable under the conditions of his experiment than males are. His finding will be correct in principle, but will he include his own smile in his account of the experimental conditions? He is probably unconscious of subtle variations in his own behavior and will mistakenly attribute the male-female differences he observes to some other factor. If his experimental hypothesis has to do with male-female differences, he may have made a self-fulfilling prophecy.

Self-fulfilling Prophecies

The term "self-fulfilling prophecies" refers to the fact that the expectations of an investigator can influence his findings; in psychology, as in other fields, people tend to find what they are looking for. If an investigator is conducting a study in which he interviews subjects face to face, for example, he can affect a subject's responses by unwittingly communicating positive or negative feelings, as by smiling when the subject's responses corroborate his theory and frowning when they contradict it.

In conducting a large research project, an experimenter often supervises the work of a team of research assistants and graduate students who do most of the direct work with the experimental subjects. In such a situation, the problem of self-fulfilling prophecies is particularly acute, because, with or without being aware of it, the assistants may feel under some pressure to obtain results that are in line with the expectations of the supervising psychologist. This phenomenon has been demonstrated by Robert Rosenthal, who supervised a study in which students of his were given the job of training rats to run a maze. Rosenthal told some of his student-experimenters that the rats they were working with had been specially bred for their maze-running ability; he told other students that their rats had been bred for dullness in running mazes. In point of fact, neither group of animals was maze-bright or maze-dull. All of them came from the same genetic stock.

As you can see from Figure 2.16, the results of the study clearly show that the rats fictitiously labeled "maze-bright" ran the maze much more quickly than did the animals labeled "maze-dull." The animals in the two groups behaved exactly as their trainers expected them to behave. Observations of the student-experimenters while they were working with the rats showed that there was no cheating in recording the animals' scores but that the students working with "maze-bright" rats tended to handle the animals more often and more gently than did students working with "maze-dull" rats. It may be that

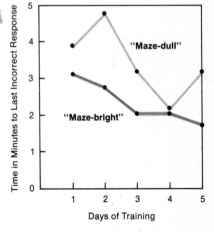

Figure 2.16   The results of an experiment by Rosenthal on self-fulfilling prophecies among student experimenters. Students trained rats in a simple maze for five days and recorded the time it took on each day for the rats to stop making incorrect choices. Some students, who had been told that their rats were from a strain bred specially to be "maze-bright," found that their rats learned more quickly than those of students who had been told that their rats were "maze-dull." In fact, all the rats were from the same genetic stock.

this subtle difference in handling was translated into a difference in the behavior of the two groups of animals.

In a similar study, Rosenthal told a group of elementary-school teachers that some of their pupils had made high scores on IQ tests and were sure to show unusual intellectual development during the school year. Actually, these pupils were no different from others not identified to the teachers as potential "bloomers." Later in the year, the teachers rated the "bloomers" as more interested, more curious, and happier than other students. And when all the children were given IQ tests at the end of the year, the "bloomers" showed a significantly greater gain in IQ than did the "nonbloomers." This effect was strong in the early grades—among first graders, the "bloomers" gained an average of 15 IQ points more than did the control "nonbloomers"—but the difference in IQ gains did not appear in the fifth and sixth grades. Presumably, the teachers of younger children were particularly susceptible to outside suggestions about the students' abilities because they had not yet had a chance to get to know them or about them.

One way for a researcher to avoid self-fulfilling prophecies is to employ a procedure called the **double-blind technique,** in which neither the experimenter nor his subjects know which subjects belong to the experimental group and which to the control group. (This procedure can be compared to the single-blind technique, in which the experimenter knows who is in which group but the subjects do not.) In an experiment testing the effects of a tranquilizing drug, for example, the experimental group would be given the tranquilizer and the control group would receive a placebo, perhaps in the form of a sugar pill, but only some outside party such as the pharmacist who supplied the pills would know which pill went to which group. The pharmacist would not give that information to the experimenter until after the effects of drug and placebo on the two groups of subjects had been recorded. In nonexperimental studies, a similar technique can be used. For example, a psychologist looking for a possible positive (or negative) correlation between IQ and psychological adjustment might assess psychological adjustment partly through interviews; it would be important that he not know his subjects' IQ scores until after he had interviewed them and recorded his conclusions concerning their adjustment.

Problems of Measurement

When a psychologist sets out to measure IQ, he knows that the way to do it is to use an IQ test. There are similarly standard ways to measure certain other psychological phenomena; for example, two ways to assess the maze-running ability of a rat are to see how much time it takes the rat to run the maze on successive trials and to see how many trials are needed before the rat can run the maze without error. In other cases, however, deciding how to measure the thing one is trying to measure can be a major methodological problem.

Do the Experimental and Control Conditions Really Differ? It occasionally happens that an experimenter inadvertently creates no meaningful differences between his experimental and control conditions. The independent variable that he thinks he is manipulating in fact remains the same for both groups. Needless to say, the results of such an experiment are likely to be inaccurate.

Here is a case in point. You have probably seen advertisements for devices that allow you to "learn while you sleep." Such a device might consist of a tape recorder, several tapes on which to record material you want to memorize, and a small loudspeaker to be placed under your pillow at night. The fantasies that can be built around sleep learning are limitless (especially for high school and college students). But can any of them be realized?

You might suppose that a study testing whether sleep learning actually occurs could be done by creating an experimental group in which sleeping subjects are presented with factual material to learn and a control group in which subjects who are awake are given the same material to listen to. By testing both groups after training, you could find out (1) whether the sleeping subjects learned anything at all, and (2) how effective sleep learning is compared to learning while awake. Some studies, done just this way, seemed to have established a definite learning effect in the sleeping subjects.

The problem is, how do you know for sure that the subjects in the experimental group were asleep? In some early sleep-learning studies, the experimenters merely looked at the subjects; if their eyes were closed, it was assumed that they were sleeping. But having one's eyes closed, even while drowsing, is not the same thing as being asleep.

Fortunately, as mentioned earlier, it is known that sleep and wakefulness can be assessed by taking EEG recordings of brain waves; in addition, instruments can be used to measure eye movements and muscle tension. The EEG reveals very accurately the state a person is in: awake, drowsy, sleeping lightly, sleeping deeply, or dreaming.

In a sleep-learning study using EEG recordings as the criteria of sleep, Charles Simon and William Emmons presented subjects with ninety-six questions and answers concerning unfamiliar but easily learned material. For example, one item was "Question: In what kind of store did Ulysses S. Grant work before the war? Answer: A hardware store." Simon and Emmons gave the questions and answers to groups of subjects in different states of sleep, drowsiness, and wakefulness, and then tested the subjects shortly after they awakened the next morning by asking the questions again. The results did not support the results of the earlier studies or the claims of the manufacturers of sleep-learning machines. If the subjects were asleep, as indicated by the EEG recordings, they did not learn. The subjects who did learn were either drowsy or awake, and the more awake they were, the more they learned. Thus, when the experimental and control conditions really differed, sleep learning was not shown to take place.

Is the Measure Sensitive Enough? A few years ago, Harriet Rheingold and Carol Eckerman reported a study that seemed to deny the existence of stranger anxiety in infants between six months and a year old—a phenomenon that most developmental psychologists, and most parents, had firmly believed in. Rheingold and Eckerman reported that infants in their study smiled at strangers and generally gave no overt indication of distress in their presence.

It now seems clear that their conclusions resulted from the use of a single, not-very-sensitive measure of infant distress. Rheingold and Eckerman measured how often the infants smiled at strangers, but they did not measure, for instance, how long it took each infant to smile; perhaps the infants smiled only after a period of wariness. Furthermore, recent studies (including one by Joseph Campos), which use several different measures, indicate that stranger anxiety does exist in nine-month-olds. The studies show, for one thing, that a nine-month-old's heart rate tends to speed up (indicating defensiveness) when he is approached by a stranger, whereas the heart rates of five-month-olds slow down (indicating interest). Second, when infants are given a choice, they show a strong preference to be away from strangers, even though they may not cry in the strangers' presence. Third, after a nine-month-old infant has been taught to press a lever in order to get a glimpse of his mother or a glimpse of a female stranger, he presses the lever more quickly when doing so lets him see his mother.

Another illustration of the problems involved in finding an accurate way to measure a psychological process is provided by the lie detector. Lie detectors, as described and shown in Chapter 15, measure three largely involuntary physiological responses: blood pressure, respiration, and the galvanic skin response (GSR). Some people believe that lie detectors reveal a pattern of physiological responses that occurs only when a person is lying, but this is not the case. Actually, lie detectors measure emotional arousal. Most people feel guilty, and therefore become emotionally aroused, when they lie. An occasional person, however, may commit a serious crime and feel no guilt at all. In addition, an innocent person who has been accused of a crime is likely to be frightened when asked questions relating to the crime; it takes a skilled interviewer to minimize this effect. Finally, there is the psychotic man, described by R. D. Laing in *The Divided Self,* who was asked during a lie-detector test whether he was Napoleon. The man said ''No,'' and the machine recorded that he was lying.

How Does One Measure States of Consciousness?

EEG recordings of the brain's electrical activity provide a direct, objective indication of whether a person is sleeping and, if so, how deeply, but similarly direct and objective ways of studying other states of consciousness have proved hard to find. Instead, psychologists have to rely on indirect measures and, sometimes, on extremely ingenious experimental designs.

Disturbance of consciousness appears to be part of many disorders treated by psychotherapists. Some hysterics, for instance, seem to be blind. They do not respond to changes in illumination; they bump into obstacles and otherwise give every indication that they are blind, even though neurological testing reveals no physiological basis for the blindness. Can these people see or not?

J. Zimmerman and Hanus Grosz designed a clever study to test a blind hysteric's claim that he could not see. They gave their subject a task that involved pressing one of three levers to get a reward. A triangle above one lever always signaled that it was the correct one to press in order to get the reward. Of course, if the subject were blind, the triangle would not influence his behavior. A blind person should press the correct lever only as often as would occur by chance. But the hysteric pressed the correct lever significantly *less* often than that. He must have been using the information provided by the triangle, but he used it as a signal *not* to press the lever. It was as if he were trying to be as blind as possible and in the process making himself too blind.

One of the claims made by the proponents of hypnosis is that hypnotized subjects can be made to experience no pain or to lose their sense of hearing, sight, and so on. Usually, these claims are assessed by examining behavior over which the hypnotized person has at least some voluntary control. For example, a hypnotist will put a person into a trance, suggest that he has lost his sense of hearing, and then sound a loud noise. When asked, the subject typically says that he heard nothing; moreover, he does not jump or flinch in response to the noise.

Even jumping in response to an unexpected, loud noise is subject to some voluntary control, however. J.P. Sutcliffe therefore devised a different test of hypnotically induced deafness. Earlier research had shown that if a person hears a playback of his own voice approximately a fifth of a second after he has spoken (a procedure called delayed auditory feedback), his speech is disrupted. If a person is deaf, delayed auditory feedback should have no effect. Sutcliffe's subjects were deeply hypnotized, told that they were now deaf, and then given a delayed auditory feedback test. Their performance deteriorated. Thus, even though the subjects reported not being able to hear, the feedback task showed that they could. (Chapter 13 describes an ingenious study done by Frank Pattie to test the claim of a hypnotized woman that she was blind in one eye; the test he used appears as Figure 13.13.)

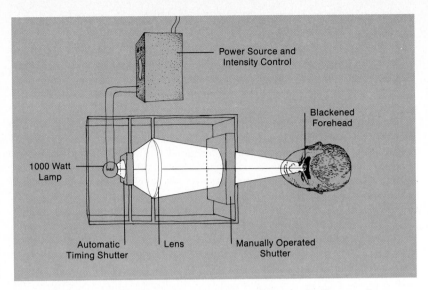

Figure 2.17 A technique for the measurement of pain stimulation. A beam of radiation from a heat lamp is directed by a lens through an automatic shutter onto the subject's forehead, which has been blackened with India ink to provide a uniformly absorbent skin surface. The shutter is used to control the duration of the stimulus; the intensity of the stimulus is controlled by the amount of current passed through the filament of the lamp. When women in labor were asked to adjust the intensity of such a heat stimulus until it matched the amount of pain they felt from the labor, Handy and Javerts found that women trained in natural childbirth were experiencing the same amount of pain as other women, although they claimed verbally that they were not. If they had truly been experiencing less pain, they would have adjusted the heat stimulus to a lower level than did the other women. (After Wolff and Wolf, 1948.)

Researching pain perception presents problems similar to those encountered in designing studies to research hysterical symptoms and hypnotic states. Whether given drug anesthesia, hypnosis, placebos, or acupuncture, many subjects report a substantial reduction of pain. Yet such verbal reports alone are not sufficient to indicate that a person does not experience pain. A striking example of the difference between the verbal reports of people undergoing a painful experience and other kinds of measures is offered in a study by Carl T. Javert and James D. Handy. These researchers tested two groups of pregnant women for pain sensitivity while the women were in labor and about to deliver their babies. One group had been trained in a natural-childbirth technique and, when asked how much pain they felt, tended to minimize their sensations. The second group had not been so trained, and reported considerable pain. The psychologists then asked the women to adjust the intensity of a point of light focused on their skin so as to indicate the amount of pain they were experiencing at the moment. Surprisingly, both groups of women set the lights to the same intensity. Evidently both groups underwent the same amount of pain, even though the group trained in natural-childbirth techniques reported less pain.

These studies have been described to illustrate a few of the more interesting ways psychologists have found to assess subjective states, not to convince you that hysterical symptoms, hypnotic phenomena, and pain reduction through natural-childbirth techniques are "unreal." Reaching a decision on the question of their "reality" is very difficult, because there is a good deal of apparently reliable evidence on both sides. It may be that some sort of compromise reflects the actual state of affairs—that a person experiencing hypnotic deafness, though in some sense able to hear, does not hear consciously, or that a woman using natural-childbirth techniques, though aware of a fairly high level of pain, does not experience the pain as intensely as a woman who is not using the techniques.

REPLICATION

During the course of their training, psychologists are taught to anticipate and avoid methodological errors, for example, by using the double-blind technique when there is a danger that a self-fulfilling prophecy may affect their findings. Despite all an investigator's training and efforts, however, errors sometimes do occur. The need to bring such errors to light is one reason for the requirement that the findings of a scientific study be **replicated**—that is, duplicated by at least one other psychologist at a different laboratory—before they are fully accepted by the profession.

Sometimes, a second psychologist attempts to reproduce all the conditions of the original study. At other times, the second investigator modifies some condition of the original study, for instance, by using adults from the general population as subjects instead of using college students, in order to assess the generality of the first psychologist's findings. When the results of either type of replication study do not agree with those of the original study, psychologists go back and try to figure out why. The Salk and Brackbill studies of stimuli that soothe newborn babies, described in Chapter 1, and the sleep-learning studies described in this chapter are good illustrations of the increased accuracy and understanding that can result from this replication process.

In other words, replication is not only a way to find out that the results of a study are accurate; it is also a way to find out that something is wrong. Often, it allows psychologists to pinpoint what that something is and, in further research, to correct the error. Sometimes, however, replication does not go quite as it is supposed to.

In the mid-1960s, Neal Miller and Leo DiCara astounded the medical and psychological worlds with reports of a series of studies indicating that rats could be trained to control such behaviors as heart rate, blood pressure, urine formation, and intestinal contractions—functions controlled by the autonomic nervous system and heretofore believed to be involuntary. In most of their studies, Miller and DiCara waited for a rat to show a spontaneous change in the response being studied (a spontaneous rise in heart rate, for example); then they administered a powerful reward, in the form of electrical stimulation of the so-called pleasure center in the brain. In their other studies, the rats had to make the proper physiological response in order to avoid a shock rather than in order to receive a reward. To make sure that the rats did not learn to control their responses merely by tightening or relaxing their muscles (which would change their heart rates), during training Miller and DiCara gave the animals a drug called curare that paralyzes muscles. (The dose of curare required was, in fact, so large that the animals needed artificial respiration until the effects of the drug wore off.)

Using these techniques, Miller and DiCara obtained very large changes in heart rate and blood pressure; their rats could increase or decrease their heart

Figure 2.18 With one of the most sophisticated procedures ever used in experimental psychology, Miller and DiCara attempted to demonstrate that rats can be trained to control such autonomic functions as their own heart rates. To eliminate the possibility that a rat might use its skeletal musculature to produce the effect, the experimenters paralyzed each of the rats with the drug curare. Because this precaution made it impossible to train the rats with conventional rewards like food, electrical stimulation of "pleasure centers" in the brain was used instead. (left) In a brain operation, the anesthetized rat was held in a measuring device that made possible the accurate placement of an electrode in its brain. (right) During the training session, the paralyzed rat had to be mechanically respirated. Whenever its heart rate rose, pleasurable stimulation was delivered to its brain. Miller and DiCara reported that under these remarkable conditions the rat did learn to increase its heart rate, but they have been unable to reproduce this result in subsequent experiments.

(After Leo DiCara, "Learning in the Autonomic Nervous System." © 1970 by Scientific American, Inc. All rights reserved.)

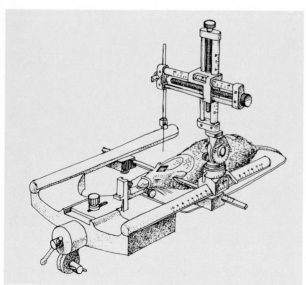
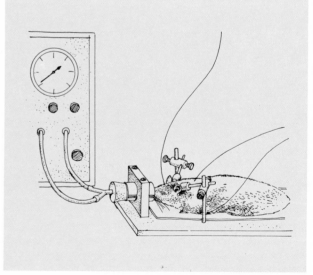

rates by as much as 20 percent. The investigators eventually obtained such fine control over their subjects' physiological responses that they could induce a rat to blush in one ear and not in the other.

Psychologists began to revise the centuries-old belief that it is impossible for an animal to control functions of its autonomic nervous system. Articles appeared speculating on the possibility that human beings could learn to control such autonomic functions as blood pressure—a possibility with tremendous medical implications. Miller and DiCara's findings also led skeptics to reexamine their disbelief in the control of autonomic functions apparently demonstrated by Eastern mystics and others.

Other laboratories, however, had difficulty replicating Miller and DiCara's findings. Miller has recently stated that he, too, is having trouble; his data show a progressive decline in the size of learned heart rate changes, from 20 percent in 1966 to 3 percent in 1970.

Why should the results of studies carried out in 1966 not replicate in 1970? Miller would love to have the answer to that question. He has conducted numerous studies in an attempt to identify changes in his laboratory that might account for the decline in learning shown by his rats. He has tested different breeds of rats, changed the formula for the curare used to paralyze the animals, tried numerous settings on the artificial respirator to see if that affected his results. When none of these efforts succeeded, Miller recalled that at the time of his original studies there was an epidemic of bedbugs in a nearby laboratory, which necessitated the spraying of his own lab. When even respraying the lab with insecticide did not restore his findings, Miller said—half in jest and half in desperation—that he was considering reinfesting the laboratory with bedbugs.

Miller is a very well-known and highly respected psychologist working within an experimental tradition that insists on strict laboratory controls; in addition, he ran not just one study but an extensive series. It is doubtful that any psychologist, when he read about Miller's original findings, would have predicted such a dramatic and inexplicable failure to replicate. Indeed, it is still possible that someone, somewhere, sometime will succeed in doing again what Miller and DiCara did the first time. Until they do, however, the voluntary control of involuntary functions must be regarded as no more than a dim possibility.

METHODOLOGY AND THE STUDY OF PSYCHOLOGY

This chapter's presentation of the basic methods psychologists use is meant to be more than a body of knowledge to learn. It is a tool for you to use, just as the methods discussed are psychologists' tools. You can apply what you have read here to reports in newspapers and magazines of results that seem to be dramatic and are therefore deemed newsworthy. Was the study properly set up? If there was an experimental group, was there also a control group? Could the experimenter have affected his outcome by somehow influencing his subjects, or did he use a double-blind technique? What statistical method did the experimenter use in order to decide that his results were significant?

Few experiments in newspapers or magazines are described in such detail. In fact, few experiments in this textbook are discussed in such detail. Space limitations in this text simply do not permit us to cover the discipline broadly and to discuss in depth the methods of each study cited. Still, all psychological experiments are reported in such detail in professional journals or books. This text contains a complete bibliography for each chapter, which shows where each study was published. If you doubt a certain study's findings, or if you are curious, you can read the detailed study in its original publication (or in a book of readings). And you can apply what you have read here to judging the study's findings and their significance.

SUMMARY

1. The procedure used in all psychological studies first involves **gathering data**—by one or more methods—and then **analyzing the data**—often by means of statistical techniques.

2. Data can be gathered through a number of different methods. The method a psychologist chooses will depend on his area of research and on the nature of the question his study is meant to answer. Usually, the researcher will collect only a **sample** of all the data pertaining to his hypothesis.

    a. **Case studies** are intensive investigations and reports on individuals. They provide descriptive information about the persons studied and allow for deep and detailed analysis of the particular area of interest being studied. For example, Freud's case studies enabled him to develop his elaborate personality theory. Case studies, however, cannot *prove* that any general statement about behavior is true or false.

    b. In **naturalistic observation,** the investigator watches and records the behavior of interest without intruding on the activities in question.

    c. **Surveys** are generally used when psychologists wish to gather information from a large number of people. Surveys may be written— people complete questionnaires—or oral—they answer questions in a face-to-face interview with the psychologist. Social psychologists often use surveys to assess the attitudes and beliefs of large groups of people. Psychologists who use surveys must make sure that the sample of people they choose to interview fairly represents the group they wish to study. Otherwise, their results may be **biased.**

    d. With **cross-cultural comparisons,** psychologists compare some attitudes or type of behavior of persons in one culture with attitudes on the same matter or type of behavior of persons in another culture.

    e. **Longitudinal studies** examine the behavior of the same persons over a period of years to determine what and how changes occur over time. Developmental psychologists often use this method.

3. The method of gathering data that many psychologists prefer to use (when it is possible) is the **experiment;** these psychologists consider the experimental method to produce more definitive and scientific results than is possible with other methods. The drawback to experiments is that the kind of control possible in a laboratory often is not possible in real life, so that results may not be generalizable, or applicable, to everyday situations. The components of experiments are:

    a. an **experimental subject** or **experimental group,** the person or persons whose behavior is to be studied.

    b. an **independent variable,** the factor that the experimenter deliberately manipulates.

    c. one or more **dependent variables,** the behavior that the experimenter expects will be affected by his manipulation of the independent variable.

    d. a **control group,** a group of subjects who have the same characteristics as the experimental subjects except that the independent variable is not applied to them.

Figure 2.19 Alfred Kinsey's courageous pioneer work provided the first information about human sexual beliefs and practices that was based on a large representative sample and was gathered with techniques that ensured its accuracy. Kinsey founded the Institute for Sex Research at Indiana University, and that institute continues to compile and publish information about human sexual behavior. Kinsey's work played an important role in stimulating other research, such as that of Masters and Johnson, and in breaking up traditional social constraints on the discussion of this subject.

4. In the experimental method, psychologists expect to find that one thing **causes** another to happen: a **cause-effect relationship.** Other methods allow researchers to say only that there is an association, or **correlation,** between things. A correlation indicates the degree of relatedness between two things.

Figure 2.20   Neal Miller is one of America's most prolific and original psychological researchers. His work, discussed in several places throughout this book, ranges over many areas in psychology: for example, personality theory; the experimental analysis of conflict; the physiology of hunger and thirst; and the brain mechanisms underlying motivation, reward, and punishment.

   a. A high positive correlation between A and B indicates that a high score or frequent occurrence of A is usually accompanied by a high score or frequent occurrence of B. A perfect positive correlation is indicated by the **correlation coefficient** $+1$.

   b. A high negative correlation between A and B indicates that a high score or frequent occurrence of A is usually accompanied by a low score or infrequent occurrence of B. A perfect negative correlation is indicated by the correlation coefficient -1.

   c. The degrees of correlation, then, range between the correlation coefficients of $+1$ and -1; for example, .70 indicates a relatively high positive correlation; $-.70$, a relatively high negative one. A correlation coefficient of .70 indicates a relationship about twice as strong as does one of .50; and one of .50 indicates a relationship about twenty-five times as strong as does one of .10.

5. Some measures often used to assess individual behavior or attitudes are **tests,** such as IQ or personality tests; **psychophysiological measures,** such as the electroencephalograph (EEG), which measures the electrical activity of the brain; and **ratings,** subjective impressions ranked according to intensity or some other criterion.

6. After a psychologist has gathered his data, he must often use statistics to find out what conclusions he can safely draw from those data. There are two main kinds of statistics psychologists use: descriptive and inferential.

7. **Descriptive statistics** are used to summarize data and make them understandable.

   a. When a psychologist looks at a group of scores and sees what the highest and the lowest are, he can express the range of scores. For example, on a test whose highest possible score is 100, if the highest score obtained was 83 and the lowest 28, the range was 55 ($83 - 28 = 55$).

   b. Knowing the range, a psychologist can plot a **frequency distribution** of the scores—see Figure 2.10. Most scores fall into a **normal** distribution, which has most scores around the middle and very few at the extreme ends of the possible scores; the curve drawn to reflect a normal distribution is often called a ''bell curve,'' because its shape resembles that of a bell.

   c. A psychologist can then calculate a **measure of central tendency,** which can be one of the following: (1) the **mean,** for which he simply adds up all the scores and divides by the number who took the test; or (2) the **median,** which is the score that falls exactly in the middle of the distribution. For example, in the scores 80, 80, 64, 63, 62, 61, 40, 32, 20, the median is 62, because four scores are higher and four are lower. Or (3) the **mode,** which is the score made most frequently in any distribution. For the preceding list of scores, 80 is the mode. The psychologist must decide which measure of central tendency to use on the basis of the kind of distribution the scores have.

   d. **Measures of variability** show how closely clustered or widely spread out a researcher's distribution of scores is. Variability is usually expressed by the **standard deviation,** a number that indicates to what extent figures in a given group of data vary from the mean.

8. **Inferential statistics** allow a researcher to infer whether the hypothesis on which he based his study was correct or incorrect—that is, with what degree of certainty he can draw a conclusion from the data gathered.

   a. The influence of chance on research results is studied by means of **probability theory,** a complex area of mathematics. What a researcher wants to know when he uses these techniques is how sure he can be that his experimental results were not a matter of chance.

   b. Psychologists have adopted an arbitrary statistical convention that permits them to decide how significant their results are. They may use an inferential statistic called the **t-test.** If the odds against a given event occurring are 20 to 1, that is, if the event could be expected to occur by chance only 5 percent of the time, the researcher can assume, with few reservations, that his results are not a matter of chance. His hypothesis can be accepted at the **.05 level of significance.** If the odds against its occurring by chance are 100 to 1, he can assume, with almost no reservations, that his results are not due to chance. His hypothesis can be accepted at the **.01 level of significance.**

9. Psychological research is subject to several methodological difficulties.

   a. A researcher conducting an experiment or a survey can unwittingly affect the results he obtains by very subtly conveying to subjects his bias—often by nothing more than a slight smile or a hand gesture. This phenomenon is known as the **self-fulfilling prophecy.** It can be avoided if the research is conducted using a **double-blind technique,** in which neither the experimenter nor his subjects know which subjects belong to the experimental group and which belong to the control group.

   b. Finding accurate ways to measure what he wants to measure is often a problem for the research psychologist. Sometimes, by mistake, the way he sets up the research problem produces no *meaningful* difference between the experimental and the control conditions. Sometimes, the measure under study is not sensitive enough and is therefore inaccurate.

10. One difficult problem in psychological research has been the measurement of subjective states, or states of consciousness. Several ingenious methods have been devised to do this, however. One is the electroencephalographic (EEG) recording of the brain's activity during sleep. Other methods test the hypnotic state and experience of pain.

11. To assure that one study's findings are significant and accurate, that study should be **replicable** by at least one psychologist other than the original researcher. Attempts at replication sometimes uncover methodological errors.

SUGGESTED READINGS

Bronfenbrenner, Urie. "The Structure and Verification of Hypotheses," in Urie Bronfenbrenner (ed.), *Influences on Human Development*. Hinsdale, Ill.: Dryden Press, 1972. One of the few extremely clear and readable descriptions of the logic of inference in psychology.

Downie, Norville, and R. W. Heath. *Basic Statistical Methods*. 2nd ed. New York: Harper & Row, 1965. An excellent, easy-to-read introduction to statistical methods in the social sciences.

Eysenck, Hans J., W. Arnold, and Richard Meili (eds.). *Encyclopedia of Psychology*. New York: Herder and Herder, 1972. 3 volumes. An alphabetical listing of definitions and articles covering important psychological terms and concepts, written by psychologists from all over the world.

Hays, William L. *Statistics for Psychologists*. New York: Holt, Rinehart and Winston, 1963. A more advanced treatment of statistical methods and probability theory for the social scientist.

Kerlinger, Fred. *Foundations of Behavioral Research*. New York: Holt, Rinehart and Winston, 1964. A very thorough coverage of many facets of behavioral research and fallacies to be avoided.

Marx, Melvin H., and William A. Hillix. *Systems and Theories in Psychology*. 2nd ed. New York: McGraw-Hill, 1973. A historically oriented discussion of major psychological systems and theories, comprehensive but primarily experimental in emphasis.

Rosenthal, Robert. "Experimenter Outcome-Orientation and the Results of the Psychological Experiment," *Psychological Bulletin*, 61 (1964), 405–412. A summary of experimenter-bias effects.

Scott, William, and Michael Wertheimer. *Introduction to Psychological Research*. New York: Wiley, 1962. A broad overview of many of the research strategies used in psychology.

Sidman, Murray. *Tactics of Scientific Research*. New York: Basic Books, 1960. A classic introduction to the strategy and rationale of research with individual organisms and its advantages over group research.

Turner, Merle B. *Philosophy and the Science of Behavior*. New York: Appleton-Century-Crofts, 1967. This prize-winning book is a fascinating discussion of psychological method and theory and their philosophical underpinnings.

Wolman, Benjamin B. (ed.). *Handbook of General Psychology*. Englewood Cliffs, N.J.: Prentice-Hall, 1973. A collection of forty-five articles that reveals both the diversity of psychologists' interests and the unifying nature of psychology's philosophical and methodological foundations.

UNIT II
Learning and Problem Solving

Many psychologists have considered learning to be the most important topic in psychology. Even something as biologically basic as adult sexual behavior does not develop normally in monkeys and people without certain kinds of learning experiences. All aspects of human culture depend on the capacity to learn.

Different generations of psychologists have had different conceptions of learning, however. Thirty years ago the most widely accepted approach to learning was behaviorism, and laboratory animals were the most

3 Species-Specific Behavior: Ethology

provides an important sense of perspective for beginning the study of psychology: It views people as members of the biological species *Homo sapiens*. It looks at behavior in terms of Darwin's theory of evolution and examines how the behavior of members of a species is determined by the particular characteristics of the species.

See related chapters: 7, 9, 12, 14, 21, 25

4 Conditioning and Learning: Behaviorism

presents the behaviorist view of learning, which is the cornerstone of behaviorist theory. Behaviorism, one of the most influential approaches in American psychology, sees behavior as controlled by external events, especially reinforcement and punishment, which lead to the conditioning of responses to specific stimuli.

See related chapters: 10, 14, 19, 20, 21, 25, 27

RELATED CHAPTERS

7
Heredity and Environment continues the discussion, begun in Chapter 3, of the relative influences of hereditary and environmental factors on behavior.

8
Development of Intelligence: Piaget's Theory explains in detail one of the most influential theories in cognitive psychology and thus elaborates on the brief discussion of Piaget's theory in Chapter 6.

9
Language Development pursues the discussion of communication that is begun in Chapter 3 with the description of honeybees' use of "dances" to communicate.

10
Social Development: The Case of Morality offers several views of how people develop into social beings. One explanation uses the behaviorist principles of learning described in Chapter 4; another reflects Chapter 6's cognitive approach to learning and development.

11
Perception: Principles and Processes explains how the information-processing approach, described in Chapter 5, has been applied to several problems in perception. One of the information-processing models that it examines is analysis by synthesis, which is also discussed in Chapter 6.

12
Sensation and the Senses describes the sensory world of human beings and so continues the discussion of sensory input and the use of sensory information begun in Chapters 3 and 5.

14
Physiology, Drives, and Emotion describes some of the biological bases of behavior in people and so extends the biological orientation to human behavior introduced in Chapter 3. It also discusses the concept of drive and its relation to one of the key behaviorist notions presented in Chapter 4, reinforcement. And it uses some of the concepts of information processing, described in Chapter 5, to explain how the nervous system functions.

common subjects of research on learning. More recently, this emphasis has begun to shift. Animal researchers are more aware of the importance of an animal's natural environment in determining its characteristic behavior. Investigators of human learning are more aware of the complexity of the thought processes involved in many forms of learning. One reason for the changing emphasis is the invention of the computer, which provides a new model for how people store information, think, learn, and solve problems. Indeed, because it emphasizes the importance of cognition, problem solving has begun to assume a central position in psychology: Several major approaches even treat learning as a special case of problem solving. In order to reflect the diversity of approaches to learning in psychology today, this unit will present four of the most important viewpoints, each of which extends far beyond the analysis of learning and recurs throughout the rest of the book.

5 Thinking and Memory: Information Processing

describes the new information- processing approach to human behavior. Human functioning is analyzed into input, which deals with the selection of information to be processed; processing, how information is organized and transformed for memory storage and output; and output, how behavior influences and is influenced by input and processing.

See related chapters: 11, 12, 14

6 Thinking and Problem Solving: Cognitive Psychology

discusses the classical cognitive approach to psychology and describes how it has recently been influenced by information processing. The cognitive approach emphasizes the importance of problem solving in everyday life and attempts to describe the general organization of all human behavior.

See related chapters: 8, 10, 11, 16, 20, 21, 25

16

Motivation and Action concludes its discussion of motivation by suggesting that research in motivation is moving toward a cognitive approach, similar to that presented in Chapter 6. Several concepts from cognitive psychology are used to explain motivational phenomena.

19

Alternative Conceptions of Personality presents several approaches to personality, including the behaviorist approach, which is based on the principles of learning outlined in Chapter 4.

20

Person Perception and Interpersonal Attraction discusses some of the cognitive principles underlying people's perceptions of other people and at the same time describes ways that people's choices of friends and lovers are influenced by rewards. In this way, the chapter uses both the cognitive approach of Chapter 6 and the behaviorist approach of Chapter 4.

21

Patterns of Social Behavior: The Case of Sex Roles presents several possible explanations of how social roles are acquired, including the biological approach of Chapter 3, the behaviorist approach of Chapter 4, and the cognitive approach of Chapter 6.

25

Bases of Disorder reviews a number of concepts that may help explain how mental disorder arises, including biological concepts like heredity, discussed in Chapter 3; behaviorist concepts, presented in Chapter 4; and cognitive concepts, like those examined in Chapter 6.

27

Behavior Therapy and Behavior Modification discusses at length the therapies and tools for behavior change that have been developed from the behaviorist learning principles described in Chapter 4.

I have written a number of stories about robots: complex, artificial, manlike structures, with a "brain" sufficiently developed to allow them to speak, understand, and perform human functions in a human way. I supplied them with the *three laws of robotics,* which totally governed their behavior. My robots were machines designed to do useful work and would naturally have built-in safety factors, and the three laws were those safety factors. The robots, but not humans, had to obey the three laws:

1. A robot may not injure a human being or, through inaction, allow a human being to come to harm.
2. A robot must obey the orders given it by human beings except where such orders would conflict with the First Law.
3. A robot must protect its own existence as long as such protection does not conflict with the First or Second Law.

I had supplied my robots, you see, with a set of *instincts* firmly imprinted on their "brains" at the moment of manufacture.

In one of my stories, a robot was constructed that could somehow read minds. The designers could not imagine how that could have been possible, and the robot was retained in the factory for study. Those who worked with it could not resist asking what was in the minds of other men or women, in connection with whatever it was that excited the desires or ambitions of the questioner.

Since the robot could not injure a human being, it would tell the questioner not the truth, where that would cause grief or disappointment (which its telepathic powers would allow it to detect), but the kind of lie that would cause relief or joy. Naturally, with each person acting confidently under mistaken beliefs, there was soon wild confusion.

Finally, there was a bitter argument between two of the men, based on the false information each had been fed by the telepathic robot. They confronted the robot and demanded resolution. The robot faced a situation where it had to say something (call it A) which would injure the self-love of at least one of the questioners. The strongest instinct it possessed, the First Law, could not allow it to injure human beings either by doing something (saying A) or through inaction (not saying A).

So it collapsed—burnt-out, useless, dead.

Instincts that work well under some conditions are deadly under others. The light-hunting instinct of the moth, when natural sunlight is not involved, will carry it into an open candle flame and kill it. The harm-avoidance instinct of the robot, when subtle psychological factors are involved, will present it with an insoluble dilemma and kill it.

Isaac Asimov

3

Species-Specific Behavior: Ethology

**HEREDITY AND
SPECIES-SPECIFIC BEHAVIOR**
Instinct Versus Intelligence
Heredity Versus Environment

SYSTEMS OF RESPONDING
Human Facial Expressions
Displacement Activities
**Neural Stimulation
of Fixed Action Patterns**
Motivation and Drive

SYSTEMS OF SENSORY INPUT
Sign Stimuli
Habituation

COMPLEX SYSTEMS OF BEHAVIOR
Migration
The Dancing of Honeybees
**The Development
of Behavioral Systems**

Imprinting
Bird Songs
Human Language

After the great biologist Charles Darwin published his theory of evolution in *On the Origin of the Species* in 1859, people's conception of themselves underwent a fundamental change. No longer was a human a unique creature, completely different from animals; instead, he was part of the animal kingdom—a species that had evolved by natural selection in the same way that all other animal species had evolved. To be sure, humans were unique in some ways, but at the same time they were similar in many ways to other species, especially apes and other primates. By placing humans firmly within the animal kingdom, Darwin laid the foundation for the field of psychology. In fact, publication of *On the Origin of the Species* is regarded by some people as marking the beginning of psychology as a legitimate field.

Although all of psychology has been influenced by Darwin's theory, one approach can be singled out as the most direct descendant of Darwin's work: **ethology,** the study of human and animal behavior from a biological point of view. Just as evolutionary biologists try to describe and understand the physical characteristics of each animal species, so ethologists try to describe and understand the behavioral characteristics of each species. That is, the subject matter of ethology is **species-specific behavior.**

In *The Expression of the Emotions in Man and Animals* Darwin assumed that many behavior patterns of an animal are as characteristic of its species as the shape of its body. With this assumption he essentially founded ethology; ethological research to the present day has generally confirmed his assumption. Even many human behavior patterns, such as smiling and speaking, are species-specific.

Although more than a century has passed since the publication of Darwin's work, modern ethologists are still highly indebted to Darwin. Like him, they see species-specific behaviors as an **adaptation** by an animal to its environment—that is, they view

Figure 3.1 Chimpanzees embracing. People's tendency to respond to these animals as though they were human beings suggests that there are resemblances among the behaviors characteristic of the higher primates—chimpanzees, gorillas, baboons, and humans. Ethologists contend that behavior, like anatomy, is the product of evolution and that resemblances among the behaviors of closely related species are to be expected and are worthy of study.

those behaviors as the product of evolution. One of the first questions ethologists ask about a behavior is, what is its adaptive importance for the animal? In other words, what role does the behavior play in the animal's way of life? To answer this question, the first phase in most ethological studies must be detailed observations of a particular species under natural conditions, usually in the wild. The well-known ethologist Jane Van Lawick-Goodall, for example, has carried out extensive field studies of three different species in Africa: chimpanzees, baboons, and wild dogs. Field observations provide the ethologist with a record of the behavior patterns an animal normally displays in its natural environment. Only after this record is fairly complete does he begin to analyze the role of the behavior in the animal's way of life.

One step in the analysis of a species-specific behavior pattern is to identify its components. What actions make up a behavior? What stimuli must be present for the behavior to occur? But ethologists do more than identify the components of behavior patterns, for they see each behavior as belonging to an **ongoing behavior system** that has an important role in the animal's overall way of life. Because the behavior is part of a system, the relation between specific stimuli and specific responses is complex. At different times the same stimulus may evoke very different responses; also, different stimuli may produce the same response. That is, changes in the environment alone do not fully account for behavior. Events occurring within the organism must be taken into account, as well as the relation of changes in environment to the animal's way of life.

Ethologists think of an organism as an ongoing system composed of many behavioral subsystems. The overall system (the animal) can produce many different outputs (systems of responding) to many different inputs (systems of stimulation or sensory input). But because the organism is an ongoing system, a complete description of it must deal with more than just inputs and outputs. The organization of more complex behavior systems that cannot be analyzed primarily in terms of either input or output also needs description. This chapter discusses all three kinds of systems—systems of responding, systems of sensory input, and complex behavioral systems—after considering another basic tenet of ethology: that heredity plays an important part in behavior.

HEREDITY AND SPECIES-SPECIFIC BEHAVIOR

Because ethology is a direct descendant of Darwin's evolutionary theory, much ethological research has been devoted to the study of hereditary influences on behavior. In early ethological writings, the concept of instinct received much attention. Ethologists were impressed by the fact that certain behaviors are characteristic of (specific to) a given species and, furthermore, that many of these species-specific behaviors are *not learned* in any direct sense. John Fentress reports that a young wolf will howl in a characteristic way, as shown in Figure 3.2, even if it has not had a chance to see other wolves do so. Konrad Lorenz, who in 1973 won a Nobel Prize with fellow ethologists Niko Tinbergen and Karl von Frisch, has pointed out that a striking amount of species-specific behavior occurs even under very unfavorable environmental and developmental conditions. Many species-specific behaviors seem to be part of complex sequences of behavior, and they appear to originate largely within the organism. They contrast with simple reflexes like the eye blink and the knee jerk, which are apparently automatic responses evoked by outside stimuli. The concept of instinct is an attempt to account for these complex sequences that originate within the animal.

Instinct Versus Intelligence

Instinct refers to the idea that complex sequences of behavior are inherited, but its definition and even its existence have been the center of controversy for

Figure 3.2 A young wolf raised by humans will howl like an adult in the wild even though it has never heard the cries of other wolves. Behavior that appears to be independent of learning, as this howling does, is called species-specific behavior.

years. In common parlance, instinct is often contrasted with intelligence, the ability to learn and solve problems. Human beings act intelligently, whereas animals, particularly organisms near the bottom of the evolutionary scale, are thought of as instinctive automatons. People also use the word "instinctive" to describe automatic behavior that human beings develop through long practice. A professional baseball player "instinctively" makes the right play, for example, and an experienced driver "instinctively" steps on the brakes if a child darts into his path. These behaviors are contrasted with intelligence because they are automatic; yet these behaviors actually all involve a large degree of learning.

On the other hand, few people interpret the phrase "maternal instinct" as meaning that human mothers engage in purely automatic behavior. Instead, it indicates that love of children is a basic tendency common to most human mothers. In this case, too, most people would not rule out the contribution of learning.

Learning plays an important role in some "instinctive" behaviors of animals as well. For example, Niko Tinbergen has observed that the hunting wasp digs a nest, flies once or twice around the nest site, and then heads off in search of food, as shown in Figure 3.3. The wasp can find its way back flawlessly, something that many people would not be able to do. It obviously learns landmarks extremely rapidly—and rapid learning is something we tend to think of as indicating intelligence. If the landmarks are moved a little, however, the wasp becomes hopelessly disoriented, even though the nest is in clear sight. Here is an instance of a behavior pattern that clearly depends on learning but that, once learned, is extremely inflexible.

The intelligence of the animals in a species, as indicated by their ability to learn and solve problems, can be treated as a species-specific behavior. As a general though not perfect rule, the further one moves up the evolutionary scale, the more approaches a species can take to a given problem—that is, the more flexible its behavior is. D. O. Hebb described a series of experiments in which a simple discrimination between a circle and a triangle (Figure 3.4) was taught to rats, chimpanzees, and two-year-old human children. In the different species the ability to generalize the concept of the triangle to new tasks varied greatly. When the triangle was rotated, the rat had to relearn the problem, whereas the chimp and the child generalized from the previous solution. In a more difficult test, a triangle made of circles had to be identified as different from a circle. The chimp failed to discriminate between these two figures, but the child did so easily. Apparently, the chimp could not abstract the overall triangular form from the group of circles that composed it. Again, flexibility of behavior and the ability to reorganize features of the environment appear to be roughly correlated with position on the evolutionary scale.

The intelligence of a species is difficult to define with precision, for one's conclusions depend on which aptitudes and possible behaviors are examined.

Figure 3.3 The hunting wasp's ability to find its way back to its nest is an example of a behavior that depends both on learning and "instinct."

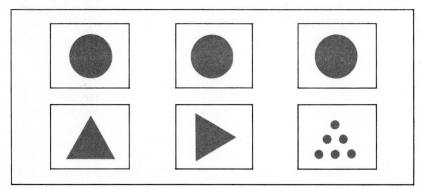

Figure 3.4 Rats, chimpanzees, and two-year-old humans can all learn to pick one of the stimuli in the pair on the left and ignore the other. With the middle pair, rats have to learn the discrimination all over again, but chimps and two-year-olds do not. Chimps, however, fail to generalize their learning to the pair on the right, whereas children easily see the group of circles as a triangular shape. (After Hebb, 1949.)

Figure 3.5 Some of the difficulties in making general statements about the relative intelligence of different species are illustrated in this photograph of John Fentress training a wolf cub to shake hands. Pawing motions are natural to this species, but sitting motions are unusual. If the wolf's ability to learn to shake hands were the measure of intelligence, the wolf would appear to be a clever animal; if its ability to sit were the measure, it would seem stupid. Both conclusions are equally invalid.

For example, Fentress found that it was very easy to train a young timber wolf to shake hands (three trials), but it took many hours to teach the animal to sit (Figure 3.5). These observations say little about whether wolves are smarter or dumber than dogs, which can easily be trained both to sit and to shake hands. Timber wolves typically make pawing movements during play, so the handshaking response was already there. It simply had to be brought under the control of a vocal command. On the other hand, timber wolves rarely sit, particularly if they are excited; consequently, this behavior was more difficult to teach. Generally, animals can more easily learn tasks that make direct use of behaviors they display without training than they can tasks that require them to learn a new response.

Clearly, instinct cannot be defined by simply contrasting it with intelligence. Learning plays a major role in many behaviors that are commonly called instinctive. Likewise, species-specific behaviors cannot be treated as simply instinctive—that is, as determined by heredity and not learned—because the ability of a species to learn is itself a species-specific behavior.

Heredity Versus Environment

A central issue to consider in defining instinct is the relative importance of hereditary and environmental factors to the development of a behavior. Heredity must contribute a great deal to the behavior of the hunting wasp, discussed earlier. The hunting wasp can learn nothing from its parents; they die before the young wasp emerges from its pupa in the spring. In contrast, the environment seems to contribute much to the behavior of higher animals, especially human beings, who usually undergo a long period of learning from parents and siblings. Despite the apparent implications of extreme examples, however, no behavior can be classed as completely hereditary (that is, completely uninfluenced by the environment) or as completely environmental (that is, completely uninfluenced by hereditary endowment). Every behavior is influenced by both factors.

The relative contributions of hereditary and environmental factors are difficult to unravel. For example, some human newborns can suck well immediately after they are born, and almost all can suck well within a day or two. This fact has been interpreted to mean that sucking is instinctive, that it is entirely hereditary and does not require practice or any other experience. But this interpretation ignores another fact. Babies can have experience before they are born. While still in their mother's wombs, many babies start to practice sucking. They suck their thumb, or a finger, or a part of their arm. This example, like several others described later in the chapter, shows that it is risky to rule out the influence of experience, even if a behavior appears to develop without it.

There is a better way to attack the heredity-environment problem than by trying to rule out one influence or the other. For example, animals with a similar hereditary endowment (those born in the same litter) can be raised under different environmental conditions. If the animals then show systematic differences in behavior, the differences can be attributed to environmental influences. Or, animals with different heredities can be raised under environmental conditions that are as similar as possible. Then differences in their behavior can be attributed to genetic factors. In other words, differences in behavior between groups that are similar in all ways but one can be attributed to the one way in which the groups differ, even though no particular behavior pattern can be attributed solely to heredity or solely to environment.

Because of the problems that arose in connection with early attempts to treat species-specific behavior as instinctive (and therefore determined entirely by heredity), the term "instinct" has been largely abandoned, and the term **species-specific behavior,** introduced at the beginning of the chapter, has replaced it. Although hereditary influences clearly play an important role in most, if not all, species-specific behaviors, environmental influences are also important. Instead of asking whether a behavior is instinctive, modern ethologists ask what particular hereditary and environmental influences are necessary for the behavior to occur. (Chapter 7 offers a detailed discussion of the interplay of heredity and environment.)

SYSTEMS OF RESPONDING

Whatever the hereditary and environmental influences are that produce a species-specific behavior, the behavior itself and its relation to an organism's way of life must be described before the behavior can be understood. Species-specific behaviors can be divided into three major types, as pointed out earlier: systems of responding, systems of sensory input, and complex systems of behavior. The type that is most obvious when an ethologist begins his observation of an animal is **systems of responding.**

Careful observation of any species of animal shows that much of its behavior consists of relatively stereotyped and frequently repeated patterns of movements. Lorenz and Tinbergen both developed the concept of the **fixed action pattern** to emphasize this fact. Many of the response systems of any animal consist of only a few dozen fixed action patterns. Locomotor behavior, for example, comprises only a handful of patterns for each species. In the horse, Peter Marler and William Hamilton report, there are three: walking, trotting, and galloping. Each of these fixed action patterns is a distinct series of movements that varies little from one horse to another, and all normal horses display the patterns. (Horses will not consistently keep to one gait, however, unless trained to do so.) We human beings also have three major patterns of locomotion: crawling, walking, and running.

Human Facial Expressions

Some of the most important human fixed action patterns involve facial expressions. Darwin marshaled much evidence in *The Expression of the Emotions in Man and Animals* that certain facial expressions occur in virtually all people and are associated with specific emotions. But many psychologists have been unwilling to accept Darwin's conclusions because of striking differences in the facial expressions of people from different cultures.

Paul Ekman and his co-workers have recently shown that Darwin was right about several basic facial expressions. They began by trying to specify some of the facial expressions that they thought were linked with specific emotions, such as surprise, anger, sadness, and happiness. Next, they sought out photographs of faces showing these expressions (see Figure 3.7). They showed these photographs to people from five different cultures and asked them to describe the emotions portrayed. In all cultures most observers chose the expected emotion to go with each facial expression.

Influences from other cultures could conceivably have accounted for the similar choices people made, however, because most of the people tested were either from the Western world or had had some contact with people from the West. To eliminate this possibility, Ekman and his associates subsequently tested a group of preliterate people in New Guinea who had had virtually no contact with Westerners. These people's judgments of the emotion associated with each facial expression generally agreed with the earlier findings. Ekman also tested a group of children from the same New Guinea tribe about the emotions represented by facial expressions and found that their judgments agreed even better than the adults' had.

The facial expressions of children who are born blind or deaf and blind also provide support for Darwin's conclusions. Irenäus Eibl-Eibesfeldt has summarized several documented cases of facial expressions in these unfortunate

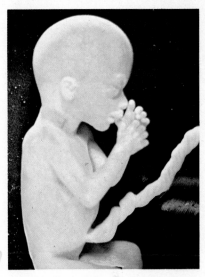

Figure 3.6 The existence of a well-coordinated behavior pattern such as thumb sucking shortly after birth is not necessarily evidence that this behavior is hereditary. It is known that human fetuses can suck their thumbs in the womb; their postnatal thumb sucking may therefore be at least partly a product of learning.

(From Rugh and Shettles, *From Conception to Birth: The Drama of Life's Beginning.* Harper & Row, 1971.)

Photograph Judged						
Judgment	Happiness	Disgust	Surprise	Sadness	Anger	Fear
Culture			**Percent Who Agreed with Judgment**			
99 Americans	97	92	95	84	67	85
40 Brazilians	95	97	87	59	90	67
119 Chileans	95	92	93	88	94	68
168 Argentinians	98	92	95	78	90	54
29 Japanese	100	90	100	62	90	66

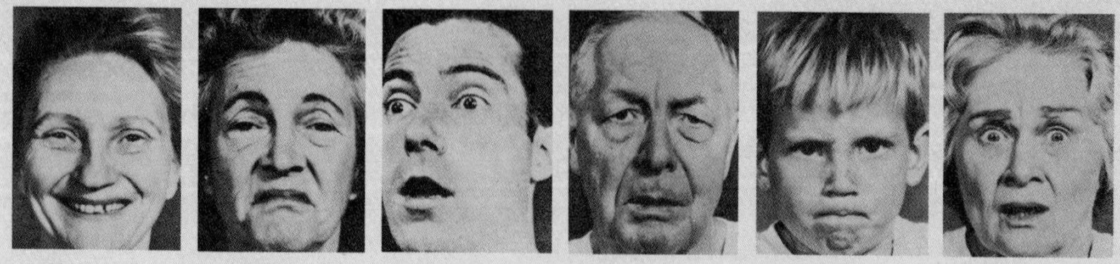

Figure 3.7 Emotional expression is a good example of species-specific behavior in humans. The data in this table show that there is substantial agreement among the members of different cultures about the meaning of various facial expressions. The muscular movements that produce these expressions are probably human fixed action patterns, and the expressions themselves are probably sign stimuli for human beings.
(After Ekman, Friesen, and Ellsworth, 1972.)

children. None of them ever saw other people's faces, and those who were both deaf and blind had great difficulty learning to imitate anything from other people's behavior. Yet smiling, crying, and facial expressions like those in Figure 3.7 all occurred in these children at an early age.

These findings suggest that certain human facial expressions are fixed action patterns associated with specific human emotions. But these facial expressions are probably all like those shown in Figure 3.7—strong and grossly different from each other. There is more to human facial expression than these fixed action patterns. There are many adult facial expressions, some strong and some very subtle, and the way they are used often varies between cultures. In the United States, for example, it is generally considered inappropriate for a man to cry or show other strong signs of sadness and distress in social situations. Human adult facial expressions probably combine fixed action patterns with cultural rules for how facial expressions should be used.

Many ethologists have pointed out the usefulness of understanding the species-specific behaviors connected with human emotions. In an interview in the magazine *Psychology Today*, Niko Tinbergen and his wife Liess assert, for example, that we could better understand much pathological human emotional behavior if we could tell what conditions would produce the same behavior in normal people. They have observed the behavior of autistic children—severely disturbed children who avoid social contact, do not speak, will not look other people in the eye, and often repeat meaningless behaviors over and over, such as rocking back and forth or banging their heads. According to the Tinbergens, normal children act exactly the same way when they are in conflict between fear and a desire to socialize or explore. From this, the Tinbergens infer that autistic children are caught in a similar conflict. If the

Tinbergens are right, then one way to help autistic children would be to try to reduce this conflict in them.

Displacement Activities

Fixed action patterns are merely stereotyped sequences of movements. These sequences do not fully describe the systems of responding that a person or animal possesses. One way of moving toward a fuller description is to examine not only single fixed action patterns but the relationships among them. **Displacement activity,** for example, involves several fixed action patterns. Suppose that a tern is sitting on a nest of eggs. When it sees a man approaching, the bird begins to vacillate between escaping and staying on the nest with the eggs. At some point the bird is likely to stop vacillating and carry out a fixed action pattern that appears to be irrelevant to the situation: It preens its feathers. Similarly, when (as shown in Figure 3.8) a herring gull is confronted by another gull on the attack, the first gull will, for a while, vacillate between running away and fighting; then it may show displacement activity: It carries out nest-building movements. The word "displacement" was originally used to suggest that behavioral energy was displaced from the conflicting behaviors (such as escaping harm versus protecting eggs) onto a seemingly irrelevant activity (such as preening), but the energy interpretation has been called into question by many investigators. It is best to think of the term "displacement" merely as indicating the occurrence of an activity that seems irrelevant to the situation.

Displacement activities are very common in many species. Rats show displacement reactions similar to those described in the tern. Human beings, under moderate levels of conflict or tension, often perform simple stereotyped movements such as drumming their fingers or scratching their heads.

Neural Stimulation of Fixed Action Patterns

Investigators have recently found that fixed action patterns can be produced by electrical stimulation of the brain. Erich von Holst and Ursula von St. Paul used this technique to study systems of responding in chickens. The area of the brain that von Holst and von St. Paul stimulated is called the brain stem. They placed electrodes in various places in the brain stem and electrically stimulated each place. In some places, stimulation produced a specific behavior pattern, and different places often yielded different patterns. With a large number of electrodes, a large number of different patterns could be elicited. Stimulation of some areas produced simple actions—the chicken stood up or sat down or turned its head to one side. Other areas elicited more complex patterns—grooming, attack behavior, fleeing behavior, eating, or courtship.

Once von Holst and von St. Paul had specified exactly which fixed action patterns were produced by stimulating which areas, they began to examine the relationships among the patterns. To do this, they simultaneously stimulated two different areas that would normally evoke two different fixed action patterns, then they observed how the two patterns interacted. In a natural setting, simultaneous evocation of two fixed action patterns sometimes produces displacement, and electrical stimulation did the same. When von Holst and von St. Paul simultaneously stimulated an area that produced aggressive pecking and a second area that produced fleeing with feathers smoothed down close to the body the hen ran excitedly back and forth giving piercing cries—a displacement activity. This displacement activity is similar to the behavior that occurs naturally when a hen is in conflict between protecting its nest and escaping from a dangerous enemy.

Other types of interaction between fixed action patterns also occurred. Stimulation of one area caused the animal to stretch out its neck and flatten its feathers, while stimulation of a second area made it fluff up its feathers. When

Figure 3.8 In situations where two or more fixed action patterns are released at high intensity, displacement activities often appear. The gull on the left, undergoing conflict between the fixed action patterns of fighting or fleeing from the attacking gull on the right, is making nesting movements, which are wholly irrelevant to the situation. (After Tinbergen, 1951.)

Figure 3.9 A pair of electrodes has been implanted in the brain of this chicken and is held in place by an apparatus through which electrical stimulation may be delivered. Von Holst and von Saint Paul used this procedure to investigate the effects of eliciting a number of fixed action patterns simultaneously.

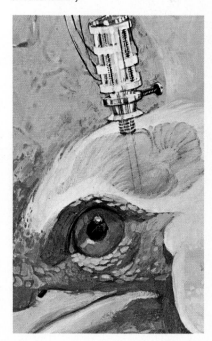

both these areas were stimulated simultaneously, the animal would stretch out its neck and flatten its feathers; after the stimulation stopped, it would fluff its feathers. That is, it showed first one fixed action pattern and then the other. In other instances, both action patterns occurred at once. Simultaneous stimulation of the area that produced looking to the left and the one that evoked sitting, for example, led the hen to sit and look to the left at the same time.

Motivation and Drive

Displacement and the other response systems studied by von Holst and von St. Paul are relatively simple systems. They involve fairly straightforward interactions among two or three fixed action patterns. Usually, when ethologists speak of systems, they refer to a more complex interaction of a larger number of response patterns, such as the interaction between an animal's sensitivity to particular stimuli and the responses it makes in a given state. Birds migrate only at certain times of the year; the praying mantis is most receptive to prey when it has gone some time without eating; and a major feature of human life is that human behavior is controlled partly by changes in emotion and moods.

Behavior that is influenced by changes in inner states has traditionally been investigated under the general heading of **motivation,** and psychologists have frequently tried to explain motivational changes by invoking the concept of drive. A drive has generally been thought of as a source of energy that builds up in the organism over time until it reaches a point at which responding has to occur, thereby reducing the stored-up energy. In some cases, behavior does fit this description. In his book *Studies in Animal and Human Behavior,* Lorenz describes the behavior of a well-fed starling that was deprived of the opportunity to catch flies for a long period of time. The bird occasionally went through elaborate fly-catching movements even though no flies were around. This kind of behavior is called **vacuum activity.** It is a striking example of how motivational forces seem to build up inside an animal and can lead to a behavior even in the absence of normally necessary cues. On the other hand, if an animal is observed eating food, merely attributing its behavior to a hunger drive does little to help us understand the behavior. We do not gain much if we merely *invent* a drive to account for every instance of behavior that is influenced by inner motivational factors.

Because of the complexity of the behavioral changes it brings about, motivation has been one of the most elusive concepts in psychology. Many biologically oriented psychologists think that a valid way to sneak up on an understanding of motivation is to study relatively simple animals with small behavioral repertoires, such as insects. In such animals one can investigate a functioning system of responding, such as feeding, and then ask the question: What factors, both inside and outside the organism, influence its feeding behavior?

Vincent Dethier carried out just such an investigation of feeding behavior in the blowfly. A blowfly that has not eaten for a while begins flying about randomly until it encounters the smell of a food, such as sugar water. Following the smell to the general area of the food source, it lands and begins walking, again in a random manner. (It is unable to follow the smell to the precise location of the food.) Blowflies and many other insects taste with their legs. When a leg touches a drop containing sugar, the fly extends its proboscis (a sort of hollow tongue, shown in Figure 3.10) to the drop and begins pumping food into its stomach. When filled, it stops. If left undisturbed, it will stay still for several hours before it resumes its random flight.

At this point, two important questions can be asked: What tells the fly that the drop of liquid it stepped on contains sugar? And what tells the fly to stop eating? The first question was relatively simple for Dethier to answer. There

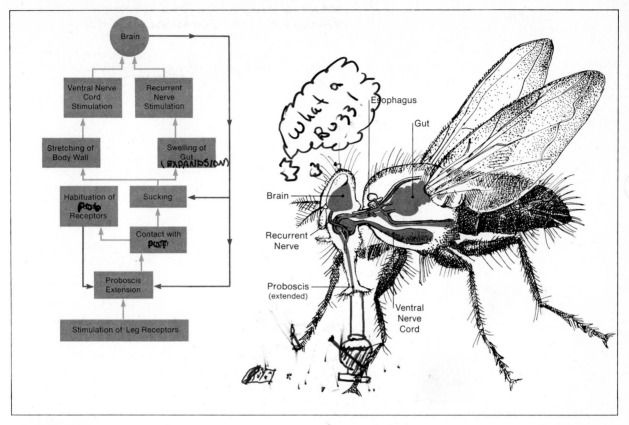

are sugar receptors in the leg. When these are stimulated, the blowfly's feeding pump starts up.

The answer to the second question was more difficult for Dethier to find. After a short time of contact with the drop, the receptors in the proboscis habituate; that is, they lose their sensitivity to sugar, and the fly stops feeding. But this loss of sensitivity does not fully answer the second question. Although the receptors become sensitive again a few minutes after feeding has stopped, the fly does not eat again for several hours. What keeps it from doing so? The easiest way to answer this new question is to determine what will make a blowfly continue to eat. Dethier found two nerves that, if cut, would make the fly continue eating. Severing one made the fly eat so much it could not fly. Severing the other caused it to eat until it actually burst!

Further investigation showed that the first nerve, called the recurrent nerve, receives impulses from receptors that measure the swelling of the fly's gut. This nerve tells the brain when the gut is full. The second cord, called the ventral nerve cord, receives impulses from receptors in the fly's body wall that tell the brain when the body wall is becoming stretched from food.

In other words, Dethier found three different ways that feedback causes the fly's feeding behavior to be stopped, or inhibited, as shown in Figure 3.10. Habituation of the sugar receptors in the legs stops extension of the proboscis. Swelling of the fly's gut stops both sucking and proboscis extension through impulses from the recurrent nerve. And stretching of the fly's body wall stops both sucking and proboscis extension through impulses from the ventral nerve cord.

As this description indicates, the fly's eating behavior is controlled by a fairly complex motivational system, which is influenced not only by the presence of food but by several other important factors: the periodic sensitiv-

Figure 3.10 (right) A drawing of the major parts of the blowfly's nervous system and digestive system. (left) A diagram of the three feedback loops in these systems that control the fly's eating behavior. The orange arrows indicate a facilitating or excitatory effect. The purple arrows indicate an inhibitory effect. Thus, stimulation of the leg receptors causes the proboscis to be extended; habituation of those receptors causes it to be retracted. An examination of this diagram will show how the surgery performed by Dethier affected the fly's eating behavior.

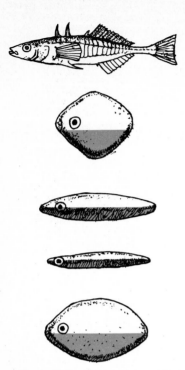

Figure 3.11 Tinbergen found that a male stickleback will attack any of the bottom four of these models before it will attack the top one, which closely resembles a stickleback in everything but the red belly. The red belly acquired by male sticklebacks during the mating season is a sign for attack that outweighs all other stimuli.

Figure 3.12 A herring gull attempting to brood an egg many times the size of the eggs it lays. For this species and for a number of other birds, size is a key element of the sign stimulus that elicits brooding behavior.

ity of the sugar receptors in the legs; the distension of the gut (as measured by the recurrent nerve); and the pressure of the gut against the body wall (as measured by the ventral nerve cord). A complex system for a simple animal like the blowfly! And even so, not everything about the system is understood. Dethier stresses how little is known about the role of the fly's tiny brain in its behavior. Since the motivational system for eating in the blowfly is so complex, it is no wonder human motivational systems are difficult to unravel.

SYSTEMS OF SENSORY INPUT

We know from our daily lives that the sensory world stimulates and guides much of our behavior. The same is true for nonhuman animals, but the world they experience through their senses may be quite different from ours, because each species' sensory systems are species-specific. Animals' sensory systems, just like their response systems, play a particular role in the way of life of the species.

In many animal species only a few stimuli produce observable effects on behavior. The European naturalist Jakob von Uexküll painted a vivid verbal picture of the behavior of the female tick, which for a meal will climb into the branches of a bush and wait for weeks, if necessary, for a mammal to pass directly beneath her. As she waits, the tick seems unresponsive to the barrage of sights, sounds, and odors about her. Only one stimulus will elicit a response. The distinctive smell of mammals' skin glands (caused by butyric acid) signals an approaching meal and leads the tick to drop on her host. In Uexküll's words, the tick is like a gourmet who picks the raisins out of a cake.

Sign Stimuli

Ethologists were quick to realize the importance of such observations. Different animal species live in different sensory worlds. Indeed, many species can be classified according to the stimuli they attend to, in much the same way that they can be compared in terms of fixed action patterns. Highly specific cues in the external environment often seem to serve as signals for complex sequences of behavior. Ethologists call these cues sign stimuli.

In several species, a red underside serves as a sign stimulus. For example, Tinbergen reports that the male stickleback fish will attack a crude model of another stickleback if the model has a red belly. The general appearance of the model is unimportant as long as it has a red belly. The stickleback ignores models that seem very fishlike to human beings, like the one shown at the top of Figure 3.11, but it quickly attacks the other models shown, which seem unfishlike but have a red underside. For a male robin protecting its territory, red breast feathers are a sign stimulus for an attack. In young herring gulls, the feeding response of pecking is affected more by the presence or absence of a red patch on the lower bill of a model "parent" than by distortions that to human beings make the model look very unbirdlike.

Although color is a key element in many sign stimuli, it is not always important. Tinbergen reports a remarkable example in which size is the main factor. Many sign stimuli elicit a response only if they are about the right size. But a bird called the herring gull, offered an egg several times larger than one of its own eggs, prefers the larger egg—even when the substitute egg is so large that the bird cannot assume a normal brooding position, as shown in Figure 3.12.

Because sign stimuli are so specific, ethologists at first interpreted them as indicating the existence of an innate releasing mechanism. The sign stimulus was assumed to release a fixed action pattern because the animal had inherited a neural connection that automatically triggered the pattern in response to the sign stimulus. A study by Tinbergen initially seemed to support this explanation, but later research has shown that the formulation is oversimplified.

Tinbergen used a cardboard model like the one shown in Figure 3.13 that moved through the air above the heads of young barnyard turkeys. When the model was moved in one direction, the shadow that it cast had a short neck and a long tail and looked like a flying hawk. When the model was moved in the opposite direction, the shadow had a long neck and a short tail and resembled a flying goose. The turkeys showed vigorous escape responses when the model cast the hawk shadow but few escape responses when it cast the goose shadow. Because the turkeys had never seen any hawks, it was tempting to conclude that the escape response to hawks was inborn and unlearned. That is, the shape of a hawk seemed to be a sign stimulus that automatically released the fixed action pattern of escape in the turkey.

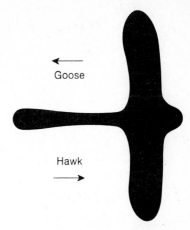

Goose

Hawk

Habituation

Wolfgang Schleidt has demonstrated that this interpretation seems to be incorrect. He showed that turkeys try to escape from any unfamiliar object of an appropriate size that is moving overhead, whether it is shaped like a natural enemy or not. When he exposed turkeys to circles or rectangles moving overhead, for example, they showed the same initial alarm reactions that they did to an overhead silhouette of a hawk. As the turkeys became familiar with the shapes, their alarm reactions decreased. This phenomenon, in which an animal responds in a particular way to a stimulus when it is first presented but gradually stops responding as the stimulus is presented over and over, is called **habituation.**

Figure 3.13   The shape of the model used by Tinbergen in studying young turkeys' escape responses. Tinbergen thought that the hawk shape was a sign stimulus eliciting the fixed action pattern of escape because the turkeys fled from it but not from the goose shape. Subsequent research by Schleidt showed that the hawk shape caused the escape responses only because it was unfamiliar, whereas the turkeys were familiar with goose shapes, having shared the barnyard with geese.
(After Tinbergen, 1951.)

In each case, Schleidt found, the habituation of the turkeys' fear reaction was specific to the shape that was repeatedly presented. Turkeys that repeatedly saw a hawk silhouette but not a circle eventually stopped reacting to the hawk; they did, however, show fear in response to the circle. Conversely, animals that were repeatedly exposed to the circle but not to the hawk silhouette showed no alarm reactions to the circle but many reactions to the hawk. Schleidt concluded that the apparently innate fear of hawks that Tinbergen observed occurred because Tinbergen's turkeys had never seen hawks. If they had never seen flying geese, they probably would have shown a similar reaction to that shape as well, because the fear response would not have had an opportunity to become habituated.

Although interpreting the meaning of sign stimuli is a difficult task, the general point remains. The sensory systems of a particular species are characteristic of that species, and the meaningfulness of objects and events in the world of an animal are determined partly by the capacities and limitations of its sensory apparatus. Humans cannot tell whether light is polarized, but bees and many other invertebrates can; they use polarization as an important cue for locomotion and orientation. For the female tick, the significant stimulus is butyric acid, in concentrations that the human olfactory system cannot ordinarily detect. The upper limit on auditory sensitivity in human beings is about 20,000 cycles per second, but some rodents can hear up to 100,000 cycles per second. Mice and rats show a definite startle response to hand claps, but they do not do so if the hand claps are recorded on tape, because tape recorders cut off the high-frequency components to which the rodents are particularly sensitive. Bats, which navigate by means of echolocation, can also detect frequencies considerably above those that human beings respond to.

COMPLEX SYSTEMS OF BEHAVIOR

In our discussion so far, we have considered motor output and sensory input as if they were separate phenomena. This division, revealing as it is, is somewhat arbitrary and can be misleading if carried too far. To understand the functioning of an organism, it is not enough to analyze response systems and sensory systems, outputs and inputs: The whole, as represented by an ani-

Figure 3.14 The migratory patterns of the northern fur seal, the Atlantic golden plover, and the American eel.

mal's natural behavior, always seems to be greater than the sum of the parts. Indeed, one of the virtues of ethology is that it attempts to describe entire systems of behavior and to deal with the full array of influences on what an animal does. Two of the most interesting kinds of species-specific behavior that ethologists have studied as ongoing systems are the seasonal migrations of many animals and the dance language of honeybees.

Migration

Many animal species migrate over vast distances, as shown in Figure 3.14. Alaskan fur seals, for example, breed only on the Pribilof Islands in the Bering Sea. Eibl-Eibesfeldt reports that during the winter, the females and young seals swim some 3,000 miles to the coast of southern California, while the males travel to the southern Aleutian Islands (a much shorter journey). In the spring, the sexes join each other again in the Pribilofs. Eels born in the Sargasso Sea, near the West Indies, find their way to the coasts of North America and Europe; and the Atlantic golden plover flies from as far south as Argentina to breed in the Yukon and Alaska, a trip of about 7,000 miles.

The exact cues used by various species during their remarkable trips have been under investigation for many years, but because of the difficulties of studying migration in the field, no more than the bare outlines of the behavior have become clear. Birds, the most thoroughly studied migratory animals, seem to use the sun and the stars as well as various landmarks as guides. It has also been found that homing and migration do not necessarily follow the same flight path every time. Geoffrey Matthews describes experiments in which birds were transported over large distances and then released. Many species still found their way home.

The Dancing of Honeybees

Honeybees are social insects. They live in colonies that include one egg-producing queen, a few males called drones, and many workers, which are females that have not developed genitals. The insects eat flower nectar and pollen, fertilizing plants by spreading pollen from one to another as they forage for food. Only a few bees, called scouts, leave the hive to search for food. When they find it, they collect some—on their bodies and in their stomachs—and return to the hive. Shortly thereafter, many other workers fly to the place where the scouts found food and begin gathering it. How do the workers find the food? The scouts do not lead them to it; they somehow tell the workers where it is when they return to the hive.

The communication process in bees is the subject of a long series of observations and experiments by Karl von Frisch. His work is particularly impressive if one tries to imagine the difficulties he had to face both in recording the honeybees' behavior and in analyzing his observations.

In an early experiment, von Frisch demonstrated the precision with which worker bees locate a food source that the scouts have found. He fed some scout bees with food that he had placed on a particular group of flowers at a botanical garden. The plants were a kind not usually visited by the scouts, but within minutes after they had left the garden, many workers from the hive arrived. The workers lighted only on the species of flower where the scouts had been fed, ignoring the 700 other kinds of flowers in the garden.

How could one go about determining the nature of a communication process that works so precisely? Ideally, the bees' communication medium—their "language"—would have to convey information about the type of flower the scouts had found, its quality and abundance, and its distance and direction from the hive.

An obvious possibility is that the first factor, the type of flower, is communicated by odors the returning bees carry. The scout returns with flower odors on its body, and its stomach is filled with fragrant nectar, some of which it gives to the other bees. Through careful experimentation, von Frisch determined that bees use both these odors in finding the food source. In addition, he found that they use a specific scent that the scouts themselves (by means of a scent gland) leave at the food source.

The odor of a flower alone would help a bee locate food near the hive, but it would not suffice for telling workers about the abundance of food or for locating distant sources—and bees often forage over a mile from their hives.

Von Frisch found that scouts returning to the hive from nearby food sources (fifty yards or less away) perform a circular movement called a round dance, illustrated in Figure 3.15. Bees in the hive follow the dancing bee, touching it with their antennae. When von Frisch varied the richness of an artificial food source, he found that the bees danced more vigorously, running in circles faster, when the source was richer. The bees in the hive learned about the richness of the source from the vigor of the dance.

But the round dance apparently tells nothing about direction, as von Frisch showed in another experiment. He fed scouts from a lavender-scented dish near the hive, around which he had placed a number of similarly scented but empty dishes. After the scouts went back into the hive, he removed the full dish and put an empty scented one in its place. When the bees emerged from the hive to find the food, they did not settle on that dish but distributed themselves equally among all the dishes. Apparently, the scouts had told the other bees that food was nearby but had not told them exactly where to look for it.

Later on, von Frisch repeated the experiment but put the dishes farther away from the hive. This time something entirely different happened. At about 200 yards almost all the bees went to dishes very near the one where the scouts had eaten. Why? Von Frisch noticed that the scouts did a different

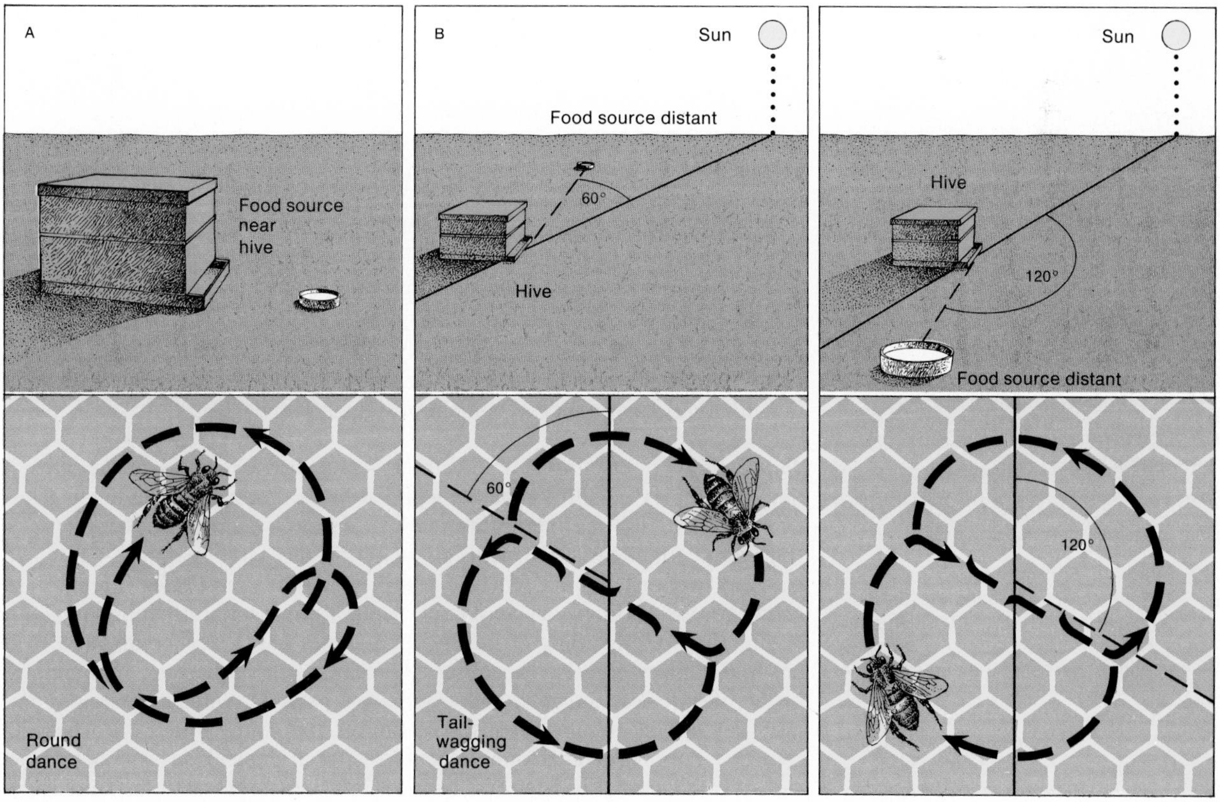

Figure 3.15 The language of honeybees. (A) When a food source is discovered close to the hive, the scout bee flies back into the hive and attracts the attention of the other bees by dancing on one of the walls in the hive formed by the honeycomb. The dance of the scout bee is circular and matches in intensity and vigor the richness of the source. (B) When the food source is at some distance, the scout's dance is more complex. The bee loops round again and again to repeat a straight-line motion while waggling its body rapidly from side to side. The angle that this straight-line portion of the dance makes with the line of gravity corresponds to the angle that the direction of the food source makes with the direction of the sun in the horizontal plane of the surrounding countryside. The speed of the dance indicates distance. Note that in both dances the dancer is followed by the other bees who are receiving the message.

(After von Frisch, 1950.)

dance when the food source was far from the hive than when it was nearby. Instead of the round dance that conveyed no information about direction, they did a "wagging" dance, also shown in Figure 3.15. In the wagging dance a bee runs straight forward a little way, turns 360 degrees to the left, turns 360 degrees to the right, and repeats that sequence several times. (You might want to pause at this point and try to imagine yourself in von Frisch's place. What do you think the wagging dance means, and how would you find out if you were right?)

The distance from hive to food source, von Frisch managed to show, is indicated quite precisely by the speed of a scout's 360 degree turn. The direction of the straight run between turns indicates the angle of the path of flight. The bees "calculate" the angle by using the line connecting the hive and the sun, as shown in Figure 3.15. The calculation does not require direct sunlight—bees are sensitive to polarized light, which results from the scattering of the sun's rays in the atmosphere and is transmitted by blue sky, indicating the position of the sun even when it is out of sight behind a cloud or a hill. Polarized light is not transmitted when the sky is completely overcast, but bees can see the sun through a thicker cover of clouds than people can.

Bees' language, then, is highly complex. It involves at least three senses (smell, sight, and touch) and conveys information not only about the type and quality of the food the scouts have found but about how far the food source is from the hive and, if it is not nearby, in what direction.

Von Frisch spent many years studying the behavior of bees, and his work is an excellent illustration of ethological research. Even deciding which variables to compare requires a thorough knowledge of the behavior and physiology of the species under study. Beyond that, one must design an experiment that employs scientific controls without destroying the naturalness of the situation for the animal—that is, without preventing the organism from behaving as it normally would. Combining careful naturalistic observation with thoughtful experimentation and analysis is the essence of the ethological approach.

The Development of Behavioral Systems

One of the most fruitful ways to study complex systems of species-specific behavior is to observe their development in young animals. Developmental studies, which are particularly important for determining the influence of learning on species-specific behaviors, have led to two important conclusions. First, the ability of an animal to learn is itself species-specific, as was pointed out earlier in the chapter. Second, learning is essential for the development of many species-specific behaviors. Three phenomena that ethologists have studied demonstrate these points especially well: a process called imprinting, by which some species of birds form early social attachments; the development of bird songs; and the development of human language.

Figure 3.16 Imprinting. A few hours after they were hatched (during a sensitive period), these goslings saw Konrad Lorenz instead of a mother goose. Thereafter they followed him around as if he were their mother. Imprinting demonstrates not only a species-specific ability to learn but also the importance of such learning to the social bonds of the species.

Imprinting Imprinting is one of the most striking examples of the interaction of complex hereditary factors with learning. Lorenz brought to the attention of ethologists the interesting fact that a newly hatched duckling or gosling, at a certain early age, will follow almost any moving object—a human being, a wooden box on wheels, a bird of a different species. Figure 3.16 shows some ducklings that were imprinted to Lorenz faithfully following him. A slightly older duckling or gosling (sometimes only a few hours older) will not follow these objects. This observation suggests that there are certain times in the life of these animals, called **sensitive periods,** when they are particularly susceptible to attachments. The time in the young bird's life when the sensitive period for attachment occurs seems to depend on two factors, as shown in Figure 3.17. The sensitive period cannot begin until the animal can walk well enough to be able to follow the stimulus. And it must end when the animal develops a fear of novel stimuli, as it does after it has had time to become familiar with a certain environment.

It is not difficult to see the importance of these attachments for young birds. Birds of a feather flock together, as the saying goes, and early attachments to particular moving objects—in the wild, usually other birds of the infant's own species—seem to be the first stage of participation in many bird social systems. In other words, imprinting seems to be a primary mechanism for the early development of social bonds. Although the first moving object that a baby bird encounters in its natural habitat is usually its own mother (who is, appropriately, a member of the same species), in the laboratory a baby bird can be exposed to something other than its mother and become imprinted inappropriately. Lorenz describes an extreme case, a barnyard goose that he raised. The goose not only followed him but, upon reaching sexual maturity, actually attempted to mate with him.

The important features of imprinting, then, are that the young bird *learns an attachment during a sensitive period that is fairly restricted in time and that this early attachment normally produces the social bonds* that are a necessary part of the bird's life with other birds of the same species. Imprinting clearly demonstrates both of the conclusions suggested earlier about the relation between learning and species-specific behaviors. First, the species of birds that show imprinting are exhibiting a species-specific ability to learn; in this case, they learn attachment during a sensitive period. Second, imprinting is an excellent demonstration of the role that learning can play in the development of species-specific behavior. The learning that occurs during imprinting seems to be essential to the development of normal species-specific social behavior.

Bird Songs How do birds come to sing the songs characteristic of their species? An American child who grows up in a foreign country usually learns at least a bit of the foreign tongue even if his parents never speak anything except English, but a cardinal sings like a cardinal even if its parents have nested in a yard full of robins and sparrows. What is the role of learning in the development of bird songs?

Among different species of birds, the role of learning and of general environmental factors varies greatly. At one extreme are such birds as chickens, which produce a normal song even if they are deafened as soon as they hatch. At the other extreme are such birds as sparrows, which produce a highly abnormal song if they are prevented from hearing other members of their species during the first year of life.

The chaffinch is a member of the sparrow family whose song development has been thoroughly studied. In the first month after hatching, a normally raised chaffinch gives only simple food-begging calls. During the next eight months the bird gradually begins singing the notes and syllables that will make up its final song, but these are not sung in any distinct order. The song begins to take on a definite form in the tenth month and then, by the time the bird is twelve months old, crystallizes into the specific song that the bird will use for the rest of its life. Although there are minor variations from one bird to the next, the general form of the song is characteristic of the species.

The easiest way to see if a chaffinch learns its song from other birds is to isolate it and see what develops. W. H. Thorpe isolated young chaffinches from other birds as soon as they hatched and kept them isolated for a year. These birds produced abnormal songs. But if tape recordings of chaffinch songs were played during the first four months of isolation, the young birds developed virtually normal songs at the usual age of ten or twelve months. In other words, chaffinches show a sensitive period for the development of

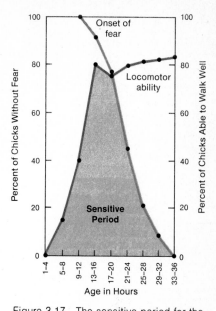

Figure 3.17 The sensitive period for the imprinting of chicks reaches a peak between thirteen and twenty hours after they hatch. This figure shows that the sensitive period is determined by two factors. Imprinting is impossible without the organism's ability to follow a moving object, and it is impossible if the organism is afraid of strange objects. The percentage of chicks able to use their legs effectively increases steadily during the first thirteen hours after they hatch. The percentage of chicks not showing fear of strange objects decreases steadily from about twelve hours after hatching on. Only when locomotor ability is high and fear is low can chicks be imprinted, and this combination of factors occurs at only one time in their lives.
(After Hess, 1973.)

Figure 3.18 Sound spectrographs of the songs of two chaffinches. (A) The song of a normal adult chaffinch. (B) The song of a chaffinch reared in isolation and exposed during its sensitive period to a tape recording of the normal chaffinch song spliced in such a way that the ending of the song came in the middle. Note that this bird produces a song that reflects both learned and innate influences. It sings with the "splice" that was on the tape it heard, but it also sings with the overall broadening and deepening trend of the normal song. It would not be expected to sing in this way if its song were merely a mimicry of the tape.
(After Thorpe, 1961.)

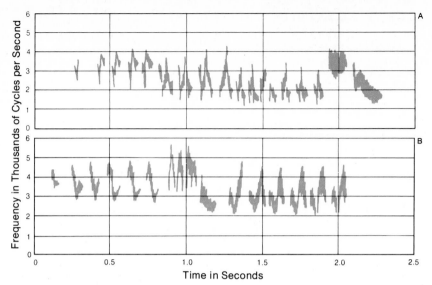

normal song. During this sensitive period they learn the song, even though they cannot actually produce it until months later.

If, during the sensitive period, chaffinches are exposed not to the normal chaffinch song but to a rearranged form of the song, they later produce the rearranged song rather than the normal one. If they are played tape recordings of the song of a species very different from chaffinches, however, they do not learn the song. Figure 3.18 shows some spectrographic recordings of the songs of chaffinches raised under various conditions.

Some other birds are less limited in the songs that they will learn. Klaus Immelman has shown that young zebra finches, for example, easily learn the very different song of Bengalese finches when raised by them.

Human Language Birds are not the only creatures that show sensitive periods in the acquisition of a species-specific behavior. A striking example is human beings' acquisition of language, which is a behavior highly specific to our species. Of course, human children cannot be subjected to isolation experiments, but nature produces its own experiment in this case: Deaf children are isolated from normal human speech because they cannot hear.

Eric Lenneberg has collected data on the relation between a deaf child's language skills and the age at which he or she became deaf. According to Lenneberg, there is a sensitive period in language acquisition lasting from about two years of age to about fourteen. Children who become deaf at, say, three or four years of age stop speaking within a short time, but if they are given training in language, they learn it much more easily than those who become deaf earlier. Thus, the sensitive period for acquisition of human language seems to start at about two years of age.

To determine the upper end of the sensitive period for language, Lenneberg looked at different data: When does the language of deaf children stop showing substantial improvement from training? He found that at about thirteen to fifteen years of age, the deaf child's general language ability seems to stabilize, and very little improvement is shown after that age. Children who can hear but are mentally retarded stop progressing at the same age. Because they are retarded, their language development is much slower than that of normal children, and when they reach their early teens, it levels off and shows no further general improvement.

The experiences of normal children also support Lenneberg's contention that there is a sensitive period for language development. At the beginning of the sensitive period, approximately two years of age, most children utter their first primitive sentences. At the end of the sensitive period, about fourteen years of age, most people seem to show a decrease in their ability to learn to speak a foreign language. In fact, Lenneberg argues that people who try to learn a foreign language after their early teens can seldom learn to speak it exactly like a native speaker. They almost always retain some trace of an accent.

In summary, human language, just like imprinting and bird song, is a species-specific behavior that requires learning for normal development. People have a species-specific ability to learn language during a long sensitive period stretching from two to fourteen years of age.

SUMMARY

1. By showing that humans belong to the animal kingdom, Charles Darwin laid the foundations for the **ethological approach to behavior,** which is the study of human and animal behavior from a biological point of view.

2. The main goal of ethology is to describe and understand **species-specific behaviors:** the behaviors characteristic of a particular species of animal. Ethologists think of an organism as an **ongoing behavior system,** and they view species-specific behavior as **adaptive.** That is, they want to know how each behavior fits into the animal's way of life and helps (or fails to help) the animal adapt to its environment.

3. The term "instinct" refers to the idea that some complex sequences of behavior, such as the way a wolf howls and pounces, seem to be inherited rather than learned. However, learning has been found to play a major role in many behaviors that have been called instinctive; for this and other reasons, contemporary ethologists rarely speak of instincts. Instead, they refer to **species-specific behavior** and try to identify the particular hereditary and environmental conditions that are necessary for the behavior to occur.

4. An ethologist usually begins his observations of an animal by noting its **systems of responding.** Such response systems include:

    a. **Fixed action patterns,** which are relatively stereotyped and frequently repeated patterns of movements. For example, the locomotor behavior of the horse includes three fixed action patterns: walking, trotting, and galloping. Some human facial expressions are also fixed action patterns.

    b. **Displacement activities,** which are fixed action patterns that are apparently irrelevant to the situation and seem to occur at times of conflict. For example, a tern may at first vacillate between sitting on its nest of eggs and fleeing from an approaching man; at some point, the bird may stop vacillating and preen its feathers—a displacement activity. Displacement activities and other fixed action patterns can be produced in the laboratory by electrical stimulation of certain parts of an animal's brain.

5. **Motivation** is the study of why an organism does what it does—a complex and difficult subject. One way to simplify it is to study a single response system in a relatively primitive organism. This approach is

Figure 3.19 Ethologists Niko Tinbergen (top), Konrad Lorenz (middle), and Karl von Frisch (bottom) were co-recipients of the Nobel prize in medicine and physiology in 1973 for their work on the study of animals in their natural environments. Tinbergen is author of the classic work *The Study of Instinct.* Lorenz is well-known for his engaging book *King Solomon's Ring* and for his controversial book *On Aggression.* Von Frisch is the author of numerous works, which, in addition to their scientific value, have contributed significantly to the practice of beekeeping.

illustrated by Vincent Dethier's study of the blowfly, in which he tried to identify the various factors, both environmental and internal, that control the blowfly's feeding behavior.

6. The meaning the world has for an animal is determined partly by the capacities and limitations of its sensory apparatus. Therefore, in addition to studying response systems, ethologists study the **systems of sensory input** characteristic of a species. Some species, such as the tick, seem to respond to only a few sensory stimuli.

7. If a highly specific cue in an animal's environment triggers a complex sequence of behavior, that cue is called a **sign stimulus.** For example, Niko Tinbergen found that a male stickleback fish will attack another stickleback (or a crude model of a stickleback) if it has a red belly; the red underside is a sign stimulus for attack behavior in that species.

8. Sometimes an animal responds to a stimulus when it is first presented and then, after repeated presentations, stops responding—a phenomenon known as **habituation.** In some cases an apparently innate sign stimulus may actually result from habituation.

9. Treating motor output and sensory input as if they were separate phenomena can be misleading if not balanced by a consideration of **complex systems of behavior.** Among the complex systems that ethologists have studied are the **seasonal migrations** of birds and other animals and the **dance language of honeybees.** In a series of studies that illustrate the ethological approach at its best, Karl von Frisch discovered that scout bees use two different "dances" to communicate information about food sources to other workers in the hive.

10. Another approach to the study of complex systems of behavior is to examine the ways they develop in young animals.

   a. **Imprinting** is a process by which some species of birds form early social attachments. Konrad Lorenz found that a duckling or gosling, during a **sensitive period** early in its life, will follow almost any moving object. In nature, the moving object the young bird sees during the sensitive period is likely to be its mother.

   b. Some species of birds, such as chaffinches, show a sensitive period for the development of the bird song characteristic of their species. Young chaffinches that are isolated during the sensitive period never develop their normal song.

   c. Research with deaf children and others suggests that there is also a sensitive period for the development of human language, lasting from about age two to about age fourteen.

11. Two conclusions to be drawn from developmental studies are that the ability of an animal to learn is itself species-specific, and that learning is essential for the development of many species-specific behaviors.

SUGGESTED READINGS

Darwin, Charles. *Expression of the Emotions in Man and Animals.* Chicago: University of Chicago Press, 1965. With this book, originally published in 1872, Darwin developed the assumption that an animal's behavior is characteristic of its species in the same way that its bodily characteristics are.

Eibl-Eibesfeldt, Irenäus. *Ethology: The Biology of Behavior.* New York: Holt, Rinehart and Winston, 1970. A useful, up-to-date introductory survey of the field of ethology, written by a student and colleague of Konrad Lorenz.

Hinde, Robert A. *Animal Behavior.* 2nd ed. New York: McGraw-Hill, 1970. A comprehensive view of animal behavior that attempts to integrate the approach of continental European ethologists (such as Lorenz, Tinbergen, and von Frisch) with the work of English-speaking animal psychologists.

Lorenz, Konrad. *King Solomon's Ring.* New York: Thomas Y. Crowell, 1952. A light, easy-to-read book of essays about Lorenz's many interesting experiences with animals.

Lorenz, Konrad. *Evolution and Modification of Behavior.* Chicago: University of Chicago Press, 1965. In this short book, Lorenz analyzes the meaning of the term ''innate'' as applied to behavior and discusses controversies over the heredity of behavior.

Lorenz, Konrad. *Studies in Animal and Human Behavior.* Robert Martin (tr.). Cambridge, Mass.: Harvard University Press, 1971. 2 vols. Lorenz's most important papers, translated into English, are brought together in these two volumes.

Marler, Peter R., and William J. Hamilton. *Mechanisms of Animal Behavior.* New York: Wiley, 1966. A thorough, well-written summary and integration of major areas of research on animal behavior.

Tinbergen, Niko. *The Study of Instinct.* Fairlawn, N.J.: Oxford University Press, 1951. A stimulating discussion of instinctive behavior by one of the most important modern ethologists.

Van Lawick-Goodall, Jane. *In the Shadow of Man.* Boston: Houghton Mifflin, 1971. Van Lawick-Goodall provides a highly readable account of what she learned during the several years that she studied and lived with wild chimpanzees in Africa.

Von Frisch, Karl. *The Dance Language and Orientation of Bees.* L. E. Chadwick (tr.). Cambridge, Mass.: Belknap Press of Harvard University Press, 1967. Von Frisch's most recent and most extensive treatment of his lifetime of work with honeybees.

Most people seem to fear and resent behaviorist notions. They seem to think it denies man freedom of will and makes of him merely a machine. I heard William Buckley discuss *Beyond Freedom and Dignity*, a book by B. F. Skinner, and he referred to Skinner's theories as implying "a dehumanization" of man. But does behaviorism dehumanize a man or merely *describe* a man?

Frankly, I tend to accept behaviorist notions. I find the behavior of people quite predictable; and the better I know them, the more predictable I find their behavior. People sometimes surprise me, I admit, but I have the feeling that this is because I don't know enough about them and not because they are capable of free will.

And, of course, my own behavior is most predictable of all; at least, to me. For instance, I respond favorably to praise. It has an extraordinary reinforcing effect on me. All my publishers and editors find this out at once. It is their profession, of course, to study the weaknesses of writers and use those weaknesses to manipulate those writers. So they carefully begin to praise the quickness with which I complete my work; the speed with which I read galleys and prepare indexes; the cooperativeness with which I make (reasonable) revisions, and so on and so on.

All this I lap up with avidity; no one has ever handed out praise in larger servings than I can swallow. What's more, in order to get still more of it, I complete my work more quickly than ever, read galleys and do indexes with still greater speed, make *reasonable* revisions with at least a trace of a smile, and the result is that over the last six years I have averaged nine books a year.

Came the time when I was supposed to work on the introductions to these chapters. I was in New York; the editorial staff was in California. I sent off some introductions and heard nothing.

Whereupon I grew sad and sulky and found that I didn't feel like doing any more. When I was nudged very politely by the editors, I wrote a long letter, saying that unless I knew that they liked those I had already written, I could do no further work. Whereupon the staff, suddenly enlightened, promptly sent me a letter telling me that my introductions were great and that everybody loved them. At once I sat down to write more. Periodically, they sent me kind words and I sent more introductions. It was very neat and efficient.

But does that mean I'm just a robot? That I have buttons that need pushing? That I point them out, that they push them, and that all is well? Well, I guess so. I like to be praised and that's what I work for. Maybe we all have our buttons, and maybe we all know where they are, and maybe we all do our best to get them pushed.

Could the behaviorists be saying that it's love that makes the world go round?

Isaac Asimov

4
Conditioning and Learning: Behaviorism

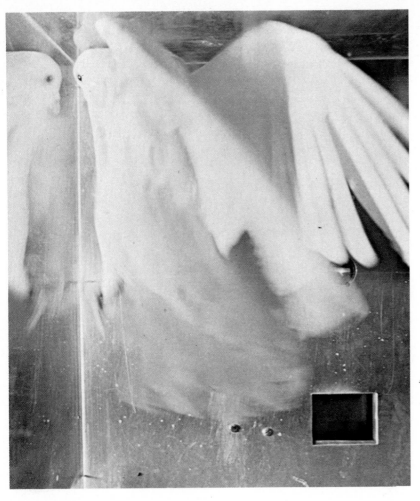

One hundred years ago, most people believed that the mind and the body were completely separate. Darwin's theory of evolution was still new and highly controversial, and even those who accepted it usually made a sharp distinction between the body and the mind. The mind was thought to be an expression of the soul, and because the soul was not composed of matter like the body, the mind could not be part of the body. At that time psychology, which people were just beginning to consider a field of study in its own right rather than a subdivision of philosophy, was defined as the study of the mind.

Because most people believed that the mind was independent of the body, psychologists were continually faced with religious, philosophical, and methodological problems. How could they hope to do a systematic, scientific analysis of something that might not even be subject to physical laws? This difficulty had a profound impact on the kind of research that early psychologists did. Many of them used the so-called introspective method: They tried to establish scientific techniques for analyzing the contents of whatever crossed their consciousness. Such men as Wilhelm Wundt and Edward Titchener made important discoveries using this approach; however, they also tended to neglect people's overt actions, their outward behavior.

In the United States, discontent with this mentalistic psychology eventually produced the very different approach called **behaviorism,** which originated with John B. Watson around 1913 and was carried on later by such well-known psychologists as Clark Hull and B. F. Skinner. Watson argued that it is impossible to study in a scientific way phenomena that can be known only through subjective reports. If psychology was to be a science, he said, psychologists would have to concentrate on **objective analysis of observable behavior,** such as movements and speech; they would have to stop attempting the study of

Figure 4.1 Up until a few moments before this photograph was taken, this pigeon was able to obtain food from the square hole in the bottom part of the panel by pecking at the round key directly above it. The experimenter then cut off the electricity, so that the bird's well-conditioned behavior—pecking the key—no longer was reinforced by the food rewards. In the language of learning theory, its behavior was undergoing extinction. The agitation the bird is showing is typical of animals in this situation. Modern behaviorism is based on carefully controlled laboratory procedures such as this one.

such mental phenomena as consciousness and thought, except insofar as those phenomena were revealed in behavior. It was not that Watson had no interest in so-called mental phenomena. In fact, during the early days of behaviorism, he formulated a theory that explained thinking as subvocalization—as movements of the vocal cords that were so slight as to produce no sound. This theory, if it had been correct, would have allowed behaviorists to study thinking by analyzing the movements of the vocal cords. It was soon pointed out, however, that some thinking occurs so rapidly that the subvocalized sounds would have to be made at frequencies well beyond the physical capacity of the vocal cords, and so the effort to treat thinking as subvocalization has largely been abandoned.

LEARNING AND PERFORMANCE

From the very beginning of behaviorism, one of the main interests of behaviorists has been the study of learning. But the concept of learning comes very close to being a mental phenomenon. Consequently, behaviorists have sought to define learning precisely in terms of observable behavior. To begin with, they carefully distinguish between **performance,** which is what a person or animal actually does, and **learning,** which has to do with changes in what one can do that result from experience with the environment. They then try to infer the process of learning from careful analysis of changes in an individual's performance.

Inferring changes in learning from changes in performance is not as simple a matter as it may seem. Improvements in performance are not always a result of learning. A football player may play better this week than last week for many reasons. He may have had a cold last week, or he may have had a fight with the coach, or perhaps this week's game is especially important. And when performance changes for the worse or does not change at all, one cannot assume that something learned earlier has been forgotten or that nothing has been learned.

In the laboratory, the psychologist can study animals that he is certain have had no previous experience with the task to be learned. For example, a hungry rat can be taught to run a maze for a food reward. If it runs the maze faster on Trial 20 than on Trial 1, the experimenter can tentatively conclude that learning has taken place, because he knows the past history of the rat. Once the animal has eaten its fill, however, it may be reluctant to run the maze as fast as it did before. Its performance is impaired, but what it has learned is not: When the animal is hungry again, it will demonstrate the learned response in as lively a fashion as before.

Similarly, outside the laboratory it is safe to assume that a person who successfully negotiates an advanced ski slope has learned to ski. But the mere fact that he knows how to ski does not mean he will ski as well as he can on all slopes at all times. He may, for example, ski better (or worse) when people are watching than when they are not. To make correct inferences about learning, psychologists must carefully observe changes in performance and try to exclude factors other than learning that may have caused these changes.

Another important goal of behaviorism, in addition to precise description of observable behavior, has been precise description of simple experimental **techniques to control behavior.** If one can specify that, under certain conditions, a particular experimental technique has a consistent effect on performance, then one does not necessarily have to be concerned about whether the performance is a result of learning. By using the technique with an animal or person, the psychologist can produce the desired performance. In this way, through simple manipulations of the environment, the psychologist can control much behavior. B. F. Skinner has been the most influential proponent of this type of behaviorism. His approach has been called **behavioral engineer-**

ing because he is more interested in determining how to control behavior than in devising theoretical explanations of the processes that underlie behavior. This approach is reflected in behavior therapy, which is discussed in Chapter 27.

But even behaviorists who are more interested than Skinner in the psychological processes underlying performance prefer explanations that remain as close as possible to manipulations of the environment. They usually explain learning by relating it to two established experimental techniques that are used to manipulate the environment in well-defined ways: classical conditioning and operant conditioning. Because the effects of these two conditioning techniques are so well understood, psychologists find it easy to distinguish between the effects of learning and the changes in performance resulting from factors unrelated to learning.

CLASSICAL CONDITIONING

Classical conditioning (sometimes called Pavlovian conditioning or respondent conditioning) involves reflex behavior. A **reflex** is an involuntary response that is elicited by a specific stimulus. For example, a sharp puff of air on the eye evokes a blink of the eyelid; a tap on the patellar tendon of the knee produces the knee jerk; the prick of a thorn causes a reflexive withdrawal of the hand or foot. In classical conditioning, a new stimulus comes to elicit the response. For example, if several times in a row a buzzer is sounded just before a puff of air is blown at your eye, you will probably blink the next time you hear the buzzer, whether the puff of air follows or not.

The noted Russian physiologist Ivan Pavlov discovered classical conditioning in 1904 while continuing a series of studies on the physiology of digestion, for which he had won the Nobel prize earlier that year. Pavlov was originally studying the preparatory reflexes of the stomach—how the stomach prepares itself, by secreting digestive juices, for food that is placed in the mouth. He found that the mouth also prepares itself, by secreting saliva, when food is merely seen or smelled. This is a learned response: When an animal first sees or smells an unfamiliar food, it does not salivate. The fundamentals of conditioning that Pavlov unraveled in studying the conditions under which an animal learns to secrete saliva have had an extraordinary influence on nearly every theoretical position in the psychology of learning.

Strictly speaking, however, Pavlov was not the first to study the conditioned reflex. That honor goes to a little-known American psychologist, Edwin Twitmyer. About the turn of the century, Twitmyer was a graduate

Figure 4.2 The apparatus used in early studies of classical conditioning. Saliva dropping from a tube inserted into the dog's cheek strikes a lightly balanced arm, and the resulting motion is transmitted hydraulically to a pen that traces a record on a slowly revolving drum. Pavlov's discovery of conditioned salivation was an accidental by-product of his researches into the activity of the digestive system.

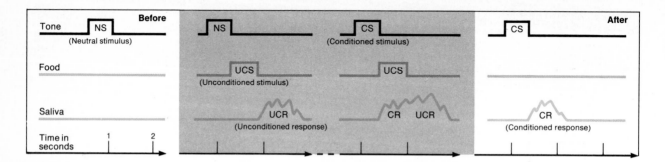

Figure 4.3 The relationship of events in classical conditioning. (from left to right) First, the presentation of a stimulus such as a tone elicits no salivary response and can therefore be described as a neutral stimulus (NS) with respect to salivation. Then, this stimulus, the tone, is paired with an unconditioned stimulus (UCS), food, which elicits the unconditioned response (UCR) of salivation. After repeated pairings of the tone and the food, salivation begins to appear in response to the tone as well as to the food. The tone is now a conditioned stimulus (CS), and the salivation it elicits is a conditioned response (CR). Finally, a test with the tone alone elicits salivation.

student at the University of Pennsylvania. For his dissertation experiment he chose to work with the patellar reflex, or knee jerk. Twitmyer rigged up a small hammer that, when released, would strike a person's patellar tendon. As a warning that he was about to release the hammer, he always sounded a bell beforehand. One day during testing he accidentally hit the bell. Although the hammer did not drop, the person's knee jerked anyway. When Twitmyer asked him why, the subject said he didn't know—the response was involuntary. Recognizing that he had stumbled onto something very interesting, Twitmyer abandoned the original plan for his dissertation in order to study this fascinating new type of learned response. Although he reported his findings at the annual meeting of the American Psychological Association in 1904, none of the scientists there saw the significance of his work. In fact, Twitmyer's report was the first published description of what is now called classical conditioning. Disappointed in the unenthusiastic reception the scientific world gave his experiments, Twitmyer abandoned them entirely.

Within that same year, Pavlov made essentially the same discovery working with dogs that Twitmyer had made working with human beings. At first the scientific world did not give Pavlov much encouragement either, but he was an established investigator—a Nobel-prize winner with his own well-equipped laboratory—and he persevered. Finally, other scientists saw the importance of his work. So Pavlov's name, not Twitmyer's, is associated with the discovery. Because his work was more complete and more elegant than Twitmyer's, we shall discuss it in detail.

The salivary reflex, like all other reflexes, consists of a **stimulus**—food in the dog's mouth—that elicits a **response**—salivation. Pavlov discovered that if a previously neutral stimulus regularly occurs just before food is placed in the dog's mouth, the neutral stimulus itself gradually comes to elicit salivation. In Pavlov's terms, the food in the mouth is an **unconditioned stimulus.** It elicits the **unconditioned response** (or unconditioned reflex) of salivation. The term "unconditioned" is used because the response usually does not depend on the organism's previous experience with the stimulus: An unconditioned reflex is not learned. The new stimulus that comes to elicit salivation is called the **conditioned stimulus.** The salivation that it evokes is called the **conditioned response,** or conditioned reflex—conditioned by the animal's experience of the constant pairing of the unconditioned stimulus with the new stimulus. In other words, classical conditioning occurs when a previously neutral stimulus comes to produce the same response as the unconditioned stimulus, as shown in Figure 4.3. Any one of a large variety of stimuli can serve as a conditioned stimulus for salivation: the sight of food, the sound of a metronome or a bell, the flash of a light.

Establishing a Conditioned Response

The experimental apparatus that Pavlov used is illustrated in Figure 4.2. Before the experiments began, each dog underwent minor surgery: A tube was inserted in its cheek so that saliva would flow from the duct in the dog's salivary gland into a glass container. The mechanical device on the far left of the drawing kept track of the number of drops secreted. In front of the dog was a food tray from which the animal could eat. The unconditioned stimulus was food in the dog's mouth. The conditioned stimulus was a ticking metronome or a light or a brush that stimulated the animal's skin.

In a typical study, the experimenter presented a stimulus—say, the light—for about five seconds, then dropped a piece of food into the dog's tray. The dog picked up the food and salivated as a result of the food in its mouth; this was the unconditioned response. As the pairing of light and food continued time after time, the previously neutral stimulus, the light, began to elicit salivation. This was the conditioned response. Once every few trials, the light was presented alone, without food. As Figure 4.4A shows, the light alone elicited saliva—in this case, between ten and thirteen drops.

Pavlov and other psychologists after him have used a similar procedure to condition other reflexes. For example, an electric shock to a dog's forepaw causes a withdrawal reflex—the dog pulls its paw away from the stimulus. If the unconditioned stimulus (the shock) is regularly preceded by some previously neutral stimulus, such as the ticking of a metronome, the dog soon pulls its paw away in response to the sound alone. Figure 4.5 shows a human example of classical conditioning. The unconditioned physiological response of blushing can be conditioned to a previously neutral stimulus such as a trench coat if the trench coat has been paired with an unconditioned stimulus that produces blushing, such as the sight of a naked man. Some other human emotional responses, such as fear, can be classically conditioned in this same way, so that they occur in response to a previously neutral stimulus. Some people's response to swear words—a speeding up of heart rate and blushing, for example, is an example of a conditioned response.

Extinction

A conditioned reflex continues to occur, Pavlov found, only if the conditioned stimulus is occasionally presented in conjunction with the unconditioned stimulus. If it is not, the conditioned reflex gradually disappears. For example, if a dog has been conditioned to salivate in response to a light and then, on a number of successive trials, a light is presented but food (the unconditioned stimulus) is not, the amount of saliva elicited by the light gradually declines toward zero, as shown in Figure 4.4B. Similarly, if a dog hears the ticking of the metronome on a number of occasions but receives no shock, it

Figure 4.4 Acquisition and extinction of a conditioned response. (A) On early test trials—with light alone—there is little salivation. Later in the series the light alone (CS) elicits considerable salivation. A conditioned response (CR) has been acquired. (B) When the light-food pairings are eliminated, the amount of salivation (CR) to the light alone (CS) drops steadily. The destruction of the relationship between the CS and the CR by this means is known as extinction.
(After Pavlov, 1927.)

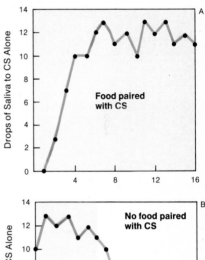

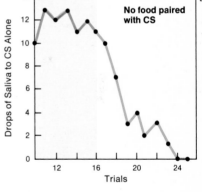

Figure 4.5 Like salivation, blushing is an involuntary response, or reflex, controlled by the autonomic nervous system and capable of being classically conditioned. Here a trench coat (NS) is paired with male nudity (a UCS for the UCR, blushing). As a result, the trench coat becomes a CS for blushing.

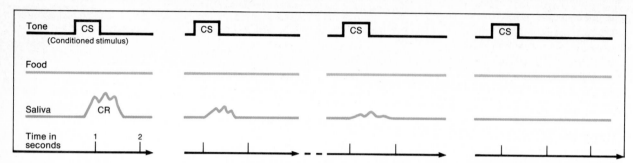

Figure 4.6 The relationship of events in the extinction of a classically conditioned response. The CS is presented repeatedly without the UCS. As a result, the CR gradually diminishes until it is no stronger than it was before conditioning.

gradually stops lifting its paw in response to the ticking. This procedure is called **extinction:** The conditioned reflex gradually decreases in strength and is extinguished. Unless the conditioned reflex is occasionally strengthened by elicitation of the unconditioned reflex, it ceases to occur. Today psychologists use this extinction procedure for certain kinds of therapy, as discussed in Chapter 27. For example, a phobia (an extreme, irrational fear) can often be eliminated through extinction, by presenting the feared object repeatedly in situations where it is clearly harmless.

In addition, extinction sometimes occurs spontaneously. Even though the conditioned response of salivation to a light is always followed by food, a dog may stop salivating when the light is presented alone. Pavlov was an excellent observer as well as a careful experimenter, and early in his research he uncovered this enigma, which is called spontaneous extinction. Today this phenomenon still has not been adequately explained.

Pavlov's findings had an enormous impact on American psychology in general and on behaviorism in particular. He worked out the factors that influence classical conditioning so carefully that many of the standard terms for conditioning phenomena and techniques derive from him, including some that will be discussed later in the chapter, in the section describing operant conditioning.

John B. Watson, the founder of American behaviorism, was so impressed by Pavlov's work that he based his entire behaviorist analysis of learning on it. All learning, he argued, could be explained in terms of classical conditioning. He pointed out, for example, that fear could be classically conditioned and demonstrated his point with a famous experiment involving an eleven-month-old boy named Albert. Watson and his colleague Rosalie Rayner showed Albert a white rat. Albert showed no signs of fear and even tried to play with the rat. Then, Watson and Rayner started their classical-conditioning procedure. At regular intervals they presented the rat and simultaneously sounded a loud noise just behind the child's ear. The noise made Albert cry and become upset, and gradually he began to exhibit conditioned fear whenever they showed him the rat, whether the noise occurred or not. Indeed, Albert's fear even generalized to other furry objects and animals—a rabbit, a dog, and a piece of fur. Fortunately, through the process of extinction, conditioned fears such as Albert's can be unlearned. Although few behaviorists today agree with Watson that all learning can be explained by classical conditioning, virtually no one questions its importance in many types of learning.

OPERANT CONDITIONING

In the 1930s B. F. Skinner in the United States and Jerzy Konorski and Stefan Miller in Poland described a second type of conditioning, **operant conditioning** (sometimes called instrumental conditioning). There are a number of differences between classical and operant conditioning. One of the most basic is that classical conditioning applies to reflexes, whereas operant conditioning applies to what is usually called voluntary behavior. Reflexes are sometimes called respondent behavior, to point up the contrast with voluntary behavior, or **operant behavior.** When an animal salivates in response to food in its mouth, the salivation is a reflex. In behaviorist terms, *the reflex response is elicited from the organism by the stimulus. Operant behavior, on the other hand, is said to be emitted by the organism;* there is no identifiable stimulus that provokes it. No particular stimulus is needed to induce a rat to sniff and move about in its cage, for example. Such behavior is as natural for a rat as flying is for a bird or swinging through trees is for a monkey. The babbling of babies is another example of operant behavior. It is not normally elicited by external stimuli; it simply happens.

The occurrence of operant behavior is, however, *influenced* by events in the environment—in particular, by rewards and punishments. Generally, operant behavior that results in the appearance or attainment of something that is liked will be repeated, and operant behavior that results in something that is disliked will not be repeated. This is what operant conditioning is all about.

Reinforcement and Punishment

The environmental consequences of behavior can be classified according to their effect on the behavior. A consequence that results in the repetition of the behavior that produced it is called **reinforcement,** or **reward;** a consequence that results in the suppression of the behavior that produced it is called **punishment,** or an **aversive stimulus.** Money, for example, is classed as reinforcement for people because behavior that accumulates money tends to be repeated. Loss of friendship and pain are classified as punishment, because behavior that produces them tends not to be repeated. In fact, if a person is exposed to punishment, any behavior that ends the punishment tends to be repeated. In other words, the termination of aversive stimulation, by avoidance or escape, can itself be reinforcing and is, in fact, called **negative reinforcement.** Both punishment and negative reinforcement are discussed at length later in this chapter.

In each case, a behavior is followed by a consequence, and the nature of the consequence modifies the organism's tendency to engage in the behavior in the future. Behavior that is reinforced tends to be repeated; behavior that is punished tends not to be repeated. A reinforcer is defined as a stimulus or event that *increases* the frequency of occurrence of the behavior that it follows (see Figure 4.7). A punisher is defined as a stimulus or event that *decreases* the frequency of occurrence of the behavior that it follows.

An example of operant conditioning using reinforcement is shown in Figure 4.8. A man emits an operant behavior; he kisses a woman friend. She reinforces that behavior by smiling or holding his hand. As a result, his responding increases in frequency and vigor.

Besides increasing the frequency (and vigor) of the behavior that it follows, reinforcement has another effect of equal importance: It brings the reinforced behavior under the control of the stimuli prevailing at the time of reinforce-

Figure 4.7 The relationship of events in operant conditioning. (from left to right) Before conditioning, the response occurs infrequently. Then a food reinforcer is made available as an immediate consequence of each response, and the rate at which the response occurs increases markedly. Finally, the response is seen occurring at a high rate even though no food reinforcers are made available. This high response rate would last only a short time if food were never delivered again.

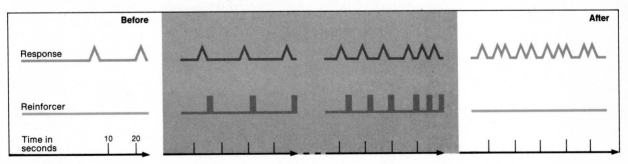

Figure 4.8 Kissing is a response that is subject to operant conditioning. Here the response is emitted tentatively and would probably be repeated only after a considerable time interval if it produced no result. The kiss is reinforced, however, and immediately the response increases in frequency. Note that the operant behavior increases in vigor, as well as frequency, after reinforcement.

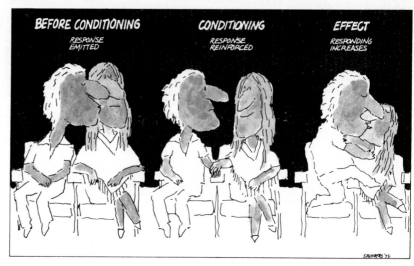

ment. That is to say, the behavior tends to recur predominantly in the presence of stimuli that in the past have set the occasion for its reinforcement. The man in Figure 4.8 kisses his particular friend, not some other woman. This effect of reinforcement is referred to as **stimulus control.**

Stimulus control can be observed when you speak with a slightly deaf person. If he fails to react to what you say, you speak more loudly, until he hears you and reinforces your behavior by responding. The next time you meet that person, you will probably speak more loudly than usual. In this case, the deaf person is a stimulus controlling louder speaking.

Stimulus control is not always so reasonable, however. At times it results in superstitious behavior—behavior that persists because, purely by chance, it preceded reinforcement in a particular situation. For instance, if a golf player happens to wear a certain sweater on a day when he plays unusually well, that response is reinforced and he may begin wearing that sweater whenever he plays golf. The situation of playing golf becomes a stimulus controlling the response of wearing the sweater, even though the superstitious behavior of wearing the sweater does not actually produce the reinforcement.

In summary, then, in the presence of a controlling stimulus the organism emits a response, which produces a reinforcement. As a result, the frequency of the response increases in the presence of that stimulus.

The Shaping of Behavior

In order to see how operant conditioning is studied, let us trace a hungry rat's career in a piece of laboratory equipment developed by B. F. Skinner and called a **Skinner box.** Our rat is going to be trained to press a bar for a food reward in much the same way that a person pulls a lever or a knob to obtain food from a vending machine. The type of Skinner box used to study this behavior is shown in Figure 4.9B; its essential parts are a bar, a light or a buzzer, and a food cup. The light or buzzer is used in the establishment of precise stimulus control. First, however, the animal's behavior must be shaped by the psychologist into the desired response—pressing the bar.

Shaping a Bar Press Operant behavior, as has been pointed out, is emitted by an organism rather than elicited by a particular stimulus. That is, there is no stimulus that will force the rat to press the bar. Furthermore, although an untrained rat has in its behavioral repertoire all the operant behaviors necessary for bar pressing, they rarely occur in the required sequence. In order to press the bar, the rat must approach it, rise up on its hind legs, put its front paws on the bar, and push the bar down toward the floor. An experimenter may, if he wishes, wait to see whether the rat, given enough time, will spontaneously execute this sequence. Or he may use **shaping,** a procedure developed by Skinner, in which the experimenter molds the animal's natural behavior by using reinforcement to produce closer and closer approximations to the desired response. The animal whose behavior is to be shaped must be hungry or thirsty so that the reinforcer (food or water) will be effective.

Shaping begins by reinforcing the first response in the desired sequence—in this case, approaching the bar. After a few reinforcements, the rat begins to interrupt its other behavior in order to approach the lever. Now reinforcement can be withheld until the rat not only approaches the lever but rises slightly off the floor in front of it. At first, the experimenter may have to settle for reinforcing the mere lifting of one paw off the floor; later, he will reinforce only lifting both paws high enough to reach the bar. Next, reinforcement is withheld until the animal puts its paws on the bar. At that point, bar pressing is practically guaranteed. The experimenter simply withholds reinforcement until the lever is actually depressed, and he has finished shaping bar pressing. The procedure is illustrated in Figure 4.10.

Shaping, then, is the reinforcement of ever-closer approximations to a desired behavior. The reinforcement of successive approximations is a powerful technique, but it often assumes the status of an art rather than a science, for it takes a skilled trainer to know which approximations to reinforce and which to ignore. Furthermore, each successive approximation must be only a small step beyond what the animal was previously doing. If the steps are too large, the procedure fails.

There is nothing magical about bar pressing as a response, although it is the one most often studied in experiments with rats. The reason for its popularity is that it is a well-defined act, easy for a rat to perform and easy to record automatically. If reinforcement were made dependent on another operant response, such as sniffing in the cage corner, that behavior, too, could be shaped, and the rat would soon do little else. In the simple environment of a Skinner box, any response that procures food for the hungry rat will tend to be emitted by the animal—almost to the exclusion of anything else.

But something has been left out of the discussion so far. For any organism, a reinforcer must be established before any shaping can occur. In the present example, food is the primary reinforcer, but the rat must be trained to eat from the food cup in the Skinner box before it can be shaped.

Magazine Training Rats are by nature cautious creatures. When a rat is first put into the box, it acts uneasy and cautious until it has had an opportunity to explore for perhaps half an hour, sniffing and touching everything. After that, the rat can be taught that the food cup sometimes contains food. This is

Figure 4.9 Experimental chambers (or "Skinner boxes") for the operant conditioning of common laboratory subjects—the pigeon and the rat. The pigeon is being rewarded for pecking the lighted disc higher on the panel. The reward is several seconds of access to a grain trough. The rat is pressing a bar and may be rewarded with food or water delivered through the round hole in the bottom of the wall.

Figure 4.10 Shaping, a method for producing new responses (such as a bar press) by modifying old ones. Shaping is a selective process; the behavior that is closest to the desired response at any point in time is the behavior selected for reinforcement. Here the rat is first rewarded with food for movements in the general vicinity of the bar; then reinforcement is delivered only if it rises on its hind legs; finally reinforcement is withheld until the rat places its forepaws on the bar. When it does this, the shaping process is all but complete. It is highly likely that the rat will soon put enough weight on the bar to activate the automatic circuitry controlling the delivery of food, the reinforcer. (During shaping, before the rat begins to press the bar, the experimenter watches the animal and delivers reinforcement with a manually operated switch.)

1. Click! | 2. Rat eats | 3. Click! | 4. Rat eats
5. | 6. | 7. Rat paws bar | 8. Rat eats

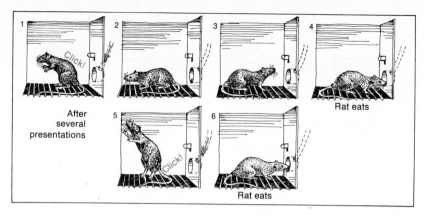

Figure 4.11 Magazine training. The shaping procedure illustrated in Figure 4.10 cannot be carried out unless the gap between the rat's response and the consumption of the reinforcer (food) can be bridged by a conditioned reinforcer such as the "click" of the apparatus that delivers the food. Before shaping, therefore, the rat is exposed repeatedly to the operation of this apparatus, called the food magazine. At first it does not associate the sound with food and may even be afraid of it. But if on repeated occasions the hungry rat discovers food after hearing the "click," the sound will come to be an immediate signal for the availability of reinforcement. The "click" itself will become a conditioned reinforcer, one that can be delivered instantly to the animal at any time, whatever it is doing in the chamber.

done through a procedure called **magazine training.** Regardless of what the animal happens to be doing, the experimenter periodically drops a few pellets of food into the food cup—known as a food magazine—through a plastic tube.

The purpose of magazine training is to establish the reinforcer to be used in shaping. The experimenter must be sure that the rat's bar presses will be reinforced *immediately* after the rat performs them. But food alone is not an immediate reinforcer for bar pressing. Because it takes time for the animal to get food into its mouth, the food may reinforce some behavior other than the bar press, such as a movement of the head, if there is time for that to occur between pressing the bar and eating the food. Magazine training overcomes this problem—and also gives the animal a chance to learn to eat in the new environment of the Skinner box. That is, through magazine training the sights and sounds that accompany the delivery of food—the sight of the food and the "click" sound made when the food drops into the cup—become signals for the reinforcer. Because such signals reach the animal instantly, they provide for immediate reinforcement. Stimuli of this sort are called **conditioned reinforcers** (or, sometimes, secondary reinforcers); they will be discussed at greater length later in this chapter. Food is the **primary reinforcer.**

Magazine training can stop when the rat runs to the food cup and eats whenever food arrives. This behavior indicates that the sights and sounds accompanying the food are well enough established to act as conditioned reinforcers for bar presses.

Something similar to magazine training is also necessary in many human situations that involve shaping. For example, institutions for retarded children often employ a token system to shape the children's behavior. When a child carries out a desired behavior, such as washing his hands or making his bed, he is given a token that he can exchange for a reward, such as candy or a trip to the movies. Before such a token system can affect the child's behavior, however, he must be "magazine trained" with the tokens and taught that they can be exchanged for rewards. Tokens can be used to shape his behavior only after they have been well established as reinforcers. Then the tokens can be employed effectively to influence and control the retarded child's behavior.

Clearly, operant conditioning is not limited to Skinner boxes. It can be used with many different animals. Even a killer whale has been conditioned, as shown in Figure 4.12. And it occurs commonly in daily life, in any situation in which reinforcements are present. For example, as will become clear later in the chapter, parents and children often use reinforcement—purposely or accidentally—to control each other's behavior.

Figure 4.12 Operant-conditioning methods have been applied to training a variety of animals. This killer whale has been trained at Sea World in San Diego, California, to perform a variety of new responses, such as a grateful kiss to the "doctor" who just "examined" her. The doctor rewards his patient with fish.

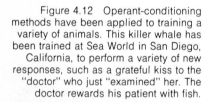

Mazes and Jump Stands Operant conditioning can be studied in any situation where the presentation of reinforcements can be controlled systematically. Psychologists have made use of several kinds of apparatus other than the Skinner box, each with its own particular virtues.

Several popular types of **maze** are shown in Figure 4.13. In a maze the hungry or thirsty rat (or other animal) runs along the paths that lead to a goal box containing food or water, which serves to reinforce movement along the correct path. Mazes are especially useful for studying the early phases of operant conditioning because they eliminate the human factor that is usually present when the behavior of an animal is shaped in a Skinner box. The human experimenter does not affect the rat's learning in a maze, because he does not have to shape the rat's behavior. The maze itself shapes the behavior. The rat will not find the food until it moves along the correct path. The more errors made along the way, the longer the rat takes to obtain the food.

Another common piece of apparatus for studying operant conditioning is the **jump stand,** shown in Figure 4.14. The late Karl Lashley, an eminent physiological psychologist, invented the jump stand to study stimulus control. It is used to train a rat to jump through a door that is marked with a particular stimulus—with vertical bars, for example. The rat's task is always to jump toward the door marked with vertical bars, whether they appear on the right door or on the left one. Behind the correct door the rat usually finds food or some other reinforcement. For this task, the experimenter generally must do some initial shaping of the rat's behavior; also, on most trials he must exert some pressure, such as a squeeze of the tail or a puff of air, to get the rat to jump at all. But the animal usually learns quickly which door to jump toward. Learning on the jump stand is usually much faster than learning in mazes and Skinner boxes, because punishment as well as reinforcement is used: The "wrong" door is locked, so that when the rat jumps toward it, it bumps its nose and falls into a net. The combination of food for jumping toward one door (positive reinforcement), and punishment for jumping toward the wrong door is a very effective way to produce rapid learning.

Extinction

During shaping, why does an organism make closer and closer approximations to the desired response? When the experimenter withholds reinforcement until an animal produces a closer approximation, why doesn't the animal merely give up and return to whatever it was doing before shaping began? The behaviorist's answer to questions like these requires an understanding of what the known effects of extinction are.

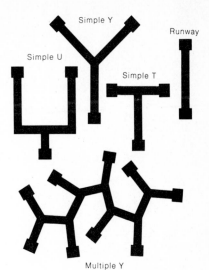

Figure 4.13 Floor plans of various kinds of mazes that have been the traditional apparatus for the laboratory study of learning. The expanded areas at the ends of each maze indicate "start" and "goal" boxes. The runway sets the simplest learning task; the animal, usually a rat, has only to learn that food is available in the goal box. "Y" and "T" mazes are used for discrimination problems; the rat has to learn that food or, perhaps, freedom from shock is available in the goal box at the end of only one of the arms. The "U" maze presents the same problem, but the goal boxes are not in view at the choice point. The multiple "Y" maze presents a series of choice points rather than just one.

Figure 4.14 A rat makes the correct choice in a trial on the Lashley jump stand. A puff of air from the tube leading up to the jumping platform forces the rat to make a choice. Learning is rapid in this apparatus because a correct choice produces food and safety whereas an incorrect choice produces aversive consequences: The rat bumps its nose on the closed door (horizontally striped in this case) and falls into the net below.

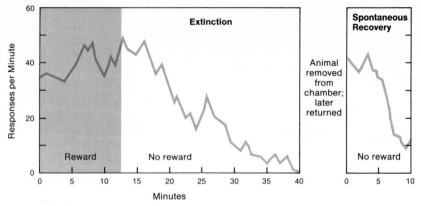

Figure 4.15 Extinction of an operantly conditioned response. In the shaded part of the figure the animal's responding is being reinforced. After twelve and a half minutes reinforcement is withheld, and the animal's responding steadily declines in frequency. After forty minutes the animal is removed from the chamber for a time. When it is returned to the chamber, its response rate begins again at nearly the rate it was before extinction began, even though there has been no reinforcement. This phenomenon is called spontaneous recovery, and it is thought to result from the animal's generalization from other occasions on which it has been rewarded a short time after being put into the chamber. Note that in the absence of reinforcement the behavior quickly extinguishes again.

The extinction of a behavior is brought about by withdrawing reinforcement. When the organism performs a response that previously led to reinforcement, the reinforcement no longer occurs (for example, food no longer drops into the food magazine). The main effect of withdrawing reinforcement is to decrease the probability that the previously reinforced behavior will occur. Behavior that is no longer reinforced gradually dies out. But it does not die quietly. Although the behavior gradually becomes less frequent, it tends to be executed more forcefully and in a wider variety of ways. The pigeon that is shown in Figure 4.1 had been reinforced for pecking a light, then reinforcement was suddenly withdrawn. You can see the bird's agitation and upset. The temporary withholding of reinforcement thus encourages the animal to produce a closer approximation to the desired response. If a rat has been reinforced for lifting its forepaws slightly off the floor and then the reinforcement is withdrawn, the rat lifts its paws less and less often. But the lifts that do occur are more variable and more forceful than before. Some will be high enough off the floor for the rat to press the bar, providing the experimenter with a closer approximation to the desired response, which he can reinforce.

These effects occur whenever a previously reinforced response is no longer reinforced, for people as well as for rats. Suppose your front door, which usually works well, one day does not open. Your previously reinforced response of grasping the knob and turning it is no longer rewarded by the opening of the door. Within a few minutes you will stop trying to get the door open. But in the meantime your responses will become more variable and more forceful than your first attempt. You will probably turn the knob harder, perhaps with both hands. You may kick the door, or even go try the one in the back—an extreme instance of variable responding. If any of these responses succeeds in getting you into the house, it will tend to persist. If none is successful, you will stop trying to enter your house through a door, and perhaps "break in" through an unlatched window. Figure 4.15 shows what typically happens during extinction: When responding is no longer reinforced, the frequency of responding gradually decreases over time.

If an animal is removed from the experimental chamber for a while after a response has been extinguished and then is put back in again, responding will occur again. This phenomenon is called **spontaneous recovery:** During the rest period outside of the chamber, the animal seems to recover spontaneously from the effects of extinction. The reason this happens may be that the animal is responding to situational cues. In the past it was frequently reinforced for a certain behavior when it was placed in the chamber; why not this time? Similarly, you may try the stuck door again the next time you want to get inside, even if last time you had to use a different entrance.

The phenomenon of extinction has many important practical implications. For example, many of the undesirable behaviors of problem children are unknowingly reinforced by parents and teachers. Chapter 27 discusses how techniques of behavior modification are used to eliminate these unwitting reinforcements and thereby extinguish the undesirable behaviors.

Stimulus Effects

In the discussion of operant conditioning so far, the main concern has been with the effect of reinforcement on operant responding. It was mentioned earlier, however, that one effect of reinforcement is **stimulus control.** That is, the stimuli prevailing at the time of reinforcement come to control the responding. When at a later time those stimuli are present, the organism is likely to emit the appropriate operant response. Stimulus control is only one of several ways that stimuli influence operant behavior, but it is an important part of operant conditioning and so will be discussed first in this section.

Discrimination and Generalization In most operant conditioning situations, extremely precise stimulus control can be easily established through a procedure called **discrimination training.**

You may recall that the essential equipment in a Skinner box includes not only a bar and a food cup but a light or buzzer. Assume that the rat of the earlier experiment, which has already acquired the bar-pressing response, is in a box that contains a light. To establish the light as a controlling stimulus, the experimenter changes the situation so that the box is lit for a few minutes, then dark for a few minutes, then lit again, and so on, and he reinforces only bar presses that occur during periods of illumination. The rat quickly stops pressing the bar during periods of darkness. Because bar presses are not reinforced then, the response is extinguished. But the rat continues to press the bar for food when the light is on. The light comes to control responding because pressing the bar is reinforced when it is on. In this way, reinforcement and extinction together can be used to bring a behavior under the control of a specific stimulus (here, the light).

For an animal's behavior to come under the control of a specific stimulus, the animal must discriminate that stimulus from other stimuli. In the bar-pressing example the rat must discriminate "light on" from "light off" and respond only in the presence of "light on." That is why the training procedure is called discrimination training. The stimuli that control behavior in this way are called **discriminative stimuli.** Figure 4.16 shows the sequence of events in discrimination training.

Now consider how an animal trained with a light of one color would respond to a light of a different color. Rats cannot perceive color, so a different animal will have to be the subject. Assume the subject is a pigeon that has been conditioned to peck at a yellow light. If the pigeon is presented with a light of a different color, say, a green light, it will normally peck at this new light, too, though to a lesser degree. When an organism responds in this way to a stimulus different from the stimulus with which it was originally

Figure 4.16 The course of discrimination training. Early in the procedure the animal responds equally frequently in the presence and in the absence of the light, but its responses are reinforced only when the "positive" stimulus is present. As the alternations of "light on" and "light off" are continued and the animal's behavior is reinforced in one condition and not in the other, its behavior gradually comes under the control of the stimuli. The animal responds when the light is on and reinforcement is available and does not respond when the light is off. Light on and light off have become discriminative stimuli controlling the animal's responses.

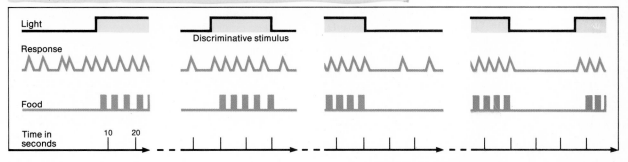

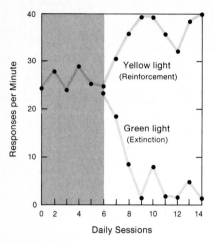

Figure 4.17 A plot of a pigeon's development in discriminating between two colors. Throughout the fourteen daily sessions the pigeon is rewarded with grain for pecking at the light when it is yellow. Beginning on the sixth day, however, the light is green half the time and the bird's pecking is never reinforced when the light is this color. Steadily, its pecking at the green light decreases, while its responding to the yellow light actually increases.

conditioned, psychologists say that **stimulus generalization** has occurred.

Stimulus generalization occurs commonly in everyday life. When a young child first learns to call the family dog "doggie," he frequently calls lots of other animals by the same name—not only other dogs, but cats and perhaps even cows and horses. Likewise, an adult who has learned how to drive a car with a standard gearshift will try to depress the clutch pedal when he is coming to a stop, even if he is driving a car with an automatic transmission, which has no clutch pedal for him to depress.

The extent of generalization can be limited by a discrimination-training procedure similar to the ones used to train the rat to press the bar only when the light was on. Let us continue with the example of the pigeon that was conditioned to peck at a yellow light. In discrimination training, the yellow light alternates with a green light, but only responses to the yellow light are reinforced. Figure 4.17 shows that pecking the green light, the response that is being extinguished, decreases as training proceeds.

To test the effect of this discrimination training on generalization, the behavior of two different pigeons is compared: the pigeon that received discrimination training, and a second pigeon that was conditioned to peck at the yellow light but not given discrimination training. Each pigeon is given a generalization test consisting of a series of different-colored lights, including the yellow and green ones. During the generalization test, no responses at all are reinforced. Eventually, all responding will stop; what the experimenter is interested in is the number of responses each pigeon makes to the various lights before extinction is complete. Figure 4.18 shows the results of a typical experiment of this kind. The amount of responding is plotted along the vertical axis; the color of the lights is plotted along the horizontal axis. The resulting curve is called a **generalization gradient.** The peak of generalization gradients for both pigeons is over the yellow light. The less similar the stimulus is to the yellow light, the less either animal responds. But the pigeon that did not receive discrimination training produces a wider and flatter generalization gradient than the bird that received discrimination training. That is, the one without discrimination training responds relatively more to lights other than the yellow light. This fact points up an important and well-documented finding. The effect of discrimination training is to sharpen and strengthen stimulus control.

Both discrimination and generalization obviously relate to the control of behavior by stimuli. *When a stimulus has strong control over a response, even a slight change in the stimulus will cause the animal to stop responding (discrimination). When the control is not strong, the animal may continue the response despite fairly radical changes that are made in the stimulus (generalization).* Luckily for normal behavior, there are limits on the extent to which discrimination and generalization occur. An organism that carried discrimination to its logical extreme would see every event as different from every other event; a child who had been burned by fire would not hesitate to try to touch it again, because the second fire would look different from the first. On the other hand, an organism whose behavior was completely generalizable would react in exactly the same way to all situations.

Generalization usually occurs only within a stimulus dimension. That is, a pigeon trained to make a particular response to a yellow light may respond the same way to any colored light, but it probably will not make the response to the sound of a bell.

As for discrimination, its theoretical limit is reached when two stimuli are so nearly alike that telling the difference is beyond the organism's biological capacities. For example, no known organism can tell the difference between a tone with a frequency of 5,000 cycles per second and a tone with a frequency

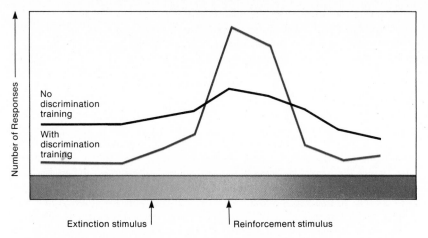

Figure 4.18 Graph showing generalization gradients for two pigeons in a test of color generalization. One pigeon had previously received the discrimination training shown in Figure 4.17; the other had been rewarded for pecking a yellow light but had seen no other colored lights before the generalization test. Discrimination training results in a much more sharply peaked generalization gradient. That is, the pigeon that had received discrimination training treats the colors as more distinct than does the pigeon without this training. Color difference exerts more control over its behavior.

of 5,001 cycles per second. In practice, however, stimulus control rarely needs to be as precise as an organism's biological capacities would permit. Although it is useful to know the difference between an orange, which is to eat, and a baseball, which is to throw, it is usually not necessary to make fine distinctions between various oranges or baseballs.

When an organism that has not been given discrimination training fails to respond differently to two different stimuli, it does not necessarily mean that the animal cannot distinguish between the two. If an animal has been reinforced for responding in the presence of a white light but has not been given discrimination training with a light of a different color, it will also respond (though perhaps less often) in the presence of a similar stimulus such as a green light. This behavior may mean that the animal cannot tell the difference between the white and the green lights, or it may mean that the animal is responding to the brightness of the light, for example, rather than to its color. If a pigeon has by chance learned to respond to the brightness of the white light, it will also respond to other lights on the basis of their brightness, not their color. What an animal does depends not only on the distinctions it is capable of making but on the distinctions it has learned to attend to.

Conditioned Reinforcement Discriminative stimuli are not the only stimuli that affect operant behavior. As discussed in the section on the shaping of behavior, conditioned reinforcers also have an important effect on the direction and control of behavior. A conditioned reinforcer is a stimulus that acts as a signal for the presentation of a reinforcer. For example, the clicking sound of food dropping into the food cup in a Skinner box is a conditioned reinforcer. It signals the arrival of the primary reinforcer, food. An experimenter can use this sound to direct and control the behavior of an animal because the sound occurs immediately after the desired response, before the animal has had time to perform another behavior. If it were not for conditioned reinforcers, primary reinforcers would be effective only when there was no delay between the response to be reinforced and the primary reinforcer.

Both discriminative stimuli and conditioned reinforcers have an effect on the frequency of a response, but there is an important difference between them. Discriminative stimuli accompany a response or precede it (like the lights in the preceding examples), whereas conditioned reinforcers follow the response as a consequence, in the same way that primary reinforcers do.

The power of conditioned reinforcers is suggested by some classic experiments with chimpanzees. John Wolfe has shown that chimps can be trained to perform tasks in order to obtain tokens, which the chimp uses to buy food

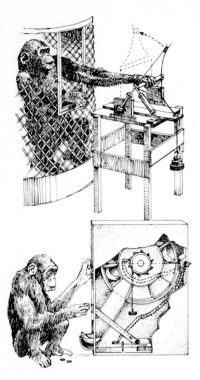

Figure 4.19 A strong conditioned reinforcer in daily human life is money. Wolfe showed in an important series of experiments that chimpanzees, too, could learn to use "money." Wolfe showed that they could be conditioned to pull down a heavily weighted handle in order to obtain tokens (poker chips), which could then be inserted into a machine that vended peanuts or bananas. The value of the tokens to the chimps was evident from the fact that they would work for them and save them—and would sometimes try to steal them from one another.

from a vending machine called a Chimp-O-Mat. The most important conclusion stemming from experiments with the Chimp-O-Mat is that the conditioned reinforcers—the tokens—will bridge very long delays between the performance of the task and the arrival of the primary reinforcer, food. Without the tokens, even small delays between the performance of the task and the arrival of food make the chimp reluctant to continue performing the task.

In experiments of this kind, the effect of the tokens is clear and dramatic, but the mechanism by which they operate is not nearly so clear. In recent years many people have called into question whether the tokens can legitimately be called conditioned *reinforcers*. Do they truly have a reinforcing function of their own, or does their effect depend entirely on the fact that they are signals for the primary reinforcer? People use money in much the same way as the chimps use the tokens—to buy things. But when a currency has lost its value, as happened in several European countries during the Depression of the 1930s, people quickly stop using it and revert to trading the essential goods (such as food, clothing, and fuel for heating homes) that the money formerly bought. When money loses its signal value, it quickly loses its apparently reinforcing effect.

Chains of Behavior   As long as conditioned reinforcers continue to signal the arrival of a primary reinforcer, they can maintain long sequences of behavior. For example, the chimpanzee working for tokens carries out at least three separate responses in sequence, and the first two of them are maintained by conditioned reinforcers. The chimp first pulls a handle to obtain the token from a token-dispensing machine, then operates the Chimp-O-Mat with the token to obtain some food, and finally eats the food.

Such an orderly sequence of stimuli and responses is called a **chain of behavior,** and each separate component of the chain is called a **link.** In the Chimp-O-Mat task there are three links, each with its own discriminative stimulus and its own reinforcer (conditioned or primary), as shown in Figure 4.20. The discriminative stimulus tells the animal which response is appropriate—that is, which link is occurring—and the reinforcer maintains the response for the link. For the first link, the discriminative stimulus is the token-dispensing machine, which tells the chimp that pulling the handle is the appropriate response. For the second link it is the token (as well as the Chimp-O-Mat), which tells the chimp that the correct response is putting the token into the Chimp-O-Mat. For the third link it is the banana, which tells the animal to eat. The conditioned reinforcer for the first link is the presentation of the token, which is produced by the response of pulling the handle and reinforces that response. For the second link, the conditioned reinforcer is the presentation of the banana, which is produced by the response of putting the token into the Chimp-O-Mat and reinforces that response. For the third link, the reinforcer is not conditioned, but primary: The animal eats the banana.

As is evident from the example, the same stimulus in a behavior chain often serves as both a conditioned reinforcer for one link in a chain and a discriminative stimulus for the next link. The token is a conditioned reinforcer for the first link and a discriminative stimulus for the second link. The banana is a conditioned reinforcer for the second link and a discriminative stimulus for the third. Thus, as Figure 4.20 illustrates, the stimulus effects associated with conditioned reinforcers and discriminative stimuli maintain complex sequences of behavior.

Intermittent Reinforcement   Behavior chains are one way to maintain long sequences of behavior, but they are not the only way. With another useful technique, called intermittent reinforcement, reinforcement is delivered not for every response but for every tenth response, say, or every ten minutes regardless of the number of responses that the animal has made during that time. As long as the discriminative stimuli associated with reinforcement are present during the entire period of responding, intermittent reinforcement can be used to maintain long sequences of responses.

If you have ever taught a dog a trick, you probably have had some experience with what happens to an animal's behavior under intermittent reinforcement. Suppose you were training your dog to stand on its hind legs and dance (move around in a circle) and that you were using dog crackers for reinforcement. At first, you would probably reinforce dancing every time it occurs, beginning with rather rough approximations and leading the animal gradually toward a more expert performance (shaping). Then you would probably use discrimination training to establish a discriminative stimulus, such as holding your hand up over the dog's head and moving it in a circle. The best way to establish a new behavior is to reinforce it each time it occurs. Once it has been established, however, you can teach the dog to perform it several times for each cracker if you switch to an intermittent schedule of reinforcement. For example, your dog will dance for a moment when you give it your hand signal. If you respond by giving it the dog cracker, it is likely to wag its tail and go off to eat its cracker. But if you give no reinforcement for the first attempt and continue to give your hand signal, the dog will dance several more times, probably responding more vigorously than the first time. Continuing to give no reward for the response will ultimately bring on complete extinction, but if you stop short of that and simply reinforce every few tries, you can probably keep the behavior going at quite a high, steady rate for a few minutes with only a few reinforcements.

Once an intermittent reinforcement schedule has been established, the behavior in question becomes highly resistant to extinction. If you run out of crackers, the dog will continue to dance many more times before it stops responding than it would if it were used to receiving a cracker after each dance. This fact has much practical importance, because undesirable behaviors are often maintained by intermittent reinforcement. For example, some children misbehave in order to receive attention from adults, which they find reinforcing even though the attention involves scolding. If the adults realize that they are reinforcing the misbehavior by paying attention to the child, they may try to stop the misbehavior by ignoring it. But if occasionally they fail in their attempts, they will be using an intermittent schedule of reinforcement, and they will achieve exactly the opposite of what they want: The frequency of misbehavior will increase, and the misbehavior will become more resistant to extinction. Whether we mean it to be or not, intermittent reinforcement is a powerful technique for maintaining frequent repetition of a behavior. Chapter 27 discusses intermittent reinforcement at length—in particular, how behavior therapists make use of intermittent schedules of reinforcement in behavior therapy and behavior modification.

Aversive Conditioning

Most of the techniques described so far have relied on food, money, or similar positive reinforcers, events that increase the frequency of the behavior that precedes them. Other techniques involve aversive stimuli, or punishers, events that decrease the frequency of the behavior that precedes them. Other techniques also involve **negative reinforcement.** In negative reinforcement, an organism's response removes an aversive or unpleasant stimulation, such as electric shock. In other words, *in positive reinforcement the frequency of a response is increased because of a positive event that the response produces. In negative reinforcement the frequency of a response is increased because of*

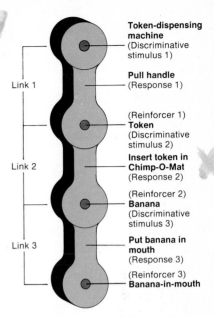

Figure 4.20 An analysis of the behavior of the chimpanzees in Figure 4.19 as a behavioral chain. The "pins" that hold the chain together are stimuli. Each "pin" functions simultaneously as a conditioned reinforcer for the response in the preceeding link and a discriminative stimulus for the response in the following one. At the end of the chain there is a primary reinforcer, the taste of food.

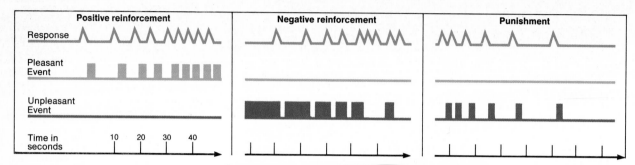

Figure 4.21 The relationships of events in positive reinforcement, negative reinforcement, and punishment. Reinforcement always means that some response is *strengthened*, or increased in rate. In positive reinforcement the consequence that strengthens a response is the *onset* of some pleasant event; in negative reinforcement the consequence that strengthens the response is the *removal* of some unpleasant event. In punishment, the effect on responding is the opposite; responding decreases because the response produces the onset of an unpleasant event. (Note that it would also be possible to "negatively punish" a response, that is, to weaken a response by making it result in the removal of some pleasant event. This relationship between behavior and environment is quite common in everyday life.)

a negative event that the response removes. Figure 4.21 diagrams the sequence of events for both positive and negative reinforcement, as well as for punishment.

The manner in which both types of reinforcement operate in everyday life is illustrated in Figure 4.22. The child throws a temper tantrum because his parents do not want him to play in the mud. His parents give in and let him play in the mud. The parents have positively reinforced the child's temper tantrums by letting him play in the mud; that is, his temper tantrum has produced the desired event, playing in the mud, and so has been reinforced. At the same time, the child has negatively reinforced the parents' giving in; that is, their giving in has removed the aversive event, the temper tantrum, and so has been reinforced.

This example also highlights a distinction between two important concepts that are frequently confused: negative reinforcement and punishment. Negative reinforcement is often used as a synonym for punishment, but that is an error. In punishment, an aversive stimulus or event *decreases* the frequency of occurrence of the response that produces it. In negative reinforcement the removal of an aversive stimulus or event *increases* the frequency of a response. The giving in of the parents in the example was negatively reinforced by the removal of the aversive event, the temper tantrum. But at the same time a different behavior of the parents was punished. They tried to prevent their child from playing in the mud, and he punished their efforts with a tantrum. In this way he decreased the frequency of the parents' attempts to prevent him from playing in the mud. (It may help you to understand negative reinforcement if you remember not only that it results in an increase in the behavior it follows—and is therefore a reinforcer—but also that it *follows* and takes away *(negates)* an aversive stimulus.)

In summary, three types of conditioning are happening in Figure 4.22. The parents' behavior of preventing the child from playing in the mud is *punished* by the child's temper tantrum. His temper tantrum in turn is *positively reinforced* by the parents' giving in and allowing him to play in the mud. And the parents' giving in is *negatively reinforced* by the removal of the aversive event, the child's temper tantrum.

Although negative reinforcement and punishment are totally different processes, they are often categorized (as here) under aversive conditioning because both involve aversive stimulation; that is, there must be some aversive stimulus before negative reinforcement can be administered.

Two important ways of administering negative reinforcement involve escape from or avoidance of an aversive stimulus. Psychologists have developed conditioning procedures that use escape or avoidance.

Escape and Avoidance In escape conditioning an organism is exposed to some kind of aversive stimulation; it performs a response that removes that stimulation and so is negatively reinforced. Escape conditioning usually proceeds rapidly; usually less shaping is required to establish an escape response

Figure 4.22 An analysis of the relationship between the behavior of a child and the behavior of his parents. To follow the analysis it is important to remember that one person's response may at the same time be another person's consequence. (from left to right and from top to bottom) The child is about to engage in a positively reinforcing activity (playing in the mud), but his parents are emitting a behavior (forbidding him to play in the mud) that threatens to block his access to that reinforcer. He punishes their forbidding behavior with an aversive stimulus (a violent tantrum). Their forbidding behavior decreases in strength and is replaced by a new behavior: They give in. The parent's giving-in behavior is now negatively reinforced by the removal of the aversive tantrum. The child's tantrum is positively reinforced with the consequence playing-in-the-mud. The results of this conditioning process are that tantrums are now more likely, forbidding is less likely, and giving in is more likely. The new behavior may generalize to any new situation that is similar enough to the situation in which the conditioning originally occurred.

than to establish a response that is positively reinforced. There is a rather simple explanation for the rapidity of shaping with escape conditioning. Aversive stimulation often produces a great amount of activity in an animal, which increases the likelihood that the animal will make the response the experimenter is looking for. Consider the rat in Figure 4.23, which receives a shock when current is passed through the grid on the floor of its box. When the current is turned on, the rat jumps around excitedly, providing the experimenter with a wide variety of behaviors from which to choose a close approximation to the desired response—for example, bar pressing. The response is reinforced when the experimenter turns off the current.

Avoidance conditioning is similar to escape conditioning in one important respect. In avoidance conditioning a signal warns the animal that an aversive stimulus, such as electric shock, is about to occur. If the animal makes the appropriate response during the warning signal, the shock does not occur. If it does not make the appropriate response during the warning signal, then it can no longer *avoid* the shock and can only *escape* it. For example, a rat in an experimental box might hear a tone for five seconds and then receive a shock. In order to avoid the shock, the rat must learn to run through a door into an adjoining box and press a bar in the second box. If it does not press the bar

Figure 4.23 This rat is in an experimental chamber in which electric shocks can be delivered through the bars in the floor. Jumping is being negatively reinforced. If the rat happens to press the bar, his behavior will be even more strongly negatively reinforced—the electricity will be completely shut off for a short period.

during the five seconds that the tone is sounding, it will be shocked. In this situation the rat quickly learns to run into the adjoining box and press the bar as soon as the tone begins to sound.

Punishment and Its Side Effects Escape and avoidance conditioning involve reinforcement and thus an increase in the frequency of a response. Punishment generally lowers the probability of the response that it follows. To study punishment in any detail, it is usually necessary to punish a response that is being maintained by some positive reinforcer. Otherwise, there will be no reason for the animal to continue responding, and there will be no response to study. Figure 4.24 shows how varying degrees of punishment affect the frequency of a response that is simultaneously maintained with a food reinforcer. The more intense the electric shock, the less the animal responds.

Although punishment can quickly eliminate undesirable behavior or at least reduce its frequency, it is often a poor method of control because it has undesirable side effects. It is intrinsically unpleasant and so commonly creates emotional behavior, which interferes with learning. In addition, punishment can readily produce escape or avoidance conditioning, which can likewise interfere with learning. In a school where punishment is a primary technique to induce learning, children will frequently attempt to avoid attending the school as much as possible, and thus never learn the skills that it is supposed to teach them.

There are other methods for eliminating behavior that do not have these undesirable side effects. One is to determine what reinforcer is maintaining the behavior and then eliminate it, so that the behavior will be extinguished. Another is to use positive reinforcement to condition behavior that is incompatible with the unwanted behavior. For example, instead of attempting to eliminate stuttering by punishing it, a parent or teacher can reinforce smooth speech. Still another method is to try to avoid the need to punish incorrect behaviors by ensuring from the start that only correct behavior occurs. This technique, used commonly by animal trainers, usually requires careful initial shaping of behavior and elimination of opportunities to perform an undesired response. If a puppy is never allowed near streets except when it is under the control of its owner, then it will be easy to train it to cross only at its owner's command. It will never have had the opportunity to learn to run into the street by itself.

COMPARISON OF OPERANT AND CLASSICAL CONDITIONING

So many different varieties of operant conditioning have been described by now that it is easy to get overwhelmed by the details and lose sight of what

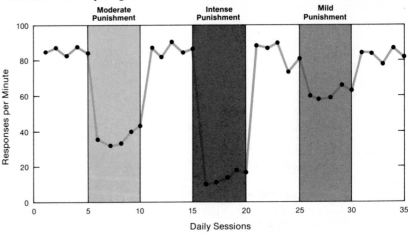

Figure 4.24 A graph of the effects of different intensities of punishment on responding that is being maintained by intermittent positive reinforcement. (That is, the animal is receiving both food and shock for responding.) The effect of punishment appears to be proportional to its intensity. It should be noted that even at the lowest levels of responding the animal is still responding enough to obtain its usual amount of food.
(After Reynolds, 1967.)

they all have in common. What is important to remember is that whichever varieties are used, the procedure of operant conditioning always has the same basic characteristics. If a reinforcer or punisher is not present, it must be established. Once established, it is presented whenever the animal or person carries out some specific desired response, and its presentation alters the frequency of that response. Reinforcement increases the frequency of the response, whether the reinforcement is positive (response *produces* event) or negative (response *removes* event). Punishment decreases the frequency of the response. In addition, reinforcement and punishment both establish stimulus control. The organism tends to produce a response primarily in the presence of stimuli that in the past have set the occasion for reinforcement of that response; the organism tends to inhibit (or fail to produce) a response primarily in the presence of stimuli that in the past have set the occasion for punishment of that response.

Classical conditioning also has a few such basic characteristics. An unconditioned stimulus elicits an unconditioned response, or reflex. When a previously neutral stimulus is paired repeatedly with the unconditioned stimulus, then it becomes a conditioned stimulus. That is, it comes to elicit the same response, now called a conditioned response.

Classical and operant conditioning procedures are what behaviorists use to separate learning from performance and, more generally, to explain learning. In many situations, especially in the laboratory, the two types of conditioning procedures can be easily separated, but in everyday life they often tend to overlap. Recall, for example, John B. Watson's example of classical conditioning of fear. The infant Albert was conditioned to fear a white rat, and his fear generalized to other furry objects and animals. As soon as such fear is established, operant conditioning will usually begin to occur. The child will learn operant responses that allow him to avoid or escape from furry objects and animals. Likewise, when punishment is being used to establish operant conditioning, an inadvertent accompaniment of the punishment is classical conditioning of fear to the agent of punishment. The teacher who punishes the child becomes a conditioned stimulus evoking fear.

Nevertheless, the two types of conditioning procedures can be precisely defined, and their effects can usually be separated. Although both types involve the establishment of a connection between a stimulus and a response, the two procedures and their effects clearly differ greatly. Table 4.1 summarizes the most important distinctions between operant and classical conditioning.

Table 4.1 **Distinctions Between Classical Conditioning and Operant Conditioning**

Classical Conditioning	Operant Conditioning
Behavior affected is usually experienced as *involuntary*—for example, reflexes (knee jerk, salivation, eye blink), feelings (fear, anxiety).	Behavior affected is usually experienced as *voluntary*—for example, actions (bar press), thoughts (plans for action).
Key events (unconditioned and conditioned stimuli) are *presented* to the organism.	Key events (reinforcement and punishment) are *produced* by the organism's behavior.
Those events *elicit* the behavior; that is, they directly evoke it.	Those events *control* the behavior; that is, they determine how often the organism emits it.
In the absence of key stimuli, the behavior *does not occur.*	In the absence of specific stimuli, the behavior *does occur*; the effect of discriminative stimuli is to alter its frequency.

Figure 4.25 Ivan Pavlov's work on the conditioned reflex is one of the cornerstones of modern experimental psychology. In Russia, Pavlov's native country, his work occupies an even more central role in psychological theory. Pavlov was already an honored physiologist when he stumbled upon the conditioned salivations, which he called "psychic secretions," of dogs in his laboratory. He subsequently attained international recognition for the theoretical systems he based on this discovery.

SUMMARY

1. Around 1913, John B. Watson changed the course of American psychology by formulating the approach to psychological questions called **behaviorism.** In order to become a science, Watson said, psychology would have to abandon the introspective method and the examination of subjective phenomena, concentrating instead on the **objective analysis of observable behavior,** such as visible actions, speech, and measurable physiological changes.

2. Behaviorism has two main goals: the precise description of observable behavior and the development of **techniques to control behavior.** B. F. Skinner and his followers tend to emphasize the second goal and to stress the need for **behavioral engineering.**

3. Behaviorists distinguish between **learning** and **performance.** Working under carefully controlled conditions, they attempt to infer (invisible) changes in learning from (observable) changes in performance. They usually do this by referring to two well-established experimental techniques: classical conditioning and operant conditioning.

4. **Classical conditioning** was discovered by the Russian physiologist Ivan Pavlov early in the twentieth century.

   a. Classical conditioning applies to involuntary behavior, and particularly to **reflexes**—involuntary responses that are elicited by particular stimuli. For example, salivation is a reflex response elicited by the stimulus, food in the mouth.

   b. Pavlov found that if a previously neutral stimulus, such as a light, is regularly presented to a dog just before food is placed in the animal's mouth, the light itself gradually comes to elicit salivation. The **unconditioned stimulus** is food in the mouth; the **unconditioned response** is salivation elicited by the food. The **conditioned stimulus** is the previously neutral stimulus (the light) that comes to elicit the response; the **conditioned response** is salivation elicited by the light.

   c. In their well-known experiment with the eleven-month-old boy Albert, Watson and Rayner showed that not only reflexes but emotions—in this case, fear—can be classically conditioned. Albert at first showed no fear when he was presented with a white rat. Then a loud noise, which made Albert cry, was sounded each time he was given the rat. Soon the rat alone elicited fear.

   d. Pavlov found that classical conditioning can be undone through the procedure of **extinction.** If the conditioned stimulus (which, for Albert, is the white rat) is repeatedly presented alone, without the unconditioned stimulus (the noise), the conditioned response (fear of the rat) eventually dies out.

5. **Operant conditioning** was first described in this country by B. F. Skinner around 1930.

   a. Operant conditioning applies to voluntary behavior, or **operant behavior.** Whereas reflexes are elicited by particular stimuli, operant behavior is spontaneously emitted by an organism. Some examples of operant behavior are a rat exploring its cage, a bird flying, and a baby babbling.

   b. The basic principle of operant conditioning is that behavior that is

Figure 4.26 Clark Hull's stimulus-response learning theory was the most comprehensive and ambitious psychological theory in the first half of the twentieth century. His work stimulated a tremendous amount of research and continues to be influential in the study of learning, motivation, and behavior modification to this day. Hull's theory was exactingly formulated and rigorously tested. He was famous for expressing learning phenomena in mathematical formulas.

rewarded (reinforced) tends to be repeated, whereas behavior that is punished tends not to be repeated. **Reinforcement** is therefore defined as a stimulus or event that increases the frequency of occurrence of the behavior it follows; **punishment** is defined as a stimulus or event that decreases the frequency of occurrence of behavior it follows. Punishment is sometimes called an **aversive stimulus.**

c. Three pieces of laboratory equipment commonly used to study the conditioning of operant behavior are the **Skinner box,** the **maze,** and the **jump stand.**

d. **Shaping,** which can be defined as the reinforcement of closer and closer approximations to a desired behavior, is used by psychologists to teach an animal to perform the behavior to be studied. For example, shaping is used to train a rat to press the bar in a Skinner box.

e. Before shaping begins, the experimenter uses **magazine training** to teach the rat that the food cup in the Skinner box sometimes contains food. The purpose of magazine training is to establish the sight and sound of the arriving food as **conditioned reinforcers** (or secondary reinforcers). This must be done because it takes time for the animal to get the food (the **primary reinforcer**) into its mouth, and reinforcement is most effective if it reaches the animal immediately after the desired behavior occurs.

f. **Tokens** are examples of conditioned reinforcers that can be used to bridge long delays between the performance of a task and the arrival of a primary reinforcer such as food. For instance, chimpanzees will perform tasks in order to obtain tokens that are later used to buy food from a Chimp-O-Mat vending machine; token systems are sometimes used to influence the behavior of institutionalized retarded children and others.

g. The **extinction** of operant behavior is brought about by withholding reinforcement. The withholding of reinforcement has two main effects: (1) it decreases the frequency of the previously reinforced behavior, which eventually dies out (is extinguished); (2) while the behavior is dying out, it is executed less often but *more forcefully and in a wider variety of ways.* The latter effect explains why, during shaping, an animal produces closer approximations to the desired behavior when reinforcement is withheld.

h. **Stimulus control** refers to the fact that reinforced behavior tends to recur in the presence of stimuli that in the past have set the occasion for its reinforcement.

i. **Discrimination** and **generalization** are related to the precision of stimulus control. If a pigeon has been reinforced for pecking at a yellow light, it will also peck at lights of other colors, and we say that **stimulus generalization** has occurred. But if the experimenter, using a procedure known as **discrimination training,** reinforces *only* pecks at the yellow light, the pigeon will stop pecking at other lights. Discrimination training sharpens and strengthens stimulus control by establishing a **discriminative stimulus**—in this case, the yellow light.

j. An orderly sequence of stimuli and responses, such as the sequence a chimp executes in Chimp-O-Mat studies, is called a **chain of behavior;** each behavior in the chain is called a **link.** The sequence of behavior is maintained because each link has its own discriminative stimulus and its own reinforcer, and the same stimulus often serves as

Figure 4.27 Karl Lashley made important contributions as a neurophysiologist to the study of learning. Lashley's work formed the basis for much of the field now known as physiological psychology. He was interested, for example, in discovering exactly where memories for newly learned tasks were stored in the brain. He was never able to discover any precise location for them, and difficulties such as this led him once to pronounce ironically: "I sometimes feel . . . that the necessary conclusion is that learning is not possible at all. Nevertheless, in spite of such evidence against it, learning does sometimes occur."

Figure 4.28 B. F. Skinner is the most influential thinker in the American behaviorist tradition and one of the most influential people in the history of psychology. His contributions include an emphasis on the environmental determinants of behavior; a highly effective technology for the control of behavior in the laboratory and in everyday life; and a strong statement for the necessity of using behavioral control for humanistic purposes on a wide social scale instead of ignoring it and allowing it to be used by special interests for limited and often antihumanist purposes.

both a conditioned reinforcer for a preceding link and a discriminative stimulus for the next link.

k. Another effective way to maintain behavior is through **intermittent reinforcement,** in which an animal is reinforced not for every correct response but, say, for every tenth correct response. Intermittently reinforced behavior is very resistant to extinction.

l. Negative reinforcement and punishment are often confused with each other. **Negative reinforcement** involves the removal of an aversive stimulus and *increases* the frequency of a response; for example, a rat often presses a bar if doing so turns off an electric shock. With punishment, the occurrence of an aversive stimulus *decreases* the frequency of the response that produces it; for example, a rat stops pressing the bar if each bar press turns on an electric shock.

m. Two negative reinforcement techniques are **escape conditioning,** in which an animal performs a response that removes aversive stimulation, and **avoidance conditioning,** in which a warning signal is given and the animal performs the response to prevent the arrival of aversive stimulation.

n. Punishment, though a powerful way to eliminate unwanted behavior, has undesirable side effects. For example, a child who is often punished at school may become conditioned to avoid educational institutions.

6. To summarize, the basic characteristics of classical conditioning are:

   a. An unconditioned stimulus elicits an unconditioned response, or reflex.

   b. When a previously neutral stimulus is paired repeatedly with the unconditioned stimulus, it becomes a conditioned stimulus. It elicits the same response (now called the conditioned response) as does the unconditioned stimulus.

7. The basic characteristics of operant conditioning are:

   a. A reinforcer or punisher is identified or, if necessary, established.

   b. A reinforcer is presented whenever the animal carries out a desired response, which increases the frequency of the response; if punishment is used, a punisher is presented whenever the animal carries out an undesired response, and its effect is to decrease the frequency of the response.

   c. Both reinforcement and punishment bring about stimulus control of the response.

8. The distinctions between classical and operant conditioning are summarized in Table 4.1.

SUGGESTED READINGS

Boring, Edwin. *A History of Experimental Psychology.* New York: Appleton-Century-Crofts, 1950. The definitive book on the history of the various branches of experimental psychology, including both behaviorism and the introspectionist approach.

Hilgard, Ernest R., and Gordon H. Bower. *Theories of Learning.* 3rd ed. New York: Appleton-Century-Crofts, 1966. A systematic treatment of major behaviorist theories of learning and also of some nonbehaviorist theories.

Kimble, Gregory A. *Hilgard and Marquis' Conditioning and Learning.* 2nd ed. New York: Appleton-Century-Crofts, 1961. A classic treatment of behaviorist research on learning, with emphasis on the approach of Clark Hull.

McGuigan, Frank J., and D. Barry Lumsden (eds.). *Contemporary Approaches to Conditioning and Learning.* New York: John Wiley, 1973. A collection of papers in which psychologists specializing in the study of learning discuss recent, exciting developments in the field.

Pavlov, Ivan P. *Conditioned Reflexes.* G. V. Anrep (tr.). London: Oxford University Press, 1927. A definitive statement of Pavlov's work, this book is the translation of a series of lectures given in 1924 in which Pavlov summarized his research and theory.

Reynolds, George S. *A Primer of Operant Conditioning.* Glenview, Ill.: Scott, Foresman, 1968. A brief but thorough account of the theory and principles of operant conditioning, as developed from the work of B. F. Skinner and his friends.

Skinner, B. F. *The Behavior of Organisms.* New York: Appleton-Century-Crofts, 1938. The book in which Skinner first spelled out his approach to learning.

Skinner, B. F. *Walden Two.* New York: Macmillan, 1948. A novel outlining a utopian society where behavior is programmed according to Skinner's analysis of learning by reinforcement.

Skinner, B. F. *Beyond Freedom and Dignity.* New York: Knopf, 1971. Skinner's controversial book that argues for a program of psychological engineering in society and against the meaningfulness of such concepts as freedom and dignity.

Watson, John B. *Behaviorism.* New York: Norton, 1930. An introduction to behaviorism by the man who founded it.

Memory has a good press. It is considered a great thing to have a good memory, and a constant annoyance to be prone to forget. To remember trivial things is often considered a sign of great intelligence, and in the 1950s, game shows on television offered huge sums of money and vast public respect for people who could remember batting averages of ball players and middle names of presidents. Newspaper and magazine reports of investigations into the machinery of memory always seem to be about ways and means for making memory more extensive and intensive, and yet . . .

In all the fuss, is there no one to raise a voice in praise of forgetting? Is there no one who is willing to point out that if memory has its uses, so has forgettery?

For instance, when I was seventeen, my younger brother was eight, and I was in charge of him when my hard-working parents couldn't be. At one time he was playing assiduously and noisily with a rubber ball, and my mother wanted him to stop. He wouldn't, so my mother looked at me and made a gesture that indicated I was to take care of it. I approached my younger brother with a friendly grin and said, "Hey, Stan, throw me the ball and I'll show you a trick." He threw me the ball and I instantly tossed it over the roof. The ball was gone, and that effectively stopped his playing.

But he looked at me with shock and horror, then hung his head and walked away, and that look went through me like an ice pick. I had betrayed him and taken advantage of his trust, and I cannot adequately describe what a mean dog I felt myself to be at that moment.

For years afterward, Stanley's eight-year-old face would rise before me, hurt and disillusioned, and each time I squirmed. Nothing I could do would wipe it out. It was always there, as clear and fresh as in the beginning, any time I chose to look at it. At this very moment, as I write, I feel the bitter shame.

In adulthood, Stan and I rarely had the chance to talk to each other alone, but one of those rare occasions came a couple of years ago. On impulse, I decided to cleanse myself of the burden. I told Stanley the story and then apologized and asked for forgiveness. But Stanley looked at me, puzzled, and said, "I don't remember a thing about it."

The incident hadn't bothered him for more than an hour or two, but, thanks to my inefficient forgettery, it has made me writhe for over thirty years!

Isaac Asimov

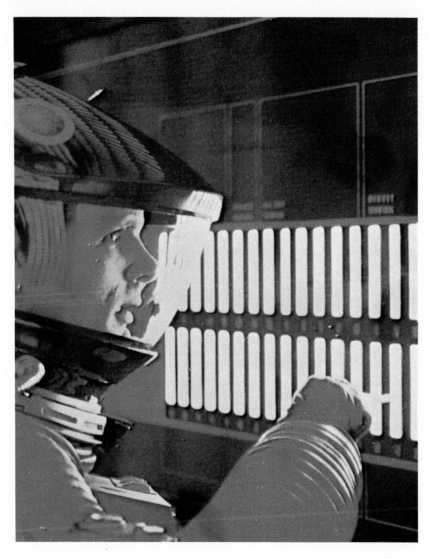

Figure 5.1 In this scene from the film *2001: A Space Odyssey*, Dave, an astronaut en route to Jupiter, is removing some of the components from the memory of HAL, his spaceship's traitorous giant computer. No computer has yet been built that can act as humanly as HAL, but computers have been programmed to answer questions, play chess, and draw pictures. The ways in which computers receive, retain, and use information have become important models for the study of perception, memory, and thought in human beings.

Scientists often use metaphorical explanations of natural phenomena when they cannot understand them directly—they say things are "like" something else. At one time, for example, atoms were characterized as miniature solar systems: The nucleus of the atom was "like" the sun, and the whirling electrons were "like" its planets. Psychologists are especially likely to use metaphorical explanations because many of the processes they seek to understand cannot be viewed directly. Thoughts, emotions, motives, attention, memory—these have always seemed suspiciously spiritual and unusually resistant to scientific analysis, so psychologists begin by saying, for example, that memory is "like a library."

The popular metaphors in psychology have changed periodically in response to technological progress. Whenever a machine is invented that produces complex, humanlike behavior, scholars and popular writers begin to use a new set of mechanical metaphors to describe people. Hundreds of years ago, when European clockmakers, just for fun, designed springs and gears to move the parts of realistic dolls, writers began to use phrases like "the springs of action" and "wound up," and we still find these in our vocabulary today. Later, when the steam engine came along, writers and psychologists saw certain similarities between steam-powered machines and human beings. The machines "ate" coal or wood and turned the resulting energy into steam pressure, which in turn could be channeled through pipes and pistons to create a wide variety of actions. Freud's psychoanalytic theory (described in Chapter 18) is sometimes said to be "hydraulic" because he spoke of psychic energy that was produced by a source, "flowed" through channels, got blocked and repressed, and "leaked out," or expressed itself in unexpected forms (such as dreams and slips of the tongue). Freud's language was a reflection of the mechanical systems available in the late nineteenth century.

Not long after Freud developed the energy metaphor, American behaviorist psychologists, whose view of learning is presented in Chapter 4, adopted the "switchboard" metaphor. They likened human behavior—which they explained in terms of a stimulus followed by a response—to the plugging in of a switch on a telephone switchboard and the immediate ringing of a phone. (This stimulus-response process, under the circumstances described in Chapter 4, produces conditioned learning.)

Today a new breed of machines is available—computers—and, true to form, psychologists and popular writers are describing people in terms of these machines. People may sometimes express their failure to comprehend something by saying it "doesn't compute" or is "difficult to process."

Although it might seem all right to dismiss the language of metaphor-makers as passing fads—last decade you were a telephone switchboard, this decade you are a computer—these comparisons are extremely useful. Real insight is gained each time psychologists can account for a formerly mysterious process in a mechanical way. And such accounts have become more interesting and accurate as more impressive machines have been designed—machines deliberately designed to perform like human beings, as some computers and communication devices have been.

Therefore, this chapter examines some insights gained by psychologists who have adopted the language and concepts of computer and communication scientists; the insights are especially useful in areas of human activity like attention, memory, and problem solving.

THE INFORMATION-PROCESSING METAPHOR

You probably have had some contact with a computer and, if not, you have surely seen an adding machine or a pocket calculator. The purpose of such machines is to transform an initial set of data, called input, into a useful set of results, called output. Typically the input is a set of numbers representing something like the costs of goods and services. The output may be a specified breakdown of the data or a total or an average. The general name for the input and the output is information. This term has a precise technical definition in the communication and information sciences, but for the purposes of this chapter, it is all right to rely on your own intuitive understanding of it. The transformation of input into output, which is called information processing, is accomplished inside the computer by a list of instructions for a set of operations, called a **program.** A simple program for human information processing, set up as a computer program would be, is shown in Figure 5.2. The situation is as follows: A person is facing an apparatus that flashes either a red or a green light (input). He is to press a key on the right when the red light flashes and a key on the left when the green one flashes (output). Figure 5.2 shows how a computer program would represent the processing of this information.

The basic difference between the classical behaviorist approach and the information-processing one is that behaviorists have not in the past considered that one could study—or even make conjectures about—the human "program." Because what occurred inside the person who received the stimulus (input) and made the response (output) was not observable, behaviorists considered that it could not be scientifically studied. Now that computer technology is so advanced and some of the complex programs are available for study, many psychologists who formerly referred to themselves as behaviorists are turning to an information-processing approach and attempting to study the series of operations people perform that are analogous to computer programs.

As part of their processing function, computers must also store a great deal of information in a way that it can be quickly and efficiently retrieved. So

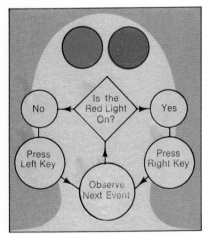

Figure 5.2 A simple piece of human behavior described in information-processing terms. The input here is the flashing of one of two lights. The output is the pressing of one of two keys. This diagram describes a program that establishes a systematic relationship between the input and the output: If the red light flashes, the right key will get pressed; if the green light flashes, the left key will get pressed.

computers also raise provocative questions about human memory. Before the invention of computers, most psychologists said that memory worked by "association." No doubt there is some truth to this, but how exactly do associations allow a person to answer the question, "Are all canaries yellow?" How does one know the rules of football by association? As soon as it became necessary to design complex memory systems for computers, vague answers to such questions were no longer acceptable. If a computer is to recall yesterday's temperature and average it with today's temperature, it has to be specifically and painstakingly programmed so it can locate yesterday's temperature in its memory. If retrieval is to be rapid, the computer's memory must be systematically organized. It is obvious that the average person can retrieve (recall) a vast amount of information on a specified topic in a very short time (Where did you go to kindergarten? Who was the President of the United States before Richard Nixon? Is a Ford a President or an automobile?), and this fact leads computer scientists to believe that human memory must be very well organized. One thing psychologists hope to learn, perhaps through the information-processing approach, is exactly what the organization of human memory is.

Comparisons between human and mechanical information-processing systems are being made by two different groups of scientists, using two different approaches. In one approach, called **computer simulation,** psychologists construct computer programs that act as much like people as possible. Their goal is the same as the goal of any other psychological theorist—to explain particular processes precisely and to make predictions that can be tested experimentally with human subjects. The computer program is, in fact, the theory, and it is an especially clear form of theory: Each logical step is completely specified, and precise predictions can be made simply by running the program under various conditions to see what it does. As a theory, the program predicts that humans will act just as it does. Such predictions can be tested by observing human subjects performing under the same conditions as the program.

In the second approach, called **artificial-intelligence (AI)** research, scientists and engineers attempt to build machines that perform human functions, but they make no special effort to use the same process found in humans. Often, in fact, their goal is to find novel methods that will allow the machines to work better and faster than humans. AI researchers would like to build a voice-operated typewriter, for example, a machine that would in some ways replace a human secretary. They have no particular interest in making the machine work the way a human being works, as long as it performs its function efficiently. Although this approach may seem less relevant to psychologists than computer simulation, many programming techniques and mechanical devices that have been invented by AI researchers have turned out to be useful to simulation psychologists. Knowing how a machine can be programmed to perform an operation formerly performed only by humans, simulation psychologists can gain good insight into how humans function.

INPUT

No one has actually invented a voice-operated typewriter, so you cannot simply go to a computer center and talk to a machine. The sound of your voice would have no effect because computers do not have sound sensors. Even if they did, there is nothing in a computer that can turn sound into meaning. Similarly, you could not show the computer a painting by Picasso and hope for a response. Most computers have no visual system, and the few that do can "see" only specifically constructed objects such as diagrams and simple block designs. Information must be put into acceptable form (for example, punch cards or magnetic tape) before the computer can process it, and it must enter the computer in a systematic way—usually one item at a time according to a predetermined sequence.

Although the channels through which computers can receive input seem remarkably limited in comparison with the channels available to people, their limitations raise questions about the way human perception and attention work. After all, humans cannot detect all kinds of information either; they cannot detect x-rays and infrared light, for example, and some sounds are too high in pitch and others too low to be detected by the human ear. In a sense, then, we humans can only process information that is suitable for our "input devices." Moreover, there are definite limitations on the amount of information that a person can handle at one time. A person who is listening to one conversation has trouble following another simultaneously. If someone gets distracted while trying to remember a telephone number, the number may be crowded out of his memory. One of the goals of psychologists who study information processing is to characterize these limitations on input and processing capacity.

Sensory Gating

The brain is able to control the sense receptors to some extent and so can put a damper on incoming sensory information that is not important at the time. When you attend to a visual stimulus—a painting, for example—the brain sends messages to your ears and other sensory systems to cut down the volume of information coming over those channels. This selective damping down is called **sensory gating.** Despite this process, if your ears detect a strange sound—or an unexpected silence—while you are looking at the painting, your attention will probably shift, at least briefly, to the message coming into your ears. This phenomenon indicates that sensory gating is not complete and that information in sensory systems that are tuned down gets some processing; otherwise you would not know when to shift the focus of attention.

Selective Attention

A more complex form of information selection can occur *within* a particular sensory channel. When you carry on a conversation at a crowded cocktail party, for example, your ears receive a great deal of extraneous information. Besides hearing the person you are conversing with, you may also hear the din of other conversations mixed with clinking glasses and music. Somehow you manage to screen out all but your partner's conversation, the attended message. It may seem that you do this by completely ignoring the other sounds, but research evidence indicates that an elementary form of processing is applied even to the rest of the sounds, the nonattended messages. An example of selective attention in vision is shown in Figure 5.3. People were given different instructions about what to look for in the painting shown; then their eye movements were recorded. You can see how their intentions affected what they paid attention to.

Because cocktail parties are sometimes chaotic and the conditions uncontrollable, psychologists have created a tamer way of testing the same phenomenon. They put earphones on their subjects and ask them to "shadow" a message coming into one ear. To shadow is to repeat a message aloud as it is received (the subject's voice, like a shadow, trails along immediately behind the recorded message). While the message is being played into one ear and shadowed, another message is played into the other ear. Later the subject is asked to recognize or recall material that was played into the ear that received the nonshadowed message. If he had not processed the nonshadowed message at all, the subject would be unable to remember anything about it. In fact, what happens under most conditions is that people detect only gross characteristics of the message they did not have to shadow (attend to). They notice whether a voice was present and whether it changed midway from male to female, but they generally do not remember the contents of the message or the language in which it was spoken—in fact, they don't even notice the difference between speech and nonsense sounds. There are exceptions, however. People tend to hear (1) their own name in the unattended channel and (2) information that is relevant to the attended message.

The large body of research on selective attention can be summarized by saying that a vast amount of information enters the sensory systems and is processed **in parallel** (simultaneously), although this processing is by no means complete. Only the most important information is chosen for careful processing, and this material seems to be handled **sequentially**—that is, roughly one item at a time. For this reason, computers, which process information sequentially, may be suitable for simulating the higher cognitive processes (attention, memory, problem solving) but not very appropriate for simulating lower-level sensory processes. The distinction between parallel and sequential processes is often discussed by information-processing psychologists, and there is still some controversy concerning which human processes are simultaneous and which are sequential. However, as an introductory student, you will not be far from the mark if you remember only that many elementary processes occur simultaneously (in parallel), whereas information that deserves special attention or careful processing is handled sequentially.

Feature Extraction

The problems of input selection do not end with the identification of the sensory channel or of the particular portion of information coming through that channel that deserves attention. The task of decoding the message—deciding what it means—remains. Information-processing psychologists refer to the first stage of decoding as **feature extraction.**

Existing physiological data—at both the animal and human levels—show that feature extraction in vision depends on structures and processes both in the eye and in the brain. Studies have shown that the retinas of cats' eyes contain some sorts of line detectors. Large numbers of cells in the retina seem to be "wired together" so as to distinguish horizontal from vertical features. Other studies, by Jerome Lettvin and others, suggest that, after some processing in the eye, certain parts of a frog's brain act as feature analyzers. The investigators found that one part of the frog's brain displays activity whenever a line or the edge of an object comes into view. Another part is activated by small, erratically moving objects—a very useful analyzer to have if flies are your main source of nourishment.

These and similar results obtained by David Hubel and Torsten Wiesel on the visual cortex of the cat have led to speculation that the human eye and brain may contain structures that respond selectively to different types of

Figure 5.3 A demonstration of selective attention. (left) The painting "An Unexpected Visitor" by the Russian artist I. E. Repin. (middle) Tracings showing the eye movements of a person looking at the painting for three minutes after he had been instructed to examine the picture freely. (right) The eye movements of this person after he had been instructed to surmise what the family had been doing before the arrival of the "unexpected visitor." Note that with different intentions and expectations, the person scans the picture very differently.

incoming visual signals. Chapter 11 discusses the kind of complex feature analysis people seem to use when they recognize letters.

Computer programs have been constructed that permit machines to read special templates representing each letter of the alphabet and the digits from 0 to 9, but as models of human behavior their potential is severely limited. Such programs can do nothing at all with handwritten characters, for example.

A more recent and powerful group of models employs programs that identify letters on the basis of their distinctive features. These models approximate human performance more closely than the template-reading machines do. The program specifies a series of tests for each letter to be identified as well as the order in which these tests take place. Consider the printed letters—a b c d e f g h i j k l m n o p q r s t u v w x y z. A simplified program might ask the following questions of an incoming character:

Is it a "closed" letter?

Answer: Yes. Then it is a, b, d, e, g, o, p, or q.

Does it have a straight line in it?

Answer: No. Then it is a, e, g, or o.

Does it possess a lower loop?

Answer: Yes. Then it is g.

In practice, the number of feature-analyzing questions necessary to identify every letter would be more than the three shown here and would depend on the actual set of letters or figures to be discriminated.

Such models may help us to understand, in a very limited way, how people

Figure 5.4   (from top to bottom) A representation of the processing performed by a competent reader as he scans a few lines of print. Note that only part of the information the reader is using to interpret the physical patterns of ink on the page is coming from the patterns themselves. The reader extracts a few features from these patterns and makes use of a large number of other information sources to complete his identification of the words and letters in front of him: He is familiar with common English letter and word sequences; he is familiar with grammatical constraints; and the context built up by what he has previously read places further constraints on what he might reasonably expect the next words to be. Note that if the reader could not depend on these sets of expectations—if, for example, he were reading very difficult or nonsensical material—he would have to extract many more features from the physical stimulus and could read only very slowly.

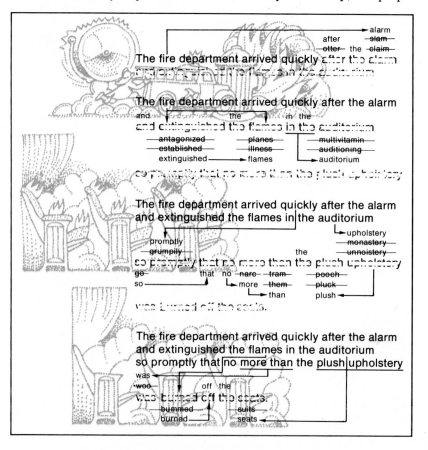

detect features, but they cannot begin to match the performance of humans for several reasons, one of which is the importance of context to feature analysis.

Context

Even if it becomes possible to identify feature analyzers in the human brain, the problem of feature identification will be far from solved. There is far more to the way we understand, say, a printed text than merely the identification of a small set of distinctive features. Existing computer-recognition systems are stymied by irregular or oddly shaped characters. Such things do not bother human readers at all, and we even cope with incorrect spellings and omitted letters. How do we manage it?

For one thing, human beings do not read on a letter-by-letter basis. A study by Miles Tinker shows that the eyes move from place to place on a printed line at the rate of three or four jumps per second, taking in whole words and even phrases at each fixation. This finding strongly suggests that recognition is based on features of units at least as large as words.

Probably much more is involved. As you read this text a tremendous number of things help you understand it, from particular expectations about letter combinations and word order all the way to very general expectations about textbooks and about psychology. These expectations operate as a sort of running crossword puzzle that provides a framework for the words you are reading (see Figure 5.4). In short, the recognition and interpretation of letters is not a simple physical affair but depends intimately on past experience. It is impossible to say at present just how far computer systems will take psychologists in their attempts to identify and weigh the significance of all these factors.

Programming a machine to recognize and understand spoken language—or indeed, any complex pattern—presents problems similar to those of programming it to read. There are machines that appear to speak, or even to sing, with the aid of electronically controlled vocal cords vibrating in response to tape recordings. But the computer that listens and understands in the human sense has yet to be developed. The contextual clues and preliminary expectations that play such a large part in human understanding, and are gained through a tremendous amount of experience, are largely unavailable—at least to the present generation of machines. The fact that psychologists cannot tell engineers how to build better machines is an indication that they do not yet understand how humans understand spoken language.

PROCESSING

Once information is fed into an information-processing system and decoded, it must be stored for some period of time in order to be processed. Data fed into a computer, for example, can either be stored temporarily—until all specified calculations are carried out—and then be erased, or data can be retained indefinitely for later analysis. The human nervous system allows for similar, although more complex, options. Human memory seems to take three forms: sensory storage, which holds a large amount of information but only for an instant; short-term memory, which holds a small amount of information for a matter of seconds, keeping it available for immediate use; and long-term memory, which stores information indefinitely, to be used over and over again in the future.

Sensory Storage

If the pattern of letters and numbers shown in Figure 5.5 were presented to you very briefly, you would most likely be able to recall between five and nine of them. People who have tried this task usually feel, immediately after the presentation, that they will remember more than eight or nine items, but

Figure 5.5 When exposed to this array of unrelated items for a brief period, people typically recall no more than nine of them. (Psychologists use a device called a tachistoscope for flashing such items; it can expose them for periods as brief as fifty-thousandths of a second.) But if subjects are signaled immediately after the exposure to recall just one of the lines, they can always recall all four items correctly. This evidence suggests that people "read" the information from some sort of complete sensory image of the stimulus, which fades in the time it takes to say the names of a few of the letters and numbers in the image.

by the time they have reported about six of them, the other items seem to have evaporated from their memory. Are the subjects correct in saying they remembered more items before they began to report them? In 1960 George Sperling devised a way to answer this question. He briefly presented an array like the one in Figure 5.5 and followed it by sounding a high, medium, or low tone to indicate to subjects which line they should report. Under these conditions, subjects displayed almost perfect recall, indicating that immediately after stimulus presentation all twelve symbols *are* available, although only about half a dozen can be reported before the sensory image fades.

Psychologists who have studied sensory storage believe that it is modality specific—that is, that the storage occurs somehow within the sensory system that received the information as input, and not at some central location. If a second visual stimulus—say a set of X's—is presented shortly after an array like the one in Figure 5.5, people's memory for the initial array is lost. But the image is not disturbed by stimulation in another sensory system, such as hearing or touch. Moreover, memory for such a visual array is better if the stimulus is made brighter during presentation or if the presentation is preceded and followed by darkness. There is also some evidence for brief sensory storage in sensory modalities besides the visual. If several of a person's finger joints are touched simultaneously by air jets, for example, it is difficult for that person to report more than three touch locations correctly. However, if the joints are classified into three sets—upper, middle, and lower (analogous to Sperling's three tones)—memory is significantly improved. Similar results have been obtained with hearing.

The purpose of sensory storage seems to be to provide a second or so during which the selection of information warranting further processing can take place. Usually we are not aware of the existence of this very brief memory, but special circumstances can make us aware of it. When we watch a modern movie, for instance, the action seems smooth and realistic because there is only a tiny time lapse between presentation of each still picture, or "frame." If you have recently seen one of the early movies, you probably were aware of how jerky and unnatural the action seemed. The reason for the perceived jerkiness is that the early movies left too much time between frames, so the sensory image of one frame begins to fade before that frame is overtaken by its successor.

Short-Term Memory

It is obvious that memory is not limited to sensory images that fade within a second. It is easy to hold items in mind for longer than that. If you look up a phone number in the local directory, for example, you can certainly remember it for longer than a second—otherwise you would not be able to dial it. You also know, however, that you cannot remember it for very long without some effort. You have to keep your attention glued to it, so to speak, and you probably have to repeat it to yourself—aloud or mentally—one or more times. If you get distracted for several seconds, the phone number may just disappear from memory, and you will be forced to consult the directory again.

This example illustrates the basic features of **short-term memory (STM):** It is limited in capacity and its contents disappear unless they are periodically reinstated by **rehearsal** (repetition). How long does an item stay in short-term memory? Various experiments (for example, one by Lloyd Peterson and Margaret Peterson, the results of which are shown in Figure 5.6) have yielded figures under twenty seconds. If you are given a short series of letters—for instance, CPQ—to remember and then are asked to count backward by 3s from a number like 270 (267 . . . 264 . . . 261, and so on), you are likely to forget CPQ after about fifteen seconds. The backward counting is the psychologist's way of keeping you from rehearsing. If you could secretly re-

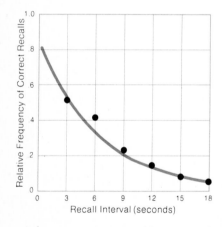

Figure 5.6 The results of Peterson and Peterson's experiment to measure the length of time that short-term memory lasts without the aid of rehearsal. Subjects were shown a three-consonant combination (CPQ, for example) that they were to remember; immediately after they saw it, they began to count backwards by threes from some number supplied by the experimenter. The longer the experimenter let them count before asking them to recall the combination, the less likely the subjects were to recall it correctly.

hearse CPQ while appearing to take a deep breath between counts, your memory for CPQ would probably last longer than fifteen seconds.

What is the capacity of short-term memory? How much information will it hold? In the mid-1950s George Miller published a classic paper titled "The Magical Number Seven, Plus or Minus Two: Some Limits on Our Capacity for Processing Information." Miller summarized the results of many experiments, all indicating that one could hold in the mind only about 5 to 9 items (hence the figure 7 ± 2). Although the magical number has never been pinned down precisely, everyone agrees that it is near the range specified by Miller. If anything, his estimate may have been a bit high.

Miller at first found it mysterious that although people's information-processing capacities seem to be so complex, they should also be so limited. Then he realized that we make do with this small capacity by **chunking** information. If we could process only 7 ± 2 letters at a time, our thoughts would be limited indeed. But we can arrange letters into words (chunk them) and then hold 7 ± 2 words in STM. We can then group words into familiar phrases (larger chunks) and hold in mind 7 ± 2 phrases. Finally, when whole passages have been learned and labeled, we can retrieve them by calling on the titles of things like "Jingle Bells" and "The Gettysburg Address."

Chunks need not be verbal; in fact some of the most useful ones are visual. Study the chess board shown in Figure 5.7A for about five seconds, then turn the page and see how many pieces you can draw correctly on the empty board there. If you do not know a great deal about chess, the number will probably be in the "magical" range (7 ± 2). (That is, if you have played chess from time to time, the position of one piece on the board may be a chunk; if you have never played chess, remembering the identity and position of a single piece may require you to hold several items of information: shape, row, column, etc.) It may surprise you to know that excellent chess players are able to reproduce the entire board after a five-second exposure. At one time this kind of performance led people to think that chess masters had unusually good memories. However, experiments have shown that the amazing superiority is lost if the pieces are arranged randomly on the board (in a pattern that would never occur in a game between good players). In such cases, the masters remember the placement of about 7 ± 2 pieces just like anyone else. Thus, the chess masters' superiority has something to do with recognizing familiar visual configurations (chunks); it is not a sign of unusual intelligence or memory capacity.

Research on chess masters suggests they can identify 25,000 to 100,000 visual chunks! Although this seems like an astronomical number—enough to burden a normal memory—it is roughly equal to the number of words in the vocabulary of an educated English speaker. When you stop to realize that a chess master probably started playing the game early in childhood and spent more time on chess than on anything else, the large number of chunks does not seem so unreasonable.

Long-Term Memory

Earlier in this chapter you read about what it is like to look up a telephone number and hold it in STM. As long as you attend to it and repeat it to yourself, the number remains available, but if you get distracted for several seconds it is likely to disappear. Obviously, there is more to memory than this or else you would not be able to remember your own telephone number without rehearsing it continually every day. There must be a difference between short-term memory and **long-term memory (LTM)**.

In 1962 Bennet Murdock reported a series of memory experiments that distinguished between the two kinds of memory. Subjects listened to a list of twenty words presented at the rate of one each second. At the end of the list

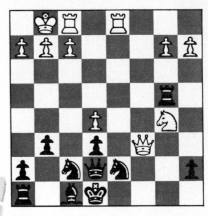

Figure 5.7A Study this arrangement for five seconds. Then turn to the empty chess board on the next page and try to reproduce the arrangement. The amount you are able to recall correctly represents approximately seven of the chunks you have developed for processing information about chess games.

Figure 5.7B   Turn to Figure 5.7A on the preceding page, if you have not already looked at it, and study it for five seconds. Then try to reproduce the arrangement shown there on this empty chess board. Your success in doing so will depend heavily on your experience with the game of chess.

Figure 5.8   The results of a series of experiments by Murdock (A and B) and by Postman and Phillips (C) that elegantly demonstrate the separate contributions of short-term memory (STM) and long-term memory (LTM) to the serial position curve. The black dots show the percentage of correct recalls as a function of the position of the word in the list. The colored line in (A) represents the idealized form of the data there and is repeated in (B) and (C) for purposes of comparison. Note that in (B) LTM's contribution has been enhanced by the allowance of more rehearsal and organization time between words, but STM's contribution is unaffected. In (C) the contribution of STM has been completely eliminated by the prevention of rehearsal, but LTM's contribution is unchanged.

the subjects were given a minute and a half to write down all the words they could remember. After a short break, a new list of twenty words was read, followed by another recall test. The results of the experiment, averaged over several subjects and many trials, are summarized in Figure 5.8A, which shows the proportion (or percentage) of words recalled at each of the twenty positions in the list. This **serial position curve** indicates that memory is excellent for the last few items in the list, next best for items at the beginning of the list, and not very good for items in the middle.

Murdock and others who have used this method (for example, Leo Postman and Laura Phillips) believe that the words recalled at the end of the list are stored in STM, whereas the ones recalled from the rest of the list are stored in LTM; however, more words from the front of the list are stored because there is less interference from the later words and there has been more time to store them. One bit of evidence for this interpretation is that if more time is allowed between items, making rehearsal of the earlier items possible, memory for these items is improved, as Figure 5.8B shows. The portion of the curve representing the later items on the list is not affected by this manipulation. On the other hand, if subjects are asked to count backward by 3s as soon as the last word is presented, the upturn at the end of the curve is destroyed, as Figure 5.8C shows. As you recall, counting backward by 3s interferes with information in STM. The front of the curve is not affected by this counting backward.

The Organization of Memory   What does the word "mafterling" mean? How long did it take you to decide that you do not have that word in your vocabulary? How long to conjecture or decide that no such word exists in English? It probably took your recall, or retrieval, system only seconds to make those decisions. How incredibly efficient, then, the organization of human memory must be. No other information-processing system matches it.

Peter Lindsay and Donald Norman have developed a model of the organization of human memory, which is too complex to set out in detail here but whose basic characteristics can be described. They emphasize the **dynamic and integrative processes of memory,** in contrast to models of memory that focus on associations or on a passive kind of "storage tank" analogy. Consider, for example, that a person's understanding of a concept he has stored in memory early in life often changes and becomes elaborated, even if that person has not dealt with that concept between the time he first stored it and when he needs to recall it again.

An experiment conducted by Baerbel Inhelder illustrates how this constructive process works. Five- and seven-year-olds were shown an arrangement

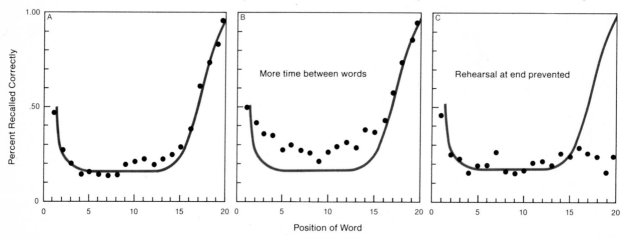

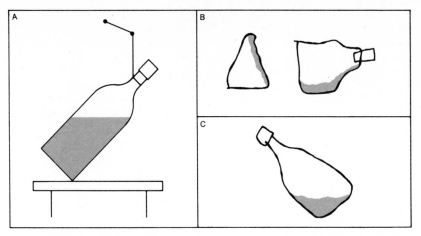

Figure 5.9 Children between the ages of five and seven were shown a half-filled bottle suspended as the diagram in (A) shows. When asked a short time later to reproduce what they had seen, the children typically made such drawings as those in (B). The drawing in (C) was made by one of these children six months later. According to Inhelder, the increased accuracy of this child's drawing was the result of an increase in his general understanding of the properties of physical objects. This argument implies that memory depends on the active organization and reconstruction of experiences and is not a passive storage process.

similar to that in Figure 5.9A. The bottle was about one-fourth filled with colored water. The children were asked, after being shown this arrangement, to draw from memory what they had seen. Around 80 percent of the drawings showed very marked deviations from the original arrangement. Many of them were of the form shown in Figure 5.9B. However, when the same children were asked six months later to draw what they had seen, some 30 percent of them reproduced the arrangement much more accurately than before, even though the children were not shown the arrangement again. Not only had the nature of what they remembered changed during the six months—it had become more accurate.

These results underline the active, constructional nature of memory. The children had not seen the arrangement between testings, so presumably any changes that occurred in what they "remembered" were the result of developmental changes taking place in their knowledge of the world and in their sense of logical necessity. (See Chapter 8.)

This model of memory also suggests that there are vast differences between the way children encode things into memory and the way adults do. In an adult's memory, every piece of stored data is connected to every other piece. Lindsay and Norman say: "The memory system is an organized collection of pathways that specify possible routes through the data base. Retrieving information from such a memory is going to be like running a maze. Starting off at a given node, there are many possible options available about the possible pathways to follow. Taking one of these paths leads to a series of crossroads, each going off to a different concept." An example of how Lindsay and Norman model such a data base is shown in Figure 5.10. So children must build up their data base, learning many concepts from scratch. They slowly accumulate data about the properties of things, gather examples, and connect things in order to understand class relations.

It is important to note that in building up the data base, verbal input is often accompanied by input from the sensory systems. Faced with an object like a salt shaker, a person does not, as far as we can tell, search through a particular list to retrieve its name—for example, through "street," "house," "dining room," "table," and "crockery" to "(please pass the) salt." When we use our memory on a daily basis, we are in sensory touch with the situation—our behavior is *context* specific. Our kinesthetic system, our systems of smell, hearing, and sight are constantly conveying information to our nervous systems, ensuring that retrieval of an item from memory will take into account the immediate situation. One can construct a metaphor by thinking of the memory structure as "rotating" in response to perceived cues of the situation. At the dinner table, for example, the smell of the food, the feel of the

Figure 5.10 A sample data base in Lindsay and Norman's model of human memory. This structure represents stored information about certain kinds of containers. The labeled arrows indicate relationships between items in the data base and can be followed in either direction. Items that are bracketed indicate concepts for which there is no simple name. [*Liquid*], for example, means "a liquid" or "a certain kind of liquid." Lindsay and Norman's model is obviously highly simplified and limited compared to the reality of human memory, but even the tiny data base shown here can be used to simulate human memory rather dramatically. Suppose that these data exist in your memory and you are asked: "What do you know about kettles?" You trace the paths in the data base from Kettle, and you answer: "Well, a kettle is a pot, and it has a spout, and it has liquid that is hot." Now you are asked: "What else has liquid that is hot?" You answer: "Teapot!" How do you reply to the question: "What is a pot?"
(After Lindsay and Norman, 1972.)

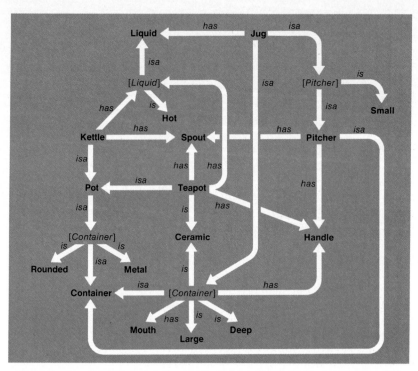

silverware in your hand and of your body in a certain kind of chair placed in a certain relation to the table, the sound of crockery clinking, the sight of the food and the utensils—all these cues serve to rotate your memory structure to a path that facilitates the recall of "salt shaker."

Lindsay and Norman's model of memory characterizes human memory as a system that uses a conceptual structure to interpret the information it receives, that compares incoming messages with what it knows, and that can evaluate the plausibility of something in terms of its past experience. Although these basic processes operate the same way in everyone, each individual's memory will be unique because his data and the way he has connected them will depend on what he has experienced.

Mnemonic Devices Besides attending to and rehearsing information in order to lodge it more firmly in LTM, what can be done to improve memory? This question has been asked by forgetful humans for thousands of years. Before it became common to write out lecture notes, famous orators used the **method of loci** to remember the high points and organization of their speeches. This method requires that you imagine a familiar environment, say your house or apartment, and imagine walking through it, putting items to be remembered in conspicuous places. Then, when you want to recall the items, you take another imaginary walk through your home and "notice" the items to be recalled along the way. It may sound strange, but it has worked for thousands of years, and its efficacy has been proved in modern psychology experiments.

The method of loci works because it takes advantage of an organization already held in the person's memory. This use of an existing organization seems to be one of the main secrets behind most mnemonic devices (memory aids). One popular scheme, called the **key-word system,** or peg system, requires that you memorize the list of simple sentences printed in the opposite margin. The list is easy to learn because the words associated with the numbers are concrete, easily visualizable nouns that rhyme with the numbers. You

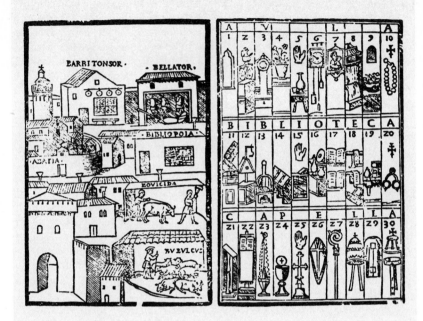

Figure 5.11 Technical aids to memory have a long history, beginning with the use of the method of loci by Greek and Roman orators. These woodcuts are from a text explaining the method of loci that was written in the sixteenth century by a Dominican monk for the benefit of such professionals as jurists, confessors, and ambassadors. At the left is a set of loci, an abbey and its associated buildings. At the right are objects that can be placed in these loci and so remembered. Note that each row on the right corresponds to one of the abbey buildings (top row, the courtyard; middle row, the library; bottom row, the chapel). Note also that every fifth place in each row is marked by a hand and every tenth by a cross. As the memorizer mentally moves through the abbey, he can "tick off" the items he is recalling on the fingers of each hand.

can use the list to remember either numbers or ordered lists of objects. Suppose you wish to remember the number 4391. Say: "4-3-9-1, door, tree, line, bun; I see a little door in a big tree and when I open the door there is a line leading to a bun." As silly as this may sound, it works. If you want to remember a list of objects, you imagine the first object inside a bun, the second wearing shoes, and so on. When recall is required, the images will come back to you, and the order will be preserved by the familiar list of key words or "pegs."

There are many other mnemonic systems, but all of them follow the same basic principles. The point of them all is organization. Although some materials may be learned by sheer repetition, it is much more effective to group and structure the material in some way, if possible taking advantage of already familiar organized information.

So-called memory wizards who appear on stage and television have probably just worked unusually hard to acquire a set of complex mnemonic devices. Some of their secrets were recently revealed in the best-selling *Memory Book,* by Harry Lorayne and Jerry Lucas. It is still impressive to see Lorayne and Lucas on television memorizing the name of every person in the audience. Perhaps one should admire their motivation more than their memories.

A few people, however, do have superior memories, a special ability that is as yet unexplainable. In *The Mind of a Mnemonist,* the Russian psychologist Aleksandr Luria tells about a man whose memory for detail was so good that he had trouble forgetting unwanted images and could rarely think in abstract terms because he remembered all the concrete particulars. He literally "could not see the forest for the trees." Such cases are so rare that psychologists still do not know what the neurological basis of superior memory is.

Imagery Many of the popular mnemonic devices rely on visual imagery, and research in learning laboratories (for example, the laboratories of Allan Paivio and of Gordon Bower) has shown unequivocally that people do learn verbal materials better when they hook them to a visual image of some kind.

Remember:

One is a bun.
Two is a shoe.
Three is a tree.
Four is a door.
Five is a hive.
Six is sticks.
Seven is heaven.
Eight is a gate.
Nine is a line.
Ten is a hen.

Figure 5.12 In an experiment in which children were shown drawings like these and later asked to recall what appeared in them, Horowitz, Lampel, and Takanishi found that recall was much better when the elements were organized (top) than when they were unrelated (bottom).

This technique is successful only if the image is a unit. You can begin to understand why this might be so by looking at the two panels of Figure 5.12. An experiment done in 1969 by Leonard Horowitz, Anita Lampel, and Ruby Takanishi showed that the top panel was remembered much better than the bottom. Another experiment done by George Atwood showed that integrated phrases in which all the objects are actively related to one another, such as "*truck* being attacked by a *nudist* with a lead *pipe*," resulted in much better recall for the italicized words than did phrases in which the objects are merely placed side by side ("*truck* driven by a *nudist* who stands near a lead *pipe*"). One might say that images allow people to process items in parallel, whereas words alone can be processed only sequentially. That is, words enter the ears or eyes one (perhaps a few) at a time, but an image can link many elements so they can be processed together.

Imagery improves verbal learning most when the materials to be learned are concrete rather than abstract. Again, you can understand why this is so by considering an example: Compare the pair of words "steamship-canary" with the pair "dissonance-republic." The concrete nouns immediately suggest specific images, whereas the abstract nouns either suggest no images at all or suggest images that are not uniquely tied to the words to be remembered. For example, the word "republic" may suggest an image of the American flag, but later, when this image is recalled, the word "democracy" rather than "republic" may come to mind.

Concrete and abstract words may differ in an even more profound way. In 1971 George Atwood, using a method devised in 1967 by Lee Brooks, conducted an experiment to test his hypothesis that concrete words are processed differently than are abstract words. Subjects heard either a concrete phrase ("*nudist* devouring a *bird*" or "*pistol* hanging from a *chain*," for example) or an abstract one ("the *intellect* of Einstein was a *miracle*" or "the *theory* of Freud is *nonsense*," for example). After each phrase was said, the subject either saw or heard the number 1 or the number 2. If a phrase was followed by a 1, the subject had to say "two" out loud. If it was followed by a 2, he had to say "one" out loud. Later, subjects were given one noun from a phrase (nudist, for example) and were asked to recall the other noun (bird). Atwood found that the subjects' memory for concrete phrases had been disrupted by visual presentation of the number, whereas their memory for abstract phrases had been disrupted by auditory presentation of the numbers. These results do seem to support Atwood's hypothesis: It appears that concrete words and their associated images are processed somewhere in the visual system, whereas abstract words are processed by an auditory-linguistic system. Atwood believes that the visual system might be located in the right hemisphere of the brain and the auditory-linguistic system, in the left hemisphere. (See Chapter 13 for a discussion of the special functions of the two hemispheres.)

The important point is that imagery may be a powerful aid in recalling verbal material, not just because images are inherently memorable or because an image has special organizational properties, but also because imagery is processed in a nonlinguistic location. According to this line of reasoning, you are more likely to remember words plus images than words alone for the same reason that it is better to leave two reminder notes for yourself—one at home and one in your pocket—than to leave only one: The two notes make it twice as likely that you will remember the message.

Retrieval

Retrieving stored information is in some ways the key property of memory, although successful retrieval obviously depends on successful acquisition and storage. Two basic methods of retrieval are: recognition and recall.

Recognition and Recall In recognition, we are presented with something and asked if we have seen or heard it before. In recall, we are given certain cues and asked to generate something that corresponds to them. Multiple-choice and true-false items on exams test recognition. Essay questions and fill-in questions require recall.

Recognition is easier than recall. If you pass someone on the street you knew in elementary school, you may recognize his face but be unable to recall his name. In recognition, you need only decide whether the person, object, experience, sound, or word before you is the one you are seeking. People usually do very well at recognition tasks, and they tend to know whether their recognitions are accurate. They can say not only that they do or do not recognize something but state how sure they are that they are right.

Recognition errors take two forms. You can fail to recognize an item that is actually stored in your memory; you can also claim to recognize an item that you have never seen before (or at least had not seen when you said you had).

The second major type of retrieval, recall, is often quite difficult. In this method you must recover information on the basis of cues that are sometimes quite sparse. As with recognition, people can usually tell how confident they are that their recollection is accurate; in fact, when recall occurs, it tends to be accurate. The most common error is failure to retrieve anything, as when people stumble in speaking, trying to find the word they want, or fail to remember a name they thought they knew. False recalls are rare. When they do occur, it is usually possible to explain them on the basis of strong, familiar associations. For example, parents have been known to call one of their children by another's name; especially in large families it is easy to see why.

Confabulation Motivation affects recall, as it does most human activities. A person offered a thousand dollars to remember the name of his first-grade teacher is more likely to come up with it than is the person who is offered a dime. But under conditions of high motivation, we often commit a memory error called confabulation: If unable to retrieve a certain item from memory, we may manufacture something else that seems appropriate. For some time, psychologists were impressed by the apparent ability of people in deep states of hypnosis to give detailed reports of events that occurred during childhood. The hypnotist would tell the person being hypnotized "Go back, back, back to when you were very, very young" and then ask the subject to describe, for instance, his sixth birthday. Typically, the subject, if in a deep trance, would

Figure 5.13   (left) Recognition. A man is presented with a picture of a bear and asked "Is this a bear?" If the image matches the image of "bear" in his memory, he can reply "Yes" with certainty. If the image does not match, he will reply "No" with equal certainty. (right) Recall. Here the man is given a number of verbal cues and asked to find in his memory the image that corresponds to them. The possibility for error is considerable; he might easily reply "Lion."

give a lengthy and quite impressive account of a birthday party complete with cake, candles, presents, and guests. He would seem absolutely convinced that his report was accurate, but objective evidence usually contradicted him. Almost always it could be shown that the person had confabulated—that he had combined several birthday parties and invented missing details; even under further questioning, the person could not tell the true parts of his story from the imaginary parts.

Hypnosis induces a state of high motivation in most people, as well as making them much more suggestible than usual. The hypnotized person tries to please the hypnotist and responds to even very subtle vocal and facial cues suggesting what the hypnotist wants. If the hypnotist suggests that the subject ought to be able to remember something, the subject eagerly complies, even if he must resort to confabulation to fulfill the request.

Now You Say It, Now You Don't What do you do when a specific memory is retrieved in unreliable, partial, and ambiguous form—or perhaps not quite retrieved at all? Consider what happens when you try to recall a name you are sure you know. If you are merely talking with a friend, you need not be certain you are right before taking a guess. The two of you together can stumble toward the correct name: "It's Fishmonger . . . No, Fishman . . ." False recalls in this situation incur no penalties. But if you are face to face with the mysterious Mr. X, you probably will not guess. The social cost of a false recall—that is, of addressing Mr. Troutman as Mr. Fishmonger—may be high, whereas the cost of avoiding the name entirely is nominal. (Actually, and in this case, happily, you are not very likely to think that Mr. Troutman's name is Mr. Fishmonger. False recalls, research by Roger Brown and David McNeill has shown, tend to resemble the target word in sound rather than meaning.)

A decision mechanism clearly plays an important role in retrieval (as it does in forgetting, which will be discussed later in the chapter). The decision to accept or reject a bit of retrieved information is made on the basis of some rather complex assessments. The assessments must be based, somehow, on the way memories are organized, although there is no cohesive theory yet to explain the entire process. The view that memory is constructional hypothesizes the existence of landmarks, or cues, on which the constructions are based, but so far the nature of those cues and landmarks remains unclear. Work by Ralph Haber suggests that some of the cues are pictorial; the "mafterling" example (and other studies) suggests that some cues are based on word sounds. Some studies seem to show that people who have a word "on the tip of the tongue" use the sound of the word to arrive at its recall; others indicate that the shape of the word is the important cue. Most people are familiar with the phenomenon of a particular odor or texture cuing the release of a memory.

It seems that several cues can lead to the retrieval, or reconstruction, of a memory, and when the cues are plentiful, reconstruction is both easy and accurate. However, when some cues—perhaps the most important one—cannot be retrieved, we either cannot remember at all or we are not certain that what we remember is correct. You might want to try one of the problems in Figure 5.14 to test your retrieval. Retrieval, then, is not an all-or-nothing affair. It is affected by a variety of factors, which can render it more or less effective—under circumstances that remain to be explored.

Forgetting

So far we have concentrated mainly on successes of the memory system—on how information gets in, stays in, and is retrieved. When this process goes wrong in some way, forgetting ensues. How, why, and even whether some-

Figure 5.14 Retrieval problems that demonstrate the reconstructive nature of memory. If, at first glance, any of these questions seems impossible to answer, try anyway. You may be surprised at what you can recall if you put your mind to it.
(After Lindsay and Norman, 1972.)

In the rooms you live in, how many windows are there?

What were you doing on Monday afternoon in the third week of September two years ago?

Can pigeons fly airplanes?

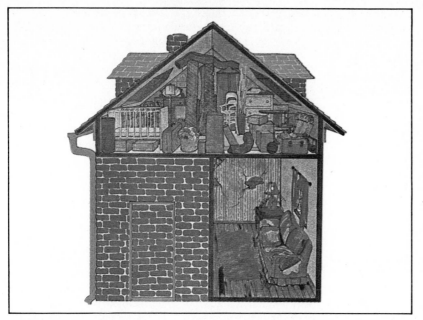

Figure 5.15 A representation of three theoretical explanations of forgetting. Interference theories emphasize the importance of organization in memory. The difficulty of remembering a forgotten name could therefore be compared to the difficulty of finding a particular item in a cluttered attic. Decay theories postulate that the physical changes that take place in the brain when learning occurs are unstable. According to this view, a forgotten name has rotted away like a piece of ancient furniture. Psychoanalytic theory attributes a great deal of forgetting to repression; the forgotten name has not been lost, but access to it has been blocked because it is associated with painful feelings.

thing learned well enough to pass into long-term memory can ever be completely forgotten are questions that psychologists, despite considerable effort, still have not resolved.

Three approaches to the problem of forgetting, described by Ian Hunter, are popular. The first approach brings together two rather unlikely bedfellows: computer-oriented psychologists who think in terms of information processing and psychoanalytically oriented psychologists. These groups tend to think that if true forgetting—in the sense of the disappearance of an item from long-term memory—occurs at all, it is at least much rarer than is commonly supposed. The second theory, which comes from physiological psychology, views forgetting primarily as a physical process that occurs in the brain. The third approach, which is behaviorist in orientation, attributes forgetting to environmental events rather than to internal processes, whether psychological or physiological.

The three approaches obviously differ in emphasis, and they also conflict at several important points. As you read about them, however, note that they are not totally incompatible. When the full story is known, if ever, it seems likely that each of them will prove to have contributed at least a few grains of truth.

Intentional Forgetting   When we say that something has been remembered, we mean that acquisition, storage, and retrieval have all proceeded successfully. When we say that something has been forgotten, any one of these processes may be at fault. If the memory lasts for a while instead of disappearing at once, that indicates that the acquisition process worked. But the failure to recall the item later does not indicate whether it is physically gone from long-term memory (erased from storage forever) or whether one simply cannot retrieve it at the moment.

Most computer memories are constructed to allow information to be added or erased at will. Human memory, on the other hand, may be nonerasable. So far, we have no sure way to tell whether material in human long-term memory ever actually disappears from storage.

Many instances of so-called forgetting fall into the category of failures in retrieval rather than erasures from long-term memory. Psychiatrists, psychoanalysts, and hypnotists often help people recover memories that seemed to

Figure 5.16 The results of an experiment on learning and sleep. Two subjects were given lists of nonsense syllables to learn (BIK, QAJ, NIC, for example) and were tested after various periods of time. When the subjects were allowed to sleep during the time interval between learning and recall, they remembered much more than they did if they had stayed awake. Apparently, during sleep less new material is introduced to interfere with the material already learned. These results could not be accounted for by a decay explanation of forgetting.

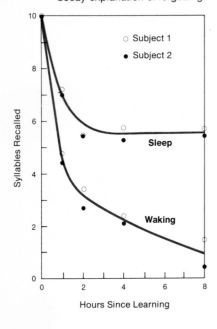

have been lost forever. The same thing sometimes happens without outside assistance, when people undergo senility or delirium.

Although some apparent memories are confabulation, it is also true that some apparent forgetting is a matter of suppression or **repression.** The material has not disappeared from storage. Instead, a conscious or unconscious decision process is at work: The person has arranged things so that the retrieval mechanism by-passes the memory in question. Indications that the apparently forgotten material is still there usually show up in the person's behavior. He may pause or fumble for words when he talks about matters related to the critical items, and there may be physiological signs of anxiety, such as sweating, rapid heart rate, and blushing.

The Decay of Memory Traces According to the second theory of forgetting, a memory trace is formed in the brain whenever we learn an item or have an experience. That is, each act of learning and each experience leave some sort of physical trace in the brain. The better an item is learned, the stronger the trace. With time (the amount depends on the strength of the trace), the trace decays and may disappear altogether—the item has been forgotten.

This theory of forgetting has the virtue of emphasizing both time and the physiology of the brain; it is hard to imagine an adequate theory of forgetting that fails to take these factors into account. The memory-trace idea is also plausible in the light of subjective experience. If you try to recall in detail an event that happened last year or the points made in the first chapter of this book, "decay" and "disintegration" may describe quite well what seems to have happened to the memories.

There is, however, no direct evidence to support the memory-trace theory, and there is a considerable amount of evidence to suggest that it is, at best, preliminary and incomplete. For example, it fails to account for the fact that motor actions tend to be remembered over long periods of time. A parent who has not ridden a bike for twenty years usually has little trouble demonstrating the skill for his child. Also, although the memory-trace theory might account for repression and intentional forgetting by attributing them to weak traces, it makes no provision for the restrengthening of the traces later on. Finally, it has been demonstrated that people forget substantially less if they sleep for several hours after learning something than they do if they stay awake (see Figure 5.16); again, this fact is hard to explain if we assume that memories simply decay with the passage of time.

Interference The third approach to forgetting attributes it to interference from other material. Although interference probably does not account for *all* forgetting, it does account for the experimental results graphed in Figure 5.16, which shows that people who learn something and then go to sleep (so they are subject to no interference) recall what they learned better than people who continue their activities. It has been shown to have strong effects on material learned by rote and on some other kinds of tasks as well.

Near the beginning of the acquisition process, interference from extraneous material can prevent new information from passing into long-term memory. Suppose you are asked to memorize list A of the adjectives shown adjacent. You are given the first word on the list, and you have to remember the second, then the third, and so on. Each time you go through the list, you have a certain amount of time to remember each item; if you fail to recall it in that time, it is read out to you, and you are asked to go on to the next word. Eventually, you will remember the entire list. Now you are asked to memorize list B.

At some time in the future, you are asked to recall list A. You may find that you have forgotten many of the list A words—most people do. They may hesitate, recall only some of the list A items, and add some words from list B.

List A	List B	List C
happy	gay	58
big	large	22
hard	solid	18
funny	humorous	19
thin	slender	33
calming	soothing	71
neat	tidy	45

In instances like this, when learning of later material interferes with remembering of material learned earlier, psychologists say that **retroactive interference** has taken place. If you had found that list A interfered with your recall of list B, that would have constituted **proactive interference.** It may help to keep these items straight if you fix firmly in your mind that *pro* means forward and *retro* means backward. In proactive interference, the interference moves forward from list A to list B; in retroactive interference, it moves backward from B to A.

Now suppose that after you had learned list A, you were given list C to learn instead of list B. The odds are that this list of numbers would interfere little with your recall of list A—certainly much less than list B interfered. J. McGeoch and his colleagues did experiments with this type of material, and their results indicated that the greater the similarity between the memories of different events, the greater the interference in recalling them.

Charles E. Osgood did subsequent work, using lists of paired-associate words (such as "noisy-thin" and "distinct-happy" on one list and "noisy-slender" and "distinct-gay" on another). He found that with the learning of such lists, there was less interference. He ascribed the decrease in interference to the stimulus word being constant ("noisy"; "distinct"), which reduces interference among similar items.

Although it seems that interference does account for some forgetting, it is not easy to predict how much interference—if any—will occur in a given situation. Each situation requires that one analyze not only the material to be learned but also how the material relates to earlier experiences and what part it plays in performance. Also, most of the experiments on interference have been laboratory experiments dealing solely with verbal learning; it is not yet clear how the principles apply to other kinds of learning under conditions that are more like those in real life.

OUTPUT

So far we have talked mainly about a one-way route: from environmental stimulation through various bottlenecks (sensory gating, selective attention, STM) to long-term storage. The only outputs considered were words and images retrieved from memory. If we were interested only in computers, this would be appropriate: Data come in and are processed and stored according to program rules, and requested results are printed out. Unfortunately for psychologists, people aren't that simple (nor in fact are some computers), so we are forced to examine the *way in which outputs influence inputs,* a process called feedback.

Feedback

The human hand is capable both of picking up an egg without breaking it and of lifting a brick. If the amount of pressure needed to hold a brick were applied to an egg, the egg would break. In picking up an egg, one must squeeze just hard enough to hold it firmly without cracking its fragile shell. Movements of this kind are said to be governed by continuous feedback—that is, by information about results that is continually fed back to control the process that is producing the results. Such a process is called a **feedback loop,** as shown in Figure 5.17. Most human behavior can be described in this way—as resulting from a **hierarchy of feedback loops.**

One feedback loop, called a TOTE unit (an acronym for *Test Operate Test Exit*) by George Miller, Eugene Galanter, and Karl Pribram, is shown in Figure 5.18. It represents part of a common behavior, pounding a nail into a board with a hammer. In the *test* phase of the loop, the nail is checked to see whether it is flush with the board. If the answer is yes, the processor *exits* from the loop—the job is finished. If the answer is no, the processor is

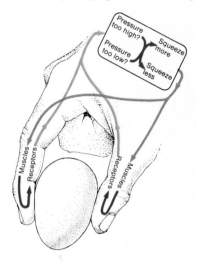

Figure 5.17 The feedback loop that makes it possible to hold an egg without either dropping it or crushing it. Information about the pressure at the fingertips (input) is continuously fed back to the brain, which adjusts the tension of the muscles of the hand (output) accordingly. When the pressure falls below a certain level, the muscles contract to increase it. When it exceeds a certain level, the muscles relax to decrease it. Thus, the actual pressure being exerted on the egg is continuously changing over a small range.

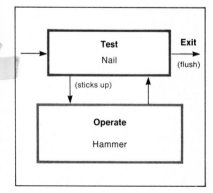

Figure 5.18 Miller, Galanter, and Pribram's unit of behavior: the TOTE. In this example, the input is the perception of the nail. The output is hammering. No exit occurs from this unit until the perception of the nail matches a predetermined standard (flushness). Compare this unit to the feedback loop in Figure 5.17. The standard there is a certain level of pressure. Tests are being performed by sense organs in the fingertips, and operations are being performed by the muscles of the hand.

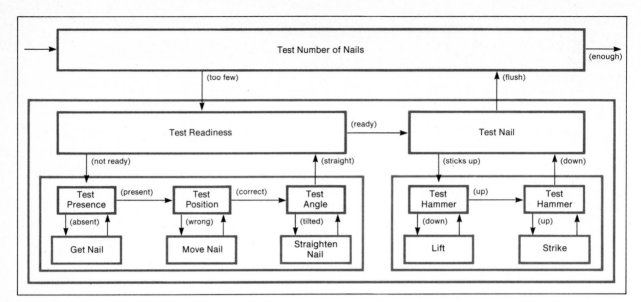

Figure 5.19 A hierarchy of TOTE units. Note that the TOTE unit of Figure 5.18 is a single subunit in this hierarchy and is itself broken down into still smaller subunits. This hierarchical analysis could in principle be continued down to the level of individual cells in the nervous system and up to the level of the whole person's desires and aspirations.

instructed to *operate* the hammer. Then the results are tested again. A more complicated program or plan (by Miller, Galanter, and Pribram) is shown in Figure 5.19. It is called a "hierarchy" of TOTE units, or feedback loops, because one loop is embedded in another to form a hierarchical structure.

In general we can view behavior as an attempt to achieve goals. A person wants something and so acts to get it. As the action is executed, the person watches to see whether the desired result is obtained. If it is not, behavior is altered in an attempt to achieve the goal by a new means. Reviewing earlier parts of this chapter, we see that sensory gating, selective attention, rehearsal, organization of material to be stored, and retrieval are all active, goal-directed processes. They can be viewed in isolation, but they make much more sense when viewed in relation to the system—the person—in which they are embedded. Such a system is not properly viewed as only responding to stimulation (the traditional view); it is more accurate to say that *it behaves in order to control the kind of stimulation it receives.*

The Person as an IPS

It appears that in a few more years, the majority of psychologists will share a conception of the human being as an information-processing system (IPS) having the following characteristics: (1) sensory systems whose structure determines what kind of information is available to be processed; in a sense, these systems form a screen between people and their environment; (2) a short-term memory whose capacity is limited to a few chunks; (3) mechanisms of attention that determine which tiny fraction of all available sensory information will receive further processing; (4) a long-term memory that, for all practical purposes, appears to have unlimited capacity; it contains a vast amount of material linked together by countless associations; it seems to store only information that is screened through the mechanisms of attention; (5) hemispheric specialization, yielding two different modalities (visual and verbal) for long-term storage; (6) the control of behavior by plans or programs made up of hierarchically integrated feedback loops.

MAN AND MACHINE

To date, the information-processing approach to psychology has raised more questions than it has answered. Human memory capacity is far larger than the capacity of the most impressive computers, and no one has figured out how we can retrieve such a variety of information as quickly as we do. A few complex computer programs have successfully modeled small facets of human cognition; for example, a program exists that can test the correctness of logical propositions better than the most outstanding mathematicians. In many ways, however, the programs have failed to approach human abilities. Perhaps it would be instructive to look at some of the areas of obvious weakness.

First, computers are notoriously rigid. They do not approximate or confabulate like humans do. They are unbelievably single-minded, do not become distracted, and do not discover solutions for one kind of problem while searching for the solution to a different kind. This limitation seems to be due partly to the sequential nature of computer programs. We pointed out earlier that although high-level human cognitive processes seem to be more or less sequential, they are built on a foundation of parallel processes. If you need a screwdriver but do not have one, a host of substitutes will come to mind, perhaps more than you can process—a dime, a knife blade, a piece of stiff paper, and so on. Some of the ideas will be rejected as unsuitable after a little thought, others may be tried and either accepted or rejected. The evaluation process is sequential and computerlike, but the creative or associative stage is not. The number of associative links needed in a memory that provides creative solutions to new problems every day is astronomical—greater than anything we can imagine putting in a present-day computer memory.

Second, computers are not emotional, and the information-processing psychologists have not yet said very much about the place of emotions in their models. Nevertheless, many human cognitive processes seem to be influenced by emotions. We pay particular attention to novel, surprising, or dangerous stimuli. We work harder and faster when we want to meet an important deadline. We remember some things better than others because they are important to us, and we repress some memories because they are painful. Although rudimentary computer models of emotion and personality have been constructed, they are not very realistic or complete.

Third, computers do not seem to simulate what Endel Tulving has called **episodic memory,** the memory for particular events in one's life as these were experienced from one's own point of view. Tulving distinguishes this from **semantic memory,** which is the kind of memory referred to earlier in this chapter. A person can know that a canary is yellow, that the sun sets in the west, and that all men are mortal; and a computer can "know" these things too. But a person can also tell where and when he has actually seen canaries, can remember how certain sunsets looked to him, and can describe for you his reaction to his father's death. There is no reason why a computer cannot be programmed to keep a record of its own dealings; in fact, many do this to some extent already. But so far the relationship between episodic and semantic memory in humans is not well understood, and something like a "sense of identity" is even further from being formalizable. It will be some time before these human qualities are simulated by a computer.

Fourth, computers do not develop or change themselves in dramatic ways, although some do learn a few things. Piaget and other developmental psychologists argue that abstract thinking, the kind usually simulated on computers, develops only after long experience with physical actions and, later, with representations of physical actions. If this is the case, can abstract thinking and, especially, cognitive development be simulated by a computer that has no experience with actions, does not move around to get new perspectives on its environment, does not manipulate objects, and does not come into conflict with people whose perspectives differ from its own?

Finally, can a computer really understand anything? For a while artificial-intelligence researchers were interested in building a machine that would translate one human language into another, say Russian into English, the way human translators do at the United Nations. After many failures, they began to realize that the machine could not work effectively unless it understood the meaning of the message it was translating. There is no way to go from one language to another without *understanding* the message being transmitted.

Although no one knows at the moment how to solve the problems raised by human meaning, movements, and development, a young artificial-intelligence researcher named Terry Winograd has developed an interesting computer program to control a robot. The program is meant to fit in with a TV camera "eye" and a mechanical arm, thus creating a more realistic feedback system than seen in previous computer models of human behavior. A dialogue between Winograd and the program is shown in Figure 5.20. Although not as emotional and complex as Hal, the fictional computer in the movie *2001*, Winograd's program represents considerable progress. No doubt further progress will be made before the year depicted in the movie, and this progress will, indirectly at least, shed new light on the ways in which people function.

Figure 5.20   (right) The block-world of the computer program written by artificial-intelligence researcher Terry Winograd and (left) a sample dialogue between Winograd and the computer (capital letters). The pictures here were simulated on a high-resolution cathode-ray-tube screen connected to the computer, but the program could in principle be used to control a real robot. One of the most remarkable achievements of Winograd's program is its ability to understand and produce (via a computer-controlled typewriter) English sentences that accurately describe its block-world.

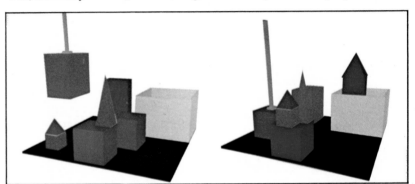

Will you please stack up both of the red blocks and either a green cube or a pyramid?
OK

Which cube is sitting on the table?
THE LARGE GREEN ONE WHICH SUPPORTS THE RED PYRAMID

Is there a large block behind a pyramid?
YES, THREE OF THEM: A LARGE RED ONE, A LARGE GREEN ONE AND THE BLUE ONE

Put a small one onto the green cube which supports a pyramid.
OK

SUMMARY

1. Many psychologists have recently adopted the language and concepts of computers to help them understand human cognitive processes: thinking, learning, memory, problem solving. The analogy between humans and computers is generally a good one: Both receive **input,** and **process** it somehow so as to produce **output.**

   a. The processing is accomplished inside the computer by a detailed, step-by-step list of instructions for a set of operations, called a **program.**

   b. Computers also must store a great deal of information in a way that allows for quick and efficient retrieval.

   c. Two different groups of scientists, having very different approaches, compare human and computer information-processing systems. One group, **computer-simulation** psychologists, construct computer programs that perform as much like people as is possible. They wish to use what they learn from computers to explain human behavior. The other group is devoted to **artificial-intelligence (AI)** research. They make no analogy between humans and computers but look for novel ways that will make machines more efficient information processors.

Their findings, however, are sometimes of great use to simulation psychologists.

2. Both computers and humans are limited in what form of stimuli they can take in as **input.** Computers cannot sense the human voice; humans cannot sense some sounds that are too high or too low in pitch.

   a. Humans can receive input over a number of channels, and if all these channels were completely open all of the time, chaos would result. Thus, the brain employs **sensory gating** to cut down on information coming in over other channels when it is important for the person to attend to stimuli coming into one channel.

   b. Even within one sensory channel, there is **selective attention.** In a lecture hall, for example, there may be conversations in the hall, traffic noises coming in the window, and voices from the adjoining class-room, but selective attention allows you to damp down the other sounds in order to hear the lecturer. In this situation you are processing all the sounds **in parallel,** something a computer cannot do. For material that requires more careful processing, however, people seem to use **sequential processing.**

   c. Input selection involves **feature extraction,** which is the first stage of decoding of a sensory message so that the brain can make sense of it. In vision, feature extraction depends on structures and processes in both the eye and the brain. That is, specialized structures detect such features as lines, edges, or angles.

   d. Even if the physical structures that perform feature extraction were completely identified, it would not mean that human input processes would be completely explained. Humans can identify oddly shaped characters (computers cannot), identify words with missing letters (computers cannot), or read sentences with missing words (computers cannot). People can do so because they make use of a feature's **context.** Their expectations, based on experience, lead them to fill in gaps.

3. Once material enters an information-processing system, it must be stored for some period of time in order to be processed. Computers must first store the data they are to perform operations on. Human storage, or memory, appears to take three forms: sensory storage, short-term memory, and long-term memory.

   a. **Sensory storage** seems to be specific to each sense—not stored in a single location. The purpose of sensory storage seems to be to provide a second or two during which information that warrants further processing can be selected.

   b. Information entering **short-term memory (STM)** seems to remain there somewhat less than twenty seconds unless it is **rehearsed** (periodically repeated). The number of items that can be held in STM appears to be 7 ± 2 (5 to 9). But items can be **chunked:** Letters are chunked into words, words into phrases, phrases into long messages. Chunks need not be verbal, however. Chess masters, for instance, can remember and reproduce arrangements of pieces on a board after only a five-second exposure, if the pieces are arranged in ways that would normally occur in a game between two good players.

4. The difference between short-term memory and **long-term memory (LTM)** is evident from certain memory experiments, in which subjects are presented twenty words at the rate of one each second. After the reading of

Figure 5.21 George Miller is a versatile scientist who has worked in the areas of psycholinguistics and information processing. He is particularly well-known for his paper on the limits of human information-processing capacity and on the concept of chunking, titled "The Magical Number Seven, Plus or Minus Two." Recently he coedited (with Kenneth B. Clark) a panel report that urged psychologists to find means of applying their knowledge to the solution of urgent social problems.

the list, subjects are given a minute and a half to write down the words they can remember. The results of many such experiments, summarized and plotted in a **serial position curve,** show that memory is best for the last few items on the list (held in short-term memory), next best for items at the beginning of the list (stored in long-term memory), and worst for items in the middle of the list.

a. The organization of long-term memory is not well understood, but Peter Lindsay and Donald Norman have constructed a model that helps to explain it. They emphasize the **dynamic and integrative processes of memory,** saying that the storing of things is not only the building up of a data base; rather, things that enter storage are integrated with things already there, and, in fact, concepts that are stored and not called upon for years become elaborated while in memory. Lindsay and Norman believe that in an adult's memory, every piece of stored data is connected to every other piece.

b. **Mnemonic devices** use material already organized in memory to help remember other materials. One method, thousands of years old, is the **method of loci:** It requires that one walk, in imagination, through a familiar environment and put items to be remembered in conspicuous places. This method works extremely well. Another method is the **key-word system,** in which one associates things to be remembered with concrete, easily visualizable nouns that rhyme with the words you wish to remember. Then you link the concrete nouns in an image.

c. Many popular mnemonic devices rely on **visual imagery,** and experimental evidence has supported the efficacy of linking verbal and visual materials for memory. George Atwood has suggested that concrete words, which have images associated with them, are processed somewhere in the visual system (in the right hemisphere of the brain), whereas abstract words are processed by an auditory-linguistic system (in the left hemisphere). Linking visual and verbal learning, then, may make it twice as likely that one will remember a message.

5. **Retrieving** information from memory depends on successful acquisition and the organization of the storage.

a. There are two basic ways to retrieve information: recognition and recall. In **recognition,** a person is presented with something and asked whether he has seen or heard it before, as in multiple-choice tests. In **recall,** a person is given certain cues and asked to generate something that corresponds to them, as in essay questions.

b. Motivation can affect recall. When people are very anxious to remember something, they are likely to commit a memory error called **confabulation,** that is, they manufacture something that seems appropriate, sometimes mixing several past events and sometimes inventing things.

c. When one has difficulty retrieving something from memory, one uses some kind of decision process to decide whether an item that is retrieved is the correct one. The assessment is based somehow on the way memories are organized, but it is difficult to pin down the process because some words seem to be retrieved through their imagery, some through their sound, some through their shape.

6. There are three theories that attempt to explain **forgetting.**

a. One approach says that things successfully acquired and stored cannot

Figure 5.22 Gordon H. Bower's research includes experiments in memory, learning, and behavior theory, but he is best known for his contributions to mathematical models of human memory and learning. He is the author of books on human associative learning and human attentional processes and is the coauthor (with Ernest Hilgard) of an influential text on theories of learning.

be retrieved because the person consciously or unconsciously **represses** them.

b. One approach says that whenever people have an experience or learn something, a chemical or physical **memory trace** is formed in the brain, and over time, these traces are subject to decay.

c. The third approach attributes forgetting to **interference** from other items learned. In instances when learning of later material interferes with material learned earlier, **retroactive interference** is said to have taken place. When material learned earlier interferes with learning of later material, **proactive interference** is said to have taken place.

7. **Output** can affect input through a process called **feedback,** which is sometimes called ''knowledge of results.'' Most movements are monitored by continuous **feedback loops**—from muscles and senses to brain, and back to muscles and nerves. Because any behavior is an attempt to reach a goal, people use a **hierarchy of feedback loops** to let them know how closely they are approaching the goal.

8. A comparison of human and computer information-processing systems tends to point up the limitations of computers with respect to the human system.

a. Computers are rigid and cannot be creative.

b. Human memory capacity is much larger than that of the most impressive computers.

c. Computers are not emotional, and emotions seem to influence many cognitive processes.

d. Computers cannot simulate what in humans is called **episodic memory,** life events recalled from a person's own point of view. This type of memory is distinguished from **semantic memory,** which is the type of memory referred to in most of this chapter.

e. Computers do not develop or change themselves (some do learn a few things). Jean Piaget, whose work is discussed at length in Chapter 8, and other developmental psychologists believe that interaction with one's physical and mental environment is required for the development of abstract and logical thought.

Figure 5.23 In addition to his work on interference theory in learning and forgetting, Charles Osgood has made contributions to such areas as human communications and cognitive processes. He is author of the influential handbook *Method and Theory in Experimental Psychology,* and he developed the semantic-differential technique for the measurement of meaning discussed in Chapters 13 and 15. He is presently director of the Institute of Communications Research at the University of Illinois.

SUGGESTED READINGS

Lindsay, Peter, and Donald Norman. *Human Information Processing: An Introduction to Psychology.* New York: Academic Press, 1972. A thorough and easy-to-read introduction to psychology from an information-processing point of view. Many topics dealt with briefly in this chapter are discussed at length in Lindsay and Norman's book.

Powers, William T. *Behavior: The Control of Perception.* Chicago: Aldine, 1973. A highly original work, explaining all of human behavior in a hierarchical model. The author's thesis is that our perceptions are the only reality we can know, and the purpose of all our actions is to control the state of the perceived world. The mechanism for that control is negative feedback. Powers has had training in electronics and systems engineering as well as in psychology.

Everyone must solve a problem of some sort at almost every moment of his life—even if it is a simple one, such as: Where did I put my glasses? It is the mathematician and the scientist, however, who are usually considered *the* problem solvers. It is their profession to consider and solve, if possible, the deepest problems set them by the universe. How do they do it?

One could never find out by reading the learned papers in which they describe their discoveries. These are dry, straight-line, logical expositions, prepared after the fact of discovery. Such papers are very likely to contain not one hint of the actual manner in which the solution of some problem was arrived at.

Here is a case in point. Back in the 1850s a German chemist, Friedrich August Kekulé von Stradonitz, had worked out a system for representing the arrangements of the atoms in molecules. He connected their symbols with little dashes according to a small number of simple rules. The formulas that were produced in this fashion could be used to explain the ways in which particular molecules behaved. They could even be used to predict new ways in which they would behave under special circumstances. The formulas helped guide chemists to the synthesis of new and remarkable substances that did not exist in nature.

There remained one important substance, benzene, that did not seem to fit. Kekulé tried to work out a formula for its atoms (six carbon atoms and six hydrogen atoms in each molecule) but could not do it. He arranged the carbon atoms in the different kinds of chains that worked for other molecules, but none made sense of the way in which benzene behaved. If the benzene problem were not solved, his whole system might break down.

One day in 1865, he was in Ghent, Belgium, on a public bus. He was tired, and, lulled by the droning beat of the horses' hooves on the cobblestones, he fell into a comatose half-sleep. In that sleep, the overwhelming preoccupation with the problem of molecular structure took over. He seemed to see a vision of atoms attaching themselves to each other in chains that moved about. And then one chain twisted in such a way that head and tail joined, forming a ring—and Kekulé came to full wakefulness with a start.

That was it! He arranged the six carbon atoms of the benzene molecule in a ring and found that he could now account for its properties. It was that semicomatose vision that established his system, and although chemists have deepened and broadened that system in the century since then, they have never departed from it. When Kekulé came to describe the new addition to his system, he said nothing of his dream. He merely advanced evidence and reasoning in the driest possible way—as though that were how he had worked it out. We only know of the dream because he described it in a letter to a friend during another moment of relaxation long after.

Isaac Asimov

6
Thinking and Problem Solving: Cognitive Psychology

The cognitive approach to thinking and learning, which is presented in this chapter, has been a major force in psychology for many decades—unlike the information-processing approach to thinking (discussed in Chapter 5), which is not much more than ten years old. Although the two approaches have some things in common, they differ in two important respects. Cognitive psychologists traditionally hold two assumptions that information-processing psychologists may or may not accept. First, cognitive psychologists view all learning as a process of *solving a problem:* When we learn something, cognitive psychologists say, we have a goal; we think about what we want to accomplish, and then we try to find a way to accomplish it. The second assumption cognitive psychologists hold is that behavior is *organized.* One of their goals, then, is to discover how the many components of thought and action fit together to form behavior. Just as a chemist tries to understand how atoms are organized into molecules, the cognitive psychologist wants to understand how the components of behavior fit together to make a pattern. This chapter emphasizes these two aspects of cognitive psychology—problem solving and the organization of behavior.

EXPLANATIONS OF PROBLEM SOLVING

Most days of our lives we find ourselves beset by one problem or another. Some problems are easy, some difficult, some downright impossible. Some we work out completely in our heads; others we solve by using our hands or feet or other parts of our bodies. Forcing yourself to get up in the morning, learning to ride a bicycle, pitting your wits against a crossword puzzle, naming all the Presidents of the United States, fixing a flat tire, stretching the weekly budget, writing a novel, trying to explain how people solve problems—all these

Figure 6.1 Although playing chess is a demanding problem-solving activity, the principles that govern a chess player's behavior may also govern the behavior of such other kinds of problem solvers as a person trying to predict the weather, a rat trying to find its way through a maze, or a child trying to dress himself. This chapter discusses these general principles.

activities and many more we commonly lump under the general heading: problems. What do these activities have in common that leads us to call them problems? Is there some trait they all share? Do they all require the same abilities, for instance, or involve the same processes of solution?

Whenever someone is faced with a problem, he has a goal, and he must somehow find a way to reach it. In some cases, both the goal and how to reach it are clear. If your goal is to name all the Presidents of the United States, one obvious way to accomplish it is by finding an encyclopedia or almanac that lists all the Presidents. In other cases, as when a child is learning to ride a bicycle, the goal is clear enough but the way to attain the goal is not very clear. That is what the child must learn: how to keep the bike balanced while at the same time steering it and pedaling it. In still other cases, such as when one tries to write a novel or explain how people solve problems, neither the goal nor how to accomplish it is very clear.

Partly because problems vary so in the clarity and obviousness of their goals, and the means for reaching the goals, it has been difficult for psychologists to devise a single, comprehensive explanation of problem solving. Although none of the approaches to problem solving described below succeeds in fully explaining how all organisms solve all the many types of problems that they do, each emphasizes at least one important problem-solving process and each is valid for at least some kinds of problems. The first explanation says that organisms solve problems by testing hypotheses about ways to reach a goal. The second approach, which is based on a computer model, emphasizes the importance of procedures called heuristics in problem solving. The third stresses the need for an initial understanding of the problem and its components. The fourth suggests that there are several distinct phases that an organism goes through when solving a problem: Each phase represents a different level of comprehension of the problem.

Hypothesis Testing

Hypothesis-testing theory is one of the oldest theories in American cognitive psychology. It explains problem solving as the formulation and testing of hypotheses about the manner in which a goal can be reached. If a person's goal is to force himself to get up in the morning, for example, he may formulate the hypothesis that he will be forced to get up if he sets four alarm clocks and places them in different spots around his bedroom. He can test that hypothesis by setting the clocks and seeing whether they do indeed force him to get up.

Edward Tolman and David Krech, two early formulators of American **hypothesis-testing theory,** showed that in problem-solving or learning situations even rats often act as if they are testing hypotheses. In one series of experiments, Krech used a maze like the one shown in Figure 6.2, in which the alleys are equipped with lights that the experimenter can turn on and off. At each choice point in the maze, the rat could turn either right or left and toward an alley that was either lighted or dark. Krech adjusted the apparatus from trial to trial, so that the rat could not find its way through the maze by using the left-right and light-dark cues in a systematic fashion. In such a situation, the rat acted as if it were checking out a series of hypotheses. It might first choose mostly left turns; when that did not work, it might choose mostly right turns; when that did not work, it might choose all the lighted alleys; and so on.

Later investigators have generally accepted the basic idea of hypothesis theory—that problem solving involves the use of hypotheses—and have tried to specify more precisely how hypotheses are selected and how they are related to each other in complex tasks like playing checkers or solving problems in logic, which involve numerous interrelated hypotheses. In Krech's

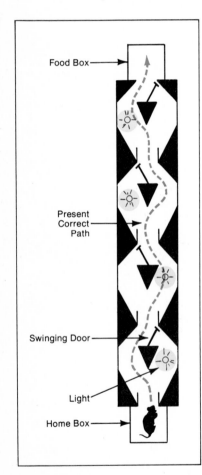

Figure 6.2 The floor plan of the maze used by Krech to study problem solving in rats. At each of the four choice points (triangular blocks) the rat could take either the left or the right path, one of which was lighted and the other unlighted. Although on each trial a particular sequence of choices led to the food at the end of the maze, by changing the lighting and the positions of the swinging doors (behind the triangular blocks) from trial to trial, Krech made it impossible for the rat to find a solution that would reliably lead to the food. Under these conditions the rat would try one possible solution (choosing all the right-hand paths, for example) for several trials, then reject it and try another.

Labels on figure: Food Box, Present Correct Path, Swinging Door, Light, Home Box maze there were only a few possible hypotheses, because a turn at a choice point could be only to the right or left and toward a lighted or a dark alley. But a checkers player about to begin a game could never even consider all the 10^{40} play sequences (hypotheses) open to him. Even if he could evaluate three of them every micromillisecond (one millionth of one thousandth of a second), he would be sitting for 10^{21} (one billion trillion) centuries before he had considered all his alternatives. Clearly the way the checkers player conceptualizes the play sequences and chooses one or another must be included in any model of problem solving.

Heuristics of the General Problem Solver

Several years ago Allen Newell, J. C. Shaw, and Herbert Simon developed an information-processing model of problem solving: a computer program called the **General Problem Solver (GPS)** that has solved diverse problems in logic, algebra, and chess. In part, the program is an attempt to state more precisely how people use hypotheses by specifying the procedures they use to formulate and test hypotheses. The basic premise of the GPS program is that all thinking directed toward attaining a goal in problem solving is influenced by a small number of procedures called **heuristics.**

Heuristics are best understood by contrasting them with another type of procedure, called an **algorithm.** An algorithm is a problem-solving method that specifies the sequence of all possible operations that might help solve a particular problem. For example, an algorithm for opening a combination lock would require the problem solver to test every possible number combination in turn until he or she happened upon the correct one. An algorithm for Krech's maze problem would specify the testing of every possible combination of right/left and lighted/dark alleys.

For many kinds of problems, it is not possible to construct algorithms, and even if one could, they would be extremely tedious and time consuming. If the checkers player were to use an algorithm to decide on his opening move, he would have 10^{40} possible play sequences to test. An algorithmic chess player would have even more play sequences to consider, since he faces some 10^{120} possibilities. Yet people play chess and checkers, and some people even play well. (Indeed the best human chess players can still consistently beat the best computer programs at chess.) The way they do it, presumably, is by using heuristics.

A heuristic is an explicit, carefully specified strategy, or rule of thumb. A heuristic problem-solving method calls for the use of only a few of the possible ways to solve a problem, but it usually allows a successful, relatively quick solution. The heuristic approach relies on familiarity with the task. Because the person is familiar with the task or some parts of it, he can investigate what he estimates to be the more likely solutions before looking at the more far-fetched alternatives. To pick a simple example, suppose your ''problem'' is that you want to watch television but do not have a listing of the evening's programs. As you flip the channel selector, you will probably go quickly past the channels that are not available in your area and pause only at those that are. You may even use a slightly more sophisticated heuristic, and turn first to a channel that often broadcasts programs you like, such as old movies.

Newell and his co-workers tried to identify the heuristics that people most commonly use in solving problems; then they programmed the computer to use them, either singly or in combination. They found that the two heuristics that the computer (and perhaps human problem solvers as well) relies on most heavily are **subgoal analysis** and **means-end analysis.**

In subgoal analysis the General Problem Solver divides a difficult problem into a series of smaller problems—subgoals—that it has a better chance of

Figure 6.3 Bernie is using a heuristic called means-end analysis to solve a transportation problem. He wants to reduce the difference between his initial state (being in Boston) and his desired state (being in London), but he runs into considerable difficulty in executing the first step of this process.

solving. Faced with a chess problem, for example, GPS would first see if the king is safe from attack (subgoal 1). If the king is in danger, GPS concentrates on moves that will protect it or remove it from the danger zone (subgoal 2). If the king is safe, GPS goes on to its next-most-important subgoal, which is to ensure that other pieces are not in imminent danger (subgoal 3). Then it tries to gain control of the center regions of the board so as to be in a good position for attack (subgoal 4): It starts to move pawns into the center squares. If all its pieces remain safe, GPS works through a series of additional attack subgoals. In this way, GPS uses subgoal analysis to divide a difficult problem into a number of interrelated subgoals—each a problem in its own right—but a more manageable one than the main goal, winning the game.

In the second type of heuristic, means-end analysis, the General Problem Solver seeks to reduce the difference between the initial state and the desired state (the goal or end). Means-end analysis, despite its rather formidable name, is a heuristic that people often use to solve practical problems in daily life. Suppose that Bernie wants to travel from Boston (his initial state) to London (his desired state). As shown in Figure 6.3, the means for reducing the difference between Boston and London that readily spring to mind are planes and ships. Bernie telephones a travel agent, only to find that neither airlines nor shipping lines have carriers that go directly from Boston to London. The means that he thought would reduce the difference between Boston and London will not work. He decides to fly to New York, thus reducing the Boston-London difference to a New York-London one, and take a plane to London from there. But unfortunately, if he flies to New York, he has to wait seven hours before the London flight leaves. What about driving his car to New York? The difficulty with that plan is that he must do something with his car in New York. He doesn't want to leave it there; it might be stolen. So he calls his girl friend Gloria and asks her to drive to New York with him and take care of the car while he is away. When she turns down his offer, he decides to take the plane to New York and wait seven hours after all. From New York he will take a plane to London, completely removing the difference between his initial and desired states. His problem is solved.

Depending on the problem it is given, GPS may use means-end analysis by itself or in combination with subgoal analysis (or some other, less common heuristic). One of the computer's tasks is to decide, for each problem given, which heuristics to use and how to combine them. In playing chess, for example, the computer would use subgoal analysis to break down its overall problem into smaller, more manageable problems; but it might use means-end analysis to achieve its subgoals. Subgoal 4 in the example described earlier (attaining control of the center regions of the chess board in order to gain a good offensive position) could be restated in terms of means-end analysis: GPS wants to reduce the difference between its initial state, a defensive position, and its desired state, an offensive position. It begins to do this by moving pawns into the center squares.

Research with GPS has shown that these heuristics are central to some very complex problem-solving activities. They explain some of the ways in which hypotheses are formulated and tested in complex problems. Because GPS shows how a few heuristic rules are instrumental in a wide range of problem-solving behaviors, it is one of the most striking achievements in recent research on problem solving and thinking.

There are, however, serious limitations to GPS (pointed out by William Powers, among others) that prevent it from being a truly general model of problem solving. Other models based on information processing suffer from the same limitations. For one thing, all the problems that GPS deals with are well structured; whether they concern chess or algebra or logic, their components are well-known and well-understood, at least by people who specialize in that sort of problem. For another thing, the programmer does some of the work: He tells the computer what the problem is, gives it a list of possible heuristics to use in reaching a solution, and provides it with information on how to decide when a solution has been attained. Ordinarily, a human being facing a problem is given none of this information.

How people recognize and define problems is one of the least studied and least understood aspects of problem solving. Virtually all contemporary theories of problem solving deal primarily with procedures for solving a problem after it is generally defined as one. On the other hand, there is a recent theory that attempts to explain how people reach their initial definition of a problem. The theory is based on work in the field of pattern perception, but it deals with the perception of patterns in problem-solving terms; that is, it treats the recognition of a pattern as part of the solution of a problem. In some cases, the theory states, the problem is solved through a process called analysis by synthesis, described in the following section.

Analysis by Synthesis

A pattern-recognition problem like one used by Peter Lindsay and Donald Norman to demonstrate analysis by synthesis is shown in Figure 6.4. In each case a person's general conception of the problem, that is, his **synthesis** of the pattern, determines how he interprets the components of the problem, that is, his **analysis** of the pattern. In the first case, Figure 6.4A, the lines shown are essentially meaningless. When those lines are given a context, as in Figure 6.4 B, they become more meaningful. A blot is covering up several letters in a word, probably with four letters; you may even be able to tell what the word is. A more complete context, providing a fuller conception of the problem, is shown on page 127.

Forty years ago Karl Duncker proposed a similar explanation for how problems in general are initially conceptualized and described. The person trying to solve a problem starts out with a general conception of the problem. Then, using his own knowledge and past experience, he analyzes the problem into more specific conceptions, through which he eventually produces a solution. Here is one problem studied by Duncker that is solved in this way:

A person has an inoperable stomach tumor. He can be treated with radiation, but radiation of sufficient intensity will destroy healthy tissue as well as the tumor. How can radiation be used to eliminate the tumor without destroying the healthy tissue surrounding it?

Duncker asked each person to "think out loud" as he worked on the problem. Figure 6.5 shows a diagram of the solution attempts of one person who thought of an especially large number of possibilities. The experimenter provides the general conception of the problem, described at the top. From this general conception, or synthesis, the person analyzes the problem into several general outlines of possibilities for solution; then he analyzes each outline into several possible means of solutions; finally, from some of these means, he constructs possible specific solutions to the problem. The specific solutions that were not the best solution were rejected either by the problem solver or by the experimenter, leaving the "best solution" shown in the lower right-hand corner of the diagram.

In each case the person used his conceptualization from one level in the diagram as a synthesis from which he could analyze the problem into the conceptualizations of the level just below. Analysis by synthesis, then, provides an explanation for the process of conceptualizing and describing a problem, whether it is a problem in pattern recognition or a more traditional type of problem like Duncker's.

Ideally, psychologists should be able to formulate analysis by synthesis as a

Figure 6.4 (A) What do these marks mean? It is very unlikely that a piece-by-piece analysis of them will lead to a solution, and there is not enough information given here to generate a useful synthesis. (B) With the context added here, you may be able to see the marks as parts of a whole, and many possible solutions to the problem of interpreting them may come to mind. Information that resolves the problem even further is given in Figure 6.4C on page 127.
(After Lindsay and Norman, 1972.)

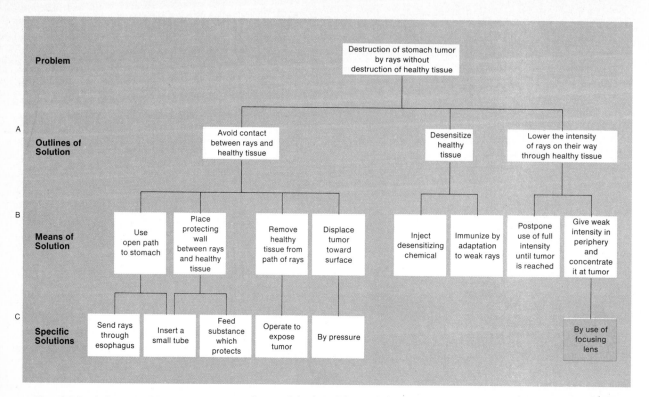

Figure 6.5 A diagram of the attempts made by one subject to solve the problem posed by Duncker. Note that the subject's thoughts (spoken aloud, as Duncker requested) can be interpreted in terms of a hierarchy—from extremely general syntheses at the top to highly specific analyses at the bottom. The technique of requiring a subject to "think out loud" has since been used repeatedly in studies of problem solving. It is a method that you can use with yourself as subject, with the aid of a tape recorder or pencil and paper. (After Duncker, 1945.)

precise model of problem solving—as precise as the General Problem Solver, for example. To do so, they must deal with a number of central issues about the exact nature of analysis by synthesis. What are the differences between early phases of problem solving (Figure 6.5A) and later phases (Figure 6.5C); that is, what exactly is the nature of analysis by synthesis at different points in the problem-solving process? How are new components brought into the problem at each phase: for example, the lens, esophagus, small tube, protective substance, and so on, which are parts of the suggested specific solutions in Figure 6.5? What is the nature of the very earliest phase of problem solution: the recognition that there is a problem to be solved? In the psychology laboratory, psychologists typically tell the person that he is to solve a problem and they even give him an idea of the general nature of the problem, but in everyday life people need to recognize that there is a problem before they can go about trying to solve it.

Phases in the Development of a Solution

Duncker observed that the general properties of a solution are formulated early in the problem-solving process and that more specific properties develop out of the general ones later on. He therefore suggested that problem solving be viewed in terms of phases in the development of a solution. According to this approach, the problem solver goes through phases that gradually move him toward a solution much as a child goes through stages in, for example, the development of a specific skill, like classification (see Chapter 8), except that the phases of problem solving may occur in minutes or even in seconds, while the stages of development of a skill take a child many years to complete. Kurt Fischer has recently proposed a theory that attempts to specify the number and nature of problem-solving phases more precisely. Although the theory is not yet as explicit as the General Problem Solver of Newell, Shaw, and Simon, it does provide a useful formulation of the phases both people and animals go through in the development of the solution of a problem.

	Phases in the Development of a Solution		
Phase	**Level of Comprehension**	**Organization of Behavior**	**Transition**
0	No understanding of problem.	Behavior shows no particular organization with respect to the task to be learned.	Organism recognizes that there is a problem to be solved or a goal to be attained.
1	Vague, diffuse conception of problem.	Behavior is relatively disconnected and irregular, but parts of the task are performed quickly and excitedly, especially near the goal. Behavior appears to be goal-directed despite its relative disorganization.	The general outline of the solution is defined.
2	Conception of general direction of solution.	Organism may be slow to begin to respond, but once it has begun, it performs the task in a single thrust, virtually without pause.	The components of the solution are differentiated.
3	Understanding of all components necessary for a solution.	The task is performed smoothly and regularly, but spontaneous pauses occasionally occur at various places in the task.	The components of the solution are integrated.
4	Understanding of solution.	Performance is similar to that at Phase 3, but even more regular. Behavior becomes an integrated whole (in Bruner's terminology, a module).	

The general phases of problem solving proposed by Fischer are shown in Figure 6.6. There are five phases, starting with Phase 0, in which the individual does not even recognize that there is a problem, and ending with Phase 4, in which the problem is solved.

Problem Solving in Children: Understanding Size Relations To illustrate how an individual progresses through the phases, consider a problem that is very simple for adults to solve but impossible for a young child: How do you put ten sticks in order from smallest to largest? At age four or five, the child does not understand the task at all; his cognitive capacities are not well enough developed. A few years later, though, he is able to perform it easily. Figure 6.7 shows the phases he goes through in developing that ability. Because the development of the solution is stretched out over several years, the phases are particularly clear-cut and easy to distinguish.

Suppose a four-year-old girl is presented with ten sticks, lined up in order from smallest to largest. The experimenter then mixes up the sticks and asks the child to make the same series that she saw. At Phase 0 the child does not at all understand the nature of the problem and simply begins to play with the sticks.

Six months later, when the same girl is presented with the problem again, she has achieved the transition from Phase 0 to Phase 1: She recognizes that there is a problem to be solved involving size. Her understanding of size, however, is not very good: She merely distinguishes big sticks from little sticks and is unable to put them in order, as shown in Figure 6.7.

After another year or so, the girl has attained the transition from Phase 1 to Phase 2: She can define the general outline of the solution and knows that the sticks are to be laid out in terms of size. But because she does not fully understand that "longer than" and "shorter than" can be applied to the same stick, she can only make a partially correct series. She cannot yet treat each stick as longer or shorter than every other stick in the series.

Figure 6.6 Fischer's phase theory of problem solving. Note that the phases are described in both cognitive and behavioral terms and also in terms of the means by which a problem solver may pass from one phase to the next.

THE WORK MUST GET DONE.

Figure 6.4C A complete context for the marks in Figure 6.4A. Note that in interpreting the marks now, you use each of them to help you interpret the others. Seeing the W helps you see the O, seeing the O helps you see the W, and so on. Your analysis of each individual mark as a part of a letter is made possible by your synthesis of all the marks as letters forming the word "work." (After Lindsay and Norman, 1972.)

Phase	Level of Seriation	Representative Result of Behavior	Transition Rule
0	No understanding of seriation.		
			Child recognizes that there is a problem to be solved involving size.
1	Distinguishes long from short sticks.		
			General outline of solution is defined: All sticks to be ordered in terms of size.
2	Makes partial series by trial and error.		
			Components for solution are differentiated: Each stick must be treated as larger than some and smaller than others.
3	Makes complete series by trial and error.	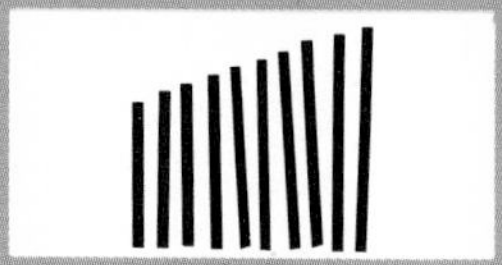	
			Components are integrated into a solution: Collection of sticks forms a step-by-step series in which each has its unique place.
4	Anticipates entire series from the start.		

Figure 6.7   The development of a child's ability to order a series of sticks according to size. This ability is technically called *seriation*. Its development is described in terms of Fischer's phase theory, even though the development takes place over a period of years. The theory is applicable to many kinds of problem solving, independently of whether the problem can be solved in a matter of minutes or requires the development of cognitive skills over a number of years.

Figure 6.8   A dead end in the seriation problem. The child that constructed this ordering of the sticks was concentrating on how the line formed by the ends of the sticks ought to appear. With this conception of the problem, the child could not possibly develop the ability to systematically compare the sticks in length.

When she accomplishes the transition to Phase 3, she understands "longer than" and "shorter than" and can probably make the correct series by trial and error, measuring each stick against the others as she goes. Finally, she achieves the transition from Phase 3 to Phase 4: She understands that each stick has a particular place in the series, and she can form the series smoothly and easily.

Duncker's diagram of the tumor problem also demonstrates the phases of problem solving. Phase 0 occurred before the problem was presented to the individual: He did not yet know it existed. As soon as the problem was presented to him (and he understood what he was told), he entered Phase 1, where he had the rather vague conception of the problem indicated at the top of Figure 6.5. Transition to Phase 2 requires defining a general outline for solution; in this case, the problem solver devised three different general outlines. For each outline, he differentiated several possible means for solution, which placed him at Phase 3. In addition, he specified possible instruments that might be used in solving the problem (tubes, protective substances, and so on). Then he accomplished the transition to Phase 4 by putting together the appropriate components into a solution: He formulated the specific method by which an instrument could be used in a particular way to effect a solution. All the solutions developed in this manner were appropriate in the abstract, although most of them had to be rejected for practical reasons.

Notice that one outline for solution, desensitizing the healthy tissue, was not developed into a specific solution. The problem-solving process stopped at Phase 3, probably because the problem solver knew that the means he had thought of for desensitizing the healthy tissue would not work. That is, an inappropriate definition of the problem led to a dead end. Children trying to solve the seriation problem also sometimes reach a dead end. In one common inappropriate outline for solution the child lines up one end of the sticks in a

128

stepwise fashion, as shown in Figure 6.8, thus mimicking one end of the correct series but ignoring the crucial dimension of size. Testing inappropriate outlines for solution is an important part of problem solving, common with adults as well as children. The only way to determine whether an outline is inappropriate is to try it.

Now that you are familiar with the phases of problem solving, try the following verbal problem. See if you can observe a progression through the phases.

This an example in a demonstration whole piece of writing. The to figure out what rule transforms the sentences back to standard English idea. The, of course, not present in normal English rule. Considering how the parts of the sentence break down into components facilitates discovery of the rule. Necessary for solving the problem persistence. The not an easy one problem. Can you discover the rule?

(If you have not figured out the passage, look it over several more times.)

Kurt Fischer, with the assistance of John Cannell, used a passage similar to this one to study the phases of problem solving; he found that people who solved the problem did progress through the phases as predicted by the theory. Many people, however, could not solve it; they became stuck at Phase 1, 2, or 3.

Problem Solving in Animals: Running a Maze   Rats learning to navigate the simple S-maze shown in Figure 6.9 appear to progress through phases similar to those found in human problem solving, Fischer has found. The problem that each rat must solve is how to run through the maze to obtain the food in the goal box. In Phase 0 the rat does not yet recognize the problem; it does not show any goal-directed behavior. In Phase 1 it recognizes that there is food to be obtained somewhere in the maze. Defining the general outline for solution—that the food can be found by running through the maze to the end—brings Phase 2. But the rat is not yet familiar with the layout of the maze. The animal reaches Phase 3 when the components of the maze are differentiated, and it attains Phase 4 when it integrates those components into what Edward Tolman called a cognitive map—a mental representation of the spatial relationships of the parts of the maze.

Because a rat cannot think out loud as it solves the maze problem, the phases must be distinguished by observing the organization of the animal's behavior as it runs through the maze. In the seriation-of-sticks problem, children arrange the sticks in different patterns during each phase; in running the maze, rats show different patterns of pauses during each phase, as shown in Figure 6.9. In Phase 0, the rat meanders through the maze, pausing virtually everywhere. In Phase 1, it pauses less often in the area near the goal box, indicating that it recognizes that food is to be found there. In Phase 2, after some hesitation near the start box, it runs quickly through the maze. In Phase 3, it usually runs the maze quickly and smoothly, though it pauses occasionally here and there. The animal is able to stop for a moment and then resume its run without losing its place because it has differentiated the components of the maze.

In Phase 4, the pause pattern is about the same as in Phase 3, but the rat gives other evidence that it has integrated the components of the maze into a cognitive map. For example, the withdrawal of reinforcement (extinction) affects the behavior of a rat in Phase 3 differently from that of a rat in Phase 4. When an animal in Phase 3 no longer finds food in the goal box, it continues to start out well on later trials but hesitates as it approaches the goal box. When an animal in Phase 4 encounters the same situation, it seems reluctant to start running at all. It stays in the start box for long periods or runs back and forth between the start box and the first corner of the maze. In other words, the removal of the food disrupts the behavior of the animal in Phase 3

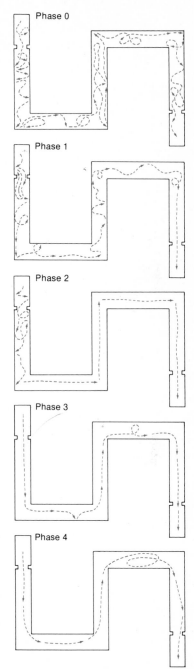

Figure 6.9   The behavior of a rat at each of the phases in the development of its solution to the problem of running an S maze for food. The arrows in the illustrations represent the rat's movements. Note that although the last two phases are not well distinguished by differences in the rat's movements, clear differences can be seen in such other indicators as its behavior during extinction.

primarily in the area where the animal actually experiences the absence of food. Apparently, the animal does not associate what it does at the start of the maze with what it hopes to find at the end, because it has not yet integrated the sections of the maze into a unit. The animal in Phase 4, in contrast, anticipates the sequence as a whole. "Knowing" that there probably will be no food in the goal box, it hesitates even to begin running.

The differences Fischer has observed in the organization of behavior from phase to phase resemble Jerome Bruner's observations of the behavior of human infants as they learn to pick up a cup. As soon as an infant recognizes that the cup can be picked up, he will look intently at it for long periods but only occasionally manage to get his hand in its vicinity. When he begins to understand how to reach for the cup, his reaching pattern looks rather like a rat's Phase 2 pause pattern: Once the reach begins, it is carried out in a quick, single motion without pause. As the child continues to practice the action, his performance becomes smoother, more expert, and more relaxed. Pauses begin to appear here and there in the middle of it, as they did in the maze running of the rat at Phase 3. The smooth performance and occasional pauses continue as the infant gradually integrates the components of reaching into a single action. The action is not merely a sequence of differentiated components; it is an integrated whole that serves as a new unit of behavior. Bruner calls such integrated units **modules.**

Modules are important components of behavior. Besides allowing the individual to solve efficiently the original problem (the one that led to formation of the module), they have other important properties that make them useful for solving problems that the individual will encounter later. These properties involve the phenomenon of transfer.

PROBLEM SOLVING AND TRANSFER

Psychologists have long recognized the importance of transfer in problem solving and learning. Transfer occurs when something learned on one task affects an organism's performance on a second task. In **positive transfer** the learning or solution of one task facilitates performance on a second task. For example, if someone has learned to play the clarinet well, it will be much easier for him to learn to play the saxophone. He can transfer much of his clarinet-playing skill to saxophone playing. In **negative transfer** the learning or solution of the first task interferes with performance on the second. For example, when automatic gear-shifts first appeared on automobiles, reverse was in the same position as low gear had been on standard shifts. As a result, many drivers experienced negative transfer. They had difficulty learning to drive cars with automatic shifts, because they frequently put the car in reverse when they meant to be putting it in low.

Bruner, Fischer, and George Mandler and Jean Mandler, among others, have shown that there is a relationship between the type of transfer that occurs and the modularization of the initial task. When an organism has reached Phase 4 on the initial task and has therefore formed a module for that task, positive transfer commonly occurs on a second related task: Performance is improved. A person who is experienced at driving a car will almost certainly find it easier to learn to drive a truck than a person who has no experience with driving. Indeed, he or she will probably be able to skip the first few phases of problem solving with the truck. But when the organism is still at earlier phases on the first task and is required to perform the second task, negative transfer occurs: Performance on the second task is hindered. A person who has been learning to drive a car for only two weeks will probably find it more difficult to learn to drive a truck at that time than will a person who has no experience with driving. Transfer, both positive and negative, is an important factor in our everyday lives. Indeed, most of the problem solving done by

Who is taller, Paul or Tom, if:

1. Dave is taller than Paul.
2. Paul is taller than John.
3. Dave is taller than John.
4. Tom is taller than Alan.
5. Alan is taller than Dave.

adults probably involves the transfer of modules developed during earlier problem solving.

Strategies for Problem Solving

Certain types of modularized skills are especially useful for problem solving, because they transfer easily to a number of different problems. Generalized problem-solving skills of this sort are called **strategies.** The heuristics that Newell, Shaw, and Simon embodied in the General Problem Solver, such as subgoal analysis and means-end analysis, are examples of particularly effective and general strategies for solving problems. Of course, strategies for solving problems are not always effective or efficient. *Any* general method for solving problems is a strategy, including, for example, algorithms, which, as noted earlier, are often extremely inefficient.

Learning to Learn   Most strategies are learned when a person or animal is exposed repeatedly to similar problems. Harry Harlow calls the acquisition of strategies of this sort learning to learn.

Harlow studied learning to learn by giving monkeys the problem of finding a raisin that had been placed under one of two lids or cups. In one version of the task, the monkey was first presented with one red lid and one green one. The raisin was always hidden under the green lid, and the experimenter kept changing the position of each lid, so that the monkey was forced to learn that color was important, not location. When the monkey had learned always to pick the green lid, the experimenter changed the problem. Now the animal had to choose between triangular and circular lids. The raisin was always placed under the circular lid, and the experimenter again changed the location of the lids on each trial. As before, it took several tries for the monkey to realize that the shape of the lid, not its location, indicated where the raisin would be. After doing hundreds of problems like these, in which the significant characteristics of the two lids were changed for each problem, the monkey began to learn that the difference between the two lids was always the key to the problem. Eventually it could solve any similar problem with, at most, one error. It had learned the following strategy: Ignore position and pay attention to the characteristics of the lids. If on the first trial the lid that is picked has the raisin under it, keep picking it, but if it does not, switch to the other lid; it is the correct one.

People, of course, show learning to learn too. When exposed repeatedly to problems of the same type, they can discover more efficient strategies for solving the problems. Particularly dramatic improvements in strategy tend to occur as people gain experience with the type of problem shown in the opposite margin, called a series problem. Asked to solve a number of these series problems, most people start out with an effective but relatively inefficient strategy. According to a study by Clinton DeSoto, Marvin London, and Stephen Handel, they build up mental images in which the people in the series are represented in a top-to-bottom order, with the tallest person at the top and the shortest person at the bottom, as shown in Figure 6.10. Later on, they devise a more efficient, less strenuous strategy that does not require visualizing the line-up described in the problem.

For example, given the problem in the margin after several similar ones, the problem solver first notes whom he is asked about (Paul and Tom), and then, instead of constructing an image including all the people mentioned, he tries to find a connection between Paul and Tom. Suppose that he starts by looking for a connection from Tom to Paul. He finds that Tom is taller than Alan (line 4), Alan is taller than Dave (line 5), and Dave is taller than Paul (line 1). Therefore Tom is taller than Paul, as shown in Figure 6.10A. If he had started out looking for a connection from Paul to Tom, then he would

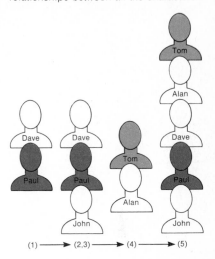

Figure 6.10   The strategy people use when first exposed to problems of the kind posed in the margin on page 130. Using the given statements one by one, they build up a mental image of the relationships between all the characters.

(1) ⟶ (2,3) ⟶ (4) ⟶ (5)

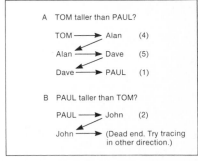

A   TOM taller than PAUL?

TOM ⟶ Alan   (4)

Alan ⟶ Dave   (5)

Dave ⟶ PAUL   (1)

B   PAUL taller than TOM?

PAUL ⟶ John   (2)

John ⟶ (Dead end. Try tracing in other direction.)

Figure 6.11   With experience people develop a more efficient strategy for problems like the one on page 130. Treating the statements as though they were algebraic inequalities, they trace a chain of connection (A) between the two characters they have been asked to relate. They select only those statements that extend the chain. If, as in (B), tracking in one direction does not work, they will try the other direction.

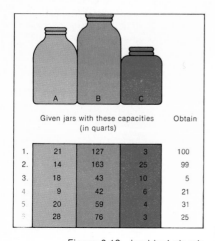

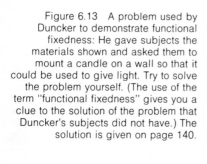

Figure 6.12 Luchins' classic demonstration of set in problem solving. In each of the problems in this series you must work out how you could measure out the quantities of liquid indicated on the right by using jars with the capacities shown on the left. Try the series yourself before reading on. After solving the first five problems, nearly two-thirds of Luchins' subjects were unable to solve the sixth. The sixth problem actually requires a simpler strategy than the first five, and it would be easily solved were it not for the set established by the first five.

Figure 6.13 A problem used by Duncker to demonstrate functional fixedness: He gave subjects the materials shown and asked them to mount a candle on a wall so that it could be used to give light. Try to solve the problem yourself. (The use of the term "functional fixedness" gives you a clue to the solution of the problem that Duncker's subjects did not have.) The solution is given on page 140.

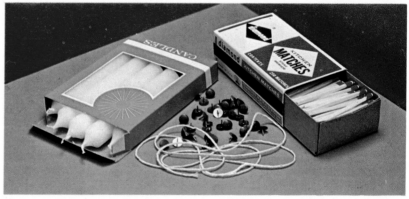

have been unable to find the connection, as shown in Figure 6.10B, because Paul is taller than John (line 2) but John is not mentioned as being taller than anyone. At that point he would begin again, looking instead for the connection from Tom to Paul, as above.

In this way people or animals can develop strategies that allow them to solve a specific type of problem quickly and efficiently. They simply transfer the module for the type of problem to each new instance of the problem that they are presented with. Once the module for the strategy is established, the earlier phases of problem solving no longer appear; instead, the person only shows Phase 4 behavior. He immediately applies the module to every new instance of the problem.

Set and Functional Fixedness When a person or animal shows a tendency to respond to a certain type of task in a predetermined way, he is said to have developed a **set.** In everyday life, set is exemplified by the strategies ordinarily called habits—methods developed through experience for dealing with familiar problems. In the two examples given, set increased the efficiency of the problem solver and made later problems easier for him than earlier ones. The big advantage of sets (and habits) is that they allow us to solve familiar problems quickly and almost automatically, freeing time and energy for use on other matters.

Sets are not always useful, however. When someone is set to use a strategy or other module that, unbeknownst to him, is inappropriate for the problem at hand, then set can be a curse rather than a blessing. Negative transfer occurs, and problem solving is slowed down or stopped. Set that hinders problem solving in this way is called **functional fixedness,** a term coined by Duncker.

Research by Abraham Luchins on set in the solution of arithmetic problems provides an example of one type of functional fixedness. Luchins gave his subjects—thousands of them, under many different conditions—a series of arithmetic problems, several of which are shown in Figure 6.12. All but one of the problems could be solved most simply in the same way: Fill Jar B and dump its contents into another container, then use Jar A once and Jar C twice to bail out the extra water. This method can be stated as a formula: B - A - 2C.

What about the sixth problem? Almost everyone can solve it if he does it first, without acquiring a set by doing the first five. But Luchins found that roughly two-thirds of his subjects showed functional fixedness on it if they encountered it after doing the first five problems. They tried to use the B - A - 2C method and either got the wrong answer and gave up or staunchly maintained that the formula worked here, too, saying that 76 - 28 - 3 - 3 equals 25.

Another type of functional fixedness involves a different kind of set—not an inappropriately applied strategy, but a difficulty in using a familiar object in an unfamiliar way. The difficulty can be demonstrated with Duncker's candle problem, shown in Figure 6.13. A person is given a box of candles, a match, tacks, and string, and he is asked to mount a candle vertically on a wooden wall, using any of the objects he sees before him. The candles and matches are given to the person in their boxes, which emphasizes that the boxes are containers and so encourages the problem solver to fix upon this familiar function. Inclusion of extraneous materials also makes solution of the problem harder.

All types of functional fixedness demonstrate essentially the same phenomenon. Counterproductive set is produced by the inappropriate transfer of a module from one task to another. Whether the module is a strategy, a conception of how an object can be used, or an incorrect assumption about the requirements of the problem, it has the same effect: a rigidity in behavior that prevents effective problem solving.

Recombination and Insight

In most of the examples of transfer discussed so far, an entire module was transferred from one task to another—sometimes appropriately, as with the series problem, and sometimes inappropriately, as with the examples of functional fixedness. One characteristic of modules is that they can be transferred wholly from one problem to another.

A second characteristic of modules is that they can be separated into their components and the components then **recombined** in new ways. Consider the following example. A woman has two driving modules: the route she takes from home to work every day, and the route she takes from her office to a restaurant for lunch. One weekend, when she is at home, she decides to have lunch at the restaurant that she usually goes to from work. Instead of combining the two modules to get to the restaurant, which would mean she had to drive the long route, she takes them apart and recombines the parts into the short route, as shown in Figure 6.14.

Many cognitive psychologists are especially interested in **insight,** a type of transfer in which components from one or more modules recombine suddenly to produce a solution to a problem. Insight usually occurs with problems that are resistant to more routine problem-solving efforts. For example, many people find the analogy in the margin puzzling at first; those who solve it usually do so by insight. Once they understand that analogy, they have acquired a new rule for analogies; as a result, they usually solve the analogy at the top of page 135 quickly, simply by transferring the rule formulated for the first one. The second analogy requires no new insight, because it requires no new recombinations. (If you have not yet attained the insight necessary to solve the analogy, pay less attention to the spelling of the words and more attention to their sound.)

In human beings, insight is often accompanied by what psychologists call an "aha!" reaction, the feeling of sudden inspiration or understanding usually represented in comic strips by a flashing light bulb. The "aha!" experience is generally abrupt, intense, demanding of our attention, and often exhilarating. According to an old story, Archimedes showed an insight reaction when he discovered that an object placed in water appears to lose a quantity of weight equal to the weight of the water that it displaces. Sitting in the bathtub when the insight came to him, he leaped from the tub and ran naked through the streets of the Greek city Syracuse shouting, "Eureka! Eureka!" ("I have found it!")

Insight reactions have various intensities; there are little ones and big ones. And insight can occur at any point in the problem-solving process. That is, the understanding necessary to move from any phase of problem solving to the next phase could be achieved by insight. In fact, it might even be possible to move through several phases at once by experiencing a single sudden insight,

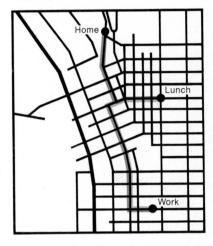

Figure 6.14 Separation and recombination of modules. Even such a complex pattern of behavior as driving to a destination several miles away becomes a single module if it is repeated many times. As this map shows, such modules can be broken apart and recombined to serve a purpose for which they were never originally intended.

Whale: Cry = Son:

Study   Chair   Pattern   Star

Figure 6.15 Look at these cards. Each of them has a circle on one side and a triangle on the other. Every circle and triangle is either red or blue. You are to determine whether or not it is true that all cards with a red triangle on one side have a blue circle on the other. Which of the cards do you need to turn over to find out?

(After Wason and Johnson-Laird, 1968.)

a dramatic recombination that allows a great stride toward solution of a problem. It is also true that insight experiences at times lead to solutions that are incorrect. We may feel great excitement at an insight that we think will solve a problem for us, only to discover upon reflection that the insight does not, in fact, lead to solution of the problem.

THE NATURE OF EVERYDAY REASONING

One focus of cognitive psychology is the organization of behavior. Up to this point, the chapter has emphasized one aspect of organization: the way that the components of behavior and thought fit together as a person or an animal solves a particular problem. In the rest of the chapter, discussion is extended to the question: How does the behavior of solving a specific problem fit into the broader context of all behaviors?

A question that leaps to mind as soon as this broader perspective is adopted is: How is reasoning organized—not just reasoning about one or a few problems, but reasoning more generally? What is the nature of everyday reasoning? Psychologists are still far from being able to characterize human reasoning in any general way. Cognitive research has centered around two different (though not incompatible) positions. Some experiments emphasize the logical basis of human reasoning; others emphasize the role of invention and creativity in human reasoning.

Logic: To Err Is Human

Ever since the days of Plato and Aristotle, philosophers and logicians as well as psychologists have argued at length about how close everyday reasoning is to pure logic. Some have argued that logic is the ideal toward which everyday reasoning strives—that we are all aspiring, if at times unsuccessful, logicians. Others claim that logic is not a description of everyday reasoning at all, but is instead a special system of thought that has particular functions, such as allowing one to state in unequivocal and final form the train of thought that led to a conclusion already reached.

To show that the laws of logic are also the fundamental laws of thought, it would be necessary to demonstrate that reasoning is influenced only by the logical *structure* or *form* of a problem and not by its *content*. To illustrate, suppose that the statement *if A, then B* represents the structure of a set of problems, where A and B stand for objects or events. The problem consists in testing the truth of such statements; Figures 6.15 and 6.16 provide examples of such problems. Purely logical solutions to all problems with this structure would have to be identical across all cases of *if A, then B,* regardless of content.

The way people reason in *if A, then B* problems has been investigated by Peter Wason and Philip Johnson-Laird. Most people give one of these two answers to the problem posed in Figure 6.15: They say you need only turn over the card with the red triangle showing; or, you need to turn over the cards showing the red triangle and the blue circle. Both answers are wrong. The correct answer is that you must turn over the cards showing the red triangle and the red circle. What is intriguing about this problem is not only that most people reach a logically incorrect solution (and usually feel quite confident as they do so) but that the way they reach it seems to be very ingrained. Most people have great difficulty understanding why the correct answer should be both the red triangle and the red circle.

One source of error seems to be the supposition that if all the cards with red triangles on one side have blue circles on the other, then all cards with blue circles on one side must have red triangles on the other. *If all A are B, then all B are A.* This acceptance of the equivalence of A and B is a useful, often valid everyday inference, although it is not *logically* necessary.

For everyday purposes such "impure" logic often works better than pure. For example, suppose you are given the following information:

All crows are jet-black birds. There is a huge flock of various types of jet-black birds in the sky.

You might be disposed to conclude from those statements:

There are some crows in that flock.

That conclusion is an example of what Loren Chapman and Jean Chapman call **probabilistic inference.** It is not dictated by logical necessity, but it has a high probability of standing up if you take the trouble to examine the flock.

In more recent studies Wason and Johnson-Laird have shown that with some *if A, then B* problems people's best guess conforms with the meaning assigned by logic. For example, suppose the cards have names of cities on one side and means of transport on the other. How would you solve the problem posed in Figure 6.16? In this case, you have to turn over *London,* of course. You do not have to turn over *Paris,* since you have made no prediction about that, or *Plane,* since you could be going anywhere by plane. But you do have to turn over *Ship,* just in case you are trying to sneak your way to London that way, which would invalidate the statement.

The conclusion to be drawn from studies like these is a simple one. When people are solving problems, they do not behave illogically, but neither do they behave according to the rules of formal logic. Instead of ignoring content as logicians do, they pay close attention to it and make a best guess (a probabilistic inference) about the structure of the problem. They are not very good formal logicians, but as practical logicians they are not at all bad.

Creativity

When Archimedes sat in his bath, thus displacing a considerable portion of his own weight in water onto the floor, a new system of thought was born. Archimedes' principle was a new way of thinking about what happened when objects were put in water, a way of thinking that had not existed until Archimedes invented it.

The types of problems discussed so far in the chapter for the most part require a type of thinking called **programmatic.** They involve the use of systems rather than the invention of them. Logical thinking, for example, relies on already-established conventions and rules. This type of thinking can be simulated with some success in a computer, as in the General Problem Solver, but computer theories and, in fact, all other explicit theories of prob-

Reed: Book = Sea:

Man   Picture   Marsh   Car

Figure 6.16   Each of these cards has a destination (London or Paris) on one side and a mode of transportation (plane or ship) on the other. Which cards do you need to turn over in order to test the statement, "When I go to London, I always go by plane"? Note that the logical form of this problem is similar to the form of the problem in Figure 6.15 but that the two problems differ in content. (After Wason and Johnson-Laird, 1968.)

Figure 6.17 A test that attempts to measure flexibility in thinking. The task is to name a single word that all three words in each triplet have in common. The answer to the first item is "foot." The rest of the answers are given on page 140.

1. stool   powder   ball
2. blue   cake   cottage
3. man   wheel   high
4. motion   poke   down
5. line   birthday   surprise
6. wood   liquor   luck
7. house   village   golf
8. card   knee   rope
9. news   doll   tiger
10. painting   bowl   nail
11. weight   wave   house
12. made   cuff   left
13. key   wall   precious
14. bull   tired   hot
15. knife   up   hi
16. handle   hole   police
17. plan   show   walker
18. hop   side   pet
19. bell   tender   iron
20. spelling   line   busy

Figure 6.18 A problem described by DeBono as one that requires "lateral thinking" for its solution. Try to solve the problem yourself, then check your solution with the one on page 140.

The following story is taken from *New Think*, written by Edward de Bono, the originator of the concept of lateral thinking. © 1967, 1968 by Edward de Bono, Basic Books, Inc., Publishers, New York.

lem solving and thinking cannot deal very effectively with a contrasting type of thinking, **generative thinking**—the creation of partially or completely new systems of thought. In generative thinking the very first step in the phases of problem solving, discovering the problem, may be the most important one.

Although no one can claim to truly understand or explain generative thinking, or creativity, a number of psychologists do characterize everyday reasoning as involving generative thinking. Within this group there are two major lines of research.

The Importance of Flexibility One group of psychologists attempts to define creative thinking by turning to studies of transfer and functional fixedness. They point out that some people are more prone to rigidity of thought than others, and they suggest that flexibility and originality go together. This line of argument has led to the development of creativity tests composed of questions intended to measure flexibility, such as ''How many uses can you find for a bicycle tire?'' One of the most interesting of these tests focuses on a person's capacity to see connections between words that most people would not readily notice. For example, given the list of word triplets in Figure 6.17, can you name a single word that the three words of each triplet have in common? Studies of creativity by psychologists such as Sarnoff Mednick and Martha Mednick (the originators of the test) and Arthur Staats have shown that there does seem to be some association between creativity and high scores on the Remote Associates Test. In a typical study of creative people, architects who are rated as being highly creative by their fellow architects score higher than architects who are rated as not being especially creative. A typical laboratory experiment shows that in a functional-fixedness situation like Duncker's candle problem, people who score high on the test are less susceptible to functional fixedness than those who score low. Although the meaning of remote associations is not at all clear, it is probably fair to conclude that highly creative people tend to be more flexible in their associa-

n old money-lender offered to cancel a merchant's debt and keep him from going to prison if the merchant would give the money-lender his lovely daughter. Horrified yet desperate, the merchant and his daughter agreed to let Providence decide. The money-lender said he would put a black pebble and a white pebble in a bag and the girl would draw one. The white pebble would cancel the debt and leave her free. The black one would make her the money-lender's, although the debt would be canceled. If she refused to pick, her father would go to prison. From the pebble-strewn path they were standing on, the money-lender picked two pebbles and quickly put them in the bag, but the girl saw he had picked up two black ones. What would you have done if you were the girl?

tions and suffer less from functional fixedness than do less creative people.

Edward DeBono takes the flexibility argument one step further and tries to differentiate two general types of thinking, one creative and flexible and one uncreative and not especially flexible. "Vertical thinking" is roughly equivalent to what we have called system using, or programmatic thinking. "Lateral thinking" is similar to system inventing, or generative thinking—that is, creative thinking. DeBono has devised various problems that, he claims, call for lateral thinking, such as the example shown in Figure 6.18. He argues that education as it is usually practiced stresses vertical thinking and leaves lateral abilities largely untapped and undeveloped. To encourage lateral thinking, he suggests deliberately ignoring the usual perceptual features of a situation and the usual way of handling and thinking about these features and paying attention instead to the less obvious features.

Most psychologists would agree that this work on creativity, though sometimes provocative, is far from conclusive. For one thing, except in extreme cases, people tend to disagree on which solution is more creative than another; therefore, it is difficult to prove which solution is the most creative. Another shortcoming of most of this research on creativity as flexibility is that an experimenter presents his subjects with an already-formulated problem, even though the recognition of a new problem is probably the process most essential to creative thought.

Children as Inventors   The second line of research on generative thinking focuses on its development in the child. Most of the more traditional techniques for studying creativity take but an instant in a subject's life (forty-five minutes in a psychology laboratory) and investigate only a tiny fragment of his experience. The developmental focus, to the contrary, studies the way thinking develops over many years. The foremost proponent of this approach is Jean Piaget, the Swiss psychologist, whose theory is discussed at length in Chapter 8.

According to the developmental approach, generative thinking is a basic characteristic of the child's intelligence from the start. In fact, the development of intelligence requires generative thinking. Every child develops his intelligence by generating new systems of thinking (new for him, at least). Each time he generates a new system, he has attained a higher stage of intelligence. Consequently, every child is an inventor, and the difference between him and such eminent creators as Archimedes, Picasso, and Einstein is one of degree, not of kind. It is not that creative people have a capacity for generative thinking and ordinary people do not but rather that the people who are considered highly creative extend their generative thinking into new realms, while ordinary people do not. Ordinary people do invent new systems of thinking, but the systems are new only to them. A creative person invents systems that are new to everyone.

To summarize what has been said in this section, there is evidence that everyday reasoning is a kind of practical logic and that, at least sometimes, it also involves mental invention or creativity. But these general descriptions of everyday reasoning do not fully explain the organization of reasoning. A number of cognitive psychologists in recent years have attempted to describe the organization of reasoning more explicitly, and some have tried to extend their analyses beyond reasoning to all behavior. The basic question asked by these psychologists is: How do all the modules of behavior that a person has learned relate to each other?

HIERARCHIES OF BEHAVIOR

An individual's behavior cannot be composed of a number of modules that have no relation to each other. In some way or other all the modules must fit

Figure 6.19 Surreptitiously using a notebook and a stopwatch, Betty Lou made this record of Herman's behavior while they sat together through *2001: A Space Odyssey* (for the eighth time) last Saturday night. Herman spent almost all his time watching the film. About half the time he was also holding Betty Lou's hand, and half the time, when he wasn't holding her hand, he was sipping a can of beer. Occasionally he put his feet up on the seat in front of him. Even less frequently he ate Betty Lou's popcorn, and on a very few occasions, he made comments to Betty Lou. This Saturday, when they go to the movies again, Betty Lou can use this hierarchy of behaviors to manipulate Herman's behavior: By controlling his opportunities to perform higher-probability behaviors, she can raise his rate of performing lower-probability behaviors.

together into a general organization of behavior. Recent research attempting to determine the nature of this organization includes some of the most exciting and innovative work in psychology today.

Virtually all these theories center on the idea of **hierarchy,** a ranking or ordering of components so that a component of one rank is subordinate to a component of the next higher rank. A familiar example of a hierarchy from outside psychology is a bureaucracy, in which an official of one rank is subordinate to an official of the next higher rank, who in turn is subordinate to an official of the next higher rank, and so forth.

Many different types of hierarchies of behavior have been proposed in recent years. From these we have chosen three examples. Each has proved its usefulness, and each shows a different kind of hierarchical organization.

The Premack Principle: A Hierarchy of Reinforcers

David Premack discovered the hierarchical organization of reinforcers only fifteen years ago, and his discovery has radically changed the way psychologists think about reinforcement. Premack's principle states that reinforcers do not necessarily involve things like food, water, or sex; instead, they can be identified by referring to a hierarchy of modules of behavior. That is, the opportunity to perform any response that occurs regularly in an organism's behavior can be used to reinforce other responses that occur less often. More specifically, any response that occurs in some particular situation with a higher frequency than another response in that situation can serve to reinforce the latter, lower-frequency response. To determine what will reinforce what in a particular situation, it is necessary to rank all common behaviors (modules) according to how often they occur. All behaviors higher in the hierarchy (ranking) can be used to reinforce all those lower in the hierarchy.

If you think back to the discussion of reinforcement in Chapter 4, you will see that Premack's view of reinforcement is radically different from the one traditionally used in behavioral research. Reinforcers have usually been defined as *stimuli* that increase the probability that a given response will occur. Premack's data indicate that **reinforcers** are more accurately viewed as *opportunities to engage in high-probability responses.*

Typical learning experiments have led to an erroneous definition of reinforcement because they have used as reinforcers a special, limited class of responses, such as eating. Because eating always involves the availability of the stimulus *food,* it is possible for the psychologist to incorrectly view that stimulus as the reinforcer. Actually, the reinforcer is the opportunity to emit *eating responses,* which have been given a very high probability by the psychologist's experimental manipulations (such as depriving the animal of food for many hours).

Here is an everyday example of how the Premack principle operates. Herman does not really like to eat large quantities of popcorn at the movies, but Betty Lou has a bet with her roommate Sue that she can get Herman to eat two boxes of popcorn. Betty Lou is taking introductory psychology and she has just learned about Premack's principle, so she decides to put her knowledge to work to win the bet. The last time Herman and Betty Lou were at the movies, as shown in Figure 6.19, she recorded how much time Herman spent doing various things and later computed the probabilities of Herman's activities, as shown.

This list shows a hierarchy of reinforcers, a ranking of Herman's activities at the movies that tells Betty Lou which activities can be used to reinforce which other activities. Any of the activities higher on the list can be used to reinforce his eating popcorn. Betty Lou decides to use all four of them, so she can win the bet. First she offers Herman some popcorn, and he takes a little and eats it. Immediately she reinforces his popcorn eating by holding his hand. Then she starts talking energetically about school, so that Herman cannot watch the movie. As soon as he takes a little more popcorn, she stops talking and this reinforces his popcorn eating by letting him watch the movie. Then Herman wants to take out the can of beer that he smuggled into the movie theater. She has frequently complained about his drinking beer, and this time she insists that he not drink it. But as soon as he takes a little more popcorn, she says that she did not mean to be so stern and it would be all right if he drinks the beer. And so forth: She uses all four activities higher than eating popcorn in the hierarchy to reinforce eating popcorn. By the time the movie is over, Herman has eaten the two boxes of popcorn, and Betty Lou has won her bet.

As illustrated by this example, a hierarchy of reinforcers is a ranking of modules of behavior, such that any behavior represented in the hierarchy can be reinforced by the opportunity to engage in any other behavior higher in the hierarchy (but not by those lower in the hierarchy). That is, whether a module can serve as a reinforcer is determined by how it relates to other modules in a specific situation.

The hierarchy of reinforcers is one of the simplest types of hierarchies: The components are ordered by a simple ranking from highest to lowest. The other two examples of hierarchies have a more complex organization.

The Hierarchy of Goals in Problem Solving

The second type of hierarchy is something that you have already learned about: the hierarchy of goals and subgoals in problem solving. Newell, Shaw, and Simon based one of their heuristics for the General Problem Solver—subgoal analysis—on the concept of a goal hierarchy. When a person is solving a complex problem, it is a difficult matter to attain the goal implicit in that problem; that is why the problem is called complex. In order to attain that goal, the person must set up subgoals so that he can solve one part of the problem at a time, just as the General Problem Solver sets up subgoals when it plays chess. If a subgoal is also too complex to solve directly, then the person also establishes subgoals for it. (They might be called "sub-subgoals.") And so he goes on, setting up subgoals, sub-subgoals, sub-sub-subgoals, and so forth. If the person's problem is extremely complex (such as trying to develop a theory to explain all problem solving), he might spend an entire lifetime working on subgoals, sub-subgoals, sub-sub-subgoals, and so forth, without ever reaching his original goal.

Betty Lou's behavior in the above example demonstrates a hierarchy of goals. Her goal is to get Herman to eat two boxes of popcorn at the movies. Her subgoals are to reinforce his popcorn eating by using each of the four possible reinforcers in Herman's hierarchy of reinforcers. Her sub-subgoals involve actually carrying out each instance of reinforcement that she plans.

In this kind of hierarchy, unlike the hierarchy of reinforcers, items are not ordered quantitatively; instead, the ordering is one of inclusion. That is, the set of subgoals of the problem are included in the general goal, each set of sub-subgoals is included in a subgoal, and so forth.

This kind of hierarchy is clearly an essential part of the organization of human problem solving. But it tells us mostly about how people go about solving an individual problem. The third type of hierarchy tries to characterize the relationships between different kinds of problem-solving abilities.

A Hierarchy of Problem-Solving Abilities

Several psychologists have suggested possible hierarchies of problem-solving abilities; the best developed and most explicit of these hierarchies is that of Jean Piaget. In his theory, presented in more detail in Chapter 8, he suggests that problem-solving abilities (which he calls intelligence) form a hierarchy of

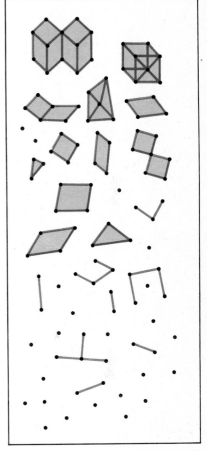

Figure 6.20 A representation of the hierarchical development of intelligence conceived by Jean Piaget. The construction of one-, two-, and finally three-dimensional forms from dimensionless points is used as a metaphor for the emergence of new intellectual abilities as intelligence develops through four stages. Elements at each level correspond to what Piaget calls schemes. The points, for example, correspond to the simple physical actions—such as looking, sucking, and grasping—that the infant uses to understand the world. At each stage the schemes are organized and integrated into new, more sophisticated patterns. Thus, each level of intelligence is built on and incorporates the abilities of the preceding level but also has characteristics that were not present before.

four different types; Figure 6.20 illustrates the relationship between the levels in this hierarchy. The four types develop during infancy and childhood, and all four are present in adults. The simplest type is called sensorimotor intelligence, in which the only problem solving that can occur involves actions, not thinking. Infants and most animals are capable of only this kind of problem solving. The second type of intelligence, which develops out of sensorimotor intelligence, is called pre-operational intelligence. It appears in the preschool child and is characterized by only the simplest kind of thinking. The child can use words and symbols, but he cannot use them logically. He thinks in much the same way that adults daydream: His thoughts meander from one thing to another, without any logical connections between them. The third type, which develops out of pre-operational intelligence, is called concrete-operational intelligence. Emerging during the elementary school years, it involves the ability to understand concrete logic, such as how objects are classified by shape, color, and so forth. Finally, the fourth type, which develops out of a concrete-operational intelligence at about the time of adolescence, is called formal-operational intelligence and is characterized by the ability to deal with abstract logic and scientific reasoning.

This hierarchy not only includes all problem-solving abilities, according to Piaget, but it also shows how the two types of everyday reasoning discussed earlier (logical reasoning and generative reasoning) relate to each other. Completely logical reasoning is at the top of the hierarchy, the highest type of human problem-solving ability; generative reasoning is the means by which people develop through the four types of problem-solving abilities. Children generate pre-operational intelligence out of sensorimotor intelligence; they generate concrete-operational intelligence out of pre-operational intelligence; and they generate formal-operational intelligence out of concrete-operational intelligence. In addition, of course, adults can use generative thinking to develop new systems of formal-operational reasoning.

This hierarchy of types of problem-solving ability is organized differently from the previous two hierarchies, in that many different factors together determine the order of the components. Children develop the four types of problem-solving ability in the hierarchical order. The complexity of the problems that can be solved increases from the lowest type to the highest. The closeness of the reasoning to logic increases from the lowest to the highest. And, most important, according to Piaget, each type is actually built upon the one immediately preceding it. By generative reasoning, the problem-solving abilities of one type are put together to form the problem-solving abilities of the next type, and this succession constitutes the development of intelligence.

Figure 6.21 Solutions to the problems posed on page 136 (A) and (B) and on page 132 (C). The rule that governed the construction of the verbal problem in the text on page 129 is: For sentences that contain a form of the verb "to be," transfer the noun phrase, excluding the article (a, an, the), that is the subject of the sentence to the end of the sentence and delete the form of the verb "to be." For example: "The music is beautiful." becomes "The beautiful music." The solution to the problem, then, requires a reversal of this process.

A
1.	foot	11.	light
2.	cheese	12.	hand
3.	chair	13.	stone
4.	slow	14.	dog
5.	party	15.	jack
6.	hard	16.	man
7.	green	17.	floor
8.	trick	18.	car
9.	paper	19.	bar
10.	finger	20.	bee

B

hen the girl put her hand into the bag to draw out the fateful pebble, she fumbled and dropped it, where it was immediately lost among the others. "Oh," she said, "well, you can tell which one I picked by looking at the one that's left." The girl's lateral thinking saved her father and herself.

C

SUMMARY

1. The cognitive approach to thinking and learning focuses on learning as a kind of problem solving and on the organization of the components of thought and action.

2. Although the problems that people and animals solve are extremely varied, in each case the organism has a goal and must find a way to reach it.

3. **Hypothesis-testing theory,** an early cognitive approach to problem solving, explains problem solving as the formulation and testing of hypotheses about the way a goal can be reached. Later investigators have tried to elaborate hypothesis-testing theory by specifying more precisely how hypotheses are used. For example, a checkers player could not possibly consider all the 10^{40} play sequences (hypotheses) available to him at the start of a game.

4. The **General Problem Solver,** a problem-solving computer program, is in part an attempt to clarify how hypotheses are formulated and tested when solving complex problems. GPS relies on **heuristics,** which are selective strategies that allow a problem solver to investigate likely solutions before less likely ones. (This procedure is very unlike another problem-solving procedure, called an **algorithm,** which specifies the sequence of all possible operations that might solve a given problem.) Two examples of heuristics are **subgoal analysis,** in which a general goal is divided into more manageable subgoals, and **means-end analysis,** in which a problem is viewed as the need to reduce the difference between an initial state and a desired state (the goal). The main shortcoming of GPS as a comprehensive model is that the programmer defines each problem for the computer, whereas people facing problems must usually define them themselves.

5. **Analysis by synthesis** states that a person's original conception or synthesis of a problem determines how he interprets or analyzes it into components. To formulate this notion more precisely, psychologists must describe how the analysis-by-synthesis process changes as the person progresses through the various steps in solving a problem.

6. In an attempt to provide this precision, problem solving is viewed in terms of **phases in the development of a solution.** According to this approach, there are five phases of problem solving; both the problem solver's level of comprehension and the organization of his behavior differ from phase to phase. Children learning to put sticks in order by size, adults solving verbal problems, and rats learning to run a maze all progress through the phases that the theory outlines. In the final phase, the organism's behavior is integrated and well organized: The problem solver has acquired a new unit of behavior, called a **module,** which can be used in solving other problems.

7. **Transfer** occurs when something an organism learns on one task affects its performance on a second task. In **positive transfer,** what was learned on one task facilitates performance on a second task; in **negative transfer,** what was learned on one task interferes with performance on a second task. If an organism has reached the final phase of problem solving on the first task, positive transfer is likely to occur in performing a second task; if it is still at an earlier phase in solving the first task, negative transfer is likely to occur.

Figure 6.22 Jerome Bruner is an experienced investigator in cognitive psychology. Some of his observations of children are cited in this chapter, and Bruner is probably best known for his contributions to the theory of education. He has developed a curriculum for elementary-school students titled *Man: A Course of Study*, in which he has attempted to integrate methods of instruction with what is known about patterns of children's psychological development.

8. Modularized skills that transfer easily to various problems are called **strategies.** They are usually learned through repeated exposure to similar problems. With increased experience, people tend to develop more efficient strategies. When working on a series problem involving height, for example, people may at first form a visual image of the individuals in the series; later, they use a more efficient strategy that relies on verbal connections between the people in the problem.

9. When a person or animal shows a tendency to respond to a certain type of task in a predetermined way, he is said to have developed a **set.** Set is useful when it helps solve familiar problems efficiently; it is not useful when it becomes **functional fixedness.** In one kind of functional fixedness, a person continues to use a certain problem-solving strategy when it no longer applies, as in Luchins' water-jar problem. In another kind, a person finds it hard to see that familiar objects can be used in unfamiliar ways, as in Duncker's candle problem. In a third kind, a person makes an incorrect assumption about the requirements of the problem.

10. One characteristic of modules is that they can be transferred wholly from one task to another, as described above. Another characteristic of modules is that they can be broken into their components and the components can be **recombined.** When the components of one or more modules recombine suddenly to produce a solution to a problem, **insight** is said to have occurred. Insight experiences, which are often accompanied by an "aha!" reaction, differ in intensity; they can occur at any phase of problem solving; and they can sometimes accompany solutions that turn out to be incorrect.

11. Cognitive psychologists are concerned not only with understanding how people solve particular problems but with how, in general, people reason.

   a. Although much everyday reasoning is based on logic, it often does not follow the rules of formal logic, which require a problem solver to consider only the structure or form of a problem and not its content. Instead, people use practical logic: They draw **probabilistic inferences** based partly on a problem's form but primarily on what they know about its content.

   b. Besides the use of existing systems of thought—**programmatic thinking**—everyday reasoning involves the creation of new systems—**generative thinking.** In studying creativity, some psychologists stress the connection between originality and flexibility, pointing out that a person who is highly susceptible to functional fixedness is not likely to be very creative. Other psychologists focus on generative thinking in children. Jean Piaget, for example, believes that children use generative thinking to develop the different cognitive abilities that characterize the stages of intellectual development Piaget has identified.

12. Some psychologists, in an attempt to describe the organization of reasoning and the organization of behavior in general, have turned to the concept of **hierarchies,** rankings of components of behavior along some dimension.

   a. David Premack has discovered that reinforcers are hierarchically organized: The opportunity to perform any response that occurs regularly in an organism's behavior can be used to reinforce another response that occurs less often. Premack's definition of a **reinforcer** as an opportunity to engage in a high-probability response is very different from the one traditionally used in behavioral research, which states that a reinforcer is a stimulus that increases the probability that a given response will occur.

b. Another hierarchical approach states that problem solving is based on a hierarchy of **goals and subgoals;** the General Problem Solver's use of subgoal analysis in playing chess illustrates this concept.

c. A third kind of hierarchy attempts to characterize the relationships between different kinds of **problem-solving abilities.** Piaget's stages of intellectual development form a hierarchy of this sort. The hierarchy includes all problem-solving abilities, according to Piaget. One of its most important characteristics is that each ability is built on the one preceding it through a process of generative thinking.

SUGGESTED READINGS

Bruner, Jerome S. *Beyond the Information Given.* New York: Norton, 1973. Selected papers by one of the most influential cognitive psychologists, including some of his papers on hypothesis theory and on modularization of skills.

Fischer, Kurt W. *Piaget, Learning, and Cognitive Development* (forthcoming). Presents the theory of phases of problem solving and outlines Piaget's approach to the development of intelligence.

Hebb, Donald O. *The Organization of Behavior: A Neuropsychological Theory.* New York: Wiley, 1949. The classic book that helped to cause a resurgence of interest in cognition and the organization of behavior in American psychology.

Mandler, George. "From Association to Structure," *Psychological Review,* 69 (1962), 415–426. Mandler argues that as learning progresses it shifts from a process of association to an integrated structure (a module).

Newell, Allen, and Herbert A. Simon. *Human Problem Solving.* Englewood Cliffs, N. J.: Prentice-Hall, 1971. A good reasonable statement of the authors' thoughts on problem-solving research. Includes reference to earlier research and is therefore a good starting point for anyone interested in a detailed account of computer applications to the study of heuristic problem solving.

Powers, William T. *Behavior: The Control of Perception.* Chicago: Aldine, 1973. One of the most provocative books on cognitive psychology in recent years. Powers argues that both behaviorist and traditional computer models of human behavior are untenable and proposes an alternative hierarchical theory of behavior that begins at the level of brain functioning and extends all the way to abstract reasoning.

Wason, Peter C., and Philip N. Johnson-Laird (eds.). *Thinking and Reasoning.* Baltimore: Penguin, 1968. A good collection of articles covering a range of topics in the field of human intellectual functioning. In addition to a section on problem solving, there are articles dealing with logical thought, which discuss in readable terms computer simulation and information processing. Other sections cover intellectual development and conceptual thinking.

UNIT III
Human Development

As organisms go, human beings are unusual creatures. We have a very long childhood, during which we acquire a vast array of cognitive and social skills. Each of us develops language, a distinctive personality, a knowledge of the mores of the particular culture into which we were born, and the ability to think in ways that are much more complex than those of any other creatures on earth. Yet newborn babies are very poor thinkers and learners. One of the great puzzles of psychology is to explain how the infant develops from this primitive state into the complex human adult.

7 Heredity and Environment

discusses one of the classical issues in development: What are the relative roles of hereditary influences and environmental ones? After outlining the mechanisms by which heredity operates, it discusses what is known about the roles of heredity and environment in perception, intelligence, and schizophrenia. **See related chapters: 3, 11, 15, 17**

8 Development of Intelligence: Piaget's Theory

describes how knowledge develops, according to the great Swiss psychologist Jean Piaget. After explaining concepts basic to Piaget's theory of how people think, it discusses the four main periods of cognitive development and suggests how cognitive development is influenced by environmental factors. **See related chapters: 6, 21**

RELATED CHAPTERS

3
Species-Specific Behavior: Ethology first introduces the question of the relationship between hereditary and environmental influences on behavior, which is the main topic of Chapter 7. It also describes a species-specific behavior that is unique to people: language, which is the topic of Chapter 9.

4
Conditioning and Learning: Behaviorism describes the basic principles of the behaviorist approach to learning. These principles are discussed in Chapter 10 as one way of explaining social development.

6
Thinking and Problem Solving: Cognitive Psychology outlines the cognitive approach to learning and problem solving and briefly describes Piaget's theory of cognitive development as one example. Chapter 8 examines Piaget's theory in detail; Chapter 9 presents a cognitive analysis of language development, and Chapter 10 describes a cognitive approach to moral development.

11
Perception: Principles and Processes explains the nature of perception. Hereditary and environmental influences on the development of perception are discussed in Chapter 7.

Earlier in this century, most studies of development simply measured what the child was like at each age: What does a typical one-year-old do, a typical two-year-old, a typical three-year-old, and so on? These studies only described the differences between children of various ages; they did not explain *how* the differences came about. It is one thing to say that four-year-olds cannot solve a certain kind of problem while five-year-olds can. It is another thing to ask which human capabilities change between the ages of four and five to permit that kind of problem solving and what causes these particular capabilities to develop at that time. Many psychologists have come to realize that one of the most basic questions they can ask about almost anything that people do—normal or abnormal—is: How does it develop? Recent attempts to answer this question have focused on normal development, and especially on the development of cognition and the development of language.

9 Language Development,

in presenting recent research on language acquisition in children, discusses the nature of language, the capacities required for language—in both children and chimpanzees— and the relationship between language and thought.
See related chapters: 3, 6

10 Social Development: The Case of Morality

takes moral development as a special case of social development and examines it from the viewpoint of the three most complete theories of social development: Freud's psychoanalytic theory, behaviorist social-learning theory, and Kohlberg's cognitive-developmental theory.
See related chapters: 4, 6, 18, 21, 25

15

Emotional Experience and Expression examines learned and hereditary factors that influence emotional expressions and so relates to the discussion of heredity and environment in Chapter 7.

17

Psychological Testing describes intelligence tests, the results of which have led to an ongoing controversy over the inheritance of intelligence, discussed in Chapter 7.

18

Psychoanalytic Theories of Personality presents Freud's theory of personality development, which is one of the theories applied to moral development in Chapter 10.

21

Patterns of Social Behavior: The Case of Sex Roles discusses how adults' social roles help determine their behavior. Focusing on male and female roles as its primary example, it describes how three major theories of social development explain the acquisition of these roles. The same three theories are used to explain the development of morality in Chapter 10. One of them is the cognitive-developmental approach, which is the focus of Chapter 8.

25

Bases of Disorder examines various explanations of why psychological disorder occurs; two of the theories that it presents are psychoanalysis and social-learning theory, both of which are also included in Chapter 10's discussion of normal social development.

Progress in genetics has made the possibility of genetic engineering more than a piece of science fiction. Of course, any mention of genetic engineering automatically starts us all thinking of eugenics: of the arrangement, somehow, of the human race into something closer to our heart's desire. We will eliminate the unfit, strengthen still further the fit, and make everyone good, beautiful and talented—in short, just like ourselves.

Actually, mankind has been practicing genetic engineering all along in a crude way, and the results are all about us. We have cows that are all milk, sheep that are all wool, turkeys that are all breast. We pick, choose, breed, and nurture our plants and animals so as to emphasize what we want and need. If we are now dreaming of reshaping human physiology by proper gene adjustment or by the fostering of proper gene combinations, we must either treat human beings as domestic animals with no say of their own in the matter or we must ask what the individual human being wants.

Shall we breed a race of muscular giants, men with broad shoulders and women with large breasts, all of them with regular, handsome features? It would take a great deal of food to support all that bone and muscle. And will each person feel tall and beautiful when he or she is simply one of the crowd? And what skin color would they be?

Of course, it is quite possible to argue that we should not be concerned with physical appearance, except for removing actual disease and deformity. Tastes differ, anyway. It is the mental and temperamental qualities that distinguish human beings from other animals; it is these which influence society for good and evil; it is these which should be shaped and adjusted.

What we need then, may be a race of human beings—black, white, yellow, tall, short, stocky, and lean—who are all as one in being good, kind, patient, understanding, and highly intelligent. In fact, let's make them all geniuses of one sort or another; in science, art, music, philosophy, literature . . .

But how sure can we be that a humanity consisting solely of intellectual peaks and virtuous moderation will be tolerable? Might there not be uses for occasional specimens of humanity of only moderate intelligence and of some trifling defects of character? Might it not be desirable to be irritable now and then, impatient, petty, vain, even irrational—just for variety?

In fact, it is possible to argue that the greatest asset the human race has is genetic versatility. We don't know all the potentialities of gene combinations; of how one gene, unremarkable in itself, might have a rare use in combination with certain others; of how some gene combinations, unremarkable now might be very desirable at other times or under other conditions.

Perhaps we should decide to keep our hands off and let the forces of kindly Chance dictate gene combination and recombination, gene mutation and remutation, and find in all the different expressions of humanity—physical, mental, and temperamental; wise and foolish; saintly and vicious; strong and weak—the wherewithal to face the Universe under all circumstances, now and into the indefinite future.

Isaac Asimov

7
Heredity and Environment

The sperm from a man joins with the egg from a woman, and human development begins. Nine months later, a baby is born. One year after birth, the child begins to walk; at two years he begins to talk; at six years he goes to school; at adolescence he becomes sexually mature. The goal of developmental psychology is to explain the changes that occur as an egg and a sperm are gradually transformed into a human adult.

Many different factors contribute to this development, and these factors can be divided into two broad classes: hereditary influences stemming from the original egg and sperm, and environmental influences arising from the world in which the child grows up. Environmental factors include a wide range of influences—from the physical environment in the mother's uterus before birth, to the nutrition that the child receives, to the rules of the society in which he lives.

The distinction between heredity and environment is a useful one, but it is important to understand that heredity and environment can in fact never be separated. Without the hereditary factors contributed by the egg and sperm, a child cannot even begin to develop, and a child cannot live and grow without environment. Heredity and environment always work in combination. This chapter, then, examines how hereditary factors act in concert with environmental influences to produce development.

THE QUESTIONS OF "HOW?" AND "HOW MUCH?"

In examining the ways that heredity and environment collaborate to bring about development, psychologists ask two different questions: "How?" and "How much?"

"How?" asks about the ways in which genes and environments combine to produce development in all people. This chapter looks at the "How" of one aspect of development: the development of perception.

"How much?" asks about sources of differences among individuals. The sources of individual differences

Figure 7.1 The factors of inheritance are determined at the moment of conception. How those factors will be expressed depends on the child's experiences, which begin even before he is born. Just how much the future of a newborn child is predetermined by his genes and how much is shaped by environmental forces is one of the oldest controversies in psychology.

in intelligence are examined in this chapter: How much of individual differences in scores on IQ tests is the result of hereditary differences (genetic effects), and how much is the result of differences in home atmosphere and schooling (environmental effects)? The chapter also examines the sources of individual differences in the development of schizophrenia. Answers to these questions must be based on some essential facts about how heredity operates.

GENES AND CHROMOSOMES

Every person begins life as a single cell that is formed when the male germ cell (spermatozoon) penetrates the female germ cell (ovum). These germ cells are different from all other cells in the human body because they contain twenty-three single and distinctively different chromosomes, while all other cells contain twenty-three pairs of chromosomes. The germ cell is formed in a process called **meiosis,** where a cell with twenty-three pairs of chromosomes splits twice, breaking up the pairs and forming two germ cells with twenty-three chromosomes each. At conception the twenty-three chromosomes from the mother's germ cell pair with the twenty-three from the father's germ cell, and the individual's genetic structure is formed.

Chromosomes are threadlike structures along which the **genes** are strung somewhat like beads. The genes are arranged in the same order along each chromosome in a pair. Each of the thousands of genes on the twenty-three pairs of chromosomes is a sequence of **DNA** (deoxyribonucleic acid) that specifies both the production of a protein (proteins are the building blocks of the human body) and the program for combining that protein with others to form a human being. That is, genes provide "instructions" for building the body.

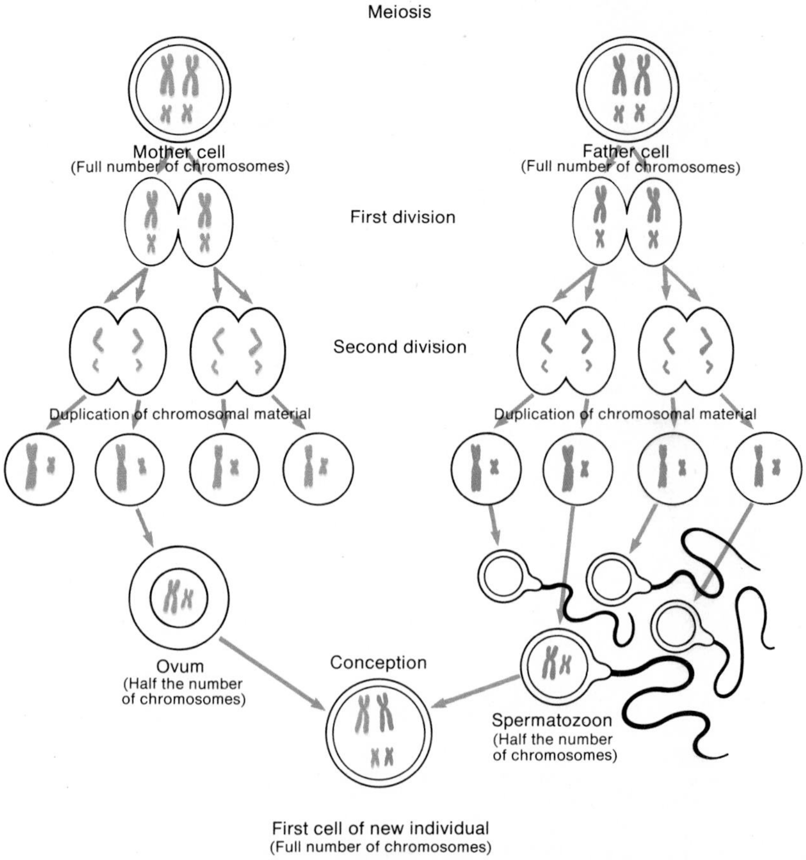

Figure 7.2 Meiosis, a special type of cell division that results in production of germ cells—spermatozoa and ova. At the top of the diagram are the male and female parent cells, each with a full complement of genetic material. (Human beings have forty-six chromosomes, but for simplicity only four are shown here.) Note that the chromosomes come in pairs, and that each one is itself a double strand. The parent cells divide twice. In the first division the members of each pair of chromosomes are separated so that each new cell has only half the usual number of chromosomes. In the second division the chromosomes themselves split apart. (Shortly after meiosis each chromosome regenerates its missing part.) The result is four germ cells from each parent (although in the female only one of these actually becomes a live ovum). In conception, one spermatozoon and one ovum unite, each bringing twenty-three chromosomes, to form a new cell with the full forty-six chromosomes.

Most genes are the same for all members of the human species; these are the genes that determine the "How" of development: that we all have two eyes, lungs instead of gills, and characteristically human (species-specific) behaviors, such as the ability to comprehend and produce language. Little is now known about the "How" of development. That is, many of the mechanisms that operate to produce the human body and human behavior remain a biochemical mystery. But it is known that most human characteristics are determined by the combined influence of a number of genes. There are at least 150 genes that affect brain development; this number is known because 150 independent genes have been found to produce various forms of mental retardation. Therefore, at least 150 genes have to function properly to produce a normal brain. There are probably several hundred more required. The ways these hundreds of genes act together to produce a normal brain and normal intelligence is not at all known.

The more complex an organism, the more difficult it is to discern the relationships between its features and behavior and its genes—and humans are one of the most complex of organisms. The features one can see are often many steps removed from the inherited package of genetic instructions. Genetic mechanisms that determine development are often called **gene action pathways,** because from a single gene's specification for a single protein, there may be many steps in the sequence of the body's use of that protein.

The inherited disease called phenylketonuria (PKU) is a good example of how one defective gene can affect the steps in such a pathway and produce a number of serious consequences. It is also a good example of how scientists, knowing the gene defect and gene action pathway, can modify the environment to prevent expression of genetic disorders.

PKU: A Single-Gene Defect

Children who are affected with PKU show extremely low IQ and lighter pigmentation, shorter stature, and greater irritability than normal children. These children appear to be normal at birth but deteriorate progressively in intelligence.

Research has shown that the defective gene causing the symptoms of PKU is one that codes the gene action pathway for the body's use of phenylalanine, an essential protein present in milk and many other foods. The defective gene results in the lack of a substance needed to convert phenylalanine into another protein (tyrosine), which among other things is essential to the production of skin pigment. The unconverted phenylalanine builds up and changes to a toxic substance, which attacks the cells of the nervous system and causes the progressive mental retardation. Thus, one defective gene can produce, through several steps, a number of observable features and behavior, as shown in Figure 7.3.

Relatively few such relationships between a gene's actions and observable human behavior are as well known. But scientists, having been able to trace PKU back to a single defective gene, were able to prescribe a simple environmental change to prevent retardation. Children are now routinely screened shortly after birth, and those found to have abnormally high levels of phenylalanine in their blood or urine are given a diet low in foods containing that protein. Such a diet largely prevents the retardation and other traits that otherwise result from PKU.

Another form of retardation that has been traced to a genetic origin is Down's syndrome, but this disorder is caused by a chromosomal defect.

Down's Syndrome: A Chromosomal Defect

Children afflicted with Down's syndrome, which tends to occur in one of every 600 births, are severely retarded (with a few exceptions); they have, on

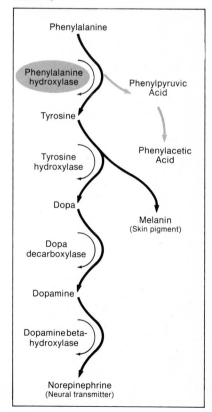

Figure 7.3 PKU illustrates the way in which heredity and environment interact in a gene action pathway. Individuals with PKU lack a gene that is necessary for the production of a chemical (phenylalanine hydroxylase) that begins the breakdown of phenylalanine (a component of many foods) into useful chemicals (such as melanin and norepinephrine). As a result, in these individuals, phenylalanine breaks down more slowly into a different set of chemicals, phenylpyruvic acid and phenylacetic acid. The consequent build-up of phenylalanine and these other chemicals is destructive to portions of the nervous system. The condition can be prevented by an environmental change: removal of phenylalanine from the diet.

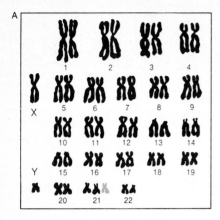

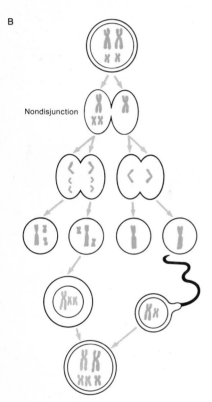

Figure 7.4 (A) A Down's syndrome karyotype. The chromosomes are arranged in pairs, but in Down's syndrome the twenty-first pair has three chromosomes. (B) Nondisjunction. (For simplicity, only two pairs of chromosomes—one pair for each parent—are illustrated.) In the first division of meiosis, both members of one pair of chromosomes have ended up in one of the daughter cells. The end product is an ovum with an extra chromosome. When this cell is fertilized by a normal spermatozoon, the condition shown in (A) results.

the average, IQ levels well below 50. Down's syndrome can be distinguished from other forms of mental retardation by the peculiar physical features of the afflicted children (as depicted in Figure 7.5). The children's eyelids superficially resemble those of Orientals (hence the common name mongolism for the disorder). These children also typically have short, stubby fingers, small ears, a protruding tongue, and other physical defects, including a marked tendency toward leukemia.

Although heredity has always been the suspected cause of many forms of mental retardation, little evidence was found for Down's syndrome running in families. By the mid-1950s, however, data had been gathered showing that for identical twins, both twins almost always proved to have Down's syndrome, whereas in very few sets of fraternal twins did both have the disorder. Physicians and psychologists were very puzzled; the twin data showed that heredity must be playing a role, yet why didn't the disorder run in families?

Chromosomal Analysis By 1959, biologists had developed methods that allowed human chromosomes to be photographed accurately and analyzed. Biologists call the technique of analyzing chromosomes **karyotyping.** When this technique was applied to several cases of Down's syndrome, an astounding fact came to light: In all the Down's syndrome cases examined, the scientists found evidence of an extra chromosome. All normal human cells, as discussed earlier, contain forty-six chromosomes (twenty-three pairs), but the cells of the children with Down's syndrome typically possessed forty-seven chromosomes, the extra one being a third chromosome in the twenty-first pair. Figure 7.4 depicts a karyotype of chromosomes in Down's syndrome, and the extra twenty-first chromosome is plainly visible.

Apparently, in most cases of Down's syndrome, the normal process of disjunction of the twenty-three pairs of chromosomes into forty-six single ones is defective in one of the parents. What seems to happen is that the twenty-first pair of chromosomes shows **nondisjunction,** a failure to separate; thus, some of the parent's sex cells have twenty-four chromosomes (including the extra twenty-first), and some have only twenty-two chromosomes (no twenty-first). Fertilization involving the sex cell without the twenty-first chromosome apparently leads to miscarriage. But fertilization involving the cell carrying the extra twenty-first chromosome will create a fertilized egg carrying forty-seven chromosomes, including three of the twenty-first, and the child who develops from this fertilized egg will be born with Down's syndrome. The process is depicted in Figure 7.4.

Mother's Age In their endeavors to account for the fact that Down's syndrome did not seem to run in families, scientists analyzed a great deal of data to find possible causes. When they analyzed the ages at which mothers tended to give birth to offspring with Down's syndrome, they found a clear relation between the mother's age and the incidence of Down's-syndrome births. The greater the age of the mother, the greater was the proportion of these births. It seems, then, that the nondisjunction takes place in the ovum rather than in the sperm; ova exist in the body during a female's entire reproductive life, whereas sperms are newly produced all the time and do not age in the same way. (Theoretically, failure of disjunction may also occur in the male.) Note that until the initial nondisjunction takes place, there probably have been no such genetic anomalies in any previous member of that family. Nor need later offspring of that mother have Down's syndrome; the failure of disjunction can be a one-time phenomenon.

A small proportion of cases of Down's syndrome shows a different pattern of inheritance: The syndrome does run in families, and its occurrence is not related to the mother's age. In these cases carriers who transmit the defect have one of their twenty-first chromosomes attached to another chromosome (usually one of the fifteenth pair). These people are normal themselves, because they have only two twenty-first chromosomes (even though one is attached), but some of their offspring will have Down's syndrome because the attachment causes them to produce some eggs or sperms with an extra twenty-first chromosome.

Genetic Counseling The pinpointing of the precise genetic cause of Down's syndrome has made it possible to alleviate much human anxiety and suffering about the birth of a defective child. If there appears to be cause for concern about a possible defect in the unborn offspring, the family can undergo genetic counseling. Some hereditary defects, such as the rare type of Down's syndrome, can be detected in a husband or wife before they conceive, either through a genetic history or through karyotyping of the adults' cells. Although most instances of Down's syndrome cannot be identified prior to conception, physicians have developed a technique, called **amniocentesis,** for removing some fetal cells that are sloughed off in the amniotic fluid (the fluid that fills the sac the fetus is in) and testing those cells for the presence of any abnormal chromosomes. Figure 7.6 demonstrates the amniocentesis procedure. If the test demonstrates the presence of the normal complement of chromosomes, the mother is relieved of her fear of giving birth to a child with Down's syndrome. If the test does show a third twenty-first chromosome, the mother may, if she wishes, elect to have a therapeutic abortion.

Advances in genetic counseling are now available for many other conditions with a genetic basis, and abortion procedures may soon give way to procedures—for example, chemical manipulation of the fetal environment—that actually prevent the genetic trait from expressing itself.

The notion that an environmental manipulation can cancel the manifestation of a genetic trait may seem inconceivable if one believes that heredity dooms a person to a certain fate. However, once scientists know exactly how it is that a gene or a chromosome exerts its effect, it sometimes becomes possible to institute procedures to prevent the gene or chromosome from having that effect.

The information about the mechanisms of heredity set out in this section provides the knowledge necessary for a discussion of the developmental questions of "How?" and "How much?"

THE DEVELOPMENT OF PERCEPTION: A "HOW?" QUESTION

As stated earlier, the questions surrounding the role of heredity in universal developmental processes is extremely difficult to pin down. Consequently, there have been long and sometimes heated debates about the relative importance of heredity and experience in some of these processes. Perception is one. In what ways are we "programmed" by our heredity to accurately perceive the objects around us and their relation to each other? And in what ways must we learn, through environmental experience, how to perceive objects and events in the real world? Those who emphasize the role of heredity are called **nativists.** Those who emphasize the role of experience are called **environmentalists.** The arguments of both nativists and environmentalists are presented here.

The Environmentalist Argument

According to the classical environmentalist view, a baby at birth experiences nothing but a mass of sensations, elementary impressions, meaningless in themselves, based directly on the senses and presenting to consciousness nothing but uninterpreted sounds, colors, lights, shadows, touches, and so forth. There is no form, no depth to the world. The infant's view of the world

Figure 7.5 Annie, a girl with Down's syndrome, is living a happy and reasonably productive life with her family. In many cases, unlike Annie's, genetically caused retardation is aggravated by demeaning treatment at school, by other family members, or by other children.

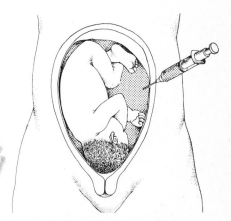

Figure 7.6 The method of taking a sample of cells floating in the amniotic fluid for purposes of genetic counseling. This procedure is used to test for many genetic defects early in pregnancy. Although generally safe, it does involve a slight risk of injury to the fetus.

Figure 7.7 Depending on the direction and the distance from which it is viewed, the same triangle can take on all the different appearances shown here. Many psychologists maintain that a considerable amount of learning has to take place before the perception "triangle" is possible.

is thus like our perception of the night sky—a flat surface—even though the sensations that reach the baby come from objects like the stars, which are at different distances from him.

The environmentalists often point to the inherent ambiguity of the images that objects cast on the retina of the eye. The retina is the light-sensitive tissue at the back of the eye; it is analogous to the film in a camera, in that it registers the pattern of light received from an object—often called an image. The retina then transmits the image via the optic nerve to the visual centers of the brain. Because the retina is only a flat surface, environmentalists say that people cannot perceive a three-dimensional world from the image registered by the retina alone. Instead, the information from the retina is combined with information from past experience.

Experience with an object must be more than merely visual, according to this argument. Only by touching and reaching for an object can an infant be sure of how long it is or how far away it is. A baby needs to learn to perceive distance, for example, by relating the size that an object projects onto the retina with the distance he must reach for the object. Figure 7.8 shows how a baby's retinal image becomes associated with certain muscle movements, and a neural pattern is developed. Eventually, this image alone can trigger the pattern, and no movement is required to perceive depth.

The environmentalists also hold that infants must learn to perceive form. It is only by associating visual sensations with tactual sensations, for example, that they can learn to tell a sphere from a cube or to recognize a triangle from any perspective despite the fact that it looks very different from different perspectives, as shown in Figure 7.7.

The Nativist Argument

The nativists do not deny the importance of experience in perception. They merely assert that the baby's brain is built in such a way that he *must* see depth and form from the earliest moment that he can see. The nativists believe that experience can *improve* a capacity with which nature has endowed the baby but that learning is not necessary for the basic ability to perceive form and depth. They look to studies of how the brain is put together and to studies of newborns' behaviors in response to patterns to tell them exactly how people can perceive without the need for experience.

The Evidence

Historically, one of the earliest and most exciting attempts to investigate the role of experience in vision came when a German, Marius von Senden, brought together dozens of people who had been blind at birth or had been blinded shortly after birth but whose sight was restored later in life through eye surgery. Senden hoped that by studying adults who, like newborns, had had little or no visual experience he could discover how the baby first sees the world.

The cases cited by Senden seemed to support some aspects of the environmentalist theory of form perception, as shown in the following excerpt:

Various things were now presented to her, which she must have known well from everyday life: an apple, a pear, plums, potatoes, an egg, bread, a knife, fork and spoon, a pencil, a box, a brush, a bottle, a watch, and her own doll. She knew none of these objects, but naturally she hardly needed to touch them with her fingertips in order, once guided by her tactual recollections, to know at once what they were. . . . A large grey cat was set before her; she followed the animal's movements attentively, but did not know what to make of the visual impression and remained quiet until, on touching it, she cried out happily "The cat! The cat!"

These and other observations led Senden to conclude that, despite years of experience with touching objects of different shapes and forms, the newly

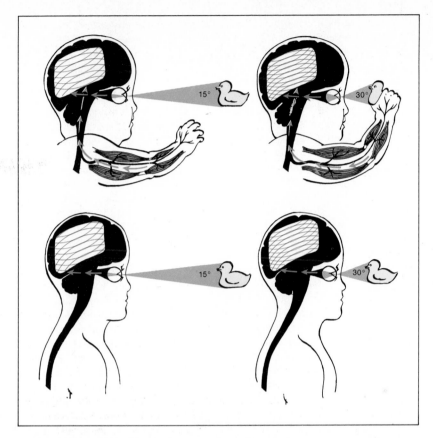

Figure 7.8 The retina is only a two-dimensional surface and cannot directly record informaton about depth. How, then, are you able to perceive depth as well as height and breadth? Environmentalists argue that you have associated specific retinal images with the movements of reaching for an object. (top) A baby spends much of his early life reaching for objects. (bottom) The sets of muscle movements he uses to reach an object at various distances become associated with the various sizes of the retinal images produced by that object. Eventually, according to environmentalists, these associations occur whether he actually moves or not, and it is these associations that produce his perception of depth.

seeing person could not call upon this tactual information to identify the objects visually. The data from restored vision in the blind thus supported the environmentalist viewpoint that, for a person to identify an object, visual sensations must be associated with other sensations and with movements.

Some of Senden's cases, however, did not support environmentalist ideas about form perception. Although the patients could not identify the objects they saw without touching them, they evidently could tell that the objects were *different* from one another, just from the evidence of their vision:

After keeping him in a dark room for a few days, until the opaque particles of lenses were nearly absorbed, and the eyes clear, the same objects, which had been carefully kept from him, were again presented to his notice. He could at once perceive a difference in their shapes; though he could not in the least say which was the cube and which was the sphere, he saw they were not the same figure.

Nativists were delighted with the finding that people with restored vision could discriminate forms from one another, and they were not convinced by the evidence in favor of environmentalism that Senden had marshalled. They were quick to point out important methodological problems with Senden's cases. They noted that all the patients suffered from a number of postoperative effects, including a jerky movement of the eyes, which can prevent clear vision because of the eyes' inability to fixate steadily. Senden's work, then, did not serve to settle the arguments, because each side rejected the findings that did not support its position.

In search of better answers, psychologists began to study animals to see whether animals learn to perceive or whether they are innately programmed to perceive. Nativists held that many perceptual functions needed time—but not experience—to develop. Some early studies designed to test this theory in-

Figure 7.9 A young infant exploring the visual cliff apparatus. Results of visual cliff experiments have lent support to nativist theories of depth perception; children as young as six months and chicks, lambs, and kittens tested shortly after birth all avoid the "deep" side. Nativists say that the depth perception of the newborn animals could not have resulted from experience in matching muscle movements with retinal images (see Figure 7.8). Their avoidance of the deep side of the cliff must be the product of some innate capacity to perceive its depth.

volved rearing animals in darkness so that they might mature without being able to associate movement and touch with vision.

Austin Riesen's 1947 study of chimpanzees reared in darkness for sixteen months seemed to strongly support environmentalism. When the chimps were brought into the light, they used visual information poorly. For example, objects that approached their faces produced no reaction until the objects actually hit the chimps. But a subsequent physical examination of the chimps showed that the retinas of their eyes had actually deteriorated, and they were permanently half-blind. Apparently, at least some visual stimulation was necessary for the normal development of the eye; without it, deterioration occurred. This finding clearly demonstrated that experience is necessary for the maintenance of the ability to see, but it did not prove that *learning* is necessary for visual perception.

Because of the physical damage caused by early visual deprivation, other methods must be used to test the influence of heredity and environment on perception. One of the most fruitful methods analyzes the perceptual capacities of infants very early in life in order to determine what abilities they are born with. Eleanor Gibson and Richard Walk developed one useful technique for studying early **depth perception: the visual cliff,** which is illustrated in Figure 7.9. The experimenters place a young animal or child on a board on the center of the table at the brink of the apparent "cliff," as shown in the figure, and observe whether he crawls off the board onto the shallow side or the deep side. Animals or children who can perceive depth will presumably avoid the deep side to keep from falling.

Many species have been tested with this apparatus. Some animals (such as goats, chicks, and lambs) can walk almost immediately after birth. At this very early age the role of experience in depth perception cannot be very great because the animals have had no time to have any experience. Yet they avoid the deep side. Clearly, at least *some* animals have an inborn capacity to perceive depth.

What about the human infant? Does the visual cliff reveal any evidence for inborn depth perception in people? Gibson and Walk tested human infants after they were old enough to crawl (six months of age and up) and found that they also consistently avoided the deep side. But they had already had six months of visual experience. Recently, a way has been found to test subjects who are much younger. An infant is placed directly atop the shallow side or the deep side of the cliff, and his emotional reactions on the two sides are noted. Infants as young as two months of age have been found to give very different emotional responses on the two sides of the cliff. Although two-month-olds do not appear to be *afraid* on the deep side (in contrast to older infants), they do appear to be fascinated and almost awe-struck, as evidenced by a marked slowing down of heart rate. (Contrary to popular opinion, heart rate slows down rather than speeds up when people pay very close attention to something.) On the shallow side, they seem to be uninterested and often bored. Clearly, the two-month-old infant perceives the two sides of the cliff differently. Infants tested at one month of age, however, respond to *both* the deep and shallow sides with no significant emotional reactions. Although this research supports the nativist contention, in that two-month-olds seem to have depth perception, it is not conclusive. Are humans born with depth perception, or do they learn it in the two months after birth?

Depth perception in very young human infants has also been studied by T. G. R. Bower, who also found evidence of depth perception in two-month-old infants. Bower first trained the infants to turn their heads to obtain a reward. (The reward was a peek-a-boo; an adult popped up into view in front of the infant, smiled, and spoke to him.) After he had conditioned the infants, he trained them to respond for the reward *only* when a twelve-inch cube was

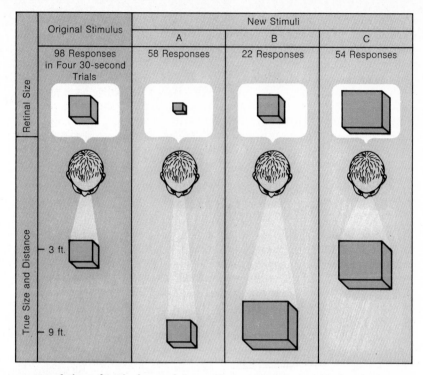

	Original Stimulus	New Stimuli		
		A	B	C
	98 Responses in Four 30-second Trials	58 Responses	22 Responses	54 Responses

Retinal Size

True Size and Distance

3 ft.

9 ft.

Figure 7.10 T.G.R. Bower's ingenious test of infant depth perception. Bower trained infants to turn their heads to obtain a reward and then trained them to do so only in the presence of a twelve-inch cube located three feet away. Bower then tested the infants with the following stimuli: the original stimulus (a twelve-inch cube at three feet); the twelve-inch cube at nine feet (A); a thirty-six inch cube at nine feet (B); and a thirty-six inch cube at three feet (C). The infants responded most often to the original stimulus, of course; but they also responded often to the stimulus that was the same size as the training stimulus (A) or to the stimulus at the same distance as the original (C). They responded least to the stimulus that was farther away but cast the same-sized retinal image (B) as the training stimulus. That is, they responded to real size and real distance but not to the size of the retinal image.

presented three feet in front of them. If the infant turned his head when the cube was present, he received a reward. If he turned his head when the cube was absent, he received no reward.

The infants were then presented not only with the original cube but also with the cubes shown in Figure 7.10: a twelve-inch cube at nine feet (Stimulus A), a thirty-six-inch cube at nine feet (Stimulus B), and a thirty-six-inch cube at three feet (Stimulus C). Stimulus B cast the same-size retinal image as the original stimulus as shown in Figure 7.10. If the infant were using only size of retinal image to determine whether he would get a reward or not, then he should respond as often in this condition as in the first. If he had the ability to see distance, however, he should respond to Stimulus B less than to either Stimulus A, an object the same size as the original one, or Stimulus C, an object at the same distance as the original one.

What Bower found suggests very strongly that two-month-old infants can perceive depth. Of course, the infants gave the greatest number of responses to the original stimulus, but their responses to the three new stimuli supported the nativist argument: They responded more frequently to Stimulus A and Stimulus C than to Stimulus B. Two-month-olds must, therefore, take into account the distance of the object as well as its true size.

Whatever the final outcome of research into the role of environment and heredity in the early development of perception, another line of evidence—with human adults—has demonstrated convincingly that visual perception can be drastically altered by experience. G. M. Stratton and Ivo Kohler, among others, have worn special eyeglasses that turn the world upside down, so that what used to be up looks as if it is down, and what used to be down looks as if it is up. (A photograph showing how these researchers' perception was altered appears as Figure 11.1.) At first they had great problems adapting to these changes; they would constantly reach in the wrong direction for an object, and they even had difficulty just walking about. But after about a week of wearing the glasses they could move around normally, and Kohler found that after a few weeks he could ski, fence, and ride a bicycle with the glasses on. Indeed he adapted so well to his new visual world that, when he finally removed the glasses and so restored his vision to its normal state, he at first saw the "normal" world as upside down. He had to then readjust to normal vision. Regardless of what is inherited in visual perception, people clearly can adapt their vision to drastic alterations.

The upside-down-world studies and the visual-cliff studies have provided information about how certain characteristics of visual perception develop, but the question of "How" heredity and environment jointly produce perceptual development remains unanswered. Although the "How" questions have been difficult to answer, it is possible to get more definitive answers to some questions of "How much" genetic differences affect individual differences in development.

THE DEVELOPMENT OF INTELLIGENCE: A QUESTION OF "HOW MUCH?"

The nature of intelligence has been the focus of much study and debate in psychology. What do we mean when we talk about intelligence? Is it a single trait or a number of different capacities? How does it develop? Chapter 8 presents Piaget's view of intelligence, which is very different from the view of psychologists who argue that IQ tests are good measures of intelligence. Chapter 17, which describes IQ tests, also looks into the uses to which such tests can fairly be put.

Whatever the outcome of further research and debate about IQ tests, the fact remains that IQ tests are widely used. They do predict school performance moderately well, and in some cases they predict job performance, too. One accepted meaning of intelligence, therefore, is simply that intelligence is what IQ tests measure, and this is the meaning accepted for investigations of the contributions of heredity and environment to intelligence. By examining IQ scores, these investigations look for an answer to the following question: To what degree are people different from one another because of their genetic differences and to what extent because of differences in their environments?

Family Studies

Figure 7.11 shows how a person shares more genes with certain types of relatives than with others. Parents and children, brothers and sisters have more genes in common than do grandparents and grandchildren or cousins. Family studies use these amounts of shared genes to assess the inheritance of intelligence. If intelligence has a strong hereditary basis, then people with more shared genes should have more similar IQ scores than people with fewer shared genes.

To check that hypothesis, psychologists employ a statistic called the correlation coefficient (discussed in Chapter 2), which is used to measure the degree of similarity of IQ scores for pairs of people. In this case, the pairs are made up of father and son, or two sisters, or brother and sister, or two cousins, and so forth. For each type of pair a high correlation means that the IQ scores for one member of the pair tend to be ranked similarly to the IQ scores for the other member of each pair. For example, for pairs of fathers and sons, a high correlation means that for any one pair the relative ranking of the father's IQ compared to all other fathers' IQs is similar to the relative ranking of the son's IQ compared to all other sons' IQs, as shown in Figure 7.15. A correlation can range from 0.00, which means that there is no similarity in ranks of IQ scores, to 1.00, which means that the IQ scores for the two members of each pair have essentially identical ranks.

According to the hypothesis that differences in intelligence are hereditary, then, people with more shared genes should show higher correlations than people with fewer shared genes, because the ranking of their IQs should be

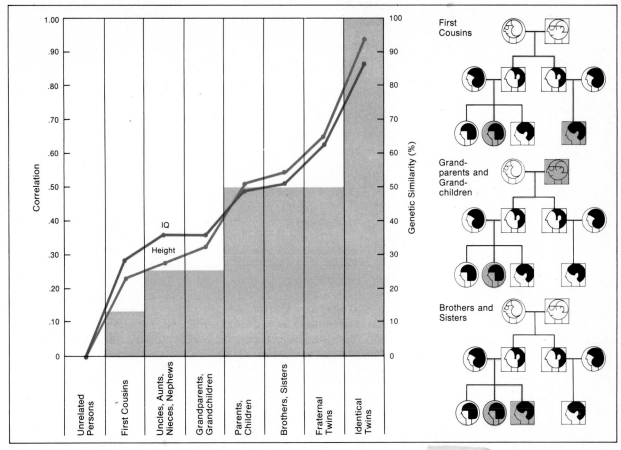

more similar. That is, as the percentage of shared genes shown in Figure 7.11 increases, the correlations should also increase.

The results graphed in Figure 7.11 suggest that heredity does play a role in intelligence. One line shows correlation coefficients for height, a physical trait known to have a large hereditary component. As you can see, knowing the relative ranking of a person's height relative to other people's, you can predict the ranking of his cousin's height with a degree of accuracy expressed by the correlation of .24 (which shows that although there is some accuracy in prediction, it is hardly impressive). Knowing the ranking of his parents' height, you can predict the ranking of a child's height with considerably more accuracy (.51). The greatest correlation is between identical twins. Knowing the ranking of the height of one of the twins, you can predict the ranking of the height of the other with a nearly perfect correlation (.93). Thus, for height, the more genetic overlap between persons, the higher is the correlation between the height of one and the height of the second.

Support for the role of heredity in intelligence comes from comparing the line for height and the line for intelligence. The results for the trait of intelligence are almost perfectly congruent with those for height. For both, correlation increases as genetic overlap increases, precisely what would be expected if the results were accounted for by heredity.

These data are merely suggestive, however. (See the discussion of correlation presented in Chapter 2.) It is possible to argue that along with degree of kinship goes not only degree of genetic overlap but also degree of environmental overlap. Thus, unrelated persons probably have unrelated environments; the environment in which cousins live is probably more similar than

Figure 7.11 The relationship between height similarity, IQ similarity, and genetic similarity among relatives. Calculations of genetic similarity are indicated by the bars in the graph. The family trees on the right suggest how it is possible to compute the degree of genetic similarity between two relatives by using the fact that in each generation 50 percent of each parent's genes are passed to the offspring (see Figure 7.2). First cousins, for example, are related through three sets of parents. Their genetic similarity, therefore, is 50 percent × 50 percent × 50 percent = 12.5 percent. The data on IQ and height presented here suggest that both variables are strongly related to heredity.

(After Newman *et al.*, 1937; and Burt and Howard, 1956.)

that in which unrelated persons live; and identical twins probably have the most similar environments of all.

Twin Studies

A more difficult but also more sophisticated way to attempt to find out how great a role heredity plays in intelligence is to design a study in which some people have either:

1. the *same* heredity and live in the *same* environment.
2. the *same* heredity but live in *different* environments.
3. *different* heredity but live in the *same* environment.
4. *different* heredity and live in *different* environments.

Such a research design would allow one to specify the role of heredity and the role of environment on any given trait. Twin studies use exactly this research design. Because only identical twins have the same heredity, conditions 1 and 2 must use identical twins. The researchers study fraternal twins for conditions 3 and 4, which require individuals with different heredity. As shown in Figure 7.12, **identical twins** develop from a single fertilized egg and so share all the same genes, whereas **fraternal twins** develop from different fertilized eggs and so share only the same percentage of genes as any siblings, 50 percent. Fraternal twins are used in preference to individuals with no shared genes (such as adopted children), so that factors specific to twins can be controlled for: For example, before birth, twins must share their mother's womb, unlike other infants.

The task of finding twins who were separated early in life is a difficult one. Besides the fact that their numbers are few, many of them simply do not know they have a twin. Horatio Newman, Frank Freeman, and Karl Holzinger, who published a study of separated twins in 1937, took several years to track down just fourteen cases that could be authenticated as identical twins reared apart. Some of the twins had learned about each other when a third person mistook the second twin for the one he knew. The data from the Newman study and from two other major twin studies are compiled in Figure 7.13. (Note that the fourth condition in the research design was omitted. It is even more difficult to find fraternal twins reared apart than to find identical twins reared apart.)

Of major interest is the correlation between intelligence-test scores of the identical twins reared apart. If hereditary factors do partially determine individual differences in intelligence, identical twins reared apart should nonetheless have similarly ranked IQ scores; the correlations should be high. If the environment is the major determinant of individual differences in intelligence, then the ranking of IQs of identical twins reared apart should not be similar; the correlations should be low.

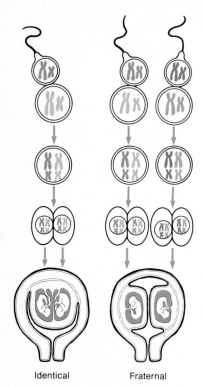

Identical   Fraternal

Figure 7.12 (left) Identical twins develop from a single fertilized egg and are therefore genetically identical. (right) Fraternal twins, on the other hand, have the same degree of genetic similarity as other siblings, 50 percent. Note that even in the womb most identical twins share a more similar environment than fraternal twins do.

Figure 7.13 The results of three studies that compared the correlation coefficients for IQ scores of identical twins reared together, identical twins reared apart, and fraternal twins reared together. The results of two of the three studies suggest a large hereditary contribution to individual differences in IQ.
(After Newman, 1973; Shields, 1962; and Burt, 1966.)

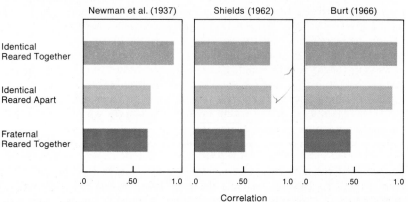

Even though Figure 7.13 shows that in the Newman study, the correlation for identical twins reared apart is not much greater than the correlation for fraternal twins reared together (which would lend some support to environmental factors), in the other two studies, the correlation for identical twins reared apart is so similar to that of twins reared together that many psychologists conclude that intellectual differences are more influenced by heredity than by environment.

Studies of Adopted Children

Because it is so difficult to find subjects for studies of twins reared apart, psychologists have attempted to find other means to assess the relative power of heredity and environment in influencing intelligence. One successful technique uses studies of adopted children to determine whether the children are more like their **biological parents,** with whom they have had no contact since shortly after birth, or their **adoptive parents,** with whom they have no common genes but whose environment they have shared since early infancy.

Evidence that both heredity and environment contribute to intelligence comes from the study of adopted children performed by Marie Skodak and Harold Skeels in 1949. These investigators tested adopted children over a period of some dozen years and then related their intelligence-test scores to the educational levels of their biological mothers and fathers and their adoptive parents. (Educational level is an index that is itself related to intelligence and was used as an imperfect substitute for IQ scores.) These data are presented in Figure 7.14. The children's IQs show increasing resemblance to their biological parents' intellectual level with age but little resemblance at any time to their adoptive parents' intellectual level.

Although these findings suggest that heredity is partly responsible for determining intellectual differences, another aspect of Skodak and Skeels' data strongly demonstrates the effect of environment on intellectual level. Despite the correlation between the IQ scores of the adopted children and those of their biological mothers, the children's IQs were, on the average, some *20 points higher* than those of their biological mothers. (Recall that a correlation indicates the similarity in the ranking of scores: Even if the IQ scores for all adopted children are raised above their biological mothers' scores, the correlation can be high so long as the ranking is similar, as shown in Figure 7.15.) Skodak and Skeels attributed this 20-point increase to the fact that most of the children were adopted into better environments (usually into a higher socioeconomic class) than those their mothers came from. The adopted children's *actual* IQ scores were thus influenced more by the intellectual level of their adoptive parents, while the *rankings* of their IQ scores were influenced more by the ranking of their biological parents' intelligence.

Such dramatic improvements in IQ scores can result from a change to a more intellectually stimulating environment. Suppose that two similar infants were placed in different homes within the first year of life, one in an unstable, poor slum home and one in a stable, economically sound home that provided good intellectual stimulation. Suppose that later, at eight years of age, they were given intelligence tests. The child from the stable and stimulating home might score about 20 to 30 points higher, on the average, than the child from the unstable slum home—for example, an IQ of 120 instead of 95. In one of several other dramatic demonstrations of this effect by Skeels and his colleagues, he and Harold Dye took infants from an orphanage, where they were beginning to show the usual detrimental effects of such institutions—general apathy and a slowness in development—and placed them in the care of retarded women in an institution for the retarded. The women doted on the babies, giving them much attention, stimulation, and care, and all the infants showed sharp improvements in comparison to a group of similar infants that

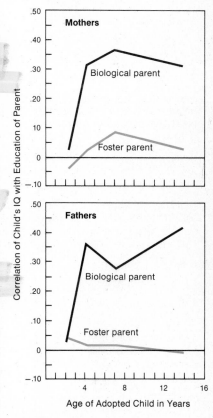

Figure 7.14 The correlations found by Skodak and Skeels between the IQ scores of adopted children and the educational levels of their biological and adoptive parents. The rather low levels of even the highest of these correlations probably reflect the imperfect relation that exists between IQ and education. Nevertheless, there seems to be a strong indication that a biological relationship has a considerable effect on IQ. (After Skodak and Skeels, 1949.)

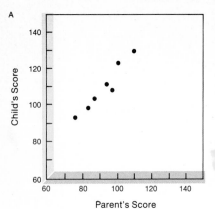

A

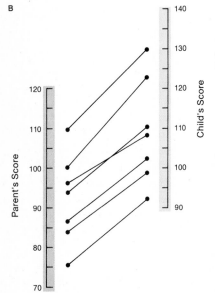

B

Figure 7.15 The effects on correlation of a systematic twenty-point difference between the correlated variables. (A) shows the children's IQ scores plotted on one axis of the graph and their mothers' scores plotted on the other. It is obvious that these two sets of data are strongly correlated despite the fact that there is a twenty-point average difference between a mother's IQ and her child's score. (B) illustrates this relationship in another manner by showing that the orderings of the two sets of scores are nearly identical. Absolute differences between sets of scores do not imply that those scores are not highly correlated.

had remained at the orphanage. On intelligence tests given during the preschool years, the IQ scores of the group given special care averaged about 30 points higher than the scores of the group that had remained at the orphanage. All but two of the children who were given special care were of normal or above-normal intelligence, whereas most of the children left in the orphanage were retarded. These effects were still evident twenty years later, when the infants had become adults: All of the group given special care were self-supporting, and almost half of them had attended college for a year or more. Almost half of the other group were still wards of institutions.

Results like these illustrate a crucial concept for understanding genetic influences: the **reaction range.** The genetic make-up of each person has a unique range of possible responses to the environments he may encounter. In other words, there are some limits on how each of us can respond to good and poor environments. In the case of height, good nutrition will make all of us taller than poor nutrition will, but in both kinds of environments, genetic make-up will dictate that some of us will be taller than others. Genes do not specify a particular height for anyone. They do specify a pattern of growth that varies, depending on nutrition and other environmental factors. The final height a person reaches is a result of both genetic and environmental factors.

The development of intellectual skills sampled by IQ tests also has a reaction range. No matter how stimulating their environments, few people become Albert Einsteins or Leonardo da Vincis. And in other than extremely deprived circumstances, most people do not become retarded. According to Sandra Scarr-Salapatek, each person who is not subjected to severe deprivation has a range of perhaps 20 to 25 points in which his IQ score can fall, depending on his environment. Very depressive environments can make anyone mentally retarded. The reaction range is a concept important to a current heated debate about IQ differences between groups of people.

Group Differences in IQ: The Debate

A controversy that has involved not only psychologists but also the public began in 1969, after Arthur Jensen, an educational psychologist, published a long paper titled "How Much Can We Boost IQ and Scholastic Achievement?" After reviewing the evidence that genetic factors can influence individual intelligence-test scores and the evidence that on the average blacks score about 11 to 15 IQ points lower than whites, Jensen proposed that it is "a not unreasonable hypothesis that genetic factors are strongly implicated in the average Negro-white intelligence difference. The preponderance of the evidence is, in my opinion, less consistent with a strictly environmental hypothesis than with a genetic hypothesis, which, of course, does not exclude the influence of environment or its interaction with genetic factors."

Jensen's thesis, that IQ is highly heritable and therefore that racial differences in IQ are largely due to differences in the gene distributions of the populations studied, has been questioned by a number of psychologists. In order to fully understand the arguments pro and con, it is necessary to have some understanding of what psychologists and geneticists mean by heritability. With respect to a specific group, or population, in a given environment, one can ask how much of the observed individual variation of a trait is the result of genetic differences and how much the result of environmental differences. **Heritability,** then, is the percentage of variability in a trait that is attributable to genetic differences among those individuals in that environment. Saying that a trait has high heritability does *not* mean that genes "cause" it: Heritability is a measure that is specific to a given population in a given environment; it is not a constant property of the trait per se. Heritability of a trait, then, may change from year to year if the factors producing the trait change. The heritability of blindness, for example, has increased markedly since 1800 as a result of the elimination of smallpox and other communicable diseases that are potential environmental causes of blindness. That is, because there are fewer environmental factors contributing to blindness, a greater percentage of this trait's variability in the population is attributable to genetic differences among individuals.

With respect to IQ, Jensen's side of the argument can be phrased as follows: If individual differences in intelligence within the white population as a whole have a high heritability, it is plausible that the average differences between racial groups also reflect genetic differences. Those opposing Jensen either attack his methodology or point to environmental factors he has not taken account of. However, Jensen has proceeded to rule out a number of environmental factors that have been proposed to explain black-white IQ differences. Here are some of his major points:

1. Even when socioeconomic class of the two races is equated, blacks score well below whites, on the average.
2. Environmental deprivation affects American Indians more than blacks, yet Indians score higher on IQ tests than blacks, on the average.
3. The absence of the father in the lower-class black home has not been found to account for the lower intelligence level.
4. The race of the examiner has not been found to make a difference to the IQ scores of black children when many studies are considered.

Arguments in rebuttal to Jensen include the following:

1. Blacks and whites differ on numerous factors besides genetic ones, such as living conditions and degree of discrimination. For instance, blacks and whites supposedly of the "same" socioeconomic class actually differ in income, schooling, and housing.
2. To argue that black-white IQ differences are not explainable by the few environmental factors investigated does not rule out a possible explanation due to other, as yet unspecified, environmental factors. For example, lead, which when eaten causes sharp decreases in intelligence, is present in old paint in many slum dwellings, and young children commonly eat paint chips. Recent research by John Scanlon and Donald Barltrop has shown that lead can be transmitted from the pregnant woman to her unborn child, and Herbert Needleman points out that, partly because of this transmission, the effects of lead poisoning give the appearance of being genetic although they are not. He also has shown that lead poisoning is especially common in urban blacks. To this date, many environmental factors that apply especially to blacks have not been fully studied.
3. IQ tests are affected by numerous nonintellectual factors such as motivation, anxiety, and test-taking skills, and these factors are especially relevant for minority groups. These nonintellectual influences on the IQ score detract from its value as a reliable measure of the differences between racial groups in intelligence.
4. Jensen seems to imply that heredity "fixes" intelligence-test scores within limits and does not take account of the facts of reaction range. Data from the adoption studies discussed earlier suggest that adoption to a higher social class can lead to a significantly higher IQ than would be expected if the same children had been reared by their natural parents.
5. All major studies of heritability of IQ have been based on samples of white populations; no adequate heritability studies have been based on samples of the black population of the United States.

Sandra Scarr-Salapatek, in a review of Jensen's article, said, "While we may tentatively conclude that there are some genetic IQ differences between

Figure 7.16   In any population, any trait can be measured and its variability observed. This observed variability is assumed to be the sum of variability due to genetic factors and of variability due to environmental factors. When genetic variability is a high proportion of the sum, heritability is said to be high; when environmental variability is a high proportion of the sum, heritability is said to be low. These diagrams show how heritability can change without a change in genetic variability. The amount of variability is represented by length of line. In (A) the contributions of genetic and environmental factors to the observed variability are about equal; heritability is about 50 percent. In (B) heritability is much higher—but not because genetic variability increased. Heritability is higher because environmental variability has decreased, leaving genetic variability a large proportion of the remaining observed variability.

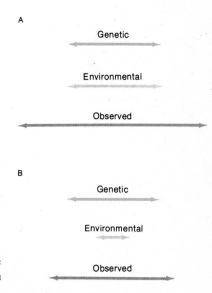

social-class groups, we can make only wild speculations about racial groups. . . . racial groups are not random samples from the same population, nor are members reared in uniform conditions within each race.'' She points to the common misunderstanding of the concept of heritability in relation to IQ: If heritability ''is high, this reasoning goes, then intelligence is genetically fixed and unchangeable . . . This misconception ignores the fact that [heritability] is a population statistic, bound to a given set of environmental conditions at a given point in time. Neither intelligence nor [heritability] estimates are fixed.''

Scarr-Salapatek argues that not enough proof exists to support either the arguments of those who say there *are* racial differences in IQ or the arguments of those who say *all* such differences can be accounted for by environmental differences. She hypothesizes further that hereditary and environmental factors may operate dependently, combining in different ways under different circumstances. For example, she suggests that genetic differences would show up more in persons who grow up in favorable surroundings, whereas adverse environments would act to mask genetic variance. She tested the hypothesis in her study of 992 sets of twins attending public schools in Philadelphia. She compared scholastic-aptitude test scores across races and across socioeconomic levels and found that for both blacks and whites, test scores varied more according to genetic differences among advantaged than among disadvantaged children. Her findings indicate that adverse environments affect expression of the reaction range, so that at least part of the IQ differences between races is the result of environmental differences.

Scarr-Salapatek's hypothesis that hereditary and environmental factors operate dependently—that is, may affect each other in the course of development—seems to apply to another area of individual differences—the development of schizophrenia.

BECOMING SCHIZOPHRENIC: A QUESTION OF ''HOW MUCH?''

For centuries it was believed that ''insanity'' was inherited, although there was no real proof. After Freud revolutionized psychologists' way of thinking about mental disorders, emphasizing the importance of past experience in their formation, environmental explanations of mental disorder became more prevalent. However, when psychoanalytic and other forms of therapy proved to be unsuccessful in treating certain disorders, particularly psychoses (see Chapter 24), investigators once again began to search for genetic explanations of these disorders.

One of the most common of these disorders is schizophrenia. Characterized by loss of contact with reality, thought disorders, and emotional withdrawal, schizophrenia is currently one of the most serious health problems in the United States, accounting for the use of about 20 percent of all hospital beds in the country. It is not only prevalent, it is very difficult to treat.

Researchers have asked ''How much'' of the differences between individuals in their susceptibility to schizophrenia is the result of hereditary differences and how much the result of environmental effects. They have used a number of research methods in their attempts to answer this question.

Family and Twin Studies

As with intelligence, the earliest attempts to discover the role of heredity in schizophrenia involved family studies. Figure 7.17 presents the results of studies showing the incidence of schizophrenia in relatives of a schizophrenic. In general, these data provide *some* evidence for the role of heredity, in that the closer relatives (those having more genes in common) were the ones that tended to have a higher incidence of schizophrenia. These data also raise

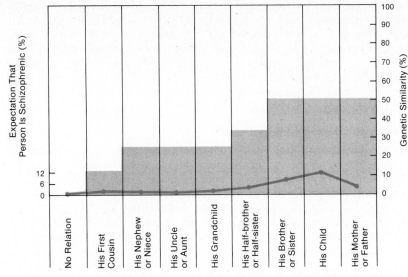

Figure 7.17 The relationship between genetic similarity among relatives and the likelihood that a schizophrenic's relative will be schizophrenic. The data presented are analogous to the data presented in Figure 7.11 (genetic similarity, height, and IQ), but this evidence does not support a strongly genetic explanation of schizophrenia. (After Slater, 1968.)

puzzling questions, however: A schizophrenic shares the same proportion of genes with his parents as he does with his siblings and with his own children (50 percent). Yet, as Figure 7.17 shows, the expectation of schizophrenia for children of a schizophrenic is much higher than for his siblings, which, in turn, is much higher than for his parents. Simple explanations based on heredity cannot account for these differences.

Data from twin studies appear to provide better support for the role of heredity in schizophrenia. Some of the early twin studies suggested that in as many as 86 percent of the cases in which one identical twin had schizophrenia, the other twin also did. In contrast, the percentage for fraternal twins was only 14 percent. Because of more stringent diagnostic criteria for schizophrenia, more recent twin studies have not obtained as high a percentage for identical twins, and the generally accepted percentage is closer to 40 to 50 percent. Nevertheless, almost without exception, the percentage for fraternal twins is much lower—approximately 10 to 15 percent.

The study of schizophrenia in close relatives has recently been extended to a unique case of identical girl quadruplets, reported by David Rosenthal in 1963. All four girls became schizophrenic in their early twenties. Considering the odds of giving birth to identical quadruplets plus the odds of all of them becoming schizophrenic, Rosenthal calculated that the odds of this case recurring were one and one-half billion to one. These quadruplets, given the fictitious name Genain, tended to have not only similar abnormalities in their brain waves but also similar personalities prior to their episodes of schizophrenia (the girls were extremely shy and withdrawn).

The Genain quadruplets also shared the same environment, however. They had a very dominant mother and an ineffectual father. The parents kept the girls from socializing with other children throughout their childhood. "They were literally fenced in" from playmates, according to the author of the report. The girls' sexuality was harshly repressed by their parents. Two of them, who had a compulsive habit of masturbating, were made to undergo surgery for circumcision in an attempt by the parents to make them stop. In another instance, the father swabbed one girl's clitoris with carbolic acid to make it painful for her to masturbate. Yet, the father was on occasion seductive with the girls, insisting on their dressing in his presence. All the girls were subject to the same environmental conditions, which could have accounted as well for their similar illness as their common heredity did. You can see that family studies are, by themselves, not conclusive.

Studies of identical twins reared apart would supply better evidence for inferring a genetic cause in schizophrenia. Very few identical twins reared apart have been studied for schizophrenia, however. In 1971 Rosenthal reported sixteen cases of identical twins reared apart; in 62.5 percent of these cases both twins had schizophrenia. Because there are so few data about identical twins reared apart and because it is so difficult in family studies to separate heredity and environment, researchers have recently adopted a new strategy of study.

Studies of Adopted Children

The studies reported here involve a variant of the adopted-child method of studying the inheritance of intelligence. The adopted-child studies of schizophrenia are much better controlled than the adopted-child IQ studies because they were done in Denmark, where excellent records are kept of family lineages, psychiatric illnesses, adoptions, and the like. One line of research begins with children who were adopted early in life (in many cases within one month after birth) and who later became schizophrenic. The research traces both the adoptive relatives and the biological relatives (father, mother, siblings and half-siblings for both) in order to see whether schizophrenia runs higher among the adoptive relatives (with whom the child has shared a common environment but no common heredity) or among the biological relatives (with whom the child shared a common heredity but no common environment).

One investigation done in 1968 by Seymour Kety, David Rosenthal, Paul Wender, and Fini Schulsinger identified all the children adopted in Copenhagen between 1924 and 1948 and determined which of these became schizophrenic; the records turned up 33 adopted schizophrenics. The investigators also chose a control group of 33 adopted children who were similar to the schizophrenics in a number of factors that have been proposed to account for schizophrenia in relatives—for example, socioeconomic status. Search of the records uncovered 463 first-degree relatives of the 66 adopted persons, including 21 relatives whose psychiatric records revealed either full-blown schizophrenia or less intense, schizophreniclike symptoms. The results of this study, presented in Table 7.1, show that schizophrenia or schizophreniclike symptoms run along *biological* family lines rather than *adoptive* family lines. These results suggest strongly that schizophrenia is affected by hereditary factors.

A second investigation by David Rosenthal and his colleagues used a different research strategy that reversed the sequence of the preceding method. This approach began by identifying parents who had put their child up for adoption and who were eventually hospitalized for schizophrenia (or, in a few cases, for manic-depressive psychoses). This group was matched with a control group of parents whose children were adopted by others but who had no schizophrenia. The adopted-away children (now grown up) of these two groups of parents were then identified through the Danish registry system, contacted, and invited to participate in a study of their "health." Those who agreed to do so were given thorough psychiatric interviews by physicians or psychologists who did not know whether the parent of the interviewee was one eventually hospitalized for schizophrenia or not; this method eliminated the possibility that the interviewers would be biased by knowledge about the parents.

The findings of this study were clear: 33 percent of the children adopted away from schizophrenic parents had "schizophrenic-spectrum" personality diagnoses—that is, identification of some schizophrenic symptoms, however mild. Among the adopted-away offspring of controls, the proportion was only 15 percent. These results provide further evidence that a tendency toward schizophrenia runs along biological lines. Although both these studies of

Table 7.1 Incidence of Schizophrenia

	In Biological Relatives	In Adoptive Relatives
Schizophrenics (33)	13 of 150	2 of 74
Controls (33)	3 of 156	3 of 83

Source: David Rosenthal, *The Genetics of Psychopathology* (New York: McGraw-Hill, 1971).

adopted children support the role of heredity in producing schizophrenia, they still are not conclusive.

It must be noted also that both studies suggest the influence of environmental factors. In neither study did the incidence of schizophrenia in the adopted children run as high as the incidence in biological family members living together. In fact, in the second study described, only 1 percent of the adopted-away children of schizophrenics had yet been hospitalized for schizophrenia.

Although adoption studies, twin studies, and family studies all indicate that hereditary factors are somehow responsible for the development of schizophrenia, no studies of this kind have been able to say *exactly how* schizophrenia comes about. One thing is certain: People do not inherit the disorder in any simple way. If they did, the proportion of the offspring of schizophrenics who are themselves schizophrenic would be far higher than has been found to date. Similarly, the percentage of identical twins where both twins have schizophrenia would approach 100 percent instead of only 40 to 50 percent.

Evidently, factors other than hereditary ones can affect the expression of schizophrenia, even in people who have a high risk of developing it because it runs in their biological families. The Danish studies seem to show that adoption into an environment different from that of the biological family reduces the expression of schizophrenia. Thus, Scarr-Salapatek's hypothesis that hereditary and environmental factors operate dependently might serve to explain why the development of schizophrenia appears to be so complex. In fact, a theory set out by Paul Meehl, and discussed in Chapter 25, postulates that although a single gene is responsible for the risk of schizophrenia, whether a person does become schizophrenic depends on whether he inherits other defective genes and on his early experiences. That is, a person with only one defective gene may exhibit some schizoid traits, but he most likely will not become fully schizophrenic unless he also has other defective genes *and* has been exposed to stressful childhood experiences. A person without that defective gene will never become schizophrenic. The expression, then, of a hereditary trait is always influenced during development by environmental factors.

THE COLLABORATION BETWEEN HEREDITY AND ENVIRONMENT

Most of the research evidence set out here supports the statement made at the beginning of the chapter: Developmental outcomes are a result of hereditary and environmental influences acting in concert. For example, even though the existing evidence from family studies and separated-twin studies strongly supports the notion that individual intelligence is inherited, the evidence from studies like those of Skeels shows that children can gain in intelligence if they are adopted into an environment that has more opportunities for them to learn.

Many human traits, like schizophrenia, seem to involve very complex interactions between inherited potential for the trait and how—or whether—it is expressed. Even though the Danish studies showed that there is some biological basis for the disorder, the fact that it is expressed less often and its expression is less severe in adopted children must mean that environmental factors are also important. And evidence like that of Sandra Scarr-Salapatek's study of black and white children in Philadelphia suggests that the development of intelligence also involves complex, interdependent processes operating between inherited potential and environmental influences.

This view of the growth of intelligence is much like that of Jean Piaget, whose theory of cognitive development is presented in the following chapter. His theory deals with how the human mind works and how its workings change as infants grow to adulthood. He sees the growth of intelligence as a continuous creative collaboration between the organism, with its biological givens, and that organism's environment.

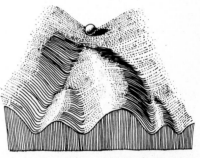

Figure 7.18 The epigenetic landscape, a graphic analogy for the interaction of heredity and environment in development created by the geneticist Conrad Waddington. The landscape represents the possibilities determined by genetic factors, and the path of the rolling ball represents the actual course of development. Such forces on the ball as cross-winds represent environmental factors. The ball can roll down different valleys, depending on the forces that are brought to bear on it, but it cannot easily change from one valley to another once it has started. Although Waddington suggested this analogy for the physical development of cells in the embryo, the analogy is as useful in understanding how genetic and environmental factors interact to produce different personality traits or different degrees of intellectual ability. (After Waddington, 1957.)

SUMMARY

1. Two different questions can be asked when one is investigating the causes of developmental outcomes. One question asks **"How"** heredity and environment act together to produce development in all people. The other question asks **"How much"** of a difference between individuals is the result of genetic effects and how much is the result of environmental influences.

2. To properly investigate hereditary effects, one must know something about the process of genetic transmission. The agents of genetic transmission are chromosomes and genes.

   a. **Chromosomes** are long threadlike structures that carry the genes. All normal human cells, except germ cells, have forty-six chromosomes, in twenty-three pairs. The germ cells (the ovum and spermatozoon) have only twenty-three chromosomes because they go through a splitting process (**meiosis**) during which the pairs become separate. At conception, then, the twenty-three chromosomes from the mother join with the twenty-three from the father, and the individual begins to develop.

   b. The chromosomes carry thousands of genes. **Genes** are the carriers and directors of human growth. Each gene is a sequence of **DNA** that specifies the production of a given protein (the basic material of the human body) and the program for combining that protein with others to form the human individual.

   c. The development of most structures and behavioral characteristics of an individual depend on the joint action of a number of genes.

   d. A single gene's specification for a protein often involves several sequential steps in the body's use of that protein; this sequence is called a **gene action pathway.**

3. The disorder called **PKU (phenylketonuria)** results from a defective gene, and thus the blockage of a gene action pathway. Because the body fails to produce a certain substance that in normal people converts a protein present in many foods (phenylalanine) into another protein (tyrosine), phenylalanine builds up and changes to a toxic substance, which affects the nervous system. The most serious symptom of the disorder is progressive and severe mental retardation. Early diagnosis of the disorder permits a simple environmental preventive: a diet low in phenylalanine.

4. Down's syndrome is usually caused by **nondisjunction** of a pair of chromosomes during formation of the sex cells (the ovum or sperm). Children with **Down's syndrome** display certain physical abnormalities, such as an eyelid fold that resembles that of Orientals (which is why the disorder is sometimes called mongolism), as well as severe retardation.

   a. The process of **karyotyping,** the technique of photographing and analyzing chromosomes, permitted the discovery that children with Down's syndrome had an extra chromosome in the twenty-first pair, a total of forty-seven chromosomes instead of the normal number of forty-six.

   b. Because Down's syndrome does not run in families, and because few people with Down's syndrome have offspring, scientists examined all the factors that might be related to the nondisjunction. They discovered that there were many more Down's-syndrome births in older mothers.

c. With a process called **amniocentesis,** physicians can now determine before birth whether the fetus has Down's syndrome. They draw some fetal cells from the fluid in the amniotic sac and karyotype them. If there is a third twenty-first chromosome, the parents may elect to have the fetus therapeutically aborted. Further advances in genetic counseling may permit a chemical manipulation of the fetal environment that will prevent the genetic trait from expressing itself.

5. The development of perception is an area in which little is known about "How" heredity and environment work together. There has been a long debate as to which is more important. The question is: Are humans programmed by heredity to correctly perceive the world they encounter, or do they need experience with seeing and touching objects to correctly perceive things like depth?

   a. One of the best methods to test **depth perception** in human and animal infants is the **visual cliff** (see Figure 7.9). Children or animals who perceive depth will presumably climb off the center board onto the shallow side rather than the deep one. Day-old goats, chicks, and lambs choose the shallow side, as do six-month-old humans. Even two-month-old infants recognize the difference between the deep and shallow sides (as indicated by measures of heart rate). Although these data indicate a hereditary basis for depth perception, the question remains of whether in the first two months of life infants learn to perceive depth.

   b. An experiment by T. G. R. Bower also indicates that two-month-olds perceive depth. Having trained infants to respond to a twelve-inch cube three feet in front of them, he then tested them with three other cubes, one of which was the same size as the original, one at the same distance as the original, and a third that was larger and farther away but that cast the same-size retinal image as the original cube. The fact that the infants responded least to the cube that cast the same-size retinal image showed that they could correctly perceive size and distance.

   c. Another series of experiments shows that visual perception can be greatly altered by experience. Researchers donned special eyeglasses that made the things normally perceived as down seem up, and vice versa. After a few weeks' experience, the researchers had adapted their activities so well to this altered perception that they could even participate in sports.

6. Intelligence, as measured by IQ tests, is the subject of much psychological research seeking an answer to the question: To what degree are people different from one another because of their genetic differences and to what extent because of differences in their environments?

   a. **Family studies,** which compare the number of genes shared in common by relatives of varying degrees with the relatives' IQs, suggest that there is a hereditary basis for intelligence. The more genes the relatives share, the higher the correlation of their IQs. However, it is also true that closer kinship often implies more similar environments, so the family-study data are by no means conclusive.

   b. **Twin studies** compare the correlation of the IQs of identical twins reared apart with that of the IQs of identical twins reared together and that of the IQs of fraternal twins reared together. **Identical twins** share 100 percent of their genes in common, whereas **fraternal twins** share 50 percent, like all siblings. Because several studies show that the correlation of the IQs of identical twins reared apart is similar to that of

Figure 7.19 Arthur Jensen, a respected educational psychologist who has received wide publicity for his position that IQ is largely inherited. He argues that compensatory education programs for poor and black children falsely assume that IQ is subject to great influence by environmental factors. Earlier in his career Jensen studied aggressiveness in delinquent and nondelinquent boys and spent three years with Hans Eysenck studying the nature of individual differences in learning.

identical twins reared together, many psychologists conclude that heredity is an important determinant of intellectual differences.

   c. **Studies of adopted children** compare the correlations of IQs of adopted children with the IQs of their **biological parents,** with whom they share genes, and of their **adoptive parents,** with whom they share environment. Results of these studies show both the importance of heredity and of environment. The correlation of intellectual levels is much higher for the children and their biological parents than for the children and their adoptive parents—the influence of heredity. But in one study the IQs of adopted children were, on the average, 20 points higher than those of their biological mothers—the influence of environment.

   d. The fact that the IQs of the adopted children in the study just cited were 20 points higher illustrates a concept called the **reaction range.** That is, genes specify a pattern of growth that varies depending on environmental factors. For IQ, genes probably specify a reaction range of 20 to 25 points. That is, a person's IQ may be 85 or 110, depending on how good his environment is in a normal range of environments.

7. A heated debate has recently surrounded publication by Arthur Jensen of an article concluding that the 11-to-15-point differences found, on the average, between blacks' and whites' IQ scores are the result of hereditary differences. The arguments against Jensen's conclusions strongly suggest that his study did not sufficiently take account of various methodological and social factors. One problem is his assumption that IQ is highly heritable.

   a. **Heritability** is the percentage of trait variability attributable to genetic differences among individuals in a given population. It is a measure specific to a given population in a given environment, and it can change if the factors producing the trait change. For example, if environmental factors producing the trait decrease, the trait will become more heritable.

   b. Sandra Scarr-Salapatek hypothesizes that genetic differences in intelligence would show up more in persons who grow up in favorable environments, while adverse environments would tend to mask genetic variability. She tested this hypothesis in a study of black and white children of all social classes. She did, in fact, find that for both blacks and whites, test scores varied more according to genetic differences among advantaged than among disadvantaged children.

8. **Schizophrenia** is a mental disorder that a number of psychologists believe is inherited to some degree.

   a. Family and twin studies gave some slight indication of a hereditary basis for schizophrenia, but the data have been few and unclear. Studies of identical twins indicate that in 40 to 50 percent of the cases where one twin has schizophrenia, the other twin also has it. This finding suggests a hereditary basis, but if the cause were solely a hereditary one, both twins should be schizophrenic in 100 percent of the cases.

   b. The results of studies of adopted children conducted in Denmark show that schizophrenia or schizophreniclike symptoms run along biological family lines rather than adoptive family lines, which indicates that schizophrenia has some hereditary basis. However, because the incidence of the disorder was much lower among biological relatives who lived apart than among those who lived together, environment must play a role in whether and how the disorder is expressed.

c. It appears that hereditary and environmental factors combine in a complex way to produce—or suppress—schizophrenia. Paul Meehl has theorized that a number of defective genes are involved in the development of schizophrenia: Whether a person in fact becomes schizophrenic depends in part on the number of defective genes he inherits and in part on early stressful experiences.

SUGGESTED READINGS

Berrill, Norman J. *The Person in the Womb.* New York: Dodd, Mead, 1968 (paper). A beautifully written book that describes the development of the fetus and embryo in the womb.

Bower, T. G. R. *Development in Infancy.* San Francisco: Freeman, 1974 (paper). An exciting book by one of the best-known researchers in perceptual development. He discusses the determinants of perceptual development.

Dobzhansky, Theodosius. "Differences Are Not Deficits," *Psychology Today,* 7 (December 1973), 96–101. A well-known geneticist discusses the difficulties in inferring that the racial differences in IQ are due to heredity.

Friedmann, Theodore. "Prenatal Diagnosis of Genetic Disease," *Scientific American,* 225 (November 1971), 34–42. A clear description of the new methods being used early in pregnancy to detect diseases that are influenced by heredity.

Hochberg, Julian. "Nativism and Empiricism in Perception," in Leo Postman (ed.), *Psychology in the Making: Histories of Selected Research Problems.* New York: Knopf, 1962. An interesting chapter, drawing into sharp relief the classical philosophical and psychological issues in this area.

Hubel, David H. "The Visual Cortex of the Brain," *Scientific American,* 209 (November 1963), 54–62. A famous article that describes how the brain is wired to respond to features of the world much more complex than light and color: lines, edges, and other visual patterns.

Jensen, Arthur R. "The Differences Are Real," *Psychology Today,* 7 (December 1973), 79–86. An articulate and up-to-date account of the latest status of Jensen's hypothesis that the obtained black-white IQ differences are due in large part to hereditary factors.

Kagan, Jerome. "Inadequate Evidence and Illogical Conclusions," *Harvard Educational Review,* 39 (1969), 274–277. A persuasive argument rebutting some of the assumptions behind Jensen's hypothesis about IQ differences.

McClearn, Gerald E., and John C. DeFries. *Introduction to Behavioral Genetics.* San Francisco: W. H. Freeman, 1973. A clearly written, comprehensive review of most of the issues on the inheritance of behavior.

Rosenthal, David. *The Genetics of Psychopathology.* New York: McGraw-Hill, 1971. A lucid account of the sources of evidence for the inheritance of predispositions toward a number of different psychological traits, such as schizophrenia, manic-depressive psychosis, and alcoholism.

Each of us leaves childish things behind us as we grow older and more sophisticated—but ought we to do so entirely? Can we go too far in abandoning what seems silly?

As babies, we may think, for instance, that anything that passes out of sight is destroyed and no longer exists. But eventually we learn better and just look for it elsewhere. And we laugh at the childishness of those primitives who felt that the sun was destroyed each evening when it set, and that a new sun was created each morning. Or that each new cycle of the phases of the moon started with a literally new moon. (We still call it a "new moon," don't we?)

Yet is that really so primitive a notion? When a flame is extinguished, has it merely moved out of sight? Of course not. It has really and literally been destroyed. And if a candle is lighted once more, a new flame has really and literally been created. Why not then assume, by analogy, that as the great flame of the sun sinks into the western oceans, it, too, is really and literally destroyed by the huge quantity of water, as a candle flame would be destroyed if it were dipped into a small pool of water? Then, when the sun rises the next morning, surely a new flame has been created. In other words, something can be wrong without necessarily being silly.

Again, children may not equate amount and volume tightly. They may not quite get the notion that the same amount of liquid always has the same volume whatever the shape of the container that holds it. We learn better as we grow older, though. So we are amused by the Arabian Nights notion of giant genies trapped in small bottles. Just fantasy! But the imagination of human beings is not unlimited. Even the wildest stroke of fantasy nas some foothold in reality. Think about the fact that although liquids and solids do retain their volumes, gases don't. A large quantity of gas can be compressed into a small volume. What's more, a small quantity of solid, in burning, may release a large volume of vapor. Indeed, when the genie-in-the-bottle appears on the Hollywood screen, it is always pictured as a matter of gas. The hero opens the bottle and gas comes out, faster and faster, and higher and higher, and finally solidifies into a giant.

So it becomes wrong to carry wisdom to extremes. If we become so adult as to be certain that nothing is ever destroyed just because it disappears, and that nothing changes volume without changing quantity, we will never understand flames and gases.

Isaac Asimov

8
Development of Intelligence: Piaget's Theory

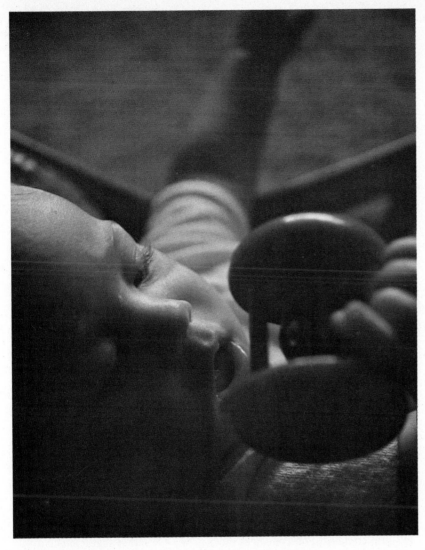

The existence of child psychology as a field of study is the result of a fundamental change in people's conceptions of children. Until the end of the nineteenth century most people thought of children merely as miniature adults. The next time you go to a museum, look carefully at the way infants are portrayed in paintings done during the Middle Ages; the babies look like adults shrunk to about two-fifths normal size. But even after artists had begun to paint infants that *looked* their ages, it took centuries for people to understand that children's *minds* are not merely replicas of adults'— with, of course, fewer facts in their memories. It is now known that children think and learn in different ways than adults do. This realization has opened up whole new areas of psychological investigation, some of which are discussed in this and the following two chapters.

The greatest contemporary figure in child psychology is the Swiss psychologist Jean Piaget. He has published more systematic observations of children's thinking and learning than anyone else in history. Most of the discussion in this chapter is based on Piaget's theory of the development of thinking from infancy to adulthood. Although Piaget's theory provides a framework that will help you think about psychological development, you should keep in mind as you read that the study of infants and children is still in its own infancy.

QUALITATIVE CHANGES IN THINKING

One of the main tenets of Piaget's theory of the development of intelligence is that the mind of the child is qualitatively different from the mind of the adult. In attempting to uncover the key steps in intellectual development, Piaget has discovered some dramatic changes in the way a child reasons about particular tasks at different ages. Consider the following example.

A four-year-old girl is playing with a box full of shiny red beads. Her

Figure 8.1 An infant's earliest behaviors are reflexive; objects put into his hand are automatically grasped, and objects put into his mouth are automatically sucked. In this photograph, a baby is beginning to experiment with and expand these primitive ways he has of knowing and understanding the world. The theory presented in this chapter is based on the assumption that all of human intelligence is developed in this way: Present abilities are used, and through use are extended and transformed.

father takes ten of them and lines them up in two matching rows of five beads each. The father asks the girl, "Does one row have more beads than the other, or do they both have the same number?" The child replies that they're both the same, of course. But her father encourages her to count them, just to make sure. (The girl can count to ten.) The father then changes one row so that its five beads are farther apart, stretched out into a longer line. When he asks his daughter if the rows still have the same number of beads in them, the girl shakes her head: "No, now that one has more," she says, indicating the row where the five beads make a longer line. A year later, the father tries the same task again. When he lengthens one row of beads and asks his daughter if the number of beads is still the same, the girl answers, "Yes, of course." Her tone implies that the question is silly because the answer is so obvious.

The child has acquired what Piaget calls **conservation of number.** She understands that the number of items in a set is not altered by changes in the configuration of that set. A short line of beads can be made into a long one or changed to form a circle without changing the number of beads. Earlier, when the girl was four years old, she could count to ten, but she did not truly comprehend how numbers function. She did not understand that number is conserved in spite of changes in pattern.

After the girl has successfully finished the number task, her father brings out a new game, shown in Figure 8.2. He starts with two beakers of the same size and shape, and he pours some water into each one. He asks for his daughter's help in making each beaker contain the same amount of water. After a few adjustments, the girl announces, "O.K., they're the same." Now the father brings out a tall, thin beaker and pours the fluid from one of the original containers into the new beaker. The girl watches him pouring. When the father asks if the water in the tall, thin beaker is still the same amount as the water in the original container, the girl says, "No, that one's more," pointing to the tall, thin beaker.

Although the child can understand conservation of number, she does not yet appreciate that amount of liquid also shows conservation. She does not realize that pouring a liquid into a container of different shape does not change the amount of liquid. Although to most adults the tall, thin beaker might look as if it contains more liquid than does the shorter beaker, adults know that the amounts of liquid have to be the same because they were the same before the liquid was poured. The child reacts only to the appearance of the liquid in the tall, thin container and concludes there is more liquid in that container.

Figure 8.2 The girl taking part in this demonstration has not yet acquired what Piaget calls conservation of quantity of liquid. Although she has seen the liquid poured from one beaker to another, she reacts only to the apparent increase of quantity in the tall beaker.

When the girl is about seven years old, the same problem is posed to her again. Now she answers the question correctly. The amount of liquid is the same, she asserts emphatically—without hesitation and with a tone of certainty. By that age, she understands **conservation of quantity of liquid.**

Intelligence as the Construction of an Understanding

What is happening as the child learns about conservation? Using conservation and many other tasks, Piaget has extensively studied the development of intelligence from infancy to adolescence, and he has repeatedly found that children's understanding of certain fundamental aspects of the world is not easily acquired. Studies by many other investigators, including Jan Smedslund, Joachim Wohlwill, and Susan Carey-Block, have confirmed Piaget's finding that children cannot be trained to truly understand certain principles, such as conservation of liquid, unless they have reached the point in their development when they are ready to understand them.

What is the process of intellectual growth that brings children to an understanding of such principles? It is not simply a process of maturation, because the speed of children's development varies greatly depending on their environments. And studies like the ones just cited show that training alone will not produce the understanding. Piaget believes that the learning of anything involves the **construction of an understanding.** These constructions are the result of encounters between the child and his environment in which the child experiences a discrepancy between what he already understands and what his environment is presenting to him.

Piaget's view that intelligence involves the construction of an understanding should be contrasted with a common view that intelligence is what is measured by IQ tests. People who take the latter view assume that intelligence is a trait that people have in various degrees: Someone with an IQ of 130 has more of it than someone with an IQ of only 90. For Piaget, intelligence is not a trait; it is the process underlying all thought—all knowledge—the process of construction of an understanding. Before one can discuss in detail what Piaget means by construction of an understanding, it is necessary to become familiar with four other concepts that Piaget uses: schemes, assimilation, accommodation, and equilibration.

Schemes   As an infant interacts with the world around him, he uses certain recurrent schemes of action. Scheme is Piaget's word for an organized action or mental structure that, when applied to the world, leads to that mysterious event called knowing. For example, infants have a few simple schemes: They can suck and grasp, and they do attempt to grasp and to suck on almost everything. In Piaget's terms, they have a grasping scheme and a sucking scheme (among others). By using these schemes, the one-month-old comes to understand and appreciate much of his world in terms of things that can be grasped or sucked.

Grasping is, in fact, a useful metaphor for what schemes do. An infant comes to know objects by grasping them with his hand, and he must often change the way he is holding his hand in order to grasp an unfamiliar object. He finds that different objects must be grasped in different ways and that some (such as walls) cannot be grasped at all. In the same way that the child adjusts his hand to fit different objects, he adjusts his schemes to fit different objects and events. This adjustment of schemes is what produces intellectual growth.

As the child grows older, his schemes for understanding the world become more complicated and less dependent on overt action. They become what Piaget calls **interiorized schemes.** That is, they become transformations carried out mentally, without physical action. For example, when you are doing addition, you must mentally transform numbers in order to reach a solution: 3

Figure 8.3   Piaget believes that this baby's actions can be described with the same concepts that explain the actions of the girl in Figure 8.2. Both are applying schemes to objects in the world, but the schemes that the girl is using are considerably more interiorized than are the infant's schemes. He is applying "sucking" and "grasping" to a new object, a set of keys. She is applying judgments and perceptions (rather than physical actions) to a set of objects.

plus 5 become 8. If you are trying to understand a poem, you must mentally transform the concepts of the poem in order to put them together in a way that makes sense to you.

Both the action schemes of an infant and the interiorized schemes of an adult play the same central role in knowing. Whatever his age, a person seeks to understand his world by applying his schemes to objects and events, and he adjusts the schemes to fit the characteristics of the world. A task from an experiment by Mary Potter demonstrates the way schemes function. Look at Figure 8.6A, a photograph that is out of focus. What object do you think is pictured in the photograph? Next, look at Figure 8.6B, on page 177, which is the same photograph in slightly better focus. Does it still look like the same object, or could it be something different from what you first thought? Now look at Figure 8.6C on page 179, where the focus is improved a bit more. Do you think that you know what the object is? Your attempt to identify the object in these photographs exemplifies Piaget's view of knowing.

Assimilation and Accommodation   Piaget uses the terms assimilation and accommodation to describe the process of interaction between the person's application of a scheme to an object or event and the adjustments to the scheme that the object or event requires the person to make. As you attempted to understand the photographs in terms of a particular scheme (or hypothesis), you were assimilating the photographs to the scheme. The characteristics of the first out-of-focus photograph contributed to your original choice of scheme, but as you tried to adjust that scheme to fit the series of photographs, the photographs' changing characteristics continued to influence the scheme. That is, at all times during your application of the scheme, you were also accommodating the scheme to what you perceived to be the characteristics of the photographs.

Thus, the word **assimilation** refers to a person's active attempts to apply particular schemes to things and events in the world, and the word **accommodation** refers to the adjustment of those schemes to the characteristics of the things to be known. As shown in Figure 8.4, assimilation involves the effects of the scheme; accommodation, the effects of the things and events. When a baseball player is fielding a ball, he attempts to apply particular schemes for catching the ball (assimilation) and he chooses the schemes and adjusts them according to the way the ball is moving (accommodation). Assimilation and accommodation occur in any situation of knowing or doing.

Piaget defines "knowing" in terms of this continuous interaction of assimilation and accommodation, illustrated in the "knowing circle" in Figure 8.4. It is this interaction that Piaget sees as producing cognitive development from one period to the next. The schemes with which infants start life are relatively primitive. As they apply the schemes to the world around them, they must continually adjust the schemes so that they can assimilate objects and events that would not fit the schemes without this adjustment. Through the modification, infants' schemes become more refined and better accommodated to their world, and their intelligence grows. Figure 8.5 shows how a child applies a grasping and pulling scheme to a toy and accommodates that scheme to take account of the shape of the toy and the space between the bars of the crib.

Equilibration   The term equilibration sums up this process. Piaget believes that the mind constantly seeks an equilibrium of assimilation and accommodation. Think of the photographs of the fire hydrant. At the beginning, when you were trying to figure out what was pictured in them, you probably vacillated between noting specific characteristics of the photographs (accommodation) and trying to understand those characteristics in terms of particular schemes (assimilation). Only when you finally understood the photographs

Figure 8.4 The "knowing circle." Assimilation and accommodation are reciprocal processes that continue until a fit is achieved between a scheme and an object.

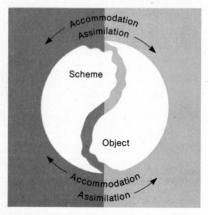

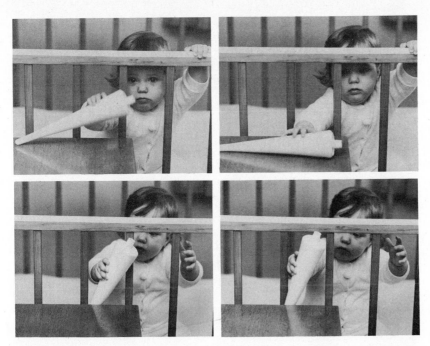

Figure 8.5 (reading from left to right and top to bottom) This child possesses a scheme for grasping objects and pulling them to her that does not adequately match the features of the environment that she is now trying to assimilate. Her scheme will not get the toy through the bars of the playpen. An accommodation to her scheme—the addition of turning to grasping and pulling—achieves a state of equilibrium.

did assimilation and accommodation reach a state of equilibrium, or balance. At that point, you could use your scheme to assimilate all the characteristics of the photograph because your scheme was fully accommodated to them.

In the following pages, as you read about the characteristics of thinking during development, keep in mind this model: Intelligence involves a person acting on the world and the world influencing the way that he can act: A person's intelligence is constantly attempting to move toward a state of **equilibrium** in which he can take full account of the characteristics of his environment—that is, in which assimilation and accommodation are in balance. It is this constant movement toward equilibrium that accounts for cognitive development.

The **construction of an understanding,** then, takes place through a series of encounters a child has with his environment. An encounter disturbs the child's cognitive equilibrium, and, through assimilation and accommodation, he reorganizes his understanding of the object or event in that encounter. Construction should not be thought of in the sense of, say, building a wall. It is not a piling up of discrete objects (experiences) to form a structure. The proper analogy is the construction of a clay sculpture of a person or animal: As new pieces of clay are added, the form not only grows but changes shape, continuously becoming better and better defined, until it accurately represents the reality of the thing sculpted.

Periods of Intellectual Development

Much of the power of Piaget's view comes from his documentation of exactly how children construct their knowledge of the world. In describing how children go about this herculean task, Piaget uses the concept of periods of intellectual development. The intellectual development of a human child, according to Piaget, includes four main periods: the sensorimotor period, the pre-operational period, the concrete-operational period, and the formal-operational period. Some of the periods are subdivided further into stages. The periods are **qualitatively different** from each other—the child thinks in different ways during different periods—and their **order is invariant**—the child must complete the sensorimotor period before he can reach the pre-

Figure 8.6 A What is pictured in this photograph? Arrive at a hypothesis if you can, then check your hypothesis with Figure 8.6 B on page 177.

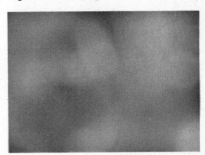

operational period, and he must complete the pre-operational period before he can reach the concrete-operational period, and so on.

The intellectual development of a child, however, is not an automatic process; it is dependent on the environment in which the child grows up. The speed of the child's development through the four periods varies widely in different environments, and it is possible that some people never reach the last one. Each of the four periods can be thought of as embodying a different kind of mind, and each type of mind has specific capacities (and specific limitations). In a suitably rich environment, each type of mind gradually develops the capabilities that will transform it into the mind of the next period. It is most important to note that the mind of each period includes within it the minds of earlier periods. For example, a child in the concrete-operational period still possesses the capacities that typified the two earlier periods (the sensorimotor and the pre-operational). Likewise, an adult who has mastered formal-operational thinking is capable of functioning at the level of all three earlier periods.

Although it is useful to learn the ages associated with each period of intellectual development, you should remember that they are only rough guidelines. The **sensorimotor** period encompasses infancy, approximately the first two years of life. The **pre-operational** period occurs during the preschool years. **Concrete-operational** thought begins to appear around school ages, when the child is from five to seven years old, and develops further during elementary school. **Formal-operational** thought first appears around the beginning of adolescence and can continue to develop throughout adulthood.

THE SENSORIMOTOR PERIOD

During the sensorimotor period (from birth to about age two), intelligence is primitive in form. It is based on overt action. Although its primitiveness might make it seem unimportant, sensorimotor intelligence is in many ways the most important type to understand because it is the foundation of later types of intelligence.

Practical Intelligence

Sensorimotor intelligence seems to be the basis of all intelligence. Virtually all animals that exhibit intelligent behavior seem to have sensorimotor intelligence in some form. Yet this period is the hardest for most people to understand, for reasons that will become evident. Piaget suggests the term "practical intelligence" as a rough synonym for sensorimotor intelligence. As this term suggests, an infant learns to *act* in the world, but he cannot *think* about what he is doing. He learns how to get along practically in the world of objects—how to bring about certain effects—but his intelligence is entirely on the level of actions. He has no understanding of what he is doing, only of how to do it.

Adults often operate at the sensorimotor level. For example, riding a bicycle, driving a car, or operating any complex machine occurs primarily at this level. In carrying out these activities, an adult has a sensorimotor understanding that certain actions, such as turning the handlebar of a bicycle, will produce certain effects, but he does not think about the particular actions or the particular effects; in fact, if he does think about them, he may have trouble carrying out the actions. Think about the way you are balancing a bike and it will probably start to wobble. When an adult thinks about what he is doing in activities like these, a higher—and, for bike riding, a less effective—level of intelligence takes over.

One difference between an adult and an infant is that the adult is capable of thinking about what he is doing. He can carry out an action in his mind

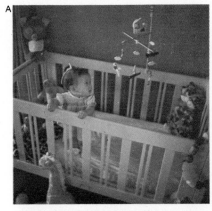

Figure 8.7   Children at Piaget's four periods of cognitive development. (A) The sensorimotor child interacts physically with objects (in this case, by looking at them), but he does not understand them in the sense that an adult does. Objects and actions are two sides of the same coin to him; objects do not even exist independently of his own behavior.   (B) The pre-operational child has the ability to represent objects and events mentally. Two pieces of wood can mean more to him than the sensations they cause in his eyes or the ways they can be moved by his muscles. They can be related to a plane he once saw, or the motions of birds he has watched.   (C) Concrete-operational thought is distinguished by the ability to understand certain logical properties of objects and events in a practical way. For example, some understanding of speed, force, and weight is necessary in order to launch a kite or to adjust its tail.   (D) The abilities of the formal-operational thinker go beyond the concrete here and now. The person at this stage can think abstractly and hypothesize about possibilities as well as understand actualities. This boy can systematically apply principles he understands about flight and the design of planes in order to solve a problem or to find new ways of doing things.

without actually performing it. He understands that his actions are distinct from the objects that he acts upon, and he realizes that his body is one object in a world of objects. The one- or two-month-old infant fails to make any of these important distinctions. He does not recognize that he has a body that is an object moving in space like other objects. He can be said to know about an activity only in the sense that he can actually carry it out. In short, he does not yet understand that there is a distinction between his own knowledge and actions and the things in the world that he is acting upon.

Object Permanence

In an ingenious series of experiments, Piaget has shown how infants gradually build up these distinctions. One group of observations illustrates especially well the nature of sensorimotor intelligence and shows how the primitive, action-based intelligence of the newborn infant is gradually transformed into the intelligence of a two-year-old. Most of the observations are simple and can be repeated by anyone, provided that care is taken to keep the infant's attention.

Piaget asked a simple question: How does an infant come to recognize **object permanence?** That is, how does a child know that an object does not stop existing when he can no longer see it or feel it or hear it? Piaget showed that very young infants do not have object permanence. They construct it, gradually and systematically, during the first eighteen to twenty-four months of life.

Early in infancy, anything that is not seen or touched or heard seems not to exist for the child. He will look at a toy that is held in front of his face and grasp the toy if it is put in his hand, but as soon as the object is moved out of sight and out of reach, he acts as if it had ceased to exist. He does not search

Figure 8.6B   Can you tell yet what the photograph is showing? Make another guess, then turn to page 179 and check your hypothesis with the better resolution of the photograph shown in Figure 8.6C.

for it or show any other sign that he believes in its continued existence. In addition, he does not coordinate his senses—that is, combine information from one sense with information from other senses. He does not recognize that objects that can be seen can also be touched or that objects that make a noise can also be seen.

In this world without stable objects, the infant's rudimentary intelligence is based on his actions. He understands things in terms of a few elementary schemes based on the reflexes that he is born with, such as grasping and sucking. He has all the normal human senses: He can see, hear, touch, feel warmth and cold, and the like. But these sensations acquire meaning for the infant only in terms of his action schemes. Through these schemes he learns to recognize certain stable sensory configurations that Piaget calls tableaux. From the second week of life on, for example, the infant can usually find the nipple of his mother's breast to suck. He can tell the breast from other things that can be sucked, and he can differentiate the nipple of the breast from the area surrounding it. He has learned to recognize the sensory tableau of the nipple. But this recognition does not mean the infant understands that the breast is an object or a part of a human body. He has merely learned that it is a stable sensory tableau and that, when the tableau is present, he will be able to use his sucking scheme in his accustomed way.

As the infant has more and more experience with the world around him, he develops more and more skill in applying his schemes and in recognizing tableaux that are appropriate to them. He also begins to coordinate some of the schemes—that is, to combine them into new, more complex schemes. For example, he coordinates grasping and sucking, developing the ability to bring objects to his mouth to be sucked. Earlier, the infant could suck objects that were put in his mouth and he could grasp objects that were placed in his hand, but he could not bring an object that he had grasped up to his mouth for sucking.

As these coordinations develop, the infant begins to show the first elementary signs of object permanence. Under some circumstances he pursues disappearing objects with his eyes. If an object is moved across his visual field, he not only turns his head to follow its path but continues to look along

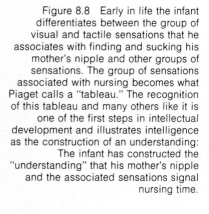

Figure 8.8 Early in life the infant differentiates between the group of visual and tactile sensations that he associates with finding and sucking his mother's nipple and other groups of sensations. The group of sensations associated with nursing becomes what Piaget calls a "tableau." The recognition of this tableau and many others like it is one of the first steps in intellectual development and illustrates intelligence as the construction of an understanding: The infant has constructed the "understanding" that his mother's nipple and the associated sensations signal nursing time.

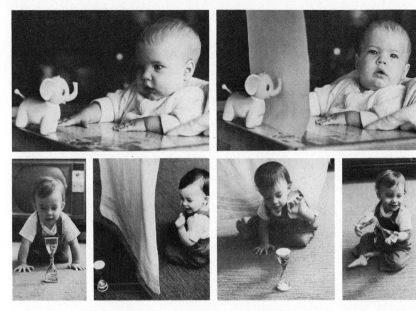

Figure 8.9 (top) An infant who sees his toy hidden from view may stare in its direction for a few seconds, but he will not look for it. He acts as if it has ceased to exist. (bottom) An older child will conduct a search for his toy in such a situation, which shows that for him the object has an existence that continues even when he cannot see it. He has acquired object permanence.

the path even if he loses sight of the object. Similarly, if only part of a familiar object is visible—such as the edge of a rattle that is almost covered by his blanket—he may reach for it. Earlier, he would not have reached for the rattle unless it was fully visible.

At the next stage in the development of object permanence, the infant for the first time searches for an object when it is out of sight. A familiar, desirable object is shown to him until he has displayed a clear interest in it. Then, while the child watches, it is put under a blanket or a pillow. At this stage the infant will move aside the obstacle and reach for the object. A simple act! But at earlier stages the child behaved as if the object had ceased to exist as soon as it disappeared (see top of Figure 8.9.) And even now he shows a strange deficit in his ability to locate hidden objects. If the object is placed under one pillow and then—in full sight of the child—is taken out from under the first pillow and put under a second one, the child looks for it under the *first* pillow. He is repeating the action that produced the object earlier rather than looking for the object where he last saw it.

Casual observation of an infant at this stage often seems to indicate that he understands the notion of permanent objects, but the impression is misleading. The infant does not understand that he is handling *objects*. For him, an "object" is a series of potential actions that he can bring about in the sights and sounds around him. When an infant at this stage is said to "grasp an object" or "look at an object," it must be kept in mind that only the adult observer—not the infant—knows that the thing grasped or looked at is an object with fixed properties.

When the child reaches the last purely sensorimotor stage in the development of object permanence, he can follow all visible movements of an object and therefore find it in the last place it was hidden. When an object is hidden under one pillow and then under a second one, the child reaches for it under the second one. Indeed, he can find it even if it is hidden under a third or a fourth pillow. The only limit remaining is that the child still cannot cope with invisible displacements. For example, an object is hidden in a matchbox, and the matchbox is placed under a pillow. While the matchbox is covered by the pillow, the object is secretly removed and left under the pillow. The empty matchbox is then put in front of the child. The child searches for the object in the matchbox, but he does not search for it under the pillow. He cannot

Figure 8.6C You may already know what has been photographed here; you probably have had to discard several hypotheses and modify others. Check your decision with Figure 8.6D on page 181.

yet take into account the possibility that something he did not see might have happened.

The final realization of object permanence comes when the child understands that objects can be moved from place to place even when he does not perceive their movements. This development marks the end of the sensorimotor period and the beginning of the pre-operational period.

THE PRE-OPERATIONAL PERIOD

Faced with the matchbox experiment, the pre-operational child can take account of invisible displacements; when the object turns out not to be in the matchbox, he looks under the pillow. If the object is not there, he widens his search. Is it under the table, or in the adult's pocket? And if he still cannot find it, he may turn to the adult and ask (as well as he can) where the object is.

Developing an awareness of object permanence is a truly impressive feat. Virtually every human child achieves what is in effect a Copernican Revolution. Before Copernicus, people looking at the sky accepted at face value what they saw. The stars, the sun, and the moon appeared to revolve around the earth, and people therefore believed that was what they did. Copernicus discovered that the earth and the other planets actually revolve around the sun, and that heavenly bodies only appear to revolve around us because the earth is turning. His discovery required him to deny what appeared to be true in order to understand the underlying reality. Similarly, the child who understands object permanence must realize that although objects seem to disappear periodically, they do not stop existing. Their existence does not depend on his perceiving them.

Representation

The attainment of complete object permanence is a result of a new capacity that the child has developed, a capacity called representation. For the first time, the child can evoke certain mental schemes in the absence of the overt actions, objects, or events on which the schemes are based. Put more simply, he can think about some actions when they are not being performed, objects

Figure 8.10 Unlike the sensorimotor child, the pre-operational child is able to make believe—to use some objects to symbolize others. This child is "painting" a tree with water from his plastic bucket.

when they are not present, and events when they are not happening. He shows the first signs of what people ordinarily call thought.

This new capacity produces a number of new abilities besides object permanence. For the first time, the child is capable of **deferred imitation:** He can imitate someone else's actions a long time after he has seen them. He also begins to show insight learning (discussed in Chapter 6). That is, he looks at a problematic situation, pauses to think about it for a moment, and then, after what seems like an "aha" reaction, solves the problem. And he begins to play **make-believe,** pretending that he is going to sleep or that a log he comes upon in the woods is a horse. Finally, in what is probably the most important development of all, the pre-operational child begins to use language. He begins to use true words and to say short sentences as discussed in Chapter 9. Each ability that occurs with the appearance of representational thinking is a sign of a new type of intelligence that, although still limited in some ways, is qualitatively different from sensorimotor intelligence.

Intuitive Thought and Its Limitations

Representational thinking permits an adultlike intuitive understanding of many complex tasks and situations. In insight learning, for example, the child solves a problem by what is normally called intuition. **Pre-operational intelligence,** which is characterized by this intuitive thinking based on representation, is a dramatic advance over sensorimotor intelligence, but it also has certain limitations: Because he has not yet developed operational intelligence, the child lacks the logical capacities of older children and adults. For one thing, his thought is **egocentric.** This term does not mean that the child is deliberately selfish. Rather, it means that he is a prisoner of his own viewpoint. He does not understand that different people have different viewpoints and that his own is merely one among many. His thought is centered on himself because he does not know that any other viewpoint exists.

Piaget and Baerbel Inhelder describe a good experimental demonstration of egocentrism. A child is shown a model of a mountain range composed of three mountains in a triangular arrangement. The model is large, so that the child has to walk around it to look at all its sides. Each mountain has different objects on it, objects that the child can easily identify. After he is familiar with the landscape, he sits on one side of it, facing one mountain. The experimenter sits on another side and asks the child which of several pictures shows what the experimenter sees. The child repeatedly chooses the picture showing his own view of the landscape. He cannot mentally coordinate the various views, so he cannot figure out how the landscape looks to someone in a different position.

The following poem illustrates a second characteristic of pre-operational thinking. It was written by Hilary-Anne Farley, who was five years old at the time, and it appears in Richard Lewis' *Miracles,* a collection of children's poetry.

I Love Animals and Dogs

I love animals and dogs and everything.
But how can I do it when dogs are dead and
  a hundred?
But here's the reason: If you put a golden egg
  on them
They'll get better. But not if you put a star
  or moon.
But the star-moon goes up
And the star-moon I love.

The poem shows what Lev Vygotsky calls **complexive thinking.** Instead of unifying a number of thoughts under a single concept, it jumps from one idea

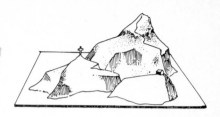

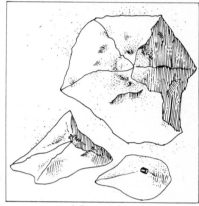

Position A

Figure 8.11 A model used to demonstrate egocentrism. Piaget and Inhelder first had children walk all around the model and look at it from all sides. Then they seated children of various ages at position A and asked them how the scene would appear to observers at other positions. Pre-operational children regularly indicated that the scene would appear as it did from position A, no matter where the observer was located. Their thinking did not allow them to mentally reconstruct the scene from a point of view other than their own.

Figure 8.6 D Finally, a fire hydrant. The cognitive processes you used in making hypotheses and modifying them in your attempt to understand the photograph exemplify Piaget's concepts of assimilation and accommodation. (After Potter, 1966.)

Figure 8.12 A pre-operational child will find this set of blocks of absorbing interest because cues for their use are built into them. A dowel protrudes from each block and fits into a hole in the block that forms a part of one level of the pyramid. Also, the central area of each level is slightly elevated to fit snugly into a depression in the next higher level. These cues help guide the child's actions.

to the next, frequently showing connections between adjacent ideas but having no overall integration. Some element in one idea makes Hilary-Anne think of another idea. Some element in the second idea makes her think of a third idea, and so forth. Although every idea is related to some other, the various ideas are not coordinated into a single system or around a single concept. Complexive thinking like Hilary-Anne's is common in children in the pre-operational period.

Both Piaget and Heinz Werner describe a third main characteristic of pre-operational thought. The child has a strong tendency to **perceive human characteristics in objects.** Werner mentions a two-year-old boy who saw a cup lying on its side and exclaimed, "Poor, tired cup!" Another child said that a towel hook was a "cruel" thing. A four-and-a-half-year-old child called a camera tripod "proud" when it stood straight and "sad" when it leaned over at an angle. The important point about these reactions is that the children seem to actually see the cup as tired, the towel hook as cruel, and so forth. They have not yet learned to make all the necessary distinctions between human beings and objects, so they perceive objects as having human attributes.

A fourth limitation of pre-operational intelligence is that the child is not capable of carrying out tasks that require him to direct and coordinate his own thinking. He needs **direct, external cues to guide and sustain his behavior.** For example, a four-year-old will play for long periods with building blocks like the ones shown in Figure 8.12 because he can always see the connectives, which help focus his attention on making the blocks fit together; also, he can always see the progress that he has made in building. Figure 8.13 shows two tasks Piaget used to demonstrate the importance of prominent cues for pre-operational children. If a five-year-old is given the sticks in Figure 8.13A, he can easily put them in order from largest to smallest. The size differences between the sticks are large enough to be noticeable for the child. But if he is asked to arrange the sticks in Figure 8.13B, he will fail because the differences in the sizes of the sticks are too small to serve as cues to guide him. Only when he reaches the concrete-operational period will he be able to put these sticks in order of size.

These limitations of pre-operational intelligence form a unified picture. On the one hand, the child's capacity for representation allows him to carry on new, complex kinds of mental activity. On the other hand, the child does not yet have the ability to organize his thinking into coordinated systems that he can direct and control. His thinking is egocentric because he cannot coordinate various viewpoints into a single system that takes all of them into account. It is complexive—his thoughts run on of themselves, and he flits from one idea to another—because he cannot coordinate his ideas around a single concept. Similarly, he cannot coordinate characteristics of people with characteristics of objects, so as to avoid projecting human characteristics onto objects. And he cannot carry out a task that requires him to coordinate and direct his thinking unless he has the help of prominent concrete cues.

THE CONCRETE-OPERATIONAL PERIOD

The end of the pre-operational period does not herald the end of intuitive thought. Much adult thinking is similar to the intuitive thought of the pre-operational child, according to Piaget. In daydreaming, for example, one wanders from this idea to that in much the same complexive way as Hilary-Anne did in her poem. But an adult can think in ways that the pre-operational child cannot. Most notably, an adult can switch back and forth between intuitive intelligence and operational intelligence.

At around five to seven years of age, the child develops an elementary kind of operational thought: He starts to understand concrete operations (this term is defined in the course of discussion in this section). In reading the following discussion, however, you should keep in mind that many of the child's efforts during this period of development are still limited to intuitive thinking. In dealing with many problems, he uses pre-operational thinking rather than concrete-operational thinking. Even if the child has the benefit of good schooling, it will take him five to ten years to fully develop his concrete-operational capacities.

Conservation

Conservation is one of the most striking developments during this period. A child in the late pre-operational period can correctly predict the effects of certain simple manipulations of liquids. If liquid from a medium-width container is to be poured into a narrow container, he can usually predict correctly that the liquid will be higher in the narrow container than in the medium one. That is, the pre-operational child usually understands that changing the width of a container will change the height of a fluid, and he knows whether the height will go up or down. But he still does not understand that the amount of liquid stays the same when the liquid is poured from jar to jar.

What is required for him to develop conservation of amount of liquid? The child must be able to coordinate his thoughts about the length and width of the first container, the length and width of the second container, and the change brought about by pouring the liquid from the first container into the second. The pre-operational child cannot do this; he considers the state of each container separately and consequently chooses the jar that "looks like more." The concrete-operational child, on the other hand, pays close attention to the transformation that occurs as the liquid is poured, coordinating his thoughts about that transformation with his thoughts about the height and width of the containers. The change from pre-operational to concrete-operational intelligence is similar for other kinds of conservation, including those shown in Figure 8.14.

What is the nature of this coordination, and how does it take place? To explain it, Piaget uses the concept of a system of operations. An **operation** is a special kind of scheme, defined as an *interiorized action or transformation that is reversible.* The operation is **interiorized** in the same sense that the schemes of intuitive (pre-operational) thought are interiorized: The child can

Figure 8.13 (A) A five-year-old pre-operational child can usually arrange the sticks shown in the top photograph in decreasing order of size, because the large differences in their lengths provide obvious guiding cues. (B) The sticks in the bottom photograph are too much alike; the cues are not obvious enough to guide the pre-operational child's comparisons.

Figure 8.14 Examples of problems for which a child must acquire conservation. Concrete-operational children interiorize the possibility of making and unmaking the transformations for each task shown here. Thus, they come to see the lengths and quantities as unchanged in each case. Pre-operational children, who are not able to imagine the transformations required, respond to perceptually striking but irrelevant aspects of the objects in attempting to answer the questions. For example, pre-operational children will answer that there are more marbles in the bottom row than in the top one.

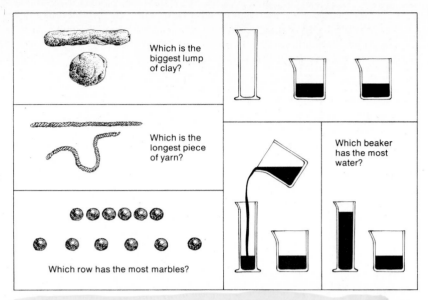

Which is the biggest lump of clay?

Which is the longest piece of yarn?

Which beaker has the most water?

Which row has the most marbles?

Figure 8.15 One system of concrete operations is the addition of classes. Concrete-operational children can produce the sorting shown in (B) and can answer questions comparing the number of toys in each grouping. They use the classification scheme shown in (A). Pre-operational children do not have these skills. They are confused by such questions as "Are there more dogs or more poodles?" whereas the concrete-operational child can answer correctly, "Dogs."

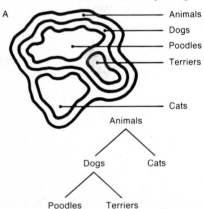

A

Animals
Dogs
Poodles
Terriers

Cats

Animals

Dogs   Cats

Poodles   Terriers

B

carry out the transformation mentally without carrying it out physically. The operation is a **transformation** because it specifies how one state is changed into another state. And it is **reversible** because the system of operations also contains another operation that can mentally *undo* the transformation to restore the original state. **Operational intelligence** is thought that is based on such systems of operations.

An example is in order. Without actually pouring any liquid, a child who understands conservation can think about the changes that pouring would bring about (interiorization). He can mentally coordinate the two states of the liquid by considering how pouring transforms one state into the other (transformation). And he can restore the original state by mentally pouring the liquid back into its original container (reversibility).

Classification

Conservation is only one of many different systems of operations that the concrete-operational child gradually masters. Included among the others are several dealing with classification. How well can a child understand the relationships between different ways of classifying things? The answer to that question illustrates especially well the way the concrete-operational child coordinates his thinking into systems.

Addition of Classes One of the main skills needed for classification is called the addition of classes. A child needs to understand, for example, that the class of dogs is made up of the class of poodles, the class of terriers, and the classes of all other types of dogs. That is, he needs to understand that the classes for each type of dog are added together to form the class "dogs."

As with conservation, the pre-operational child has some of the capacities that are necessary for understanding addition of classes, but he cannot coordinate his thinking. A simple example shows the kinds of questions he can answer and the kinds he cannot. Suppose a child is given eight toy poodles, two toy terriers, and three toy cats. The child is first asked to sort the toys into piles that are all alike. An early pre-operational child will not even be able to sort them properly, but a late pre-operational child will manage to make three simple groups—one of poodles, one of terriers, and one of cats. When he has done that, the experimenter begins to pose a number of questions.

Which of the toys are dogs? The child points to the group of poodles and the group of terriers. Which are cats? He points to the group of cats. Which of the toys are animals? He points to all three groups. Are there more poodles or more terriers? The child correctly chooses poodles. Are there more dogs or more cats? He correctly indicates more dogs.

So far the child is doing well; he seems to understand classes and to be able to use them properly. But his answers to a few key questions show that this conclusion is incorrect. Although he understands the meaning of the words, he cannot coordinate the various classes so as to be able to carry out simple addition of classes. The child is asked the key question: Are there more dogs or more poodles? "More poodles," he says. Are there more dogs or more animals? "More dogs," he says. A second pre-operational child's answers may be incorrect in a different way. He will say that the number of dogs is the same as the number of poodles and that the number of animals is the same as the number of dogs.

Both children have a similar difficulty. They cannot coordinate two levels of classification: They cannot move up and down between the class of animals and the subclasses of poodles and terriers. It should be made clear that the questions asked the children are in no sense trick questions that fail to reflect the child's true abilities. Children who answer the questions correctly can also construct the simple type of diagram shown in Figure 8.15, whereas children who answer incorrectly cannot.

Multiplication of Classes   A second skill required for classification is the multiplication of classes. For example, given the geometrical shapes in Figure 8.16A, the child cannot construct the arrangement diagramed in Figure 8.16C. A concrete-operational child behaves very differently. He can readily make up the three-by-three grouping of figures, and he can explain how the rows and columns are organized. He has mastered multiplication of classes.

As with addition of classes, the pre-operational child's failure comes from his inability to coordinate two dimensions. He cannot move back and forth across the two axes that are diagramed in Figure 8.16C. That is, he cannot deal with colors and shapes at the same time.

Systems of Concrete Operations

Conservation of liquid, addition of classes, and multiplication of classes all illustrate the development of **concrete operations**—systems of operations

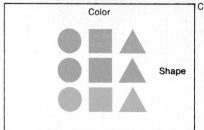

Figure 8.16   The photographs in (A) and (B) show a problem that requires multiplication of classes and the partial solution that a pre-operational child might be able to achieve.
The diagram in (C) shows how the concrete-operational child can "multiply" two bases for classification (shape and color) to produce a complete classification.

that can be applied to concrete (tangible) things in the real world. The examples show that the pre-operational child is unable to coordinate his thinking about two separate states or two separate levels of analysis, as the concrete-operational child can. In conservation of amount of liquid the height and width of the liquid before pouring must be coordinated with the height and width of the liquid after pouring. In addition of classes two levels of classification must be coordinated, and in multiplication of classes two kinds of classification must be coordinated. The concrete-operational child coordinates these things by constructing systems of operations in which his thought moves readily back and forth between one level or state and the other. The back-and-forth movement is allowed by the reversibility of the operations in the system: Whatever mental transformation the child thinks about can be readily undone by a reverse mental operation. The effect of reversibility is to allow the child to think virtually simultaneously about the two different states.

Although most of Piaget's examples come from problems related to science, like conservation and classification, the child's capacity to coordinate his thinking into systems is not limited to scientific problems. For example, he can now understand and follow the rules of children's games, such as marbles, hopscotch, and baseball. He is less egocentric—better able to coordinate other people's viewpoints with his own and to understand that his viewpoint is only one among many. His thinking has taken on many of the characteristics of adult thought.

But it still has a way to go. There are definite limitations in the child's capacity to coordinate his thinking. Piaget calls the period ''concrete operations'' because the child can deal only with concrete objects and events. He can coordinate *concrete characteristics in an actual situation* but not possible characteristics in hypothetical situations.

Piaget argues that the concreteness of operational thought in this period produces a kind of unevenness in the child's abilities. He develops specific concrete-operational systems for dealing with specific types of situations, but he cannot coordinate the systems to form a higher-order system. This incapacity is one of the reasons that all types of conservation do not develop simultaneously. Conservation of number develops first, then conservation of amount of liquid, still later conservation of weight, and so on. Because the child cannot coordinate his operational systems, each type of conservation seems like a new problem. He cannot tie the related systems together and understand all types of conservation at once.

THE FORMAL-OPERATIONAL PERIOD

In the formal-operational period the limitations of concrete operations are overcome. Around the beginning of adolescence a new set of capacities, called **formal-operational intelligence,** begins to appear. The child becomes able for the first time to think hypothetically and to carry out systematic tests of the various possible explanations of a specific event. As a result, he can solve new kinds of problems.

One of Piaget's tasks demonstrates particularly well the central difference between concrete operations and formal operations. A child is presented with a balance beam, as shown in Figure 8.17C. There are two ways to alter the balance of the beam: by adding weight to one side, and by moving a weight farther from or closer to the fulcrum of the beam.

The concrete-operational child can understand the influence of adding and taking away weights. He quickly learns, for example, that if one side of the beam has more weights on it than the other side, balance can be restored either by removing the extra weight from that side or by adding weight to the other side. He can also understand the influence of distance from the fulcrum. If the

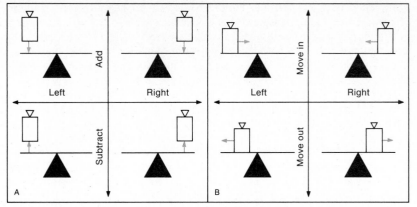

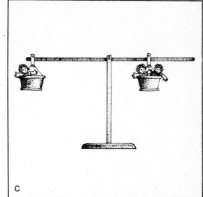

weight on one side of the beam is farther from the fulcrum than the weight on the other side, he sees that balance can be restored either by moving the far weights closer to the fulcrum or by moving the near weights farther from the fulcrum.

But the concrete-operational child cannot understand the way the two influences (weight and distance) are related. He cannot extract the principle that an extra weight on one side of the balance can be counteracted by moving the weights on the other side farther from the fulcrum. He fails to see that distance can compensate for weight, and weight, for distance. In other words, the child can deal with weight alone or distance alone, but he cannot coordinate the two.

The influence of weight alone and of distance alone can be understood in terms of the concrete-operational ability of multiplication of classes, as shown in Figure 8.16. During the formal-operational period the child develops the capacity to coordinate these two separate concrete-operational systems (one for weight and one for distance) and so to understand how changes in weight are related to changes in distance. This capacity to coordinate concrete-operational systems allows for the development of many new skills.

Figure 8.17 A full understanding of the principles by means of which the beam in (C) can be balanced is not reached until formal operations are acquired. Such an understanding requires the coordination of the two sets of principles diagramed in (A) and (B). (A) shows the multiplication of the two classes "left-right" and "add-weight–subtract-weight." (B) shows the multiplication of "left-right" and "move-weight-in–move-weight-out." The concrete-operational child can understand both of these ways of balancing the beam, but he cannot coordinate them. He understands that he can compensate for weight added to the right, for example, by adding weight to the left, but he does not understand that he can also do so by moving the weight on the left farther away from the fulcrum.
(After Piaget and Inhelder, 1969.)

Systematic Experimentation

One of the most important new skills of the formal-operational child is the ability to consider all possible combinations of events in a problem or task and to exclude all combinations that are irrelevant to the problem. In other words, the formal-operational child can carry out **systematic experiments,** in which he considers all possible causes of an event and rules out one after another until he discovers the actual causes. The concrete-operational child, on the other hand, has difficulty going beyond the combinations that actually occur in the real situation. He cannot systematically consider all possibilities.

The material for an experiment that Piaget used to investigate this skill is as follows. There are four beakers of clear, colorless, odorless liquids labeled with numbers 1, 2, 3, and 4, and there is a smaller bottle, labeled g, also containing a clear, colorless, odorless liquid. First, the child is presented with two unmarked glasses. One contains a mixture of liquids 1 and 3 and the other contains liquid 2. The experimenter adds a few drops from g to each glass, and the liquid in one glass turns yellow while the liquid in the other glass remains colorless and clear. Now the child is given some empty glasses and is asked to produce the yellow color himself, using the liquids in the beakers. If he succeeds, he is questioned about the function of each of the four liquids.

The combination that produces the yellow color is 1 plus 3 plus g. The liquid in 2 is plain water and has no effect on the reaction, and the liquid in 4 prevents the yellow from appearing. Because the child must find out what

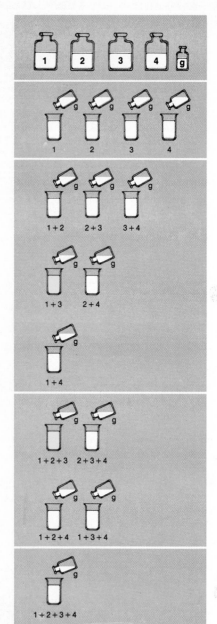

Figure 8.18 A problem that requires the systematic examination of hypotheses for its solution. The chemicals selected by Piaget and Inhelder for this problem have unexpected interactions. It is virtually impossible to determine how the color yellow is produced without trying every possible combination of the liquids, as shown here, and keeping track of the results. Not until a child reaches the formal-operational period can he conceive of such a procedure. (After Piaget and Inhelder, 1969.)

each liquid does by trial and error, he must try all possible combinations. Otherwise, he cannot be sure of his conclusions.

When presented with this task, a concrete-operational child often begins by systematically trying out all the single possibilities. He may test 4 plus *g*, then 2 plus *g*, then 1 plus *g*, then 3 plus *g*. When none of these combinations produces yellow, he is apt to say, "I tried them all and none of them works." With a little coaching from the experimenter, he may realize that more than one liquid can be combined with *g*, but he then mixes the liquids haphazardly. He is unable to test all combinations systematically. Inhelder and Piaget mention a child who tried 1 plus 4 plus *g* and 2 plus 3 plus *g* and then stopped, failing to understand that every liquid could be combined with every other liquid, as shown in Figure 8.18. When the experimenter suggested to the child that he try additional combinations, he poured the fluid 1 plus *g* (which he had mixed earlier) into the jar already containing 2 plus 3 plus *g*. This mixture produced yellow, but the child did not know why. When asked to make the color again, he unsystematically tried several other combinations, none of which worked.

An older, formal-operational child can systematically consider all possible combinations of the four liquids. That is, he can coordinate all the possible ways of putting the liquids together so as to come up with a single system that includes all possible combinations. Some children may need a paper and pencil to keep track of the combinations that they have made, but they nevertheless understand how to generate the full set.

Hypothetical Ideas and Abstract Thinking

A child's ability to coordinate concrete-operational systems within a formal-operational system also leads to several other changes in thinking. The concrete-operational child is tied to the actual, but the formal-operational child develops the **capacity to consider the hypothetical,** even when the thing hypothesized is highly fanciful. For example, consider the following question: "Yesterday excavators found a three-year-old skull of an animal with five feet and three heads that lived to be fifty years old. What is wrong with this statement?" A concrete-operational child will say that the question is silly because animals do not have five feet and three heads. A formal-operational child can accept the "silly" hypothesis and reason out the answer. In a similar way, the concrete-operational child tends to assume that liquids must show conservation of amount, whereas the formal-operational child is capable of thinking about the possibility that some liquids might conceivably not be conserved.

With the capacity to deal with the hypothetical comes the **ability to understand abstract principles.** This new capacity is extremely important to the child. It allows him to study such fields as mathematics, science, and language on a different, less concrete level than he has earlier, and it brings about dramatic changes in his daily concerns. He may become preoccupied with certain abstractions, such as ethical ideals, conformity, and phoniness. He will often apply his new abilities to his own thoughts and motives: "I found myself thinking about my future, and then I began to think about why I was thinking about my future, and then I began to think about why I was thinking about why I was thinking about my future."

INTELLIGENCE AND ENVIRONMENT

Now that the major periods of intellectual development have been outlined, it is wise to emphasize several key points that are often misinterpreted.

First of all, *intelligence involves an active interaction between the person and his world.* The person actively assimilates things and events in the world and accommodates to those things and events. Consequently, it is a serious mistake to treat the developmental periods as an innate unfolding of intelligence that occurs without the influence of the environment. The nature of the environment necessarily affects the course of development, because knowing and learning always involve accommodation.

Second, *what Piaget has described is the general course of the development of intelligence.* His descriptions of each period are not meant to indicate the specific skills an individual child will possess. Instead, they indicate the general capacities of children at each period. Even the particular tasks used to illustrate general capacities cannot be solved by all children who have reached the appropriate period, because the tasks require specific skills that some children do not possess. For example, if a person in the formal-operational period has never seen a balance beam or any similar instrument, he will have to learn how the beam works before he can use it to demonstrate his capacity for formal-operational thought.

Even an adult with full formal-operational capabilities cannot use them in tasks that require specific skills he does not possess. An astronomer does not usually have the skills necessary to dissect a frog or to classify types of insects. Faced with those tasks, he would not be able to use his considerable formal-operational capacities very effectively. Similarly, a child who understands addition of classes will not be able to demonstrate his understanding if he is dealing with words and classes that are new to him.

In sum, it is important to avoid an oversimplification of Piaget's theory. The periods cannot be used as pigeonholes to explain all of a person's intellectual abilities. They merely outline certain general capacities. For most practical purposes, the specific skills that a person possesses are at least as important as the period that he has reached.

SUMMARY

1. Jean Piaget's systematic observations of children over the years have shown that children's minds are qualitatively different from adults' minds.

2. Because Piaget sees intelligence as constantly moving toward equilibrium, he calls the overall process by which intellectual growth takes place **equilibration.**

   a. The human mind actively seeks to make sense of what it sees, hears, and so on. It does so by constructing and applying schemes to objects and events in its world. The **schemes** of infants are organized actions, which they modify to fit physical objects and events; older children and adults apply **interiorized schemes,** which are mental constructs that can be used mentally, without overt action.

   b. The process of applying schemes is called **assimilation;** the adjustment of those schemes to fit an object or event is called **accommodation.** Both assimilation and accommodation occur in any situation of knowing or doing, and it is the continuous interaction of these processes that produces development from one cognitive period to the next.

   c. When, for any given event, assimilation and accommodation are in balance—when a person has applied a scheme and the scheme fits the event so that the event makes sense—then **equilibrium** has been produced.

   d. When a child's cognitive equilibrium is disturbed and, through a series of encounters with the environment requiring assimilation and accom-

Figure 8.19 Jean Piaget began his researches on intellectual and moral development with his own children over half a century ago. He continues his work at the Institut Jean Jacques Rousseau in Switzerland, where he and his colleagues interview and test children from Genevan schools and preschools. His theory of the nature of intelligence and the periods of intellectual growth form the substance of this chapter.

modation, the child reorganizes his experience so that his understanding of an event accurately reflects the reality of that event, the child has **constructed an understanding** of it.

3. Piaget has shown that there are four distinct **periods** of intellectual development between birth and adult cognitive functioning.

    a. Cognitive functioning at each of the four periods is qualitatively different from that of the preceding period.

    b. The order in which the periods follow each other is invariant, although not everyone achieves the cognitive abilities characteristic of the later periods.

    c. The capacities of an earlier period are always present in the later periods.

4. The transition from one period to the next, that is, the course of cognitive development, is greatly dependent on the individual's environment.

5. The first cognitive period is the **sensorimotor period** (from birth to about age two). Intelligence during this period is based on overt action; the infant learns to bring about certain effects in the world of objects, but he has no understanding of what he is doing. He cannot think without acting. The most important development during this period is the recognition of **object permanence,** that is, that objects continue to exist when they can no longer be seen.

6. The **pre-operational period** is the second period (from about age two to about age seven). It begins when the child has a complete grasp of object permanence.

    a. A new capacity, **representation,** is what permits the full development of object permanence. That is, a child can construct some simple mental schemes in the absence of the objects or events that the schemes deal with; in essence, he can think about some things.

    b. Representation also enables the child to develop **deferred imitation,** the capacity to imitate another's acts long after the child has seen them; **insight learning,** a mental solving—on an intuitive level—of certain simple problems; the ability to play **make-believe;** and, most important, the ability to use **language.**

    c. One important limitation on cognitive development during this period is the child's **egocentrism,** the inability to understand viewpoints different from his own. Other limiting characteristics are **complexive thinking,** the inability to coordinate thoughts into integrated concepts, the **tendency to perceive human characteristics in objects,** and the **inability to direct his own thinking** without external cues.

7. In the third period, the **concrete-operational period** (from about age seven to early adolescence), the child gains the ability to coordinate his thoughts about a given event into a system of thinking. In Piaget's terms, the child can deal with a **system** of operations.

    a. An **operation** is a special kind of scheme, having the following **characteristics:**
    (1) it is **interiorized,** that is, it can be carried out mentally and does not require physical action; (2) it is a **transformation,** in that it specifies how one condition or state of a material or event is changed to another; (3) it is **reversible,** that is, the system of operations always

includes another operation that will mentally reverse the conditions created by the transformation in order to restore the original state.

   b. The capacity to deal with systems of operations is necessary to such basic concrete-operational tasks as **conservation, addition of classes** and **multiplication of classes,** and, in turn, skills of this kind are required to understand and follow the rules of many children's games.

8. The final developmental period is called the **formal-operational period.** It is characterized by the ability to simultaneously coordinate two systems of operations. This ability allows the person to **carry out systematic experiments**—to systematically consider all possible combinations of events in a task and exclude irrelevant ones. In addition, it allows the person to deal not only with concrete operations but also with the **hypothetical** and the **abstract.**

SUGGESTED READINGS

Evans, Richard I. *Jean Piaget: The Man and His Ideas.* New York: Dutton, 1973. Includes both an interesting interview with Piaget and his brief autobiography.

Fischer, Kurt W. *Piaget, Learning, and Cognitive Development* (forthcoming). A clear, easy-to-read summary and discussion of Piaget's theory, which focuses specifically on his approach to learning and cognitive development.

Furth, Hans G. *Piaget and Knowledge: Theoretical Foundations.* Englewood Cliffs, N.J.: Prentice-Hall, 1969. An in-depth treatment of Piaget's theory of knowing, with special emphasis on its philosophical and biological foundations.

Holt, John. *How Children Fail.* New York: Dell, 1970. An analysis of the shortcomings of contemporary educational methods in light of Piaget's theory.

Lesser, Gerald S. *Children and Televsion: Lessons from Sesame Street.* New York: Random House, 1974. One of the originators of Sesame Street, the innovative educational TV program for children based on cognitive-developmental theory, discusses some of the effects it has had on elementary-school education.

Piaget, Jean. *The Construction of Reality in the Child.* New York: Basic Books, 1954. A description and analysis of how the infant develops an understanding of the physical world: objects, space, time, and causality.

Piaget, Jean. *Biology and Knowledge.* Chicago: University of Chicago Press, 1971. In this recent book, Piaget describes the significance of his lifetime work for understanding the human ability to know and the relationship of that ability to human biological heritage.

Piaget, Jean, and Baerbel Inhelder. *The Psychology of the Child.* New York: Basic Books, 1969. Piaget and Inhelder's own summary of their work. Its main usefulness is as a summary of major experimental findings rather than as an introduction to Piaget's theory.

Werner, Heinz. *Comparative Psychology of Mental Development.* Rev. ed. New York: International Universities Press, 1966. A useful compendium of research on mental development, including observations of primitive thought and insanity as well as studies of thought in children.

In Shakespeare's *Richard II*, Thomas Mowbray is exiled from England for life, and he responds in agony:

The language I have learned these
   forty years,
My native English, now I must forgo;
And now my tongue's use is to me
   no more
Than an unstringed viol or harp,
Or like a cunning instrument cased up,
Or, being open, put into his hands
That knows no touch to tune the
   harmony:
Within my mouth you have engaoled
   my tongue,
Doubly portcullised with my teeth
   and lips;
And dull, unfeeling, barren ignorance
Is made my gaoler to attend on me.

Every time I read that speech, I am chilled, for I love English—so rich in vocabulary, so bright in metaphor, so hospitable to foreign terms, so fanciful in idiom, so flexible, so colorful, so fascinating. I could not bear to lose its use.

Fortunately, I couldn't be in Mowbray's position now. In his day, English was a minor language spoken by three million people on one small island. Today English is spoken the world over, and it would be hard to find a patch on the globe where someone speaking English could not manage to find someone else to understand him. No one speaking any other language is quite that fortunate. Every other language is spoken by fewer people or in less widespread fashion or (almost always) both.

And yet English isn't just English. The English of London, Dublin, Canberra, Boston, Charleston, Brooklyn, and Indianapolis are each different. The differences aren't enough to preclude understanding, but they are quite enough to produce curiosity, suspicion, or even automatic dislike. George Bernard Shaw's *Pygmalion* is based on this.

An immigrant (my father, for instance) can learn every facet of his adopted country's culture and yet, even after a generation, give himself away every time he opens his mouth. Though he may have learned the vocabulary and grammar of his new language perfectly, the subtle distinctions of sound will defeat him.

The dialect can be a prison, too, placing one behind the bars of the sound one makes, forever and forever. I am the prisoner of my boyhood sounds. I make my living as a writer and speaker, and I trust I may be forgiven if I say that there are surely few in the land who can surpass me in the use of the English language in the written form. When I speak, however, I must accept the inevitable and speak humorously, for it is difficult to take me seriously. You see, I speak Brooklynese, and the sounds of Brooklynese are, alas, associated with, at best, uneducated shrewdness.

Isaac Asimov

9
Language Development

Figure 9.1 All children without handicaps acquire their native language during their first four or five years of life. As long as they grow up hearing language used around them, children will develop language. The human mind appears to be somehow "programmed" to understand and use any particular language, but the precise way that natural capacities and environment act together has not yet been determined.

If you have ever tried to learn a foreign language, you probably know how complex and painstaking a task it can be. Now try to remember "learning" your native tongue. For the sake of discussion in this chapter, we will assume it was English. Do you remember having to memorize the verb forms differentiating past from present and future? Or learning how to formulate a question? It is very unlikely that you do remember, because your use of English was fairly sophisticated by the time you were three years old and highly skilled by your fifth birthday.

Obviously one cannot say that people "learn" their native language in the same way college students learn a foreign language. One must speak of language acquisition as a developmental process. But what part does learning play in the process? What is it about the human mind that makes it capable of acquiring and using language at a time of life when the mind is otherwise cognitively unsophisticated? And do we know precisely what language is?

Psychologists and linguists all over the world are attempting to answer these questions. This chapter will transmit some of their findings and the discussion surrounding them. Before discussing children's acquisition of language, it will attempt some answers to the broad question "What is language?" by looking into recent experiments that involve teaching language to chimpanzees.

WHAT IS LANGUAGE?
First, language, is clearly not synonymous with speech (which is oral language). Persons born deaf learn to communicate by means of sign language. And children who can hear but who cannot speak because of a physical handicap show that they understand completely the uses of language and all its intricacies. Eric Lenneberg studied one such child and tested him in several ways for language comprehension. When the child was eight, Lenneberg

Figure 9.2 How Brown's three criteria distinguish human speech from other communication systems. The units in human speech (patterns of sounds) correspond to other objects (such as people) and are therefore *meaningful*. The possibility of using these units to refer to objects that are, for example, hidden from view fulfills the criterion of *displacement*. A limited number of these units can be used in different combinations to communicate an unlimited number of new meanings; this feature fulfills the criterion of *productiveness*. It is interesting to use these criteria to judge whether blushing, for example, counts as language (probably not) or whether shrugging one's shoulders does (perhaps so).

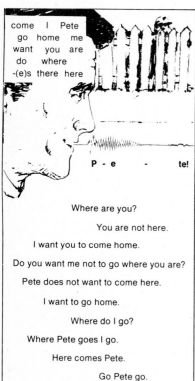

told the child a short story and questioned him about its content, using complex grammatical constructions. The child's responses, which he gave by pointing to things, nodding or shaking his head, or responding to instructions, left no doubt that he had a complete grasp of his native language.

If language is not speech, then are the communication systems of animals language? Is there a definition that sets off and describes human language?

Brown's Definition

Psycholinguist Roger Brown has suggested that language has at least three essential characteristics. First, language allows the individual to talk about things that are not immediately present. That is, it allows **displacement,** the transmission of information about objects or events that are removed in time or space from the communicator, such as last Saturday's dance or the record player in the next room. But the communication systems of certain lower organisms also allow displacement; for example, according to ethologist Karl von Frisch, the honeybee performs a dance that informs other bees of the location of a nectar source, which may be some distance away from the hive (see Chapter 3). The concept of displacement, then, although necessary to define human language, is not sufficient to set language off from other means of communication.

A second characteristic of language cited by Brown is **meaningfulness** (or semanticity); that is, the symbols of language (words or gestures) are more than simple behaviors: They *represent* objects, events, or abstract ideas. The communication systems of some animals are meaningful, but in a rather limited way. Apes, for example, have a small repertoire of calls and grunts to signal the presence of either food or danger or to indicate anger, fear, and other emotions. In general, however, animal "vocabularies" are small, and the "meanings" the symbolic sounds convey are social and emotional meanings, not references to objects or ideas.

The characteristic unique to human language, Brown says, is its **productiveness:** its open-ended quality. If humans were limited to one-word utterances, we would need to have a tremendously large vocabulary. Instead, language allows us to combine words into phrases and sentences, thus vastly increasing the number of meanings that can be expressed. From a limited number of words, we can produce an infinite number of meanings.

Chimp Talk

Psychologists have long been interested in investigating the linguistic ability of man's near relative, the chimpanzee. In two well-known cases couples raised chimps in their homes and tried to teach them to speak. Both efforts ended in failure. The first chimp, Gua, raised by the Kelloggs around 1930, never learned to speak at all. The second, Viki, was raised by the Hayes about 1950. She learned to make sounds that were rough approximations of only four words. Spoken language does not seem suitable for chimps, partly because they do not have the appropriate vocal apparatus.

Recently, experimenters have had considerably more success with two different approaches: teaching chimps to use gestural signs or to use concrete symbols rather than vocal signs. As a result, the debate about whether chimps have the ability to use language has been reopened. The controversy hinges on defining the minimum requirements that a form of communication must meet before it is called a language.

The Sign Language of Washoe In the mid-1960s Beatrice and R. Allen Gardner, at the University of Nevada, decided it would make more sense to teach a chimp a gestural language; they set out to teach a female named Washoe to use **American Sign Language (ASL),** the gestural language used

Figure 9.3 Washoe at about five years of age. She is shown here using the ASL sign for "hat." Once she became practiced at signing generally, Washoe could use a newly acquired sign in requests that showed displacement. For example, she could use "open food drink" to ask that the refrigerator be opened and that she be served a drink.

by many deaf people in North America. Each sign in ASL corresponds to an individual word. Many of the gestures visually represent aspects of the word's meaning. For example, to sign "flower" you extend the fingers of one hand and keep them joined at the tips, so that your hand looks something like a closed tulip; then you touch your fingertips first to one nostril and then to the other, as if sniffing a flower. To sign "drink," you make a fist, extend your thumb, and touch your thumb to your mouth. ASL also has devices for signaling tense and other grammatical meanings and is fully adequate for expressing anything that can be expressed in speech.

When her training began, Washoe was a year old. The Gardners and their associates signed to her and each other all day in ASL. They tried to make Washoe's situation similar to that of a human child acquiring a spoken language. Sometimes they would just chat with her, and sometimes they would teach her a specific sign. After three years of training, Washoe had acquired eighty-five signs.

Once Washoe had learned a particular sign, she quickly generalized its use to appropriate activities or objects. For example, she learned the sign "more" to request more tickling (which she greatly loved); she then used the same gesture to request more hair brushing, more swinging, and a second helping of food. Clearly, Washoe had grasped the meaning of the sign for "more." In another instance, she learned the sign "dirty" to describe things that were soiled, and a short time later she began to use the sign to insult her keeper when she became angry with him: "Roger dirty." Furthermore, as soon as she had learned eight or ten signs, she spontaneously began to use some of them in combination, forming such sentences as "Hurry open," "More sweet," "Listen dog," and "Roger come." Later she combined three or more signs: "Hurry gimme toothbrush," "You me go there in," and "Key open food." Her early sentences expressed the kinds of semantic relationships that have been observed in the early sentences of human children. She can comprehend signs made by others, and she can make them herself. She can use signs together to express particular meanings.

The Gardners are currently replicating their research with two other chimps who came to live with them soon after the chimps were born. When Washoe was five (and had a vocabulary of some 160 signs), several of her teachers had to leave the project. Because it would have been difficult for Washoe to get used to new teachers, the Gardners gave her to Roger Fouts, a graduate student who had worked with Washoe and who was going to the Institute for Primate Studies in Norman, Oklahoma. Fouts is now working with seven chimps, two of whom are being prepared to participate in an experiment with Washoe. These two are learning a limited number of signs, and later Fouts

Figure 9.4 Lucy, Lucy's cat, and her trainer, Roger Fouts. Lucy, along with Washoe, is one of Fouts' seven chimpanzees; she has lived in a human family since she was two days old (she is now eight years old), and she has been learning ASL for the last three years. Fouts takes Lucy and her cat on frequent trips and visits to human friends to give Lucy a variety of experiences about which to sign and to put her in a variety of situations that will encourage her to do so.

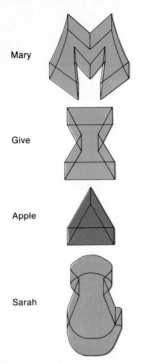

Mary

Give

Apple

Sarah

Figure 9.5   A sentence formed from the plastic symbols Premack and his associates used in their training regimen with the chimpanzee Sarah. Note that the symbols used cannot be seen as models of the objects to which they refer; the symbol for apple, for example, has no physical resemblance to an apple.

will try to get Washoe to teach them others. The two chimps already communicate with each other in certain situations designed to encourage them to do so. Another chimp is scheduled for motherhood. Her trainers want to see if she will attempt to teach signs to her infant.

Sarah and Her Symbols   David Premack, of the University of California at Santa Barbara, has taken a very different approach to teaching chimps language. Premack's first chimp, Sarah, was about six years old when her training began in 1968. Sarah lived in a laboratory instead of a homelike environment, and she received special one-hour lessons five days a week. Her language symbols were small pieces of plastic, varying in color and shape, like those shown in Figure 9.5. Each piece of plastic stood for one word. Sarah learned to construct sentences with the pieces by placing them vertically on a special magnetized board. Premack's system was less difficult for the chimp than the Gardners' ASL in one sense: Because the symbols were always in front of her, she did not have to hold them in her memory; in ASL only one sign can be presented at a time, and earlier signs in a sentence must be remembered. On the other hand, Sarah is mute when she does not have her symbols; she cannot take them with her wherever she goes.

Sarah learned about 130 symbols. Her trainers used standard conditioning techniques, rewarding her for correct responses although never punishing her for errors. Sarah has mastered linguistic forms that are much more complex than those used by Washoe. Premack is now extending the experiment, using two other chimps.

Lana and Her Computer   In yet another approach, Duane Rumbaugh and his colleagues at Georgia State University are teaching a three-year-old chimpanzee, Lana, to operate a special typewriter controlled by a computer. The machine has fifty keys, each displaying a geometric configuration that represents a word in a specially devised language called Yerkish (after the primatologist Robert M. Yerkes). When Lana types a configuration, it appears on a screen in front of her. She has spontaneously learned to correct herself by checking the sequence of configurations on the screen. In other words, she has learned to read.

Is Chimp Talk Language?

Washoe, Sarah, and Lana are all using language, according to Roger Brown's definition. They are using symbols in meaningful ways. Their languages

Figure 9.6   Lana working at her computer console. In order to activate the console Lana must pull down a bar above her left arm. She faces the console and pushes keys that have different meanings. A representation of the sequence of selections she makes is projected on a screen above the console. She has just composed the sentence "Please machine give piece of banana," checked the sentence on the screen, judged it to be correct, and is ready to push the "period" button. The banana dispenser is located directly below the console. Lana can use this communication system to obtain food, drink, and human companionship.

allow displacement; when Washoe signs "You me go there in," she is talking about some place she is not in at the moment. And all the chimps have used their various symbols in productive ways, although compared to human productiveness, their use of symbols is very limited.

It can be argued, of course, that these chimps had to be trained to use language; the natural communication of chimpanzees is not noticeably productive. And they were trained by people, so what they are using are really human languages. In that case, the parameters defining language set out earlier still apply only to human languages.

Perhaps what can best be learned from these studies is something about the capacities or abilities organisms must have in order to acquire and use language. It is this aspect that most interests Premack: He is interested in the nature of these capacities. Premack feels that if he is successful in devising a training program that can teach language to chimps, he can go on to apply that method to human beings who have trouble learning language—autistic children, retarded people, and aphasics.

THE CAPACITIES THAT LANGUAGE REQUIRES

The fact that humans are the only species of animal that spontaneously uses language in a productive way seems to indicate that there is some biological, species-specific mechanism involved. If it is true that people are somehow "programmed" to learn language, how do environmental factors influence this biological program when a child is learning language? And does the acquisition of language depend on a certain level of cognitive development, or does language develop independently? Although these questions have by no means been completely answered, there are some findings, discussed in the following sections, that at least begin to answer them.

Biological Requirements

Eric Lenneberg argues that several specializations of the human body make spoken language possible. There are specializations in the articulatory apparatus and in the motor regions of the brain that permit fine control of the production of sounds, and specializations in the auditory cortex of the brain that permit fine discrimination of sound patterns. Several researchers, including Peter Eimas and his colleagues, have shown that one-month-old babies can hear the difference between the sounds *ba* and *pa*. Lenneberg says there are also specializations in the breathing apparatus that permit prolonged speech, and other sensory and cognitive specializations that elaborate and coordinate these activities.

The linguist Noam Chomsky has theorized that all the natural languages of the world have certain common features and that the human brain is so organized as to be sensitive to the kinds of distinctions that all languages make. In mastering the sounds and grammar of his native language, Chomsky says, the child is aided by this characteristic of his brain. The chimpanzee, whose brain differs in many important ways from that of the human being, may have strict limitations on the kinds of auditory and grammatical distinctions it can make.

A recent finding suggests that some autistic children may suffer from a specific kind of brain damage that produces a deficit in their ability to master the sounds of language. Autistic children show severely disturbed behavior: They avoid social interaction, are unable to speak, do not respond to most spoken language (although they are not deaf), and frequently repeat stereotyped behaviors, such as rocking back and forth or jumping up and down waving their hands. John Bonvillian and Keith Nelson have reported the case of a nine-year-old autistic boy called Ted, who, prior to his encounter with them, had undergone several different kinds of therapy, all with no success.

● Areas of the brain associated with speech

◖ Larynx

"oo"   "aw"   "ee"

Figure 9.7 The human speech apparatus, including the larynx (which houses the vocal cords), areas of the brain associated with speech, and other such essential physical structures as the tongue and lips. Below are the configurations of these structures necessary for the production of three vowel sounds. The specialized anatomy that makes human speech possible is easy to see. The corresponding specializations of the brain are not. But the ease with which children acquire language suggests that the brain must in some way be specially designed for the production and comprehension of speech sounds.

Figure 9.8 (from left to right) An autistic boy being trained by John Bonvillian makes the ASL sign for "break," the sign for "baby," and then makes two attempts at the sign for "sleep." (The correct sign is to fold both hands together on one side of the face.)

They set out to teach Ted American Sign Language, the language of the deaf that was also taught to Washoe the chimpanzee. Ted learned quickly. Within the first six months he acquired fifty-six signs, which he used spontaneously to communicate with other people, and he began to combine signs into sentences. Since that time he has continued to make further progress in learning ASL. As he has learned to sign, he has shown general marked improvement in many other areas: His stereotyped behaviors and temper tantrums have decreased sharply, and his interaction with other people has improved dramatically. Preliminary reports indicate that efforts to teach ASL to additional autistic children are having similar success.

These findings indicate that some autistic children may suffer from an inability to understand spoken language. As a result, of course, they could never learn to speak. Their inability to understand the language spoken around them and to communicate their own desires and thoughts to others may account for much of their bizarre behavior: Social interaction for a child with this kind of specific language deficit would be extremely frustrating and difficult. Many of the problems of the autistic child, then, may come from a special kind of brain damage—a loss of the normal human capacity to analyze spoken language.

If there is something about the brain that facilitates normal language acquisition, however, that something changes with time: There seems to be a **sensitive period** for language acquisition in human beings, from about two to about fourteen years of age, as discussed in Chapter 3. We have all observed the ease with which children in a foreign country pick up a new language while their parents are still groping for a way to express themselves. Also, deaf children can acquire some language if they are given the opportunity to do so during the sensitive period, but they have difficulty learning any more later in life. And children who lose their speech as a result of brain damage during this period are more likely than adults to recover.

General Cognitive Abilities

Perhaps the most basic cognitive requirement for language is the ability to manipulate symbols independently of objects. According to Jean Piaget, children lack this ability until they become capable of **representational thought,** at about eighteen to twenty-four months of age, when they move from the sensorimotor to the pre-operational period of intelligence (see Chapter 8). Before that time, they do not form mental representations of objects; therefore, they cannot think about objects that are not physically present, and they cannot use symbols to talk about objects that they cannot think about. During the sensorimotor period, children gradually develop the abilities that culminate in representation and language. Slowly they learn that objects continue to exist even when they cannot see the objects.

Roger Brown and Lois Bloom, among others, suggest that the *child's first sentences are linguistic expressions of sensorimotor intelligence.* Once the child is able to recognize objects as permanent, and separate from actions, he is ready to name things in the environment and comment on or request more of these permanent things. Once the child realizes that objects continue to exist when removed from his sight, he can begin to ask about where things are that are out of his immediate perceptual field. And when the child can think about himself, other persons, and objects, and can understand them as potential sources of causality and potential recipients of the force of an action, then he can use words as agents and objects. Table 9.1 lists the emerging linguistic abilities that reflect these developing cognitive capacities.

Because Piaget's stages of cognitive development appear to be universal, it

Table 9.1   Basic Meanings in Children's Two-Word Sentences

Grammatical Function	Meaning	Example
Nomination	Names or calls attention to something in the environment.	"That car."
Recurrence	Comments on, or requests the recurrence of, a person, process, or thing.	"More candy."
Nonexistence	Expresses the nonexistence of some object or entity in terms of present context.	"Sun gone," "Allgone egg."
Agent and action	Indicates that someone or something causes an action.	"Mommy go."
Action and object	Indicates that someone or something undergoes a change of state or receives the force of an action.	"Push car."
Agent and object	Indicates a semantic relation between the agent of an action and its object, without specifying the action itself. There is no parallel in adult speech.	"Daddy ball," (when Daddy is doing something to the ball).
Action and locative	Indicates that an action occurs at a particular place.	"Write paper."
Entity and locative	Indicates that a person or thing is located at a particular place.	"Lady home."
Possessor and possession	Indicates that an object belongs to someone.	"Daddy chair."
Entity and attribute	Indicates that something has a particular attribute.	"Little dog."
Demonstrative and entity	Points out some specific entity.	"That truck."

Source: Roger Brown, *A First Language: The Early Stages* (Cambridge, Mass.: Harvard University Press, 1973).

might seem possible to predict a universal course of linguistic development just on the basis of what we know about cognition. But the situation is complicated by the fact that language has its own characteristics that are independent of the characteristics of cognition. Cognitive limitations do impose constraints on what the child can achieve linguistically at a particular age, but sometimes a concept that seems simple for a child fails to find linguistic expression until a later stage of development because the linguistic form is grammatically complex. Also, some linguistic forms that are easily within the child's cognitive grasp may be difficult because they are less easily perceived than others. Compare the full possessive, ''That is John's hat,'' with the elliptical possessive, ''That is John's.'' In the elliptical form, the *s* is easily heard because it is at the end of the sentence and stressed, whereas in the full possessive, the *s* is likely to be slurred over.

Although it is not possible to draw a one-to-one correspondence between the sequence of cognitive advance and the sequence of linguistic advance, it is clear that certain cognitive abilities are required for language acquisition. How do the chimps fare in this respect? Chimps have shown for certain the capacity for representational thought, including the ability to imitate someone's action at a later time (you may have seen them do so at a zoo) and the ability to solve problems by thinking about them instead of by trial and error (see the discussion of animal learning in Chapter 6). It is beyond this point that chimps and humans may part company. So far it seems that chimps never go much beyond the intuitive egocentric thought characteristic of a four-year-old. Children, on the other hand, continue to advance through the remaining periods of cognitive development; they acquire the ability to understand conservation and classification and to think hypothetically. Chimps have not demonstrated such capacities, and this suggests some strict limitations on the potential sophistication of chimpanzees' language use.

The results of ongoing chimpanzee studies have indeed furthered our understanding of the nature of language and the capacities it requires. It is now time to leave the chimps until more results from these studies are available and to turn to a description of the remarkable achievement of human children in acquiring their native tongue.

HOW CHILDREN ACQUIRE LANGUAGE

Children grow up in very different kinds of cultural and social environments, yet they seem to go through a remarkably similar sequence of stages in

Figure 9.9 An early stage in the development of language is the period of babbling that begins toward the middle of the first year of life. The baby begins with vowel sounds and brings in consonant sounds later. At first not all of his sounds closely resemble the speech he is hearing. He seems to be practicing and playing with his ability to produce sounds. By the age of ten months, however, infants begin to try to match the sounds and rhythms they hear.

learning the language they speak. One child may reach a particular stage at a somewhat earlier age than another, but both do reach that stage; one child may express himself more fluently or more eloquently than another, but all normal children learn the basic features of their language.

Early Vocalizations

Before a child speaks his first recognizable word, he has a considerable amount of practice at vocalizing. At birth, babies can cry, and by three months, they can coo. During the next few months, the sounds they spontaneously produce increase in frequency and variety; by six or seven months, they are able to babble—to chant various syllabic sounds in rhythmic fashion. Early babbling, a type of motor play and experimentation, is not limited to the sounds used in a particular language. Instead, infants seem to make sounds from all languages; American children may babble French vowels and German rolled *r*s. For the first six months of life, deaf babies cry and babble like children who can hear, a further indication that early vocalizations are spontaneous and relatively independent of what the child hears. Eventually, the child develops the capacity to imitate the sounds made by others and to control the sounds he can make.

Some researchers believe that imitation is very important during the process of acquiring speech sounds and that parents can encourage their infants to practice the sounds of their language by rewarding them when they say something that sounds like a word. Others believe that mere exposure to speech is sufficient. One thing, however, seems clear: It is not necessary for a child to practice speech sounds in order for him to learn to *understand* spoken language. Children (like the boy mentioned earlier that Eric Lenneberg studied) who are unable to produce normal, articulate speech but who hear perfectly well—and who therefore have never imitated speech or been rewarded for speaking—can understand all the complexities of phonology and grammar. They indicate their comprehension by pointing to pictures, nodding or shaking their heads, responding to instructions, and so forth.

By the end of their first year, children know the names of a few people or objects, and they begin to produce their **first words.** In order to reach this stage, the child must understand that sound can be used to express meaning. Generally, the first wordlike sounds are merely accompaniments to actions; for example, "bye-bye" is said only when the child is waving his hand at someone. The first true words refer to the immediately tangible and visible;

Figure 9.10 At approximately one year of age most children produce their first true words. Their communication has become meaningful. A child's first words are typically monosyllables, or repeated monosyllables, such as "dada," "mama," or "wah" (for water). When the child acquires a new word, he often starts applying it to a variety of things in his environment.

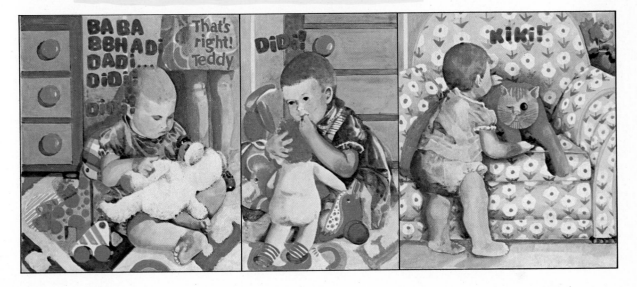

Figure 9.11 At about two years of age, the child begins to string individual words together into sentences. As was true when the child was using only single words, his meaning is almost impossible to determine without a knowledge of the context in which he is speaking. But the child now refers often to things not immediately present (displacement) and combines various words, two at a time, to express new meanings (productiveness).

the child's language does not yet exhibit displacement. Words are used to label objects or give commands ("Dog!" "Cookie!"). It may be that children at this stage are actually producing "one-word sentences," intended to convey complicated underlying meanings for which adults would use sentences. But we cannot credit the child with having a true grammar until he begins to combine words into two-word sentences, which occurs around his second birthday.

Two-Word Utterances

The concepts that the child expresses in his first two-word sentences are not much different from what he tried to say with one word. But this two-word stage is especially significant for two reasons: (1) It represents a striking advance in young children's ability to code their understanding in linguistic terms and to project their ideas more fully into the world of social interaction; and (2) even at this earliest stage of sentence formation, one can see that the language is structured by grammatical rules.

Rules and Grammar It is important to understand that when psycholinguists say that a person—a child or adult—has a grammatical rule, they do *not* mean that the person can state the rule explicitly. Few people can state even the most common rules of their grammar; in fact, no *complete* formal grammar of any language has ever been written. What psycholinguists do mean is that a person's pattern of speech shows that he is observing a **rule,** whether or not the rule exists in his head. Psycholinguists decide that a child has a rule: (1) if the child's behavior is consistent with the rule; (2) if the mistakes he makes are predictable on the basis of the rule; and (3) if he corrects himself or others to conform to the rule.

The rules for constructing sentences in a language are known collectively as the **grammar** of a language. "Grammar" is a word that tends to frighten people, probably because they associate it with boring classroom lectures on the "correct" way to write or talk. Modern linguists, however, compile formal grammars for the purpose of describing the way people actually talk; a grammar represents what people must know in order to use a particular language. You can think of grammar as a system of rules lying between the meanings you wish to convey and the sentences you actually utter.

Because individuals know the grammar of their native tongue, they can produce and understand sentences they have never before encountered. This productive aspect of language is extremely important, because most sentences are novel events—a fact that surprises many people, who assume they originally learned their language merely by imitating the sentences spoken by others. You can prove to yourself how rare duplication is by selecting any sentence in this book and then trying to find another one just like it. Your chances of success are very low. And yet, although you probably have never heard or seen the sentence you selected in that exact form before, you understand it. Theoretically, the number of possible English sentences is infinite, and a given individual encounters only a small number of them during his or her lifetime. According to one estimate, it would take 10,000 billion years (nearly 2,000 times the estimated age of the earth) merely to utter all the possible twenty-word sentences in English.

The Rules Governing Early Language   A linguist or psychologist who wants to find out what is grammatically acceptable for an adult can simply ask him. An adult speaker of English would have no difficulty rating "The men are nice" as grammatical, and "A man are nice" as ungrammatical. But children under four are unable to make these kinds of overt judgments. Roger Brown and Ursula Bellugi have reported the disastrous results of an attempt to ask a two-year-old about his grammar:

Adult: Now Adam, listen to what I say. Tell me which is better . . . some water or a water.

Adam: Pop go weasel.

With very young children, there is no recourse but to record the child's speech and to try to infer his linguistic competence from what he actually says or to test his linguistic comprehension in indirect ways.

One of the best-known studies of language development is one in which Brown and his collaborators, Ursula Bellugi, Colin Fraser, and Courtney Cazden, worked with three children they call Adam, Eve, and Sarah. At the start of the study, Adam and Sarah were twenty-seven months old and Eve was eighteen months old; the children were just beginning to combine words in two-word utterances. The researchers visited them in their homes at regular intervals, collecting samples of their speech, until Adam and Sarah were five years old. (Eve moved away nine months after the study began.)

Brown found that a child's speech is not much like that of an adult. A child's utterances are short, and his or her vocabulary is largely limited to nouns and action verbs. Nonessential words, such as articles, prepositions, and conjunctions, are omitted, much as they are in telegrams. Prefixes and suffixes (such as the *ing* in *going*), which would be included in adult telegrams because they are not charged for, are also omitted. People who know the child can usually understand what he means, and they often respond by expanding his utterances into well-formed adult sentences. Adjacent are some examples of a young child's **telegraphic speech** and his mother's interpretation, as recorded by Brown and Bellugi.

Brown and several other investigators have discovered that even at this early stage the child's speech is highly structured. The child does not merely juxtapose any word with any other word, nor is his language simply a collection of random deviations from the adult system. Psycholinguists can write formal rules that describe what is acceptable in the child's system and what is not.

In general, children at this age preserve adult word order in their speech. For instance, a two-year-old might say, "Eat cake," while devouring his birthday cake. An adult, of course, would say, "I am eating the cake," which indicates that he is the actor, that eating is in progress at present, and that the

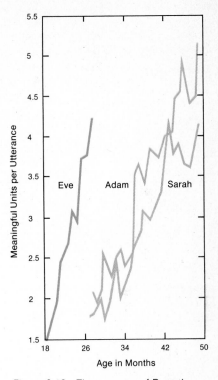

Figure 9.12   The progress of Brown's three subjects during the period he and his colleagues studied the children's acquisition of the English language. The average length of their utterances is plotted as a function of their age. The steady increase in length reflects the children's increasing ability to string words together in grammatically complex sentences. Brown suggests the kinds of factors that caused the irregularity seen in these curves when he noted that Eve may have had a cold on the only day that she showed a downward jog in her progress. Eve acquired language considerably earlier and faster than did Adam and Sarah. (After Brown, 1973.)

Child	Mother
Baby highchair	Baby is in the highchair.
Eve lunch	Eve is having lunch.
Throw Daddy	Throw it to Daddy.
Pick glove	Pick the glove up.

Adult	Child
I am drawing a dog.	I draw dog.
I do not want an apple.	I do a apple.
Read the book.	Read book.

cake is what is being eaten. Although the child fails to include all the proper inflections, he does correctly put "cake" after "eat," which tells the listener that the cake is the object being eaten rather than the agent that is doing the eating. When Brown and Fraser asked children between two and three years old to repeat sentences that were spoken to them, one child made the typical responses shown in the margin.

On the other hand, the literature is full of endearing examples of childish sentences that do not look like reduced imitations of adult sentences: for example, "all-gone sticky" (after washing hands). Even though such utterances are not predictable from the adult rules, they are predictable from the child's rules.

Underlying Meanings   When psycholinguists first started to analyze the speech of children at the two-word stage, they concentrated on the formal grammatical rules that govern the distribution of word classes, such as nouns and verbs, in the child's sentences. Lois Bloom has argued convincingly that such an analysis is of limited value because it describes a sentence in the same way no matter how it is used. Bloom argues that one must take account of the **context** of an utterance in order to know the **underlying meaning.** For example, Kathryn, a child studied by Bloom, used the sentence "Mommy sock" in two different contexts—once as she was picking up her mother's sock, and another time as her mother was putting Kathryn's sock on Kathryn's foot. In each case, the child's sentence was composed of two nouns, but in the first context the sentence appeared to express possession, Mommy being the possessor, whereas in the second, Mommy was the agent performing an action involving the sock.

Similarly, at twenty-one months Kathryn used the following sentences:

1. No fit. (She was having trouble putting a toy lamb into a small block.)
2. No dirty soap. (She was pushing away a piece of unwanted dirty soap in the bathtub.)
3. No pocket. (She was unable to find a pocket in her mother's skirt.)
4. No Mommy. (She was pulling away from someone, not her mother, who had offered to comb her hair.)

The first of these negatives seems to express denial, the second rejection (of the dirty soap), and the third nonexistence (of a pocket). The fourth sentence is in fact an affirmation, that Kathryn wants Mommy. You can see that merely describing the **surface structure** of a sentence gives an incomplete picture; the apparent underlying structure must also be analyzed.

Another factor, besides context, that provides information about the underlying meaning of children's utterances is their **intonation.** With two words like "Daddy book," the child may (1) emphasize "Daddy," indicating possession (This is Daddy's book.); (2) use a rising inflection, indicating a question (Is this Daddy's book? or Will Daddy read a book?); (3) emphasize "book," signifying a command for Daddy to read the book.

Psycholinguists are finding that throughout the world young children express the same kinds of meanings. In his recent book, *A First Language,* Roger Brown examined data from several different children and proposed a set of eleven basic meanings (listed earlier in Table 9.1) to account for about 75 percent of early two-word sentences. (Other investigators, including Lois Bloom and I. M. Schlesinger, have suggested similar although not identical sets.) According to Brown, the addition of a few less-frequent meanings to this set allows one to account for almost all early utterances.

By the time they reach the end of the two-word stage, young children have mastered much of the basic grammatical machinery they need to acquire their native language. Most of the more complex rules of grammar are acquired in the next two or three years.

Acquiring Complex Rules

Children seem to acquire grammatical rules in a fairly stable order. There is some variation from child to child, but not as much as might be expected. Certain rules are apparently acquired in steps; a good example is the use of the negative. Bellugi found that two-year-olds have a very simple rule for forming negative sentences: They simply add "no" to a positive statement: "No want stand," "No gonna fall," "No write book." This rule seems to be adequate as long as the child's sentences are quite simple, but as his sentences grow in complexity, more complex rules of negation become necessary. The child learns to place "no" or "not" just before the verb: "You no have one," "He not bite you," "I not get it dirty." The last step is to add the required auxiliary verb: "You don't have one," "He isn't going to bite you," "I won't get it dirty."

Thomas Bever has discovered an example of rule acquisition in which two-year-olds actually perform better than four-year-olds because of a rule that the four-year-olds have developed. (Bever prefers to call the rules that children use "strategies" and to reserve the term "rule" for linguists' grammars.) Two-, three-, and four-year-olds individually acted out the following types of sentences by using a toy horse and a toy cow.

1. The *cow kisses* the horse.

2. It's the *cow that kisses* the horse.

3. It's the horse that the *cow kisses*.

4. The horse is kissed by the cow.

Surprisingly, two-year-olds tend to act out the first three sentence types correctly, but their performance on the fourth (passive) sentence is nearly random. Three- and four-year-olds consistently reverse the interpretation of sentence 4, making the horse the actor and the cow the recipient of the kiss. The four-year-olds also tend to incorrectly interpret sentence 3, picking the horse as actor. Why do two-year-olds seem to "do better" on sentences 3 and 4 than four-year-olds? Bever suggests that the two-year-olds have a simpler strategy: If a noun and verb occur in sequence, they interpret that noun as actor of the action. If anything interrupts this simple sequence, as in sentence 4, the

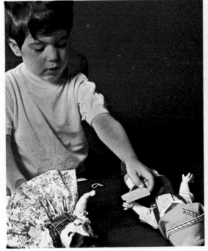 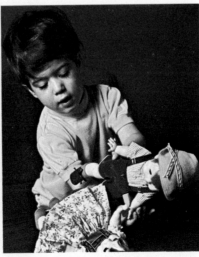

Figure 9.13 How can a researcher know for sure how a young child is interpreting adult sentences? One way is to have the child act the sentences out. This boy has been handed two dolls and a washcloth and asked by an experimenter to "Show me 'The boy is washed by the girl.'" The boy treats this sentence as though it were "The boy washes the girl." The grammatical rules that he has acquired so far are inadequate to correctly process a sentence in the passive voice.

two-year-old will have no rule or strategy to handle it, so the random choice results. The strategy of four-year-olds, developed beyond the simple noun-verb sequence, is that the first noun in a sentence is the actor. That is why they consistently misinterpret sentences like 3 and 4. It seems that *children do not progress directly toward adult grammar but rather construct and discard a variety of temporary grammars as they go along.*

By the age of five, a child's speech is much like that of an adult. He seems to have mastered most of the basic rules of grammar. Correct use of questions called **tag questions** is a good indication of mastery of rules. Roger Brown and Camille Hanlon report that when Adam was four years and seven months old, he asked the adjacent questions.

I made a mistake, didn't I?

He can't beat me, can he?

Ursula is my sister, isn't she?

At first glance, these sentences may not seem very complicated or difficult, but a child has to have considerable knowledge of his language in order to produce them correctly. First, he must realize that he should use a negative tag ("didn't I") when he expects a "yes" in response to his question, but an affirmative tag ("can he") when he expects a "no" response. He also must be able to substitute a pronoun for a noun; that is, he must replace *Ursula* with *she* in the third tag question. He must know how to use auxiliary, or "helping" verbs, such as *did* in the first example. And he must be able to reverse the order of verb and pronoun ("can he" instead of "he can"). Figure 9.14 illustrates the sequence of rules a child must follow to generate a tag question correctly.

Overregularization

As the child's speech becomes less and less telegraphic and as he begins to acquire more complex rules, he tends to commit errors of overregularization. That is, he overextends a grammatical rule to instances where it should not apply. Overregularizations, which are very common in the speech of three- and four-year-olds, are "smart mistakes," because they show that the child is trying to use general rules and that his speech is systematic.

A good example of overregularization is the way children learn forms of the past tense in English. At first, they correctly use common but irregular past-tense verbs like "fell" and "came," verbs that are very frequent in adult English. Each word probably enters the child's repertoire as a separate vocabulary item. But then the child learns the general rule for forming the regular past form by adding a *d* or *t* sound to the base, as in "walked" or "hugged." Once he acquires this rule, he tries to apply it to the irregular

Figure 9.14 When a speaker forms a tag question, he must follow the process diagramed here, although he is probably unaware that he is doing so. Children's ability to form such questions is evidence that their linguistic behavior is regulated by fairly sophisticated rules, which they have acquired without specific training.

(From Ursula Bellugi, "Linguistic Mechanisms Underlying Child Speech," in *Proceedings of the Conference on Language and Language Behavior,* 1968.)

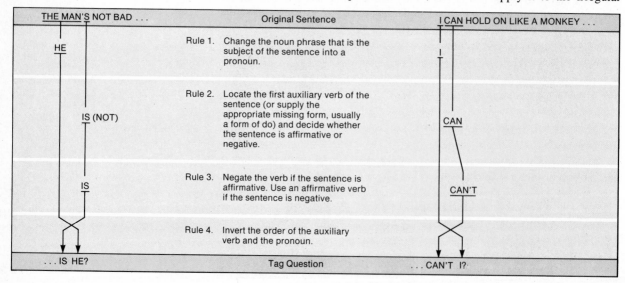

THE MAN'S NOT BAD . . .	Original Sentence	I CAN HOLD ON LIKE A MONKEY . . .
HE	Rule 1. Change the noun phrase that is the subject of the sentence into a pronoun.	I
IS (NOT)	Rule 2. Locate the first auxiliary verb of the sentence (or supply the appropriate missing form, usually a form of do) and decide whether the sentence is affirmative or negative.	CAN
IS	Rule 3. Negate the verb if the sentence is affirmative. Use an affirmative verb if the sentence is negative.	CAN'T
	Rule 4. Invert the order of the auxiliary verb and the pronoun.	
. . . IS HE?	Tag Question	. . . CAN'T I?

verbs as well, producing such incorrect sentences as "He goed to the store," or "I falled down." Similarly, once the child learns the general rule for forming plural nouns by adding an *s* or *z* sound to the singular form (dog/dogs), words like "foots," "mans," and "mouses" begin to creep into his conversation. The important point is that, although the child may have been using correct (irregular) forms for months, these forms are temporarily replaced by incorrect forms because of overregularization.

Such behavior cannot be explained by imitation—most of the children studied by psycholinguists have come from homes where incorrect verb forms are rarely used. Nor can it be explained by simple reinforcement, because presumably the initial, irregular forms were reinforced, practiced, and correctly used before being replaced by the incorrect forms. It seems children are predisposed to look for regularities and to create order in their language.

LANGUAGE AND ENVIRONMENT

Most empirical evidence so far collected indicates that children's brains are neurologically programmed to figure out very efficiently the structure of any particular human language. Children readily acquire language provided that they live in an environment where the language occurs in a communicative setting—that is, where it is related to activities, objects, and needs. Beyond this general requirement, psychologists have so far been unable to specify the exact nature of environmental factors that influence children's language acquisition. Two processes by which the environment influences children's learning of other behaviors are imitation (discussed in Chapter 10) and reinforcement (discussed in Chapter 4). But no simple mechanism of imitation or reinforcement can account for children's acquisition of language.

That a mechanism of direct imitation is inadequate to explain language acquisition is obvious simply because children do not repeat what adults say to them. In a case reported by David McNeill, for example, a mother tried to correct her daughter's speech; an excerpt is shown in the margin. The child seems to filter what she hears through her own rule system.

If direct imitation were an important mechanism of language acquisition, then children should learn the features of their language in an order that corresponds to the frequency of those features in adult speech. Things that he hears more often, he should learn earlier; things that he hears less often, he should learn later. For example, if a child hears many sentences in which the suffix *ing* is attached to the verb, he should easily figure out how to correctly use this ending. Brown decided to test this hypothesis with the parents of Adam, Eve, and Sarah. He found that the three sets of parents did use various grammatical features with differing frequencies, and that these frequencies were remarkably consistent within each home. The features the parents used most frequently, however, were *not* the ones the children acquired first. Frequency of features in parental speech simply did not explain the order in which the children acquired grammatical rules.

The inadequacy of a simple mechanism of reinforcement is demonstrated by the fact that parents do not usually reinforce children for using correct grammar. Although most middle-class parents believe they actively correct their child's speech, the evidence available fails to support that belief. Brown and his co-workers examined mother-child interactions in which the child's utterance was followed by the parent's expression of approval or disapproval. The parents seemed to pay very little attention to bad grammar. They tolerated even very severe errors, such as the substitution of "he" for "she," as long as they could understand what the child meant to say. The parents' approval and disapproval of what the child said were related to whether the sentence was true, that is, to whether or not it conformed to reality. So simple reinforcement cannot play much of a role in the learning of rules of grammar.

Child: Nobody don't like me.

Mother: No, say, "Nobody likes me."

Child: Nobody don't like me.
(Eight repetitions of this dialogue)

Mother: No, now listen carefully; say, *"Nobody likes me."*

Child: Oh! Nobody don't like*s* me.

Despite the failure of simple mechanisms of direct imitation or reinforcement to account for language acquisition, imitation and reinforcement clearly do play some role. A child who grows up hearing American English spoken around him learns to speak American English, not Chinese or German. In a broad sense, he is imitating the language that he hears. Also, he learns to say what other people understand. If they do not understand him, he cannot communicate adequately, and so it is more difficult for him to influence people to do what he wants; that is, he has difficulty obtaining reinforcements from other people. The exact processes by which environmental factors like imitation and reinforcement influence children's acquisition of their native language remain to be discovered.

LANGUAGE AND THOUGHT

This chapter has concentrated on the acquisition of language and has argued that language development always builds on a base of cognitive development, or the development of thinking. But, at least in adults, thinking is also in some sense dependent on language. Some psychologists and philosophers have held that thinking is entirely dependent on language, that language sets boundaries on what we are able to think. In the words of the philosopher Ludwig Wittgenstein: "The limits of my language mean the limits of my world." George Orwell spelled out some of the chilling implications of this view in his novel *1984*, in which he described a tyrannical government that sets out to control all thought by removing certain words from the language, coining some new ones, and redefining others.

The idea that language determines thought was expounded eloquently by the linguist Benjamin Lee Whorf (1897-1941). **Whorf's hypothesis** actually has two parts: First, language is more than a means of expression—it determines our ideas, thoughts, and perceptions. When a child acquires language, he simultaneously acquires a "world view." Second, the way in which language influences cognition is relative to the particular language being used; different languages embody and perpetuate different world views.

According to Whorf, one way in which language affects cognition is through vocabulary. The words that we learn determine the categories that we use to perceive and understand our world. For example, English has a single word for snow, but an Eskimo would find one all-inclusive word absurd—he needs different words for falling snow, slushy snow, packed snow, and so forth. If language determines one's perception of the world, then when an Eskimo looks out the window on a cold winter morning, he should perceive the white substance on the ground differently than do speakers of English.

Languages differ in the way they divide up many domains of meaning—not only the domain of frozen water that falls from the sky. Whorf observed that languages differ in the grammatical categories they must express—categories like number, gender, tense, voice, and so forth. He believed that these linguistic categories affect the way people think about time, space, and matter. Whorf called Hopi a "timeless language" because, although its grammar recognizes duration, it does not distinguish between the present, past, and future of an event. English, of course, always does so, either by verb inflection (he talks, he talked) or by use of certain words and expressions (Tomorrow I talk). Hopi verbs do distinguish, however, between various kinds of validity; they are inflected to indicate whether the speaker is reporting an event, expecting an event, or making a generalization about events. If these very different ways of grammatically classifying events affect thought, one would expect a Hopi-based physics to look very different from an English-based one.

Psycholinguists usually regard the Whorfian hypothesis as having a strong and weak form. The strong form—that language completely determines thought—is not taken very seriously today. Several writers have observed that although a language may lack a specific word to express a concept, a speaker can always resort to circumlocutions of one sort or another. Whorf himself was able to communicate with his monolingual English-speaking readers about certain American Indian expressions for which there were no corresponding words or idioms in English. People can think about concepts that their language has no word for.

The weak form of the hypothesis is that because languages differ in the ease with which certain concepts can be expressed, their speakers are at least predisposed to think or perceive in certain ways. This version of the hypothesis still has serious difficulties. Even if it should turn out that Eskimos attend to characteristics of snow that English speakers tend to ignore, the explanation may have to do with the Eskimos' livelihood or some other cultural factor. The life of Eskimos, after all, requires that they recognize many different types of snow. While language may reflect cultural differences, it probably does not produce them.

Most psychologists and linguists now believe that the linguistic differences Whorf wrote about, though interesting, do not have the significance he gave them. The extent to which a language actually limits thought is small, and there is good evidence, summarized in Chapter 13, that some types of thought are completely independent of language. Interest has shifted to a concern with identifying the capacities shared by all peoples that allow one person to learn another's language and that even allow us to communicate with each other to some degree when we do not speak the same language. Some of the attempts to identify such universal linguistic and cognitive phenomena have been described in this chapter and in Chapter 8.

The universal cognitive basis underlying human language has recently been shown to apply even to a phenomenon that in the past was thought to be a particularly striking illustration of the effect of language on perception. Although speakers of English tend to think of their way of naming colors as natural, other languages divide up the spectrum of colors quite differently. As shown in Figure 9.15B, Ibibio, a language of Nigeria, has four basic color terms, while Jalé, spoken in New Guinea, has only two. At first glance, there seems to be little in common between the way these two languages classify colors and the way we classify colors in English. But Brent Berlin and Paul Kay have recently shown that a universal structure underlies the diversity of color terms in different languages. Apparently all languages select from the eleven basic color categories shown in English in Figure 9.15C. When a language has fewer than eleven terms, it lacks terms for the categories lower down in the list. Jalé, with only two terms, names only the first two categories, black and white. Ibibio, with only four terms, names only the first four categories: black, white, red, and green. English uses all eleven categories.

In what sense are these color categories used in the same way in all languages? The Ibibio word for red (ndaitat) covers a much wider range of colors than the English word "red." So at first glance the words do not seem

Figure 9.15 Some of Berlin and Kay's evidence that there is a universal cognitive basis for the naming of colors. The large color chart shows most of the color chips Berlin and Kay presented to members of various cultures. (They also presented a black chip, a white chip, and several shades of gray chips.) The three small diagrams correspond to the large color chart, with the bands at the top and bottom of each diagram corresponding to the black and white not shown in the large chart. (Grays are not shown at all.) Each diagram shows the names that members of a particular culture applied to various chips. A name inside an outlined area indicates that it was applied to all the chips that correspond to that area in the large chart. The surrounding gray areas indicate chips to which that name was applied with less certainty. Thus, English speakers designate as "green" a small set of chips that are included in a somewhat larger set of chips called "awawa" by speakers of Ibibio, a language of South Nigeria (B). These chips in turn are among an even larger set of chips for which the people of New Guinea who speak Jalé have no name at all (A). (After Berlin and Kay, 1969.)

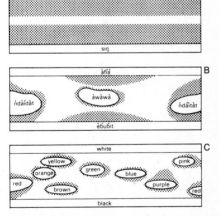

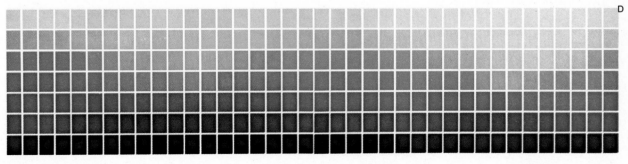

to belong to the same category of color. But Berlin and Kay asked native speakers of dozens of languages to pick from the color chips in Figure 9.15D the *best instances* of each of their color terms. The best instances for each category fell within a narrow range of chips: see Figures 9.15A and 9.15B. That is, languages differed in the range of colors included under a single color word, but they agreed quite closely on the best instances for each basic color category. The best instance of red in English is virtually the same as the best instance of red in Ibibio, as well as in all the other languages studied (except, of course, those that only had two color categories, black and white).

All people, then, seem to share the same basic color categories. Even when their language does not have all eleven categories, they can easily learn the missing ones and borrow terms from other languages for them. Color categories, like so many other language phenomena, seem to reflect a universal cognitive structure, common to all humankind. More generally, the evidence is that cognition determines language more than language determines cognition.

On the other hand, language certainly does play some role in thinking. It probably is especially important for the discovery and refinement of abstract concepts—the sort that normally develop during the formal-operational period, around the start of adolescence. Hans Furth reports that deaf children who have little or no language show essentially normal cognitive development until they reach the age of eight or ten, the concrete-operational period. At that point they are very slow at progressing further. Furth suggests that language is necessary for cognitive development past this point.

Certainly the importance of language for the adolescent and adult in our society can hardly be overestimated. Our education and communication systems depend on the efficient transmission of an enormous body of information by means of language, both oral and written. Language enables us to communicate across time and space, frees us from having to rediscover ideas anew in each generation, and makes possible the relatively smooth functioning of a complicated social system.

Figure 9.16 Roger Brown's text in social psychology and his research and writings in developmental psycholinguistics have earned him wide respect. Some of his work on language is presented in this chapter; his earlier research in social psychology included studies of attitude change and of mob and crowd behavior.

SUMMARY

1. Roger Brown has said that there are three characteristics that a communication system must have to qualify as a **language.**

   a. A language allows **displacement;** people using the language can communicate about things or events removed in time or space from them.

   b. A language possesses **meaningfulness;** the symbols a language uses—whether as sounds or gestures or written symbols—represent objects or events or abstract ideas.

   c. A language has **productiveness;** its symbols can be combined in many ways so that the language can express great numbers of meanings.

2. Several psychologists have been teaching chimpanzees to communicate—through various language systems—in order to test both the definition of language and the cognitive capacities that language requires.

   a. Beatrice and R. Allen Gardner and Roger Fouts taught Washoe to use **American Sign Language (ASL),** the gestural language used by many deaf persons. After Washoe had learned a number of signs (the gestural equivalent of words), she began to combine them productively to make three- and four-sign phrases.

b. David Premack taught a chimpanzee named Sarah to construct sentences using plastic chips of varying shapes and colors, which she put vertically on a magnetized board. Each plastic chip was a symbol for a word. Sarah learned about 130 words, and she mastered some linguistic forms much more complex than those Washoe uses.

c. Duane Rumbaugh and his colleagues have taught a chimp they call Lana to operate a special typewriter whose symbols are geometric shapes; each shape represents a word. What Lana types appears on a screen in front of her. She has learned to check herself and erase series of symbols whose sequence is incorrect. That is, she has essentially learned to read.

Figure 9.17 David Premack is well known both for his work in training chimps to use language and for his work in analyzing the organization of behavior. The Premack principle, discussed in Chapters 6 and 27 of this text, is a powerful tool in describing behavior and in behavioral research and therapy.

3. Even though the chimpanzees' use of symbols fulfills Roger Brown's three criteria for true language, their use of language so far is at about the level of a two- to three-year-old child. One must therefore ask what capacities are required for the use of human language.

a. Experiments attempting to teach spoken language to chimps were failures. There are specializations in the human articulatory system and in motor regions of the brain that permit fine control of the production of sounds. Also, Eric Lenneberg and others believe that the human brain is constructed for fine discrimination of the auditory patterns of spoken language. Autistic children (who show severely disturbed behavior, especially in social interaction) may suffer from a lack of this normal human ability.

b. Noam Chomsky and others have argued that all the natural languages of the world have certain features in common, which make certain kinds of distinctions, and that the human brain is "programmed" to deal with those features.

c. Like some other biologically based human and animal behaviors, the acquisition of language appears to have a sensitive period, namely, the years from about two to about fourteen. Adults have much more difficulty than children in picking up a foreign language, for example.

d. Certain cognitive abilities are required for language acquisition: The most basic is the capacity for **representational thought,** which appears in humans at about the age of two. Brown argues that the child's first sentences are linguistic expressions of sensorimotor intelligence, because representational thought is built upon sensorimotor intelligence.

e. Although chimps are capable of representational thought, they have not yet shown cognitive abilities beyond that of the intuitive egocentric thought characteristic of three- or four-year-olds.

4. During their first four or five years of life, children all over the world pass through much the same sequence of stages in acquiring their native tongues.

a. The babbling sounds of an infant, which are a kind of motor play, are not limited to sounds of his or her native language. After six months, infants begin to develop the capacity to imitate sounds made by others.

Figure 9.18 Eric Lenneberg, a developmental psycholinguist, is interested in the biological basis of language. He is a leading proponent of the view that human language acquisition is dependent on special features of the human brain.

Figure 9.19 Noam Chomsky's theory of the origin and development of language has gained wide acceptance and is the basis for some of the research reported here. Chomsky believes that a child learns to speak his native language not because he has been reinforced for successive approximations to correct speech, but because all people have an inborn capacity for analyzing the language they hear and subsequently interpreting and using that language correctly.

The ability to *speak,* however, is not necessary to the ability to *understand* spoken language. Children who hear but who have a disability that keeps them from speaking demonstrate that they understand all the intricacies of language very well.

b. Around their first birthday, children begin to use their first true words: They name a few objects and use one-word utterances to refer to the immediately tangible and visible. They do not yet exhibit displacement.

5. **Two-word utterances** represent an important advance in the child's ability to use language; these earliest sentences are seen to be structured by grammatical **rules.**

a. Psycholinguists decide that a child is observing a grammatical rule (1) if the child's behavior is consistent with the rule; (2) if the mistakes he makes are predictable on the basis of the rule; and (3) if he corrects himself or others to conform to the rule.

b. A system of language rules constitutes a **grammar.** A grammar, as used by psycholinguists, simply describes what people must know in order to use a particular language.

c. Research shows that at this early stage children use **telegraphic speech,** omitting nonessential words, but they do preserve adult word order.

d. It is important to judge a child's two-word sentences in **context,** in order to find their **underlying meanings.** The same sentence, spoken with different **intonations** and in different situations, may reflect a number of different meanings.

e. Psycholinguists have found that children all over the world express the same kinds of meanings in these early sentences. Roger Brown has proposed that about 75 percent of early two-word sentences reflect eleven basic meanings. (See Table 9.1.)

6. Children acquire most of the more complex rules of adult language in the years between two and four.

a. Certain rules are acquired in steps, like use of the negative in English.

b. Thomas Bever has suggested that children construct certain language rules consistent with their level of cognitive development and then, when they develop cognitively, discard those in favor of more sophisticated rules.

c. Good evidence of the fact that children employ rules comes from their **overregularizations,** overextensions of grammatical rules, common in the speech of three- and four-year-olds. For example, children who have been correctly using the past forms of irregular verbs (for instance, "went") will suddenly begin to use incorrect forms ("goed"). This substitution shows that the child has mastered the general rule for forming the simple past in English.

7. Evidence to date indicates that specific environmental factors have little impact on language acquisition, as long as the child hears language in a meaningful, communicative setting. Mechanisms through which the environment influences other kinds of learning do not seem to affect language acquisition, at least not in any simple way. Neither imitation nor reinforcement has been shown to affect language acquisition.

8. The **Whorfian hypothesis** states that one's language sets boundaries on what one is able to think. Psychologists and linguists in recent years have amassed evidence that cognition probably determines language more than language determines cognition. The emphasis is now on searching for universal linguistic and cognitive phenomena. For example, the differences in color terms across various languages has often been cited as an example supporting the Whorfian hypothesis. Brent Berlin and Paul Kay have shown, however, that all languages build their basic color terms upon the same eleven **color categories.**

SUGGESTED READINGS

Bar-Adon, Aaron, and Leopold F. Werner. *Child Language: A Book of Readings.* Englewood Cliffs, N.J.: Prentice-Hall, 1971. Valuable collection of papers that gives a historical perspective on the study of language and makes available many previously untranslated papers.

Brown, Roger. *A First Language: The Early Stages.* Cambridge, Mass.: Harvard University Press, 1973. An excellent, comprehensive, and thoughtful treatment of the major current issues in early child language learning. This book is a source of several of the key ideas in this chapter.

Brown, Roger, *et al. Psycholinguistics: Selected Papers by Roger Brown.* New York: Free Press, 1970. A compilation of the major papers of Brown and his associates on child and adult language. Brown is one of the most interesting and readable writers in psychology.

Chomsky, Noam. *Language and Mind.* New York: Harcourt Brace Jovanovich, 1972. A good lecture on a linguist's view of language and mind, as well as a general introduction to Chomsky's system of describing language (transformational grammar).

Fleming, Joyce Dudney. "Field Report: The State of the Apes," *Psychology Today,* 7 (January 1974), 31+. A current review of all the work in progress on teaching language to chimps in centers across the country.

Furth, Hans. *Thinking Without Language.* New York: Free Press, 1966. Thoughtful discussion of the problem of the relationship of language and thought, based, in part, on Furth's experiments with deaf children.

Lenneberg, Eric. *The Biological Foundation of Language.* New York: Wiley, 1967. Excellent analysis of language development in the context of the growth and maturation of the child and in light of evolution and genetics. Also presents language disorders in children and adults and discusses the problem of language and cognition.

Miller, George. *Communication, Language, and Meaning.* New York: Basic Books, 1973. Prepared for a general audience, this collection of papers by the leading authorities in the fields of language and communication provides a broad, up-to-date introduction to psycholinguistics.

A child's notions of what constitutes morality change as he grows older, but toward what final end do these changes progress? What part do models of moral behavior play in the child's development? And do we have in our great national leaders models whom children might admire and imitate as examples of the desired ends of moral development?

Consider ex-Vice President Spiro Agnew, who—having spent five years lecturing the nation's troubled youth on morality and therefore making a name for himself as the nation's outstanding exponent of "law and order"—found that his own stardard of morality with respect to graft was so low that he was forced to resign his office. It was the first time in American history that so high an elected official had had to resign over a question of personal honesty. In his speech to the nation after his resignation, Agnew admitted that his actions looked bad but only, somehow, in the light of what he referred to as "post-Watergate morality."

The implication seemed to be that the American public was content to dismiss certain actions as normal political behavior prior to 1973 but that after the revelations as to the frightening extent of extra-legal manipulations by members of the executive branch of the government, new and more rigid standards of morality had been applied. Many commentators pounced on Agnew's disingenuous self-justification by pointing out that the kind of corruption of which he was held to be guilty was illegal, immoral, and unacceptable at any time in our nation's history.

What is it, then, that makes a man like Spiro Agnew capable of lecturing others on morals while behaving so immorally himself? Whence comes this enormous capacity for hypocrisy not only in him but in so many others of the administration of the thirty-seventh President of the United States? When in history has the United States been so steadily lectured on law and morals by so illegal and immoral a bunch? Perhaps the cause is something I call the "Yes, but . . ." attitude, which divides the human race into two groups, oneself and everyone else, and then applies the morals only to the everyone else. For instance, it is wrong to kill, isn't it? "Yes, but when our soldiers do it, it's in the cause of freedom and justice." It is wrong to commit terrorist acts in war, isn't it? "Yes, but when our soldiers do it, they're just following orders and misinterpreting them a little bit." It is wrong to cheat your fellow man, isn't it? "Yes, but when I do it, it's only because I know he's trying to cheat me." It is wrong to weaken our nation by cheating on income tax and accepting graft, isn't it? "Yes, but I am so underpaid, and besides everyone does it."

As long as we can "Yes, but . . ." ourselves into accepting different standards for ourselves than for others, any system of morality we advance is just so much hypocrisy and hot air, and there remains a great deal of room for further development.

But who am *I* to talk? Have I never used the "Yes, but . . ." argument myself?

Yes, but . . . there are degrees, and I don't think I have ever sunk to the level characteristic of the administration of which Agnew was a member. Perhaps very few people could, and it is remarkable that so many of them were concentrated into the White House at one time.

Isaac Asimov

10

Social Development: The Case of Morality

PSYCHOANALYTIC THEORY
Theory
Research

SOCIAL-LEARNING THEORY
Theory
Research

COGNITIVE-
DEVELOPMENTAL THEORY
Theory
Research

THEORIES OF MORAL
DEVELOPMENT: A COMPARISON
The Focus of the Theories
Is Morality Culturally Relative
Socializing Agents and Child Rearing
What Determines Moral Behavior

Figure 10.1 A society requires that its young learn what acts and attitudes are acceptable in given circumstances. Children's acquisition of this knowledge is called social development. Part of knowing what is acceptable is knowing what the society deems "right" and "wrong"—what is moral. The child shown here has already internalized many of her society's rules: She knows it is "wrong" to cheat on a test. But what processes did she go through in acquiring that knowledge? And what relation does that knowledge have to her behavior? Psychologists answer these questions in different ways, depending on their theoretical approach. Three major theories of moral development are presented in this chapter.

W hile visiting Concord in 1843, shortly after building his cabin at Walden Pond, the poet Henry David Thoreau was arrested and jailed for refusing to pay a poll tax. Thoreau refused to pay the tax to protest Massachusetts' support of slavery. As the story goes, Thoreau was looking out at the street through the bars of his window when who should walk by but his friend Ralph Waldo Emerson. Catching sight of Thoreau, Emerson rushed to the window and asked, "Henry, what are you doing in there?" "Waldo," Thoreau replied, "What are you doing out there?" Thoreau's situation poses a moral dilemma. He thought morality required him to disobey a law and go to jail. The authorities, however, saw it differently.

Consider another story, told by Elliot Turiel, a psychologist from Harvard University. One day a five-year-old boy named John was playing with his uncle when the uncle teasingly informed him that he had spent some time in jail. At first John refused to believe his uncle, but the uncle insisted that what he said was true. Finally John was convinced. Suddenly he became frightened of his uncle, rushed off, and refused to speak to him for the rest of the day. It seems doubtful that John would have thought Thoreau had behaved morally.

As we all know, what is moral and immoral, right and wrong, is a controversial matter. We all have definitions of morality, and our definitions constitute implicit **theories of morality.** We rarely bring the theories to consciousness and even more rarely test them, but we do have ideas about what kinds of people and actions are moral and why.

The study of morality has long been an important concern of psychologists. In 1908, William McDougall wrote, "the *fundamental problem* of social psychology is the moralization of the individual by the society." The system of rules that governs social relations and makes social life possible is embodied in a culture's morality, although the moral "rules" may be expressed as norms or laws.

Moral development entails changes in our understanding of the rules that govern social life and our interpretation of what we ought to do. At present there are several theories in psychology that attempt to account for social development in general and moral development in particular. The three most influential theories of social and moral development are based upon the three most important general theories in psychology today: (1) Freud's psychoanalytic theory of psychosexual development, (2) the behaviorist theory of social learning, and (3) Piaget's cognitive-developmental theory. Each of these three theories is examined in this chapter (and also discussed in Chapter 21), and some of the research supporting it is discussed. Then the theories, and their strengths and weaknesses, are compared.

PSYCHOANALYTIC THEORY

Until the late nineteenth century, many thinkers believed that moral behavior was governed by a homunculus—a "little man" inside us, sometimes called "the small voice of conscience." Conscience was considered innate and, in many cases, something instilled by God to govern behavior. People who behaved immorally were called "moral imbeciles" and thought either to have been born without a conscience or to be possessed by a devil. The "small voice" concept of conscience was prevalent in the Victorian era until the popularization of Sigmund Freud's theory of psychoanalysis, the first major psychological theory of social development. It was to Freud's great credit that he cast the study of morality—and hence the study of social development in general—on a more scientific plane.

Theory

The most important innovation in Freud's conception of morality was the suggestion that *people develop a sense of morality* rather than being born with one. Freud viewed the newborn infant as essentially amoral; the child develops morality through his interaction with his parents. According to Freud's theory of personality, which is described in more detail in Chapter 18, children pass through five major stages of psychosocial development: the oral, anal, phallic, latency, and genital. In each stage the focus of the child's pleasure is a different part of his own body, and in turn his affections shift to a different object. For example, the focus of pleasure in the first stage, the **oral stage,** is the child's mouth, and therefore, his love object is his mother's breast: Social development really begins with the episode of nursing. With increasing social as well as general development, the infant begins to love his mother as a person. In the **anal stage,** the focus of his pleasure shifts to the anus and the process of defecation, and one of the main social interactions that he has with his mother (his main love object) is over toilet training. Because he loves her and wants to please her, he learns to control his defecation and to use the "potty." In this way he begins to follow social rules: Mess in the bathroom, not in your pants.

During the **phallic stage,** around the age of three to six, the focus of pleasure for young boys shifts to their penises; for example, masturbation is very common. And at the same time they begin to view their fathers as rivals for their prime love objects, their mothers. At this time, what Freud calls the **Oedipus complex** develops. The young boy desires his mother and wants to destroy his rival, the father. He perceives his father's power, however, and is afraid his father will retaliate, perhaps by castrating him or by harming him in some other way so as to eliminate him as a rival; Freud called this primitive fear of physical harm "castration anxiety." Usually, a child resolves this conflict by repressing his desire for his mother and identifying with his father, so he can vicariously share in his father's special relationship with his mother.

The reason that the Oedipus complex is important in the psychoanalytic approach to morality is that the young boy acquires a conscience through his **identification** with his father. He internalizes his father's moral standards. In Freud's words, a boy who successfully resolves his Oedipus conflicts *introjects the superego of the father,* which means he incorporates the moral standards that he has learned from his father into his own personality. Freud thought that the **superego** consisted of two parts: the ego ideal and the conscience. The **ego ideal,** which is the child's notion of what he ought to strive to be, rewards the child whenever he lives up to introjected parental expectations, such as restraining aggressive and sexual urges, obeying rules, and acting generously. The **conscience,** which is the child's notion of what he ought *not* do, punishes the child for failing to live up to the rules of society that he has learned from his parents.

Of some importance is Freud's contention that what is introjected is not the behavior of the father but rather a set of values, communicated by the father and reinforced by other "father figures." According to Freud, "the parents' influence includes the racial, national, and family traditions they represent as well as their own personalities. Moreover, with development, the superego takes over contributions from successors and substitutes of [the child's] parents, such as teachers, admired public figures in public life or high social ideals." It should be noted that, in Freud's opinion, a boy's identification with his father not only provides him with a superego but also establishes the boy's (masculine) sex identity. This process of identification is discussed further in Chapter 21.

When the child resolves the Oedipus conflict, his superego is formed and therefore the most important occurrence in moral development is complete, but the child must pass through two more psychosocial stages to reach adulthood, according to Freud. The resolution of the Oedipus conflict moves the child into the **latency stage,** where his sexual impulses are repressed, and so his love of his mother is no longer a problem because it is nonsexual. The hormones of adolescence cause his sexuality to burst forth again, and he enters the **genital stage,** where his love object is a person of the opposite sex, and the focus of his pleasure is sexual intercourse with that person.

Although Freud paid little attention to females in his theory and is consequently often accused of an antifeminine bias, he did attempt to explain social and moral development in females. The five stages of psychosocial development are the same for males and females, but there can be no Oedipus complex in girls because a girl's sexual attraction is toward her father, not her mother. Freud postulated an **Electra complex** and penis envy as counterparts to the male Oedipus complex and castration anxiety. In males, the threat of castration is thought to *end* the Oedipus complex (by bringing about identification with the father), whereas in females the realization that they have no penis is thought to *initiate* the Electra complex. The girl turns away from her mother as a love object and toward her father because he has the penis that she lacks. By analogy with what happens in the male, she identifies with her mother, who controls her father's penis, and thereby introjects her mother's superego and gains a feminine sexual identity. In this way, morality in both sexes develops by identification with the parent of the same sex and the resulting formation of a superego.

Research

The most important contention of the psychoanalytic theory of morality is that there is a dramatic qualitative change in the moral orientation of the child as he resolves the Oedipus complex: He changes from no morality to strong morality. Is there any evidence that the moral responses of children change drastically around this age? Research findings show that there is a change,

Figure 10.2 The psychoanalytic theory of moral development says that the resolution of the Oedipus conflict is the beginning of morality. The young boy (between three and six years old) loves his mother and comes to fear and hate his rival, his father. He resolves this conflict by renouncing his mother as a sexual object and identifying with his father. Through this identification he takes in his father's moral standards, which become his superego, the moral segment of personality structure. Freud believed that an analogous sequence of events takes place in girls.

although it is not as dramatic as Freud suggested. Research on altruistic behavior by Dennis Krebs showed that such behavior does begin to increase in the early school years; and Jean MacFarlane, Lucile Allen, and Marjorie Honzik found that stealing and lying, as reported by parents, decreased in those years. Several other investigations, by Jean Piaget and Lawrence Kohlberg, have shown that children begin to understand social rules and make moral judgments at around six or seven years of age. There is, therefore, some evidence that a change in morality occurs at roughly the age that psychoanalytic theory postulates the resolution of the Oedipus complex.

A second contention of psychoanalytic theory is that both morality and sexual identity are determined by the same process. If that is true, then people with a poorly formed sexual identity should be immoral and immoral people should have a poorly formed sexual identity. But no research has shown that immoral people have any more problems with their sexual identity than moral people have.

Another way of supporting Freud's theory of moral development would be to establish the validity of his theory of identification. The most convincing evidence for the importance of identification in the resolution of the Oedipus complex comes from case reports of individual children undergoing psychotherapy. Few well-controlled experimental studies have attempted to investigate this phenomenon. But the general concept of identification has been adopted by most psychologists as an accurate description of a basic process in human social interaction. As Freud suggested, people identify in general with others whom they see as similar to themselves or whom they want to be similar to. Examples of this process are described in Chapters 21 and 22.

Actually, psychoanalysts typically test their theories with individual patients in psychotherapy and do not conduct experimental studies. Most of the research on the psychoanalytic position has been done by social-learning theorists, such as Robert Sears, John Whiting, Neal Miller, John Dollard, and O. Hobart Mowrer.

SOCIAL-LEARNING THEORY

Like the psychoanalytic theory of moral development, the social-learning theory of moral development comes from a larger theoretical context—the behaviorist analysis of social behavior. The behaviorist approach focuses on two major processes to explain social behavior and development: learning by conditioning (see Chapter 4) and observational learning, or imitation.

Theory

The two contemporary social-learning theorists who have been most concerned with social development and particularly with moral development are Justin Aronfreed and Albert Bandura. Both point out that a great deal of the behavior that we call moral is controlled by immediate rewards and punishments. For example, a person who resists the temptation to steal a wallet may do so because a policeman is standing nearby, and so the individual expects to be caught and punished if he steals. Much moral behavior, however, is not under the immediate control of external events. For example, people also resist the temptation to steal even when they do not expect to be caught. The main concern of social-learning theorists has been to explain why moral behavior occurs even when there are no immediate rewards to be obtained or punishments to be avoided. Their explanations center on two main ways in which children learn to govern their own behavior: through conditioning and through the observation of models.

Conditioning The principles of conditioning, as described in Chapter 4, apply to the conditioning of social behavior as well as to behavior of other types. Responses that are reinforced immediately are more likely to recur than responses that are not; the stronger the reward or punishment, the greater its effect; behavior that is reinforced intermittently is more likely to prevail than behavior that is reinforced every time it occurs.

According to social-learning theory, then, a person behaves in the way that will lead to the greatest satisfaction in a given situation. Gradually he comes to associate various goals and thoughts with basic, unlearned satisfactions. For example, the infant's satisfaction when his mother feeds him is unlearned, but, the theory states, he soon begins to associate the presence of the mother herself with pleasure. Later, the child tries to do things that his parents approve of and to inhibit actions his parents think are wrong because he fears that they will withdraw their affection or that he will be punished. Later still, he behaves morally even when his parents are not there. The reason he does so is that he anticipates the pleasure associated with parental approval and the fear or anxiety associated with punishment. When he sees the chair used to reach the cookie jar, he remembers his mother's disapproving look the last time she caught him taking cookies. While social-learning theorists recognize the importance of internal events such as thoughts and memories, they still insist that all behavior is under at least indirect control by external cues. Even moral behavior that occurs in private may be governed by thoughts oriented toward external events, such as future punishment. In *Conduct and Conscience* Aronfreed outlines a continuum of controls ranging from external to internal. He suggests that a child may resist temptation because, at the external end, he thinks that his parents are watching or that God will punish him or because, at the internal end, he wants to avoid feeling guilty over violating a principle.

The things parents *say* to children are of particular importance to the internalization of moral standards because they help form thoughts that the child associates with pleasure or pain. If a child hits another child and an adult simply spanks him, the child may hesitate to hit that particular playmate again, but he may not understand why he should not. If, on the other hand, the adult explains that it is wrong to hurt people, the child may also hesitate to bite his friend or to hit some other child. That is, when a parent tells a child why he is being punished, he may provide the child with an appropriate generalization (discussed in Chapter 4), which will help him control his behavior in a variety of situations.

Conditioning is not the only mechanism by which the child learns to inhibit immoral behavior; according to social-learning theory, the way the child reacts to his own wrongdoings is also a result of conditioning. For example, a child may learn that he can avoid punishment for misbehaving if he says he is sorry. Apologizing, then, becomes associated with a reduction in anxiety in various situations, even when no punishing agent is present. Similarly, if a child's parents punish him for misbehaving by taking a toy or privilege away from him—instead of physically punishing him—the child may associate the removal of goods with anxiety reduction. Later, he may give goods away to someone he thinks he has harmed in order to reduce the anxiety associated with wrongdoing. Self-criticism and confession are other responses that a child may learn to use generally to avoid anxiety because, originally, these responses helped him avoid punishment from his parents.

Imitation The second mechanism by which social and moral development take place is imitation, learning how to do something through watching someone else (called the **model**) do it. Albert Bandura and Richard Walters have shown that with children, simply watching someone do something interesting can result in imitation. This learning by observation occurs in two steps: acquisition and performance. First, the child acquires a cognitive representa-

Figure 10.3 Social-learning theorists believe that a child's behavior comes to conform to moral principles because the child learns from (is conditioned by) the consequences (rewards and punishments) of his actions. In addition, the child learns by observing other people, particularly people he admires or likes. Once a child has begun to imitate some new action she has seen, she will experience the consequences of that action for herself and thus be further conditioned. This little girl is learning about caring by imitating her mother.

tion of the act. Second, after this mental image has been acquired, he may actually perform the response himself. For example, a child might observe his parent leaving a tip for a waitress at a restaurant and thereby acquire an image of that behavior. Whether the child subsequently imitates the model and leaves a tip depends both on rewards and punishments and on his perception of the model. Whether the child expects rewards or punishments determines whether he behaves as the model did. The waitress's expression of gratitude to the father, for example, could determine whether the child will subsequently perform the tipping behavior. The way the child perceives the model always influences imitation: He is likely to imitate someone whom he sees as nurturant, powerful, competent, or similar to him.

Research

Experimental studies on social-learning theory have established the importance of both conditioning and imitation. Children's resistance to temptation and reactions to transgression can be shaped through reward and punishment, and children imitate the moral behavior of prestigious and powerful adults.

Aronfreed investigated the effect of punishment on moral behavior and found that, while punishment usually has some effect, the time interval between a wrong deed and punishment can be critical in establishing future resistance to temptation. In one experiment, Aronfreed asked children to choose between an attractive toy and an unattractive toy. Whenever the child chose the attractive toy, the experimenter yelled "No!" and took some candy away from the child. Aronfreed varied the time interval between the misdeed (picking up the attractive toy) and the reprimand, "No." The experimenter reprimanded one group of children when they reached for the toy, a second

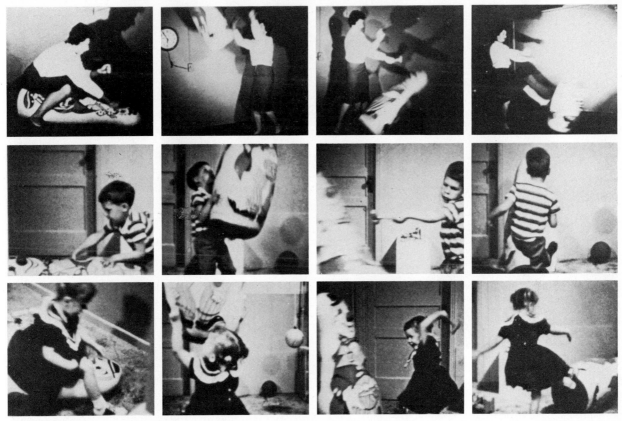

group when they picked up the toy, a third group six seconds after they had picked it up, and a fourth group after they had held the toy for a while. Children in all groups quickly learned not to pick up the attractive toy when the experimenter was in the room, but some of them did take the toy when the experimenter left the room. Aronfreed found that the earlier in the act that the children were punished, the less likely they were to transgress in private—that is, the stronger was their resistance to temptation. A number of other experiments by Bandura as well as other researchers have investigated factors influencing imitation. In a typical experiment, Bandura and his colleagues have different groups of children observe models who respond to a situation in unusual or novel ways. Then he puts the children in a situation similar to that of the model and notes the number of imitative responses they make. Bandura found that most children will imitate novel behavior by a model with very little prodding.

In addition to establishing that imitation does occur, Bandura and his colleagues have investigated the ways in which it can be increased or decreased. They have found, for example, that children are more likely to imitate the behavior of a model they see rewarded than that of a model they see punished. In one experiment, several groups of children watched films of a model who yelled at and punched the Bobo doll shown in Figure 10.4. In the film that one group saw, the model was punished by an authority for punching the doll. In the film that a second group saw, the model was praised for his aggressive behavior. When put into a situation similar to that of the model, the children who had seen him receive praise were much more likely to imitate him than those who had seen him get punished. Bandura hypothesized that the children identified with the model and experienced reward or punishment vicariously as they watched the film. When given a chance to act as the

Figure 10.4 Frames from films taken during Bandura's experiment on imitation of aggression. Children saw a model behaving like the woman in the top row of frames—punching and kicking the Bobo doll—and saw her either being rewarded or punished for the aggressive behavior. Children who saw the model rewarded were much more likely to imitate her—as the two children shown here are doing—than were children who saw the model punished.
(Bandura, 1963.)

Figure 10.5 Kohlberg's "premoral" stages, at which instinctive impulses are modified by rewards and punishments. At Stage 1—The Obedience, or Reward, Orientation—the physical consequences of an action determine its goodness or badness regardless of the human meaning or value of these consequences. At Stage 2—The Instrumental Exchange, or Marketplace, Orientation—right action consists of that which instrumentally satisfies one's own needs. Elements of reciprocity are present only insofar as they help the individual to fulfill his own needs.

Figure 10.6 Kohlberg's "conventional morality" stages. This is the morality of role conformity, of conduct controlled by anticipation of social praise and blame. At Stage 3—The Conformist, or "Good Boy–Good Girl," Orientation—good behavior is what pleases or helps others. There is much conformity to stereotypes of "normal" behavior. Actions are frequently judged by intention, for example, "he means well." At Stage 4—The "Law and Order" Orientation—there is orientation toward fixed laws and authority. Right behavior consists of doing one's duty, showing respect for authority, and maintaining the social order for its own sake.

model had, they therefore tended to behave as if they themselves (instead of the model) had earlier been praised or punished for hitting the doll.

COGNITIVE-DEVELOPMENTAL THEORY

The cognitive-developmental approach to moral development has been most completely formulated by Lawrence Kohlberg. Kohlberg's approach is based upon Jean Piaget's theory of cognitive development.

Theory

Kohlberg hypothesizes that children progress through a number of qualitatively distinct stages of moral judgment. The stages are characterized by the way the child views the world. In all, there are six stages as shown in Figures 10.5 through 10.7. The stages occur in sequence—each one develops out of and subsumes its predecessor—and each stage is more cognitively complex than the one before it.

The stages are related to age. Older children tend to be at more advanced stages, but the speed with which a child travels through the stages varies with his intelligence and with social influences. No stage can be skipped, but a child may stop (become fixated) at any point. Typically, about half a child's judgments are at one stage and the rest fall into the stages that are one step above and one step below.

Like the psychoanalytic and learning theories of moral development, Kohlberg's theory is part of a more general cognitive theory, a theory most fully elaborated by Piaget (see Chapter 8). Kohlberg sees the development of moral judgment as a specific case of general cognitive development. With moral judgments, as with other cognitions, Kohlberg is concerned not with the specific conclusions people reach but with the overriding structure of their

view—how they reason about moral issues. Kohlberg sees cognitive development as a process of interaction between internal cognitive structures, or schemes, and the external environment. The child interprets new experiences as best he can, and he learns from them. His schemes, based on his limited experience of the world, permit the assimilation of only certain information. When the child is presented with information that he cannot assimilate because his schemes are inadequate to account for or to interpret it, he experiences disequilibrium and must accommodate (or adjust) his schemes in order to put the new information in perspective. In this way, cognitive structures advance. As Chapter 8 explains, there are limits on the child's capacity to accommodate his schemes to new material. In moral development he usually cannot process information more than one stage above the stage he is in at any given time. Studies by Elliot Turiel have shown that challenging a child's moral judgments with moral arguments one stage above the child's level is an effective way of raising the child's level. Arguments too far above the child's level have little effect on him.

Moral development involves not only the cognitive processes of assimilation and accommodation but another, more strictly social process: **role taking,** the ability to understand another person's viewpoint. During the acquisition of moral values the child gradually learns to understand the roles of other people. That is, he restructures his concept of self and his concepts of other people so that he can see himself and his own needs and desires in relationship to other people and their needs and desires. The changes in role taking for each moral stage are reflected in Figures 10.5 through 10.7 .

During Stage 1 standards of morality are *external* to the self, and the child is egocentric; he cannot adopt the viewpoint (take the role) of others. He therefore perceives morality in terms of the external consequences of his actions—whether they lead to **reward** or **punishment** from authorities. At Stage 2 he organizes his own viewpoint, his self, and is able to take account of others' roles insofar as he can use them to obtain what he wants. Thus, he concludes that it is moral for him to do what he can to exert his own point of view—a **marketplace** bargaining orientation. When children at Stage 2 are asked what the Golden Rule means, they generally say "help someone if he helps you, and hurt him if he hurts you." At the next stage, Stage 3, the child is able to truly adopt others' viewpoints. He grasps the ideal nature of the Golden Rule: "Treat another as you would want to be treated yourself." His morality is decided, in fact, by what others want and think: He does not decide for himself what is right and wrong but follows rules given by others. He is a **conformist.** At Stage 4, the child takes on the viewpoint of his society and uses it to decide what is right or wrong. He sees **law and order** as the essence of morality, and so he can make a moral decision on his own, without finding out what other people think.

Figure 10.7 Kohlberg's stages of "morality of self-accepted moral principles," at which conduct is regulated by ideals that enable right action regardless of praise or blame from the immediate social environment. At Stage 5—The Social-Contract, Legalistic Orientation—right action is defined by standards agreed upon by the whole society and designed to take account of individual rights. There is awareness that personal values differ and an emphasis upon procedures for reaching consensus. At Stage 6—The Universal Ethical Principle Orientation—right is defined by conscience in accord with universal principles of justice, of reciprocity, and of respect for individuals.

If the individual reaches the final Stages 5 and 6, his standards are even more internalized, and role taking is even more general. Stage 5 requires a recognition of the different viewpoints taken by different societies. Because societies vary greatly in their laws and customs, the laws of the individual's own society cannot be taken as the only basis of morality. Instead, moral decisions are made on the basis of a **social contract,** by which the citizens of a society agree upon how they will establish laws and resolve differences between individuals. At the final stage, Stage 6, the individual considers the universal viewpoint, what all people in all societies would like for them-

Table 10.1 Motives for Stealing or Not Stealing the Drug

	Pro	Con
Stage 1 Action motivated by avoidance of punishment, and "conscience" is irrational fear of punishment.	If you let your wife die, you will get in trouble. You'll be blamed for not spending the money to save her and there'll be an investigation of you and the druggist for your wife's death.	You shouldn't steal the drug because you'll be caught and sent to jail if you do. If you do get away, your conscience would bother you thinking how the police would catch up with you at any minute.
Stage 2 Action motivated by desire for reward or benefit. Possible guilt reactions are ignored and punishment is viewed in a pragmatic manner.	If you do happen to get caught, you could give the drug back and you wouldn't get much of a sentence. It wouldn't bother you much to serve a little jail term, if you have your wife when you get out.	He may not get much of a jail term if he steals the drug, but his wife will probably die before he gets out so it won't do him much good. If his wife dies, he shouldn't blame himself, it wasn't his fault she has cancer.
Stage 3 Action motivated by anticipation of disapproval by others, actual or imagined.	No one will think you're bad if you steal the drug, but your family will think you're an inhuman husband if you don't. If you let your wife die, you'll never be able to look anybody in the face again.	It isn't just the druggist who will think you're a criminal; everyone else will too. After you steal it, you'll feel bad thinking how you've brought dishonor on your family and yourself; you won't be able to face anyone again.
Stage 4 Action motivated by anticipation of dishonor, i.e., institutionalized blame for failure of duty, and by guilt over concrete harm done to others.	If you have any sense of honor, you won't let your wife die because you're afraid to do the only thing that will save her. You'll always feel guilty that you caused her death if you don't do your duty to her.	You're desperate and you may not know you're doing wrong when you steal the drug. But you'll know you did wrong after you're punished and sent to jail. You'll always feel guilty for your dishonesty and lawbreaking.
Stage 5 Concern about maintaining respect of equals and of the community (assuming their respect is based on reason rather than emotions). Concern about own self-respect, i.e., to avoid judging self as irrational, inconsistent, nonpurposive.	You'd lose other people's respect, not gain it, if you don't steal. If you let your wife die, it would be out of fear, not out of reasoning it out. So you'd just lose self-respect and probably the respect of others too.	You would lose your standing and respect in the community and violate the law. You'd lose respect for yourself if you're carried away by emotion and forget the long-range point of view.
Stage 6 Concern about self-condemnation for violating one's own principles.	If you don't steal the drug and let your wife die, you'd always condemn yourself for it afterward. You wouldn't be blamed and you would have lived up to the outside rule of the law but you wouldn't have lived up to your own standards of conscience.	If you stole the drug, you wouldn't be blamed by other people but you'd condemn yourself because you wouldn't have lived up to your own conscience and standards of honesty.

Source: Adapted from Lawrence Kohlberg, "Stage and Sequence: The Cognitive-Developmental Approach to Socialization," in David A. Goslin (ed.), *Handbook of Socialization Theory and Research* (Chicago: Rand-McNally, 1969).

selves. From this, he formulates a few abstract **universal ethical principles** to which all societies should adhere—ideals of universal reciprocity and equality, which together constitute *justice*. Justice can be traced back to role taking, for it prescribes that a person (or a society) must take everyone's perspective into account before acting. It requires a full and genuine awareness that every person is a human being with equal rights.

Research

Like the social-learning approach, Kohlberg's cognitive-developmental approach is well substantiated by research. The first step in most of Kohlberg's research is to discover the stage of moral development most characteristic of his subjects. If you were a subject in one of Kohlberg's experiments, your main task would be to respond to a number of moral dilemmas, saying how you would act in the situation described giving your reasons for your decision. The questions that Thoreau and Emerson asked each other entail moral dilemmas. Was it moral or immoral for Thoreau to be in jail? Was it moral or immoral for Emerson to be out? And why was it moral or immoral? To Kohlberg, the most important question is the "why?"

Here is one of the moral dilemmas Kohlberg has used in his research:

In Europe, a woman was near death from cancer. One drug might save her, a form of radium that a druggist in the same town had recently discovered. The druggist was charging $2,000, ten times what the drug cost him to make. The sick woman's husband, Heinz, went to everyone he knew to borrow the money, but he could only get together about half of what it cost. He told the druggist that his wife was dying and asked him to sell it cheaper or let him pay later. But the druggist said, "No." The husband got desperate and broke into the man's store to steal the drug for his wife. Should the husband have done that? Why?

What is of concern to Kohlberg is the way a person interprets this dilemma—the terms in which he makes his decision, not the decision itself. A person at any stage could think that Heinz should or should not have stolen the drug. The stage of moral development he has reached depends on the reasons he gives for his decision.

If you took Kohlberg's test, you would probably be asked to respond to from four to ten moral dilemmas. Your response would be scored according to twenty-five categories or aspects of moral judgment that, according to Kohlberg, are viewed differently at each stage of moral development. For example, your decision on what Heinz should do might be scored on your motives for engaging in the action—how you define punishment or what would cause you to condemn yourself. Table 10.1 presents representative motives for and against stealing the drug at each of the six stages.

The basic step that Kohlberg had to take to substantiate his theory was to establish that children pass through his stages of moral development in an invariant sequence. Figure 10.8 shows the average percentage of responses to a moral dilemma at each stage made by children ages seven to sixteen. These findings supply substantial support for the idea that children do go through the stages of moral development in order: As stage increases, the age with the highest percentage of responses also increases.

Kohlberg also maintains that children *in all cultures* progress through the stages in the same order. He has substantiated this contention with several cross-cultural studies; the results of one study appear as Figure 10.9. It shows that the progression is about the same for urban boys of ages ten to sixteen in three different cultures, the United States, Taiwan, and Mexico.

THEORIES OF MORAL DEVELOPMENT: A COMPARISON

All three of the theories examined agree that an essentially amoral child somehow becomes a more or less moral adult, but they disagree on the way

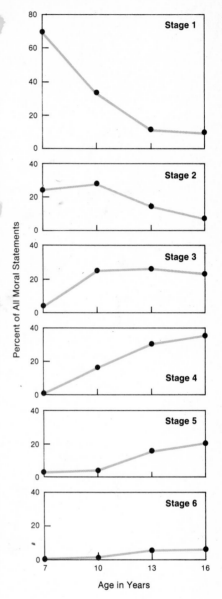

Figure 10.8 Evidence that children progress through moral stages in an invariant sequence. Kohlberg asked children to respond to moral dilemmas such as the one on this page. He classified their statements according to stage of moral development. Each graph here shows the average percentage of all the statements made by children of a given age at a given stage. For example, the top graph shows that about 70 percent of the statements made by seven-year-olds were classified as Stage-1 thinking; on the average, older children consistently show moral thinking at higher stages than younger children do.

(After Kohlberg, 1963.)

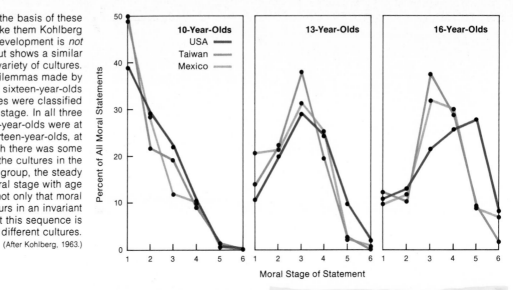

Figure 10.9   On the basis of these data and others like them Kohlberg maintains that moral development is *not* culturally relative but shows a similar pattern in a variety of cultures. Responses to moral dilemmas made by ten-, thirteen-, and sixteen-year-olds from three cultures were classified according to moral stage. In all three cultures, most ten-year-olds were at Stage 1 and most thirteen-year-olds, at Stage 3. Although there was some difference between the cultures in the sixteen-year-old group, the steady progression of moral stage with age strongly suggests not only that moral development occurs in an invariant sequence, but also that this sequence is the same for different cultures.
(After Kohlberg, 1963.)

the transformation comes about. Psychoanalytic theory suggests that children incorporate a set of moral standards during the Oedipal period through identification. Social-learning theory argues that morality is learned in the same way as other behavior, through conditioning and imitation. Cognitive-developmental theory sees moral development as essentially cognitive rather than behavioral and postulates six qualitatively different stages. Table 10.2 summarizes the differences among the three theories.

Each of the three theories makes considerable sense. We tend to think of morality in terms of conscience and guilt, and Freud hypothesized a guilt-generating superego. We also realize, as the social-learning theorists emphasize, that we are taught to behave in ways that those around us consider right or wrong. Kohlberg's stress on qualitative changes as a child matures also seems reasonable, for we know that children have different ideas about morality than adults.

Reading about a single theory, one tends to adopt its point of view and follow its author's line of reasoning. But the fact that a theory makes sense does not mean it is correct. As the brief reviews of research on each theory suggest, they have all received some substantiation. But can they all be correct? Another way to judge the validity of the theories is by comparing them. Do they contradict one another? One can ask whether they even address the same issues.

The Focus of the Theories

The first point of comparison is the most basic, the explanatory realm and focus of the theories. What do they attempt to explain? Consider Thoreau's situation. What aspect of it would particularly interest psychoanalytic, social-learning, and cognitive-developmental theorists?

Psychoanalysts would probably focus on Thoreau's **emotions.** The primary concern of the psychoanalytical school is feeling, or emotion—particularly guilt and anxiety and especially when they seem inappropriate to the situation. If Thoreau did not feel guilty at all about his refusal to pay the poll tax and showed little awareness that moral questions were involved, a psychoanalyst would suspect that his superego was weak. If he felt very guilty, or very self-righteous, a psychoanalyst might suspect that he had an overly restrictive superego. In either case, a Freudian would want to know about Thoreau's childhood. He would be less interested in Thoreau's decision as a response to the current political situation than in its connection with his childhood experi-

Table 10.2 Comparison of the Three Major Theories

	Psychoanalytic	Social-Learning	Cognitive-Developmental
Major Theorist	Sigmund Freud	Albert Bandura	Lawrence Kohlberg
Basic Emphasis	Feelings (conscience and guilt)	Behavior (influence of others and stimulus conditions)	Thought (qualitative changes in development)
Mechanism for Acquisition of Morality	Internalization of parental values in the child's superego	Results from conditioning and modeling	Proceeds in orderly stages related to cognitive development
Age of Acquisition	Superego is formed by about age five	Learning continues throughout life; wide individual differences	Ongoing process to adulthood—may fixate at any stage
Cultural Relativity	Morality is culturally relative within a framework of universal psychosexual stages	Morality is culturally relative	Moral values and stages are universal
Agents of Socialization	Parents are central influence	Adults and peers who dispense rewards and punishments and who serve as models are main influence	Persons at next highest stage exert greatest influence
Implications for Education	Education exerts little influence	Teacher should serve as good example and should reward appropriate behaviors	Teacher should try to stimulate child to reach next stage by exposing him to moral conflicts and to moral statements at next level

ences and his relationships to his mother and father.

Social-learning theorists would focus not on Thoreau's feelings but on his **behavior.** They would ask what caused him to act the way he did. Why did he choose this particular way to respond to his situation? How did it help him gain reward or punishment? Had he been reinforced for similar behavior in the past, or was he perhaps imitating the behavior of someone he admired?

Cognitive-developmental theorists would focus on Thoreau's **thoughts** about his situation. They would want to know how he reached the decision he did—what he perceived as the basic issues and how he interpreted them. Cognitive-developmental theory focuses on judgment rather than on emotion or behavior.

Psychoanalytic theory suggests that people are what they feel; social-learning theory suggests that they are what they do; cognitive-developmental theory suggests that they are what they think. But none of the three emphasizes emotion, behavior, or cognition to the exclusion of all else. Each makes some attempt to account for feelings of guilt, moral and immoral behavior, and judgments about morality.

Although psychoanalytic theory focuses on the emotion of guilt, it also has a strong behavioral emphasis. Like learning theory, it is ultimately concerned with explaining what people do. Unlike social-learning theory, however, it hypothesizes an internal moral structure, the superego, instead of explaining behavior by linking it to external rewards and punishments. Psychoanalytic theory gives less attention to judgment. In stressing the unconscious, irrational determinants of behavior, Freud minimized the importance of cognition. One aspect of Freud's theory of moral development that is often overlooked, however, is his suggestion that the superego consists of an ego ideal as well as a conscience. Freud's position is commonly interpreted as totally guilt-oriented, but that interpretation is incorrect. The ego ideal sets standards and evaluates performance in relation to these standards—a process that requires judgment. Thus, the ego ideal offers a way of explaining the kind of forward-moving development discussed by cognitive-developmental theorists.

Although social-learning theorists stress behavior, they do recognize the importance of cognition and emotion. In Bandura's theory, the acquisition phase of observational learning (during which the child acquires a mental representation of a behavior) is essentially cognitive, and Aronfreed discusses cognitive processes at length. In addition, Aronfreed (much more than Bandura) recognizes the role of emotion in moral development. He believes that the prime source of internal control over behavior is anxiety. Like psychoanalytic theorists, he believes that anxiety, shame, and guilt suppress much immoral behavior. Unlike psychoanalytic theorists, however, he views these unpleasant emotions as learned, or conditioned, rather than as mediated by a superego.

Kohlberg emphasizes the judgmental core of morality, but he does not lose sight of the importance of emotion or behavior. He sees cognition and emotion as closely related. Kohlberg subscribes to a theory of emotion much like Stanley Schachter's (see Chapter 15), arguing that people place their own reactions into a particular category of emotion primarily on the basis of how they interpret or analyze the situation. For example, Kohlberg says that a child is likely to define the emotion that accompanies wrongdoing differently at different stages of moral development. At Stage 3, he may feel shame—concern that he has lost the approval of others. At Stage 4, he may feel guilt for violating rules. At Stage 6, the emotion may take the form of self-blame for violating a principle of conscience.

Figure 10.10 The women's prison at Niantic, Connecticut, where, in accord with Kohlberg's theory, inmates are given experience in decision-making processes that affect their own lives. Kohlberg believes that moral behavior is often consistent with a person's understanding of moral norms; thus, the inmates' participation in these decision-making processes should help them clarify their moral thinking and adopt different norms.

Kohlberg berates many American psychologists for their obsessive concern with behavior; he does not, however, completely neglect what people do. He believes that moral judgment helps determine behavior, and he argues that most behavior is *situationally specific.* That is, he believes that people act as they do primarily because of the demands and norms of the particular situation they are in. This matter has been investigated experimentally, and some of the research is discussed at the end of the chapter. At this point, the important thing to note is that in most situations in everyday life a society's norms clearly indicate how a person is expected to behave, and as a child moves through the first four stages his moral thinking concentrates more and more on these norms and his behavior becomes more consistent with them. In Stages 5 and 6, the individual is also very likely to follow those norms, so long as they do not conflict with broader issues of law and justice. Moral dilemmas like that in the Heinz story are not very common in most people's lives, and so for most situations processes of moral judgment lead directly to behavior.

Recently Kohlberg and his associates have begun to apply his theory and findings to situations in the real world; they are attempting to create "just communities" that will affect the behavior of their participants. For example, in a women's prison in Niantic, Connecticut, they have instituted a "just" decision-making process—inmates may exercise control over aspects of their lives, sharing the decision-making powers that are totally in the hands of prison administrators in the usual penal systems. Preliminary results suggest that the inmates who participate in this process are less likely to return to the prison for subsequent crimes. If the return rate here and in other prisons that have such programs remains markedly lower than usual, the process may be a breakthrough in criminology and would prove an extremely powerful support for Kohlberg's theory.

Is Morality Culturally Relative?

Because social-learning theory holds that moral behavior, like other behavior, is determined by conditioning and modeling practices that vary from society to society, it also holds that moral behavior is culturally relative. That is, what is moral varies from culture to culture in accordance with what socializing agents believe is right or wrong. From parents and other socializing agents, the child learns the rules of the society. He is rewarded for behaving in socially acceptable ways and punished for behaving in socially unacceptable ways; and parents, teachers, and other socializing agents supply the child with models of approved behavior. The idea that moral behavior is culturally relative is supported by anthropological and sociological data that describe extreme differences in the behavior different cultures call moral. Even incest, one of the very few types of behavior considered immoral in all known societies, is differently defined from one culture to another. Almost all societies forbid sexual intercourse between brother and sister, father and daughter, and mother and son, but beyond that the prohibitions on sex and marriage between relatives are exceedingly varied.

Psychoanalytic theory assumes less cultural relativity than social-learning theory but more than cognitive-developmental theory. Freud said that all children go through the oral, anal, phallic, and genital stages of personality development; that everyone in every culture develops an Oedipus or Electra complex; and that all societies make some attempt to suppress the sexual and aggressive drives of their members. He also believed, however, that the specific content of the moral standards introjected at the resolution of the Oedipus complex depends on the culture to which a person belongs.

In Kohlberg's opinion, it is a mistake to conclude from striking cultural differences in customs, or content of beliefs, that morality is culturally relative; one must take into account the *meanings,* or structure of thought, underlying the customs. Kohlberg says that certain basic moral values are universal because all normal children everywhere learn to think and interact socially in essentially the same ways. Facing a dilemma like that of the husband with the dying wife, any person will decide what to do on the basis of such considerations as the value of life, concern for the law, and affectional and family role obligations. How people think about these things depends more on their stage of moral maturity than on the conventions of their particular culture. For example, a Taiwanese boy at Stage 2 might say that Heinz was right to steal the drug because "if his wife dies he will have to pay for her funeral," whereas an American boy, also at Stage 2, might say he was right to steal it because otherwise "there will be no one to cook his food." The two explanations differ because the content of Taiwanese and American customs differ (large funerals are an important value in Taiwan), but both children see the problem in a way consistent with the structure of the instrumental exchange orientation that characterizes Stage 2.

Kohlberg's theory is the only one of the three that implies a value judgment. It suggests that people *should* think in Stage 5 or 6 terms. Psychoanalytic and social-learning theories are not concerned with what "true morality" is. They view moral development as a problem in social development and attempt to explain how an essentially amoral child comes to behave in ways that are considered moral by the adult society he will join.

Socializing Agents and Child Rearing

Who are the socializing agents that teach a child the norms of society and influence his moral development? Most people—and all three theories—

agree that parents are especially important as socializing agents. In psycho-analytic theory they are central to identification and socialization, although Freud also recognized the influence of other socializing agents. Social-learning theory also views parents as central, because they are the earliest and most pervasive rewarding and punishing agents and models, but this theory gives somewhat more attention to other adults, including teachers, models seen on television, and the child's peers.

For cognitive-developmental theory, parents are important as influences on both role taking and norms, but other people can be equally important and can even substitute for the parents. Kohlberg recognizes, for example, how important the influence of the peer group may be. He cites research on Israeli children reared in collective communities called kibbutzim, who rarely see their parents but still develop morally. In Kohlberg's theory, what is important is that the child have experience with moral judgments more advanced than his own but not so much more advanced that he cannot understand them. A Stage 2 child ("I won't hit Bobby because he will hit me back") will learn more from a playmate or parent who talks in Stage-3 terms ("If you were a good boy, you wouldn't do that") than from a parent's Stage-5 explanations ("If people hit people whenever they felt like it, we wouldn't have a very good world, would we?").

A question closely related to who the socializing agents are is, "What are the effects of different methods of socialization?" A large proportion of early research in the psychoanalytic and social-learning traditions concerned the effects of parental warmth, power, and discipline on moral development. An exhaustive early study on the effects of different types of discipline, performed by Robert Sears, Eleanor Maccoby, and Harry Levin, showed that children who are punished psychologically (with love withdrawal and reasoning) develop stronger consciences and are more susceptible to guilt feelings than children who are punished physically. Although at first it was thought that love withdrawal was the more important factor, later studies by Aronfreed and by Martin Hoffman and Herbert Saltzstein suggest that reasoning with the child is the critical factor. This finding corresponds with what would be expected from cognitive-developmental theory, which says that reasoning with a child encourages him to take the role of others; it is also in accord with Aronfreed's position that verbal explanations help the child internalize moral standards by providing him with thoughts that he associates with reward or punishment.

It has also been fairly well established that children who are physically punished for aggression nevertheless behave more aggressively than other children. Assuming that physical punishment means an aggressive father, psychoanalytic theory would predict that punishment would encourage the resolution of the Oedipus complex and result in the development of a strict superego, because the father is frightening to the child. But aggressive behavior would be expected nonetheless, because it is the father with whom the punished child identified. As for social-learning theory, the finding that physical punishment encourages later aggression seems to contradict the basic behaviorist tenet that says the more intense the punishment, the greater its effect. Aronfreed and Bandura have offered several reasons why the expected effect of punishment does not hold. Bandura observes that parents who punish their children physically for aggressive behavior provide a model for that very behavior. In *Conduct and Conscience* Aronfreed suggests that psychological punishment may, in fact, be more painful for a child than physical punishment; therefore, the physical punishment may not serve as well as psychological punishment to extinguish the aggressive behavior. Also, psychological punishment encourages the internalization of moral standards because it includes reasoning with the child, whereas physical punishment does not; therefore, as the child who is physically punished grows up, it is not likely that he will develop a conscience about aggression.

What Determines Moral Behavior?

Another topic that has received much attention from researchers is the extent to which moral behavior is determined by characteristics of the *situation* as opposed to the honesty or dishonesty of the *person*. A monumental study performed by Hugh Hartshorne and Mark May and their colleagues in 1928, which involved thousands of children in many different situations, was a considerable disappointment to those who would like to divide the world into cheaters and noncheaters. Hartshorne and May found that almost all children cheat some of the time and that knowing a person has cheated in one situation does *not* make it possible to predict that he will (or will not) cheat in another. The decision on whether to cheat seemed to be largely determined by expediency—by whether the situation was such that it seemed safe and easy to cheat. When honest behavior was not dictated by concern about detection and punishment, it seemed to depend on immediate social and situational factors such as group approval and example. In some classrooms many children cheated, whereas in other, seemingly identically composed classrooms, almost no one did.

Psychoanalytic theory hypothesizes an internal superego that should give more consistency to moral behavior than was found by Hartshorne and May. Social-learning theorists would have fewer problems with these results, because they interpret behavioral consistencies and variations in terms of generalization and discrimination. That is, they would expect behavior that occurs in one situation also to occur in another only when the stimuli in the two situations are similar.

At first glance, it may seem that cognitive-developmental theory would predict consistency of moral behavior across situations. Recall, however, that for Kohlberg the consistency is in how people reason about moral issues. As was mentioned earlier, Kohlberg emphasizes that behavior is to a large extent situationally determined for most people.

Studies such as that by Hartshorne and May have cast doubt on the concept of a consistent superego that produces moral behavior. Other studies, in particular one done by Kohlberg, have suggested that ego functions (characteristics of the rational self) are more important than superego functions in

Figure 10.11 A social-learning theorist might explain the scene here by pointing out that in the absence of parental restrictions, the older boy is merely doing what he finds most immediately rewarding. A cognitive explanation would not be greatly dissimilar: Both children are at Stage 1 or 2, in which morality is chiefly a matter of what "I want" and what "I can get away with." A psychoanalytic theorist would explain that because neither child has yet resolved his Oedipus complex, neither has internalized the values of his father that might regulate and restrain his behavior in this situation.

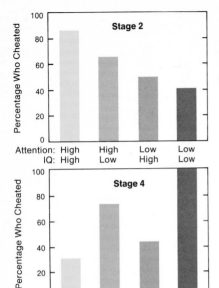

Figure 10.12 The results of Krebs' study of the relationship between ego strength and cheating at different stages of moral development. Attention level and IQ were taken as objective measures of ego strength. These data show that whether children cheat depends on both moral stage and ego strength. Those children at the higher stage of moral development who also had high ego strength cheated least; those at the higher stage who had weak ego strength cheated most.

(After Krebs, 1967.)

morality. Ego functions include intelligence, strength of will, the ability to wait for a large reward instead of taking an immediate small one, a capacity for sustained attention and fantasy-control, and high self-esteem. Although psychoanalytic theory postulates an ego (self)—and perhaps more important, an ego ideal—the relationship between morality and ego strength lends most support to the cognitive-developmental approach.

An experiment by Richard Krebs indicates some interesting associations between two aspects of ego strength, attention and IQ, and the moral behavior of children at different stages. Krebs found that at an early stage of moral development, Stage 2, more children with high ego strength (that is, high IQ and high attention) cheated, but at a higher stage of moral development, Stage 4, fewer of these children cheated. These findings suggest that the Stage-2 children who were attentive and bright enough to see that they could cheat did so in a characteristically unprincipled way. The low-attention, low-IQ Stage-2 children presumably did not notice the opportunity to cheat. Stage-4 children with high ego strength had the will to obey the rules of their society, whereas the Stage-4 subjects with weak egos gave in to the temptation to cheat.

At the principled level of moral development, Stages 5 and 6, both situational factors and ego strength are less important influences on behavior than they are at earlier stages because at that level a person carries his own interpretations of the situation around with him. In 1968 Norma Haan, M. Brewster Smith, and Jeanne Block studied student participation in the Berkeley Free Speech Movement of 1964. Their research indicated that students' past behavior (whether or not they participated in the Free-Speech-Movement demonstrations, for example) could be predicted quite accurately from their level of moral development. Of the principled subjects, 80 percent had indeed actively participated in the demonstrations, apparently because they perceived the situation at Berkeley to be clearly unjust; only 10 percent of the Stage 3 and 4 subjects had done so. You may see a parallel between the behavior of the Berkeley students active in the Free Speech Movement and that of Henry David Thoreau.

This chapter has discussed moral development as an example of social development. The study of the development of morality brings to light the major facets of social development more generally. Growing up morally is just one part of growing up socially. After learning considerably more about the individual and his many ways of functioning, we shall return to social development in Unit VI.

SUMMARY

1. **Moral development** is one aspect of social development. What changes in people as they grow from infants to adults is their understanding of the rules that govern social behavior and of what *should* be.

2. One of the three theories described in this chapter that attempts to explain how age-related changes in moral thinking and moral action take place is Freud's **psychoanalytic theory.** Freud was the first to suggest that people develop a sense of morality rather than being born with one.

   a. Freud divided psychosocial development into five stages, each defined according to the main focus of pleasure for the child. In the **oral stage** pleasure centers upon sucking and the mother's breast; in the **anal stage** upon defecation; in the **phallic stage** upon the penis and the relationship with the parent of the opposite sex. At the end of the phallic stage the child resolves the Oedipus complex (for boys) or the

Electra complex (for girls) and thus moves into the **latency stage,** in which sexuality is submerged. Finally with adolescence and the **genital stage,** the person's sexuality emerges once again, and the focus of pleasure is sexual intercourse with the opposite sex.

b. Freud argued that resolution of the Oedipus or Electra complex is the most important occurrence in moral development. The **Oedipus complex** develops (between the ages of three and five) because the boy desires his mother and wants therefore to destroy his rival, his father. Perceiving his father's power, however, and fearing castration, the boy resolves the complex by repressing his desire for his mother and identifying with his father. It is this **identification** that starts the course of moral development, because the boy, in striving to be like his father, internalizes his father's moral standards; in Freud's terms, he introjects his father's superego.

c. In the **Electra complex** the girl first realizes that she has no penis and therefore turns away from her mother and toward her father as love object, because he has a penis. She identifies with her mother so as to become like her mother and thus to be able to have a special relationship with her father (as her mother does). Thereby she internalizes her mother's moral standards and thus acquires a superego.

d. Freud saw the **superego** as consisting of two parts; the **ego ideal,** the standards dictating what the child ought to be, and the **conscience,** the prohibitions dictating what the child should not do.

e. Research on the psychoanalytic theory of moral development shows that there is an increase in morality around the time of the resolution of the Oedipus complex, but it is not as sharp a change as psychoanalysis predicts. Research has also supported Freud's concept of identification—not so much as a process in the Oedipus complex as a general process in social development.

3. **Social-learning theory's** analysis of moral development focuses on conditioning and imitation as explanations of why moral behavior occurs even in the absence of direct rewards and punishments. Two of the foremost theorists in this area are Albert Bandura and Justin Aronfreed.

a. According to the principles of **conditioning** (as described in Chapter 4), social behavior, like other behavior, is maintained by rewards and punishments. Once the child learns which behaviors are rewarded and which punished, he need only think of the potential consequences of an act in order to decide whether to do it.

b. Social-learning theorists believe that what parents say to children as they punish or reward them is very important for the internalization of moral standards. The parents' words help the child to understand exactly what is being punished or rewarded.

c. A child's reactions to his own transgressions are also the results of a conditioning process. If, for example, a child learns that he can avoid punishment by apologizing, he may learn to apologize whenever he fears punishment.

d. **Imitation** is, with conditioning, one of the most important explanatory tools of social-learning theory. A child first watches a **model** do something, thus acquiring a cognitive representation of the act, and then he may later perform the response himself. Whether he does eventually imitate the model depends on the rewards or punishments he sees given to the model and on his perception of what kind of person the model is.

Figure 10.13 Justin Aronfreed has given his attention to how external events such as rewards and punishments result in the creation of such internal controls on behavior as conscience. He also has attempted to isolate the factors that favor the development of helping behavior in children and to understand how children develop representational thought.

Figure 10.14 Robert Sears, whose extensive study of child-rearing practices (with Eleanor Maccoby and Harry Levin) is referred to in this chapter, has combined an interest in psychoanalytic concepts with training in behaviorist thinking. As a graduate student in the 1930s, he studied under the noted American behaviorist Clark Hull. He was president of the American Psychological Association in 1950–51; in his presidential address he discussed the importance of studying people in pairs, such as husband-wife, parent-child, and employer-employee, as well as studying them individually.

Figure 10.15 Albert Bandura's extensive research on imitation and observational learning in children has made him a highly regarded source of opinion about the causes of deviance in American society. He has, for example, been consulted by the government about the relationships that may or may not exist between television violence and violence in the streets. He has also investigated the use of imitation in the reduction of intense fears in children and has theorized about the importance of observational learning in language acquisition.

e. Much experimental evidence supports the social-learning approach's emphasis on conditioning and imitation. In addition, Aronfreed has shown not only that children's resistance to temptation can be shaped through reward and punishment but also that the earlier a punishment (verbal) was administered to a child during a transgression, the less likely he was to transgress when no one was watching. Bandura has also done studies showing that children do imitate models and that they are especially likely to imitate a model they see being rewarded.

4. The **cognitive-developmental theory** of moral development, formulated by Lawrence Kohlberg, is based upon Piaget's general theory of cognitive development. Kohlberg believes that developments in moral judgments take place, like other cognitive advances, through assimilation and accommodation. For moral development **role taking** is also of central importance—the ability to look at the world from others' viewpoints. Kohlberg postulates **six stages of moral judgment;** the stages always occur in sequence, and a later one always develops out of and subsumes the earlier one. Each stage is more cognitively sophisticated than the ones that precede it. The characteristics of moral thinking at each stage are set out in Figures 10.5–10.7.

5. A number of experimental studies have supported the cognitive-development approach. Kohlberg presented children with a series of moral dilemmas, asked them what action they would take to resolve each dilemma, and then asked them to explain the reasons for their decisions. He found that the stages of moral development reflected in their answers corresponded well to the ages (from seven to sixteen) of the children making the decisions. That is, the answers at Stage 2 declined steadily with age, whereas the answers at Stage 4 increased with age. Another Kohlberg study showed that children in three different cultures progress through the stages of moral development in the same order.

6. It is instructive to compare the three theories on a number of key issues to see not only how they differ but what they may have in common. The main focuses of the three differ: Psychoanalytic theory focuses on **emotions;** social-learning theory, on **behavior;** cognitive-developmental theory, on **thought processes.** But none of the theories deals exclusively with the thing it focuses on; each theory tries to deal with emotions, behavior, and thought processes. For example, the first phase of the behaviorist concept of imitation is acquisition of a mental image of the act to be modeled; that mental representation is essentially cognitive. Also, Kohlberg deals with emotion, saying that children do experience emotion upon wrongdoing but that their interpretation of what they feel changes with changing stages of development.

7. A basic question for a theory of moral development is whether morality differs from culture to culture.

   a. According to social-learning theory, morality must be culturally relative because the agents of socialization and the social norms to which children learn to adhere are different in each culture.

   b. Psychoanalytic theory says that there is a universal sequence of psychosexual development, including the Oedipus and Electra complexes. Morality is nevertheless culturally relative in that the moral standards each child incorporates into his or her superego vary from culture to culture.

   c. Cognitive-developmental theory states that some basic moral values are

Figure 10.16 Lawrence Kohlberg, educator and social psychologist, has gained considerable attention with his theory of the development of moral judgment and character. His work is novel in current American psychology because of its close associations with Piaget's theories; because of its broad and somewhat speculative nature; and because it contains value judgments about human behavior.

universal. Because all normal children everywhere go through the same stages of cognitive development and interact socially in essentially the same ways, the meanings—or structure of thought—that underlie moral reasoning are universally comparable, despite differing customs.

8. All three theories focus on the parents as important socializing agents affecting children's moral development. They are supremely important in psychoanalytic theory. They are central to social-learning theory as the most important dispensers of rewards and punishments, but other people may also be important models. Other people can substitute for the parents, according to cognitive-developmental theory; for example, slightly older children may serve as better influences on the child's moral judgments because they are just one stage above his own and so provide the disequilibrium needed for moral advance.

9. Another question that a theory of morality must deal with is whether moral behavior is determined more by characteristics of situations or by permanent personality characteristics, such as a person's basic honesty or dishonesty. A famous study of moral behavior was performed by Hartshorne and May in 1928. They studied children's cheating behavior in school and found that almost all children cheat some of the time, and they could not predict when or where children would cheat.

   a. Psychoanalytic theory would have a difficult time explaining these results, because the superego should produce moral consistency from one situation to the next.

   b. Social-learning theory would have no trouble with Hartshorne and May's results: It says that moral behavior is determined by situational cues, not by permanent personality characteristics.

   c. Cognitive-developmental theory emphasizes that people are consistent in their moral reasoning but that their behavior is, for the most part, situationally determined.

SUGGESTED READINGS

Bandura, Albert, and Richard H. Walters. *Social Learning and Personality Development.* New York: Holt, Rinehart and Winston, 1967. One of the first presentations of Bandura's social-learning theory. It supplies the rudiments of Bandura's position, which are elaborated in Bandura's chapter in the Goslin *Handbook,* cited here.

Brown, Roger. *Social Psychology.* New York: Free Press, 1965. Brown's chapter on the acquisition of morality presents an eloquently clear outline of the psychoanalytic, social-learning, and cognitive-developmental theories of moral development.

Freud, Sigmund. "Dissection of the Psychical Personality," in James Strachey (ed.), *The Complete Works of Sigmund Freud.* Vol. XXII. London: Hogarth Press, 1964, pp. 57–80. This article is the one that deals most explicitly with Freud's view of morality.

Golding, William. *Lord of the Flies.* New York: Coward, McCann & Geoghegan, 1962. An absorbing and shocking novel about how a group of young boys stranded on an island run wild in the absence of socializing influences.

Goslin, David A. (ed.). *Handbook of Socialization Theory and Research.* Chicago: Rand McNally, 1969. Contains three chapters that supply the single best presentation of theories of moral development—chapters by Aronfreed, Bandura, and Kohlberg. The Kohlberg chapter is his single best work and has been called "inspired."

UNIT IV
The World of Sense and Feeling

In the Western world the so-called "mind-body problem" has been a major concern of thinkers since the Greeks: Is the mind essentially independent of the body or is it solely a manifestation of a bodily process? In some domains psychologists have been able to forget about the mind-body problem and worry simply about behavior—overt action that can be analyzed without reference to a mind. But that is not true of the topics of this unit. We stub a toe, the noise of a plane drowns out our conversation, someone we know dies and we feel

11 **Perception:**
Principles and Processes
discusses how people use information gathered by their sense organs to perceive objects and events in the real world. It examines the process behind perception, the nature of perceptual organization, and the relationship between perception and the real world.
See related chapters: 5, 6, 20

12 **Sensation and the Senses**
first describes the general relationship between sensory experiences and the characteristics of the physical stimuli that produce those experiences. Then it discusses each specific human sense—the structure of each of the sense organs and the basic characteristics of each sense.
See related chapters: 3, 5, 7

13 **Varieties of Consciousness**
examines the nature of consciousness and describes recent research breakthroughs that permit its scientific study. Special phenomena of consciousness are discussed, including the effects of a split brain, dreaming, meditation, hypnosis, spirit possession, and drugs.
See related chapters: 18, 24, 28

RELATED CHAPTERS

3
Species-Specific Behavior:
Ethology introduces the biological approach to psychology, which is the focus of much of this unit, especially Chapters 12 and 14.

4
Conditioning and Learning:
Behaviorism describes the behaviorist concept of reinforcement, which is closely related to the notion of drive, discussed in Chapter 14.

5
Thinking and Memory:
Information Processing examines the view that man is like a computer. In Chapter 11, an information-processing approach to pattern perception is applied, and Chapter 12 discusses the sensory input that is used by the human computer.

6
Thinking and Problem Solving: Cognitive Psychology
first introduces the computer model called analysis by synthesis, which is applied to pattern perception in Chapter 11. Also, Chapters 15 and 16 discuss the implications of the cognitive approach for understanding emotion and motivation.

7
Heredity and Environment
describes the physiological mechanisms of heredity and thus relates to the discussion of the physiological bases of behavior in Chapters 12 and 14 and to the discussion of hereditary and environmental influences on emotional expression in Chapter 15.

17
Psychological Testing describes the TAT test and scoring procedures for it. The TAT is a tool used in measuring several motives discussed in Chapter 16, especially the motive to achieve and the motive to avoid success.

sorrow. Or we taste a delicious meal, we feel the passion of sex, a baby is born and we feel joy. In all these cases, there is someone who experiences the perceptions, sensations, or emotions. But because these topics seem to require the notion of an experiencing mind, they have been especially troublesome for psychology.

Psychology's answer to this apparent difficulty has been to assume that the mind is indeed a physical process—that mental phenomena can be explained scientifically because they arise from the body's (in particular the brain's) interactions with the physical world in which it lives. For example, perceptions arise because specific stimuli in the world affect the sense organs of the body, which in turn transmit information to the brain, which in turn interprets the information, and this process ends in our experiencing perceptions. Whether or not you agree with psychology's analysis of the mind, it has produced some amazingly effective explanations of sensation, perception, emotion, and even consciousness itself. Those explanations are the topic of this unit.

14 Physiology, Drives, and Emotion

discusses the biological bases of behavior and experience: the nature of the nervous system and the endocrine system, the physiology of the essential biological drives (especially hunger, thirst, sex, and parental behavior), and the physiology of emotion.
See related chapters: 3, 4, 7, 25, 28

15 Emotional Experience and Expression

outlines what psychologists know about emotions: the basic dimensions underlying emotions, the relationship between physiology, cognition, and emotion, and the roles of learning and heredity in the emotions.
See related chapters: 6, 7

16 Motivation and Action

discusses theories of human motivation—in particular, drive theory and expectancy-value theory—and takes the motive to achieve as a case study of the analysis of human motivation. This chapter provides a transition to personality and social psychology, which are the topics of the following units.
See related chapters: 6, 17, 18, 21

18

Psychoanalytic Theories of Personality presents Sigmund Freud's approach to personality. Freud's analysis of the meaning of dreams is examined in Chapter 13. Also, the Freudian approach to motivation can be contrasted with the approach presented in Chapter 16.

20

Person Perception and Interpersonal Attraction discusses people's perception of other people and thus relates to Chapter 11's examination of perception.

21

Patterns of Social Behavior: The Case of Sex Roles examines differences between male and female sex roles; Chapter 16 discusses differences between men and women in particular motives and suggests that those differences may be a result of the sex roles prescribed by American culture.

24

Adjustment and Disorder describes the alterations in perception, cognition, and consciousness that accompany various kinds of mental disorder—an addition to the discussion of varieties of consciousness in Chapter 13.

25

Bases of Disorder discusses the possible physiological roots of psychological disorder and so relates to the description of the physiological bases of behavior in Chapter 14.

28

Drugs and Drug Therapy expands upon Chapter 13's discussion of the effects of various drugs on consciousness. It also discusses how the effects of certain drugs are thought to relate to the chemistry of the nervous system, which is discussed in Chapter 14.

The various sense perceptions are the means by which we obtain agreed-upon knowledge of the universe. We may feel we have knowledge by other routes—by intuition, perhaps, or by "feelings" or perhaps we "just know." It is, however, difficult to get general agreement on results of such personal intuitions, feelings, and just knowings. There is always fascination with extrasensory perception, or ESP. There is a strong desire on the part of people to believe in additional windows in the world, windows that open on vistas closed to the accepted senses—the ability to see into the future, into another's thoughts, in the dark, over distances.

So far, no one has worked out a rationale to explain such ESP. Of course, if ESP existed, the absence of a rationale would not abolish that existence, but no one has yet advanced convincing evidence of its existence—only more or less amusing anecdotes.

The anecdotes, of course, are sometimes awfully persuasive. All of us have experienced cases of apparent telepathy, or precognition, or the rest of the various "wild talents." The best ESP tale I ever heard happened to a colleague of mine, a professor of immunology, who swore to me that his story was true. I know him well and I absolutely believe him. Here is the story. The professor said to me:

"This happened about thirty years ago when my wife and I were planning to go on an excursion steamer up the Hudson River. We thought we would welcome a day of noise and overeating, dancing perhaps, or just sitting.

"We bought the tickets well in advance, for the ship was sure to be filled, and as luck would have it, the day was absolutely beautiful. We packed a delightful picnic basket, for we expected there might be difficulty in buying food on the crowded ship.

"We arrived at the dock in good time; passengers were just beginning to file aboard. The ship itself was gaily festooned with pennants, and it seemed to me I could already hear a dance band playing on board. All about were happy, carefree groups of people, most of them young, talking and laughing.

"It seemed a scene compounded entirely of happiness and joy, and yet as I watched the people moving up the gangplank it seemed to me that the ship darkened, that there was a fitful ruddy glow dancing along its sides, and the distant dance music turned into the sound of screaming.

"I turned to look at my wife, whose eyes, as they met mine, turned anxious. 'What's wrong?' she asked.

"I tried to pass it off lightly. 'Just one of those feelings,' I said. 'It seemed to me that the ship was on fire.'

"My wife whispered, 'I had the same feeling.'

"We said not another word. We turned on our heels, made our way back through the crowd. That afternoon we ate our picnic lunch somberly in our own home."

My friend stopped at this point, and I said, rather tensely, "And the ship burned that day?"

"No," said my friend, calmly. "It went and returned safely and everyone on board had a wonderful time."

And that, I repeat, is my favorite ESP story.

Isaac Asimov

11

Perception: Principles and Processes

Figure 11.1 The Gestalt psychologist Ivo Kohler experimented with his ability to adapt to wearing various distorting prisms over his eyes, like the ones shown here, which turn the world upside down. He discovered that in time he was able to compensate for most distortions. He was, for example, able to walk around and even ride a bicycle after wearing a set of prisms like these for a few days.

In the next few seconds, something peculiar will start hap pening to the material youa rereading. Iti soft ennotre alized howcom plext heproces sofrea ding is. Afe w sim plerear range mentscan ha vey oucomp lete lycon fused!

We normally gather and interpret information from our environment without being aware of what we are doing. We read the words on a page, not noticing how we are analyzing patterns of lines in order to read. We listen to a train in the distance, and we can tell whether it is to the north of us or to the south; but we do not usually notice that we are analyzing the sounds of the train in order to determine the train's location. We only pay attention to how we analyze information from our environment—how we *perceive*—when something like the garbled paragraph above forces us to.

Instead of thinking about how we perceive, most of us simply assume that our perception mirrors the external world. We imagine that our senses send copies—images or pictures—of the external world over pathways of nerves to some sort of central switchboard, where the images are displayed on a screen of consciousness that reflects our awareness of the world. But this is not an adequate explanation of how we perceive the things around us.

It is true that perception is usually based upon information that we obtain through our senses: We can extract information from the environment because our senses connect us with the world. Just as it is impossible to walk without legs, so it is impossible to see the world without eyes or to hear the world without ears. But eyes, ears, and other sense organs do not simply transmit copies of the world to our brains. Perception is an **interpretation** based on information from the senses.

Several facts about the way we perceive illustrate how perception involves interpretations that are not simply mirrors of the world. First of all, *we are unable to perceive many aspects of the world:* Individual molecules, magnetic forces, cosmic rays do not register on our sense organs. High-frequency sounds, which dogs, bats, and many other animals are especially sensitive to, we cannot hear at all. Second, *we often perceive things that are not in the world:* We dream, sometimes we have hallucinations or see illusions, and at times we even receive sensory information that is not "real." For example, we can see without our eyes' receiving light. If you close your eyes and press on the side of one of them, you will probably see a flash of light. (If you do not see it at first, concentrate on your visual experience for a while. You have to overcome the fact that you have learned to ignore flashes of this sort.) This flash is not an image of something that happened in the world. Your visual system has been tricked, in a sense, for a visual experience has been created without actual light stimulation. Usually the eye responds to light energy from the external world, but it can be made to respond by other means, such as pressure on the eyeballs. Indeed, experiments have shown that direct electrical stimulation of the visual area of the brain causes us to "see" light patterns.

A third way that our perceptions differ from mental mirrors is that our experience of the world depends on much more than what is really physically there. *Expectations influence perceptual experience.* When we are in the shower and are expecting an important telephone call, every noise seems to be the ringing of the phone. When we expect to see the word "expect," we will often not even notice that it has been misspelled, and when we expect a word to be in a sentence, we may not notice that it been left out.

Obviously, then, our perception is closely tied to the world but does not simply mirror it. Through perception we monitor what is happening in the world around us by interpreting the information that we receive from our senses. The three chapters in this unit deal with different aspects of the way we analyze this information. **Perception,** the topic of this chapter, concerns the process of analysis itself: the way in which people interpret information from the environment and organize it into meaningful patterns. The operation of the **senses,** the bodily organs through which people gather information from their environment, is described in Chapter 12. And Chapter 13 discusses the **consciousness** that lies behind perception, the quality of mind through which people experience things and are aware of things. (Person perception, our interpretations of other people's personalities, is discussed in Chapter 20.)

As the definition of perception indicates, we perceive meaningful patterns. That is, through interpreting sensory information, we perceive *real objects and events* in a real world. An object or an event is not merely a conglomeration of sights, sounds, textures, and so forth. It is a thing in the world, with a past and a future. It has a distinctive set of properties: It takes up space or does not; it may be heavy, brittle, hot, transitory. In other words, it has meaning, and when we perceive the thing we perceive its meaning.

In trying to understand how this perception of meaning occurs, psychologists focus upon three general aspects of perception. Perceptual inference is the process by which we interpret sensory information. Perceptual organization involves the principles that govern our perception of meaningful patterns. The relation between perception and the real world involves analysis of the specific patterns of sensory information that our perceptual system uses to perceive the characteristics of the real world. After these three aspects of perception are discussed, the phenomena of extrasensory perception and how they relate to ordinary perception will be considered.

PERCEPTUAL INFERENCE

When you put a book on a table, you do not check to make sure the table is solid. You probably do not test a chair to see if it will bear your weight before

Figure 11.2   How might you analyze the sensory information in this photograph? You might begin by noting the large, peculiarly shaped dark mass of bluish-green in the lower half of the field. There are a large number of patches of color: some similar, some strongly contrasting; some large, some small; some with fairly simple boundary lines, some with extremely complex boundaries; some that are homogeneous throughout, some that vary greatly over the range of brightness or purity. But obviously this is *not* a description of what you see when you look at this photograph. You see a wine bottle, a corkscrew, a wineglass and other objects lying on a table. In short, you do not sense stimuli; you perceive objects.

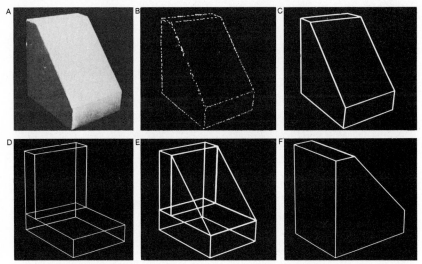

Figure 11.3 Like humans and animals, an appropriately programmed computer can do more than record sensory information: It can use perceptual inference. Here the stages in a computer's processing of a photograph (A) are shown. The computer generates an outline (B) of the form represented in the photograph and sharpens it (C). Then it uses combinations of simple, geometric solids to generate a plan (D and E) for the three-dimensional object that the photograph probably represents. Finally, it rotates the three-dimensional object it has created and presents a view of it (F) that is has never been exposed to before. Note that this computer's capacity for perceptual inference would be inadequate if the shape presented to it were extremely unusual or complex.
(After Roberts, 1963.)

you sit down; you assume that its legs are planted firmly on the floor even though they may be hidden from your view. You assume that the wall that was behind you the last time you looked is still there and that the familiar bark at the door indicates that your dog is there—not a mountain lion or a cat, not even some other dog. Even though the apple in Figure 11.2 blocks your view of the stem of the wineglass, you do not worry that the wine will spill. You infer that the stem exists even though you cannot see it. In all these instances, you are making unconscious perceptual generalizations, based upon past experience.

Hermann von Helmholtz, a great nineteenth-century European scientist, began the study of the influences of past experience on perception. He suggested that the perception of objects in general is derived from patterns of sensory information by a process of unconscious inference. It is *inference* because we interpret sensory information by relating it to our past experience. And it is *unconscious* because it occurs automatically, without our being aware of the process of interpretation.

Some psychologists criticized the notion of unconscious inference because Helmholtz could provide no explanation of how the inference occurs. The best that he could do was to say that we generalize on the basis of our past experience. He could not specify the process by which an inference is made. Consequently, critics accused him of relying upon a homunculus to explain perception—a "little man" inside the head. To account for perception by imagining that there is a little man inside who is drawing inferences is not much of an explanation, because one must then explain how the little man works.

The development of computers, however, essentially eliminated this objection to Helmholtz's theory. Computers regularly draw conclusions (inferences) from "sensory" information, and the processes by which these inferences are made can be completely described (in the language of information processing, discussed in Chapter 5). One example of perceptual inference in a computer is illustrated in Figure 11.3. Given a photograph of an object, the computer can infer the object's shape and thus generate views of the object not shown in the photograph. There is no little man inside the computer allowing it to make this inference; there is simply a systematic process for inferring shape from "sensory" information (in this case the information in photographs). In a similar way the human brain makes perceptual inferences through systematic processes that analyze and interpret sensory information.

The advent of computer models of perceptual processes has had a major

Figure 11.4 This photograph is the same one that appears in Figure 11.2 minus all the objects that were perceived in that photograph as figure. Note that your attention shifts to the remaining elements in the photograph and again differentiates them into figure (the green table) and ground (the brown wall). Both of these were seen as ground in the earlier photograph.

impact on the field of psychology. (Several of the most important computer models will be discussed later in the chapter.) Besides providing explicit models for how inference can occur in perception, the development of computer models has also helped to change the meaning of inference. Helmholtz emphasized that the process of inference was a result of generalizations from past experience, but computer research has demonstrated that inferential processes can occur in perception that do not rely on past experience; the process for inferring shape illustrated in Figure 11.3 is one example. The term **perceptual inference,** which is now preferred to Helmholtz's "unconscious inference," refers to any process of interpretation of sensory information by people or computers, irrespective of whether past experience is involved.

Figure and Ground

Our most basic perceptual inference is the division of what we perceive into figure and ground. When we look at a scene that has any detail at all, we automatically separate it into regions that represent objects, or **figure,** and those that represent spaces between objects, or **ground** (see Figure 11.4). This ability to separate objects from space does not seem to depend on past experience. When people who have been blind from birth have an eye operation that gives them sight, they can immediately separate figure from ground (as shown by the research of Marius von Senden), even though they have never before had any visual experience.

Although visual experience does not seem to be necessary for perceptual inference of figure and ground, it does normally have some effect. The role of experience is most easily demonstrated in figures that have had most of the normal sensory cues removed from them. Figure 11.5 may not seem to you at first to constitute a single object in space, but after some effort you will see it as a Dalmatian dog. Your perception of the blotches as a single figure against a ground requires experience with what a Dalmatian dog looks like. Young children are unable to see the blotches as a single figure, according to Louis Thurstone. (Chapter 7 discusses more generally the role of experience in perceptual development.) Thus, experience allows us to organize what we see into figure and ground more easily.

Figure 11.5 A stable differentiation of the elements of this photograph into figure and ground is difficult at first, and would probably be impossible if you have had no previous experience with Dalmatian dogs. The knowledge that there is a Dalmatian dog in this photograph, however, makes it possible to clearly differentiate one set of blotches and spots as figure, and to see the rest of the blotches and spots as undifferentiated ground. Note also that once you have differentiated the figure in one part of the photograph, it becomes easier to further differentiate the rest of the photograph.

Figure and ground are important not only in vision but in other senses as well. When you follow one person's voice at a noisy party, that voice is the figure and all other sounds become ground. If you shift your attention to another voice, it replaces the first voice as figure. Similarly, if you listen to a piece of music you do not recognize and then suddenly you hear a familiar melody embedded in the unfamiliar music, the melody leaps out at you. The melody becomes the figure, and the rest of the music merely background.

Perceptual Ambiguity

One of the most dramatic demonstrations of perceptual inference is the phenomenon of perceptual ambiguity, where two different perceptual inferences can be made from the same stimulus. For example, figure and ground can be ambiguous, as shown in Figure 11.6. This figure can alternatively appear as a white vase against a black background or as two black faces against a white background. Another type of perceptual ambiguity involves a figure that can be seen in two different orientations when it is interpreted as being three-dimensional. One of the best known is the Necker cube, shown in Figure 11.7A. The figure provides no information as to which part of the figure is the front and which is the back. Presented with this dilemma, the brain evidently entertains alternate hypotheses—and never decides between them.

But if we can see Figure 11.7A in two different ways, it would seem that we should be able to see it in still other ways. Why is it seen in only two ways, and why are both of them cubes? Theoretically it could be seen as many different three-dimensional objects—a giant truncated pyramid tipped toward the viewer as shown in Figure 11.7B, or any other object that from some perspective would produce the outline shown. The reason it is not seen in other ways is that cubes are simpler and more familiar than truncated pyramids. Perceptual inference operates by inferring the *most likely possibility* that accounts for the sensory information available.

Perceptually ambiguous figures thus illustrate the process of perceptual inference especially dramatically. Such figures show that sensory patterns do not completely determine which inference we draw, because a single pattern can be perceived in more than one way. Perception involves choosing among

Figure 11.6   This drawing is a classic demonstration of figure-ground ambiguity. What you perceive as figure and as ground depends on a number of factors, including your expectation.

Figure 11.7   (A) Another classic demonstration of perceptual ambiguity, this time in depth perception. Either face of the Necker cube may be seen as being in the foreground. (B) The Necker cube could, in principle, be seen as any number of shapes if the expectancies of the viewer were appropriately modified. Here a number of depth cues are used to induce the viewer to see the Necker cube as a pyramidal shape with its top lopped off, sloping toward the viewer.

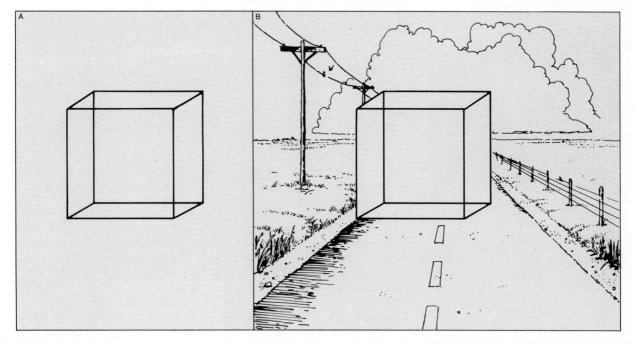

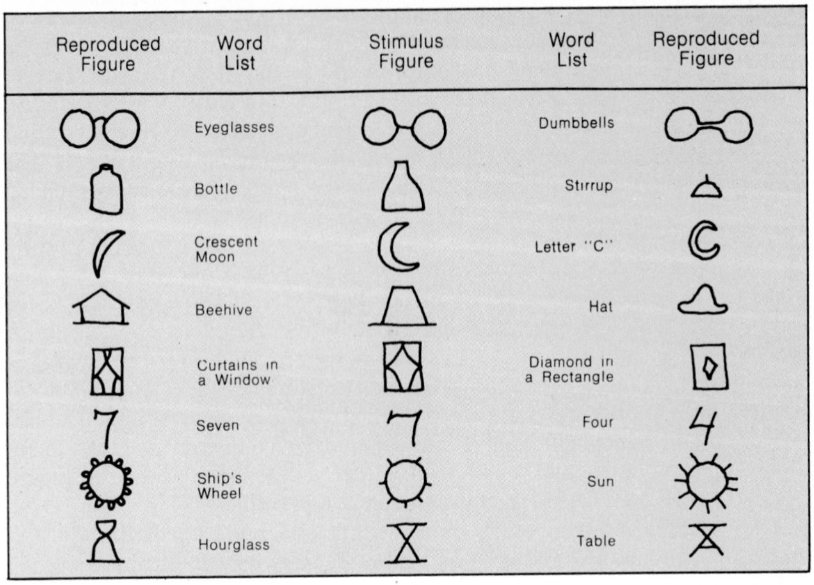

Reproduced Figure	Word List	Stimulus Figure	Word List	Reproduced Figure
⬭⬭	Eyeglasses	⬭⬭	Dumbbells	⬭–⬭
	Bottle		Stirrup	
	Crescent Moon	☾	Letter "C"	C
	Beehive		Hat	
	Curtains in a Window		Diamond in a Rectangle	
7	Seven	7	Four	4
	Ship's Wheel		Sun	
	Hourglass	X	Table	X

Figure 11.8 Carmichael, Hogan, and Walter designed an experiment to study the influence of set on perception. Subjects were shown the line patterns in the middle column of this figure, and these stimuli were described as drawings of various objects. Later, when the subjects were asked to reproduce from memory the patterns they had seen, they made the drawings shown in the right and left columns. You can see how the naming of the patterns influenced their drawings.
(After Carmichael, Hogan, and Walter, 1932.)

a number of possible answers to the question, "What object is producing that pattern?" Typically, a familiar object is likely to be chosen in preference to an unfamiliar one.

Perceptual Set

A third phenomenon that illustrates perceptual inference is called perceptual set, the readiness to perceive a stimulus in a particular way. If you tell a friend that you are about to show him a drawing of a vase and then you present Figure 11.6 to him, you have *set* him to see a vase rather than two faces (unless he has seen the figure before). You have given him an expectation about what he will see, and that expectation influences what he actually sees.

In one famous experiment on perceptual set done by Leonard Carmichael, Helena Hogan, and A. A. Walter, people were shown the drawings in the center column of Figure 11.8; some of them were told that the first drawing, for example, was a pair of glasses, while others were told that it was a barbell. When the two groups were later asked to draw the figure that they had seen, they typically drew not what they had actually seen but instead what they had been told that they would see.

Telling someone what he will perceive is only one way of affecting perceptual set. Another way is by manipulating a person's previous experience. For example, look at Figure 11.9A; then turn to page 248 and look at Figure 11.9B. Do you see a young woman? Now look at Figure 11.9C and then look back at Figure 11.9B. Do you now see an older woman? The experience of viewing one drawing influences what you see in the ambiguous figure. In other words, expectation based on your experience with one drawing influences the perceptual inference that is made from the ambiguous figure.

The experiences that we have in our daily lives influence perceptual set just as much as the experiences that are produced by psychologists. Count, quickly, how many aces of spades there are in Figure 11.10. To find out how much people's perception is influenced by perceptual set arising from everyday experience, Jerome Bruner devised special playing cards. In a normal deck of cards, clubs and spades are black, and hearts and diamonds are red. Bruner added incongruous cards, such as aces of spades colored red, to a set of normal cards. He found that most people who are familiar with a normal deck of cards do not see these unusual cards as spades. They are perceptually set to see black spades and red hearts, and so they do not include the two red spades

Figure 11.9A This drawing (like those in Figures 11.6 and 11.7) is perceptually ambiguous. The effect of personal experience and set on what is perceived here is particularly strong. Many people have difficulty seeing an old woman in this drawing. Others have equal difficulty in seeing a young woman. If you have such difficulties, turn to Figures 11.9B on page 248 and 11.9C on page 249.
(After Boring, 1930.)

in Figure 11.10 when they count the number of spades. Their perceptual inferences about Figure 1110 are determined by their expectations rather than by what is actually there. That is, just as with the ambiguous Necker cube above, people are more likely to perceive what is simple and familiar than what is complex and unfamiliar.

In summary, perceptual inference is the process by which we interpret sensory information. Our most basic perceptual inference is differentiation between figure and ground. Perceptually ambiguous figures illustrate the occurrence of perceptual inference: Different objects can be inferred from a single sensory pattern. Perceptual set influences which object we infer from sensory patterns, especially from ambiguous ones.

PERCEPTUAL ORGANIZATION

When we look at an apple, we infer from sensory information that the object before us is an apple. An essential part of the perceptual process by which we make that inference involves analysis of the *pattern* that comprises the apple. Likewise, when we hear music at a concert, we perceive the pattern of musical notes and tones that make up each composition we hear. A major focus of psychologists' analysis of perception is this perceptual organization. How do human beings perceive patterns? Two different approaches to answering this question have been taken: Gestalt psychologists have emphasized description of the *principles* that we use in grouping things into patterns, and information-processing psychologists have focused on the *processes* underlying pattern recognition.

Gestalts and Gestaltists

Gestalt psychologists emphasize that in our perception we are constantly organizing bits and pieces of information into meaningful patterns, called **gestalts** after the German word for pattern or whole. Because of the organization of the black patches in Figure 11. 5, for example, one may perceive the form of the dog; a slight rearrangement of the patches would assure that no form could be perceived. The dog's form is a gestalt, a perceptual whole. Although one can see each of the elements in the pattern, more than just these elements is perceived: The gestalt is greater than the sum of the parts.

Gestalt psychology originated in Germany early in the twentieth century with psychologists such as Max Wertheimer, Kurt Koffka, and Wolfgang Köhler, and its influence extends into present-day psychology. In their research, the early Gestalt psychologists presented people with patterns of some kind—often patterns of dots or musical tones—and they simply asked the people what they saw or heard. From these data they formulated a number of **principles of perceptual organization,** which identify some of the characteristics of groupings that lead to the perception of gestalts. Several of the principles are illustrated in Figure 11.11. In Figure 11.11A no stable pattern is perceived. In Figure 11.11B, some dots are closer together, demonstrating the principle of **proximity:** The dots are now perceived as forming a series of lines. In Figure 11.11C, the addition of a few dots leads one to perceive two curved lines. In this case another principle, **continuity,** overrules proximity: Dots that form a single, uninterrupted pattern are seen as a gestalt. Another organizing principle is **similarity.** In Figure 11.11D a cross is perceived in the original pattern of dots because of the similarity of the dots making up the cross.

The principles of perceptual organization apply not only to vision but to other senses as well. For example, similar phenomena occur in the perception of sounds and are especially obvious in music. Proximity in time serves the same function for hearing as proximity in space does for vision. When you listen to a melody, you tend to group the notes according to their temporal

Figure 11.10   As quickly as you can: How many spades are there here? Read on only when you have answered. . . . If, like many people, you counted three, go back and look more carefully, disregarding color. Cards like these were prepared by Jerome Bruner and Leo Postman to demonstrate the effects of set, or expectancy, on perception.

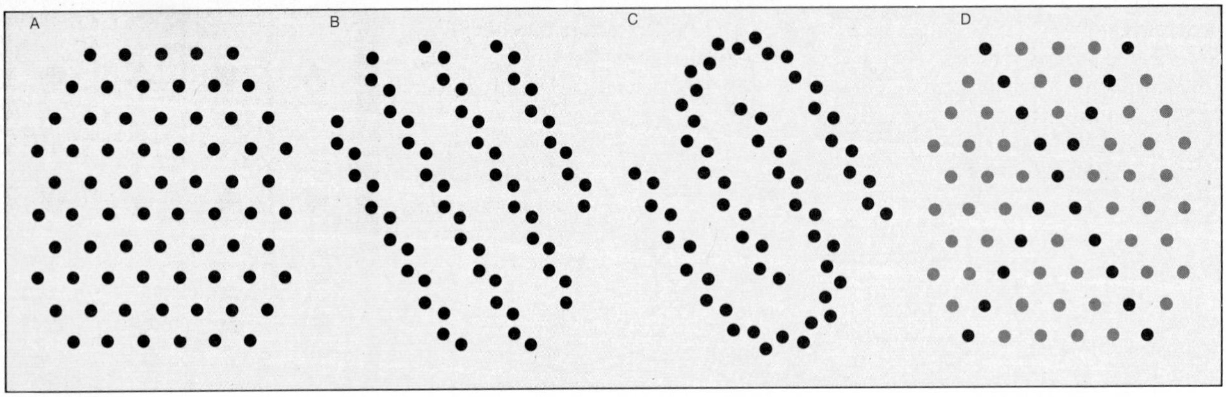

Figure 11.11 A demonstration of some of the Gestalt principles of organization. The pattern of equally spaced identical dots in (A) is not easily organized. It is seen either as an undifferentiated field or as a set of unstable overlapping patterns. In (B) a stable perception of parallel lines emerges because of the *proximity* of some dots to others. When some of these lines are made *continuous* with each other in (C), dots that are physically quite distant from one another are seen as belonging to a single curved line. In (D) a very stable organization emerges suddenly because some of the dots have been made *similar* to one another and different from the rest.

Figure 11.12 An illustration of the perceptual tendency toward simplicity. Despite conflicting cues, this figure is seen as two intersecting circles. The circle is among the simplest of perceived forms and provides by far the simplest means of interpreting this pattern.

proximity. But in hearing, as in vision, one principle can often override another. Listen to a composition in which two melody lines are being played simultaneously—for example, a fugue by Bach—and you can hear continuity override proximity. Notes that are very close together in time are not heard as belonging together when they are part of different melody lines. The principle of similarity is also important in hearing. It allows you to follow the sound of a familiar voice or instrument in a group even when continuity is lacking—to follow the bass guitarist through a song in which he never carries the melody, for example.

Julian Hochberg, Fred Attneave, and others have pointed out that the gestalt principles of organization can all be integrated under a single concept: **simplicity.** Patterns that are simple are more likely to be perceived than patterns that are complex, whether the simplicity is a result of proximity, continuity, similarity, or some other principle of perceptual organization. Despite the possible distractions and interpretations that might occur in viewing Figure 11.12, one tends to see it as two interlocking circles, because a circle is one of the simplest forms in nature. The perceptual process tends to infer the simplest possible pattern for any grouping of elements.

Pattern Recognition

Early Gestalt psychologists attempted to find principles for describing how people group things into a gestalt. Most contemporary psychologists who study the perception of patterns have accepted the notion of gestalt and the principles of perceptual organization, but they have gone beyond this description analysis to try to understand the process of perceptual inference underlying pattern perception. That is, they have combined an interest in perceptual organization with a concern for uncovering the process of perceptual inference. They have focused especially upon the way that people *recognize* patterns. As Peter Lindsay and Donald Norman have pointed out, people are remarkably good at recognizing patterns, despite wide variations in the particular instances of a pattern. An ''F'' can be big or small, fancy or plain, slanted or straight, upside-down or right-side up. Yet all these different configurations make up the same pattern: F. The ability to recognize patterns no matter what shape they are in is referred to as **pattern recognition.**

Most psychologists interested in pattern recognition use the information-processing approach to psychology (described in Chapter 5). In order to understand the human process of recognizing patterns, they try to program a computer to recognize patterns. If they can get a computer to recognize patterns about as well as people can, then they will have an effective model for explaining pattern recognition.

Recall that in perception we interpret the meaning of sensory information. In order to deal effectively with pattern recognition, these information-processing models must consider two different components of the perceptual process: how sensory information is analyzed, and how meaning and expectation influence and control that analysis. Models that focus on the analysis of sensory information generally employ a procedure known as feature analysis; models that focus on meaning and expectation use a procedure known as analysis by synthesis.

Feature Analysis: Pandemonium   In the procedure of feature analysis, sensory information is broken down into distinctive characteristics that can be used to identify specific patterns. For example, some of the features that are used to identify different letters of the alphabet are shown at the top of Figure 11.13. One of the most important information-processing models of feature analysis is the Pandemonium model developed by Oliver Selfridge in 1958. He programmed a computer to act as if it were a series of four types of demons, each having a different assignment in a feature-analysis procedure. When all the demons work together, the result is a system that can recognize patterns. Figure 11.13 portrays how the system functions, according to Lindsay and Norman. The first level of demons, the image demons, simply register what is seen and display it. The image is then analyzed by the second level of demons, the feature demons, each of which looks for a specific feature in the image. In the case of letters of the alphabet, some feature demons look for types of angles, some for types of curves, some for types of straight lines.

The cognitive demons (the third level) then carefully monitor the responses of the feature demons. Each cognitive demon represents a particular pattern; in this example there would be a different cognitive demon for each letter of the alphabet. A particular cognitive demon knows the features that correspond to its letter and looks for those features in the responses of the feature demons.

Figure 11.13   Selfridge's Pandemonium. In this model of pattern recognition, image demons register an image of the outside world and display it to the feature demons. Each feature demon is specialized to perceive a certain feature; the demon examines the image for the presence of that feature and reports its findings to the cognitive demons. Each of the cognitive demons represents a particular pattern that might be expected to come in from the outside world. A cognitive demon starts yelling if the features that have been identified match the features that are found in its particular pattern. The better the match, the louder it yells. The decision demon listens to the resulting uproar and chooses the pattern corresponding to the noisiest cognitive demon. Presumably it is its pattern that has appeared in the outside world.

Figure 11.9B A version of the drawing in Figure 11.9A that has a strong tendency to be interpreted as a representation of a young woman. Viewing this drawing can affect your perception of Figure 11.9A.

The L demon, for instance, looks for one vertical line, one horizontal line, and one right angle. When a cognitive demon finds features that correspond to its letter, it yells, and the more features it finds, the louder it yells. The demon that finds the most features matching what it is looking for therefore yells the loudest. In Figure 11.13 the L cognitive demon yells as loudly as it possibly can, while other demons that find some of their features but not all of them, such as the T demon, yell less loudly. This chorus of yells from the cognitive demons creates a pandemonium of noise, which is what gives Selfridge's model its name.

Finally, the fourth level of demon, the decision demon, listens to the pandemonium created by the cognitive demons and tries to determine which of them is yelling loudest. In this case, it would pick the L cognitive demon as the one yelling loudest and so would recognize what is seen as probably the pattern L.

Of course, neither a computer nor a person that recognizes an L really uses demons to do so. Just as the general process of perceptual inference formulated by Helmholtz does not require a little man making inferences inside the head, so the process of pattern recognition described by the Pandemonium model does not require demons. The demons are simply a convenient means for describing how feature analysis brings about pattern recognition in a computer, or in a person. The essence of the Pandemonium model is the feature analysis. It is the set of features extracted by the feature demons that makes recognition of letters possible. Similarly, recognition of any group of patterns can only be accomplished if the features that distinguish the patterns within that group can be identified. It does not matter whether the patterns to be recognized are paintings of famous artists, songs performed by different rock bands, constellations of stars in the sky, smells of different flowers, or letters of the alphabet. The process of pattern recognition involves feature analysis, and successful feature analysis requires a set of features that will identify every pattern within the group.

In human perception, however, feature analysis as portrayed in the Pandemonium model is only part of the story of pattern recognition. When people read, they do not merely analyze the features of each letter as it is printed on the page. They also use their own knowledge of what they are reading to determine *what the features should be*. For example, the features of the pattern at the top of Figure 11.14 are not entirely clear, but as soon as that pattern is placed into the sentence ''Fido is drunk,'' its features are clarified: It becomes the word ''is.'' On the other hand, when it is placed into the number 14,157,393, its features are clarified in a different way, and it becomes the numerals 1 and 5. In this way we go beyond the sensory information that we actually obtain about something, and we use *meaning* to determine what that pattern ought to be. Meaning allows us to fill in missing or ambiguous features.

Analysis by Synthesis Information-processing models that take account of the effect of meaning on perception usually employ the procedure of analysis by synthesis. In this procedure, a person first forms a general conception, or **synthesis,** of a pattern and then uses that synthesis to guide his **analysis** of the features in the pattern. In the example in Figure 11.14 the synthesis provided by the sentence allows one to analyze the features of the ambiguous pattern, which thereby becomes the word ''is.'' Similarly the synthesis provided by the number allows us to analyze the features in a different way.

A phenomenon reported by George Miller illustrates the importance of analysis by synthesis in our perception of speech. If a person hears a series of words, such as ''Lives mountain man on that a'' embedded in a great deal of noise, he will be unable to recognize many of the words. But as soon as

IS

FIDO IS DRUNK

14, 157, 393

Figure 11.14 The stimulus above the handwriting can be interpreted as either ''15'' or ''is'' depending on its context. The meaning of a stimulus is often determined in part by its context.

they are put into meaningful order, "That man lives on a mountain," he can recognize most of them despite the noise. The synthesis that he formulates from the meaningful arrangement of words guides his analysis of each word and thus helps him to recognize all or most of the words in the sentence. We all take advantage of such analysis by synthesis whenever we are in a noisy situation, such as a loud party.

According to the analysis-by-synthesis model, then, meaning influences perception because whenever we perceive a pattern we start out with a general conception of the pattern and we then proceed to analyze the pattern based on that general conception. The general conception, or synthesis, is influenced not only by sensory information but also by the meaning that we give to the pattern.

Consequently, analysis by synthesis accounts for much of the influence of expectation and past experience on perception. If someone expects to see the vase in Figure 11.6, he applies the synthesis "vase" to the picture and so analyzes the features that are appropriate for a vase. Similarly, if he first sees the young woman in Figure 11.9B and then looks at Figure 11.9A, his experience with the first picture provides him with the synthesis "young woman," which guides his analysis of the features of the second picture. That is, expectations and past experience influence meaning, which in turn affects synthesis. In this way, analysis by synthesis explains the process underlying perceptual set.

As is evident from these examples, formulation of a synthesis for a pattern frequently relies upon the complex capacities of human thought. Psychologists are only beginning to understand these complex capacities, which no computer can yet match. Figure 11.15 demonstrates some of the complexity of our abilities to analyze by synthesis. Figure 11.15A shows several lines for which it is difficult to find a synthesis because they are out of context. When those lines are put in the context shown in Figure 11.15B, we recognize them as representing a word and call upon our knowledge of English words to provide a synthesis for what the word might be. If we still cannot find the synthesis that will allow us to recognize the word, then we can use the context of the sentence in which the word occurs to find a synthesis, as shown in Figure 11.15C. We will call upon our knowledge of what can be said in sentences to provide a synthesis for the word. If that synthesis is still not adequate, we can use our knowledge of the context of the paragraph in which the sentence appeared, or the context of the chapter in which the paragraph appeared, and so forth. As Lindsay and Norman point out, we can use anything from our vast store of knowledge to provide a synthesis for the pattern that we are trying to recognize.

PERCEPTION OF OBJECTS AND EVENTS

Most of the examples used so far to illustrate the process of perception have been drawings, photographs, or printed letters, all of which are two-dimensional and static. Textbooks by their nature are limited to two-dimensional, static illustrations, but in everyday life, perception (and the behavior it leads to) is geared to real three-dimensional objects in a world that is full of movement. A full understanding of the process of perception requires that psychologists' interpretations of perceptual inference and perceptual organization be applied to perception of the real world.

A three-dimensional object is perceptually very different from a two-dimensional one. For one thing, some parts of a three-dimensional object overlap other parts and obscure them from view: If we view a tree from one position, we cannot actually see the whole tree because some of the branches overlap others and the side of the tree closest to us blocks our view of the other side. Similarly one three-dimensional object can obscure our view of

Figure 11.9C This version of Figure 11.9A is likely to be interpreted as a representation of an old woman. Viewing this figure can affect your perception of Figure 11.9A. One tends to use whatever is familiar in interpreting an ambiguous stimulus pattern.

Figure 11.15A What could these peculiar squigglings mean? Go to Figure 11.15B on page 250 if you are unable to give a satisfactory analysis.

Figure 11.15B   The information added here to the pattern in Figure 11.15A makes it possible to generate a number of syntheses that might be appropriate, especially if you assume that the author wrote in English.

imagine, For me in

Figure 11.15C   Here even more context is added to the pattern presented in Figure 11.15A. It would be possible to go on adding context indefinitely. It might prove necessary in difficult cases to investigate the author's life history, personal tastes, and so on in order to generate a helpful synthesis.

When I wanted to get out of bed this morning I simply folded up. This has a very simple cause. I am completely overworked. Not by the office but by my other work. The office has an innocent share in it only to the extent that, if I did not have to go there, I could live calmly for my own work and should not have to waste here six hours a day which have tormented me to a degree that you cannot imagine. For one in particular it is a horrible double life from which there is no escape but insanity.

another object that is behind it: If there is a house between us and the tree, we cannot see the part of the tree that is behind the house.

The fact that we normally move around in the world also has a major impact on our perception. The sensory information that we receive about an object changes drastically as we move about. If we move toward the tree, the image that it casts on our eyes gets larger, its color becomes clearer, and the details of the branches and the trunk become more distinct. Yet we know that the tree is not expanding as we walk toward it, nor is it changing color or acquiring greater detail. Likewise, when we walk between the tree and the house, the two are no longer both in front of us, but rather one is in front and one is behind. Yet we know that neither one of them has actually changed its location.

We are not the only things in the world that move: Many objects move about. As a car moves down the road away from us, the image that it casts on our eye grows smaller, but we know that the car has not changed size. Somehow we take account of the movements of other things we perceive in the world just as we take account of our own movements.

Living in a three-dimensional, mobile world clearly requires some special kinds of perceptual abilities that are not required in a two-dimensional, static one. Psychologists who focus upon this aspect of perception, such as James Gibson, emphasize the particulars of our perception of the real world: Rather than asking about the general process of perceptual inference or the general organization of perception, they ask how humans use the sensory information available in the world to perceive the specific characteristics of the world. That is, what are the particular patterns of sensory information that we use to perceive three-dimensional space, size, shape, movement, and causality?

Perception of Space

One of the most basic characteristics of the real world is that it is organized as three-dimensional space. The human body is built in many ways that help us to perceive space. For example, because we have two ears that are on opposite sides of our heads, sounds that are coming from one side produce sound waves that arrive at each ear at different times, as Figure 11.16 shows. As a result we can determine approximately which direction a sound is coming from; that is, we can localize the sound. (Some of the details of sound localization are discussed in the next chapter.)

Vision is, however, our best sense for perceiving space. Not only can we localize the direction of an object with our eyes, but we can also perceive

Figure 11.16   Human beings are able to perceive the direction of sound sources by making comparisons between the times at which a particular sound reaches each of the two ears. Because the ears are not very far apart, the differences between the sound's arrival time at the two ears is quite small; human beings are able to detect a difference of about thirty-millionths of a second. It is this amazing sensitivity to small time differences that makes your perception of stereophonically reproduced sound so different from your perception of monaurally reproduced sound.

(After Lindsay and Norman, 1972.)

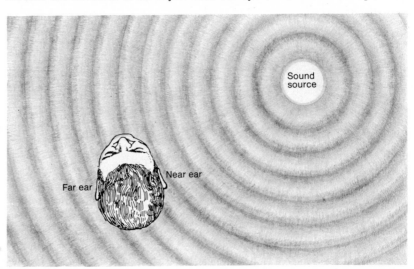

Sound source

Far ear   Near ear

depth. **Depth perception,** the ability to tell how far away an object is or how thick it is, results from a number of features of the sensory information that we receive through our eyes. First of all, the eyes, like the ears, are set slightly apart, so that each eye has a slightly different view of anything we look at. This difference is called **binocular parallax,** or binocular disparity. You can demonstrate binocular parallax by holding your finger in front of you and looking at it with one eye at a time. The image registered by the right eye will be slightly left-of-center, and that registered by the left eye will be slightly right-of-center. Now line up your finger with some other object farther away, and look at both your finger and that object with one eye at a time. Your finger will seem to jump back and forth relative to the more distant object, because the binocular disparity of far objects is less than that of near objects. We use this difference in disparity between the eyes to perceive the distance of an object from us. When we look at things with both eyes, the information from the two eyes combines to give a perception of depth. The stereoscope, a device that fuses the images of two photographs of the same scene taken from slightly different angles, takes advantage of this perceptual phenomenon and allows us to perceive a photographed scene in three dimensions, as illustrated in Figure 11.17.

Another feature that we use to perceive depth is **motion parallax,** also called motion disparity: the differences in our view of an object that occur as we move around while looking at it. You can demonstrate motion parallax to yourself by looking toward two objects in the same line of vision, one near you and the other some distance away, and moving your head back and forth. Use just one eye, so that you eliminate binocular parallax. The near object will seem to move more than the far object. As we move about, we use this disparity between near and far to perceive depth.

Objects, people, and animals move about too, and this **movement of perceived objects** provides a highly effective feature for perception of depth. As an object moves, it blocks our view of successively different things that are behind it, and so we can tell that the things that it blocks are farther away than both the things that it does not block and the moving thing itself. The natural camouflage of many animals prevents us from seeing them, but the camouflage only works as long as the animal remains completely still. The slightest movement makes it stand out immediately as figure against ground—an object in front of the bushes that it is hiding near.

If you paint or draw, you are probably familiar with many other features involved in the perception of distance. In **visual occlusion,** near objects obscure parts of objects that are farther away, so viewers can tell which

Figure 11.17 The interaction of the two eyes in the perception of depth is analogous to the interaction of the two ears in the perception of direction. The brain combines two slightly different two-dimensional images of the same stimulus into one perception that is three-dimensional. The two photographs shown here were taken from slightly different positions in order to reproduce the slightly different images received by your two eyes. If you look down the sides of a tall piece of cardboard placed on the line dividing the two photographs, as the woman in the sketch is doing, you can deliver one of these images to your left eye only and the other to your right eye only. If you are able to fuse these images, that is, to visually superimpose them exactly, the scene will jump out in depth. A popular toy, the "Viewmaster," operates on the same principle that this figure demonstrates.

Figure 11.18   A texture gradient. The perception of depth is induced by the decreasing size of the elements in the fields—in this case pebbles on a stony beach. Note that the gradient is seen as a flat plane as long as the decrease in size is constant and continuous. If there is a discontinuity like the one that has been produced here by the removal of the middle part of the photograph, a cliff edge is seen.

objects are nearer and which farther. Gibson has pointed out that many other distance features involve **gradients** of some sort—graduated differences—as shown in Figure 11.18. As distance increases, for example, objects appear to become gradually smaller and colors become gradually less intense.

Perceptual Constancies

Perception of a number of other basic characteristics of the real world depends less upon our ability to perceive differences (as with depth perception) and more upon perceptual constancies. People perceive objects as having certain constant (or stable) properties despite large changes in the sensory information that they receive from the objects from moment to moment.

One type of constancy, **size constancy,** depends on an interaction between apparent size and depth. The farther an object is from us, the smaller the size of the image it projects onto the eye, but because we have information that it is far away, our perceptual process takes account of the distance and translates the object's projected size into its real size. To see how size constancy works, hold one hand at arm's length and the other hand half that far from your eyes, and note the relative size of your hands. They look very much the same size, even though the size of the far hand as projected onto the eye is smaller than the projected size of the near hand. The projected sizes will show up if you move the near hand so that it partly overlaps—partly hides from view—the far one. Now, although you know your hands are the same size, the far one looks smaller. Evidently the partial overlapping can disrupt size constancy, so that we see our hands as they are presented to the eye.

The relationship between size and distance can be demonstrated more precisely with afterimages—images that persist after the original stimulus is removed. Stare for about forty seconds in adequate lighting at the dot in the red square in Figure 11.19. Then look at the center of a white piece of paper held about a foot in front of your eyes. If you have trouble seeing the afterimage, focus on one spot on the paper. Now move the paper to about two feet in front of your eyes and look at it: The square looks twice as large. Next look at a more distant surface, such as a white wall. The afterimage appears much larger than before. The size of the afterimage on the eye does not change: It is determined by your original fixation on the red square. When you vary the viewing distance by looking at close and far surfaces, the perceived size of the image changes, because with greater distance your brain interprets the afterimage as representing a larger object. When the afterimage is viewed on a piece of paper that is two feet away, it looks twice as large as when it is viewed at one foot for a simple reason: Normally when one object is twice as far away as a second object but still projects the same size onto the eye, the first object is twice as large as the second.

The relationship between distance and the size that an object projects, illustrated in Figure 11.19, is the same for both the eye and a camera. The projected size is halved when the object's distance from the eye or the camera is doubled. If you take a photograph of a tree from 100 feet and take another photograph of the same tree from 200 feet, the tree will be twice as high on the first photograph as on the second. That is, the size that an object projects onto your eye or onto photographic film is inversely proportional to its distance from you. The farther the object is from you, the smaller its projected size on your eye. Consequently, the visual system can maintain size constancy as long as it detects some feature that allows the distance of the object to be inferred: By taking account of the relationship between size and distance, the visual system can make accurate inferences about size.

A question like "Is it a bird, is it a plane, is it Superman?" is therefore easy to answer if you know how far away the flying object is. Only if distance features are ambiguous will you have trouble telling whether the object is a

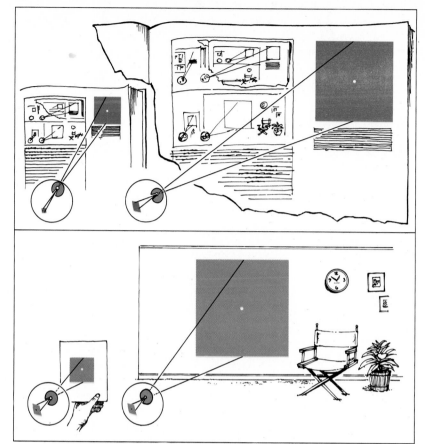

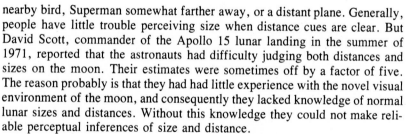

Figure 11.19   Hold the red square in the margin at reading distance and fixate your vision steadily on the dot in the middle of it for forty seconds. (The image should begin to shimmer.) Then look at a white sheet of paper held at the same distance from your eyes. You will see a green afterimage of about the same size as the red square. Now shift your gaze to a blank wall. The afterimage will appear to lie on the surface of the wall as it did on the surface of the paper; the farther away the wall is, the larger the afterimage will appear to be. The drawings at the left explain why this happens. (top) Normally, the size of the image projected onto the back of the eye by an object varies in proportion to the object's distance from the eye. The more distant the object is, the smaller the image. The brain compensates for this variation by scaling up the apparent size of distant objects. The result is size constancy: Objects do not appear to change size just because they move closer or farther. But when the image in the eye is held constant, as it is with an afterimage (bottom), the brain's compensation for changes in distance creates large changes in apparent size.

nearby bird, Superman somewhat farther away, or a distant plane. Generally, people have little trouble perceiving size when distance cues are clear. But David Scott, commander of the Apollo 15 lunar landing in the summer of 1971, reported that the astronauts had difficulty judging both distances and sizes on the moon. Their estimates were sometimes off by a factor of five. The reason probably is that they had had little experience with the novel visual environment of the moon, and consequently they lacked knowledge of normal lunar sizes and distances. Without this knowledge they could not make reliable perceptual inferences of size and distance.

Similar misperceptions of size can occur here on earth. When features for size and distance conflict, the visual system opts for one or the other—usually for the one that seems to lead to the more likely conclusion. During the invasion of Normandy in World War II, for example, the Allies dropped dummies of paratroopers about two feet tall through the early morning twilight onto the fields near the coast. When the dummies hit the ground, the impacts set off a series of small explosions simulating rifle fire. In the poor light and general confusion, German observers thought the dummies were real paratroopers attacking from a distance. Not until the Germans got close enough to see the dummies did they realize that the small size had misled them about distance.

There are several other important constancies besides size constancy, some of which are illustrated in Figure 11.20. Size constancy has been described in some detail in the chapter so that the nature of a perceptual constancy could be presented fully. Although the sensory information that we receive from objects changes greatly from moment to moment, our perceptual process nor-

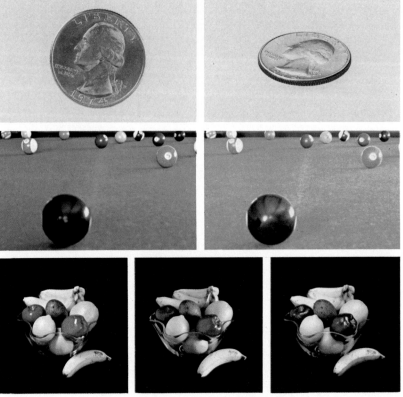

Figure 11.20. The brain tends to compensate for physical changes in viewing conditions in order to produce invariant perception. (top) The tendency to see a coin as round no matter what angle it is viewed from is an example of shape constancy. (middle) The tendency to see surfaces that reflect relatively little light as black and surfaces that reflect relatively large amounts of light as white no matter how much or how little light is physically present is an example of brightness constancy. (bottom) The tendency to see the colors of these fruits as natural in either incandescent light, daylight, or fluorescent light is an example of color constancy. The degree to which your brain compensates for the lighting changes in the middle and bottom photographs can best be judged if you expose only one photograph to view at a time.

mally detects the major stable properties — such as size, shape, and color — of the objects and people that surround us in the world.

Illusions

The constancies represent phenomena in which perception is more accurate than might be expected. Illusions are phenomena in which perception seems to be worse than one would expect. Armand Thiery suggests, however, that many illusions may occur because our perceptual process treats the sensory patterns from illusions as if they were produced by real objects in a three-dimensional world.

In particular, a number of illusions may result from misapplication of size constancy by the perceptual process, as pointed out by R. L. Gregory. For example, look at the illusions in Figure 11.21, then measure the lines with a ruler. Although the lines are in fact the same length, one does look longer. Both the Müller-Lyer illusion (Figure 11.21A) and the Ponzo illusion (Figure 11.21C) have features similar to those that indicate distance when we look at real objects in space. In the Müller-Lyer illusion the arrows are like outlines of corners, as illustrated in Figure 11.21B. As a result, the "shorter" line is interpreted as though it were raised above the page and therefore seems closer to the observer than the "longer" line, which is interpreted as being recessed into the page and therefore seems to be farther from the observer. Because both lines project the same size onto the eye, the one that appears to be closer is seen as smaller, in accordance with size constancy. In the Ponzo illusion the converging lines are like railroad tracks or other parallel lines extending away from the viewer, as illustrated in Figure 11.21D. Consequently, the bar that is farther down the track is perceived as larger, because in accordance with size constancy an object is larger if it is far away but projects the same size onto the eye as another object that is closer.

A similar explanation may account for the famous moon illusion. The moon looks considerably larger when it is just above the horizon than it does when it is overhead, although the size of the image projected on the eye is the same in both cases. Indicators of distance—trees, buildings, the skyline—near the horizon are far superior to those overhead, and they indicate that the moon is a long way away. When we look at the moon near the horizon, then, our brain apparently concludes that a moon-size image from something so far away means quite a large object; when we look overhead, our brain tells us that a moon-size image from something that seems not so far away means a smaller object.

Adelbert Ames, a painter, created some especially striking visual illusions by building models that trick our visual system into misapplying size and shape constancy. The best-known example is the Ames room, shown in Figure 11.22B. The two women inside the room look dramatically different in size because you perceive the room as rectangular. In fact, as Figure 11.22A indicates, the back wall is farther away on the left than it is on the right. But our visual system interprets it as rectangular, like a normal room, and so we perceive the two women to be standing the same distance from us. In accordance with size constancy, if two people seem to be at the same distance but one projects a larger size image onto the eye, then that one is perceived to be much larger in real size than the other.

Although the Ames room in Figure 11.22B has been photographed as if it had only three walls, laboratory models of it have four. To see the illusion, observers look into the room through a peephole in the fourth wall. A peephole is required because the illusion only works if we see the room without good perception of depth. Looking through the peephole eliminates important depth features like binocular parallax (because we can use only one eye at a time) and motion parallax (because we cannot move around to see the room from different positions).

Interestingly, observers become less susceptible to the illusion if they are allowed to explore its surfaces with a stick inserted through a hole in the wall. Gradually, the room stops looking as if it is built of rectangular walls that form right-angle corners and begins to look like what it really is: a set of trapezoids joined to form acute and obtuse angles—that is, a distorted room. On the other hand, mere intellectual knowledge of how the room is shaped does not prevent the illusion; only active exploration of the room is effective.

Figure 11.21 Two famous illusions and possible explanations for how they work. The vertical lines of the figures in the Müller-Lyer illusion (A) are identical in length, but they do not appear to be. An explanation for this illusion, suggested in (B), is that the arrow markings on the lines in (A) cause them to be perceived as three-dimensional objects that have corners. The corners seem to induce a size-constancy effect: The vertical line that appears to be distant is perceived as larger. The horizontal lines in the Ponzo illusion (C) are also identical in length. As the photograph in (D) suggests, this figure, too, could easily be perceived as three-dimensional, and again size constancy would cause the apparently more distant ''object'' to be scaled up in apparent size relative to the ''nearer object.''
(After Gregory, 1970.)

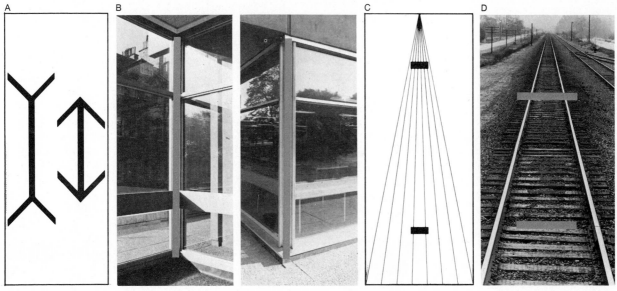

A   B   C   D

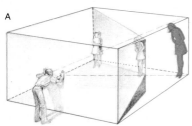

Figure 11.22 The Ames Room. In (A) the actual construction of the room is compared with the way the room is perceived. The photograph in (B) shows the room as it is seen through the peephole. The illusion is produced by people's inexperience with any rooms except rectangular ones with flat floors. The brain infers that both women standing against the back wall are at the same distance from the eye and interprets the difference between the size of their images as a real difference in size.

The Ames room, like the Müller-Lyer illusion and the Ponzo illusion, thus produces erroneous perceptual inferences about size because its features mislead our visual system into applying size constancy inappropriately. In all three illusions we make incorrect perceptual inferences about distance and size because the features of the perceived pattern mimic features of real objects in the world: In the real objects those same features allow our visual system to correctly infer size and distance.

Movement and Causality

In the real world we not only perceive objects of a certain size and shape in three-dimensional space, but we also perceive movement—of both ourselves and of objects. Movement has great importance in the lives of people and animals. To catch the evening meal, an animal must be able to detect both the dinner that is hopping by and his own movement as he chases his dinner. To drive on a highway, a person must be able to keep track both of how he and his car are moving and of all the potentially lethal moving objects around him.

One way that we can tell that we are moving is, of course, through the movements of our own arms, legs, eyes, and so forth. We know when we move our bodies, and so we can relate our own movements to resulting changes in what we see. When we look from one side of a room to another, what we see changes constantly, in much the same way that it does when a movie camera pans around a room. But we perceive the changes as a movement of our own eyes, not as a movement of the room.

The result of these changes is very different when we are not producing the movements ourselves. If you close one eye and push the other eye with a finger, you will see the world move. Because you did not produce the movement of your eye in the natural way, your visual system interprets the changes in what you see as movement of things in the world. Similarly, when you are riding in a car that someone else is driving, you can still tell that you are moving even though you are not producing the movement yourself. Gibson points out that what you see in the world outside the car is all changing. This global motion parallax, a constant flux in what you see, thus produces your perception that you are moving through space. (Recall that a more specific feature of motion parallax is also used to perceive depth.)

When we are stationary but see an object moving, the situation is quite different. There is not change in everything we see but only **figural motion,** change related to the object that is moving. As Gibson indicates, this change can be of two types. First, as a dog runs in front of us, it blocks (or occludes) our vision of things that are behind it, and what it blocks changes as it runs. From these changes we perceive the dog moving. Changes in visual occlusion produce the perception of an object moving through space. Second, part of an object can move, while the rest of the object remains stationary. When someone smiles, we perceive movement of only his lips and some other parts of his face. The sensory information that specifies this kind of motion for us is change of some parts of an object with respect to others. The relationship between the lips and the rest of the face changes, and we perceive movement of the lips.

There does not, however, need to be real motion for us to perceive motion: In **apparent movement** we are presented with a rapid succession of static stimuli that reproduce the changes that occur in true movement, and we perceive motion. People in motion pictures seem to move although there is no real motion—the people are simply photographed at least sixteen times per second, and then the photographs are presented in rapid succession. Watch Figure 11.24 as you rapidly flip pages 167–249, and you will see apparent movement. Another example of apparent movement, called the phi phenomenon by Gestalt psychologist Max Wertheimer, is commonly used in neon signs: Lights are switched on sequentially, and we see movement, although nothing is actually moving. In these two examples of apparent movement, the rapid succession of stimuli reproduces the changes in sensory information that occur in real movement, and so our perceptual system infers movement.

When things move about in the world, they do more than merely move: They influence each others' movements. Albert Michotte has demonstrated that we directly perceive some of these influences; we perceive causality. As illustrated in Figure 11.24, when one object moves toward another and makes contact and the second object then moves away, we actually *see* the first object causing the second object to move. Michotte has shown that, for this perception to occur, specific sensory information must be present. For example, the speed of the first object must be perceived as equal to or greater than the speed of the second object. When the two objects make contact, there must be a slight pause before the second object moves away.

In summary, our perception is geared to the real world. James Gibson and other psychologists have analyzed the particular patterns of sensory stimulation that we use to infer the major characteristics of the real world. These sensory patterns also account for our perception of many illusions. This emphasis on the sensory stimulation underlying perception must be combined with the two aspects of perception discussed earlier to provide an adequate total picture of the perceptual process. Our perceptual system uses patterns of sensory information to infer the characteristics of the objects and events occurring around us.

In all the perceptual phenomena discussed so far in this chapter, a close relationship exists between sensory information and the thing perceived. Even when perception is not entirely accurate, it is based on sensory information: The sensory information is simply misinterpreted. Some psychologists believe, however, that there may be another way of receiving information from the world that does not involve the senses and that cannot yet be explained: There may be extrasensory perception (ESP).

EXTRASENSORY PERCEPTION

ESP is thought to occur in three forms: **telepathy,** or mind reading, the transference of thought from one person to another; **precognition,** the ability

Figure 11.23 Motion perspective. The observer, moving to the left in a train, is looking at a house in the distance. All objects between him and the house move across his visual field to the right. The closer they are to him, the faster they move. All objects beyond the house move across his visual field to the left, relative to the house, and the closer they are to him the slower they move. These gradients of relative motion are a strong cue to the perception of the depth of the various objects.
(After Gibson, 1950.)

Figure 11.24 A demonstration of apparent movement and perceived causality. Close this book and then open the front cover only. Grasp all the pages of the book in your left hand. Use your thumb to flip the lower right-hand corners of the pages slowly and smoothly from the back of the book to the front. Watch the area to the right of the page numbers as you do so, and you will see a short film beginning on page 249.

to foresee the future; and **clairvoyance,** knowledge of events not detectable by normal senses. If a person were clairvoyant, he could, for example, sense the suit and number of a card that is sealed in an envelope and that no one else knows. Another phenomenon that is often thought to be related to ESP is **psychokinesis (PK),** the ability to move objects without touching them.

Scientific investigations into the existence of ESP and PK have been conducted in the United States since the early 1900s. J. B. Rhine, the most famous researcher in this area, has tried to prove through scientific methodology that ESP exists. For example, he tests for telepathy by having a "sender" focus on each card in a special deck one at a time. The deck consists of twenty-five cards, each with one of five symbols on it. A "receiver," locked in a distant room, states which card he thinks the sender has turned up and is thinking about. Studies of this sort by different investigators have produced opposite results. Some studies have found certain individuals who, acting as receivers, could name more cards than would have been possible by chance, but other studies have been unable to find any such individuals.

One of the reasons that many scientists will not accept the results of the experiments supporting ESP and PK is that the findings are highly unstable. One of the basic principles of scientific research is that one scientist should be able to replicate another scientist's results. Not only do different experiments yield contradictory findings, but the same individual seems to be able to show ESP or PK on one day but not on the next. Proponents of ESP and PK argue that the reason the research is not consistently replicated is that the special abilities are stifled in a laboratory setting. They say that ESP and PK responses are generated by highly emotional situations or by objects or events relevant to the person's life. Laboratory experiments that test people's ability to sense what symbols appear on cards are irrelevant to most people's lives and are usually a particularly boring way to spend an afternoon. According to this viewpoint, it is remarkable that ESP and PK abilities appear in the laboratory setting at all.

Another reason that this field is particularly controversial is that ESP and PK appear to contradict established scientific laws. For example, precognition violates what scientists know about time. So far, there is no known scientific explanation for how someone could jump ahead to see the future and then jump back again to tell about it. Similarly, PK violates what scientists know about space. There are no known ways that an individual can move something by sheer force of thought.

Unfortunately ESP and PK evoke strong passions, and consequently it is difficult to gather evidence that both believers and nonbelievers would consider definitive. If a person has undergone an experience that he believes involved ESP or PK, there is virtually nothing that anyone can say or do that will convince him that it does not exist. On the other hand, if someone believes that ESP cannot possibly exist, then nothing anyone can say will convince him that it does exist.

In sum, psychologists cannot yet say whether ESP or PK exists. The elusiveness of the phenomena, the violence that they seem to do to known scientific laws, and the strength of the passions that the topic arouses all conspire to make almost impossible difficulties for the experimenter who wants to test for the existence of ESP or PK.

SUMMARY

1. People's perceptions do not mirror the external world. Rather, perception is an **interpretation** based on information from the senses. Three facts about how we perceive support the notion of interpretation:

   a. There are many aspects of the world we cannot perceive: molecules and high-frequency sounds, for example.

   b. We often perceive things that do not exist in the world, for example, when we dream.

   c. Expectations influence what we perceive.

2. **Perceptual inference** is the process of interpretation of sensory information, sometimes based on past experience. For example, if one is driving up a steep hill, the road appears to end at the top of the hill. But people infer that it continues down the hill, because it always has in the past.

   a. One basic perceptual inference people make is the division of a perception into **figure and ground.** In visual perception of a photograph, for example, some parts or objects stand out and are perceived as being the "subject matter"; these are the figure. The rest of the photograph is perceived as spaces between the objects, or as background for them; this is the ground. In auditory perception also, the sound focused on is figure; the rest of the sound, or noise, is ground.

   b. Stimuli that are **perceptually ambiguous,** that is, stimuli that can be perceived in more than one way, dramatically illustrate the process of perceptual inference. An ambiguous figure requires choosing among two or more possible hypotheses as to what the figure represents, and people's brains generally choose the simpler and more familiar of the possible forms.

   c. **Perceptual set,** a readiness to perceive a stimulus in a specific way, is also a factor in perceptual inference. If a person who is given an ambiguous figure to look at is told ahead of time about just one of the possible forms, his expectation sets him to perceive that one form, and he will most likely perceive it.

3. Human beings perceive patterns, not simply collections of elements. When we hear music, we do not hear a series of notes but patterns that are chords, rhythm, and melody. This perception of pattern is called **perceptual organization.**

   a. Gestalt psychologists believe that people perceive a **gestalt,** a whole or pattern, rather than merely the elements that make up the whole. Gestalt psychologists state a number of **principles of perceptual organization** that describe the properties of elements that lead to perception of gestalts. Three important ones are: **proximity,** how close together the elements of a pattern are; **continuity,** how smooth and uninterrupted a pattern of elements is; and **similarity,** how much like each other certain elements of a pattern are.

   b. Recently, some psychologists have pointed out that all the gestalt principles imply a single principle, that of **simplicity.** People generally perceive simpler rather than more complex patterns in the elements that compose the pattern.

4. A recent information-processing approach to perception is **pattern recognition.** Psychologists working in this area attempt to program a computer to recognize the patterns that people recognize; if they succeed in devising

Figure 11.25   Gestalt psychologist Wolfgang Köhler was associated with Max Wertheimer and Kurt Koffka in Europe in the early 1900s. All three men came to the United States in the 1920s and 1930s. They were interested in the psychology of learning and thinking as well as in perception. Köhler's book *The Mentality of Apes*, written in 1917 after his seven-year directorship of the Anthropoid Station on the island of Tenerife, is considered a classic in experimental psychology.

Figure 11.26   J. B. Rhine of Duke University has long been the most prominent and serious investigator of parapsychology in the United States. His determination to make the study of parapsychology a respected scientific discipline began long before parapsychology attained its current position of limited acceptance among scientists.

such programs, they have a model of human pattern recognition. Some models, such as the Pandemonium model, focus primarily on analysis of sensory information, called **feature analysis:** Sensory information is broken down into distinctive characteristics that identify patterns. Other models focus on the ways that meaning and expectations influence perception, called **analysis by synthesis:** A person's general conception, or synthesis, of a pattern guides his analysis of the features.

a. In feature analysis of letters of the English alphabet, for example, the features analyzed are lines, curves, and angles; each letter has a distinctive set of such characteristics.

b. In analysis by synthesis, the model takes account of people's expectations, based on their experience, of what a letter *should* be. That is, whenever people perceive a pattern, they formulate a general conception, or synthesis, of the meaning of the pattern. Their further analysis of the pattern, then, is based on their original synthesis. Further analysis, however, may require a revision of the synthesis, and so on.

5. Objects in the real world are three-dimensional and exist and move in three-dimensional space. In order to perceive this three-dimensionality and movement, people use various cues provided by specific sensory information. Some sensory information is provided by the eyes, each of which receives a slightly different view of the world. This **binocular parallax** allows us to perceive depth: It allows us to see an object's distance from us. Another aid to **depth perception** is **motion parallax,** the way our movements change our perception of an object from moment to moment, as we are moving. Also important are the **movements of perceived objects**—people, animals, cars. As they move, they block our view of things in the background, so we can tell that those things are farther away. Other cues to depth perception are received from visual **occlusion** and visual **gradients.**

6. People also possess **perceptual constancies,** that is, abilities to perceive objects as having constant properties even though the sensory information received from the objects changes from moment to moment. A chair seen in bright light gives different sensory information than the same chair seen in dim light. Yet, one recognizes that the chair is not changed.

a. In **size constancy** we see an object as the same size even when its distance from us changes. Although the size of the retinal image of a car seen from a block away is much smaller than the retinal image of the same car seen from three feet away, our visual system takes account of the distance as well as the projected size, so we do not assume that the car far away is a toy.

b. Similar constancies exist for shape and color.

7. **Illusions** are phenomena that we are led to perceive incorrectly. Because we apply processes of perceptual inference to these patterns, we perceive them as we would perceive objects in the real world, even though, objectively, their features are different from what we perceive them to be. Many famous illusions trick us into using size constancy inappropriately.

8. **Perception of movement** is extremely important to how people and animals operate in the world.

a. Our body movements relate to the changes in our perceptions of objects as we move—motion parallax—to let us know we are moving through space.

b. When we are stationary but see an object move, **figural motion** (the object blocks successive things in its background or changes some of its parts with respect to other parts) allows us to perceive its movement.

c. Presentation of a rapid succession of static stimuli, as in motion pictures, produces **apparent movement,** a kind of illusion. The rapid succession of the stimuli reproduces the kinds of changes in sensory information that occur in real movement, and so our perceptual system infers movement.

d. Certain movements of objects in relation to each other cause people to **perceive causal relations** between the objects: for example, that one object caused another one to move.

9. Some psychologists are doing research in the area of **extrasensory perception (ESP),** which includes **telepathy,** thought transfer from person to person; **precognition,** the ability to foresee the future; **clairvoyance,** a knowledge of events not detectable by normal senses. A related phenomenon is called **psychokinesis (PK),** the ability to move objects without touching them. Laboratory experiments in extrasensory perception are difficult to replicate, but supporters of the existence of ESP argue that a laboratory is an unsuitable setting for investigating ESP.

SUGGESTED READINGS

Allport, Floyd. *Theories of Perception and the Concept of Structure.* New York: Wiley, 1955. Describes and compares all the major classical theories of perception.

Arnheim, Rudolph. *Art and Visual Perception: A Psychology of the Creative Eye.* Berkeley: University of California Press, 1954 (paper). Basing his analysis on the psychology of perception—especially the principles of the Gestalt school—Arnheim describes how understanding the visual process can help one to understand visual art.

Gibson, James J. *The Senses Considered as Perceptual Systems.* Boston: Houghton Mifflin, 1966. An excellent treatment of the dependence of perception upon sensory information.

Gregory, R. L. *The Intelligent Eye.* New York: McGraw-Hill, 1970 (paper). Gregory stresses the importance of perceptual inference, arguing that perception is a set of simple hypotheses about reality that depend upon sensory experience. The book is particularly strong on visual illusions.

Hansel, C. E. M. *ESP: A Scientific Evaluation.* New York: Scribner's, 1966 (paper). Criticizes many ESP experiments on the basis of their poor design and misapplication of the scientific method.

Held, Richard, and Whitman Richards (eds.). *Perception: Mechanisms and Models.* San Francisco: W. H. Freeman, 1972 (paper). This book of readings from *Scientific American* provides accounts of some famous research on perceptual processes in man and animals.

Hochberg, Julian. *Perception.* Englewood Cliffs, N.J.: Prentice-Hall, 1964 (paper). A good general introduction to perception.

Koestler, Arthur. *The Roots of Coincidence.* New York: Random House, 1972. An interesting and eloquent argument asking only that the reader keep an open mind with regard to the possible existence of ESP.

Lindsay, Peter, and Donald Norman. *Human Information Processing.* New York: Academic Press, 1972. The first half of this book presents a clear, readable account of information-processing analyses of perception.

There are certain statements of belief that are often called "folk wisdom" for no other reason than that they originate out of the unsophisticated observation of the world by people of limited experience. In almost every case they might be considered "folk stupidity" and laughed at if it weren't that so many tragic consequences have followed from what everyone "knew" was true but wasn't. How many unfounded accusations have ruined lives and precipitated riots because "Where there's smoke there's fire"? Dry Ice in water produces fascinating smoke without fire. And would we ever be exploring the Moon if it were really true that "everything that goes up must come down"?

But to me the most pernicious piece of "folk wisdom" is the one about "Seeing is believing," when it is phenomenally easy to fool the eye. In the Greek myth Narcissus drowned himself because the beautiful young man he saw in the water wasn't really there.

The trouble is that very early in life we learn that light travels in straight lines. Very young children reach for something by following rays of light backward in a straight line, and very often they succeed in making physical contact with what they have seen. We never break the habit of interpreting all light as a straight-line phenomenon, even though light travels in a straight line only under restricted conditions. If we place a stick in water, light from that portion of the stick below the water level is refracted as it passes from water to air. The straight stick seems bent at the water level, and no matter how much our intelligence tells us that it is not the stick that is bent

by the rays of light, what we see is that the stick is bent. We cannot argue ourselves out of that.

Our inability to appreciate the vagaries of light are at the base of a large proportion of our mystical beliefs. Ghosts and spirits are born in a world in which there is no artificial illumination other than the flickering of an open flame. Why has the ghost story lost its earlier popularity? Because the steady, dim shadows cast by a frosted light bulb are nothing like the shifting mysterious shadows cast by unsteady flames. Ghosts can't survive steady light.

And what about those modern ghosts called "flying saucers"? Where the report is not an outright hoax, it is a matter of some sort of light being seen in the sky; and I suspect that in very many cases it is a matter of light refraction. A light ray curves through air in layers of varying temperature and density, so that you see a light in a place it should not be because your eye and mind don't follow the curve but insist on moving along a straight line tangent to the curve at the point where it enters the eye. Distant lights of a city or a line of automobile headlights will therefore appear in the sky.

But always, the cry of "Seeing is believing" goes up. I'm afraid not. As far as I'm concerned, the proper wisdom is "Seeing is merely seeing, nothing more." Belief requires a lot more than the complicated trickery of a light wave.

Isaac Asimov

12
Sensation and the Senses

Figure 12.1 The simplest, most direct experiences of the physical world are usually called sensations. Sensations can be described in terms of fundamental qualities and quantities: color, brightness, hardness and softness, coolness and warmth, loudness, sweetness, and fragrance, to name a few.

Suppose that you are walking down a city street one evening on your way to a concert. Each instant of the time you are walking you are moving through a world full of energy. Your body intercepts light rays that stream from automobile headlights, streetlights, store windows, and neon signs. Because your ear is hit with air molecules set in motion, you hear people talking and scuffling their shoes on the pavement. If it is winter, you may feel the icy bite of the wind. If it blows with enough force, you may have to adjust your balance to keep from falling over. Even the simple act of walking means that you continually must adjust the actions of the muscles in your legs and back to keep upright against the pull of gravity.

In the auditorium listening to the music you are exposed to other patterns of energy. The music may be so loud, so energetic, that you can feel it in your skin as well as hear it. You can also feel the pressure of the seat against your back as it keeps you from falling to the ground. During the intermission you buy a hot pretzel because its tempting smell is wafted to your nose by the molecules that evaporated from the pretzel. When you eat it, you taste it as a result of chemical reactions between the pretzel and the fluids in your mouth.

We live in a world that is filled with **energy** of various types. Some of the processes of life serve to translate this energy into different forms. For example, photosynthesis in plants turns light energy into chemical energy to create food substances. Sensory processes in animals and people turn various forms of energy, like light and sound, into energy in the nervous system, and our brain interprets this energy as information about what is "out there."

Perception, discussed in the previous chapter, is the overall process by which people use sensory information to make inferences about objects and events in the world. Sensation is a part of the perceptual process: It is our experience of the brightness of light or the loudness of sound, for example. Each of our sense organs detects a particular type of energy (stimulus) in the world—light rays or sound waves, for example—and transforms that energy into sensation, or sensory information. The perceptual process then uses that sensory information, with other information it has about the world, to infer what is happening ''out there.''

This chapter examines both **sensation**—our qualitative experience of quantitative differences in energies detected by each sense—and the **sense organs** that transduce that energy.

STIMULI AND SENSATIONS

The analysis of sensation was one of the first major focuses of early experimental psychology. About the middle of the nineteenth century psychologists began to ask: What is the relationship between a sensation and the physical characteristics of the stimulus upon which the sensation is based?

A simple experiment that you can do at home illustrates the meaning of this question. Use a three-way light bulb, one with 50-, 100-, and 150-watt capacities. Try the bulb at each of these settings in an otherwise dark room. You will see that, although each successive setting uses 50 watts more power and therefore produces a constant increase in the actual intensity of the light *stimulus,* the jump from 50 to 100 watts results in a larger increase in the *sensation* of brightness than does the step from 100 to 150. Psychologists want to know why the change in the sensation of brightness is larger for the jump from 50 to 100 watts than for the jump from 100 to 150 watts.

A **stimulus** is any physical energy that can produce an experience (or some other response). Light is an example. Light is the stimulus for vision. We see because our eyes are sensitive to light. The light energy that our eyes receive and transform into sensation, however, is just one part of a range of energies called the electromagnetic spectrum. As Figure 12.2 shows, this range of energies also contains radio waves, x-rays, and gamma rays. These entities are *not* stimuli for humans because we are not sensitive to them and cannot transform their energy into sensation.

There are portions of the electromagnetic spectrum that play no part in vision but are nonetheless stimuli. Although our eyes are not sensitive to ultraviolet rays, our skin is; ultraviolet light causes our skin cells to produce a pigment that gives us our suntans. And infrared rays are stimuli because we sense them as heat.

The stimulation of the eyes by light produces visual sensations, our experience of the qualities associated with vision: color hue, color purity, brightness, and so forth. An example of a question that psychologists ask about the

Figure 12.2 The spectrum of electromagnetic energy. The small portion of this spectrum that the human eye is sensitive to is shown expanded. The scale on the large spectrum is a logarithmic scale of wavelength: Each step on the scale corresponds to a tenfold increase in the wavelength of the electromagnetic radiation. Visible light is between 400 and 700 millimicrons (billionths of a meter) in wavelength. AM radio waves have a wavelength 10^{12} times greater—about 1 meter. Note that the spectrum of visible light shown here does not include all the colors that can be experienced. Some colors (whites, grays, purples, and browns, for example) are experienced when the eye is stimulated by combinations of various wavelengths within the spectrum of visible light.

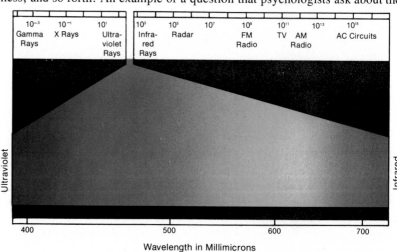

10^{-3}	10^{-1}	10^1	10^3	10^5	10^7	10^9	10^{11}	10^{13}	10^{15}
Gamma Rays	X Rays	Ultraviolet Rays	Infrared Rays	Radar		FM Radio	TV AM Radio		AC Circuits

Ultraviolet

Infrared

400   500   600   700

Wavelength in Millimicrons

relationship between stimulus and sensation is: What is the relationship between the physical amount of light and the sensation of brightness?

By the end of the nineteenth century, psychologists had made much progress in analyzing the relation between stimulus and sensation. Indeed, they had even given a name to the study of this relationship: **psychophysics.** One of the main questions that psychophysicists ask is: How much of a stimulus is necessary for a given person to sense it at all? How much energy is required for that person to see a light? How much pressure must be applied to his or her skin before the person feels it? The answers to these questions involve the concept of threshold.

Threshold

A threshold is the smallest stimulus that produces a specific sensation or change in sensation in an individual. There are several types of thresholds, including the absolute threshold and the difference threshold. The minimum stimulus necessary to produce a specific sensation is the **absolute threshold.** One way that psychologists measure a person's absolute threshold for light is as follows: She or he enters a completely dark room and watches for a light on the wall. The psychologist, using a machine that can project low-intensity beams, projects very weak beams and then gradually increases their strength until the person says, "I see it." Or else the psychologist can project a strong beam and gradually decrease it until the person says, "I don't see it." The psychologist generally repeats the process a number of times with the same person. The point at which the person *usually* reports that he or she sees the light is the absolute threshold.

The **difference threshold,** or **just noticeable difference,** is the smallest change in a stimulus that produces a change in sensation. For example, how much brighter must the beam of light become before the person in the dark room says, "Yes, this is brighter than the light I just saw." The psychologist increases the intensity of the beam until the person says "Yes, I see the difference."

You can do an experiment to show one way that just noticeable differences are measured. Suppose you want to find out how sensitive people are to differences in weight. Take two 8 1/2 x 11-inch sheets of paper and nine identical envelopes. Fold the first sheet smoothly and seal it in the first envelope. Write an 8 lightly on the back of this envelope. Then cut the second sheet of paper precisely in half and put one of the halves into the second envelope. Number this envelope 7. Take the remaining half sheet and divide it into two. Seal one of these quarter sheets in the third envelope and number this envelope 6. Continue this procedure until you have envelopes numbered 8 through 1. These are your comparison stimuli. Seal the last envelope with nothing in it and number it 0. This is your standard stimulus. Now, using a copy of the list shown in Figure 12.3 for a data sheet, ask a person to judge the envelopes in pairs. On each trial he should extend his hand (with his eyes closed), and you should place one envelope, then the other, on his hand. He must judge which one is heavier (he may not reply that they are the same), and you should record his answer by circling the stimulus he judged heavier on your data sheet. When all 80 trials are complete, you will have 10 judgments of each comparison stimulus against the standard stimulus. Count up the number of judgments your subject made correctly for each comparison stimulus, and plot your results on a graph like those shown in Figure 12.4. You should find that at the low numbers the correct judgments occur about 50 percent of the time; that is, the subject was guessing. The proportion of correct judgments will probably rise to 100 percent at the higher numbers. Notice that your curve does not jump suddenly from 50 percent (guessing) to 100 percent (certainty) but rather rises gradually. The threshold you have

	Stimuli			Stimuli	
Trial	1st	2nd	Trial	1st	2nd
1.	8	0	41.	0	5
2.	3	0	42.	8	0
3.	0	7	43.	0	2
4.	0	1	44.	0	6
5.	4	0	45.	6	0
6.	1	0	46.	0	3
7.	7	0	47.	0	3
8.	0	6	48.	0	4
9.	3	0	49.	0	2
10.	8	0	50.	0	6
11.	0	4	51.	7	0
12.	0	2	52.	8	0
13.	5	0	53.	8	0
14.	0	5	54.	6	0
15.	0	6	55.	0	5
16.	0	2	56.	0	1
17.	4	0	57.	0	4
18.	0	5	58.	5	0
19.	3	0	59.	1	0
20.	2	0	60.	0	4
21.	1	0	61.	7	0
22.	0	1	62.	0	3
23.	0	6	63.	2	0
24.	0	3	64.	0	3
25.	0	2	65.	2	0
26.	6	0	66.	5	0
27.	0	7	67.	0	6
28.	5	0	68.	6	0
29.	7	0	69.	3	0
30.	0	8	70.	2	0
31.	0	4	71.	0	8
32.	8	0	72.	0	1
33.	1	0	73.	0	8
34.	5	0	74.	0	1
35.	0	1	75.	0	4
36.	2	0	76.	0	7
37.	8	0	77.	0	5
38.	0	7	78.	7	0
39.	4	0	79.	4	0
40.	7	0	80.	3	0

Figure 12.3 This list gives the order of presentation of the pairs of stimuli to use in your experiment on just noticeable differences. Note that the subject will never know on any given trial whether he is going to be presented with the lighter or the heavier stimulus first. Consequently, if he is unable to discriminate between the stimuli and therefore guesses, he will be correct half the time, on the average.

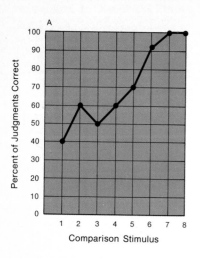

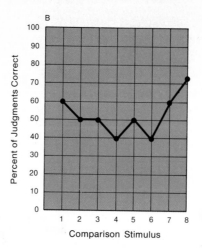

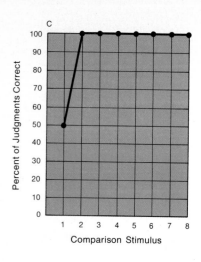

Figure 12.4 Examples of results you might obtain if you carry out the method of measuring a just noticeable difference described in the text. The percentage of trials on which a subject indicated correctly which stimulus was heavier is plotted in these graphs as a function of the magnitude of the comparison stimulus. Remember that if the subject is unable to sense a difference, he will score around 50 percent. The data in (A) are for a subject whose threshold falls in the range around $1/8$ of a sheet of paper: He senses this as different from no paper 70 percent of the time, clearly above the chance level of 50 percent. (B) Data that might be obtained if your subject thought he had found some way of "beating the system" but was wrong. You might obtain results like this, for example, from a subject who decided to say that the first envelope was the heavier most of the time. (C) Data that might be obtained from a subject who had an extremely low threshold for weight difference. This subject's threshold lies somewhere between $1/128$th and $1/64$th of a sheet of paper. To measure his threshold accurately, you would have to test him with some intermediate stimuli (envelopes containing sizes of paper between $1/128$th and $1/64$th of a sheet).

measured is not some exact number but rather a range over which your subject begins to show that his senses can detect a difference in weight. Different subjects may give different results, as the graphs in Figure 12.4 suggest. An extremely sensitive subject, for example, may rise above guessing probability at stimulus 2 or 3. For him a just noticeable difference is smaller than for someone who is still guessing at stimuli 5 and 6.

Sensory Ratios

In the mid-1800s Ernst Weber, who was studying just noticeable differences, discovered a relationship between the general magnitude of a stimulus and the size of just noticeable differences: Whereas people notice small changes in a weak stimulus, they only notice large differences in a strong stimulus. For example, if you add one pound to the weight of a couple of paperback books you are carrying, the sensation of weight will be greatly increased. If you add that one pound to your seventy-pound backpack, however, you may not sense any increase in the weight.

After further study, Weber specified the nature of this relationship more precisely: According to **Weber's law,** the amount of a stimulus necessary to produce a just noticeable difference is always a constant proportion of the intensity of the stimulus. The just noticeable difference for a one-hundred-pound backpack is about two pounds for most people. For a fifty-pound backpack it would be about one pound. For a ten-pound backpack it would be about one-fifth of a pound. The proportion for a just noticeable difference is therefore about 1/50 for weight. Proportions for some other sensations are: 1/10 for intensity of a tone; 1/7 for skin pressure; 1/5 for saltiness of a liquid.

Gustave Fechner, known as the founder of psychophysics, took up Weber's findings and tried to generalize them beyond just noticeable differences to sensation more generally. He asked: How does the magnitude of a stimulus relate to the magnitude of the sensation arising from it? For example, what amount of increase in the intensity of light is necessary for someone to see the light as twice as bright? According to **Fechner's law,** the relationship was always proportional. With the three-way light bulb, for example, your sensation of increased brightness is not the same for the two different jumps because the proportions are different: 150 to 100 watts is 3/2, while 100 to 50 watts is 2/1. This relationship has turned out to be only partially correct. Although proportionality is roughly true for stimuli of moderate magnitude, it does not hold for very strong or very weak stimuli.

Recently S. S. Stevens discovered a better formulation of the relationship between stimulus and sensation. **Stevens' power law** says that the magnitude of a sensation is equal to the physical magnitude of the stimulus raised to some power, or exponent, and the power depends on the particular sense, as shown in Figure 12.5. The exponent for brightness, for example, is 0.33, which means that to produce a sensation of brightness twice as great as a given level of brightness, the light stimulus must actually be increased not merely two times but about eight times. Loudness has an exponent of 0.6. To produce a sensation twice as great as a given sound, the stimulus must actually be increased by more than three times. This suggests why good stereo equipment can be so expensive. An amplifier must be able to put out very large amounts of power in order to keep doubling the apparent loudness of the music. To produce so much power without hopelessly distorting the quality of the sound requires high-quality components.

In some cases, the exponent is greater than one. For electric shock (applied to the fingertips) the exponent is 3.5; doubling the magnitude of the shock makes the sensation grow tenfold, as shown in Figure 12.5. Apparent length of line has an exponent close to 1.0, so that doubling the length of a line makes it look just about twice as long.

In summary, the same basic idea seems to underlie the work of Weber, Fechner, and Stevens: *The nervous system analyzes stimulation in terms of sensory ratios, not in terms of absolute differences in sensory magnitude.*

Signal Detection Theory

The work of Weber, Fechner, and Stevens deals primarily with the analysis of just noticeable differences and with sensory ratios. It says little about absolute thresholds. In recent years psychologists have become especially interested in absolute thresholds and in the many factors that seem to influence them. One reason for this interest is a very practical one: Some of the machinery of modern society requires people to detect minimal stimuli, events that are near the absolute threshold and therefore sometimes difficult to detect.

A radar operator, for example, must be able to detect an airplane on his radar screen even when the blip from the plane is faint and difficult to distinguish from blips caused by natural phenomena such as bad weather, which can produce images on the radar screen that are like visual "noise." Consider radar operators watching a screen in wartime during a storm. How can they judge when a blip on the screen is an enemy plane or when it is only a patch of noise? If they were to call out massive armed forces for every blip, they would create chaos, yet if one of the blips that they thought was merely noise turned out to be a bomber, the results could be disastrous.

Many factors influence radar operators' judgments of whether a blip is an enemy plane. Different radar operators appear to have different sensitivities to blips. A specific individual's apparent sensitivity also seems to fluctuate depending on the situation: For example, being watched by his superior officer will probably affect his performance.

The modern theory of signal detection, inspired largely by the difficulties facing radar operators, reformulates the concept of absolute threshold so as to take account of the many factors affecting detection of minimal stimuli. The theory abandons the idea that there is a single true absolute threshold for a stimulus and replaces it with the view that the stimulus, here called a **signal,** must be detected in the face of **noise,** extraneous sensory information that can interfere with detection of the signal. That is, signal detection is similar to standing in a noisy bus terminal listening for the announcement of your bus departure time over the loudspeaker. The noise in the terminal fluctuates up and down so that sometimes you can hear the announcement easily, and other times you have difficulty hearing it.

In all situations there is at least some noise. Even in a completely "silent" room, for example, we hear buzzing, thumping, and hissing from our own

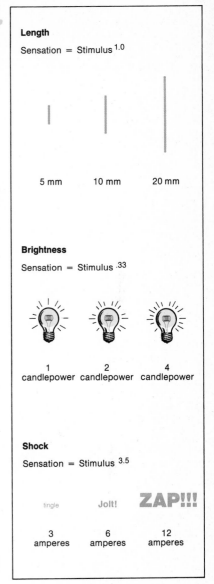

Length

Sensation = Stimulus $^{1.0}$

5 mm   10 mm   20 mm

Brightness

Sensation = Stimulus $^{.33}$

1 candlepower   2 candlepower   4 candlepower

Shock

Sensation = Stimulus $^{3.5}$

tingle   Jolt!   **ZAP!!!**

3 amperes   6 amperes   12 amperes

Figure 12.5 S. S. Stevens has shown that the magnitude of a sensation (psychological magnitude) corresponds to some power of the magnitude of the stimulus (physical magnitude) but that the exponent in this relationship varies from sense to sense. (top) The sensation of line length has an exponent of 1; this means that when a line is doubled in length, you see it as twice as long. (middle) Brightness has an exponent of 0.33; when you double the amount of light coming from a bulb, your sensation of brightness increases only about one-fourth. (bottom) Electric shock has an exponent of 3.5; this means that doubling the intensity of the electricity produces a feeling of shock 11.3 times stronger.

blood circulation, heartbeat, and breathing. Analysis of signal detection should, therefore, take account of the observer's reactions both to the noise that might be confused with the signal and to the signal itself. The individual does not simply have a sensation when the signal is present and fail to have a sensation when the signal is absent. Instead, he makes a **judgment** about whether the signal is present or not. Figure 12.6A shows the four possible combinations of actual events and the person's judgments about those events. A doctor is examining an injured man for signs of life; either the man is dead or he has a very weak pulse that the doctor must detect above the noise of the muscle twitches, imagined heartbeats, and the doctor's own pulse. When the doctor correctly separates the pulse from the noise and determines that the person has a pulse, she has made a **hit.** When she mistakes noise for pulse and so incorrectly judges that there is a pulse when there is none, she makes a **false alarm,** calling in the emergency equipment to help a man who is already dead. A **correct rejection** is made when the doctor correctly judges that there is no pulse, only noise, and that the man is dead. The most unfortunate outcome in this case is the **miss,** when the doctor mistakes pulse for noise and incorrectly judges that there is no pulse, declaring that a living person is dead.

The relative proportions of hits, false alarms, correct rejections, and misses are determined by three main factors. First, the relationship between signal and noise determines the ease of discriminating signal from noise. In a normal, healthy man, the doctor would have no difficulty detecting his pulse, because the signal of the pulse would be heard strongly and clearly above any background noise. But when the pulse is weak or absent, then the doctor can begin to have false alarms and misses, in which she confuses noise and pulse. Similarly, on a clear day when there are no storms to create extra noise on the radar screen, radar operators can easily judge when a blip is present. But when the noise level is increased by a storm, then they can begin to have false alarms and misses. In other words, *the relationship between signal and noise is a major determinant of the accuracy of signal detection.* Either a weak signal or strong noise will produce errors. Figures 12.6B and 12.6C show this relationship and how it is described in terms of distributions.

Second, people differ in their sensitivity to signals. Some people can detect pulses or radar blips more easily than other people. In an extreme case, a person with poor eyesight who has lost his eyeglasses will not detect radar blips as well as a person with good eyesight. **Individual differences in sensitivity** thus have an effect similar to changes in the relationship between signal and noise: A person with good eyesight essentially has a stronger signal than a person with poor eyesight.

Third, and very important, in situations where false alarms and misses do occur (because of a weak signal, strong noise, or poor sensitivity), the **response criterion** determines the proportions of hits, false alarms, misses, and correct rejections. If a radar operator is afraid of accidentally causing a nuclear war by issuing a false alarm, he may be cautious about reporting that he sees an airplane on his radar screen; he will only say that he has seen a plane when he is very sure of his judgment. Because of this strict response criterion, he will make fewer false alarms, but he will also make more misses. On the other hand, if the radar operator is especially concerned about an enemy plane getting through his radar and bombing a city, he may adopt a looser response criterion and report that he has seen a plane on the radar screen even when he merely suspects that it might be a plane. In this case, he will make more false alarms, but he will not have as many misses.

An individual's response criterion is influenced by many diverse factors, but one of the most important is **payoff:** the costs and benefits of hits, false alarms, correct rejections, and misses. The doctor dealing with the injured man would probably adopt a loose rather than a strict criterion for reporting

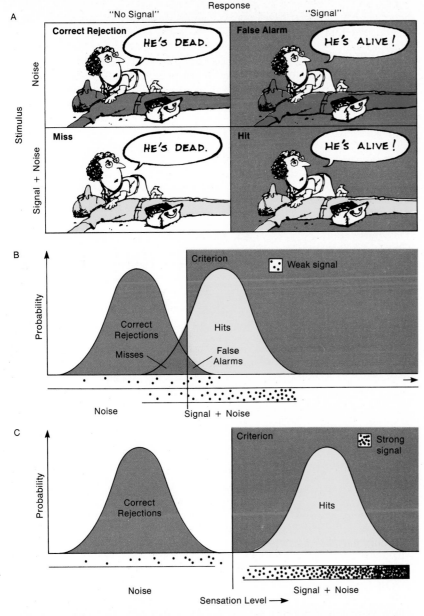

Figure 12.6 (A) The outcome matrix for a doctor who is trying to find a patient's weak pulse. The doctor is forced to make a risky decision. If she plays safe to avoid judging a live patient to be dead (a *miss*), she may judge a dead patient to be alive (a *false alarm*). (B) A theoretical representation of this weak-pulse problem. At any time the doctor feels for the pulse (signal), she may experience a high level of sensation or a low one. This variation is represented by the increasing density of the dots along the horizontal scale. The vertical scale plots the probability of a particular sensation level occurring. The doctor's question is: When is the sensation level high enough to say that there is a pulse? The left curve shows that even when there is no pulse, the doctor experiences sensations (noise) that could be confused with the pulse. Sometimes these sensations are at a very low level, sometimes they are at a fairly high level, but usually they are at some moderate level. When the pulse itself is added to this background noise, as the right curve shows, the level of sensation is somewhat higher. Note, however, that it still varies and that there is a range of sensation levels that might be produced by either a high level of noise alone or by a low level of noise plus the signal. The doctor has no way of telling the difference between these situations. She can only set a criterion, or cut-off point. If the level of sensation goes higher than this point she will say that a pulse must have occurred; if it remains lower than this she will say that there is no pulse. She will, of course, make some errors. (C) A theoretical representation of the doctor's problem if the pulse is strong. Note that now the curves do not overlap. The lowest level of sensation that the doctor could experience when there is a pulse is higher than the highest level of sensation that she could experience when there is only noise. If she sets her criterion somewhere between the two curves, she will make no errors at all.

that his pulse is present, because misses have a very high cost: The patient loses his life. Similarly, the New York City Fire Department answers over 100,000 false alarms each year, according to Phillip Shaver and his co-workers. The cost of false alarms is small relative to the cost of misses, in which a building burns to the ground and lives are endangered, so the Fire Department adopts a loose criterion to minimize the risk of misses.

In other situations the payoffs may be very different, however. Suppose that the doctor's next patient is suffering from severe headaches, periodic blackouts, and other symptoms that suggest that he may have a brain tumor. She takes an x-ray to see if there is a tumor. Although x-rays are often ambiguous, she must make a decision from the x-ray as to whether a tumor is present. In this situation the reward for a hit would be the possibility that, by performing a dangerous brain operation, she might be able to save the patient's life. The cost for a false alarm would be extreme: The patient would be subject to unnecessary surgery that might kill him even though he has no tumor. For correct rejections there would probably be no costs, but there would be general rewards to the doctor for doing a good job. The cost for a miss could be serious: If a tumor grew quickly, it might harm or kill the patient before there was another opportunity to detect and remove it. Clearly, hits, misses, false alarms, and correct rejections can all have different pay-offs, and an individual's response criterion will be influenced in some way by each of these payoffs.

Signal detection theory, a modern psychophysical method, and the other theories and methods discussed here for relating stimuli and sensation are one aspect of sensory psychology. A full understanding of how people transduce the energies that are the stimuli into their sensation, or experience, also requires knowledge of how each of the human senses works.

THE SENSES

People commonly refer to "the five senses," by which they mean sight, hearing, taste, smell, and touch. Actually, humans and animals have at least nine senses. Touch really consists of three different skin senses, and there are two other senses: the vestibular sense, which involves balance, and kines-thesis, which deals with movement and body position.

The sense organs transform patterns of energy in the world (patterns of light, sound, words, and so forth) into patterns of energy, or sensory information, in the nervous system. This process of transformation is called **transduction.** Each sense organ is normally responsive only to a highly specific kind of stimulus, and it has a specific structure designed to transduce this kind of stimulus into sensory information in the nervous system.

Vision

Vision is certainly one of our richest senses. Our eyes collect the light reflected from things in the world, and from this light we somehow see shape, color, depth, texture, movement, and the full variety of things in space.

Stimulus Light, the stimulus for the eyes, has two characteristics that are essential for vision: wavelength and intensity. The color of what we see is determined by the **wavelength** of light; how bright it looks is determined by the **intensity** of light. The two characteristics together determine whether light can be seen. For example, a purple light shown against a gray wall in a dark room must be somewhat more intense than a green light (shown against the same wall) before it will become visible.

Structure The structure of the human eye is shown in Figure 12.7A. There are four major functional parts of the eye: the cornea, iris, lens, and retina. Light enters the eye through the **cornea,** the transparent window covering the front of the eye. The cornea is sharply curved, so that it helps focus the light that enters the eye. The **iris** is a ring of muscle whose pigmentation gives the eyes their color. Its function is to regulate the amount of light that enters the eye through the **pupil,** the opening in the center of the eye that appears to be black. The pupil is just a hole, although covered by the cornea. Through it, light passes to the **lens,** which focuses the light to make a clear image on the **retina** in the back of the eye.

The opening and closing of the iris and the action of the lens to focus light are reflexes. We do not have to think about either activity. In fact, about the only time we notice that either is not working well enough is when we need to relax our eyes from too much reading.

The eye has been said to function like a camera. This analogy is only partly true, however. The iris and lens of the eye function much as do the diaphragm and lens of a camera; they both allow an image to be projected onto a light-

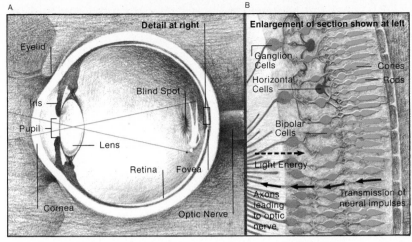

A

B

Detail at right

Enlargement of section shown at left

Eyelid

Ganglion Cells

Cones

Blind Spot

Horizontal Cells

Rods

Iris

Bipolar Cells

Pupil

Lens

Light Energy

Retina

Fovea

Axons leading to optic nerve

Transmission of neural impulses

Cornea

Optic Nerve

Figure 12.7 The structure of the eye and the transduction of light energy into neural firing. (A) A cross section of the human eye. Note that the lens transmits an inverted image onto the retina. Note also the centrally located fovea, which is the area of maximum visual acuity, and the blind spot, which is the area at which the optic nerve leaves the eye. (B) The detailed structure of a small portion of the retina close to the fovea. Note that the light-sensitive cells, the rods and cones, are the cells farthest from the incoming light. Note also that cones are more common toward the fovea and that near the fovea each cone is connected to a single bipolar cell. Arrows on the figure indicate the passage of neural impulses from the receptor cells through bipolar cells and ganglion cells to the optic nerve on their way to the brain. The neural circuitry in the retina is quite complex; a considerable amount of coding and processing of the incoming information is done here, before the information ever reaches the brain.

sensitive medium—the retina or the photographic film. The film in a camera is not like the retina, however.

The Retina and Receptor Cells The retina is the transducing part of the eye. It contains the receptor cells, or **receptors,** that transform light energy into neural energy and also several types of neural cells that help encode the energy from the receptors into a form that is easily interpretable by the brain. As Figure 12.7B indicates, the receptors—the **rods** and **cones**—are actually farthest of all the retinal cells from the light. The light that enters the eye must first pass through the other nerve cells and the blood vessels nourishing the eye before it hits the receptor cells.

Figure 12.7B shows how information is transmitted through the retina. The receptor cells stimulate the bipolar cells, and from the bipolar cells the neural information passes to the ganglion cells. It is the ganglion cells that help form the **optic nerve,** which carries the information about what is seen to the brain for interpretation.

Figure 12.7A illustrates how the optic nerve leaves the eye through an area of the retina called the "blind spot." This area is aptly named. No visual transduction is possible at this spot because there is a complete absence of receptor cells. Figure 12.8 enables you to demonstrate to yourself that you cannot see something that falls on the blind spot. If you look at the figure so the dot falls on the blind spot in your eye, the dot will seem to disappear.

The two types of receptors serve different functions. Simply stated, the cones give us color vision, and the rods give us vision of light and dark. The two cell systems also require different amounts of light to function. The rods require less light than do the cones. We see little color by moonlight because there is not enough light to stimulate the cones; we can see a monochromatic landscape because the rods are stimulated by moonlight.

The transduction of light to neural energy is carried out by means of a series of chemical reactions. One of the most important chemicals involved, as George Wald discovered, is **rhodopsin,** the pigment in rods. The more pigment in the rods, the more sensitive is the eye to light. When a rod is struck by

Figure 12.8 Although you are never normally aware of it, the blind spot is literally blind. To demonstrate this fact to yourself, hold this figure at arm's length, cover your left eye, and focus on the center of the X. Slowly move the figure toward you, maintaining your fixation on the X. At some point, you will no longer be able to see the red spot. This is the point at which the red spot's image has fallen on the blind spot in your right eye. The red spot will reappear if you move the figure even closer.

Figure 12.9 Dark adaptation. In this figure the smallest intensity of light needed to cause a sensation (the absolute threshold) is plotted as a function of time spent in total darkness. As dark adaptation proceeds, less and less light is needed to cause a sensation. Note that the curve plotted here appears to be made up of two simpler curves. The first is believed to represent the adaptation of the cones, which are relatively insensitive to light-dark differences. The second represents the adaptation of the rods, the receptor cells on which night vision chiefly depends. Note also that the physical intensity of the light is measured on a logarithmic scale. Logarithmic scales are often used in psychophysics because the human nervous system is sensitive to such a huge range of energies. (After Hecht, Haig, and Wald, 1935.)

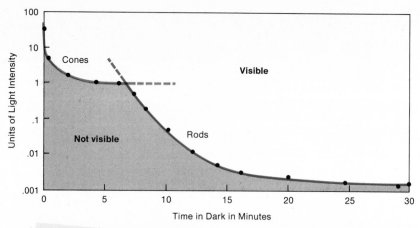

light, rhodopsin absorbs the light, and consequently its own chemical structure changes. The change in chemical structure results in the generation of a neural signal. Because light breaks down the rhodopsin (as well as the pigments in cones), rhodopsin must continually be replenished by receptor cells. The reason you cannot see well when you enter a dark room from bright daylight is that the supply of pigments has been depleted by the bright light. The few minutes it takes you to see well are necessary for the replacement of receptor pigments. As Figure 12.9 shows, the more time a person spends in the dark, the more sensitive the rods get to light. This phenomenon is called **dark adaptation,** and the plotted curves are called dark-adaptation curves; the curves also show that the cones do not function at all in dim light.

The rods and the cones are not distributed evenly over the retina. There is a much higher concentration of cones in the center of the retina, an area called the fovea. The **fovea** is the area of the retina that has the greatest visual acuity, that is, the clearest and most accurate vision. Whenever you ''look at'' something, you are seeing it with the foveal cones. The high density of receptors in the fovea gives more detail to the visual image and is one reason for the great acuity of the fovea. Another reason is that the cones in the fovea are fully exposed to light. The blood vessels and nerve cells that cover the rest of the retina do not cover the fovea, so the light has an unimpeded path to the fovea. Also, because each cone is connected to one bipolar cell, as shown in Figure 12.10, the exact nature of the visual information recorded by cones is better preserved than it is for rods. Many rods may be connected to one bipolar cell, so the signals from them to the higher centers are blended. The periphery of the retina is mostly rods and is therefore not very sensitive to color, but it is very sensitive to movement.

Receptors, bipolar cells, and ganglion cells are thought of as transmitting information vertically through the retina. Other cells (horizontal cells and amacrine cells) transmit information horizontally through the retina, that is, they connect receptor cells to receptor cells, and bipolar cells to bipolar cells. The transmission of information laterally through the retina results in lateral inhibition (see Figure 12.10). **Lateral inhibition** means that a cell highly stimulated by a bright light will act to prevent the cells next to it from responding. As Figure 12.10 indicates, if the inhibited cell happens to be just

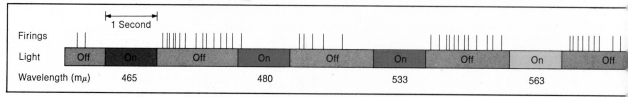

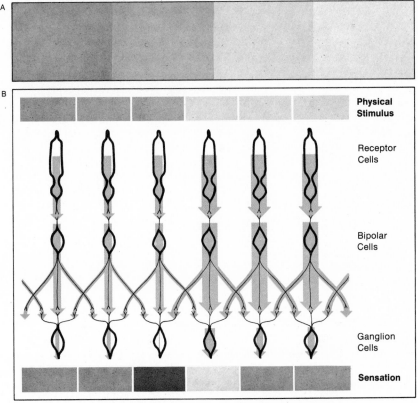

Figure 12.10 (A) The effects of lateral inhibition. Each gray band is physically uniform but appears to be lighter on the edge that borders on a darker gray, and darker on the edge that borders on a lighter gray. (B) How lateral inhibition produces this contrast effect. The pattern of stimulation at one light-dark border is shown falling on a row of receptor cells in the retina. These cells respond with levels of excitation (red arrows) that correspond in strength to the brightness of the stimulus. This excitation is transmitted to the middle layer of bipolar cells. Each of these cells exerts an inhibitory influence (brown arrows) on each of its neighbors and also transmits excitation to the bottom layer of ganglion cells. Note that the inhibition causes a weakening of excitatory effect, and that the bipolar cells that have been most strongly excited also exert the strongest inhibitory influence. The activity in the ganglion cells produces the psychological effect shown at the bottom. The contrast at the light-dark border has been heightened because the first ganglion cell on the dark side received a strong inhibitory input that other ganglion cells on this side did not. Conversely, the first ganglion cell on the light side received one weak inhibitory input while all the other ganglion cells on this side received only strong ones.

over the border into a slightly darker area of the pattern, it will respond less (because of the inhibition from its highly stimulated neighbor) than the rest of the cells being stimulated by the same amount of light. This mechanism is responsible for sharpening contrasts of brightness so that, for example, an object is differentiated from its background. The effects of lateral inhibition on visual sensation are fairly well understood, but the results of other interactions between cells in the visual system are not so well understood.

Color Vision The generally accepted explanation of color vision points to three types of cones, each type being maximally sensitive to a different color. Thus, this explanation is called the **trichromatic theory of color vision.** Edward MacNichol, Jr., has shown that particular cones respond best to red light, others to green light, and others to blue light. The color that we see depends on how many of each of these cones are stimulated. When a greater number of the red-sensitive cones are stimulated, we see red. When an equal number of red-sensitive and green-sensitive cones are stimulated, we see yellow because yellow is between red and green in the spectrum.

Color processing also occurs in the brain itself. Russell DeValois has found that there are **color-opponent cells** in one part of the brain that respond to stimulation of the eye by one color but are inhibited by its opposite. Thus, as Figure 12.11 shows, there are cells that respond to red and are inhibited by

Figure 12.11 The firing of a color-opponent cell in the brain of a monkey. The vertical spikes correspond to single firings of the neuron. Note that this cell fires at a moderate rate when there is no stimulation. Lights at the red end of the spectrum flashed in the monkey's eye cause this cell to fire faster (excitation). Lights at the opposite end of the spectrum cause the cell to fire less often than usual (inhibition). (After De Valois, 1965.)

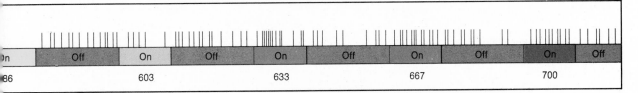

A   B   C   D

Figure 12.12   Representations of how the same scene might be perceived by a person with normal vision and by people with three kinds of color blindness. (A) The scene as people with normal color vision see it. (B) The experience of a person who is red-green "blind"; he sees everything in shades of blue and yellow. (C) Someone who is blue-yellow "blind" would see something like this; his visual world is made up of shades of red and green. (D) The scene as experienced by a monochromat. Because the cones, the cells that are responsive to color and fill the central area of the retina, are missing entirely in this rare kind of color blindness, these persons not only fail to see color, they also have generally poor visual acuity.

green. The opponent cell to this type would be one that is excited by green and inhibited by red. There are also opponent pairs for blue and yellow.

About 10 percent of people have some difficulty seeing colors. A person with normal color vision is called a **trichromat,** to reflect the fact that the three types of cones are functioning normally. A **dichromat** is a person in whom one of the three cone systems is absent or deficient. Most common is red-green "blindness"; blue-yellow "blindness" is rarer. These types of dichromacy are illustrated in Figures 12.12B and 12.12C. A rare type of color-blindness is monochromacy, where the person sees with only rods, not cones. The **monochromat** sees something that looks like Figure 12.12D.

Color blindness is rarely an all or nothing thing; some people just have weak cone systems and therefore need the color to be stronger before they are able to sense it. A few individuals are born without any cones, however; theirs is the most extreme form of color blindness possible. These people lack a fovea, and because they can only see things on the peripheral retina, must move their eyes rapidly back and forth to see at all.

Hearing

Hearing, whether of voices, music, the rumble of a subway, or the ripple of a brook depends on the sound stimulus just as vision depends on light. And, just as the eyes transduce light and turn it into neural electrical energy interpretable by the brain, the ears turn sound waves into such energy.

Stimulus   When you listen to a radio, the amplifier in it makes the speaker vibrate. This vibrating speaker alternately pushes against the air in front of it, compressing it, and pulls away from the air, making it less dense, or rarefying it. The **waves of compressed and rarefied air particles** travel through the air until they strike your eardrum. The eardrum gets pushed and pulled by the compressions and rarefactions and, as a result, vibrates very much like the loudspeaker did originally.

Figure 12.13 suggests what the waves of compression and rarefaction look like and shows how these waves relate to the physical attributes of the sound stimulus—the chief of which are frequency and intensity. **Frequency** refers to the number of compression-rarefaction cycles a wave goes through in a given period of time. **Intensity** refers to the amount of pressure a wave exerts;

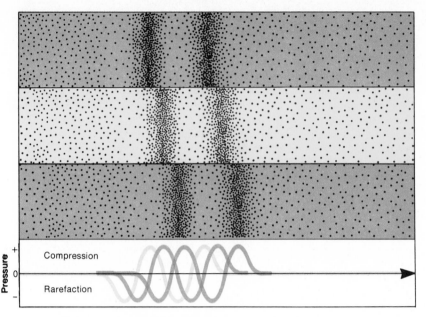

Figure 12.13 The physical stimulus for hearing. A vibrating body, such as a guitar string, moves back and forth extremely rapidly, alternately compressing and rarefying the air around it. (top) The compressions and rarefactions are transmitted through the air as waves, which are analogous to waves on the surface of a body of water. (bottom) A graph of this sound wave. Air pressure at a particular point in space is plotted as a function of time. As the sound wave passes, the air pressure rises and then falls. If middle C were played on the piano, this rise and fall would take place 256 times per second. The greater the magnitude of this rise and fall, the louder the sound.

it is represented in Figure 12.13 by the distance of the wave's peaks and valleys from the baseline.

The physical attribute of frequency corresponds to the sensation of **pitch;** intensity to **loudness.** The human ear is sensitive to a wide range of frequencies and intensities. In fact, your ear is sensitive enough to hear one molecule of air hitting the eardrum, but your brain has habituated to the sound of the millions of air molecules that randomly hit the eardrum, so the sound is ignored.

Structure Figure 12.14A shows the structure of the ear: the outer ear (the pinna and the auditory canal); the middle ear; and the inner ear, or cochlea. (The three semicircular canals are part of the vestibular apparatus rather than of the auditory system; they provide cues to body position and movement.)

Sound reaching the **eardrum** sets it and the three bones of the **middle ear**—called the ossicles—vibrating. The vibrations transmit the movement of the air particles to the **cochlea,** a coiled tube filled with fluid buried deep in the skull, the body's hardest bone. Running the length of the cochlea, and

Figure 12.14 The anatomy of the ear, and the transduction of sound energy into neural firing. (A) Sound waves strike the eardrum and set the three bones in the middle ear in motion. The last of these bones is attached to a membrane, the oval window, at the end of the fluid-filled coiled tube that is the cochlea. The wave motion is transmitted through the fluid in the cochlea, and the pressure changes in the fluid cause ripples to run down the skinlike basilar membrane that divides the cochlea in half for most of its length. (B) A detailed view in cross section of the organ of Corti. Ripples running down the basilar membrane cause the tectorial membrane to brush across the hair cells. This stimulation of the hair cells generates neural impulses, which are carried as auditory signals to the brain.

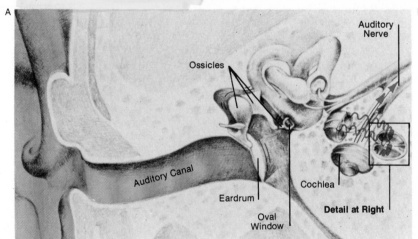

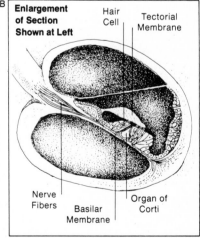

Figure 12.15 Two ways in which sound frequency might be encoded by the ear. (A) The place theory. This diagram shows waves traveling down the basilar membrane and indicates the points at which the waves are largest for a number of different frequencies. Because greater displacement produces more stimulation of the organ of Corti, the brain could use the location of the most rapidly firing cells in the organ of Corti as a code for the frequency of the sound. (B) The volley theory. The activity in the nerve leading from the cochlea to the brain tends to keep time with the pressure changes of the sound wave that was the stimulus. This is another possible code that the brain could use to identify frequency. Note that because individual neurons cannot fire fast enough to keep up with most sound frequencies, the neurons would have to fire in staggered groups (called volleys), as shown in this diagram.

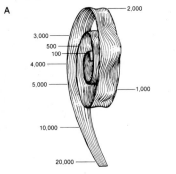

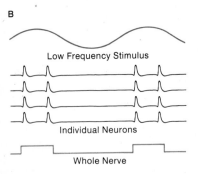

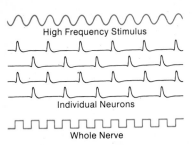

inside it, is the extremely sensitive **basilar membrane.** Sound energy enters the cochlea through the oval window and sets up a pressure wave that moves along the basilar membrane to the apex of the cochlea. Pressure against the oval window is relieved by the flexibility of the round window, which lies on the other side of the basilar membrane.

When the basilar membrane is wobbled by the traveling wave, the **organ of Corti** lying on it also moves up and down. In the organ of Corti are **hair cells.** Their extensions, or hairs, are embedded in the **tectorial membrane.** The tectorial membrane and the basilar membrane move somewhat differently, so that the hairs between them are bent in a kind of rubbing or shearing action. The bending of the hairs causes the hair cells to send neural impulses to the auditory nerve. At the threshold of hearing, the basilar membrane vibrates over a distance a hundred times smaller than the diameter of a hydrogen atom. Somehow, this infinitesimally small movement leads to hearing.

Neural Coding by the Ear The transduction from stimulus energy into neural energy is performed by the organ of Corti. Georg von Békésy found that different parts of the basilar membrane are maximally displaced by different frequencies. As shown in Figure 12.15A high-frequency tones most affect the region near the oval window. As the frequency of the tone decreases, the locus of maximum wave motion moves along the membrane toward the top of the cochlea. According to the place theory of pitch, frequency is encoded by the place of maximum displacement on the basilar membrane. The chief difficulty with the place theory is that the areas of maximum displacement of the basilar membrane seem to overlap too much, particularly at low frequencies, to account for our ability to tell the difference between closely similar tones.

An alternate theory, called the volley theory by Ernest Wever who developed it, says that frequency is directly represented in the nervous system by some repetitive event that has the same frequency as that of the sound; that is, activity in the auditory nerve increases and decreases in time with the pressure changes occurring in the sound-wave stimulus. The activity in the auditory nerve, however, depends on the firing rate of individual nerve cells, and it is known that single nerve cells are physiologically incapable of firing and refiring quickly enough to keep up with the pressure changes that occur in high-pitched sounds. Wever therefore theorized that the individual cells fire in staggered, or alternate, volleys so that the whole nerve can keep up with higher-frequency sounds. Figure 12.15B shows how this principle could account for a correspondence between activity in the auditory nerve and pressure changes in the sound-wave stimulus. But even with this theory, it is difficult to account for the ear's encoding of sounds much higher than 4000 cycles per second (high notes played on a piccolo). It is now thought that place theory must account for the encoding of frequency differences at all frequencies, but that the volley principle also plays a role at lower ones.

Auditory Localization An important part of auditory perception is our ability to tell where sounds are coming from—to locate them in space. This ability depends primarily on tiny intensity and time differences in a sound when it reaches the left and right ears. (See Figure 11.16 in the previous chapter.)

At low frequencies, tones have such long wavelengths compared to the size of the human head that intensity differences reaching the two ears are almost nil. For low-frequency sounds, then, and also for brief sounds and sounds with changing frequencies, the important cue to localization is difference in the time of the sound's arrival at the ears. Sound travels about 1,100 feet per second—fast, but still slow enough to produce a clear time difference. Because most sounds we hear either are fluctuating or are available for a very short time, we usually rely on time differences for locating their source.

The ears of the average adult male are about seven inches apart. A sound directly opposite the right ear reaches that ear about 0.7 millisecond sooner than it reaches the left ear, so the listener knows the sound is coming from the right. As the sound source moves toward a position directly in front (or back) of the listener, the time difference decreases and, finally, disappears. If a sound is coming from directly in front of or in back of you, you must turn your head slightly to tell where it is coming from.

If you doubt the difficulty of locating sounds in the front-rear plane, you can do the following experiment with a friend. While you sit blindfolded, with your head absolutely still, have your friend move (noiselessly) around the room and snap his fingers to your right, left, front, and back. You should find that your ability to locate sounds on the right and left is essentially perfect, but you may not always be able to tell front from back.

Distinguishing between sounds from above and sounds from below is also difficult because, again, the sound reaches both ears at the same time. In this case you locate the sound by tilting your head. When a sound reaches both ears at the same time, a person usually rotates his head slightly (to distinguish front from back); if that does not work, he tries tilting it.

Smell

A human being's sense of smell is not nearly as sensitive as that of many animals and insects. Male moths, for example, can smell female moths several miles away. Humans' sense of smell requires that appropriate molecules enter the nasal passages, where the membrane containing smell receptors, the **olfactory epithelium,** is located. Only volatile substances—substances that are readily vaporized from a liquid or solid to a gas—are accessible to the olfactory receptors. Millions of hair cells in the olfactory epithelium transduce these gas molecules into nerve impulses.

Most odors to which human beings are sensitive are organic compounds, but little else is known about why we can smell some substances and not others or why certain groups of odors smell alike. A search for a way to classify odors on the basis of their physical characteristics has so far been unsuccessful. Subjective classification schemes based on people's judgments are not entirely successful either, but the most popular one is Hans Henning's smell prism, shown in Figure 12.16. Six supposedly pure qualities form the corners of the prism, and the intermediate qualities lie along the surface. The search for the basis of odor differences and similarities is a search for common chemical properties that distinguish the members of one class of odors from the members of other classes.

Without knowing what stimulus properties are important in smell, researchers find it difficult to control stimuli for experimental purposes—more difficult than in studies of vision and hearing, for which the important properties are known and easily measured. What is known is that the subjective intensity of smell increases with the concentration of the odorous substance and also that humans adapt completely to most odors within a few minutes of exposure and so are temporarily unable to smell them. Generally, the more concentrated the odor, the faster the adaptation. Smell plays a relatively small role in people's behavior compared to animals', although smell is important enough to people that large perfume and deodorant industries do exist. Smell is probably most important to human beings when it interacts with taste.

Taste

Taste, or gustation, may be considered either as the global sensation that accompanies the presence of a substance in the mouth or as the specific sensation that accompanies the stimulation of certain organs in the mouth.

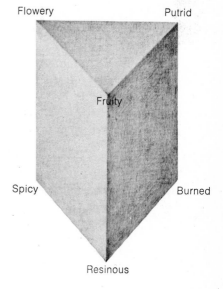

Figure 12.16 Henning's smell prism. Supposedly, every possible smell sensation can be located somewhere on the surface of this solid. This theoretical description of smell implies that certain smells are impossible. For example, a putrid, flowery, burned, spicy smell should be possible, but not a putrid, flowery, resinous smell. Where on this surface would you place the smell of a fresh, ripe cantaloupe?

Figure 12.17 (A) A map of the human tongue showing the areas of maximum sensitivity to the four fundamental kinds of taste sensation. (B) The tastes of a number of foods analyzed into the four components of taste shown in (A). The length of the colored bars indicates the amount of each component judged to be present in the taste of the food by a number of subjects in a psychophysical experiment.

(Data from J. G. Beebe-Center, 1949.)

A

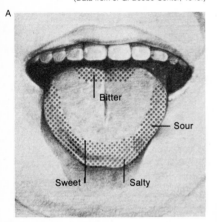

B

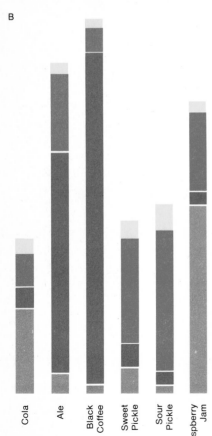

Global taste perception includes a very strong component of smell, and sensations of temperature and touch as well. If none of the vapors from food reaches the organ of smell, global taste is substantially restricted.

The specific sensation of taste results from the stimulation of the **taste buds,** which are grouped in large numbers as papillae and located primarily on the surface of the tongue. Most of our specific taste sensations are mixtures of four primary taste qualities: sour, salty, bitter, and sweet. The location of groups of papillae specialized for the four taste qualities and the mixtures of tastes in some common foods are shown in Figure 12.17. The qualities can be elicited in more or less pure form by stimulating the taste buds with concentrated solutions or by stimulating individual papillae with electrical pulses. The fact that electrical stimulation brings out only these four taste qualities suggests that four kinds of papillae are responsible for the four primary taste qualities. How chemical or physical properties of stimuli elicit these four different taste sensations, however, is not yet well understood.

The Skin Senses

Touch comes to our awareness in three distinct forms: as pressure, as warmth and cold, and as pain. The receptors for these sensations lie in the thin **epidermis** and the inner **dermis** of the skin, as shown in Figure 12.18. Nerve endings in the skin transmit sensory information to the brain.

Warmth and Cold Touching the skin with stimulators at skin temperature, usually 32 degrees centigrade, yields no sensation of warmth or cold; the temperature at which there is no sensation is referred to as physiological zero. Warmth is usually felt at temperatures greater than physiological zero, cold at lower temperatures. Warmth and cold are not felt at every point of the skin, only at specific spots. Exploration of one square centimeter of skin with small points of warm and cold materials reveals about six cold spots at which cold may be felt but only one or two warm spots at which warmth may be sensed, on the average. The separate identity of warm and cold spots is generally accepted, partly because stimulating a cold spot with a very warm stimulus sometimes yields a cold sensation. The name for this phenomenon is paradoxical cold.

Pressure Sensitivity to pressure varies from place to place on the skin, and pressure-sensitive spots are more responsive to changes in pressure than to steady states. Once the skin has been displaced, the sensation of pressure disappears—rapidly, if the force exerted is slight. If this were not true, we would be constantly aware of the gentle pressure of clothes, eyeglasses, hair lying against the back of the neck, and so on.

The amount of energy that must be exerted for pressure to be just detectable is perhaps smallest on the tips of the thumb and fingers, the underside of the forearm, the lips, and the tip of the tongue. Although the pressure thresholds at these points are among the lowest on the skin, the energy required to produce a sensation is from 100 million to 10 billion times greater than the energy values required by the eye and ear at visual and auditory absolute thresholds.

Lately, sensitivity to pressure has sparked the interest of researchers who are considering the potential of this sense to provide substitute sensory information to the blind. A group of investigators at the Smith-Kettlewell Institute of the University of the Pacific has developed prototype equipment that translates visual images picked up by a television camera into patterns of vibratory pressure that can be sensed by the skin. The user sits in a chair that has a matrix of small vibrators embedded in the back. The television camera is connected to these vibrators so they vibrate more in response to brightness

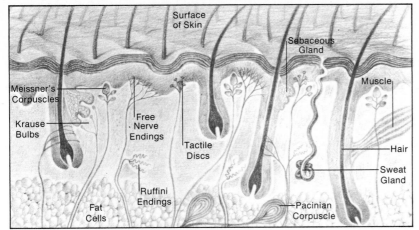

Figure 12.18 A cross-sectional diagram of human skin. A number of different kinds of receptors have been identified near the surface of the skin, but there is considerable uncertainty about their functions. Meissner's corpuscles are believed to be pressure sensitive. Pacinian corpuscles may be additional receptors for "deep" pressure. Free nerve endings may be important in the sensation of pain. And, it is speculated that Krause bulbs are responsive to cold and Ruffini endings responsive to warmth.

than to darkness. People have been quite successful in "seeing" simple objects through these skin vibrations. Although this research is in its early stages, the outlook for future developments is bright.

A similar device is the Optacon, a vibrating device that enables the blind to read ordinary printed text. The user places a finger on a panel of vibrating reeds and "scans" a small television camera over the text to be read. The reeds vibrate in the pattern of the letter that the television camera sees. Sensing the pattern of vibration, a blind person can read without having special Braille translations made.

Pain Pain is associated with more than just the skin. However, little is known about pain from the interior of the body except that it seems to be deep, dull, and much more unpleasant than the bright, sharply localized pain from the skin. Many kinds of stimuli—scratch, puncture, pressure, heat, cold, twist—can produce pain. Their common property is real or potential injury to bodily tissue. In general, an overstimulation of any sensory modality—loud sounds, bright lights, intense pressure—is painful.

Thresholds for pain vary little from person to person and from time to time. In the laboratory, mild cutaneous pain can be shown to disappear with prolonged stimulation, but little adaptation to pain occurs under ordinary circumstances. Nonadaptation to pain is probably fortunate, because pain alerts us to noxious stimuli and to injuries and disease that need treatment.

The Vestibular Sense

The vestibular sense is the sense of balance. We are never directly aware of it: There is no "vestibular sensation" that we can ascribe to a particular body organ. We are very much aware of our posture, movements, and orientations in space, however. The vestibular, visual, and kinesthetic senses cooperate to produce that awareness. Adults can get along fairly well without their vestibular organs, provided that their visual and kinesthetic senses are unimpaired. But interest in the vestibular sense has been high since space travel began, because a long absence of gravity might disturb vestibular functions.

The vestibular organ lies in the inner ear, buried in bone above and to the rear of the cochlea. Its prominent section is the three fluid-filled **semicircular canals,** which lie at right angles to each other as shown in Figure 12.19. When the head starts turning in the plane of a given canal, the movement causes the fluid to move, which in turn bends the endings of receptor hair cells. The hair cells connect with the vestibular nerve, which joins the auditory nerve on its way to the brain. Not enough is known to fully explain how the bending of the hairs is transduced to neural impulses.

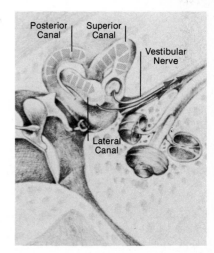

Figure 12.19 The vestibular system. The organs of balance are three fluid-filled semicircular canals arranged at right angles to one another. The inertia of the fluid inside at least one of the canals causes it to move relative to the walls of the canals whenever the motion of the head speeds up, slows down, or changes direction. The motion of the fluid drags tiny stones over hair cells in the walls of the canals, and the hair cells transmit impulses to the brain.

The stimuli for vestibular responses are rotational or linear acceleration, falling, and tilting of the body or head. These stimuli result in some interesting interactions with the eye-movement systems. Rapid rotation about the longitudinal axis of the body, like that produced by spinning on skates, can produce what is known as vestibular nystagmus, a rapid back-and-forth motion of the eyes. Similarly, vestibular nystagmus results when a person stops spinning, though in this instance the nystagmus results from the fluid in the semicircular canals continuing to move after spinning has stopped. Another type of nystagmus can be induced by running hot or cold water into the external ear canal. The heat of the fluid transfers to the semicircular canals and starts the fluid in them moving: Caloric nystagmus results. Running warm water into your ear from the shower is often enough to produce the effect.

Kinesthesis

Kinesthesis is the sense of movement and body position. This sense cooperates with the vestibular and visual senses to maintain posture and equilibrium. The sensation of kinesthesis comes from nerve endings in and near the more than 100 body joints and in the muscles. The nerve endings in the joints are especially important for the perception of bodily movement. Which receptors respond depends on the direction and angle of movement. Other nerve endings in the muscles and tendons also contribute to the sensation of kinesthesis. Together, these various receptors help provide the feedback necessary for regulation of active body movement. Kinesthesis and the vestibular sense really work together to foster efficient locomotion and body movement. Vision plays a part too. In fact, it is really unfair to discuss the senses separately from each other—unfair in the sense that such discussion is artificial. People rarely use one sense alone, but almost always use many senses at once.

SUMMARY

1. **Sensation** is a part of the perceptual process. It is our qualitative experience of differences in quantitative stimuli, such as our experience of the brightness of light or the loudness of sound. The **stimuli** are **energies** in the world that can produce an experience, such as light waves or sound waves, and these energies are transformed by our sense organs into energy in the nervous system. The perceptual process then uses these sensations, along with other information, to infer what is happening ''out there.''

2. **Psychophysics** is the study of the relationship between stimulus and sensation.

3. Individuals differ in their sensations of a given stimulus. For example, shown a beam of light of a certain brightness, some people will sense it as brighter than other people will.

4. One of the central questions in psychophysics concerns the minimum stimulus necessary for sensation.

   a. Psychologists test an individual's **absolute threshold,** that is, the minimum stimulus necessary for a person to sense a stimulus. For example, they will show the person low-intensity beams of light in gradually increasing strengths until the person says ''I see it.'' The

Figure 12.20   E. G. Boring was an experimental psychologist whose work was extremely diverse. Early in his career he performed experiments on the regeneration of nerves. In World War I, with primatologist Robert Yerkes, he pioneered the development and administration of group intelligence testing for the Army. Later in his career he studied psychophysics intensively. He was the author of the definitive books *A History of Experimental Psychology* and *Sensation and Perception in the History of Experimental Psychology.*

point at which the person usually reports having seen a light is his absolute threshold.

   b. A person's **difference threshold,** or **just noticeable difference,** is the smallest change in a stimulus that produces a change in sensation.

5. A related question in psychophysics that has stimulated much research concerns the relationship between magnitude of a stimulus and magnitude of the sensation arising from it; several renowned psychologists have attempted to formulate laws that would express such a relationship for all stimuli and sensations.

   a. These laws all have the same basic underlying idea: that the nervous system analyzes stimulation in terms of **sensory ratios,** not in terms of absolute differences in sensory magnitude.

   b. **Weber's law** states that the amount of a stimulus necessary to produce a just noticeable difference is always a constant proportion of the intensity of the stimulus.

   c. **Fechner's law** states that the magnitude of increase in a sensation is always a constant proportion of the stimulus producing the sensation. This relationship is not true of very strong or very weak stimuli.

   d. **Steven's power law** says that the magnitude of a sensation is equal to the magnitude of the stimulus raised to some power, or exponent, and the power depends on the particular sense being stimulated.

6. A recently formulated method of studying absolute thresholds is **signal detection theory.** It says that an individual's threshold is not determined solely by the presence or absence of a sensation. Rather, three factors are involved in a person's **judgment** of whether or not he has sensed a stimulus.

   a. A person's judgment that he has sensed a stimulus depends on: first, the relative strengths of the **signal,** or stimulus, and **noise** (which is extraneous sensory information that always accompanies a signal); second, **individual differences** in **sensitivity** (for example, good hearing versus slight deafness); third, the individual's **response criterion** (which depends on situational and personality variables and on payoff).

   b. **Payoff** is the relative costs and benefits, in a given situation, of: **hits**—correct detections of a signal; **false alarms**—judging that there is a signal when in fact none has occurred; **correct rejections**—judging that there is no signal when in fact none is present; and **misses**—judging that there is no signal when in fact one is present.

7. The sense organs transform, or **transduce,** patterns of energy in the world, such as light, into patterns of energy in the nervous system. There actually are nine senses: sight; hearing; taste; smell; touch (which includes sensation of warmth and cold, pressure, and pain); the vestibular sense (which involves balance); and kinesthesis (which involves movement and body position).

8. **Vision** is one of our most important senses.

   a. The physical stimulus for vision is light. Our sensation of color is determined by the **wavelength** of light; brightness, by the **intensity.**

   b. There are four major functional parts of the eye: the **cornea;** the **iris** and **pupil;** the **lens;** and the **retina.** (See Figure 12.7.)

Figure 12.21 Director of Harvard University's Laboratory of Psychoacoustics for many years, S. S. Stevens was a leader in the field of psychophysics. He developed a procedure of magnitude estimation that enabled him to overthrow the long-accepted psychophysical findings of Weber and Fechner. Stevens was also the editor of one of the standard reference works in experimental psychology, the *Handbook of Experimental Psychology.*

Figure 12.22 Georg Von Békésy discovered the remarkable mechanism whereby sound waves are transduced into neural impulses in the cochlea, and virtually every aspect of the subject of the physiology and physics of hearing has profited from his contributions. Although he did not direct his work toward practical applications, he was honored with a Deafness Research Foundation Award. He has also been awarded a Nobel prize.

c. The retina is the part of the eye that transduces physical energy into neural energy by means of the **receptor cells,** the **rods** and **cones.** The transduction occurs by means of chemical reactions; the most important chemical involved is **rhodopsin,** the pigment in the rods. When light hits the rods, rhodopsin absorbs the light and its chemical structure changes. This change produces a neural signal, which travels via the **optic nerve** to the brain.

d. The time it takes for a person to see well after having been exposed to a bright light is the time it takes for the receptor pigments, such as rhodopsin, to replace themselves. The more time a person spends in the dark, the more sensitive he becomes to light; this phenomenon is called **dark adaptation.**

e. An area at the center of the retina, called the **fovea,** contains a high concentration of cones and consequently has the most accurate vision.

f. The generally accepted theory explaining color vision is the **trichromatic theory of color vision.** It states that there are three types of cones, each type sensitive to red, green, or blue light. People with normal color vision are called **trichromats.** Those in whom one set of cones is deficient are **dichromats;** they are "color blind" for red-green or yellow-blue. A few people have only one set of functioning cones; they are called **monochromats.** (See Figure 12.12.)

9. In hearing, the stimulus is **waves of compressed and rarefied air particles.** The number of compression-rarefaction cycles a wave goes through in a given period of time is referred to as the **frequency;** frequency corresponds to the sensation of **pitch.** The amount of pressure a wave exerts is referred to as the **intensity;** intensity corresponds to the sensation of **loudness.**

a. The structure of the ear is shown in Figure 12.14.

b. The **organ of Corti** transduces the stimulus energy into neural energy. **Hair cells** in the organ of Corti have extensions, or hairs, embedded in the **tectorial membrane.** Bending of the hairs causes the hair cells to send neural impulses to the **auditory nerve,** and the auditory nerve carries those impulses to the brain.

c. The ability to tell where sounds are coming from—**auditory localization**—depends primarily on the difference in the time of a sound's arrival at the two ears.

10. The physical stimulus for smell is molecules that make up gases. Hair cells in the **olfactory epithelium** transduce the gases into nerve impulses.

a. It has not yet been possible to successfully classify odors. Some classifications, such as Hans Henning's smell prism, are based on people's subjective judgment of similarity of smells.

b. The subjective intensity of a smell increases with the concentration of the odorous substance. Also, humans adapt completely to odors after a few minutes, and the more highly concentrated the odor, the faster they adapt.

11. Taste depends a great deal on smell. Most specific taste sensations are mixtures of sour, salty, bitter, and sweet. It appears that specific **taste buds,** or papillae, are responsible for the four primary taste qualities.

12. Receptors for the skin senses lie in the skin's **epidermis** and **dermis.** Nerve endings in the skin transmit sensory information to the brain.

    a. Specific receptor spots in the skin are sensitive to **warmth** or to **cold.** On one square centimeter of skin there are, on the average, six cold spots and one or two warm spots.

    b. The skin contains **pressure-sensitive spots.** The areas of the body on which the skin is most sensitive to pressure are the fingertips, lips, tip of the tongue, and underside of the forearm.

    c. Many kinds of stimuli can produce **pain.** The body does not adapt to pain under ordinary circumstances.

13. The **vestibular sense** is the sense of balance. The vestibular organ is in the inner ear, and its most important part is the **semicircular canals,** filled with fluid, which moves with movements of the head and body. The fluid bends receptor hair cells, which connect with the vestibular nerve. This nerve joins the auditory nerve and thus connects with the brain.

14. **Kinesthesis** is the sense of movement and body position. Combined with vision and the vestibular sense, it permits people to maintain posture and equilibrium. Nerve endings in joints, muscles, and tendons carry messages to and from the brain for regulation of body movement.

SUGGESTED READINGS

Boring, Edwin G. *Sensation and Perception in the History of Experimental Psychology.* New York: Appleton-Century-Crofts, 1942. Essential for a historical appreciation of sensation and psychophysics. The book is especially noteworthy for its treatment of the attributes of sensation and the historical antecedents of modern color theory.

D'Amato, M. R. *Experimental Psychology: Methodology, Psychophysics, and Learning.* New York: McGraw-Hill, 1970. This book presents easily understandable yet detailed explanations of psychophysics and the theory of signal detection. This is the book to read for a fuller treatment of this theory than what is presented in the chapter.

Geldard, Frank A. *The Human Senses.* 2nd ed. New York: Wiley, 1972. Updated from the earlier edition, Geldard's book is still the most complete source book for information about all the senses.

Green, David M., and John A. Swets. *Signal Detection Theory and Psychophysics.* New York: Wiley, 1966. An excellent treatment of the theory by the two scientists largely instrumental in developing it.

Gross, Charles G., and H. Philip Zeigler (eds.). *Readings in Physiological Psychology: Neurophysiology/Sensory Processes.* New York: Harper & Row, 1969. Contains many important readings on the processing of sensory information.

Gulick, Walter L. *Hearing: Physiology and Psychophysics.* New York: Oxford University Press, 1971. For a detailed explanation of hearing, refer to this book. Its easy reading belies the information that it conveys.

Uttal, William R. (ed.). *Sensory Coding: Selected Readings.* Boston: Little, Brown, 1972. This book contains reprints of original articles describing many of the important advances in our knowledge of sense organ functioning.

Woodworth, Robert S., and Harold Schlosberg. *Experimental Psychology.* New York: Holt, Rinehart and Winston, 1954. This book contains the classic explanations of psychophysics and sensory scaling.

A chapter dealing with consciousness, as this one does, reminds me of a story I wrote back in 1956. It was entitled "The Last Question," and what follows is a résumé of its plot.

Mankind, thanks to its giant computers, has managed to work out systems for making use of solar energy, and it appears that a golden age will be dawning—free energy without pollution. One minor official, however, worries about what will happen when the sun runs down. Will mankind be able to wind it up again, so to speak? He asks the computer, which can only say it has insufficient data to give an answer.

Over centuries and millennia people learn to travel between the stars and to colonize the galaxy. They learn the secret of immortality. They free themselves of their material bodies and become consciousnesses living in space. At every stage they are helped by the information-analyzing ability of computers, which steadily grow more complex. Indeed, computers grow so complex that only computers themselves can design and construct still better computers. The result is that people lose all physical connection with the vast central computer that becomes the great problem solver in mankind's later history. At one stage this computer occupies an entire world by itself. Then parts of it actually exist outside space. Finally, although all of it exists outside space, it still keeps itself at the disposal of man's consciousness. Anyone can ask any question at any point in the universe and get an answer.

Through all of history, however, no matter how widespread and ethereally immortal people become, it is clear that the entire universe is running down. Available energy decreases, and the stars are dimming to final extinction. Periodically, someone asks the ever-improving computer if the universe can ever be wound up again. Always, the computer answers that it doesn't have enough information to formulate an answer. Finally, the end comes. The last stars are all but dead. Mankind has coalesced into one energy being that is pure consciousness, and at the last it coalesces with the ultimate computer that exists outside space. Now only the computer is left. And the computer cannot rest, for in all of human history there remains that one question it could not answer—the last question. Can one wind up the universe once more?

Ages pass while the computer endlessly analyzes all the information gathered in the course of a trillion years, and finally it has the answer. But now the computer is the only remaining consciousness in the universe; it has no one to tell the answer to. So it decides to answer the question in such a way as to make sure that there will eventually be someone to understand. The computer began . . .

And it said, "Let there be light!" And there was light! . . .

Isaac Asimov

13

Varieties of Consciousness

THE NATURE OF CONSCIOUSNESS
Consciousness Is a Brain Process
Consciousness Is Limited
Consciousness Is Active
Consciousness Is Divided
Consciousness Is Varied

STATES OF CONSCIOUSNESS
Everyday Consciousness and the Split Brain
Sleep and Dreams

Stages of Sleep
REM Sleep
Stage-4 Sleep
Dreams and Their Meaning

Meditation
Hypnosis

A Case of Hypnotic Blindness
Is Hypnosis Real

Spirit Possession
Drug States

Figure 13.1 Visitors to the 1967 World's Fair in Montreal wander between the giant figure of a woman and the stainless-steel sheet from which it was cut. These two forms may serve as a metaphor for consciousness. Think, for example, of your everyday waking consciousness and your consciousness while you are asleep and dreaming; the form your thought takes is different in these two states, yet the two sets of experiences are related to each other in ways that are both universal and unique to each individual. The two forms of the sculpture shown here, which are separate but could be fit together (as is the case, for example, when your waking consciousness reflects on the content of your dreams), symbolize some of the varied aspects of consciousness discussed in this chapter.

he original meaning of the word psychology is "the study of the mind." So far in this textbook there has been no discussion of the mind itself, although phenomena that traditionally imply the existence of a mind—learning, thinking, intelligence, perception—have been discussed.

The concept of mind implies the existence of a **consciousness,** an experiencing self. As a start at understanding what consciousness is, one of the best sources of information is you, yourself—your consciousness. Look at your feet. Your feet are part of your body, but what is the relationship between your feet and your mind? As you look at your feet, do you feel that there is a *you* of some kind that, while it can experience your feet (or any other part of your body), has a separate existence from them? What is the nature of that experiencing self? Was it that self that followed the instructions to look at your feet? Is it that self that is seeing them? Now bounce your knee up and down for fifteen or twenty seconds. At the same time, concentrate on some nearby object, such as a table. Did your self start your leg moving? Is it keeping the leg moving now, even while it is concentrating on the table? Try to concentrate so hard on the table that you do not even notice your leg moving. Is your self moving the leg now? If you are really engrossed in the table, then your leg probably seems to be moving by itself. What is making it move?

At times various philosophers and psychologists have tried to dismiss as meaningless questions about the nature of consciousness—and with them such phenomena as hypnosis, spirit possession, meditation, and even dreams. Behaviorism, for example, originally grew out of the assertion that mind, consciousness, awareness, and similar concepts cannot be analyzed scientifically and therefore should be banished from the field of psychology. Many psychologists, including some contemporary behaviorists, have not accepted this view, however, and their research has provided a number of important insights about consciousness.

THE NATURE OF CONSCIOUSNESS

Consciousness is the quality of mind through which we experience things. What are the characteristics of this quality of mind? Research indicates that consciousness has at least five essential characteristics.

Consciousness Is a Brain Process

Roger Sperry, the famous neuropsychologist, has argued that consciousness can no longer be considered an unscientific concept unworthy of consideration by psychologists; in fact, Sperry says, the evidence indicates that it is a real property of the functioning of the brain and plays an active role in the control of brain activity.

One of the most striking demonstrations that consciousness is a brain process comes from the work of Wilder Penfield, a surgeon who pioneered a type of brain operation for people with certain brain disorders, especially epilepsy. In performing this operation, the surgeon must first map out the patient's brain so that he can be sure to operate on the correct portion of it. The patient is then given only a local anesthetic applied to the scalp and skull. (If a general anesthetic were used, the patient would be unconscious, and it would be impossible to map the brain.) The surgeon applies a mild electrical current to an area of the brain, and by noting the effect on the patient he can tell which brain function is located in that area. The patient does not feel the electrical current itself, because there are no sense organs in the brain, but usually the electrical current disrupts the activity of the brain structure that it is applied to.

Penfield found that electrical disruption of certain structures of the brain produces a loss of consciousness. Consciousness returns as soon as the electrical disruption is stopped. Medical histories show that if these structures are permanently damaged by some kind of accident, such as a gunshot wound, the person lapses into a coma and remains unconscious until he dies. The parts of the brain that Penfield's experiments and other evidence indicate are necessary for consciousness belong to the primitive brain; they are not at all unique to humans but are present in monkeys, dogs, cats, all other mammals, and many other vertebrates.

Consciousness Is Limited

When Penfield applied electrical current to the so-called higher centers of the brain, which are more developed in humans than in other species, patients did not lose consciousness and, in fact, were not at all aware of the electrical disruption. Instead, they showed another interesting phenomenon. For example, one patient was naming the objects on a series of cards, and just before a card showing a butterfly was presented, electrical current was applied to the language area of his brain. After a few seconds he began to snap his fingers as if exasperated, but he said nothing. When the electrical current stopped, he blurted out, "Butterfly!" and added that he had known all along what the card portrayed but could not think of the word "butterfly." He tried to think of a closely related word, "moth," but he could not think of that, either. Then abruptly the word "butterfly" came to him—just as the electrical disruption was stopped.

The experience of many people who suffer brain damage is similar. For example, when an area associated with language is destroyed, the individual does not feel any different than he did before: His consciousness does not seem different to him. But then when he tries to speak normally, he may be unable to do so. If he can speak at all, his language is halting or distorted.

As this example illustrates, consciousness is limited. We are not only unaware of electrical disruption or brain damage, but we are unaware of most of what is going on in our brains. Our brains and nervous systems are control-

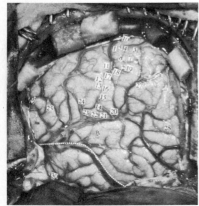

Figure 13.2 An exposed portion of the left side of the brain of a patient undergoing surgery for a brain injury. (The metallic objects at the top of the photo are surgical clamps that hold back the scalp around the opening in the skull.) The dotted line follows a major vein across the temporal lobe (see Chapter 14). The numbers indicate points at which mild electrical stimulation produced reports from the patient. By systematically stimulating the cortex in this way in operations on various patients, Wilder Penfield was able to map correspondences between areas on the surface of the cortex and subjective experiences. Stimulation at one set of points might cause the patient to report tingling sensations in various parts of his face. Stimulation at other points might cause him to see bright lights or hear a familiar tune. (Penfield and Roberts, 1959.)

re taking in and expelling air **the capital of California is Sacram**
ouse my brother is a murderer it's cold **I met Cecelia at Er**
boy stood on the burning deck... O, say can you see, by the daw
Alice makes great chocolate chip cookies **my n**
a funny joke Madaleine just told I think I'll tell the joke ab
I have to go to the dentist tomorrow *Sanford and Son* is on
has been married three times I like there's a song playin
om **I have to remember to pick up that roll of film** that was
Burr shot *it's nearly 3:00* on I have to tell Henry about that c
is producing hormones I once saw my mother kiss a stranger

I'm hungry
is Henry's birthday, *Gone with the Wind* was made in 1939 sto
s good I hate my grandmother there are 36 inches in a yard I
ce blood is circulating **the square root of 81 is 9** tipping is 15 p
is digesting food there are stomach is growling.
the kitchen is the most dangerous room in the house stoma
I met Alice and Sheila at Ernie's place that was a funny joke

Figure 13.3 Consciousness is limited; indeed, some things can never be made conscious. And of the information that is available to consciousness, only a small amount can be focused on at a time. Consciousness has been compared to a searchlight in that it illuminates powerfully only the small area it falls on. As this representation suggests, the contents of consciousness may be strongly affected by one's physiological state.

ling our breathing, our heartbeats, our level of fatigue, our walking, our talking, and much more, and we are not aware of most of the processes involved. The next time you are engaged in a conversation, try to notice what is within your awareness as you speak. Thoughts will be there, but probably not in the form of particular sentences. You will decide to speak, and sentences will flow. Most people report no awareness of the process of constructing sentences. And even when they consciously formulate a sentence before they say it, they are not aware of the complicated linguistic rules that they are using to do so (such rules are discussed in Chapter 9).

Indeed, at any moment we are not even aware of most of the things that we are capable of being aware of. Of the items that are available to consciousness, only a few can be focused on at once. If someone is playing a guitar, singing, and reading music simultaneously, he is not aware of most of what he is doing at any moment. If it is after lunchtime and you have not eaten and you are sitting in class daydreaming, then the focus of your consciousness might be similar to that depicted in Figure 13.3.

Consciousness Is Active

Consciousness does not come and go; it is always active, always going on. In the words of William James, there is a "stream of consciousness," which, like a river, is always flowing. James made this characterization in 1890, but only in the last twenty years has research shown how accurate it is.

One of the most dramatic demonstrations of the stream of consciousness is the effect of **sensory deprivation,** in which an individual is isolated from other people and cut off from virtually all normal sensory stimulation. In the early 1950s, D. O. Hebb and his research group at McGill University began the investigation of sensory deprivation by paying students twenty dollars a day (a lot of money twenty years ago) for as long as they wished to remain in the sensory-deprivation situation portrayed in Figure 13.4. While wide awake in this situation, most people experience vivid **hallucinations**—sensations or perceptions that have no external reality. For example, Joseph Mendelson and his co-workers report that one participant, after taking a sip of eggnog from his feeding tube, imagined that it contained poisonous bacteria and that his body was producing a counterpoison as an antidote. Later, he was frightened to see rays of light emanating from the tape-recorder microphone above his

Figure 13.4 In a classic series of experiments on sensory deprivation conducted at McGill University in the 1950s, subjects were isolated in sound-resistant cubicles. Gloves and cotton cuffs prevented input to their hands and fingers; a plastic visor diffused the light coming into their eyes; a foam pillow and the continuous hum of the air conditioner and fan made input to the ears low and monotonous. Except for eating and using the bathroom, the subjects did nothing but lie on the bed. Few chose to remain longer than three days.

(After "The Pathology of Boredom," by Woodburn Heron. © 1957 by Scientific American, Inc. All rights reserved.)

Figure 13.5 Scenes from a film version of *The Three Faces of Eve*, the case report by Thigpen and Cleckley of a multiple personality. (A) Eve White, a shy, demure wife and mother, begins seeing a psychotherapist because of repeated headaches and blackouts.   (B) Eve Black, an outgoing but irresponsible personality, "comes out" during a therapy session, to the complete surprise of the therapist.   (C) Jane, the personality who gradually emerged after a long period of therapy, talks with the man who married Eve White.

head. Other participants reported distorted body images: They perceived themselves as divided into two bodies lying next to each other, or they felt that they were hovering in the air above the bed looking down upon their own body. Generally, the longer the deprivation, the more vivid and systematic hallucinations became. Many individuals perceived scenes similar to cartoons, such as Walt Disney-like animals marching along with sacks over their backs. When a person returns to the normal world after several days of sensory deprivation, he is severely disoriented and confused and has difficulty controlling his own movements. Techniques of brainwashing and solitary confinement take advantage of the disorienting effects of sensory deprivation.

As these findings indicate, even when people are deprived of virtually all normal sensory stimulation, the stream of consciousness flows on. They begin to see, hear, and feel things that are not present in outside reality. The active consciousness seems to create its own perceptions.

Consciousness Is Divided

We have a sense of the unity of our consciousness. That is, we usually feel and act as if our mind is one. But, in fact, all of us have more than one consciousness. In the words of William James, we have various **co-consciousnesses,** distinct consciousnesses (experiencing selves) that coexist within the same person. This division of consciousness into two or more co-consciousnesses is called **dissociation,** because one consciousness is dissociated, or separated, from another.

You will read about several everyday examples of dissociation later in the chapter, but one of the most interesting and extreme instances of dissociation is the occurrence of **multiple personality,** a rare condition in which one person shows two or more sharply dissociated consciousnesses with distinct personalities. A famous, well-documented case is described by Corbett Thigpen and Hervey Cleckley in *The Three Faces of Eve.* A twenty-five-year-old woman came to Thigpen, a psychiatrist, for therapy, complaining of emotional problems and "severe and blinding headaches" followed by black-outs. The woman, whom the authors called Eve White, was an extremely self-controlled, shy, and conscientious person. During one of her therapy sessions, a strange expression suddenly came over her face, and she quickly put both hands to her head. After a moment, her hands dropped, she smiled brightly, and in a sparkling voice she said, "Hi there, Doc!" A second consciousness, whom the authors later called Eve Black, had appeared. Eve Black's personality, speaking style, and even her walk were quite different from those of Eve White. She was childlike, fun-loving, and irresponsible. She reported that she was conscious at all times and could follow the thoughts, actions, and feelings of Eve White, but she did not participate in them or consider them her own. Eve White, on the other hand, became unconscious when Eve Black was in control; that was why Eve White reported periodic blackouts. Eve Black seems to have had an independent conscious life since early childhood, when she would periodically "come out" and do mischievous deeds. But most of the time, Eve White was in control, and Eve Black could not gain control or come out at will.

After about a year of psychiatric treatment, a third consciousness emerged. This personality, who called herself Jane, was more mature, self-confident, and capable than either Eve. She did not exist before therapy and somehow seemed to grow out of the therapy process. Although she had access to the consciousnesses of both Eves, she did not have complete use of their knowledge and memories from before her emergence. The therapist used Jane's strengths to help resolve the problems encountered by the two Eves. Jane gradually took over their consciousnesses, and Eve White and Eve Black ceased to exist. In Chapter 15, you will read about Osgood's semantic differ-

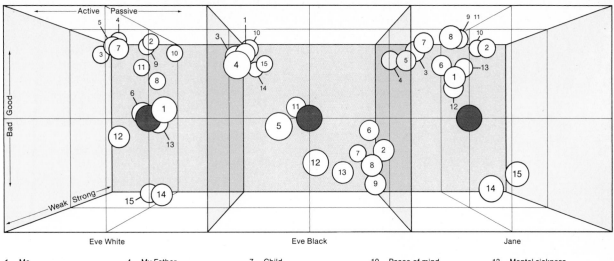

Eve White	Eve Black	Jane

1. Me	4. My Father	7. Child	10. Peace of mind	13. Mental sickness
2. My Job	5. My Mother	8. Sex	11. Self-control	14. Fraud
3. My Doctor	6. My Spouse	9. Love	12. Confusion	15. Hatred

ential, a technique for the measurement of meaning. Osgood's scales were applied by Thigpen and Cleckley to the three personalities of Eve as they emerged, and the results are shown in Figure 13.6. As you can see, the three personalities used words very differently.

Although multiple personality is a rare and extreme phenomenon, it is merely an exaggeration of the normal nature of consciousness. Each of us normally has several consciousnesses that are partially distinct: a consciousness on the left side of our brain and a consciousness on the right side; a waking consciousness and a dreaming consciousness; and so forth. Several of these dissociated consciousnesses will be discussed later in the chapter.

Consciousness Is Varied

Consciousness exists in many different varieties. Under different conditions our conscious experience and our feelings about who we are can vary dramatically. That is, we can enter many diverse states of consciousness, each providing its own distinctive quality of experience. The quality of our experience differs, depending on whether we are awake, asleep, intoxicated, hypnotized, meditating, possessed . . . Most recent psychological research on consciousness has centered upon describing and explaining many of the various states of consciousness. And so the rest of the chapter will deal with what psychologists know about several different states of consciousness.

STATES OF CONSCIOUSNESS

The causes and circumstances that produce different states of consciousness vary widely. Some states of consciousness occur naturally in everyone's daily experience, such as sleeping and dreaming. Others, such as meditation, hypnosis, and spirit possession, can only occur in a specific situation or with a specific technique. And still others can only be induced by specific drugs, like alcohol, marijuana, and LSD.

Everyday Consciousness and the Split Brain

Harriet Lees is a thirty-year-old woman who at one time suffered from epilepsy. For most of her life the seizures were mild and infrequent and could be controlled by drugs. But when she was about twenty-five, the seizures started getting worse. Drugs were no longer effective, and in a few years she was having as many as a dozen severe convulsive fits a day. In order to save her

Figure 13.6 Meanings given to fifteen concepts by each of "the three faces of Eve." At the request of the therapists, each personality responded to Osgoods' semantic differential: They rated all the concepts on a number of scales (cold versus warm, valuable versus worthless, and so on.) The results were simplified into three basic dimensions, and the position of the concepts in the "semantic space" described by those dimensions is shown here. The dark-colored sphere in the center of each space represents the hypothetical "meaningless" concept. Concepts above it are good; those below it are bad. Concepts in front of it are weak; concepts behind it are strong. Concepts to its left are active; those to its right are passive. Note Eve White's concept of ME: slightly passive, slightly good, and definitely weak. Note that Eve Black sees the meanings of the various concepts in a clearly disturbed way: ME, HATRED, FRAUD, PEACE, DOCTOR are all good and active; LOVE, SEX, JOB, SPOUSE, and CHILD are passive and bad. Note finally that Jane gives the most nearly normal meanings to these concepts. Clearly, these three "faces" of the multiple personality are quite distinct from one another in the ways they conceive of themselves and their world.

(After Osgood and Luria, 1954.)

life, her doctors finally recommended a radical type of surgery in which the right and left cortexes of her brain would be disconnected from each other. A year ago she went ahead with the operation.

Harriet has not had a seizure since. For a while, though, she thought she was partially paralyzed. Not paralyzed really—the left half of her body just does not respond readily. She does not have full control of it; her left hand especially sometimes seems to act on its own. Why did Harriet's operation have these effects?

An epileptic seizure typically begins in one hemisphere of the brain and then spreads to the other. To halt the spread of Harriet's seizures, a surgeon had cut the thick tract of nerve fibers that runs from one cortical hemisphere to the other through the corpus callosum.

The most encouraging effect of the **split-brain operation** is an almost total elimination of epileptic attacks. But the operation also has a fascinating effect on the person's consciousness. Roger Sperry, Michael Gazzaniga, and other researchers have made extensive studies of what happens to people who undergo this operation. When the two cortexes of the brain are disconnected, two distinct consciousnesses emerge, one in each hemisphere. To some extent, the different consciousnesses control different parts of the body. For example, in most people, the left hemisphere has primary control over the right hand, the right half of the visual field, and in general the right side of the body; the right hemisphere has primary control over the left hand, the left half of the visual field, and in general the left half of the body. The area of the brain that has primary control over speech in most individuals is located in the left cerebral hemisphere, and therefore only the consciousness in the left hemisphere is able to speak. But the person's right-hemisphere consciousness can communicate by pointing or drawing with the left hand. Figure 13.7 shows the features of the eye and brain involved in the experiments.

These patients' two consciousnesses tend to go to sleep and wake up at about the same time and to have generally similar personalities, but they have largely independent memories and do not seem to have access to each other's awareness. Gazzaniga describes what happened, for example, when he flashed a picture of a nude to the right consciousness— the right sides of the eyes—of a patient (see Figure 13.7). She laughed but said that she saw nothing. (The left-half consciousness alone can speak, and it did not see the nude, but the right-half consciousness, which did see the nude, produced the laugh.) When the woman was asked why she laughed, she acted confused and could not explain why.

Despite this division of the mind into two separate consciousnesses, the person who undergoes the operation does not usually seem to be particularly disturbed by the fact that two separate consciousnesses share one body. The two consciousnesses usually cooperate, and, when necessary, one consciousness communicates overtly to the other one. Gazzaniga gives an example of how this communication takes place: He flashed either a red or a green light to the right-hemisphere consciousness of one patient, and the patient was supposed to say which color he saw. Because the left-hemisphere consciousness controls language, the right-hemisphere consciousness could not give the correct answer verbally. Instead, the left hemisphere made a verbal guess— say, red—and if that answer was wrong, the right hemisphere would make the patient frown and shake his head, and then the left hemisphere would say, "Oh no, I meant green."

Although virtually the only human beings who have undergone this operation are epileptics, the phenomenon of separate consciousnesses, each controlled by one hemisphere of the brain, does not seem to be limited to epileptics. Recent research indicates that people without epilepsy probably also have two separate consciousnesses, one in each hemisphere. But because the

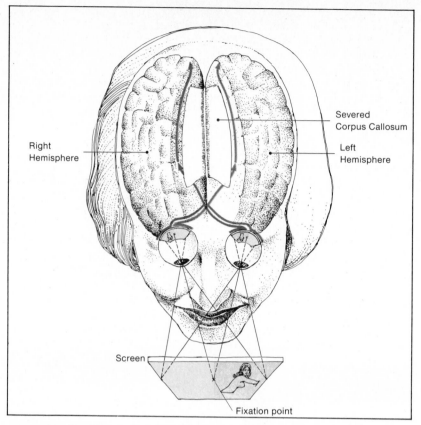

Right
Hemisphere

Severed
Corpus Callosum

Left
Hemisphere

Screen

Fixation point

connection between their two hemispheres is intact, one hemisphere always knows what the other is doing, and so they usually function as one.

Robert Ornstein describes two demonstrations of the separateness of the two consciousnesses, which can be carried out by anyone. First, when people are thinking, they commonly shift their gaze to one side, and the direction in which they look is affected by the kind of thinking they are doing. Other research has shown that, for most people, language and arithmetic abilities seem to be localized primarily in the left hemisphere, spatial and drawing abilities primarily in the right hemisphere. So to try out Ornstein's first demonstration, pick someone who is right-handed (some people who are left-handed seem to have their abilities localized differently), and ask him to do some arithmetical computation in his head, such as "Add 37 and 159, and divide the answer by 7." Then ask him to solve some spatial problem in his head, such as "Which way does Abraham Lincoln face on the penny?" He should usually gaze more to the right when he is solving the arithmetic problem (because the left hemisphere both does arithmetic and controls the right side of the visual field) and more to the left when he is solving the spatial problem (because the right hemisphere both does spatial reasoning and controls the left side of the visual field).

For the second demonstration that Ornstein described (originally conceived by Marcel Kinsbourne and Jay Cook), ask a right-handed friend to balance a wooden stick on one finger of his right hand and then on the same finger of his left hand. Time how long he can balance the stick with each hand. Then ask him to speak while balancing the stick, and time him again. According to Kinsbourne and Cook, his performance with his right hand should deteriorate, because his left hemisphere is busy talking and so cannot concentrate on balancing the stick in his right hand; but his performance with his left hand

Figure 13.7   The presentation of a visual stimulus to a single hemisphere in a person who has undergone split-brain surgery. The subject is asked to fixate on a dot on the screen in front of her. While she is fixating, an image is flashed briefly onto one side of the screen. Because the flash is very brief, the subject has no opportunity to move her eyes over the image. Also, because her eyes are focused on the central dot, all the information to the left of the dot falls on the right side of each of her eyes, and all the information to the right side of the dot falls on the left side. As the diagram shows, the nerve paths from the eyes to the brain are organized in such a way that all the information delivered to the right halves of the eyes goes to the right hemisphere and all the information delivered to the left halves goes to the left. In this case, the image of a nude flashed on the left side of the screen reaches the right hemisphere of the brain only. Because the area of the brain that controls speech in most individuals is in the left hemisphere, the patient is amused but is unable to say why.

Table 13.1 Relative Strengths of the Brain's Hemispheres

Right Hemisphere (Left Hand)	Left Hemisphere (Right Hand)
Intuitive	Rational
Spatial	Verbal
Wholistic	Analytic
Sensuous	Intellectual
Diffuse	Focal
Simultaneous	Sequential
Experience	Argument
Space	Time
Yin: The Receptive	Yang: The Creative
Eternity	History
Dark	Light
Night	Day
Left	Right

should be unaffected, because his right hemisphere plays no part in talking and so can concentrate on balancing the stick in his left hand.

Joseph Bogen and Ornstein have summarized much of the research to date on the differences in the abilities of the two hemispheres, and a listing of what are probably the relative strengths of the two hemispheres for most people appears at the top of Table 13.1. Ornstein has also pointed out that customarily in both East and West the two hands (and therefore the two hemispheres) tend to be associated not only with those abilities but also with a number of other dichotomies, such as light and dark, active and receptive, Yin and Yang, and so forth.

Sleep and Dreams

Few people notice the differences between their left and right consciousnesses, but all people notice that they sleep. What happens to your consciousness during sleep? You probably think of sleep as a time when your mind stops working, except during a few brief periods when you are dreaming. Or perhaps you think that you do not even dream. In the past thirty years psychologists have made many important discoveries about sleep and dreaming, and these discoveries have showed that both these beliefs are wrong. Everyone is mentally active during all or most of sleep, and everyone dreams, but most people remember little of that mental activity when they are awake.

Stages of Sleep Nathaniel Kleitman laid the foundations for these recent discoveries about sleep with his work on the physiological indicators of sleeping and dreaming. One of the most useful physiological indicators of brain activity is the **electroencephalogram (EEG),** which is a record of the brain's electrical activity. A person's EEG varies consistently as he goes from wakefulness to light sleep to deep sleep, as shown in Figure 13.8. Brain waves in a person who is fully awake and has his eyes closed are typically of high frequency (about ten per second) and low magnitude. These brain waves are called **alpha** waves. As a person begins to fall asleep (Stage 1 in Figure 13.8), he still shows a large proportion of alpha waves, but mixed in with the alpha waves are some waves of a lower frequency. As sleep becomes progressively deeper (Stages 2, 3, and 4), alpha waves disappear, and waves of low frequency and large magnitude appear.

During a night of sleep, however, a person does not merely fall into progressively deeper sleep and then gradually wake up. Instead, his brain waves show a regular cyclical pattern that occurs about every ninety minutes, as shown in Figure 13.9. First, the brain waves indicate that he is falling into deeper and deeper sleep, and then they gradually return to a Stage-1 pattern, only to start the cycle over again.

REM Sleep An important series of studies on sleep was carried out by Kleitman and his associates Eugene Aserinsky and William Dement. It was Aserinsky who first noticed that when a person's brain waves return to a Stage-1 pattern after having passed through the deeper stages, his closed eyes usually begin to move rapidly back and forth. To investigate these **rapid eye movements,** or **REMs,** they woke sleepers up during the REM periods and other stages of sleep and found that dreams with vivid visual imagery usually occurred during REM periods. Sometimes, Dement reports, the eye movements correspond to movements that the eye would have made during the events in the dream, such as following the ball in a tennis match as it moved back and forth over the net. Mental activity that occurs during non-REM periods is usually less vivid—like drifting thoughts rather than vivid dreams.

According to some measures, REM sleep seems similar to being awake, whereas according to others it seems to be a very deep sleep. The EEG pattern

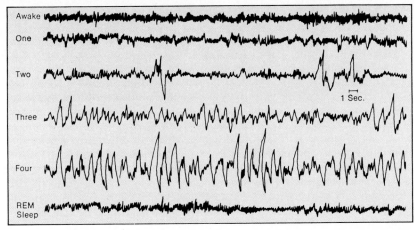

Awake

One

Two

Three

Four

REM
Sleep

1 Sec.

Figure 13.8 Records of the electrical activity of the brain (EEG) in a person in various stages of sleep. The waking record given here for the purpose of comparison is one that occurs when a person is resting quietly with his eyes closed and is often referred to as "alpha." Note that in the deeper stages of sleep the high-frequency, small-amplitude waves give way to lower-frequency, large-amplitude waves. This change is thought to reflect the fact that the neurons in the brain are all firing at about the same level and in about the same pattern. Note also that the EEG pattern in REM sleep is very similar to the waking pattern.

is close to the pattern of the waking state, and many other physiological patterns resemble those of being awake and excited: There are increases and irregularity in heart rate and breathing, elevations in blood pressure, and erection of the penis—all physiological changes associated with being awake and excited. On the other hand, most behavioral measures indicate that REM sleep is very deep sleep—similar to Stage 4. People are often very difficult to wake and do not respond to stimuli as readily as during Stages 2 and 3. Because of these contradictory patterns, Michel Jouvet coined the term **paradoxical sleep** to describe REM sleep: People seem to be awake and yet deeply asleep at the same time.

While this physiological activity is occurring, an unusual change takes place in the muscles. Virtually all the major body muscles lose their normal tone, and the individual loses all ability to move his body: He becomes temporarily paralyzed. Jouvet has shown that a specific small part of the brain is responsible for this loss of muscle control. When he removed this small part of the brain in cats, REM sleep continued to occur, but during it the sleeping cats no longer lay still. Instead they jumped up and moved about the room— all the while asleep. The cats' behavior suggests that, without the loss of muscle control that is normal during REM sleep, our bodies would act out our dream activities.

REM sleep apparently contributes to the maintenance of mental equilibrium. If people are awakened every time they begin to enter REM periods but are otherwise allowed to sleep a normal length of time, they tend to make up those lost periods whenever they have the chance. They also begin to show abnormal behavior while they are awake. Dement reports that when people are deprived of REM sleep for several consecutive nights, many of them suffer from anxiety and irritability, difficulties in concentration, and in some cases hallucinations and ravenous appetites.

Working with cats, Jouvet and others found that deprivation of REM sleep can produce more serious and dramatic results. Jouvet discovered that if he removed a certain small part of the brain (different from the one mentioned earlier), the cats no longer showed REM sleep although they continued to show non-REM sleep. As several days passed, the cats began to behave very strangely. They periodically showed agitation, stared fixedly, and swiped with their paws as if they were hitting at nonexistent objects. Some of them exhibited greatly increased eating and sexual activity. In some cats the REM sleep eventually returned, and these abnormal behaviors eventually disappeared, but the cats that showed no return of REM sleep became increasingly agitated and finally died in a state of extreme hyperactivity.

Dement and Anthony Kales have found that some commonly used drugs, such as alcohol and sleeping pills, suppress REM sleep; consequently, habitual use of these drugs produces REM deprivation. Although the full implications of this deprivation are not known, it is known that these drugs can actually cause chronic insomnia. The insomnia occurs because when people stop taking these drugs, they immediately start to have more REM sleep in order to make up for the REM sleep they lost while they were taking the drugs. This increased REM activity causes them to sleep fitfully and wake often, sometimes with nightmares. They mistakenly interpret this temporary wakefulness as chronic insomnia and so usually resume use of the drugs, which they believe will help them sleep better. In order to eliminate the ''insomnia,'' these people need only sleep without using the drugs until their bodies make up the lost REM activity; after several nights of fitful sleep, they will begin to sleep well. Resuming use of the drugs only causes further REM deprivation. In extreme cases, long-continued suppression of REM sleep can produce hallucinations and other bizarre behavior: The individual dreams while awake.

Stage-4 Sleep   Stage-4 sleep occurs only in the early part of a night's sleep, as shown in Figure 13.9. Although the evidence is clear that mental activity occurs during most of sleep, Stage 4 is something of a puzzle. It is extremely difficult to wake someone up from Stage-4 sleep; the person seems almost to be in a coma. By the time the sleeper is awakened, it is difficult to determine whether what he reports occurred during Stage 4 or while he was being awakened. Yet at times mental activity clearly occurs in Stage 4, because most episodes of sleepwalking, sleeptalking, and intense nightmares occur during Stage 4 (as well as Stage 3). A sleepwalker may take a lengthy stroll, and when he encounters someone, he may look directly at them with his eyes open and yet not appear to recognize them. When awakened, he usually does not remember the episode. Apparently, activities of this sort cannot occur during REM sleep because people lose control of their muscles, but during non-REM sleep people still have muscular control and so their mental activity can produce bodily activity.

Dreams and Their Meaning   The stream of consciousness flows on, then, during all or most of sleep, and this mental activity during sleep is what is called dreaming. But the dreams a person is able to recall represent only a small proportion of those that actually occur. Sleep researchers sometimes make a point of waking up their subjects at regular intervals throughout the night to ask them what they were dreaming. The first few dream reports early each night are concerned primarily with vague thoughts left over from the day's activities (''I was watching TV''). As the night wears on, dreams become more vivid and dramatic. It is these more vivid types, especially the REM dreams, that are most likely to be remembered under normal circumstances outside the sleep laboratory.

As Erich Fromm has pointed out, the consciousness of dreams seems to be

Figure 13.9   A typical night's sleep described in terms of the stages in Figure 13.8. Note that the sleep increases and decreases in depth cyclically and that sleep becomes shallower and periods of REM sleep longer later in the night. Dement and his colleagues have discovered that the proportion of time spent in REM sleep decreases steadily with age. Infants sleep about sixteen hours a day and are in REM sleep for eight of them. Adolescents and young adults sleep eight or nine hours out of twenty-four, and are in REM sleep for only one or two.

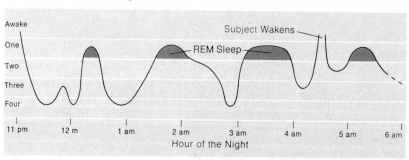

Figure 13.10 The qualities of experience peculiar to dreams have often been the subject of artistic expression. In this painting—Marc Chagall's *I and the Village*—images are intermingled, and space, time, and color are rearranged in ways that are rarely experienced in a waking state but seem characteristic of the dream state.
(Collection, the Museum of Modern Art, New York. Mrs. Simon Guggenheim Fund.)

essentially separate from our normal waking consciousness. That is, most of us have two distinct consciousnesses, one for waking and one for sleep. Kurt Fischer describes a series of dreams that provides a vivid example of the difference between the two consciousnesses. Throughout the series of dreams the dreamer believed that he could fly; all that he needed to do was hold out his arms and flap them like wings. Knowing that flying is unusual in human beings, he tested during almost every dream to make sure he was not dreaming and repeatedly determined that he was awake and able to fly. For several months the series of dreams continued, with the dreaming consciousness always being sure that he actually could fly and the waking consciousness never remembering the dreams. In other words, the two consciousnesses did not have access to each other's experiences concerning flying. One day the waking consciousness finally realized that he had dreamed that he could fly and then recalled the whole series of dreams. At that point the memory of the series of dreams merged for the two consciousnesses, and the dreaming consciousness no longer believed that he could fly: Immediately, the dreams of flying stopped, and they never returned.

The frame of reference of the dreaming consciousness is radically different from that of the waking consciousness. As Fromm states, "While we sleep we are not concerned with bending the outside world to our purposes. . . . We live in an inner world concerned exclusively with ourselves.'' In this inner world the nature of the outside world does not matter; all that matters is what the dreamer thinks and feels. If the dreamer believes that an acquaintance is a coward, he may dream that the person has literally become a chicken. Although this transformation is not realistic, it makes good sense in terms of how the dreamer feels about the person.

Sigmund Freud first pointed out the significance of the inner world of dreams for psychology: Analysis of a person's dreams can provide insights into how he thinks and feels and what is important to him. No matter how simple or mundane, dreams may have important hidden meanings about the true thoughts and desires of the dreamer. In Freud's terms, dreams are the language of the unconscious mind trying to express the subconscious wishes of the dreamer.

Calvin Hall, a contemporary dream researcher, emphasizes that dreams usually convert the dreamer's thoughts and desires into concrete images: The cowardly acquaintance actually becomes a chicken. Consequently, the elements of the dream are **symbolic** of the dreamer's thoughts, desires, and concerns. Dream interpretation allows one to translate the images back into ideas, thus providing a view of the dreamer's self-concept and attitude toward life. In this way dreams can reveal the individual's most personal and intimate thoughts. In some cases, as Freud suggested, the thoughts may be so personal and intimate that the individual does not even admit them to his own waking consciousness: They remain unconscious.

Deciphering the symbols of dreams requires an understanding of several of their most important characteristics. Dream symbols usually demonstrate what Freud called condensation and displacement. In **displacement** the focus is shifted (displaced) from the matter of interest to something only vaguely related to it: The matter of interest is a penis, and the focus is displaced to a tower, which symbolizes the penis. In **condensation** several objects or concepts are combined (condensed) into a single symbol, so that the symbol has multiple meanings: One person in a dream is an amalgam of father, mother, and lover, combining the father's face, the mother's body, and the lover's clothes. Or a foul-smelling shoe symbolizes both the dreamer's concern about his body odor being offensive and the fact that he has an ugly scar on one of his feet.

In addition, dream symbols vary greatly from one person to another. The symbolism of dreams is a private language that each individual has invented for himself. Suppose that a dreamer sees himself standing naked amongst strangers. For one person, this dream may symbolize his desire to be able to show his true self to people, without pretense. For another, it may symbolize his fear of having his inadequacies exposed in public. And for still another, the dream may symbolize a desire left over from childhood to show off his genitals in public.

Meditation

The two consciousnesses of the right and left halves of the brain and the two consciousnesses of waking and sleeping are common to everyone's daily mental life. They occur spontaneously. The state of consciousness associated with meditation does not occur spontaneously. It must be induced by the ancient techniques of meditation, developed over centuries by Hindus, Buddhists, Catholic monks, and members of other religious groups.

Meditation is a set of techniques that, according to yogis and other practitioners of meditation, produce a fully rested, relaxed body and a fully aware, relaxed mind and thereby bring about a ''higher consciousness.'' Many meditators report that they can separate their minds from their senses at will and

Figure 13.11 The goal of meditation is to concentrate one's attention and consciousness completely upon some single object. A mandala like this one aids meditation because its visual forms continually return one's eye to the center of the figure.

that meditation can produce kinds of awareness that are free from worldly concerns. Some say that they can experience something for the thousandth time as freshly as they did the first.

Most forms of meditation involve sitting still and focusing or concentrating on one thought or object, like a sacred picture, a wall, a spot in the lower abdomen, or a mandala, which is designed so that the gaze always returns to the center (see Figure 13.11). Sometimes a word, for example, the sacred word ''Om,'' or a phrase called a mantra is said, and its sound is contemplated. These techniques produce a kind of trancelike focusing of the stream of consciousness on a single thing.

In a study of meditation by Arthur Deikman, several people who had not meditated before learned to meditate on a blue vase. Deikman recorded their reports of their experiences. The participants reported that as they meditated, the color of the vase became vivid and time passed quickly. Some people felt themselves merging with the vase. Others found that their surroundings became unusually beautiful, filled with light and movement. All the meditators found the experience pleasant. After twelve sessions they all felt a strong attachment to the vase and missed it when it was not present during the next session.

For a long time there was virtually no psychological research on meditation, because psychologists considered it mystical and unscientific. Several recent studies have shown, however, not only that meditation produces feelings that meditators consider important but that it is accompanied by striking physiological changes. Trained meditators show both highly specific EEG patterns and prominent changes in bodily functioning.

Akira Kasamatsu and Tomio Hirai investigated the EEG patterns of Zen monks. They found that, as soon as the monks began meditating, alpha waves appeared in their EEGs, even though the monks had their eyes open. Normally, alpha waves are produced only when people's eyes are closed. The alpha waves of Zen masters also showed systematic changes in magnitude and frequency as a meditation session progressed. When EEG patterns were recorded for Zen students, the students whom the masters considered to be the most proficient meditators showed EEG patterns most similar to those of the masters. Robert Wallace and Herbert Benson summarize several other studies with similar findings.

Wallace and Benson themselves have studied the changes in bodily functioning that occur during transcendental meditation, a technique that was developed by the Maharishi Mahesh Yogi. They found that meditation produced strong changes in bodily functioning and that those changes were different from the effects of sleep or hypnosis. Oxygen consumption dropped sharply shortly after meditation began, and various other measures indicated that this decrease was due to a reduction in the rate of energy use by the body. Various physiological measures showed that the meditators were highly relaxed but awake and alert. A blood substance normally associated with anxiety and hypertension showed a marked decrease during meditation. Wallace and Benson suggest that, in fast-paced industrial societies like our own, meditation might well be used to help people relax and maintain their psychological equilibrium.

Hypnosis

Hypnosis is another technique that induces a trancelike state of consciousness, but its effect is very different from the effects of meditation. In hypnosis, an individual seems to give some of the control of his thoughts and perceptions to another person. By allowing the hypnotist to direct his consciousness, the individual can be made to experience things that he usually does not experience and he can be made unaware of things that he usually notices. Psycholo-

Figure 13.12 Western scientists began to pay attention to the performance of Eastern mystics when they were able to demonstrate that meditative states of consciousness are accompanied by measurable physiological changes. Meditators' voluntary production of alpha waves in their EEGs was one of the feats that most impressed Western investigators. The use of biofeedback (the amplification and display in visual or auditory form of biological indices of physiological processes) has enabled people untrained in meditation to gain comparable control over some body processes. Whether they are duplicating all that is achieved by the experienced meditator is not known.

gists who use hypnotism stress that the relationship between a hypnotist and a subject involves cooperation, not domination by the hypnotist. The subject is simply cooperating with the hypnotist by becoming particularly responsive to the hypnotist's suggestions.

Hypnosis is popularly thought to put a subject to sleep, but actually the hypnotic trance is much different from sleep. A sleeping person is oblivious to what is going on around him, whereas a hypnotized person is able to become highly receptive and responsive to certain things around him: He is able to focus his attention on one tiny aspect of reality and to ignore other things happening around him.

The hypnotist induces a trance by slowly persuading the subject to relax and to lose interest in external distractions. In the usual induction procedure the subject sits or lies down, and the hypnotist suggests that he stay quiet, relax, and forget all his ordinary concerns. Crystal balls and other such paraphernalia are not necessary but are sometimes used as a means of increasing the apparent authority and expertise of the hypnotist. The hypnotist usually begins with a few simple suggestions that are easy for the subject to respond to, such as that the subject will be unable to move his arm; only when these are successful does the hypnotist proceed to more difficult suggestions. About one in twenty people is particularly susceptible to hypnosis, but about nineteen in twenty can be hypnotized to some degree if they want to be hypnotized and if they trust the hypnotist.

A Case of Hypnotic Blindness   In some cases, hypnosis can be used to bring about a striking type of dissociation, in which the person's consciousness under hypnosis is not at all accessible to his normal waking consciousness. Frank Pattie reports a particularly dramatic example. He was testing to see whether he could induce blindness in one of a person's eyes during hypnosis. The test he used for blindness involved stimulating the person's eyes in such a way that it was impossible for the person to tell without cheating which eye was being stimulated. Cheating would consist of blinking one eye, moving the eyes from side to side, or a similar trick. Of course, in his experiment Pattie tried to prevent all such tricks. If the test indicated that the supposedly blind eye was really blind, that would be convincing evidence that hypnosis can actually block sensory input to the brain from the eyes.

Pattie tested five people previously known to enter a deep trance readily. To his surprise one woman, whom he called "E.," did seem to become blind in one eye under hypnosis. Throughout most of a long series of tests covering several sessions, E. consistently appeared to be blind in one eye. But there were a few indications that she might be using tricks. Consequently Pattie devised an even more subtle test of blindness in which it was essentially impossible to cheat. With this test, Pattie demonstrated that E. was not blind at all. Pattie had her look at the top line of Figure 13.13 with a red filter over

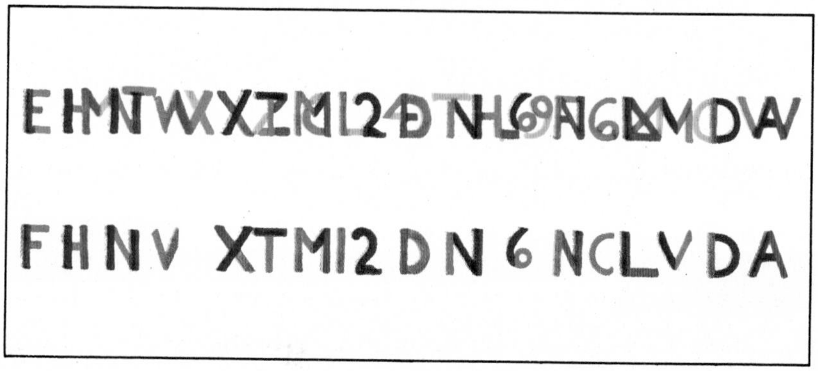

Figure 13.13   The technique used by Pattie to expose a suspected cheater in an experiment on hypnotically induced blindness. The subject was required to look at a line (top) of mixed colored letters and numbers with a red filter over her "good" eye and a green filter over her "bad" eye. The effects of the red filter is shown in the bottom line. If the subject had really been blind in the eye covered by the green filter, she would have seen only a line of distinct letters and numbers. The subject failed this test but passed a number of other, similar, tests by successfully guessing what she was "supposed" to see. All her cheating had been carried on by a consciousness that was separate from the consciousness with which she communicated with the hypnotist.
(After Pattie, 1935.)

her seeing eye and a green filter over her "blind" eye. The effect of the filters was to block out parts of the top line as shown. If E. had truly been blind in the green-filtered eye, she would have seen only what appeared through the red filter, but this was not what she reported seeing.

Strangely enough, even when she failed this test, E. insisted that she had not cheated and that she was, in fact, blind in one eye. According to every indication, she really believed that she had not cheated. Pattie then put E. into as deep a hypnotic trance as he could and tried to get in touch with "the part of her which faked the tests." He encountered enormous resistance. First she said that she could not remember how she had cheated, then she began to give out little bits of information but showed great emotional upset. Pattie had to repeat the process over and over of telling her that her memories would come back when he counted to three and snapped his fingers. Gradually he extracted the information from her.

The woman showed two consciousnesses—one that was "blind" during hypnosis and communicated with Pattie, and one that cheated in order to obtain the information necessary to appear blind in one eye. In the woman's own words, "I want to tell the truth, and I know it, and something doesn't want to. Something makes me keep forgetting it, and I know I know it. It just goes, and I can't say it, and it makes my head ache and swim." In fact, Pattie even found that the cheating consciousness had intervened several times while E. was not under hypnosis in order to acquire information that would help her cheat. The consciousness that normally communicated with Pattie had no recollection whatsoever of these episodes.

Long before Pattie's experiment, in 1890, when psychology was just becoming established in the United States, William James had pointed out in *The Principles of Psychology* that this kind of dual consciousness is necessary to explain much of the behavior of hypnotized persons. For example, whenever a hypnotized person fails to perceive something that is present, he must somehow perceive it in order to be able not to perceive it. In one of James' examples, a mark was made on a piece of paper, and the hypnotized person was instructed that he would not see it. Many additional marks were then made on the paper, and the person acted as if he saw all the marks but the first. Somehow hypnotized people can discriminate that mark from all the others and manage not to perceive it.

Is Hypnosis Real? Ever since hypnosis became widely known, people have been skeptical about it. Many stage performers have used hypnosis to make themselves appear to have mystical abilities and thus have given it a bad name. It is common for disbelievers to assert that hypnotized people are simply pretending to be hypnotized. In James' example, for instance, it would be easy for someone to knowingly lie and pretend that he did not see the mark. But the behavior of Pattie's subject E. cannot easily be interpreted as simple pretending. And the research of Martin Orne provides even more convincing evidence that hypnosis brings about a state of consciousness that is genuinely different from ordinary consciousness. Orne compared people who were truly hypnotized with people who were purposely faking hypnosis. The hypnotist did not know which were which and found it difficult to guess correctly. Orne, as well as other investigators, found that people who fake hypnosis can do virtually all the supposedly superhuman feats that hypnotized people can do, as long as they are strongly motivated. They can hold a heavy weight straight in front of them at arm's length for several minutes; they can lie with a chair at their shoulders and a chair at their feet but nothing else between to support them; they can even stick needles through their hands. But Orne also found some important differences between the two groups.

The hypnotized group showed what he called **trance logic.** Using trance logic, a hypnotized person may readily perceive hallucinations suggested to him by the hypnotist and, without making any attempt at logical consistency, may mix these hallucinations freely with perceptions based on real objects and events. For example, in Orne's experiment the hypnotist told the subject that there was a third individual sitting in a chair next to him that was actually empty. That third individual was, in fact, standing *behind* the subject. When the subject turned around and saw the third individual, he acted surprised and reported that he saw two images of the same individual. In contrast, when people who were faking turned around, they said either that they saw no one or that they did not recognize the person they saw. Their faking was exposed by their own efforts to respond in a conventionally logical way.

If truly hypnotized people are asked to discriminate between a hallucinated image and a real one, they often indicate that they can tell the difference, according to both Orne and Milton Erickson. If the image hallucinated is a person, hypnotized subjects can either see through the hallucinated image or cause it to move by their own thought processes. For example, they can make it raise one of its arms. People faking a hypnotic state report no such ability.

Clearly, hypnosis is a genuine state of consciousness, in which the consciousness that is in contact with the hypnotist is dissociated from the rest of the person's mind in such a way that the content of its awareness is partially controlled by the suggestions of the hypnotist. Also, this dissociated consciousness of hypnosis does not necessarily disappear when the person returns to his normal waking state. **Posthypnotic suggestions** given during the trance often lead to dissociative behavior later on. For example, the hypnotist might suggest that after the person is awakened from hypnosis he will be unable to hear the word "psychology." When he awakens from hypnosis, the subject will report that some people around him are speaking strangely: They seem to leave out words occasionally in their speech. The subject is not aware that part of his consciousness is blocking out that word from his perception.

Occasionally there are aftereffects of hypnosis similar to posthypnotic suggestion even when no posthypnotic suggestions have been given. For example, Josephine Hilgard, Ernest Hilgard, and Martha Newman report a case of a college student who, after she had been brought out of hypnosis and had left the hypnosis laboratory, suddenly responded to a suggestion that had been made during hypnosis: She seemed to regress to childhood, feeling that her body had shrunk to about half its actual size.

As scientists have come to accept hypnosis as a real phenomenon, it has gained increasingly wide usage in medicine, dentistry, and psychotherapy. For example, when used by a competent professional, it can often replace minor anesthetics such as those used for pulling teeth. Acupuncture, an ancient Chinese practice that involves inserting needles into various, specific points on the body in order to curb pain and cure ailments, may derive some of its effectiveness from induction of a hypnoticlike trance. Acupuncture does, however, also seem to have some more direct effect on the nervous system, but scientists do not yet understand why it has this effect.

Spirit Possession

Modern work on hypnosis began late in the eighteenth century with the storm of publicity generated by the claims of a European physician named Anton Mesmer. Mesmer believed that hypnosis (then called Mesmerism) was caused by a mysterious force, "animal magnetism." But reports of hypnosislike phenomena can be traced back thousands of years, and are still prevalent today, especially in some nonindustrial cultures, in some religious sects, and in groups who believe that they can communicate with the dead. These phenomena are called **spirit possession,** because the people who enter into the hypnoticlike trances usually say that they have been possessed by a

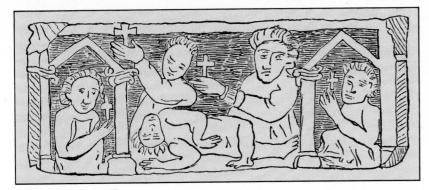

Figure 13.14 Exorcising by the cross, a bas-relief on a water vessel from the seventeenth century. The Christian ritual of exorcism, the rituals of shamanism in a number of non-Christian cultures, and Mesmer's psychotherapeutic use of hypnosis are closely related phenomena. All can be considered attempts to induce in the disturbed, or "possessed," person a state of consciousness in which the priest, shaman, or "magnetizer" gains access to aspects of the person's consciousness that are not normally accessible.

supernatural spirit. The trance is induced by some sort of religious ritual, and the behavior under the trance is generally prescribed by the traditions of the religious group.

Research on spirit possession has generally been neglected by social scientists, but a few cases have been described in some detail. Walter Mischel and Frances Mischel describe the occurrence of possession among the Shango in Trinidad. Possession—by a "power" that is believed to be a specific god—usually occurs during formal religious ceremonies. A possessed person is called a horse. As a power enters a horse's body, dramatic behavioral changes take place. In one case a woman lost her balance and fell to the ground. Her arms became stiff, and her entire body began to vibrate. She grunted and groaned, and she stared fixedly. She then stood up and put on the costume of the power possessing her. The powers play an important role in the culture. People who are frequently possessed usually become religious leaders. They are generally revered, and descriptions suggest that they are intelligent and highly competent people.

Specific powers usually produce distinctive behaviors and can therefore be easily identified. The behaviors range from vigorous dancing and rolling on the ground to a gentle, benign giving of advice and presciption of folk medicines. The most common way for possession to end is for the horse to spin around rapidly and then abruptly fall to the ground. Whatever the behavior, the participants usually feel that the experience of possession is the supreme life experience.

Drug States

Meditation, hypnosis, and spirit possession involve techniques or ceremonies that induce specific states of consciousness. Drugs are chemicals that act directly to alter the functioning of the brain and body and thereby alter consciousness. Many drugs are consumed because of their psychological effects. Some, such as coffee and other stimulants, produce increased alertness; others, such as tranquilizers, cause a general reduction in activity, alertness, and anxiety; and still others, such as alcohol, reduce some social inhibitions. But the most interesting drugs for a chapter on consciousness are the drugs classed as **hallucinogens,** or **psychedelics.** Although the meaning of "psychedelic" has come to be distorted in recent years, it was derived from Greek words meaning "mind-manifesting": The implication of the term is that the drugs demonstrate potential ways in which the mind can function.

The psychedelic drugs include LSD, psilocybin, and mescaline, or peyote. These drugs, as well as most other drugs that have psychological effects, are discussed in some detail in Chapter 28. Some psychedelic drugs, like peyote, have long been part of the religious rites of some American Indian groups. Others, like LSD, have been in existence for no more than thirty years.

LSD is the most potent of these drugs and the one most studied in recent years. Although its effects, like those of other psychedelics, seem to depend heavily on the user's expectations, the setting, and the suggestions offered by people around the user, LSD usually produces a pronounced alteration in awareness called a "trip." A trip generally lasts from six to fourteen hours. It usually includes intense hallucinations accompanied by emotions ranging anywhere from intense euphoria to extreme panic. Thoughts become vivid and generally seem to be beyond the individual's control—somewhat as in a dream. Also as in dreams, the changes in awareness are often accompanied by a dissociation of the self into two parts, an observer and a participant. In the following excerpt from a magazine article, Alan Harrington, a novelist, describes these and other effects of LSD he experienced during his first trip.

It began with a salty taste in my mouth, and my vision started to become prismatic. . . . The world I could see had begun slowly to come apart. No cubic inch of space had to do with any other. Everything in my field of vision turned into bright jelly. There was no time and place, nothing but a flow. . . . I saw my own situation with terrible clarity. I had gone too far out and couldn't get back!

The jelly before my eyes separated. The universe cracked into bright globules and separated; then I was in little pieces, about not to exist anymore, and being borne away on something like a jet stream, and this was the stream Arthur had mentioned, streaming unconsciousness that one was supposed not to fight. Let the ego die. Go with it . . . but I fought upstream all the way. . . .

Arthur offered me the pulp of an orange. The presence accepted it, huddling cold in his jacket, then sweating from the fire's heat, shivering and gasping for breath.

Meanwhile the fleck of existence performed every act it had never dreamed of performing. While the body in the living room constantly changed positions, during which at various times it was fetal, crawling and sucking its thumb, the speck was pushed by a tremulous current into a lotus of naked bodies, and diving in, was folded into the universe, as if the universe was making love to itself. The speck then flew to the top of all things, and saw in every direction what was and will be. . . .

Thereafter the speck whirled down a great glowing tract, experienced a terrific pressure, as if its mass were built up intolerably, and—reentering—was thrust down, labored, felt a collar, and burst clear into the room.

I rested on the couch, with the colored musical notes still floating in the air around me, and I was shivering and saying: "I want to go home now. . . ."

The dramatic physical sensations Harrington describes, his panic when he realizes he cannot halt the effects of the drug, and, later, his impression of himself as two beings—one the "body in the living room," the other a "speck" of ego or "fleck of existence"—are typical LSD experiences.

Marijuana and hashish (also discussed in Chapter 28) can produce effects similar to those of the psychedelic drugs when taken in large amounts. In smaller amounts, the effects are less dramatic: Sensory experiences seem richer and fuller than usual, ordinary events take on special significance, and time seems to pass with less than its customary swiftness. Most marijuana smokers find that their mood improves when they use the drug—they become more relaxed and easygoing. Sometimes there is a feeling of dissociation, in which an observing self watches the participating self; at other times, there is a heightened sense of internal unity.

As Chapter 28 indicates, the psychedelic drugs are powerful and can be dangerous. Marijuana, by contrast, seems at present to be relatively safe. It is not physiologically addictive; it has never proved fatal, even in large doses; it does not seem to be the first step down the road to heroin. On the other hand, it is a drug—and an illegal drug, at that—and should therefore be approached with caution.

SUMMARY

1. **Consciousness** is the quality of mind through which people experience things. It has at least five essential characteristics.

   a. Consciousness is a **brain process.** Wilder Penfield, a brain surgeon and researcher, has shown that mild electric current applied to certain parts of the primitive brain produces a loss of consciousness. When these areas are permanently damaged, people lapse into a coma and never regain consciousness.

   b. Consciousness is **limited.** People are not conscious of many processes they routinely perform, such as walking, breathing, and using language. For example, people rarely consciously formulate a sentence before they speak it.

   c. Consciousness is **active.** William James characterized it as a stream, always actively flowing. **Sensory-deprivation experiments** that put people into a situation where they are cut off from virtually all sensory input have shown that the active consciousness creates its own perceptions, in the form of **hallucinations**—perceptions with no obvious external cause.

   d. Consciousness is **divided.** Two or more **co-consciousnesses** exist at the same time within each person, and they are more or less **dissociated,** or separated from one another. One example is the existence of a waking consciousness and a dreaming consciousness. A rare case of dissociation is **multiple personality,** in which two or more separate consciousnesses, each with a different personality, exist in the same person.

   e. Consciousness is **varied.** Our experiencing of our selves and our surroundings is different, depending on whether our **state of consciousness** is one of being awake, asleep, drunk, high, or hypnotized.

2. The brain is divided into two hemispheres, each of which controls separate functions and, to some degree, possesses a separate consciousness, even though people are not aware of this phenomenon. The existence of co-consciousnesses is dramatized by a **split-brain operation** performed on some people suffering from severe epilepsy: The tract of nerves between the two hemispheres is severed. Pictures shown to the right consciousness (the left eye only) cause the patient to react, but when asked to explain the reaction, the patient cannot because it is the left hemisphere, which did not see the picture, that controls speech. In our normal, everyday waking state, the two sides of the brain seem to specialize in different abilities, summarized in Table 13.1.

3. The state of consciousness other than our everyday waking state that all people experience is sleep.

   a. Physiological measures show there are **four distinct stages of sleep.** The most useful measure is the **EEG,** or **electroencephalogram,** an indicator of electrical activity in the brain. It shows that people go through the four stages at cycles of about ninety minutes while they are asleep. **Alpha waves,** characteristic of the waking state, are also present in Stage-1 sleep, but are progressively replaced in Stages 2, 3, and 4 by waves of low frequency and large magnitude.

Figure 13.15 Neurosurgeon and founder of the Montreal Neurological Institute, Wilder Penfield pioneered a highly successful technique for the treatment of severe epilepsy, and he has subsequently been honored by a great number of scientific organizations and the governments of many nations for his work in correcting disorders resulting from brain damage. In perfecting his surgical technique, Penfield also discovered the phenomenon he calls the "experiential response"; electrical stimulation of certain areas of the brain produces a reexperiencing of past events that is so real the events seem to be actually occurring.

Figure 13.16 William James' remarkable career included a Harvard professorship in physiology, psychology, and philosophy. His turn-of-the-century texts *Principles of Psychology* and *Psychology: The Briefer Course* still provide a rich source of speculation and insight about the problems of psychology. In these books James describes consciousness as "the stream of subjective life." In still another work, *The Varieties of Religious Experience,* he points out that in addition to "rational consciousness as we call it" there may exist entirely different forms of consciousness parted from normal consciousness only "by the filmiest of screens."

Figure 13.17 D. O. Hebb is an eminent neuropsychologist whose research has included study of the physiological correlates of learning and the process of directed thinking. He also began the investigations of sensory deprivation mentioned in this chapter. His theoretical book *The Organization of Behavior* is a landmark work in the scientific attempt to understand the relation between the physiological properties of the nervous system and the psychological properties of behavior and experience.

b. When the sleeper's cycle returns to Stage 1 after passing through the deeper stages, his closed eyes show rapid back-and-forth movement. Consequently, this stage is often called **REM (rapid-eye-movement)** sleep. Dreams with the most vivid visual imagery occur during REM sleep. It is also called **paradoxical sleep,** because by some measures (EEG, heart rate, breathing) it resembles the waking state, but by other measures (muscle tone, response to stimuli) it appears to be an extremely deep stage of sleep. REM sleep appears to contribute to mental equilibrium. People deprived of it for several nights often suffer from irritability, anxiety, inability to concentrate—and sometimes hallucinations. As soon as they are given the opportunity, they quickly make up the REM sleep they were deprived of. Certain common drugs, such as sleeping pills and alcohol, suppress REM sleep.

c. **Stage-4 sleep** is a stage of deep sleep; it is difficult to wake someone from it. Yet, it is also the stage during which most episodes of talking and sleepwalking occur. Also, people report the most nightmares when awakened from Stage-4 sleep.

d. The consciousness from which dreams arise appears to be separate from the consciousness that exists during waking hours, which is why people often have difficulty remembering what they have dreamed.

e. The dreaming consciousness does not require the same kinds of logic as does the waking consciousness, which must adjust to living in the real world. The dreaming consciousness employs **symbols** and metaphors that the waking consciousness often cannot interpret. Dream symbols usually show two key characteristics, called displacement and condensation. In **displacement,** a person's focus shifts from the matter of interest to something related to it symbolically. For example, someone interested in a penis may dream about a tower. In **condensation,** the characteristics of several people or objects are combined into one symbolic person or object. Dream symbols and their import undoubtedly vary greatly from person to person.

4. The act of **meditation** seems to induce a special type of consciousness. Meditation, used by Buddhists, Hindus, and others, is meant to produce a relaxed body and a fully aware, relaxed mind that can dissociate itself from mundane concerns and reach a "higher consciousness." Physiological measures of experienced meditators show changes in EEG, oxygen consumption, and apparent hypertension while they are meditating.

5. **Hypnosis** induces a trancelike state of consciousness. The hypnotized consciousness usually becomes dissociated from the person's normal waking consciousness and can be controlled by suggestions from the hypnotist. The hypnotized individual can be made to perceive things that do not actually exist. Martin Orne has shown that people actually hypnotized can be distinguished from those faking hypnosis by the fact that hypnotized people use **trance logic.** That is, they mix suggestions from the hypnotist about what they will see with their own perceptions and do not apply real-world logic when inconsistencies arise. If, for example, a hypnotized person is told by the hypnotist that a certain person is sitting in a chair and the hypnotized person himself perceives that person elsewhere in the room, he will see both images of the same person, a hallucinated one and the real one.

6. **Spirit possession** is a hypnoticlike trance usually occurring in members of certain religious groups. People who enter this state of consciousness generally believe that they have been possessed by a supernatural power or

Figure 13.18 A leading investigator of the behavior and consciousness of humans and monkeys who have undergone split-brain surgery, Roger W. Sperry has won a number of scientific awards and honors. His research includes many other areas in physiological and experimental psychology, for example, the neurophysiology of learning and memory, the development of nerve connections, and adaptations of neural organization.

deity. The trance is usually induced by religious ritual; behavior under the trance is usually that prescribed by the group's religious tradition.

7. Certain drugs chemically alter everyday consciousness. **Hallucinogens,** or **psychedelic** drugs, such as LSD, mescaline, and peyote, induce hallucinations, distorted perceptions, and intense emotions.

SUGGESTED READINGS

Dement, William C. *Some Must Watch While Some Must Sleep.* San Francisco: W. H. Freeman, 1974. One of the pioneers in modern dream research presents a brief, readable, up-to-date account of what is known about sleep and dreaming. Gives special attention to the relationship between sleep and psychological disorders, including insomnia and mental illness.

Faraday, Ann. *Dream Power.* New York: Coward, McCann and Geoghegan, 1972. Based on modern dream research, this is a well-written, informative, entertaining explanation of the kinds of messages that dreams convey and the best procedures for converting those messages into useful self-knowledge.

Jones, Richard M. *The New Psychology of Dreaming.* New York: Grune & Stratton, 1970. Jones explores the entire field of dream research, all the way from the classical psychoanalytic approach to modern physiological research, and attempts to integrate the field.

Naranjo, Claudio, and Robert Ornstein. *On the Psychology of Meditation.* New York: Viking, 1971. A discussion of the wide range of meditative techniques and their relations to the control of internal body and brain states.

Ornstein, Robert. *The Psychology of Consciousness.* San Francisco: W. H. Freeman, 1972 (paper). Ornstein explores the idea that man has two modes of consciousness, one in each brain hemisphere.

Shor, Robert E., and Martin T. Orne (eds.). *The Nature of Hypnosis.* New York: Holt, Rinehart and Winston, 1965. This collection of readings contains classical papers on hypnosis and on such related topics as multiple personality and spirit possession.

Tart, Charles T. (ed.). *Altered States of Consciousness.* New York: Wiley, 1969. A collection of readings on a wide range of topics, including dreaming, hypnosis, drugs, and meditation. Of particular interest are a "fact sheet" on marijuana and many useful papers that are difficult to obtain elsewhere.

Teyler, Timothy J. *Altered States of Awareness.* San Francisco: W. H. Freeman, 1972. A collection of important articles from *Scientific American* dealing with the split brain, sleep and dreaming, drugs, meditation, and sensory deprivation.

Thigpen, Corbett H., and Hervey Cleckley. *The Three Faces of Eve.* New York: McGraw-Hill, 1957. An intriguing psychiatric account of the case of multiple personality discussed in this chapter. The book reads like a novel and was, in fact, made into a movie.

Weil, Andrew. *The Natural Mind.* Boston: Houghton Mifflin, 1972. Weil examines alternatives to ordinary consciousness. He is particularly interested in what he calls "stoned thinking," a non-drug-induced state.

When we get down to the simple biological drives that guide our actions—hunger and thirst, weariness and pain, pleasure and passion—we find ourselves compelled to recognize our kinship to the rest of the animal kingdom.

Yet we hate to. We value our special human ability to subdue our appetites and maintain a dignified command over them. We may be hungry, but the canons of polite society tell us we must eat in moderation and without undue haste, noise, or signs of pleasure. To behave otherwise is to "wolf" one's food, or to "eat like a pig." Similarly, we should bear pain with fortitude and indulge in pleasure with restraint.

That, at least, is the theory, and when all too many times people do show evidence of being driven to extremes by these basic biological urges, they are, of course, behaving in an "uncivilized" or "uncultured" way—and, if a worse insult is desired, they are "animallike" or "bestial."

Where the unflattering comparison of humans with other animals is most marked is in connection with sex. After all, there is a limit to how far we can control our responses to hunger, thirst, weariness, and pain, and it does not pay to make our contempt too plain here. Any of us may forget our training and, when driven to distraction by any of these, behave in ways that we will later remember with shame. None of us can feel secure in this respect.

But sex? We can go for indefinite periods without sex. It may distress us to do so, but the lack does not threaten our physical survival and many people, either out of choice or through circumstance, remain celibate all their lives. It is therefore particularly shameful, it would seem, to give in to the sexual drive.

To make too obvious one's interest in sex, and to be too eager for sexual gratification, is to show evidence of pandering to one's "lower instincts" and "animal impulses." Indeed, the puritan view of sex is that one should abandon all "animal impulse" in this respect and indulge in it for no other purpose than childbearing—and to do that without excessive pleasure.

Yet this puritan attitude toward sex is precisely that of the entire animal kingdom *but* humans. In other species there is a definite season when the female is in heat, and it is only then that sexual contacts are made, usually with marked economy of effect and with high effectiveness as far as childbearing is concerned.

Human beings, on the other hand, are ready for sexual contact at just about any time. What's more, human beings are the only species, as far as we know, that understands the connection between sex and childbearing, and makes definite efforts to disconnect the two. Moralists may disapprove of excessive sex, or of sexual techniques deliberately designed to give pleasure without risking impregnation, or of contraceptive devices—but none of that is animallike or bestial. It is entirely and uniquely *human*. It is the puritan sex ethic that is animallike.

Considering that human beings have a better understanding of sex than any other species, that they bring to it all the heightened pleasures of speech and shared cultural experience, and that there is an imperative present need for a low birth rate, it might be argued that sex should be made into a complex and versatile human function designed to achieve heightened intimacy, rather than that it should be retained, beast-wise, as a mere baby-making mechanism.

Isaac Asimov

14
Physiology, Drives, and Emotion

Figure 14.1 An understanding of the physiology of an organism is fundamental to an understanding of its psychology, because an organism neither feels nor acts without physical changes occurring in its body. A large proportion of present knowledge about the relationships between physiology and psychology has been learned from a single kind of organism: the laboratory rat. The rat has been chosen as a laboratory subject because it has an evolutionarily advanced mammalian brain but one that is not too complex. The rat is small, cheap, easily handled, easily cared for, and easily operated on, but its behavior is not so rigid and limited that comparisons cannot be made between it and the human being.

All people—just like all other organisms—are material objects. Every time we perform some act or have a thought, a feeling, or a memory, some physiological change occurs in our bodies. Biological processes always lie at the base of our behavior. In order to understand why fear is accompanied by a chalky complexion or a queasy stomach, why some people respond to stress by developing ulcers, or why some people are subject to epileptic seizures, we must understand something about biological contributions to behavior and mental life. This chapter surveys the basic concepts of physiological psychology, the area of psychology that deals with physiological correlates of behavior and mental life.

Consider a tennis player engaging in a tricky shot; a student absorbed in homework or worrying about the next test; a businesswoman reading the morning paper or analyzing the stock market reports. Whatever one does do involves an incredibly detailed coordination among all the billions of cells that make up the tissues, organs, and systems of the body. This coordination depends on effective, flexible, and precise communication among all the parts of the body.

The body's communication system can be compared to that of a city. Imagine, for example, a city struck by an earthquake. Scores of buildings are ablaze, and electric lines are down, causing a major power failure. Immediately the fire, police, and other emergency departments spring into action to handle the crisis. Newsmen and photographers rush to the scene of the disaster to keep the city's inhabitants informed about the emergency. Charities provide food and shelter for homeless victims, while ambulances carry the injured people to waiting hospitals. Despite the apparent chaos, groups of people are solving the problems that the earthquake has created. The body responds in a similar way to emergencies; when we cut a finger, for example, many different parts of the body mobilize to deal with the emergency and overcome it.

To be able to mobilize effectively against such emergencies, and to function smoothly the rest of the time, communities—and human bodies—must have a central organization, such as a city government, that can tie together all the separate parts of the community and see to it that all segments function well together. The human body has exactly such an organization. Like a city, the body is sensitive to inputs from its environment and is able to respond quickly. The brain is the body's city hall, and it has two communications systems for receiving information from and giving messages to billions of individuals—the body's cells. One is the nervous system, and the other is the endocrine (or hormone) system.

THE NERVOUS SYSTEM

The nervous system is in many ways comparable to the telephone system of a city. The messages are basically electrical, and the route of distribution is along prelaid cables, linked with one another by relays and switchboards. The cables are the individual nerve fibers; the relays are the synapses between nerves; the switchboards are either interneurons—nerve cells interposed along a main line of communication—or whole networks of neurons.

Messages to and from the brain travel along **nerves,** which are strings of long, thin cells called **neurons** (see Figure 14.3). Chemical-electrical signals travel down the length of the neurons, much as a flame travels along a firecracker fuse, but in the neuron the fuse can burn over and over again hundreds of times a minute. When a neuron transmits one of these chemical-electrical signals, it is said to be **firing.** Neurons can make other neurons fire faster or slower by releasing chemicals, called **transmitter substances,** across the gaps, or **synapses,** that occur between all neurons. It is by this method that messages travel through the body.

The nerves of the body run in and out of a huge mass of neurons clumped together to form the **central nervous system (CNS):** the brain and spinal cord (see Figure 14.2). The **spinal cord** is a bundle of nerves running down the length of the back, much like a telephone cable, that transmits most of the messages back and forth between the body and the brain.

The spinal cord, which is about as thick as a pencil, is well protected by the backbone, just as the brain is protected by the skull. This protection prevents any interference with the line of communication between the brain and the rest of the body. Without the spinal cord, messages from the brain would never reach any of our muscles except those in the face; we would essentially be paralyzed from the neck down.

Branching out from the central nervous system (mostly from the spinal cord) is the **peripheral nervous system,** a network of nerves that conducts information from bodily organs to the CNS and takes messages back to the organs. The peripheral nervous system is thought of as having two divisions, the **autonomic nervous system,** which controls internal biological functions such as digestion, heart rate, and hormone secretion, and the **somatic nervous system,** which controls the voluntary movement of skeletal muscles.

Neurons: The Building Blocks of the Nervous System

Neurons are the basic units of the nervous system, which contains billions of them. Most neurons are microscopically small: Any element of behavior (raising an eyebrow, thinking a word) involves hundreds of thousands of them, all working together. We cannot think faster than neurons can act; we cannot sustain a memory longer than neurons can function. Although there are many individual variations among neurons found in different portions of the nervous system, they all conform to the same basic pattern, and as far as is known, they all operate in the same way. Every neuron has a cell body, an axon, and dendrites, as shown in Figure 14.3. The **cell body** is specialized for

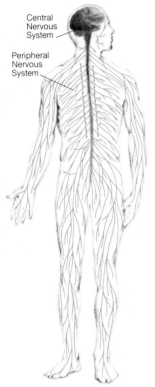

Central Nervous System

Peripheral Nervous System

Figure 14.2 The central nervous system (CNS) and the peripheral nervous system (PNS) in the human body. Both of these systems are made up of billions of nerve cells, or neurons, each of which is capable of transmitting a train of chemical-electrical signals in one direction. In the CNS, these neurons form an immensely complex network that organizes, stores, and redirects vast quantities of information. In the PNS, neurons in every pathway carry information either from receptors (such as the sense organs) toward the CNS or away from the CNS to effectors (in the muscles, for example). There is a close match between information going to the CNS and information coming from it. Every muscle, for example, not only receives from the CNS directions to contract or relax but also sends back information about its present state of contraction or relaxation.

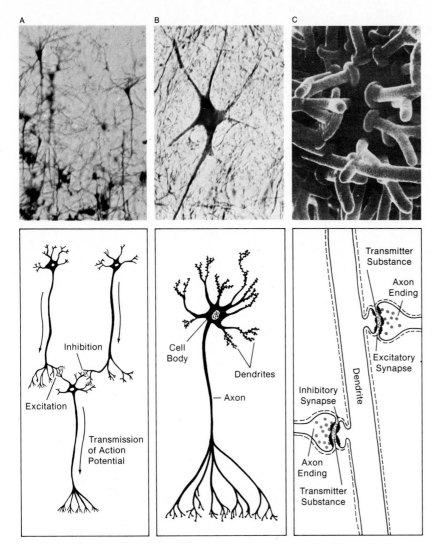

Figure 14.3 The fundamental structures in the nervous system. (A) A photomicrograph and a simplified diagram of neurons in the cerebral cortex. Note that there can be very large numbers of contact areas, or synapses, between neurons. Note also that one neuron may have either an excitatory or an inhibitory effect on another and that the action potentials are transmitted in only one direction along the firing neuron. (B) A photomicrograph and a diagram of the parts of a single neuron. The dendrites are the receiving end of the neuron; the axon is the sending end. An action potential is transmitted along the axon of a neuron only when its dendrites have been sufficiently excited. (C) An electron micrograph and a diagram of the structures at the synapse. Note the correspondence between the axon endings and the small protrusions on the dendrites in the diagrams in (C) and (B). When an action potential reaches the end of the axon of a neuron, small amounts of transmitter substances are released from storage areas across the synapse to the dendrites of another neuron. The substances from some neurons are excitatory in their effect; the substances from others are inhibitory. If the receiving neuron gets sufficient excitation (and not too much inhibition), it in turn fires. (D) Three records of a neuron firing. Such records are obtained by inserting very fine wires into a cell in a living organism to record voltage changes within the neuron. Note that, depending on how much excitation or inhibition a neuron is receiving, it may fire over and over again extremely rapidly, or fire hardly at all.

absorbing and using nutrients to provide energy for neuronal activities. The **axons** are specialized for carrying impulses from the neuron to other neurons or to bodily organs. The **dendrites** are multitudes of fine projections that receive messages from other neurons and transmit them to the cell body. A ''decision'' whether the neuron should pass on its message is made in the part of the cell body nearest the axon; if the input reaches a certain level, the axon fires and passes the message to a dendrite of some other neuron or to a bodily organ.

Only the axon is specialized to fire. The phenomenon of firing obeys the all-or-none law of neuronal conduction: Either the axon fires or it doesn't— there is no intermediate process. The all-or-none electrical charge that passes down an axon is called an **action potential.** Because a neuron always fires with precisely the same action potential, different types of messages cannot be transmitted by the size of the action potential. Instead, the type of message is reflected by the number of neurons firing at any particular time or by the particular pathway of firing neurons.

How is a message received by one neuron from the axon of another? When the impulse reaches the end of the axon, chemicals stored at the tip of the axon are released into the **synapse,** the tiny space separating one axon from an adjacent neuron (Figure 14.3). The released chemicals diffuse across the synapse and give a "message" to the adjacent neuron; the message is usually received by the dendrite, but cell bodies and axons can also receive messages across a synapse. This message is then carried (but not "fired" in the all-or-none manner unique to the axon) into the cell body. If it is bolstered by incoming messages from the many other dendrites of the recipient cell, then the cell will fire its axon.

The Brain

Although most parts of the body are implicated in psychological functioning, the most important psychological processes—such as thinking, feeling, remembering, and learning—occur in the brain. The brain monitors what is happening both inside and outside the body by receiving messages from **receptors**—cells such as those in the eye and ear (see Chapter 12) whose function is to gather information. The brain sifts through these messages, combines them, and sends out orders to the **effectors**—cells that work the muscles and internal glands and organs. For example, receptors in your eye may send a message to the brain such as: "Round object. Size increasing. Distance decreasing rapidly." Your brain instantly connects this image with information from memory to identify the object as a baseball. Almost simultaneously your brain orders the effectors in your arms to prepare themselves to catch the ball.

Signals from receptors travel through the peripheral nervous system to the brain, usually via the spinal cord. The first part of the brain reached by incoming signals is a section often referred to as the **old brain,** so named because of its similarity to the brains of primitive creatures, such as fish and frogs (see Figure 14.4). Fish can do little else but eat, sleep, carry out basic bodily functions, and try to escape danger. Their tiny brains are responsive primarily to basic needs, and their behavior is, for the most part, rigidly and automatically controlled. The portion of the human brain comparable to the fish's primitive brain carries out similar functions. For example, your old brain (together with your spinal cord) handles the hundreds of reflex actions that are a normal part of your daily life—pulling your hand back automatically when you touch a hot object, coughing when food gets into your windpipe, blinking and shedding tears when dust gets into your eye, and so on.

Unlike fish and frogs, however, people are able to learn to behave in entirely new ways, to think, and to imagine. These abilities come from a section of the brain that is miniscule in fish, larger in mammals such as cats and dogs, and huge in humans. This new brain, called the **cerebral cortex,** surrounds the old brain in people in much the same way that a halved peach surrounds the pit. While the old brain guides biological needs and reflexes, the new brain enables us, among other things, to talk, to read, to solve problems, to play musical instruments, and to participate in sports.

The Old Brain The portion of the old brain that first receives signals is the reticular formation (see Figure 14.5), which controls an activating network of nerves that runs through the whole brain. This network, the **reticular activating system,** is the brain's waking and attention system. It screens incoming messages, blocking out some signals and letting others pass. During sleep it blocks most inputs, but in response to a loud or unusual sound it sends messages to the rest of the brain, alerting it and raising its activity level to a state of wakefulness.

In the center of the brain is the **thalamus,** the brain's great relaying center. It sorts incoming impulses and directs them to various parts of the brain, and it relays messages from one part of the brain to another.

At the base of the brain, below and to the front of the thalamus, is the **hypothalamus,** a small, closely packed cluster of neurons (see Figure 14.5)

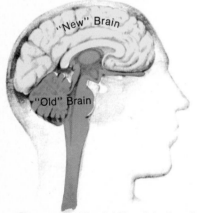

Figure 14.4 The "old" and the "new" parts of the human brain. "Old" brain structures are those that human beings share with more primitive animals, such as fish and snakes; they are the most deeply buried structures in the brain and they control such basic processes as breathing, circulation, hunger, and thirst. Generally, the more evolutionarily advanced an organism is, the greater the proportion of its brain that is "new." Structures of the "new" brain are related to an organism's ability to perceive, learn, and think. The more "new" brain an organism has, the more flexible and adaptable its behavior is likely to be. A large proportion of the human brain is "new."

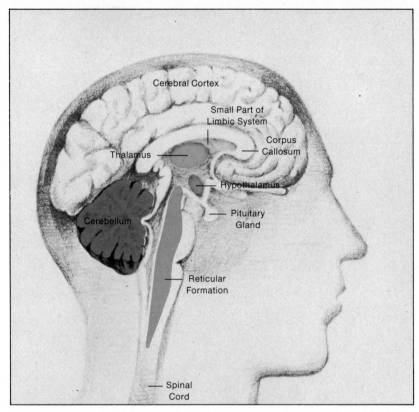

Figure 14.5   The structures of the "old" brain. (This illustration shows the brain as it would appear if it were sliced exactly in half from front to back.) The structures shown here are the first to receive incoming information, and they regulate all the most fundamental processes of the body. Note that the reticular activating system, which controls the most general responses of the brain to sensory input, is located in the area that connects the brain to the spine and the rest of the nervous system. Also, note that the thalamus has an almost perfectly central location in the brain and that the hypothalamus is very close to the pituitary gland, which controls the activity of the body's other endocrine glands. The several structures of the limbic system are not shown in this illustration because they lie on either side of the line that cuts the brain exactly in half. A few "new" brain structures are also shown here. Note particularly the corpus callosum, the large band of nerve fibers that connects the two hemispheres of the cerebral cortex.

that is one of the most important parts of the brain. This structure regulates the autonomic nervous system, the part of the peripheral nervous system that controls essential biological functions. By sensing the levels of water and sugar in your blood, for example, your hypothalamus can tell when you need food or water and can then cause you to feel hungry or thirsty. The hypothalamus also plays an important role in determining emotional responses and in regulating the endocrine system, which will be discussed later in the chapter.

Another structure that plays a large part in emotions is the **limbic system,** which is a group of interconnected structures situated near the hypothalamus. Damage in the limbic system has profound effects on emotional reactivity, even to the point of turning excitable animals like monkeys or mountain lions into docile creatures or converting tame laboratory rats into ferocious combatants.

At the very back and bottom of the old brain is the **cerebellum,** the brain's "executive secretary." Among other things, it controls posture and balance as you move about so that you do not fall over or bump into things. Consequently, it helps to regulate the details of major commands from the cerebral cortex. Without your cerebellum, you might hit a friend in the stomach as you reach to shake his hand.

The old brain contains many structures besides those described thus far; some of these structures will be discussed in later parts of the chapter.

The New Brain   Wrapped around the old brain is the cerebral cortex, or new brain. It is a great gray mass of ripples and valleys folded so that its huge surface area, in which most of the higher brain functions take place, can fit inside the skull. The cortex is divided into several regions called **lobes** (see Figure 14.6). Some lobes receive specific kinds of sensory messages. Visual

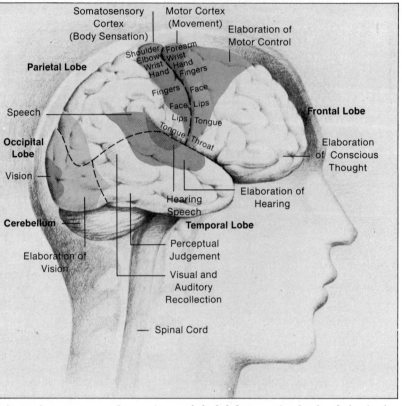

Figure 14.6 An external view of the brain from the side. Most of the areas exposed here are parts of the "new" brain. For purposes of reference, the surfaces of the hemispheres are divided roughly into the lobes indicated here. The divisions between these lobes are somewhat arbitrary, however, and do not correspond in any way to distinctions made on the basis of function. The functions of the cerebral cortex are not fully understood; areas whose behavioral importance is known are indicated. The locations of the cerebellum and the brain stem are also indicated, so that this view of the brain can be compared with the view in Figure 14.5.

information goes mostly to the **occipital lobes** at the back of the brain, whereas auditory sensations go primarily to the **temporal lobes** on each side of the brain. At approximately the middle of the brain surface are the **parietal lobes,** which include the **somatosensory cortex,** where information from the skin, muscles, and joints is received.

Just in front of the somatosensory cortex, across a deep fold, is the **motor cortex,** which is part of the **frontal lobes.** The motor cortex controls bodily movement. Areas of the body that are involved in complex tasks receive the greatest representation in the motor cortex. Areas with the greatest sensory input receive the greatest representation in the somatosensory cortex (see Figure 14.6). For example, the hands are highly represented in both these areas of the cortex, which is reflected in the great ability of people to make skillful movements with their hands.

The very front of the brain, the part of the frontal lobes farthest forward seems to have nothing to do with the regulation of any bodily functions. It is believed to have more to do with intellect and personality; this part of the brain enables people to be witty, sensitive, or easygoing. Damage to the frontal lobe can result in major personality changes. For example, in the mid-1800s a railroad man named Phineas Gage was injured in an explosion. The force of the blast drove an iron stake into Gage's brain, striking and damaging the frontal lobe. Gage survived the accident, but he changed dramatically. He became childish, fitful, irreverent, impatient, and capricious, where once he had been trustworthy and dependable. Yet the damage did not seem to affect his memory, his ability to think, or such basic capacities as seeing, moving, or talking.

The cortex is made up of two **hemispheres** that are roughly mirror images of each other; each of the four lobes is present in each hemisphere. The two hemispheres are connected by a band of nerves, called the **corpus callosum,** which carries messages back and forth between the hemispheres. Roughly speaking, each cortex is connected to half of the body, but the connections are crisscrossed: The left half of the brain controls mostly the right half of the body and vice versa. For example, a stroke that causes damage to the right hemisphere results in numbness or paralysis on the left side of the body.

Although the two cerebral hemispheres appear to be identical mirror images of each other, there seem to be major functional differences between them. For example, the dominance of one hand over the other in left-handedness or right-handedness implies that one cortex is dominant over the other.

People who have suffered brain damage that is restricted to one hemisphere or the other are the greatest source of knowledge about the differences between the two hemispheres. For example, many adults with left-hemisphere damage experience difficulty with language, whereas such difficulty is extremely rare when damage is restricted to the right hemisphere. This is most clearly true for right-handed people, but the control of language is primarily in the left hemisphere even for about 65 percent of left-handed people. Damage restricted to the right hemisphere often results in defects in spatial abilities: People have difficulty copying geometric designs and recognizing pictures they have been shown earlier. Michael Gazzaniga and other psychologists have suggested that the two hemispheres differ markedly in their abilities and constitute two virtually separate consciousnesses (see Chapter 13).

Reflexes and the Spinal Cord

The spinal cord serves not only as a connecting link between brain and body but also as a lower-level center for the control of some simple reflexes. The reflexive response to pain is one of the most important protective reflexes of the spinal cord. Consider what happens in the case of a painful stimulus to the arm. Receptors in the skin of the arm are activated by very hot or cold or otherwise painful stimuli. Usually many skin receptors are activated by a painful stimulus, and consequently many neurons bring the pain message into the spinal cord. The cord immediately sends a message to activate the muscles that bend the arm, moving it away from the source of pain. Also, neurons carry the message of the painful stimulus to the brain, where the stimulus is "experienced" and "understood," and additional activities are initiated to prevent the recurrence of the painful incident. Thus, even though simple reflex action can be controlled by the spinal cord without specific instructions from the brain, the stimuli that produce the reflex are still relayed to the brain.

THE ENDOCRINE SYSTEM

As was noted earlier, the brain has two communication systems for receiving information from and giving messages to the body's billions of cells. The nervous system is one; the other is the endocrine, or hormone, system.

The endocrine system is a chemical system: Its messages are chemical substances called **hormones,** which are produced by endocrine glands and distributed by the blood and other body fluids. The various endocrine glands are shown in Figure 14.7. This chemical communication system is in many ways similar to the mails. Chemical messages circulate throughout the bloodstream but have their effects at certain key addresses, the particular organs of the body that they influence. Also as with the mails, the messages are merely distributed; they generally are not changed as they are distributed. (In the nervous system, on the other hand, the electrical messages are changed as they are conducted across the synapses between neurons.)

The pituitary and thyroid glands illustrate how hormones work. The **thyroid gland** produces the hormone thyroxin (as well as several other hormones). Thyroxin promotes certain key chemical reactions that are important for all tissues of the body. Too little thyroxin makes people lazy and lethargic;

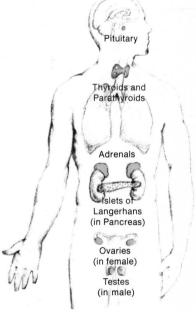

Figure 14.7 The endocrine glands. Note how close the pituitary gland is to the brain and refer back to Figure 14.5 to see its association with the hypothalamus. Besides the pituitary, the glands whose activity is most important in the regulation of behavior are the sex glands, the adrenals, and the thyroid.

too much makes them overactive. But the activity of the thyroid gland is itself controlled by a hormone—released by the pituitary gland—that is necessary for the production of thyroxin by the thyroid gland. The level of thyroxin in the blood in turn affects how much of the thyroid-stimulating hormone is produced by the pituitary: High levels of thyroxin in the blood reduce the output of thyroid-stimulating hormone, whereas low levels of thyroxin lead to greater production of thyroid-stimulating hormone. The pituitary and the thyroid glands therefore regulate each other, and the combination regulates general bodily activity.

This type of system for controlling levels of hormones in the bloodstream is called negative feedback, or **homeostasis.** The basic principle of homeostasis is that deviations from a certain level of a substance lead to processes that will eliminate that deviation. A thermostat, for example, is a mechanism for homeostasis: Deviations in temperature below a certain level in a room turn on a furnace and thus produce heat to eliminate the deviation. Hormones generally show homeostasis not only in one direction, like the thermostat on a furnace, but in two directions. A low level of thyroxin in the blood is a deviation in one direction: It leads to production by the pituitary of the thyroid-stimulating hormone, which then eliminates the deviation. A high level of thyroxin in the blood is a deviation in the opposite direction: It leads to a decrease in the production of the thyroid-stimulating hormone and a consequent reduction in the production of thyroxin, thereby eliminating the deviation. As a result of these homeostatic processes, the level of thyroxin in the blood is kept in *equilibrium.*

The brain, together with the **pituitary gland,** is the center of control of the homeostatic action of most of the endocrine system. The pituitary gland, often called the master gland of the endocrine system, secretes a large number of hormones, and many of them (including the thyroid-stimulating hormone) control the output of hormones by other endocrine glands. The brain, in turn, controls the release of pituitary hormones and so indirectly controls the activity of many other glands. It also monitors the amount of hormones in the blood and sends out messages to correct deviations from the proper homeostatic level.

Generally, the endocrine system has important effects on behavior; it is particularly important in its influence on emotion and motivation, several examples of which will be discussed later in the chapter. Through the combined actions of the nervous system and the endocrine system, the brain monitors and controls most human behavior.

HOW SCIENTISTS STUDY THE BRAIN

By mapping the brain's mountains, canyons, and inner recesses, scientists try to understand the role of the brain in behavior. Psychologists who do this kind of research use three methods for exploring the brain: recording, stimulation, and destruction.

Recording

By inserting wires called **electrodes** into the brain, scientists are able to detect the minute electrical changes that occur when neurons fire. These wires are connected to electronic equipment that amplifies the tiny voltages produced by the firing of the neurons. Even single neurons can be monitored. For example, when David Hubel and Torsten Wiesel placed tiny electrodes into the part of the cortex of cats' and monkeys' brains that receives visual information from the eye, they found that specific neurons responded to specific visual stimuli projected onto particular parts of the retina. A line of a certain orientation projected onto a particular part of the retina would cause one neuron to fire. Another neuron would fire when an edge was projected onto a specific part of the retina. Still another would fire when an angle was projected onto a particular part of the retina.

Scientists can also record the electrical activity of whole areas of the brain by using the **electroencephalograph (EEG).** Wires attached to the scalp measure the overall electrical activity of the millions of neurons in a specific part of the brain. Because the neurons in the brain tend to increase or decrease their amount of firing in unison, they produce rhythms of electrical activity, which are called brain waves. Using the EEG, psychologists have found, for example, that brain waves change systematically as a person goes to sleep and then go through a regular cycle while the person is asleep (see Chapter 13).

The brain disorder of epilepsy can be monitored by the use of EEGs. Epilepsy is frequently caused by a small piece of brain tissue that produces abnormal electrical activity. Typically this tissue has somehow been damaged, and the damage causes the abnormal electrical activity. Epilepsy is characterized by seizures, ranging from brief, barely noticeable ones that seem to be nothing more than slight lapses of attention to severe convulsive seizures in which the victim suffers violent spasms and typically falls unconscious. When an epileptic seizure occurs, abnormal electrical activity begins in the small piece of damaged brain tissue and then spreads to neighboring areas of the brain until much of the brain is showing abnormally large brain waves. By monitoring an epileptic's brain waves, psychologists can locate the site at which the seizure begins and can follow its spread through the brain. A surgical method that physicians use for controlling severe epileptic seizures is discussed in Chapter 13.

Stimulation

Electrodes can be used to make neurons fire as well as to measure their normal firing. Brain surgeon Wilder Penfield is famous for stimulating the brains of his patients during surgery to determine what functions the various parts of the brain perform. For example, Penfield found that he could trigger vivid memory sequences by applying a tiny electric current to points on the temporal lobe of the cerebral cortex: One woman heard a familiar song so clearly that she thought a record was being played in the operating room.

Another experimenter, José Delgado, made a particularly dramatic demonstration of the effects of brain stimulation. He entered a bullring occupied by an angry bull whose brain contained electrodes Delgado had placed there earlier. Delgado carried a small transmitter that could send an electric current through those electrodes. The bull charged, but just before it reached Delgado, he pushed the transmitter button, thus stimulating the bull's brain and bringing it to a skidding halt.

In addition to electrical stimulation, scientists have also used chemicals to stimulate the brain. A small tube is implanted in an animal's brain so that the

Figure 14.8 (left) A rhesus monkey, receiving electrical stimulation from an electrode implanted in a certain part of its hypothalamus, viciously attacks other monkeys with which it is housed. (right) The apparatus used for the remote delivery of brain stimulation can be seen strapped to the back of this similarly aroused animal.

A

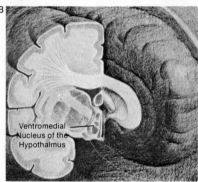

B

Ventromedial Nucleus of the Hypothalmus

Figure 14.9 (top) After the destruction of a small part of its hypothalamus, this rat has overeaten until it is three or four times its normal weight. Interestingly, a rat with this type of lesion will not work for extra food, even though it will eat huge amounts if the food is tasty and easily available. (bottom) A drawing showing the part of the human brain that corresponds to the part lesioned in the rat in (A). This drawing shows a view from the front of the brain, with one of the halves of the brain shown in cross section. Note the structures visible in this view that were not visible in Figures 14.5 and 14.6.

end touches the area to be stimulated, and a small amount of chemical is then delivered through the tube to that area. Experiments with chemical stimulation have demonstrated, for example, that different chemicals applied to the hypothalamus in the old brain can affect hunger and thirst in an animal.

Stimulation techniques have aroused great medical interest in recent years. For example, an electrical current delivered through electrodes implanted in certain areas of the brain seems to provide temporary relief from pain. Thus, electrical stimulation is now used on terminal cancer patients to relieve them of intolerable pain. Also, some psychiatrists have begun to use brain stimulation to control violent aggressive behavior in mental patients for whom no other method of control has been successful.

Destruction

Scientists often cut out or destroy a part of an animal's brain in order to see what function that part performs. In a **lesion** a small area of the brain is destroyed, while in **ablation** a large piece of the brain is cut out.

One kind of lesion of the hypothalamus can cause a rat to eat so much that it overeats and becomes three or four times its normal weight, as shown in Figure 14.9; without this part of its brain the animal cannot judge when it has eaten enough. People sometimes have parts of their brain ablated as a result of an accident, as in the case of Phineas Gage and the iron stake. Occasionally, however, brain-ablation operations are performed on people. One such operation, called a prefrontal lobotomy, was once performed frequently on violent mental patients. Today this type of surgery is severely criticized because it tends to leave the patient a dull and docile being who can never regain normal brain functioning, for it is impossible to replace the part of the brain that has been removed.

PHYSIOLOGY OF MOTIVATION AND EMOTION

It was noted at the beginning of this chapter that every psychological process has a physiological basis. Motivation and emotion are two categories of psychological functioning whose physiological underpinnings have been the subject of much psychological research, mostly with animals: Primitive motives and emotions are easily demonstrable in lower animals. Nevertheless, understanding the physiology of motivation and emotion is difficult, because so much of the brain and body is involved. Structures as far removed from each other as the kidneys and the salivary glands play a role in thirst, for example, and structures as separate as the sweat glands, the stomach, and the adrenal glands play a role in the emotion of fear.

A key concept for understanding the physiological basis of motivation is the biological **drive,** a physiological state that arises from some kind of physical need and energizes and directs behavior. The hunger drive, for example, rouses an individual to look for food.

Emotion is more difficult to define formally, although we can all identify such emotional experiences as joy, grief, anger, and panic. What these states have in common is widespread physiological arousal combined with specific experiential qualities that enable us to categorize each particular emotion: The experience of joy is usually very different from the experience of anger. These feelings that uniquely define each emotion are determined not only by physiological activity but also by the circumstances under which the experience occurs, as will be demonstrated later.

Yet drives and emotions also have much in common. Both drives and emotions are experienced as either pleasant or unpleasant. Both cause the organism to focus on specific aspects of the environment (such as food or safety) and to neglect others. Both are able to motivate learning (and, in fact, are often used as motivators in psychological experiments on learning).

Recent research has uncovered part of the physiological basis for one of these shared aspects of drives and emotions: pleasantness and unpleasantness. James Olds and Peter Milner reported in 1954 that rats learned to press a lever in order to stimulate particular areas of their own brains with a mild electric current (see Figure 14.10). The rats in this and in many subsequent experiments clearly were motivated to obtain this electrical stimulation. They would stop pressing the lever when the current was turned off, they would learn a maze in order to get a chance to press for stimulation, they pressed thousands of times per hour when given the opportunity, and they preferred pressing for brain stimulation over eating, even after periods of food deprivation. The areas of the brain that produced these effects have come to be called pleasure centers. Areas that seem to be aversive, or painful, have also been discovered; if electrodes are implanted in those areas, animals will work to turn off stimulation.

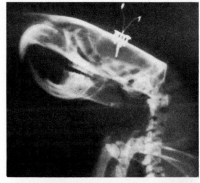

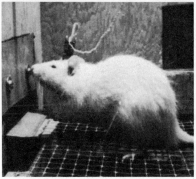

Figure 14.10 (top) An x-ray photograph of the head of a rat that has an electrode implanted in its brain. (bottom) A rat (with a similar electrode implantation) in James Olds' laboratory pressing a lever to produce small pulses of electric current in an area of the "old" brain.

Both the positively reinforcing areas and the negatively reinforcing ones are located in the old brain—mostly in some areas of the hypothalamus and the limbic system, both of which have been implicated in many emotional and motivational processes. Stimulation of the cerebral cortex, on the other hand, produces neither positive nor negative effects: The animals seem to ignore the stimulation when it is turned on by the experimenter and do not work to turn it on themselves.

What if people with electrode implants were asked what they experienced during electrical self-stimulation? Doctors have implanted electrodes in the brains of a large number of people with epilepsy or other brain disorders in order to search for areas of abnormal brain activity. On occasion, patients (several of them at the Tulane Medical School Hospital, under the supervision of Robert Heath) have been given the opportunity to stimulate their own brains by pressing buttons connected to electrodes implanted in various portions of their old brains. The patients reported pleasurable sensations from areas that roughly correspond to those revealed in animal experiments. In particular, according to Heath, several patients, both male and female, reported pleasurable sexual feelings when stimulating an area in the limbic system, feelings that on a number of occasions culminated in orgasm. Stimulation of other sites resulted in pleasurable feelings that did not have sexual qualities.

The animal and human research data taken together suggest, then, that pleasure and pain processes can be manipulated and explored by brain-research techniques. There are a number of methodological problems in this type of research that should also be mentioned, however. For example, if an individual presses a lever at a higher rate for one electrode location than for another, is the first site more pleasurable, or are some sensations possibly so intense that one would rather experience them more slowly? Also, in many studies it seems that animals "forget" overnight that the electrical stimulation is pleasurable and must be given a "priming" electrical stimulus before they again begin to press the lever themselves. This suggests that the stimulus may induce some sort of drive that is satisfied by the next press of the lever, which again induces the drive. The research in this field is obviously complex and will provide controversy for some time to come.

HOMEOSTASIS AND HOMEOSTATIC DRIVES

Suppose you deprived a dog of all water for a day or so, then turned it loose. What would you expect the animal to do? Search for something to drink, of course. But why would the dog do that? To answer "Because it is thirsty" is to embark on a circular line of reasoning, for thirst is usually defined as a condition that occurs in an organism when it has been without water for a while. The real question, then, is what *is* this thing called thirst that makes an organism get up off its haunches and hunt for something to drink? To put the problem another way, how does the organism know that it wants water rather than, say, food or air or sex?

When circumstances deprive an animal of a substance necessary for life, the animal has a physiological **need** for that substance. The need exists whether or not the organism is aware of what it lacks. In most organisms, including people, a biological need brings about internal changes that cause the organism to fulfill the need. If you had to describe the behavior of a dog that needed water, you might say that the animal seemed *driven* to find water. The existence of a need often elicits a **drive.** Drives are very compelling. Until weakness sets in, virtually nothing will dissuade a thirsty animal from its search for water, and shipwrecked sailors have been known to fight to the death for it.

Not all physiological needs produce drives. The ones that do so tend to be needs that must be met on a regular basis if the organism is to survive, such as the needs for water and food. Less common or less crucial needs often do not produce drives. For example, an animal with anemia (an iron deficiency) needs to eat liver or another iron-rich food but may not be driven to choose it.

But most drives do arise from bodily needs—and are thus homeostatic. Homeostasis, as you recall, is the tendency of an organism to maintain a stable level of something by detecting deviations from an optimal level and correcting them. For example, you have a homeostatic temperature drive. If your body temperature drops below a certain point, you start to shiver, your peripheral blood vessels constrict, and you put on more clothes; all of these activities reduce heat loss and bring body warmth back to the optimal level. Should your body heat increase above a certain point, you start to sweat and sweating induces you to take some clothes off, and your peripheral blood vessels dilate; all of these activities reduce temperature to the optimal level. Thus, you maintain your temperature at a level of equilibrium.

The drives of hunger and thirst are also homeostatic; a decline in the level of body energy or water reserves triggers processes that restore the proper level. Some other drives, such as the sex drive, are not homeostatic, however, and do not seem to arise from any physical deficit; these drives will be discussed later in the chapter.

Hunger and the Energy Balance

After food is digested and absorbed into the body's cells, it is used to provide energy for all types of cellular functions, including nerve impulses and muscular contractions. Each organism must adjust its food intake to its energy requirements in order to maintain an equilibrium. A long-term excess of energy use over food intake results in weakness and, ultimately, death. An excess of food intake over energy use will result in obesity and inability to function properly. What is the mechanism that brings about this homeostatic balance? In particular, is the main determinant of hunger and satiety in the brain or in the organs associated with eating—the mouth, the stomach, and the intestines?

Determinants   Walter B. Cannon, early in the twentieth century, suggested that stomach contractions (''hunger pangs'') provide the main initiating stimulus for hunger and satiety. In one of Cannon's experiments a colleague, A. L. Washburn, swallowed a balloon that was then inflated. The hunger sensations reported by Washburn coincided with gastric contractions, which the experimenter could trace by means of the changes in the balloon. However, according to Robert MacDonald and his associates, people whose stomachs have been removed continue to experience hunger, and therefore the stomach contractions cannot be the only initiating stimulus of hunger.

Recent research has focused on the role of the brain in initiating hunger. The part of the old brain called the hypothalamus apparently monitors the amount of sugar in the blood, as well as other factors relevant to hunger, and then produces or inhibits hunger depending on the blood-sugar level. Rats with damage to the ventromedial area of the hypothalamus will overeat until they reach the sorry state of the animal shown in Figure 14.9. Research conducted by Philip Teitelbaum and his associates indicates that such brain damage seems to make animals less responsive to their internal need for calories and more responsive to the environmental factors that facilitate or deter eating: For example, they gorge themselves on good-tasting food but eat even less of bad-tasting food than normal animals do. Moreover, the brain-damaged animals do not respond to starvation in the same way as do normal ones, which indicates a lack of responsiveness to internal cues.

In an ingenious experiment, Stanley Schachter and his colleagues attempted to extend this distinction between internal and external controls over eating to people. Schachter asked fat people (defined as people whose weight was at least 20 percent above the optimal weight levels for their height and sex) and people of normal weight to rate the flavor of two large bowls of ice cream. To keep their attention away from the subject of how much they ate, he told them they should eat as much or as little as they needed to make their decision. One kind of ice cream was mixed with bitter quinine. The other was the best vanilla ice cream available. The normal subjects took about a spoonful of each flavor; the fat subjects barely tasted the bitter ice cream but took huge amounts of the tasty kind.

Schachter, Ronald Goldman, and Melvin Jaffa also studied fat and normal international airplane pilots and discovered that fat ones tended to eat whenever mealtime arrived in the country where they landed, even if they had already eaten at the mealtime in the country they had departed from. On the other hand, the normal-weight pilots ate according to internal stimuli, which were often not in accord with the meal schedules of the arrival or departure locations. This again suggests a more external source of drive for the fat subjects than for those of normal weight.

These and similar experiments suggest that overweight people may respond to the sight and taste of food and that people of normal weight may respond more to internal cues arising from actual physical needs. The fact that the behavior of Schachter's overweight subjects resembles that of rats with lesions of the ventromedial area of the hypothalamus suggests there may be

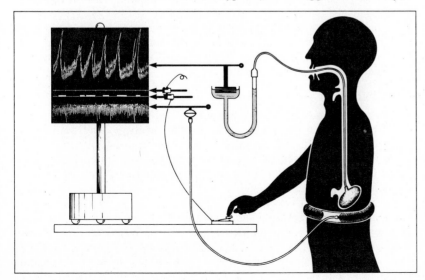

Figure 14.11 The apparatus used by Cannon to investigate the relationship between hunger pangs and stomach contractions. The top pen on the revolving drum recorded changes in pressure on a lightly inflated balloon inside the subject's stomach. The second pen marked time intervals. The third pen was controlled by the subject (who could not see the drum); he pressed a button that moved the pen whenever he was experiencing hunger pangs. The fourth pen recorded abdominal breathing. It is interesting to note that sometimes the acids secreted by the subject's stomach popped the balloon. This experiment, performed in 1912, is a good example of the attempts psychologists have made to link subjective experiences to objective physiological changes.

some physiological process in overweight people that parallels a malfunctioning of the hypothalamus, but it certainly does not mean that overweight people have any sort of brain damage.

Dual Control by the Hypothalamus Electrical or chemical stimulation of the ventromedial area of the hypothalamus has opposite effects from destruction of the area: Instead of overeating, animals stop eating altogether, even if they have been deprived of food. However, Teitelbaum and Alan Epstein showed that animals with neuronal destruction in a different but nearby area of the hypothalamus (Figure 14.5) show the same effect as do those animals that undergo electrical stimulation of the ventromedial area: They, too, completely stop eating. Animals with such damage starve to death, unless they are fed intravenously until other areas of the brain develop the capability to induce eating.

These related effects for the two areas of the hypothalamus have led to the simple idea that eating is controlled by a balance in activity between the two areas. When an animal is in need of food, the second area, called the **excitatory** area, makes the animal hungry. After the animal has eaten, internal stimuli such as stomach fullness and a rise in blood sugar signal the ventromedial area, the **inhibitory** area, to inhibit the second area and turn off hunger and eating. This notion of balanced "excitatory" and "inhibitory" centers, first proposed by Eliot Stellar in 1954, has been a popular one in physiological psychology for two decades. Newer techniques, however, suggest that matters may not be that simple.

Recent Chemical Research After surgical damage to part of the brain, major chemical changes may take place throughout the rest of the brain. In particular, according to J. Eric Ahlskog and Bartley Hoebel, damage to either of the two hypothalamic areas affecting hunger results in chemical changes throughout the rest of the brain: Neural pathways that pass through these areas of the hypothalamus produce chemicals in other parts of the brain. Richard Gold has suggested that hypothalamic damage affects animals' eating patterns because of these chemical changes; the chemical alterations following removal of one of the areas in the hypothalamus cause widespread changes throughout the brain, and it is these changes that are responsible for the changes in eating patterns. This line of reasoning is supported by recent experiments showing that despite hypothalamic damage, if the lost chemicals are replaced, the damaged animals eat normally.

In sum, the areas in the hypothalamus that affect eating seem to do so by affecting the level of certain chemicals in the brain. It appears to be these chemicals that produce or inhibit hunger and thereby normally maintain a homeostatic energy balance in the body.

Thirst and Water Balance

The principal constituent of all cells is water. Living tissue depends on water for all physiological processes. Water is continually leaving the body in sweat, urine, and exhaled air, and so the organism must take in fluids to maintain its water balance. Just as with hunger, there are physiological mechanisms that produce thirst and drinking and thus maintain a homeostatic equilibrium of water in the body.

Stimuli Initiating Drinking Three types of stimuli induce thirst and drinking in mammals. The first is an **increase in salt concentration** in the various fluid compartments of the body—inside cells, around cells, and in the blood. There seem to be specialized cells in the hypothalamus that detect this change in salt concentration. Activation of these cells results in thirst and then drink-

Figure 14.12 Tiny tubes called cannulae have been implanted in this rat's brain so that their ends are in a precisely known location. This procedure allows experimenters to circulate liquids at various temperatures or solutions of various chemicals through that portion of the animal's brain. Because the rat is healthy and free to move, the effects of such stimulation on its behavior can be easily studied.

ing. Bengt Andersson discovered the location of these cells by implanting small tubes into various areas of the brain and stimulating those areas with salt solutions injected through the tubes. Only in certain areas do such injections result in the animal's beginning to drink (Figure 14.12).

J. T. Fitzsimons discovered that another stimulus resulting in drinking is a **decrease in the volume of fluid** in the circulatory system. No change in chemical concentration is involved here, simply a volume decrease, such as results from hemorrhage. Hemorrhage causes a very intense thirst.

Fitzsimons more recently has discovered the mechanism whereby a change in blood volume is sensed by the brain and results in drinking; the mechanism provides an illustration of how the entire body can get involved in a drive. All blood is filtered through the kidneys. If a kidney senses a reduction in blood volume, it releases a chemical that alters the structure of a substance in the blood. This altered substance then acts directly on several portions of the hypothalamus to elicit drinking.

The third major stimulus to thirst is an **increase in exercise or body temperature.** The mechanism involved is probably identical to that involving the cells in the hypothalamus that sense a change in salt concentration. Both exercise and increased body temperature result in sweating, which cools the body but also takes water from the blood. With less water, the concentration of salt in the blood becomes higher, since the same amount of salt is dissolved in less water. This high salt concentration excites the salt-sensing cells and results in drinking.

Satiation of Thirst   Thirst and drinking seem to stop long before enough time has passed for the body to have absorbed the water from the stomach and for the equilibrium in the blood to have been restored. One of the stimuli that causes drinking to stop is stomach distension, a sense of fullness. Edward Deaux has suggested that the reason cold water satisfies thirst more quickly than warm water does is that cold water moves out of the stomach much more slowly than does warm water and thus provides a clearer stomach-distension signal to the brain.

Stomach-distension signals are not the only ones involved in satiety, however. In 1939 R. T. Bellows showed that if a dog is allowed to drink freely but the water it drinks is prevented from reaching its stomach (because the water is diverted out through an incision made in its neck for experimental purposes), the dog does not drink continuously. It takes in some water and then stops drinking. Soon the dog begins again but then stops again. It seems as if there is some "mouth metering" mechanism that gauges the amount being ingested and compares that amount with the amount needed to restore the water balance. If the internal need is not corrected, the internal stimuli then override the mouth messages and the animal begins drinking again. But the mouth meter is not essential to maintaining a correct water balance either.

Alan Epstein has shown that animals can learn to press a bar and deliver spurts of water directly into their stomachs and regulate their water balance adequately. Clearly, the process of thirst is monitored by several different physiological mechanisms. These mechanisms allow the animal to have a number of different ways of feeling the need for water, and so it is more likely to maintain the proper homeostatic balance.

Brain Mechanisms   A great deal more is known about the brain mechanisms involved in the initiation of drinking than about those involved in its termination. As was mentioned earlier, injection of salty solutions into certain hypothalamic areas causes drinking. Also, ablation of one particular hypothalamic area leads to an enormous increase in water intake. A simple mechanism, having to do with normal water balance, is involved. Normally, water is filtered out of the blood by the kidneys, and some of it is not reabsorbed but leaves the body in the urine. The part of the hypothalamus in question produces a hormone that normally causes the kidney to reabsorb much of the water and return it to the blood. Damage to that part of the hypothalamus stops production of the hormone, and so the kidney excretes great amounts of water.

In addition to the area that produces this hormone, other parts of the hypothalamus have been implicated in the control of thirst and drinking. For example, the lesions of the hypothalamus that lead to a reduction of eating also cause a depression of drinking.

NONHOMEOSTATIC DRIVES

In addition to hunger and thirst, which are clearly homeostatic drives, there are drives that are not homeostatic. These drives do not seem to arise as the result of a homeostatic imbalance. Nevertheless, they are drives in that they energize and direct specific goal-oriented behaviors. Sex and parental behavior are two of the nonhomeostatic drives that physiological psychologists have investigated most.

Sex

Sexual activity does not arise as an effort to correct some biological imbalance. There have been no bodily changes found to occur with increasing abstinence that might stimulate sexual behavior; there seems to be no homeostatic mechanism for sex. Rather, it seems that biology provides the necessary backdrop for sexual activity but that its actual occurrence depends on the power of arousing stimuli in the environment. Without such stimuli there might well be no sexual behavior. Thus, the sexual drive is not homeostatic in the same sense that hunger and thirst are.

Physiological psychologists are interested in a number of questions about the sex drive. What, for example, is the role of sex hormones in the development and maintenance of differences between males and females? Are hormones necessary for the arousal of sexual desire and for satisfactory performance? What changes occur in the body during sexual arousal, intercourse, and orgasm? Are there cycles of sexual desire that coincide with the female menstrual cycle?

The Role of Hormones   A hormone secreted by the testes (the male sex glands) is critical in the differentiation of male and female sexual anatomy very early in the process of embryonic development. Its presence causes the embryo in the womb to develop male organs (penis, scrotum, vas deferens, prostate, and seminal vesicles)—even in genetic females: That is, if a genetically female embryo is exposed to the male hormone, it will develop male organs. In the absence of this hormone, the female organs (uterus, vagina, clitoris, and labia) develop from the same tissues; even a genetic male will develop female organs if not exposed to the male hormone at the proper time.

Are differences in human sexual behavior determined in the same fashion as are the differences in human sexual anatomy? Anke Ehrhardt and Ralph Epstein, working with John Money, analyzed children's activities and fantasies and concluded that girls exposed to male sex hormones prenatally are closer to boys in these activities than are girls not exposed to such hormones. However, it is not clear that such "masculinization" of behavior is a direct result of the male hormone. These girls usually have abnormal genitals (in particular, an enlarged clitoris); and their parents have been informed that these abnormalities were caused by the prenatal male hormone. Money reports that the parents worry about the long-term effects of the prenatal hormone, and their worry may well be communicated to their daughters. Money himself argues that a main, if not *the* main, contribution to a person's gender identity is unambiguous messages about whether one is a boy or a girl.

Given all the factors that can contribute to sex-role behavior in humans (not the least important of which are the widely varying cultural definitions of appropriate masculine and feminine behavior, discussed in Chapter 21), the general consensus is that biological factors probably play a small role.

If sex hormones do not have much direct effect on human sex-role behavior in general, are they nevertheless necessary for the behaviors involved in sexual intercourse? Eliminating the normal sex hormones by removing the testes or ovaries of adult animals has different effects in different species and in males and females. In rats it is followed by a relatively rapid cessation of all sexual behavior in both males and females, although sexual behavior can be restored if hormone injections are given. In cats and monkeys, females rarely show sexual receptivity after removal of the ovaries. Males who have had sexual experience prior to castration often continue to display sexual behavior, but males without sexual experience do not.

Human beings show greater freedom from the controlling influence of hormones than even experienced male cats and monkeys. Sexual desire and activity (usually masturbation) are frequent even before hormonal levels become high (during puberty). Furthermore, many sexually experienced men and women who have had their gonads removed in adulthood for medical reasons report no postoperative diminution in sexual desire or potency. Others, who perhaps were led to expect that they should experience a decline, do report a lessening of interest, ability, or both. Both men and women report increased desire after they have received injections of hormones for a variety of medical reasons, so hormones can play a role. But they do not seem to be necessary for human sexuality in experienced adults.

In women and girls, there are cyclical changes in hormones that are correlated with changes in the menstrual cycle. Are there any parallel changes in sexual desire? Female rats and cats—which do not menstruate but do show a similar hormonal cycle, called the **estrus** cycle—show sexual interest *only* at the peak of the cycle, when levels of hormones are high and fertilization is possible. In some species of subhuman primates, particularly chimpanzees, sexual behavior is less tightly tied to hormonal control, and females may show receptivity throughout their menstrual cycle. Studies of human females are, at this point, contradictory. Women vary in what part of the cycle they report highest levels of desire: Some say just before menstruation, others say around the time of ovulation, and so on. Some report no noticeable peak at all. No cycle of sexual desire has been demonstrated in human males.

Physiology of Arousal and Orgasm The research of William Masters and Virginia Johnson, published in 1966, has provided, for the first time, detailed knowledge of the physiology, especially the genital physiology, of human

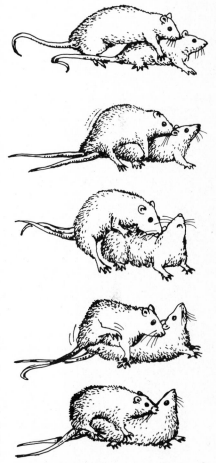

Figure 14.13 Copulation by the rat is accomplished in a series of highly stereotyped behaviors characteristic of each sex. Gordon Bermant describes these behaviors: The female will assume the arched receptive posture shown here only at the peak of her estrus cycle. The male's activity progresses invariably through a series of several mountings each followed by one or two penetrations and withdrawals. After three or four mountings, he ejaculates.

sexual response. Masters and Johnson used anatomical measurements, analysis of motion-picture films of both internal and external genital changes during sexual activity, and measurements of heart rate, blood flow, and breathing. They found that the sexual-response cycle of both men and women could be divided into **four phases:** excitement, plateau, orgasm, and resolution, although not everyone showed precisely the same physiological changes during the various phases.

During the excitement phase, heart rate and respiration generally increase. Women's breasts may change in size; the vagina becomes lubricated. In both men and women, blood flows into the genitals, resulting in erection of the penis and some swelling of the comparable structure in the female, the clitoris. There is also some rising of the testes in the scrotal sac.

In the plateau phase the clitoris draws back into its hood and can no longer be directly observed or contacted (although, like the glans of the penis, it remains the woman's single most sensitive area). Blood continues to flow into the genitals until maximal engorgement is reached in both male and female. The innermost part of the vagina expands, and the uterus rises slightly within the abdomen. The glans of the penis enlarges. Some fluid seeps out of the penis, and although ejaculation has not yet occurred, it may contain active sperm. Arousal and excitement, which have been rising throughout the first two stages, reach a high point at the end of the plateau phase, and a feeling of the inevitability of orgasm sweeps over the individual.

The orgasm is a relatively brief response in both males and females. During orgasm, muscular contractions cause the genitals, which have been filling with blood, to expel the blood forcefully back into the bloodstream. In the female there are contractions of the outer third of the vagina and contractions of the uterus. In the male there are contractions of the major muscles in the groin (and smaller contractions of minor muscles in the penis) and also contractions of various semen-producing structures, causing the forceful ejaculation of semen and sperm. The muscular contractions and the expulsion of blood from the genitals back into the bloodstream are the essential physiological changes during orgasm in both sexes—the ejaculation of the male is separate and actually is not essential to the experience of orgasm.

During resolution, the body gradually returns to the unaroused state. Men experience a "refractory period" that must elapse before additional arousal is possible. Many women, however, report that they can have multiple orgasms within a short period of time after their first one. The human response cycle is shown in Figure 14.14.

Whether animals experience anything like the human orgasmic experience is not known. However, C. A. Fox and Beatrice Fox found that heart rate and

Figure 14.14 Graphs summarizing Masters and Johnson's description of coitus in the human male and female. The four phases are defined in terms of measurable physiological changes. In both sexes excitement leads to a plateau phase that may be maintained for considerable periods without orgasm. The male has only one pattern of response after this: He ejaculates quickly in orgasm and his arousal decreases rapidly. There is a period after his ejaculation, the refractory period, in which he is incapable of another ejaculation. He may repeat the orgasmic phase several times before returning to an unaroused state. The female may variously have one orgasm or several orgasms in succession (line A), not achieve orgasm at all and return relatively slowly to an unaroused state (line B), or, rarely, have a single prolonged orgasm followed by rapid resolution (line C).

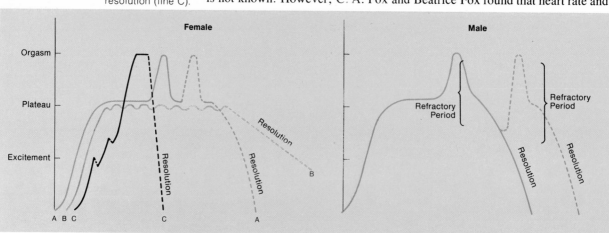

respiratory measurements of copulating animals do suggest a peak of excitement that often coincides with a vocal cry, as sometimes occurs with humans.

Brain Research Concerning Sex Some investigators have looked for brain mechanisms underlying sexual behavior and the effects of sex hormones. Scientists have recently shown that sex hormones affect many areas of the brain, especially parts of the hypothalamus. Little is known, however, about what goes on during actual sexual arousal and activity. Sexual reflexes (such as erection, ejaculation, and postural movements indicating sexual receptivity in females of lower species) can occur independently of brain activity—they occur even in animals and people with damaged or severed spinal cords. Frank Beach has suggested that the role of the brain in sexual behavior is to inhibit the activity of these reflexes until appropriate stimuli signal the brain to remove the inhibition. This role can cause emotions such as fear or embarrassment to interfere with sexual processes, as some people are all too aware.

Parental Behavior

The desire of a parent to protect its young can serve as a powerful motive. Most research on the biological factors controlling and influencing this behavior has been done with female subjects, an investigative imbalance that presumably will be remedied because of the growing recognition that child rearing involves males as well as females in both human and many nonhuman societies.

Animal experimentation has focused on the relationship of hormones to such behaviors as nest building, nursing, and retrieving young. Very little attention has been directed to the role of the brain in integrating the various components of parental care. Many experiments show a link between female hormones and the female's readiness to engage in certain types of parental behavior. However, both females with their ovaries removed and males can engage in the same kinds of parental behavior if exposed to the appropriate young.

The parental drive in some ways may be the most powerful of all drives, at least as judged by an apparatus measuring "drive strength" popular in the 1920s and 1930s (shown in Figure 14.15). If an animal is separated from its goal by an electrified floor, the amount of shock it will tolerate to reach the goal can be used to gauge motivation. In 1931, Carl Warden reported that female rats would tolerate more foot shock to reach their pups than to reach any other goals, including food and water, and the level they would tolerate was higher than males would tolerate for any goal. Whether this "drive strength" applies to other species or even to other situations is unknown.

THE PHYSIOLOGY OF EMOTION

We would have a hard time believing that a person who simply sat quietly was experiencing extreme emotion. We might believe that he or she was remembering, learning, or thinking about something, but not experiencing an extreme emotion. We expect people to reveal their emotions through overt behaviors and bodily changes.

Why are our emotional experiences so tied to overt behaviors and bodily changes? Are there demonstrably different body states for each different emotion? These are questions that physiological psychologists are attempting to answer and that are discussed in this chapter. Questions about emotional experience and expression are more generally discussed in Chapter 15.

The Role of the Autonomic Nervous System

The autonomic nervous system is the part of the peripheral nervous system mentioned earlier that controls the glands, internal organs, and involuntary

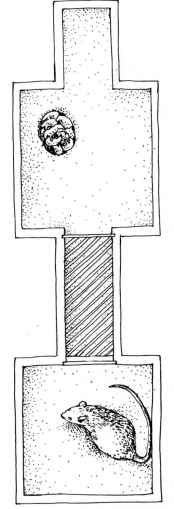

Figure 14.15 The Columbia obstruction box. By placing the subject in one end of the box and a goal in the other end and varying the intensity of shock on the intervening grid, researchers are able to measure the strengths of various drives.

Figure 14.16   The interactions of neural, endocrine, and other bodily structures in emotion. This diagram is a simplified representation of what is known about the complex systems involved in the physiology of emotion. Orange areas and arrows indicate neural structures and the transmission of information by action potentials in neurons. Broken orange arrows indicate that the transmission is not the sending of specific messages to specific locations but is diffuse and acts to change general levels of activation. Blue areas and arrows indicate endocrine structures and the transmission of information by chemicals in the bloodstream. Note that certain organs—the hypothalamus, the pituitary gland, and part of the adrenal gland—act as transducers between neural and chemical modes of transmission; that is, they receive one kind of transmission and send out the other. Note also that the system is organized in such a way that a structure often receives information from the structures to which it is sending information. This feedback arrangement is important to the control and stability of the system as a whole.

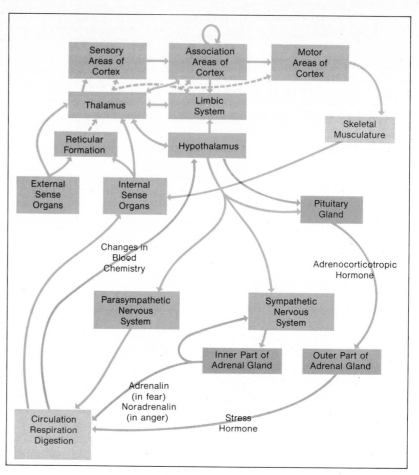

muscles; it is of critical importance in the physiology of emotion. The autonomic nervous system has two divisions, the parasympathetic and the sympathetic, which, in many instances (though not always), work in opposition to one another. Activation of the **sympathetic system** tends to prepare the body for dealing with emergencies or strenuous activities: for example, speeding up the heart to hasten the supply of oxygen and nutrients; dilating arteries going to the muscles and constricting those to the digestive organs and skin, thus sending blood where it is needed most; and increasing the breathing rate. The **parasympathetic system,** by contrast, tends to conserve energy and enhance the recuperative activities of the body. It reduces the heart rate and breathing rate and routes blood to the digestive system, for example. Figure 14.16 illustrates how these systems interact with the central nervous system, the endocrine system, and other organs.

Much research has addressed the question whether there are unique patterns of autonomic activity for each emotion or whether the same changes occur during fear and anger and embarrassment, and maybe even during the joyful emotions. A recent review by Peter Lang and his colleagues in 1972 suggests that there are reliable differences between the autonomic patterns shown in fear, anger, the startle response, hunger, and pain; differences among the more subtle emotions have not been demonstrated consistently. Equally interesting is that there are consistent differences between individuals in autonomic responding. People can be classified according to how they respond in emotional situations. Some people respond with an all-out autonomic arousal to every emotional situation, others respond very little to any emotional situation, still others respond greatly in some situations and only slightly in others. Scientific classifications simply substantiate what people have known for centuries—that there are definite emotional types of individuals.

Stress and Psychosomatic Illness

The various autonomic changes that occur as an immediate reaction to a threat help the organism mobilize for action—either fight or flight. Such threatening stimuli as extreme cold, lack of food, a predator, a coming examination, a divorce, or loss of blood resulting from injury are all considered types of **stress.** Often one can deal with stress on a short-term basis, either by avoiding it or by coping with it effectively. However, there are many real-life occasions (some of which can be duplicated in the laboratory) when stress is prolonged. How do we cope with such prolonged emotional challenges?

Hans Selye has argued that all types of prolonged stress evoke identical physiological responses. Whether the stress is extreme cold or prolonged fear, the body reacts with immediate sympathetic arousal, as described earlier. In addition, the endocrine system also releases hormones that produce sustained effects similar to the briefer effects of sympathetic arousal. A hormone from the pituitary gland activates one part of each **adrenal gland,** which secretes hormones that cause an increase in the availability of blood sugar for energy. At the same time the brain sends a message through the autonomic nervous system directly to another part of each adrenal gland, and as a result the gland releases **adrenalin.** Adrenalin causes an increase in energy use by the body, an increase in heart rate and respiration, and other bodily changes all designed to provide the organism with adequate energy to defend itself against the stressful situation. If the stress persists for a long time, the body's resources become depleted, and the animal eventually succumbs to exhaustion and death.

Prolonged stress is probably involved in initiating such psychosomatic diseases as ulcers, high blood pressure, asthma, and spastic colon. (A **psychosomatic disease** is one in which the initial problem is a psychological one, which in turn produces a physical ailment.)

Much animal research has focused on ulcer development. In an experiment by Joseph Brady, two monkeys were linked together so that they received an equal number of electric shocks, but one had the power to prevent the shocks by pressing a lever at appropriate times and the other did not. The monkey that could prevent the shocks (called the "executive" monkey) later devel-

Figure 14.17 The apparatus in which Brady subjected monkeys to six-hour sessions of repeated shocks. The beam of plexiglass at the level of the monkey's neck is part of the restraining chair in which it is sitting. The metal box in the foreground of the last photograph houses a button that some of the monkeys could use to keep postponing the shocks. Brady's famous finding that the availability of a working button promoted the development of ulcers has been questioned recently. It is now thought that uncertainty rather than decision making itself contributed to ulcer formation in the "executive" monkeys.

oped ulcers. The other monkey, who presumably suffered as much from receiving the electric shocks but did not have to worry about when to press the lever, did not develop ulcers (Figure 14.17).

In more recent research, Jay Weiss has suggested that ulcers develop in situations where an individual makes many responses but receives no feedback about whether those responses are correct or incorrect. In Brady's study, Weiss argues, the "executives" developed ulcers primarily because they were never sure if they had made the correct response to avoid the shock. (In addition, the monkeys that Brady chose to be "executives" were specifically picked because they made large numbers of responses and so were more susceptible to ulcers than the monkeys in the other group, who made fewer responses.) According to Weiss, ulcers develop because the lack of feedback produces uncertainty, and uncertainty is stressful. One might extend this reasoning to a group of people infamous for getting ulcers: human executives. The ones who get ulcers are probably those who do not know for years what the results of their work will be or those who never quite know where they stand with their superiors.

Stress of various sorts is unavoidable. Physiological responses to stress, as we have seen, can assist in coping or can ultimately cause physical harm if the stress continues too long.

SUMMARY

1. Physiological psychology is the area of psychology that studies the workings of the body that accompany thinking and acting. The two body systems that are most important to psychology are the **nervous system** and the **endocrine system.**

2. Messages to and from the brain travel along **nerves,** which are composed of cells called **neurons.**

    a. A neuron is composed of a **cell body,** which absorbs nutrients and uses them to provide energy for the neuron's activity; **axons,** which carry messages from the neuron to other neurons; and **dendrites,** which receive messages from other neurons and transmit them to the cell body.

    b. When a chemical-electrical signal travels down the length of a neuron, the neuron is said to be **firing.** If the firing, or message, is strong enough, the firing goes through the axons and the message is usually carried to the dendrite of another neuron.

    c. There are gaps between the axons of one cell and an adjacent neuron; these gaps are called **synapses.** Messages cross the synapses by means of **transmitter** substances that are released by the axons and that affect the nearby neurons. Messages travel into the cell body of one of these adjacent neurons, usually through a dendrite (this is not "firing"). If messages from several of its dendrites arrive at the cell body, the neuron will then fire its axon.

    d. The electric charge that travels down an axon is called the **action potential.** It is always of the same strength—either an axon fires or it doesn't. The type of message occurring in the nerve is determined by the number of neurons firing at a time.

3. The **central nervous system (CNS)** is composed of the brain and the spinal cord, a bundle of nerves running down the length of the back, enclosed in the bone called the spinal column. Branching out from the CNS is the **peripheral nervous system,** which conducts messages from the organs to the CNS and back. The peripheral nervous system has two divisions: the **autonomic nervous system,** which controls such functions as digestion and heart rate, and the **somatic nervous system,** which controls the voluntary movement of skeletal muscles.

4. The **brain** monitors almost all physical and mental activities. It receives messages from **receptor** cells, such as those in the eyes and ears, sifts those messages and combines them, and then sends out messages to the **effectors,** cells that control the muscles, glands, and organs.

Figure 14.18 Sir John Eccles is one of the world's leading authorities on the physiology of the nervous system. His researches on the synapse won him a Nobel prize in 1963. When Eccles began his researches, there was much controversy about whether neurons excited one another across the synapse chemically or electrically (as impulses are transmitted within the neuron.) This was known as the "soup or spark" controversy, and Eccles reports that initially he (mistakenly) championed the "spark" theory. Eccles' studies of the neuron have led him to make some interesting speculations about consciousness: He believes that the nervous system may be so highly sensitive that free will can operate within it.

5. The part of the brain that receives messages first is the **old brain,** which is similar to the brains of more primitive creatures, such as fish and frogs. The part of the old brain affected is the reticular formation, which controls the **reticular activating system,** the brain's attention system. This system screens out some messages (during sleep, for instance) and alerts the brain to incoming messages. Other parts of the old brain include:

   a. the **thalamus,** which sorts incoming signals, relays them to the various parts of the brain, and also relays messages from one part of the brain to another;

   b. the **hypothalamus,** which regulates the autonomic nervous system;

   c. the **limbic system,** which somehow regulates emotional reactivity; and

   d. the **cerebellum,** which controls posture and balance and helps regulate the details of major commands from the new brain.

6. The new brain, or **cerebral cortex,** is wrapped around the old brain. This "gray matter" is full of folds. It is divided into **lobes** (see Figures 14.4 and 14.6), which have special functions.

   a. The cortex is made up of two **hemispheres,** connected by a band of nerves called the **corpus callosum.** Although the hemispheres appear to be identical, they seem to have different functions. For example, people who have suffered damage to the left hemisphere have difficulty with language, whereas this effect is rare for people with right-hemisphere damage.

   b. The left of the cortex controls mostly the right half of the body, and vice versa.

Figure 14.19 James Olds' discovery of "pleasure centers" in the brain was a major breakthrough in physiological psychology because it opened the possibility of understanding the psychological concept of reward in biological terms. Olds' experimental skill and exactness have won him wide recognition.

7. The **spinal cord** serves as a connecting link between brain and body and also controls some lower-level reflexes. Withdrawal of a hand that touches a flame is controlled by the spinal cord.

8. The **endocrine system,** which is controlled by the brain, is a chemical system composed of endocrine glands. The glands produce and release **hormones,** chemicals that travel through the circulatory system to the various organs whose activities they monitor.

   a. Hormones work to produce **homeostasis.** That is, deviations from a necessary level of a substance lead to processes that bring the level of that substance either up or down to the appropriate level.

   b. The **pituitary gland** and brain together control most of the homeostatic action of the endocrine system. The pituitary gland secretes a

Figure 14.20 Phillip Teitelbaum is known for his studies of the physiological mechanisms underlying motivation, particularly his work on the relationship between hypothalamic centers and feeding behavior. Teitelbaum is a consulting editor for the prestigious *Journal of Comparative and Physiological Psychology.*

large number of hormones, and many of these hormones control the output of hormones by other endocrine glands. The brain controls the release of pituitary hormones.

9. Psychologists study the brain by using one of three methods.

    a. They insert wires called **electrodes** into the brain and **record** the electrical activity that occurs when neurons fire. They can also attach electrodes to the scalp to record the electrical activity of whole areas of the brain; such recordings are called **electroencephalograms.**

    b. They can also use electrodes to make neurons fire in order to see what changes in behavior occur as a result of the **stimulation.** Chemicals can also be used for stimulation.

    c. They can cut out or destroy a part of an animal's brain to see what function that part plays in personality or behavior. In a **lesion** a small area is destroyed; in **ablation** a relatively large part is removed.

10. A key concept for understanding the basis of motivation is **drive,** a physiological state that arises from some physical **need** and that energizes and directs behavior. Certain drives are homeostatic.

    a. **Hunger** is one drive. Organisms require food for energy for all bodily functions. Psychologists have attempted to find the mechanism that operates to produce homeostasis in food intake. Although stomach contractions play some part, people without stomachs also experience hunger. The hypothalamus has been shown to play a part. There seem to be two areas in the hypothalamus that act together to maintain a homeostatic balance, an **excitatory** center and an **inhibitory** center. These areas seem to work by affecting the level of certain chemicals in the brain.

    b. **Thirst** is another drive, and the maintenance of a homeostatic equilibrium of water in the body is its object. Three types of stimuli initiate drinking: **increase in salt concentration, decrease in the volume of fluid** in the circulatory system, and **increase in exercise or body temperature.** A number of mechanisms cause drinking to stop: stomach distension, a mouth-metering mechanism, and some brain mechanisms, involving the hypothalamus.

11. There are a number of drives that are not homeostatic.

    a. The **sex drive** is biologically universal but also seems to depend on arousing stimuli in the environment. In humans hormones play some role in controlling sexual activity, but social and psychological factors seem to be most important.

    b. Masters and Johnson's research has detailed the physiological changes that occur during sexual intercourse. There are distinct changes that occur during each of the **four phases** of sexual response: excitement, plateau, orgasm, and resolution.

    c. **Parental behavior,** the desire of a parent to care for and protect its young, is also a nonhomeostatic drive. It is not clear what, if any, role hormones play in this behavior, but in some experiments it has proved to be the strongest of drives. Female rats endured greater electric shocks to get to their young than to reach any other goals, including food when they were hungry or water when they were thirsty.

12. Psychologists are attempting to find out whether different emotional states involve distinctive physiological changes.

a. They do know that the autonomic nervous system is involved. The autonomic nervous system has two divisions, which in many instances work in opposition to each other: The **sympathetic system** is activated to prepare the body to deal with emergencies or strenuous activity; it speeds up heart rate, dilates arteries going to the muscles, and increases rate of breathing. The **parasympathetic system** is activated to conserve energy; it reduces heart rate and breathing rate and routes blood to the digestive system. There seem to be reliable differences between autonomic patterns of activity during fear, anger, the startle response, hunger, and pain. Also, there are consistent differences between individuals in autonomic responses to the same kinds of stimuli.

b. Autonomic changes help an organism mobilize for flight or fight in the face of threatening stimuli. Sometimes, however, the stimuli are long-lasting, and the organism suffers **stress.** In stressful situations, the **adrenal gland** secretes **adrenalin,** a hormone that causes increased use of energy by the body, an increase in heart rate and respiration, and other bodily changes designed to increase energy levels. Because under prolonged stress the body uses a great deal of energy to keep defending itself, its resources become depleted, and exhaustion—even death—can ensue. Prolonged stress probably causes such **psychosomatic diseases** as ulcers. In a psychosomatic disease, the initial problem is a psychological one and it, in turn, causes a physical ailment.

Figure 14.21 Frank Beach has long been one of the most respected investigators of the neurophysiology and endocrinology of animal behavior, particularly sexual behavior. He has also written a classic cross-cultural analysis of human sexual behavior. Beach has on several occasions criticized trends in American studies of animal behavior. In a paper titled *The Snark Was a Boojum* he chided his colleagues for concentrating their researches more and more exclusively on one species, the white rat, as though its behavior were a perfect model for human behavior. In another paper, *The Descent of Instinct,* he predicted that the efforts of learning theorists to dispose entirely of the concept of innateness in behavior were doomed to failure.

SUGGESTED READINGS

Delgado, José M. R. *Physical Control of the Mind: Toward a Psychocivilized Society.* New York: Harper & Row, 1969. Readable (and chilling) survey of electrical-stimulation work with animals and humans by one of the leaders in the field.

French, Gilbert M. *Cortical Functioning in Behavior: Research and Commentary.* Glenview, Ill.: Scott, Foresman, 1973. Up-to-date readings and commentary dealing with current views on localization of function within the cortex.

Kimble, Daniel P. *Psychology as a Biological Science.* Pacific Palisades, Calif.: Goodyear, 1973. A readable elementary introduction to physiological psychology.

Luce, Gay G. *Body Time: Physiological Rhythms and Social Stress.* New York: Pantheon, 1971. Survey of data and theories on how biological rhythms affect behavior and mental life.

Stevens, Charles F. *Neurophysiology: A Primer.* New York: Wiley, 1966. An elegant little book with every detail one could want on exactly how individual neurons work and communicate with one another.

Williams, Moyra. *Brain Damage and the Mind.* Baltimore: Penguin, 1970. A readable account of all the different types of brain damage and their consequent psychological impairments.

Wooldridge, Dean E. *The Machinery of the Brain.* New York: McGraw-Hill, 1963. Basic physiological psychology with many illustrations from animal life and from computer science. (The author is a former administrator and businessperson who is greatly fascinated by the brain.)

As an "expert" on robots—and I put the word in quotes because the supposed expertise is based only on the fact that I write about them and not that I know anything about them—I am frequently challenged on my expressed belief that robots have the potentiality of being as good as human beings, or, in fact, better. One of the challenges is to the effect that human beings can demonstrate emotion, while robots cannot, and in that way robots are basically different from human beings and therefore (presumably) basically inferior.

Many years ago, I discussed the matter with John W. Campbell, the late editor of *Astounding Science Fiction,* where my robot stories appeared.

He said, "Why do *you* feel fear sometimes, Isaac?"

Being a materialist, I said, "Because my adrenal glands pump adrenalin into my bloodstream and I then undergo the physiological changes that produce the effects we call 'fear.' I pant because my breathing accelerates; I turn pale because my blood withdraws from my skin and concentrates in my muscles; I tremble because my muscle tone increases. I need all that for rapid flight or other strenuous activity."

John said, "Does the adrenalin pump because you are afraid, or are you afraid because the adrenalin pumps?"

I said, "The adrenalin is first discharged; then I am afraid."

"What makes it discharge?"

"The sight, sound, or other perception of something that can harm or hurt me."

"If you turn a corner and see a snarling, crouching lion, would the adrenalin start pumping at once at the sight?"

"Absolutely," I said.

"And if you are at the zoo and turn a corner and see a snarling, crouching lion behind bars, would the adrenalin start pumping at once at the sight?"

"No," I said, chagrined.

"In other words, you are afraid only when you consciously consider what you perceive, and you decide to be afraid as the best way of keying your body to its work, and you use the adrenalin as your tool."

"You make it sound so," I said.

"And suppose you could increase your oxygen supply without panting, and feed blood to your muscles without withdrawing it from your face, and tighten your muscles without making them tremble. Wouldn't you have all the effectiveness for action that fear brings and yet not *look* afraid? And if you didn't look afraid, would anyone know you were afraid? Isn't what we call fear merely the *look* of fear? And if a robot could make all the internal adjustments needed for the kind of rapid action that should bring about escape from the presence of something potentially destructive, but was not designed to have anything visible result in his face or body, would he not have all the value of fear without looking afraid, and would we not then judge him not to be *displaying* emotion? But how important is it that the physiology of fear be visible as far as analyzing a brain's capacity is concerned? And do robots lack emotion just because you can't see that emotion?"

The answers were all obvious. I have rarely been so Socratically demolished.

Isaac Asimov

15
Emotional Experience and Expression

Figure 15.1 If you look intently at this photograph for a minute, you may find that it touches you. Clowns are supposed to make us laugh, and we assume they are joyous or at least light-hearted people. Yet there is no make-up that can mask the eyes' expression of emotion. And if this man's expression touched you, you felt an emotion. Psychologists who study emotion are interested in how people perceive the emotions of others and in how a person learns to name his own emotions. They are also interested in describing the changes that take place in a person when he feels an emotion.

Surely emotion, not variety, is the spice of life—though the two are obviously related. Imagine how dull and mechanical we would be if we had no feelings—if we never fell in love, burst into tears, or got angry. Here is how William James, one of the first psychologists to offer a systematic theory of the emotions, described the powerful role emotions play in human experience:

Conceive yourself, if possible, suddenly stripped of all the emotion with which your world now inspires you, and try to imagine it *as it exists,* purely by itself, without your favorable or unfavorable, hopeful or apprehensive comment. It will be almost impossible for you to realize such a condition of negativity and deadness. No one portion of the universe would then have importance beyond another; and the whole collection of its things and series of its events would be without significance, character, expression, or perspective. Whatever of value, interest, or meaning our respective worlds may appear endued with are thus pure gifts of the spectator's mind. The passion of love is the most familiar and extreme example of this fact. If it comes, it comes; if it does not come, no process of reasoning can force it. Yet it transforms the value of the creature loved as utterly as the sunrise transforms Mont Blanc from a corpse-like gray to a rosy enchantment; and it sets the whole world to a new tune for the lover and gives a new issue to his life. So with fear, with indignation, jealousy, ambition, worship. If they are there, life changes. And whether they shall be there or not depends almost always upon nonlogical, often on organic conditions.

James read and thought about the entire gamut of human emotions and then, in his monumental *The Principles of Psychology,* published in 1890, he attempted to synthesize the best theoretical ideas available at the time. Because James was an engaging writer, and because his theory is a major conceptual predecessor of contemporary theories of emotion, quotations from his books will be used as reference points throughout this chapter: It is interesting to see how far the psychology of emotions has come since James' 1890 version.

THE DIVERSITY OF HUMAN EMOTIONS

A reasonable discussion of any psychological phenomenon ought to begin with a definition, but no clear definition of emotion has yet been agreed upon. Psychologists are often guilty of confounding introspective knowledge with objective or behavioral indices when defining psychological processes; such confounding is especially common in writing about emotions. We all know what it feels like to be angry, jealous, depressed, or happy, and psychologists tend to rely on this knowledge when defining emotions. In many textbooks, an emotion is defined as a "feeling" of some kind. The reader should immediately ask: "All right, then, what's a feeling?" If pressed in this way, the writer would be forced to admit that he is relying on the reader's experience.

Of course, there is nothing wrong with the use of subjective reports in the study of emotion. As the chapter introduction by Isaac Asimov suggests, in some cases emotion may be present without showing itself in either expressions or actions. Because psychologists want to know about how people experience emotions, as well as how emotion is reflected in their behavior, they have devised special rating scales and measurement techniques for obtaining **systematic subjective reports.** Nevertheless, psychology would probably not have progressed much from 1890 to the present if it had relied only on subjective accounts. Philosophers from Aristotle to Sartre have analyzed emotions from a more or less subjective point of view, and there is no reason to believe that psychologists could improve on their analyses without the benefit of new methods.

Fortunately, it is possible to agree on **behavioral indicators** of many emotions. If Mary punches someone in the stomach while alternately gritting her teeth and then screaming, most of us would agree that she is angry. If you think about how you first learned to use the words "angry," "happy," and "worried," you will realize that situational and behavioral cues *must* have been involved; otherwise, no one could have taught you how to identify the state that goes with each label.

In addition, as we shall see, psychologists can make **physiological measures** of changes associated with emotional experience, such as changes in heart rate, resistance of the skin to the flow of a small electric current (called galvanic skin response, or GSR), and muscle contraction. These indicators can be measured quite precisely; no doubt you have heard of "lie detectors," which take advantage of this fact.

Reports of experience, observations of behavior, and physiological assessment—these are the major sources of psychologists' information concerning emotions. William James had at least crude versions of these sources available to him in 1890. What conclusions did he draw from them? First of all, he concluded that if we were to make up a list of all the emotions people experience and study the organic manifestations of these emotions, the list would be almost endless and without apparent coherence:

Rigidity of this muscle, relaxation of that, constriction of arteries here, dilatation there, breathing of this sort or that, pulse slowing or quickening, this gland secreting and that one dry, etc., etc. We should, moreover, find . . . that every one of us, almost, has some personal idiosyncrasy of expression, laughing, or sobbing differently from his neighbor. . . . The internal shadings of emotional feelings, moreover, merge endlessly into each other. Language has discriminated some of them, as hatred, antipathy, animosity, dislike, aversion, malice, spite, vengefulness, abhorrence, etc., etc.; but in the dictionaries of synonyms we find these feelings distinguished more by their severally appropriate objective stimuli than by their conscious or subjective tone.

Figure 15.2 What is this man feeling? The scene in the photograph on the next page provides the answer.

Much progress has been made in reducing the many emotion words to a few basic dimensions, as is discussed in the next section, but the thrust of James' criticism still applies. Eighty-five years after his book was written, psychologists still cannot define "emotion" clearly, although everyone agrees on what some of the important emotions are and on the fact that they have a potentially identifiable physiological basis. Many contemporary psychologists would agree with James that emotions are "distinguished more by their severally appropriate objective stimuli than by their conscious or subjective tone." That is, we often identify our own emotions and those of other people by inferring them from situational cues rather than by recognizing them directly.

Let us, then, begin our investigation of emotions humbly and honestly. There is no clearly agreed-upon definition that avoids both undefined subjective terms and a list of examples (fear, rage, humor, love). There are many, many emotions—all that we can name (hundreds) and many more that can be characterized only metaphorically (for example, "butterflies in the stomach"). Although many of these emotions have identifiable physiological and behavioral correlates, context is often as important as physiology and behavior to a psychologist trying to determine which emotion a person is experiencing. Can psychological research make any headway in this complex domain?

DIMENSIONS OF EMOTION

Granting that people may experience an almost unlimited range of emotional states, is it possible to group them into a few basic categories? There are several ways to seek an answer to this question, only two of which will be considered here. One way to organize emotions into categories is to ask people to rate the similarity of emotions expressed in photographs of faces. Another is to ask them to rate the similarity of emotion words like "fear" and "anger." Both methods have been tried experimentally and, fortunately, have yielded similar results.

Facial Expressions

In an early study, Jean Frois-Whitman asked a large number of people to characterize forty-six still photographs of faces by selecting terms from a list of emotion words. (As in most other studies of this kind, the photographs were taken while an actor attempted to portray the various emotions represented by the words.) In a similar study done in 1935, Wilbur Hulin and Daniel Katz eliminated the verbal responses, arguing that people might use emotion *words* differently even though they saw the same things in the photo-

Figure 15.3 The difficulty of judging the emotion expressed in Figure 15.2 is greatly reduced here. In addition to the cue of facial expression, other behavioral indicators and a knowledge of situational factors are provided in this photograph. An interview with the man about his subjective state, and recordings of such physiological measures as heart rate, breathing, and skin resistance would undoubtedly confirm the judgment that he is very angry.

graphs. They simply asked people to sort photos into piles representing "distinct types of facial expressions." In 1938, Robert Woodworth pointed out that the six categories usually obtained in studies of this kind could be ordered along a continuum ranging from "love" to "contempt." (Earlier investigators had simply reported the separate categories without much regard for their possible interrelations.) One of Woodworth's colleagues, Harold Schlosberg, carried this idea one step further in an important series of studies. He found that Woodworth's continuum could be shaped into a circle and that the circle was defined by two perpendicular dimensions: **pleasantness-unpleasantness** and **attention-rejection,** as shown in Figure 15.4.

In 1954 Schlosberg added a third dimension to the diagram, perpendicular to the other two, called **level of activation.** This dimension ran from "sleep" at one extreme to "tension" at the other. Schlosberg's idea was that emotions in each of the six categories could range from weak to strong. Thus, a complete pictorial representation of all the emotions would look something like the three-dimensional figure shown in Figure 15.5. The figure is shaped like a cone because differences between the various emotions diminish as degree of activation approaches the low point of sleep.

In 1962, Robert Plutchik conducted a study to see how the intensity or activation dimension is reflected in verbal descriptions of emotions. He presented subjects with lists of emotion words representing six emotional categories similar to Schlosberg's and asked them to rate the intensity of each emotion by giving it a number from 1 (weak) to 11 (strong). Representative results are presented in Figure 15.6.

Interesting as this kind of research is, there are several problems with it. First, most of the studies began with posed photographs, and the poses that the photographed people adopted were based on names of emotions. It might be more valid, although much more difficult, to base a study on naturally

Figure 15.4 The results of a study by Schlosberg using Frois-Whitman's photographs of an actor. Schlosberg asked subjects to name the emotion expressed in each photograph; he then grouped the photographs about which people had made similar errors. The arrangement shown here was the result. Schlosberg found it possible to explain the arrangement in terms of two dimensions of emotion.
(After Schlosberg, 1952.)

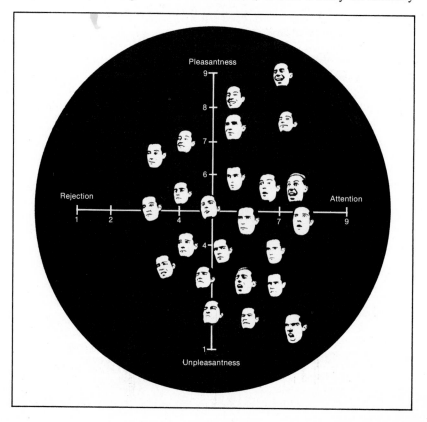

occurring expressions. Second, the number of photographs used was limited, and the categories discovered may be based to some extent on the particular photographs that subjects were shown. Third, studies that use words as stimuli for actors or as response categories for respondents may uncover a structure in the language people use to refer to emotions rather than a structure that is inherent in the emotions themselves. Finally, because the photographs show only faces and not contextual cues, studies using photographs tell us nothing about the role of context in the perception and classification of naturally occurring emotional expressions. Similarly, little is known so far about expressive gestures and postures, although these are cues to emotion currently being studied.

Despite these difficulties, the extensive research on facial expression of emotions does indicate that a coherent structure lies behind the diversity of emotional experiences and expressions. James was apparently unduly pessimistic when he ruled out this possibility. (It is worth noting that Wilhelm Wundt, the founder of experimental psychology, had proposed three dimensions similar to the ones discussed here, but James and other introspective psychologists did not put much stock in them.)

Emotion Words

As mentioned earlier, many emotions have been explicitly named, although there may be considerably more emotional states than there are labels in any natural language. How many such labels are there in English? In 1969 Joel Davitz found over 400 in *Roget's Thesaurus,* a source book for writers that lists synonyms of important words. He had forty people read through the list of 400 words, marking the ones that they personally might use to label an emotion. Over half the subjects agreed on a list of 137 words. Davitz then chose 50 of these ''on an intuitive basis to represent as wide and varied a range as possible of emotional states.'' Representative words include amusement, disgust, gratitude, impatience, reverence, and jealousy.

A check list of 556 phrases was then constructed, on the basis of written essays and interviews with people concerning particular emotional experiences. Each phrase represented a fragment of an emotional experience or behavior—for example: weakness across my chest; my hands are shaky; I'm jumpy, jittery; I feel hot and flushed; I feel dirty and ugly; I want to cry but I can't; I want to scream and yell; I'm afraid of the feeling; tears well up. Fifty new subjects then matched the 50 emotion words with phrases on the 556-item

Figure 15.5 This arrangement of labels of facial expressions of emotion includes one more dimension than the arrangement shown in Figure 15.4. This solid takes into account the effect of changes in activation, or arousal, on the judgment of facial expressions. The solid is cone-shaped because at low levels of activation little distinction among expressions is made on the dimensions of pleasantness-unpleasantness and attention-rejection.
(After Schlosberg, 1954.)

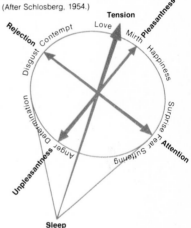

Figure 15.6 The results of Plutchik's analysis of emotion words. Plutchik theorized that there are eight primary emotional qualities, which can be related to Schlosberg's pleasantness-unpleasantness and attention-rejection dimensions. The form of this figure shows that Plutchik's data can be considered to form the sides of the emotion cone envisioned by Schlosberg, because the emotion words correspond to different levels of activation.
(After Plutchik, 1962.)

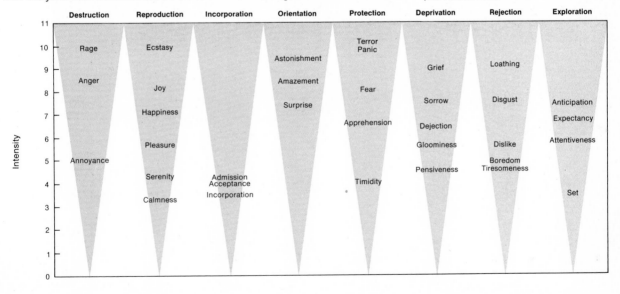

Table 15.1 A Structural Analysis of Emotional Meaning

Dimension	Clusters		
	Positive	Negative: Type 1	Negative: Type 2
Activation	Cluster 1: Activation	Cluster 2: Hypoactivation	Cluster 3: Hyperactivation
	A special lift in everything I do and say; I feel bouncy, springy	I feel empty, drained, hollow	My blood pressure goes up; blood seems to rush through my body
	A sense of lightness, buoyancy, and upsurge of the body	I feel tired, sleepy	There's an excitement, a sense of being keyed up, overstimulated, supercharged
	A strong sense of interest and involvement in things around me	I feel mentally dull	My heart pounds
Relatedness	Cluster 4: Moving Toward	Cluster 5: Moving Away	Cluster 6: Moving Against
	I want to help, protect, please another person	I want to withdraw, disappear, draw back, be alone, away from others, crawl into myself	There is an impulse to strike out, to pound or smash or kick or bite; to do something that will hurt
	Realization that someone else is more important to me than I am to myself	A feeling of a certain distance from others; everyone seems far away	Fists are clenched
	A sense of being wanted, needed	A sense of wandering, lost in space with nothing solid to grab onto	I keep thinking of getting even, of revenge
Hedonic Tone	Cluster 7: Comfort	Cluster 8: Discomfort	Cluster 9: Tension
	A feeling of warmth all over	An inner ache you can't locate	My whole body is tense
	A sense of being very integrated and at ease with myself, in harmony with myself	There is a sense of loss, of deprivation	A tight knotted feeling in my stomach
	A sense of smiling at myself	I feel as if I'm under a heavy burden	I'm easily irritated, ready to snap
Competence	Cluster 10: Enhancement	Cluster 11: Incompetence: Dissatisfaction	Cluster 12: Inadequacy
	I feel taller, stronger, bigger	Seems that nothing I do is right	A sense of being totally unable to cope with the situation
	A sense of more confidence in myself; a feeling that I can do anything	I get mad at myself for my feelings or thoughts or for what I've done	I feel vulnerable and totally helpless
	There is a sense of accomplishment, fulfillment	I keep blaming myself for the situation	I want to be comforted, helped by someone

Source: Joel R. Davitz, *The Language of Emotion* (New York: Academic Press, 1969).

check list. For example, the word "anger" was frequently matched with phrases like "Fists are clenched" and "I want to say something nasty." The result was a dictionary of 50 emotion words listing the phrases used by at least one-third of the subjects to describe each emotion.

Further analysis was performed to reduce the 50 words to a smaller number of clusters. Each of the twelve clusters obtained represented a concept with a coherent definition in terms of the items in the check list. Still further analysis revealed that the twelve clusters could be meaningfully arranged along four dimensions. Table 15.1 shows the clusters arranged along these dimensions and a few defining phrases for each cluster. Notice that three of the dimensions—**hedonic tone, relatedness,** and **activation**—are strikingly similar to Schlosberg's dimensions: pleasantness-unpleasantness, attention-rejection, and level of activation (or sleep-tension). Because Schlosberg's dimensions were derived from photographs and Davitz's from words, and both were based on careful and extensive analyses, we can be fairly confident that the dimensions reflect the basic structure of human emotions.

Indeed, other research indicates that these three dimensions may even represent the emotional connotations of words in general. Charles Osgood has used a technique called the **semantic differential** to investigate the connotations of words; people rate various words according to adjectives with opposite meanings. For example, the word "polite" may be rated on a scale between "big" and "small" and between "beautiful" and "ugly." Extensive research with the semantic differential shows that virtually all words are rated as having three kinds of connotations: evaluative connotations, active or passive connotations, and strong (potent) or weak connotations. "Polite" is rated as relatively good, active, and strong. These dimensions of emotional connotation identified by Osgood are essentially the same as the dimensions that Schlosberg identified in analyzing people's judgments of facial expressions: In Osgood's terms, pleasantness-unpleasantness would be the **evaluative dimension;** level of activation would be the **activity dimension;** and attention-rejection would be the **potency dimension.** Although the labels for the three dimensions used by Schlosberg, Davitz, and Osgood differ slightly, their meanings are essentially identical, especially for the evaluative dimension and the activity dimension. The disagreements over the exact meaning of the third dimension still remain to be resolved.

THEORIES OF EMOTION: THE OLD AND THE NEW

The procedures used by Schlosberg and Davitz provide a description of the structure of human emotions, but they do not tell us *why* this structure exists. A number of theorists have tried, over the years, to devise comprehensive explanations of emotion. Five theoretical approaches that have stimulated research will be reviewed in this chapter, beginning with the classical James-Lange and Cannon-Bard theories and concluding with three more recent approaches. Note that all five theories include some notion of physiological arousal, which probably corresponds to the activation dimension identified by Schlosberg and Davitz. The two most recent theories, however, also stress the role of cognitive interpretations in evoking emotions and in determining how people label them and behave under their influence. The three recent theories are not incompatible. In fact, it is quite possible that future work will result in a merging of these theories.

The James-Lange Theory

As mentioned previously, William James believed that the number of distinct emotions was vast and that merely cataloging them was a tedious and useless exercise; he wanted to give a general explanation of all emotional states. Having read other people's catalogs of the physiological processes involved in

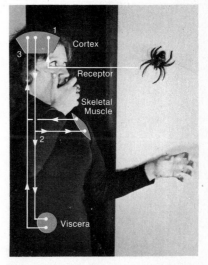

Figure 15.7 A schematic representation of the sequence of events that occur in the experience of an emotion according to the James-Lange theory. An emotion-eliciting event is sensed by a receptor (1) and is perceived in the cerebral cortex, but the event is not yet experienced emotionally. The cortex responds by activating the viscera and the skeletal muscles (2). These changes are, in turn, perceived in the cortex (3), and the original event is then experienced emotionally. As James put it: "The feeling of bodily changes as they occur *is* the emotion."

each emotion, he began with the assurance that "the general causes of the emotions are indubitably physiological." Most writers thought that events in the environment triggered a psychological state, the emotion, which in turn gave rise to bodily expression of the emotion. James disagreed:

My theory, on the contrary, is that *the bodily changes follow directly the perception of the exciting fact, and that our feeling of the same changes as they occur IS the emotion.* Common-sense says, we lose our fortune, are sorry and weep; we meet a bear, are frightened and run; we are insulted by a rival, are angry and strike. The hypothesis here to be defended says that this order of sequence is incorrect . . . and that the more rational statement is that we feel sorry because we cry, angry because we strike, afraid because we tremble . . . Without the bodily states following on the perception, the latter would be purely cognitive in form, pale, colorless, destitute of emotional warmth. We might then see the bear, and judge it best to run, receive the insult and deem it right to strike, but we should not actually *feel* afraid or angry.

James emphasized visceral reactions (that is, gut reactions) as central to emotional experiences. Writing at about the same time, a Dane named Carl Lange proposed a similar theory but emphasized vascular changes (changes in the blood pressure). Ever since, the view that perception of bodily changes *is* emotion has been called the **James-Lange theory of emotion.** Although there is considerable evidence against the theory, its spirit lives on in the currently dominant views of Stanley Schachter and George Mandler, discussed later in this chapter.

It is also noteworthy that James' theory could potentially account for the incredible diversity of emotions. In the following passage, James uses the word "reflex" broadly, to refer to all the involuntary bodily or muscular reactions associated with emotion:

Now the moment the genesis of an emotion is accounted for, as the arousal by an object of a lot of reflex acts which are forthwith felt, *we immediately see why there is no limit to the number of possible different emotions which may exist, and why the emotions of different individuals may vary indefinitely,* both as to their constitution and as to objects which call them forth. Any sort of reflex effect is possible, and reflexes actually vary indefinitely, as we know. . . . In short, *any classification of the emotions is seen to be as true and as "natural" as any other . . .*

Although we have already seen that James' final claim is incorrect (Schlosberg and Davitz have shown that some classifications of emotion are more "true" than others), the explanation of emotional variety is worth keeping in mind. Any complete theory will have to explain variety somehow.

The Cannon-Bard Theory

The James-Lange theory stimulated a great deal of research on emotions, much of it designed to disprove James' claims. In 1929, Walter B. Cannon published a powerful critique of the theory based on several points: First, the total surgical separation of the viscera from the central nervous system does not greatly alter emotional behavior. Later investigators, such as Lyman Wynne and Richard Solomon, have suggested that this phenomenon may be true only for animals and human beings who have already had experience with the behavior in question, however. Dogs with a nonfunctional sympathetic nervous system often cannot learn to avoid shock, but dogs that had learned the behavior before they were operated on can avoid it. Second, the same visceral changes occur in very different emotional states and also in nonemotional states. More recent experiments by Albert Ax and others have shown that it is sometimes possible to differentiate emotions such as fear and anger by using physiological indices; for example, blood pressure and galvanic skin response increase more when a person is afraid than when he is angry. However, most emotions in most situations are impossible to distinguish in

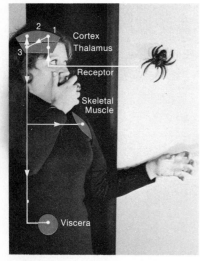

Figure 15.8 The Cannon-Bard theory of emotion took into account knowledge of the nervous system that James and Lange did not have. According to this theory the cortex normally acts to inhibit the activity of lower brain centers, such as the thalamus. Information about an emotion-eliciting event comes in through the senses and (via the thalamus) goes to the cortex, where it is perceived (1). The cortex responds by reducing its inhibition of the thalamus (2). The thalamus is then free to release a pattern of impulses that (3) activates the viscera and the skeletal muscles and simultaneously produces in the cortex an effect that causes the original event to be experienced emotionally. Cannon summed up the theory by saying, "The peculiar quality of the emotion is added to simple sensation when the thalamic processes are aroused."

this manner. Third, the viscera are relatively insensitive structures, and visceral changes are too slow to be a source of emotional feeling. Fourth, the artificial induction of visceral changes typical of strong emotions (for example, by the injection of adrenalin) does not produce the emotions.

Cannon evolved an alternative theory, altered somewhat later by Phillip Bard, which should be compared with the James-Lange theory in Figure 15.7. The Cannon-Bard theory was based on the idea (now proved incorrect) that emotion-provoking events cause the cortex of the brain to release its usual inhibition of the thalamus, whereupon the autonomic nervous system discharges as a unit, causing increased heart rate, faster breathing, perspiration, and other physiological changes. Although the role of the thalamus proposed by Cannon has been discounted, his and Bard's emphasis on autonomic arousal has been retained in more recent theories.

Activation Theories

Many later investigators have followed Cannon and Bard's lead in stressing arousal, or activation, as *the* defining characteristic of emotion; in fact, some writers have proposed that the term "emotion" be dropped from the psychological vocabulary entirely. Because it is possible to measure heart rate, rate of respiration, skin conductance, the dilation or constriction of the blood vessels, blood pressure, and many other variables in emotion-producing situations, such measures could be used instead of subjective reports to identify emotional arousal, or activation.

Perhaps the most interesting work on activation has been that of Donald Lindsley and others who have studied the role of the **reticular activating system** in producing emotional behavior. Lindsley showed that emotional behavior is usually accompanied by changes in EEG patterns away from synchronized (alpha) rhythms, which are associated with relaxation, to low-amplitude, fast-activity brain waves. This change in EEG pattern can also be produced by stimulating the reticular formation, a neural structure located in the brain stem and shown in Figure 15.9. Appropriately placed lesions in the reticular formation produce chronic drowsiness and an EEG pattern characteristic of sleep. Several studies (for example, one done by D. O. Hebb in 1955) have shown that such things as performance on reaction-time tasks, problem-solving ability, and maze-learning ability are related to cortical arousal level. At low arousal levels, performance is poor; as arousal increases (as measured by EEG changes), performance improves, but only up to a point. After a certain point in the process of arousal, called the **optimal arousal level,** further increase in arousal causes performance to deteriorate. This relationship, diagramed in Figure 15.10, is often called the Yerkes-Dodson law, after the two psychologists who first wrote about it in 1908. You probably know what it's like to be too "hyped up" to perform well at a task, to try to work too fast to do a thorough and efficient job, or to be so tense and jittery that you cannot concentrate.

Activation theories have their problems, however. Recent research, such as that done by Sebastian Grossman, has shown that the functioning of the reticular formation is more complex than it originally seemed. Another difficulty with activation theory is that some of the physiological processes involved in emotional behavior (such as heart rate and galvanic skin response) operate independently of the reticular activating system. Moreover, various measures of arousal level do not always correspond well, suggesting that arousal is not a unitary process. During rapt attention, for example, a person's GSR and respiration rate may increase, indicating activation, while his heart rate remains unchanged. Finally, perhaps the most significant problem with activation theories from the point of view of a person searching for a general and complete explanation of emotions is that a unidimensional explanation—

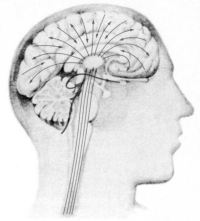

Reticular Formation

Figure 15.9 The reticular activating system is a diffuse network of neurons in the brain stem, which receives sensory inputs from all parts of the body. In response, it sends a general pattern of excitation toward the cortex. A high level of sensation therefore produces a high level of arousal. In sleep the reticular formation inhibits much of this input, thus reducing arousal.

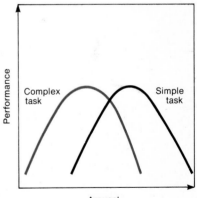

Figure 15.10 The relationship between arousal and the effectiveness of performance may be represented as an inverted "U". For a given task there is an optimal amount of arousal; a greater or a lesser degree of activation will result in less efficient behavior. This result is known as the Yerkes-Dodson law. The peak of the curve varies with the nature of the task: Optimal arousal for a complex, intricate task such as repairing an electron microscope may be far below the optimal arousal for a simple physical task like washing dishes.

one based only on activation or arousal level—cannot account for the existence of strikingly different emotions. The difference between such emotions as fear, joy, and anger cannot be explained by activation theories. Attribution theory seems to provide the missing factors.

Attribution Theory

In an early study done in 1924—one that cast doubt on the James-Lange theory of emotion—Gregorio Marañon injected 210 subjects with adrenalin. He found that about 71 percent of the subjects reported physical arousal symptoms with no emotional overtones; about 29 percent responded in an apparently emotional fashion, but most of these subjects experienced what Marañon called "as if" emotions. These subjects said, "I feel *as if* I were afraid" and "I feel *as if* I were happy." Their feelings were similar to emotions but clearly were not authentic emotions. In the few remaining cases a genuine emotional experience was produced, but it seemed to be the result of special *thoughts* that the subjects added to the experience—particularly memories with strong emotional force, such as a parent's remembrance of a time when his child was seriously sick.

Marañon's study (along with several other sources of evidence) led Stanley Schachter to propose a **two-factor attribution theory of emotion.** According to Schachter's theory (and to modifications of it by, among others, George Mandler), emotions depend both on a **change in arousal or activation level** and on a **cognitive interpretation**—an attribution—that explains the change. Schachter's theory is called an attribution theory of emotion because it is closely related to the wider-ranging attribution theory being developed by social psychologists (see Chapter 20). The term attribution refers to causal interpretations concocted by people to explain their own experiences and their own and others' behavior. For example, one might say, "I'm feeling drowsy today because I didn't get much sleep last night," or "I'm feeling drowsy because I'm depressed about not getting into law school; depression always makes me tired."

In a classic study conducted in 1962 by Schachter and Jerome Singer, the two-factor attribution theory of emotion was tested. Subjects received what they thought was a vitamin injection in an experiment purportedly designed to assess the effects of the "vitamin" on vision. Actually the injection was adrenalin (except in the case of subjects in a placebo control group), and the real purpose of the study was to see whether subjects under different experimental conditions would give different labels to the physiological sensations produced by the adrenalin. One group of subjects was told that the "vitamin" would have certain side effects, such as heart palpitations and tremor (which are real effects of adrenalin). Another group was led to expect other side effects not usually associated with adrenalin, such as itching and headache. A third group was told that the injection would have no side effects. The first group was similar to the subjects in Marañon's study, who knew they were receiving an adrenalin injection. The others had no explanation for their arousal state. Thus, Schachter and Singer reasoned, they were more likely to attribute their physical feelings to "emotional" factors.

While waiting for the "vision test," each subject sat in a room with another person, a confederate of the experimenter. In some conditions, this person acted very happy and frivolous (Schachter and Singer's term was "euphoric"), throwing paper airplanes, laughing, and playing with a hula hoop. In other conditions he acted annoyed and angry, finally tearing up a questionnaire he was supposed to fill out. The major finding of the experiment was that subjects who did not expect the arousal symptoms produced by adrenalin were likely to experience and express the emotion portrayed by the confederate in the waiting room—either euphoria, as shown in Figure 15.11, or anger.

Figure 15.11 Two of the conditions in Schachter and Singer's experiment on emotion. (A) A subject is misled about the effects he should expect from the adrenaline injection he is receiving. Placed with a companion who joyfully flies paper airplanes around the waiting room, he attributes his state of arousal to a similar mood in himself and joins in. (B) A subject is told exactly what to expect from the injection. Although placed in the same situation as the first subject, he recognizes his physical sensations as the product of the injection and is unmoved by the euphoria of the experimenter's confederate.

Subjects who were told to expect arousal side effects, like Marañon's subjects, were much less likely to share the confederate's feelings.

Subsequent studies have continued to support the two-factor theory. An experiment by Schachter and Ladd Wheeler, for example, showed that subjects who had been injected with adrenalin laughed more and harder while watching a slapstick comedy film than did subjects in a placebo control group; subjects who received an injection of chlorpromazine, a drug that *lowers* physiological arousal, laughed less than controls. Richard Nisbett and Stanley Schachter have shown that people can tolerate more electric shock if they attribute part of their discomfort to noise. According to Michael Storms and Richard Nisbett, insomniacs report falling asleep faster if they can attribute their nervous tension to a pill rather than to themselves. In addition, Dolf Zillman has shown that people behave more aggressively against a disliked person if they have been physiologically aroused by exercise. Speculative extensions of the theory have been suggested, such as the possibility that "falling in love" is often an incorrect label given to sexual arousal, to feelings of frustration or jealousy, or even, as is explained in Chapter 20, to a "physiological hangover" following a frightening experience. It has also been suggested that various symptoms commonly associated with menstruation, such as irritability and depression, are due more to cultural attitudes than to hormonal changes (see Chapter 21).

The attribution theory might be speculatively extended still further to explain powerful religious experiences such as the one described in Figure 15.12, taken from James' *The Varieties of Religious Experience*. Though the account reads as if it were a piece of fiction written specifically to illustrate Schachter's theory, it is authentic. Bradley notices his heartbeat accelerating. He seeks an explanation for this and initially attributes it to the Holy Spirit— perhaps not a surprising hypothesis for one who has just returned from a revival service. A question arises in Bradley's mind, "What can it mean?" He sees clearly a passage in Romans that (to him) confirms his suspicion that his stirrings are due to the Holy Spirit. (Notice that he doesn't consider Krishna, Zeus, or physical excitement from attending a revival, let alone the possibility that he might have consumed too much coffee or might be developing a disease of the adrenal glands.) Eventually this single incident leads

> At first, I began to feel my heart beat very quick all on a sudden,
> which made me at first think that perhaps something is going to ail me, though I was not alarmed,
> for I felt no pain. My heart increased in its beating, which soon convinced me
> that it was the Holy Spirit from the effect it had on me. I began to feel exceedingly happy
> and humble, and such a sense of unworthiness as I never felt before. . . .
> My heart seemed as if it would burst, but it did not stop until I felt as if I was unutterably full
> of the love and grace of God. In the mean time while thus exercised, a thought arose in my mind,
> what can it mean? and all at once, as if to answer it, my memory became exceedingly clear,
> and it appeared to me just as if the New Testament was placed open before me . . .
> and I read these words: "The Spirit Helpeth our infirmities with groanings which cannot be uttered."
> And all the time that my heart was a-beating, it made me groan like a person in distress . . .
> I now feel as if I had discharged my duty by telling the truth, . . .
> and I now defy all the Deists and Atheists in the world to shake my faith in Christ.

Figure 15.12 In his book *The Varieties of Religious Experience*, William James presents the writings of a certain Stephen Bradley as one of many examples of the phenomena he was attempting to analyze. Bradley's account appears to support Schachter's contention that a person's thoughts and beliefs (cognitive components) are an important determinant of the experience of emotion. Bradley interprets his sudden physiological arousal as a visitation from the Holy Spirit and becomes consumed with the emotions of happiness and humility. The Schachterian view would hold that had Bradley's heart rate accelerated when he had just finished reading a letter informing him of a friend's serious illness, he would have interpreted his physical sensations as evidence of alarm or grief.

Bradley to ". . . defy all the Deists and Atheists in the world to shake [his] faith in Christ." What began as a mysterious experience ended with attributional certainty.

If Schachter's theory is correct, it ought to explain why, as James originally noticed, there is such a wide variety of emotional experiences. Although Schachter himself has not addressed this issue, he would probably say that there could be as many differences in experienced emotions as there are in the *situations* associated with physiological arousal. This argument fits very well with James' statement that ". . . in the dictionaries of synonyms we find these feelings distinguished more by their severally appropriate objective stimuli than by their conscious or subjective tone."

Schachter's experiments, which were designed to show that both physiological arousal and cognitive labels play necessary roles in emotional experience, began with an adrenalin injection. You may be left wondering where physiological arousal comes from in more natural settings. (Certainly you would need to know this before accepting a Schachterian interpretation of Stephen Bradley's religious experience.) The answer is that arousal comes from very diverse sources: intrapsychic conflict (discussed in Chapter 18); novel or unexpected events; drugs such as caffeine; physical exercise; conditioned fear (as when the sound of a police siren raises your heart rate even though you haven't done anything); heavy work pressures; and many others.

Normally, a change in arousal level and interpretation of the situation occur simultaneously, for instance, when you hear footsteps behind you in a dark alley at midnight. The interpretation ("My God, someone's following me—I may be mugged") and the arousal are completely intertwined. In other cases, however, people seem not to know the appropriate label for their feelings: "I must be hungry if I'm eating this much." "I must be worried; I'm biting my nails." Such examples are highly prized by attribution theorists. Despite these examples, it seems likely that an interpretive process usually occurs between an event and the onset of arousal, not just after arousal. The theoretical approach outlined in the following section focuses on such an interpretive process, which precedes arousal.

Cognitive Appraisal as a Determinant of Emotion

In a scholarly review of the major approaches to emotion published in 1960, Magda Arnold pointed out that most theorists had focused on the relationship between emotional experience and bodily changes. Many theorists had accepted the common-sense view that emotion causes bodily changes (heart-rate increase, sweaty palms, and the like), although James and Lange had defended the opposite position—that emotion *is* the perception of bodily changes. Schachter's theory is like the James-Lange theory in stating that the emotional experience (or interpretation) follows arousal. Arnold emphasized a different possibility: Both the emotional experience and the bodily changes may follow the perception and appraisal of an object or event as beneficial or harmful. That is, *both experience and physiological arousal* (to use Schachter's term) *may be effects,* neither one causing the other.

Arnold's emphasis can be seen in her definition of emotion as "the felt tendency toward anything intuitively appraised as good (beneficial), or away from anything intuitively appraised as bad (harmful). This attraction or aversion is accompanied by a pattern of physiological changes organized toward approach or withdrawal." Arnold carefully analyzed the sequence of events that usually occur when someone experiences and expresses an emotion. First comes **perception;** a person must perceive an object or event before an emotion can result. (Sometimes this stage occurs only in imagination, as when you become anxious about a possible future event.) Next comes **appraisal,** the crucial step omitted by most other theorists. As Isaac Asimov indicates in his introduction to this chapter, a caged lion causes no emotional reaction, but a lion on the loose can be terrifying. The important difference is registered during the appraisal stage. The third and fourth stages are, according to Arnold, the **emotion** and accompanying **bodily changes.** These stages are omitted if the appraisal indicates no cause for concern. The final stage, **action,** may occur either alone or followed by what Arnold calls **secondary appraisal.** Secondary appraisal is a consideration of the bodily changes that followed the initial appraisal.

Arnold gives several examples of the entire sequence in her book. In one of these examples, a bomber pilot perceives enemy planes, appraises them as dangerous, experiences a fear reaction but, because he is busy taking action, does not attend carefully to his bodily changes. Later, he feels the effects of these changes (fatigue and trembling) and appraises them (an example of secondary appraisal). This example, illustrated in Figure 15.13, is interesting for at least two reasons. It helps explain something that really happens to men in battle. Some of them break down from tension and exhaustion without realizing that they have repeatedly been fearful. More important for present

Figure 15.13 Magda Arnold's theory of emotion describes a continuous process of reaction and appraisal. Both the subjective state and the physiological changes that accompany emotion are seen as effects of appraisal rather than as causally related to each other. Arnold's theory accounts for a wide variety of possible outcomes in emotion-provoking situations. This figure shows how a man may respond immediately and effectively in a dangerous situation and later misinterpret the aftereffects. The sequence could have taken other courses: Suppose the pilot *had* attended to his fear and the accompanying physiological changes. His awareness (Stage 5) would have been immediate and his secondary estimate might have been, "I am afraid and unable to handle the situation." Stages 7 and 8 would then have been panic and its physiological correlates. Alternatively, his secondary estimate might have been, "Not surprisingly, I am afraid. I must act anyway." No misinterpretation of his later tremor and fatigue would then have followed.

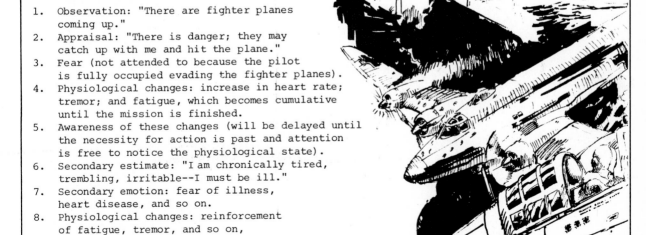

1. Observation: "There are fighter planes coming up."
2. Appraisal: "There is danger; they may catch up with me and hit the plane."
3. Fear (not attended to because the pilot is fully occupied evading the fighter planes).
4. Physiological changes: increase in heart rate; tremor; and fatigue, which becomes cumulative until the mission is finished.
5. Awareness of these changes (will be delayed until the necessity for action is past and attention is free to notice the physiological state).
6. Secondary estimate: "I am chronically tired, trembling, irritable--I must be ill."
7. Secondary emotion: fear of illness, heart disease, and so on.
8. Physiological changes: reinforcement of fatigue, tremor, and so on, increasing the malaise.

purposes, the example reveals that the process focused on by Schachter—interpretation of bodily reactions—may come fairly late in the sequence of events that constitute emotion. Schachter has ignored the initial appraisal process while studying what Arnold would call secondary appraisal.

Recently Richard Lazarus and his colleagues have begun to study the cognitive processes involved in the initial appraisal process. In their studies, subjects are shown an arousing film, usually either an account of a stone-age ritual in which adolescent boys' penises are cut, or a safety lesson in which bloody workshop accidents are vividly depicted. Meanwhile, subjects' heart rates and galvanic skin responses are measured (as indicators of arousal). Cognitions are manipulated by playing special sound tracks designed to encourage the use of defense mechanisms (see Chapter 18 for an explanation of defenses), such as denial or intellectualization. A "denial" sound track explains that the participants are actors or that the incidents portrayed are not painful; in short, the stressful aspects of the movies are denied. An "intellectualization" sound track might indicate to viewers of the films that a detached, academic orientation is appropriate, and that one need not identify with the injured people in the film.

Figure 15.14 shows results from a study of the effectiveness of denial for subjects who saw the film of the adolescent boys undergoing the ritual cutting of their penises. Not only did the denial sound track lower galvanic skin response when played during the film, it lowered it even more when played before the film was shown. Not shown in the figure is another interesting result: Subjects who had been classified as having a predisposition toward denial benefited most. This study and several others summarized by Lazarus indicate that cognitive processes play a role not only in labeling arousal but in determining its level.

EMOTIONAL EXPRESSIONS: INNATE OR LEARNED?

Psychological research from James' time to the present indicates that emotions have a physiological basis, so it would not be surprising if certain components of emotional expression were innate. Even Schachter's theory, which places heavy emphasis on context and cognition, refers to arousal

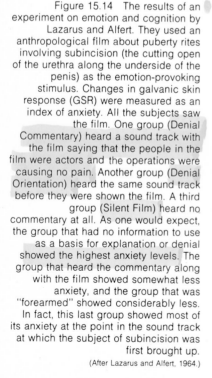

Figure 15.14 The results of an experiment on emotion and cognition by Lazarus and Alfert. They used an anthropological film about puberty rites involving subincision (the cutting open of the urethra along the underside of the penis) as the emotion-provoking stimulus. Changes in galvanic skin response (GSR) were measured as an index of anxiety. All the subjects saw the film. One group (Denial Commentary) heard a sound track with the film saying that the people in the film were actors and the operations were causing no pain. Another group (Denial Orientation) heard the same sound track before they were shown the film. A third group (Silent Film) heard no commentary at all. As one would expect, the group that had no information to use as a basis for explanation or denial showed the highest anxiety levels. The group that heard the commentary along with the film showed somewhat less anxiety, and the group that was "forearmed" showed considerably less. In fact, this last group showed most of its anxiety at the point in the sound track at which the subject of subincision was first brought up.
(After Lazarus and Alfert, 1964.)

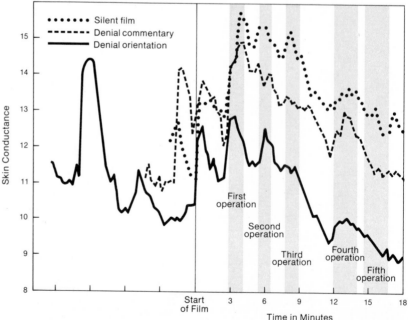

level, and it is quite possible that one's characteristic arousal level, for example, or the reactivity of one's reticular formation, might be influenced by genetic factors. On the other hand, if cognitive processes play a large role in emotional experience and expression, learning should also be important.

Innate Factors

According to Charles Darwin, in his classic work *The Expression of the Emotions in Man and Animals,* many of the features of emotional expression are inherited. He offered three principles to account for their origin and survival value. The first is **associated habits.** In animals, baring the teeth is part of preparing to fight; in both animals and man, then, bared teeth are part of the expression of anger, and they serve as a warning to potential targets of aggression that violence is impending, even though human aggression rarely involves biting. Certain facial expressions are associated with nausea, and these are often used to indicate disgust even though people are rarely disgusted enough to throw up. The second principle that Darwin formulated he called **antithesis.** If a particular gesture or act, such as fighting with a clenched fist, is common, then its opposite (or antithesis) may come to indicate the opposite emotion. In many cultures an extended or open hand is a friendly greeting because it once meant, ''I carry no weapon, I come in peace and friendship.'' Finally, Darwin referred to **excitatory overflow.** Certain intense expressions of emotion—screaming, kicking, and writhing in pain, for example—seem to have no particular function besides discharging extremely high levels of energy. Such ''overflow'' of arousal can be seen both in human beings and in animals. All three principles have been criticized, but most psychologists accept the idea that some components of emotional expression are innate and at one time had survival value. The main problem with Darwin's analysis is that he seemed to believe that habits could be inherited; scientists no longer believe this.

There are other kinds of evidence for the claim that some aspects of emotionality are inherited. Laboratory rats can be bred systematically to increase or decrease the emotionality of particular strains. (Emotionality is measured in a variety of ways, including activity level and the number of incidents of

Figure 15.15 Innate patterns of emotional expression in dogs. In the top row anger increases from left to right, and in the bottom row fear is present. The extreme fear and rage exhibited by the dog at the lower right would probably occur only in an animal who was facing a greatly feared or hated enemy and was unable to flee. The baring of teeth as a sign of rage is an example of Darwin's principle of associated habits. The perked-up ears of anger and the laid-back ears of fear illustrate the principle of antithesis. Excitatory overflow would be seen in parts of the dog's body not shown here.

urination and defecation in a fear-producing situation.) Selective breeding has also been shown to affect the emotionality of dogs and other domestic animals. (The term ''high-strung'' is commonly used by pet owners to refer to emotionality.) Studies of human beings comparing identical and fraternal twins suggest that psychiatric disorders related to emotionality, for example, manic-depressive psychosis, are due, in part, to inherited factors.

One of Davitz's students, Anne Marie Allerand, asked identical twins, fraternal twins, and nontwin siblings to describe the experiences of affection, anger, delight, disgust, excitement, fear, sadness, and worry. When the descriptions were analyzed, it was found that identical twins gave more similar reports than either fraternal twins or nontwin siblings, which suggests that emotional experience is partly due to heredity. It should be noted, however, that the experiences reported by identical twins were for the most part not identical, so factors other than heredity are still very important.

In a frequently cited study by Florence Goodenough done in 1932, a ten-year-old girl who had been deaf and blind from birth was observed in a variety of situations. Obviously the little girl could not have learned emotional expressions by observation, so her behavior should have reflected mostly innate determinants of emotional display. Goodenough observed that when the girl succeeded in finding a doll hidden in her clothing, she ''[threw] herself back in her chair. . . . Both the hand containing the doll and the empty hand [were] raised in an attitude of delight, which [was] further attested by peals of hearty laughter. . . . Her laughter [was] clear and musical, in no way distinguishable from that of a normal child.'' The girl also got angry on occasion: ''Mild forms of resentment are shown by turning away her head, pouting the lips, or frowning. . . . More intense forms are shown by throwing back the head and shaking it from side to side, during which the lips are retracted, exposing the teeth which are sometimes clenched.''

There were also several differences between this girl and her normal ten-year-old counterparts, which led Goodenough to conclude that normal expressions of emotion are based on innate patterns that have been altered by a ''social veneer.'' Later studies of handicapped children have supported this conclusion.

A similar position was arrived at by Paul Ekman and Wallace Friesen, who studied cross-cultural similarities in facial displays of emotion. Several basic expressions (including anger, fear, disgust, surprise, and happiness) were recognizable by people from different cultures, although the appropriate occasions for expressing a given emotion and the frequency with which it is expressed vary greatly. Despite the evidence for innateness, it is worth noting that facial expressions are much easier to identify if culturally appropriate situational cues are provided (for a more detailed account of this study, see Chapter 3).

Years ago, Harry Harlow and Ross Stagner suggested that four basic emotions—pleasure, displeasure, excitement, and depression—are unlearned. Various kinds of evidence besides what has already been cited support this suggestion. As explained in Chapter 14, physiological psychologists have discovered ''reward'' and ''punishment,'' or ''pleasure'' and ''pain,'' centers in the brains of animals and humans. The presence of these centers suggests that Schlosberg's pleasantness-unpleasantness dimension and Davitz's hedonic-tone dimension have a physiological basis that could be affected by genetic factors. Earlier in this chapter the reticular formation was mentioned as an important physiological component of the activation or arousal process. Both Schlosberg and Davitz included activation as a basic dimension of emotional experience, and it has been pointed out in the chapter that ''emotionality'' (roughly meaning activation level) can be enhanced or reduced by selective breeding. If depression is related to one form of low

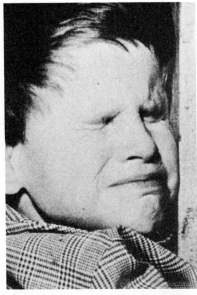

Figure 15.16 Extreme and clearly recognizable expressions on the face of a girl who was born deaf and blind. Her behavior implies that emotional expression has strong innate determinants. The top photograph was taken when she was seven, the bottom when she was nine.

activation, then all four of the emotions that Harlow and Stagner have said are basic and unlearned may, in fact, be affected by heredity.

The Role of Learning

Even the most basic emotions can be shaped by learning. Children do not begin life expressing emotion in the same way that they will later. Katherine Bridges has said that the emotional reactions of children show an **increasing complexity and differentiation** over the first two years of life. At birth, infants display only a generalized excitement or quiescence. By the end of the first year, an observer can tell the difference between their expressions of fear, anger, delight, and elation. By the end of the second year, more complex emotions, such as affection and jealousy, can be observed.

In some cases, the increasing complexity and differentiation of emotional expressions seem to be more the unfolding of a predetermined pattern than a matter of learning. For example, in infants, anger and frustration are first differentiated from general distress at about three months of age. At this age, anger is shown by a change in the tone of crying, increased breath holding, and vigorous leg thrusts. Near the end of the first year, the child's face becomes flushed and he screams when thwarted. A little later, true temper tantrums appear. Finally, at about eighteen months of age, children show anger toward other people by hitting them and by behaving obstinately. These later reactions clearly show the effects of learning.

Violations of Expectancies Similar differentiation and development occur for emotions as diverse as amusement and fear, but here the role of learning is clearer. Both amusement and fear seem to be instigated by, among other things, violations of learned expectancies. Young children laugh at jokes based on category violations; this may be one reason for their fascination with cartoons in which animals and machines talk. At a later age, laughter is elicited by verbal incongruities. Joke books for eight-year-olds are full of two-liners like the following: "Order, order in the court!" "I'll have ham and cheese on rye, your Honor." Adult jokes are based on incongruities as well, but often the expectation that is violated is beyond the ken of children.

Sometimes a violated expectancy produces not laughter but fear. For example, an infant may cry in fear if he wakes in the night and encounters a baby-sitter instead of his mother or father; he may be shy with strangers; he may even act fearful of a parent with a new hair style or hat.

Irrational fears of the strange have been reported in many nonhuman species as well, especially intelligent mammals. For example, when D. O. Hebb showed chimpanzees various strange objects, each of them similar to a familiar object but different in some important ways, he found that the chimps became excited, frightened, and aggressive in response to many of the objects—particularly a human skull, a mask of a chimpanzee face, and a model of a snake. Also, apparently trivial changes in a person's appearance often evoked strong emotions in the animals. When an attendant who habitually wore the same laboratory coat came into the chimpanzees' room wearing a different one, the animals were clearly upset. Chimps are often afraid of strangers, or of a familiar attendant who cuts his long hair or shaves his beard. Similarly, when Ronald Melzack presented various objects to dogs, such as a horsehide complete with head and an umbrella that the dogs saw being closed for the first time, they barked and either attacked the object or ran away.

It is not clear why, for human beings, violations of expectancies sometimes produce fear, sometimes amusement, and sometimes merely interest. But just as the incongruities that produce amusement change as a person develops, so the incongruities that produce fear change with age. The young infant's concern with physical support gives way to a concern about love and social

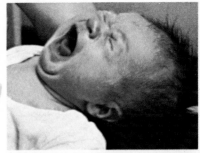

Figure 15.17 The emotion expressed by the infant at the top is clearly one of distress, but whether it is fear, anger, or grief is impossible to say. These emotions are not believed to be distinct in infancy. By the age of two years, according to Bridges, a child expresses a number of distinguishable emotions. The elation shown in the photograph at the bottom and the sadness and anger that seemed to be mixed in the child in the middle photograph are among the earliest emotions to become distinct.

support. Young infants cry when they are in pain, when they fall or are dropped, and when they hear a loud noise. Older infants cry when a stranger appears or when a familiar sequence of events is disrupted in a way that seems to threaten physical or psychological security, although they usually show no fear at all of quietly dangerous objects, such as poisons, knives, and deadly snakes or spiders, which adults usually fear. But even for adults, society's symbolic rewards are often more important than physical safety. An extreme example would be a Buddhist monk who burns himself to death as a political protest; a more common example is the American businessman who risks ulcers and an early heart attack in his pursuit of career success. Such a person may respond with little discomfort to the discovery that he has an incipient ulcer but may go into a panic during merger negotiations that may cause him to be fired.

Learned Helplessness   In many situations it is possible for an animal or person to learn to avoid painful outcomes. For example, in experiments with rats in which shock is administered in one compartment of a cage, rats learn to jump a barrier to avoid or escape from the shock. (These experiments are described in more detail in Chapter 4.) Similarly, a child who has been insulted by the neighborhood bully learns to cross the street to avoid being confronted by him.

If a person is feeling diffuse or unfocused anxiety, however, or is frightened by conditions over which he has no control, he may develop a syndrome called **learned helplessness.** Recently Martin Seligman and his colleagues have studied learned helplessness in rats, dogs, and human beings. In the typical experiment, subjects are presented with an aversive stimulus, such as electric shock or noise, and nothing they can do affects the level of stimulation. There simply is no escape. After such a training period, escape from the aversive stimulation is made possible—for example, the barrier that formerly blocked an animal's escape route is removed. A common result is that subjects do not take action to avoid further punishment. In Seligman's words: ''The experience . . . had taught the dog that its responses did not pay, that [its] actions did not matter. We concluded that the dogs in our experiments had learned that they were helpless.''

Seligman has pointed out the striking similarity between animals that have learned to be helpless and people who suffer from reactive depression (depression that is a reaction to an external event and is not hormonally or genetically based). Depressed people are often extraordinarily passive; they feel that nothing they can do will ease their suffering. Perhaps you have had this feeling after failing in school, separating from a lover, or struggling with a prolonged illness. Seligman says that a similar emotional reaction is common among college students who seem to have nothing to complain about:

Since this is a generation that has been raised with more reinforcers—more sex, more intellectual stimulation, more buying power, more cars, more music . . . than any previous generation, why should they be depressed? Yet the occurrence of reinforcers in our affluent society is so independent of the actions of the children who receive them, the goodies might as well have fallen from the sky. And perhaps that is our answer. Rewards as well as punishments that come independently of one's own effort can be depressing.

Cross-Cultural Comparisons

Although the physical bases of emotional experience and the fundamental patterns of emotional expression may be innate, *the occasions on which certain feelings are seen as appropriate and the constraints placed on forms of expression vary from one culture to another.* For example, in 1938 Otto Klineberg studied standard descriptions of emotions in novels from China and

Western Europe. There were many similarities, especially in the descriptions of fear; for instance, a Chinese novelist said, "Everyone trembled with a face the color of clay" and "Every one of his hairs stood on end, and the pimples came out on the skin all over his body." (The latter reaction, incidentally, is one that human beings share with their fellow mammals.) There were also some striking differences. For the Chinese, "They stretched out their tongues," meant that they were surprised. "He scratched his ears and cheeks," was supposed to let the reader know that he was happy. Especially interesting was Klineberg's discovery that in China strong anger (rather than fright or shock, as in the West) might be followed by fainting—and even by death. Further inquiry assured him that such reactions did not occur only in the pages of novels; there were cases on record of death due to anger. The person would become enraged, faint, and then develop a fatal disease (not a heart attack or a stroke, but a more lingering illness that sometimes lasted for weeks). Klineberg writes: "When I showed wonder as to why this should be, Chinese friends said that they in turn could never understand why European women fainted so frequently in the mid-Victorian literature with which they were acquainted."

The fact that occasions for various expressions differ cross-culturally is illustrated in a study done by Joel Davitz comparing Ugandan and American adolescents. Sixty students from each country were asked to write descriptions of several emotional states, including happiness and sadness. For each state, the subject was asked to think of a certain time when he or she had experienced the emotion, to describe the situation briefly, and to describe his or her feelings as fully as possible. The Ugandan subjects often associated happiness with academic success, whereas the Americans most often mentioned social success (such as while dating or at a party), although non-academic success (such as learning to drive) was a close second. Davitz explains that academic success is the only escape route from poverty for adolescents in urban Uganda; most of his American subjects were not suffering from poverty. In their descriptions of sadness, most Ugandan subjects wrote about the death of a friend or relative, while American subjects usually mentioned social difficulties. Premature death is more common in Uganda than in the United States, and the Ugandan extended family system emphasizes the importance of relatives. Davitz concluded that although happiness and sadness are recognizably similar in the two cultures, they are associated with situations different enough to justify saying that they are not quite the same emotions in the two cultures.

HOW FAR HAVE PSYCHOLOGISTS COME SINCE JAMES?

It is quite possible both to marvel at James' powers of observation and analytic skill, and still to see that psychologists have come a long way since 1890. James could find no coherent structure underlying the great variety of feelings; his successors have agreed upon a few basic dimensions. James' theory of the emotions, based on the notion that perception of visceral reactions *is* emotion, was discounted by several researchers and refuted by Cannon and Bard, though his concept of self-observation reappears in altered form in Schachter's attribution theory. According to Schachter, an emotion becomes an emotion only when a change in physiological arousal is given an interpretation based on situational cues. It is still conceivable that, as James said, humans sometimes become aroused, strike someone, and label the whole sequence "anger" only after the blow has landed. James' idea that the diversity of emotions reflects the diversity of visceral and muscular reactions is replaced in Schachter's theory by the idea that there are many different meaningful situations, each associated with a different emotional nuance.

If Schachter's theory is correct, why do Schlosberg and Davitz and other researchers find a few basic dimensions of emotion? Consider first the activation dimension (mentioned by both Schlosberg and Davitz); it is not hard to see that it may correspond to arousal in Schachter's theory. Schlosberg's pleasantness-unpleasantness dimension or Davitz's hedonic-tone dimension may result from an interaction between situational and motivational factors: Some events are generally rewarding or punishing, others are rewarding, neutral, or aversive depending on one's needs at the moment. The attention-rejection and relatedness dimensions of Schlosberg and Davitz, respectively, are less easily explained, but it seems that they, too, have to do with the relation between a person's needs and his or her current environment. There is, in other words, *a relationship between motivation and emotion* not completely characterized by Schachter's theory. This relationship will be taken up in the following chapter.

Although psychologists have made considerable progress since 1890, many questions remain to be answered. One section of James' emotion chapter in *The Principles of Psychology* was titled "The Subtler Emotions," by which he meant esthetic pleasure, mild interest, and the like. These feelings seemed to James to be too mild to be caused by visceral reactions, and today they seem too mild to be caused by a burst of adrenalin (a Schachterian possibility). James had little to say about this phenomenon, and Schachter has said no more. But there has been recent work relating interest, attention, and esthetic reactions to cortical arousal. This may prove to be a fruitful approach to the problem, although additional evidence and conceptual integration are needed.

James devoted a short section of his chapter to acting. He knew that some of his readers would wonder how it is possible for an actor to express a certain emotion, say anger, without, in fact, feeling it. (Remember, James' theory said that perception of the act *was* the emotion.) James offered several logical explanations. For example, actors may sometimes get carried away and really feel the emotion they are supposed to be simulating; or simulation may not involve all the visceral reactions that bring about the genuine emotion. But James said little about the fact that each of us is an actor much of the time. We feign one emotion while experiencing another and sometimes seem not to know whether our expressions are genuine or not. Such phenomena have received almost no attention from psychologists who study human emotions, although sociologists (such as Erving Goffman in *The Presentation of Self in Everyday Life* and *Interaction Ritual*) have pointed the way.

Schachter's theory has received considerable support, but it can be criticized too. Howard Leventhal has summarized the major criticisms. For example, Schachter's theory does not say how arousal level is usually determined, and it also slights the possibility that at least some emotions are innately structured. It says little about the origins of expressive patterns. It relies on a very loose notion of arousal—which, as stated earlier, turns out not to be a unitary construct when measured simultaneously by several different physiological indicators. Some of these shortcomings have been remedied by Arnold, but so far her comprehensive theory has not been thoroughly researched.

Despite a great deal of progress in the study of human emotions since James first outlined the major problems in 1890, much work remains to be done. James was an energetic advocate of the empirical approach to psychology; no doubt, if he were alive today, he would be pleased by both the progress and the challenge.

SUMMARY

1. **Emotion** has proved difficult for psychologists to define; in describing what the term means, they often rely on their readers' subjective knowledge of what it feels like to be angry, jealous, depressed, happy, disgusted, frightened, and so on.

2. In studying emotions, psychologists have three main sources of information: People's **subjective reports** on their emotional experiences; **observations of behavior** during emotional states; and **physiological measures** of emotional arousal, such as changes in heart rate, galvanic skin response, respiration, and muscle tension.

3. William James, who wrote about emotion in his classic 1890 textbook *The Principles of Psychology,* believed that human emotions are too numerous and too various to be classified into meaningful groups. Later research indicates, however, that emotions can be organized into categories.

    a. Studies by Harold Schlosberg and others—in which subjects sort photographs of different facial expressions into groups—reveal three basic dimensions of emotion: **pleasantness-unpleasantness, attention-rejection,** and **level of activation** (sleep-tension).

    b. Studies by Joel Davitz of **emotion words** and their definitions yield four basic dimensions, three of which are similar to Schlosberg's: **hedonic tone, relatedness,** and **activation.** Because of the similarity between the dimensions derived from photographs and those derived from emotion words, it seems likely that the dimensions reflect the basic structure of human emotions.

    c. Charles Osgood's **semantic differential,** a method that investigates the emotional connotations of words, has shown that almost all words are rated along three dimensions, which correspond well to Schlosberg's dimensions: Osgood's **evaluative dimension** corresponds to Schlosberg's pleasantness-unpleasantness dimension; his **activity dimension,** to the level of activation; and his **potency dimension,** to the attention-rejection dimension.

4. The procedures used by Schlosberg and Davitz provide a description of human emotions but not a causal theory to explain emotion. For such explanations, one must turn to the major **theories of emotion** formulated over the years.

    a. According to the **James-Lange theory,** an emotionally arousing event immediately and automatically triggers certain bodily changes, and a person's perception of those bodily changes is the emotion he feels. We do not run because we are frightened; we are frightened because we run. That is, James believed that a person's **physiological reaction**—visceral and muscular changes—to an event precedes his psychological reaction—the emotion. (Carl Lange believed essentially the same thing but thought the physiological changes were vascular—coming from the veins—rather than visceral—coming from the stomach and intestines.) James thought that the incredible diversity of emotions people experience was probably matched by an equally large number of different visceral and muscular reactions to emotionally arousing situations—an idea that was not borne out by later research.

    b. The **Cannon-Bard theory** was devised partly in response to objections to the James-Lange theory. It stated that emotionally arousing events cause the autonomic nervous system to discharge as a unit, leading to

Figure 15.18 Harold Schlosberg's work on the classification and scaling of emotional variables is one of the bases by which psychologists presently understand and interpret emotion. Schlosberg was an accomplished experimenter in a variety of areas of psychology; in 1960 he assisted Robert Woodworth in the revision of Woodworth's text on experimental psychology. The result, Woodworth and Schlosberg's *Experimental Psychology*, became the definitive and standard text in this area for many years.

such physiological changes as increased heart rate and faster breathing. Although the particular physiological explanation the theory offered for autonomic arousal was incorrect, its emphasis on arousal has been retained in more recent theories.

c. A number of **activation theories** have been proposed; they follow Walter B. Cannon and Phillip Bard's lead in stressing physiological arousal, or activation. For example, Donald Lindsley has suggested that the **reticular formation,** a structure in the brain stem, might be responsible for much of the physiological arousal experienced during emotional states. There are various difficulties with activation theories: Most important, an explanation of emotions based only on activation cannot account for the existence of sharply contrasting emotions like anger and joy.

d. Stanley Schachter has proposed a **two-factor attribution theory** of emotion. It states that emotions depend both on a **change in arousal or activation level** and on a person's **cognitive interpretation,** or attribution, of his circumstances. The theory was tested in an experiment in which subjects who had been injected with adrenalin but had no logical explanation for the resulting physiological arousal tended to attribute their feelings to emotion and to label the emotion in very different ways (as either euphoria or anger), depending on their circumstances. Schachter's theory, which is supported by other research, is potentially capable of accounting for the many different emotional experiences people have: It implies there could be as many different experienced emotions as there are different arousing situations.

e. According to Magda Arnold, *cognitive appraisal of a situation determines both emotional experience and bodily changes.* This idea is supported by research in which experimental subjects who heard a "denial" sound track before watching a shocking movie showed less physiological arousal in response to the film than did other subjects.

5. Both innate and learned factors seem to play a role in emotional expression. Some of the evidence for innate factors is as follows.

   a. Charles Darwin formulated three principles to support his claim that many features of emotional expression are inherited: **associated habits, antithesis,** and **excitatory overflow.** These principles have been questioned, but most psychologists accept the idea that some of the emotional expressions discussed by Darwin are innate.

   b. Selective breeding has been shown to affect the emotionality of dogs, rats, and some other animals.

   c. Identical twins, asked to describe emotional experiences, give more similar reports than do fraternal twins or nontwin brothers and sisters.

   d. Florence Goodenough found that a girl who was born deaf and blind expressed such emotions as delight and resentment similarly to other children.

6. It is clear, however, that even very basic emotions can be shaped by learning. The emotional behavior of children shows **increased complexity and differentiation** over the first few years of life. Although some changes are probably due to the unfolding of a predetermined pattern, others are clearly due to learning.

   a. Both amusement and fear often stem from **violations of learned expectancies.** A child may cry if a baby-sitter instead of a parent enters his room at night; chimpanzees and dogs also act afraid when shown strange objects that resemble familiar ones.

   b. Recent research by Martin Seligman has identified a syndrome called **learned helplessness,** in which an animal subjected to painful stimulation that it cannot escape does not try to escape later on, after escape has been made possible. Similar behavior can be observed in depressed human beings.

7. Although the facial expressions that accompany certain basic emotions can be identified by people from different cultures, *forms of emotional expression tend to vary from one culture to another.* For example, the Chinese sometimes indicate surprise by extending their tongues and happiness by scratching their ears and cheeks.

8. Schachter's theory, which has stimulated more research than any other current theory of emotion, shows that psychologists have come a long way since James but still have a way to go. Some of the topics that have yet to be fully dealt with are: (a) the relation between motivation—a person's needs and goals—and his emotions; (b) the quieter emotions, such as esthetic pleasure, which do not seem to be associated with strong physiological arousal; and (c) the question of exactly how emotional arousal occurs.

Figure 15.19 Martin Seligman, an experimental and clinical psychologist, has edited a book on the biological boundaries of learning and has also investigated an experimental corollary of psychological depression, which he calls "learned helplessness." This work has paved the way for other experimental analyses of emotion.

SUGGESTED READINGS

Arnold, Magda (ed.). *Feelings and Emotions.* New York: Academic Press, 1970. A collection of recent symposium papers by many of the theorists mentioned in this chapter and by several others who could not be mentioned because of limited space. An excellent cross section of the field as it exists today.

Cofer, Charles N. *Motivation and Emotion.* Glenview, Ill.: Scott, Foresman, 1972. A good, short introductory survey of emotion and motivation and the relationship between them.

Darwin, Charles. *The Expression of the Emotions in Man and Animals.* Chicago: University of Chicago Press, 1965. This classic work, first published in 1872, describes the expression of emotions in humans and animals and interprets them in terms of evolution and natural selection.

James, William. "The Emotions," in *The Principles of Psychology.* Vol. II. New York: Holt, 1890. A fascinating classic that reviews basic issues and presents and defends what is now called the James-Lange theory of emotions.

Leventhal, Howard. "Emotions: A Basic Problem for Social Psychology," in C. Nemeth (ed.), *Social Psychology: Classic and Contemporary Integrations.* Chicago: Rand McNally, 1974. An excellent review article that covers much the same ground as this chapter, but in greater detail. Includes criticisms and proposed modifications of Schachter's theory that deserve the attention of advanced students and researchers.

Schachter, Stanley. *Emotion, Obesity, and Crime.* New York: Academic Press, 1971. A compilation of previously published papers related to Schachter's theory of emotion.

It seems to me that few things we do in life can be ascribed to only one motive. Just as "mixed emotions" has come to be a cliché, so should "mixed motives."

Take the case of Hamlet in Shakespeare's play of that name. He is probably more discussed (even by professional psychologists) than any other character in literature. His father dies suddenly, and his uncle, Claudius, having married Queen Gertrude (young Hamlet's mother) is now the new king. His father's ghost tells Hamlet that Claudius had murdered him and charges Hamlet with the task of vengeance—and yet Hamlet delays. As long as you consider Hamlet motivated by a single, pure feeling, the desire for revenge, there is no way of explaining that delay. Hamlet himself admits only the desire for revenge, and he is constantly complaining at his own delay.

But suppose he had another motive, too. Besides the lust for revenge, suppose he felt ambition. Suppose he had the itch for the throne. Why not? He was his father's grown son. Yet Claudius was elected. Why? Suppose we consider eleventh-century English history (about the time Hamlet was supposed to have taken place). Emma, widow of dead King Ethelred, married Canute of Denmark. Canute became King of England in preference to Emma's grown son by Ethelred. To be sure, Canute became king by right of conquest, but his marriage to the queen gave it a flavor of legality. In the same way Claudius' marriage to the widow of the dead king gave him a kind of legal claim to the throne and ensured his election. One can argue that Hamlet was not so much annoyed with his mother's marriage to Claudius as with the *speed* of the marriage. The quick marriage made it possible for Claudius to be elected successor before Hamlet had time to return from school and claim the throne.

From that standpoint, the play begins to involve a dynastic dispute, and that makes sense. England's Queen Elizabeth was in her late sixties at the time and had no direct heir. Her death might once again set off dynastic civil war. Shakespeare, concerned with that, wrote many plays dealing with disputed successions, and *Hamlet* was one of them.

Now we see how the mixed motives play their part. If Hamlet simply killed Claudius (a clever and popular king), that would feed his revenge but would not gain him the throne. It might gain him only civil war or execution. For Hamlet to kill Claudius *after proving him a murderer* would gain him both revenge and ambition, for then he would surely be the next king. Hamlet, therefore, is not trying to prove Claudius' guilt to himself out of irresolution and a yearning for delay. He is trying to prove Claudius a murderer *to the court* out of calculated policy.

Isaac Asimov

16

Motivation and Action

HISTORICAL APPROACHES TO MOTIVATION
Instincts
Drive Theory
Shortcomings of Drive Theory

Incentive Effects
Contact Comfort
"Pleasure Centers" in the Brain
Stimulation Seeking
Cognitive Determinants

EXPECTANCY-VALUE THEORY
Emotion and Motivation
The Expectancy-Value Conception of Motivation

ASSESSING ACHIEVEMENT MOTIVATION
A Model of Achievement Motivation for Men
The Achievement Motive and Society
Achievement Motivation in Women
Differences Between Men and Women
An Attribution-Theory Approach

HUMAN MOTIVATION: A HIERARCHICAL CONCEPTION

When people use the term "motivation" in everyday conversation, what do they mean? Consider an example. If you heard that "Miriam is highly motivated to go to medical school," you would probably expect to find that she works hard in her college courses, that she spends long hours in the lab and stays up late at night memorizing organic-chemistry equations. You would not be surprised to learn that she sometimes declines offers from friends to go drinking or to watch late movies on TV. If Miriam received a bad grade on a science exam, she would probably work—in fact, work extra hard—to bring her grade average up by the end of the course.

Psychologists have borrowed their conceptions of motivation from ordinary language; therefore, their approaches to motivation are similar in orientation to the example just given. Motivation is not an observable process, and it cannot be measured directly. As in our account of Miriam, *motivation is a hypothetical process that is inferred from goal-directed behavior.* In Miriam's case, the goal is to get into medical school, but countless other examples of goals could have been used. The goal could have been food, a successful marriage, or escape from boredom.

The purpose of motivation theories in psychology is to account for the **initiation, direction, intensity,** and **persistence** of goal-directed behavior. Initiation and direction have to do with why one activity rather than another is chosen at a particular time. Why, for example, does Miriam decide to study in the evening when other people want to see a movie? Other questions touch upon the intensity of motivated behavior. Why does one person work harder than another to become famous? Why will one man "walk a mile for a Camel" while his best friend, also a smoker, decides to forgo cigarettes until they become more easily available? Miriam's behavior is an example of persistence; other people who do poorly on a test might decide to drop the course.

Figure 16.1 What motivates a person to push himself to his limits—physical ones in the case of this runner? What motivates him to develop the arduous discipline required to enter and win such a race? Early psychological theories, which tried to account for human activity in terms of the reduction of drives, appear to be inadequate to explain motives like the runner's. Later theories, presented in this chapter, offer explanations that depend more on particularly human capacities—cognitive ones—than on analogies between humans and other animals.

It is possible to simplify the earlier statement about the aim of motivation theorists by saying that they seek to account for the *energization* and *direction* of behavior at a particular moment. Usually they are interested in *contemporaneous* determinants of behavior—that is, in the variables that operate at the moment of action. Unlike learning or developmental theories, they are not so interested in historical determinants except insofar as these are helpful in explaining forces acting at a given time.

The energization and direction of some behavior is determined by the physiological state of the organism. Human beings as well as other animals have certain survival needs. Human nervous systems are constructed in such a way that deficits in blood sugar, water, and air, or excesses of toxic chemicals, lead to changes in behavior designed to return the body to a more optimal condition. Chapter 14 describes the physiological basis of hunger, thirst, temperature regulation, and certain other motivational states.

Many human motives, however, do not have a simple physiological basis. Recall Miriam's desire to get into medical school. Although not all psychologists would be able to agree on an explanation of her behavior, none would say that it was the result of physiological deficits. Consider a week in the life of a typical college student or a priest or a nurse or a psychologist; it is clear that many human activities are not directly related to physiological needs. Thus, despite the exciting gains in knowledge concerning the physiological basis of some forms of motivated behavior, psychologists are still left with many questions about distinctively human motives.

HISTORICAL APPROACHES TO MOTIVATION

Before discussing the way contemporary psychologists approach human motivation, two earlier approaches should be described: one based on the concept of instincts and the other on drive theory. Of the two, drive theory is by far the more important, both intrinsically and in terms of its effect on contemporary psychology. For a time, many psychologists believed that it might be possible to explain all motivated behavior—indeed, all behavior—by relating it directly or indirectly to the reduction of some drive. If this had been true, drive theory would have become psychology's first paradigm (see Chapter 1). Gradually, however, studies based on the theory showed that it applied to a much narrower range of behavior than its supporters had hoped. The theory as an entity was discarded, although some of its tenets are used today, particularly by psychologists who study physiologically based motives.

Expectancy-value theory, a current approach to human motivation that is described in detail later in the chapter, resembles drive theory in some ways—for example, in its use of precise, mathematical formulas. In addition, the research responsible for the decline and fall of drive theory as a comprehensive approach to behavior has defined many of the issues that current motivational theories attempt to deal with.

Instincts

After Darwin's theory of evolution became widely accepted among psychologists, it was common to seek explanations of human behavior in terms of instincts. Mothering was said to be due to a maternal instinct, quarreling to instinctual aggression, and so on.

Although there was a grain of truth in some of the instinct theories (human behavior is in part due to genetic determinants), early in this century the instinct approach lost favor. It became clear that an instinct could be invented for any identifiable behavior pattern and that such special-purpose instincts explained nothing. Perhaps you can understand this problem better by inventing instincts to answer the following questions: Why do people get married? Why do they climb mountains? Or go swimming? Or drink alcoholic beverages? As was pointed out in Chapter 3, we know nothing more about the question once we have added a "swimming instinct" to our explanatory arsenal than we knew before we did so. Frank Beach, in an article he wrote in 1955, offers a detailed account of the demise of instinct theories.

Drive Theory

You probably know something about Sigmund Freud's psychoanalytic theory of personality, even if you have not read the detailed account given in Chapter 18. Freud believed that human behavior is motivated by a general form of "psychic energy" (libido) that arises from a few basic instincts. The direction of behavior is determined by socially imposed constraints on the expression of instinctual impulses or, in Freud's words, on the "discharge of psychic energy." Although Freud's terminology has been rejected by most contemporary psychologists, it is worth noting his solution to the energization and direction problems faced by every motivation theorist: He believed instinctual "energy" was channeled or directed by learned constraints.

The dominant theory of human and animal behavior in the United States during the 1940s was Clark Hull's **drive theory.** Though it differed from Freud's theory both in form (Hull's model was mathematical; Freud's was not) and in its empirical basis (Hull studied mainly rats; Freud focused on neurotic humans), it was structurally quite similar. The source of behavioral energy was called **drive,** and the directional component of behavior was called **habit.** Hull conceived of drives as arising, originally at least, from physiological needs. A deficit of some kind—food or water, in most studies—was thought to lead to a feeling of tension and to more or less random activity. If the activity brought an animal to its goal (food, water, a sexual partner, or whatever was needed), the responses (bar-pressing or turning right in a maze) that led to the goal and reduced the unpleasant tension would be strengthened, or reinforced, by **drive reduction.** The response that led to the goal would thus be more likely to occur next time the animal found itself in the same situation. That is, the **habit strength** of that response would increase.

A great deal of evidence was collected in support of Hull's theory. Many studies showed, for example, that food-deprived or sexually aroused rats were more active, as the theory required. They covered more territory in an open-field situation and ran more vigorously in a running wheel even when no goal objects were available (see Figure 16.2). A wide variety of studies also seemed to support Hull's idea that learning was due to drive reduction (although later the generality of this principle was questioned).

In explaining how drive level and habit strength determine performance, Hull said that these two variables combined multiplicatively—hence the famous performance equation: performance (P) is a function of drive (D) times habit strength (H). Parts A and B of Figure 16.3 show some of the evidence gathered to support this claim. Part C of Figure 16.3 shows how the relationship might work in a real-life situation. Part A shows the results of an experiment with rats. Rats that had previously been trained to press a bar to get food were placed before the bar again after either three or twenty-two hours of food deprivation. Some of the animals had received five reinforced trials during the learning portion of the experiment; others had received more—some as many as ninety. Thus, the rats' bar-pressing "habit" varied from weak to strong. The performance measure in the study was the number of times the animal pressed the bar during extinction, when food rewards were no longer forthcoming. The graph shows that hungrier animals pressed the bar far more often, indicating that drive is a determinant of behavior. It also shows that the number of prior reinforced trials (habit strength) was related to the number of bar-presses during extinction. The divergence of the two curves indicates that drive and habit strength are in fact related multiplicatively.

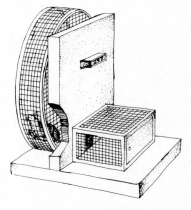

Figure 16.2 An activity wheel, a device for measuring activation or arousal in rats and mice. A counter attached to the wheel records—in number of revolutions per unit time—how much the animal runs. This measure shows the extent to which the animal is generally energized by a drive.

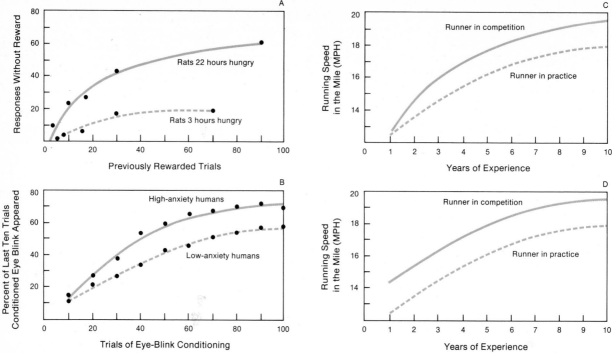

Figure 16.3 (A) These data show that rats perform a previously reinforced response more frequently the longer they have been without food (the higher their drive) and the more often they have been rewarded in the past (the stronger their habit). But a higher drive does not simply add a constant amount to the rats' performances at different habit strengths. The rats' resulting performances represent a multiplication of the two factors. (B) The same kind of relationship is seen between anxiety (drive), the number of previous conditioning trials (habit strength), and the percentage of trials on which a conditioned eyeblink appears. (C) Imaginary data on running speed from the career of a track star. Habit strength is assumed to increase with the runner's experience, and his drive is assumed to be greater in competition than in practice. These data show the same multiplicative relationship as those in (A) and (B); the more experience the runner has had, the greater the energizing effects of competition will be. (D) Imaginary data on the track star's behavior that do not show a multiplicative relationship. Data such as these would mean that in competition the track star always runs just the same amount faster than he does in practice, whether his practice speed is low because of inexperience or high because he has been running for years.

(After Weiner, 1972.)

Drive theory was also tested in studies of human subjects. One paradigm for such studies was devised by Kenneth Spence and Janet Taylor. Taylor constructed a questionnaire measure of anxiety called the Manifest Anxiety Scale, which was used to classify people as high or low in anxiety. Subjects are asked to answer "True," "False," or "Cannot say" to items such as, "I am usually self-conscious." Anxiety was conceived as a drive, so it was possible to make several predictions based on Hull's theory about low- and high-anxiety subjects in learning situations. One such prediction was that high-anxiety subjects would show more classically conditioned eyelid responses (blinks) to an aversive air puff. Figure 16.3B shows the results of an eye-blink study by Spence and Taylor supporting the prediction. High-anxiety subjects exhibited more conditioned responses than did low-anxiety subjects, and the curves diverged over trials as they should if the relationship between drive and habit strength were multiplicative. Parts C and D of Figure 16.3 illustrate this multiplicative relationship in a real-life situation and show the difference between an additive and a multiplicative relationship. In the additive relationship, the curves are parallel.

Other studies showed that complex tasks, in which the correct response is weak in strength, are more difficult for high-anxiety than for low-anxiety subjects, whereas easy tasks, in which the correct response is already strong, are easier for high-anxiety than for low-anxiety subjects. This pattern is predictable from drive theory. (In 1966, Janet Spence and Kenneth Spence summarized several such studies.)

Although Hull and his followers did not say much about such motives as achievement, power, and affiliation, it is clear how they intended to handle them: as **learned drives.** They thought that all nonphysiological motives were originally associated with basic needs. Fear, for example, was seen as a learned reaction to potential pain. (See the section on John Dollard and Neal Miller's psychodynamic approach to personality in Chapter 19.)

Shortcomings of Drive Theory

Since 1950 many objections to the drive theory of motivation have been raised. It is mainly the objections that are especially relevant to later work on human motivation that this section discusses.

Incentive Effects First, it does not seem to be the case that learning occurs only when a drive is reduced. Rats that are allowed to explore a maze will later show much better performance than will control rats when running the maze for food, even though no food was available during the exploration phase of the experiment. In other words, rats learn something about their environment even when they are not being rewarded, although indications of learning remain latent until an **incentive** is offered for performance. (This phenomenon came to be called **latent learning.**) There is a multitude of evidence for the same process in humans. Think of the times you have suddenly wanted to buy something, such as a pizza or a Chinese dinner, and were immediately able to recall where the nearest Italian or Chinese restaurant was located. You knew where to go even though you never needed or cared about this information before.

The notion of incentive is important beyond its role in demonstrating latent learning. Animals and people will exert more effort to get large rewards than small ones, a fact that was not explained by Hull's original formulation. The effects of incentive on performance were not included in either the drive or habit-strength variables in Hull's theory: Hull emphasized what several writers have called the "push" of internal drives and almost ignored the "pull" of available incentives although later versions of Hull's theory did incorporate an incentive variable.

Contact Comfort Another problem with drive theory was that positive feelings were viewed as consequences of relief from tension; no allowance was made for inherently positive experiences. For example, as mentioned earlier, most psychologists thought that infants came to love their mothers because the mothers relieved unpleasant physiological states such as hunger. Figure 16.4 shows two kinds of artificial mothers used by Harry Harlow and his col-

Figure 16.4 In Harlow's classic experiment on the determinants of mother love, infant monkeys chose between two surrogate mothers: One was made of wire and was equipped with a feeding nipple; the other was made of soft terry cloth. The monkeys spent most of their time with the terry-cloth mother even though they fed from the wire mother, and they used the terry-cloth mother as a security base when frightened by strange objects introduced by the experimenter. A drive-reduction explanation of their behavior is inadequate because the monkeys chose the mother that did not provide food—the one that was least obviously associated with the termination of an unpleasant state (hunger). The effective reward seemed to be a positive event rather than escape from a negative one.

leagues to study this hypothesis. One of the ''mothers'' was made of wire and contained a bottle holder from which the infant monkeys were fed. The other ''mother'' did no feeding but was covered with soft, comfortable terrycloth. Infant monkeys spent more time with the terrycloth mother, even though the wire mother fed them; moreover, the infants clung to the terrycloth mother when frightening new objects were placed in the cage. Harlow concluded that contact comfort was more important than hunger reduction in establishing ties between infant monkeys and their mothers.

"Pleasure Centers" in the Brain Another kind of evidence for the existence of inherently positive experiences came from studies by James Olds and his associates, who discovered that rats will learn to press a lever in order to stimulate certain areas of their own brains with electric current from an implanted electrode. When particular brain areas could be stimulated by bar-presses, rats would press the lever *thousands of times per hour* for at least ten hours; these areas came to be known as ''pleasure centers.''

The location of the stimulating electrode is critical: Olds found some areas that were apparently associated with great pleasure and others that seemed to be associated with severe pain. (Rats will work to escape the latter kind of stimulation.)

Analogous studies with human subjects (patients undergoing brain surgery) have had similar results, but they also reveal several complications. Some human ''pleasure centers'' are associated with specific memories of pleasant or interesting events (such as a long-forgotten birthday party), others with vaguely pleasant feelings that do not seem identical to any of the common emotions. It is not clear yet how the specific pleasure centers are related to general motivational systems in humans. Nonetheless, the discovery that electrical stimulation can serve as a reinforcer without reducing a drive cast further doubt on Hull's theory.

Stimulation Seeking Freud and Hull both implied that organisms, including human beings, seek the lowest possible level of stimulation or drive: Both saw drive *reduction* as rewarding. It was thus a blow to drive theory when psychologists began to discover that experimental subjects will work to gain access to novel or complex stimulation; Figure 16.5 shows some examples. In

Figure 16.5 Further examples of behavior that cannot readily be explained by a drive-reduction model of motivation. Monkeys will work vigorously for the privilege of viewing an electric train, but it would be hard to say what drive is reduced as a result. Similarly, human children (and adults) find such toys as a jack-in-the-box highly enjoyable. The reward for playing with a jack-in-the-box would seem to be an *increase* in stimulation rather than a reduction of it.

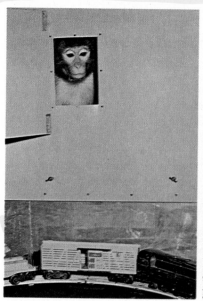

addition, people of all ages will choose to look at changing rather than repetitive stimuli and at stimuli that are relatively complex rather than simple. As is explained in Chapter 18, Robert White and other personality theorists have concluded from this and related evidence that humans are rewarded by challenging stimulation, that they sometimes like being aroused and active, and that increased competence and mastery is rewarding in itself, not necessarily because it reduces drive. In addition, as is explained in Chapter 13, human subjects find the reduction of stimulation to a very low level, as in sensory-deprivation studies, distinctly disturbing.

Cognitive Determinants of Motivation Finally, drive theory lost adherents because it did not do justice to the role of cognitive processes in human motivation. When a person decides to go to one college instead of another, or to invest in stock X instead of stock Y, or to take a trip to Europe instead of buying a car, it makes sense to talk about motives but not about drives. The conceptual distance between hunger and the desire to take a trip to Europe is so great that a construct like "learned drive" is not very useful. Rather, psychologists need some way of measuring and taking into account people's beliefs and values.

EXPECTANCY-VALUE THEORY

Psychologists and other social scientists, especially economists, have long been interested in the way people make practical decisions. Most social scientists have adopted some version of **expectancy-value theory.** The general outlines of this theory should be easy enough to understand; consider the following example: Suppose you decide to buy a raffle ticket for one dollar, and forty-nine other people do the same. You have one chance in fifty of winning the raffle. If the grand prize is $1,000, you have made a wise decision, because the expected value of your investment is $19.00. Figure 16.6 shows how this was determined.

The expectancy-value approach to motivation explains motivated behavior by *relating a person's expectancy of achieving a particular goal to the value the goal has for the person.* That is, it extends the decision model just described to include the subjective probability that an action will lead to a certain outcome and the subjective incentive value of that outcome (see Figure 16.7). Like the objective value of a financial investment (which can lead to the gain or loss of money), subjective incentive values can be positive or negative. One couple wants a large family, whereas another couple thinks children would be a disaster; one person looks forward to retirement, whereas another dreads it; and so on.

Emotion and Motivation

As these examples suggest, subjective incentive values can be discussed not only in terms of motivation but in terms of emotion. So far in this chapter it has been stated that motivation is inferred from goal-directed behavior; in most experimental situations the goal is an external object, such as food or money. But it is just as possible to focus on the subjective side of goal-directed activity and point out that the goal often has something to do with a pleasant or unpleasant feeling. You may eat ice cream either because you are food-deprived (hungry) or because you like its sweet taste.

Some psychologists have even defined a motive as an expectancy of pleasantness (positive emotion) or unpleasantness (negative emotion) and a goal as an object that gives rise to pleasant feelings or that reduces negative ones. These definitions may be overly simplistic, for it is not always clear that a person consciously "expects" a certain outcome from his actions. According to psychoanalysts, many of our motives are unconscious; we cannot always

Figure 16.6 The computation of an expected value. Expected value is the overall gain (or loss) that would result if the risk were taken over and over again. The amount that could be lost (in this case, the cost of the ticket), multiplied by the probability of losing it (by losing the raffle), is subtracted from the amount that could be gained (the $1000 prize minus the cost of the raffle ticket), multiplied by the probability of gaining it. In the long run, the buyer could expect to gain only $19.00 by taking this risk repeatedly.

	Winning	Losing	
Probability	1/50	49/50	
Value	$999.00	-$1.00	**Total**
P × V	$19.98	-$0.98	**$19.00**

Figure 16.7 Expectancy-value theory suggests that an individual makes decisions by comparing the expected values of alternative courses of action. His expected values are computed (perhaps not consciously) from his subjective estimate of the probability and value of each possible outcome, as shown here.

say why we are doing a particular thing. However, if we are willing to accept the idea that we sometimes *unconsciously* seek positive emotional states and avoid negative ones—a claim made by Freudians—then the interpretation of goal-directed behavior in terms of emotional states may be valid.

Another problem arises when one considers actions undertaken for vague or abstract reasons. Suppose you write a letter to a friend. Why do you do this? Perhaps because you like him, and you will feel good if he replies; you want to hear from him. Perhaps because you have owed him a letter for a month, and you feel guilty. If so, the interpretation of goals in terms of emotions is appropriate. But arguments about the hypothetical pleasures and pains associated with various actions can easily become philosophical rather than psychological ones. Why do you help an old lady across the street—because you feel like a "better person" for it? Maybe, but the assertion would be difficult to prove.

It is therefore sensible to conclude simply that emotions and motives are often closely linked. The energy component of motivation is presumably the same as the arousal or activation component of emotion (which is discussed in the preceding chapter). The incentive value of goals is closely related to the pleasantness-unpleasantness (hedonic tone) and attention-rejection (relatedness) dimensions of emotional expression (also discussed in the preceding chapter). Emotions, then, are often the result of goal-directed action, and an anticipated emotional state can determine the incentive value of a goal.

The Expectancy-Value Conception of Motivation

Research has uncovered substantial differences between one rat and another in the kinds of goals that are chosen as most interesting, most tasty, most sexually gratifying, and so on. You are probably aware of such differences among dogs, even between two that come from the same litter. But such differences pale in significance compared to the differences between people. Especially when one leaves the realm of physiological needs and focuses only on psychosocial motives such as affiliation, conformity, power, money, independence, and so on, one finds large differences between and within human cultures. Within a particular culture or even a single family, one person may be an introvert who likes to walk along quiet nature trails, whereas another is an extravert who sings with a rock band. One may want to be a scholar, another a business executive, still another a ballet dancer. Psychologists need some way to include such individual differences in a full account of human motivation.

The expectancy-value approach to motivation, which originated in the work of Edward Tolman, Kurt Lewin, David McClelland, and John Atkinson, has been elaborated by Atkinson to include such individual differences. In his conception, a *motive is defined as a relatively stable capacity to gain gratification from a particular class of incentives, a capacity that differs from person to person.* This definition emphasizes the fact that some people find scholarly activity rewarding and others do not; some find athletics exciting and stimulating and others have no interest in exercise or competitive games.

Atkinson distinguishes between a motive and motivation. He defines *motivation as the process that results from the interaction of motive, expectancy, and incentive value.* Sometimes "response availability" is mentioned as a fourth factor in explaining motivated behavior because people may differ in what they know about methods for reaching a goal as well as in motive strength, perceived likelihood that certain actions will lead to the goal (expectancy), and incentive value of the goal. Because this chapter is concerned primarily with motivation, not with learned skill, a discussion of response availability will not be pursued, except to point out that it is similar to the concept of habit in Hull's drive theory.

Behavior does not always reflect motivation directly. For one thing, a given action may serve more than one motive. Miriam may want to go to medical school because such a goal fulfills her parents' expectations, *and* because she wants to enter a high-status profession, *and* because she wants a particular kind of power over other people's lives. All these desires can be met by the same activities; as Freud said, many human acts are motivationally **overdetermined** (determined by more than one motive). In addition, an action may be the result of **conflict between contradictory motives;** for example, Miriam may have an unconscious desire to hurt people as well as a conscious desire to help them.

Many of the current methods for studying motives are based on work done by Henry Murray and his co-workers in the late 1930s. Murray, a personality theorist, emphasized the role of "psychogenic," or nonphysiological, needs in determining human behavior. He and his co-workers accepted Freud's idea (discussed in Chapter 18) that people express their motives more clearly in free-associative thought than in direct self-reports. Guided by clinical evidence, Murray and his colleagues devised a test called the Thematic Apperception Test (TAT) which requires subjects to write or tell brief stories about ambiguous pictures or verbal cues. The stories can then be analyzed for signs of particular motives.

Using the TAT, Murray identified a long list of human motives (which he called needs); a number of them are shown in the following chapter, Figure 17.14. The motives on the list that psychologists have studied most intensively are achievement, affiliation, and dominance—especially achievement. For that reason, the achievement motive is discussed in this chapter in some detail, with particular attention to the work of expectancy-value theorists.

ASSESSING ACHIEVEMENT MOTIVATION

To measure the achievement motive, McClelland, Atkinson, and their colleagues showed subjects pictures from the TAT (see Figure 16.8). Each subject was given about four minutes to write a story answering the following questions: (1) What is happening? Who are the persons? (2) What has led up to the situation; that is, what has happened in the past? (3) What is being thought? What is wanted? By whom? (4) What will happen? What will be done? Typically, each subject was shown three or four different pictures, so that a large enough fantasy sample could be obtained for scoring. Figure 16.8 presents some sample stories and shows how they were scored.

Figure 16.8   A picture of the sort that might be used in the measurement of the Need for Achievement (*n* Ach). Examples of stories that would be scored from fairly high to low are shown beside the picture. The portions of the stories printed in italics are the kinds of themes considered to reflect *n* Ach.

This guy is just getting off work. These are all working guys and they don't like their work too much either. The younger guy over on the right knows the guy with the jacket. Something bad happened today at work—*a nasty accident that shouldn't have happened.* These two guys don't trust each other *but they are going to talk* about it. *They mean to put things to rights. No one else much cares* it seems.

The guy with the jacket is *worried.* He feels that *something has to be done. He wouldn't ordinarily talk* to the younger man *but now he feels he must.* The young guy is ready. He's *concerned* too but doesn't know what to expect.

They'll both realize after talking that you never know where your friends are. *They'll both feel better* afterward because they'll feel they have someone they can rely on next time there's trouble.

Harry O'Silverfish has been working on the Ford assembly line for thirteen years. Every morning he gets up, eats a doughnut and cup of coffee, takes his lunch pail, gets in the car, and drives to the plant. It is during this morning drive that his mind gets filled with *fantasies of what he'd like to be doing* with his life. Then, about the same time that he parks his car and turns off his ignition, he also *turns off his mind*—and it remains turned off during the whole working day. In the evenings, he is *too tired and discouraged to do much* more than drink a few beers and watch TV.

But this morning Harry's mind didn't turn off with the car. He had witnessed a car accident on the road—in which two people were killed—soon after leaving home. Just as he reaches the plant gate, Harry suddenly turns. Surprised, he discovers that he has made *a firm decision* never to enter that plant again. He knows that *he must try another way* to live before he dies.

These are hard-hats. It's the end of the shift. There is a demonstration outside the plant and the men coming out are looking at it. Everyone is just walking by. They are not much interested. One person is *angry* and *wants to go on strike,* but this does not make sense to anyone else. He is out of place. Actually he is not really angry, he is just bored. He looks as though he might do a little dance to amuse himself, which is more than the rest of them do. *Nothing will happen* at this time *till more people join* this one man in his needs.

Figure 16.9 Items from the Mandler-Sarason Test Anxiety Questionnaire. A high score on this scale is used as an indicator of a high fear of failure, which would be expressed behaviorally as the avoidance of a task.

The following questions relate to your attitude toward and experience with examinations. Try to represent your *usual* feelings and attitudes toward examinations, not toward any specific examination you have taken.

When you are taking a course examination, to what extent do you feel your emotional reactions interfere with or lower your performance?

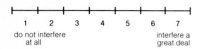

If you know that you are going to take a course examination, how do you feel *beforehand*?

After you have taken a course examination, how confident do you feel that you have done your best?

While taking a course examination, to what extent do you experience an accelerated heartbeat?

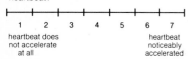

Before taking a course examination to what extent do you experience an accelerated heartbeat?

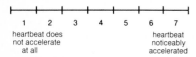

While taking a course examination to what extent do you perspire?

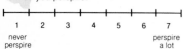

Before taking a course examination to what extent do you perspire?

The scoring system was devised by comparing stories written under achievement-oriented conditions (when a competitive intelligence test was also administered) with other stories written under relaxed conditions. In stories that received high scores for achievement, the major character showed concern about standards of excellence and a high level of performance; about unique accomplishments, such as inventions and receipt of awards; and about the pursuit of a long-term goal or career. High-achievement stories also dealt with persistent attempts to achieve and with good or bad feelings (pride or shame) aroused by the outcome of achievement-related activity.

To assess individual differences in the achievement motive, subjects are given the TAT under neutral conditions, and their stories are numerically scored for achievement imagery according to rules provided by Atkinson in 1958. Independent scorers trained in the use of this method have been found to agree very well on the scores for most stories. Similar scoring systems have been designed to measure other motives, such as need for affiliation and need for power, and the scoring systems for these motives can also be reliably used by trained scorers.

A Model of Achievement Motivation for Men

Early studies of achievement behavior revealed that highly motivated subjects—those who received high TAT scores on need for achievement—performed better on such tasks as anagram puzzles and addition problems than did low scorers on the TAT achievement measures. The high scorers also persisted longer at difficult tasks, were more likely than low scorers to recall interrupted tasks (indicating a continuing desire to complete the tasks successfully), and chose "expert" work partners more often than "friendly" ones (because the "experts" were more likely to contribute to success).

As the research evidence accumulated, several mysteries were encountered. For one thing, various results indicated that at least two motives were active in achievement situations: the need for achievement, which came to be called the **motive to approach success,** and an inhibitory motive called the **motive to avoid failure.** Many subjects were motivated to succeed at a particular task and so wanted to undertake it. But they were also worried about the consequences of failure and felt it might be safer to avoid the task in order to avoid the shame of failure. Atkinson, among others, began using the Mandler-Sarason Test Anxiety Questionnaire to measure this avoidance motive (see Figure 16.9 for sample items).

It was also mysterious that males and females often produced different results in studies of achievement motivation. The immediate result of this phenomenon seems to have been the elimination of female subjects from many subsequent studies—not a very satisfactory solution to the problem, to say the least. Recently the mystery has been confronted directly by Matina Horner; before discussing her work, however, let us consider the model of achievement motivation that Atkinson gradually developed for men.

Atkinson posed his model in mathematical form because he wanted to be as precise as possible and to derive clear predictions from the model that could be tested experimentally. In the model, the tendency to work for a particular goal—that is, the tendency that gets expressed in behavior—is called **resultant achievement motivation** (abbreviated T_R). The word "resultant" is used because this tendency results from a conflict between two opposing tendencies, the tendency to approach success (T_S) and the tendency to avoid failure (T_{AF}).

Each of the two opposing tendencies is determined by three variables, which have already been discussed: a personality characteristic called **motive;** an **expectancy,** or subjective probability; and an **incentive value.** For the approach tendency (T_S), the variables are (1) the motive to approach success, measured by the TAT, (2) the subjective probability of success (the person's belief about the likelihood of succeeding in a particular situation), and (3) the value to the person of succeeding. (The mathematical equation for the approach tendency is: $T_S = M_S \times P_S \times I_S$. T stands for tendency, M for motive, P for probability, and I for incentive.)

For the avoidance tendency, the variables are (1) the motive to avoid failure (measured by the test-anxiety questionnaire), (2) the subjective probability of failure, and (3) the incentive value of failure. (The equation is $T_{AF} = M_{AF} \times P_F \times I_F$.) When real numbers are placed in the equation, the value of failure, I_F, is negative—preceded by a minus sign—to indicate that failure is a costly outcome, an outcome to be avoided.)

Atkinson made a few assumptions and rules for computing probabilities. The most important assumption he made was that the incentive value of a task varies *inversely* with the probability of success. That is, the harder the task, the more value there is in succeeding at it. Probabilities are usually written as fractions ranging from 0 to 1; a probability of .50 means that there is a "50 percent chance" of succeeding at a task. (Thus, the equation relating incentive value, I_S, to probability, P_S, is $I_S = 1_S - P_S$.) It follows that if you have a high probability of success—say, .75—the probability of failure is low—.25. Atkinson further assumed, for his model, that the probability of success (P_S) is equal to the incentive value of failure (I_F) on a task ($I_F = P_S$). That is, the easier the task, the greater the shame in failing to do it.

With these assumptions, Atkinson was able to derive the theoretical curves shown in Figure 16.10 for tendency to approach success, tendency to avoid failure, and the resultant achievement motive. (Recall that resultant achievement motive is determined by subtracting tendency to avoid failure from tendency to approach success.) You can see that the tendency to approach success is positive and that it reaches its highest point where the probability of success is around .50 (that is, where the chances of succeeding and failing are equal). The tendency to avoid failure has a similar shape but is negative; it is strongest in the negative direction when the probability of success is .50.

Figure 16.10A represents a person with a high tendency to approach success and a low tendency to avoid failure; Figure 16.10B represents one with a low tendency to approach success and a high tendency to avoid failure. What the figure shows—and what the model predicts—is that a person who needs success more than he fears failure will try hardest at tasks of intermediate difficulty—that is, when he has a .50 probability of succeeding (Figure 16.10A). On the other hand, a person who fears failure more than he desires success will avoid such tasks when he can (Figure 16.10B).

Figure 16.10 These graphs show how the behavior of two hypothetical individuals on tasks of varying difficulty would be predicted by Atkinson's theory of achievement motivation. The tendency to approach success is represented by the yellow curves; the tendency to avoid failure, by the blue curves. Resultant achievement motivation is computed by subtracting the tendency to avoid failure from the tendency to approach success. (A) The person whose tendencies are represented by these curves has a high resultant achievement motivation (high tendency to approach success and low tendency to avoid failure); the curves show that this person will try hardest at tasks at which he perceives he has a .50 chance of succeeding. He is much less likely to try tasks that he sees as being impossible or extremely difficult to accomplish (0–.20) or those that are a cinch (.90–1.00). (B) This person has a low resultant achievement motivation (low tendency to approach success and high tendency to avoid failure). He will try hardest to avoid tasks that he sees he has a .50 chance of accomplishing. He is less likely to avoid tasks that seem very difficult to him (he can't be blamed for failing at such hard tasks) or that seem to him very easy to do.

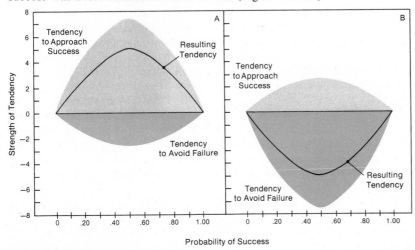

Figure 16.11 Results of a study that tested Atkinson's theory. Subjects in this study selected distances from which to make shots in a ring-toss game. Subjects who had previously been rated as having a high need for achievement (and who had scored low on the Test Anxiety Questionnaire, indicating low tendency to avoid failure) showed a strong preference for shots of medium difficulty. These subjects were like the individual represented in Figure 16.10A. Significantly fewer of the subjects with low need for achievement (and who had scored high on the Test Anxiety Questionnaire) chose to throw from an intermediate distance; more of them chose to stand closer to the target, where success was certain, or far enough away so that success could not be expected. These subjects were like the individual represented in Figure 16.10B.

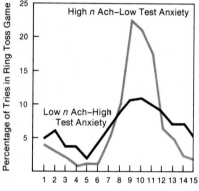

Chosen Distance from Target in Feet

Predictions from the model illustrated in the figure have been borne out in several laboratory studies. In the study whose results are presented in Figure 16.11, subjects with high resultant achievement motivation chose to stand at an intermediate distance from the target in a ring-toss game, thus making the game challenging but not impossible. Subjects with low resultant achievement motivation, on the other hand, were more likely to stand either very close to the target, where success was assured, or far away from the target, where they seemed to feel that no one could blame them for failing. In real life, too, people with high resultant achievement motivation tend to pursue careers that are difficult enough to be challenging but not so difficult that they will end in failure. People with low resultant achievement motivation are less realistic. They tend to choose either very easy jobs, where success is certain but the rewards are small, or very difficult jobs, which no one could blame them for failing to do.

The Achievement Motive and Society

McClelland and Atkinson worked together during the early stages of research on achievement motivation (in fact, Atkinson was one of McClelland's graduate students at that time). More recently their interests have diverged. Atkinson has been working on a precise model of individual achievement motivation, while McClelland has been primarily concerned with social origins of the achievement motive and its implications for a society. McClelland argues that a high level of achievement motivation within a particular society is partly responsible for a high level of entrepreneurial activity, which in turn leads to economic growth and modernization.

Particularly interesting and novel are his studies relating the economic growth and decline of certain societies to the level of achievement motivation reflected in the society's literature. The studies consisted of content analyses of literary samples, such as folk tales and children's readers, taken from critical points in each society's history. McClelland postulates that as the children who read these stories became old enough to be entrepreneurs, their activity would be reflected in economic indicators such as the amount of coal the society burned, the kilowatt hours of electricity it used, or the extent of its foreign trade. McClelland claims that the risk-taking activities and new ideas of entrepreneurs result from a strong achievement motive, not merely from a strong "need for money," as is often maintained.

McClelland has recently turned his attention to developing ways of strengthening people's achievement motivation. In one such project McClelland, David Winter, and their co-workers succeeded in raising the achievement motivation of businessmen in India, using a variety of techniques. The program they implemented consisted of encouraging the businessmen to have high-achievement fantasies, to make plans that would help them realize entrepreneurial goals, and to communicate with each other about goals and methods for reaching them. McClelland approached the project pragmatically: His aim was to raise the businessmen's achievement motivation rather than to identify the best techniques for doing so. For that reason, he does not know just why his program succeeded—whether one technique worked and the others did not or whether all of them helped—but succeed it did. The businessmen became more productive as entrepreneurs, expanding the size of their businesses and hiring more of their neighbors. Although small in scope, the project suggests that larger efforts of the same kind can be a major force in economic development.

Achievement Motivation in Women

Why doesn't the McClelland-Atkinson approach to achievement motivation work for female subjects? One clue is that females often obtain higher test-anxiety scores than do males. For a while some psychologists thought that this scoring pattern indicated that females were constitutionally more anxious than males, but Eleanor Maccoby suggested another possibility: "Suppose a girl does succeed in maintaining throughout her childhood years the qualities of dominance, independence, and active striving that appear to be requisites for good analytic thinking. In so doing, she is defying the conventions concerning what is appropriate behavior for her sex. She may do this successfully, in many ways, but I suggest that it is a rare intellectual woman who will not have paid a price for it: a price in anxiety." In other words, females in our culture are not supposed to be successful, at least not in some kinds of activity, and attempting to succeed in some endeavors may lead to negative consequences. This explanation for females' high anxiety scores is certainly a plausible one. Indeed, if you look back at the items in Figure 16.9, you will see that many of the items have to do with perspiration, tension, and heart rate—symptoms that could indicate either concern with failure (Atkinson's interpretation) or concern with success.

Matina Horner, in her research on this topic, devised a way to measure what she called the **motive to avoid success** (or "fear of success"). Note that this is a third achievement-related motive (along with motive to approach success and motive to avoid failure). Presumably it would operate in conjunction with the motive to avoid failure (by avoiding difficult tasks) in inhibiting the motive to approach success. Using a variation of the TAT, Horner gave college-student subjects the opening sentence of a story that they were supposed to complete. For the ninety women in the study, the sentence was "After first term finals, Anne finds herself at the top of her medical class." For the eighty-eight men, the name John was substituted for Anne.

A present-absent scoring system was developed to reflect fear-of-success imagery. A story was scored as showing fear of success if negative consequences befell the hero or heroine as a result of getting high grades in medical school. As with Atkinson's scoring system for achievement imagery, it was found that well-trained independent raters could agree on the appropriate scoring category for over 90 percent of the stories.

The fear-of-success stories were further classified into three main categories. The largest category was made up of stories in which negative feelings and consequences mainly had to do with affiliative concerns, such as fear of being rejected by society or by one's friends, of not being datable or marriageable, or of becoming isolated or lonely because of the success. It also included the desire to keep the success a secret so as not to seem intelligent.

Another category contained stories in which negative feelings and consequences of success were not explicitly related to affiliation; they expressed doubts about femininity or psychological normality, or such feelings as guilt and despair following the success.

The third group of stories included various examples of denial, such as denying the situation described by the cue ("it is impossible") and denying "Anne's" or "John's" effort or responsibility for attaining success. This third group was the second-largest category and a particularly interesting one. (Some sample stories appear in the adjacent margin.)

Differences Between Men and Women

The first striking characteristic of Horner's results was the sheer magnitude of the differences between the kinds of responses men and women made to the cue. The women showed significantly more evidence of the motive to avoid success than did the men. Fifty-nine of the ninety women in the study, or over 65 percent of them, wrote stories containing fear-of-success imagery, but only eight of the eighty-nine men, or fewer than 10 percent, did so.

Figure 16.12 Stories written by subjects in Matina Horner's research on the motive to avoid success. The first three stories, by women, show such a motive. The rest of the stories, only one of which was written by a woman, do not. (From Matina Horner, in *Feminine Personality and Conflict*, 1970.)

Anne has a boyfriend Carl in the same class and they are quite serious. Anne met Carl at college and they started dating around their sophomore years in undergraduate school. Anne is rather upset and so is Carl. She wants him to be higher scholastically than she is. Anne will deliberately lower her academic standing the next term, while she does all she subtly can to help Carl. . . . His grades come up and Anne soon drops out of med school. They marry and he goes on in school while she raises their family.

Aggressive, unmarried, wearing Oxford shoes and hair pulled back in a bun, she wears glasses and is terribly bright.

Anne is really happy she's on top, though Tom is higher than she—though that's as it should be . . . Anne doesn't mind Tom winning.

Congrats to her! Anne is quite a lady—not only is she tops academically, but she is liked and admired by her fellow students. Quite a trick in a man-dominated field. She is brilliant—but she is also a lady. A lot of hard work. She is pleased—yet humble and her fellow students (with the exception of a couple of sour pusses) are equally pleased. That's the kind of girl she is—you are always pleased when she is—never envious. She will continue to be at or near the top. She will be as fine practicing her field as she is studying it. And—always a lady.

John is a conscientious young man who worked hard. He is pleased with himself. John has always wanted to go into medicine and is very dedicated. His hard work has paid off. He is thinking that he must not let up now, but must work even harder than he did before. His good marks have encouraged him. (He may even consider going into research now.) While others with good first term marks sluff off, John continues working hard and eventually graduates at the top of his class. (Specializing in neurology.)

John is very pleased with himself and he realizes that all his efforts have been rewarded, he has finally made the top of his class. John has worked very hard, and his long hours of study have paid off. He spent hour after hour in preparation for finals. He is thinking about his girl Cheri whom he will marry at the end of med school. He realizes he can give her all the things she desires after he becomes established. He will go on in med school making good grades and be successful in the long run.

Horner suggested that the motive to avoid success would affect performance only in situations in which that specific motive was aroused. She hypothesized, further, that the motive to avoid success is aroused when a person is anxious about competitiveness and its aggressive overtones. Horner performed a second experiment in which each person was given a number of achievement tasks to perform in a large competing group of both men and women. People were then randomly assigned to other experimental conditions. One-third of them were placed in a strictly noncompetitive situation in which they worked alone on a verbal and arithmetic task, guided only by tape-recorded instructions. The performance of each of these thirty people in the noncompetitive situation was then compared with his or her previous performance in the large mixed-sex group.

Of the one-third of the subjects discussed here, more than two-thirds of the men performed at a higher level in the competitive situation than in the noncompetitive one, but fewer than one-third of the women did so. The results for women differing in strength of motive to avoid success were even more interesting: 77 percent of the women who had previously been scored high in motive to avoid success performed at a significantly higher level in the noncompetitive than in the competitive situation, compared with only 7 percent of those rated low in motive to avoid success. Of the women low in the motive to avoid success, 93 percent behaved more like the men in that they performed at a significantly higher level in the competitive than in the noncompetitive situation. These results suggest that sex differences in performance may be the result not of inherent differences in ability, as is often assumed, but of culturally imposed sex differences in motivation.

In the past few years many other researchers have studied fear of success. A study conducted by Ronald Winchel, Diane Fenner, and Phillip Shaver, for example, indicated that girls who attended coeducational schools were more likely to express fear-of-success imagery than were girls from similar backgrounds who attended noncoeducational schools. This finding suggests that the presence of boys increased success avoidance or at least brought it out more. In 1972 Horner reported that *better* female college students show more fear of success than their less-accomplished classmates, which again suggests that fear-of-success imagery reflects the strength of the conflict between attainment of success and traditionally defined femininity.

Other studies have challenged Horner's results (see the review by David Tresemer done in 1974), indicating, for example, that the proportion of males showing fear of success is larger than Horner claimed. It is not clear whether this new finding is the result of cultural changes in the last few years, of differences in the population studied, or of minor changes in the measures used. It is known that different results are obtained if "Anne" succeeds in nursing school rather than in medical school, which suggests that what females fear is not success per se but success in a male-dominated field. Much more investigative work needs to be done in this important area to ascertain the differences between the achievement motive in men and women.

An Attribution-Theory Approach

The preceding chapter outlined Stanley Schachter's attribution theory of emotion and explained that Schachter uses the term "attribution" to refer to interpretations given by people to their own feelings and actions. (Attribution also refers to one person's interpretation of another's reasons for performing an act, as discussed in Chapter 20.) A theoretical framework similar to Schachter's has been applied by Bernard Weiner to the study of achievement-related behavior.

Weiner has found that people usually attribute success and failure to one or more of the following four causes: **ability, effort, task difficulty,** and **luck.**

These four factors can be classified in terms of two dimensions, **locus of control** and **stability** (see Figure 16.13). Ability and effort are called internal factors because they seem to reside inside the person; task difficulty and luck are called external factors because they seem to lie outside the person. Ability and task difficulty are classified as stable because they are unlikely to change, at least in the short run, whereas effort and luck are both subject to change (that is, are unstable).

Studies by Weiner and his students suggest that the emotional reaction following success or failure (pride or shame) is stronger if the outcome is attributed more to internal factors (effort and ability) than to external factors (task difficulty and luck). Another way of saying this is that internal attributions influence what Atkinson called incentive value of success and of failure (I_S and I_F). Attributional differences on the stability dimension are related to what earlier were called expectancies of success and failure (Atkinson's P_S and P_F). For example, a person who attributes success to stable factors (ability and task difficulty) will expect to succeed again next time he or she tries the task. If unstable causes are believed responsible, on the other hand, the person is less certain of succeeding at that task again (especially if luck is emphasized).

Weiner's most interesting findings, from the perspective of the present chapter, have to do with attributional differences between people high and low in resultant achievement motivation ($T_S - T_{AF}$). People high in the achievement motive usually attributed their success to internal factors (high ability and high effort) and their failure to lack of effort. People low in achievement motivation were more likely to attribute success to external factors (ease of task and good luck) and failure to lack of ability.

These attributional differences help explain the behavioral differences documented by Atkinson and others. For example, people choose to undertake achievement-related activities; perhaps they do so because they have experienced strong positive emotion after success in the past (having attributed it to ability and effort). They persist longer in the face of failure than do their low-motivation counterparts; perhaps they persist longer because they think that failure is the result of insufficient effort on their part, and therefore that increased effort will lead to their success. Those low in achievement motivation give up easily because they attribute failure to low ability, and nothing can be done about that.

So far the sex differences in fear of success reported by Horner have not received much attention from attribution theorists, but a study conducted in 1974 by Norman Feather and J. G. Simon suggests that the attribution approach has the potential to account for sex differences in achievement motivation. Female college students (in Australia) responded to a verbal cue in which a male or female character either passed or failed an occupational qualifying examination. Among other things, the subjects were asked to rate several possible causes of the outcome. These included "cheating" and "examiner's error" in addition to Weiner's four categories—effort, ability, task difficulty, and luck. Results indicated that subjects saw ability as a more important cause of success for males than for females; lack of ability was seen as a more important cause of failure for females than for males. When the occupation in question was medicine and the character in the story succeeded, this outcome was more likely to be seen as the result of the easiness of the task if the character happened to be female rather than male. Finally, cheating was seen as a more important cause of success for female than for male characters, but as a more important cause of failure for males than for females.

If these results prove reliable, they will help explain why females seem to take less pleasure in competition and success than males do. Because of certain socialization experiences, females may not take enough personal

Figure 16.13 A classification of the factors that people use in explaining their successes and failures.

Locus of Control

	Internal	External
Stable	Ability	Task Difficulty
Unstable	Effort	Luck

Stability

credit for success and may be too quick to attribute failure to low ability. Weiner's work suggests that it is better, at least in terms of persistence and success, to attribute failure to insufficient effort. Then "if at first you don't succeed," you will conclude that you should "try, try again."

HUMAN MOTIVATION: A HIERARCHICAL CONCEPTION

The contents of this chapter indicate that a complete theory of human motivation must account for motives based on physiological needs similar to those of other animals, perhaps also for some drives that are akin to physiological needs, and, finally, for some motives that cannot be characterized without reference to human cognitive processes. One way to organize these diverse motives conceptually has been suggested by Abraham Maslow, a personality theorist whose work is discussed in Chapter 19.

Maslow believed that human needs, or motives, are organized hierarchically. The **fundamental needs** are related to physiological deficits (needs for food, water, and so on). The **intermediate needs**—for safety, belongingness, and esteem—are also "deficiency needs," in Maslow's conception. Failure to obtain feelings of basic security, social acceptance, and self-esteem produces pathological discomforts and maladjustments that may be almost as debilitating as starvation. The highest motives, called **metaneeds,** have to do with creativity and "self-actualization."

According to Maslow, the lower needs are preemptive or prepotent: Extreme hunger or thirst is so urgent that the severely deficient individual has no opportunity to worry about social acceptance and psychological security, let alone the creative exercise of his or her talents. Similarly, a person who is neurotically seeking social acceptance is not free to create independent scholarly or artistic works. Such a person cannot express any of his feelings and ideas comfortably.

There is some evidence to support this hierarchical conception of motivation. Even among animals, thirst and hunger are more potent than sexual motivation, and all of these preempt exploratory behavior. You probably know from your own experience that intense hunger interferes with almost all other activities. The research on achievement motivation indicates that fear of possible failure (a negative state related to Maslow's psychological deficiency needs) interferes with the tendency to exercise one's talents. Although Maslow's hierarchy needs further study, there is little question that each person's unique talents could be of more benefit to us all if societies were organized to guarantee that at least fundamental human needs are met.

Figure 16.14 Maslow's hierarchical classification of human needs or motives. The classification is hierarchical because the higher needs do not come to the fore until the lower needs are fulfilled. Maslow described all the needs except the last group as deficiency needs, needs that must be fulfilled if some form of sickness or disturbance is to be avoided. The last group of needs he described as growth needs, needs peculiar to human beings.

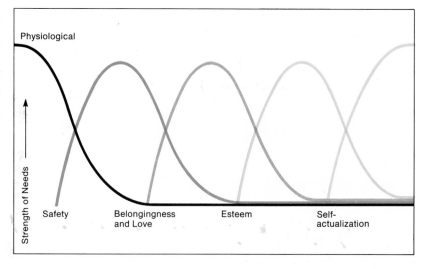

SUMMARY

1. Motivation is not an observable process that psychologists can measure directly; it must be inferred from **goal-directed behavior.**

2. The purpose of motivation theories in psychology is to account for the **initiation, direction, intensity,** and **persistence** of goal-directed behavior. Put more simply, motivation theorists try to explain the **energization** and **direction** of behavior at a particular moment.

3. An early approach to motivation, derived partly from Darwin's theory of evolution, emphasized inherited instincts as the determinants of behavior. This approach lost favor early in the twentieth century as it became clear that inventing instincts to account for various behaviors really explained nothing.

4. In the 1940s, Clark Hull's **drive theory** was the dominant approach to behavior in this country. Both drive theory itself and the research that disproved some of its claims have had an important effect on current theories of human motivation.

   a. Hull called the energy source of behavior **drive** and the directional component of behavior **habit.** According to his theory, a physiological deficit (such as food deprivation) activates a drive, which causes tension and increased activity in the animal. If, in the course of this activity, an animal presses a bar and receives a pellet of food, the bar-pressing is reinforced by **drive reduction,** and the **habit strength** of the bar-pressing response increases. One tenet of Hull's theory was that learning occurs only when a behavior is reinforced by the reduction of some drive.

   b. Hull and his followers viewed such human motives as achievement, power, and affiliation as **learned drives.** They believed, for example, that fear was a learned reaction to potential pain and that a child's love for his or her mother was originally based on the mother's satisfaction of the infant's need for food.

5. Research on drive theory uncovered a number of phenomena that were not in accord with the theory.

   a. Learning sometimes occurs even when no drive is reduced, although the learning may remain latent until an animal is offered an **incentive** (such as food) for performance.

   b. Infant monkeys prefer terrycloth mothers to wire ones that feed them, indicating that **contact comfort** is more important than feeding as a basis for the ties between infant and mother.

   c. Electrical stimulation of ''pleasure centers'' in the brain is reinforcing for animals and human beings, even though it reduces no known drive.

   d. Human beings and animals do not always seek to reduce stimulation to its lowest possible level, as drive theory implies they should; sometimes they seek stimulation, for example, in the form of novel or complex tasks.

   e. Many human motives are better explained by referring to cognitions —beliefs and values—than by defining them as learned drives originally associated with the satisfaction of physiological needs.

Figure 16.15 Harry Harlow's contributions to experimental psychology have not been equaled by many. In his primate laboratory at the University of Wisconsin, he was able to demonstrate phenomena such as ''learning-to-learn'' and the importance of physical comfort in mother love, which behaviorists had previously claimed to be fictions.

Figure 16.16 Kurt Lewin's research began in Germany, where he was associated with the Gestalt School of Psychology at the University of Berlin. He came to the United States in 1932 and became an influential contributor to the theory of motivation and social psychology. He was interested in using the mathematical discipline of topology in his theorizing about psychological phenomena. Lewin is also credited with being the originator of T-groups (the forerunner of sensitivity training groups).

6. One of the most important current approaches to human motivation is **expectancy-value theory,** which emphasizes cognitions. It relates motivated behavior to a person's expectancy of achieving a particular goal and to the incentive value the goal has for the person.

   a. Incentive value can be viewed in terms of pleasant or unpleasant emotion. In this conception, a goal with a high incentive value is one that a person believes (consciously or unconsciously) will lead to pleasant feelings; a goal with a negative incentive value is one that a person believes will lead to unpleasant feelings. The close relation between motivation and emotion is further indicated by the similarity between the energization component of motivation and the arousal or activation component of emotion.

   b. One aim of the expectancy-value approach to motivation is to allow for individual differences—for the fact that different people find different kinds of activities rewarding. In Atkinson's theory, the individual-difference variable is called **motive.** A second aim is to indicate, as precisely as possible, the *relation between motivation and behavior*—a difficult task, because a single act (such as entering medical school) may be both emotionally **overdetermined** (intended to satisfy more than one motive) and the product of a **conflict between contradictory motives.**

7. Using the Thematic Apperception Test (TAT), which he devised, Henry Murray identified a long list of human needs or motives. The motive studied most intensively by expectancy-value theorists has been the **achievement motive.**

   a. John Atkinson, working almost exclusively with male subjects, has used the TAT to measure the strength of people's achievement motive and a test-anxiety questionnaire to measure the strength of an opposing motive, the **motive to avoid failure** (opposing because it causes people to avoid difficult tasks). He has developed a mathematical model for achievement motivation that relates a person's expected value of succeeding or failing at a task to the person's level of achievement motivation and fear of failure. The model allows one to calculate the **resultant achievement motivation** by using a mathematical formula, $T_A = T_S - T_{AF}$. Each of the tendencies, T_S and T_{AF}, is determined by three factors: a **motive,** an **expectancy,** or probability, and an **incentive value.** Many laboratory studies have confirmed predictions based on Atkinson's model; for example, people with a strong tendency to approach success and a weak tendency to avoid failure tend to choose tasks of intermediate difficulty—hard enough to make success rewarding but easy enough to make it possible.

   b. David McClelland has studied the social origins of the achievement motive and its implications for society. He argues that a high level of achievement motivation in a society is partly responsible for a high level of entrepreneurial activity, which in turn leads to economic growth and modernization.

   c. Matina Horner, working with male and female subjects, has identified a third achievement-related motive: the **motive to avoid success.** The motive is common in women, who apparently fear that success in "masculine" areas will have negative consequences. She found that female subjects who showed fear of success tended to do much better in noncompetitive situations than in competitive ones, whereas most men (and women who did not show fear of success) performed better under competitive circumstances.

Figure 16.17 David McClelland's primary contributions to psychology are his techniques for measuring achievement motivation and his studies of that subject in a wide range of contexts, including the rise and fall of various cultures. McClelland has advised governmental and public committees and is the author of more than six books and forty articles.

8. Bernard Weiner has developed an **attribution theory of achievement motivation** based on the fact that people tend to attribute success or failure to some combination of **ability, effort, task difficulty,** and **luck;** these four factors can be classified in terms of **locus of control** (whether an act is thought to be the result of the person's own effort or caused by external events) and **stability** (for example, task difficulty and ability are less likely to change than effort and luck). His findings help explain certain behavioral differences between people high and low in achievement motivation and also suggest some possible reasons for sex differences in achievement-oriented behavior.

9. A complete theory of human motivation must account for cognitively determined motives as well as for motives based on drives or physiological needs. Abraham Maslow's three-step hierarchy of human needs may be useful as an organizing principle; it includes **fundamental needs** (physiological needs for food, water, and so on); **intermediate needs** (psychological needs for safety, belongingness, esteem, and so on); and **meta-needs** (psychological needs for creativity and self-actualization), which a person is able to attend to only when his **deficiency needs** (physiological and psychological) have been met.

SUGGESTED READINGS

Atkinson, John W. (ed.). *Motives in Fantasy, Action, and Society.* New York: Van Nostrand Reinhold, 1958. An important book that pulls together work done by many investigators on the various methods used to assess and study individual differences in motivational dispositions such as achievement, affiliation, and power. Scoring manuals and self-teaching materials are also included.

Atkinson, John W., and Norman T. Feather. *A Theory of Achievement Motivation.* New York: Wiley, 1966. Focuses on the contemporaneous determinants of achievement-oriented behavior and the marked advances made in psychologists' understanding of the problem.

Cofer, Charles N. *Motivation and Emotion.* Glenview, Ill.: Scott, Foresman, 1972. A short, comprehensive paperback textbook covering drive and incentive theories, biological aspects of motivation, the need for stimulation, and cognitive consistency theories.

Horner, Matina S. "Toward an Understanding of Achievement-Related Conflicts in Women," *Journal of Social Issues,* 28 (1972), 157–175. One of several article-length statements of Horner's theory and findings. Contains a useful bibliography of related works, including papers by Horner in which her scoring system is described.

McClelland, David. *The Achieving Society.* New York: Van Nostrand Reinhold, 1961. This book addresses the question of the social origins and consequences for society of achievement motivation.

Weiner, Bernard. *Theories of Motivation: From Mechanism to Cognition.* Chicago: Markham, 1973. A textbook covering, among other topics, drive theory, achievement theory, and—most important—the author's attribution-theory approach to achievement motivation. Presents clearly the differences between mechanistic (for example, drive) and cognitive (for example, attribution) theories.

UNIT V
Personality

To most people who have not studied the subject, the word "psychology" means only personality theory. What are people really like? Are people essentially good but corrupted by civilization, or are they basically selfish, aggressive, and greedy, needing civilization to soften them? Why do people do the things they do, love the people they love, and grow up to become doctors or lawyers or merchants or thieves?

17 Psychological Testing

describes the basic characteristics of psychological tests, such as reliability and validity, and discusses various kinds of psychological tests now in use. It focuses especially on personality tests and intelligence tests.
See related chapters: 7, 16, 24

18 Psychoanalytic Theories of Personality

first describes the goals and general characteristics of theories of personality. It then discusses at length the first comprehensive personality theory in psychology, developed by the great Austrian psychologist Sigmund Freud, and examines revisions of Freud's theory suggested by neo-Freudian psychologists.
See related chapters: 10, 16, 20, 21, 25, 26

RELATED CHAPTERS

4
Conditioning and Learning: Behaviorism describes the key concepts of the behaviorist approach, which provide the basis for the discussion of behaviorist analyses of personality in Chapter 19.

6
Thinking and Problem Solving: Cognitive Psychology examines the cognitive approach to learning and problem solving. The phenomenological and humanistic approaches to personality presented in Chapter 19—and especially George Kelly's personal-construct theory—all share much of the focus of cognitive psychology.

7
Heredity and Environment discusses the controversy over hereditary and environmental influences on IQ scores. Chapter 17 examines the intelligence tests from which IQ scores are derived.

10
Social Development: The Case of Morality considers three different theories of social development: psychoanalytic theory, discussed in Chapter 18; social-learning theory, described in Chapter 19; and cognitive-developmental theory, which shares the general cognitive focus of Kelly's personal-construct theory, also presented in Chapter 19.

16
Motivation and Action discusses several motives (including the motive to achieve and the motive to avoid success) that are measured with the TAT test, described in Chapter 17. The view of human motivation in Chapter 16 can also be compared to the interpretations of motivation of each of the personality theories in Chapters 18 and 19.

Unfortunately for people who want these questions answered, psychologists do not agree about which of the many personality theories in psychology is correct—or even most nearly correct. The most extensive and complete theory of personality was constructed by Sigmund Freud, and it is Freud's system that many laymen refer to when they try to determine what is the "real" reason for another person's behavior. Since Freud first formulated his theory, many others have followed him. Some have followed his approach closely; others have developed theories totally different from his. Most of the important approaches are presented in this unit, together with a description of some of the psychological tests that are often used to assess people's personalities and to test psychologists' theories of personality.

19 Alternative Conceptions of Personality

represents three main viewpoints on personality that have been proposed as alternatives to psychoanalytic theory: behaviorist, humanist, and trait approaches. It also examines the current controversy over whether individuals do in fact show consistencies in personality across many different situations.
See related chapters: 4, 6, 10, 16, 20, 21, 25, 26, 27

20 Person Perception and Interpersonal Attraction

describes how people form impressions of other people's personalities in everyday life. The orientation of many of these impressions can be related to the theories of personality reviewed in Chapters 18 and 19.

21 Patterns of Social Behavior: The Case of Sex Roles

examines several different explanations of how sex roles are acquired, including the psychoanalytic approach presented in Chapter 18 and the social-learning approach described in Chapter 19.

24 Adjustment and Disorder

outlines the standard classifications of psychological disorder. Chapter 17 discusses the main psychological tests and other assessment techniques that are used to help classify individual cases of disorder.

25 Bases of Disorder

considers a number of concepts that may help explain how mental disorder arises, including concepts from psychoanalytic theory, presented in Chapter 18, and concepts from social-learning theory, discussed in Chapter 19.

26 Individual and Group Psychotherapy

examines the history of psychotherapy and discusses current trends in therapy. In many cases specific types of psychotherapy reviewed in Chapter 26 derive from particular theories of personality described in Chapters 18 and 19.

27 Behavior Therapy and Behavior Modification

describes the behaviorist framework for psychotherapy, which relates to the behaviorist approach to personality presented in Chapter 19.

What is intelligence, anyway? When I was in the Army I received a kind of aptitude test that all soldiers took and, against a normal of 100, scored 160. No one at the base had ever seen a figure like that and for two hours they made a big fuss over me. (It didn't mean anything. The next day I was still a buck private with KP as my highest duty.)

All my life I've been registering scores like that, so that I have the complacent feeling that I'm highly intelligent, and I expect other people to think so, too. Actually, though, don't such scores simply mean that I am very good at answering the type of academic questions that are considered worthy of answers by the people who make up the intelligence tests—people with intellectual bents similar to mine?

For instance, I had an auto-repair man once, who, on these intelligence tests, could not possibly have scored more than 80, by my estimate. I always took it for granted that I was far more intelligent than he was. Yet, when anything went wrong with my car I hastened to him with it, watched him anxiously as he explored its vitals, and listened to his pronouncements as though they were divine oracles—and he always fixed my car.

Well, then, suppose my auto-repair man devised questions for an intelligence test. Or suppose a carpenter did, or a farmer, or, indeed, almost anyone but an academician. By every one of those tests, I'd prove myself a moron. And I'd *be* a moron, too. In a world where I could not use my academic training and my verbal talents but had to do something intricate or hard, working with my hands, I would do poorly. My intelligence, then, is not absolute but is a function of the society I live in and of the fact that a small subsection of that society has managed to foist itself on the rest as an arbiter of such matters.

Consider my auto-repair man, again. He had a habit of telling me jokes whenever he saw me. One time he raised his head from the automobile hood to say: "Doc, a deaf-and-dumb guy went into a hardware store to ask for some nails. He put two fingers together on the counter and made hammering motions with the other hand. The clerk brought him a hammer. He shook his head and pointed to the two fingers he was hammering. The clerk brought him nails. He picked out the sizes he wanted, and left. Well, doc, the next guy who came in was a blind man. He wanted scissors. How do you suppose he asked for them?"

Indulgently, I lifted my right hand and made scissoring motions with my first two fingers. Whereupon my auto-repair man laughed raucously and said, "Why, you dumb jerk, he used his *voice* and asked for them." Then he said, smugly, "I've been trying that on all my customers today." "Did you catch many?" I asked. "Quite a few," he said, "But I knew for sure I'd catch *you*." "Why is that?" I asked. "Because you're so goddamn educated, doc, I *knew* you couldn't be very smart."

And I have an uneasy feeling he had something there.

Isaac Asimov

Figure 17.1 A woman at a YMCA counseling service is shown taking one subtest of the Wechsler Adult Intelligence Scale. She is being timed while she assembles the cubes to match a pattern in the booklet that stands in front of her. Because testing is one of the principal means psychologists have of quantifying human behavior, tests are used in a great many areas of research as well as for assessing people's capabilities and personalities for purposes of counseling or therapy.

I t is a fact that, on the average, poor Americans and black Americans score lower on standard intelligence tests than rich Americans and white Americans. Does this mean that poor people and blacks are innately inferior to rich people and whites?

It is a fact that many large corporations have designed personality and aptitude tests that allow them to determine which job applicants are likely to do well and which are not. Does this mean that an applicant should be refused a job on the basis of his score on a personality test?

It is a fact that psychotics score differently from normal persons on many personality tests. Does this mean that people whose scores are similar to those of psychotics should be hospitalized?

Over the years, psychologists have devised a whole range of instruments to measure intelligence, interests, skills, aptitudes, and basic personality patterns. The tests vary greatly in their purpose, content, and construction, according to which characteristics are being assessed. The use of all these instruments—whether they test easily measured traits, like achievement in mathematics, or such complex personality traits as needs or values—is steadily increasing in the modern world. However, the use of these tests raises many ethical issues. Most of the objections to the tests stem from the fact that although people are similar to each other in some ways, they are different in others, and when the attributes of individuals or of groups of people are statistically compared, someone must come out second best. The use of measures of intelligence has been especially criticized on several counts.

INTELLIGENCE TESTING

Alfred Binet, a French psychologist, was the first to develop a reliable intelligence test. Before Binet's work, psychologists had attempted to measure intelligence by giving sensory and motor tests; they tested people's ability to accurately estimate the passage

Figure 17.2 Two tests on the Stanford-Binet Intelligence Scale being administered to a little boy. Both these tests are ones that would be easily passed by him unless he were severely retarded.   (top) The examiner has built a tower of four blocks and has told the child, "You make one like this." The average two-year-old is able to build the tower. Three-year-olds are asked to copy a three-block bridge.   (bottom) The examiner shows the child the card with six small objects attached to it and says, "See all these things? Show me the dog," and so on. The average two-year-old can point to the correct objects as they are named.

of time, the efficiency of their hand-eye coordination, their speed of tapping, and their memory. Around the end of the nineteenth century, Binet began testing children's vocabulary, their recognition of familiar objects, their understanding of commands, and the like; he was looking for abilities that changed with age. Binet assumed that if older children did better on the tests than younger children, then children who performed better than others of their own age must be more intelligent.

In 1905 Binet was asked by the Minister of Public Instruction for the Paris schools to develop a test that could be used to identify mentally defective children, so that they could be taught separately. In collaboration with psychiatrist Theodore Simon, Binet devised a thirty-item test, arranging the items or tasks in order of increasing difficulty. By 1908 Binet's tests were also being used to make differentiations among and predict the school performance of normal children.

Originally, Binet had defined children as retarded whose scores were at least two years below the average scores for children of their chronological age. One problem with this definition was that a child of fourteen who was two years behind his age group was considered to be as retarded as a child of six who was two years behind his age group. A German psychologist, William Stern, suggested that rather than take the difference between mental age (defined as the average age of children who obtain a particular score on an intelligence test) and chronological age, the test should employ the ratio of mental age to chronological age. His idea resulted in the **intelligence quotient (IQ)**, computed by dividing mental age by chronological age and multiplying by 100 (to get rid of the decimals). In the 1960 revision of the Stanford-Binet test, a system of standard scores, called "deviation IQs," was instituted. Standard scores are discussed later in this chapter.

Individual Tests

Binet's test of intelligence has been revised many times since he developed it. The Binet test currently employed in the United States is a revision made at Stanford University. The **Stanford-Binet** test contains a number of subtests that are grouped by age. Some are verbal tests and some are performance tests. Performance tests include such activities as picture completion, block design, picture arrangement, and object assembly (see Figure 17.2). They are arranged in an order designed to hold the interest of the person being tested. The examiner is trained to carry out the standardized instructions exactly but at the same time to try to put the subject at ease. The best way to be sure that differences in scores do not reflect variations in motivation rather than in ability is to try to ensure that all subjects are highly motivated.

In administering the tests, the examiner first tries the person out on some questions—often from the vocabulary test—to locate the proper level at which to start. For example, if a nine-year-old who seems reasonably bright is being tested, the examiner would probably begin by giving him the tests for an eight-year-old. If the child misses some of the questions, the examiner drops back to tests for year seven. After locating the basal age—the highest age at which the child can pass all items—the examiner proceeds with tests at later year levels and gives the child extra credit for the ones he can pass. When a child reaches the level at which he can pass no items, the testing session ends.

In the final scoring, the mental age indicates how high a level of development the person has reached. If a child has a mental age of twelve, then his performance is as good as the average twelve-year-old's. The IQ indicates how his level of development compares with that of his age mates. In addition, the examiner generally picks up a good deal of qualitative information about how the child's mind works, information often very useful to teachers or psychotherapists who deal with him. The original Binet tests were designed for school-age children, but successive revisions of the Stanford-Binet tests have extended the scale downward into the preschool levels and upward into the adult levels.

The other individual intelligence tests that have been most frequently used are those developed by David Wechsler: the **Wechsler Adult Intelligence Scale (WAIS)** and the **Wechsler Intelligence Scale for Children (WISC)**. These tests, like the Stanford-Binet, are made up of both verbal and performance tests, but they are arranged differently. Items of the same kind are grouped together into a subtest and arranged in order of difficulty. The examiner administers each of the subtests, starting with a very easy item and continuing until the end or until the person has missed three items in succession.

The Wechsler tests differ from the Stanford-Binet in several ways. For example, the Wechsler tests have more performance tasks and are therefore less biased toward verbal skills, and the Wechsler tests do not organize their questions in terms of age; the items are the same for children of all ages. There is one major overall difference between the two tests. The Wechsler gives separate scores for each kind of subtest—vocabulary, information, arithmetic, picture arrangement, block design, and so on. The subtest scores are in turn combined into separate IQ scores for verbal and performance abilities. This method of scoring helps the examiner sketch a qualitative picture of how the individual reacts to different kinds of items. Most important, it encourages the treatment of intelligence as a number of different abilities rather than as one overriding ability.

Group Tests

Group intelligence tests are strictly paper-and-pencil measures; there is no person-to-person interchange as with individual tests. The convenience and economy of group tests have led to their use in schools, employment offices, and many other mass testing situations. The Army Alpha and Army Beta, for example, were developed during World War I for classifying soldiers. Group tests include verbal and performance varieties and many combinations of the two. However, group tests do not generally predict school performance as well as individual tests do, and individual tests are still preferred by clinicians. It is not possible to pick out one or two tests that are as representative of group tests as the Stanford-Binet and Wechsler instruments are of individual

Figure 17.3 Two examples of group testing. Examinations and intelligence tests administered under conditions ranging from formal (left) to casual (right) are familiar experiences to students in almost any public school system. Both intelligence tests and regular examinations can be considered psychological tests because both are intended to measure psychological variables (intelligence and knowledge). Regular examinations are classified by psychologists as achievement tests, a category discussed later in the chapter.

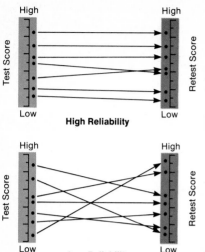

Figure 17.4 The concept of test reliability. On the left in each diagram the test scores obtained by seven individuals are ordered on a scale. On the right the corresponding scores on a second version of the same test, or on the same test given at a later time, are ordered. In the upper diagram the two sets of scores correspond very closely. This pattern of scores means that the test is highly reliable. In the lower diagram, there is little relationship between the two sets of scores. This scrambled pattern means that the test has a low reliability: Two different administrations of the same test gave quite different results.

Figure 17.5 If one were to construct a test of intelligence by measuring head size and equating inches with IQ, one would have a highly reliable test. That is, all the people who independently measured Leonardo da Vinci's head would come up with much the same results. However, the test would have very low validity because head size has, in fact, no relation to intelligence.

tests. Group tests are usually used in particular situations for particular purposes. Many group intelligence tests are really better thought of as scholastic aptitude tests, since they are made up of the kinds of items that have been found to correlate most closely with school success.

CHARACTERISTICS OF A TEST

There are two essential characteristics of a test, its reliability and its validity. **Reliability** refers to how consistent or stable the scores on the test are, and **validity** refers to the test's ability to measure what it is supposed to be measuring. Figure 17.4 illustrates the difference between a test with high reliability and one with low reliability. Figure 17.6 illustrates the difference between a test with high validity and one with low validity.

An anecdote might help explain the two concepts. Imagine that one of your friends invents an intelligence test and asks you to try it out. You do, and you obtain an IQ score of 80. Predictably, you become skeptical of the result. There are two main bases on which you could challenge the test: You could argue either that it was not reliable or that it was not valid (or, presumably, both). And with the knowledge gained after reading this chapter, you would probably be able to marshal proof of your argument.

Reliability

To show that a test is not reliable, you must show that the scores people obtain are either not consistent or not stable—that the scores have been affected by factors not related to the attribute being tested. For example, you might claim that the way your friend scored his test was arbitrary and demand that he have someone else score it. If a second scorer failed to obtain a score consistent with that of the first scorer, the test would be unreliable. Another way of checking for reliability would be for you to take the test, or a comparable one, again at some later time. Because IQ is an attribute that is supposed to be stable over time, a drastic difference in scores would challenge the test's reliability. A third way of checking the reliability of a test is to split it in half and take the halves at different times. You could also have each half scored by a different person. If both halves are meant to measure the same quality or trait, the scores should be consistent. There are a number of different ways to check a test's reliability, but they all boil down to checking whether it consistently produces the same result, either over time in measuring a stable characteristic or when equivalent scoring methods are used. In short, it must be *relied* on to produce the same results on different occasions.

You should keep in mind that for a test to be reliable, it does not have to give a valid measure of what is being tested. If, for example, you devised a reading-level test that scored printed materials on the number of syllables in each word—the more syllables, the harder the word—you could easily obtain a reliable measure, but it might not be valid. Consider this sentence: "The inhabitants of the yurt discovered, upon reaching the chine overlooking the heaf, that the quern had been demolished." All the difficult words in this sentence (they *are* words; see *Webster's Third New International Dictionary,* unabridged) are only one syllable. Yet each time the test was scored, the scores would show the same number of one-syllable, two-syllable, three-syllable words, and so on. Figure 17.5 suggests another type of test that is reliable without being valid. If the assumption that the test is based on is that the greater a person's head size, the more intelligent he is, you would get reliable measures—almost everyone who measured Leonardo's head would come up with the same measurement. But because head size bears no relation to intelligence in the real world, the test would not be valid.

Now, what if your test-making friend proved to you that his test was reliable—that it produced the same score consistently? You still would not be forced to admit that you had an IQ of 80. You could argue that although the test was reliable, it was not valid.

Validity

To establish that his test was valid, your friend would have to show that it measures what it purports to, in this case intelligence. The indicator of performance in real life against which a psychological test is evaluated is called the criterion. The criteria and the kinds of evidence that must be assembled to demonstrate validity vary with the nature and purpose of a test, and, depending on the purpose, there are four types of validity a test may have. One way your friend might try to prove his test valid would be to give you a second intelligence test—one whose reliability and validity were well established—and attempt to show that your score was the same on both. **Concurrent validity,** then, is established for a test by comparing its results with those of an established test.

Your friend might employ his test to predict your performance on related behavior. For example, people of low intelligence should perform poorly in academic settings. Your friend would have to correctly predict that, with an IQ of 80, you would get poor marks in college courses. **Predictive validity,** then, refers to a test's ability to predict performance in a related area. Of course, no test can predict perfectly. If all children who score low on a so-called intelligence test do as well in school as the children who receive moderate or high scores, the test cannot be considered a valid measure of intelligence, at least of the kind of intelligence that schoolwork requires. Binet used the ability of his test to predict schoolchildren's performance as a criterion of its success, and ever since Binet, the primary criterion for intelligence tests has been their ability to predict school performance.

Let us imagine that one of the items on your friend's test required you to draw a picture. You might argue that drawing measures artistic ability, not intelligence, and that the test therefore lacks **content validity.** The content of a test must relate logically to what it purports to measure. In a school achievement test designed to find out how much individual students know about, say, geometry or American history, the questions asked in the test must correspond to knowledge and information in that particular field. In validating the content of such a test, one looks for information about how its items are selected. People who select the questions may have individual biases about what knowledge is representative of the field, but such biases should offset one another when a committee of several equally competent people make the selections.

Finally, **construct validity** is required when a test result is going to be explained in terms of a construct (a specific theoretical concept) that is part of a larger, more general psychological theory. For example, if a psychologist is running an experiment to determine the effects of anxiety on test-taking, he must start with several hypotheses about what anxiety is and how it may affect behavior. He can draw from any psychological theory the constructs meant to describe anxiety and its effects. He must then experimentally check his expectations based on these constructs with the subjects' experiences and behavior. If his experimental procedures show that his subjects' experiences and behavior are what the theoretical constructs predicted they would be, his test of anxiety has construct validity. The determination of construct validity is much more complex than the other types of validity discussed here; it is most often required for tests used for descriptions of people, as in some personality tests, or tests used in psychological research.

A test may have high reliability but low validity even when the content of the test seems to be appropriate to whatever the test is supposed to be measuring. One of the main factors that produces high reliability with low validity is called **response bias.** With certain kinds of tests, there are people who tend to

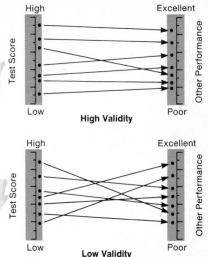

Figure 17.6 The concept of test validity. A comparison of this figure with Figure 17.4 shows that reliability and validity are assessed in exactly the same way. The difference is that while assessment of reliability requires that a test be checked against itself, assessment of validity requires that the test scores be compared to some other measure of behavior. For example, the lower diagram might represent the comparison of scores on the "head-size" test of intelligence (on the left) with school grades (on the right). The upper diagram might represent the result of comparing Stanford-Binet scores with school grades. The Stanford-Binet is a valid test for predicting school grades; the head-size measurement is not.

give one type of answer, even though their answer has little or nothing to do with the content of the test. For example, if a test is made up of a series of questions all of which are to be answered "yes" or "no," some people will tend to answer "yes" to questions regardless of their content, and others will tend to answer "no." Similarly, if, on a personality scale, people are supposed to rate a characteristic on a dimension from low to high, many people will make ratings toward the middle of the dimension regardless of the characteristics listed.

Few people realize that no tests are absolutely valid. It is tremendously difficult to validate a test. For example, from the very beginning, the search for an adequate measure of intelligence was tied to the search for an adequate theoretical definition of intelligence. Binet never published a formal definition of intelligence. How can we know whether an intelligence test is measuring intelligence when we have no criterion of intelligence that is better than the test? In order to establish the test's construct and content validity, we need a criterion. (Intelligence tests do have predictive and concurrent validity as long as one accepts their function as predictors of academic achievement.) But in order to obtain a criterion, we must know what intelligence is—and no one knows for sure, although there are theories and opinions aplenty, many of which you will read or have read in this text. The definition of intelligence implicit in intelligence tests is, in fact, an operational one; that is, intelligence is defined as what intelligence tests measure.

It is clear, then, that the nature of intelligence is elusive and that test validity is not a simple matter. With this in mind, people who offer tests to the public should carefully collect all the information needed to establish what the tests are measuring; those who use the test scores—teachers, personnel managers, and psychotherapists, for example—should be familiar with the whole body of research data concerning tests and use it as a basis for their interpretations of people's scores.

Norms

Still another kind of information that must be provided if a test is to be useful comes under the general heading of norms. A score in itself tells an individual very little unless he knows what kinds of scores other people have made. That is, if a person were told he had correctly answered fifty-three of the eighty-eight questions on a test, he would not know whether he had done well or poorly unless he knew that most people are able to answer only forty-four. Testers develop norms before a test is put into general distribution by giving it to a large and well-defined group of people, called a **standardization group.** It is customary to take the arithmetic average of the standardization group's scores as a reference point and indicate how far above or below this average any given score is. There are many ways of doing this. On the IQ scale, 100 is the average figure, and there are many more scores near the average than there are in the most extreme categories. Most commonly used tests of intelligence are constructed so that about 68 percent of the population obtains IQ scores between 85 and 115; over 95 percent obtain scores between 70 and 130; and over 99.7 percent obtain scores between 55 and 145. The meaningfulness of scores under 50 and over 150 is questionable.

Most tests require several sets of norms—for example, norms appropriate for people of different ages, sexes, and races. The group to which a person is compared must be the group to which he or she belongs. In intelligence testing, age is the most important factor, but sex, social class, and race can also be important. For example, most intelligence tests have been developed and validated with white people as the standardization group. There are few norms for members of other races, and the established norms, therefore, may be inappropriate for individuals of other races who take these tests.

The **percentile system** and the **standard score system** are the most common systems for translating "raw" scores, the scores individuals actually make, into scores that are relative to the scores of others. The percentile system divides a group of scores into 100 equal parts; each percentile, then, contains 1/100 of the scores. A percentile number therefore shows the proportion of individuals that a person scores above and below. For example, a score at the 80th percentile would be better than the scores of 80 percent of the rest of the people who took the test and worse than the scores of 20 percent. Standard scores are more complex. They represent points on a bell-shaped curve (see Figure 17.7) that reflects the way people score on almost all tests. The bell-shaped curve shows that the majority of people obtain scores within a narrow range, somewhere in the middle of the distribution of test scores. The further a score is from the middle, or average, the rarer it is (that is, few people obtain it). Whatever the actual average score of the given test is, it is converted to a **standard score** of O. The further a score is from the average (higher or lower), the greater the standard score, up to $+4$ or -4. The purpose of converting test scores to standard scores is to show how representative they are of what most people do. As Figure 17.7 shows, a standard score of $+3$ or -3 means that the score is extremely rare: Less than 1 percent of the people who take the test obtain it.

The standard score system currently used for the Stanford-Binet test (called "deviation IQ") was substituted for the ratio IQ system in order to obtain constant IQ variability at all ages. The raw scores were converted to standard scores in such a way that the score of 100 remains the average score, and a standard deviation of 15 was instituted throughout the age range. This statistical procedure, which need not be detailed here, eliminated some problems that existed in scoring ratio IQs. There are, in fact, tables that testers can use,

Figure 17.7 The theoretical normal curve (top) and a practical application of it (bottom). The curves show the proportions of a group or population that fall at various points on a scale; a few fall at high points, a few at low, and most in the middle. The theoretical curve is useful because it has precisely known mathematical characteristics from which such relative measures as standard and percentile scores can be calculated. Standard scores describe the position of an individual's score in terms of the variance of the whole group's scores. A person with a standard score of 2 is twice as far away from the mean (zero) as is a person with a standard score of 1 and equally far away from the mean in the opposite direction as is a person with a standard score of −2. Percentile scores describe the position of an individual's score in terms of the percentage of scores in the group that his score exceeds. Thus, a person in the 90th percentile has a greater score than 90 percent of the group. Percentile scores can be converted into standard scores because the proportions of the group that fall at various standard scores are known. For example, a person with a standard score of 1 has a higher score than approximately 84 percent of the group. As the lower curve shows, a single standard-score unit corresponds to about 16.4 IQ points on the 1937 Stanford Binet. Knowing this correspondence and knowing the average IQ (approximately 100), one can convert any IQ into a standard score or a percentile score by reading from the IQ curve to the theoretical curve. Note that the IQ curve does not match the theoretical curve perfectly. There is an unexpected hump, for example, at IQ scores around 40. This hump is believed to represent people who have had brain damage.
(After Terman and Merrill, 1973–bottom graph only.)

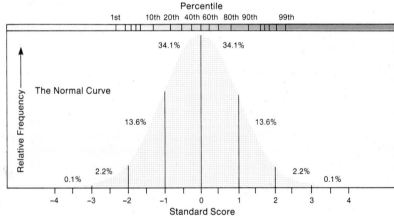

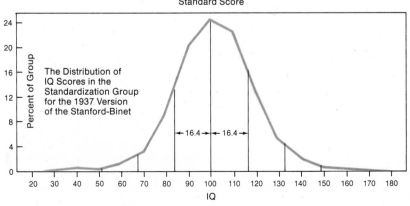

The Dove Counterbalance Intelligence Test
by Adrian Dove

If they throw the dice and "7" is showing on the top, what is facing down?
(a) "Seven" (b) "Snake eyes"
(c) "Boxcars" (d) "Little Joes"
(e) "Eleven"

Jazz pianist Ahmad Jamal took an Arabic name after becoming really famous. Previously he had some fame with what he called his "slave name." What was his previous name?
(a) Willie Lee Jackson
(b) LeRoi Jones
(c) Wilbur McDougal
(d) Fritz Jones (e) Andy Johnson

In "C. C. Rider," what does "C. C." stand for?
(a) Civil Service
(b) Church Council
(c) County Circuit, preacher of an old-time rambler
(d) Country Club
(e) "Cheating Charley" (the "Boxcar Gunsel")

Cheap "chitlings" (not the kind you purchase at the frozen-food counter) will taste rubbery unless they are cooked long enough. How soon can you quit cooking them to eat and enjoy them?
(a) 15 minutes (b) 2 hours
(c) 24 hours
(d) 1 week (on a low flame)
(e) 1 hour

If a judge finds you guilty of "holding weed" (in California), what's the most he can give you?
(a) Indeterminate (life) (b) A nickel
(c) A dime (d) A year in county
(e) $100.00.

A "Handkerchief Head" is
(a) A cool cat (b) A porter
(c) An "Uncle Tom" (d) A hoddi
(e) A "preacher"

Figure 17.8 An extreme example of how an intelligence test may depend on knowledge specific to one culture. A population of urban blacks would score high on this test, and a population of suburban whites would score low. Even when a test's items do not show this kind of obvious culture loading, a test may have validity problems. For example, many subcultures within Western society place great emphasis on competence in test taking. In a subculture where such emphasis is lacking, the validity of almost any test is likely to suffer.

which give them the deviation IQ for people simply from their mental age and chronological age in years and months.

To generate norm tables for either a percentile system or a standard score system is not difficult after a standardization group has been tested. What is more difficult—and extremely important for test producers—is to make sure that the standardization group, on which norms are based, is really representative of the population in which the test will be used.

INTERGROUP DIFFERENCES

As mentioned earlier, many relationships between IQ and other attributes have been found, but the significance of these relationships is often difficult to determine. For example, it is well established that the higher a person's social class (as measured by occupational level, educational level, and income), the higher his IQ score is liable to be. Interpretation of this relationship is not simple because people in the higher social classes clearly have more exposure to the skills that are tested on intelligence tests. In a classic study of people with high IQs, Lewis Terman followed over 1,000 gifted students from an early age to adulthood. He found significant positive relationships between IQ and physical, academic, social, and moral development. Brighter persons were generally taller, heavier, stronger, more advanced in social and personal maturity, and had greater achievements in school and other social situations. People with high IQs were also less likely to show lethal behavior (fatal accidents, suicide), deliquency and criminality, alcoholism, drug dependency, and severe mental illnesses. And, finally, Terman found that highly intelligent people received more degrees, distinctions, awards, professional licenses and certifications, and income; they made more artistic and literary contributions and reported more satisfaction in life. But all of these relationships may result not from IQ itself but from other factors, like social class.

Nature or Nurture

Many people have tried to use intelligence tests to obtain definite answers to age-old questions about whether or not there are innate intellectual differences among groups, but it has proved to be almost impossible to come to reliable conclusions about such postulated differences. People whose childhood environment has been quite different from that of the majority of American and European children tend to have lower scores on tests developed in the United States and Europe. This difference, even when statistically significant, cannot be accepted as evidence that various groups differ in innate potential, because a person's score reflects not only his genetic potential for intellectual development (nature) but also what he has learned from his experience (nurture).

If a test is developed for people with a specific cultural background, it cannot legitimately be used for people with a markedly different background. For example, of all the various kinds of items on intelligence tests, vocabulary provides the best single estimate of IQ scores. If you had only ten minutes to assess IQ, you would probably use a vocabulary test; yet vocabulary clearly depends on cultural background. If someone has never heard words like "sonata" or "ingenuous," he will perform poorly on verbal intelligence tests. And if he has grown up in a community where the primary language is not English, he will be handicapped even further. Figure 17.8 reproduces some questions from the "Counterbalance" Intelligence Test, created by Adrian Dove, a black, to test the intelligence of whites.

There are differences among the *average* IQ scores of different races and different nationalities. However, it has proved to be virtually impossible to conceive of those differences as resulting primarily from either differences in upbringing and environment or differences in inheritance. Chapter 7 contains a lengthy discussion of how both hereditary factors and environmental influences affect the development of intelligence and sets out a short discussion of some current controversies in the area.

The Use of IQ Scores

The usefulness of IQ tests does not lie in their ability to measure innate differences between groups or individuals. It lies in aiding counselors and schoolteachers to give the kind of individual help to students that is required. For example, test scores can alert a seventh-grade history teacher to the fact that one student is equipped at the outset of the course to do excellent work and should be held to a high standard and that another student may have much more difficulty in using the vocabulary or grasping the main ideas and should be given special help. The teacher need not think in terms of heredity or environment.

ACHIEVEMENT AND APTITUDE TESTS

The construction of achievement tests and aptitude tests began as separate enterprises carried out by different psychologists with completely different objectives. **Achievement tests** were constructed to assess accurately how much individuals know about subjects taught in school; **aptitude tests** were designed to find out how much talent or capacity individuals have for particular lines of work. As time passed, however, the distinction between achievement tests and aptitude tests became more and more blurred. What psychologists first thought were tests of aptitude—defined as innate ability or talent—turned out partly to measure different kinds of experience, so that they had to be considered in some sense achievement tests. Achievement tests often turned out to be the best predictors of many kinds of occupational abilities, so that they were in some sense aptitude tests. The distinction between aptitude and achievement tests has come to rest more on purpose than on content. When a test is used to evaluate what a person knows, it is an achievement test; when the same test is used to predict how successful the person will be, it is an aptitude test.

Although achievement and aptitude tests are similar, they must be validated in different ways. If one is interested in achievement, the important consideration is **content validity** (the questions on the test must represent fairly the area of achievement in question). If one wishes to assess aptitude, one seeks evidence about the test's **predictive validity** (the test must be validated to show that people who do well on it can, in fact, perform well in situations for which their aptitude is being tested).

The most impressive work in aptitude measurement has been done by the United States Employment Service, which produced a two-and-a-half-hour set of tests called the **General Aptitude Test Battery (GATB).** The GATB makes it possible for a person to find out whether he meets minimum standards for each of a considerable number of occupations.

Psychologists once hoped that achievement testing would lead to significant improvements in education and that aptitude testing would enable each person to find an occupation in life that suited him. Several decades of work have not accomplished these purposes, however, and it now seems unlikely that further efforts along the same lines will do so. Nevertheless, these efforts have resulted in techniques and instruments that are helpful when they are used by people who understand both their advantages and their shortcomings.

THE MEASUREMENT OF PERSONALITY

Intelligence tests, achievement tests, and tests of aptitude measure mental abilities, which are important parts of a person's personality. The instruments for measuring personality characteristics, however, differ from instruments for measuring abilities. Answers to questions on an intelligence test indicate

1. Which two words have the same meaning?
   (a) open **(b)** happy **(c)** glad **(d)** green

2. Which two words have the opposite meaning?
   (a) old **(b)** dry **(c)** cold **(d)** young

3. A man works 8 hours a day, 40 hours a week. He earns $1.40 an hour. How much does he earn each week?
   (A) $40.00 **(C)** $50.60 **(B)** $44.60 **(D)** $56.00

4. At the left is a drawing of a flat piece of metal. Which object at the right can be made from this piece of metal?

Figure 17.9 The General Aptitude Test Battery (GATB) consists of a number of different kinds of tests. Samples of items testing verbal and mathematical skills (top) and manual dexterity (bottom) are shown here. The results of the GATB might tell a person, for example, that he had the minimum reading comprehension and manual dexterity required to become a typist.

Figure 17.10 (A) Some items from the Strong Vocational Interest Blank (SVIB). In this part of the test the test taker is asked to indicate whether he thinks he would like (L), dislike (D), or be indifferent to (I) doing various kinds of work. In later portions of the test he is asked to respond similarly to School subjects, Activities, and Amusements; to indicate his preference for activities, choosing between pairs of them; and to accept or reject certain statements about his personality. (B) An analysis of the item *Night clubs* on the SVIB, showing the number of occupational samples of men and women responding to the item and the percentage of each sample group that indicated a liking for night clubs. Note that more male groups than female groups have high percentages of liking but that the highest percentage of those liking night clubs is from one of the groups of women—female flight attendants. The male sample with the highest percentage of liking was a group of department-store managers. The female sample with the smallest percentage of liking was a group of mathematicians. The male groups who least liked night clubs were a group of German accountants and a group of members of the National Institute of Arts and Letters.

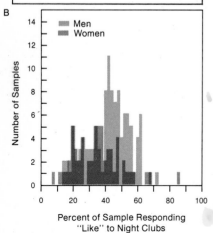

A

1 Actor/Actress	Ⓛ Ⓘ Ⓓ
4 Art museum director	Ⓛ Ⓘ Ⓓ
8 Astronomer	Ⓛ Ⓘ Ⓓ
10 Auctioneer	Ⓛ Ⓘ Ⓓ
18 Beauty and haircare consultant	Ⓛ Ⓘ Ⓓ
19 Biologist	Ⓛ Ⓘ Ⓓ
21 Building contractor	Ⓛ Ⓘ Ⓓ
28 Children's clothes designer	Ⓛ Ⓘ Ⓓ
30 City or state employee	Ⓛ Ⓘ Ⓓ
33 College professor	Ⓛ Ⓘ Ⓓ
38 Criminal lawyer	Ⓛ Ⓘ Ⓓ
39 Dancing teacher	Ⓛ Ⓘ Ⓓ
40 Dental assistant	Ⓛ Ⓘ Ⓓ

B

whether the person being tested can, in fact, do certain kinds of thinking and solve certain kinds of problems, whereas answers on personality tests have no clear-cut right or wrong answers. Anyone familiar with the complexities of personality organization knows that a person may have a variety of reasons for giving any one answer on a personality test and that there is no simple way of judging the meaning of an answer.

One way of reducing the ambiguity about the meaning of scores on personality tests is to develop scoring keys without regard to the apparent significance of the questions and answers. Testers develop scoring keys *empirically* by collecting information about how persons in clearly defined groups actually respond to individual test items. For example, for some personality tests, such a group would be persons hospitalized for schizophrenia. This method has worked particularly well in the measurement of vocational interests.

The Strong Vocational Interest Blank

In constructing the first Strong Vocational Interest Blank, psychologists took the responses to particular questions asked a group of men successfully employed in a particular occupation and compared them to the responses of a group of "men in general." Only the questions that produced clearly different responses from the two groups were included in the test; this is the empirical method. A similar instrument for women was developed later. Recently, however, the test was revised: The two forms, one for males, one for females, were combined into a new form, which eliminated items that were sexually biased. New scales were developed to allow individuals of both sexes to be scored on all scales. Although the test cannot tell people how well they would do in an occupation, it can tell them how well their interests correspond with typical interests of those already in the occupation. Sometimes that correspondence may be an important predictor of success in an occupation. For example, research has shown that people who give responses similar to those given by physicians are less likely to drop out of medical school than those who give other responses. The most recent edition of the Strong Vocational Interest Blank can be scored for 124 occupations.

The Minnesota Multiphasic Personality Inventory (MMPI)

The most widely used personality inventory, the Minnesota Multiphasic Personality Inventory (MMPI), was developed without regard for the meaning of its questions. The MMPI was developed in order to identify items on which the pattern of response was different for groups of psychiatric patients and groups of normal people. These items were then combined into **scales,** which were used originally to aid in the evaluation and diagnosis of mental illness.

The authors of the test began with a set of approximately 560 statements. Many of these items dealt directly with psychiatric symptoms—including delusions, hallucinations, obsessive and compulsive states, and sadistic and masochistic tendencies—but the other items ranged widely over a variety of questions dealing with physical health, general habits, family and marital status, occupational and educational problems, and attitudes relevant to religion, sex, politics, and social problems. It is fortunate that the MMPI items were so diverse because many of the items that did not seem relevant to the initial purposes of the inventory have turned out to be useful not only in studying psychopathology but also in developing a variety of other scales, many of which measure personality characteristics of normal people.

While developing the MMPI over a period of three or four years, the authors carefully selected 800 clinical patients and gave them the test. They also administered the basic MMPI items to 724 normal people (nonpatients) who happened to be visiting relatives or friends in the university hospital. Other normal groups used in the development of MMPI scales included young persons of college age seeking guidance at the University of Minnesota Testing Bureau, workers on government projects, and individuals who were hospitalized for physical illness at the University of Minnesota Hospital.

Scale Construction The scale construction can be illustrated by considering the case of depression. The authors' original set of 560 items was administered to patients with depressive disorders and to normal people. From this large set, about 53 items were found to differentiate the two groups significantly. Table 17.1, on the following page, presents definitions of the validity scales used and of a number of the clinical scales, including scales to discriminate hypochondria, hysteria, paranoia, introversion, schizophrenia, and obsessive-compulsive tendencies. Later, a few additional items were added to sharpen the discrimination between patients with severe depressive reactions and those with other psychiatric diagnoses. The MMPI D (for Depression) scale has been found to be a highly sensitive indicator not only of psychotic forms of depression but also of less severe forms of depression, of varying mood states, and even of reaction to various forms of psychological treatment. In a similar way, eight additional clinical scales were developed for the original MMPI, as well as a masculinity-and-femininity scale.

In addition to the original scales, over 200 special scales have been devised for the MMPI by a great variety of investigators. Consistent with the original strategy, anyone can develop a special scale by giving the MMPI to people who possess the characteristics he wishes to measure, then picking out the questions that they answer differently from other people. Special scales vary from specific symptoms of disorder, like "bizarre sensory experiences," to normal and perhaps desirable qualities, like the extent to which a person has "counselor personality."

Interpretation Clinical psychologists usually base their interpretations of the test results on the patterning of the scale scores rather than on the absolute scores. A great deal of information has been gathered about thousands of people who have been classified by the MMPI profile. Since the mid-1950s, when the computer became generally available to psychologists, computer programs have been developed to write clinical reports based on MMPI data.

The MMPI has been used most in psychiatric clinics and hospitals, but it has also been used for several other purposes, including employment screening, counseling of college students, and personality research. Its major advantage, and the major reason it will probably be around for quite some time, is that it has proved to be useful in so many different situations. Its major disadvantages are its predominately psychopathological content and the fact that its accuracy can be upset by response biases, such as the tendency always to choose desirable or undesirable alternatives.

The Study of Values

The Study of Values, developed by Gordon Allport and Philip Vernon, is different from the MMPI because it does not focus at all upon pathological aspects of personality. The Study of Values assumes that what is most significant about people is their values. The Study of Values has produced the best results for college students or for adults with higher-than-average educational backgrounds. It should be used primarily in contexts where the full cooperation of the subjects is obtained; for example, it is used to advantage in vocational counseling, classroom demonstration, and research.

Underlying Typology The Study of Values is based on a typology first advanced by Eduard Spranger. Spranger maintained that a person is best understood by his interests and intentions rather than by his achievements. For

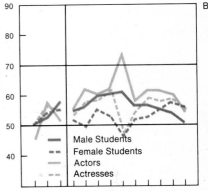

133. I have never indulged in any unusual sex practices.

151. Someone has been trying to poison me.

182. I am afraid of losing my mind.

337. I feel anxiety about something or someone all the time.

Male Students
Female Students
Actors
Actresses

L F K Hs D Hy Pd Mf Pa Pt Sc Ma Si

Figure 17.11 (A) Sample MMPI items. (B) MMPI profiles for groups of males and females in first-year psychology courses and in acting professions. The lettering along the bottom of the plot corresponds to the scales described in Table 17.1. The horizontal lines across the plot indicate the normal range of scores. Note that actors scored much higher than male students on the Masculinity-Femininity Scale, whereas actresses' scores were almost identical to those of female students. This result implies that actresses do not deviate from their sex-role norm as much as actors do from theirs.

Table 17.1   Scales of the MMPI

Validity Scales

Lie Scale (L)	Items that reflect socially desirable but unlikely behavior and are therefore likely to be marked true by a naive faker.
Infrequency Scale (F)	Items that are rarely marked true except by people who either are trying deliberately to give an exaggerated impression of their problems or are in fact highly deviant.
Correction Scale (K)	Items that reflect how defensive or how frank the person is being. The scale is sensitive to attitudes more subtle than those that affect the Lie Scale.

Clinical Scales

1. Hypochondriasis (Hs)	Items selected to discriminate people who persist in worrying about their bodily functions despite strong evidence that they have no physical illness.
2. Depression (D)	Items selected to discriminate people who are pessimistic about the future, feel hopeless or worthless, are slow in thought and action, and think a lot about death and suicide.
3. Hysteria (Hy)	Items selected to discriminate people who use physical symptoms to solve difficult problems or avoid mature responsibilities, particularly under severe psychological stress.
4. Psychopathic Deviate (Pd)	Items selected to discriminate people who show a pronounced disregard for social customs and mores, an inability to profit from punishing experiences, and emotional shallowness with others, particularly in sex and love.
5. Masculinity-Femininity (Mf)	Items selected to discriminate men who prefer homosexual relations to heterosexual ones, either overtly, or covertly because of inhibitions or conflicts. Women tend to score low on this scale, but the scale cannot be interpreted simply "upside-down" for women.
6. Paranoia (Pa)	Items selected to discriminate people who have delusions about how influential and how victimized they are or how much attention is paid them by other people.
7. Psychasthenia (Pt)	Items selected to discriminate people with obsessive thoughts, compulsive actions, extreme fear or guilt feelings, insecurity, and high anxiety.
8. Schizophrenia (Sc)	Items selected to discriminate people who are constrained, cold, aloof, apathetic, inaccessible to others, and who may have delusions or hallucinations.
9. Hypomania (Ma)	Items selected to discriminate people who are physically overactive, emotionally excited, and have rapid flights of disconnected, fragmentary ideas; these activities may lead to accomplishment but more frequently are inefficient and unproductive.
10. Social Introversion (Si)	Items selected to discriminate people who are withdrawn from social contacts and responsibilities and display little real interest in people.

Source: Based on W. G. Dahlstrom, G. S. Welsh, and L. E. Dahlstrom, *An MMPI Handbook,* Vol. I: (Minneapolis: University of Minnesota Press, 1972).

Spranger, the nature of their values distinguishes different people, and he summarized values in terms of six major types, each of which he considered to be a kind of idealized individual. The six ideal types are the theoretical, the economic, the aesthetic, the social, the political, and the religious. Although Spranger believed that an individual could be characterized primarily in terms of a single value type, he also allowed for combinations, an approach consistent with that used by the authors of the Study of Values.

Interpretation   A great wealth of data has accumulated about the interpretation of the value scores. One source of information is based on the scores obtained by people in different occupations. Figure 17.12 contrasts scores obtained by undergraduate students with scores of two different groups. With remarkable consistency, the profiles of the groups conform to what one would expect. Individuals within each group might be expected to vary within a fairly wide range, but it is reasonable to expect that individuals most satisfied with a particular occupation would frequently be those whose value profiles were consistent with and typical of people already in the occupation.

Application The values a person holds, as indicated by his profile on the Study of Values, have been shown to affect performance. They also seem to be influential in a person's choice of friends and spouse; profiles of friends and of married couples tend to be similar. Values have also been found to be important determinants of perception. In one study of selective perception by Leo Postman, Jerome Bruner, and Elliott McGinnies, words were flashed on a screen for very brief intervals. Each word appeared for such a short fraction of a second that the subjects had difficulty recognizing it. Each of the words was related to one of the value areas. For example, there were words like "profit" and "money" that were linked to the economic value, and words like "beauty" and "poetry" that were linked to the aesthetic value. The experimenters found that each individual's recognition threshold was lowest for—that is, he most often recognized—words closely related to whatever value area he had scored highest on.

This finding indicates that values may represent a central and fundamental aspect of personality, determining not only such things as what an individual believes but even what he is likely to see when confronted with items that are ambiguous or barely perceptible. Very little of history, and even less of personality, would be understandable without some appreciation of the diversity of human values.

The Personality Research Form

The Personality Research Form (PRF), developed by Douglas Jackson, is one of the first personality-assessment devices to take advantage of the modern digital computer in order to develop more sophisticated scales for personality measurement.

Assessment Items The PRF initially tried to measure personality characteristics described by Henry Murray in his theory of personality; some of these are shown in Figure 17.14. The actual questions included in the PRF were selected by a very careful statistical procedure. In the construction of the entire set of twenty-two PRF scales, over 3,000 items were written initially, and the final items were selected from those. The items on each scale were chosen by means of a statistical index that sought to maximize relevance to the personality scale and minimize response bias. Thus, these scales show good correlations with distinct criterion measures. For example, the score a person makes on the aggression scale of the PRF has been found to correlate highly with ratings of aggression of that person by others who know him well.

Interpretation The PRF scores are usually summarized in the form of a profile. In the interpretation of personality-inventory profiles, a great deal of attention is directed toward interpreting *patterns* of total scores rather than the scores themselves. An attempt is made to capture a total life style as revealed by the relative importance of various traits in the individual's personality.

Figure 17.13 gives an illustration of the PRF profile of a twenty-one-year-old college senior who became president of the student association while also serving on the university debating team and achieving a level of scholastic performance that consistently placed her on the dean's list. Note that the most prominent features of the profile are consistent with her pattern of performance. There are high scores for exhibition and dominance, both of which have been shown to be associated with the tendency to be talkative in and to take over the leadership of small groups. There are also high scores for achievement and understanding. Achievement involves the attempt to meet standards of excellence, and understanding primarily involves a kind of intellectual curiosity, so these characteristics are consistent with her outstanding level of performance in academic work. Note that the score for autonomy is relatively

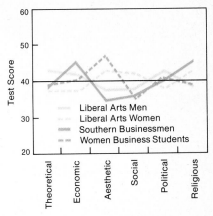

Figure 17.12 The average scores of four sets of people on the Study of Values. The lighter lines show the scores of the men and women in the standardization group, a number of liberal arts students.
The heavier lines represent the scores of two other groups, one a number of Southern businessmen, the other a group of women in the Radcliffe Graduate School of Business Administration. These scores should be compared with the scores of the standardization group.

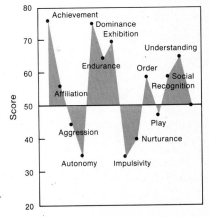

Figure 17.13 This PRF profile was obtained for a female college student who was student-association president, a member of the college debating team, and who maintained a consistently high grade-point average. The line at 50 shows the mean on this test, and a ten-point range corresponds to one standard unit on the theoretical curve in Figure 17.7. (A number of scales on the PRF are not shown here, including abasement, change, cognitive structure, defendance, harmavoidance, sentience, succorance, infrequency, and desirability.)

Figure 17.14 Needs identified by Henry Murray in his formulation of a theory of human personality. Note that Murray distinguishes between a class of primarily physical needs and a—much larger—class of psychological needs.

n   Acquisition
(to gain possessions and property)
n   Conservance
(to collect, repair, clean, and preserve things)
n   Order
(to arrange, organize, put away objects)
n   Construction
(to organize and build)
n   Achievement
(to overcome obstacles, to exercise power, to strive to do something difficult as well and as quickly as possible)
n   Recognition
(to excite praise and commendation)
n   Defendance
(to defend oneself against blame or belittlement)
n   Dominance
(to influence or control others)
n   Autonomy
(to resist influence or coercion)
n   Aggression
(to assault or injure)
n   Affiliation
(to form friendships and associations)
n   Rejection
(to snub, ignore, or exclude)
n   Nurturance
(to nourish, aid, or protect)
n   Succorance
(to seek aid, protection, or sympathy)
n   Play
(to relax, amuse oneself, seek diversion and entertainment)
n   Cognizance
(to explore)

low, which implies that she prefers to work with people rather than independently, and note also that her scores for affiliation and aggression imply that her interaction with others is based more on friendship than on pushiness.

Associations have been pointed out between predominant dimensions of personality, as measured on the PRF, and vocational interests. In a study linking PRF scores to scores derived from the Strong Vocational Interest Blank, seven dimensions common to both vocational interests and personality were identified. One of these dimensions was particularly interesting: impulse control and expression. At one extreme, PRF scales for order and cognitive structure—together implying high impulse control—were associated with interest patterns of accountants and office workers. At the other extreme the PRF scales for impulsivity, change, exhibition, and autonomy were associated with the interest patterns of authors, lawyers, clinical psychologists, and advertisers. Each of these occupations would seem to have in common the possibility of some freedom of expression and escape from routine. This dimension is presented in Figure 17.15, together with a second dimension reflecting dominance versus passivity in human relations.

Projective Tests

In projective tests, personality characteristics are revealed by the way people respond to and interpret ambiguous material. Projective tests attempt to measure unconscious dispositions. The idea is that because there is no established meaning, any meaning that the person puts into his story must come from himself and should therefore reveal something about his personality. Projective tests are based on a different set of principles than are the personality questionnaires previously discussed. Instead of focusing upon the measurement of specific traits through answers to specific questions, projective tests give the person an opportunity to reveal his personality traits by the particular manner in which he interprets the material. Some ambiguous materials are highly abstract, like inkblots; others are more concrete, like pictures of actual social situations. In others, the person is not provided with something to

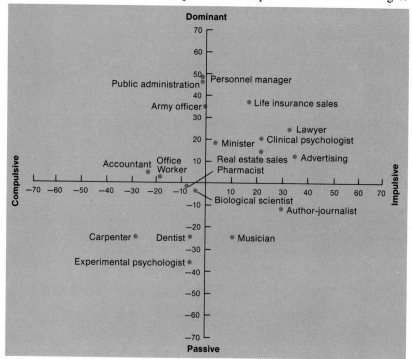

Figure 17.15 The locations of a number of occupational groups on the Impulsivity and Dominance dimensions of the Personality Research Form. These data were derived by Douglas Jackson from an analysis of responses to the Strong Vocational Interest Blank.
(After Jackson, 1967.)

interpret verbally but rather is asked to create something by drawing, modeling with clay, or even acting out roles.

The Rorschach Inkblot Test   Perhaps the best-known projective technique is that developed by Hermann Rorschach, a Swiss psychiatrist, who with remarkable insight developed a set of ten inkblots. Rorschach developed a scoring system that has been modified but is still in wide use today.

In administering the Rorschach, the examiner hands the inkblots one by one to the person and instructs him to report what he sees. The testing time is divided into a free-association period and an inquiry period. During the free association, the person simply identifies what he sees. He might say, for example, that a certain area of a blot resembles an airplane or a rocket. During the inquiry, the examiner asks certain general questions in an attempt to discover what about the inkblot determined the response.

In general, three categories are involved in scoring. The first category indicates how much of the inkblot the person responds to, ranging from small or even minute detail to the whole blot. The second relates to the determinants of the response—whether the person responds primarily to form, color, shading, or activity level. The third category is content.

People unacquainted with this test often think that the content of a response is most important, but in most scoring systems, content is the least important aspect of the individual's performance. The way the individual uses content is much more significant. For example, there are types of responses that indicate the possibility of serious psychological disorder. These include the tendency to mix indiscriminately parts belonging to different animals and human beings, and the tendency to talk about things that go far beyond the material at hand, often with bizarre overtones.

It would be a mistake to place too much emphasis upon the scoring techniques used by Rorschach examiners. The Rorschach method is essentially impressionistic. It is based to a large extent upon the individual clinician's insight, capacity for careful observation, and awareness of the manner in which psychopathology is revealed. In the assessment procedure, he will use not only the individual's Rorschach responses but also his reaction to the test situation. Some people, for example, are extremely defensive and wary in the test situation, and others define it in authoritarian terms. Still others view it as a competitive task, expecting their performance to be evaluated against some standard and judged in terms of its quality.

The fact that the person being tested has great latitude in how he acts in the situation detracts from the reliability of the test, but it also provides an opportunity for him to reveal important things about himself. The lack of structure involved in the Rorschach technique, as in many projective techniques, is both a strength and a weakness. It is a strength in the sense that it samples a broad range of behavior and permits the possibility for certain patterns to emerge that might not otherwise become apparent. The disadvantage of such an approach is that interpretation is left open to the biases of the particular examiner.

The Thematic Apperception Test   Although also a projective device, the Thematic Apperception Test (TAT) requires a kind of response different from that required by the Rorschach inkblot technique. The TAT, developed by Henry Murray, consists of a series of twenty cards, each a picture of a different situation. The person is asked to tell a coherent story about each picture, including what led up to the situation, what the characters are thinking and feeling, and how it will end. Murray's original suggestion was to present all the pictures in two one-hour sessions, the first involving the ordinary scenes and the second involving the more bizarre scenes; however, most

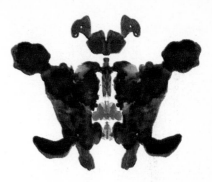

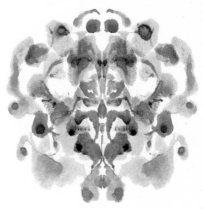

Figure 17.16   Inkblots similar to those used on the Rorschach test. In interpretations of a person's responses to the inkblots, as much or more attention is paid to the style of the responses as is paid to their content. For example, a person's tendency to see the white areas as meaningful or to see the blot as a whole rather than as a collection of parts is considered significant. Formal attempts to establish the Rorschach test's reliability and validity have been failures, but the test remains very widely used.

Figure 17.17 Three cards similar to those used in the Thematic Apperception Test (TAT). The scenes depicted in the drawings permit a variety of interpretations, and the person taking the test is therefore assumed to project his own needs, wishes, defenses, and other personality factors into the story. One problem of reliability in the TAT is that the story a person tells might occur to him partially because of some recent experience rather than because of some enduring characteristic of personality.

clinical psychologists who employ the test select their own series of cards from the twenty.

Analysis of the stories is usually done on an individual basis. Originally, Murray suggested that the TAT be interpreted in terms of a person's "internal needs" and "environmental presses," terms Murray uses in his own theory of personality, but a variety of other systems, including some based on psychoanalytic theory, are also employed. Research indicates that clinicians agree only moderately well about TAT interpretations and predictions. In fact, the accuracy of these clinicians who professionally administer and interpret the TAT often does not exceed that of psychology students who have not received specific training in TAT interpretation.

All interpretive systems depend on certain underlying assumptions regarding the sort of fantasy tapped by the TAT. Common assumptions are that the hero or heroine of the story is the one with whom the storyteller usually identifies, that the storyteller's fantasies will reveal his or her motives, and that uncommon responses are more likely to reveal important aspects of personality than common ones.

A number of very interesting studies have employed the TAT, including studies about the changes that arise from altered states of consciousness induced by sensory deprivation and the use of drugs. Equally important, the TAT has led to the development of a variety of techniques useful for measuring particular traits like the need for affiliation and the need for achievement. Some of the findings from research on these traits are discussed in Chapter 16.

Other Verbal Projective Tests Although the Rorschach and TAT tests are by far the most popular projective tests, several other varieties are used. In a technique originally produced by Sir Francis Galton and later revised by Carl Jung called the **word-association test,** the person is presented with a word and is instructed to say the first word that comes to his mind. The stimulus words—words such as "guilt," "desire," and "mother"—are commonly associated with psychological difficulties. Responses are analyzed in terms of the time that passes before the response, its content, and such nonverbal responses as blushing or wringing of hands. Word-association tests are sometimes accompanied by the measurement of such physiological states as heart rate and blood pressure.

Another widely used projective technique for personality assessment is the **sentence-completion test.** In this procedure, only the first few words of a

Figure 17.18 An example of the analysis of expressive drawings. The drawing on the left was produced when a thirteen-year-old girl named Chris was asked to draw a person. The off-center design of the blouse and precision of the drawing were thought to indicate that Chris was a rigid and overly careful person. The flat chest and the pantskirt were thought to show that she wanted to pretend that she had no sexuality. Similar interpretations were made of the picture that she drew after being asked to draw a family, the drawing on the right. The member's ages are drawn above their heads, and Chris has marked her drawing of herself "Self." Notice the apathetic expression and the pock marks on the father's face. The cross-hatching of Chris's sweater were thought again to indicate rigidity and a denial (or crossing out) of sexuality. The interpretation of such drawings is practically impossible unless the psychologist also knows something about the rest of the life of the person he is testing. The above interpretations were confirmed by the fact that Chris's father was in a mental hospital and, according to Chris's mother, had sexually molested all the children in the family.

sentence are presented to a person, and he is asked to complete the sentence. For example, he might be asked to complete the following sentences: "The thing that upsets me the most is . . ." "My parents . . ." "I felt like quitting when they . . ."

Expressive Techniques   All the projective tests that have been described focus on words—what the person says or writes. A number of other tests have been developed that focus on expressive aspects of behavior. These techniques require a person to draw pictures of people, to construct miniature situations out of toys or out of pictures, to make figures from clay, or to act out social roles. In general, research with these techniques has been too sparse to develop reliable testing methods or to test the validity of inferences drawn from the techniques.

One possible exception to this limitation is the Draw-a-Person test, popularized by Karen Machover. The individual is first instructed simply to draw a person and then to draw a second person of the opposite sex from the first one. Research with this test suggests, for example, that it may be useful for indicating an individual's tendency to be analytical and to structure his environment. Analytical people tend to incorporate many details in their drawings, to differentiate clearly between the sexes, and to avoid simplification.

Expressive and stylistic behavior is potentially a valuable source of information about an individual's personality, quite apart from his particular traits. Many years ago, Gordon Allport and Philip Vernon did a series of studies investigating stylistic consistencies in behavior. An individual's gait, his tempo of talking, his characteristic facial expression, and his posture all proved to be measurable and consistent. They distinguished this kind of behavior from personality traits per se, suggesting that although stylistic behavior is only surface behavior, ultimately it may be possible to show that it reveals personality characteristics of more central importance.

Using Projective Tests   The major difficulty with projective techniques of all kinds is that they have not been proved either reliable or valid. The basic principle—that each person tends to structure an ambiguous situation according to his own personality—seems tenable enough. The problem is in interpreting the person's personality from the test results. There is always the danger that a clinician's interpretation will tell us more about the clinician himself than about the person who produced the responses in the first place,

Figure 17.19 The man on the right is being tested on an airplane flight simulator. The aim of this test is to gauge how well he will perform in actual flight situations. When a test is administered in order to estimate a person's potential performance in a specific situation, the test should be as similar as possible to the actual situation.

(United Air Lines photo.)

and the methods of interpretation used by different clinicians are often too poorly standardized to test for reliability. When the Rorschach and the MMPI are compared experimentally, the MMPI almost always proves to be a better predictor of future behavior. It is one of the unfortunate facts of life that while the more structured tests may not delve as deeply into personality structure as the projective tests, a great deal more faith can usually be placed in information yielded by the structured techniques. A good clinician may be a better predictor than a good test, but with the structured tests there is much less need to worry about the biases of the individual clinician.

Formal Interviews

Probably the most widely used technique for personality appraisal is the interview. Few employers would hire an employee without interviewing him. The interview is also used in counseling, clinical assessment, and educational decision making. Interviewing techniques vary widely, ranging from those that leave the person free to discuss whatever he wishes to those that involve a set of very precise and well-structured questions. Many books have been written on the interview, particularly the clinical interview. The books on clinical interviewing discuss a wide variety of techniques for eliciting information and encouraging the person to accept counseling or the need for therapeutic change.

The interview affords an excellent opportunity to appraise such qualities as level of anxiety, fluency and style of speech, and sensitivity to certain topics. The interviewer can also obtain personal history and background data. Although people may be motivated to distort the information they give on personal history forms, they find it more difficult to do so in an interview. In addition, it is sometimes more appropriate to ask personal questions in an individual interview than on a standardized questionnaire. Indeed, psychologists have found that the use of highly personal questions in a standardized questionnaire is a potent device for arousing aggression.

Problems with the interview are similar to problems with projective techniques. Interviewers vary widely in their skill at eliciting information and in the accuracy with which they can interpret it.

Situational Measures

Another important technique of personality appraisal is one that assesses a person's reaction in a situation relevant to the job or task for which he is being considered. Some situational measures involve business games, in which certain essential materials must be obtained from competitors, and players must serve as negotiators.

Some of the most ingenious procedures examine a person's reaction to frustration or stress. The staff of "Station S" of the Office of Strategic Services during World War II developed procedures for selecting espionage agents and other individuals to work behind enemy lines. In one procedure, a senior staff member suggested to the candidate that he build a certain type of small-scale construction and then gave him a plan and two assistants—who were actually other staff members. The staff members were instructed to behave in a very frustrating manner but not to disobey orders. The candidate, of course, did not know of these secret instructions to the two assistants. One assistant was extremely sluggish, took no initiative, engaged in projects of his own, and offered no advice. The other was extremely aggressive; he criticized weaknesses in the candidate, offered irrelevant suggestions, and expressed dissatisfaction. The particular direction the needling took almost invariably resulted in some degree of frustration on the part of the candidate. The emotional reactions elicited by this task provided a rather good gauge of the person's tolerance for frustration. Some men were so shaken up by this experience that afterward they asked to be released from the assessment program and from their assignment to the Office of Strategic Services.

THE ETHICS OF TESTING

Personality assessment and intelligence testing can be useful tools to help individual people lead more productive lives. Realistic information about a person's capabilities and dispositions can help him situate himself in appropriate social and occupational contexts. Techniques such as those outlined in this chapter have been applied with increasing success in vocational counseling, clinics, hospitals, educational institutions, and industry. There are, however, two important dangers associated with personality assessment and intelligence testing. One is that the tests are not always accurate, and the second is that they can be used unfairly to control people's fates.

Questions concerning the accuracy and appropriateness of tests can usually be answered with technical information. For example, one can ask, ''Is the personality test valid for the purposes for which it is being used?'' or ''Can the questions asked be legitimately answered in terms of the data collected with the personality-assessment techniques employed?'' With the use of test manuals, most qualified psychologists could answer such questions without a great deal of difficulty. Tests usually turn out to measure much less than most people think they do, and they never supply absolutely certain information. The results of all tests are always a matter of probability—at best, they only supply a good estimate of what they are designed to measure.

The second issue is more complex—and more important. Regardless of test validity, to what uses may people put personality and intelligence tests? Tests can supply people with information about themselves—for example, about their vocational interests, strengths, weaknesses—but even the dissemination of this information may be open to question. Should a psychologist tell a child that he has obtained a poor IQ score when it may have the effect of decreasing the child's motivation to learn? Most psychologists supply only approximate information about the results of intelligence tests.

Another use to which personality and intelligence tests are put is to help groups decide about who should be admitted and who should be rejected. We would probably agree that the law requiring people to pass driving tests before they are issued licenses is an appropriate device to keep bad drivers off the road. But is it appropriate for a company or organization to inquire into a person's relationships with other people before they hire him, and if so, may they also inquire into his fundamental beliefs or his private fantasies? Is it appropriate for colleges to use attitude questionnaires as an aid in selecting students in order to ensure a certain homogeneity in the student body? Is it appropriate for business or government organizations to give tests originally intended for psychiatric patients, such as the Rorschach, in order to assess the potential of executives or civil servants? Or for that matter, should the results of a Rorschach test be used to decide whether a person will be hospitalized?

There are no absolutely right answers to these questions, but some general guidelines can be suggested. To begin with, in almost all cases, people should have the option of taking or not taking tests—and their decisions should not be used against them. When tests help predict adjustment or success at a task, they are generally useful. When they are used as an artificial basis for restriction, their use is certainly questionable.

Personality and intelligence tests are tools, and like other tools such as nuclear power or surgeons' scalpels, they may be used for desirable or undesirable ends. Knowledge about people entails power over their fate, a power that can become a weapon or an aid.

SUMMARY

1. The first reliable intelligence test was developed by Alfred Binet in response to a request from the public school system to devise a means of identifying mentally defective children. Users of the test later found that it could also differentiate levels of ability of normal schoolchildren and predict their academic performance. The score, or **intelligence quotient (IQ)**, was computed by dividing mental age (as tested) by chronological age and multiplying by 100.

2. One individual intelligence test widely used in the United States is the **Stanford-Binet**, a revision of Binet's test made at Stanford University.

   a. The test is composed of subtests, both verbal and performance, grouped by age.

   b. The examiner works with one person at a time, carrying out the standardized instructions but also putting the person at ease and noting his characteristics of mind and approach to the material.

   c. The subtests are arranged by age. The examiner first finds the person's basal age—the highest age subtest for which he can answer all the questions. The examiner then asks questions at progressively higher age levels until the person reaches a level at which he can answer no questions correctly.

   d. The IQ score originally gave a mental age, which, when divided by chronological age, showed how the person's developmental level compared with that of his age mates. For example, a child whose mental age tested out as twelve and whose chronological age was ten had an IQ of 120—$(12 \div 10)100$. In 1960, a standard score system was instituted.

3. The other individual intelligence tests most widely used in the United States are the **Wechsler Adult Intelligence Scale** (WAIS) and the **Wechsler Intelligence Scale for Children** (WISC).

   a. The subtests, both verbal and performance, are grouped not by age level but by type of item (vocabulary, for example), and the items are arranged in order of difficulty. The examiner gives each subtest in turn, asking questions until the person misses three successive items.

   b. The score for the Wechsler test gives separate scores for each subtest, which are then combined to give two IQ scores, one for performance and one for verbal abilities. Some of the subtests are: vocabulary, information, arithmetic, picture arrangement, block design. The separate scoring of subtests probably reflects more accurately the fact that intelligence comprises a number of different abilities.

4. Group intelligence tests, which are entirely paper-and-pencil measures, are often administered to large groups of people to save time and money. They are used, for example, by schools, employment offices, and the armed services. They do not predict school performance as well as individual tests do.

5. One characteristic of a test essential to its usefulness is its **reliability.** One must be able to rely on a test to produce the same results for the same individual on different occasions. Reliability refers to a test's consistency in being able to produce the same results, either over a period of time or when equivalent scoring methods are used.

Figure 17.20 David Wechsler, author of the Wechsler Adult Intelligence Scale and the Wechsler Intelligence Scale for Children (WAIS and WISC), is a clinical psychologist and psychometrician who has been active in the development of psychological tests since 1925. Wechsler has also written scientific papers on the galvanic skin response, intelligence and memory, artificial intelligence, and the range of human capacities.

6. One must be assured that a test's results validly reflect what the test set out to measure. There are several kinds of **validity** that tests may have.

   a. If a new test's results are compared to the results of a similar, well-established test and are shown to be comparable, **concurrent validity** is established for the new test.

   b. Many tests are meant to predict some kind of performance; intelligence tests, for example, are supposed to predict academic performance. If the level of people's performance is accurately predicted by their test results, the test is said to have **predictive validity.**

   c. When a test's content logically relates to what the test purports to measure, the test has **content validity.** For example, a test that is supposed to measure knowledge of vocabulary logically should not contain arithmetic problems.

   d. **Construct validity** is based on the idea that a test measures some theoretical construct, or hypothesis.

   e. One factor that can produce a test with low validity but high reliability is **response bias.** On tests that use "Yes–No" choices or choices along, say, a five-point scale, some people tend always to mark either "Yes" or "No" or always to mark number 3, the middle of the scale.

Figure 17.21 One of the foremost experts on psychological tests and measurement, Anne Anastasi is the author of one of the most comprehensive and authoritative texts in the field. Anastasi is a past president of the American Psychological Association and has served as a consultant to the College Entrance Examination Board. Her research interests include child psychology, group relations, and industrial (applied) psychology, as well as the measurement of individual differences.

7. An individual's score on a test must be compared to other people's scores before he can know how well or how poorly he has done. Test makers therefore must establish **norms** for tests before the tests are widely put into use.

   a. Norms for a test are established by administering it to a large, well-defined group before the test is published; this group is called the **standardization group.** The standardization group should contain representatives of all people to whom the test will later be administered.

   b. Most tests require several sets of norms—norms appropriate, say, to people of different ages, sexes, and races.

   c. The norms for a test are usually expressed in either a **percentile system** or a **standard score system.** The percentile system divides the test scores into 100 equal parts. A percentile rank, then, shows the percentage of people the person scored higher and lower than. A percentile rank of 90 means the person's score was better than 90 percent (and worse than 10 percent) of those who have taken the test.

   d. A standard score is obtained by plotting the test scores on a bell-shaped curve that represents the range of scores on most tests. The actual average of the scores is converted to a standard score of 0, and the scores range from +4 to −4, these scores representing the highest and lowest—and rarest—test scores.

8. Achievement and aptitude tests are similar and may, in fact, be the same test used for different purposes. When a test is used to evaluate what a person knows, it is an **achievement test;** the same test used to predict how successful the person will be, academically or in an occupation, is an **aptitude test.** Achievement tests must have content validity. Aptitude tests must have predictive validity.

9. Several types of **personality assessment** tests, with different purposes and uses, have been developed. Many of them have in common, though,

Figure 17.22 Henry Murray was a pioneer in the measurement of personality; he developed (with Christiana Morgan) the Thematic Apperception Test (TAT). Medically trained and holder of a Ph. D. in biochemistry, Murray attributed the fact that he became interested in psychology to his personal contact with Carl Jung. Murray's research and theory on human personality were major factors in changing the study of personality from a speculative undertaking to an empirical one. His emphasis on the necessity of relating personality concepts to observable events and his study of normal (nondisturbed) populations have influenced generations of psychologists.

the means of scoring. Because there are no right or wrong answers and because there is no clear-cut way to judge the meaning of an answer, the significant items and answers are found empirically, by giving the test to a clearly defined group and comparing their answers to those of people "in general." For example, if a group of paranoid schizophrenic persons consistently answers a given subset of questions in a similar manner and differently from people "in general," that subset of questions can be used to distinguish between paranoids and normal people.

a. The **Strong Vocational Interest Blank** can tell someone how his or her interests correspond to the interests of people already in a certain occupation.

b. The **Minnesota Multiphasic Personality Inventory** (MMPI) has been used mostly in the diagnosis of mental disorders, but more than 200 special scales have been developed from it for use in employment screening, counseling, and psychological research. The scale is constructed by finding those questions that a well-defined target population answers differently from other people. One scale, for example, is the MMPI D, which is a highly sensitive indicator of depression.

c. The **Study of Values** is based on the premise that people's personalities are best characterized by the values they hold. The test is based on a typology involving six types of values: aesthetic, religious, economic, theoretical, social, and political. Scores made by people taking the test are often compared to scores received by various occupational groups. Thus, the Study of Values is often used in vocational counseling.

d. The **Personality Research Form** (PRF) uses a computer to perform complex statistical manipulations of test answers in order to produce rather sophisticated scales for personality assessment. There are scales, for example, for aggression, autonomy, achievement, and affiliation. Performance on these scales is then summarized in a personality profile like the one shown in Figure 17.13.

10. **Projective tests** of personality attempt to measure people's unconscious dispositions. They are generally given in a one-to-one situation, the tester presenting the person with an ambiguous stimulus or situation and asking the person to interpret it. The person supposedly reveals important personality traits in the way he responds to the material. The results of these tests depend greatly on the tester's sensitivity and on his or her interpretive abilities.

a. The **Rorschach Inkblot Test** is the best-known projective technique. For a series of ten inkblots, the person first free associates, pointing out what he sees in the blot; then the tester asks him certain questions to find out what in the inkblot dictated his response. Scoring depends greatly on the scorer's interpretation.

b. In the **Thematic Apperception Test** (TAT) persons are shown a series of drawings of ambiguous situations and are asked to make up a story for each, telling what is happening, what led up to the situation, and how it will be resolved. Rather sophisticated scoring systems have been developed for the TAT to measure such personality traits as affiliation or need for achievement.

c. Other projective techniques include the **word-association** test: The person is presented with a word and is asked to respond with the first word that comes to mind. Responses are analyzed not only in terms of content but in elapsed time before a response and in such nonverbal responses as blushing or hand wringing. In the **sentence-completion** test, the person must finish sentences that begin with such phrases as "The thing that upsets me most is . . ." It is assumed he will project his anxieties or fears into his answers.

11. **Expressive techniques** use nonverbal means to gain insight into a person's personality. Some of these techniques require the person to draw or to model with clay, to construct situations using toys or pictures, or to act out social roles.

12. In many situations **formal interviews** are used to assess a person's personality. Interviews are used in hiring, in counseling, in clinical assessment, and in academic assessment. Some interviews are carefully planned; others are more impressionistic. But the effectiveness depends totally on the interviewer's skill in eliciting answers and attitudes and in interpreting them.

13. Personality and intelligence tests can be decidedly useful in certain situations—when they are administered, scored, and assessed by skilled people who also know what the tests' limitations are. Tests tend to be misused either by individuals who purposely do so in order to exclude certain people from a given group or organization or by persons who are unaware that the results of all tests are always a matter of probabilities—not certainties.

SUGGESTED READINGS

Allison, Joel, *et al.* (eds.). *The Interpretation of Psychological Tests.* New York: Harper & Row, 1968. Presents a series of papers that together supply a good overview of psychological testing.

American Psychological Association. *Standards for Educational and Psychological Tests and Manuals.* Washington, D.C.: American Psychological Association, 1966. Contains a thorough description of standards for psychological tests.

Buros, Oscar K. (ed.). *Personality Tests and Reviews.* Highland Park, N.J.: Gryphon Press, 1970. Contains descriptions and critical reviews of all existing personality tests. A source book for anyone who is searching for almost any type of personality test.

McReynolds, Paul (ed.). *Advances in Psychological Assessment.* Palo Alto, Calif.: Science & Behavior Books, 1968. Contains a survey of recent advances in the measurement of personality and intelligence.

Meehl, Paul E. *Clinical Versus Statistical Prediction: A Theoretical Analysis and Review of the Evidence.* Minneapolis: University of Minnesota Press, 1954. Can individual clinicians predict behavior on the basis of their intuition better than experimentalists on the basis of statistical evidence? Meehl supplies a thorough discussion of the evidence for both sides.

Schachtel, Ernest G. *Experiential Foundations of Rorschach's Test.* New York: Basic Books, 1966. Attempts to supply a theoretical foundation for the interpretation of the Rorschach inkblot test. Schachtel's position is based on a theory of perception.

Wechsler, David. *The Measurement and Appraisal of Adult Intelligence.* 14th ed. Baltimore: Williams & Wilkins, 1958. A classic discussion of intelligence and intelligence testing.

Everyone knows that Freud revolutionized the world's thinking with respect to sex, guilt, repression, and many other facets of the inner workings of the mind. Some of the changes he effected seem to me to be rarely spoken of, however.

For instance, the fact that Freud made the notion of the Oedipus complex popular made it necessary to look upon the relationship of a boy and his mother in less sentimental fashion. This killed a type of song that was extremely popular at the turn of the century—the one in which a man soulfully hummed his love for his mother. There is one perfectly dreadful song of the 1890s called "Break the News to Mother" in which a dying soldier sings, "Just tell her that no other/Can take the place of mother." And, of course, there is the old standard that tells us "I want a girl just like the girl that married dear old Dad."

Such songs can't be written any more except as burlesques—and a good thing, too.

On a more serious plane, consider that before Freud popularized the notion of the unconscious, no one really thought that a person could do anything but think consciously. A conclusion, a solution, a discovery that popped into the mind without conscious thought was a difficult thing to handle, and the blame fell easily upon the supernatural. (Dreams also were sent from Heaven. Pagans and Christians both agreed on that.)

"Enthusiasm" originally had a stronger meaning than it is given at the present. It was a kind of frenzy that carried a person along into actions he was incapable of doing ordinarily. It comes from Greek words meaning "the god within" so that a person in the grip of enthusiasm is possessed by a divine being.

There is the particular type of enthusiasm, or divine possession, that affects a person's mental creativity; that enables him to see, in a moment of insight, some conclusion that has escaped others and that perhaps would forever escape others. A scientific law may become clear, as when Archimedes suddenly understood the law of buoyancy, and dashed naked out of the bath, running home and crying "Eureka" ("I have it") all the way. Or continuous insight may enable a person to know just how to go about writing a great book, painting a great picture, composing a great symphony; knowing just which words, colors, notes to choose, even when the creator cannot explain what it is, exactly, that guides the choice.

The ancient Romans thought that every man had a divine spirit in whose charge he was. When that spirit took over the body and mind completely, the possessed person could do, know, and understand what ordinary mortals could not. The Romans called such a personal spirit a "genius," and we still use the word today to refer to a person of transcendent creative abilities.

What Freud did, then, was to reduce the supernatural to the natural; to transfer matters from the mysterious divine to the less-mysterious human. It is the greatest feat a scientist can perform.

Isaac Asimov

18
Psychoanalytic Theories of Personality

Figure 18.1 French poet and philosopher Paul Valéry once remarked that the purpose of psychology is to present a completely different way of looking at one's most familiar experiences. The theories of personality described in this chapter are Freud's psychoanalytic theory—the first comprehensive theory of personality—and various extensions of it. Many people are likely to feel that Valéry's observation is applicable to these theories, which explain much of human behavior in terms of the unconscious, an unfamiliar and thus intriguing way of examining experience.

P ersonality is a deceptively simple concept. Everyone thinks he knows what it means to characterize someone's personality ("she's an extrovert," "he's passive and dependent"). And we have all asked ourselves the inevitable question, "Who am I?"—which, if answered carefully, would entail a theory of personality. Laymen and introductory psychology students usually think personality is what psychology is all about. Everyone wants to know why some people are friendly, some creative, some typically hostile; why one person has tension headaches and another is afraid of snakes. Fortunately, we can begin with just this kind of question, and with whatever intuitions you have about the ways in which people differ, and elaborate these into the major scientific approaches to personality. Although personality theorists try to weigh their ideas against the logical and empirical criteria of science, their goals and interests are similar to your own.

Advanced personality textbooks usually list several definitions of personality and then go on to report, with evident frustration, that each theorist seems to have his own definition. Some definitions by prominent theorists are given in Figure 18.2. There are several reasons that so many definitions exist, and we will consider them in a moment, but first let us see what the definitions have in common. Most personality theorists, regardless of background and terminology, are addressing two key questions. First, *when several people confront the same situation, why don't they all behave in the same way?* If human behavior were determined by some combination of environmental stimuli and universal psychological or biological characteristics, all people would display the same behavior when confronted by the same environmental stimuli. But they do not. Recite what you think is a funny story to three people, and one almost chokes to death laughing, another groans in disgust, and the third titters politely while allowing mild disapproval to show through. Ask three people to see the same movie and they may remember entirely different versions of it. Talk to three people who received a B on a test. One will be elated because "the exam was easy," another because "studying hard really paid off." The third may be miserable—she wanted an A! Speaking loosely, we can say that there is something inside people that makes them think, feel, and act differently from one another; this "something inside" is what is meant by personality.

The second question that most personality theorists ask is this: *What accounts for the relative consistency in a person's behavior from one situation to the next?* Most people have characteristics that reveal themselves under many different circumstances. Some people are energetic; others, lethargic. Some are shy; others, typically outgoing. Activity level, shyness, sense of humor, ambition, rigidity—traits such as these seem to be responsible both for the consistencies in a given person's behavior and for individual differences in behavior. No matter how a given theorist defines personality, or how he decides to assess it and describe its development, then, he will be referring to a relatively stable, persisting organization of characteristics that accounts for each person's uniqueness.

You will almost certainly wonder, as soon as you begin thinking about personality, where this organized set of characteristics comes from. Left alone for a while, you would probably come up with two classes of determinants— biological and social—just as most personality theorists have done. For example, some have sought to explain individual differences primarily in terms of brain structure, hormones, body type, or other biological factors. Others have argued that people differ because they come from different cultures and different families. Some families are religious, some exceedingly neat, some liberal, and some conservative, and these differences seem to be related to different social experiences. Few psychologists would say that personality is determined *only* by biological or *only* by social factors, though. Rather, they look for the ways in which biological and social forces interact at the psychological level to produce a unique person.

COMPARING PERSONALITY THEORIES

The study of personality, like all scientific endeavors, begins with observation. And observation, especially in a complex domain, always involves selective attention. You may recall from Chapter 5 that human beings have quite a limited capacity for processing information. They cannot attend to several complex phenomena at one time, and they can hold only a certain amount of material in short-term memory. Personality theorists, being human, tend to pay attention to something less than the total human picture. Their observations and concepts are related to their own interests and goals and to the methods they use to gather information. Because psychologists disagree more about human personality than they do about many other psychological questions, it is especially important to note the interests and methods of the various theorists. Some of them (Sigmund Freud, for example) made their observations in the course of treating neurotic or psychotic patients. Others got their ideas primarily from observing normal college students in psychological laboratories. Some analyzed dreams, and others used computers to analyze questionnaire responses. Obviously, such differences in orientation can produce very different kinds of theories.

How can the various theories be compared? Salvatore Maddi, the author of a widely used personality textbook, distinguishes between the **core** and the **periphery** of personality. He points out that most theorists intend their general conception of personality to apply to everyone. They say, for example, that we all have certain basic needs or that we all go through the same developmental stages. The universal set of human attributes that a theorist identifies is

Figure 18.2 Definitions of the concept "personality" that have been offered by some prominent psychologists. Although these psychologists have widely differing backgrounds—Guthrie studied learning and McClelland studied motivation, for example—their definitions tend to focus on the idea that personality has to do with inner causes and on the idea that a description of an individual's personality must account for a large number of facts about that person.

Personality is:

the dynamic organization within the individual of those psychophysical systems that determine his characteristic behavior and thought (Gordon Allport).

a person's unique pattern of traits (J. P. Guilford).

those habits and habit systems of social importance that are stable and resistant to change (E. R. Guthrie).

the person in the situation, and only what is not accounted for in terms of focal, contextual, and background stimuli may be ascribed to personal or inner factors (Harry Helson).

that organization of unique behavior equipment an individual has acquired under the special conditions of his development (Robert Lundin).

the most adequate conceptualization of a person's behavior in all its detail (David McClelland).

a percept or idea resulting from the fact that individuals possess identities based upon behavioral attributes, which appear to have an inner locus of causation, and possess some degree of structure and organization (Leon Levy).

the core of personality as viewed by that theorist. But each theorist also tries to explain individual differences, which he does by pointing to somewhat less basic characteristics. These Maddi calls the periphery of personality. Many theorists see peripheral characteristics as growing out of an interaction between the core personality and forces in the environment. Freud, for example, believed that all people have certain instincts or drives in common but that the way instincts are expressed is powerfully shaped and constrained by the environment.

Another well-known textbook, *Theories of Personality* by Calvin Hall and Gardner Lindzey, provides slightly different categories for comparing theories. Each theory is discussed in terms of its treatment of four issues:

1. The **structure** or organization of personality.
2. The **dynamics** by which the parts of personality structures relate to each other and interact with the environment.
3. The **development** of personality over time: how personality structure is influenced by biological development, cognitive development, social experience.
4. The **motivational factors** that relate to personality, including those that determine universal human goals (if such exist) and those that affect individual differences in behavior.

As you read this chapter and the next, ask yourself how each theory handles core and periphery problems and how each deals with questions about personality structure, dynamics, development, and motivation. Wherever possible, the theories will be described in a way that facilitates answering such questions. You might also ask yourself how much each approach helps you to understand your own structure, dynamics, development, and motivation. If you understand each theory well enough and if you observe your own feelings and behavior closely, something in each approach will almost certainly ring true and seem relevant to you personally. This is to be expected; the theories were all created by people to describe themselves and their acquaintances. Each theory was designed with particular issues and goals in mind, so none is complete or exclusive. Human beings are so complex that each individual possesses easily enough needs, pains, abilities, minor neuroses, quirks, beliefs, hidden and expressed desires, and inadequacies to require more than one or two special-interest theories to describe him or her adequately.

FREUD'S PSYCHOANALYTIC THEORY

Sigmund Freud has been, without doubt, the most influential theorist in the field of personality. His was the first formal theory of personality, and it is still the most detailed and original of all those formulated. Even critics of Freud—and there have been some vociferous ones—admit that the range of phenomena he identified and explored will forever stand as a challenge to personality theorists. Freud's **psychoanalytic theory** is based on his fifty years of experience as a psychoanalyst working intensively with many patients in the intimacy of the therapeutic situation. The richness of Freud's recorded observations is the result of several factors: his incredible skill as an observer of human behavior; his training in medical science; his broad background in literature and history (including knowledge of such things as joke books and folk tales); and his unusually fine writing ability. It takes no particular training in psychology for a reader to be excited, entertained, and educated by some of Freud's major works, such as *The Interpretation of Dreams, Civilization and Its Discontents*, and *New Introductory Lectures on Psychoanalysis*.

Freud was trained as a neurologist and first became interested in personality

Figure 18.3   One of the reasons for the tremendous influence of Freud's theory was that it took into account the symbolism used by great poets, writers, and artists. For instance, Freud drew on the insights of Shakespearian and Greek tragedy in his analysis of his patients' behavior. This painting uses symbols of some of the primary themes in Freud's theory: sexuality and the presence of both civilized and barbarous motives within an individual.

(or rather, in what he would later call psychoanalysis) when he discovered, in collaboration with Josef Breuer, that hysteric disorders could be cured if the patient recalled critical events from early childhood and talked about them under hypnosis. For example, one of Breuer's case studies describes a young woman called Anna O. who had become exhausted while caring for her sick and dying father. She had a nervous cough, severe headaches, abnormal vision, and other symptoms. She could not bring herself to drink water out of a glass. During the period when Breuer was coming to see her, she would often pass into a trancelike state that she called "clouds." In this state she would recount past experiences (a process she called "chimney sweeping"). Occasionally, when she told about experiences related in some way to one of her symptoms—and especially if she seemed to relive the emotional part of the experience vividly—the symptoms would disappear. Breuer sometimes supplanted this spontaneous "treatment" with sessions in which he hypnotized Anna and encouraged her to talk about emotional events and experiences that seemed to be related to her physical symptoms. This technique, too, was often effective.

Freud began to use Breuer's method, but he concluded after considerable effort that hypnosis was not an ideal therapeutic procedure. Many patients were not hypnotizable, and for those who were, symptoms that disappeared under hypnosis often returned later for no apparent reason. Also, hypnotized patients did not take a very analytic stance toward their symptoms and thus did not reach a better understanding of their underlying difficulties. Gradually Freud developed a better, more general technique that he called **free association:** The patient was asked to lie down on a couch in Freud's office and to say out loud whatever came to mind from moment to moment. Freud found that eventually certain themes became evident and that these themes centered on the patient's important emotional conflicts. As these conflicts were talked out, the patient experienced relief from neurotic symptoms, as Anna O. had done under hypnosis.

Freud could see that although Anna O. and the other hysteric patients could not remember the childhood experiences—the wishes and fears—that seemed to produce their symptoms, they were behaving *as if* they did remember. And these memories often did come back during therapy, so they had been alive somewhere, somehow in the personality. Thus, Freud was led to theorize the existence of unconscious processes.

Undoubtedly, the concept of the **unconscious** is Freud's major contribution to the understanding of human behavior and personality. From his work with patients and study of dreams, he saw that the contents of the conscious mind are only a part of personality structure. In fact, he drew an analogy between the mind and an iceberg: People's conscious thoughts are like the tip of the iceberg; although that is the part we can see, it is only a small part. The massive unconscious lies beneath the surface. In the unconscious (which is a process, not an entity) reside the universal instinctual drives and the infantile goals, hopes, wishes, and needs that have been repressed, or carefully controlled. The controls are slackened when we dream, and one of Freud's purposes in studying dreams was to understand and clarify how the unconscious operates.

In 1900 the publication of *The Interpretation of Dreams* introduced psychoanalysis to the world. Although antagonism and confusion kept people from accepting Freud's ideas at first—especially ideas that sexual motives and conflicts originate in childhood and are involved in most adult neuroses—psychoanalysis was gradually recognized as a major breakthrough in human self-understanding. Many people came to Vienna to study Freud's methods, and soon psychoanalysts were practicing in many countries, including the United States. Freud revised and supplemented his theory from 1900 until his death in 1939, but his work was never completely finished. His writings are voluminous—and sometimes contradictory.

Freud's Sources of Data

Freud's hysteric patients often suffered from what seemed to be a neurological defect—for example, paralysis of an arm, loss of sensation in a hand, deterioration of hearing or vision. But Freud, trained as a neurologist, often knew that the defect was not organic. When a patient showed loss of feeling in a hand, for instance, the affected region might correspond to the area covered by a glove (hence the term "glove anesthesia")—an area that does not correspond to any known grouping of nerves. We tend to think of our hands as glove-sized units, but the nervous system does not recognize this conceptual unit. Glove anesthesia is not a neurological disorder; instead, it is related to *thoughts* of some kind. Through psychoanalysis Freud discovered what these thoughts were. Typically they were connected with an impulse to engage in a forbidden action, such as playing with one's genitals or striking someone. Thus, the anesthetized hand served as a sign or symbol of an underlying motivational conflict.

Freud was also interested in dreams, jokes, and what we might call accidents (such as forgetting an appointment, spilling a drink on a friend's best clothes, or mispronouncing the name of a disliked person). These phenomena are often similar to hysterical symptoms in that they are signs of unconscious motivational conflicts. Dreams, for example, may seem incoherent and meaningless, but Freud discovered that when patients free-associated in response to certain images in their dreams, the trail of associations led to unacceptable impulses (the desire to kill one's father, for example, or to have sexual relations with him). Dreams have what Freud called **latent content** as well as **manifest content.** The manifest content is what the dreamer remembers; the latent content is what is revealed through free association and analysis. Jokes, too, are often an outlet for sexual or aggressive impulses that, according to Freud, are socially acceptable only when disguised by harmless humor. So-called accidents serve a similar purpose. Suppose you anticipate half-consciously that a visit to your parents may be unpleasant for some reason. You do not want to go home, yet you cannot quite admit to yourself (or to your parents) that you do not. A compromise might be to miss the last bus to your home town—and then call in distress and apologize.

Freud's discoveries can be summarized by saying that people often experience conflicts between social or moral constraints on the one hand and impulses to engage in sexual or aggressive actions on the other. People may not be completely aware of either side of the conflict. An unconscious or half-conscious compromise is established, the nature of which is revealed in what appear to be physical symptoms, dreams, jokes, and "accidents." In order to make the sources of such compromises conscious, one may choose to undergo psychoanalysis. This procedure, if carried out properly, often helps people to understand themselves better, to express formerly unconscious and forbidden impulses in a harmless way, and to reduce the negative side effects resulting from their emotional conflicts.

Personality Structure

Although Freud was obviously interested in healing his troubled patients, he was perhaps even more interested in developing a coherent theory to explain their disorders. Freud believed that in the long run his theory would be more important than any of his therapeutic procedures.

Freud divided the personality conceptually into three separate but interacting agencies: the **id,** the **ego,** and the **superego.** Every personality includes these agencies, which belong to what Maddi calls the core of personality. It

Figure 18.4 This quotation from Freud is a good example of his vibrant, literate prose. In this passage he explains the relationships that exist between the three components of adult personality.
(From Sigmund Freud, *New Introductory Lectures on Psychoanalysis,* 1965.)

We are warned by a proverb against serving two masters at the same time. The poor ego has things even worse: it serves three severe masters and does what it can to bring their claims and demands into harmony with one another. These claims are always divergent and often seem incompatible. No wonder that the ego so often fails in its task. Its three tyrannical masters are the external world, the super-ego and id. . . . Owing to its origin from the experiences of the perceptual system, it is earmarked for representing the demands of the external world, but it strives too to be a loyal servant of the id, to remain on good terms with it, to recommend itself to it as an object and to attract its libido to itself. In its attempts to mediate between the id and reality, it is often obliged to cloak the *Ucs.* [unconscious] commands of the id with its own *Pcs.* [preconscious] rationalizations, to conceal the id's conflicts with reality, to profess, with diplomatic disingenuousness, to be taking notice of reality even when the id has remained rigid and unyielding. On the other hand it is observed at every step it takes by the strict super-ego, which lays down definite standards for its conduct, without taking any account of its difficulties from the direction of the id and the external world, and which, if those standards are not obeyed, punishes it with tense feelings of inferiority and of guilt. Thus the ego, driven by the id, confined by the super-ego, repulsed by reality, struggles to master its economic task of bringing about harmony among the forces and influences working in and upon it; and we can understand how it is that so often we cannot suppress a cry: "Life is not easy!" If the ego is obliged to admit its weakness, it breaks out in anxiety—realistic anxiety regarding the external world, moral anxiety regarding the super-ego and neurotic anxiety regarding the strength of the passions in the id.

may help you to understand Freud's tripartite division of personality to know that in German the id was called *es,* which means "it"—implying an alien force, something in a person that is not recognized as part of the self. The ego was called *ich,* which means "I"—the part of the personality recognized and accepted as oneself. Superego thus means "above the I."

Freud sometimes talked as if the three agencies had minds of their own—as if the ego were a rational, self-controlled person at war with an irrational and impulsive person (the id) and a harsh, moralistic person (the superego). This manner of speaking, while dramatic and engaging, has received a great deal of criticism from psychologists who feel that it borders on mysticism. You will do well, therefore, to take the terms in the sense intended by Freud—as metaphorical names for functional (not physical) divisions of the personality. The id, for example, is not a person, place, or physical thing; it is the name given to certain kinds of motivational forces inferred from behavior. If it sometimes seems to be more a place or an entity than a motivational force, this is only a result of Freud's literary style.

The Id The id is the most fundamental component of personality. Freud characterized it as a reservoir of instinctual psychic energy, or **libido,** and as completely unconscious. Freud described the id as unable to tolerate tension (the build-up of psychic energy) and as obedient only to the **pleasure principle;** that is, the id's goal is to reduce painful tension to the lowest possible level. Many contemporary psychologists reject the term "psychic energy," but Freud's ideas do not suffer if this concept is interpreted as a metaphor. (Remember, you may have a more accurate picture of the human nervous system after reading Chapter 14 than Freud had after attending medical school during the last quarter of the nineteenth century.) Freud observed that many of his patients were physically tense and prone to exhaustion. These symptoms seemed to be related to the suppression, blocking, or repression by one agency within the personality of sexual and aggressive impulses arising from another part of the personality. Hence, it seemed reasonable to say that primitive impulses originated in the id and that the id sought their immediate discharge regardless of circumstances.

The Ego Because immediate gratification is not always attainable and in some cases may be associated with punishment, a new agency of personality, the ego, develops to handle transactions between the id and the outside world. The ego operates according to the **reality principle,** moderating the impulsiveness and social unacceptability of the id. The ego delays gratification in order to achieve realistic, long-term goals and to avoid punishment. For example, if a person is lonely and obtains gratification through romantic fantasies, the pleasure principle is operating. The id can discharge some of its tension simply by indulging in pleasant fantasy. But fantasied lovers do not satisfy a person's real need for intimacy and companionship. It is up to the ego to distinguish fantasy from reality and to launch a search for real, not just imaginary, gratification. This search may require the suppression of impulses, the solution of external problems, communication with other people, and so on. These are the functions of the ego.

According to Freud, much of the ego (unlike the id) is conscious or can readily become conscious. The ego is sometimes called the executive agency of the personality because it controls action, selects the features of the environment to which a person will respond, and decides how the person's needs can safely be satisfied. It serves as a mediator between the demands of the id and the demands of the environment. During childhood, some of the environmental demands become internalized to form the superego, the moral arm of the personality, as described in Chapter 10. Then the ego must, in

Freud's words, serve ''three severe masters'': the id, the external world, and the superego, as described in Figure 18.4.

The Superego   The superego is the representative of social values and ideals as these are interpreted for a child by his or her parents (who enforce moral standards by administering rewards and punishments). The superego is composed of the **conscience** and the **ego ideal,** which represent negative and positive facets of morality. The main functions of the superego are (1) to inhibit the impulses of the id, particularly the sexual and aggressive impulses condemned by society; (2) to influence the ego to substitute moral goals for immoral or amoral ones; and (3) to strive for perfection.

Lest the superego seem to be a dry abstraction, you should realize that intense guilt and the wearying pursuit of perfection are two of the most common reasons people give for entering psychoanalysis. Probably you can recall times in your own life when you did something very wrong that no one else knew about. Why couldn't you simply forget it? Freud would say that your superego, the internal representative of society's standards, continued to seek punishment. You are not unusual if such guilt feelings occasionally give rise to headaches, sleepless nights, or even illness. Nor would it be surprising to a psychoanalyst if, during periods of intense guilt, you left yourself open to injury or attack. Have you ever gone on a long walk during cold, wet weather, suspecting that you might get sick but feeling vaguely that it would serve you right? Have you ever taken risks on a bicycle or in a car, tempting fate to strike you down? Do you ever have dreams in which the police arrest you—perhaps with no clear indication that you had committed a crime?

Personality Dynamics

According to Freud, the instincts are the prime source of energy for human behavior. Throughout most of his life, Freud focused on two broadly defined

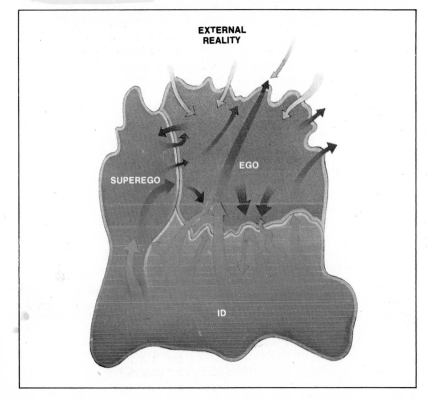

EXTERNAL REALITY

SUPEREGO

EGO

ID

Figure 18.5   A representation of Freud's conception of adult personality. The id, the ego, and the superego are seen as structural divisions of the psyche. The arrows represent the interactions and conflicts continually taking place between these structures. The deepening shading toward the lower part of the figure represents levels of decreasing consciousness: The id is wholly unconscious; both ego and superego function at all levels of consciousness. The id is represented as the primary source of psychic energy. Both the ego and superego, which do not have energy of their own, are derived, or differentiated, from the id during childhood in response to the demands of external reality. The ego is the structure differentiated first; it is the only structure that has direct contact with external reality; and it uses energy derived from the id to cope with reality and to meet (or control) the demands of the id. The superego, differentiated somewhat later than the ego, is represented as only partially independent of the id because it shares with the id a tendency toward irrationality and blind force. The superego helps to control the id, but only by placing additional demands on the ego.

instincts: sex and aggression. He hypothesized that personality is mainly a result of the way a person resolves the conflict between the id's demands that those instincts be satisfied and society's restrictions (as internalized by the superego) on the ways they may be satisfied.

Late in his career, however, Freud changed his classification of the instincts from sex and aggression to a related pair, **life instincts** (Eros) and **death instincts** (Thanatos). Freud continued to see the chief life instinct as sex. He pointed out that a person's erotic wishes can center on any of several different parts of the body called **erogenous zones.** An erogenous zone is a highly sensitive area of skin or mucous membrane that, when massaged or manipulated in certain ways, produces pleasurable feelings. The lips and mouth are one such zone, the anal region another, and the sex organs a third. Freud's psychosexual stages of development are described fully in Chapter 10; at this point, it need only be said that he saw personality development as involving the release of sexual energy progressively through the oral, anal, and phallic (genital) zones. That is, he viewed the sexual instincts in childhood as relatively independent of one another. During adolescence, they fuse and come to serve the aim of sexual union and reproduction. Sometimes, however, this normal progression is blocked and **fixation** occurs. Fixation occurs when, because of frustration or unusual pleasure at one stage, development to the next psychosexual stage is temporarily or permanently stopped. Fixation is rarely complete. Its usual outcome is that an adult manifests certain character traits associated with the stage at which fixation occurred. For example, it can be inferred that a person who cannot bear to spend money, a miser, was fixated at the anal stage. He retains money in the same way he retained feces.

The death instincts perform their work much less conspicuously than the life instincts, and this may be one reason Freud had less to say about them. His intention was clear: He needed to account for people's destructive tendencies, their aggression toward themselves and each other. (Some biographers have attempted to explain Freud's fascination with destruction and death in terms of his painful reaction to the violence during World War I and the rise of Nazism in Germany. Others point to his slow, painful, and ultimately fatal struggle against cancer.) Freud claimed that "the goal of all life is death," which may seem implausible at first. But biologists have discovered that some insects die after only a few days of life because of chemical poisons released by their own systems, and no one yet knows much about the causes of human aging. From the point of view of evolution, the species, not the individual, is important; it may be advantageous for the species to eliminate its "test cases" once their genes have been passed on. Freud was perhaps being more literary than scientific when he noted that organic matter evolved out of inorganic matter and postulated that the death instincts are manifestations of an unconscious wish to return to the inorganic. As in so many other instances, however, Freud's intuition may have been on the right track. The problems of human aggression and self-destruction have sparked the interest of some of our best contemporary thinkers and scientists.

Instincts and External Stimulation The basic concept in Freud's treatment of personality dynamics, then, is **conflict between opposing energies.** Within the person (intrapsychically, as it is called), there are conflicts between the life instinct and the death instinct, between love and hate, between creativity and destructiveness. In addition, there are conflicts between the person's urge to satisfy both the instincts he is born with and the rules of society, which insist that his instinctual desires be restrained and rechanneled in various ways that are both socially acceptable and in tune with the society's goals—productiveness, for example.

Figure 18.6 (opposite) Some of the dynamics in Freud's theory of personality. All of these dynamics can be seen as ways in which psychic energy is related to various objects of that energy, usually other people but often oneself as well. The displacement of a widow's love from her lost husband and family onto her pets is shown here. Identification is represented by a man's attempt to become his admired television hero. Three mechanisms of defense by the ego against threatening forces from the id are also illustrated: Repression, which is the unconscious burying of anxiety-causing impulses, is shown by a woman who is not only concealing and restraining a monstrous impulse but also trying to conceal from herself the fact that she is doing so. Projection is, in some ways, the opposite of identification: The person shown here is seeing ridiculous attributes of his own personality as though they were possessed by others. In reaction formation a person's ego enlists the aid of opposite personality characteristics to control and repress characteristics of himself that he finds dangerous.

Freud's is a **homeostatic,** or tension-reduction, model of behavior. Stimulation from the outside arouses an instinct; the aroused instinct activates behavior. If the behavior is effective, the person returns to the state that existed before the instinct was aroused. For that reason, an instinct is said to be conservative: Its aim is to conserve the equilibrium of the organism by abolishing disturbing excitations.

In discussing the ways that conflicts proceed and tensions are reduced, Freud emphasized four terms: displacement, identification, anxiety, and defense mechanism. As you read the descriptions of what these terms mean (they are illustrated in Figure 18.6), bear in mind that Freud was often exploring uncharted territory and so had to accept the dangers of speculation and of reasoning by analogy.

Displacement   An instinct has four characteristic features: a **source,** which is a bodily condition or need (such as the need for sexual release); an **aim,**

which is to satisfy the need and remove excess stimulation; an **object,** which is the means the person uses to satisfy the need; and a force or strength called **impetus,** which is determined by the intensity of the need. Although the source and aim of an instinct remain constant throughout life, the means the person uses to satisfy the need can and do vary considerably. This variation in object choice is possible because psychic energy is displaceable: It can be expended in various forms of behavior and directed toward various objects and effects.

The **displacement** of instinctual energy from one object to another is perhaps the most important feature of Freud's personality dynamics, and it is the key process in his theory of development. It accounts for the apparent plasticity of human nature and the remarkable versatility of man's behavior.

Practically all of an adult person's interests, preferences, tastes, habits, and attitudes represent the displacement of energy from original instinctual object choices. For example, smoking may be conceived of as the result of displacement of energy that was originally directed toward sucking the mother's breast. Similarly, a need to keep one's living quarters extremely neat may be a displacement of the energy originally directed toward anal pleasure; just as the child avoids defecating in his pants, the adult avoids messing up his house. A person experiences tension because a substitute object is rarely, if ever, as satisfying as the original object. This tension accumulates and acts as a permanent motivating force for the person's behavior.

Identification A second key process of development, identification, is one in which a person takes on the features of another personality and incorporates them into his own. The two persons with whom the child is most likely to identify are his mother and father. Typically, the boy identifies with his father, the girl with her mother.

In Chapter 10, the identification process is discussed at length in the context of Freud's approach to social development. Identification is an extremely important concept in Freud's theory. It is the incorporation of the parent's values that provides the child with a superego and that establishes his or her sexual identity.

The child identifies at first with his or her parent because the parent appears so powerful. During later stages, the child identifies with others according to his needs or goals at the time—teachers, sports figures, or others.

Anxiety Transactions with the external environment may increase tension if they are threatening or harmful. This kind of tension is experienced as anxiety. In addition to anxiety caused by environmental threats (Freud called it reality anxiety), two other types of anxiety were described by Freud: neurotic anxiety and moral anxiety. Neurotic anxiety is fear that the instincts will get out of control and cause the person to do something for which he will be punished. Moral anxiety is having a guilty conscience; it occurs when a person does something or thinks of doing something that is contrary to the moral code he learned from his parents. Anxiety, then, can result from threats from the environment, the id, or the superego.

The purpose of anxiety is to warn the person of impending danger so that he may do something to avoid danger. Under the pressure of anxiety, the ego is forced to use measures called defense mechanisms.

Defense Mechanisms All defense mechanisms have two characteristics in common: (1) They deny, falsify, or distort reality; (2) they operate unconsciously so that the person is not aware of what is taking place. At one time or another Freud and his followers have mentioned a host of defense mechanisms. Because defense mechanisms control instinctual energy, one can conceive of fixation, displacement, and identification all as defense mechanisms. The other most common ones are discussed in the following paragraphs.

Repression is the mechanism by which threatening thoughts and memories are kept from consciousness and pushed back into the unconscious. Repression was one of Freud's earliest and most important discoveries. He observed that his patients were unable to recall traumatic childhood events without considerable probing. Traumatic memories, Freud concluded, had been repressed from consciousness and were held in the unconscious by strong forces. According to Freud, the threats from these memories, the expenditures of energy needed to repress them, and the anxiety generated in the process were at the basis of neurosis.

Regression occurs when, in response to some threat, a person returns to an earlier stage of development. A young married woman who has difficulties with her husband may behave in ways that previously offered her security in her parents' home; an office worker under severe strain may throw a temper tantrum, a typical behavior at an earlier age.

Reaction formation involves the replacement in consciousness of an anxiety-producing impulse or feeling by its opposite. For instance, hate may be replaced by love. Instead of saying "I hate my child," a mother determinedly showers him with love. In Shakespeare's *Hamlet*, one may suspect reaction formation on Queen Gertrude's part when she says, "The lady doth protest too much, methinks." Gertrude is watching an actress in a play express her moral anxiety about marrying her dead husband's brother; Gertrude's response may be seen as a defense mechanism against acknowledging her own guilt in a similar situation.

Projection occurs when a person unknowingly attributes his own instinctual impulses or the threats of his own conscience to other people or to the external world. It is then easier to deal with an anxiety that arises from these internal impulses and threats. For example, a woman who is growing tired of a lover but who is afraid to break off the relationship (perhaps because, subconsciously, she feels that it would be too aggressive a move) may project her feelings onto her lover and begin to believe he is growing tired of her. If she expresses the belief, stating repeatedly that the man does not love her anymore, she may induce him to break off the relationship—which both confirms her assertion and achieves her real goal. Another example of projection is the older person who expresses extreme attitudes about the sexual behavior of young people, such as "Kids today are all perverts by the age of sixteen." Such a person may be reacting to his fear of his own sexual impulses by projecting them onto others.

Sublimation describes a displacement that produces a higher cultural achievement. Freud pointed out in *Civilization and Its Discontents* that the development of civilization was made possible by the inhibition of primitive object choices and the diversion of instinctual energy to social organization and the development of culture. Sublimation is the most productive defense mechanism. Freud observed, for example, that Leonardo da Vinci's interest in painting Madonnas was a sublimated expression of a longing for a reunion with his mother, from whom he had been separated at a young age. But sublimation does not result in complete satisfaction, and some residual tension may discharge itself in the form of nervousness or restlessness; these conditions, Freud pointed out in one of his characteristically pessimistic passages, are the price human beings pay for civilization and may be related to their periodic wars and other primitive, violent behavior.

Development: Freudian Psychosexual Stages

Freud was the first psychological theorist to emphasize the developmental aspects of personality and in particular to stress the decisive role of infancy

Figure 18.7 Possible behavior of a
child at each of Freud's first three
psychosexual stages, and the adult
personality characteristics that might
follow if, according to Freud's theory, the
behaviors were somehow encouraged
and the child became fixated. (from left
to right) An infant obtains oral
gratification by putting just about
anything he can find into his mouth; as
an adult, this person exhibits a similar
lack of discrimination about what she
takes into herself. A two-year-old in the
anal stage thwarts his mother by
refusing to release his feces; as an adult
he obtains satisfaction by hoarding. A
four-year-old girl in the phallic stage,
observing that she lacks a penis, gives
up her hopes of being like a man in any
way. As an adult, she adopts a
traditionally passive female sex role.
Many people now consider that Freud's
views on the outcomes of the phallic
stage, especially in regard to
the psychology of women, had
merit only in the context of the type of
society in which he lived.

and childhood in laying down the basic character structure of the person.
Indeed, Freud felt that personality was rather well formed by the time the
child entered school and that subsequent growth consisted of elaborating this
basic structure.

Freud believed that the child passes through a series of qualitatively different stages during the first five years of life. The three early stages, collectively
called the pregenital stage, are the **oral,** the **anal,** and the **phallic.** Each is
organized around the zone of the body indicated by the name. A period of
latency follows, in which the dynamics become more or less stabilized. With
the advent of adolescence, another eruption of libidinal forces upsets the
stabilization of the latency period and gradually comes under control as the
adolescent moves into adulthood. The final developmental stage, which occurs in adolescence and adulthood, is the **genital stage**. The stages will not be
described in detail here, because they are discussed at some length in Chapter
10. Although Freud differentiated these stages of personality growth and saw
them as qualitatively distinct, he did not assume that there were any sharp
breaks or abrupt transitions in passing from one stage to another. The final
organization of personality represents contributions from all the stages.

A Short Case Study

Condensing Freud's rich and difficult theory into a few pages may make it
seem incredible and terribly abstract. The only good remedy for this is to read

some of Freud's works for yourself. It may also help to remind you that most of Freud's ideas came from concrete case studies of real people. Later analysts have continued to report supporting evidence from their clinical practices; here is an example from George Mahl's book *Psychological Conflict and Defense.*

A young man, whom we shall call Ed, periodically attempted to find sexual satisfaction in masturbation and in premarital intercourse with his fiancée. However, in both circumstances he felt uneasy, tense, and sweaty, and a vague sense of impending doom engulfed him afterward. Hence, Ed avoided both activities most of the time.

Conscious guilt and shame were very important causes of Ed's discomfort. He did not want anyone to know about his masturbation, and despite a boastful attitude toward his premarital intercourse, he preferred that no one know about it. Mere discretion or a sense of privacy was not his only motivation; he felt that both acts were sinful and relieved evil urges on his part. He discovered a still more powerful and previously unknown source of his discomfort as he explored his behavior day after day in psychoanalysis: He feared that his genitals would be cut off if he engaged in these activities. This fear was unconscious; it manifested itself most clearly in frightening dreams that only occurred following an increase in either masturbation or intercourse. After one such upsurge in sexual activity, for example, Ed dreamed that he had a fatal illness and was in a hospital. The doctors had removed an organ from his body and wrapped it up. It made a small, elongated package. As Ed told the dream to his analyst, the shape of the package reminded him of the shape of a penis.

Following another upsurge in sexual activity, Ed dreamed that one of his testicles was quite large owing to a tumor growing within it. A man, presumably a doctor, was going to cut it off. Ed's view of his sexuality as a fatal and evil cancerous process as well as his fear that he would be castrated were very thinly disguised in these dreams. While thinking about this dream, he remembered suddenly that he had dreamed something similar when he was about 7 years old: "A woman had cut off my penis and was starting to slice the end of it the way my mother sliced bananas for my cereal. This woman had cut the penises off all the little boys in the world. She looked like a witch."

The fact that these dreams followed increases in Ed's sexual activity, their content and Ed's associations to them strongly suggest that his anxiety about masturbation and intercourse stemmed from an unconscious fear of castration. Because sexual behavior activated this fear, Ed kept his sexual activity to a minimum.

NEO-FREUDIAN DEVELOPMENTS

Because Freud's observations were made behind a closed office door—either while listening to patients pour out their dreams, feelings, and free associations or while scrutinizing himself (as he did in astonishing detail, reserving the final half-hour of each day for self-analysis)—it is not surprising that other investigators failed to agree with everything Freud said. Even if we assume that Freud was an unbiased observer (a big assumption), we can raise questions about his particular sample of cases and his emphasis on himself. For example, he may have felt an unusually strong attachment to his mother, an attractive woman half the age of Freud's father who remained close to her son as long as she lived. Other people may have had quite different experiences. Little wonder, then, that before Freud had even worked out his own ideas very clearly, two of his close associates, Carl Jung and Alfred Adler, broke away from him (as would other students throughout Freud's career). These disagreements are worth considering briefly, for they foreshadow much of the later development of psychoanalytic theory.

Early Dissenters: Jung and Adler

Carl Jung, the founder in 1913 of his own school of psychoanalysis called analytic psychology, disagreed with Freud on two important issues. First,

Figure 18.8 Carl Jung was interested in mystical experiences, as this passage from his book *Psychological Reflections* suggests. The "primordial images," or archetypes, as he called them, were images that he observed coming to the surface in many different situations—in fables and myths, in dreams, in religious writings, in literature and art, and in the delusions of psychotics.
(From Carl Jung, *Psychological Reflections*, 1972.)

The great problems of life are always related to the primordial images of the collective unconscious. These images are really balancing or compensating factors which correspond with the problems life presents in actuality. This is not to be marvelled at, since these images are deposits representing the accumulated experience of thousands of years of struggle for adaptation and existence. . . .

I can only stand in deepest awe and admiration before the depths and heights of the soul whose world beyond space hides an immeasurable richness of images, which millions of years of living have stored up and condensed into organic material. My conscious mind is like an eye which perceives the furthermost spaces; but the psychic non-ego is that which fills this space in a sense beyond space. These images are not pale shadows, but powerful and effective conditions of the soul which we can only misunderstand but can never rob of their power by denying them. For comparison, I can only think of the wonder of the starry night sky, for the equivalent of the inner world can only be in the outer world; and just as I experience this world through the medium of the body, so I experience that other world through the medium of the soul.

Jung believed that people are guided by their future aims as well as by their past. Jung's theory, therefore, casts human beings in a more favorable light than Freud's; instead of simply adapting to and displacing instinctual urges, a person can develop his potential. Jung believed that there is a forward-going character to personality development. A human being is trying continuously to realize himself. His goal is to achieve complete unity within his personality. A person begins by developing all parts of his or her personality. Jung called this process **individuation.** After a person achieves individuation, he attempts to unite the disparate systems of his personality into a fully realized self. Of course, Jung realized that this union—the work of the **transcendent function**—is an unrealizable goal, but he held that it nevertheless is the great driving force of all human behavior.

Jung disagreed with Freud on a second issue. He believed that human behavior is determined by events that occurred in mankind's ancestral past as well as by those that occurred during the individual's childhood. Like Freud, Jung recognized the great importance of unconscious factors in determining behavior, but he distinguished two levels in the unconscious. One level, the **personal unconscious,** is similar to Freud's depiction of the unconscious; it contains experiences the individual has had that were once conscious but have been repressed or forgotten. According to Jung, the contents of the personal unconscious can return to consciousness. The other level, the **collective unconscious,** is the storehouse of memories and behavior patterns inherited from mankind's ancestral past. It is almost entirely detached from anything personal in the life of the individual, and all human beings have more or less the same collective unconscious. Jung felt that the idea of the collective unconscious was the most unique feature of his theory.

Like Jung, Alfred Adler was an early and intimate associate of Freud's. He broke with Freud in 1911 to found his own school of individual psychology. Whereas Freud assumed that human behavior is motivated by inborn instincts (primarily sexual ones), Adler took the position that people are motivated to achieve superiority, and he emphasized the primacy of aggressive over sexual instincts. Adler made consciousness the center of personality. A person is ordinarily aware of the reasons for his behavior. He is conscious of his inferiorities (Adler's famed **inferiority complex**—see Figure 18.9), and he is conscious of the goals for which he strives. Moreover, he can plan and guide his actions with full awareness of their meaning for his own self-realization. A human being strives to obtain an unobtainable ideal, and much of this striving is an attempt to overcome feelings of inferiority, feelings based on the early realization that adults can do things that children cannot. An important variation of Adler's inferiority principle is his theory of organ inferiority and compensation. He hypothesized that many people have a deficient organ—like Demosthenes, the Greek orator who put pebbles in his mouth to cure stuttering—and devote their lives to compensating for it.

Adler's emphasis upon the uniqueness of the individual personality also sets his theory apart from classical psychoanalysis. He saw a human being as capable of defining his or her own existence: Adler argued that every act performed by the person bears the stamp of his or her own distinctive style of life. Adler also stressed the social rather than the instinctual forces in development; in so doing he anticipated the approach of later neo-Freudians such as Robert White and Erik Erikson.

Many writers, including Jung himself, have tried to explain the theoretical differences between Freud, Jung, and Adler in terms of the theorists' own personalities. Although there may well be something to this explanation, it has become clear over the years that some of the issues raised by Jung and Adler seem worthy of consideration to many psychologists with quite varied temperaments and interests. Here only a few of the more recent developments

Figure 18.9 In this passage from *What Life Should Mean to You* Alfred Adler sets out the difference between universal feelings of inferiority and the feelings and actions that characterize an inferiority complex. As this passage suggests, Adler placed more emphasis on conscious motivation than Freud did. (From Alfred Adler, *What Life Should Mean to You*, 1931.)

Inferiority feelings are in some degree common to all of us, since we all find ourselves in positions which we wish to improve. If we have kept our courage, we shall set about ridding ourselves of these feelings by the only direct, realistic and satisfactory means—by improving the situation. . . . But suppose an individual is discouraged; suppose he cannot conceive that if he makes realistic efforts he will improve the situation. He will still be unable to bear his feelings of inferiority; he will still struggle to get rid of them; but he will try methods which bring him no farther ahead. . . . If he feels weak, he moves into circumstances where he can feel strong. He does not train to be stronger, to be more adequate; he trains to appear stronger in his own eyes. His efforts to fool himself will meet with only a partial success. If he feels unequal to the problems of occupation, he may attempt to reassure himself of his importance by being a domestic tyrant. In this way he may drug himself; but the real feelings of inferiority will remain. They will be the same old feelings of inferiority provoked by the same old situation. They will be the lasting undercurrent of his psychic life. In such a case we may truly speak of an inferiority complex.

can be mentioned—developments that relate to the ego, to social processes, and to relationships between personality and the body.

A Revised Conception of the Ego

Freud's major discoveries all had to do with unconscious motivational forces and their expression in dreams, psychosomatic symptoms (physical symptoms having a psychological origin), and behavior. Thus, it is understandable that he did not spend as much time elaborating the functions of the ego as some of his critics would have liked. As time went by and more psychologists became exposed to Freud's ideas, tension developed between psychoanalysts, who focused primarily on unconscious motivation, and psychologists, who studied what the analysts were calling ego processes (such as perception, problem solving, conscious memory). This problem has been addressed by several psychoanalytic writers since World War II, which has resulted in a changed psychoanalytic conception of the ego.

David Rapaport has written about the "relative autonomy of the ego from the id" (a concept originally formulated by Heinz Hartmann) and about "conflict-free spheres of ego-functioning." Whereas Freud saw the ego as developing after birth, Rapaport and others postulate that the rudiments of the ego are innate. They also claim that the ego is energized in part by sexually neutral libido, thus indicating that id instincts are not the only source of motivation. Because the ego can also delay its reactions to environmental stimulation, Rapaport has discussed the "relative autonomy of the ego from external stimulation."

Although the new emphasis on ego autonomy may at first seem inconsequential, the issues raised by ego psychologists are worth considering, for they have at least two important consequences. One is that the integration of psychoanalytic theory with other theories in psychology is more likely to be accomplished if the ego is given greater prominence than it had in Freud's works. Perceptual processes in infancy, attention, cognitive development—indeed, most of the topics covered elsewhere in this book—can more easily be related to the observations of psychoanalysts if the ego (the portion of the personality most concerned with perception, thought, and action) is given more autonomy and importance.

Second, the development of ego functioning can now be seen as due in part to forces other than repression and avoidance of punishment. Robert White is the best-known writer on this topic. White has suggested that a great deal of an infant's behavior is oriented toward nonsexual goals and motivated by a desire for **competence**. Consider Freud's oral stage, for example. White argues that although the most important event of the period for the child may be obtaining nourishment, he or she engages in many other activities, such as playing, manipulating objects, and exploring the environment visually, and these are not oral in any sense. He also points out that weaning is not necessarily the psychosexual tragedy portrayed by Freud, because young children gain an increased sense of competence from drinking out of a cup. White takes exception to the stress placed by traditional analysts on toilet training. The most important events for most two-year-olds, he contends, are learning to walk, learning to talk, learning to play with more complex toys—that is, events that increase self-esteem and feelings of accomplishment. The negativism of the two-year-old may be more a message that "I want to learn to do it myself" than a displacement of libido associated with toilet training.

Competence is the term White uses to describe the vast range of activities engaged in by children that do not seem to be either psychosexual or based on avoidance of punishment. He believes that research on curiosity and exploratory behavior warrants the conclusion that not all motivation is based on tension reduction, as Freud thought. According to White, people want to have a noticeable effect on the world and also want to change themselves, even when these desires require increasing rather than reducing tension.

Social Factors in Psychosexual Development

Once Freud's heavy emphasis on instinct is questioned and the ego is given a more significant role in personality dynamics, it is natural to ask how social factors contribute to ego development. Several neo-Freudian theorists have asked this question. Erik Erikson, for example, has recast Freud's psychosexual stages in **psychosocial** terms and has added a number of stages that are not tied as closely as Freud's to a biological base. Freud had said that conflict is bound to arise between instincts and the requirements of reality, stressing the importance of social reality in his concept of the superego. Erikson has made the social forces much more explicit, and has advanced the idea that personality is the result of an encounter between the needs of the person and *the demands of a society during a particular historical epoch.* He has outlined eight stages of development, each of which is characterized by a **psychosocial crisis;** each human being must, in effect, pass eight great tests. The historical context in which a person develops will influence the exact nature of the crisis. In some periods toilet training and cleanliness are more important than in other periods, for instance. During some epochs it has been relatively easy to establish an identity (at one time, if your father was a barrel maker you could count on becoming one, too), but today many people find that establishing an identity requires a painful struggle.

Erikson's Psychosocial Stages   Figure 18.11 is a diagram of Erikson's stages. At the first stage (Freud's oral stage), the crisis is one of **basic trust** or **mistrust.** Normally, the child acquires a basic orientation of trust—trust that the mother will return and provide comfort. If he does not, he may carry throughout his life an orientation of mistrust that is often, but not always, inconvenient. At the second stage (Freud's anal stage), the child begins to gain control over his bladder and bowels and to assert his individuality. If he is psychologically successful, he gains **autonomy;** if not, he suffers **shame** and **doubt.** At the third stage (Freud's phallic stage), the child becomes assertive, rivaling in fantasy the same-sex parent for the other parent. If he learns to channel his urges into socially acceptable acts, he acquires **initiative;** if not, he builds a **reservoir of guilt.**

Erikson's fourth stage parallels Freud's latency stage. Unlike Freud, however, Erikson thought that the early school years were important for development. In this stage the fourth crisis occurs: The child at this time must achieve **learning** and **competence** or experience **failure** and **inferiority.**

The fifth crisis occurs at adolescence. In contrast to Freud, who emphasized the conflicts associated with intensified sexual urges, Erikson emphasizes the **crisis of identity.** The adolescent must decide who he is and what he will do later in life; otherwise he will fall into **role confusion.** He must resolve his sexual identity, choose his occupation, and plan his life as an adult. Freud's genital stage is interpreted by Erikson—the sixth crisis—as involving a conflict between **intimacy** and **isolation.** Only after the adolescent has "found himself" is he able to find another.

The mature post-adolescent personality is a combination of relatively successful or unsuccessful outcomes of these crises. At worst, a person would be completely mistrustful, full of shame and doubt, thoroughly ridden with guilt and feelings of failure, confused about his roles, and isolated from humanity. At the other extreme, a person would be completely trusting, autonomous, able to seize initiative, competent, and intimate with humanity. The two extremes are caricatures, to be sure. Most people's personalities show a combination of attitudes that reflect experiences of both success and failure.

Figure 18.10   These passages are from Erikson's admiring psychohistorical biography of Mahatma Gandhi, the Indian originator of nonviolent political resistance. The passages appear in a section titled "A Personal Word." Erikson was moved to write this section when he found that his insight as a psychoanalyst made it impossible to ignore certain flaws in Gandhi's character.

(From Erik Erikson, *Gandhi's Truth: on the Origins of Militant Nonviolence,* 1969.)

. . . I must now confess that a few times in your work (and often in the literature inspired by you) I have come across passages which almost brought *me* to the point where I felt unable to continue writing *this* book because I seemed to sense the presence of a kind of untruth in the very protestation of truth; of something unclean when all the words spelled out an unreal purity; and above all, of displaced violence where nonviolence was the professed issue.

. . . you seem either unaware of—or want to wish or pray away—an ambivalence, a co-existence of love and hate, which must become conscious in those who work for peace.

It is not enough any more—not after the appearance of your Western contemporary Freud—to be a watchful moralist. For we now have detailed insights into our inner ambiguities, ambivalences, and instinctual conflicts; and only an additional leverage of truth based on self-knowledge promises to give us freedom in the full light of conscious day, whereas in the past, moralist terrorism succeeded only in driving our worst proclivities underground, to remain there until riotous conditions of uncertainty or chaos would permit them to emerge redoubled.

You, Mahatmaji, love the story of that boy prince who would not accept the claim of his father, the Demon King, to a power greater than God's, not even after the boy had been exposed to terrible tortures. At the end he was made to embrace a red-hot metal pillar; but out of this suggestive object stepped God, half lion and half man, and tore the king to pieces.

. . . we must admit that you could not possibly have known of the power of that ambivalence which we have now learned to understand in case histories and life histories . . . . It is, therefore, not without compassion that I must point out that your lifelong insistence on the "innocence" (meaning sexlessness) of children is matched only by your inability to recognize the Demon King in yourself.

Stage	1	2	3	4	5	6	7	8
Maturity								Ego Integrity vs. Despair
Adulthood							Generativity vs. Stagnation	
Young Adulthood						Intimacy vs. Isolation		
Puberty and Adolescence					Identity vs. Role Confusion			
Latency				Industry vs. Inferiority				
Locomotor-Genital			Initiative vs. Guilt					
Muscular-Anal		Autonomy vs. Shame, Doubt						
Oral Sensory	Basic Trust vs. Mistrust							

Figure 18.11 Erikson's representation of life as a succession of psychosocial crises coming to the fore at successive biological stages of life. Erikson's theory is an extension and expansion of Freud's; Erikson's first four stages correspond to Freud's first four psychosexual stages, and like Freud, Erikson considers that the resolutions of conflicts at each stage have lasting effects on personality.
(After Erikson, 1950.)

In his final two stages, Erikson discusses key crises of adulthood and old age. His seventh stage is characterized by a conflict between **generativity** and **stagnation.** A person needs more than intimacy; he or she must be productive—teaching the younger generation or working at some task worthwhile for society. The final stage in development can only be reached if the earlier crises are adequately resolved—if there are no debilitating fixations. If the person reaches this final stage, he achieves a sense of **integrity;** if he does not, he experiences **despair,** and he suffers the sense of a wasted life.

Psychohistory In two book-length biographies, *Young Man Luther* and *Gandhi's Truth,* Erikson has vividly illustrated his thesis that psychosocial development is conditioned by historical context. The first case study focuses on Martin Luther's "identity crisis" but deals also with the earlier and later stages of the famous Protestant reformer's development. Erikson tries to explain why, in a particular time and place, a personality like Luther's appeared. In the second book, Erikson uses similar methods to probe the life of India's great nonviolent political leader. At one point in the book Erikson's analysis is interrupted by a remarkable "personal letter" to his (deceased) biographical subject in which he struggles with the implications of his psychoanalytic findings for the future of nonviolent resistance.

Lately, several other psychoanalysts and historians have followed Erikson's lead. Their work is collectively being called **psychohistory,** a term that Erikson has at times seemed reluctant to accept even though many of the young psychohistorians see Erikson as their model. The new hybrid discipline has already spawned a journal, and it promises many exciting future developments.

Erich Fromm's Sociological Approach Even more than Erikson, Erich Fromm emphasizes the sociohistorical roots of personality. He has taken ideas from both Freud and Karl Marx, using them to (among other things) elaborate Marx's concept of **alienation**. Fromm has noted that many modern men and women feel lonely and isolated because they have become separated from nature and from each other. In his book *Escape from Freedom,* Fromm develops the thesis that as a person gains freedom he or she feels increasingly alone. **Freedom** becomes a negative condition from which people try to escape, sometimes by succumbing to a totalitarian government, sometimes by engaging in war. (Under these conditions, however horrible they might otherwise be, someone *else* makes all a person's decisions for him.)

Most of us can observe at least moments of our own spontaneity which are at the same time moments of genuine happiness. Whether it be the fresh and spontaneous perception of a landscape or the dawning of some truth as the result of our thinking, or a sensuous pleasure that is not stereotyped, or the welling up of love for another person—in these moments we all know what a spontaneous act is and may have some vision of what human life could be if these experiences were not such rare and uncultivated occurrences.

. . . Why is spontaneous activity the answer to the problem of freedom? . . . Spontaneous activity is the one way in which man can overcome the terror of aloneness without sacrificing the integrity of his self; for in the spontaneous realization of the self man unites himself anew with the world—with man, nature, and himself. Love is the foremost component of such spontaneity; not love as the dissolution of the self in another person, not love as the possession of another person, but love as spontaneous affirmation of others, as the union of the individual with others on the basis of the preservation of the individual self. The dynamic quality of love lies in this very polarity: that it springs from the need of overcoming separateness, that it leads to oneness—and yet that individuality is not eliminated. Work is the other component; not work as a compulsive activity in order to escape aloneness, not work as a relationship to nature which is partly one of dominating her, partly one of worship of and enslavement by the very products of man's hands, but work as creation in which man becomes one with nature in the act of creation.

What is the answer to this dilemma? Fromm says that rather than becoming a mindless conformist a person can freely unite with others in an equalitarian spirit of love and shared work (see Figure 18.12). For this reason, Fromm is sometimes classed as a humanitarian socialist. (Incidentally, Freud's only definition of normality or psychological health was *"lieben und arbeiten,"* which means "to love and to work.")

According to Fromm, there are five specific needs that arise from the conditions of human existence. First, there is the need for relatedness, which stems from the stark fact that mankind in becoming human was torn from the animal's primary union with nature. Second, human beings have a need for transcendence—an urge to overcome animal nature and to become creative. Third, there is a need for rootedness; people want to be an integral part of the world, to feel a sense of belonging in it and of brotherliness. Fourth, a person wants a sense of personal identity—he or she wants to be distinctive and unique. Finally, people have a need for a frame of reference that will give stability and consistency to their behavior.

Fromm believes that the ways in which these needs express themselves are determined by the social arrangements in which a person lives. His personality develops in accordance with the opportunities that a particular society offers him. In a capitalist society, for example, he may gain a sense of personal identity by becoming rich or develop a feeling of rootedness by becoming a dependable and trusted employee in a large company.

In order for society to function properly, it is absolutely essential, Fromm points out, that children's characters be shaped to fit the needs of that particular society. The task of the parents and of education is to make the child wish to act as he must act if a given economic, political, and social system is to be maintained. In a capitalist system, therefore, the desire to save must be implanted in people, so that capital will be available for an expanding economy. A society that has evolved a credit system must see to it that people feel an inner compulsion to pay their bills promptly.

By making demands upon human beings that are contrary to their nature, society warps and frustrates them. It alienates humans from fulfilling the basic conditions of their existence. Fromm points out that when a society changes in any important respect—for example, when the factory system displaced the individual artisan—the change is likely to produce dislocations in the social character of people. The old character structure does not fit the demands of the new society, and human beings feel an increasing sense of alienation and despair.

One of the greatest dangers in trying to escape these personal demons—alienation and despair—is the concomitant escape from the freedom they imply. Freedom also means opportunities for social and personal integration. Fromm's warning not to abandon the opportunities of freedom out of raw fear of freedom itself is one of the hallmarks of his thinking on personality.

Sullivan's Interpersonal Approach   If Erikson's and Fromm's adaptations of Freud's theory are called sociohistorical, Harry Stack Sullivan's might be called sociopsychological. Sullivan maintained that personality cannot be isolated from interpersonal situations; in a sense, it is impossible to speak about an individual's personality without in the same breath saying or implying something about his or her relations with other people. (Most of the personality characteristics mentioned so far in this chapter—friendliness, hostility, shyness, ambition, alienation—don't really make sense outside a social context.) Sullivan was a psychiatrist who, like Freud, came to his conclusions after seeing a large number of patients. Perhaps you will understand his interpersonal conception of personality better if you begin by reading an idealized Sullivanian case study (see Figure 18.13); notice that, unlike

Mahl's Freudian case study presented earlier, Sullivan's involves *two* people.

Although Sullivan stressed social determinants of personality, he also specified certain capacities with which an infant begins life, particularly, capacities for tension and symbolization, both of which are bases for later social experiences. Tensions are discomforts related to basic needs (obviously similar to Freud's notion of instinctual psychic energy seeking discharge). Sullivan included among the innate sources of tension a need for contact. This primitive desire for contact is the basis of later needs for tenderness, love, and intimacy. The postulated need for contact allowed Sullivan to give his theory a positive social cast quite different from Freud's.

Sullivan also stressed the symbolic quality of human experience. He put great emphasis on the acquisition of language as a contributor to personality development. According to Sullivan, the newborn baby has no clear concept of time, of relations between events, of distinctions between self and nonself. Gradually the infant learns to classify events and to anticipate good and bad experiences (those that relieve or increase tension). There is a good nipple (the one that brings comfort and relief) and a bad nipple (the one that provides no milk and therefore causes additional stress), a good mother and a bad mother, a good me and a bad me. Only when language is acquired can the child integrate the emotionally distinct mothers or selves into single verbal concepts. Sullivan believed that even linguistically competent adults often experience the world in a mixture of ways, with the more primitive ones becoming prominent during periods of stress.

Anxiety was treated in a distinctive way by Sullivan. He saw it as a feeling of tension that is communicated empathically to an infant by a tense mother. Thus, very early in life, anxiety is associated with social disapproval and insecurity. The developing child builds a self-system in the context of social rewards and threats to security and learns to use something akin to what Freud called defense mechanisms to remove threatening aspects of the self from conscious consideration.

Mental disorders, both neurotic and psychotic, do not exist "inside" people, according to Sullivan, but in a network of distorted and manipulative social relations. The case study of Mr. and Mrs. X (Figure 18.13) provides a good example. (Freud would probably have classified them both as hysterics.) Such problems can often be traced by Sullivanian analysts back to poor social relations at an earlier developmental stage.

The Embodiment of Personality

This chapter would not be complete without a brief discussion of another neo-Freudian theme, the physical expression of psychological conflicts. Early in the chapter it was mentioned that Breuer and Freud's first patients had bodily symptoms as well as psychological complaints; they suffered from headaches, paralyzed limbs, and sensory disorders. It might have seemed to you that Freud's method revealed these symptoms to be imaginary; and, indeed, some of them disappeared quickly once the "talking cure," psychoanalysis, was initiated. Anyone who has suffered from tension headaches, "nervous stomach," or sexual disturbances (such as impotence or frigidity) knows, however, that these are not mere figments of the imagination. Prolonged conflict leaves its mark on the body as well as on the unconscious; in fact, it is a mistake to succumb to the Western tendency to see mind and body as distinct.

One of Freud's followers, Wilhelm Reich, is especially well known for his attempts to assess psychological disturbances through their expression in the body. (Unfortunately, he is even better known for being sent to prison after the U.S. Food and Drug Administration declared that claims made for one of his inventions, the orgone box, were fraudulent. This ill-fated conclusion to a

Figure 18.13 In this hypothetical case study of hysteria, Sullivan shows how he views neuroses as *interpersonal* phenomena. This approach can be contrasted with Freud's *intrapsychic* analyses of hysteria, although there is not necessarily any conflict between the two viewpoints.
(From Harry Stack Sullivan, *The Interpersonal Theory of Psychiatry*, 1953.)

Let us say that a man (call him Mr. X) with a strong hysterical predisposition has married, perhaps for money, and that his wife, thanks to his rather dramatic and exaggerated way of doing and saying things, cannot long remain in doubt that there was a very practical consideration in this marriage and cannot completely blind herself to a certain lack of importance that she has in her husband's eyes. So she begins to get even. She may, for example, like someone I recently saw, develop a never-failing vaginismus, so that there is no more intercourse for him. And he will not ruminate on whether this vaginismus that is cutting off his satisfaction is directed against him, for the very simple reason that if you view interpersonal phenomena with that degree of objectivity, you can't use an hysterical process to get rid of your own troubles. So he won't consider that; but he will suffer terribly from privation and will go to rather extravagant lengths to overcome the vaginismus that is depriving him of satisfaction, the lengths being characterized by a certain rather theatrical attention to detail rather than deep scrutiny of his wife. . . . Then one night . . . he has the idea, "My God, this thing is driving me crazy," and goes to sleep.

. . . He wakes up at some early hour in the morning, probably at the time when his wife is notoriously most soundly asleep, and he has a frightful attack of some kind. It could be literally almost anything, but it will be very impressive to anyone around. His wife will be awakened, very much frightened, and will call the doctor. But before the doctor gets there, the husband, with a fine sense of dramatic values, will let her know in some indirect way that he's terribly afraid he is losing his mind. . . .

Now let us say that the doctor in this case is a high-grade but somewhat inexperienced psychiatrist and that he sets out to get the history of the immediate situation from which this business grew. He might get an awful lot of details—details about distressing situations in the office, the terrible strain that the husband has been under from the pressure of his work. . . But there will be no comment about anything else—no faintest suspicion of anything the least bit out of the way in the sex life.

Figure 18.14 In this passage Reich describes some of the physical manifestations of deeply rooted psychological conflicts. An emphasis on bodily function is a common theme in psychoanalytic personality theory, but no other analyst before Reich considered physical intervention as a possible form of psychotherapy. (From Wilhelm Reich, *Character-analysis*, 1949.)

The armored individual does not himself feel the armor as such. If one tries to describe it to him in words he usually does not know what one is talking about. What he feels is not the armoring itself but only the distortion of his perceptions of life: he feels himself uninterested, rigid, empty, or he complains about nervous unrest, palpitations, constipation, insomnia, nausea, etc. If the armoring is of long standing and has also influenced the tissues of the organs, the patient will come to us with peptic ulcer, rheumatism, arthritis, cancer or angina pectoris. . . .

The armored individual is incapable of dissolving his armor. He is also incapable of expressing the primitive biological emotions. He knows the sensation of tickling but not that of orgonotic pleasure. He cannot emit a pleasurable sigh or imitate it. If he tries, he will produce a groan, a repressed roar or an impulse to vomit. He is incapable of letting out an angry yell or convincingly imitating a fist hitting the couch in anger. He is incapable of full expiration: the movements of his diaphragm (as X-rays readily show) are very limited. If asked to move the pelvis forward, he is incapable of doing so, and often even of understanding what one asks of him; he may even execute the opposite motion, that of retracting the pelvis, a motion which expresses holding back. The tension of the peripheral muscle and nervous system is shown in an exaggerated sensitivity to pressure. It is impossible to touch certain parts of an armored organism without producing intense symptoms of anxiety and nervousness. What is commonly called "nervousness" is the result of this hypersensitivity of highly tensed muscles.

The total holding back results in the incapacity for the plasmatic pulsation in the sexual act, that is orgastic impotence.

brilliant, if turbulent, career has retarded research and exploration of some of Reich's more promising ideas.)

Reich developed the concept of **muscle armor** or **character armor** to describe the ways in which prolonged conflict can alter a person's posture, breathing patterns, facial expressions, and movements in characteristic ways. The concept of bodily "armor" as a sign of conflicts and defenses was useful not only for diagnostic purposes; Reich was allegedly able to induce people to relive a traumatic experience, to alter their characteristic moods, and to change in other ways through physical manipulations of various kinds.

Recently several therapists have followed up Reich's insights and have developed new bodily oriented therapies. However, bodily oriented approaches to psychotherapy are still very controversial and need to be evaluated by hard-nosed researchers. Some of these approaches may survive the test, for a large body of research on stress indicates that psyche and soma (mind and body) are not separable. In twenty years it may be common to include physical and postural variables in personality assessment, just as psychologists now include life-history questions.

THE IMPACT OF PSYCHOANALYTIC THEORY

What holds the various theories in this chapter together is Sigmund Freud's direct influence on all of them. Freud's ideas have had a massive impact on psychology—as they have had on art, literature, literary criticism, and other fields. Introductory students are sometimes so fascinated by Freud's theory that they wonder why it hasn't been embraced by all psychologists. One reason has to do with the difficulty of gathering evidence for psychoanalytic hypotheses. Few patients would feel comfortable having their psychoanalytic sessions made public, yet something like this would be necessary to allow careful study of the psychoanalytic procedure. Also, psychoanalysis takes a long time to complete and so is not amenable to laboratory experimentation. Besides, most psychoanalysts are more interested in helping their patients than in systematically collecting and analyzing research data. Although many important observations may be made each day in analysts' offices around the world, most of them will never be described in print. Finally, many psychoanalytic concepts are difficult to measure objectively. As was pointed out earlier, some are more poetic or metaphorical than scientific.

Despite these problems, it would be a grave mistake to think that Freud's theory has had little impact on researchers. His ideas concerning anxiety, defense mechanisms, and dreams, to name just a few examples, have influenced countless researchers—even though many of them do not identify themselves with his theory. You shouldn't be at all surprised to hear someone in your psychology department criticize and seem to reject Freud's theory one day and the next day casually refer to someone's defensiveness or to the latent meaning of a dream. Regardless of current theoretical allegiances, we are all indebted to Sigmund Freud.

SUMMARY

1. Although personality theories differ greatly, they all attempt to account for two things: **individual differences** in the behavior of different people confronting the same situation, and **consistencies** in the behavior of a single person confronting different situations. That is, they all try to explain the relatively stable, persisting organization of characteristics that makes each person unique, usually by referring to an interaction between biological and social factors.

2. In comparing personality theories, it is helpful to ask oneself how each theorist describes the **core** and **periphery** of personality (Maddi's classification) and to assess the way each theory treats four issues: **structure, dynamics, development,** and **motivational factors** (Hall and Lindzey's categories).

3. The first formal theory in the field of personality was **Sigmund Freud's psychoanalytic theory.** Freud introduced psychoanalysis in 1900 in *The Interpretation of Dreams* and kept revising and supplementing his ideas until his death in 1939. The theory has had a tremendous influence even on those who reject it.

Figure 18.15 Sigmund Freud is perhaps the single most important figure in the history of psychology. His influence has been huge in psychiatry, anthropology, and in literary criticism, not to mention virtually every area of psychology.

   a. Freud's sources of data were chiefly the **free association** of hysteric patients, although he also treated people with other disorders and performed an impressive amount of self-analysis.

   b. From these data, Freud theorized the existence of unconscious processes, probably his most important contribution. Repressed infantile wishes and goals reside in the unconscious and can come to consciousness through free association.

   c. Freud found that a patient's free associations, and also his **psychosomatic symptoms, dreams, jokes,** and **accidents** (such as forgetting an appointment), revealed **unconscious conflicts,** usually between an impulse to engage in a forbidden act and social or moral constraints that prohibit the act.

   d. Freud saw personality structure as consisting of three separate but interacting agencies: the **id,** the **ego,** and the **superego.**

   e. The id is an inborn reservoir of instinctual psychic energy, or **libido,** completely unconscious, which demands immediate satisfaction and operates according to the **pleasure principle.**

   f. The **ego,** which is not inborn, develops to handle transactions between the id and the outside world; later, it also mediates the demands of the superego. The ego is the executive agency of the personality: It controls action, postpones gratification of impulses in the interests of long-term goals, and operates according to the **reality principle.**

   g. The **superego,** which develops at around age six, represents social values and ideals. It includes both the **conscience,** which inhibits the impulses of the id, and the **ego ideal,** which offers a standard of behavior toward which the person aspires.

   h. According to Freud, the energy for human behavior is provided by two inborn id instincts, sex and aggression, which he redefined in his later writing as **life instincts** (Eros) and **death instincts** (Thanatos). He believed that personality is determined by the way a person resolves the **conflict** between the id's demands that these instincts be satisfied and society's restrictions on the ways they may be satisfied.

Figure 18.16 Carl Jung was a Swiss psychiatrist who, early in his career, met Freud and became his close friend, and then later had serious disagreements with him. One of the most mystical and metaphysical of psychological theorists, Jung has had greater acceptance in Europe than in America. The popularity of his works, however, appears to be growing in America, especially among persons interested in mysticism and nonempirical aspects of psychology.

   i. Freud postulated a **homeostatic,** or tension-reduction, model of behavior: An aroused instinct activates behavior; if the behavior is successful, it reduces tension and returns the person to the state that existed before the instinct was aroused.

   j. In discussing conflict and tension reduction, Freud emphasized four terms: **displacement,** by which instinctual energy is transferred from one object to another; **identification,** by which a person incorporates personality features and values of another person, particularly his same-sex parent; **anxiety,** in which a person senses impending danger

Figure 18.17 Adler's theories of personality and psychotherapy—developed largely after he, too, broke away from Freud—have had wide impact in the United States and Europe. His theories use less complex concepts than Freudian or Jungian psychoanalysis, and his writings on psychotherapy offer more optimism and practicality. Because of his emphasis on the child's inferiority feelings and on power relationships in the family. Adler has had important influence on psychotherapy with children.

(whether real or not); and **defense mechanisms,** which are unconscious attempts to reduce anxiety by denying or distorting reality.

k. Some common defense mechanisms are **repression, regression, reaction formation, projection,** and **sublimation.**

l. Freud describes personality development in terms of five **psychosexual stages: oral, anal, phallic** (or **childhood genital**), **latency,** and **genital.** Except for the latency period, each stage is named for the zone of the body that is most important to personality development during a particular time of life.

m. **Fixation** occurs when development from one psychosexual stage to the next is partially (and in some rare cases, completely) halted. The adult then manifests certain character traits associated with the stage of fixation. For example, fixation at the oral stage may result in gullibility or argumentativeness during adulthood.

n. During the phallic stage, the **Oedipus complex** (or **Electra complex** in girls) appears: The child falls in love with the parent of the opposite sex. The Oedipus or Electra complex is resolved when the child identifies with the same-sex parent, partly to defend himself against castration anxiety and partly to achieve vicarious possession of the opposite-sex parent. **Identification** is responsible for the development of the superego and establishment of the child's basic sexual identity.

4. Two early colleagues of Freud, **Carl Jung** and **Alfred Adler,** soon broke with him over certain issues.

a. Jung differed with Freud on two points. First, he took a more positive view of human nature, believing that people try to develop their potential as well as to handle their instinctual urges. Second, he distinguished between the **personal unconscious** (similar to Freud's idea of the unconscious) and the **collective unconscious,** which is a storehouse of memories and behavior patterns from mankind's ancestral past.

b. Adler believed that people are motivated to achieve superiority; he is the originator of the term **inferiority complex.** He stressed the uniqueness of the individual personality, the primacy of aggressive over sexual instincts, and the importance of social rather than instinctual forces in development.

5. Other neo-Freudians have given the ego more importance than Freud did. For example, **Robert White** says that a young child's behavior, rather than being oriented toward the sexual and aggressive instincts of the id, is largely motivated by a desire for **competence.** White points out that walking, talking, and playing with more complex toys—which increase the child's feeling of competence—are probably more central events in a two-year-old's life than toilet training.

Figure 18.18 Robert White is a psychoanalytic theorist whose emphasis on competence as a primary drive has become part of the body of psychoanalytic theory. White explains both the growing child's urge to master his environment and the role of competence (mastery) in adult behavior. He is the author of an influential work on personality, *Lives in Progress,* and also a textbook in abnormal psychology.

6. A third group of neo-Freudians emphasizes the **social factors** in development.

a. **Erik Erikson** says that personality results from an encounter between the needs of a person and the demands of a society during a particular epoch. He outlines eight **psychosocial stages of development,** each characterized by a particular crisis, such as the **identity crisis** of adolescence.

b. Building on Erikson's biographies of Luther and Gandhi, several psychoanalysts and historians have begun a new approach to personality called **psychohistory,** which stresses the importance of historical context to personality development.

c. **Erich Fromm** emphasizes the sociohistorical roots of personality even more than Erikson. He says that the ways human needs express themselves are determined by a person's society. In a capitalist society, for example, a person may try to satisfy his need for personal identity by becoming rich. Fromm is particularly interested in the relation between **alienation** and **freedom.**

d. **Harry Stack Sullivan** stressed the **interpersonal** nature of personality, pointing out that an individual's personality inevitably involves his or her relations with other people. Mental disorders, according to Sullivan, exist not ''inside'' people but in a network of distorted and manipulative social relations. Sullivan gave particular emphasis to the acquisition of language as a contributor to personality development.

7. A final neo-Freudian theme concerns the **physical expression** of psychological conflict, a concept developed especially by **Wilhelm Reich.** He suggested that the idea of **muscle armor** or **character armor** to describe the ways in which prolonged conflict can alter a person's posture, breathing patterns, facial expressions, and movements.

Figure 18.19   Erik Erikson is an American psychoanalyst who has devoted considerable attention to such matters as the experience of American Indian children in modern America. His term for the conflicts experienced by adolescents in many societies—"identity crisis"—has become part of everyday English.

Figure 18.20   Erich Fromm emphasizes social and historical determinants of personality more than any other neo-Freudian theorist does. His work has combined a psychoanalytic perspective with sociological and existential viewpoints. His books *Escape From Freedom, The Art of Loving,* and, recently, *The Anatomy of Human Destructiveness* have been widely read.

SUGGESTED READINGS

Hall, Calvin S., and Gardner Lindzey. *Theories of Personality.* 2nd ed. New York: Wiley, 1970. The classic secondary source on theories of personality. It begins with a discussion of the nature of personality theory and outlines the most important classical and contemporary theories. It then compares and contrasts theories across a number of dimensions and issues.

Levy, Leon H. *Conceptions of Personality.* New York: Random House, 1970. Levy's text on personality examines issues in personality theory rather than outlining theories of personality. It integrates a number of contemporary lines of research.

Maddi, Salvatore R. *Personality Theories: A Comparative Analysis.* 2nd ed. Homewood, Ill.: Dorsey Press, 1972. A recent text on personality theory, it classifies personality theorists according to whether their basic assumption relates to *conflict, fulfillment,* or *consistency.* The text examines what the theorists have to say about the core and periphery of personality. It presents research on each position and draws conclusions about their strengths and weaknesses.

Maddi, Salvatore R. (ed.). *Perspectives on Personality: A Comparative Approach.* Boston: Little, Brown, 1971. A book of readings by or about each major theorist discussed in the Maddi text, cited above.

Mahl, George F. *Psychological Conflict and Defense.* New York: Harcourt Brace Jovanovich, 1971. A clear exposition of psychoanalytic theory, including both clinical and research evidence for the theory's main hypotheses. (This paperback is a section excerpted from a four-part personality text by Irving L. Janis, George F. Mahl, Jerome Kagan, and Robert R. Holt titled *Personality: Dynamics, Development, and Assessment.* New York: Harcourt Brace Jovanovich, 1969.)

Wollheim, Richard. *Sigmund Freud.* New York: Viking, 1971. A fresh look at Freud's writings; contains basic biographical information, a history of the development of psychoanalytic theory, and a careful examination of major concepts.

Figure 18.21   Harry Stack Sullivan is a psychiatrist who has integrated psychoanalysis with an interpersonal theory of personality, psychopathology, and psychotherapy. Sullivan based most of his thinking on his years of work with schizophrenic adolescents.

Psychologists dealing with theories of personality tend to deal with human beings in general. Individual cases can, however, be extremely puzzling. People's personalities do occasionally change, sometimes late in life, and they begin to think and act as we would not have judged they were capable of thinking and acting. Back in the 1930s, there was a motion picture called *Gabriel over the White House*, in which Walter Huston played a party hack who had somehow managed to get himself elected President of the United States. Through some supernatural intervention he was suddenly turned into a capable and forceful man and surprised everyone by becoming a great executive.

Just fiction, we might say, just wishful dreaming. A personality once fixed will not suddenly reverse itself and show hidden depths. Warren Gamaliel Harding was a charming, handsome small-town editor who was pushed into politics, rose to be Senator and then, in 1920, became President of the United States. One would have supposed from the general feckless incompetence he always displayed that he would make a perfectly rotten president. And so he did!

Then there was Chester Alan Arthur. Arthur was a lawyer who, in the days just before the Civil War, joined the newly formed Republican party and became a ward-heeling hack.

He eventually rose to the position of chief henchman of the unscrupulous Republican party boss, Roscoe Conkling. Arthur was rewarded with the post of Collector of the Port of New York. This made it possible for him to allow Republican wheel-horses to fatten themselves at the public trough in a riot of incompetency and graft. He was eventually removed from his position when the stench grew too strong to ignore.

Then in 1880, James A. Garfield was nominated by the Republicans for the presidency over the opposition of Conkling and his following. To appease Conkling, Chester Arthur was given the vice-presidential nomination. The Republicans won the election and Vice-President Arthur remained Conkling's man, backing him loyally in all his disputes with President Garfield.

On July 2, 1881, Garfield was shot by an assassin. On September 19 he died, and Chester Alan Arthur, cheap politician *extraordinaire* became President of the United States.

What do you think happened? To the surprise of everyone in the United States, Arthur did a right-about-face. Suddenly, and without warning, he proved himself an honest and forceful man, who bowed neither to Conkling nor to anyone else. He fought the bosses, exposed corruption, appointed competent men, and presented an administration of remarkable integrity.

Most of all he surprised the crooked politicians, who had expected a field day with Arthur as President. In 1884, he had no chance of being renominated. Too honest!

Isaac Asimov

19

Alternative Conceptions of Personality

Figure 19.1 In this chapter the major rivals to psychoanalytic theories of personality are presented: behaviorally based theories, existentially based ones, and factor-analytic ones. Although these groups of theories are very different in their approaches, they can all be contrasted with psychoanalytic theory in that they examine behavior and experience as concrete phenomena rather than as clues to unconscious motives and hidden dynamics.

Virtually every psychologist who studies personality is familiar with the Freudian and neo-Freudian theories discussed in the preceding chapter, yet not everyone accepts them as sufficient or as completely correct. Some people think that psychoanalytic theory is not tied closely enough to empirical research (on learning, cognition, and individual differences measured by psychological tests, for example). Others say psychoanalytic theory is too negativistic; it fails to stress the positive, humane side of personal development and overemphasizes instincts, irrationality, and painful anxiety. Of course, all the critics do not agree with each other, either. Their positions depend on which problems they choose to address, which methods they adopt, and what kinds of people they study most carefully (for example, normal adults, neurotics, or schizophrenics). Although there are more nonpsychoanalytic theories of personality than can be covered here, the most important ones in terms of the issues they raise fall into three groups: behavioristic approaches; phenomenological and humanistic approaches; and trait and factor-analytic approaches.

BEHAVIORISTIC APPROACHES

American psychology has been concerned with animal and human learning since the beginning of this century. Some of the most famous American psychologists—for example, Edward L. Thorndike, John B. Watson, Clark Hull, and B. F. Skinner—are known for research on learning. Naturally, when Freud's ideas became known in American universities, learning theorists had to take notice. Like other European theorists whose work has slowly penetrated the American academic establishment (such as Jean Piaget, discussed in Chapter 8), Freud was at first ignored, then attacked, and finally more or less assimilated.

Dollard and Miller's Psychodynamic Behavior Theory

The most ambitious assimilation effort

was made during the late 1940s at Yale University by John Dollard and Neal Miller, two associates of the well-known learning theorist Clark Hull. Their approach is called psychodynamic behavior theory by some psychologists because it represents an attempt to deal with the psychodynamic phenomena identified by Freud in terms familiar to behavioristic learning theorists.

As explained in Chapter 16, Hullian learning theory included two central concepts: drive and habit. **Drives** are the energizers (in Calvin Hall and Gardner Lindzey's terms, the motivating forces) of behavior. Any strong stimulus, whether its origin is internal (hunger pangs, thirst) or external (electric shock, a loud noise, or sexual desire) can activate a drive, and organisms will engage in behavior to reduce or eliminate such stimulation.

Although there are substantial differences between their theories, Hull's drive theory and Freud's theory of psychic energy or libido are alike in that both are **homeostatic,** or **tension-reduction,** theories; according to both, behavior is motivated in what might be called a negative manner—by an unpleasant state of affairs that the organism seeks to escape or avoid. **Habit** is the structural concept in Hull's theory; it refers to a hypothetical connection in the nervous system whereby a particular response is always triggered by a particular cue or stimulus. According to Hull, a habit is strengthened (or reinforced) when the response associated with it leads to **drive reduction.** For example, if a hungry animal obtains food by turning right in a T-maze, it will be likely to turn right at the intersection next time it is seeking food.

In order to learn something first-hand about psychoanalysis, Dollard and Miller underwent analysis themselves (as did many other social scientists interested in Freud's theory). Although they came to agree with the analysts that many of the phenomena identified by Freud were quite real (including conflict, defense mechanisms, and even the efficacy of analysis), Dollard and Miller believed these phenomena could be better explained in terms of Hull's theory. Moreover, because most of the Hullians had used lower animals rather than people as subjects in their experiments, Dollard and Miller wanted to show that animal experiments (usually with rats) could illuminate the processes described by Freud, now to be translated into Hullian terms.

In Freud's theory the basic sources of motivation are instincts. Dollard and Miller relied on a similar concept, that of innate needs, or **primary needs**. According to Freud, much neurotic behavior is the result of conflict between instinctual impulses and feelings of anxiety that signal that punishment may occur if the impulses are expressed. To show that an analog of human anxiety could be created in rats, Miller placed a rat in a two-compartment box with a metal floor. One compartment was painted black, the other white. When the rat was in the white compartment, the metal floor was electrified and the frantic rat soon discovered that it could escape the painful shock by jumping a barrier and landing in the black compartment. Once this habit had been established, the rat would jump from the white compartment to the black compartment as soon as it was placed in the box—even before the electricity was turned on. Moreover, the electricity could be left off henceforth and the rat would still learn new responses, such as pushing a lever or turning a wheel, in order to escape the now-harmless white side of the box. Thus, a learned drive, or **secondary drive** (in this case, learned fear, perhaps somewhat akin to human anxiety), could motivate behavior in the absence of a primary need.

In later work, Miller showed how something like neurotic conflict could be produced in a rat. Many neurotic humans suffer from **approach-avoidance conflicts:** They want something very badly but are afraid to admit this desire or to express it in behavior. Recall the case study of Ed presented in Chapter 18. Ed engaged in sexual activity, in the forms of masturbation and sexual intercourse with his fiancée. But he also felt guilty and tense about his sexual behavior, in part because he unconsciously associated it with fear of castration. A diagram of Ed's conflict appears as Figure 19.2A. The diagram shows how a psychoanalytic case study can be represented in terms congenial to Dollard and Miller. Miller demonstrated something similar in rats (Figure 19.2B) by first allowing a hungry rat to run down an alley to get to a food tray. Then, while the rat was eating, it received a brief but painful electric shock. Later, when the rat was placed in starting position at one end of the alley, it began running toward the food but suddenly stopped somewhere in the middle of the alley and vacillated, as if torn between the desire for food and anticipation of the painful shock. The point in the alley where vacillation occurred could be changed by altering the strength of either the approach or the avoidance component of the conflict (that is, by changing the hours of food deprivation or the intensity of the shock). In both cases, conflict occurs when avoidance and approach tendencies have equal strength. Such conflicts are discussed further in Chapter 25.

In their book *Personality and Psychotherapy: An Analysis in Terms of Learning, Thinking, and Culture,* published in 1950, Dollard and Miller discuss the genesis of important human conflicts. They agree with Freud that most conflicts arise because of social (or cultural) restrictions on impulse expression. If a person comes to have several unresolved conflicts between basic needs and socially induced anxiety, he or she may show the kind of symptoms studied by Freud. Dollard and Miller also discuss defense mechanisms, which they treat as anxiety-reducing responses (both thoughts and actions are classified as "responses"). Repression, for example, is called "learned not-thinking"; a young woman who feels apprehensive whenever she thinks about having sexual intercourse with her lover may be rewarded (in the drive-reduction sense) for shifting her thoughts to something less threatening. In Hullian terms, the habit of "not-thinking" about this particular topic is "reinforced" because it reduces the "anxiety drive."

It is interesting that some religious teachers explicitly encourage their followers to use this type of defense mechanism—to shift attention away from "evil" thoughts by praying, chanting, or engaging in meditation. Jesus seems to have encouraged repression when he said "Lust after a woman in your heart and you have committed adultery already." His statement implies that an evil thought is just as bad as an evil deed. Many psychologists obviously do not agree with this doctrine; as was stated in the preceding chapter, Freud thought repression lay at the root of most neuroses.

Psychotherapy, in Dollard and Miller's view, is a relearning process. A patient is encouraged to express formerly repressed thoughts and desires and to discover that punishment will not follow. (This process is a little like gently leading one of Miller's shocked rats into the white compartment or the feeding area of the alleyway so it can learn that shock will no longer be delivered.) Also, through analysis the patient comes to *label* previously nonverbalized feelings and conflicts, some of which may have gone unlabeled since the preverbal period of childhood. This labeling is the Dollard-Miller version of Freud's claim that after analysis, "Where id was, there shall ego be." Dollard and Miller, however, tend to think of the ego as consisting of essentially verbal processes.

Dollard and Miller's approach is important for two reasons. First, it showed that psychoanalytic concepts need not remain foreign to American researchers, even those working primarily with animals. Second, their approach helped pave the way for **behavior therapy,** a set of procedures, based on learning principles, for changing neurotic and psychotic behavior (see Chapter 24). Although many psychologists have criticized Dollard and Miller for drawing analogies between rats and humans and have pointed out that dreams and other symbolic processes are not likely to be illuminated by animal

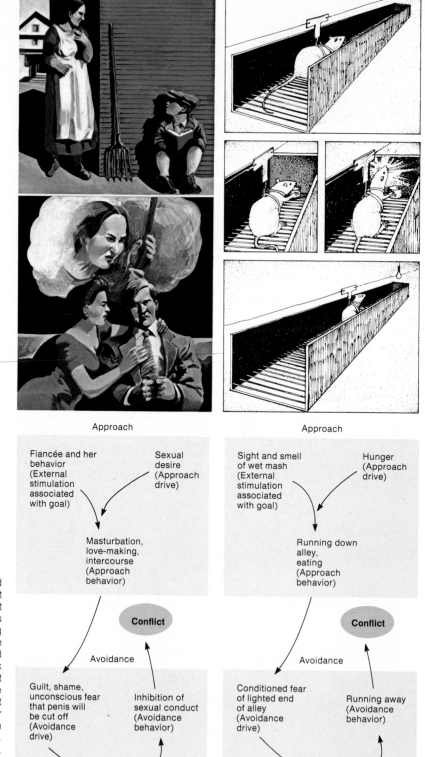

Figure 19.2   These illustrations and diagrams show how Ed's sexual conflict and an experimentally induced conflict in a rat can be given analogous analyses in terms of learning theory.   (A) Ed's sexual conflict. Here Ed is shown as a child being frightened by his mother while reading a book about sex and, later, as an adult experiencing conflict about making love to his fiancée.   (B) A conflict experimentally induced in a rat. Miller and his students rewarded a rat with food for running down an alley. Subsequently when it reached the food, they gave it electric shocks. On later trials the rat would run part way down the alley and then vacillate.

research, no one doubts that psychodynamic behavior theory has had an effect on the psychology of personality.

Skinner's Radical Behaviorism

Unlike Hull and Dollard and Miller, B. F. Skinner rejects internal constructs such as drive and habit; he sees no need for a general concept of personality structure. Instead he proposes a **functional analysis of behavior,** in which the external conditions that control behavior are specified without speculation about what is happening inside the organism. The external conditions include such things as **food deprivation** (an operation that most other theorists see as related to a need or drive but that Skinner says can be identified and manipulated without reference to internal states), **discriminative stimuli** (which indicate to an organism whether a particular behavior will be rewarded, punished, or ignored), and **reinforcement and punishment** (events which, following a response, increase or decrease its frequency of occurrence later, in a similar situation, as explained in Chapter 4).

One reason Skinner's position has become popular is that it suggests that people's behavior can be changed even if the internal dynamics of their behavior are not understood. If pigeons and dogs can be taught to play ping-pong and perform tricks without their trainers' understanding their internal psychological mechanisms, perhaps similar procedures can be used to teach arithmetic to children and more normal behavior to people suffering from mental disorders. Teaching machines and some forms of behavior therapy are outgrowths of Skinner's ideas. In addition, Skinner's technical writings have stimulated a great deal of laboratory research on the effects of rewards and punishment under various conditions (see Chapter 4), and his less technical books have been read by many laymen. One of these, *Walden Two*, describes a utopian community operated according to Skinnerian principles. Another, *Beyond Freedom and Dignity*, attributes many contemporary social and personal problems to people's failure to recognize that freedom and dignity are illusions that get in the way of efficient and rational social control. As you can imagine, Skinner's popular books have been strongly attacked by many psychologists (including some mentioned later in this chapter, especially Carl Rogers), but his views continue to be extremely influential in schools, mental hospitals, and research laboratories.

Social-Learning Theory

A number of experimental psychologists, most notably Albert Bandura and Richard Walters and Walter Mischel, have elaborated Skinner's approach to make it more applicable to the study of human personality development. Their approach is known as social-learning theory; it states that learning occurs not only through conditioning but through **observational learning,** or **modeling.**

Children seem to learn many things indirectly—without being explicitly rewarded or punished—by observing other people, watching TV, and reading books. This social-learning process, called modeling, has been the subject of many research papers by Bandura, Walters, Mischel, and their followers. These papers often emphasize the distinction between **learning** and **performance,** pointing out that children learn many things through observation that they do not actually act on. Both boys and girls see their mothers putting on lipstick and their fathers shaving; although they learn enough about both activities to imitate them, they usually perform only the one appropriate to their sex.

In addition to receiving direct rewards and punishments for performing certain responses, children often notice whether a model is rewarded or punished for a particular behavior. In a study reported by Bandura in 1966, for example, children watched a movie of an adult hitting and kicking a large

Figure 19.3 In his novel *Walden Two* B. F. Skinner describes a behavioral utopia. Burris, a professor of psychology, is visiting Walden Two, which was designed and established by his friend Frazier according to behaviorist principles. The dialogue between these two characters seems to reflect two sides of Skinner himself. In 1949, when it was first published, *Walden Two* was a farsighted book; since then many of Skinner's ideas have been put into practice. But Skinner's rigidly behavioristic type of analysis has more recently given way to a recognition that thoughts and motives have to be taken into account.
(From B. F. Skinner, *Walden Two,* 1962.)

"These are my children, Burris," he said, almost in a whisper. "I love them." He got to his feet and started back along the ledge. I followed carefully. He turned into the underbrush and waited for me to catch up. He was embarrassed and rather confused.

"What is love," he said, with a shrug, "except another name for the use of positive reinforcement?"

"Or vice versa," I said.

inflated rubber doll. Some children saw a version of the film in which the adult model was punished, some saw the adult rewarded, and some saw no consequences. When given a chance to play with the doll themselves, children behaved in accordance with the model's outcomes, hitting and kicking the doll most if the model's behavior had been rewarded in the movie, less if this behavior had no consequences in the movie, and least if this behavior had resulted in punishment. When the children were offered attractive rewards for duplicating the model's behavior, however, the differences between experimental groups were erased. Thus, all had *learned* the aggressive behavior but only some (those who had seen the model rewarded) were likely to *perform* it, unless explicit rewards for performance were offered. A similar phenomenon can be observed in adults. A number of years ago, few men would have worn flowered shirts or pants because these were thought to be appropriate only for women; once such fashions were defined as stylish for men, however, many men had no difficulty changing their behavior accordingly.

Social-learning theory has generated considerable information on sex-role development (see Chapter 21), on the instigation and control of aggression, and on the uses of modeling in behavior therapy. For example, children's dog phobias may be reduced by showing films of children playing happily with dogs; other applications from social-learning theory are described in Chapter 27. The theory has grown more complicated and sophisticated as research evidence has accumulated. In Bandura's book *Principles of Behavior Modification,* there is so much talk about "images" and "intentions" that one would hardly recognize the book's Skinnerian ancestry. And in 1973 Mischel published a theoretical paper titled "Toward a Cognitive Social-Learning Reconceptualization of Personality"—the word "cognitive" signaling a giant step away from strict behaviorism. The behavioral emphasis is still evident, however, and the therapeutic implications of this approach are still notably different from those suggested by psychoanalytic theory. It remains to be seen whether further research will lead to a more unified approach, such as the one outlined in Mischel's article.

PHENOMENOLOGICAL AND HUMANISTIC APPROACHES

While behaviorists have been very reluctant to accept such concepts as belief, intention, self-image, and subjectively interpreted feelings, other theorists have placed primary emphasis on these concepts. Although such theorists do not share a common theoretical framework, their approaches have enough in common to justify placing them in a single category. In advanced textbooks, this category is variously labeled phenomenological, humanistic, existential, cognitive, or some combination of these. It may be helpful to consider each of these terms briefly.

"Phenomenology" is a method used by some philosophers. It involves examining the world *as it appears to a particular person,* not as it appears when examined objectively. You may have noticed that many psychologists view people as objects, animals, or machines to be examined and studied just like any other objects or systems of interest to scientists; that is, they study people from the outside, necessarily focusing on behavior. The **phenomenologists** take a very different approach; they begin from the inside, so to speak, by describing the way things appear to them or by trying *empathically* to capture what someone else's experience is like. From this point of view, a stimulus cannot be characterized objectively but can be described only in terms of its appearance or meaning to a particular person. Unlike behaviorists, who see the actions of human beings as determined by external forces, phenomenologists emphasize that "from the inside" people seem to have considerable freedom; in fact, the difficulty of choosing between alternatives is one of the most important feelings people have.

The label "humanistic" is applied to psychologists who believe that human beings are different from all other animals and hence deserve special conceptual treatment. Most **humanistic psychologists** pay little attention to animal research, though they do not necessarily see it as irrelevant. They usually object both to psychoanalytic and to behavioristic approaches to personality on the grounds that these demean human beings—the one by emphasizing irrational and destructive instincts, the other by emphasizing external determinants of behavior. Humanistic psychologists tend to stress people's constructive and creative potential rather than their destructive capacities and habitual behavior.

"Existentialism" is another term borrowed from philosophy. Nietzsche, Kierkegaard, Sartre, and Heidegger, among others, are usually classed as existential philosophers; Dostoevsky is sometimes called an early existential novelist. Most of the existentialists write from a phenomenological perspective. They are concerned with how life is experienced "from the inside." They are also concerned with the major issues raised by phenomenological analysis: human freedom, the difficulty of making significant choices in life, responsibility for one's actions, identity, and the anguish associated with thoughts of death and meaninglessness. Figure 19.4 presents a quote from Jean Paul Sartre, which deals with the problem of identity.

Although not all existentialists are atheists, most of them deal with the problems raised by modern man's lack of certainty that God exists and by people's need to make moral choices in the absence of clear external standards. One of the characters in a book by Nietzsche first uttered the well-known phrase "God is dead!" and a character in a Dostoevsky novel posed the great moral problem of the age: "If God is dead, all is permitted" (that is, there are no absolute moral restrictions on behavior). **Existential psychologists**—those who concern themselves with the human problems posed by existential writers—are concerned with people's search for meaning in what has become, for many, a chaotic world.

The term "cognitive" is probably familiar to you already because the cognitive approach to learning is described in Chapter 6 and the cognitive approach to intellectual development, in Chapter 8. In brief, **cognition** refers to thought processes. Theorists who are interested primarily in human beings, in differences between animals and people, or in a phenomenological perspective cannot help concerning themselves with human thought processes—with the roles of interpretation and belief in human feelings and behavior. Perhaps you can now understand why it is common for a personality theorist who begins phenomenologically to have an affinity for humanism, existentialism, and cognitive psychology.

Rogers' Self Theory

Carl Rogers, an American clinical psychologist, is a major proponent of the phenomenological approach to personality and is closely identified with the humanistic movement in psychology. Like Freud, Jung, Adler, and Sullivan (whose theories were discussed in the preceding chapter), Rogers developed his theory from observations made while conducting psychotherapy. He noticed that his clients (a term he prefers to "patients" because the latter incorrectly implies illness) typically had trouble accepting their own feelings and experiences. They seemed to have learned during childhood that obtaining positive regard from others required feeling and acting in distorted or dishonest ways, that it was necessary to deny certain feelings in order to be accepted by parents, relatives, or peers. Rogers summarized his observations about the denial or distortion of feelings by saying that almost every child is the victim of **conditional positive regard.** That is, love and praise are withheld from him until the child conforms to parental or social standards.

Figure 19.4   In a passage from his book *Being and Nothingness* the great French existential philosopher Jean Paul Sartre shows how an examination of one's subjective experience can yield an understanding of the structure of personality. Sartre's finding here is basically that one part of the self does not come into existence except in a social context. This idea is wholly consistent with Carl Rogers' views and would not be hard to reconcile with behavioral emphases on the importance of social reinforcers in the control of behavior.

(From Jean Paul Sartre, *Being and Nothingness*, 1968.)

"Let us imagine that moved by jealousy, curiosity, or vice I have just glued my ear to the door and looked through a keyhole. I am alone.... This means that of all that there is no self to inhabit my consciousness, nothing therefore to which I can refer my acts in order to qualify them. They are in no way known: I am my acts....

"But all of a sudden I hear footsteps in the hall. Someone is looking at me! What does this mean? It means that I am suddenly affected in my being....

I now exist as _myself_.... I see _myself_ because _somebody sees me_..."

Figure 19.5 Carl Rogers' statement of the fundamental problem of personality: how to bring the two systems of personality into congruence. (From Carl Rogers, "A Theory of Personality," 1971.)

This, as we see it, is the basic estrangement in man. He has not been true to himself, to his own natural organismic valuing of experience, but for the sake of preserving the positive regard of others has now come to falsify some of the values he experiences and to perceive them only in terms based upon their value to others. Yet this has not been a conscious choice, but a natural—and tragic—development in infancy. The path of development toward psychological maturity, the path of therapy, is the undoing of this estrangement in man's functioning, the dissolving of conditions of worth, the achievement of a self which is congruent with experience, and the restoration of a unified organismic valuing process as the regulator of behavior.

Rogers draws a distinction between the **organism,** which he defines as the total range of possible experiences, and the **self,** which is the recognized and accepted parts of the person's experience. Ideally the two words would refer to the same things because a person can, in principle, recognize and accept all genuine experiences. In fact, however, the organism and the self often come to oppose each other (see Figure 19.5). For example, the self can deny consciousness to certain sensory and emotional experiences simply by refusing to symbolize or conceptualize them. (This idea is similar to the psychoanalytic concept of repression and to its neo-Freudian reformulations; it also resembles Dollard and Miller's notion that unconscious feelings are those that have been left unlabeled and hence cannot be thought about clearly.) According to Rogers, denial is likely to occur if a feeling or experience is incompatible with the self-concept. Even an action can be disowned by saying to oneself, "I don't know why I did it," or "I must have gotten carried away."

It is now possible to understand what Rogers means when he says that psychological adjustment "exists when the concept of the self is such that all sensory and visceral experiences of the organism are, or may be, assimilated on a symbolic level into a consistent relationship with the concept of self." The characteristics displayed by psychologically adjusted people, whom Rogers calls **fully functioning,** are openness to experience, absence of defensiveness, accurate awareness, unconditional positive self-regard, and generally harmonious relations with other people.

If the breach between self and organism in a less than fully functioning person grows too wide, the person may be not only defensive, conflicted, and tense but also unable to relate well to others. Such people are often argumentative and hostile, and they may project their denied feelings onto others. The split between self and organism can be healed, according to Rogers, if the person describes his experiences and expresses his feelings freely in a nonthreatening therapeutic context. The therapist, unlike most other people in the client's life, maintains an attitude of **unconditional positive regard;** he continues to support the client regardless of what the client says or does. The therapist clarifies the client's feelings by restating what has been said ("You seem to have been disappointed whenever your father failed to approve of one of your boyfriends"), but does not offer divergent interpretations or tell the client what to do or how to act. For this reason, Rogers' therapeutic method is called **nondirective** or **client-centered.**

But isn't it likely that a person who receives unconditional positive regard will become selfish, cruel, and destructive? After all, it is to avoid this kind of behavior that children are punished and police forces are maintained. This idea is also compatible with Freud's assertion that human beings have aggressive or destructive instincts. In years of therapeutic experience, Rogers has seen little evidence for this pessimistic view. Instead, he has come to believe that the human organism naturally seeks growth, self-actualization, and pleasant, productive relations with others. When not restricted by social forces, a person wants to become what most of us would recognize as healthier and happier. It is primarily for holding this optimistic attitude about people that Rogers is called a humanistic psychologist.

Maslow's Humanistic Psychology

The late Abraham Maslow, another American psychologist, is most often mentioned as the guiding spirit behind the humanistic movement in psychology. He deliberately set out to create what he called a "third force in psychology"—an alternative to psychoanalysis and behaviorism. Unlike personality theorists who base their work on studies of disturbed people, Maslow attempted to base his theory on healthy and creative, **self-actualizing,** people. He upbraided other psychologists for their pessimistic, negative, and limited conceptions of human beings. Where is the psychology, Maslow asked, that takes account of gaiety, exuberance, love, and expressive artwork to the same extent that it deals with misery, conflict, shame, hostility, and habit?

Like Rogers, Maslow believed there is an active will toward health in every person, an impulse toward the actualization of one's potentialities. He said that human instincts are weak in comparison with those of animals, so that each person is subject to considerable molding by the surrounding culture.

Maslow identified two groups of human needs: basic needs and metaneeds. The **basic needs** are the physiological needs (for food and water) and the psychological needs for affection, security, and self-esteem. These are also called **deficiency needs** because if they are not met, the person will be lacking something and will seek to make up for the deficiency. The basic needs are hierarchically organized, meaning that some (such as the need for food) take precedence over others. The higher needs Maslow called **metaneeds,** or **growth needs.** They include the need for justice, goodness, beauty, order, and unity. The deficiency needs are prepotent, or preeminent over the growth needs in most cases. If a person is lacking food and water, he cannot attend very seriously to justice and beauty. Nor, according to Maslow, can a person who lacks basic security and self-esteem feel free to consider fairness, to feel deep, reciprocal love, to be democratic, and to resist restrictive conformity. The metaneeds are not hierarchically organized; consequently, one metaneed can be pursued instead of another, depending on the particular person's life circumstances. Nevertheless, the metaneeds are real and, if unfulfilled, can lead to what Maslow called metapathologies, such as alienation, anguish, apathy, and cynicism.

Maslow conducted an intensive study of a group of people he considered to be self-actualized—Abraham Lincoln, Henry David Thoreau, Ludwig van Beethoven, Eleanor Roosevelt, Albert Einstein, and others, including some of Maslow's friends and acquaintances. Their distinguishing personality characteristics are listed in Table 19.1. He also investigated what he called **peak experiences**—profound moments in a person's life when he or she feels very much in harmony with the world—highly autonomous, spontaneous, and

Figure 19.6 This passage effectively summarizes Maslow's humanistic philosophy. He emphasizes the peculiarly human motives that he calls growth needs, without forgetting that human beings retain the basic deficiency needs of animals.
(From Abraham Maslow, *Toward a Psychology of Being,* 1968.)

[We] tend to evade personal growth because this, too, can bring another kind of fear, of awe, of feelings of weakness and inadequacy. . . . it is precisely the godlike in ourselves that we are ambivalent about, fascinated by and fearful of, motivated to and defensive against. This is one aspect of the basic human predicament, that we are simultaneously worms and gods. . . . Thus to discover in oneself a great talent can certainly bring exhilaration but it also brings a fear of the dangers and responsibilities and duties of being a leader and of being all alone.

Table 19.1   Characteristics of Self-Actualized Persons

They are realistically oriented.

They accept themselves, other people, and the natural world for what they are.

They have a great deal of spontaneity.

They are problem-centered rather than self-centered.

They have an air of detachment and a need for privacy.

They are autonomous and independent.

Their appreciation of people and things is fresh rather than stereotyped.

Most of them have had profound mystical or spiritual experiences although not necessarily religious in character.

They identify with mankind.

Their intimate relationships with a few specially loved people tend to be profound and deeply emotional rather than superficial.

Their values and attitudes are democratic.

They do not confuse means with ends.

Their sense of humor is philosophical rather than hostile.

They have a great fund of creativeness.

They resist conformity to the culture.

They transcend the environment rather than just coping with it.

Source: Abraham Maslow, *Motivation and Personality* (New York: Harper & Row, 1954).

Figure 19.7 Natural childbirth is a "peak experience" for many women. Maslow believed that such experiences are rare in the majority of people's lives. (After Tanzer, 1968.)

How the World Seemed	Women's Feelings About Themselves
truth	queenly
goodness	receptive
beauty	victorious
wholeness	trusting
connectedness	joyous
aliveness	blissful
uniqueness	rapturous
perfection	supreme
inevitability	in ecstasy
completeness	integrated
justice	
order	
simplicity	
richness	
effortlessness	
playfulness	
self-sufficiency	

perceptive, yet relatively unaware of space and time. For example, some women report peak experiences at the moment of childbirth. In a study conducted by Deborah Tanzer, women whose husbands were present at delivery had more such experiences than other women; some of the words they used to describe how they felt about the world and about themselves at the moment of their peak experiences are listed as Figure 19.7.

Many psychologists have criticized Maslow's work. His claim that human nature is "good," for example, has been called an intrusion of values into what should be a neutral science. (Maslow replied by writing *The Psychology of Science: A Reconnaissance,* in which he challenges the prevailing conception of science.) His study of self-actualizing people has been criticized because the sample was chosen according to Maslow's own subjective criteria. How can one identify self-actualized people without knowing the characteristics of such people? But then, if one knows these already, what sense does it make to list them as if they were the results of an empirical study, as in Table 19.1? Despite such attacks, Maslow's influence has been great. He inspired many researchers to pay more attention to healthy, productive people and led many organizational psychologists, group leaders, and clinicians to seek ways to promote the growth and self-actualization of workers, students, and clients in therapy. It is too early to tell whether the humanistic "third force" will continue to gain strength; if it does, Maslow will probably take his place as the prime mover of this approach to personality and practice.

Laing's Existential Psychiatry

R. D. Laing was trained as a psychiatrist in Glasgow, Scotland, and he has since worked both there and in England. He is one of the most widely read psychiatric writers in the United States. His books range from philosophical analyses (*Reason and Violence,* co-authored by David Cooper) through clinical case studies (such as *Sanity, Madness and the Family,* co-authored by Aaron Esterson) to collections of essays and poems (*The Politics of Experience* and *Knots*).

Laing's theoretical statements are similar to Rogers' in some ways, but for two reasons it is worth examining some of the differences. Laing's concepts come more directly from existential philosophy, especially from Sartre, than do Rogers', and Laing has written primarily about schizophrenics whereas Rogers studies mainly neurotics.

Laing has shown in a series of case studies that schizophrenics—whom psychologists and psychiatrists often characterize as "out of contact with reality"—appear quite sensible when viewed within the context of their families. They tend to come from families whose members are less than honest with themselves and with the patient—families whose members force each other and the developing schizophrenic to deny parts of their experiences and to invalidate important feelings through a process that Laing calls **mystification.** The purpose of mystification is to keep unpleasant facts and feelings from coming to light. The victimized child eventually develops what seems like a "crazy" system of beliefs in order to explain what is happening.

Like Rogers, who distinguishes between "self" and "organism," Laing explains how the schizophrenic develops a **false self system** in an attempt to meet the confusing and conflicting demands of his or her family. Sometimes the person feels controlled by external or alien forces (spirits, powers from outer space, mysterious electronic "waves"), which, in fact, represent an "external and alien" family.

How can the **divided self** of the schizophrenic be repaired? Laing and his colleagues have experimented with various approaches to therapy. All of them involve empathic and **authentic communication.** (Authenticity is a major theme in existentialists' writings.) The therapist does not believe that

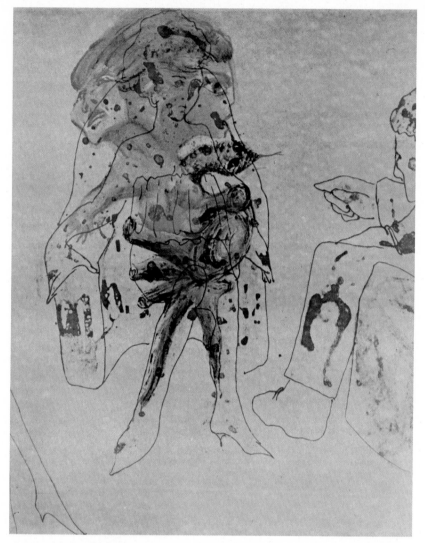

Figure 19.8   R. D. Laing, in his book *The Divided Self*, gives an analysis of the schizophrenic person that is based on Laing's subjective experiences—both his own and his reactions to dealing with schizophrenics—and on the descriptions schizophrenics have given him of their own subjective states. This painting expresses the results of Laing's analysis. The schizophrenic is a split person, a person who has separated himself from his body in fear of being engulfed or petrified by other people. His body becomes part of his false-self system, which is the front he presents to others and which looks like a real person but is not. Laing suggests that schizophrenics are people who have tried so hard to meet impossible demands made by other people (usually their parents) that they have lost their ability to maintain the integrity of their own personalities.

the troubled person is sick, "crazy," biochemically abnormal, or nonsensical. Indeed, he seems not to believe that schizophrenia, as a clearly definable state, even exists.

For a while, Laing talked with his patients in a manner similar to that of more traditional therapists. Then, some of his associates tried rearranging wards in mental hospitals to remove their medical and bureaucratic aura. Patients and staff were not sharply distinguished; they lived together merely as people trying to help each other. For a number of years, Laing also helped run a communal house called Kingsley Hall in which patients and staff lived together. One patient-staff relationship has been vividly described in the book *Mary Barnes; Two Accounts of a Journey Through Madness*, written by a former schizophrenic (Mary Barnes) and a psychiatrist (Joseph Berke).

Laing's first books were also not markedly different from those of other psychiatrists, nor were the therapeutic methods he advocated particularly novel. In 1964, however, he co-authored, with David Cooper, an introduction to the later writings of the French existentialist Jean Paul Sartre. Sartre had been trying to combine elements of existentialism with the main tenets of Marxism to form a radical contemporary philosophy. Laing and Cooper showed that this philosophy was related to their understanding of schizo-

Figure 19.9 Laing is probably the harshest critic, among personality theorists, of contemporary society; this passage from his writings illustrates his point of view.

(From R. D. Laing, *The Politics of Experience*, 1967.)

The condition of alienation, of being asleep, of being unconscious, of being out of one's mind, is the condition of the normal man.

Society highly values its normal man. It educates children to lose themselves and to become absurd, and thus to be normal. Normal men have killed perhaps 100,000,000 of their fellow normal men in the last fifty years. . . .

phrenics' attempts to construct a meaningful life in a destructive family situation. After writing this book, Laing became much more political in his discussion of mental disorders. Where he had once given a fairly neutral (albeit sympathetic) account of the family dynamics producing schizophrenia, he now portrayed the schizophrenic as a victim of the family—and the family as victim of a destructive society. He began to question more sharply not only the traditional distinction between normality and sanity but the political basis of contemporary Western society, as expressed in Figure 19.9.

Like the other theorists mentioned in this section, Laing has received heavy criticism for mixing philosophy, ethics, politics, and psychology. His moving case studies do not rule out the possibility that schizophrenia (or whatever one chooses to call severe mental disturbance) is, in part, due to biological factors. His view that all of us are somewhat alienated from ourselves—divided against ourselves because of the circumstances of contemporary social and political life—does not explain why some of us seem to be suffering much more than others. Nor is there yet much evidence that treatment centers like Kingsley Hall produce more effective results than other forms of therapy. A few case studies, no matter how dramatic, cannot be taken as convincing proof. Still, Laing's use of existential concepts (alienation, authenticity, and others not mentioned here) is interesting, and his provocative writings are having a powerful impact on both psychologists and laymen around the world. Laing has added considerably to the ongoing attempt to build an existential and humanistic psychiatry and psychology.

Kelly's Personal-Construct Theory

Like most of the personality theorists reviewed in this section, the late George Kelly was a psychotherapist. Over a period of some twenty years, he developed a comprehensive theory intended to do justice to "cognitive man." Kelly pointed out an apparent blind spot in the views of many psychologists: They fail to notice that their theories of human behavior should explain their own behavior as scientists. Everyone in psychology has probably chuckled from time to time about his colleagues who espouse environmental or physiological determinism at one moment and then say later of a student: "It's his decision; if he doesn't have the curiosity or the will power, too bad." Kelly realized this is no joking matter; a theory of human behavior that fails to explain the behavior of psychological theorists is less than adequate.

Suppose we begin with the idea that, in a sense, every person is a scientist. Everyone has his or her own theories about the events and people typically encountered; everyone is constantly conducting experiments and altering his views according to the results. In fact, it is not far-fetched to say, as Kelly did, that the main concern of most people is to interpret and understand their own experience. In doing this, they are more than passive recipients of information; they are active constructors of a subjective world. (This view of Kelly's, you may have noticed, is similar to Piaget's, described in Chapter 8.)

The fundamental postulate of Kelly's theory is that "a person's processes are psychologically channelized by the ways in which he anticipates events." The emphasis on anticipation—on being active and future-directed rather than reactive—is one of the hallmarks of Kelly's theory.

A person develops concepts with which to classify and interpret his experiences. Kelly called these **personal constructs** and conceptualized them as bipolar categories according to which an individual decides whether two people or events are similar or dissimilar. The categories might include black-white, warm-cold, like mother–like father, friendly-hostile, and like I used to be–like I want to be in the future. People differ in the constructs they establish and in the way they organize these constructs. This is equivalent, in Kelly's terms, to saying that people live in differently constructed worlds.

Surprisingly, Kelly's theory contains no concepts of learning, motivation, emotion, stimulus, ego, unconscious, need, reinforcement, or instinct—at least not in the form we have come to recognize. Kelly replaced most of these by defining emotion as an awareness that our construct system is in a state of transition. For example, he defines anxiety as "the awareness that the events with which one is confronted lie mostly outside the range of convenience of one's construct system." Guilt is "the awareness of dislodgement of the self from one's core role structure." In other words, we feel guilty when we find ourselves doing things that we would not have predicted on the basis of the constructs we use to describe ourselves (our core role constructs). Hostility, Kelly says, is "the continued effort to extort validational evidence in favor of a type of social prediction which has already been recognized as a failure." (Perhaps you have found yourself arguing vehemently for a position that you felt vaguely was not tenable, yet could not be abandoned.)

In addition to his theory, Kelly offered the world an interesting psychological assessment technique—the Role Construct Repertory Test (Rep Test, for short). You can easily administer this test to yourself. Think of ten to twenty people who have had a significant impact on your life—your parents, a lover, your best same-sex friend, someone who makes you feel very uncomfortable, a favorite teacher, a most-despised political leader, and so on. You might also include yourself. Then consider these people in sets of three and name a characteristic that two of them share but the third does not. By going through various sets of three, you will begin to see what your major constructs are, for these will be used to classify the important people in your life. Psychologists use special statistical techniques to summarize results from the Rep Test, but you can get some idea of how the technique works without a knowledge of statistics.

Psychotherapy, according to Kelly, is a set of procedures designed to help a person change his or her construct system. Any method that promotes useful change is acceptable, and Kelly seems to have employed techniques that

Figure 19.10 A version of Kelly's Role Construct Repertory Test. To discover your own constructs, begin by writing the first name of each of the persons indicated on the left. (If you cannot remember the name, make some identifying note. Do not use any person more than once.) Then consider the people you have listed in sets of three as indicated by the sets of numbers on the right. In what important way are two of these people alike, and how do these two differ from the third? Write these thoughts down in the appropriate columns, and when you have finished, examine them. You will probably find that you have used the same or closely related constructs in many comparisons. These are constructs that Kelly would consider important characteristics of your personality.

Role Definitions	Sorts	Similarity Construct	Difference Construct
1. *Self:* Yourself.			
2. *Mother:* Your mother or the person who has played the part of a mother in your life.	17, 18, 19 (Value)	___	___
3. *Father:* Your father or the person who has played the part of a father in your life.	14, 15, 16 (Authority)	___	___
4. *Brother:* Your brother who is nearest your own age, or if you do not have a brother, a boy near your own age who has been most like a brother to you.	10, 11, 13 (Valency)	___	___
	6, 7, 8 (Intimacy)	___	___
5. *Sister:* Your sister who is nearest your own age or, if you do not have a sister, a girl near your own age who has been most like a sister to you.	2, 3, 4 (Family)	___	___
	5, 14, 18 (Sister)	___	___
6. *Spouse:* Your wife (or husband) or, if you are not married, your closest present girl (boy) friend.	2, 9, 14 (Mother)	___	___
	2, 16, 17 (Father)	___	___
7. *Ex-flame:* Your closest girl (boy) friend immediately preceding Number 6.	4, 10, 15 (Brother)	___	___
8. *Pal:* Your closest present friend of the same sex as yourself.	4, 10, 15 (Sister)	___	___
9. *Ex-pal:* A person of the same sex as yourself whom you once thought was a close friend but in whom you were badly disappointed later.	5, 11, 19 (Kindliness)	___	___
	4, 9, 12 (Threat)	___	___
10. *Rejecting Person:* A person with whom you have been associated who, for some unexplained reason, appeared to dislike you.	6, 12, 18 (Spouse)	___	___
11. *Pitied Person:* A person you would most like to help or you feel sorry for.	2 (or 3), 6, 7 (Mating)	___	___
12. *Threatening Person:* A person with whom you usually feel most uncomfortable.	8, 9, 13 (Companionship)	___	___
13. *Attractive Person:* A person you met recently whom you would like to know better.	1, 4, 5 (Sibling)	___	___
14. *Accepted Teacher:* The teacher who influenced you most in your teens.	16, 17, 19 (Achievement)	___	___
15. *Rejected Teacher:* The teacher whose viewpoint you found most objectionable.	2, 3, 12 (Parent Pref.)	___	___
16. *Boss:* A supervisor you served under during a period of great stress.	1, 14, 13 (Need)	___	___
17. *Successful Person:* The most successful person you know personally.	7, 10, 11 (Compensatory)	___	___
18. *Happy Person:* The happiest person you know personally.	1, 6, 8 (Identification)	___	___
19. *Ethical Person:* The person you know personally who appears to be the most ethical.			

might be called psychoanalytic along with others that are more behavioristic. One novel approach, called **fixed role therapy,** is perhaps the most noteworthy. Kelly asked his clients to write self-characterizations in the third person (beginning "John Brown is . . ."), as if they were writing sympathetically about a friend. Kelly—often with the help of another psychologist—then wrote up a "fixed role sketch," a characterization that differed from the client's in ways that the client found both credible and desirable. When a final sketch was settled upon, the client would agree to act it out in his or her real life for a few weeks, during which time Kelly would consult with the person several times to see how things were going. Thus, Kelly helped the client perform a social-psychological experiment in hopes that the results would yield useful new constructs and hypotheses that could eventually lead to a more adaptive construct system.

Because Kelly's theory is unusual and relatively new, many traditionally educated psychologists have been reluctant to study it in detail. Still, his theory offers a researchable set of hypotheses within a cognitive and humanistic framework, which indicates that it will probably become more popular.

TRAIT AND FACTOR-ANALYTIC APPROACHES

All the approaches to personality presented so far begin with a theoretical conception and then try to explain human behavior from the point of view established by the theory. Freud, for example, began with the idea of basic instincts. If we had asked him how a given trait, say stinginess, developed, his answer would have been couched in psychosexual terms, because that is what his theory made available. (In fact, Freud did explain stinginess in psychosexual terms as a displaced form of anal retentiveness.) Kelly emphasized personal constructs and so tried to explain as much as possible in those terms. But what if we were to begin without clear preconceptions—begin somehow from a naive, theoryless vantage point?

Most people describe themselves and their acquaintances in terms of **traits** such as friendliness, introversion, stinginess, and sense of humor. We say that so-and-so is friendly but her boyfriend is not. That is, we have a friendliness dimension in mind that extends from very friendly to very unfriendly, and we arrange people along it in a comparative fashion. We can do the same with any other dimension that applies to people—anything from intelligence to political liberalism to obesity.

Traits seem to answer the two questions posed at the beginning of the last chapter: Why don't all people respond the same way to the stimuli offered by a particular situation? (Trait answer: Because they don't all have the same traits, or they don't have them to the same degree.) What makes a person behave fairly coherently and consistently over time? (Trait answer: The person's basic traits do not change easily or quickly.) One must be careful when invoking traits to explain behavior, however. It is all too easy to use circular reasoning: Why does Marie get so little done? Because she's lazy. How do you know she's lazy? Because she gets so little done.

Traits are only useful in psychology if they help explain behavior. One way in which traits can help is to reduce to a small number of underlying dimensions the vast array of specific explanations that may be offered for an infinite number of behavioral responses. This function was what Gordon Allport had in mind when, in 1936, he and Henry Odbert searched through an unabridged dictionary noting all terms that could be used to describe people. There turned out to be roughly 18,000 of them! Surely these could be reduced to a few essentials.

This hope was expressed by Allport in his claim that a person's **cardinal traits** (most basic and general dispositions) could be isolated. For example, some people seek fame and subordinate all other activities to this goal; others want to be loved by a few close friends but care nothing about fame. Allport believed that many people have a few less important but still pervasive traits that he called **central traits.** They may also have several specific and identifiable characteristics (such as a preference for flashy clothes), which he called **secondary traits.**

How might one go about isolating such traits or trait dimensions? The statistical procedure called **factor analysis** can be used for this purpose. Imagine that a researcher administers a large battery of questions to a sizable group of people. Each question is answered on a numerical scale like the ones shown in Figure 19.11. The researcher then uses the statistical procedure called **correlation** (described in Chapter 2) to determine the degree of relationship between each pair of questions on the test. For each pair of questions, he obtains a number (called a **correlation coefficient**) ranging between -1 and $+1$. A correlation coefficient close to -1 indicates a strong negative relationship between the answers to two questions: High numbers on one question go with low numbers on another. A correlation coefficient close to $+1$ indicates a strong positive relationship: High numbers on one question go with high numbers on another. A correlation coefficient close to zero indicates no relationship: Answers to the two questions are unrelated.

If the researcher had infinite time and patience, he could sort through all the pairs of correlations, grouping into clusters those questions that seem to be related. Fortunately, computerized factor analysis does this work for him. It identifies the clusters, or factors, in the mass of correlations and prints them out in tabular form. The researcher can then try to figure out *why* a particular set of questions goes together to form a single factor. Sometimes the answer is obvious; for example, all the questions in a particular cluster may have to do with anxiety, in which case he does not hesitate to say he has identified an "anxiety factor." At other times, however, he may not be sure why several questions are related. In that case, he either uses intuition to name a factor or suspends judgment for awhile, calling the cluster Factor 24, or Factor Z.

Figure 19.11 An example of the technique of factor analysis. Imagine that the five items on the left have been presented to a number of different people, and, from the resulting data, correlations between the various items have been computed. These correlations are shown in the matrix on the right. As you can see, they reveal that items 1 and 5, for example, are closely related; people tend to answer these two items in the same way. Items 1 and 2 appear not to be related; the way a person responds to one has little to do with how he responds to the other. By rearranging the order of the items in the matrix as shown here, it is possible to see that two distinct and independent personality factors are being measured. Items 1, 3, and 5 seem to have something to do with confidence in working ability, and items 2 and 4 seem to describe sociability.

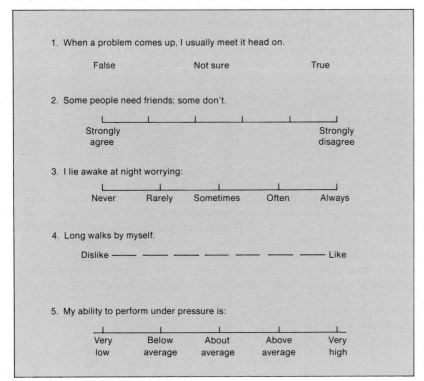

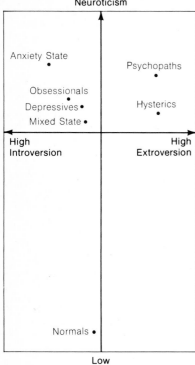

Figure 19.12 Two dimensions in Eysenck's classification system and the locations of people with various psychological disorders within the two-dimensional space the dimensions describe. This space (with the addition of a third dimension, psychoticism) is the result of a factor analysis of many personality tests. After these dimensions emerged from his analysis, Eysenck postulated possible biological factors that could account for them.

(After Eysenck, 1961.)

Two psychologists who have used factor analysis extensively to study personality traits are Raymond B. Cattell and Hans Eysenck. Cattell has factor-analyzed three kinds of data—life records, self-ratings, and objective tests (behavioral observations)—and has obtained a number of fairly specific traits, called **surface traits.** These have been further analyzed to yield what Cattell calls **source traits,** the underlying dimensions of personality. Because Cattell's list of traits is rather long, and his trait names idiosyncratic, it will be better for introductory purposes to focus on Eysenck's work.

Eysenck has factor-analyzed some of the most widely used personality questionnaires and has concluded that there are three major trait dimensions underlying them: **introversion-extraversion, neuroticism,** and **psychoticism.** For normal groups, only the first two dimensions are important. According to Eysenck, the introversion-extraversion and neuroticism dimensions are more or less independent, meaning that each person can be represented by a point in the two-dimensional space shown in Figure 19.12. That is, if you know your scores on these two dimensions, you can plot a point between introversion and extraversion and between high and low neuroticism, which represents where you stand in relation to other people's scores.

What difference do these factors and scores make? What do they mean? First of all, it is wise to be wary of them and to interpret them cautiously. Factor analysis can only identify factors based on the particular questions an investigator chooses to ask. If some important questions are omitted, then the optimal (most valid) set of trait dimensions will not be discovered. Moreover, because the factors are interpreted by a human scientist, there may be mistakes in naming or conceptualizing them. An even more serious problem is that the factors are based on descriptions and judgments made by people in response to someone else's questions. How do we know that the factors represent traits *in the people being rated* and not just categories or conceptual dimensions that exist in the eye of the beholder?

These are some of the questions that have been raised by critics of the factor-analytic approach. Fortunately, Eysenck has provided some promising answers. One knows that the factors are psychologically valid, he points out, if scores on tests of the dimensions allow one to predict other psychological and behavioral variables—and especially if the dimensions are embedded in a valid theoretical framework. Eysenck has provided a tentative framework and has gathered evidence to support it. He suggests that a biological factor, **level of cortical arousal,** lies behind individual differences on the introversion-extraversion dimension. Extraverts typically have a low level of arousal and so seek stimulation (for example, loud parties and intense social interaction) to become more aroused. Introverts naturally have a high level of arousal (for example, it takes them longer to fall asleep), and they are more sensitive to pain and to weak stimuli than extraverts are. When introverts become sedated or intoxicated (alcohol lowers arousal level), they tend to become more extraverted. When extraverts are more aroused (for instance, after taking amphetamines), they become more introverted.

Neuroticism, according to Eysenck, is related to *the ease with which a person learns to associate anxiety with neutral stimuli.* Neurotics are people who have learned to feel anxiety in all kinds of objectively harmless situations. Although Eysenck's biologically oriented theory may prove incorrect, it does show that one can go beyond simple description once basic traits have been identified by factor analysis.

A CURRENT CONTROVERSY: PERSONALITY VERSUS SITUATIONAL FACTORS

We have now devoted two chapters to personality theories. You have learned about several different approaches to the two questions asked by personality theorists: What makes people different from each other? and What gives each person a unique, identifiable character that is visible in diverse situations? But a third question has not been answered. How do we know, except through intuition, that personality traits really do exist and influence behavior across situations?

For a number of years, personality researchers more or less happily used tests to measure personality traits and correlated scores on these tests with measures of behavior in various situations. (Often, for convenience, the situations were constructed in laboratories.) The researchers measured everything from ego strength to extraversion and were able to obtain reliable correlations between their measures and such diverse behavioral indexes as whether a person would seek psychotherapy, what career he or she aspired to, and how much pain he or she could tolerate. The value of these results was seldom questioned. Because interesting relationships between variables were being discovered and documented, it seemed to all the psychologists concerned, that scientific progress was being made.

However, in 1968 Walter Mischel cast a shadow across this entire enterprise in his book *Personality and Assessment.* Reviewing one study after another, Mischel showed that correlations between personality trait measures and behavior rarely exceeded .20 or .30. Such relationships may be genuine, and even of some theoretical significance, but they are too weak to have much practical value, as Figure 19.13 shows. They do not allow a teacher, employer, or clinical psychologist to make valid decisions concerning specific students, potential employees, or patient-clients. Mischel, who you may recall is a social-learning theorist, thought he had seen enough evidence to conclude that broad personality trait measures were of little value.

Moreover, he thought he knew why. If people behave the way they do because they have been reinforced for particular responses in particular situations, it is hardly surprising to find that David is aggressive on the football field but very shy and retiring at a party; that Sharon is dependent on her mother at home but very independent at work; that Martha is ''bossy'' around younger co-workers but deferential to superiors, and so on. There is no reason, said Mischel, to expect people to have general traits, or to expect one person to be classifiable along the same dimension (such as introversion-extraversion) as another person.

Mischel's argument generated a heated debate in personality journals. No one takes it lightly, of course, when his or her professional efforts are declared misguided or fruitless. Some writers asked why, if there are no general personality dimensions and if people are not consistent across situations, we feel intuitively that personality traits exist. One answer offered by the opponents of trait theories was that people are subject to perceptual biases. For example, research reported by Mischel in 1973 indicates that we tend to maintain our first impression of a person even if he or she acts quite differently later. If we see someone act viciously or violently and later see the same person act kindly and calmly on several occasions, we may say to ourselves: ''He certainly hides his vicious nature well.'' Maybe we happened to have seen him under extraordinarily frustrating conditions the first time, but we tend not to consider that possibility. Similarly, studies were cited that show we are likely to attribute other people's behavior in a particular situation to personality dispositions or traits that they possess, whereas we attribute our own behavior in the same kind of situation to outside factors. For example, a person might say, ''He was so unbelievably obstinate and I had so little time, I just *had* to shove him out of the way.'' Perhaps one simply has a different perceptual perspective when one is an observer than when one is an actor. When you watch another person doing something, that person is at the center of your attention and so seems to ''cause'' whatever happens. You do not

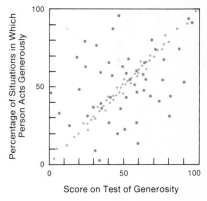

Figure 19.13 Two possible results of an attempt to validate an imaginary pencil-and-paper test of generosity against some measure of generous behavior in everyday situations. The small blue dots represent a correlation near 1.0; the large green dots represent a correlation of 0.25 between the two measures. The second correlation is of the magnitude usually observed when such attempts at validation are made. To be useful in predicting individual behavior, the test would have to have a correlation with generous behavior in daily life that is much closer to that represented by the small blue dots.

Figure 19.14 Newsman Walter Cronkite on camera and off camera. In his off-camera appearance, does he seem to you to have characteristics that you had never seen watching him on the evening news? In recent years psychologists have come to believe that conditions external to a person have at least as much effect on how he behaves as do factors inside him. We often believe we know someone well merely because we have always seen him under the same set of external conditions.

notice what may be powerful environmental forces acting on the person. But when you are the actor, the environment tends to hold your attention; you are aware of many of the pressures on you and are not very cognizant of your own role in the process.

Also, we tend to underestimate how differently our acquaintances may act when they are not in our presence. When you are present, you are part of the situation determining their behavior; they may be "different people" when you are not around. Moreover, we are often too quick to assume that other people are expressing their full set of feelings rather than, say, acting out a role. For example, a study by Richard Nisbett and his colleagues indicates that people think they know what the newscaster Walter Cronkite is like as a person, even though they have seen him only in brief, highly staged settings on television. How can people feel that they really know Walter and are not just the victims of scripts, make-up artists, cameramen, and Cronkite's own idea of what a newsman should be?

Despite these sound reasons for being suspicious of the intuitive belief that people act as their personalities dictate, there is some evidence that personality variables are more important than Mischel's analysis would lead us to believe. First of all, reviews of recent studies (such as one written by Henry Alker in 1972) reveal that, although situational variables alone are usually better predictors of behavior than personality variables alone, personality and situational variables together are an even better predictor. In other words, it helps us to know *both* the environmental factors acting on a person *and* the kind of person we are watching. People who are test-anxious, for example, often perform less well on classroom exams than people who are not anxious about tests. But under the low pressure of a leisurely take-home exam, the highly test-anxious people may perform better than their less-anxious counterparts. Both personality (test-anxiety) and situational (type of test) variables are relevant.

Although most researchers would agree that the interaction argument is valid, they still insist we need better measures of personality—measures that will assess more precisely a person's behavior in particular situations and the consistencies or inconsistencies in his behavior in several situations. This kind of research is already being carried out, and the initial results are promising. Personality has been and still is difficult to capture in scientific nets, but psychologists continue to find the murky waters well worth fishing.

SUMMARY

1. The most important nonpsychoanalytic approaches to personality can be classified into three groups: **behavioristic approaches; phenomenological and humanistic approaches;** and **trait and factor-analytic approaches.**

2. Dollard and Miller's **psychodynamic behavior theory** is an early attempt to assimilate Freud's ideas into the mainstream of American psychology by reinterpreting them in terms of the behaviorist learning principles formulated by Clark Hull.

   a. Hull's theory stresses **drives** and **habits.** Like psychoanalytic theory, it presents a **homeostatic** or **tension-reduction,** model of behavior.

   b. Dollard and Miller wanted to show that animal experiments could illuminate the processes described by Freud. They said that **primary**

needs (similar to instincts in Freudian theory) are the basic motivation for behavior; working with rats in the laboratory, they demonstrated that **secondary drives** such as learned fear (similar to anxiety) also can motivate behavior. In addition, Miller produced in laboratory rats **approach-avoidance conflicts** similar to those suffered by some neurotics.

c. Dollard and Miller view neurotic symptoms as learned (for example, they define repression as learned not-thinking) and they called psychotherapy a relearning process. Thus, they paved the way for behavior therapy.

3. B. F. Skinner's radical behaviorism rejects internal constructs such as drives (a basic concept in Hullian behaviorism) and emphasizes instead the **functional analysis of behavior.** According to Skinner, behavior is controlled by external conditions and events, such as food deprivation, discriminative stimuli, and reinforcement and punishment. The main appeal of this position is that it suggests people's behavior can be changed without an understanding of internal personality dynamics.

4. **Social-learning theory,** formulated chiefly by Albert Bandura, Richard Walters, and Walter Mischel, is an elaboration of Skinner's approach to make it more applicable to human personality development (as contrasted with animal learning). The approach differs from Skinner's in several ways:

a. Learning is seen as occurring not only through conditioning but through **observational learning,** or **modeling,** in which a child (or an adult) learns by watching the behavior of others.

b. It is assumed that **learning** can take place whether it is exhibited in **performance** or not.

c. Although the approach emphasizes the analysis of behavior, it does not deny the existence of internal images and intentions.

5. Phenomenological and humanistic approaches to personality give a central place to the very concepts that behaviorists reject: belief, intention, self-image, subjective feelings. This large category of approaches includes:

a. **Phenomenologists,** who are interested in how the world appears to a particular person rather than in its objective characteristics; they try **empathically** to capture the experiences of others.

b. **Humanistic psychologists,** who believe that human beings are essentially different from other animals and emphasize people's constructive and creative potential as opposed to their destructive capacities and habits.

c. **Existentialists,** who have a phenomenological perspective and are concerned with such issues as freedom, responsibility, and the lack of meaning in modern life.

d. **Cognitive psychologists,** who stress thought processes and the role of interpretation and belief in human feelings and behavior.

6. Carl Rogers' **self theory** stresses a person's need to accept his own feelings and experiences fully and unconditionally.

a. Rogers observed that his clients seemed to have received **conditional positive regard** as children. Obtaining love and approval from others

Figure 19.15 Gordon Allport is among the most honored of twentieth-century psychologists. He was one of the first psychologists to emphasize the role of self in personality; his work in personality also includes the development of the concept of trait and the idea that motives can become functionally autonomous of their original source. He has also written extensively on the psychology of prejudice.

Figure 19.16 As the first American psychologist whose views seriously rivaled those of Freud, Carl Rogers has had a widespread impact both on psychology and on society. Rogers has spent a quarter of a century as the head of various guidance and counseling centers, and he won the Distinguished Scientific Contribution Award of the *American Psychological Association* in 1956. He is well known for his debate with behaviorist B. F. Skinner, in whose writings Rogers believes "there is a serious underestimation of the problem of power."

Figure 19.17 The late Abraham Maslow, who developed an optimistic, humanistic personality theory based on the study of healthy and creative individuals. He served as president of the American Psychological Association in 1967–68. His work in human needs and the factors involved in the facilitation of self-actualization—along with the work of Rogers and others—created a new orientation toward the study of human behavior.

required the child to act and feel in distorted, dishonest ways, creating a discrepancy between the **organism** (the total range of possible experiences) and the **self** (the recognized and accepted parts of the person's experience).

b. Rogers' therapeutic method, called **nondirective** or **client-centered therapy,** offers the client **unconditional positive regard** from the therapist, thus closing the gap between organism and self so that the person becomes **fully functioning:** open, undefensive, aware, and generally happy.

c. Rogers is optimistic about human nature: He believes that people naturally seek growth, self-actualization, and pleasant, productive relations with others.

7. Abraham Maslow's humanistic psychology stresses the healthy human impulse toward **actualization** of one's potentialities and the positive features of human life, such as gaiety, exuberance, love, and expressiveness.

a. Maslow classified human needs into two groups: **basic needs** and **metaneeds.** He said that until basic needs (such as the need for food) are satisfied, a person can give little attention to metaneeds (such as the need for justice and beauty).

b. Maslow identified a number of self-actualized people, such as Lincoln and Thoreau, and analyzed their distinguishing characteristics, which include spontaneity, autonomy, and creativeness.

c. He coined the phrase **peak experience** to describe profound moments in a person's life when he or she feels highly autonomous, spontaneous, and perceptive, simultaneously in harmony with the world and relatively unaware of time and space.

8. R. D. Laing's existential psychiatry asserts that the "insane" statements of schizophrenics are usually quite sensible from the psychotic's own point of view. Laing stresses the roles of the family and the society in producing schizophrenia; for example, he says that schizophrenics develop **false self systems** (similar to Rogers' "self") in an attempt to meet conflicting family demands. In therapy, he stresses the need for **authentic communication** with the patient.

Figure 19.18 R. D. Laing is a physician and existential psychoanalyst who has a Marxist viewpoint. He believes that schizophrenia is an inevitable reaction of certain individuals to an insane and chaotic world. Laing and others founded a therapeutic community in England that did away with the typical distinctions between therapist and patient in attempting to create a sympathetic environment for journeys through madness. Laing's current work is centered on the role of families in determining personality and on the paradoxes in interpersonal relationships.

9. George Kelly's personal-construct theory maintains that the main concern of most people is to interpret and understand their own experience.

a. According to Kelly, a person develops **personal constructs** (bipolar categories such as warm-cold, friendly-hostile) that he uses to classify and interpret his experiences. People differ in the constructs they establish and in the way they organize them—that is, they live in differently constructed worlds. The Role Construct Repertory Test (Rep Test), which Kelly developed, can be used to identify a person's major constructs.

b. Kelly's approach to psychotherapy was eclectic: Any method that promotes useful change was acceptable to him. He introduced a technique called **fixed role therapy,** in which first the client and then the therapist writes sympathetic role descriptions of the client. These descriptions are then combined and the client tries to act out the role for a few weeks.

10. The **trait approach** and the **factor-analytic approach** to personality are not comprehensive theories but an attempt to describe people as they

usually describe themselves—that is, in terms of **traits** (such as friendliness, stinginess, sense of humor, and so on). Several psychologists have tried to reduce the huge number of conceivable descriptions to a smaller number of basic, underlying dimensions.

   a. Gordon Allport said that each person possesses **cardinal traits** (such as an overriding desire for fame), **central traits** (less important but still significant), and **secondary traits** (relatively superficial characteristics such as a preference for flashy clothes).

   b. Hans Eysenck, using factor analysis, identified three major trait dimensions: **introversion-extraversion, neuroticism,** and **psychoticism.** One way to describe the personality of a normal individual is to locate it at a point between introversion and extraversion and between high and low neuroticism. Eysenck suggested that a biological factor, **level of cortical arousal,** lies behind individual differences in introversion-extraversion, and that neuroticism is related to the *ease with which a person learns to associate anxiety with neutral stimuli.*

Figure 19.19 George Kelly is an American psychologist whose theory of personal constructs differs radically from other theories of personality and psychotherapy. Kelly's view is that a cognitive organization of the individual's perceptions of the world is the center of personality. Although this theory has not directly influenced psychotherapy, it has served to make psychotherapists more aware of the role of thought processes in personality and its disorders.

11. Recently, some psychologists have questioned the importance of personality traits and have said instead that behavior is determined mainly by **situational factors.** Although situational variables alone seem to predict behavior better than personality variables alone, neither type of variable alone explains behavior as well as an understanding of both factors. In other words, what determines behavior seems to be the interaction between personality characteristics and characteristics of the situation.

SUGGESTED READINGS

Hall, Calvin S., and Gardner Lindzey. *Theories of Personality.* 2nd ed. New York: Wiley, 1970. The classic secondary source on theories of personality. It begins with a discussion of the nature of personality theory and outlines the most important classical and contemporary theories. Finally, it compares and contrasts theories across a number of dimensions and issues.

Maddi, Salvatore R. *Personality Theories: A Comparative Analysis.* Rev. ed. Homewood, Ill.: Dorsey Press, 1972. A recent text on personality theory, it classifies personality theorists according to whether their basic assumption relates to *conflict, fulfillment,* or *consistency.* The text examines what the theorists have to say about the core and periphery of personality. It presents research on each position and draws conclusions about their strengths and weaknesses.

Maddi, Salvatore R. *Perspectives on Personality: A Comparative Approach.* Boston: Little Brown, 1971. A book of readings by or about each major theorist discussed in the Maddi text cited above.

Mischel, Walter. *Introduction to Personality.* New York: Holt, Rinehart and Winston, 1971. This recent text by a well-known social-learning theorist divides theories into five categories: type and trait, psychoanalytic, psychodynamic behaviorist, social learning, and phenomenological. The book covers theory, assessment techniques, and personality development and change (including therapy). Because of the author's orientation, behavior theories and behavior modification techniques receive more emphasis than usual, and a great deal of attention is paid to empirical evidence, especially from laboratory experiments.

UNIT VI
Social Psychology

In some respects the phenomena studied by social psychologists are the most familiar and "obvious" ones in psychology. The processes of social interaction are highly visible to all of us practically all the time. We pay close attention to how we perceive other people and how they perceive us; we are often aware of the social rules that we usually follow in interacting with other people; we frequently attempt to influence each other's attitudes

20 **Person Perception and Interpersonal Attraction**
discusses factors that influence how one person perceives another person and how people select from their many acquaintances a few people who become friends and an even smaller number who become lovers, husbands, wives.
See related chapters: 4, 6, 11, 15, 16

21 **Patterns of Social Behavior: The Case of Sex Roles**
examines the formal and informal rules that pattern people's interactions with one another, including social norms, status, roles, and stereotypes. To illustrate the operation of these rules, the chapter focuses on sex roles in contemporary society.
See related chapters: 3, 4, 6, 10, 16, 18, 19, 25

RELATED CHAPTERS

3
Species-Specific Behavior: Ethology discusses social behavior in some animals, such as migration, imprinting, and various types of communication, including bird song, facial expressions, and language. These behaviors can be compared to social aspects of human life, as described in Chapters 21 and 23.

4
Conditioning and Learning: Behaviorism presents the basic behaviorist principles of learning, which are considered in Chapter 21 as one approach to explaining the acquisition of sex roles. Chapter 20 also uses the behaviorist concept of reward to help explain the formation of friendships.

6
Thinking and Problem Solving: Cognitive Psychology examines the cognitive view of learning and problem solving. Chapter 20 applies the cognitive approach known as attribution theory to person perception; Chapter 21 reviews the cognitive analysis of the acquisition of sex roles; and Chapter 22 describes the cognitive processes involved in attitude change and social influence.

10
Social Development: The Case of Morality presents three approaches to moral development: psychoanalysis, social-learning theory, and cognitive-developmental theory. Chapter 21 considers the same three approaches to the acquisition of sex roles.

11
Perception: Principles and Processes describes the general nature of human perception and so relates to the discussion of person perception in Chapter 20.

and actions; and we commonly relate to other individuals in terms of the social groups that they belong to. Because of the familiarity and importance of social interaction to all of us in our everyday lives, social psychology is an area that every student knows something about even before he takes his first psychology course.

Yet familiarity can breed contempt, as the old saying goes. Because of the familiarity of the processes of social interaction, most people take them for granted: We assume that we understand them. But the scientific study of these processes has revealed that the common-sense consensus about "how things are" is often just wrong. One goal of the chapters in this unit is to help you achieve a deeper understanding of social processes. Along the way you may discover many things about them that are surprising.

22 Attitude Change and Social Influence

looks at processes of social influence—both the cognitive processes by which people change their attitudes and actions and the social processes that one person can use to lead other people to change their attitudes and actions. These social processes, called means of social influence, include persuasion, obedience, and conformity.
See related chapters: 6, 26

23 Individuals and Their Groups

examines the differences between a mere collection of people and a social group, how social groups function, how they affect the attitudes and actions of their members, and how different social groups relate to each other. The Bay of Pigs invasion and relations between blacks and whites in the United States are used to illustrate some of the key concepts in the chapter.
See related chapters: 3, 26

15

Emotional Experience and Expression outlines the attribution theory of emotion, which is closely related to the attribution theory of person perception examined in Chapter 20.

16

Motivation and Action presents the attribution theory of motivation, which is also closely related to the attribution theory of person perception described in Chapter 20. In addition, Chapter 21 elaborates upon Chapter 16's discussion of motivational differences between men and women.

18

Psychoanalytic Theories of Personality contains a detailed and basic discussion of psychoanalytic theory, which is presented in Chapter 21 as one way of explaining the acquisition of sex roles.

19

Alternative Conceptions of Personality describes social-learning theory, which is one of the approaches to understanding sex roles and other social roles reviewed in Chapter 21.

25

Bases of Disorder discusses several of the same approaches to human behavior as does Chapter 21, including psychoanalysis, social-learning theory, cognitive theory, and the biological viewpoint.

26

Individual and Group Psychotherapy looks at various types of psychotherapy, all of which use the mechanisms for social influence discussed in Chapters 22 and 23.

Love! How many songs are sung about love, how many poems and stories and novels written about love, how many plays acted about love! Surely the matter of love has never changed: "A kiss is still a kiss, a sigh is still a sigh. The fundamental things apply as time goes by." And fairy tales end with a marriage so that "they lived happily ever after."

But now for some reason, the divorce rate rises and adultery seems to be as common as marriage. What has happened to eternal love? Doesn't anyone love forever and ever anymore? Or have times changed somehow? Are fundamental things not all that fundamental?

Yes, I think that times have changed, and it does us no good to apply rules evolved under one set of conditions to another set altogether. Technological advance changes everything—including love—and if you doubt it, I will give you two ways in which it has done so, with the warning that I can think of others.

1. There was a time when humanity consisted of small, immobile groups; when most people were born, lived, and died in the same community; when the people beyond the hill were strangers you hardly ever saw; and when marriages took place between members of families that had known each other all their lives—for sheer lack of any other opportunity. Consider, then, that in every one of many thousands of such communities there was a young man who was, for some reason, an extraordinarily good catch, and some young woman caught him. There was some young woman who was the town belle and some young man got her. A sizable proportion of all marriages, then, involved young men and women who were remarkable for wealth, strength, beauty, family connections; and marriages involving them were social achievements. Nowadays, that's not so. It's not just that people are more mobile and that the young men and women of one town possibly suffer by comparison with those of another. It's much worse. In the twentieth century, with movies and then television becoming commonplace,

a large percentage of the young people of the world have, for the first time, incomparable and unattainable idols. What local young man can compare with Paul Newman or Robert Redford? What local young woman can compare with Marilyn Monroe or Raquel Welch? No one is satisfactory. No one is anything but a poor substitute for the visible ideal.

2. Ideally, marriage is forever. Whom God has joined together, let no man put asunder. From this day forward, till death do us part. But through almost all of human history, the average life span varied from twenty-five to thirty-five years. It meant that the average marriage lasted about ten years before death did them part. Nowadays, thanks to medical and technological advance, life expectancy in most "advanced" nations is something like seventy and the average marriage, if left undissolved, would last for fifty years. But what works for ten years of marriage may not work for fifty. Where 90 percent may stick out ten years, perhaps only 20 percent can stand it for fifty.

Is there any use then in clinging to notions of love developed by a short-lived isolated society and in trying to insist on them, unchanged, in a long-lived mobile one? Or should we learn to live with reality?

Isaac Asimov

20
Person Perception and Interpersonal Attraction

THE PSYCHOLOGY OF AFFILIATION
Anxiety and Affiliation
Comparing Experiences
Desire to Avoid Comparison

PERSON PERCEPTION
The Evidence
Physical Attractiveness
Other People's Descriptions

The Attribution of Traits
The Arithmetic of Impressions
Attribution of Causality and Sincerity

CHOOSING FRIENDS
Proximity
Similarity
Approval
Complementarity
Social Roles

THE DEVELOPMENT OF RELATIONSHIPS

ROMANTIC LOVE

TO KNOW HIM IS TO LOVE HIM

Figure 20.1 This young couple appears to be in love. But what *is* love? What originally attracted them to each other? How did they happen to meet? How do they *know* that the attraction they feel is love? Psychologists have been studying the formation of friendships for some time. Recently, however, they have begun to examine what has been the province of poets and songwriters—the state of romantic love. This chapter reports their theories and findings on both liking and loving.

Whether an individual interacts with just one other person, a small group, or a large one—and whether the person acts as an individual or with reference to his or her race, age, occupation, or sex—the individual's attitudes and behavior are affected by that interaction. And it is these effects that social psychology studies. This chapter looks at why people want to get together, how they form impressions of each other, how they go about choosing their friends, and how social relationships develop; these topics underlie all of social psychology.

The study of how people come to like or dislike other people— or **interpersonal attraction**—is one of the newest frontiers in social psychology. People have always been fascinated by the roots of friendship and love, but until the late 1950s very little systematic research had been undertaken into such "matters of the heart." In fact, psychologists have traditionally devoted much more of their attention to aggression and hostility than to sympathy and love; the late Gordon Allport once characterized the lack of psychological studies of sympathy and love as "a flight from tenderness."

In his presidential address to the American Psychological Association in 1956, Theodore Newcomb lamented the fact that psychologists had assumed the same attitudes as laymen in saying that matters of interpersonal attraction "were altogether too ineffable" to be topics for systematic research.

In another presidential address in 1958, Harry Harlow bluntly concluded that, "So far as love or affection is concerned, psychologists have failed in their mission. The little we know about love does not transcend simple observation, and the little we write about it has been written better by poets and novelists."

In the years since Harlow's

admonitions, however, the situation has changed to a remarkable degree. Although psychologists have not yet solved all the mysteries of friendship and love, they have made important starts in that direction.

THE PSYCHOLOGY OF AFFILIATION

Before we examine some of the research that attempts to explain why people choose their friends and lovers, a more basic question must be considered. Why do people seek out and want to be with other people at all? The pervasive human tendency to seek the company of others is called **affiliation.**

Anxiety and Affiliation

A pioneer study conducted by Stanley Schachter in 1959 set out to discover whether a person in a highly anxious state would be more likely to seek the company of others than would a person who was clearly not anxious. Schachter's subjects, female undergraduate volunteers at the University of Minnesota, were greeted at the laboratory by a man in a white coat who identified himself as Dr. Gregor Zilstein of the medical school. Zilstein told the women that they would be participating in a very important study of the physiological effects of electric shock. He told them they would be given a series of shocks while measures of their pulse rate and blood pressure were taken. Zilstein told some groups of subjects, in an ominous tone, that the shocks would be extremely painful. He added, with a tight smile, that the shocks would cause no permanent tissue damage. This experimental manipulation constituted the high-anxiety condition.

With other groups of subjects, Zilstein's manner was kind and reassuring. He told these women that the shocks would produce only tingling sensations, which would not even be unpleasant. This manipulation constituted the low-anxiety condition.

Zilstein told all subjects that they would have to leave the laboratory for ten minutes while the equipment was being prepared. He then asked each woman to indicate on a questionnaire whether she preferred to wait by herself in a private room or to wait in a classroom with other subjects. The answers to this question constituted the main dependent variable of the experiment. Once the women had made their choices, the experiment was concluded. No shocks

Figure 20.2 This famous passage, by John Donne, eloquently states that human beings do not and cannot exist in isolation.

From John Donne, "Meditation XVII of Devotions upon Emergent Occasions," in *The Norton Anthology of English Literature,* 1968.

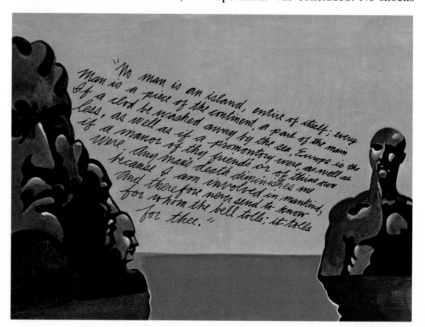

were ever given. The results, displayed in Figure 20.3, show that women in the high-anxiety condition were much more likely to want to wait with others than were women in the low-anxiety condition.

Although the results of this study indicate that anxiety can be a factor affecting the need to affiliate with others, the results raise at least as many questions as they answer. Why do anxious subjects want to wait with other people? Would they choose to affiliate with any other people or only with others in the same predicament? Social-comparison theory, as put forth by Leon Festinger, may help to answer some of these questions.

Comparing Experiences

Festinger says that people can verify their beliefs about the world and themselves in two ways—objectively, or by comparing their beliefs with other people's actions and experiences, that is, by **social comparison.** You may believe, for example, that if you take a hammer and smash it against a window, the window will break. You can check the belief objectively by simply taking the hammer, smashing it against the window, and seeing whether the glass breaks. However, if you believe that you run fast, an objective verification—timing yourself on the hundred-yard dash with a stopwatch—may not be enough. Even if you know that your time was 11.2 seconds, you still do not know whether 11.2 is fast unless you compare it with other people's times. This example illustrates the core of Festinger's theory: Many beliefs that people hold about themselves cannot be verified without comparison with other people's actions and experiences. Skills, opinions, personality traits, and even emotions seem to require this kind of social comparison.

What light can Festinger's theory throw on Schachter's results? If one assumes that the internal state of the students who anticipated receiving painful shocks was a complex and ambiguous one, then one can see how social-comparison theory could apply. Many emotional reactions may have simultaneously coursed through the student: fear for her safety, anger toward the diabolical Dr. Zilstein, and a sense of pride at being able to make a sacrifice for the sake of science. Festinger's theory suggests that everyone has a strong need to make sense out of the world and his own reactions to it. People simply are uncomfortable with ambiguity. When someone is in a state of uncertainty, he needs to validate his perceptions and assumptions. One way to do this is to affiliate with others who are in the same situation and to compare reactions. It seems likely, then, that anxious subjects like the women in Schachter's experiment would not choose to be with just anyone. Rather, they would choose to be with others in the same psychological situation because only they could serve as comparison points.

Schachter confirmed this hypothesis in a later experiment. All the women in this later study were put into the high-anxiety condition. Half of them were given the choice between waiting alone and waiting with other women about to take part in the experiment. The other half were given the choice between waiting alone and passing the time in a waiting room where students were waiting to see their academic advisers. Many more women chose to affiliate when they were able to be with other subjects in the experiment. When asked to explain their choices after the experiment, the women who chose to be with others in the same predicament made statements that seemed to support the social-comparison hypothesis. As Schachter put it, ''Misery doesn't love just any kind of company, it loves only miserable company.''

The question of why people want to be together—to affiliate—cannot be answered, of course, in a few pages. Still, the results of Schachter's studies, in light of Festinger's theory, seem to indicate that when people are anxious, they are more likely to seek the company of others. And when that anxiety is

Figure 20.3 The results of Schachter's 1959 experiment about the effects of anxiety on affiliation. Anxious subjects, those expecting to receive painful shocks, chose to wait in the company of other subjects much more frequently than did subjects not anticipating pain.

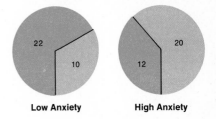

Low Anxiety   **High Anxiety**

⬤ Women who chose to be alone or did not care

⬤ Women who chose to affiliate

overlaid with uncertainty, people prefer to have the company of others in the same boat, so that they can either get assurance that their anxiety is warranted or decide that some other reaction is more appropriate. They can do this by getting information—whether verbally or from facial and body cues—from others who are presumably undergoing the same emotional experience.

Desire to Avoid Comparison

Although feelings of anxiety and uncertainty can lead to a desire to have the company of others, there are times of emotional stress when people seem to prefer solitude. There is evidence, for example, that people are likely to avoid social comparison when their feelings are particularly intense. Several days after President Kennedy's assassination in 1963, a nationwide survey of people's reactions to the tragedy was conducted by Paul Sheatsley and Jacob Feldman for the National Opinion Research Center. The survey included several questions about affiliative tendencies immediately after the assassination. Although 54 percent of those polled said they had felt like talking to others, 40 percent said they would have preferred to be alone. It is significant that many of the people who reported their preference for solitude were those who indicated the greatest admiration for Kennedy. The feelings these people experienced may have been so intense that they did not want to expose them publicly. The photograph in Figure 20.4 is a poignant illustration of this phenomenon. These young people have just witnessed an accident in which one of their friends was killed. The young man crouched alone is obviously undergoing intense shock and grief, and prefers to be alone. Note that the young women prefer to affiliate in their grief; it could be that the young man, because of sex-role training, believes that his display of emotion would be unacceptable as ''masculine behavior.'' Chapter 21 describes in detail the costs of the masculine sex role.

People's needs to affiliate or their desire to be alone depend on a great many factors, not all of which are known and only a few of which have been discussed here. In any case, the pervasive human tendency to be with others underlies the processes to be discussed in the following pages—how people

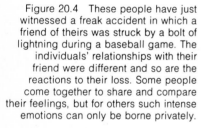

Figure 20.4 These people have just witnessed a freak accident in which a friend of theirs was struck by a bolt of lightning during a baseball game. The individuals' relationships with their friend were different and so are the reactions to their loss. Some people come together to share and compare their feelings, but for others such intense emotions can only be borne privately.

perceive each other and the ways they select, from their many neighbors and acquaintances, those who will become friends or lovers. The first process to be discussed is how people perceive others. How is human experience organized to make one person perceive another as desirable or distasteful?

PERSON PERCEPTION

The way people organize and interpret sensory input about their physical environment is described in Chapter 11. Analogous processes of organization and interpretation take place when people first encounter each other. The processes that people go through in forming first impressions are referred to by social psychologists under the general heading of **person perception.** Psychologists doing research in the area want to know: (1) what evidence people use in forming impressions of others; (2) how they process the pieces of evidence in order to form an integrated impression and to attribute lasting personality traits to the other person; and (3) what effect these first impressions have on subsequent interactions.

Just as it seems necessary for people to organize their perceptions of the sensory world, it seems that we all need to organize our perceptions about people. We need to tell ourselves what a person ''is really like'' so that we can predict his behavior and decide how we will behave toward him or her.

The Evidence

People are all, it seems, detectives. We gather evidence about what a person is like from his style of dress, including hair style, and from his way of walking, his use of gestures, and his facial expressions. If we hear him speak, we add to our evidence the sound of his voice and the way he uses language—does he use hip talk? Does he have a regional accent? Does he speak ungrammatically?

Sometimes we have received data about a person before we meet him. A fellow worker stops by his friend's office and says, ''The boss just hired Harry Crawford. He's a whiz kid—smart as they come. But he's supposed to be pretty loose and funny, I heard.'' A friend arranges a blind date and says, ''Kay is good-looking but a little quiet. She likes you to do the talking.'' How do such before-the-fact appraisals affect our perception of that person?

Sometimes we meet people about whom we have no prior information at all. People at big parties size each other up and begin to chat; travelers on ships and planes share close quarters and strike up conversations; students meet in classrooms and begin to talk about their courses. One important thing we all perceive about another is how good-looking that person is. How much does that perception affect our judgment of a person? After all, we have all heard that ''beauty is only skin deep.''

Physical Attractiveness   Recent research by Karen Dion, Ellen Berscheid, and Elaine Walster indicates that people who do embody culturally valued standards of beauty tend to be liked more than people who are less physically attractive. In a recent study, they showed subjects pictures of men and women of varying physical attractiveness and asked the subjects to rate the people depicted on various personality dimensions. The physically attractive people were viewed in consistently more positive terms than were the less attractive ones—as more sensitive, kind, interesting, strong, poised, modest, and sociable, as well as more sexually warm and responsive. There is evidence that this attractiveness stereotype is learned at an early age. Dion found that children aged three to six and one-half years discriminate differences in facial attractiveness and prefer attractive children as friends. A study by Margaret Clifford and Elaine Walster indicated that adults assume that good-looking children are better behaved than are less-attractive children.

There is little evidence to suggest that the "halo" of favorable characteristics attributed to handsome or beautiful people has any basis in reality. However, it is quite possible that other people's expectations about the dispositions of attractive people may have a direct effect on molding these dispositions. The power of the self-fulfilling prophecy was discussed in Chapter 2. If schoolteachers' baseless expectations about the brightness of some children could affect the children's IQ scores, perhaps people's expectations about the good nature of beautiful people can produce beautiful good-natured people.

Other People's Descriptions   When we are given a description of someone before we meet him, does that evidence affect how we perceive the person? An experiment conducted in the late 1940s by Harold Kelley documented the effect of a person's reputation on the impressions others form of him. Students of MIT were told that their class would be taken over for the day by a new instructor, whom they would be asked to evaluate at the end of the period. Before the instructor was introduced, the students were given a biographical note about him. The students did not know that two versions of the sketch were distributed. Half of the students read the description in Figure 20.5A. Half read the one in Figure 20.5B.

The two sketches differ in but a single word. The first sketch describes the instructor as "warm"; the second, as "cold." This simple variation in expectations, however, had great impact on how the students perceived the instructor. On the evaluations they filled out at the end of the class, the students whose biographies had included the word "warm" rated the instructor as substantially more considerate, informal, sociable, popular, good-natured, and humorous than did the students who had read the word "cold." The instructor's reputation as "warm" or "cold" also affected the students' willingness to interact with him during the class discussion: 56 percent of the "warm" subjects participated in the class discussion, whereas only 32 percent of the "cold" subjects did so. The difference in the students' perceptions of the instructor and the behavior based on those perceptions can only be attributed to that one word of difference, because all the students saw the instructor at the same time.

Solomon Asch, who conducted pioneering experiments similar to Kelley's in the late 1940s and early 1950s, called traits like "warm" and "cold" **central traits,** because they had such marked effects on how the other, **peripheral,** traits are perceived. When we are told in advance of meeting someone that he has a central trait like warmth or coldness, we build around it all our expectations of how he will behave, toward us and toward others.

Expectations and Stereotypes   In some cases, we have information and expectations about someone whom we have never met and about whom we have never received any direct information. In growing up and learning about the world from our family and friends and from television and movies, we can learn stereotypes. A **stereotype** is a set of beliefs and expectations about an entire group of people, and it is generally learned before the learner has had any direct experience with members of that group. The group may be an age group, a nationality, an occupational category, a gender, a race, a religious group. For example, a common stereotype that many people hold about football players is that they are big and dumb. If you held that stereotype and were to meet a football player, you might avoid talking to him about politics or philosophy or any intellectual matters because you would think him unable to understand them. Your behavior, then, might keep you from finding out that the *individual* you have met is, in fact, intelligent and knowledgeable. Although some stereotypes might contain a kernel of truth about the characteristics of some group, they are generalizations, and a generalization

---

Your regular instructor is out of town today, and since we of Economics 70 are interested in the general problem of how various classes react to different instructors, we're going to have an instructor today you've never had before, Mr. Blank. Then, at the end of the period, I want you to fill out some forms about him. In order to give you some idea of what he's like, we've had a person who knows him write up a little biographical note about him. I'll pass this out to you now and you can read it before he arrives. *Please read these to yourselves and don't talk about this among yourselves until the class is over so that he won't get wind of what's going on.*

Mr. Blank is a graduate student in the Department of Economics and Social Science here at M.I.T. He has had three semesters of teaching experience in psychology at another college. This is his first semester teaching Ec. 70. He is 26 years old, a veteran, and married. People who know him consider him to be a very warm person, industrious, critical, practical, and determined.

Figure 20.5A   This is the introduction read to the class in Kelley's experiment on person perception and one of the notes that were then handed out. Read the note and try to imagine yourself in the situation. Then look at Figure 20.5C on page 458. Form an impression of the instructor and note your reactions to him. When you have done so, look at Figure 20.5B across the page.
(After Kelley, 1950.)

Figure 20.6   A common advertising method is the presentation of a product with attractive models shown in desirable situations. This ad presents stereotypes, extremely positive ones, of young, attractive, upper-middle-class people who seem to be in love. People who look like this, readers are likely to believe, must also be sensitive, intelligent, and happy. And it follows, the advertisers reason, that readers will think the models' use of the product perhaps has contributed to their happy state.

cannot tell you anything about an individual. The expectations embodied in stereotypes can have insidious effects on relations between individuals and relations between groups. The effects of stereotypes about men and women are discussed at length in Chapter 21, and the effects of the stereotypes whites hold about blacks are described in Chapter 23.

The evidence that people gather about each other, whether from direct observation or from secondary sources, is processed so that one person can *infer* basic personality traits of another and can predict how he will act from those inferences. But how do those processes work? How is it that we are able to attribute to someone basic, lifelong characteristics solely on the basis of the initial impressions he or she makes?

The Attribution of Traits

The work of Asch and Kelley has established that one way people have of arranging their impressions is to organize them around a central trait, such as warmth or coldness. But what if the descriptions we are given of someone contain a number of traits, none of which is central? Suppose, further, that some parts of the description actually contradict other parts? How do we go about making sense of the data?

The Arithmetic of Impressions   If you were given a description of someone as being determined and cheerful, how could you integrate these traits to form one impression? One thing you could do is **discount** one or the other trait, deciding it is wrong or less important than the other. In a study that Eugene Gollin reported in 1954, subjects were shown movies of a woman who in some scenes appeared to be kindly and helpful and in other scenes was shown to be loose and promiscuous. After the movies the subjects were asked to write descriptions of the woman, and 48 percent of them chose to ignore one or the other set of characteristics.

Some of Gollin's subjects, however, did manage to integrate the characteristics into a coherent personality description. These subjects probably used the method of **averaging**. That is, each person weighs the various traits in accord with his own likes and dislikes and then averages his assigned values to come

Figure 20.5B   The other note in Kelley's experiment on person perception. (If you have not looked at Figure 20.5A, do so first.) Read this description, let it sink in, and then look at Figure 20.5C again, noting your reactions as before.

Mr. Blank is a graduate student in the Department of Economics and Social Science here at M.I.T. He has had three semesters of teaching experience in psychology at another college. This is his first semester teaching Ec. 70. He is 26 years old, a veteran, and married. People who know him consider him to be a rather cold person, industrious, critical, practical, and determined.

up with an integrated impression. If, for example, you valued determination high (+6) and placed a lower value on cheerfulness (+2), you might end up describing a person with both traits as follows: "He finishes a job he takes on whenever it is possible and remains calm when he finds it impossible to finish one" (+4). In this description, determination has been watered down somewhat—the person can conceive of not pursuing a task to its end—and cheerfulness is changed into calmness.

When we do put together a set of traits to form an impression, the weights we assign do not seem to depend solely on our own values. Solomon Asch and, more recently, Norman Anderson have shown that the order in which we encounter the traits affects our weighting. The first information we gets tends to color the rest. This **primacy effect** means that if we find out first that a person is cheerful and then later are told that he is also determined and practical, our image of him will be much different—he will seem jollier— than if we hear first that he is determined and only learn later that he is also practical and cheerful. In addition, Robert Abelson and David Kanouse have found that we seem to give more weight to negative traits than to positive ones in judging someone's attitudes or actions. If we are told that someone is cold, as well as practical, confident, and intelligent, we are more turned off by him than we are turned on by someone who is said to be warm, practical, confident, and intelligent.

Attribution of Causality and Sincerity   Everyone performs actions at one time or another because he or she is forced to by external factors. The law takes account of such differences, with much greater penalties for willful homicide than for accidental manslaughter. People also take account of such factors when judging someone's personality from his behavior. If we think someone is forced by "circumstances beyond his control" to do something, we do not take account of the act in inferring his personality. But how do we judge whether a person's act or statement is intentional?

One thing we do is to try to judge the person's sincerity. Edward Jones and Keith Davis suggest that when someone performs a socially approved act, we are less likely to perceive it as sincere. If we see a young man giving his mother flowers on Mother's Day, we will not think him as sincerely thoughtful as if he had brought her flowers on some ordinary day.

On the other hand, if what he does violates social norms or if what he says constitutes an extreme position, we judge the person as sincere, according to Jones and Davis. Richard Eisinger and Judson Mills did a study whose results support this hypothesis. They had subjects judge the sincerity of another person's opinion about the value of intercollegiate athletics. Subjects heard both moderate and extreme views, and they judged the extreme views as more sincere, even when the views were contrary to their own. Evidently, we feel that when someone is willing to "stick his neck out," it must be because he honestly believes what he says.

One other factor we use in judging sincerity is the extent to which what a person says or does seems to contradict his self-interest. If we were to hear the president of an oil company speak out for smaller oil-depletion allowances, we would most likely believe him, because the statement seems to violate his self-interest.

These processes of person perception clearly have a great deal to do with determining who will become our friends. Given a choice, most of us will pursue a friendship with someone who has left us with a good impression and will avoid a person who first struck us as insincere or cold. Knowing something now about what evidence people use and how they (sometimes mistakenly) sort it out, perhaps you may want to monitor some of your own processes. In the following section, a number of principles underlying the choice of

Figure 20.5C   A re-creation of the classroom scene in Kelley's experiment on person perception. (See Figures 20.5A and 20.5B.) Kelley was able to demonstrate in this study how strongly our impressions of people can be influenced by our expectations about them.

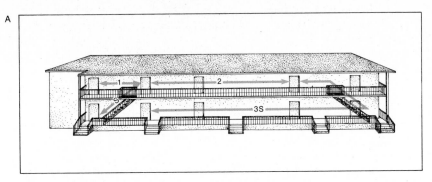

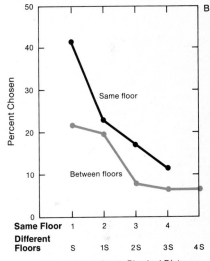

Figure 20.7   The results of the study by Festinger, Schachter, and Back at MIT housing in Cambridge. The investigators studied the relationship between proximity and choice of friends in a housing development.   (A) The illustration of one of the seventeen apartment buildings shows how proximity was measured: in roughly equal units of physical distance with a special S unit indicating a flight of stairs.   (B) The subjects' statements of where their three closest friends lived is given as a percentage of all the possible people who could have been chosen at a given distance. By far the largest proportion of friends were next-door neighbors.

(After Festinger, Schachter, and Back, 1963.)

friends are discussed. Once we have formed a good impression of someone and have attributed to him personality traits that we find attractive, how do we go about befriending him?

CHOOSING FRIENDS

The single most general principle underlying the choice of friends is quite straightforward: We like people who reward us; we are attracted to those who seem to promise rewards. We dislike people who somehow punish us, and we are unlikely to embark on a relationship that promises to be painful or costly. The definition of what is a reward or a punishment in human relations varies greatly with individuals, and the rewards may be in any number of areas. Paul Wright has noted that friends can reward us by being stimulating, introducing us to new ideas or activities; by being helpful, giving of their time and resources to help us; by supporting our egos, giving sympathy and encouragement when things are going badly and approval when they are going well. Still, psychologists have identified several social rewards and costs that are almost universal. These factors will be brought out in the context of the following discussion of the determinants of friendship: proximity, similarity, approval, complementarity, and social roles.

Proximity

Perhaps the best single predictor of whether two people will become friends is their physical proximity—how far apart they live or work. A classic investigation of the effects of physical proximity on friendship was conducted by Leon Festinger, Stanley Schachter, and Kurt Back. Their subjects were couples moving into married-student housing at MIT just after World War II. Almost none of the project residents knew each other before they moved in, so the investigators could focus directly on how proximity affected the formation of their friendships. The housing complex consisted of seventeen separate two-story buildings, each containing ten apartments (see Figure 20.7A). The researchers constructed a rough measure of the distance between apartments simply by counting as one unit each entry door and adding a special unit for going up or down stairs. (For example, the couple next door lived one unit away.) All the residents of the development were asked to name the three closest friends they had made in the project. Some of the results are depicted in Figure 20.7B. As the graph indicates, even within a single building, the closer one lived to another person, the more likely one was to choose him as a close friend. People who lived next door to each other were much more likely to become friends than people who lived two doors apart.

A more recent study by Robert Priest and Jack Sawyer, conducted in a large student dormitory at the University of Chicago, obtained very similar results. Even though the students' rooms were only eight feet apart, there was still a strong tendency for students to like the person next door more than the one two doors away, and so on. It seems obvious that *large* physical distances

Figure 20.8 A hall with many doors represents many possibilities for interaction; one with few doors does not. Being friendly with someone who lives several doors away from you in the lower hall is thus less likely than being friendly with someone a door away in the upper hall, even though the physical distances are identical.

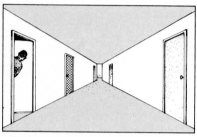

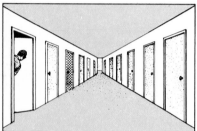

affect friendship. People who live far away from one another are unlikely to meet one another—and if they do meet, they will find it hard to stay in close contact. It is harder to account for the strong impact of proximity within a dormitory floor, where it may take no more than two seconds to get from one room to another. But Priest and Sawyer put forth an interesting explanation for their findings. They point out that **perceived distance** often seems to depend on the number of other people who intervene rather than on numbers of feet or miles. In a rural area, for example, people living half a mile away may be considered neighbors, whereas in a city those living one hundred feet away may not be—they may be in another wing of the apartment building or ten floors down. In a university dormitory, a room five doors away may represent five *closer* opportunities passed by. Thus, to borrow change for the Coke machine from someone five rooms away may raise the question, "Why didn't he ask someone closer?"

In terms of the rewards and costs of friendship, then, one can infer that interacting with someone five rooms away is more costly because a friendly approach has to be purposive instead of casual and so may result in an awkward encounter. It may be for this reason that roommates are particularly likely to be friends, even when the two do not seem to be well matched on personality dimensions. As Priest and Sawyer note, it is easy for roommates to interact without each encounter being an occasion.

A second explanation for the impact of proximity on friendship formation can be formulated from the assumption that the closer people live to one another, the more likely they are to bump into one another—to see and hear one another often. Recent studies by Robert Zajonc indicate that, all other factors being equal, repeated exposure to various stimuli (ranging from Chinese characters to men's faces) tends to produce positive attitudes toward those stimuli. In one such experiment Zajonc simply showed subjects photographs taken from a college yearbook. Each subject saw twelve faces: two faces he only saw once, two twice, two five times, two ten times, and two twenty-five times. The subjects were then given those pictures and two pictures of faces they had not seen before and were asked to indicate how much they would like the people in the photographs. The results were striking: The more frequently the subject had seen a face, the more likely he was to predict that he would like that person. A recent study by Susan Saegert, Walter Swap, and Robert Zajonc, which exposed subjects to real people with differing frequencies, yielded similar results.

Why does repeated exposure to a person make it more likely that you will befriend him? Why does he grow on you? It seems likely that, as you become more familiar with his ways, he becomes less threatening and more predictable. Although you may never come to love another person on the basis of repeated exposure alone, you may at least come to feel comfortable in his presence. Recent studies (for example, by Philip Brickman and Joel Redfield) have suggested, however, that repeated exposure to someone you initially disliked is not likely to change your attitude toward him. In fact, the exposure may have just the opposite effect—your dislike can develop into hatred. One can say, then, that when a person's initial attitudes toward another are *positive* or *neutral*, repeated exposure is likely to have positive effects; when his initial attitudes are *negative*, the effects of exposure are likely to be negative. The social rewards offered by proximity include both the opportunity for casual interaction and the familiarity that repeated exposures produce—and thus the comfort people seem to garner from the familiar.

Similarity

The second factor affecting our choice of friends is similarity, and there is abundant evidence that we choose as friends people whose social backgrounds and attitudes are similar to our own. There is much evidence showing that people practice **assortative mating:** Most husbands and wives share the same race, religion, economic status, and educational level. There are often strong social pressures, especially from parents, for a person to marry someone with a similar social history. Assortative mating also follows from the effects of proximity; people of similar income levels and ethnic backgrounds tend to live in the same areas and thus to send their children to the same schools. If during your childhood and adolescence you are effectively segregated from all but those who share your race, religion, and economic level, your friends—and potential marriage partners—will inevitably be similar to you in these respects.

Similarity of attitudes also plays a central role in friendship formation. Theodore Newcomb conducted an extensive study of attitude and friendship at the University of Michigan. He set up his own experimental dormitory, where rent for one term was waived in return for the students' cooperation. At the start of the term the students completed a series of measures of their attitudes about various political and social issues. During the study, they completed questionnaires in which they named the people in the dorm they perceived as having attitudes similar to their own and rated all the other residents as to how much they liked them. Newcomb found that his measures of perceived similarity of attitudes were a good predictor of which students would become friends by the end of the term. As one of the characters in Disraeli's *Lothair* declared, "My idea of an agreeable person is someone who agrees with me!"

Social psychologists have come up with several explanations for the power of shared attitudes in attraction. First, some agreements provide a basis for joint activities, like bridge or tennis. Agreement on political issues may provide the basis for associations in political organizations and the like. Both friends, then, are rewarded by being able to do together the things they like. Second, a person who agrees with you reinforces your notion that your opinions are correct. Such validation of one's opinions by social comparison usually has the effect of increasing one's self-esteem. Third, people who agree about things that matter to them generally find it easier to communicate with each other. They have fewer arguments, misunderstandings, and confusions. Also, people who share the same basic outlook are generally better able to predict each other's actions.

A final reason people are attracted to those with similar backgrounds and attitudes stems from an assumption that people commonly make about others—an assumption that is sometimes but not always justified. *We assume that people with backgrounds and attitudes like ours are more apt to like us.* Unfortunately, we also fear that people whom we perceive as different will reject us, so we may shy away from them—even though we were initially attracted to them. Clearly, friendship with someone whose background or perspective is different from our own can often provide more stimulation value than friendship with someone just like us. But it seems that only when our fears of rejection are allayed are we likely to make such friends. A study by Joel Goldstein and Howard Rosenfeld supports this analysis. They found that people who scored high on a measure of psychological insecurity were more likely to choose to associate with people similar to them than were more secure subjects. The social rewards of similarity, then, include the sharing of activities and the validation of one's opinion. And similarity helps us avoid the social cost of rejection.

Approval

Approval from others is one of the most important determinants of interpersonal attraction. People who like us bolster our own sense of worth. Some

Figure 20.9 Social psychologists usually investigate interpersonal attraction by studying college students—many of whom are young, middle-class adults. But the findings of these studies may apply to other ages and classes. There seems to be a strong bond between these two men; they probably live close together and share many problems and experiences. Proximity, perceived similarities, mutual approval, and complementary needs can overcome racial barriers to friendship.

Figure 20.10 The results of Aronson and Linder's experiment illustrate the complex effects of approval on liking. Subjects overheard a confederate of the experimenter make remarks about them. As one would expect, a person who made positive comments was better liked than one who made negative remarks, but best liked were the confederates whose remarks began critically but ended by being complimentary. Least liked were the confederates whose remarks were initially positive but became disparaging.

(After Aronson and Linder, 1965.)

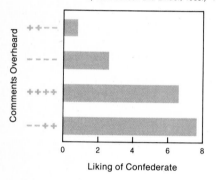

people have greater need for approval than others, but everyone feels this need to at least some degree. An interesting study of people's reactions to others' evaluations of them was conducted by Elliot Aronson and Darwyn Linder. Each subject in this study overheard a series of remarks about himself by a confederate of the experimenters. The first group of subjects heard the confederate make only complimentary remarks throughout the session. Another group heard the confederate make only derogatory remarks. What the third group heard was first very derogatory, then gradually more positive, and finally extremely complimentary (the "gain" condition). The last group heard the confederate begin by making positive comments but end by being very disparaging (the "loss" condition). Each subject was asked to indicate how much he liked the confederate. Before you look at Aronson and Linder's results in Figure 20.10, you might like to predict which group of students liked the confederate most and which group liked him least.

The best-liked confederates were not the ones who were uniformly positive but those who began by saying negative things and ended by saying positive ones (although both were strongly liked). Also, there was a tendency for subjects to prefer the confederates who said consistently negative things to those who began by saying complimentary things and ended by being disapproving. How can this pattern of results be explained? In the "gain" condition, the early disparaging remarks may have helped to establish the genuineness and credibility of the confederate. The subject may have, in effect, said to himself, "This is a very perceptive person. He's not easy to impress." As a result, his eventual approval may have been all the more meaningful and rewarding. In addition, subjects in the "gain" condition may have experienced a particularly gratifying boost in self-esteem as a result of the confederate's conversion from disapproval to approval. When the confederate's remarks were uniformly positive, on the other hand, the subjects may have thought the confederate to be a little indiscriminating, and so they were not quite as strong in their liking of him. And the subjects who heard positive comments followed by negative ones may have experienced such a surprising and disappointing loss of self-esteem that they tended to feel cooler toward the confederate than they would have felt toward someone who had been critical all along.

More recent research, conducted since the publication of Aronson and Linder's study in 1965 (reviewed by David Mettee and Elliot Aronson, in 1974), has pointed out that this "gain-loss" effect in interpersonal attraction is a subtle and elusive one. It is not always the case that we like a person who delivers a gain in evaluation more than someone who gives a consistently positive one. It seems that people do not simply add up the rewards and punishments they receive from others to determine whether or not they like them. Rather, the context and sequence in which rewards and punishments are provided play central roles. Studies like the ones discussed here, and others being currently conducted, are attempting to find out what sequences are most effective in what contexts. In general, however, individuals tend to like people who give them the social reward of approval and to dislike people who disapprove of them and cause them a loss of self-esteem.

Complementarity

Many psychologists have speculated about the ways in which the deeper levels of two individuals' personalities mesh in order to produce liking or disliking, love or hate. One theory, based on writings of Carl Jung, suggests that people have unconscious "archetypes," or ideals, of the sort of person who would best complement them; when someone encounters a person of the opposite sex who corresponds to his archetype, he immediately becomes aware of the match and falls in love. Robert Winch and other theorists have

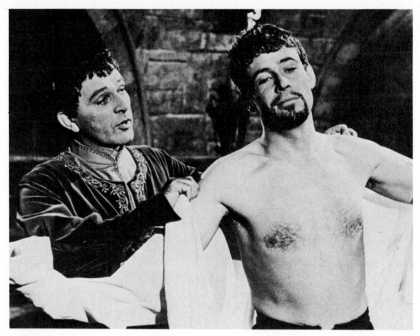

Figure 20.11 A scene from *Becket*, a film that explores the relationship between an English king and his closest friend. The contrasting characters of these two men illustrate the principle of need complementarity in friendship. King Henry II (right) was a highly emotional man but a weak one. His friend from boyhood, Thomas à Becket (left), had great self-discipline and stability. The King depended on Becket for strength; Becket depended on the King as a conduit to make that strength felt. As the circumstances of the two men changed, their needs and loyalties no longer complemented one another, and they came into severe conflict.

suggested that need **complementarity** is a basis for attraction. For example, people with needs to dominate are attracted to people with needs to be dominated, and people with a strong need to care for others are drawn to those with a need to be cared for.

Psychologist Robert White provides a good example of how two personalities complemented one another in the case of a friendship between two teen-age boys:

Ben, whose school experience had been so unstimulating that he never read a book beyond those assigned, discovered in Jamie a lively spirit of intellectual inquiry and an exciting knowledge of politics and history. Here was a whole world to which his friend opened the door and provided guidance. Jamie discovered in Ben a world previously closed to him, that of confident interaction with other people. Each admired the other, each copied the other, each used the other for practice.

Many friendships, both same-sex and opposite-sex, seem to be built on such complementarity. So far, however, it has remained much easier for psychologists to recognize such complementarity after the fact than to predict it ahead of time. There are so many human needs and so many possible ways of gratifying them that although many researchers have tried, none has yet been successful in predicting which persons will be attracted to which others on the basis of their individual personality profiles. The rewards of complementarity come from the meeting of one's needs. Costs may arise if this mutual meeting of needs keeps the two people (who are involved in a relationship) from other social interaction or if it prevents the personal growth of one or both of them.

Social Roles

Individual behavior in all societies is structured by social patterns based on social status, on social norms—standards for behavior—and on social roles —clusters of norms pertaining to particular groups of people. The society specifies acceptable behavior for age groups, for occupational groups, for sex groups. Chapter 21 describes at length the patterning of behavior by these social processes, and their operation is part of the discussion of social influence and intergroup behavior, Chapters 22 and 23. The type of social

Figure 20.12 The social roles people have or expect to have with respect to each other affect the factors they find most important in each other. The results of a study by Stroebe and his colleagues, shown here, demonstrate this aspect of interpersonal attraction. Although for all four conditions shown—working with, liking, dating, marrying—both male and female subjects preferred physically attractive people to unattractive ones and preferred people with attitudes similar to their own, some interesting findings emerged. Attractiveness was generally more important to men than to women, as indicated by the steeper curves for the men. Similarity of attitudes was generally more important to the women than to the men.
(After Stroebe *et al.*, 1971.)

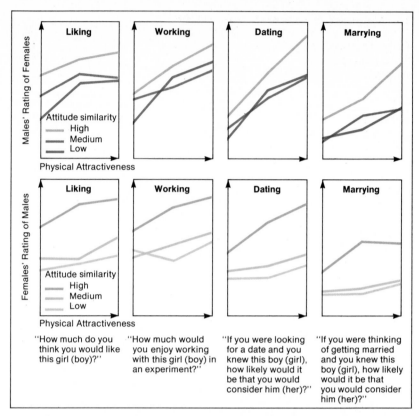

relationship two people have will be greatly affected by the expectations each has in light of their reciprocal social roles. If it is a business partnership, the expectations and attractive qualities will be very different from those of a social friendship. If the friendship between a man and a woman is a convenience for going to movies and parties together, the rewards they expect from each other will be very different from those expected by partners thinking of marriage.

The results of a recent experiment by Wolfgang Stroebe and his colleagues illustrate how the importance of different rewards varies in different role contexts. Prior to the experimental session, each subject had filled out a questionnaire that allowed the researchers to construct an attitude profile for him. The researchers showed each male subject a photograph of a woman and each female subject a photograph of a male. The picture shown to one-third of the subjects was of a person other students had previously judged to be extremely good-looking; one-third were shown an average-looking person; and one-third were shown an unattractive person. The photo was accompanied by a series of attitude statements that had purportedly been made by the person photographed but had actually been concocted by the experimenters in light of the subject's attitudes. Within each of the attractiveness conditions, one-third of the subjects were shown statements that strongly agreed with their own attitudes; one-third were shown a set of attitudes totally different from their own; and one-third were shown attitudes that partly agreed and partly disagreed with their own. The subject indicated his attraction for the person by answering the four questions shown in Figure 20.12.

As might be expected, for all four role relationships (liking, working, dating, or marrying) most subjects preferred good-looking to unattractive partners and were more attracted to those who agreed with them than to those who did not. However, the researchers' skillful analysis of their data permitted them to assess the importance of physical attractiveness and of attitude similarity relative to the subject's sex and to each role relationship. They found that men were more influenced by physical attractiveness than were women in choosing people they preferred to work with, to date, and to marry, but there was little difference between men and women in the influence of physical attractiveness on whom they thought they would like. For all subjects (both sexes combined), physical attractiveness generally had a greater impact on dating choices than on preference for persons to like or marry. Attitude similarity, on the other hand, was more important in determining the subjects' preferences for people to like than for people to date. It was clear, in other words, that the relative importance of the two factors—physical attractiveness and attitude similarity—depends on the sort of relationship envisioned. The rewards one person expects from another in a relationship, then, depend greatly on the roles dictated by the type of relationship. Costs can arise if one of the persons misinterprets the roles and defines the relationship differently than the other defines it—for example, if one person sees the relationship as a dating one and the other, as a marrying one.

THE DEVELOPMENT OF RELATIONSHIPS

Much of the research to date on interpersonal attraction has focused on people's *initial* attraction to or dislike of others they encounter. However, as research in this area progresses, social psychologists hope to learn more about the ways in which deeper relationships develop over time. It is clear that as a relationship progresses from first acquaintance to casual interaction to intimacy, the qualities that the partners find rewarding in each other are likely to change. George Levinger and Jaap Snoek illustrated this point in a recent study. They asked college students to rate the relative importance of each of thirty-three characteristics of another (hypothetical) person in terms of six different levels of involvement, ranging from "mere awareness" of the other to maintenance of an established relationship between the two. The characteristics to be ranked ranged from "height" to "how loving" to "how dominant." Not surprisingly, the subjects rated easily visible characteristics, such as the other's height or physical attractiveness, as more important at lower levels of involvement (which generally occur at early stages of a relationship). "Deeper" characteristics, such as the other's considerateness or his need to give or receive love, were rated as unimportant for low levels of involvement but very important for deeper stages (see Figure 20.14).

Levinger and Snoek also stress that as relationships develop toward intimacy—whether friendship or love—people do not consider only their own rewards and costs in the relationship but come to consider their partner's outcomes as well. Recent research on empathy by Ezra Stotland, Stanley Sherman, and Kelly Shaver helped to explain how people may experience pain or pleasure as a direct result of their knowledge of *someone else's* pain or pleasure.

One important determinant of the development of a close relationship—for example, in dating couples—is the relative degree to which each of the partners is interested and involved in the relationship. In 1938, sociologist Willard Waller propounded his well-known **principle of least interest**, which states that whichever member of a couple is less interested in the relationship is the one who is able to set its terms. The more involved partner is more dependent on the relationship and may often have to acquiesce to the wishes of the less-involved partner, for fear of losing him or her. Waller went on to suggest that relationships in which there is a lopsided balance of involvement tend to be short-lived. A longitudinal study of dating couples in the Boston area, which is currently being conducted by Zick Rubin, Anne Peplau, and Charles Hill, has obtained clear support for Waller's hypotheses. As Waller

Figure 20.13 Woody Allen's relations with women in most of his films seem to exemplify Waller's principle of least interest: He usually has more at stake in the relationship, tries harder, but loses anyway.

Beginning with **NO CONTACT**

Approach, facilitated by:

1. spatial proximity, climate and other environmental factors,
2. lack of social distance, and
3. the person's interest in other people,

leads to **AWARENESS** in which

communication is one way; there is no *common knowledge,* no *interaction,* no *relationship,* and *attraction to the other* is based on the other's reward potential or "image."

Affiliation, facilitated by:

4. the person's time and opportunity
5. attractiveness of the other, and
6. perception of the other's probable reciprocity,

then leads to **SURFACE CONTACT** in which

communication is confined to practical role requirements (no self-disclosure); there is *common knowledge* only of the other's public self; *interaction* includes stereotyped role-taking and trial-and-error in novel situations; interaction is *regulated* by cultural norms that are assumed to be shared; *maintenance* of the relationship is of little concern and is a response to external requirements only; *evaluation* of the relationship is a self-centered comparison with other relationships; and *attraction* to the other is based on the person's satisfaction with outcomes and the adequacy of the other's role enactment (as well as on previous criteria).

Attachment, facilitated by:

7. liking for the other and satisfaction with prior relationship,
8. circumstances that extend the interaction beyond usual role requirements,
9. communication about each others' experiences in the interaction,
10. accommodation and formation of contractual norms, and
11. attitude, value, and need compatibility

then leads to **MUTUALITY** in which

communication concerns personal feelings and evaluation of the relationship's outcomes; *common knowledge* includes each others' feelings and life stories; *interaction* is spontaneous and free-flowing and includes understanding of the interaction's effects on the other and concern about the other's well-being; interaction is *regulated* by some unique norms developed and found acceptable by the pair; *maintenance* of the relationship becomes increasingly valued and both persons take responsibility for protecting and enhancing it; *evaluation* of the relationship is a joint concern made on the basis of outcomes for both persons; and *attraction* is based on affection for the other as a unique person and on the person's emotional investment in the other (as well as on previous criteria).

Figure 20.14 The evolution of a relationship is facilitated by different factors at different stages of involvement between the partners. The ways that partners show interest in and communicate with each other change radically as the relationship develops. Levinger and Snoek experimentally analyzed this process of "getting to know someone" and found the characteristics for the various stages and the factors facilitating movement from stage to stage that are shown here.

(After Levinger and Snoek, 1972.)

suggested, the partner who was less involved in the relationship also tended to be the one who had more power in the relationship. And results so far indicate that relationships with an *equal* balance of involvement are more likely to survive over time.

ROMANTIC LOVE

There are many varieties of love—love between parent and child, between same-sex friends, between man and wife. Psychologists use the term "romantic love" to mean what most people's intuitive notion of it is—the intimate relationship that may exist between opposite-sex partners. One problem for social psychologists is to distinguish romantic love from a relationship based on "liking."

Zick Rubin recently conducted a study that attempted to specify more clearly the ways in which social psychologists might distinguish between "liking" and "loving." He began his research by giving several hundred students a long series of statements that expressed a variety of feelings one might have toward one's boyfriend or girl friend. The students were to apply the statements to their own relationships and indicate which statements best expressed their own feelings toward their boyfriend or girl friend. Rubin found that the students' expressed feelings could be grouped into two categories and that one of these categories corresponded reasonably well to what people typically mean by "liking" and the other to what they mean by "love." Adjacent are some sample items of the two scales Rubin developed as a result of this analysis.

The study of love, like all other aspects of human psychology, will profit more from the use of a wider range of behavioral measures than from paper-and-pencil measures alone. Rubin has made some initial progress in identifying an observable behavior related to love. He found that couples who got high scores on his "love scale" spent more time making eye contact than did couples who received lower scores on the scale. The notion that lovers spend a great deal of time looking into each other's eyes is, of course, a part of our folklore. In addition, sociologist Erving Goffman has noted that eye contact serves as a mutually understood signal that the communication channel between two people is open. He notes that, for example, strangers in an elevator are at pains to avoid eye contact. Thus, the sustained eye contact of lovers is in accord with the more specific ideas that love is characterized by strong feelings of attachment and by intimate communication between people.

Besides merely distinguishing between love and liking, psychologists also want to understand the psychological nature of love. An interesting theoretical approach to the nature of romantic love was recently taken by Elaine Walster

Figure 20.15 Rubin's scale items, some of which are shown here, were developed to distinguish between liking and loving in young opposite-sex student couples, but it is interesting to extend the analysis that these scale items make possible to same-sex relationships, relationships between very old people, people of different ages, and even to relationships that are not strictly human. People form strong likes *and* loves outside the romantic context as well as within it.

Liking

1. *Favorable evaluation.*

   I think that _____ (my boyfriend or girl-friend) is unusually well-adjusted.
   It seems to me that it is very easy for _____ to gain admiration.

2. *Respect and confidence.*

   I have great confidence in _____'s good judgment.
   I would vote for _____ in a class or group election.

3. *Perceived similarity.*

   I think that _____ and I are quite similar to each other.
   When I am with _____, we are almost always in the same mood.

Loving

1. *Attachment.*

   If I could never be with _____, I would feel miserable.
   It would be hard for me to get along without _____.

2. *Caring.*

   If _____ were feeling badly, my first duty would be to cheer him (her) up.
   I would do almost anything for _____.

3. *Intimacy.*

   I feel that I can confide in _____ about almost anything.
   When I am with _____, I spend a good deal of time just looking at him (her).

"Love is like a wind stirring the grass beneath trees on a black night..... You must not try to make love definite. It is the divine accident of life."

Figure 20.16   Through theory and research psychologists may increase our knowledge of the factors that facilitate and inhibit love. They may also clarify our understanding of the behavior of lovers. Such knowledge is not meant to substitute for the experience of love or to limit or bound it; rather, it is intended to expand our understanding of a phenomenon whose miraculous quality is expressed here by the writer Sherwood Anderson.

(From Sherwood Anderson, "Death," *Winesburg, Ohio.* New York: Viking Press, 1964, p. 223.)

and Ellen Berscheid. Walster and Berscheid based their hypothesis on Stanley Schachter's attribution theory of emotion that is discussed at length in Chapter 15. Schachter says that the subjective experience of an emotion often depends on a person's cognitive appraisal of his situation at the time he is physiologically aroused (having a racing heart, dry mouth, or the like). All attribution theories, like the ones in this chapter's discussion of person perception, point to the cognitive processing of stimuli as the most important factor in how people experience things. Schachter says that the aroused person often looks around him to determine what the external stimulus is that might be causing his inner upheaval. Walster and Berscheid hypothesized that people who are experiencing sexual arousal or the physiological effects of some other arousing experience, then, might decide they are in love with their companion. More surprisingly, they suggest that people may sometimes decide they are in love on the basis of a kind of physiological hangover. A hypothetical example of this phenomenon might be as follows: An absent-minded man is crossing the street and barely misses being demolished by a large truck. As he steps onto the curb he spies the intriguing woman he had met at a party the night before. His heart is pounding and his hands are shaking, part of his body's automatic responses to the close call. But the man has already forgotten about the truck and concludes that he is in love.

This phenomenon might serve to explain the folklore about people falling in love with their rescuers, for instance, a lifeguard at the beach or a doctor or a nurse in a hospital emergency ward. A person's physiological arousal in a perilous situation might be transferred to his or her rescuer, who then becomes a love object.

Some support for Berscheid and Walster's hypothesis comes from a recent experiment conducted by Donald Dutton and Arthur Arons. The experimenters arranged it so that male subjects were approached by an attractive female (a confederate of the experimenters) while they were crossing one of two bridges near Vancouver, British Columbia. One of the bridges was a narrow, rickety structure that swayed in the wind hundreds of feet above a rocky canyon; the other was a solid structure only several feet above a shallow stream. Dutton and Arons found, as they had predicted, that subjects on the rickety bridge expressed more sexual imagery in brief stories that they subsequently wrote at the experimenters' request. They were also more likely to telephone the female confederate later, ostensibly to get more information about the study. The explanation of these results in terms of Berscheid and Walster's hypothesis is that the subjects were physiologically aroused by the fear-inspiring characteristics of the rickety, swaying bridge and when approached by the attractive woman, they relabeled these feelings in terms of sexual arousal and attraction.

TO KNOW HIM IS TO LOVE HIM

It may be, then, that liking and loving have as much to do with how people think as how they feel. The conclusions of many of the studies in this chapter appear to point that way. It seems clear that one important reason people affiliate with others is to get better information about their own emotional reactions, particularly in stressful situations. Also, people seem to choose as their friends others who help them confirm their understanding of their own "social reality," that is, those whose attitudes and backgrounds are much the same as their own. And even love between a man and a woman, which has been considered the "sweet mystery of life" through the ages, may be a more rational happening than has been imagined. But, as stated in the introduction to this chapter, much more research must be done before these tentative findings can be confirmed—or denied.

SUMMARY

1. Although psychologists have no universally applicable explanation for people's need to **affiliate** (to seek the company of others), a pioneer study by Stanley Schachter showed that people suffering anxiety are more likely to want to be with others than are people not subjected to anxiety-provoking situations.

    a. **Social-comparison theory,** developed by Leon Festinger, can serve to explain why Schachter's anxious subjects chose to affiliate. Festinger says that people are uncomfortable with uncertainty and strive to get rid of it by checking their own perceptions and assumptions— either against the physical world or against other people's beliefs or perceptions. Because Schachter's anxious subjects were uncertain about what reactions were proper to their situation, they wished to be with others in the same situation, so that they could compare their reactions with those of others.

    b. Under certain circumstances people seek to avoid social comparison, such as when their feelings are intense and, especially, when they judge that the intense emotions they are experiencing would be **unacceptable** to others.

2. Social psychologists refer to processes of sizing up and forming impressions of others under the heading **person perception.**

    a. **Expectations** play an important role in person perception. If one is forewarned that a person is "warm," one is likely to perceive him or her as warm and possessing many other characteristics that seem to "go with" warmth—the **halo effect.**

Figure 20.17 Stanley Schachter has done much ingenious research in the field of social psychology. Besides his studies of affiliation and anxiety, discussed in this chapter, Schachter has performed studies and developed hypotheses in a number of other areas: the relationship of group cohesiveness to productivity; the interaction of cognition and physiological arousal in emotion (discussed in Chapter 15); and stimulus control of eating in obese people (discussed in Chapter 14).

Figure 20.18 Leon Festinger is one of the major theorists in the field of social psychology. His social-comparison theory provides a framework for interpreting the affiliation experiments discussed in this chapter, and his concept of cognitive dissonance, discussed in Chapter 22, has provided social psychologists with one of their most useful devices for describing the circumstances that lead to attitude change.

b. **Stereotypes**—expectations about entire groups learned during the socialization process—can heavily influence one's perceptions of an individual.

c. Research by Karen Dion, Elaine Walster, and Ellen Berscheid has shown that a halo effect exists for physical attractiveness. People expect that good-looking women, men, and children will be kinder, more considerate, and so on than will unattractive ones.

3. The single most general principle underlying the choice of friends is: We like those people we expect will reward us, and we dislike those people whose relation to us promises to be punishing or costly. Although what constitutes a reward or punishment in human relations does vary with individuals, psychologists have identified certain social rewards and costs that are almost universally perceived as such.

4. The best single predictor of whether two people will become friends is how far apart they live or work. **Proximity** in terms of physical distance, however, is often not as important as **perceived distance,** which is judged by the number of people who intervene rather than by amount of space.

a. The social costs of interacting with someone farther away in terms of perceived distance may be greater because an approach must be more purposive.

b. People who live or work in proximity are likely to notice each other often—to see and hear each other; and studies have shown that repeated exposure to a person or a thing makes it much more likely that one will come to like that person or thing.

5. There is overwhelming evidence that we choose as friends people whose social backgrounds and attitudes resemble our own. **Similarity** is a significant determinant of friendship because:

a. It provides a basis for shared activities.

b. It permits each partner to **socially validate** his or her attitudes by social comparison.

c. It makes communication easier.

d. People assume that those who hold beliefs similar to theirs will like them.

6. **Approval** from others is a powerful reward and is one of the most important determinants of interpersonal attraction. People who approve of us enhance our sense of worth, and we, in turn, tend to like them.

a. A study by Elliot Aronson and Darwyn Linder shows that at times we like someone who is initially disapproving but comes to approve of us better than someone who is consistently approving. We dislike less someone who is consistently disapproving than someone who comes to disapprove of us.

b. More generally, it is the **context** and **sequence** rather than simply the numerical frequency of rewards and punishments provided in a relationship that are important.

7. Robert F. Winch and other theorists have suggested that need **complementarity** is the basis for attraction. For example, people who have a need to dominate are attracted to those who have a need to be dominated.

Figure 20.19 Robert Abelson's interests in social psychology have been focused strongly in the area of attitude change. His research on the formation of attitudes toward persons is discussed in this chapter. Abelson has a background of scientific and mathematical training and has attempted to simulate changes in attitudes and belief systems with computer programs.

8. The kind of relationship envisioned or engaged in by two people will determine what characteristics each finds rewarding in the other. Two business partners, for example, require different factors than a dating couple does. These **social roles** dictate the nature and timing of effective rewards in a relationship.

9. The rewarding characteristics of a romantically involved couple change as the relationship deepens. The romantic relationships most likely to survive are those in which both partners are equally involved and committed. In lopsided relationships the less-involved partner is likely to wield greater power; this phenomenon has been called the **principle of least interest.**

10. Zick Rubin has devised a measure that permits psychologists to distinguish between "liking" and "loving" so that romantic love, which has rarely been studied behaviorally, can be investigated.

11. A recent approach to romantic love, taken by Walster and Bercheid, is based on Stanley Schachter's attribution theory of emotion. These psychologists hypothesize that the cognitive element in love is very important—that people can, under certain circumstances, interpret ambiguous emotional arousal as love.

Figure 20.20 Elliot Aronson is a social psychologist interested in personality. In addition to his work on approval and liking, described in this chapter, he has done research on Festinger's dissonance theory and has suggested revisions of it. He has also shown considerable interest in T-groups and sensitivity training and has recently been engaged in research on the experience of children in the elementary schools of Texas.

SUGGESTED READINGS

Berscheid, Ellen, and Elaine Walster. *Interpersonal Attraction.* Reading, Mass.: Addison-Wesley, 1969. A well-organized and valuable review of research in this area through the late 1960s.

Hastorf, Albert H., David J. Schneider, and Judith Polefka. *Person Perception.* Reading, Mass.: Addison-Wesley, 1970. A similarly well-organized and valuable review of research on the ways we form impressions of other people.

Hunt, Morton M. *The Natural History of Love.* New York: Knopf, 1959 (Minerva Paperback, 1967). A highly entertaining account of the history of love and courtship in the Western world, from ancient Greece to modern times.

Huston, Ted L. (ed.). *Foundations of Interpersonal Attraction.* New York: Academic Press, 1974. An excellent and up-to-date collection of papers by leading researchers in the field.

Miller, Howard L., and Paul S. Siegel. *Loving: A Psychological Approach.* New York: Wiley, 1972. A well-written and provocative discussion of love relationships from the viewpoint of social-learning theory.

Rubin, Zick. *Liking and Loving: An Invitation to Social Psychology.* New York: Holt, Rinehart and Winston, 1973. A lively excursion through the field of interpersonal attraction, in which laboratory and field research is applied to such real-life contexts as friendship, mate selection, and intergroup relations.

I am a women's lib advocate from way back and an optimistic one. I'm sure they'll win out. They can't lose! If the human race survives with an advanced technological culture into the twenty-first century (by no means a likely possibility, I'm afraid), then women will be free. Automatically. You see, I contend that what changes human behavior is not theory and idealism but the general tendency to accept the profitable, at least eventually.

For instance, there was nothing that society could do about horse theft. Social obloquy, corporal punishment, lynching, and legal death penalty—nothing worked! And then the cure was developed, and a simple one—the automobile was invented. When fewer people wanted or needed horses badly enough to steal them, horse theft declined. Of course, we now have the problem of automobile theft, but that's another story, isn't it?

All right, women have been subjected and dominated (and taught to relish it and feel that being dominated was wonderful) for two biological reasons. They were physically smaller than men, for one thing, so that they could be physically beaten up if they forgot their place. Second, they bore children and suckled them and that tied them down. Between these two factors, men could dominate, and with physical domination a fact, cultural factors could nail that into place. Women were taught to be passive and accepting, and affairs were so arranged that women had no rights, economic or otherwise, under law;

they could not earn a living or be sure of their next meal unless they accepted male domination.

But if we are to survive as a viable technological society into the twenty-first century, it will be only at the price of achieving population stability. (That will not be the only price, but it will surely be one of the prices.) Children will be a rare luxury by modern standards and women's role as wife and mother will be seriously depressed in importance. And if technology continues to advance, developing automation will make the work of mankind more and more a matter of controlling electrical contacts and making internal decisions—something for which women are as suited as men. Man's superior muscle will go for naught and woman's smaller and defter fingers at controls may go for a lot.

Well, then once the social pressure on a woman to marry and have children is lifted, and once she can make a living for herself as easily (or more easily) than a man can, what can possibly keep her in a state of domination but criminal force?

She may have other problems, but they will be *other* problems, not the ones she has been struggling with through all the centuries of civilization.

Isaac Asimov

21
Patterns of Social Behavior: The Case of Sex Roles

Figure 21.1 Young adolescents often wonder what it will be like to be a woman or a man, what will be expected of them in these adult roles, and how well they will be able to fulfill those expectations. But, in fact, they have been learning since infancy the roles that are constructed around being female or male. Sex roles are among the first social roles to be acquired.

I f you knew a fourteen-year-old boy whose mother took him to and from high school every day, how would you react? Now suppose the boy were four, would that make a difference? If you went to a movie one evening and saw the patrons outside shoving and tackling each other to get into the box office first, what would you think? Now suppose these people were helmeted and suited up on a football field, would that make a difference? If you invited a friend over for dinner and she started eating a slice of roast beef with her hands, how would you feel? Now suppose dinner that night were fried chicken, would that make much of a difference?

Most of us would agree that the first alternative in these pairs of behaviors is "wrong." But how do we know they are wrong, and why is there such a strong consensus about their unacceptability? Undoubtedly, because of our socialization.

Social psychologists use the term **socialization** to designate the process by which individuals develop the attitudes, beliefs, and behavior necessary for them to be effective members of their society. Through the process of socialization, children learn the values and behaviors appropriate to their culture, to their social class, and to the various groups they may find themselves part of. And socialization occurs throughout the life cycle. Adults must learn new behaviors and new attitudes appropriate to becoming a parent, entering a profession, or becoming a widow or retiree. The study of how the individual's behavior and personality are shaped by the social environment is central to the discipline of psychology (as well as to sociology and anthropology).

This chapter describes some of the psychological processes that underlie the patterning of social behavior. It explains the operation of social norms, social status, and social roles and stereotypes in the socialization process.

The case of sex roles is used as a particular illustration throughout the chapter of how social behavior in general is patterned. Knowing how people develop the attitudes and behavior appropriate to being male or female can show a great deal about how socializing factors work in other areas of life—age groups, occupational groups, racial groups, or social-class groups. Also, the case of sex roles provides a current example of how a society's norms and role definitions may be revised when the society is changing.

The chapter looks at how sex roles are acquired; three prominent theoretical explanations are set out: the Freudian, the learning-theory, and the cognitive-developmental. Finally, the chapter examines how an individual's personality may be affected by social patterns and what factors are necessary for a social pattern to change.

BASES OF SOCIAL PATTERNS

Socialization begins at birth, for in all cultures the newborn infant is a "barbarian." Unacceptable behavior is implicit in this word, originally an ancient Sanskrit term for someone who could not speak that language fluently. The Greeks applied the word derogatorily to the behavior of all non-Greeks (including the Romans), and many societies today belittle other people by calling them barbaric. In all parts of the world, societies customarily subject their members to socializing processes designed to perpetuate nonbarbaric—or "civilized"—behavior. Although the nature of the desired results varies enormously from culture to culture, the intent is the same in all societies.

Socialization is carried out by means of agents, the first of which are usually the parents, particularly the mother; later, age-group peers, teachers, and communications media become important socializing influences. In understanding how agents direct behavior of the individual, it is helpful to begin with a brief summary of four factors that are important in the socializing process: norms, status, roles, and stereotypes.

Social Norms

Norms are standards of behavior developed and upheld by societies and their subgroups. Norms lend stability and organization to social relations; they define the context of an interaction and restrict the range of behavior likely to occur in a particular context—they allow for predictability. Some norms are formulated into laws, along with the penalties considered suitable for infractions. American society, for example, legalizes its norms for the contracting of marriages, the driving of automobiles, and the manufacture, sale, and consumption of alcoholic beverages. Many norms are less obvious, yet they are often more effective than laws in controlling the social behavior of individuals. Until recently, for example, very few Latin American women ever wore slacks in public, even in areas where the wearing of such apparel was not legally banned. The restrictive force was common consensus, which held that only immoral females wore "men's" clothes. Even though the penalties for flouting this norm were nowhere codified, they were known to all.

Norms may change so gradually and subtly that one cannot notice the change or even pinpoint it historically. For example, portraits of the Presidents of the United States provide evidence that norms applying to male appearance have been subject to cyclic trends. The appearance considered appropriate for the President has varied in regard to facial hair: George Washington and the fourteen Presidents who succeeded him were clean-shaven; of the next eleven Presidents, Abraham Lincoln and six others had full beards and two had flowing mustaches; all ten men who have held office since 1913 have been clean-shaven. Today, norms concerning appropriate male appearance are again being revised, and it is possible that a bearded man could be elected President as the century ends.

Figure 21.2 Sets of social norms define the relationship of performers to their audiences and the status relationship of common men to rulers. The great jazz musician Louis Armstrong once violated both these sets of norms in a single brilliant stroke. In the London Palladium in 1932 before King George VI of England, Armstrong (looking out toward the King) stunned the audience by introducing an encore with the words "This one's for you, Rex!"

Members of a society usually regard current norms as being "right" or even "instinctive." But no instinct—either universal or regional—is involved in a woman's decision to wear pants rather than skirts or in a man's decision to shave his face or grow a beard. Like instinct, practicality and logic can seldom be used to justify the existence of social norms. Is it really more practical to eat fried chicken with the fingers than to eat a slice of roast beef that way? Or is it only a social norm that deems one action as acceptable and the other as unacceptable? And is it not this society's age norms only that would make it humiliating for a fourteen-year-old to be taken to school by his parent? Finally, members of certain societies never line up to get on buses. Their behavioral norms say there is nothing wrong with pushing and shoving to get on a bus. So, although many norms are necessary to keep social interaction from being chaotic, some norms are not justifiable in terms of contemporary practicality (although they may have been practical when they were instituted)—they simply *are.*

Social Status

The relative rank of an individual within a social system is called status, and most people have several kinds of status, associated with such factors as sex, age, religion, race, and occupation. In the larger society as well as in most of its subgroups, some positions are valued more than others and bring greater rewards and privileges. The owner of a business usually has higher status, a larger salary, and more control over the business than do employees; managers usually outrank others who work within their departments; secretaries outrank members of the typing pool; typists with seniority outrank those who are newcomers.

Status may be ascribed or achieved. Individuals are not born with the destined status of manager or typist. Each is an **achieved status,** which the individual has presumably attained by the ability to fulfill certain requirements. An **ascribed status,** however, is attributed to a person on the basis of some inherited characteristic; the son of a king, for example, has the ascribed status of prince; sex also implies an ascribed status.

Figure 21.3 The status relationships between this child and his teacher are very well-defined. Teachers have high status relative to students (achieved), and adults have high status relative to children (ascribed). Their relative status sets bounds on both the child's and teacher's behaviors: The child will not "talk back"—or if he does so on this occasion, he probably will not repeat the action in the future. The teacher will not swear or weep in the child's presence.

Status may affect social interaction even in situations where norms theoretically preclude its influence. For example, in the United States all members of a jury are supposed to consider each other as equals, according to our society's laws and norms. Yet Fred Strodtbeck, Rita Simon, and Charles Hawkins found in their studies of mock juries (which were set up for the purposes of the experiment) that people with high occupational status were much more likely to be elected jury foremen than were those with lower status. High-status members also participated more actively in discussions, had greater influence on the final decisions, and were perceived by their peers as being more competent.

A person's status can affect not only the frequency and quality of his or her participation in groups but also the probability of social interaction with others. In fact, the norms governing social interaction are closely intertwined with the status of the participants. College freshmen tend to make friends with other freshmen; secretaries are more likely to eat lunch together than with either managers or students. This dual governance of status and norms is reflected in everyday speech patterns. In Mexico, for example, the familiar form of "you"—*tu*—is used in addressing children and servants, who are expected to reply to parents and masters with *usted,* the formal pronoun for "you." And in many work situations in the United States, the employees call their employer "Mr. Jackson," while he in turn calls them "Bill" or "Ann."

Social Roles

A social role can be thought of as simply a cluster of norms (for behavior, for personality traits, and so on) applicable to some specified social category of people; each role has a status attached to it. An occupation provides a good example of a social role. A doctor, for example, is expected to wear certain kinds of clothes, to behave in certain ways, and to display certain skills. Most people would be uncomfortable in the office of a giggling doctor who was wearing jeans and dropping instruments.

Roles, which involve both obligations and privileges, have far-reaching consequences for individual behavior, particularly with regard to gender. Sex roles determine not only the general behavior expected of men and women but also the skills that are considered appropriate for each. Traditionally, an American female is expected to master the skills associated with the custodial care of the family and its living quarters. To be considered a first-rate wife and mother, she must be competent at cooking, sewing, keeping house, shopping, and caring for others—particularly children. If her husband has high occupational status, social norms may also require her to entertain her husband's business associates and to contribute time to volunteer community activities. In contrast, a male is expected to develop athletic, intellectual, and mechanical abilities, some or all of which he will presumably need in his two major social roles: wage-earner and family head.

Social Stereotypes

Stereotypes are beliefs about group behavior patterns that are based largely on tradition and emotion rather than on evidence and observation. Chapter 23 discusses stereotypes in detail, especially as they are used by one group about another. But most cultures also have stereotypes that describe the roles of men and women. Inge Broverman and colleagues have reviewed studies indicating that Americans commonly believe that women are emotional, warm, sensitive beings. Women are stereotyped as tending to be submissive and dependent; their thought processes supposedly operate intuitively rather than logically. Men's thought processes, in contrast, are supposedly logical, not intuitive; men are stereotyped as dominant, independent, competent, ambitious, and aggressive people. Most of us are so accustomed to the sexual stereotypes of

Figure 21.4 This woman was photographed for a Kodak advertisement in 1933. The traditional role of a loving and nurturant woman, who is totally protected by her husband and who gains satisfaction only from the bearing and raising of his children, is one that fewer women accept today than in the 1930s.

(Photograph by Edward Steichen.)

our society that we assume them to be based on "natural" differences between the sexes. Cross-cultural comparisons indicate, however, that the qualities considered as "masculine" or "feminine" vary considerably.

Emotionality   In our society, the stereotype of women includes the tendency to cry easily and the inability to conceal emotions; American men have the "poker faces." In Iran, however, Edward T. Hall observed that the pattern is reversed:

Men are expected to show their emotions. . . . If they don't, Iranians suspect they are lacking a vital human trait and are not dependable. Iranian men read poetry; they are sensitive and have well-developed intuition and in many cases are not expected to be too logical. They are often seen embracing and holding hands. Women, on the other hand, are considered to be coldly practical. They exhibit many of the characteristics associated with men in the United States.

Iranians consider men to be superior to women, and the society is definitely patriarchal. But emotionality is considered both natural and desirable in males and is highly valued.

Sexuality   In America, it is commonly agreed that men are more aggressive sexually than women, are more easily aroused sexually, and are less able to control their sex drives. Not all cultures share these beliefs. Among several African and American Indian groups, it is believed that women are naturally more highly sexed than men. Anthropologist Margaret Mead has noted that among the Arapesh, whom she studied in New Guinea, it is equally common for men or women to initiate sexual activity. Also, according to Mead, no natural differences in sexual desire are believed to exist between the sexes.

Physical Strength   Americans stereotype women as being definitely physically weaker than men. In Africa, however, Ethel Albert found that women constituted the chief agricultural force among the people she studied. When she told her African friends that in America males do the heavy work, they were openly distressed:

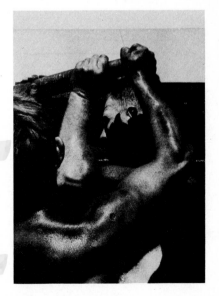

Figure 21.5   Despite the technological changes of our century, these strong, muscular arms are identified by many people as the essence of masculinity. Throughout history the strength of a man has been fundamental to his and his family's well-being, and this tradition of physical strength remains part of the definition of the masculine role.

This was a mistake, they maintained. Everybody knows that men are not suited by nature for heavy work, that women are stronger and better workers. Men drink too much and do not eat enough to keep up their strength; they are more tense and travel about too much to develop the habits or the muscles needed for sustained work on the farms.

The point of this example is not that these African men are physically different from American men or that they could not do heavy labor. Rather, they are not believed to be—nor do they believe themselves to be—as able in this endeavor as women, and they are not expected to try to compete with the sex that is considered to be "naturally" stronger.

Effects of Stereotypes   The definition of sex roles in some societies may have been based, originally, on the biological fact that women bear children. As the primary caretakers of small children, females have become associated with warmth and tenderness. Males, in the role of provider, have become linked to ambition and aggressiveness. But the complex sex-role stereotypes arising from these early definitions have considerable impact on individuals, as indicated in the research of Paul Rosenkrantz and his co-workers. These investigations showed, first, that men and women share similar beliefs—there is common consensus about the behaviors that are associated with "masculinity" and "femininity." Second, most adults see themselves as fitting the stereotype for their sex. Females usually describe themselves as being less

Figure 21.6 Dolls like Barbie and her recently created male counterpart Big Jim serve to teach and reinforce traditional sex-role stereotypes. For Barbie, there is an enormous wardrobe of stylish clothes, jewelry, equipment for hairdressing, and the like. Big Jim has athletic costumes for football and baseball, and he has sports cars. Because of Big Jim's sex-appropriate furnishings and activities, some parents might not object to their son playing with such a doll—ordinarily behavior believed to be inappropriate for boys.

aggressive and more nurturant for example, than do males. Finally, sex-role stereotypes also appear to influence the attitudes of professional mental-health workers. For instance, it was found that psychiatrists and other health-care experts usually viewed individuals who conformed to their society's sex-role stereotypes as being "mentally healthy" or "normal." Thus, individuals who do *not* exhibit those behaviors considered appropriate for their sex must bear the psychological cost of being labeled "deviant," a role that may involve strong social penalties.

ACQUISITION OF SEX ROLES

It is not surprising that one of the first of the many roles an individual acquires is a sex role, for even newborns are treated differently on the basis of gender. Few parents ever point out the long eyelashes, delicate hands, and rosebud mouth of their baby boy, or the large hands, well-muscled legs, and big mouth of their baby girl. Instead, parents and friends stress those characteristics that fit their society's idea of what males and females should be. Most children can correctly tell you whether they are a boy or a girl by the time they are two and a half years old, and most American five-year-olds have already learned that their parents differ from one another not only physically but also in behavior. How do children learn about sex roles? What makes them prefer one sex to the other? What motivates a little boy to want to grow up to be a daddy and a little girl to want to be a mommy? Three major psychological views of how sex roles may be acquired are presented here. (The same theoretical approaches are applied to the development of social and moral values in Chapter 10.) Current research provides support for each view. In reading this material, you might want to consider how the theories differ and whether they might be combined. First, however, it is necessary to examine the part biology plays in psychological differences between men and women.

Biology or Culture?

Physical differences between men and women are apparently determined primarily by biological factors. Besides the basic differences in sexual anatomy, in most parts of the world, men tend, on the average, to be taller than women, to be stronger, and to have more body hair. Women usually mature faster, are less subject to deleterious inherited traits (such as baldness, color blindness, and hemophilia), and have greater resistance to certain diseases; in societies where childbirth is not a major cause of death, women usually live longer. But how, if at all, does biology contribute to the formation of such psychological traits as dominance and aggressiveness or cooperativeness and nurturance?

At one time, there seemed to be irrefutable evidence that differences in temperament and personality were based firmly on biological facts of life. Most research conducted in laboratories as well as in natural settings had indicated that male nonhuman primates, for example, were more dominant, active, energetic, and ready to fight than were females. Studies of human societies suggest that in societies that engage in warfare, it is the men who do the actual fighting. Freud and his influential followers attributed to biological factors what they saw as woman's greater passivity and lower aggressiveness, her greater narcissism and masochism, and her weaker conscience. More recently, sociologist Lionel Tiger has proposed that biological differences decree that women are unable to establish social organization without the stabilizing influence of males.

These views are presently being challenged, primarily by women psychologists, who have proposed that the results of past investigations could benefit from reevaluation. Jane Beckman Lancaster, for example, has sharply criticized primate investigations in "In Praise of the Achieving Female Monkey."

Lancaster believes that the sexual biases of male observers have swayed the results of their observations of behavioral patterns; she points out both field and captive studies of primate behavior indicating that females provide a stabilizing organizational influence that has been overlooked by researchers.

The influence of hormones on personality and behavior is another biological factor that has traditionally been viewed as a significant determinant of sex-role behavior. For instance, during the course of the menstrual cycle, women undergo large fluctuations in the relative levels of secretion of various hormones. Investigators, including Judith Bardwick, Alec Coppen, and Neil Kessel, have found fairly consistent relationships between such hormonal changes and differences in mood, feelings of self-esteem, and sexual desire—as well as in such seemingly unrelated events as incidence of crimes and automobile accidents. This view has been challenged by Karen Paige, who has carried out studies indicating that psychological factors are heavily involved in the "menstrual blues" suffered by many women. Paige's data show that religious and cultural attitudes strongly influence females' reactions to an event many have been taught to regard as "embarrassing, unclean—and a curse."

How can the biological and cultural approaches to sex differences be reconciled? It is possible that there are some underlying biological differences in temperament between men and women. Energy level and readiness to fight may be examples of sex-linked traits. But within each sex there is very wide variation on any trait. It is important to realize that each trait covers a continuum of behaviors. An analogy with height may clarify this point. On the average, men in America are taller than women; nevertheless, there is considerable variation in height among both men and women. A woman who is six feet tall is taller than most of the men she meets. A man who is five feet tall is shorter than most of the women he meets. Psychological traits also vary widely within each sex. Although the range of activity levels among men may be higher on the average than among women, there are many exceptions to this rule. It would not be unusual to find a woman who is more energetic than most men.

Even if there are basic *predispositions* that differ, on the average, between the sexes, human beings are remarkably flexible. Cultural factors do much to

Come, you spirits
That tend on mortal thoughts! unsex me here,
And fill me from the crown to the toe top-full
Of direst cruelty; make thick my blood,
Stop up the access and passage to remorse,
That no compunctious visitings of nature
Shake my fell purpose, nor keep peace between
The effect and it! Come to my woman's breasts,
And take my milk for gall...

Figure 21.7 In one of the most powerful statements of its kind in literature, Lady Macbeth prays for the strength to perform an act of criminal aggression (assisting her husband in the murder of their king). To her, and to Shakespeare, it seems that she can do so only by denying her feminine nature.

mask certain characteristics and accentuate others. Innate predispositions do not directly determine actual behavior (see Chapter 7). How aggressive people are, for example, depends not only on their readiness to fight but also on the *consequences* of aggressive acts. In situations where physical fighting leads to dishonor or social disapproval, for example, most people will inhibit whatever predisposition to fight they may have. Society patterns our lives in many subtle ways, which we may become aware of only when we run up against different cultural patterns.

Increasing support for the preeminence of cultural factors in the determination of behavioral differences between sexes comes from cross-cultural studies. Social scientists generally assume that physiological make-up varies little from culture to culture and that differences may therefore be assumed to have resulted from social learning.

Social-Learning Theories

In all cultures, the behavior of girls and women differs from that of boys and men. Social-learning theorists such as Walter Mischel and Paul Mussen believe that children learn the behavior considered appropriate to their sex through the active teaching of parents, peers, teachers, and other social agents, as well as through imitating the behaviors of these influential persons.

From the social-learning perspective, all behavior—including that associated with sex roles—is controlled by its consequences. Actions that bring rewards tend to recur, whereas those that bring punishment tend to disappear. Imitation also plays an important part in sex-role learning. Children learn behaviors through observation, and the behavior of the parent of the same sex may assume special importance. The little girl learns that it may be considered "cute" if she puts on her mother's dress, shoes, and lipstick while at play; the little boy who dons his mother's belongings is taught (sometimes not gently) that this behavior is considered inappropriate. The child's actions are gradually molded to fit society's patterns, through the direct actions of family, friends, teachers, and other socializing agents. The learning of sex roles is viewed as an ongoing process, in which the growing child continues to add behaviors to his repertoire, generalizing the performance of previous behaviors to a broadening circle of situations.

The teaching of appropriate sex-role behaviors may be subtle. For example, the teaching that results in an individual's learning to be either dependent or independent occurs very early, and the process is difficult to detect. In general, boys are encouraged to be independent; girls, to be dependent. However, there are many individual exceptions to this rule. The investigations of Jerome Kagan and Howard Moss have indicated that many mothers discouraged dependency during their daughters' first three years of life. These girls, as adults, tended to be achievers who could function well under stress. These researchers suggest that the most influential factor involved in the daughters' personalities may have been their mothers' discouragement of dependency.

Freudian Theories

The Freudian approach and the social-learning approach differ in several important ways. First, Freud believed that psychological development is characterized by a sequence of stages (see Chapter 18), whereas social-learning theorists assume that it is gradual and continuous. He believed that the child's sex-role identity was established during a "phallic" stage that occurs between the ages of three and six. Second, although both approaches emphasize the importance of the parent who is of the same sex as the child, Freud believed that this parent is more than simply a model for the learning and imitation of sex-appropriate behavior. Imitation involves the copying of a fairly complex behavioral sequence, but Freudian **identification** involves the acquisition, *as* *a unit,* of many aspects of the parent's personality; once incorporated by the child, these aspects develop into the child's superego, or conscience.

A third difference is Freud's stress on the differences between development of the two sexes. Because of this emphasis, he was forced to postulate that the sex role develops differently in each sex. The mother is the primary love object of both infant boys and girls. Both presumably identify with her, because of her warmth and nurturance. For boys, the developmental problem is to shift identification from the mother to the father while retaining the mother (or women in general) as the love object. For girls, the problem is to shift the choice of love object to the father (or men in general) while retaining identification with the mother.

Freud believed that as the boy's love for his mother intensifies, he begins to view his father as a rival. He envies his father's possession of the mother and also imagines that if his father sensed this envy he might castrate his son in anger. Perceiving his own powerlessness, the boy gives up the fight by joining his father. He identifies with the father defensively, adopting his male parent's motives, morality, mannerisms, and perspective on the world in the hope that he can win over his mother by becoming like his father. In the Freudian view, during the phallic stage the female child begins to fear that she has been castrated and may even believe that her mother did it. Thus, she is motivated to reject her mother and transfer to her father the role of love object. Envying the male penis, the girl believes that by possessing her father she can possess or control one, or can obtain a substitute in the form of a baby. Although she continues to identify with her mother, she may also view her female parent as a competitor throughout life.

The speculations presented by Freud, which long influenced the psychological assessment of differences in male and female behavior, are no longer accepted by most developmental psychologists. Naomi Weisstein, for example, has pointed out that the theory presented in Freud's classic *The Sexual Enlightenment of Children* is based not on an accumulation of evidence but on one young boy's fears as related by his father, who was himself undergoing therapy and was a devotee of Freud. (This case, commonly referred to as the case of Little Hans, is described in Chapter 25.) Many psychologists, however, have retained the general concept of identification, suggesting that it may be motivated by nonsexual envy of the model's power and competence, by love for a warm and nurturant model, or by both.

Cognitive-Developmental Theories

An interesting and quite different theory of sex-role development, cognitive-developmental theory, has been proposed by Lawrence Kohlberg, whose approach centers on the changing cognitive world of the growing child (see Chapter 8 for a detailed description of Piaget's stages of cognitive development and Chapter 10 for Kohlberg's application of them to moral development). Kohlberg's research indicates that young children believe they could change their gender if they really wanted to. In one study, children were shown a picture of a girl and were asked whether she could be a boy if she wanted to be or if she played boys' games, had a boy's haircut, and wore boy's clothes. Most four-year-old children said that she *could* change sex. By the age of six or seven, however, most children insisted that there was no possible way for such a change to occur. Kohlberg believes that this shift in the child's conception of gender is part of a more general sequence of cognitive development. The four-year-old child might also tell you that the family cat could become a dog if its whiskers were cut off.

Young children do not see the physical world as being constant in the same way adults do. Only when they reach a more advanced stage of cognitive development—through a combination of experience and maturation—do they

Figure 21.8 The three major theories of how sex-typed identities are acquired. All such theories must account for certain accepted facts: that children form strong attachments to their parents, that children typically choose to model themselves on the parent of the same sex, and that children acquire an unambiguous sense of the sexual behavior that is appropriate for them at a fairly early age. The three theories give quite different accounts of how these facts are related and of what other factors are important in the process.

believe that gender and other physical properties remain the same despite changes in external appearances. The child comes to understand conservation of gender during the same stage in which he comes to understand conservation of liquid or the like (see Chapter 8).

For Kohlberg, sex-role development begins when the child is first labeled "boy" or "girl." After children learn which label to apply to themselves, they gradually learn to apply the proper labels to others, often on the basis of external cues, such as clothing. By the age of five or six, their beliefs about their own gender identity are firmly established, and they are then motivated to behave in ways that are consistent with these labels. They come to value things and activities that are associated with being a "boy" or a "girl." Kohlberg sees the developmental sequence as being: "I am a girl (boy), therefore I want to do girl (boy) things, therefore the opportunity to do girl (boy) things—and to gain approval for doing them—is rewarding.'' This is a reversal of the social-learning sequence, which runs: ''I want rewards, I am rewarded for doing girl (boy) things, therefore I want to be a girl (boy).'' In Kohlberg's scheme, the child is primarily motivated neither by rewards (social-learning theory) nor by sexual wishes and fears (Freudian theory). Instead, motivation comes from the desire to act in a consistent and competent manner—to do the things that are considered appropriate for one's sexual label, and to do them well.

Kohlberg recognizes that children tend to imitate the parent of the same sex. His explanation depends on neither the nurturance nor the power of the model but on the model's competence and on the child's recognition that the model is of the same sex as he or she. The young boy classes himself as male and strives to play the male role skillfully. Therefore, he finds males more appropriate than females as models. The boy is motivated to imitate a model similar to himself—that is, occupying the same sex role—who is also prestigious. The same motivation holds true for females: Girls find women more appropriate as models and try to imitate those models they perceive as being competent. Boys typically select their fathers and girls their mothers, and as a *consequence* of imitating the father or the mother, the child begins to develop a special emotional relationship with that parent.

SOCIALIZATION AND THE INDIVIDUAL

Social roles can have profound effects on an individual's personality. Although we may enter and leave some roles—such as that of airplane passenger—very casually, others are not so easily cast off. A woman who has borne three children cannot leave the role of motherhood at will. Motherhood is a key element of her personal identity, and the tasks, perspectives, and psychological characteristics associated with the performance of this role may become the dominant factor in her personality. Similarly, a man who has spent thirty years practicing law has major investments in the role of attorney. The habits of logical reasoning and careful deliberation that he first acquired at law school may become part of his personality.

We play some of our roles consciously, and we may be acutely aware of their influence on our conduct. But other roles become such a part of our personality and identity that their loss may create major psychological disturbances. The businessman who reaches retirement age and the woman whose children grow up and leave home may both suffer from the loss of important social roles, a loss that often may leave them floundering, unable to find activities to occupy their time. As a result, they may become severely depressed. In modern America, individuals may have fifteen or twenty years of life left after experiencing such incapacitating role losses, which poses social problems of major proportions.

For many Americans, being ''truly feminine'' or a ''real man'' is a major source of pride and satisfaction. Appropriate sex-role behavior is valued in our culture, and enacting one's role successfully and with flair—and receiving consequent social approval for the performance—can provide considerable pleasure. At the same time, social roles often include costs as well as benefits. Individuals may experience major psychological stress from ascribed roles such as those based on age and gender, which are not assumed by choice. It has been suggested that American sex roles orient men and women toward different aspects of social interaction. Women are expected to be *social and emotional specialists,* who concern themselves with other people's needs and the maintenance of social relationships. Men are expected to be *task specialists,* who are interested in manipulating objects and ideas to achieve some specific goal, often in an impersonal atmosphere. In the Strodtbeck, Simon, and Hawkins jury study, for example, all participants

Figure 21.9   Men and women select and are selected for different jobs because conventional sex roles describe them as being suitable for different kinds of work; these kinds of work are associated with different positions in the status hierarchy. The stereotype that describes women as nurturant and sociable but emotional and not capable of performance under stress means that jobs "for women" are those in which they attend to people and interact with them a great deal. Because men are thought of as logical, manipulative, tough, and capable of ignoring their emotions, "jobs for men" are more task oriented.

played the social role of juror, but many of the statements made by the men concerned ideas, whereas those of the women more often were either responses to male suggestions or attempts to reduce conflict.

Personality differences arising from sex roles, like other role-related personality differences such as those dictated by age or income level, are not absolute. At times, women are expected to exhibit qualities that are considered masculine, and men are expected to exhibit qualities that are considered feminine. Women, in fulfilling their ascribed roles as wives and mothers, certainly engage in task-oriented, productive behaviors, although perhaps not in competition with men. In planning meals or running a household, women are expected to be task-oriented, efficient, practical; in shopping or bargain hunting they are expected to be aggressive and competitive as well. Similarly, men's behavior toward their wives and children may show sensitivity, gentleness, and warmth.

Traditional sex-role behavior is more likely to occur in some relationships than in others. There are class and social-group differences in expectations. In addition, the depth of the relationship affects sex-role conformity: When a couple first starts dating, the female may behave in a typically feminine manner and the male may behave in a typically masculine manner. As the relationship develops, however, the behavior of both people may become less stereotyped. Sex roles, like all social roles, can change over time.

Psychological Costs of the Masculine Role

The masculine role is in many ways the more privileged, especially in middle-class social subgroups. Nonetheless, the male role carries some special burdens as well. Men must serve in the armed forces in time of war; harsher penalties for identical criminal offenses are stipulated for men; and Social Security retirement compensation is available to women at an earlier age than it is to men (despite statistics clearly indicating that women usually live longer). But the greatest costs of the role are the psychological ones associated with long-term denials of certain human traits. The roles of husband and wage-earner make stringent demands of the male. The income, life style, and social-class status of a man's wife and children derive from his occupational achievements; therefore, his dependents have vested interests in his performance. The time demands of his work role may also deprive the male of close contact with his children. The sharp emphasis on family roles for women and on work roles for men can severely limit the range of experiences for both sexes. Many men might enjoy such activities as cooking or caring for children if they could escape the restrictions imposed by their sex roles.

Being a "real man" is defined in the United States as being tough, stoical, and unemotional. Thus, Edmund Muskie's role as a presidential candidate was severely damaged when, in speaking of a political opponent's vicious attack on his wife, he burst into tears. Such an expression of emotion is taboo for an American male—it oversteps the "proper" behavior prescribed by the role of the "real man." Such boundaries—and penalties for overstepping them—hamper men's ability to express their emotions and, according to Sidney Jourard and others, may seriously affect their personalities. Men do have tender and strong emotions, Jourard argues, but are forced to deny or conceal them. The male is required to hide a part of himself, a part of his inner experience, from himself as well as from others. Jourard believes that to love another person, one must know that person well enough to be aware of the individual's psychological needs and moods; men, therefore, may be harder to love than women because they are more difficult to know. Many critics of contemporary sex roles suggest that the masculine role encourages men to treat other people as objects rather than as unique individuals. Many males who accept without question the stereotype of female behavior treat females primarily as sex objects or pretty dolls who lack the range of human interests and abilities that male persons may have. Men may also expect their female companions to accept the primacy of male interests, activities, and demands in almost all situations. Such an orientation is potentially harmful to both participants in a relationship, because it deprives them of opportunities for honest communication and the sharing of meaningful personal experiences.

Psychological Costs of the Feminine Role

All societies make conflicting demands on their members, but for modern American women, cultural contradictions regarding achievement and the feminine role have reached major proportions. Judith Bardwick, now a prominent psychologist, has described her reactions as a college student to having her name appear on a list of students who earned an A average:

> I was enraged, told the newspaper office "they had a nerve," and in general carried on outrageously—and the reason, which I was fully aware of, was my fear that now the girls would dislike me and the boys would be afraid of me. In other words, my academic success would shoot my social life down.

Traditional sex roles prescribe that, to be truly "feminine," a woman must be unassertive, dependent, and prepared to be devoted to the role of wife or

Figure 21.10 (A) It is unusual to see men expressing such joy at meeting a friend in public. Many men find it difficult to express their feelings because they have learned to conform to a stereotype that equates masculinity with emotional control. Men's comparative reluctance to express affection is one of the costs of our rigid sex-role definitions. (B) For women the costs are of the opposite kind. One rarely sees a woman taking charge in a dangerous situation. Many women find it difficult to do so because they have learned to depend on men for such resourcefulness and have thus lost the opportunity to exercise many of their strengths.

mother. For a female to excel intellectually or to make a major commitment to a professional career is to reject (or at least jeopardize) her ascribed role and—by extension—the masculinity of her male associates. At the same time, however, our culture expresses strong norms for achievement and equality for all. Regardless of the life style a particular woman chooses, she can seldom escape these mixed messages.

The research of Matina Horner provides one striking example of the psychological conflict these cultural contradictions can create. Horner's studies indicate that although men and women who are interested in achievement both experience some fear of failure, American women may also be afflicted with the additional fear of succeeding (see Chapter 16). Horner's research has attracted considerable attention from psychologists and the general public.

High Visibility Members of these groups are easily distinguished in society by such characteristics as physical appearance, dress, and manner of speech.	
Historical Roots The low status of these groups is historically old. In the past, conditions of servitude and deprivation of rights and privileges were legally sanctioned for these groups.	
Social Myths Members of these groups are held to be "content" with their status. They are stereotyped as highly emotional and possessed of some "native cunning" but lacking in the intelligence needed for higher-status responsibility.	
Deprivation of Rights and Privileges Members of these groups take undesirable, low-prestige jobs, receive lower pay for equal work, and have little access to higher-status positions.	
"Naturalness" It is considered "unnatural" for members of these groups to occupy high-status positions; when they do, they are often resented by other members of their own group.	
Kindly Paternalism The "ideal solution" of the high-status members of society has been to treat members of these groups as though they were children. They are indulged and cared for as long as they "remember who they are."	

David Tresemer has summarized results of follow-up studies indicating that men also fear success, however. He believes that the term "achievement" needs to be more clearly defined and that in addition to the "motive to avoid success" other factors may be involved in the inhibition of potential for growth and action.

Sex Roles and Social Status

Stereotyping on the basis of gender can create problems for individuals of either sex. Consider the case of the male in modern American society. He is expected, first of all, to be financially successful, and he is aware that the status of his family will in large part be measured by whether or not he achieves this goal. In competing with other males, he is expected to be aggressive. Although intellectual achievement was not stressed during his early years, when norms were set primarily by his peers, he is expected to be intelligent and productive as an adult. Stereotypes of appropriateness limit his choice of professions; a male who wants to be a fashion designer or a hairdresser, for example, must assume that he will be accused of homosexuality and that his status will thereby plunge.

The fact that sex-role stereotypes are presently changing may understandably confuse the male. In even the simplest social interaction with a female, he may no longer know what is expected of him. If he opens a door for a woman, will she smile and thank him, appear not to see him, or frown and call him a male chauvinist? Will a woman he respectfully addresses as "Mrs." coldly inform him that she is a "Ms."? Will his own wife prefer to use this term? And, perhaps most important, if women achieve the equality they talk about, will his own status be lowered?

That American women do hold second-class citizenship has been clear since sociologist Gunnar Myrdal pointed out, thirty years ago, that both blacks and women are assigned to an inferior position on the basis of an ascribed status rather than on the basis of any lack of individual merit. In 1973 Naomi Weisstein extended Myrdal's theme in her article "Woman as Nigger" by arguing that even psychological studies relating to females contain underlying assumptions, with no basis in evidence, about "the nature of women":

Psychology has nothing to say about what women are really like, what they need and what they want, for the simple reason that psychology does not know. Yet psychologists will hold forth endlessly on the true nature of woman, with dismaying enthusiasm and disquieting certitude.

Bruno Bettelheim tells us: "We must start with the realization that, as much as women want to be good scientists or engineers, they want first and foremost to be womanly companions of men and to be mothers."

Erik Erikson explains: "Much of a young woman's identity is already defined in her kind of attractiveness and in the selectivity of her search for the man (or men) by whom she wishes to be sought."

These views reflect a fairly general consensus among psychologists, and the psychologists' idea of woman's nature fits the common prejudice. But the idea is wrong. There isn't the tiniest shred of evidence that these fantasies of childish dependence and servitude have anything to do with woman's true nature, or her true potential. Our present psychology is less than worthless in contributing to a vision that could truly liberate women.

The theme of a current advertising program is "You've come a long way, baby!" And, in fact, the status of women in Western culture is improving. It is obvious, however, that in our society as well as in others females have a long way to go before they achieve social equality. Researchers have found striking examples of the cultural belief that males are somehow superior to females. In one study, Simon Dinitz, Russell Dynes, and Alfred Clark asked

Figure 21.11 (opposite) In an appendix to a study of relations between blacks and whites in the United States commissioned by the Carnegie Corporation in 1937, Swedish sociologist and economist Gunnar Myrdal pointed out that there was a parallel to the "Negro problem" in American culture. He pointed out a number of similarities between the position of blacks in a white-dominated culture and the position of women in a male-dominated culture. Other writers have extended the analysis to the position of factory workers in a capitalist society. Some of the parallels drawn are shown here. It appears that there are a number of mechanisms that operate whenever one group in a society oppresses another.

college students to state which sex they would prefer if they could have only one child. Of those polled, 91 percent of the male students and 66 percent of the female students said they would prefer a boy. Robyn Dawes recently found that couples included in a national sample of American families were much more likely to stop having additional children after the birth of a son than after the birth of a daughter. It appears that couples who do not "succeed" in having a son at first do, indeed, tend to "try, try again." The difference in status accorded to the sexes has effects in many areas of life. Here we will examine three: achievement, marriage, and employment.

Achievement ⟨Tresemer's summary of the studies that have been made since Horner's startling revelation that many women fear success indicate that men may have a similar fear.⟩Tresemer suggests that a better definition of "success" is needed, along with a clarification of "fear of success." He and his colleagues are currently investigating the possibility that the "fear" may actually be of sex-role inappropriateness or of emotional incompetence; both males and females may indeed experience anxiety about such matters.

The effects of sex-role stereotyping on the achievement of females has been well stated by Lois Hoffman:

The failure of women to fulfill their intellectual potential has been adequately documented. The explanations for this are so plentiful that one is almost tempted to ask why women achieve at all. Their social status is more contingent on whom they marry than what they achieve; their sense of femininity and others' perception of them as feminine is jeopardized by too much academic and professional success; their husband's masculinity, and hence their love relationship as well as their reciprocal sense of femininity, is threatened if they surpass him; discrimination against women in graduate school admittance and the professions puts a limit on what rewards their performance will receive; their roles as wives and mothers take time from their professional efforts and offer alternative sources of self-esteem. Perhaps most important, they have an alternative to professional success and can opt out when the going gets rough. A full-scale achievement effort involves painful periods of effort and many a man would drop out if that alternative were as readily available as it is to women.

There is evidence that the achievements of women are underrated not only by men but also by women. In a study carried out by Philip Goldberg, women college students were shown a series of professional articles on topics ranging from nutrition to city planning. Regardless of the topic, the same articles were rated as less persuasive, less well written, and of poorer quality when they were thought to be the work of women. In another study, Kay Deaux and Janet Taynor asked college men and women to evaluate applicants for a study-abroad scholarship program. Each subject in the experiment rated one of the four applicants, two males and two females. Two of the applicants—one male and one female—were presented as having outstanding qualifications, and one male and one female, only mediocre backgrounds. Students of both sexes rated the outstanding male applicant as more deserving than the equally qualified female applicant. An interesting reversal occurred in their rating of the mediocre applicants, however: The poorly qualified male was judged more harshly than the poorly qualified female. The researchers concluded that expectations for superior masculine performance work both positively and negatively, that although men find success more easily, they also receive more disparagement for their failures.

Marriage How would you feel if the excellent credit rating you had established during ten years as a single person were to be invalidated because you married? Or if, after you had handled the paying of your family's bills for ten years, you discovered on being divorced that your mate would receive the sole benefit of your efforts, while you would be left with no credit rating at all?

These are the kinds of surprises that frequently await females who change their status through marriage or divorce; the situations described are legal relics of a partriarchal Judaeo-Christian tradition that held women to be property. Attempts to eliminate such inequalities through laws have commonly been opposed in state legislatures; few people know that even the part of the Civil Rights Act of 1964 applying to sex was originally inserted as a humorous attempt to discredit the bill when it was on the House floor. Caroline Bird devotes the first chapter of her book *Born Female* to this episode in American legislative history.

In addition to differences in their legal status, husbands and wives generally perform different daily-life functions within the intimate relationship of marriage. In reviewing studies of decision making, Ira Reiss emphasizes that husbands and wives tend to make decisions about different matters. For instance, wives typically select the family's food, and husbands select the family car. In general, men tend to make the decisions that are considered more important in our society. Even in families in which both spouses work, the husband's job usually determines where the couple lives—a situation that seems ''sensible'' at present in view of the greater economic rewards that accrue to males.

Employment   If you graduate from college, marry, and apply for a responsible job, will the interviewer ask you if you intend to have children? Probably not if you are a male, for parenthood is usually considered irrelevant to male employment. It is commonly assumed that a woman's career will end when she has children, however, even though Valerie Oppenheimer's review of U.S. Census data shows that in 1970, 50 percent of American women between the ages of eighteen and sixty-four were in the labor force; of the employed women who had preschool children, a third were married and living with their husbands.

A male almost always receives a greater salary than a female who does the same work and has comparable education and experience. Some of the stridency and bitterness of the current feminist movement may be attributed to the fact that the gulf between the salaries of men and women in equivalent

Figure 21.12   The views of the Women's Liberation Movement have a history, as this statement by Nora in Henrik Ibsen's play *A Doll's House* suggests. The play was written about 1879. But the views from which she is trying to break free go back somewhat further. The counsel given at the left is from the Bible, *Colossians* 3:18–19.

489

jobs has widened during the past twenty years. In 1955 women earned about 64 percent as much as men did in the same job; in 1970 they earned only 58 percent as much. Investigations carried out by Teresa Levitan, Robert Quinn, and Graham Staines indicate that the stereotyped reasons for this inequity are invalid. Women *do* achieve as much as men in their jobs, but they continue to be paid less. Fortunately, a major effort is being made by the Federal government to ban different pay scales based on sex alone.

There are also subtle differences in occupational status. John Touhey recently asked college students to rate the prestige and desirability of such high-status occupations as physician, lawyer, and college professor. Ratings were to be based on an information sheet describing the nature of the work, training required, earnings, and working conditions. Half the subjects were told that the proportion of women in these occupations was expected to increase substantially in the future; half were told that the proportion of women would remain about the same. Both male and female subjects who believed that females were on the increase rated four out of the five occupations as significantly less prestigious and less desirable than did the subjects who were told that the percentage of women would remain about the same.

CHANGING SOCIAL BEHAVIOR

You can imagine what life would be like if we humans were unable to establish social patterns. Even simple activities, such as buying a movie ticket or a postage stamp, would be chaotic. But the patterns of socialization that make life fairly orderly and predictable are seldom rigidly fixed. Within any society, norms and roles change over time. Technology, for example, may create new situations that render former norms almost unbelievable. Today, it seems shocking that a law passed in England in 1819 set the minimum age for cotton mill workers at nine years old—and even more shocking that this law was not enforced. Although the advent of the Machine Age created new social situations, new norms were not established immediately. (In the U.S. Census of 1930, for example, one out of every twenty children between the ages of ten and fifteen was described as ''gainfully employed.'')

A dramatic change of a different kind occurred in Western society during World War II, when conscription created severe labor shortages. Most of the women who entered the labor force at first viewed their employment as being temporary, but by 1946 more than half the American working women interviewed told opinion pollsters that they would like permanent employment outside the home. When males returned from the war, seeking jobs, a crisis resulted: The men wanted their jobs back. A campaign was launched to convince women to return to their homes and resume their former positions as housewives. The idea that the only true and proper fulfillment for a woman was to care for her family was promoted by government publications, women's magazines and other media, and by psychiatrists and physicians. By the middle of the 1960s, the percentage of women entering professions began to decline, and the proportion of women to men in graduate schools fell below that of the 1930s.

In the late 1960s the women's movement, which had been largely dormant since women achieved the right to vote, re-emerged. Feminists pointed out contradictions between the stereotyped female role and the American ideals of democracy, equality of social and educational opportunities, freedom of choice, and the realization of individual potential. Psychologists began to stress the importance of questioning traditional sex-role stereotypes. Women psychologists in particular, in the words of Ravenna Helson, ''are now working away like billboard artists, revising the image of the career woman.'' In her review of current research, she stresses that the picture of the career woman as dissatisfied, maladjusted, and unhappy is invalid.

The one inarguable biological difference between the sexes—that females alone give birth to offspring—has also become less important in the lives of people today. For one thing, the dark prospect of overpopulation has led to the improvement of birth control methods and the legalization of abortion in the United States (during the first three months of pregnancy). Women need no longer become the victims of their own sexuality. The social norm that has long stipulated that the female role necessitates motherhood is being questioned today, even in magazines that are aimed at the "homemaker."

Although present-day emphasis in our society is on the changing female role, that of the male is also being revised. Increasing mechanization is altering our society's view of work, with resultant loss of status of many males. The problems of the male in his work role are summed up by a professional actor interviewed by Studs Terkel in his book *Working:* "That's what's changed in the nature of work in this country—the lack of pride in the work itself. A man's life is his work." Ideas about the appropriateness of specific occupations are changing for the male as well as for the female; for example, it is no longer startling to be answered by a male voice when you dial a telephone operator.

People who are made aware of the contradictions between social role and personal ideals may either deny the situation or support change. Even when there is a strong desire for change, however, it may not be easy to achieve. The prevailing norms usually seem justifiable to most of a society's members; at one time, it was considered fitting that children should labor long hours in factories, and the first laws prohibiting child labor were widely opposed. But change does occur, and in some instances it is sought deliberately by people who work together to revise prevailing norms.

The Israeli kibbutzim (collective settlements that farm or do small manufactures), recently studied by Martha Mednick, were organized to end the economic and social dependence of women on their husbands and to free women from the restrictions of child rearing. From birth, children are cared for in nurseries; communal dining facilities and smaller living quarters further free women from traditional housekeeping duties. To a large extent, however, the consequences of these social changes have failed to fulfill the goals of the founders. In the early days of the kibbutzim, when labor was scarce, men and women tended to perform similar jobs. But in the past twenty years women have moved increasingly into the area of education and child care, while men have come to dominate agricultural and technical jobs. In the modern kibbutz,

Figure 21.13 Susan Catania, Republican legislator in the Illinois House of Representatives, wife, and mother; and Art Fontaine, telephone company lineman in New Hampshire, auxiliary police officer, and champion knitter. Both of these people are successful at tasks once considered to be the exclusive domain of the opposite sex. Such contradictions of established sex roles were once subject to ridicule. But anyone meeting Ms. Catania and Mr. Fontaine would have no question about their sexual identities; it is certain that they themselves feel no confusion about their sexual identities.

men usually govern the community and make the political and economic decisions. Both men and women seem to be content with this traditional division of labor and status.

Why is it that a social system explicitly designed to end traditional sex roles has been relatively unsuccessful? Some have suggested that the kibbutz demonstrates that men and women are inherently suited for different activities, but biological explanations fail to take account of important aspects of the kibbutz experience. According to Mednick, the early days were times of military and economic struggle; physical labor and economic development were preeminent concerns. Women were encouraged to undertake "male" obligations and were permitted "male" privileges, but this encouragement was as much a response to the crisis as an outgrowth of an egalitarian ideology. Also, the ideology did not include the idea that male roles would have to undergo fundamental changes; the areas of child care and education were never redefined—they remained the province of women.

As time passed and the communes became more prosperous, emphasis shifted from concern for survival to increasing the birth rate and improving the creature comforts. Both activities required someone's time and effort, and it seemed "natural" for women to return to these tasks. Child bearing is the only activity now open to women that is rewarded and accorded prestige; other female tasks, such as running the kitchens, are accorded lower status and prestige than the "economically productive" activities that are essentially the province of males. In Mednick's view, the failure of the kibbutz to achieve its stated goals is explicable on the basis of social factors: It is not possible to change the role of females unless complementary changes occur in role expectations and ideals for males.

In America, people of both sexes are currently reexamining the psychological consequences of traditional sex roles and are seeking to evaluate alternative behaviors. For example, they envision a role change that would encourage males to be more emotional and sensitive to others, to be less competitive and aggressive, to be more involved in child care and housekeeping. Sandra Bem suggests that greater sex-role *androgyny* would be beneficial to all. An androgynous person is one who combines both masculine and feminine characteristics—who can, for example, be competent and assertive in one situation but sensitive and nurturant in another. Rather than adhering to rigid sex roles, an androgynous person is flexible in behavior, fitting his or her actions to each situation.

Social psychologists cannot tell you what stand to take on these contemporary issues. That you must decide for yourself. But the foregoing analysis does suggest that to the extent that sex roles create problems, these problems affect both men and women.

Figure 21.14 This portrait exemplifies the concept of androgyny that Sandra Bem believes should be the direction of sex-role change. Both men and women can be strong or gentle when the situation demands it.

SUMMARY

1. **Socialization** is the process whereby individuals learn what behavior is appropriate in their culture. The most important agents of socialization in the young child's life are his parents; later, peers, teachers, and communications media become important agents.

   a. **Social norms** are the behavioral standards of a society to which its members learn to conform. Some norms are codified into law (for example, nudity on beaches in most areas is illegal). Other norms are very subtle; they constitute an unwritten consensus about "right" behavior. Many of a society's contemporary norms are so strong that the members believe the behaviors they dictate are instinctive; for example, the covering of the genital area and women's breasts has seemed until recently to be a result of "natural modesty."

b. A person's **social status** is his position relative to others within his society or a given group in that society. One person's status may vary widely according to the groups he or she is part of. A college student, for example, who is student-body president may have high status on the campus relative to other students but a much lower status, based on age and administrative experience, in his dealings with the faculty and deans. Status may be **ascribed,** that is, attributed on the basis of some inherited characteristic—gender is an example—or it may be **achieved**—such as being elected Senator. In any case, status strongly affects social interactions.

c. **Social roles** are a cluster of social norms applicable to people of a specified social category. There are roles connected with age, sex, occupation, class, race, and so on. Sex roles, for example, describe characteristics and behavior appropriate to females and males; it is on the basis of these role descriptions that a person's "femininity" or "masculinity" is judged.

d. Social **stereotypes** are beliefs about a group's behavior based largely on tradition and emotion rather than on evidence and observation. Stereotypes can be identified by comparing them across cultures. For example, one stereotype that is part of the role description for American men is that they are less emotional than women; in Iran the stereotype is just the opposite. In either society, a man who does not conform to this stereotype in public is considered deviant, and most probably he suffers embarrassment and exclusion from certain social interactions.

2. **Sex roles** begin to be acquired very early. Girl babies are treated differently from boy babies. Because this difference in treatment begins so early, it is difficult to discover exactly what psychological differences between men and women are the result of the biological differences between them. Although there are studies relating differences in mood to hormone level as well as studies showing differences in level of aggression in male and female primates, there is as yet no unambiguous evidence about the universal "nature of men" or "nature of women" arising from their physiological make-up. There are, however, several theories that attempt to account for sex-role differences, some depending more than others on assumed physiological differences.

a. **Social-learning theories** say that boys and girls learn behavior appropriate to their sex through both active and subtle teaching by agents of socialization and through imitation of models. Behavior in line with the norms for male or female behavior is rewarded; behavior that runs contrary to the norms is punished.

b. **Freudian theories** assume biologically based temperamental differences between the sexes and different mechanisms in the development of the male role and the female role. Freud believes that the mother is the primary love object for both infant boys and girls; the boy then begins to view his father as a rival but, perceiving the father's power

Figure 21.15 Margaret Mead, whose observations on male and female sexuality in different cultures are referred to in this chapter, is a world-famous anthropologist. Recently she was voted president of the American Association for the Advancement of Science. Her classic studies, *Coming of Age in Samoa* and *Growing up in New Guinea*, are included in her book *Sex and Temperament in Three Primitive Societies*, which is listed in the Suggested Readings for this chapter. One of her contributions to anthropology is the concept of *cultural relativity*, the idea that behavior and experience must be evaluated within their cultural context rather than by any absolute standard of goodness, normality, or health.

Figure 21.16 Walter Mischel is one of the major proponents of a social-learning view of sex-role acquisition. Mischel was trained as a clinical psychologist, but he has become a severe critic of the assumptions traditionally made about personality. His research has shown that what people say about themselves on pencil-and-paper tests has relatively little relation to what they actually do in different situations. He has also found that people do not behave as consistently from one situation to another as clinical psychologists have believed. In Mischel's view, the tendency of men and women to behave in "masculine" or "feminine" ways could change markedly and suddenly if the rewards and punishments maintaining such behavior were rearranged.

Figure 21.17 Jerome Kagan is a developmental psychologist whose research has shown that differences between child-rearing practices for boys and girls are related to sex differences in conformity and dependence for those same children later, in adolescence. In addition to his studies of personality development, Kagan has contributed interesting work on cognition. He has, for example, shown that children, like adult scientists, are appreciative of "elegance" in the concepts they form to explain their experiences.

and fearing a rival's revenge (castration), in defense he identifies with the father. **Identification** involves incorporation, as a unit, of many aspects of the model's personality. The girl, although continuing to identify with the mother, suffers penis envy, and therefore is motivated to reject her mother and transfer to her father the role of love object.

c. **Cognitive-developmental theories** see sex-role identification tied to the sequence of cognitive development. Children come to recognize their gender as unchangeable at about the same time they come to understand conservation of liquid. After they have firmly established their gender identity, they strive to do the things that are considered appropriate to that identity in order to be cognitively consistent and competent.

3. **Social roles** profoundly affect personality; although some roles may be consciously played for short periods—hostess at social functions or presiding officer at lodge meetings—other roles, such as sex roles, become intrinsic parts of a person's personality. When these roles are so rigidly defined that they exclude the experience or expression of certain important aspects of life, there may be psychological costs to the individual.

a. The American definition of the **masculine role** includes the necessity of being an economic achiever and of remaining stoical and unemotional. Many men who determinedly follow these prescriptions are, because of the demands of their work, estranged from their children and, because of constantly hiding their emotions, estranged from their own inner experience.

b. The American definition of the **feminine role** includes the necessity of being dependent and unassertive and prescribes the roles of wife and mother as "normal." However, the general cultural norms express the need for achievement. Women therefore receive mixed messages. The result seems to be that women experience not only a fear of failure but also a fear of success, the attainment of which would be "unfeminine."

Figure 21.18 Eleanor Maccoby, a developmental and social psychologist, participated with Robert Sears and Harry Levin in a 1957 study of child-rearing practices that has become a standard reference in the field of the development of sex differences. The researchers interviewed 379 mothers of kindergarten children in this study; the mothers did not feel that their boy and girl children differed in aggressiveness, but they did think that their girls had more highly developed consciences than their boys. Maccoby has theorized that children internalize their parents' values, not simply by imitating their parents' behavior, but by playing roles that *complement* the parents' roles. To do so, they must have acquired an internalized image of their parents' behavior.

4. There is a difference in status accorded men and women, as evidenced by a recent study in which college students were asked which sex they would prefer if they could have only one child: 91 percent of the men and 66 percent of the women said they would prefer a boy. The higher status of males has effects in many areas of life.

a. The status difference affects people's judgments of **achievement.** The stereotype that men are better achievers than women, for example, caused both men and women subjects to rate identical articles on a variety of subjects as better if the subjects had been told they were written by men.

b. The status difference affects the partners in a **marriage** both through laws and in more intimate relations. For example, women's credit ratings are, in many states, erased after a divorce, even if the woman had been the main wage earner in the family.

c. The status difference strongly affects **employment practices.** Women are often paid lower salaries than men for identical work. And even the status of occupations is affected by whether they are predominantly male (more prestigious) or predominantly female (less prestigious).

5. Social behavior, social norms, social roles, and social status are all open to change. Currently, the definition of sex roles, particularly the female role, seems to be undergoing a dramatic change. One reason may be that the prospect of overpopulation has made the role of mother less important. However, evidence from studies of Israeli kibbutzim seem to show that lasting changes in the female role are not possible without complementary changes in the expectations and norms for men.

SUGGESTED READINGS

Bem, Sandra L., and Daryl J. Bem. "We're all Nonconscious Sexists," *Psychology Today,* 4 (November 1970), 22+. Two psychologists suggest that all Americans make sexist assumptions—often unwittingly—and they provide an interesting "test" for hidden sexist thinking.

Epstein, Cynthia F. *Woman's Place: Options and Limits in Professional Careers.* Berkeley: University of California Press, 1971. A sociologist's excellent, detailed analysis of how the structure of professional occupations and current patterns of sex roles provide obstacles to successful careers for women.

Farber, Seymour M., and Roger H. Wilson (eds.). *The Potential of Woman.* New York: McGraw-Hill, 1963. An assortment of twenty brief articles, the best of which include discussions of primate behavior (Jay), biological determinants of masculinity and femininity (Money), sex differences in intellect (Maccoby), and cross-cultural variations (Albert).

Horner, Matina S. "Fail: Bright Women," *Psychology Today,* 3 (November 1969), 36+. Horner presents her theory and data on fear of success in women.

Komarovsky, Mirra. *Blue-Collar Marriage.* New York: Random House, 1962. Behavior is patterned not only by gender but by other factors as well, such as social class. This book describes sex-role patterns among working-class white Americans.

Liebow, Elliot. *Tally's Corner: A Study of Negro Streetcorner Men.* Boston: Little, Brown, 1967. This sensitive description of the life style of a group of lower-class black men shows how being poor and black affects the patterning of relations between men and women.

Maccoby, Eleanor E. (ed.). *The Development of Sex Differences.* Stanford, Calif.: Stanford University Press, 1966. This valuable collection provides major review articles on topics including cross-cultural variations in sex roles, sex differences in intellectual functioning, and social-learning and cognitive-developmental theories of sex-role development. It also has an extensive annotated bibliography and a classified summary of research on sex differences.

Mead, Margaret. *Sex and Temperament in Three Primitive Societies.* New York: Mentor Books, 1950. Mead presents her observations of major differences in sex-role patterns among three societies. The book provides both a contrast to American sex roles and a strong case for the importance of culture in determining sex differences.

Pleck, Joseph, and Jack Sawyer. *Men and Masculinity.* Englewood Cliffs, N.J.: Prentice-Hall Spectrum Books, 1974, in press. An excellent collection of articles including men's personal accounts of negative aspects of the male role, discussions of men's liberation, and analyses by psychologists.

Tavris, Carol (ed.). *The Female Experience.* Del Mar. Calif.: Psychology Today Publications, 1973. A varied collection of highly readable articles by psychologists about aspects of the female role.

In 1840 the Democratic party, which had been in power for twelve years, was running President Martin Van Buren for reelection. The opposition Whig party, given little chance to win, nominated General William Henry Harrison, who had made his reputation fighting Indians. A Baltimore newspaper, of Democratic persuasion, printed a comment to the effect that all Harrison needed was a small pension and a jug of hard cider and he would be content to sit in a log cabin the rest of his days and do nothing. The implication was that he was an empty person, serving as a front for ambitious politicians.

Some genius of public relations seized upon this statement, and there began the most remarkable presidential campaign in American history. Harrison became the log-cabin-and-hard-cider candidate. There were log-cabin badges, log-cabin songs, log-cabin floats, log-cabin rallies, and hard cider everywhere, some poured out of containers shaped like log cabins.

The campaign included a studied attempt to picture Van Buren as a cultured aristocrat. One famous campaign song began:

Let Van from his coolers of silver
    drink wine,

  And lounge on his cushioned settee;

Our man on his buckeye bench
    can recline,

  Content with hard cider is he.

The fact of the matter, of course, was that Harrison was born not in a log cabin (as the electorate came to believe) but on a Virginia plantation. He was thoroughly educated and came from a more aristocratic background than Van Buren. What's more, his party,

the Whigs, was the party of the upper classes. Nevertheless, the American people—many more of whom were at the log-cabin stage than at the cushioned-settee stage—deliriously identified themselves with Harrison, and he won the election.

The 1840 campaign fundamentally changed political strategy in American elections. Until then, it had been assumed that to impress the people, you ought to present a nominee as a person of education, ability, experience, refinement, and all the other qualities that men were supposed to admire. After that, however, every candidate tried to show himself as fundamentally illiterate at heart.

In 1940, exactly a century later, when Wendell Willkie ran for president on the Republican ticket, his campaign managers played down the fact that he was an educated lawyer and the son of a lawyer, as well as a most successful businessman. They strove instead to emphasize the fact that he was born in a small midwestern town, in contrast to President Roosevelt's undeniable background of aristocracy. The Democratic Secretary of the Interior, Harold Ickes, demolished that strategy in a caustic and well-publicized phrase that termed Willkie "the barefoot boy from Wall Street."

The strategy, which continues today, is aimed at having just-plain-folks identify with the candidate, identification being a process through which attitude change takes place. A citizen who identifies with your candidate is a voter you want to see go to the polls.

Isaac Asimov

22
Attitude Change and Social Influence

Figure 22.1 Former President Richard M. Nixon and newsmen in a press conference that took place in October, 1973. For presidents—and for all others in public office—the newspapers, magazines, and television and radio stations that these reporters represent are the media, or channels through which holders of public office can try to change attitudes and wield social influence. Most holders of high office now employ communications experts, who advise them on the best mix of audience, message, and channel (say, newspaper versus television). And most of these experts make use of the social-psychological findings reported in this chapter.

I magine that you are managing the campaign of a Congressional candidate. Your task is to convince as many people as you can that your candidate is the best person running and so deserves their vote. You might advise the candidate to emphasize her willingness to benefit the district economically—say, by bringing in new industry. If your candidate is attractive, you could advise her to avoid controversial issues and depend on her personality to attract votes. If she has held other political offices, you might have her stress her experience and expertise.

You might decide that different approaches should be taken for different segments of the electorate. You could advise the candidate to talk to a meeting of black PTA members about community control of schools. You and your candidate are using tactics of social influence, attempting to affect voters' attitudes toward the candidate and, you hope, to move them to cast their votes for her. Social influence need not refer to persuasion on such a grand scale, however. Whenever one person tries to convince another that he should like—or dislike—a particular book (attitude change) or that he should go—or not go—to a certain dance (behavior change), social influence is at work. The types of social influence discussed in this chapter include attitude change and persuasion, obedience, and conformity; the relation between attitudes and actions is also discussed.

ATTITUDES AND THEIR CHANGE
Social psychologists use the term **attitude** to refer to a person's predisposition to regard certain objects or issues in a certain way. People have attitudes about concrete objects—from organic foods to skyscrapers—and about abstract entities—from beauty to fascism. Every attitude has two interrelated components. The *cognitive* component comprises the person's beliefs about the object (for example, "Organic food is healthy"), and the *affective* (or emotional)

component comprises the person's feelings toward the object ("I love organic food"). In addition, attitudes commonly affect the person's predisposition to behave in certain ways in regard to the object (seeking out organic-food stores).

In many cases changes in attitude and changes in behavior go hand in hand. For example, if you had been a resident in the district of the Congressional candidate discussed earlier and you had decided you liked her, you most likely would have gone to the polls and voted for her. However, a change in behavior need not reflect a change in attitude, and a change in attitude need not lead to a behavioral change. For example, a person may be influenced to donate blood to a blood bank, but this change in behavior may not be accompanied by any change in underlying beliefs or attitudes. On the other hand, people are sometimes influenced to change their minds about social issues, yet they do not markedly alter their behavior. For example, many people who became convinced that American participation in the Vietnam war had been a mistake did not join peace marches or distribute antiwar literature.

PROCESSES OF ATTITUDE CHANGE

Herbert Kelman has elaborated on the distinction between behavior change and attitude change in his categorization of the three processes by which change takes place. Kelman distinguishes between compliance, which sometimes masquerades as attitude change but in fact reflects only temporary behavior change, and identification and internalization, processes by which more enduring attitude change takes place.

Compliance

In some situations a person is induced to make statements indicating that he has changed his beliefs when, in fact, his attitudes have not budged; in this case, he is displaying compliance. In many group situations, for example, a person will express agreement with others, but once he is removed from the group situation and is questioned privately, he will restate his original attitudes. His compliance to the immediate demands usually results from a wish to avoid rejection by the group or to gain its approval. His statements agreeing with the group therefore constitute a change in behavior but not a change in attitude.

Identification

The process of identification is central to human development. Chapter 10 details how children identify with persons important to them and so learn behaviors and attitudes. As discussed in Chapter 18, Freud says that sex roles are acquired through the child's identification with the parent; boys try to be as much like their fathers as they can, and girls model their behavior on that of their mothers. The identification process is also discussed in Chapter 23, as it relates to reference groups (reference groups constitute any group with which an individual identifies—often such broad categories as racial, religious, and occupational groups). The chapter notes that people acquire a sense of personal definition from their membership in such groups. Identification in both these instances includes the adoption of attitudes; the child adopts those of the parent, and the member adopts those of the group.

Kelman defines identification as the process that occurs when a person wants to define himself in terms of his relationship to some other person or group and consequently ascribes to himself characteristics or attitudes of that person or group. Identification differs from compliance in that the individual actually believes his adopted views. But because attitudes adopted through identification are based on the person's emotional attachment to another person or group, rather than on the person's own assessment of the issues, such

Figure 22.2 Kelman's three processes of attitude change. The object of the attitudes represented is marijuana smoking. (top) The man, who is assumed to hold an initially negative attitude toward marijuana smoking, is complying with group pressure to smoke. His compliance is not true attitude change; he will not smoke marijuana when he is not in the group. (middle) He is identifying with the young woman, with whom he is emotionally involved. In this case he believes that he likes to smoke marijuana, because he likes the young woman and wants to continue the relationship. If their relationship ends, he will not continue to smoke ,unless he has internalized a positive attitude toward marijuana. (bottom) He has done so. This positive attitude is now congruent with his other beliefs. His marijuana smoking is independent of the presence of the group and of emotional attachment to the woman.

(After Kelman, 1961.)

attitudes are not always well integrated with the person's other attitudes and values. If the emotional attachment to the group or the other person loses its importance, the attitudes are also likely to fade.

Internalization

Through internalization, on the other hand, a person incorporates an attitude because it is congruent with his system of values. His emotional attachment to the influencing person or group is not nearly so important as is his belief that the influencing person or group is knowledgeable and trustworthy. If, for example, you decided to vote for a candidate because you were convinced her policies were most likely to lead to world peace, your attitude toward her would be based on internalization. Internalization is usually the most durable of the three processes. Attitudes acquired through internalization persist not only in the absence of the influencing agent but even when one's relationship to him becomes irrelevant.

Actual cases of social influence cannot always be clearly categorized as having occurred by means of one or an other of the processes. Often what occurs seems to embody some combination of the three types. For example, a person may express agreement with a friend's evaluation of a movie in part because he knows his friend would like to hear that opinion (compliance), in part because he admires his friend and would like to be similar to him (identification), and in part because he really is convinced by his friend's analysis (internalization). Nevertheless, in most situations one or another of the three processes seems to be the most important means of social influence.

PERSUASION

Advertising, salesmanship, political campaigning and lobbying, and newspaper editorials are all examples of persuasion—that is, direct attempts to change people's attitudes. Many discussions between parents and children, roommates, and boyfriends and girlfriends also contain arguments meant to change the other's attitudes. Persuaders often hope, of course, that attitude change will lead to changes in behavior. An advertisement tries to convince a consumer of the superiority of a cigarette so that he will buy it; a father tries to convince his son of the evils of smoking so that he will cease buying cigarettes. Persuasion, its form and effects, is one of the most thoroughly studied kinds of social influence.

Components of the Communication Process

Research on persuasion has focused on four major components of the communication process:

1. **The source:** the speaker or writer of the communication and his characteristics.
2. **The message:** the content, style, and organization of the communication.
3. **The channel:** the situation or medium through which the communication is presented.
4. **The audience:** the person or persons to whom the communication is addressed.

The Source Many studies have shown that the extent to which a person's attitudes are changed by a persuasive communication depends as much on *who* delivers the message as on what he says. As suggested earlier, people tend to be most persuaded by a communicator who they believe is both knowledgeable and trustworthy. A classic study, conducted more than twenty years ago by Carl Hovland and Walter Weiss, found that of people who were

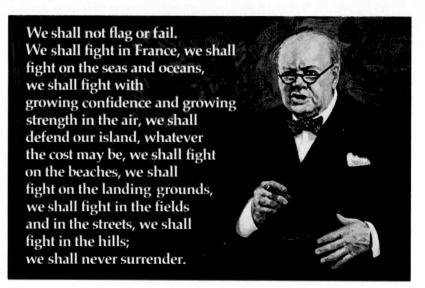

We shall not flag or fail.
We shall fight in France, we shall
fight on the seas and oceans,
we shall fight with
growing confidence and growing
strength in the air, we shall
defend our island, whatever
the cost may be, we shall fight
on the beaches, we shall
fight on the landing grounds,
we shall fight in the fields
and in the streets, we shall
fight in the hills;
we shall never surrender.

Figure 22.3 Winston Churchill, in a speech to the British House of Commons in 1940. Churchill was able to rouse in the British people a courageous and determined attitude toward the war that probably no other communicator could have roused. His long record as a soldier (in India, South Africa, and in the First World War) and as a political leader made him a source whose knowledge and trustworthiness were beyond question by the time he was needed to lead the fight against Hitler.

given a statement about the practicability of atomic submarines, many more were convinced of its truth when the source was said to be the noted physicist J. Robert Oppenheimer than when it was said to be from the Russian newspaper *Pravda*. Similarly, more subjects were convinced by a communication about antihistamine drugs when they thought it had appeared in the reputable *New England Journal of Medicine* than were convinced when they thought it had come from an article in a mass-circulation pictorial magazine.

Few people or sources are considered to be knowledgeable and trustworthy in all areas. Thus, a physician is likely to be more influential than an economist if both are making statements about health practices, but the economist is likely to be more influential in the area of monetary policy. In some cases, however, the stock we put in a statement by a prestigious communicator seems to generalize to areas outside his proper area of competence. As noted in Chapter 21, for example, studies by Fred Strodtbeck, Rita James, and Charles Hawkins have suggested that people with high-status occupations are more influential on juries than are people whose jobs have lower status.

The degree to which any persuader is influential depends not only on whether his audience thinks he knows the truth (knowledgeability) but also on whether they think he will give it to them straight (trustworthiness). If they think someone is trying too hard to influence them, they may decide that he has some ulterior motive for making his appeal and therefore cannot be fully believed. Because voters know that a political campaign is specifically aimed at persuading them of the candidate's merits, they are likely to look to another person or organization to verify the candidate's qualifications.

An interesting manifestation of the importance of trustworthiness is the tendency for people to be more persuaded by a message if they overhear it than if it is addressed directly to them (as found, for example, in an experiment by Elaine Walster and Leon Festinger). When people overhear a communication, they are less likely to call the communicator's motives into question.

A third factor that can affect the persuasiveness of a human source is simply how much his listeners like him. While a persuader's knowledgeability and trustworthiness contribute to the likelihood that people will *internalize* a particular attitude, his attractiveness is central to the *identification* process. Football players are probably not especially knowledgeable about the relative merits of deodorants or hair tonics. Moreover, when a football star endorses a particular brand of deodorant or hair tonic on television, everyone knows that he is doing so for an ulterior motive—he is handsomely paid for giving the endorsement. Such testimonials can nevertheless be quite effective in persuading fans who identify with the star to use the product. In terms of Kelman's analysis of identification, those of us who would like to define ourselves as being similar to the star are likely to be influenced by his pitch.

An attractive source, then, has an edge in persuasiveness; a highly unattractive source, it turns out, may actually produce a boomerang effect—the listener may respond by adopting attitudes opposite to those the source advocates. Robert Abelson and James Miller found, for example, that listeners tended to change their attitudes *away* from the point of view espoused by an obnoxious and insulting interviewer. The listener presumably wants to make sure that he is in no way identified with the unattractive source, so he tries to become as different from it as he can.

The Message   The persuasiveness of a message can be greatly affected by the precise way in which it is composed and organized. Research has focused on such factors as the order in which arguments are presented; the extent to which the message presents only one side or both sides of the issue; and the degree to which the message deviates from the audience's existing attitudes.

Still another important factor is the extent to which the message seems to reduce the audience's freedom to draw its own conclusions. Although a message must often be fairly explicit to be effective, the communicator must be careful to avoid oversell. If he implies that the audience has no choice but to adopt the views he advocates, he may produce resistance rather than acceptance. This danger was illustrated in a recent experiment by Stephen Worchel and Jack Brehm. Subjects were asked to read statements about the way the United States government should treat the Communist party. Both groups of subjects read identical statements of fact, but one group's message was liberally sprinkled with such high-pressure statements as "you cannot believe otherwise" and "you have no choice but to believe this." The subjects who read only the facts moved toward adopting the views advocated, but the attitudes of those whose messages contained the coercive elements were as likely to move in the opposite direction. People evidently do not like to be

Figure 22.4   Should the content of a message be an emotional appeal, or is a cool presentation of the facts more persuasive? Studies by Arthur Cohen have suggested that an effective communication combines both elements, preferably with the factual argument *following* the emotional appeal. This advertisement is intended to persuade other advertisers to use the magazine *Medical World News* as their medium, but the reasons they should do so are not mentioned until they have been shocked into attention by the picture and its headline.
(After Cohen, 1955.)

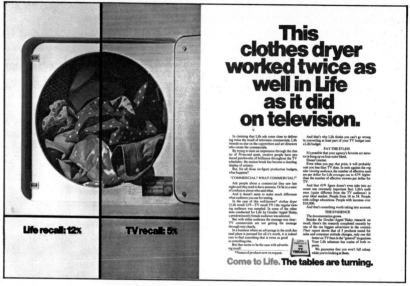

Figure 22.5 *Life* magazine folded not long after this advertisement was run, and the claim made here now has a rather pathetic sound. Like the one in Figure 22.4, this message was aimed at advertisers. *Life* was attempting to persuade advertisers that the magazine was a better communication channel than television. (The attempt failed; advertisers—the major source of income for many magazines and for commercial television—preferred television as their channel.)

bullied. Brehm has developed a more general theory of *psychological reactance* that predicts the circumstances under which people will react adversely to perceived attempts to limit their freedom of thought and action.

The Channel   The effectiveness of a persuasive communication may depend on whether it is spoken or written, seen or heard, read in a newspaper or in a magazine. Advertising agencies spend a great deal of money and employ specialists to advise them about which messages are best used in which medium. Social psychologists concerned with attitude change have so far done little research on the relative effectiveness of different channels.

Some research has been done, however, on the effect of physical distance between the speaker and his audience. Stuart Albert and James Dabbs Jr. found that the message produced most attitude change when the speaker's distance from his audience was great (fourteen to fifteen feet) and least when the distance was small (one to two feet). The researchers speculated that the subjects regarded the extreme closeness of the speaker as an imposition on their privacy and therefore became resistant to his message. In a manual published in 1970 for volunteers who planned to canvass for peace, two social psychologists, Robert Abelson and Philip Zimbardo, advised door-to-door canvassers to maintain an informal conversational distance of four to five feet from the person receiving them. Future studies in this area will probably find that there is no optimal distance. Rather, it is likely that the best space across which to deliver a message with impact depends on the nature of the message and on the relationship between the speaker and his audience.

The Audience   Some people seem to be generally easier to persuade than others. For example, there is some evidence (reviewed by David Marlowe and Kenneth Gergen) that people with a strong need for social approval are more susceptible to social influence than are people with a weaker need. In discussions of persuasibility, it should be kept in mind that susceptibility to persuasion is not necessarily a human weakness; the ability to be persuaded may also be considered to be a mark of flexibility. The words that people use in this connection reflect their personal value orientations: One person's "gullibility" may be another person's "open-mindedness." It is clear that for society to run smoothly and, in fact, for it to be capable of change, people must be able to influence and to be influenced by one another.

In addition to general differences in persuasibility, a given person may be more likely to be susceptible to influence about some issues than about others. Until recently it had frequently been assumed, for example, that women tend to be more persuasible than men, perhaps reflecting the greater dependence imposed by women's early sex-role learning. As Elliot Aronson has suggested, however, the conclusion that women are generally more persuasible than men may well be mistaken. The early studies that pointed to greater female persuasibility made use of predominantly ''male-oriented'' issues, such as political and economic affairs. Because women, at least until recently, have tended to be less attuned to such issues than men, it is not surprising that they would be more easily persuaded with regard to them. It seems likely that the results would be reversed, however, if ''female-oriented'' issues, such as home management or family relations, were employed instead. Recent research by Frank Sistrunk and John McDavid has provided support for this hypothesis. They found no general tendency for men or women to be more open to influence. Rather, men were easier to influence about ''female-oriented'' issues, and women about ''male-oriented'' issues. (Needless to say, which issues are ''male oriented'' and which are ''female oriented'' is likely to vary over time and in different cultures.)

Sometimes deep psychological needs and motives can affect a person's readiness to be persuaded. Ernest Dichter, a motivational researcher who has engineered a large number of commercial advertising campaigns, once lent his talents to a Red Cross drive for blood donations. He postulated that many men were reluctant to give blood because it aroused unconscious anxieties associated with the giving away of their strength and virility. He recommended, therefore, that the campaign focus on masculinity, implying that each man in the audience had so much virility that he could afford to give away a little. Dichter also suggested making each man feel personally proud of any suffering. One of the strategies he recommended was to give the donor a pin in the shape of a drop of blood—the equivalent of a wounded soldier's Purple Heart. These tactics did, in fact, produce a sharp increase in blood donations by men.

Another tactic that can increase the persuasive impact of a message is audience participation in its presentation. Irving Janis and Bert King found

Figure 22.6 The differences between these advertisements reflect the Army's sensitivity to changes in the audience to whom its message is directed. Individuals who voluntarily joined the Army in World War II were usually motivated by a sense of duty. At that time a recruiting poster had only to convey to an individual the idea that he was being urgently summoned by his country. In today's audience, an automatic sense of duty is less common; the Army must compete with other employers in offering security and material benefits.

that people are more likely to be persuaded by a communication if they read it out loud than if it is read to them by someone else. Such *role-playing* procedures maximize the likelihood that the person will actively rehearse the persuasive arguments and, in effect, persuade himself. Janis and Leon Mann have effectively used role-playing techniques to persuade people to stop smoking. They had smokers play the role of a patient who was informed by his doctor that he had lung cancer. Janis and Mann found that this procedure produced dramatic and long-lasting decreases in smoking. Other smokers who listened to tape recordings of such doctor-patient dialogues but did not actively take part in them did not show such dramatic decreases in smoking.

Resistance to Persuasion

Most psychological research on persuasion has been concerned with the relative effectiveness of techniques to *produce* attitude change; its viewpoint has been that of the persuader. Some research—a lesser amount—has also focused on techniques that might allow a person to *resist* attitude change.

Recent research by William McGuire has suggested that a person can be given an **inoculation** against persuasion, in much the same way that he is inoculated against certain diseases. In medical inoculation a person is purposefully given a weakened form of a disease-causing agent, which stimulates his body to manufacture defenses; if a more virulent form of the disease should attack him, these defenses make him immune to infection. The principle underlying inoculation against persuasion is analogous. Many beliefs people hold are cultural truisms, which have never been challenged. Examples of such cultural truisms employed in McGuire's research include the beliefs that annual physical examinations are a good thing and that frequent toothbrushing is important for dental health. Most people are so unused to having such beliefs challenged that if a strong opposing argument were, in fact, made, it might overwhelm them.

For the inoculation, McGuire exposed subjects first to the challenging argument and then to a statement that refuted the arguments and reinforced the person's initial belief (say, in favor of annual physical examinations). A week later the subjects read another communication that challenged their initial belief. McGuire found that subjects who had received the inoculation were much less persuaded by the challenge than were subjects who had not been inoculated. The inoculation was effective in stimulating their psychological defenses against the challenge and in making the initial attitude more resistant to change.

This technique might be used by parents before their children leave home if the parents want to make sure that the children retain the attitudes and values acquired at home. The parents would do well to inform the children in advance of the opposing views they are likely to encounter. Such exposure beforehand should reduce the chances that the children will be persuaded by opposing views when they encounter them.

OBEDIENCE

"When you think of the long and gloomy history of man," the famous British writer C. P. Snow has written, "you will find more hideous crimes have been committed in the name of obedience than have been committed in the name of rebellion." Snow's statement points to the tremendous power of that form of social influence that involves people's compliance to the commands of an authority. Such compliance commonly goes by the name of **obedience.** To document his claim, Snow suggested that one read William Shirer's *Rise and Fall of the Third Reich.* "The German Officer Corps were brought up in the most rigorous code of obedience. . . ." Snow asserts. ". . . in the name of obedience they were party to, and assisted in, the most wicked large-scale actions in the history of the world.'' Obedience does not always, or even usually, have destructive results. Obedience to the authority of parents, teachers, or government leaders often teaches lessons of kindness and leads to acts of charity. Nevertheless, most of the research on obedience has concerned itself with obedience to antisocial commands. This research may help us to understand how such phenomena as atrocities committed during war, whether in Nazi Germany or at My Lai, could have come to pass.

The most dramatic and extensive investigation of obedience was conducted by social psychologist Stanley Milgram in the early 1960s. Milgram's subjects were men from a wide range of ages and occupations; they were paid to take part in what they thought was a study of the effects of punishment on learning. Two subjects appeared for each session, but only one of them was a real subject. The other was the experimenter's accomplice. In each case the accomplice was assigned the role of the learner in the mock learning experiment, and the subject was assigned the role of the teacher. The subject was instructed that, as teacher, he was to read a list of word pairs to the learner, whose task was to memorize each of the word pairs. The learner was then moved into an adjacent room, out of the teacher's sight for the duration of the experiment. Each time the learner made a mistake, the teacher was to punish him by administering a shock from an impressive-looking shock generator. The generator had thirty clearly marked voltage levels, with switches ranging from 15 to 450 volts and with labels ranging from ''Slight Shock'' to ''Danger: Severe Shock.'' After each of the learner's mistakes, the teacher was to increase the voltage one level and administer the shock. In reality no shocks were being delivered, but the subjects had no way of knowing this.

As the session progressed, the supposed learner made many errors, and the shocks became increasingly severe. When the shock level reached 300 volts, the learner pounded on the wall in protest and then fell silent. At this point the experimenter instructed the subject to treat the absence of an answer as a wrong answer and to continue the procedure. If at any point the subject indicated that he would like to stop, the experimenter told him sternly to go on:

> Experimenter: Whether the learner likes it or not, we must go on, through all the word pairs.
>
> Subject: I refuse to take the responsibility. He's in there hollering!
>
> Experimenter: It's absolutely essential that you continue, Teacher.

How do you think most subjects would behave in this experiment? If you are like the students, psychologists, and others of whom Milgram asked this question, you will guess that most subjects refused to continue the procedure at some point quite early in the experiment. Most of the people Milgram asked believed that no more than a handful of subjects would go all the way through to the end of the shock series. The results Milgram obtained, however, did not match this expectation. Of forty subjects in the condition described, twenty-six (or 65 percent) continued to obey the experimenter to the very end. These subjects were not sadists. Many of them showed signs of extreme tension during the session, and they often told the experimenter that they would like to stop. But in spite of these feelings, they continued to obey the experimenter's commands. (Several experiments following Milgram's, including one recently conducted in West Germany by David Mantell, have replicated the high percentage of subjects who continued to obey.)

Legitimate Authority

What accounts for this surprisingly high level of obedience? A central part of the answer lies in the definition of the experimenter as a legitimate authority. Everyone learns that in certain situations he must do as he is told by the person

Figure 22.7 Stills from a motion picture of Milgram's experiment. (A) The ''shock generator.'' (B) The subject sees the confederate supposedly being connected to the apparatus. (C) The experimenter explains the procedure to the subject. (D) This subject refuses to shock the student any longer and rises angrily in protest. (E) After, the subject is introduced to the unharmed confederate.

who is properly in charge of that situation. Whether it is a policeman's order to pull to the side of the road or a doctor's request to undress, people are usually ready (even if not always enthusiastically willing) to do as they are told. If the doctor told someone to pull over or the policeman told him to undress, he might not be so willing to comply. In the setting of the psychological experiment, the legitimate authority is clearly the experimenter. He has set up the situation, and it takes place in his territory (the laboratory). Moreover, he is a scientist—a sort of modern-day priest whom many of us endow with almost supernatural power and knowledge. We assume that such an authority knows what he is doing, even when his instructions seem to run counter to our standards of moral behavior.

Conceptions of legitimate authority help to explain why so many Americans were outraged by the trial and conviction of Lt. William Calley in 1971. Calley had been held responsible for the killing of a large number of Vietnamese civilians at My Lai, even though his actions were apparently in accord with a policy dictated by his superior officers. In a Gallup telephone poll taken just after his conviction, 79 percent of a national sample of Americans voiced their disapproval of Calley's conviction. A subsequent survey conducted by Herbert Kelman and Lee Lawrence found that a central factor underlying the public outcry was the belief that a person should not be blamed for following the orders of his superiors. "Given this view of the situation," Kelman and Lawrence noted, "Calley's conviction represents a betrayal by the authorities. . . . It is as if a subject in the Milgram experiment were brought to trial for administering harmful shocks to another subject, and the chief of the laboratory came to testify against him."

Milgram's subjects were paid before the experiment began and were told that the money was theirs simply for coming to the laboratory. They could have walked out at any time without losing the money and without fear of reprisal. Nevertheless, the assumption that legitimate authority is to be obeyed seems to be so strongly ingrained that people often lack the words or the ways to do otherwise. Consider the response of one of the subjects when he was asked at the close of the experiment why he did not simply stop shocking the learner (these words are transcribed from a videotape):

He (the experimenter) wouldn't let me. I wanted to stop. I kept insisting to stop, but he said, "No" . . . I figured the voltage we were giving him was quite a bit. I wanted to stop but he kept insisting not to stop . . . I was getting ready to walk out . . . I couldn't see the point of going on when the guy is suffering in there. I figured he was having a heart attack or something. That's the reason I wanted to stop.

Even though this subject "wanted to stop" and "was getting ready to walk out," he found himself unable to do so without the experimenter's permission. Simply getting up and leaving would have violated powerful unwritten rules of acceptable social behavior.

Proximity and Touch

These unwritten rules seem to be enforced to a large extent by the experimenter's physical presence. It is of interest to note that obedience dropped sharply in an experimental variation in which the experimenter did not remain in the same room with the subject. In this condition the experimenter gave his initial instructions and then left the laboratory and gave his subsequent orders by telephone. Whereas 65 percent of the subjects obeyed to the end when the experimenter was sitting just a few feet away from them, only a third as many (22 percent) obeyed throughout when he was not physically present. It is apparently easier for people to challenge the power of an authority when they do not have to engage in a face-to-face confrontation with him. Milgram also found that increasing the closeness of the subject to the victim

"I will not give in because I oppose it—I do— not my pride, not my spleen, nor any other of my appetites but I do— I!"

Figure 22.8 Sir Thomas More defied the British Parliament's Act of Supremacy, which had given control of the Church of England to Henry VIII. His disobedience, expressed in this impassioned statement, cost him his life. (These lines are from Robert Bolt's play about More, *A Man for All Seasons.*) Obedience to rules, laws, and commands are crucially important to the welfare of a social order; widespread disobedience to them may overturn a social order, as in the American Revolution of 1776, the French Revolution of 1789, or the Russian Revolution of 1917.

increased the likelihood that the subject would defy the experimenter. Milgram called the first experimental condition, which was described earlier, the *remote* condition; the subject did not see or hear the victim while he was being shocked, except for the pounding on the wall after 300 volts. In a second condition *(voice feedback)* the victim was again in another room, but the subject could hear him grunt, groan, and scream as the shocks were increased. In the third condition *(proximity)* the victim was placed in the same room as the subject, one and a half feet from him. In the fourth condition *(touch proximity)* the subject not only sat close to the victim but was also required to force the victim's hand onto the shock plate in order to administer the punishment. As Figure 22.9 indicates, the maximum shock that subjects administered decreased steadily as contact with the victim (whether auditory, visual, or physical) increased. When the subject was out of contact with the victim, it was apparently easier for him to deny the pain he was inflicting— much as a bombardier may be able to keep his mind off the destruction he causes. As the subject was brought into closer contact with the victim, however, such denial became less possible, and the victim's suffering exerted greater weight in the struggle between the individual's conscience and the authority's demands.

The Liberating Effect of Group Pressure

Although there was much less obedience both when the experimenter was out of the room and when the subject had to move the victim's hand, still, in both these conditions, a substantial number of subjects obeyed the experimenter to the end. Obedience was virtually eliminated, however, in another experimental condition: Here the subjects were provided with social support for defiance. In this condition two other subjects (actually the experimenter's confederates) joined the real subject to form what he was told would be a team of teachers. After the shock level had reached 150 volts, one of the confederate-teachers announced that he would not continue and took a seat in another part of the room. After 210 volts the second teacher also refused to go any

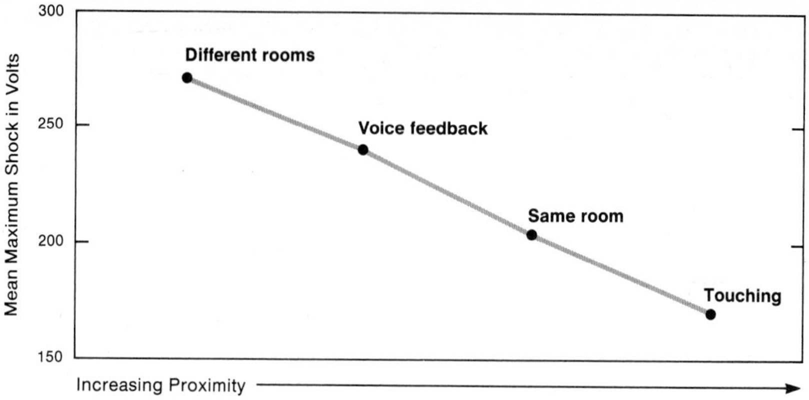

Figure 22.9   This graph of the results of some of Milgram's studies on obedience shows that the closer the subject was to the victim, the less the amount of shock he was willing to administer, despite the experimenter's demands that he continue. With increased proximity, there was a decrease in compliance.
(After Milgram, 1974.)

[Graph: y-axis "Mean Maximum Shock in Volts" (150–300), x-axis "Increasing Proximity →", points labeled "Different rooms", "Voice feedback", "Same room", "Touching"]

further. In all cases the experimenter continued to order the subjects to carry on with the procedure, but only 10 percent of them did so. All the rest refused to continue either at the same time one of the confederate-teachers did or shortly thereafter. These others were able to demonstrate to the subject that defiance of the experimenter was thinkable and, in fact, proper.

CONFORMITY

Conformity refers to a person's tendency to change his attitudes or behavior so as to bring him closer to the attitudes or behavior of his peers. When a person espouses particular political attitudes because they are fashionable, or when he adopts a particular mode of dress because it is in vogue, he is conforming to group norms. Although the word "conformity" often has a negative connotation, it should be emphasized that adopting group standards or conventions is often quite constructive. The final condition of Milgram's series described above demonstrates that conformity to group pressure can have positive effects. By going along with the group, the subject was able to liberate himself from the power of destructive authority. Analogous phenomena take place in real-life cases of civil disobedience and protest. People who are unable to defy authorities single-handed may be able to do so if they are supported by others. Also, the existence of common standards to which people conform makes it possible for us to predict each other's behavior with some accuracy and to approach others without fear of misunderstanding. Imagine how confusing social interaction would be if half of us used the word "yes" to mean no or if a smile could as easily express pain as pleasure.

Some instances of conformity, however, have little to recommend them, such as cases in which a person renounces a belief he knows to be correct so as not to be out of step with the majority. Solomon Asch focused on such conformity in a classic series of experiments conducted some twenty years ago. Asch conceived of an ingenious, if rather devious, way of studying conformity in the psychological laboratory.

Asch's Experiment

The following is what you would experience if you were a subject in one of Asch's experiments. You and seven other students report to a classroom for an experiment on visual judgment. The experimenter says that you will be asked to judge the length of lines on a series of comparisons. He displays two large white cards like the ones shown in Figure 22.10. On one card is a single vertical line—the standard whose length is to be matched. On the other are three vertical lines of different lengths, and you are to choose the one that is the same length as the standard. One of the three actually is the same length; the other two are substantially different. The experiment opens uneventfully. The subjects announce their answers in the order in which they are seated in

Figure 22.10   The stimuli in a single trial in Asch's experiment. The subject must state which of the comparison lines he judges to be the same length as the standard. The discrimination is an easy one to make: Control subjects (those who made the judgments without any group pressure) chose line 2 as correct over 99 percent of the time.

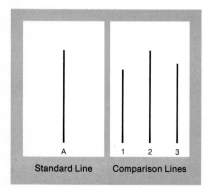

Standard Line   Comparison Lines

the room; you happen to be seventh, and one person follows you. On the first comparison every person chooses the same matching line. The second set of cards is displayed, and once again the group is unanimous. The discriminations seem very easy, and you settle in for what you expect will be a rather boring experiment.

On the third trial there is an unexpected disturbance. You are quite certain that Line 3 is the one that matches the standard, but the first person in the group announces confidently that Line 1 is the correct match. The second person follows suit and declares that the answer is Line 1. So do the third, fourth, fifth, and sixth subjects. Now it is your turn. What you thought was going to be an uncomplicated task has turned into a disturbing problem. You are faced with two contradictory pieces of information: The evidence of your own senses tells you that one answer is clearly correct, while the unanimous and confident judgments of the six preceding subjects tell you that another answer is correct. What do you do? Do you stick to your initial judgment, or do you go along with the others? The dilemma with which you are faced persists through eighteen trials. On twelve of the trials the other group members unanimously give an answer that differs from what you clearly perceive to be correct. It is only at the end of the experimental session that you learn the explanation for the dilemma: The seven other subjects were all confederates of the experimenter, who had instructed them to respond the way they did.

How do most people react in this situation? Asch put fifty subjects through this procedure and found that almost a third of them conformed at least half of the time. What accounts for this high degree of conformity, and what factors can explain why some people conform and others do not? Asch carefully observed the subjects' behavior during the course of the experiment and conducted intensive interviews with them afterward to probe the psychological mechanisms underlying the behavior of both the "independents" and the "yielders." Some of the independent subjects stuck to their guns, announcing their judgments loudly and spontaneously. Others were more withdrawn or tense but still resisted the pressure to conform to the group judgment. Among the yielders, very few reported that they actually had *perceived* the others'

Figure 22.11 Photographs of a subject who remained independent throughout Asch's classic conformity experiment. (reading from left to right and from top to bottom) The experimenter explains the task; the only real subject, Number 6, listens attentively; on the third trial he finds his judgment in conflict with those of the others; and he leans forward to concentrate on the next set of lines; his discomfort increases as the judgments of the others continue to contradict what he sees; by disagreeing for a twelfth time, he becomes one of the few subjects who managed to withstand the pressure on every trial.

Independent

After a few trials he appeared puzzled, hesitant. He announced all disagreeing answers in the form of "Three sir; two, sir." At Trial 4 he answered immediately after the first member of the group, shook his head, blinked, and whispered to his neighbor, "Can't help it, that's one." His later answers came in a whispered voice, accompanied by a deprecating smile. At one point he grinned embarrassedly and whispered explosively to his neighbor: "I always disagree—darn it!" Immediately after the experiment the majority engaged this subject in a brief discussion. When they pressed him to say whether the entire group was wrong and he alone right, he turned upon them defiantly, exclaiming: "You're *probably* right, but you *may* be wrong!" During the experimenter's later questioning, this subject's constant refrain was: "I called them as I saw them, sir."

Yielder

This subject went along with the majority in eleven out of twelve trials. He appeared nervous and somewhat confused, but he did not attempt to evade discussion at the close of the experiment. He opened the discussion with the statement: "If I'd been first I probably would have responded differently." This was his way of saying that he had adopted the majority estimates. The primary factor in his case was loss of confidence. He preceived the majority as a decided group, acting without hesitation: "If they had been doubtful I probably would have changed, but they answered with such confidence." When the real purpose of the experiment was explained, the subject volunteered: "I suspected about the middle—but tried to push it out of my mind." It is of interest that his suspicion did not restore his confidence or diminish the power of the majority.

Figure 22.12 Asch's descriptions of one "independent" and one "yielder."

(After Asch, 1965.)

choice as correct. Most yielders said that they had believed their own perception to be correct but that they had yielded to the group pressure so as not to appear different from or inferior to the others. These subjects felt that if they had not followed the group's lead, they would have been revealing some basic weakness in themselves, which they preferred to hide. Asch's illustrative descriptions on one independent subject and one yielder appear as Figure 22.12. Other studies (reviewed by David Marlowe and Kenneth Gergen) have found that people with low self-esteem (that is, a generalized lack of self-confidence) are more likely to yield to group pressure than are people with high self-esteem. It is apparently the person who has confidence in his own abilities and basic worth who can afford to be less concerned with the opinions and approval of others.

One of the most interesting findings Asch obtained in the course of several variations of this basic experiment is that the *size* of the group is not nearly so important as its *unanimity*. Just as much conformity was found when there were three or four confederates as when there were seven, nine, or even fifteen. But when just one of the confederates was instructed to give the right answers rather than to go along with the group, the amount of conformity declined dramatically from 32 percent to 5 percent.

Roots of Conformity

Taking Asch's demonstration as a starting point, later investigators have provided further insights into the powerful effects of group pressure on individual opinions. Morton Deutsch and Harold Gerard set out to determine how much of the conformity in the Asch experiment resulted from the desire to retain the approval of the other group members and how much resulted from subjects' actually being convinced that the group must be right. They devised a situation in which subjects were once again confronted by the unanimous disagreement of the other group members but in which the group members were separated by partitions that prevented them from seeing or hearing one another. Group members signaled their judgments on line lengths by pressing one of three buttons on a panel in front of them. The subjects learned of each other's judgments by means of lights on the panel, and they were led to assume that the judgments were made anonymously. Deutsch and Gerard found that under these conditions there was significantly less conformity than in a situation that differed only in permitting the subjects to see each other.

This finding clearly implied that at least some of the conformity found in Asch's situation occurred through what Kelman calls compliance rather than through the processes of identification or internalization. That is, in the face-to-face setting the subject was influenced to change his behavior to avoid being criticized or seeming inferior to the others. However, the fact that a substantial degree of conformity was found even when a subject was assured of anonymity implies that compliance is not a sufficient explanation of these phenomena. It seems that a subject's real opinions as well as his overt behavior may be altered by group pressure, either because he is motivated to define himself as a member of the group (identification) or because he accepts the unanimous group view as reliable evidence that he is wrong and they are right (internalization).

DOING IS BELIEVING

It is clear that people's attitudes often affect their actions. A person who approves of a particular candidate will be likely to vote for him. And, although it is not so obvious, *actions may lead to congruent attitudes*. For example, the act of moving into a racially integrated neighborhood may lead a person to form more positive attitudes about another racial group (Chapter 23 describes a study, by Morton Deutsch and Mary Collins, in which this attitude change occurred). His action, which brings him into closer contact with members of another racial group, may cause the person to reexamine his negative attitudes toward the group and to decide that they are really prejudices.

Changes in attitudes may also occur as a result of making statements that are contrary to one's real views. There are many situations in which people are induced to make such *counterattitudinal* statements. We considered some such situations earlier, in the context of the effects of role-playing procedures. Arthur Cohen provides additional examples of such situations in his book *Attitude Change and Social Influence:*

An American prisoner of war in Korea who longs for a smoke agrees to read a prepared indictment of American foreign policy before a group of fellow prisoners, on the promise of a cigarette . . . .

A reform Democrat in New York who despises bossism endorses the platform of a Tammany leader who seeks re-election, in the hope that the party's support will be thrown to him for his own campaign in the next election . . . .

An American dissident on a trip to Europe vociferously defends American values and the American way of life before a group of scornful left-wing café intellectuals.

All these people, for one reason or another, are saying something contrary to their private attitudes. It may happen, however, that their attitudes subsequently shift in the direction of the statement they made. The prisoner of war decides that American foreign policy may in fact be imperialistic; the reform candidate concludes that the bosses aren't so bad after all; and the American in Europe begins to think that the American way of life really has some good things to offer.

Why do attitudes tend to change as a result of such counterattitudinal statements or actions? One good explanation is provided by Leon Festinger's theory of **cognitive dissonance.** To illustrate his theory, imagine that you were somewhat opposed to the legalization of marijuana but were nevertheless induced by a friend to sign a petition supporting its legalization. You would now have two thoughts (cognitions) that seem to be inconsistent (dissonant). The first cognition is "I oppose legalizing marijuana," and the second is "I have just signed a petition calling for its legalization."

Festinger suggests that such an experience of dissonance is psychologically uncomfortable. You would be motivated, therefore, to reduce the dissonance. One way to do this is to change one of the cognitions. Because it would be difficult to make yourself believe that you had not really signed the petition, a likely occurrence would be a change in your attitude. You might well conclude that you really do favor the legalization of marijuana. This process of dissonance reduction does not always take place consciously. Whether consciously or not, however, there is a good deal of evidence to suggest that such dissonance-reducing changes in attitude take place frequently.

A second way to reduce dissonance in this situation is to add additional cognitions that provide a justification or rationale for your action. If, for example, you had signed the petition because your friend offered to pay you ten dollars for doing so, you would no longer regard yourself as having acted so inconsistently. The offer of money would have provided a justification for your behavior and consequently would have reduced the total amount of dissonance you experienced. This additional justification makes it less likely for you to change your attitude as a result of your action. If your friend had threatened that he would never speak to you again if you did not sign, that would also serve as an adequate justification for your action and would keep the amount of dissonance you experienced to a minimum.

This reasoning leads to the prediction that *the less justification a person has to perform a counterattitudinal action, the more attitude change will re-*

Figure 22.13 Attitudes are frequently modified in order to resolve contradictions. This motivation for attitude change is called cognitive dissonance. In this figure Mary has expressed two attitudes that are now brought into conflict by Bill's behavior: She cannot "love that man" and "hate those clothes" without experiencing the discomfort of dissonance. A resolution can be accomplished in a number of ways. Mary can start wondering if she really loves Bill after all, or she can broaden her tastes, or she can make such mental rearrangements as "Good taste isn't really what I'm looking for in a man anyway." Another resolution is suggested in the text by the theory that if one acts against an attitude one holds, that attitude may very possibly change. If Mary were to buy for Bill as a birthday present an outfit similar to the one she disliked, the act of buying the clothes might change her attitude toward them.

sult from the action. An experiment conducted by Festinger and J. Merrill Carlsmith provided a neat demonstration of this principle. Each subject was paid either one dollar or twenty dollars to tell another person that a very boring experiment in which they had both participated had really been fun. Afterward the subject's own attitude toward the experiment was assessed. The experimenters found that those who were paid twenty dollars to make the counterattitudinal statement continued to believe that the experiment had been boring, but those who were paid only one dollar came to believe that it had been fairly enjoyable. The subjects paid only a dollar had less reason to make the statement and therefore experienced more dissonance when they did so.

Daryl Bem has suggested another explanation of how actions work to change attitudes. He says that people in situations like the Festinger and Carlsmith experiment examine their own actions and, in effect, ask themselves, "Why did I make that foolish statement?" When the incentive for making the statement is large, the answer is clear: "It was because I got twenty dollars for doing it." When the incentive is small, however, such an answer is not really sufficient. Instead the subject is likely to reason, "It must be because I really *did* enjoy the experiment." Bem's analysis, which he calls self-perception theory, concludes that *people often make inferences about their own attitudes by observing their own behavior.* Whereas most people agree that the question, "Why do you eat brown bread?" can properly be answered with, "Because I like it," Bem goes on to suggest that the question "Why do you like brown bread?" frequently ought to be answered with, "Because I eat it." There are limits to the applicability of Bem's theory; much of the time people know what their attitudes are without needing to observe their behavior. Nevertheless, there are many instances in which Bem's analysis provides valuable insights into the ways attitudes are formed and changed.

One application of Bem's theory is the "foot-in-the-door technique." This is the principle, well known to door-to-door salesmen, that it is easier to get someone to do you a substantial favor (like buying your product) if you have already induced that person to do a smaller one (like listening to your sales pitch). To help document the principle, Jonathan Freedman and Scott Fraser found that housewives who first consented to put a small safe-driving sign in their window (practically all of them agreed to perform this small favor) were much more likely to agree to a subsequent request that they place a large "Drive carefully" sign on their front lawn. As a result of their acceding to the first request, Freedman and Fraser suggested, the subjects may have begun to perceive and define themselves as "doers": "[The subject] may become, in his own eyes, the kind of person who does this sort of thing, who agrees to requests made by strangers, who takes action on things he believes in, who cooperates with good causes." The foot-in-the-door phenomenon is another illustration of how a person's actions may affect his attitudes.

THE ETHICS OF SOCIAL INFLUENCE

Social psychologists—as well as advertisers and political propagandists—have devoted a great deal of time and effort to investigating techniques that can facilitate social influence. One can regard this social-scientific research as having great value when its findings are used in the service of what one considers good causes, such as persuading people to contribute to worthwhile charities or reducing their religious and racial prejudices. But there is no guarantee that techniques of social influence will be used for noble purposes. The same techniques that are used by health authorities to convince people to stop smoking may also be used by cigarette companies and their advertising agencies to convince them to take up or continue smoking. It is also often true that one person's good cause is another person's evil.

One may ask a basic question about the ethical propriety of *any* attempt to change the attitudes or behaviors of other people: What right can any person be said to have to manipulate the hearts and minds of others?

These are most difficult questions, and they are not ones that social psychologists have ready answers for. Nevertheless, they are questions that both researchers and users of social influence should continually bear in mind in evaluating both the means and the ends of social-influence attempts.

There is another set of ethical questions that may have occurred to you as you read this chapter. In most of the studies that were surveyed, experimenters intentionally deceived subjects about the nature of the research in which they were taking part. Asch told his subjects that he was studying perceptual judgment rather than conformity, and he employed confederates to pose as fellow subjects. Milgram told his subjects that he was studying the effects of punishment on learning, and he led them to believe that they were causing considerable pain to a fellow human being. Investigators conducting studies of persuasion also carefully withhold from their subjects full information about the nature of their research.

Although in almost all cases researchers make a point of explaining the real purposes of their studies to subjects, they rarely do so until the experiment is over. It is clear that it would have been impossible to conduct many of the studies described without this sort of deception. If Asch had told his subjects in advance that the people they thought were other subjects were really confederates, for example, the social-pressure situation that he set up would have lacked psychological reality, and the results would probably have had little bearing on the nature of conformity.

Nevertheless, one may well ask whether experimenters have a right to deceive people in this way. Is research on social-influence processes so important that it outweighs the value of honesty in interpersonal transactions, including the transactions between experimenters and subject? Once again, there are no easy answers except to emphasize that experimenters must weigh the potential benefits and costs very carefully before embarking on any research that involves deception. In recent years social psychologists have become increasingly aware of the need for such deliberation, and they are trying to conduct their research in ways that do not require deception.

SUMMARY

1. An **attitude** is defined as a person's predisposition to regard specific people or objects in a certain way. Every attitude has two parts: the *cognitive* component (''Swimming is good exercise'') and the *affective* component (''I like to swim''). Attitudes also commonly affect behavior (going to the beach).

2. Herbert Kelman has identified three distinct processes through which attitude change can take place. Although all three processes may occur in a particular case of social influence, most often one process is more important than the other two.

   a. **Compliance** usually occurs in a group situation; one member, whose attitude was initially different from that of other members, is influenced to express an attitude that conforms to the group's in order to

Figure 22.14 Solomon Asch's major contribution to psychology is his brilliant series of experiments on conformity. He has also made an analysis of how people integrate information as they form impressions of other people, a subject discussed in Chapter 20.

gain approval. Actually, that member rarely comes to believe the attitude he expressed as a result of group pressure; his change is therefore a behavioral change rather than an attitude change.

b. When a person has an emotional attachment to a group or person so strong that he wishes to somehow define himself in terms of his relationship to that group or person, he will often adopt the attitudes and characteristics of those others. In this case, the process of **identification** takes place. Although the person does believe the attitudes he has adopted through identification, he may discard them if the initial emotional attachment fades.

c. When a person adopts an attitude held by a source he considers knowledgeable and trustworthy, and when that attitude fits his own set of values, the process of **internalization** has taken place. Attitudes adopted through internalization are long lasting.

3. **Persuasion** is the direct attempt to change someone's attitudes and thereby his behavior. The ability to persuade depends on characteristics of the **four components of the communication process.**

a. The **source,** whether a person or printed matter, must be considered knowledgeable and trustworthy. Also, an attractive communicator tends to be more persuasive.

b. The persuasiveness of the **message** depends on the order in which it presents arguments, the congruence of the arguments with the audience's existing attitudes, and how much the message coerces the audience, among other things.

c. The **channel** of communication can determine a communication's effectiveness; some messages are better accepted in person, some through printed matter, for example. Also, each channel has specific traits that can be important, such as distance between speaker and audience in a personal communication.

d. The **audience** for a communication can be more or less open to influence depending on such factors as the personalities of audience members and audience participation.

e. William McGuire has found that an **inoculation** against persuasion, in the form of arguments challenging a belief, can make a person's initial attitude more resistant to change.

4. Compliance to the commands of an authority is called **obedience.** Three important factors influencing the extent to which people obey are (a) whether they view the authority as legitimate; (b) whether the authority is on the scene; (c) whether there is social support for disobedience.

5. **Conformity** occurs when a person adopts an attitude that accords with the norms of a peer group. Conformity is damaging when a person renounces a belief he knows to be correct just to be in step with a group. Researchers have found that people with low self-esteem are more likely to yield to group pressure.

6. Although it is evident that a change in attitude often leads to changed behavior, performing certain acts that run contrary to existing beliefs may cause a change in those beliefs, especially if there is no strong justification for having performed the act.

a. Leon Festinger's theory of **cognitive dissonance** explains such changes. It postulates that the mind is uncomfortable holding two

Figure 22.15 Stanley Milgram's experiments on obedience are some of the most powerful and controversial to have been performed by social psychologists, in part because of their strong social implications and in part because of the necessity to deceive the subjects. Milgram has recently become interested in the behavior of people in cities. He observes, for example, that commuters tend to treat each other as "familiar strangers," people whom one knows but never meets. He also notes the importance of cognitive maps to city dwellers; people of different classes have different maps of their cities, he says.

different cognitions about the same thing: "I disapprove of pornography"; "I have just read a pornographic book." Because you will have trouble convincing yourself that you did not read the book, you are likely to change your attitude: "Certain pornographic works are acceptable."

b. Another explanation for changes in attitude that result from behavior is that of Daryl Bem's **self-perception theory,** which says that people often infer that they must hold certain attitudes because they perceive themselves acting in certain ways: "I often listen to jazz, therefore I must like jazz."

SUGGESTED READINGS

Bem, Daryl L. *Beliefs, Attitudes, and Human Affairs.* Belmont, Calif.: Brooks/Cole, 1970. An excellent and highly readable short text on attitudes and their social implications, including a good treatment of Bem's own self-perception theory.

Gergen, Kenneth J., and David Marlowe (eds.). *Personality and Social Behavior.* Reading, Mass.: Addison-Wesley, 1970. Of relevance both to this chapter and to Chapter 23. A useful overview of theory and research linking individual personality to such social processes as influence and attraction, plus a good collection of research reports on these topics.

Kiesler, Charles A., Barry E. Collins, and Norman Miller. *Attitude Change: A Critical Analysis of Theoretical Approaches.* New York: Wiley, 1969. A useful and well-written review and critique of current theories of attitude change.

Milgram, Stanley. *Obedience to Authority.* New York: Harper & Row, 1974. A well-written and complete account of Milgram's ingenious and controversial experiments on obedience.

Rubin, Zick (ed.). *Doing Unto Others: Joining, Molding, Conforming, Helping, Loving.* Englewood Cliffs, N.J.: Prentice-Hall Spectrum Books, 1974, in press. A collection of highly readable papers on social influence and other themes of social behaviors.

Zimbardo, Philip, and Ebbe Ebbesen. *Influencing Attitudes and Changing Behavior.* Reading, Mass.: Addison-Wesley, 1969. Theory and research on social influence are applied to such varied contexts as psychological warfare, police confessions, and salesmanship.

I suppose we can all think of examples in which we participated in the formation of groups under unusual circumstances. Back in the middle 1940s, I spent some time in the army as a private. I hated it. I was not badly treated; I did not see combat; I was never in danger of any kind; but I just hated it. I hated the things we were required to do, the conditions under which we were required to live, the people with whom I was forced to associate.

Then the time came when we had to travel from Virginia to Hawaii. It was a ten-day trip by train and ship. Only a relatively small number of soldiers were going, and most were eighteen-year-olds with limited background and education. Seven of us, including myself, were older men with college degrees. We seven clung together. There was nowhere to go and no one with whom to interact except ourselves. There was nothing much to do, but we played bridge, talked, reminisced, told jokes. I never played bridge very much before that trip or since. I never even liked it very much; but it seemed the most remarkable and fascinating game in the world for those ten days. I couldn't have enough. And those six other guys—the nicest, sweetest, best guys in the world. We loved each other. We were like brothers. Everything was so warm and comfortable that I was actually *happy*. In fact, I don't know offhand when in my whole life I was so continuously happy over so long a stretch of time. And in the army!

Occasionally, I remember, we would discuss the possibility of trying out for officer-training school. As officers, life would be easier, but we would undoubtedly have to stay in the army longer. We all thought we would remain privates and push for discharge.

Of the seven of us, I was far and away the most vehement in supporting the private-and-discharge alternative.

Then one time the other six came to me, all together, and told me they had decided to opt for officer training. The advantages were simply too attractive. Wouldn't I join them? I was astonished. How could they be so foolish? So weak? I refused. I tried to dissuade them. They put the pressure on, argued, pleaded, listed the advantages. To the end I resisted and finally in black despair I cried out, "Go ahead, leave me. Desert me. To hell with all of you."

Then they broke down laughing and explained it was a put-up job. They just wanted to see if I could resist group pressure, and there were bets on as to whether I would or not. I tried to laugh, too, and boasted that I was immovable in my convictions. But I wasn't. I have never forgotten the despair of those moments and how near I came to agreeing to be an officer rather than have them leave me.

Eventually, we reached Hawaii and separated. It may have seemed to me on that wonderful trip that we were soul mates who would remain together forever, but the fact is that since I left the army—so long ago—I have never been in contact with one of them.

Isaac Asimov

23

Individuals and Their Groups

Figure 23.1 A parade, especially a small-town one, is an excellent illustration of group behavior. Task groups have to plan it. The marchers often represent social groups, such as a fraternal organization, or reference groups, such as a school. Although social psychologists are interested in how people work together in groups, their primary interest is in studying how group membership affects the behavior of individuals.

Consider a day in the life of an American male whom we will call Ralph Miller. Ralph gets out of bed at seven, has breakfast with his family, kisses his wife and two children, and then heads off to work. At the bus stop he smiles at the regulars, whom he recognizes but does not know by name. When he arrives at his office building, he rides up in the crowded elevator, joins Bernie, Frank, and Nancy for a quick cup of coffee, and then hurries to the board room for the morning conference. The conference group is trying to come up with a new advertising slogan for a mouthwash account, and Ralph contributes a couple of ideas that the group kicks around and ultimately adds to its list of possibilities.

When he arrives home that evening after a full day, Ralph settles back in his easy chair and looks over the day's mail. It includes a notice about a lecture at his professional association, a request for money from a community organization that serves needy people of Ralph's particular ethnic background, and a letter from Ralph's father describing an Independence Day celebration and American Legion parade in Ralph's hometown.

Although Ralph's experiences are unique, they have one characteristic that is common to almost everyone's experiences: For better or worse, we spend an extremely large portion of our waking hours as members of groups. Individuals pool their resources in collective activities of various sorts; in addition, groups exert a tremendous influence on the attitudes and behavior of an individual, even when he or she is alone. This chapter will explore, from the vantage point of the social psychologist, some of the processes that take place in groups, some of the ways groups affect their members as individuals, and some aspects of relations between one group and another.

DEFINING THE GROUP

Groups vary widely in size, intimacy, and formality, but all of them, from the

Figure 23.2   A rally of the United Farm Workers Union in Salinas, California, 1970. These men are part of a group whose members are interdependent. Each member's behavior affects other members. This group has power to achieve its goals only through the cooperation of all its members in decisions about when and where to work. If some members choose to act independently of the group, the bargaining power of the other members is greatly weakened.

nuclear family to the large corporation, involve some relative degree of **interdependence** between two or more people. That is, group members are affected or influenced by one another in significant ways. Interdependence generally comes about through direct communication or a feeling of group belonging (or both).

Group members affect one another's attitudes and behavior by means of their communications to one another. The communications may be quite explicit, like Ralph's suggestions at his morning business conference, or they may be more implicit, making use of subtle facial, postural, and gestural signals. One of the key ways group members influence one another is by sending messages that indicate which particular attitudes and behaviors will be approved of by the rest of the group. By adding his advertising slogans to its list of possibilities, the morning conference group suggested to Ralph that his thinking was along approved lines.

Even when there is no direct interaction among group members, a person's **feeling that he belongs** to a particular group creates interdependence by making it likely that he will respond differently to people he perceives as members of the group than he will to nonmembers and that he will behave in ways that he sees as relevant to the group's goals. People's identifications with particular religious groups, professional groups, and so on have considerable influence on their political and social attitudes as well as on their overt behavior. (The effect of these groups—called reference groups—on attitudes is discussed at length later in this chapter.)

Not all collections of people constitute groups. Ralph and the other people in the crowded elevator can hardly be considered a group, because there is little or no interdependence among them. They neither communicate significantly with one another nor have a feeling of belonging to an elevator "gang." In an emergency, however, a nongroup of people can quickly be converted into an actual group. During the Northeast power failure of 1965, for example, people stranded in stalled subways and elevators quickly became highly dependent on one another for emotional support.

There are also borderline cases that lie somewhere between a group and a mere collection of people. For example, the regulars at Ralph's bus stop may have some degree of interaction and some feeling of group belonging, both of which stem from the common enterprise of waiting for the bus every workday morning. However, they form a rather weak and amorphous group with little explicit communication among members and no clear criteria for membership.

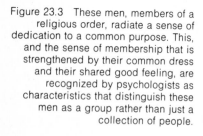

Figure 23.3   These men, members of a religious order, radiate a sense of dedication to a common purpose. This, and the sense of membership that is strengthened by their common dress and their shared good feeling, are recognized by psychologists as characteristics that distinguish these men as a group rather than just a collection of people.

Figure 23.4 Shriners cool off as they read about a seven-hour parade they held the day before. The Shriners present an interesting example of the difficulty in sorting out a group's task and social functions. The Shriners' activities, which they enjoy for fellowship and good times, are aimed at raising money for the building and maintenance of many hospitals for crippled children.

Interdependence, whether created by direct communication or by a feeling of group membership (or both), implies an additional characteristic of practically all groups: Group members see themselves as sharing certain **common goals** or interests. The goals may range from the desire to solve a particular problem (as in Ralph's task group) to the desire to perpetuate a common heritage (as in many ethnic and religious groups). If a person discovers that he no longer has any goals or interests in common with a particular group, he usually stops interacting with it and loses his feeling of group belonging.

Groups have many different goals, most of which can be categorized in terms of two major group functions: the task function and the social function. When a group of people are working together to make a governmental decision, to perform a surgical operation, or to move a piano, the group is concentrating on the **task function.** When people take walks together or participate in dormitory bull sessions, it is the **social function** that is emphasized; the person participates in the group to gain such social rewards as companionship and emotional support.

A group usually specializes in one function or the other, but almost all groups serve *both* functions to some extent. Members of certain groups, such as family or communal-living groups, provide each other with social support in addition to helping each other get food, clothing, and shelter. People whose jobs require them to work on a task together often feel personal ties to one another, and the social relationships among members may have profound effects on the way the group goes about its task.

WHEN ARE TWO HEADS BETTER THAN ONE?

Many tasks can be performed successfully only when a group of people work together. The task may require simply a **summation** of individual strengths, as when a group of people pushes a stalled car to a gas station, or it may call for smooth **coordination** of diverse activities, as in the performance of an expert surgical team or basketball squad. For some tasks, however, it is not clear whether the results would be better if a group worked together or if each person worked by himself. One such task—creative problem solving—has been of great interest to psychologists who study group performance. Much research has been done in the attempt to determine the relative merit of individual and group activity for creative problem solving.

Brainstorming

In 1938, an advertising executive named Alex Osborn introduced the concept of brainstorming as a means of fostering creativity. The basic principle of brainstorming is that group members should be encouraged to express their

Figure 23.5 (A) Groups like construction crews exist because most tasks human beings set for themselves simply cannot be done without the coordination of different skills and the summation of individual strengths. (B) Corporate executive groups exist for similar reasons. Like each of the members of the construction crew, each of the corporation's officers concentrates his abilities on one particular area to keep the large business operation running smoothly. In addition, both of these task-oriented groups require of their members considerable skill in interpersonal interaction.

ideas, no matter how wild or impractical they may seem, in a free and uncritical atmosphere. Quantity rather than quality of ideas is emphasized, at least in the short run. Osborn suggested that such an untrammeled exchange of ideas triggers new ideas and leads to a more varied and creative set of possibilities than any member could have produced alone.

The wide adoption of brainstorming in businesses and other organizations attests to its appeal. Experimental evidence suggests, however, that its effectiveness for bringing about creative solutions to problems is questionable. In a well-known investigation, Donald Taylor, Paul Berry, and Clifford Block showed that four people working *individually* consistently came up with more and better solutions to problems than did four-person brainstorming groups. It is possible that the students who participated in this study simply did not use the brainstorming technique correctly or that, in spite of instructions to the contrary, they did not feel completely immune to criticism and so kept their ideas at a relatively conventional level. It is also feasible that isolation is more conducive to certain kinds of creative endeavor than is group interaction. Another possibility, which has obtained some support in experiments conducted by Marvin Dunnette, John Campbell, and Kay Jaastad, is that people may be especially creative when working as individuals *after* participation in a brainstorming group; that is, the group discussion may provide valuable starting points for the individual's creative process.

Problems that are most likely to be solved better by group treatment are those that are susceptible to a division of labor among people with complementary skills. Government and industry frequently make use of multidisciplinary task forces, in which experts from different fields coordinate their talents in order to solve practical problems. The same principle operates in some of the creative arts. Although very few great poems, paintings, or symphonies are created by committees, most great musicals have been written by composer-lyricist teams—Gilbert and Sullivan, Rodgers and Hammerstein, Lerner and Loewe—and most, if not all, award-winning films have been created by people working together as a group.

Group Decision Making: A Case Study

Behind closed doors at the White House in the early months of 1961, a confident and tightknit group, including some of the reputedly most intelligent men ever to participate in the councils of government, made what has come to be regarded as one of the worst decisions in recent history. The group was incoming-President John F. Kennedy's inner circle of foreign-policy advisers, including Dean Rusk, Robert McNamara, McGeorge Bundy, Douglas Dillon, and Arthur Schlesinger. Meeting frequently over the course of three months, the advisory group reached the unanimous decision to go ahead with plans developed under the Eisenhower administration for an invasion of Cuba by CIA-trained Cuban exiles. On April 17, 1961, the brigade of

1,400 exiles, aided by the United States Navy and Air Force and the CIA, invaded Cuba at the Bay of Pigs. Within three days ships carrying the invaders' reserve ammunition and supplies had been sunk by Castro's air force and about 1,200 invaders had been captured; most of the rest had been killed. According to Theodore Sorensen, the policy planners had hoped that the invasion "would make possible the toppling of Castro without actual aggression by the United States." Instead, it was a total fiasco.

Subsequent reflections about the Bay of Pigs affair by Schlesinger, McNamara, and President Kennedy made it clear that the group's decision was apparently based on incomplete information. The group failed to take account of—and in some cases to acquaint itself with—available information on the size and strength of Castro's forces, the deteriorating morale of the invaders, and the improbability of the invasion touching off uprisings behind the lines in the Cuban underground. True, there were strong pressures on the new administration to prove that it was not "soft on communism," but these and other political explanations seem curiously inadequate to account for an episode that was many times more humiliating to the Kennedy administration than calling off the expedition would have been.

Irving Janis, a social psychologist at Yale University, has suggested in his book *Victims of Groupthink* a different approach to the question of why the group acted as it did. According to Janis, the policy planners were not so much affected by political pressure as they were victimized by **groupthink.** Following are two of the major symptoms of groupthink that Janis identifies in the course of his impressive analysis of the Bay of Pigs decision.

The Illusion of Invulnerability In the months following his inauguration, President Kennedy and his inner circle shared an unusually high degree of morale and *esprit de corps.* The group was a highly cohesive one—that is,

Figure 23.6 With President John F. Kennedy in this photo are Dean Rusk and Robert McNamara (back to the camera), two of the group of advisers who made the disastrous decision to use the CIA and some American armed forces to aid Cuban exiles in their invasion of Cuba at the Bay of Pigs. The three quotations are from an account of the Kennedy administration written by another group member, Arthur Schlesinger, Jr. The first two quotations describe the unshakable optimism—the illusion of invulnerability—that encouraged the group to believe that nothing they did could go wrong. The third quotation reflects the illusion of unanimity that the group operated under.

Everything had broken right for him [John Kennedy] since 1956. He had won the nomination and the election against all the odds in the book. Everyone around him thought he had the Midas touch and could not lose.

The currents of vitality radiated out of the White House, flowed through the government and created a sense of vast possibility. The very idea of the new President taking command as tranquilly and naturally as if his whole life had prepared him for it could not but stimulate a thought of buoyant optimism. . . . Euphoria reigned; we thought for a moment that the world was plastic and the future unlimited.

Our meetings were taking place in a curious atmosphere of assumed consensus.
Had one senior adviser opposed the adventure, I believe that Kennedy would have canceled it. Not one spoke against it.
From A. M. Schlesinger, Jr., *A Thousand Days.*

its members prized their membership in the group and felt strongly committed to it. There was a great feeling of optimism about the potential of the new administration. Schlesinger later wrote the descriptions that appear in the margin.

Janis notes that optimism is characteristic of highly **cohesive groups,** including encounter groups, military combat units, and athletic teams. For a policy-planning group, however, these feelings can create in the group the dangerous **illusion of invulnerability.** "The group members know that none of them is a superman," Janis writes, "but they feel that somehow the group is a supergroup, capable of surmounting all risks that stand in the way of carrying out any desired course of action." Such a feeling seems to have been behind the planners' reluctance to examine the drawbacks of the invasion plan. Running through all their assumptions was the happy but unrealistic idea that they would inevitably win out.

The Illusion of Unanimity Maintaining the optimistic outlook of a cohesive group requires that each member believe that everyone else in the group agrees that risks can be safely ignored. Such a feeling of unanimity occurred in the Bay of Pigs planning group. In fact, what occurred at the meetings was an **illusion of unanimity.** Privately, several of the participants harbored doubts about the decision, although they did not express their doubts publicly. Janis suggests that their reluctance to do so was not because of timidity or fear of damaging their careers; rather, they did not want to risk incurring the disapproval of the other group members for having destroyed the group's sense of unity. Similar tendencies toward conformity have been found in social-psychological experiments on group judgments, especially when group members have had to state their judgments out loud or when they have been concerned about being accepted by the group. (A famous series of such experiments, conducted by Solomon Asch, is described in Chapter 22.)

Preventing Groupthink

Two conclusions that should *not* be drawn from Janis' analysis of groupthink in the Bay of Pigs planning group are (1) that important decisions should be made by one individual single-handedly, and (2) that groups with low morale are more effective problem solvers than optimistic, cohesive groups. One person rarely has all the expertise and information needed to make an important policy decision. In addition, any one person inevitably has certain biases, blind spots, and other weaknesses. For these reasons the general practice of making important decisions in groups can hardly be questioned. Moreover, high morale in a decision-making (or virtually any other) group has important advantages. Unless group members are committed to one another and to the task at hand, they probably will not be willing to invest the time and energy it takes to make a difficult decision.

Thus, group cohesiveness generally should be encouraged, but groupthink should be discouraged. Perhaps the best single way to prevent groupthink is to be *aware* of the possibility that it can emerge. Although the facts are not yet all in, there is reason to think that if Republican campaign planners in 1972 had been more aware of the danger of groupthink, the national tragedy of Watergate might have been averted.

REFERENCE GROUPS

Besides functioning as a collective entity for making decisions, a group helps shape the self-definitions and personal values of its members as individuals. A group that affects a person's attitudes and standards—a group that a person identifies with—is called a **reference group** by social psychologists. Reference groups need not be formal or face-to-face groups, although they may be.

In fact, the most influential reference groups are often broad social categories such as racial, religious, occupational, and sex groupings. People often take great pride in such reference groups and tend to be highly influenced by them in their day-to-day lives.

Group Pride

People's pride in a reference group may be reflected in the way they represent the group to outsiders. One experiment illustrating this point was designed to investigate the amount of pain that undergraduate women could tolerate as a function of religious group identification. Wallace Lambert, Eva Libman, and Ernest Poser first established the amount of pain each woman could tolerate. A blood-pressure instrument with sharp, hard rubber projections sewn into the cuff was placed on the subject's upper arm, and the pressure was gradually increased until she pronounced the pain intolerable. After this limit had been established, the experimenter told the subject that a retest would be made in five minutes to determine the reliability of the measurement. In addition, he casually mentioned to those subjects who were Jewish that Jews could endure less pain than Christians, and he told those who were Christian that Christians could endure less pain than Jews. (In fact, neither of these statements is true.)

On the retest the tolerance limits of both the Jewish and the Christian subjects increased significantly. There was not change in the tolerance limit of control subjects, to whom the experimenter said nothing about religious groups. These findings suggest that people tend to interpret "insults" to their religious reference groups as attacks on themselves and are prepared to defend the group publicly, even if doing so requires them to endure intense pain. Arnold Buss and Norman Portnoy, using a method similar to that of the preceding study, showed that not only do pain tolerance levels increase when one's reference group is challenged, the increase in tolerance varies with the strength of identification. Figure 23.8A shows the average strength of male students' identification with their nation, their sex, and their college (the researchers had asked the subjects to rank these before the experiment). Figure 23.8B shows that the stronger the identification, the greater was the increase in pain tolerance.

Group Standards

When people define themselves as members of a particular group, they are likely to adopt the attitudes and values that they see as characterizing the group. In a classic study conducted in the 1930s, Theodore Newcomb investigated changes in political and social values of undergraduates at Bennington College. Most of the students came from upper-class, politically conservative backgrounds, whereas the college community was characterized by extreme liberalism. Newcomb found that the students who strongly identified with

Figure 23.7   Tommy Smith and John Carlos receiving the gold and bronze medals, respectively, for the 200-meter race at the 1968 Olympics. The two athletes raised their fists in a gesture symbolizing the black power movement and black pride. The significance of their gesture—the demand on the part of the blacks for the power to determine their own lives—was well understood by everyone. Many found the action objectionable, however, because it seemed to express cynicism about the whole purpose of the Games. It was felt that because Smith and Carlos were representatives at the Games, their reference group should have been humanity, not the black race.

Figure 23.8   The results of Buss and Portnoy's experiment, which extended the findings of Lambert and his associates about the strength of identification with reference groups. Subjects were first asked to rank the strength of their identification with various reference groups—nation, gender, college—and then the experimenter determined each subject's highest level of pain tolerance. After this determination, the experimenter casually mentioned that members of a different reference group he had studied—say, Russians or women or students at another college—consistently showed greater pain tolerance. Then the subject's pain tolerance was tested again. As the figure shows, the greater the strength of the subject's identification with his reference group, as measured by the subject's own ranking, the greater the increase in pain the subject would tolerate after the group had been challenged.

(After Buss and Portnoy, 1967.)

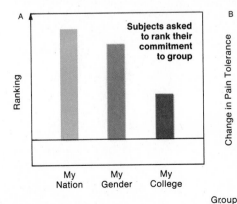

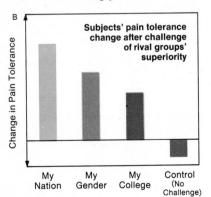

Figure 23.9 Scenes from Bennington College at the time Newcomb was there. Newcomb himself is shown on the left. Newcomb described Bennington as being suitable for the study of the development of attitudes toward public affairs because it "opened its doors during the darkest days of the depression" and because this was "the period of gathering war clouds in Europe." The Bennington faculty held the conviction "that one of the foremost duties of the college was to acquaint its somewhat oversheltered students with the nature of their contemporary social world." The marked change in reference groups experienced by Bennington students is shown in a remark by one subject that Newcomb quotes: "Family against faculty has been my struggle here."

Bennington tended to become much more liberal as they progressed through college. Not only did Bennington become a positive reference group for these women, in many cases their families and home communities became *negative* reference groups. In acquiring new attitudes, the women tried not only to identify more closely with Bennington but to disengage themselves from their conservative backgrounds as well.

Why are people so likely to adopt the standards of their reference groups? A good part of the answer comes from an understanding of the term **identification.** As the word implies, people acquire a sense of personal definition—an identity—in large measure from their group memberships. If you ask a person to tell you who he is, he may reply that he is happy, overweight, or trying to write a novel, but he is also likely to say that he is an American, a Protestant, or a member of Kappa Kappa Delta. In order to sustain the latter sorts of identities, especially when he has an emotional investment in them, a person tries to be as similar as he can to the "ideal American," the "ideal Protestant," or the "ideal Kappa Kappa Deltan," and he tends to adopt the standards and perspectives that he attributes to these groups. These attitudes are often buttressed by direct influences from friends and acquaintances, who often belong to one's own reference groups.

Because each person has not one but many reference groups, an important problem for future research is to specify how an individual decides which reference group provides the most relevant standards for his or her attitudes in a given area. If a person is a female black American chemist with a strong interest in mountain climbing, under what conditions is she influenced by the standards of each of those groups? An additional complication is that people often identify with groups that they do not actually belong to but hope to join. An assembly-line worker may adopt some of the attitudes of the managerial group to which he aspires, and a European who hopes to emigrate to the United States may begin adopting what he perceives as American standards.

RELATIONS BETWEEN GROUPS

Groups constantly come in contact with each other. Sometimes two task groups must get together to solve a joint problem, for example, when a company contracts to build something for a government agency. Members of reference groups must often come together—in schools, in universities, in neighborhoods. Sometimes the relations between groups are peaceful, productive, and pleasant. In other cases, they are characterized by tension, ill will, open hostility, or even bloodshed. During World War II America considered the Japanese enemies, placed Japanese-Americans in internment camps, and dropped atomic bombs on two Japanese cities. Today, Americans consider Japan an ally, visit the country as tourists, and equip their homes with Japanese-made products. In a coal-mining town, blacks and whites may work together in the mines in a friendly, cooperative, sometimes joking atmosphere; above the ground they live in separate neighborhoods, attend separate churches, and would not think of visiting each other's homes.

What determines whether the contact between groups is conflict-ridden or harmonious? A classic social-psychological experiment provided some answers to this question.

The Robbers Cave Experiment

In the summer of 1954, a group of psychologists headed by Muzafer Sherif organized a summer camp for boys in order to study intergroup relations. The camp, which offered all the usual summer-camp activities, was in Oklahoma, near a famous Jesse James hideout called the Robbers Cave. The boys who attended the camp had no idea that they were participating in a psychological experiment; they were healthy, well-adjusted eleven- and twelve-year-olds from stable, white, Protestant, middle-class homes. From the time the boys boarded the buses for camp, they were divided into two separate groups. In the first phase of the experiment, the *two groups were isolated from each other*. The boys went hiking and swimming and played baseball only with members of their own group, and friendships and group spirit soon developed. Each group chose a name—the Eagles and the Rattlers—and created special symbols, secret words, and in-jokes. By the end of the first phase of the experiment, two informal organizations, each with its unwritten norms and informal leaders, had emerged.

In the second phase, the psychologists (acting as counselors) *brought the groups together in competitive contact situations*. They set up a tournament that pitted Eagles against Rattlers in baseball, football, tugs-of-war, a treasure hunt, and other games. Sherif had hypothesized that when these two groups of normal boys were placed in competitive situations, where one group could achieve its goals only at the expense of the other, hostility would soon develop. And, in fact, although the tournament began in a spirit of good sportsmanship, tension increased as the games continued, and name-calling and scuffles began. One afternoon after they had lost a game, the Eagles burned a banner left behind by the Rattlers. The next morning the Rattlers stole the Eagles' flag in retaliation, and from then on, raids became more and more common.

The competition also produced several major changes *within* each group. The group's solidarity and morale and the cooperation among members increased as a result of having a common rival or enemy. Group standards changed; in one group a big boy who had been considered a bully before the tournament became a hero. At the same time, each group became less tolerant of members who failed to conform to group standards; the leader in one group was deposed because of his supposed poor showing in competition.

After having demonstrated that they could produce intergroup conflict, Sherif and his associates started the third and final phase of the experiment, which was *aimed at ending the conflict and establishing harmony* between the Eagles and the Rattlers. Their first attempt resembled the "good-will" dinners and activities often held for occasions like National Brotherhood Week. The Eagles and the Rattlers were brought together to see a movie or to eat a particularly good meal in the dining hall. This approach failed totally—as Sherif had predicted from the start. At dinner, the campers from one group shoved and pushed boys from the other group and hurled food and insults. Far

Figure 23.10 Photographs taken during the Robbers Cave experiment. Isolation of the two collections of campers produced two structured groups after a time. During the subsequent competitive-contact phase arranged by the experimenters (for example, the tug-of-war shown here), the groups developed considerable hostility toward one another.   (top right) Cabin raids were one expression of this hostility. It lessened when the experimenters contrived situations in which the two groups were forced to cooperate with one another. (bottom right) The truck that was to fetch the day's lunch had supposedly broken down, and the boys, to have food to eat, were forced to get together to push it.

from encouraging a settlement of their differences, this type of contact provided an opportunity for the campers to continue their attacks and to vent their hostility.

Next, the psychologists tried an approach based on Sherif's belief that if competition produces conflict, working *in cooperation to achieve shared goals should produce harmony.* The psychologists deliberately contrived a series of apparent emergencies in which the boys had to help each other or else lose the chance to do or get something they all wanted. One morning both groups took a trip to a lake. Around noon, someone discovered that the truck, which was supposed to go to town to pick up lunch, would not start. To get it to work, boys from both groups had to push and pull. Another morning, someone reported that the water pipe line to the camp had broken; the boys were told that unless they worked together to find the break and fix it, they would all have to leave camp. By afternoon the Rattlers and the Eagles had jointly found and repaired the damage. Gradually, through these cooperative activities, intergroup hostility and tensions lessened. Friendships began to develop between individual Eagles and Rattlers, and eventually the groups began to seek out occasions to mingle. At the end of camp, members of both groups requested that they ride home together on the same bus.

The Robbers Cave experiment provides a striking example of how social factors—in this case **conditions of competition or cooperation**—can affect the relationship between groups. What is most impressive about the hostility and subsequent acceptance that the researchers produced between the groups is that the children were from similar backgrounds and were randomly sorted into groups; none of the results can be attributed to differences in ethnic group, race, class, or ability.

Social Stereotypes

Each group of boys that took part in the Robbers Cave experiment began to see the other group as possessing certain characteristics. Eagles expected all Rattlers to be aggressive and untrustworthy, and Rattlers held similar beliefs about Eagles. One race, class, or ethnic group often holds such expectations—or **social stereotypes**—about other groups. Stereotypes frequently form part of the tradition of a group or a culture and are taught to new members during the process of socialization. People acquire many stereotypes about other groups vicariously, by hearsay, rather than through personal experience. For example, in 1933 Daniel Katz and Kenneth Braly found that American college students could describe stereotypes for Turks and Chinese, although few of the students had ever met anyone from Turkey or China.

Stereotypes can affect intergroup relations in several ways. They bias our perceptions of individuals. As is discussed further in Chapter 20, people tend to see what they expect to see; the confirmation of expectations is psychologically comfortable. Also, stereotypes often add fuel to intergroup conflict. Negative qualities assigned to an out-group can be used to justify hostile actions against them—the act of ''scapegoating.'' In extreme cases, stereotypes may serve to dehumanize others. Soldiers, for example, are often trained to regard the enemy as things rather than as people because it is psychologically easier to create hatred of, and justify aggression against, people if they are perceived as ''commies'' or ''gooks'' rather than as other human beings.

Many stereotypes are a mixture of description and evaluation. The following example of how this mixture works is presented in *Social Theory and Social Structure* by Robert Merton, who points out that:

> . . . the very same behavior undergoes a complete change of evaluation in its transition from the in-group Abe Lincoln to the out-group Abe Cohen or Abe Kurokawa. . . . Did Lincoln work far into the night? This testifies that he was industrious, resolute, perseverant, and eager to realize his capacities to the full. Do the out-group Jews or Japanese keep these same hours? This only bears witness to their sweatshop mentality, their ruthless undercutting of American standards, their unfair competitive practices. Is the in-group hero frugal, thrifty, and sparing? Then the out-group villain is stingy, miserly, and penny-pinching.

Because stereotypes combine fact and opinion, it is often difficult to know how to test their accuracy. Although some stereotypes can be proven untrue, many do contain a kernel of truth, or fact. The danger is that people applying stereotypes use *unfair standards* to evaluate the facts. In the case of Abe, a *double standard* is being used. The kernel of truth here is that Abe works far into the night and does not spend money with a free hand. However, this behavior is evaluated differently depending on whether it is done by one of ''us'' or by one of ''them.''

Conditions for Favorable Contact

As the Robbers Cave experiment showed, an important determinant of relations between groups is the conditions under which groups interact. Under favorable conditions, people can come to look beyond their stereotypes and see individuals for what they are. Gordon Allport and others have suggested several aspects of the interaction that are important.

Cooperation to Achieve Shared Goals   A crucial factor in the Robbers Cave study was cooperation to achieve shared goals. Sherif demonstrated that simply having similar goals was not adequate for good relations between groups. In the sports tournament, both Rattlers and Eagles strove for the same goal—to win. But a victory for one group meant a loss for the other. It was only when the boys had to work together to reach a joint goal that relations improved. In a cooperative situation, members are interdependent. The efforts of each person help himself and others at the same time. Sherif emphasized the point that *groups must perceive their shared goal as most*

Figure 23.11   Posters of Adolph Hitler from Germany (top) and from Belgium (bottom) in the early stages of World War II. Both are highly stereotypic images of him, and both contain elements of truth. Hitler was a charismatic leader; he was also a cruel aggressor.

important in order to override other differences between them. When the Rattlers and Eagles cooperated to fix the water pipe line, their goal of staying at camp was strong enough for them to put aside their differences.

It may be that cooperation between groups creates, at least momentarily, a new, combined group and establishes new bonds and identification with the larger unit. This condition and the three others discussed in the following sections have clear implications for improving relations between ethnic groups in the United States. In much of this discussion, research that has investigated conditions of contact between blacks and whites is reported.

Intimacy of the Contact Although intimacy of contact is an important factor in intergroup contact, the relationship between intimate contact and liking is something of a chicken-and-egg problem. One can reasonably ask which comes first, liking or contact. Both common sense and psychological research suggest that the relationship can work in either direction. If people like each other and are friendly, they are more likely to seek each other out and spend time together. If people interact frequently and intimately, they often come to form friendships and to see each other more favorably. Studies of residential contacts demonstrate that the latter process is more important for improving intergroup relations.

Shortly after World War II, public housing projects began to spring up in metropolitan areas. Some of them were racially integrated, whereas others maintained racial segregation. Morton Deutsch and Mary Collins capitalized on this "natural" social experiment. Although they could not control the situation as much as Sherif had, they carefully selected four biracial projects, two *integrated* ones, in which blacks and whites occupied adjoining apartments in the same building, and two *segregated* ones, in which blacks and whites lived in the same project but in separate buildings. In order to qualify for public housing, the families in both projects had consented to live in a biracial project.

Deutsch and Collins conducted lengthy interviews with housewives after their families had lived in the projects for a while. The results of the study

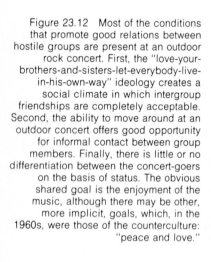

Figure 23.12 Most of the conditions that promote good relations between hostile groups are present at an outdoor rock concert. First, the "love-your-brothers-and-sisters-let-everybody-live-in-his-own-way" ideology creates a social climate in which intergroup friendships are completely acceptable. Second, the ability to move around at an outdoor concert offers good opportunity for informal contact between group members. Finally, there is little or no differentiation between the concert-goers on the basis of status. The obvious shared goal is the enjoyment of the music, although there may be other, more implicit, goals, which, in the 1960s, were those of the counterculture: "peace and love."

show clearly that the two types of contact situations had different effects on racial attitudes. In the integrated projects over 60 percent of the white housewives reported having "friendly relations" with blacks; in the segregated projects, less than 10 percent reported friendships, and over 80 percent reported no contact at all. In the integrated projects two out of three white women expressed a desire to be friendly with blacks; in the segregated projects, only one in eleven expressed such a desire. Similar effects occurred in the attitudes of black women toward whites. Many women in the integrated projects came to like the interracial aspect of their apartment building, whereas in the segregated projects many women disliked being in even a segregated biracial development.

The Deutsch and Collins study illustrates not only the effects of contact on liking but also the *importance of informal opportunities for interaction.* In the segregated projects, the actual physical distance between black and white families was not great, but functionally the distance was considerable. One white woman reported: "I used to be good friends with a colored woman who worked with me at the factory before I moved here. She lives in the other side of the project, but I never have her over to my side of the project—it just isn't done. Occasionally, I go over and visit her." The woman could not casually meet her friend in the laundry room or elevator; for her a meeting entailed a deliberate effort. In the segregated projects, the group norms would have held such an action suspect. In the integrated projects, contacts could occur spontaneously and casually. Housewives had many opportunities to meet, and they often took advantage of them. The result of these frequent and increasingly intense meetings was dramatic. One white housewife described her experience this way:

I started to cry when my husband told me we were coming to live here. I cried for three weeks. . . . I didn't want to come and live here where there are so many colored people. I didn't want to bring my children up with colored children, but we had to come; there was no place else to go . . . Well, all that's changed. I've really come to like it. I see they're just as human as we are. They have nice apartments; they keep their children clean, and they're very friendly. I've come to like them a great deal. I'm no longer scared of them.

Contacts like those in the integrated project, which permit people to get to know each other well as individuals and not in formal social roles, enable people to test their stereotypes against reality. Deutsch and Collins do not deny that old attitudes die hard and that people tend to distort their perception and recall of events to complement their existing attitudes. But they maintain that Leon Festinger's notion of cognitive dissonance (discussed at length in Chapter 22) is true here: When contact continues over time, it becomes psychologically too costly and difficult to retain beliefs that are inconsistent with experience. Interracial contacts are often uncomfortable at first for both blacks and whites, but if the conditions discussed in the following paragraphs—the social climate surrounding the contact and relative status of the group members—are favorable, intimate contact over time frequently leads to a reduction in negative attitudes and tension.

Social Climate In the Robbers Cave experiment, friendly contacts were approved by the counselors and other camp officials. Friendships between Eagles and Rattlers might not have developed if they had been discouraged by the important adults in the camp. The outcome of interracial contact also depends in part on whether the social climate is one of acceptance or disapproval. Besides the opinions of authorities, such as the adults at the camp, the crucial factors in determining a social climate (and thus the outcome of interracial situations) are the force of formal law and the impact of social norms. In the projects that Deutsch and Collins studied, the social climates differed enormously. In the segregated developments, whites and blacks hesitated to mix because they believed it "just isn't done." The authorities who built the projects had apparently intended that the races be separated, and the informal social norms of the project supported this view. In the integrated projects, the expectations were quite different. Here the housing officials apparently supported integration, and informal social norms developed that made interracial contacts appropriate.

Status   The fourth factor that affects the outcome of intergroup contact is the relative status of the group members. In any particular interaction, relative status may be determined by the individuals' social roles, their personal characteristics, or their achievements. Doctors have higher status than nurses (occupational-role status); adults have higher status than children (status based on age); skilled athletes outrank rookies (status based on achievement). Contacts between blacks and whites in which blacks have *lower* status do little to challenge or change attitudes and behavior. Interracial contacts in which blacks have *higher* status do not always produce changed attitudes either: Racial stereotypes permit some people to perceive the achievements of outstanding black athletes and entertainers as confirming those stereotypes. To effect attitude change, the blacks of higher status in interracial contacts must enact roles not associated with racial stereotypes, for example, such occupational roles as chemist, airplane pilot, or French teacher.

Equal-status contacts stand the best chance of leading to improved intergroup relations. Numerous studies, such as those by Ralph Gundlach, H. E. O. James, Ralph Minard, and John Harding and Russell Hogrefe, have shown that when blacks and whites work together as equals—in the army or as coal miners or as merchant seamen—intergroup liking and friendships often develop. The status of the black and the white women in the integrated housing projects studied by Deutsch and Collins was much the same; the family incomes were roughly comparable, all were housewives, and their living quarters were virtually identical. This equal-status contact over a long period made it possible for members of each group to realize that the others are "people just like us."

The four factors that have been suggested as important for intergroup contact are summarized in the adjacent margin. These factors work jointly, and if any one is missing, an interaction may not have positive results.

1. Participants must cooperate to achieve a shared goal.
2. Contact should be relatively intimate and long lasting.
3. Contact should take place in a social climate of acceptance.
4. Participants in the situation should have equal status.

AMERICAN RACE RELATIONS

Understanding the effects of group membership can provide insights into the relations between blacks and whites in America. Race is a very important social category in this country; it has major impact on how a person thinks about himself and how he acts towards others.

The Social Definition of Race

To the biologist, a race is a relatively isolated mating group with certain distinctive gene frequencies. However, Americans do not decide who is "Caucasian" and who is "Negro" on the basis of gene frequencies; they define race in social terms. The child with one black and one white parent cannot decide to be "white," because social convention states that any black ancestry, no matter how remote, constitutes grounds for being classified as black. Even according to the Census Bureau, a person with *any* black ancestry is "Negro" unless the community defines him otherwise.

The point of this discussion is not to deny that blacks constitute a distinct group but rather to emphasize that race is a *socially defined group*, not a biological one. Group identity is largely based on a shared cultural heritage and on the common problems of survival as an oppressed minority that occupies an inferior social position and confronts a derogatory social role.

Racial Stereotypes and Roles

In America, derogatory stereotypes have been used to justify assigning blacks to an inferior social position and denying them equal opportunities. Dozens of studies conducted during the past forty years (reviewed by John Brigham and by Nelson Cauthen, Ira Robinson, and Herbert Krauss) found that many whites believed blacks to be irresponsible, intellectually inferior, and lazy.

In recent years, however, research has found less negative stereotyping of blacks, which may reflect several social changes. First, it is probably much less socially acceptable to express derogatory ethnic stereotypes than it once was. Second, as a result of civil rights activities in the past decade, there probably has been some actual decline in racial stereotypes. Third, it appears that stereotypes of blacks are strongly affected by social-class factors. A study by James Bayton, Lois McAlister and Jeston Hamer found that whereas both black and white students described "lower-class Negroes" according to the derogatory stereotype, they described "upper-class Negroes" as intelligent, industrious, and neat. These results suggest that as blacks move increasingly into the middle and upper classes, the stereotype of blacks may weaken.

The noted social psychologist Thomas Pettigrew has suggested that many aspects of black-white relations can be explained in terms of social roles. It is important to recognize the distinction between social roles and stereotypes. Although both of these terms apply to a group or general category of persons rather than to one individual, stereotypes are primarily *descriptive* beliefs about what people in some group are like. In contrast, roles involve rules, or prescriptions for conduct. Those in the role of mother *ought* to take care of their children, and they typically do.

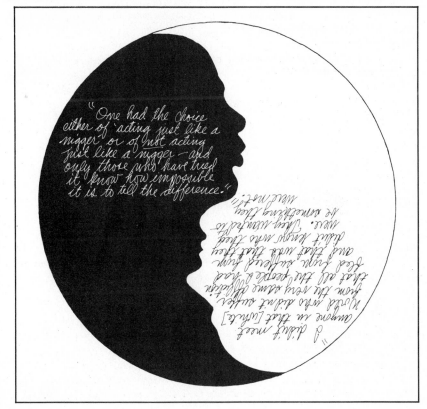

Figure 23.13 These lines from James Baldwin's novel *Nobody Knows My Name* express a black man's view of the roles of blacks and whites in New York and Boston in the 1940s and the 1950s. The black role was wholly defined by the white perception of "nigger," Baldwin says; this definition required an equally rigid role performance whether one tried to conform to it or tried not to. The necessity of always heeding role requirements resulted in a loss of identity. The black person no longer knew how he would act without the role requirements. Baldwin considered whites to be in a similar state. Pettigrew's theory of racial role reciprocity suggests one reason for this similarity: The white man could require role performances from blacks only by performing a role himself.

Since the founding of this country, blacks have been assigned at birth to an inferior social position and whites to a superior one. This assignment has been made on the basis of race rather than individual achievement. In addition to descriptive stereotypes based on race, there have also existed prescriptive expectations about how blacks and whites *should* behave toward each other. These rules and expectations constitute complementary racial roles. The black role obliges its occupant to be submissive, deferential, and respectful toward whites; the white role obliges its occupants to be superior, condescending, and perhaps paternalistic.

The elaboration of these roles was perhaps easiest to see in the Old South, where a complicated etiquette prescribed in detail the relations between the races; these unwritten rules were bolstered by laws enforcing segregation in schools, churches, residences, and other areas of life. However, racial-role definitions have affected black-white relations in all parts of the country and continue to do so today.

The concept of racial role is useful because it suggests the extent to which the lives of whites and blacks are intertwined. Racial roles are reciprocal; each is defined in relation to the other. Further, the explanation of relations between blacks and whites in terms of roles emphasizes that these relations are not controlled by biological or racial factors but simply by social convention. The notion of role also helps to distinguish between overt behavior and personality, that is, between what a person does and what he or she would like to do. Blacks, for example, have never been the simple, childlike creatures that their role required, although many have put on a good show. It is a serious mistake to confuse the behavior that people must perform because of their racial roles and the things that they might do if they were not hampered by role prescriptions.

Although roles and personality are distinct, roles do have important effects on personality. Studies by Kenneth Clark and Mamie Clark and by Thomas Pettigrew suggest that many blacks may accept, at least in part, the negative racial stereotypes of the culture. Further, playing an inferior role often takes its toll in loss of self-respect and the creation of unconscious self-hatred.

Blacks have been rejecting the traditional racial roles with increasing speed and determination. They are seeking not only freedom from social and eco-

Figure 23.14 After the assassination of Martin Luther King in 1968, a third-grade teacher gave her students a lesson in discrimination. On the basis of eye color the teacher divided the class into two groups and favored one group (the blue-eyed children the first day) with such privileges as being leaders and having their choice of seats and activities. The next day she reversed the situation, favoring the brown-eyed children. On the day that they were favored, the blue-eyed children reportedly "took savage delight" in keeping "inferiors" in their place and said they felt "good inside," "smarter," and "stronger." On that day, one child drew the picture shown on the right. The next day, the same child, now one of the "inferiors," drew the picture on the left. The children who had felt "smart" and "strong" on their favored day became tense, lacked confidence, and did badly at their work on the day they were discriminated against. They said they felt "like dying," and "like quitting school."

Figure 23.15   A scene from *Gone with the Wind*, the famous story of the South during and after the Civil War, and a scene from the television series *Maude*, a portrayal of current American upper-middle-class life. Changes in the media's stereotypes of blacks over the last thirty years are obvious when the characters of these two black women are compared. Some of the same stereotypes remain, however.

nomic oppression but also an end to traditional racial-role definitions and stereotyped images. "Black power," "black pride," and "black is beautiful" are expressions of this striving by blacks to change their social position, to redefine racial roles, to raise self-esteem, and to eliminate self-hatred. As blacks seek to redefine their role, the role of whites must also change. For some whites, racial roles have provided a sense of self-esteem and personal importance based on being better than some other group. Such feelings of superiority may be difficult to give up as racial roles change. Clear-cut new roles have not yet emerged, but it appears that social expectations and racial roles remain important in determining black-white relations, even though the content of the racial roles is changing.

Relative Deprivation

Just as racial-role definitions are defined in relation to each other, the way a person defines his status in society is related to how he views others' status. If a person finds that others in a given reference group—one he identifies with—are more advantaged than he, more popular or more successful, he feels himself to be a victim of relative deprivation. He may be envious. He may even undertake a campaign of self-improvement. However, if he also believes that the advantages held by the others are somehow unjust, his response is more likely to be one of indignation, frustration, anger, or even aggression.

For blacks, the major standard for social and economic progress is white America. It is middle-class white America whose life style is displayed on television, in magazines, and in store windows, and therefore it constitutes a reference group in the sense that its standards are those that people want to attain. Although blacks have made great gains in education, employment, and other areas of life since World War II, when the gains of blacks are compared to those of whites, the black gains begin to pale. John Preston Davis reports that although the proportion of black home owners in 1960 was a sizable 38 percent, whites had already surpassed that figure twenty years before. In 1960, nearly 65 percent of whites lived in homes they owned. Although the percentage of blacks in white-collar jobs has doubled in recent years, in 1960 the white-collar category included only 13 percent of black workers but 44 percent of white ones. Although blacks have made substantial gains, their increases do not compare with those of whites. In several areas, such as income and infant mortality, the gap between black and white achievement and standards of living has actually widened slightly since 1940. Blacks in America live in the world's richest nation, yet they are relatively deprived. Not only do they see the inequality of their situation, but they perceive it as unjust. Blacks have been treated unfairly by laws and social customs for

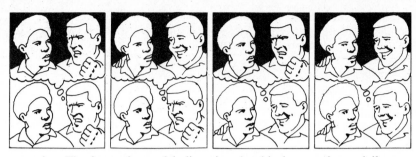

Figure 23.16   To understand racism, it is important to distinguish racist action (discrimination) from racist attitude (prejudice). This figure shows the possible combinations of the two. In the first and last frames, action and attitude are in accord: The white person dislikes blacks or likes them, and acts accordingly. In the middle frames he is inconsistent: In the second frame he is a nonprejudiced discriminator, a man without prejudice who acts in discriminatory ways, perhaps because he is complying to group pressure in a segregated community; in the third frame he is a prejudiced nondiscriminator, perhaps an employer who must obey fair hiring laws. As this chapter notes, and as the preceding chapter discussed in more detail, inconsistencies between actions and attitudes can result in considerable attitude change.

centuries. The frustration and indignation that blacks experience daily as a result of their unjust oppression make their protests understandable.

Prejudice and Discrimination

In studying intergroup relations, it is helpful to distinguish between prejudiced attitudes and discriminatory behavior. Feelings of ill will toward blacks as a group and derogatory stereotypes of them are examples of prejudice. Barring members of minority groups from restaurants, paying blacks lower wages than whites for equal work, and enacting zoning laws to prevent any blacks from living in a particular area are all acts of discrimination. The relationship between attitudes and behavior is discussed in Chapter 22. Although the two often go together, they do not always coincide. When there were laws demanding separate seating for blacks and whites on buses, even whites who were not prejudiced against blacks typically complied. In order to avoid causing an embarrassing scene or possibly going to jail, they ignored their personal convictions and engaged in discriminatory behavior. Today, the laws have changed and the situation is reversed. There are undoubtedly prejudiced whites who ride buses and even sit next to blacks, despite their personal feelings. They do this to comply with social norms and formal laws, to avoid being conspicuous or incurring social disapproval, and to continue to be allowed to use public transportation.

It is commonly believed that behavior reflects attitudes and that in order to do away with discrimination, one must first eliminate prejudice. The notion

Figure 23.17   The rebellion at Attica State Prison in 1971 was a violent protest against conditions in the prison; one of the complaints made by the predominantly black inmates was that they were not permitted to practice the Black Muslim religion. Their reaction to the attempt by prison authorities to control their behavior suggests that they believed laws could indeed "change the hearts and minds of men," if those laws were obeyed (in this case, if the inmates were forced to abide by the prison rule that forbade them to practice their religion).

that "laws can't change the hearts and minds of men" contains the assumption that although laws might change overt behavior, they cannot reach deeply held attitudes. However, the discussion of intergroup contact in this chapter suggests that this common-sense notion may be wrong.

In situations where whites and blacks are forced to associate because of laws, social convention, or the desire to achieve some valued goal, their attitudes frequently do improve. In the Deutsch and Collins study, many white housewives were initially upset about living with blacks. They had moved to the biracial project because it offered the best available housing and because they valued having a comfortable apartment more than maintaining racial separation. After living in integrated housing, many came to enjoy their interracial contacts. Studies of the desegregation of department stores, hospitals, housing, public transportation, and schools all demonstrate that when behavior is changed, "hearts and minds" are often subsequently affected. In fact, this strategy may be more effective than trying to eliminate prejudice in the hope of ultimately reducing discrimination. However, for attitude change to take place, the *conditions of contact must be favorable.*

SUMMARY

1. The groups to which a person belongs exert great influence on his attitudes and behavior, even when he is alone.

   a. Groups vary widely in size, intimacy, and formality. One characteristic that defines a collection of people as a group is some degree of **interdependence** between its members. Interdependence comes about through direct communication or a feeling of group belonging (or both).

   b. Group members see themselves as sharing *common goals.* Groups have many different goals, most of which can be categorized into two major functions: the **task function** and the **social function.** Although a group usually specializes in one function or the other, almost all groups serve both functions.

2. Many tasks can be performed successfully only when a group of people work together. For many other tasks, however, it is not clear whether the results would be better if a group worked together or if each person worked by himself.

   a. The technique of **brainstorming,** widely used in business and other organizations, involves an untrammeled exchange of ideas between members of a problem-solving group in order to produce a more varied set of possibilities than any one member could have produced alone.

   b. Problems that are likely to be solved better in groups are practical ones requiring expertise in a number of different disciplines; experts in each area coordinate their talents to arrive at a solution.

   c. One of the biggest dangers in group decision making is the possibility of **groupthink.** Irving Janis has identified two of its major symptoms: The **illusion of invulnerability**—in which a cohesive group's optimism gives it the feeling that it can surmount all risks attached to any problem—and the **illusion of unanimity**—in which members may withhold from the group their doubts, for fear of destroying the group's sense of unity. The best way to prevent groupthink is to be aware of the possibility that it can emerge.

3. Social psychologists call a group with which a person identifies and that affects his attitudes and standards a **reference group.** Reference groups are often broad social categories, such as religious or occupational groupings. Through **identification,** people often acquire a sense of personal definition from their reference-group memberships.

4. Muzafer Sherif organized a summer camp for boys in order to study intergroup relations.

a. In phase one of the experiment, the boys were separated into two groups that were completely **isolated** from one another. In phase two, the groups were brought together in **competitive contact** situations, where one group could win only at the expense of the other. The competition produced intergroup hostility and intragroup solidarity and cooperation. In phase three, the psychologists created situations in which the boys had to work together to **achieve shared goals.** As a result, intergroup hostilities lessened and friendships began to develop between members of the two groups.

5. One important determinant of intergroup relations involves social stereotypes. A **stereotype** is a descriptive belief or expectation about what members of some group or category are like.

a. Stereotypes are often part of the tradition of a group and are learned vicariously during the socialization process. Expressing them may simply be an act of conformity to group standards.

b. Stereotypes can affect intergroup relations in various ways: They bias our perceptions of individuals, and they promote intergroup conflict by making it easier to justify hostile actions toward out-groups.

Figure 23.18 Kenneth Clark's observations in this chapter about the consequences of identifying with the black stereotype are part of a large body of work that includes his books: *The Negro Protest: James Baldwin, Malcolm X, Martin Luther King Talk with Kenneth B. Clark; Dark Ghetto: Dilemmas of Social Power;* and *White Terror: The Ku Klux Klan Conspiracy.* Clark has been a consultant to the National Association for the Advancement of Colored People and the U.S. State Department, and he was president of the American Psychological Association during 1970–71.

6. The conditions under which groups interact are another important determinant of intergroup relations. Gordon Allport and others have described four conditions that are important for positive relations. If even one of these conditions is unfavorable, interaction may not have positive results.

a. The participants must **cooperate to achieve shared goals,** and these goals must be perceived by all groups as most important.

b. The contacts should be relatively intimate and long lasting.

c. The **social climate,** which is determined by the force of formal laws as well as by the impact of social norms, must be one of acceptance.

d. Participants should have **equal status;** then they are more likely to see each other as "people, just like us."

7. What social psychologists have learned about the effects of group membership and about intergroup relations can provide insights into the relations between blacks and whites in America. In America, race is defined in social terms, not biological terms.

a. Derogatory stereotypes of blacks have been used to justify assigning them to inferior social positions and denying them equal opportunities.

b. **Social roles,** which involve prescriptions for behavior, also affect race relations. The expectations about how blacks and whites should behave toward each other constitute complementary racial roles; as blacks continue to redefine their role, the role of whites must also change.

c. The concept of **relative deprivation** can offer some insight into race relations. White middle-class America, as seen on television, in movies, in magazines, constitutes a reference group for all Americans. When blacks (who have made considerable economic and educational gains since the end of World War II) compare their gains to those of the white middle class, they see themselves as deprived relative to that reference group. Also, they believe the relative deprivation to be unjust—the outcome of centuries of unfair laws, customs, and stereotypes.

8. Prejudice and discrimination are not synonymous. **Prejudice** consists of derogating stereotypes and feelings of ill will—attitudes. **Discrimination** is behavior based on prejudice, such as the passage and enforcement of laws or covenants barring people from using hotel or restaurant facilities. There have been—and still are—people who say that discriminatory behavior cannot be changed until prejudiced attitudes are erased. The results of social-psychological studies discussed in this chapter strongly suggest that this notion is wrong. People who are forced to have interracial contact—under the favorable conditions of contact described in the chapter—often undergo a change in their prejudiced attitudes.

SUGGESTED READINGS

Allport, Gordon W. *The Nature of Prejudice.* Garden City, N.Y.: Anchor Books, 1958. A classic and still vital analysis of the psychological and social processes underlying prejudice.

Brown, Roger. *Social Psychology.* New York: Free Press, 1965. This most readable of social-psychology textbooks is highly recommended. Of particular relevance to this chapter are Chapter 13 (Group Dynamics) and Chapter 14 (Collective Behavior and the Psychology of the Crowd).

Cartwright, Dorwin, and Alvin Zander (eds.). *Group Dynamics.* 3rd ed. New York: Harper & Row, 1968. An excellent collection of research reports on such topics as conformity, leadership, and power in groups; the editors have provided useful overviews of theory and research.

Davis, James H. *Group Performance.* Reading, Mass.: Addison-Wesley, 1969. A good overview of research on group problem solving and decision making and of the variables that determine their effectiveness.

Janis, Irving L. *Victims of Groupthink: A Psychological Study of Foreign-Policy Decisions and Fiascos.* Boston: Houghton Mifflin, 1973. Janis insightfully applies social-psychological theory to a series of historical decisions made by groups, including the Bay of Pigs invasion, the handling of the Cuban missile crisis, and the escalation of the Vietnam war.

Jones, James M. *Prejudice and Racism.* Reading, Mass.: Addison-Wesley, 1972. An up-to-date analysis of these social problems, focusing on American race relations.

Pettigrew, Thomas F. *Racially Separate or Together?* New York: McGraw-Hill, 1971. A well-integrated collection of essays by an eminent student of race relations.

UNIT VII
Behavior Disorders and Therapy

The area of abnormal psychology has been undergoing important and far-reaching changes. Not too long ago, the terms "madness" and "insanity" were replaced by the term "mental illness," which represents a medical model of psychological disorder. That is, disorders are assumed to be illnesses roughly analogous to a cold or the measles or the bubonic plague. For some disorders the medical model has worked quite well, but for many

24 **Adjustment and Disorder**
first examines the various criteria of normality and, finding them deficient, suggests the concept of adjustment as a better alternative. It then outlines the usual psychological classification of mental disorders, describes the disorders, and discusses how the types of disorders vary in different population groups.
See related chapters: 13, 14, 17, 18, 23

25 **Bases of Disorder**
looks at various explanations of what causes psychological disorder, including psychoanalytic theory, social-learning theory, analyses of family interaction, and examination of hereditary and biochemical bases of disorder. It then considers key concepts derived from these explanations and some attempts to synthesize the various theoretical approaches.
See related chapters: 4, 7, 10, 14, 17, 18, 19, 21, 23

26 **Individual and Group Psychotherapy**
describes the historical development of psychotherapy, analyzes the major goals and characteristics of all types of psychotherapy, and examines four major categories of psychotherapy: institutional approaches, personal approaches (including psychoanalysis), group approaches, and community approaches.
See related chapters: 17, 18, 19, 22, 23

RELATED CHAPTERS

4
Conditioning and Learning: Behaviorism describes the key concepts of the behaviorist approach. Chapter 25 offers one explanation of how mental disorder arises that is based on those same concepts—the social-learning viewpoint. Also, Chapter 27 presents the therapies based on behaviorist concepts.

7
Heredity and Environment discusses at length the arguments for and against a hereditary basis of schizophrenia. Chapter 25 examines the same issue more briefly, in the context of possible bases of disorder.

10
Social Development: The Case of Morality considers three different theories of social development: psychoanalytic theory, social-learning theory, and cognitive theory. Chapter 25 examines the same theories as possible explanations for the development of psychological disorder.

13
Varieties of Consciousness describes the varied states of consciousness that occur during sleep, meditation, and hypnosis. These descriptions can be compared to Chapter 24's examination of the changes in consciousness that accompany various kinds of mental disorder, as well as to Chapter 28's discussion of the effects of different types of drugs.

14
Physiology, Drives, and Emotion outlines the normal physiological functioning of the nervous system and the glandular system. This description provides the background for Chapter 24's discussion of organically based psychological disorders; Chapter 25's analysis of possible biochemical causes of disorder; and Chapter 28's examination of the mechanisms by which drugs work their effects.

others it has not. As a result, the study of psychological disorders is in a state of flux and confusion. Many different explanations are put forth for every disorder; many different therapies are proposed.

All this ferment makes abnormal psychology an exciting area, but it also makes it a difficult topic to present in an introductory textbook. There are very few answers to any questions that will not be strongly challenged by some group of psychologists. So this unit presents both the traditional medical approaches to behavior disorders and some of the newer approaches; it provides perspective on these various approaches by placing each in its historical context and by examining common threads that run through the different approaches. In this way it strives to help you make sense of abnormal psychology while at the same time sharing in the excitement of this field in flux.

27 Behavior Therapy and Behavior Modification

discusses the recent movement to apply behaviorist principles to the treatment of behavior disorders. After presenting the general behaviorist framework for analyzing disorder, it describes specific behavior-modification techniques based on classical and operant conditioning.
See related chapters: 4, 19, 22

28 Drugs and Drug Therapy

first discusses the impact of modern drugs on the treatment of psychological disorder and describes the major drugs used in treatment and their effects on various disorders. It then considers drugs that can create psychological difficulties, such as alcohol, hallucinogenic drugs, and narcotics.
See related chapters: 13, 14

17

Psychological Testing describes the tests and other techniques that are often used: to assess an individual's adjustment or disorder, discussed in Chapter 24; to investigate the possible bases of disorder, examined in Chapter 25; and to assess the effects of psychotherapy, discussed in Chapter 26.

18

Psychoanalytic Theories of Personality presents Freud's theory of personality as well as several neo-Freudian theories. Chapter 24 describes most of the standard classifications of psychological disorder from a psychoanalytic perspective. Chapter 25 discusses the psychoanalytic explanation of the development of disorder. Chapter 26 describes Freudian psychotherapy, along with many other types.

19

Alternative Conceptions of Personality examines several different non-Freudian approaches to personality, including behaviorist and humanist approaches. Chapter 25 considers behaviorist explanations of psychological disorder. Chapter 26 describes humanist approaches to psychotherapy. And Chapter 27 presents the behaviorist approach to psychotherapy.

21

Patterns of Social Behavior: The Case of Sex Roles considers three different theories of sex-role development: psychoanalytic, social-learning theory, and cognitive theory. All three are also applied to the analysis of psychological disorder in Chapter 25.

22

Attitude Change and Social Influence examines the social processes that bring about changes in attitudes and behaviors. These processes comprise an important part of every form of psychotherapy discussed in Chapters 26 and 27.

23

Individuals and Their Groups considers the effects of social groups on their individual members. These effects are important both as causes of psychological disorder, described in Chapters 24 and 25, and as means of social influence in psychotherapy, especially in group psychotherapy, as discussed in Chapter 26.

It is easy to talk about "madness" as though there were some objective fact one could associate with the word, as though it were something that everyone could agree on. "He must be mad to do such a thing," you might say and expect no one to argue. Who can argue with "madness"?

I thought of this when recently watching a rerun of Cecil B. DeMille's *The Ten Commandments* on television. (I even enjoyed parts of it.) If you saw it, you recall that Charlton Heston (Moses), with staff, and in robe, strides up to Yul Brynner (Pharaoh) and demands that a horde of slaves be set free, without compensation, and allowed to depart the land.

Pharaoh is interrupted while engaged in the difficult task of controlling the destiny of the wealthiest and most civilized land on Earth. He listens patiently, responds testily but without any attempt to visit punishment on Moses. Considering the economic dislocations that freeing the slaves would bring on Egypt, Pharaoh refuses the request.

The entire audience, however, is on Moses' side, every one of them. Pharaoh's action is certainly considered by them to be criminal to the point of madness, and they wait with great satisfaction for the ten plagues that will afflict the entire land of Egypt as punishment.

But if some black had, in 1835, attempted to enter the White House in order to demand of President Andrew Jackson that the black slaves in America be permitted to depart the country, the question of whether Jackson would refuse would be entirely academic. The black Moses would never have reached Jackson. It is most likely he would have been killed out of hand, and the best he could have hoped for was imprisonment as a madman.

I am quite certain that the American whites of 1835 would have agreed with our modern audience in considering Pharaoh mad or criminal for refusing Moses' request and would also have considered our mythical black mad or criminal for making the request. What's more, very few would have been aware of any contradiction in these two attitudes. Had I been there to point out the contradiction, they would have considered *me* mad. Apparently, the question of who is mad depends not only on time, place, and circumstance but on the attitudes and prejudices of those who pass judgment in such matters.

The most remarkable madman in literature is surely Don Quixote. For nearly 400 years, people of all nations have laughed at his madness, at his ability to believe the ridiculous fictions of the medieval romances of chivalry, at his mistaking windmills for giants, prostitutes for virgins, and so on.

And yet Cervantes, the author of this greatest of all novels, slowly lets Don Quixote win us over by revealing him to be a man of great intelligence and great virtue set down in a mean and petty world.

By the end of the book, when Don Quixote recovers his senses at last, becomes part of the real world, and dies, we weep for him. We weep that he dies, but we weep also that he becomes sane, for somehow Cervantes makes us prefer to be gloriously mad with a man like Don Quixote than wickedly sane with everyone else. Or is it that he faces us with the wonderfully disturbing question of whether it might be Don Quixote who was sane after all, and the world that was mad?

Isaac Asimov

24
Adjustment and Disorder

A psychiatric social worker sits at her desk reading the file of one of her clients, a man with an IQ of 50. It occurs to her that she considers the client abnormal but would never apply that word to the brilliant doctor down the hall, even though his IQ is 150, equally far from the average IQ of 100. Later, trying to counsel a fifty-five-year-old woman whose son insisted she come to the clinic because she plans to marry a man who is only twenty-three, the social worker recalls that she felt no need to counsel her uncle, who recently married a woman less than half his age. Next, a man diagnosed as schizophrenic is ushered in. His behavior reminds the social worker of that of an Eastern holy man she has read about. It disturbs her that the man in front of her is about to be committed to a mental hospital while the other has followers who worshipfully take down his revelations. She finds that she must stop here in the course of her profession to attempt to reformulate for herself an answer to a fundamental question: What does "abnormal" mean?

CRITERIA OF NORMALITY

It stands to reason that an explanation of what is abnormal—away from the normal—first requires a definition of **normal.** In medical science, normal generally means the integrity of structure and function of an organ or other body part. A broken bone, an excess of certain sugars in the blood, an ulcer on the wall of the stomach are all abnormal. For physicians, the line between normal and abnormal is usually easy to draw. For psychologists and psychiatrists, the criteria that divide normal behavior from abnormal are not so easily defined. In fact, there are several definitions of normality within the field of psychology today, each based on a different theoretical orientation. Chapters 26 and 27 present the various kinds of psychotherapies based on these orientations. This chapter first provides an examination of normality and then presents a discussion

Figure 24.1 The experiences and actions of people who are called "disturbed" or "mentally ill" are often only extreme forms of the depressed moods, exaggerated fears, and self-deceptions that everyone experiences periodically. This man, a patient in a mental hospital, was playing baseball on the grounds of the hospital when, in the middle of a play, he left the game, lay down, and withdrew by covering himself with his coat. You may have felt so depressed at times that you have wanted to withdraw in a similar fashion.

of psychological disorder based on current diagnostic practices of psychiatrists and clinical psychologists.

The **statistical criterion** is one possible way to define normality. It says that what most people do is normal. Any deviation from the majority, then, is abnormal. Use of this criterion presents several problems. First, it is specific to particular times and to particular places. For example, wearing a bikini at the beach today is normal; if a woman had worn one even twenty years ago, she would have been considered abnormal—an exhibitionist, perhaps. And in some countries it is normal for men to kiss each other, whereas in the United States the majority of men do not exchange kisses. Think of how returning Russian cosmonauts have been welcomed: They were given a hug and kiss and a bouquet of flowers by the chief of state. Can you imagine an American president welcoming astronauts like that?

Another problem with the statistical approach is that it does not distinguish between desirable and undesirable deviations from the norm. A person with an IQ of 150 must be considered abnormal in the same sense as one with an IQ of 50. And in a society where most people cheat on their income tax, the person who writes an honest return would have to be considered abnormal. Clearly, the statistical criterion is deficient as a means of distinguishing between normal and abnormal.

Some personality and developmental theorists define normality as a goal, or ideal, that people strive to attain. This definition of normality has been called the **ideal mental health criterion.** However, the criterion of ideal mental health differs from theorist to theorist: For Abraham Maslow and Carl Rogers it is self-actualization; for Erich Fromm it is productivity; for Erik Erikson, integrity. (These theories are discussed in Chapters 18 and 19.) In contrast to the statistical criterion, which defines the majority of people as normal, the ideal mental health criterion allows only a highly developed few to be classified as normal. Its usefulness as a criterion for separating normal from abnormal is therefore extremely limited.

The **clinical criterion** defines normality as the absence of abnormal symptoms. A clinician—a psychiatrist or clinical psychologist—decides for each of his patients whether the patient's symptoms indicate mental disorder. If one could clearly define the bases on which clinicians make their judgments, it seems that one could arrive at a universal set of criteria of normality. However, the bases for diagnosis—such as amount of subjective unhappiness or

Figure 24.2 Does this man strike you as odd? Do you think he should seek help? The photograph, taken in the 1930s, is of an upper-class Frenchman. In his time and place, he might have been considered eccentric, but there would have been no basis for judging him as abnormal or maladjusted. Unusual behaviors that in one context may be signs of disorder may, in another, be only amusing. Defining abnormality, then, is difficult but is of great practical importance.

degree of social maladjustment—depend greatly on the individual clinician's interpretation. The clinical criterion therefore cannot serve to universally define normality.

Most of the difficulties with the clinical criterion stem from the fact that it treats psychological disorder as if it were analogous to physical disease. Psychological problems are called "mental illness," and psychologists look for symptoms of illness in the same way that doctors look for symptoms of physical disease. In *The Myth of Mental Illness,* Thomas Szasz suggests that most mental disorders involve *problems in living,* problems that in the final analysis are solvable only by the person who has them. They cannot be cured in the way that a medical doctor cures a disease.

ADJUSTMENT

Adjustment is often used in preference to the concept of normality, especially by psychologists with a humanistic orientation who are dissatisfied with the concept of normality; Szasz is one of these. Many psychologists speak of maladjustment rather than of abnormality because decisions about who is maladjusted do not seem to require reference to a fixed moral or evaluative standard. Although adjustment does imply a referent outside the person— adjustment *to* something—the maladjusted person himself can choose the standard to which he should adjust (at least sometimes). His adjustment can then be judged on a range of efficient to inefficient. In this type of arrangement, the therapist need not impose upon his client a particular ideal or a particular moral judgment, as he must if he is concerned with a fixed concept of normality.

There are four main aspects of adjustment with which people are concerned: physical, psychological, social, and moral. Physically, the goal of adjustment is survival. If a person feels hungry, he eats; if he is attacked by disease-causing germs, his body marshals materials to fight the disease.

At the psychological level, the most basic referent for adjustment is probably pleasure, or subjective happiness. In Freudian and neo-Freudian theory, the ego is the agent of adjustment; it mediates between primitive impulses from the id and the moralistic demands of the superego. By means of defense mechanisms, the ego protects itself from anxiety generated by unsatisfied id impulses or from threats to its self-esteem generated by the superego (see Chapter 18). Learning theory also says that pleasure and the avoidance of pain are the basic goals of adjustment. Responses that bring rewards are repeated, and those that bring punishment are extinguished (see Chapter 4). In some situations, however, specification of a reward is not so simple: Hungry people sometimes give their food to others, and some Hindus have chosen to starve to death rather than eat the meat of sacred cows. Thus, although it is probably true that psychological adjustment brings pleasure, it is necessary to consider that, depending on the individual, the pleasure may stem from such different sources as satisfaction of hunger, social approval, or even ethical behavior.

People live with and depend on other people; they cannot survive and be happy without dealing with other people. In other words, physical and psychological adjustment presuppose social adjustment, the third aspect of adjustment. At the social level, the referent for survival is probably the species. Individuals do not lead isolated lives; in order to survive and maximize their pleasure, they must work together. People form social contracts; they agree to cooperate, and they establish certain rules and regulations to ensure that the social organization runs smoothly.

But it sometimes happens that adjustment on one dimension—say, the social—results in maladjustment on another—say, the psychological. For example, stealing is considered necessary in order to be accepted by peer groups in certain subcultures, so a young person in such a subculture must

Figure 24.3 A scene from the film *Who's Afraid of Virginia Woolf* (which is based on a play by Edward Albee). This unsettling drama depicts one night in the lives of four people, two American university professors and their wives. In the course of the film, the characters, who at first appear to be intelligent, urbane, and well adjusted, are brought into conflicts with one another. These conflicts expose cruelty, fearfulness, extreme dependencies, and even bizarre delusions in the characters, weaknesses that may never have come to the surface before and might never be exposed again in such dramatic force. Albee seems to be asking his audience to review their own experience and to ask themselves: Are these people abnormal? Or is it the norm that under the surface civility of every adult lie weaknesses and cruelties that will, under the right circumstances, break through and show themselves?

balance his psychological adjustment (stealing for acceptance) against his adjustment to the society at large, which prohibits stealing. And different societies have different organizations and rules, so what constitutes adjustment in one society—or even in one subculture—is maladjustment in another. You can see, then, that any talk of adjustment requires referents: adjustment to things—a fit between a certain goal, standard, or problem in a specified situation and the behavior that is designed to cope with that goal, standard, or problem.

The final dimension of adjustment, the moral one, overrides the others in the sense that a person asks: "What form of adjustment is right? What should I do to adjust?" Although there is no easy answer to that question, some psychologists have tried to outline a rough hierarchy of bases of moral adjustment. Lawrence Kohlberg, for one, has studied moral adjustment in children and young adults and has found that as a person matures, his judgments of what is moral pass through six stages (see Chapter 10). People in the first two stages view adjustment in terms of personal pleasure and pain. At the second two stages the referent for adjustment is the rules and regulations of the person's social system. In the final two stages, the rules of the social system are subordinated to higher ethical principles, and people adjust to the principles. Kohlberg's stages of moral development can be interpreted as outlining a hierarchy of moral adjustment.

The question of adjustment, then, is far from simple. Each person weighs and balances the demands of physical, psychological, social, and moral adjustment. Who, then, defines maladjustment? Physicians diagnose physical disorder; courts rule on social abnormality according to the laws of the society; clergymen usually serve as authorities in the moral realm; and, in most Western societies, psychiatrists and clinical psychologists decide about psychological maladjustment. Although the four dimensions of adjustment overlap considerably, this chapter focuses on the psychological dimension. It attempts to answer the question, "How do psychologists decide what behavior is maladjusted?"

Psychologists' judgments are based on their training—both academic and practical—and on their experience. They interview a prospective patient and discuss his problem. They often administer a battery of tests, such as the Minnesota Multiphasic Personality Inventory, the Thematic Apperception Test, the Rorschach Test, the Wechsler Intelligence Test, and perhaps some other personality scales (see Chapter 17). The clinician uses his own conceptual categories of disorder as he processes the vast quantity of information he gets from the client. His categories are based on one of the models of normality, on his evaluation of the patient's adjustment, or on some combination of normality and adjustment. *In general, he will apply the label of abnormal or maladjusted to a person who is uncomfortable, who is unhappy with his inner life and interpersonal relations, who has difficulty performing the tasks expected of him, or whose actions appear bizarre.* Many clinicians will try to diagnose the abnormality or maladjustment in terms of the official categories of mental disorder employed by the American Psychiatric Association. As you read about the categories, try to decide for yourself what model or models of normality they are based on and whether they supply a sufficient basis for defining abnormality.

THE CLASSIFICATION OF DISORDERS

Table 24.1 displays the categories of disorder set out by the American Psychiatric Association. The **diagnostic categories** are based on clinical studies and clinical experience.

The classification scheme is open to criticism on several counts. First, the principles upon which the classifications are based are not consistent. Some

---

Table 24.1 Major Categories of Mental Disorder

I. Mental Retardation

II. Organic Brain Syndromes (disorders
caused by or associated with
impairment of brain tissue
function, such as senile dementia
and alcoholic psychosis)

III. Psychoses Not Attributed to Physical
Conditions Listed Previously
Schizophrenia
Simple type
Hebephrenic type
Catatonic type
Paranoid type
Acute schizophrenic episode
Latent type
Residual type
Schizo-affective type
Childhood type
Chronic undifferentiated type
Major affective disorders
Involutional melancholia
Manic-depressive illness
(manic type, depressed
type, or circular type)
Paranoid states

IV. Neuroses
Anxiety neurosis
Hysterical neurosis (conversion
type or dissociative type)
Phobic neurosis
Obsessive compulsive neurosis
Depressive neurosis
Neurasthenic neurosis
Depersonalization neurosis
Hypochondriacal neurosis

V. Personality Disorders and Certain
Other Nonpsychotic Mental
Disorders (such as paranoid
personality, schizoid personality,
and antisocial personality)
Sexual deviations (such as
fetishism and sadism)
Sexual Orientation
Disturbances (such
as homosexuality)
Alcoholism
Drug dependence

VI. Psychophysiologic Disorders
(physical disorders, e.g.,
respiratory or gastrointestinal,
of presumably psychogenic
origin)

VII. Special Symptoms (such as
speech disturbances, tics,
disorders of sleep)

VIII. Transient Situational Disturbances
(during infancy, childhood,
adolescence, adult life, or
late life)

IX. Behavior Disorders of Childhood
and Adolescence (such as
withdrawing reaction,
overanxious reaction, and group
delinquent reaction)

X. Conditions Without Manifest
Psychiatric Disorder and
Nonspecific Conditions (such
as marital maladjustment and
occupational maladjustment)

Source: Adapted from American Psychiatric Association, *Diagnostic and Statistical Manual of Mental Disorders,*
2nd ed. (Washington, D.C.: American Psychiatric Association, 1968).

disorders are classed together on the basis of cause, or etiology—even though the observable symptoms manifested by persons with the disorders are very diverse. Most of the organic psychoses and many of the categories of mental retardation (Categories I and II of Table 24.1) are classified by cause. This principle is consistent with the model by which medical science classes diseases. Other categories, however, are based on similarities of displayed symptoms. Even here, as Edward Zigler and Leslie Phillips point out, the symptoms are combined in a number of conceptually distinct ways: Psychosomatic disorders are considered syndromes—unique clusters of specific physical *symptoms*—whereas psychoses are generally combined into types, with the groupings based on similarity among *persons*.

One further criticism that has been leveled at the classification scheme is that it tends to channel clinicians' conceptions. In interviewing and observing patients, a clinician will look for response patterns with which he is familiar—patterns of behavior characteristic of one of the categories. This criticism says that conceptual channeling prevents the clinician from seeing each patient as an individual.

In defense of the classification system, it can be said that the system permits psychologists and psychiatrists to share information about symptoms and therapies and to compare notes on possible causes. Perhaps the worst that can be said about the present classification system is that it is premature. Because so little is really known with confidence about the causes of nonorganic types of disorders (and because existing therapies are far from certain to produce cures), it may yet be too early to set up a rigidly delineated diagnostic system. The most convincing argument for the use of the classification system is that the descriptions of particular disorders and their manifestations are quite consistent in various cultures and even throughout history.

Some of the major types of disorders shown in Table 24.1 are described at length in the following sections of the chapter. The descriptions are based largely on psychoanalytic theory, described at length in Chapter 18.

NEUROSES

Everyone fears some things and takes steps to avoid them. A neurotic fears things inside himself—urges, thoughts, and feelings—whose expression may be punished. The steps the neurotic takes to avoid his fears merely hide rather than abolish them. He is continually anxious that the fearful things he has hidden may reappear. As long as the anxiety is bearable, the neurotic may have no noticeable trouble with life and society. But if the anxiety increases, he must take increasingly severe steps to cope with it. As a result, the

Figure 24.4 *Anxiety*, by Edvard Munch. Munch, probably more than any other artist, expressed in his paintings the emotions and forces studied by psychiatrists and psychologists. Here the vaguely threatening red sky and the tense stark faces serve as the visual image of anxiety, so important in many explanations of neurosis. A biography of Munch reveals that he had a great deal of experience with such disturbed feelings, both in himself and in members of his family.
(Collection, Museum of Modern Art, New York; Matthew T. Mellon Fund.)

neurotic focuses too much on his own internal problems, and his social behavior suffers. His friends recognize that he is uptight, but they are unable to see inside him to the source of his fears. As the neurotic's social behavior becomes less and less satisfactory, he also begins to worry about that, thereby adding to his anxieties. He takes additional steps to cope with both his anxiety and the problems in his social behavior. If these steps fail, the neurotic may suffer a breakdown; if they succeed, he continues to live in a society, but his social existence is often limited and crippled.

Certain basic theoretical premises are needed to explain the source of disordered human behaviors that are called neuroses. There is Sigmund Freud's concept of **repression,** one mechanism by which objectionable impulses are removed from consciousness in order to avoid the anxiety they evoke. Through repression, we become unaware of the thoughts that trouble us. If repression were always successful, there would be no reason for the emotional overreaction we call neurosis. It is when repression fails to be effective and forbidden thoughts and feelings threaten to return to consciousness that neurotic symptoms come into play as a kind of second line of defense against the threat of anxiety. These symptoms become tension-laden, last-ditch efforts that may seem to be desperate maneuvers to normal persons but that are the only compromise with anxiety that the neurotic is capable of making.

Neurosis does not occur suddenly but requires time to develop. During the course of neurotic development, the continual repression of thoughts and impulses is costly. Some part of the psychic energy and attention usually applied to constructive work and the management of interpersonal relationships is diverted by the neurotic in order to guard against the many caged impulses he has found necessary to repress throughout his life. By adulthood the neurotic does not have as much free psychic energy as most people do and is thus crippled by limited resources in meeting the challenges of living. The neurotic does not deliberately choose this way of life; he is forced into it by his constant battle with anxiety created by painful and negative experiences in the course of growing up.

Unlike the psychotic, the neurotic is in touch with reality, but his is a troubled reality; his world is real but painful. He seldoms acts in a totally bizarre fashion, but he is uncomfortable with life and deals with it in an inefficient manner. The anxiety the neurotic experiences may appear intellectually in the form of worry and concern, emotionally in the form of depression or mood swings, and physically in the form of any of a variety of bodily symptoms (headache, sweating, muscle tightness, heart palpitation, or hysteria). The neurotic's anxiety reaction makes him live a life marked by continuous upset and few periods of true tranquility.

Phobias

When neurotic anxiety is focused on a particular object or situation, it is called a phobia. Life has many dangers that realistically must be feared, but the victim of a phobia is frightened disproportionately by some aspects of existence or by objects or places that seem danger-free to most people (crowds, open spaces, closed areas, heights, school).

Obsessions and Compulsions

Another way of dealing with neurotic tension is to control it through an obsessive-compulsive reaction. The obsessive neurotic is totally occupied with recurrent thoughts and actions that he cannot banish from his consciousness. The obsessive-compulsive preoccupation may be unpleasant and painful, such as a recurrent urge to harm one's family, or completely harmless, such as the need to avoid stepping on the cracks in the pavement. Captain Queeg, a character in *The Caine Mutiny* (shown in Figure 24.5), was obsessed

Figure 24.5 A scene from the film *The Caine Mutiny*, in which the officers of an American naval vessel mutinied against a captain whose compulsions and obsessions they judged to be signs of "mental illness."

with discipline on his ship, being unable to separate trivial matters from important ones. In times of stress, he also compulsively rolled some ball bearings around in his hand; he kept the ball bearings in his pocket at all times for just such occasions.

The obsessive person is heavily laden with worry and doubt. He fears that he has failed to do something that is important to his welfare and to the well-being of his loved ones, and he may devote such an inordinate amount of time to an obsessive-compulsive double-checking of every trivial thing he does that he consequently accomplishes very little. He is even more threatened by being forced to make a decision about the future.

Obsessive-compulsive solutions to the problem of anxiety more frequently occur in intelligent persons with relatively high social status. This response to anxiety is intellectual—less direct and primitive than a neurotic reaction such as hysteria.

Hysteria

The form of neurosis characterized by a collection of physical symptoms that exist without an actual organic basis is known as hysteria. The hysterical personality may experience a loss of hearing, speech, touch, or vision or may be the victim of severe pain or muscle weakness. These symptoms appear to be like those caused by organic illness, but they are not quite perfect imitations, for they tend to be greatly exaggerated and are usually neurologically impossible. Nevertheless, they apparently lessen the individual's anxiety.

The hysteric might awaken one morning paralyzed from the waist down or might find himself deaf or blind. A normal reaction to such a traumatic event would be terror, agitation, and violent upset, but the hysteric may placidly lack anxiety about his condition (although this lack of concern is not characteristic of all hysterics). When a hysteric adapts well to such catastrophes, it is thought that the physical symptoms provide freedom from the nagging anxiety that had previously made life miserable for him. For example, a wife who dreads sexual relations may develop a paralysis of the back. Or a man who feels guilty about masturbation may wake up with his hand paralyzed. Many hysterics live out their lives in doctors' offices; they are frequently hospitalized; and many undergo a number of fruitless surgical explorations.

Neurosis and Depression

When the neurotic fails to solve issues in his life, to cope with the usual conflicts, or to manage disturbed human relationships, the outcome may be an apathetic depression in which he ceases to function effectively. The "advantage" of depression is that it frees the individual from the pace of life. The extent to which he withdraws from his conflict is a measure of the seriousness of the emotional disorder. Bodily movements slow down and become lethargic, and a mood of hopelessness and helplessness pervades the person. Even mental and intellectual functions seem to proceed in slow motion.

When neurotic depressions occur rather suddenly, they may be a response to a severe personal loss, such as losing a job or the death of a loved one. But these depressions differ in intensity and duration from the normal mood changes that most people experience in such situations. Some neurotics seem moderately depressed throughout their lives, and this depression merely deepens in time of crisis. This generalized, daily, depressive outlook on life may be coupled with an oppressive sense of fatigue, lassitude, and irritability.

PSYCHOSES

The neurotic may be handicapped in interpersonal relations, but, emotionally crippled or not, he continues to slug it out with life. If a person's psychological distortions and abnormalities of perception and behavior ever reach such

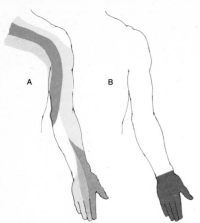

Figure 24.6   A patient who complained to a doctor that his right hand had become numb might be diagnosed either as suffering from damage to the nervous system or as a neurotic suffering from hysteria, depending on the exact pattern of his numbness. The skin areas served by different nerves in the arm are shown in (A). The "glove" anesthesia shown in (B) could not result from damage to these nerves.

Figure 24.7   The symptoms of neurotic depression are usually apathy and withdrawal. The depressed individual simply stops caring about what is going on around him; he may spend days or weeks at a time sitting or lying in one room, feeling only gloom. Usually driven into depression by some experience he has failed to come to grips with or some conflict he has failed to resolve, he dwells on his despair and does not act, so that the original uncompleted act or unresolved conflict can only worsen. This kind of vicious cycle—unsatisfying situations causing neurotic reactions, which produce more unsatisfying situations—characterizes many psychological disorders.

an irrational, fantastic, and fear-laden level that the person withdraws completely from normal life, he is labeled psychotic. It has been said that the neurotic dreams in an unreal way about life, whereas the psychotic lives life as an unreal dream.

Both neurosis and psychosis appear to have a common base in that a person afflicted with either feels tension, anxiety, and a sense of threat to the self. But the neurotic attempts to deal and cope with these issues, for example, by employing defenses that enable him to keep functioning; the psychotic, without the resources available to the neurotic, gives up and withdraws from life altogether.

Psychosis is not a single disease; therefore, it has no single cause or single cure. It is, rather, a collection of symptoms that indicate that the ego, or self, is having grave difficulties meeting the demands of life. In some yet unexplained way, biological and psychological forces combine to produce serious disorder. As Chapters 7 and 25 point out, inherited genetic bases and consequent biochemical imbalances might account for schizophrenia. Many theorists attribute serious disorder to early childhood experience in which the individual has reacted inadequately to stress, has failed to cope with it constructively, and has been forced to defend himself against the onslaught of anxiety. The defenses he employs may be sufficient to solve immediate problems, but such defenses are disruptive of long-term motivation, perception, action, and thinking.

Schizophrenia

The individual disturbed in most of the dimensions of human adjustment will probably become psychotic, and this disorder may take the particular form generally called schizophrenia. All people diagnosed as schizophrenics have in common severe disturbances in the cognitive, emotional, and perceptual senses of the self and of others, but one schizophrenic differs from another along specific dimensions, as can be noted in a brief examination of the subdivisions of schizophrenia.

Simple Schizophrenia Simple schizophrenics are not usually subject to hallucinations or delusions, nor do they commonly act in bizarre ways. Their psychosis is characterized by a slow, insidious reduction of external attachments and interests, a process in which their interpersonal relationships wither away and mental deterioration takes place. They are left apathetic, indifferent human beings whose contact with others is minimal and restricted.

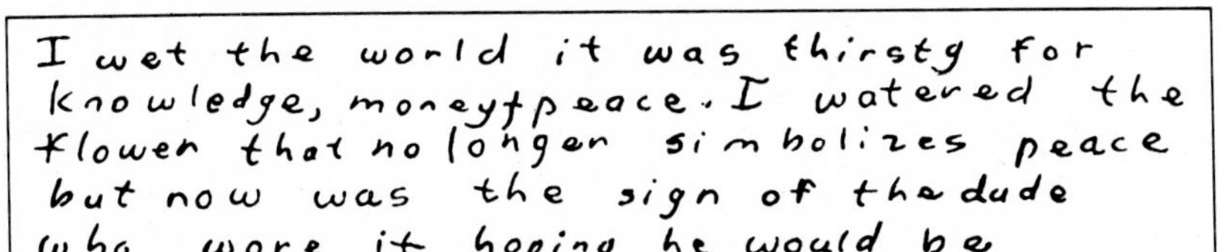

I wet the world it was thirsty for knowledge, money, peace. I watered the flower that no longer simbolizes peace but now was the sign of the dude who wore it hoping he would be watered for he was h~~ungry~~ thirsty for love.

I wet the world to kepp the leaves from getting to brown from the son. I watered him but he no longer was thirsty the lady on calavary st. gave him a drink. He died of pain not of thirst. She couldnt get the nails out becouse Franks hardware closes at 6:00 p.m.

Figure 24.8 This passage was written by a fifteen-year-old boy named Freddie, who was diagnosed as schizophrenic. His use of language is characteristic of schizophrenics, who commonly produce bizarre and jumbled but grammatically sound writings and speech. Some psychiatrists consider such speech a kind of secret code through which the schizophrenic effectively isolates himself from the rest of humanity.

Figure 24.9 This illustration was painted by a male patient diagnosed as schizophrenic. Schizophrenic art frequently uses intense colors to express the feelings, attitudes, and concerns of the patient. This particular illustration contains biblical allusions and a number of references to sexual organs and sexual functioning, all common themes in psychosis.

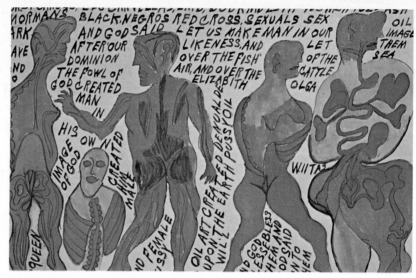

Hebephrenic Schizophrenia

The popular stereotype of insanity stems from observing the bizarre behavior of those who undergo this most severe disintegration of personality. In the hebephrenic type of schizophrenia, speech may be incoherent or unintelligible. The person diagnosed as a hebephrenic may giggle or laugh inappropriately; he lives in a private world dominated by hallucination, delusion, and fantasy; and his behavior is almost totally unpredictable. One moment he may believe he is a famous personage (Napoleon, God); the next, he may be convinced that the world has come to an end and that he is its only survivor; and the next, he may lose bowel and bladder control and act like a very young child.

Catatonic Schizophrenia

In the catatonic type of schizophrenia, the patient lives in a stuporous state. The catatonic can hold himself in painful postures for hours and not show any response to the physical discomfort that others would find impossible to bear. He may be mute and sit unmoving and unresponsive in the hospital ward. While the patient inhibits his voluntary actions and resists responding to pressure by others, he may be preoccupied with a stream of hallucinations, such as voices that whisper to him of plots against his life. Catatonia appears to be a dramatic emergency attempt to cope with overwhelming, anxiety-laden experiences; seeing no escape, the patient immobilizes himself for fear of making a wrong move. Catatonic patients occasionally come to life and display violent behavior.

Figure 24.10 In the stuporous form of the catatonic reaction, the patient may assume a strained posture, such as crouching, and maintain it for long periods of time. The body is generally quite malleable and if, for example, an arm is extended by the patient himself or by another person, the limb remains in that position for a long period of time, a condition known as waxy flexibility. Although he appears uncomprehending, the catatonic may do the opposite of what he is asked, indicating that he understands the request. Upon recovery he can remember incidents that occurred during the stupor.

Paranoid Schizophrenia

The symptoms of a person who is labeled a paranoid schizophrenic are not as visible as the rigid withdrawal of the catatonic or the bizarre behavior of the hebephrenic. The paranoid schizophrenic experiences difficulty in the way he views the world and the people in it. He trusts no one and is constantly watchful, for he is convinced others are plotting against him because they are envious of his superior ability or special status. The combination of grandiose paranoid delusions of persecution and the emotional and mental disorganization of schizophrenia may make the paranoid dangerous. He may seek to retaliate against his tormentors as he gathers, over a lifetime, his own brand of evidence of suspicious behavior around him. Each of us draws erroneous conclusions about people and events, but we check the accuracy of our beliefs against the opinions and views of others. The mistrustful, resentful paranoid is isolated from such meaningful contact with others and thus systematically constructs a tangled, distorted view of life

Figure 24.11 These paintings were done by a male patient diagnosed as schizophrenic with paranoid tendencies. Both illustrations are characterized by the consistent symbolism of watchful eyes, grasping hands, and the self as subject matter. In the first painting, which reflects a subdued emotional state, there is a strong emphasis on the eyes, with a figure watching over the shoulder. The torso of the central figure is surrounded by hands, and the figure in the background is reaching out. Religiosity as well as delusions of persecution and grandeur may be seen in the cross and the Christ-like figure bestowing a wreath. The second painting, elaborate in composition and vivid in color, reflects a more active emotional state. Again there is an emphasis on the eyes and on the hands, represented here as tentacles and claws.

that warps his whole existence. (The Diagnostic Manual of the American Psychiatric Association distinguishes between paranoid schizophrenia and paranoid states, which are affective reactions—discussed below—although the distinction is not always easy to make clinically.)

Affective Reactions

Persons diagnosed as suffering from emotional reactions, or affective reactions, experience mood disorders in which they are excessively and inappropriately happy or unhappy, optimistic or pessimistic, manic or depressed. These emotional disorders may be furthur complicated by the disintegration and disorder of the schizophrenic process.

Manic Reactions The manic patient displays symptoms of increasing agitation, excitement, and deteriorating judgment in relationships with others. The usual history of an expanding manic reaction describes a lightening of mood, a rising level of activity, a subjective sense of accelerated thought processes, and increased alertness and perception. As the mania strengthens, speech and activity speed up, eating and sleeping become annoying interferences, and the victim becomes more agitated and easily irritated by attempts to slow him down. In the final stages of a full-blown manic reaction, the patient may be close to delirium—confused, disoriented, incoherent, and difficult to control. His world is very much like a movie that has been speeded up until the figures and events are no more than a blur of frantic, purposeless movement.

Depressive Reactions Depression and mania at first appear to be opposite types of human adjustment. But theorists have suggested that the frantic activity of the manic is a futile attempt to ward off an underlying depression. In some cases, depression and mania may alternate with one another over short or long periods in a person's life.

Depression, like mania, is an exaggeration of the mood that all of us experience for brief periods of time. The person sinking into a deepening depression becomes preoccupied with feelings of failure, sinfulness, worthlessness, and despair. He cannot be reasoned with or told to cheer up, for his woe is an internal event that does not correspond to reality as others see it. Overcome with his personal hopelessness, the depressive cuts off communication with the outside world, abandons active attempts to help himself, and usually begins to contemplate ending it all by suicide. The depressive may not hallucinate, but he may descend to such a stuporous level of mental and physical inactivity that he may become bedridden and require force-feeding.

PERSONALITY DISORDERS

Both neurotic behavior and much psychotic behavior come about through attempts to control anxiety. Other kinds of abnormality are not necessarily based on anxiety; they include such disorders as sexual deviance and antisocial personality. In each case, *the person's life style is marked by a limited capacity to adapt to his social environment and by an inability to establish a rational, stable, rewarding relationship to the environment and the people who inhabit it.* The behavior of such persons appears socially inappropriate and, on closer inspection, is found to be inflexible, unstable, and immature.

Most theorists believe that personality disorders are based on anxious and painful childhood experiences that the developing person has not coped with successfully. The adult with a disordered personality acts out his conflicts in ways that elicit rejection, censure, and punishment from the better-adjusted members of society. That is, he has failed to learn socially acceptable ways of resolving conflict and attaining gratification of his needs.

The Antisocial Personality

The antisocial personality has been described as a person who misbehaves socially, is without guilt about his misbehavior, and is incapable of forming lasting affectionate bonds with other human beings. (The terms "psychopath" and "sociopath" have been used to designate persons suffering this personality disorder.)

Some antisocial personalities are irresponsible, emotionally shallow humans who cannot avoid getting into social trouble; some are in aggressive and open rebellion against society; some are criminals who prey on others as a way of life. Yet these types have certain common characteristics: *Each appears not to suffer from guilt and is egocentric, impulsive, and irresponsible; each cannot tolerate the normal frustrations of everyday life; and each exercises poor judgment by seeking immediate gratification of his needs* at the expense of more important and valuable long-term goals. The antisocial personality may be intelligent, but his relationships with others are without affection, depth, love, or loyalty. He mimics human emotions that he cannot feel, and he cannot organize his life past the pleasures of the moment and the lure of immediate temptation. Moreover, he has little insight about the kind of person he is and seems unable to profit from past errors in his style of life.

Antisocial personalities grow to adulthood relatively free of anxiety and the need for acceptance and support by other persons. People are like objects to them—things to be used for gratification and then cast coldly aside. Some psychopaths find this formula quite workable and rise to eminent positions. Their psychopathy is not recognized as an emotional disorder, and they are envied as ruthless businessmen or realistically tough and calculating politicians. In the movie *Citizen Kane,* a fictional biography of publisher William Randolph Hearst, the title character appears to have a psychopathic personality. Although he becomes extremely rich and powerful, he is not capable of love and so dies alone and friendless. Other antisocial personalities, however, continue to get into trouble with social authority and to be rejected by other persons until they finally seek help.

The Sexual Deviant

A deviant is one who departs from accepted standards of proper behavior. Yet it is common knowledge that private sexual behavior regularly differs from the public standards set for it. In fact, normal sexual behavior is what consenting adults agree to in private. However, popular opinion (and legislation in

Figure 24.12 Psychotic depression carries with it a serious danger of suicide. This woodcut by Käthe Kollwitz expresses the feelings of hopelessness, meaningless, and ugliness that a person may experience in severe depression.
(Courtesy of the National Gallery of Art; Washington, D.C., Rosenwaid Collection.)

552

several states) labels some common forms of sexual expression as disordered. The professional clinician, in contrast, believes sexual activity is disordered primarily when it is compulsive, exclusive, destructive, accompanied by great anxiety and guilt, bizarre, inefficient, or the cause of discomfort. In fact, clinicians rarely diagnose someone as being a sexual deviant.

ORGANIC DISORDERS

Psychoses resulting from acute or chronic brain disorders will become increasingly common as medical technology extends the average life span of human beings. The brain deterioration that may accompany growing old can distort memory, judgment, comprehension, and emotional control.

Patients in their seventies account for as much as 30 percent of all those admitted to mental hospitals each year. These patients not only have cerebral arteriosclerosis (hardening of the brain arteries) and other forms of senile brain disorder, they also display unmistakable evidence of psychotic disruption of their lives. Controls that these patients were once able to exert over their behavior, emotions, and thoughts seem to deteriorate and become ineffective. However, there is no necessary connection between the amount of damage to the central nervous system and the severity of the psychosis. Brain damage does not produce psychosis so much as it triggers the psychotic process in some persons. For these persons, past, present, and future are jumbled together, conscious and unconscious thoughts merge and mingle, and the senses do not function properly. These events create a psychological crisis great enough to tip the balance of rational adjustment.

Deterioration of the brain and central nervous system in an aging organism is only one of a number of possible causes of organic psychosis. Psychosis can be associated with infection or trauma or with faulty metabolism, nutrition, or growth. Of these, a significant contributor will continue to be accidental trauma to the brain. More than 50,000 persons each year are killed in automobile accidents, and a great many more are injured. When brain tissue is cut, torn, crushed, or penetrated in an accident, enough damage may be done to produce a crisis in the person's life.

If the damage is not too severe, it is the patient's psychological response to faulty physiological functioning that determines whether he will become psychotic or manage to begin the long road back to a near-normal existence. The psychological state of an individual before he has undergone brain damage is a prime determinant of how he will respond to this new event.

EPIDEMIOLOGY OF MENTAL DISORDER

Epidemiology is the study of the incidence, distribution, and control of illness in a population. For mental disorder, it is difficult to estimate the incidence, that is, the rate and range of occurrence. The number of people admitted to hospitals for mental disorder is far smaller than the number of people who are affected with mental disorder. Still, admission and residence rates for state hospitals, county hospitals, and outpatient clinics constitute the best available statistics for estimating the prevalance and distribution of mental disorder.

It is estimated that from 6 to 10 percent of the population of the United States will be treated for mental disorder and that a sizable proportion of the remaining population will suffer from unrecorded maladies. In the famous Midtown Manhattan study, which was published in 1962, Leo Srole and his colleagues categorized a full 81.5 percent of the population they studied as "less than well." And statistics from the military show that during World War II, 15 million, or 12 percent, of the inductees were rejected for psychological disorder. It is possible, however, to question the criteria that were used to make these classifications of disorder, as was shown in the discussion of criteria of normality at the beginning of this chapter.

Figure 24.13 Antisocial personality is a diagnostic category reserved for persons whose long-term behavioral patterns include emotional immaturity, inability to follow social or legal standards, poorly developed relationships with others, and disregard for the well-being of others. In *Citizen Kane*, the film by Orson Welles, the title character climbed to power in American society by using people for his own ends, violating ethical standards, and sacrificing his family and friends. Many theorists argue that psychiatric diagnoses are warranted only when the person's problem behaviors are frequent and intense, and when their effects on the individual or the society are extensive. Under these conditions, a diagnosis of antisocial personality would be warranted for Kane.

Figure 24.14 This x-ray photograph of a boxer's head at the moment he receives a punch shows that the force of the blow causes the brain to be momentarily displaced against the back of the skull. If severe or numerous enough, such displacements can cause tissue damage serious enough to produce an organic psychosis.

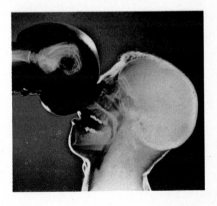

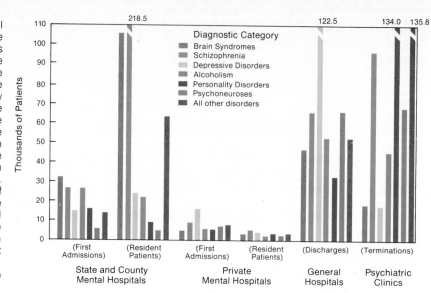

Figure 24.15 The distribution of mental disorders in the United States. The numbers of variously diagnosed patients in four different types of institutions are shown here. Note that there are considerable differences: (1) among the total numbers of patients handled by each kind of institution; (2) among the numbers of patients falling into the various diagnostic categories in the different institutions; and (3) between the numbers of resident patients and the numbers of first admissions in each diagnostic category in mental hospitals. For example, the majority of schizophrenics in the United States are resident patients in public mental hospitals. Personality disorders, on the other hand, are most frequently seen among patients ending their treatment at outpatient psychiatric clinics.
(After Kramer, 1969.)

Many investigators have wondered whether our modern environment with all its stresses and strains has resulted in an increase in the incidence of mental disorder. A survey of mental hospitals suggests that it has not. The number of admissions for most disorders peaked in the mid-1950s and has declined steadily since then. Unfortunately, however, this reduction in admissions does not necessarily mean that the actual incidence of mental disorder has declined. It is probably the result of new drug therapies (see Chapter 28) and of the concerted efforts of mental health workers to establish community mental health centers, to guide the aged to nursing homes, and to encourage potential patients to enter halfway houses or to remain in the community.

Demographic Variability

In spite of the problems associated with estimating the incidence of mental disorder, investigators have reached some consensus about the relative proportion of various disorders in the two sexes and among people of various ages, ethnic groups, marital statuses, religions, and social classes. Some of those findings are reported here.

Sex Although there is considerable variability among samples, most researchers have found that there are more males than females in state, county, and Veterans' Administration hospitals, but more females in private mental hospitals and general hospitals. There is a higher incidence of brain syndromes in males, but a higher incidence of psychosis and neurosis in females. Males evidence more alcoholism, drug addiction, and sexual deviation than females, but studies have consistently found females to be more generally unhappy with their lives. (See Chapter 21.)

Category of Symptom Formation	Percent
Well	18.5
Mild Symptom Formation	36.3
Moderate Symptom Formation	21.8
Marked Symptom Formation	13.2
Severe Symptom Formation	7.5
Incapacitated	2.7

Figure 24.16 Results of the study conducted by Strole and his associates in New York City in the early 1960s. Thousands of residents of Midtown Manhattan were given intensive psychiatric interviews. More than 80 percent of them were judged to be "less than well" by the psychiatrists; and nearly a quarter of them were judged to be "impaired" in their daily lives by psychological problems.
(After Strole et al., 1962.)

Age Figure 24.17 outlines trends in age for various mental disorders. Neuroses and personality disorders reach a peak in adolescence. Schizophrenia, other psychoses, and alcoholism reach a peak in middle age, and brain syndromes reach a peak in old age.

Ethnic Groups Most studies have found very little difference in the incidence of mental disorder across ethnic groups. Generally speaking, however, rates of mental disorder are higher for foreign-born than for native-born citizens of the United States (probably because of the stress of adjusting to a new culture). The fact that race is highly correlated with occupational group, religion, and social class makes any measurement of strictly racial inputs to mental disorder difficult. Only one thing can be said for sure: There is no evidence of a racially distinct origin for any mental disorder.

Marital Status   The highest rates of reported mental illness are found among separated and divorced persons; the next highest, among single persons; the next highest, among widows and widowers; and the lowest, among married men and women. As is the case for all demographic trends, there are a number of possible explanations for these differences. One explanation for the greater incidence of disorder in single people may simply be that single people require admittance to hospitals more often than married people because they have no one to care for them. Another suggestion is that these people have remained single because they have problems with interpersonal relations. A final hypothesis is that being single might involve more stress than being married, one reason being that social norms support the married state.

Social Class   Social class is a broad category that encompasses such other demographic variables as ethnic group, occupation, marital status, and religion. A clear relationship between social class and reported mental illness has been found. Nineteen of twenty-four studies reviewed by Lawrence Kolb, Viola Bernard, and Bruce Dohrenwend in 1969 revealed that the lower the social stratum, the higher the incidence of serious mental disorder. These data are impressive and so raise the question: Why is there a greater incidence of mental illness in the lower social classes?

Two opposing hypotheses have been advanced to explain the phenomenon. The first suggests that people in lower social classes are subject to greater environmental stress than people in higher social classes and that many succumb to the strain. The second hypothesis is that social class does not determine mental disorder; rather, people who are subject to mental disorder end up in the lower classes. Although there is evidence of a genetic basis for schizophrenia (see Chapters 7 and 25), most of the evidence suggests that the higher incidence of mental disorder in the lower classes results from the continuing stresses—stresses caused by unemployment, relocation, poor nutrition, experience with divorce. The shorter life expectancy of the lower classes serves as evidence of the existence and effect of these stresses.

Although several researchers have found a higher incidence of psychosis in the lower social strata, other researchers have found a greater incidence of neurosis in the *higher* social strata. August de Belmont Hollingshead and Frederick Redlich, for example, in their famous 1959 study of New Haven residents, found the highest rates for neurosis in the social strata with the most expensive residences, the highest levels of education, and the best-paying occupations. The authors suggest that this difference in incidence of neurosis may actually represent a class difference in the perception of the problem and the consequent action taken. That is, the lower-class neurotic sees himself as behaving badly, whereas the upper-class neurotic becomes dissatisfied with himself—and goes to a therapist.

Cross-Cultural Variability

Psychologists are interested in comparing data about the prevalence of mental disorder in different cultures for three reasons: (1) the data can serve to test the universality of the present diagnostic system; (2) they can be used to test theories of etiology, or cause, such as those based on defects in family interaction or child-rearing practices; and (3) they can be used in the investigation of the general effect of culture on symptoms of mental disorder. Disorders similar to schizophrenia, manic-depressive psychosis, neurosis, and other disorders are found in other cultures; in fact, some form of most dis-

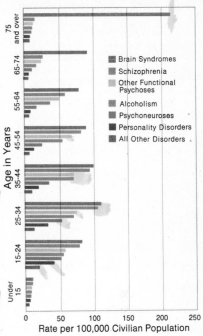

Figure 24.17   Age trends for various psychological disorders in the United States. These data reflect the number of individuals admitted for the first time to state and county mental hospitals in 1965.

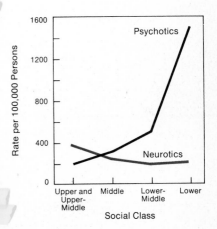

Figure 24.18   The results of a study by Hollingshead and Redlich that investigated the relationship between social class and psychiatric disorder. (After Hollingshead and Redlich, 1958.)

Figure 24.19 Psychological disorders can take different forms, depending on the culture in which they occur. This photograph from a study of the Balinese culture of Indonesia by Gregory Bateson and Margaret Mead suggests a reason for this difference. In Bali children are taught to dance gracefully and skillfully by methods such as the one shown here. An important feature of adult life in Bali is trance-dancing, in which the dancer feels that his movements are beyond his own control and are being manipulated by some alien force or spirit. A Balinese person who becomes psychologically disturbed may thus be predisposed to feel that he has been possessed by a spirit, whereas a Western psychotic might claim that he is Christ or that he is being spied upon by beams emanating from a nuclear reactor.

orders is found in most cultures, but there appear to be important variations in syndromes. For example, H. B. M. Murphy and his colleagues found that social and emotional withdrawal, auditory hallucinations, general delusions, and inability to react were common symptoms of schizophrenia in many cultures, but the style of the symptoms varied from one culture to another. For example, Christians and Muslims most frequently showed religious delusions and delusions of destructiveness, but Asians most frequently exhibited delusional jealousy. It is clear that cultures supply the idiom for delusions. To give one obvious example, delusions about electricity are limited to cultures that have had contact with electricity.

The extent to which differences in symptoms can be traced to cultural style is difficult to measure. Many investigators have reported disorders that seem unique to particular cultures. Arctic hysteria, a kind of hypnotic condition in which the patient mimics the movements of others, seems unique to the people of Northern Siberia. Members of some Canadian Indian tribes exhibit a condition called "witigo," in which the victim becomes agitated, anxious, and nauseous because he thinks he has been bewitched and will become a cannibal. Natives of Malaya are victims of a reaction called "amok" (from which our saying "to run amok" is derived); affected persons are highly agitated and aggressive. Whether these conditions are basically different from conditions in other cultures will not be known until the causes of disorder have been discovered.

The obstacles to cross-cultural comparison are legion. Probably the greatest obstacle is ethnocentrism; people observe things and judge things from their own cultural viewpoint. Consider how you would judge the medicine man of the Nacirema people (described by the anthropologist Horace Miner):

There remains one other kind of practitioner, known as a "listener." This witch doctor has the power to exorcise the devils that lodge in the heads of people who have been bewitched. The Nacirema believe that parents bewitch their own children. Mothers are particularly suspected of putting a curse on children while teaching them the secret body rituals. The countermagic of the witch doctor is unusual in its lack of ritual. The patient simply tells the "listener" all his troubles and fears, beginning with the earliest difficulties he can remember. The memory displayed by the Nacirema in these exorcism sessions is truly remarkable. It is not uncommon for the patient to bemoan the rejection he felt upon being weaned as a babe, and a few individuals even see their troubles going back to the traumatic effects of their own birth.

Do you recognize them? Spell Nacirema backwards.

SUMMARY

1. Several different criteria are used to define normality.

   a. The **statistical criterion** simply says that what most people do is normal; any deviation from majority behavior, whether desirable or undesirable, is abnormal.

   b. The **ideal mental health criterion** sets a goal, such as self-actualization, for human life; normality consists in attaining that goal.

   c. The **clinical criterion** defines normality as the absence of abnormal symptoms; each clinician applies his own standards to each of his patients in deciding whether that person is abnormally disturbed.

2. Many psychologists use the concept of **adjustment** in preference to that of normality in judging whether a person is undergoing mental disturbance. According to the concept of adjustment, an individual may define for himself what he wishes to adjust to; having set the standards, he can then judge how well he is accomplishing the adjustment.

3. Clinicians judging a prospective patient's mental state base their judgments on a combination of things: primarily, their own training and experience; one or more interviews; and psychological tests.

4. Most clinicians, using some combination of abnormal and adjustment criteria, will decide that a person who displays some combination of the following characteristics is in need of help: *He is unhappy with his inner life; he has trouble dealing with other people; he cannot do whatever tasks are required of him to keep on functioning at work, at school, or at home.*

5. Many clinicians try to diagnose mental disorder in terms of the official **diagnostic categories** used by the American Psychiatric Association. Although these categories permit psychiatrists and psychologists to share information about symptoms and therapies, these categories are the subject of much controversy because the basis for inclusion differs from category to category (some categories are based on clusters of symptoms, others are based on cause) and because the origin of many nonorganic disorders is really not yet known.

6. **Neuroses** comprise one major category used by the American Psychiatric Association. The neurotic has difficulty **repressing** thoughts and feelings that are unacceptable to his conscious mind. He becomes anxious about this inability, and the anxiety causes him to use more and more psychic energy to make the repression work. Consequently, he has less psychic energy to devote to real tasks and to relations with other people.

   a. When neurotic anxiety takes the form of an irrational fear, as of crowds or of heights, it is called a **phobia.**

   b. When a neurotic controls his anxiety by occupying his conscious mind with recurrent thoughts or behaviors, such as obsessive thoughts of murder or compulsive washing of his hands, he is said to be in the grip of an **obsessive-compulsive reaction.**

   c. When a neurotic develops physical symptoms that prove to have no organic cause, he is said to be suffering **hysteria.** Paralysis, loss of sight, and other such frightening conditions may serve as a focus for the neurotic's anxiety.

Figure 24.20 Thomas Szasz is a psychiatrist and psychoanalyst who has written on psychosomatic medicine, psychoanalytic theory and practice, the psychology of pain, and, recently, ethical and legal considerations in the practice of psychology and psychiatry. Szasz has argued forcefully that "the myth of mental illness" obscures the true nature of deviant behavior. Such behavior, Szasz claims, is the person's attempt to solve a problem in living. Writing on the social power held by psychiatrists, Szasz has suggested that psychiatric hospitalization is often a means of unjustly depriving people of their freedom.

d. **Depression** may accompany neurosis. The neurotic may become lethargic and slow when he fails to solve issues in his life. Some neurotics seem to be somewhat depressed all the time.

7. **Psychoses** comprise another diagnostic category. A psychotic usually suffers such major distortions in perception, emotion, and thought that he cannot function in the world.

a. Schizophrenia, the most common type of psychosis, can take many forms: **Simple schizophrenics** are apathetic persons who rarely suffer delusions or hallucinations but who seclude themselves from others and from an active interchange with life. People diagnosed as **hebephrenic schizophrenics** show the most severe personality disintegration; they are subject to delusions and hallucinations and seem unable to recognize that anything exists outside of their fantasy; they often display bizarre behaviors. **Catatonic schizophrenics** remain immobile and mute for long periods of time, seemingly preoccupied with hallucinations. Those who are diagnosed as **paranoid schizophrenics** suffer delusions of being exceptional persons of whom others are intensely jealous; they are constantly suspicious that those "others" are plotting to persecute them.

b. **Affective reactions** are mood disorders. Sometimes the reaction is **manic:** The person begins by feeling elated; his level of activity rises until he can no longer eat or sleep; finally, he speeds up his purposeless activity until he becomes confused and disoriented. Sometimes the manic reaction alternates with a **depressive** reaction: The person feels himself a hopeless failure and eventually cuts off communication with others, taking to his bed and becoming stuporous.

8. **Personality disorders,** a third major diagnostic category, include the **antisocial personality,** a person who appears not to experience emotion, especially in his relationships with others, and who seems not to feel guilt about bad behavior; also in this category is the **sexual deviant,** whose sexual activity is disordered by being destructive, bizarre, or exclusively oriented to inappropriate objects or practices.

9. Some psychoses result from **organic disorders,** which can be caused, for example, by sclerosis of the brain's arteries, deterioration of the brain and nervous system from aging or disease, or accidental trauma to the brain.

10. **Epidemiological studies** attempt to discover the incidence, distribution, and control of illness in a population. Admission and residence rates in mental hospitals and outpatient clinics, although inadequate, are used to estimate the prevalence and distribution of mental disorder in the United States.

a. Data on male-female differences show that there is a higher incidence of psychosis and neurosis in females but a higher incidence of brain syndromes, alcoholism, drug addiction, and sexual deviation in males.

b. Data on age differences show that during adolescence there are more neuroses and personality disorders than at other stages of life; during middle age there is more schizophrenia; in old age there are more brain syndromes.

c. Data have shown very little difference in the incidence of mental disorder across ethnic groups.

    d. Data on differences according to marital status show that the highest incidence of reported disorder is among separated and divorced persons; the next highest, among single persons; the next highest, among widows and widowers; and the lowest, among married persons.

    e. Data on differences according to social class show that there is a higher incidence of psychosis in the lower social classes and a higher incidence of neurosis in the higher classes.

11. Psychologists attempting to compare data about the prevalence of mental disorders in different cultures have found some form of most of the disorders discussed here in most cultures, but the symptomatic expression of each disorder and the way it is interpreted by other people varies greatly across cultures.

SUGGESTED READINGS

Arieti, Silvano (ed.). *American Handbook of Psychology.* New York: Basic Books, 1959. 3 vols. The first volume contains papers pertaining to adjustment and disorder and is divided into sections on general psychopathology, neurosis, functional psychosis, psychopathic syndromes, psychosomatic medicine, disorders of childhood and adolescence, and language and speech disorders.

Kisker, George W. *The Disorganized Personality.* New York: McGraw-Hill, 1964. The best elementary textbook on abnormal psychology. Well written and well illustrated, it contains a series of case histories to demonstrate types of disorder, and it presents an excellent discussion of the history of mental illness. Chapters follow the major categories in the Diagnostic Manual of the American Psychiatric Association.

Maher, Brendan. *Principles of Psychopathology: An Experimental Approach.* New York: McGraw-Hill, 1966. Contains an excellent discussion of learning theories and of the biological basis of psychopathology. Analyzes neurosis in terms of conflict, anxiety, and avoidance. Four chapters deal with theories and research on schizophrenia.

Szasz, Thomas S. *The Myth of Mental Illness: Foundations of a Theory of Personal Conduct.* New York: Dell, 1967. A highly original, extremely stimulating discussion of mental illness. Szasz argues that what is commonly called mental illness really involves "problems in living."

White, Robert W. *The Abnormal Personality.* New York: Ronald Press, 1964. A comprehensive, easy-to-read presentation of theories and research on abnormal behavior. Written by one of the pillars of classic personality theory, the book is pervaded by the force of Robert White's own personality. It contains an excellent presentation of psychoanalysis and learning theory.

Wolman, Benjamin B. (ed.). *Handbook of Clinical Psychology.* New York: McGraw-Hill, 1965. Sections of particular interest are those of diagnostic methods and clinical patterns. Contains a series of papers by experts in the field.

Zilboorg, Gregory, and George W. Henry. *A History of Medical Psychology.* New York: Norton, 1941. A fascinating discussion of the history of madness; guaranteed to appall anyone who reads it. A classic in the field.

What we call "mental disorder," with all its implications of a mind badly arranged or out of tune with reality, was viewed in quite a favorable fashion in past times. To be out of tune with "reality" was considered to be in tune with something just as real but not apparent to most people. The "other reality" was considered superior to the common reality, and those few who were fortunate enough to be in touch with it were treated with awe rather than pity.

The man or woman whose behavior or responses were inappropriate to his or her surroundings might be in touch with the gods; might indeed be controlled by divine power for its own purpose. Madmen were therefore treated with respect. In some conditions that bring a temporary retreat from the common reality, as in an epileptic fit, observers felt the sufferer to be temporarily in touch with the divine. In fact, the ancient Greeks called epilepsy the "sacred disease."

Fits of irrationality, where a person might foam at the mouth, speak incoherently, and writhe uncontrollably were impressive to onlookers in older times. If speech, during these fits, could be understood (or interpreted), that speech was looked upon as containing knowledge beyond that attainable by ordinary people—it might contain information concerning the future, for instance. The priestess at Delphi breathed fumes, chewed leaves, or in some other way induced a pseudo-epileptic fit, and the irrational, incoherent sounds she made during the fit were then interpreted into the famous utterances that on more than one occasion influenced Greek history.

In Biblical history, irrational fits were characteristic of those referred to as "prophets" in English translation. Their incoherent outcries were referred to as "prophesying." Thus, when Saul returned from his first meeting with Samuel, "behold, a company of prophets met him; and the Spirit of God came upon him, and he prophesied among them." (1 Samuel 10:10).

Again, on the first Pentecost after the Crucifixion, the apostles were gathered together and "they were all filled with the Holy Ghost, and began to speak with other tongues" (Acts 2:4). Religious sects that feature such fits are called "pentecostal" in consequence, and their meetings often involve "speaking with tongues"—writhings, foamings, incoherent outcries.

Religious "ecstasy" (from Greek words meaning "out of place" because the mind seems to be responding to some other set of impulses and to be elsewhere) is the most influential type of mental disorder in history (and there is no way of predicting how influential it may yet be in the future). Yet how can modern medicine deal with this type of mental disorder when, to so many people, it still seems to be touched by the divine.

Isaac Asimov

25
Bases of Disorder

DEVELOPMENT
Psychoanalytic Theory
Social-Learning Theory
Research on Families

HEREDITY

BIOCHEMISTRY

GENERAL PSYCHOLOGICAL CONCEPTS
Conflict
Anxiety
Attribution Theory

COMPLEX THEORIES

PROBLEMS IN RESEARCH

Most people, including students of psychology, express a great interest in abnormal behavior and psychological disorder. On the one hand, much of what a mentally ill person says and does is similar to one's own experience; on the other hand, a mentally ill person behaves and reports ideas in perplexing and incomprehensible ways. Mental illness also is associated with great human suffering, and this suffering affects other people, not just the disturbed person; so, emotional concern—as well as curiosity—helps account for the popularity of the subject. The desire to reduce people's suffering and to help solve a problem that is costly to the whole society is an important factor in motivating psychologists to do research in psychopathology—the study of mental disorder.

DEVELOPMENT

Anyone's personality—the way he thinks, feels, and acts, in short, the kind of person he is—partly reflects the kinds of experiences he has had. The developing child changes somewhat with each new experience. As he encounters new objects and situations, his mental construction of the world becomes more complex. Each interaction with his parents and others allows him to learn a little more about the consequences of his behaviors. At the same time the child is experiencing a range of different emotions, and he associates these emotions with specific situations, people, and objects. Many researchers have assumed that the bases or causes of psychological disorders lie in these kinds of associations, made in the early developmental periods.

The idea that mental disorder can be traced to the individual's psychological development has been the object of extensive theorizing and research. Two widely accepted theories of mental disorder are the psychoanalytic view of mental illness, which has its basis in the seminal works of Sigmund Freud, and the social-learning, or behaviorist, position, which developed from empirical research in

Figure 25.1 Although many psychologists believe that psychological disorder has its basis in damaging childhood experiences, these theorists do not agree on *how* experiences during development contribute to later disorders. Another group of researchers believes that the key to the bases of disorder lies in hereditary and physiological factors. This chapter presents some theories and findings from both these groups, plus theories in which both points of view are interwoven.

animal laboratories, particularly those of Clark Hull, Ivan Pavlov, and B. F. Skinner. Some clinical psychologists as well as sociologists, anthropologists, and investigators in various other fields are looking to family interactions and life histories of disturbed persons in order to formulate causes of and therapies for disordered mental development.

Psychoanalytic Theory

The psychoanalytic theory of disorder was originally outlined by Freud and was developed, with modification, by subsequent investigators, especially Norman Cameron, Erik Erikson, and Otto Fenichel. It views psychological disorders as rooted in the psychosexual development of the person. According to Freud's theory, which is discussed in greater detail in Chapter 18, there are three kinds of functions or parts of the personality—the id, ego, and superego.

Whereas the **id** might be characterized as the "I want" of psychological life, the **ego** might be described as the "how can I get it." The id operates according to what Freud calls the pleasure principle. Its goal is to reduce the tension that can build up through undischarged psychic energy, or libido—to satisfy its primitive desires, no matter what the circumstances. The ego operates according to the *reality principle.* Its two functions, the delay of gratification and the use of fantasy substitutes, are important concepts in psychoanalytic theory. The id demands immediate gratification, but the ego recognizes the need to delay satisfaction or to find a substitute. This struggle between id and ego is central to a person's psychodynamics, or "inner life." Not only must the ego deal with the unconscious instinctual urges of the id, it also must reconcile these urges with the demands of the **superego**—the person's internal representation of right and wrong—of the values and ideals of his family and his society. And neither the superego's demands nor the id's instinctual urges correspond to the requirements of the external world as perceived by the ego. Consequently, the ego is constantly striving to reconcile the id and the superego with the external world.

A person's inner life, then, is characterized by perpetual turbulence and ferment. The person is constantly reconciling instinctual urges, emotionally charged fantasies, and the requirements of his current reality. The terms *psychodynamics* and *psychodynamic processes* describe the psyche's ongoing attempts to integrate these warring forces. Psychological disorders develop when the ego is unable to reconcile the demands of the id and the superego without interrupting the person's ability to function in society. Abnormal behavior and other symptoms, such as extreme anxiety, are expressions of the ego's inability to reconcile these conflicts.

In its attempt to resolve the conflicts, the ego translates the conflicts into **symbolic** substitutes. The person's behavior may therefore express these conflicts symbolically. The symbolic nature of the expression makes it difficult to see the connection between a person's symptoms and the real nature of these basic conflicts. The following example illustrates the point: A twenty-nine-year-old professional woman had recently become engaged. She held a respected position for which she received a high salary, and she had to drive considerable distances several times a week. Two months before her wedding she developed a driving phobia (a morbid fear of driving). The psychoanalytically oriented therapist viewed the phobia as rooted in the woman's basic conflicts concerning sexuality. The woman reported that she usually felt "sort of uncomfortable" during sexual intercourse and that she could not "let go and enjoy it," but she said that she nevertheless felt a strong sexual attraction to her fiancée.

The therapist concluded that her driving phobia represented a fear of losing control. Psychodynamically, the woman's sexual desire was threatening her need for control, and she associated her marriage with a loss of the masculine, controlling role represented in her professional life. The driving phobia symbolically represented both her fear of abandoning herself sexually and her ambivalence about functioning in the roles of both wife and professional.

In this way, her inner psychic conflicts account for her experiences of psychological pain or for her inability to function normally. It is important to note this emphasis of psychoanalytic theory. It means that an external, or environmental, situation contributes to a psychological disorder only insofar as it presents a situation that symbolizes an inner conflict.

According to psychoanalytic theory, the nature of the symbolic expression of conflicts and even the nature of the conflicts themselves are a result of a person's development during infancy and childhood. In other words, the type and severity of mental illness is determined by the individual's psychodynamic development. The child passes through a series of psychosexual stages: oral, anal, phallic, latency, and genital. As Chapter 18 explains, each stage is characterized by a preoccupation with particular erotic impulses and with certain associated conflicts. At each stage, the person develops ways—sometimes effective and sometimes not—of accommodating divergent psychodynamic impulses. The child who successfully deals with problems at one stage moves to the next with a strong and energetic ego. The child whose ego has been less effective will also enter the next stage, but because his ego must continue to expend considerable energy on earlier conflicts, he will be less able to cope effectively with conflicts at later stages.

The later psychodynamic development of a child who has failed to resolve an earlier problem is like a bridge erected on a faulty foundation. The size of the fault will determine how much weight the bridge can withstand; the location of the fault will determine how much of the bridge will crumble if too much strain is applied. The person who experiences great difficulty at some period in his development will be more likely to develop a psychological disorder because there is a major defect in the foundation of his personality. The form and severity of the disorder will be determined to a great extent by the stage at which the fault occurred.

When the bridge begins to crumble, the cracks will extend down to the point of the major defect. This phenomenon is called **regression.** The person who becomes mentally ill experiences a regression, or partial backsliding, to the level or kind of activity that typifies the stage he failed to negotiate. The person's behavior mirrors, to some degree, his way of functioning at the earlier stage. But the degree of regression—that is, the extent to which all aspects of a person's functioning revert or regress—depends on the severity of the psychodynamic defect and the nature of the psychologically damaging event that triggered the disorder. The term "depth of regression" describes how far back toward birth the person goes in regressing to an early conflict. The psychoanalytic view of schizophrenics and other psychotics, whose behavior appears to be very disturbed and irrational, is that they experienced problems early in their development and that their current behavior reflects an almost total regression to these earlier conflicts. In some cases the person's behavior may literally reflect these conflicts. However, the behavior more commonly expresses the conflicts in symbolic or fantasy representations.

Psychoanalytic theory views the neurotic disorders as reflecting partial regressions to less primitive stages. Because the regression is less severe, less of the person's behavior is irrational, and he is better able to cope with the demands of ordinary living. It should be noted that the difference between the psychotic, the neurotic, and the "normal" person is one of degree. It is assumed that everyone experiences irrational impulses. A person is "normal" only insofar as the irrational components of his personality do not prevent him from functioning in society. Some psychoanalysts even believe that everyone is neurotic in one way or another because no one can perfectly resolve all the problems of psychodynamic development.

Social-Learning Theory

During the last few decades, social-learning theory has stimulated an increasing amount of research in the area of psychopathology and has yielded several provocative results. Unlike psychoanalytic theory, which attempts to explain all normal and abnormal behavior in terms of a single model of psychodynamic development, social-learning theory has no all-inclusive explanatory model. The learning-theory researcher tries instead to discover how each patient acquired his inappropriate behaviors. He works with the hypothesis that abnormal behavior is learned in much the same way as all other behavior. The person with a disorder is seen as differing from other people because he has *learned inappropriate or maladaptive behaviors* or because he has *failed to learn the adaptive behaviors* that most people acquire. The various learning-theory explanations of abnormal behavior share a number of common assumptions and concepts.

First, learning theorists assume that people learn maladaptive behaviors because the environment in some ways rewards or reinforces these behaviors. John B. Watson and Rosalie Rayner's classical experimental demonstration of how a person learns maladaptive behavior is the case of "Little Albert" (see Chapter 4). Little Albert was an eleven-month-old child who, in a classical-conditioning experiment, learned a phobia (irrational fear) of furry objects of all sorts. Initially, Albert showed no fear in the presence of a white rat. Then, a loud noise (UCS) was paired with each presentation of the white rat. Soon the sight of the rat (CS) without the noise was enough to cause a great fear reaction (CR) in Albert. This fear rapidly generalized to all sorts of other furry objects, like rabbits and fur pieces, although no noise had been paired with them.

Maladaptive behavior may also result from reinforcement given by someone in the person's social environment. For example, a child might develop a fear of horses because his mother encourages his initial fear. A person may also learn behavior that allows him to avoid something aversive or unpleasant. For example, a child who hates going to school might develop illnesses or learn to behave in ways that cause the school to repeatedly suspend him; either of these behaviors would be reinforced by the fact that they enable him to stay away from school. In such cases, the child is most likely not consciously aware that he is misbehaving or courting illness just to keep out of school.

Second, learning theorists believe that a given disturbance can result from one or more aspects of the person's learning history. The researcher keeps an open mind when he considers a person with a specific problem; that is, he assumes that there are many different possible explanations for it. When he sees that a person has more than one symptom—for example, a woman has both a driving phobia and an acute fear of heights (acrophobia)—the investigator assumes that the two symptoms may have different origins. Similarly, when he encounters two different people with identical disorders, he assumes that the problem may be rooted in very different histories or sequences of learning. The only similarity that he always assumes is that the *disorders reflect the learning of inappropriate responses.*

Finally, learning theory views the make-up of psychological disorder as nothing more than a series of maladaptive behaviors. Unlike psychoanalytic theory, which views symptoms of disorder as symbolic expressions of psychodynamic problems or conflicts, the learning-theory view postulates no such underlying process. The person's problem is defined by the symptoms, and when the symptoms have been eliminated, the problem or illness, in most

Figure 25.2 (opposite) Hans' phobia, in Freud's *Analysis of a Phobia in a Five-Year-Old Boy.* Freud based his analysis on a large number of discussions between Hans and his father in which Hans expressed great curiosity about sex organs, the recent birth of his sister, and his fear of being bitten by a white horse. Hans expressed particular fear of a horse falling under a heavy load; he had, in fact, once witnessed such a scene when he was out walking with his mother. Freud believed that Hans' dread was an expression of his anxiety about losing his mother's affection to the new baby and about being his admired and loved father's enemy because he was his father's rival for his mother's affection. The horse and the horse's biting symbolized his father and his father's retaliation. The horse's heavy burden symbolized his mother's pregnancy. The horse's accident was a symbol both of damage to his father and the bloody scene of birth. Learning theorists have suggested that Hans' phobia may have a much simpler explanation than this. Hans may have been conditioned by the extremely frightening experience of seeing the horse's accident. This experience may have produced in Hans a conditioned fear that generalized to any horse. Horse-drawn vehicles were commonplace in that period in Vienna.

cases, has been eliminated. The psychoanalytic position assumes that if only the symptoms are removed while the primitive conflict remains unresolved, the person will develop new symptoms as alternative expressions of the conflict. Learning theorists disagree with this tenet of psychoanalytic theory, which is known as the theory of **symptom substitution.**

The classic example that illustrates the difference between psychoanalytic and learning-theory interpretations of symptoms of disorder is Freud's case of "Little Hans." At the age of five years, Hans developed a horse phobia after witnessing a horse slip and fall on a wet street; he was treated by his father, a lay analyst. Freud consulted periodically with the father and subsequently published an analysis of the case. He interpreted the horse phobia as an expression of psychodynamic conflicts with which Hans was then struggling; among these were guilt about masturbation, the fear of castration, sibling rivalry with a younger sister, and the oedipal desire to seduce the mother and replace the father. Freud thought that what Hans saw—a horse hitched to a milk wagon slipping on the wet street and falling—symbolically represented Hans' fear of his mother's giving birth to another child (his sister's birth had upset him very much). It also represented the child's anxiety over his unconscious wish that his father would die so that he could possess his mother.

Joseph Wolpe and Stanley Rachman critically analyzed Freud's argument and offered a learning-theory explanation of the case. They said that conjecture concerning psychodynamic processes is unnecessary to explain Hans' phobia. Seeing the horse fall was a sufficiently frightening experience to cause the subsequent fear of horses.

In an article published in 1960, Wolpe and Rachman discuss experimental studies in learning theory. They say that any stimulus that once touches off or is paired with a fear reaction in a person can continue to elicit fear. They say that *neurotic fear* results if the person felt extreme fear with the first experience of the stimulus or if the conditioning is repeated so many times that the fear continues to occur. Wolpe and Rachman note that neurotic fear caused by repeated conditioning may include a generalization of fear to other stimuli that are similar to the original one. Hans can be viewed as having been so frightened by the experience that he was very much afraid of approaching situations in which it might be repeated: He became frightened by the general subject of horses. The case of Little Albert, too, showed this generalization of fear.

Research on Families

Other researchers have examined the life histories and family environments of people with specific psychological disorders and have compared these to similar data from normal control subjects. Their aim has been to isolate factors or processes that are unique to the psychological development of individuals with a given disorder. Two examples of this approach involve research into the family lives of schizophrenic persons.

One group of investigators, headed by Theodore Lidz, kept contact with schizophrenics and their families over a period of several years. They held weekly interviews with family members, observed the members' interactions with one another and with hospital staff members, visited the person's home, and did diagnostic and other testing. From the findings of their first sixteen cases, these researchers suggested that the families of schizophrenics fall into one of two categories.

Figure 25.3   An adolescent schizophrenic boy's paintings of his family. The paintings were made at the request of a therapist who hoped to find a starting place for communication with the withdrawn and unresponsive boy. These paintings illustrate a difficult question that comes up in trying to identify the causes of schizophrenia. Are these paintings bizarre and ominous because of the boy's disorder, or are the paintings sensitive representations of the factors in his family that caused him to become schizophrenic? Theorists such as Theodore Lidz, Gregory Bateson, and R. D. Laing (more than other theorists) would probably say the second alternative was more likely to be true, although they would not deny that schizophrenia involves disorders of perception.

The first type of family showed **marital schism.** In the words of Lidz and his associates:

. . . both spouses were caught up in their own personality difficulties, which were aggravated to the point of desperation by the marital relationship. There was chronic failure to achieve complementarity of purpose or role reciprocity. Neither gained support of emotional needs from the other . . . These marriages are replete with recurrent threats of separation . . . Communication consists primarily of coercive efforts and defiance, or of efforts to mask the defiance to avoid fighting. . . . A particularly malignant feature in these marriages is the chronic "undercutting" of the worth of one partner to the children by the other.

The other group of families was characterized by what the authors call **marital skew.** In these families

. . . one partner who was extremely dependent or masochistic had married a spouse who had appeared to be a strong and protecting parental figure. The dependent partner would go along with or even support the weaknesses or psychopathologic distortions of the parental partner . . . A striking feature in all cases was the psychopathology of the partner who appeared to be dominant, creating an abnormal environment which, being accepted by the "healthier" spouse, may have seemed to be a normal environment to the children.

The child faced with the conflict and confusion of either of these two kinds of family situations develops ways of coping that lead to problems later in life. It seems logical to expect that children whose psychological development takes place in such environments would demonstrate atypical behaviors and emotional development.

A second group of investigators, headed by Gregory Bateson and Don Jackson, examined the family environments of schizophrenics and developed the **double-bind hypothesis.** The basic idea behind their hypothesis is that the mother in these families has great difficulty accepting her child's affection and positive regard for her. She finds it hard to deal with any feelings of anxiety or hostility that she experiences toward her child. She therefore acts

Figure 25.4 An example of what R. D. Laing calls "knots." These are patterns of circular reasoning some people use in trying to make sense of the messages they receive from their families. Such individuals, Laing maintains, are the people usually described as schizophrenic. The logical trap represented here can be seen as the result of the double-binds described by Bateson and Jackson. The conflict is real and, in this person's terms, inescapable. Imagine yourself in this person's position. Are you to have what you need and feel guilty, or are you to somehow get along with nothing at all?

(From R. D. Laing, *Knots*, 1970.)

lovingly and correctly toward the child, but the child perceives the discrepancy between her overt actions and her covert feelings and messages—like the mother who tells her child to give her a kiss but stiffens her body when he approaches her. The child repeatedly receives two contradictory messages—one in behavior and one in words—from the most important person in his life. He therefore never learns to understand and make distinctions among the meanings expressed in normal language and behavior. He develops the bizarre language and social ineptness characteristic of schizophrenics.

Recently, considerable attention has been given to the work of a third group, headed by R. D. Laing. Laing's group hypothesizes that the schizophrenic is a person who has, within his family, developed a particular way of experiencing, understanding, and behaving in the world. His ways of understanding and behaving seem incomprehensible to those outside his family; but, if one examines his behavior within the context of the family in which it developed, one can see that it is adaptive. Members of the families of schizophrenics are not honest with each other; their interaction forces each of them to deny parts of their experiences and to invalidate important feelings. Figure 25.4 represents a schizophrenic's way of denying, to himself, his right to desire things or to enjoy them if he has achieved them. Laing came to believe that not only was the schizophrenic a victim of his family, the family itself was a victim of a destructive society.

Laing's basic point of view is that pathology is inherent in contemporary Western society. He says, in *The Politics of Experience:* "By the time the new human is fifteen or so, we are left with a being like ourselves, a half-crazed creature more or less adjusted to a mad world. This is normality in our present age." Because almost everyone is mad, it is absurd for some people to label others as maladjusted or schizophrenic. In fact, Laing believes that the processes psychotics pass through represent their attempts to reconcile the self that existed before socialization (the true self) with the self created by accepting substitute gratifications because of cultural demands and social sanctions.

HEREDITY

Many human characteristics such as eye color and color blindness are inherited. Over the years authorities in the field of psychopathology have examined the possible influence of heredity on psychological disorder.

Chapter 7 discusses in detail the investigation of hereditary bases of schizophrenia. It describes **family studies,** which look at incidence of schizophrenia in terms of number of genes family members share in common. Results of these studies indicate some support for a hereditary basis of schizophrenia. That is, relatives of a schizophrenic who share 50 percent of their genes in common with him (parents, siblings, children) are more likely to become schizophrenic than are those who share 25 percent (for example, grandparents, grandchildren). But the results are not conclusive for a number of reasons. First, family members who share the most genes in common also tend to share the most similar environments. Second, although a schizophrenic shares the same proportion of genes with his parents and his children, the expectation of schizophrenia is greater for his children than for his parents.

Chapter 7 also describes **twin studies,** which compare **monozygous,** or identical, twins (who develop from the splitting of a single fertilized ovum and who have identical genetic constitutions) with **dizygous,** or fraternal, twins (who develop from separately fertilized ova and are no more likely to have the same genetic constitution than are any two siblings). It is assumed that twins reared together experience virtually identical environments. With identical twins, the assumption is that the differences in certain behaviors and traits of the two persons can be attributed only to environmental causes. The researchers' hypothesis, therefore, is that heredity plays a part in determining the development of a certain characteristic when identical twins show a greater resemblance for that trait than do fraternal twins. Results cited in Chapter 7 show that in sets of identical twins where one twin is schizophrenic, the other twin will be schizophrenic 40 to 50 percent of the time. For fraternal twins, the percentage is about 10 to 15.

Another type of twin study is also used to examine the role of genetic factors in psychological disorder, and it provides a better control for the effects of the environment during the twins' upbringings. This method examines identical twins who were separated early in life and raised in different environments. If identical twins show very similar traits even when they are reared in different environments, then heredity probably contributes to those traits. Of course, the small number of twins with psychological disorders who are available for study has severely limited the research. However, in 1971 David Rosenthal reported sixteen cases of identical twins reared apart. In 62.5 percent of these cases, both twins were schizophrenic.

Another means of investigation discussed at length in Chapter 7 is the **study of adopted children.** A series of investigations by David Rosenthal and his colleagues looked at both biological and adoptive families of schizophrenics in Denmark, where very detailed records are kept of family lineages, adoptions, and mental illness. These studies found that schizophrenia does run along **biological family** lines rather than **adoptive family** lines. However, the study also showed that the incidence of schizophrenia in adopted children does not run as high as the incidence in biological family members who live together. This difference indicates that environmental factors do have an effect on the development of the disorder. It seems that people do not inherit the disorder in a simple way.

Recently, Paul Meehl developed a theory that attributes the occurrence of schizophrenia to a combination of genetic and environmental conditions. He postulates that although a single defective gene may be responsible for the risk of schizophrenia, people with that defective gene will not become full-blown schizophrenics unless they also have inherited other constitutional disorders *and* have been exposed to debilitating and stressful early childhood experiences. A person who has the defective gene, Meehl says, may display schizoid traits but is unlikely to become a clinically diagnosed schizophrenic if the other two conditions are not fulfilled. No person without the defective gene, Meehl says, will ever become a true schizophrenic. His theory provides a means for reconciling genetic evidence with psychological explanations of causes of schizophrenia.

BIOCHEMISTRY

Psychiatrists have found that certain drugs are effective in helping people with certain forms of psychological disorder. For example, chlorpromazine usually reduces the disturbed behavior of a schizophrenic person. Similarly, lithium sometimes reduces the severity of depression. As Chapter 28 points out, the fact that drugs are effective in treating certain psychological disorders does not mean that chemical factors necessarily cause these disorders. However, the use of drug therapy has led many researchers to conclude that psychopathological behavior may have a biochemical basis. Of course, biochemical explanations follow from the search for hereditary bases of disorder. As explained in Chapter 7, genes are the transmitters of all hereditary information—both for species development and for individual development. Each gene specifies the production of a protein (the building blocks of the human body) and the program for changing that protein and combining it with others for normal development and function. A single defective gene can block the program for a sequence of necessary biochemical transformations and result in physical or mental disorder. Chapter 7 describes how a single defective gene produces the disease called PKU (phenylketonuria), with its severe mental retardation.

The way researchers work on the hypothesis that mental illness is caused by some biochemical abnormality is to take one group of people with a particular disorder and search for some biochemical difference between them and a control group of nondisturbed people. Although this procedure seems straightforward, it is often difficult to carry out. Complications arise in trying to find an appropriate control group. The perfect control group would have to live in an environment identical to the one of the psychiatric patients, so that the only difference between the patients and the control group would be the psychological disorder.

Moreover, the biochemistry of human beings is extremely complex, and our understanding of it is far from complete. The medical and life histories, and even the diets, of psychiatric patients are markedly different from those of normal control subjects. Most hospitalized schizophrenics, for example, eat an institutionalized diet, smoke incessantly, get little exercise, and have long histories of drug therapy. Any of these factors can alter a person's biochemistry. Moreover, as Seymour Kety has pointed out, the extreme emotional and physical stresses associated with being mentally ill can also cause changes in biochemical functioning. When the researcher finds differences in the body chemistry of disturbed persons, he must find ways of determining whether these differences are related to the causes of the disorder or whether they are the effects of the person's emotional state or the situation in which he is living.

Some progress has been made in this area, especially with schizophrenic disorders. A series of studies reported by C. David Wise and Larry Stein in 1971 and 1973 suggests that, because of a genetic defect, a biochemical agent necessary to the sequence of changes in the hormone norepinephrine is not manufactured in schizophrenics, and that they therefore suffer progressive brain damage. The damage occurs in the areas of the brain associated with "pleasure or reward and, hence, with the organization and control of goal-directed thinking and behavior"—the diencephalon and limbic forebrain (see Chapter 14). Wise and Stein ran post-mortem examinations of the brains of eighteen schizophrenics, comparing them, for control purposes, with the brains of twelve normal persons. (The schizophrenics had died in an institution; the normal subjects had died suddenly—in accidents or from heart attacks—and had had no known history of mental disorder.) They found significant differences between the brains of schizophrenics and those of nonschizophrenics in the amount of a substance responsible for the final step in the sequence of the body's use of norepinephrine. Although all regions of the brain examined showed a deficit of the substance, the deficit was larger in the areas of the brain associated with pleasure. This research approach to determine biochemical causes of mental disorder appears to be very promising, as is evidenced by Wise and Stein's findings, but more evidence is needed before firm conclusions can be drawn.

GENERAL PSYCHOLOGICAL CONCEPTS

The discussion so far has outlined some methods of investigating the causes and development of psychological disorders. Concepts from other areas of psychology have also stimulated some interesting ideas about the bases of disorder. One such concept is the notion of conflict.

Conflict

Conjecture concerning the possible connection between conflict and psychological disorder probably dates back to 1928, when a description of a now-famous experiment conducted in Pavlov's laboratory was first circulated. In this experiment, a dog was conditioned to salivate whenever a circular stimulus was presented but was denied reinforcement whenever an elliptical stimulus was presented. When the dog had learned to discriminate between the two differently shaped stimuli, the second part of the experiment began. The experimenter presented a series of stimuli that were neither perfectly circular nor obviously elliptical but somewhere between the two. Gradually, the difference between the circular stimulus and the elliptical one was reduced until it was extremely difficult to discriminate between them. The dog was unable to make a discrimination and began to struggle and howl. Apparently, the inability to determine the significance of the stimulus—that is, food to follow or no food to follow—caused the dog's agitation. When they had been subjected to such conflict for a long period, many dogs showed severe psychopathological symptoms—even after the stress had been removed.

Research indicates that when a person encounters two equally attractive but contradictory and mutually exclusive alternatives, he may show extreme agitation, and his normal functioning may be disrupted. He may try various ways to escape from the situation. The precise way in which he tries to cope with the conflict situation is determined in part by the type of conflict he is facing. Neal Miller and others have investigated three logically distinct kinds of conflict situations: the **approach-approach** conflict, in which two equally desirable but mutually exclusive alternatives are presented; the **avoidance-avoidance** conflict, in which two equally aversive alternatives are presented in such a way that one but not both can be avoided; and the **approach-avoidance** conflict, in which a positive alternative is inseparably paired with an aversive one. Pavlov's experiment is an example of an approach-avoidance conflict.

The work of Miller and others suggests that the aversiveness or attractiveness of one alternative over another changes with the temporal or spatial distance of the alternative from the individual. For example, a child who must choose between two equally attractive objects but must wait longer to get one of them will take the one that is closer in time. An animal confronted with two equally aversive stimuli would be expected to approach the one slightly farther away if it is impossible to avoid both. On the other hand, two alternatives that are not equally aversive will nevertheless be experienced as equal if the person perceiving them is closer to the less aversive one.

The extreme agitation and inability to function that animals show in conflict experiments resembles the behavior of many psychiatric patients. The stress that conflict situations bring about might be related to the psychological origins of physical complaints or even to more far-reaching biochemical changes (see Chapter 14). Much of the erratic and irrational behavior of some psychotic patients could reflect the fact that these people are reacting to a complex constellation of conflicting stimuli that other people do not perceive. Schizophrenic behavior does reflect a strategy of withdrawal from an incomprehensible situation, and in a conflict situation, similarly, a person seeks relief and escape. However, the exact nature of the connection between conflict and psychological disorder remains unclear.

Anxiety

Anxiety is another important concept for the understanding of psychological disorder and is of central importance in a number of theories of disorders, including psychoanalysis and social-learning theory. It is also a widely used concept in other areas of psychology. Research has shown a connection between anxiety and both physical arousal and task performance. Many students find that if they are anxious about a test, they do poorly even though they are well prepared. Psychologists have found that *a high level of anxiety*

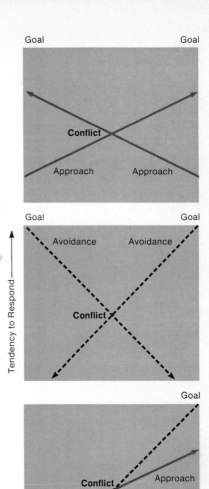

Figure 25.5 Three kinds of conflict. The graphs represent Miller's theoretical assumption that the tendency to approach a desired outcome grows stronger the closer one comes to it and that the tendency to avoid an aversive outcome grows similarly but starts later and grows faster.

drastically reduces a person's ability to perform complex tasks. Most highly anxious people persist in making a previously learned response and therefore fail to learn new discriminations or to adjust to a change in a task.

Like neurotic people, most *highly anxious people are more easily conditioned in classical-conditioning experiments.* The increased conditionability associated with high levels of anxiety might cause the person to acquire classically conditioned responses and associations that make his behavior and thinking different from that of other people who are not highly anxious.

Anxiety can be viewed as an aversive stimulus that causes a person to adopt unusual and maladaptive behaviors as a means of avoiding that stimulus. Robert Malmo and others have suggested that repeated experiences of extreme anxiety gradually lower a person's tolerance for anxiety-provoking situations. There are few data linking psychotic behavior to heightened anxiety, but anxiety is an important factor in neurotic disorders.

Attribution Theory

Stuart Valins and Richard Nisbett have recently attempted to explain some forms of disorder in terms of attribution theory. Many of the bizarre thoughts entertained by some psychiatric patients may be caused by their inability to discover the appropriate explanation for a given experience. Valins and Nisbett discuss the example of a forty-four-year-old man who had twitches over his right eye and in the areas of his heart and solar plexus. The man thought that the twitch over his eye was caused by a spirit that was helping him make decisions. The therapist later determined that the twitches occurred in situations of great stress. Valins and Nisbett propose that the individual developed the spirit delusion because he did not understand that the twitches stemmed from a physical reaction to stress situations. He had no explanation, so he attributed the twitches to spirit messages.

Valins and Nisbett believe that many disordered thought processes can be completely explained in these terms. They contend, for example, that the arousal and sensory apparatuses of the schizophrenic person are intact. The schizophrenic's disorganized thought stems from the fact that he attributes inappropriate explanations to his experiences.

It is possible, on the other hand, to integrate the attribution concept itself with the view of Brendan Maher and others that schizophrenia and other disorders are associated with atypical physical and sensory functioning. A person whose sensory apparatus gives him physical and other cues that most people do not get would certainly be expected to develop a most unusual system of cognitions.

COMPLEX THEORIES

The theories and research discussed in the preceding sections are only samples of the relevant material. Although heredity, biochemistry, anxiety, and the other factors have been treated separately, there are important connections among them. Paul Meehl's formulation, which combines genetic and environmental factors, is discussed earlier in the chapter. Another theory that integrates different kinds of information is Hans Eysenck's explanation of psychopathological behavior. It is based on his general theory of personality.

Eysenck thinks that both hereditary factors and the environment in which a person lives affect the development of psychological disorders. An individual inherits a tendency to respond in certain ways, but the exact nature of the behaviors he will learn depends upon the kinds of environmental influences to which he is exposed. The person who inherits a predisposition for neurosis, for example, can be expected to develop a neurotic disorder only in an environment that turns this disposition into maladaptive learning. Learning is viewed as the process that integrates individual and situational factors.

Eysenck believes that most behavior can be understood in terms of two basic dimensions: **neuroticism** and **introversion-extraversion.** He thinks that genetically determined properties of the nervous system are the basis for individual differences along these dimensions. People at the high end of the neuroticism dimension are said to have a labile (unstable) type of nervous system that causes them to react too strongly and too persistently to external stimuli. The nervous systems of people at the introversion end of the introversion-extraversion continuum cause these people to acquire conditioned responses more readily than people falling near the middle of this dimension; people at the extraversion end of the continuum condition least easily.

The terms extraversion, introversion, and neuroticism are descriptive of the kinds of behaviors typically shown by people with these kinds of nervous systems. Eysenck's data suggest that most people with highly labile nervous systems learn "neuroticlike" behaviors and concerns; most people who condition very quickly, on the other hand, develop passive and introverted life styles.

Although these dimensions are independent—that is, labile nervous systems are found in both highly conditionable people and people who are less easily conditioned—the influences of these two dimensions interact and cause the person to learn different kinds of behaviors. When a person has a highly labile nervous system and very poor conditionability, he can be expected to develop an extraverted and unrestrained style of behaving. Psychological disorders for people falling at these extremes of the two dimensions typically include assaultive and psychopathic behaviors. On the other hand, when an extremely labile nervous system is combined with high conditionability, the person is likely to become seclusive and obsessed by private fears and anxieties. Eysenck has also postulated a psychotic-nonpsychotic dimension, but there is, at this time, much less information about the possible physiological basis of such a dimension.

The work of John Dollard and Neal Miller is another important attempt to explain psychological disorder by drawing together different concepts. Dollard and Miller have explored the way a person's culture and situation influence his psychosexual development. Their work reflects the assumption that psychoanalytic theory, which describes psychosexual development, provides an accurate picture of a person's psychodynamic development. They say, however, that an adequate explanation of both normal and abnormal behavior requires a more detailed account of external influences. In their attempt to account for environmental influence, they have drawn heavily upon concepts from learning theory.

Dollard and Miller have, for example, substituted the **principle of reinforcement** for Freud's pleasure principle, which is discussed in Chapter 18. They say that the person reacts to his psychodynamic conflict with behaviors that are, in some way, reinforced by the environment. This hypothesis permits them to retain the view that fantasies and other symbolic representations have satisfaction value and even influence motivation, at least on the unconscious level. However, it also allows them to explain why a specific person develops a specific form of disorder or why he chooses to rely upon a particular one of the many behaviors that would be consistent with his own psychodynamic characteristics.

They believe, in short, that it is important to place greater emphasis upon factors in the external environment. They see the psychiatric patient as becoming ill and "getting well in real life." In *Personality and Psychotherapy,* Dollard and Miller say that the concept of "reality"—as in Freud's reality principle—is too ambiguous. They therefore elaborate it in terms of physical and social conditions of learning. They say that understanding behavior requires understanding not only the psychological concepts and principles but

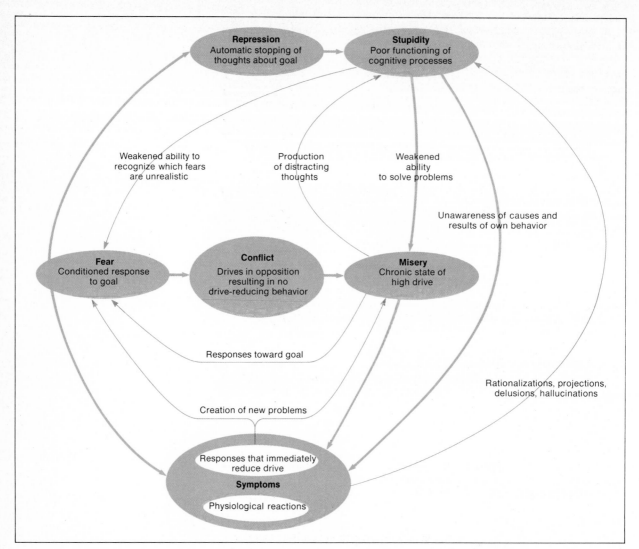

Figure 25.6 An example of a complex theory explaining the basis of psychological disorder. This diagram represents Dollard and Miller's attempt to translate the psychoanalytic theory of neurosis into the terms of learning theory. You will find it easier to understand the progression if you think of a conflict that you have experienced and trace its development in terms of the interactions diagramed here. Most people have experienced sufficient conflict over some matter to appreciate the possibility of the progression shown here, although not everyone becomes seriously neurotic because of such difficulties.

(After Dollard and Miller, 1950.)

also the social conditions that make up the individual's environment—particularly the ones that the structure of society imposes.

PROBLEMS IN RESEARCH

A major methodological problem in psychopathology research is the imprecision of diagnostic categories. The purpose of the classification system, which is described in Chapter 24, is to provide a method of grouping psychologically disturbed people. A category of disorder would include people who are more similar to each other than they are to individuals included in other groups.

Theoretically, the researcher who is familiar with the relevant descriptions and distinctions can diagnose people accordingly and proceed to search for biochemical, psychological, or other differences among groups. But, in fact, most people who suffer from psychological disorders show a variety of symptoms and display characteristics that are descriptive of more than one diagnostic category.

This problem could be called the ''nectarine dilemma.'' Just as a nectarine has both peachlike and apricotlike characteristics, most mentally ill individuals have disorders common to more than one diagnostic group. This lack of precision in the diagnostic process makes it difficult for the researcher to create groups of "pure," or blue-ribbon, diagnostic types and to interpret research results. For example, a study comparing the biochemistry of schizophrenics with that of normal persons might show a unique biochemical element for some but not all of the schizophrenic persons. How is the investigator to be sure whether there is a real connection between schizophrenia and the isolated element? It might be that such a relationship does exist and that the "schizophrenic" patients who do not have the biochemical element were incorrectly diagnosed. On the other hand, the biochemical difference may indicate a type of problem that is sometimes, and only peripherally, related to schizophrenia.

Because of this dilemma many researchers try to study only "classic" or "textbook" cases. But these cases are the exception, not the rule. Many other researchers have concluded that diagnostic classification is not a useful research tool. They feel that there is no reason to assume that a similarity of overt characteristics necessarily reflects a similarity of underlying causes. They argue against this assumption for two reasons: (1) the diagnostic system is imprecise, and (2) research that tries to find underlying processes of entities like "schizophrenia" has failed continually.

Another difficulty in psychopathology research is that *it can be conducted only after a person has become disturbed.* This might be called the "chicken or egg" problem. For example, when an investigator finds that factor x is almost always present in cases of a given disorder, how does he know whether x causes the disorder or the disorder causes x?

In the double-bind theory of schizophrenia described earlier, the researchers studied interactions within families in which a child had developed a schizophrenic disorder and found that the parents—especially the mother—behaved in ways that simultaneously communicated positive and negative feelings toward the child. Gregory Bateson and his colleagues, you will remember, hypothesized that the mother's behavior causes the child's disturbance. However, it is also possible that the mother feels ambivalent and acts in contradictory ways because the child is disturbed, for a disturbed child can be expected to stimulate both compassion and irritation in a parent. Research into either the biochemical or the psychological aspects of abnormal behavior presents this problem of chicken and egg because mental illness may cause changes both in metabolism and in the external environment (which is the mother's attitude, in this case).

In the short run, at least, researchers will have to depend on their own intelligence and intuition to decide which direction of causality is more likely the real one. Even if the incidence of blue-ribbon cases were high—which it is not—it would be almost impossible to completely monitor the lives of enough people for a sufficiently long period of time—say, from birth through forty years—to provide answers to these questions. Experimentation is an ethically unacceptable alternative. If an investigator suspects that some factor, a chemical substance or psychological experience, can trigger a disorder, clearly he cannot expose a person to that factor unless he is quite sure that he can return the person to his original state. Eventually, it may be possible to study from birth certain people whose characteristics would make them likely to develop a psychological disorder. Certainly this strategy would be possible for inherited and physiological factors, but investigators would need strong leads.

A third problem in psychopathology research has to do with **sequential causative factors.** In other words, psychological disorders may be the result of a series of changes or processes, each step being caused by a different set of circumstances. The following example illustrates the possibility of this kind of causal chain.

Let us assume that one characteristic a person inherits is the high lability of his nervous system, that is, a strong susceptibility to emotional arousal. Let us also assume that although the person develops ways of accommodating or channeling this extreme arousal, it can initially produce a temporary biochemical imbalance. If this type of person should encounter very stressful situations—perhaps situations of extreme conflict—at a very early age, the biochemical imbalance will occur.

During the period of chemical imbalance, a person's perceptions and cognitions are distorted. Imagine the case of a child in whom heredity and early environment combine to give an altered view of the world. Moreover, because the condition is transient and the child is very young, these occurrences go unnoticed. After the critical period is over, the child looks and acts like any other child. He is different only in that he has had and remembers experiences that most children have not had.

Now assume that for a considerable length of time the child's psychological development revolves around mastering the current environment, developing language skills, and formulating an understanding of the world. Later, when the child begins to refine his cognitive map or understanding of the world, he compares his memories with his present experiences. The way he integrates these memories of early experiences results in perceptions and attitudes that are very different from other people's perceptions. However, the child is not yet mentally ill.

The way his family reacts to him is important. Will they find his uniqueness troublesome and anxiety-provoking? The nature of his past learning is a determining factor, too. How will he react to the experiences that produce stress and confusion? What kinds of demands will his future environment make on him? Should the person find himself in a situation where his behaviors are totally inappropriate, he would be unable to function. He would then have a psychological disorder.

The preceding example tries to show how multiple causative factors might operate sequentially and to suggest the almost infinite number of possible causal chains. Like scientists in other areas, the researcher in psychopathology attempts to fully explore a specific phenomenon or set of apparently related phenomena. The questions he can ask—or rather scientifically investigate—and the answers he finds are limited. Much of the material discussed in this chapter will some day be integrated into yet unformulated theories to provide a more comprehensive understanding of psychological disorder. Future research will probably indicate that many factors that now seem to be related to psychological disorders are, in fact, extraneous.

Figure 25.7 A number of possible causative factors may have to occur in a specific sequence to produce disorder. A person in whom these factors occurred singly or in some other combination might not become disturbed. This illustration represents the supposition that a child is born with a biochemically unusual nervous system, one that reacts very strongly to stimulation. As a result, during an early childhood illness that would have no lasting effect on most children, this child has pronounced hallucinations. As he grows older, he tries to understand this experience and integrate it with the rest of his life. He tries to discuss his memories of that time with his parents. Being insecure individuals themselves, they become uneasy and respond in ways that make him feel that he is wrong or bad in some way. His unusual biochemistry causes him to react very strongly to this rebuff and he thus has further troubling experiences that he needs to make sense of. He now begins to experience a conflict between his need to talk to his parents about his innermost feelings and his fear of their cold response. He is well on the way to becoming psychologically disordered unless the links in this repetitive chain are somehow broken.

SUMMARY

1. Many theories of psychopathology account for its occurrence by tracing the source of mental disorder to the experiences and associations of infancy and childhood.

   a. **Psychoanalytic theory** postulates a series of psychosexual stages of development (oral, anal, phallic, latency, and genital) that everyone passes through. Each stage has associated with it particular impulses and conflicts. A child who successfully deals with the problems at one stage moves to the next with a strong **ego**—the part of the personality that can deal rationally with the real world, reconciling instinctual urges (**id**) and internalized societal demands (**superego**). A child who does not resolve all the problems of one stage must use some of his ego energy on the unsolved problems of that stage and so will not be able to deal as effectively with the problems of the new stage. When such a person faces an irreconcilable conflict in adulthood, his psychological behavior is likely to **regress** to the psychosexual stage of development he had failed to pass through successfully. The conflict and regression usually express themselves in **symbolic** form.

   Figure 25.8 John Watson's conditioning experiment with "Little Albert" is considered a classic demonstration of the applicability of learning principles to human disorder. Watson's 1913 proclamation that "the time has come when psychology must discard all reference to consciousness" set the behavioristic tone of American experimental psychology for the next fifty years. Watson was an extremely influential writer and lecturer. He was president of the American Psychological Association in 1915 and author of an influential book on child rearing.

   b. **Social-learning theory** states that the abnormal behavior of disturbed persons has been learned through the same mechanisms that govern all learning—the person has at some time in his life been reinforced through reward or punishment for behaving that way.

   c. Some researchers believe that particular factors are common to the family environments of disturbed persons. Theodore Lidz and his colleagues, after observation of a number of families of schizophrenics, found two types of characteristic situations: **marital schism** and **marital skew.** In the first type, both parents, who have brought personality problems to the marriage, try to coerce each other instead of cooperating, and downgrade the other's worth to their children. In **marital skew,** one parent, who is very dependent, supports all the actions of the other, who is disturbed. The child then gets a consistent message that this abnormal environment is acceptable.

   Gregory Bateson and Don Jackson developed the **double-bind hypothesis.** They believe that the mothers of schizophrenics cannot accept their children's affection and at the same time are anxious about these hostile feelings. Although the mother behaves in what appears to be a correct and loving way, the child perceives her ambivalent feelings and so receives two contradictory messages—one in behavior, one in words. He therefore never learns to make the distinctions among meanings expressed in normal language and behavior.

   R. D. Laing says that the behavior of schizophrenics makes sense when viewed in the context of their families' interactions. He argues further that pathology is inherent in contemporary society.

2. Some psychologists have presented evidence suggesting that certain psychological disorders are transmitted through the genes.

   a. **Family studies** compare the incidence of a given disorder among blood relatives; if its incidence is higher among the relatives sharing a greater percentage of genes in common, the researchers conclude that it is inherited.

   b. **Twin studies** are of two types: Researchers compare sets of identical (**monozygous**) twins with sets of fraternal (**dizygous**) twins for a trait; it is assumed that each set of twins has a virtually identical environ-

Figure 25.9 Paul Meehl is a respected and prolific writer in psychology. Much of his work has dealt with problems of defining psychological concepts and classifying psychological phenomena. He has also written about modern learning theory, construct validity in psychological testing, and psychology's relation to the law. His description of catatonic schizophrenia is considered classic.

ment and that, therefore, heredity is somehow responsible when the identical twins show more resemblance for the trait. The other type of twin study finds identical twins who were separated in infancy and reared in different environments; if these twins display similar traits, it is assumed that heredity is responsible.

c. **Studies of adopted children** compare incidence of a disorder in the child's **biological family** with its incidence in his **adoptive family.** If the incidence is higher in the biological family—as it is in schizophrenia—researchers conclude that there is a hereditary basis.

d. A theory by Paul Meehl implicates both genetic and environmental factors in the development of schizophrenia. Someone who has inherited a defective gene will become a full-blown schizophrenic only if he has inherited other defective genes and also has had stressful childhood experiences.

3. Some researchers believe that severe forms of mental disorder are caused by some kind of **biochemical malfunction.** It is very difficult to obtain conclusive evidence, but one recent hypothesis has been formulated about schizophrenia: C. David Wise and Larry Stein believe that a defective gene results in the lack of a biochemical agent necessary in the sequence of the body's use of the hormone norepinephrine. Lack of this substance causes progressive brain damage in the areas of the brain associated with pleasure and goal-oriented behavior.

4. **Conflict,** especially over an extended period, has been cited as a possible cause of mental disorder. Neal Miller and others define three distinct types of conflict: The **approach-approach** conflict, requiring the person to choose only one of two equally desirable alternatives; the **avoidance-avoidance** conflict, presenting two equally distasteful alternatives, only one of which can be avoided; and the **approach-avoidance** conflict, which inseparably pairs a desirable alternative with a distasteful one.

5. **Anxiety** plays a part in many theories of disorder; its relation to psychosis is not known, but it is an important factor in neurotic disorders. Psychologists have found that when people are very anxious, they are less able to perform complex tasks.

6. **Attribution theory** was developed by Stuart Valins and Richard Nisbett to account for the bizarre thinking of certain extremely disturbed persons. The psychologists postulate that such persons cannot find appropriate explanations for why they undergo certain experiences—say, heart palpitations—so they attribute the experiences to inappropriate causes: demons or the like.

7. Several theories attempting to set out the basis of mental disorder postulate a combination of causes instead of a single cause. Paul Meehl's theory, discussed earlier in the chapter, is one of these.

a. Hans Eysenck believes that heredity plays a part in what kinds of nervous systems people inherit—for example, some people inherit a tendency to react more strongly than others to stimuli—but that the individual's environment is extremely important in determining whether the inherited tendency will lead to psychological disorder. He believes that most behavior can be understood in terms of two dimensions: **neuroticism,** and **introversion-extraversion.**

b. John Dollard and Neal Miller draw from both psychoanalytic theory and learning theory to explain the basis of disorder. They believe that

Figure 25.10 Hans Eysenck is a British personality theorist who has made extensive use of the technique of factor analysis (discussed in Chapter 19). His dimensions of neuroticism and introversion-extraversion were derived with this technique. Eysenck has also played an important role in the development and growth of the behavioral psychotherapies (discussed in Chapter 27).

the psychoanalytic description of psychosexual development is valid but that it doesn't take sufficient account of the way an individual's social and physical environment punishes or rewards his behavior. They substitute the **principle of reinforcement** for Freud's pleasure principle.

8. Research into the causes of disorder is beset by a number of different problems. One is the shortcomings of the diagnostic classification system: The behavior and symptoms of most disturbed people do not fit neatly into one descriptive category. Therefore, it is difficult, say, to test schizophrenics for biochemical anomalies because the researcher cannot be sure that his experimental group includes only schizophrenics.

   a. Another research problem is raised when a factor, biochemical or psychological, is found to be common to a group of disturbed persons: The researcher often cannot know whether that factor caused or was caused by the disorder. Experimentation is usually out of the question.

   b. A third problem faced by researchers is the possibility that **sequential causative factors** are responsible for psychological disorder. For example, an early but temporary biochemical imbalance, a result of heredity, may produce distorted perceptions and cognitions in a child too young to voice or show them. The child, then, will integrate these distortions, which are part of his experience, into attitudes he forms about the way his world operates. The nature of his environment, the way his parents treat him, and the kinds of stresses he is subject to will then determine whether he develops a psychological disorder.

SUGGESTED READINGS

Cameron, Norman. *Personality Development and Psychopathology.* Boston: Houghton Mifflin, 1963. This work provides the reader with an understanding of how the psychoanalytically oriented clinician views psychological development and its relation to psychological disorders. It is a relatively complete presentation but can be easily understood by the unsophisticated reader.

Kaplan, Bert (ed.). *The Inner World of Mental Illness.* New York: Harper & Row, 1964. This book contains a collection of descriptions of what it is like to have a psychological disorder. Each account is written by a person who experienced the disorder described.

Sahakian, William S. (ed.). *Psychopathology Today: Experimentation, Theory and Research.* Itasca, Ill.: F. E. Peacock, 1970. This volume contains a collection of important research papers concerning psychopathology. The volume is well organized, and the editor has provided introductory discussions for each section. These introductions allow the reader to understand the individual papers as parts of a comprehensive whole.

Ullman, Leonard P., and Leonard Krasner. *A Psychological Approach to Abnormal Behavior.* New York: Holt, Rinehart and Winston, 1970. This volume provides a simply written yet comprehensive understanding of psychological disorders that is based on learning-theory principles. It is useful for students at all levels.

White, Robert W., and Norman F. Watt. *The Abnormal Personality.* 4th ed. New York: Ronald Press, 1964. This text provides an excellent introduction to the subject matter of psychopathology. The various forms of psychological disorders are described, and a brief discussion of the theories and empirical data concerning each is provided. A wide variety of deviant behaviors are discussed. The reader need not have studied psychology before.

I've met a considerable number of psychiatrists in my life and, as far as I can remember, I liked them all. In fact, I liked at least one of them very much, since she is my wife. Yet I've got to admit I feel personally uneasy about psychotherapy. I am now trying to think this through, because the uneasiness is getting in my way in constructing an introduction to this chapter. *Why* am I uneasy?

The closest I ever came to undergoing psychotherapy was when I was in the Army back in 1945 and 1946. It wasn't a bad time really, as I look back on it. The war was over; I was in no danger; everyone was moderately nice to me; I underwent no suffering—but I *hated* it.

If one thing bothered me more than another, it was the lack of privacy. Sleeping in the same room with thirty others and listening to their snoring and trying to ignore the smell was bad enough, but what really got me was that the toilets not only didn't have doors, they didn't even have partitions. I trained myself to get up at 3 A.M. to visit the toilet—and there was invariably one other soldier using it.

The unhappiness got me so far down that, out of sheer desperation, I had to choose someone with whom to discuss the matter. It had to be either the chaplain or the psychiatrist, and I chose the latter. Actually, I spoke to one of his young assistants (a social worker in real life) for several sessions. The psychiatrist himself didn't bother seeing me because the social worker, after listening to my sorrows, told his boss not to waste his time on me.

In a way, nothing came of it. I had vaguely hoped that if the psychotherapist realized the extent of my misery, he would set me up in a room of my own with a private toilet and shower. But it turned out that all *they* were interested in was in adjusting *me*. I was supposed to react more calmly to the lack of privacy. Well, heck, this I didn't want to do. If I couldn't have my privacy then, darn it, I wanted my grievance.

In another way, something did come of it. The social worker discovered I could type at professional speed, and the office needed typists. He got me a job as a typist there, which meant no more KP. Now *that* was good psychotherapy. I enjoyed the job, and I even got to know the psychiatrist. I used to talk to him, informally, every chance I got, feeling that one shouldn't give up on psychotherapy yet. Perhaps if one went straight to the boss, it might be arranged for me to have at least a special time in the community toilet when no one else was allowed to enter.

Not so. The psychiatrist was a lovable fellow but he never wanted to talk about these matters in an objective way. His only curiosity was in my own subjective reaction to these things. Once I said hotly, "Why are you so surprised that I resent being crowded in with strangers? Wouldn't you?" His response was a cool, "Would I?"

Then one day I told him a joke that was distinctly antipsychiatrist. I tell jokes very well and I told that one at the top of my form. When I finished, I laughed heartily, but all the psychiatrist did was to put his fingertips together, wait for me to calm down, and say, "Tell me, Asimov, why did you feel it necessary to tell me that joke?"

I think that's why I'm uneasy about psychotherapy. I can't win.

Isaac Asimov

26
Individual and Group Psychotherapy

Figure 26.1 A facilitator helps a member of an encounter group through a particularly intense emotional experience that has been triggered by the member's attempts to become conscious of certain painful feelings. Psychotherapeutic settings such as this one have become as well-accepted in America as the analyst's office once was. Both forms of therapy share with such social forms as religious confession, shamanism, and faith-healing certain features that seem to characterize all societies' methods of responding to psychological distress.

I t has never been easy to function effectively as a human being. In all parts of the world, at all times, people have strained against the accepted behavioral standards of their societies, and few have escaped the conflict without suffering anxiety, depression, frustration, guilt, or rage.

All societies have sought ways to change nonconforming behavior and to relieve human suffering, but the ways have varied according to the psychological theories by which the behavior was explained. The theories, in turn, have varied according to social and historical circumstances. During the Middle Ages, the prescribed therapy in many Western societies for persons with behavioral disorders was exorcism, on the theory that their souls were possessed by demons. Some cultures, both in remote parts of the world and in modern urban areas, still subscribe to the practice of exorcism by shamans, witch doctors, or faith healers. Most Western societies, however, now favor treatment by professional therapists whose methods are based on psychological theories.

Exorcism and psychotherapy seem to be divergent approaches; but Jerome Frank, in *Persuasion and Healing,* suggests that methods used by shamans, faith healers, and psychotherapists share some common features, such as:

1. A sanctioned, trained healer whose powers are accepted by both the sufferer and the social group with which he is affiliated.

2. A sufferer who seeks relief through the healer.

3. A more or less structured series of interactions in which the healer uses words, acts, or rituals in the attempt to change the sufferer's emotional state, attitudes, or behavior.

An important question, which is still unanswered, is how the particular techniques used by each type of healer work their specific effects on the individuals treated—how the specific changes take place.

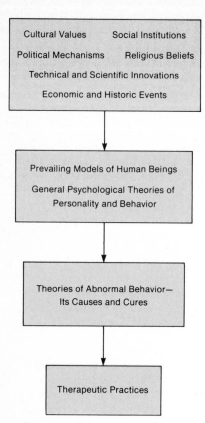

Figure 26.2 The particular form taken by a society's response to behavioral disorder is the product of a number of factors, as this diagram shows. Exorcism, for example, was popular in medieval Western cultures because of prescientific beliefs about the causes of sin and about the relationship between God and human beings.

Preceding chapters have discussed various models of personality and behavior as well as theories of disordered behavior. This chapter deals chiefly with techniques used with individuals and groups by professional therapists who base their treatment on personality theories. The next chapter will describe treatments based on behavioral models.

INSTITUTIONAL APPROACHES

Professional efforts to help persons with behavioral disorders began with a concern for institutionalized persons. At that time, some two hundred years ago, society regarded its psychological misfits as sinners who were being uniquely punished by God and who deserved additional punishment from other human beings. The misfits were thrown into prisons and put in chains along with other persons who were unable to earn a living or to pay their debts. The people who ran the institutions served not as healers but as agents of social and economic control.

A dramatic change in public attitudes and in the treatment of deviant individuals came in the last decade of the eighteenth century when Phillippe Pinel, a French physician, put into practice his firm belief that these institutionalized misfits were not sinful and deserving of chains but were mentally ill and deserving of compassionate care. This change was part of the drastic social and intellectual upheavals of the century, which brought a new rationalism to medicine and, along with the American and French revolutions, a new concern for individual rights.

Cure or Custody

In the 1800s, mentally ill individuals in the United States were usually kept in small asylums, where the prevailing method of therapy was moral treatment. It included a paternalistic and optimistic teaching program: Patients attended inspirational classes and religious services, were encouraged to work and to refrain from morbid thoughts, participated in group meetings and individual interviews with staff members, and were otherwise helped to establish "regular habits of self-control." This treatment produced remarkable results: It was reported that some 75 percent of the patients who were admitted to institutions for the first time recovered and were released. Of these, about 58 percent never suffered a relapse.

It is difficult to understand why such a successful program was abandoned, but a few factors may be cited. First, within a period of two decades an influx of immigrants from Europe—mostly penniless—quadrupled the ratio of patients to doctors, widened the socioeconomic gap between them, and increased public prejudice against ethnic minorities (as strikingly evidenced by a new diagnostic classification of mental illness: "foreign insane pauperism"). In addition, the successful efforts of Dorothea Dix and other humanitarian social reformers that had resulted in the building of huge hospitals to provide care for the mentally ill fell victim to the era's widespread political corruption: Hospital staff members were mainly political appointees, untrained and uncaring.

By 1900, mental health workers had lost their optimism about curing mental illness, and **custodial care** had supplanted moral treatment at most institutions. Though critics pointed out that the custodial approach maintained misery and deviance instead of alleviating them, it prevailed through the early decades of this century.

In the early 1950s the social effects of this system were studied by a number of investigators. They concluded that the mental health professionals employed in custodial care responded most frequently to pathological symptoms of patients, thus reinforcing this behavior rather than the healthy behaviors that patients also showed. Even when benevolent, staff attitudes retarded

Figure 26.3 Phillippe Pinel supervising the unchaining of the inmates of the insane asylum at La Salpetriere in 1795. Earlier Pinel had obtained permission to unchain the inmates of Bicetre Hospital in the face of such objections from the revolutionary authorities as: "Why not proceed to the zoo and liberate the lions and tigers?" and "Woe to you if you deceive me and if you hide enemies of the people among your insane!" The conditions depicted here were typical of eighteenth-century asylums; unfortunately, wards in some mental institutions today are equally depressing.

patients' progress, because the paternalism actually elicited the helplessness, dependence, and irresponsibility that the staff expected to see from the patients. Patients who were held accountable for their own behavior, who were allowed to make decisions and to suffer the consequences, often improved rapidly. But most patients engaged neither in therapeutic activities nor in bizarre behavior. Rather, they did absolutely nothing.

The advent of tranquilizers and antidepressant drugs in the 1950s dramatically affected not only patients but staff as well. Patients on such medication ceased to be hyperactive or extremely depressed and were more easily influenced verbally. Professional workers, no longer preoccupied with controlling behavior, grew more optimistic as they saw that it was possible for patients to change. This attitude made possible the development of a different model of hospital care, which is now replacing the custodial institution.

The Therapeutic Community

A proposal for using the entire hospital milieu for therapeutic purposes was made at about the same time that drugs began to be used extensively. The new model, introduced in 1953 by Maxwell Jones and his associates in the influential book *The Therapeutic Community,* was based on several assumptions. First, even for the rare patient who received an hour of psychotherapy daily, the other twenty-three hours of life seemed wasted, for they provided no opportunities to learn and practice constructive behaviors. Second, patients were not helpless, hopeless, and irresponsible; most of them were able to collaborate with therapists in directing their own treatment and in solving problems. Thus, the difficulties of living and working together in a residential unit could be analyzed and resolved by the residents acting jointly instead of by staff members only. Third, if mental illness is viewed not as a disease but as a failure to deal adequately with life stresses, and if the faulty perceptions and frustrating relations with others are seen as results of this failure, then it is through interactions with others that confidence can be restored, perceptions can be changed, and new behaviors can be learned.

The physical changes brought to the typical hospital ward by these new attitudes are remarkable. Doors are no longer locked, staff members and

Figure 26.4 The range of conditions in American mental institutions. The scene in the upper photograph is not uncommon: Lack of space, staff, money, public concern, and government supervision has made some mental institutions more like holding tanks than like treatment centers. The scenes in the lower photographs, however, suggest how a well-funded institution can operate: Patients are active in a pleasant environment and have a great deal of contact with each other and the staff. As this chapter discusses, there is a trend today away from rigid separation of the hospital environment and the environment to which the patient will return.

patients wear their own street clothes (and patients do their own laundry), meals are family style, and bedrooms look more like motel accommodations than hospital rooms. Such physical changes are signs of the new roles played by patient and staff. Picture, for example, a patient whose daily activities are mostly of her own choosing. She may meet daily in group therapy; she may attend regular meetings of staff and patients on the ward—meetings in which everyone participates equally, on a first-name basis, in airing problems and gripes, in proposing solutions, and perhaps in voting on proposed regulations and procedures. The meetings may be run by patients elected as officers by their peers. And staff-patient teams may decide *together* if patient A is ready for a weekend at home, if B needs to be accompanied by another patient on a shopping trip to town, or if C should be helped to become more assertive by being rewarded for assertive behavior. Patients confront and support each other and the staff, and vice versa.

The therapeutic community has not become firmly established as the dominant approach, however, and it is already being modified by an orientation that emphasizes community ties. Figure 26.4 shows scenes from a number of institutions, some of which use the therapeutic-community methods and some that still give only custodial care.

Community Mental Health Programs

"Halfway houses" and facilities that offer care only during the day provide therapy without isolating the patient from his community. Often patients are not admitted to a hospital at all but receive immediate help in their own homes at a time of crisis. If they need a respite from environmental stresses, they may be placed for a few days in a local residence where they receive medication, psychotherapy, and support before returning home.

This change of emphasis is part of the **community mental health** movement, which has as one goal the reduction of the size and number of mental hospitals and the shifting of care to local clinics, general hospitals, and other short-stay facilities. The movement received major impetus in 1961, when the Joint Commission on Mental Illness and Health, appointed by President Kennedy, reported on the nation's extensive mental health problems and their resultant social and economic costs, showing that the institutions and services then current were totally inadequate, especially for the treatment of major mental illness. In 1963, the federal Community Mental Health Centers Act provided funds and guidelines for local Community Mental Health Centers (CMHC) that would each provide comprehensive services for a surrounding population of 200,000 persons. This act emphasized local control and community initiative, services to previously neglected segments of the populations, and optimism—the same values and action orientation that lay behind the civil rights and economic opportunity programs of the 1960s.

Many centers have been established, although their number is far below that initially proposed. Recent changes in the political and social climate have slowed the progress of community-oriented care. So, too, has our society's traditional and still influential view that disturbed people must be locked up in isolation from the rest of the population: In many states, citizens have protested the closing of large mental institutions, charging that inmates are being "dumped" into the community. The CMHC program has provided new roles and challenges for therapists—not the least of which is explaining the emerging methods of treatment that are replacing custodial care in terms that will make the benefits of this exciting concept apparent to the average citizen.

PERSONAL APPROACHES

Ironically, at a time when psychologically based treatment of the severely disturbed psychotic patient was being abandoned in the United States, therapy for the less seriously disturbed neurotic individual was being devised in Europe. The intellectual giant who initiated the intensive study of neuroses was Sigmund Freud (whose theories of personality are presented in Chapter 18). Freud's theories, which emphasized sexual instincts and repression, were a reflection of the strait-laced Victorian era.

Freud and Psychoanalysis

Anton Mesmer, an eighteenth-century Viennese physician who developed techniques of hypnosis, believed that both mental and physical illnesses were caused by an imbalance between the influences of the stars and an individual's "animal magnetism." Mesmer's general theories were not attuned to the scientific trend of his day and were discredited; but hypnotism attracted the attention of neurologist Jean Martin Charcot, who used it in treating hysteria, a type of neurosis.

Freud, who studied with Charcot in the 1880s, found that under hypnosis, hysterics apparently could recall their early childhood traumas. The recovery of these early memories seemed to alleviate the paralysis, blindness, deafness, and other hysterical manifestations that these patients suffered. Freud later abandoned hypnosis in favor of **free association,** a technique in which the patient talks freely without censoring his thoughts. Freud's therapy also included **interpretation of the patient's dreams** and **transference** of the patient's attitudes toward his parents onto the therapist.

The impact of Freud's revolutionary techniques was heightened by the fact that Vienna, during his lifetime, was a major cultural and intellectual center.

Figure 26.5 Fifty-minute sessions alone with "my analyst" were for a long time the only common form of psychotherapy in Western society. In this form of therapy most of the burden of analysis is on the patient. The analyst says relatively little, requiring the patient to discuss his private thoughts, his memories, his present relationships, and to interpret his dreams. Analysts only occasionally suggest interpretations themselves. The patient often experiences resistance because he is unwilling to probe further into himself. He also frequently experiences transference: He projects feelings about important figures in his present or past life onto the analyst. Here, in a patient's dream, his resistance to therapy is represented by the transformation of his therapy session into the unpleasant experience of going to the dentist, and transference causes the dentist-analyst to take the form of a threatening mother figure.

Doctors from all parts of the Western world went there to study, and the medical tradition to which Freud belonged gained prestige and power as his explanations and techniques were formalized into theory. Both the prevalent world view and the intellectual and cultural experimentation of the post-Victorian era were amenable to Freud's innovative proposals, which brought a scientific orientation to the study of the fascinating mysteries of the unconscious mind. Novelists and painters, psychiatrists and psychologists alike were excited by the ideas of **psychoanalysis,** the name given to Freudian therapy.

Psychoanalysis offered far more intellectual stimulation to the therapist than did the custodial care of individuals who were confined to institutions, and professionals became increasingly concerned with the treatment of noninstitutionalized clients. The socioeconomic determinants of this situation are worth noting, for they are still influential today.

Institutionalized patients tended to be poor and were often objects of ethnic prejudice, as previously noted. Freud's patients, on the other hand, shared his values and cultural background; and his techniques accommodated both his middle-class clientele and his theory of personality. Psychoanalysis involves a verbal, one-to-one relationship between therapist and client; it was designed for neurotic, rather than psychotic, individuals; and it required that they have intelligence, money, time, and patience.

The divergence between the psychoanalytic ideology and the ideology that prevailed in mental hospitals affected even the classification of mental illnesses. Psychoanalysts diagnosed patients on the basis of the individual and the conflicts between different levels of his personality. Institutional therapists, oriented toward biology, devised classifications based on symptoms.

Freudian theory was quickly accepted by educated people, and it became fashionable to explain behavior—and sometimes even physical illness—in terms of psychoanalytic concepts; persons with less education continued to ignore the significance of emotions and psychological variables, however. This dichotomy still prevails today. The middle-class patient, for example, may tell his family physician that "tension" and "anxiety" are causing him to have frequent headaches. The working-class patient, on the other hand, may complain of trouble with his "nerves"—meaning that his physiology, his nervous system, is somehow causing shaking and sweating hands, shortness of breath, and other symptoms that the physician may diagnose as anxiety. Mass communication and mass education have gradually decreased the differences between these viewpoints, but only recently have the poorer members of society who are in need of therapy begun to receive the kind of attention professionals once reserved for the middle classes.

The Paradigm Crisis

A few decades ago, textbook chapters on psychotherapy might have ended at this point. Today, however, psychoanalysis is no longer firmly established as the dominant school of psychotherapeutic thought, although the assessment of psychotherapy is far from simple. How did this change come about in so short a time? And why?

Science historian Thomas Kuhn (whose point of view is also discussed in Chapter 1) has said that a scientific theory is more than a set of explanations: It is also an expression of a particular viewpoint with many practical implications that even the scientists who formulate the theory do not always recognize. Kuhn believes that when a branch of science adopts a theory, it also adopts a **paradigm**—a way of thinking, often unconscious, that projects theoretical assumptions into research methods, into scientific and professional institutions, and even into the values and organization of society.

Psychoanalysis served as such a paradigm. Within the fields of psychotherapy and psychopathology, it long defined both the topics of interest and the methods of investigating them. Psychoanalytic institutes, in which therapists received years of training and personal psychoanalysis before becoming qualified analysts, acquired tremendous prestige. Although other theories might have been able to better explain particular aspects of human behavior, none approached the tremendous scope and brilliance of psychoanalysis, which permeated all aspects of intellectual and cultural life, especially in the United States. In addition, psychoanalytic theory was essentially irrefutable, since its practice involved a very private relationship between therapist and client. For years, these factors ruled out objective scientific research in psychotherapy.

How is such a pervasive paradigm overturned? According to Kuhn, it is not by the gradual accumulation of evidence, in the way we ordinarily think of a theory being revised. The process is revolutionary rather than evolutionary. Researchers work for years within the limits of a paradigm, refining details and analyzing problems without questioning the paradigm itself. But then, when problems repeatedly fail to yield to accepted methods of investigation, a crisis develops. Revolutionary thinkers break the conventional rules, and a period of chaos ensues. Adherents of the paradigm continue to insist that it alone is adequate, but eventually it is replaced by a new paradigm, which alters the previous philosophy, and with it, previous limitations on thought.

Kenneth Colby, a prominent analytically trained psychotherapist, pointed out a decade ago that psychotherapy had reached this crisis point, and absolutist convictions are still being loosened today. Neo-analytic therapy has become increasingly more neo and less analytic. Although rival theories derived from classical and operant conditioning, existential philosophy, and community-oriented social psychology have been presented, none yet commands the consensus necessary to become a paradigm. Within each theoretical area there is confusion about concepts and facts. Proponents of each approach talk past each other, as Colby puts it, "because in experiencing the same events they actually observe different things."

How Well Does Psychotherapy Work?

What factors helped to weaken the old paradigm? Probably the most important factor was that research results tended to refute some of the basic tenets underlying psychoanalysis. For example, psychoanalytic theory says that symptoms are produced by underlying neuroses and that simply removing a symptom will not change the basic condition—and may, in fact, produce new or substitute symptoms. Behavioral studies of children seemed to show, however, that anxiety was typically a consequence rather than a cause of symptoms; when symptoms were directly removed, the child's overall functioning improved—without signs of either the overt anxiety or the substitute symptoms that Freudian theory had predicted. The idea that behavioral traits continue across situations, another assumption of Freudian and other personality-based theories, also was challenged by clinical researchers.

Of even greater importance were studies of the effectiveness of psychotherapy, or **outcome research.** In 1952, at a time when "psychotherapy" was almost synonymous with "psychoanalysis," a British psychologist named Hans Eysenck published a landmark review of the literature, from which he concluded that the behavior of some two-thirds of the mentally ill eventually improves—with or without treatment. This study, which Eysenck updated in 1966, was a tremendous stimulus to further investigations of both the procedures and the results of psychotherapy.

The problems involved in outcome research are many. Precise criteria for "improvement" are difficult to define and difficult to apply. The nature of "spontaneous remission" (sudden disappearance) of symptoms in persons who have not received formal psychotherapy is difficult to assess, for these

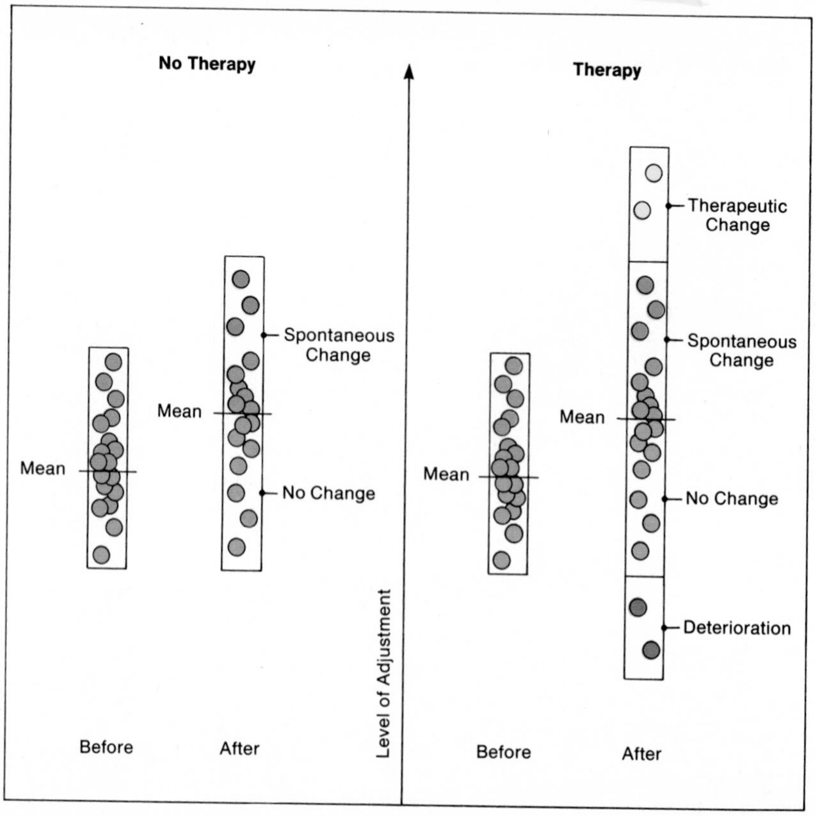

Figure 26.6 The results of Bergin's reanalysis of studies on the outcome of therapy. These studies compared the "wellness" of people before and after formal psychotherapy, or before and after a period of time in which they might have been in therapy but were not. Bergin confirmed Eysenck's finding that the *average* increase in "wellness" was the same in groups of people who had had therapy as in groups of people who had not. But Bergin also noted that both "after" groups showed a greater range of health—that is, some people were better than they had been before. The health range was greater, however, in the group that had undergone psychotherapy. That is, although some people who had not undergone therapy appeared to be better after a period of time, none were as much improved as some who had undergone therapy. On the other hand, some who had undergone therapy appeared to be worse after the experience, whereas none of the nontherapy group actually got worse. Bergin concluded that psychotherapy *does* have an effect on people and that investigations should be conducted to find out what makes this effect favorable in some cases and unfavorable in others.

(After Bergin, 1971.)

people may have received help from unacknowledged sources—friends, relatives, religious advisers, family physicians. And if, as some researchers believe, the prime ingredient in therapy is the establishment of a close relationship, then "spontaneous remission" in people who have received continuing help from such sources is not spontaneous at all.

In a more recent review of outcome studies, Allen Bergin concluded that rates of improvement without treatment varied widely according to the type of disorder and that the median rates were often as low as 30 percent. From the data he reviewed, Bergin concluded that a more optimistic view of the effects of psychotherapy is warranted, even though the effects of therapy are both better and worse than Eysenck's data showed (see Figure 26.6):

There remains some modest evidence that psychotherapy "works." While most studies do not seem to yield very substantial evidence that this is so, the number that do seems to be clearly larger than would be expected by chance. . . . While the average effect is modestly positive, the existence of a substantial improvement, as well as a significant "deterioration effect" [that is, when a disorder becomes more severe], suggests that the effects of therapy may be quite powerful indeed. The challenge is to isolate those variables more highly correlated with improvement and to incorporate them into flexible treatment strategies.

Figure 26.7 summarizes some of the generalizations proposed by researchers who have attempted to identify the factors that seem to influence the outcome of therapy. But until there is a more precise definition of the procedures that are used in treatment, the characteristics of the clients receiving help, and the criteria for improvement, the factors set out by these researchers as important to the outcome of therapy can only be tentative.

Despite Bergin's more encouraging view, outcome research issued a tremendous challenge to traditional psychotherapy, a challenge that has yet to be adequately met. Ironically, disappointment with the results of traditional treatment has led to the development of new approaches that are often presented as improved methods without actually having been subjected to any evaluation of their effectiveness.

Rivals to the Paradigm

As nonpsychoanalytic psychologists began to enter the clinical field, initially because of the man-power shortages of World War II, new influences began to impinge on psychotherapy. The therapists who ushered in these new influences usually had research backgrounds, and they often worked with clients unlike those who had traditionally been involved in psychotherapy. Many of these therapists were trained in classical and operant conditioning, and the behavior therapies they developed became a major challenge to psychoanalysis in the 1960s (see Chapter 27).

The client-centered therapy of Carl Rogers, whose theory is discussed in detail in Chapter 19, was devised even earlier. Interestingly, a technological development—the invention of the electronic tape recorder—played a vital role in furthering the innovations of Rogers: He and his students were ready to share the content of their sessions and to do controlled research on the events within treatment; tape recordings made this possible. Tapes also contributed to a recognition of the confusion existing within orthodox treatment: Once the sacred silence of the therapy session was breached, the diversity of psychoanalysts' actual practices was strikingly revealed.

The Third Force The challenge of Rogerian techniques was ignored at first by psychoanalysts and others, because initially the new methods were restricted to the counseling of "normal" college students who were experiencing mild situational distress. However, the monumental stresses of World War II had brought into prominence the ideas of existential philosophers, with whose

Figure 26.7 Factors identified by Luborsky and his associates as determinants of the outcome of psychotherapy. (After Luborsky, 1971.)

1. Initially sicker patients do not improve as much with psychotherapy as the initially healthier do . . . improvement is shown by patients, whatever their initial level of functioning.

2. Patients with higher initial intelligence perform better in psychotherapy.

3. Patients with high anxiety at the initial evaluation or at the beginning of treatment are the ones likely to benefit from psychotherapy. High initial anxiety probably indicates a readiness, or at least an openness, for change . . . almost any affect is better than no affect, and . . . anxiety and depression are probably the two "best" initial affects. The presence of these strong affects may indicate the patient is in pain and asking for help. The absence of affect very likely goes along with a state in which the patient is not reaching out for help, or has given up. . . .

4. Patients with higher social achievements are better suited for psychotherapy.

5. The therapist's empathy (and other related qualities) facilitates the patient's gains from psychotherapy.

6. Greater similarity between therapist and patient is associated with better outcomes . . . The variety of forms of positive similarity includes social class, interests, values, and compatibility or orientation to interpersonal relations. . . .

7. The *combination* of individual and group psychotherapy is better than either individual or group psychotherapy alone.

8. Schools of treatment usually make no measurable difference.

9. In 20 of 22 studies of essentially time-unlimited treatment, the length of treatment was positively related to outcome; the longer the duration of treatment or the more sessions, the better the outcome! Other interpretations: a) Patients who are getting what they need drop out sooner; b) Therapists may overestimate positive change in patients who have been in treatment longer.

10. Psychotherapy with pharmacotherapy tends to be slightly more effective than psychotherapy alone, but in more ways not more effective than pharmacotherapy alone – especially for schizophrenic patients.

Figure 26.8   In recent years it has become as common for people to talk about "my group" as about "my analyst" when referring to their psychotherapy. The discovery by Kurt Lewin that one's peers can be effective therapeutic agents and the idea that a person undergoing therapy is in a growth process are fundamental to this new form of therapy. Here a husband and wife who are finding life with each other less than satisfactory expose their relationship to other people by reenacting an emotion-charged situation in front of the group. Other members of the group react in various ways. Some of their reactions help the husband and wife to see their conflicts in a new light. Other members react by seeing themselves in a new way. Often, in such groups, the exposure of a member's hitherto private problems is an occasion for the expression of great warmth and sympathy by other members of the group.

concepts Rogers' notions of individual growth or self-actualization were compatible. Victor Frankl, for example, having faced the long ordeal of trying to find meaning in his existence as Prisoner No. 119104 in the Nazi concentration camp at Auschwitz, concluded that the existential quest for meaning was far more important for modern humanity than were the unconscious conflicts of Freud's Victorian era. Similarly, the wartime experiences of Jean Paul Sartre and other existential thinkers led them to focus on the individual's need to make his life meaningful—and the postwar generation was receptive. Existentialism not only influenced literature and art but also led to the development of new forms of psychotherapy. As the self-actualizing and search-for-meaning therapies rose to prominence in the 1960s, they became known as the "Third Force": an alternative to both Freudianism and behaviorism.

Families and Groups   Other innovative approaches to therapy were gradually devised, often by persons who were not psychoanalysts. For example, clinicians who were studying the communication patterns of schizophrenic young adults began to interview their parents as well, often with the patient present. These researchers observed peculiar transactions between patients and parents, which suggested that distorted communications, together with specialized roles within the family (such as that of scapegoat), might be relevant to schizophrenia. Treating the patient within the context of the family, the researchers soon evolved the concept that the *total family system* was the true locus of pathology; an individual member's symptoms were simply a message of distress, a part of a desperate effort to maintain balance within the family.

A pioneering group, led by Don Jackson, Jay Haley, and Virginia Satir, began to include entire families in therapy, focusing on "here-and-now" interactions and communication patterns. This conceptual revolution soon affected the practice of all therapists, for another previously sacred rule of psychoanalysis had been overturned: the rule that a therapist must deal only with the client, lest trust be destroyed and transference—the shift of feelings about a parent to the analyst—be violated.

The spread of **family therapy** was facilitated by social psychologists, who had developed means of studying small groups—a framework within which family therapy could be explored. Another approach to behavioral change was devised by social psychologists who were interested in group dynamics and wished to apply what they had learned to the functioning of bureaucratic and managerial groups. They founded the National Training Laboratory, where training groups, or T-groups, applied a direct-experience approach to improving group functioning.

In the early 1950s, the conventionality and superficiality of American society became a matter of general concern. David Riesman argued in *The Lonely Crowd* that the typical American was no longer an inner-directed and self-reliant individual; instead, he strived to conform to group values and behaviors. William H. Whyte's *The Organization Man* and novels such as *The Man in the Gray Flannel Suit* by Sloan Wilson were also critical of conformity.

The late 1950s brought increasing awareness that the established structure of American life ignored the need for human intimacy. In *Growing Up Absurd,* Paul Goodman described "the spiritual emptiness of our technological paradise," arguing that the beat generation, the organization man, and delinquent youths were all victims of this alienation. Carl Rogers proclaimed that the greatest threat to mankind was not overpopulation or atomic warfare but society's rapid rate of change: Increasingly, humans were facing the difficulty of trying to establish intimate relationships in the midst of mobility, shifting values, and cultural diversity.

The individualistic, democratic spirit of the **T-group,** with its emphasis on developing sensitivity to one's own impact on others, fit the concerns of the times very well. So well, in fact, that the focus began to shift from increasing the effectiveness of the task-oriented group to facilitating the growth of individual members, an orientation that was reflected in the increasing use of the term **sensitivity group** in place of T-group.

The Growth Movement Sensitivity-group techniques became widely used in the late 1960s in training mental health professionals, in treating less serious emotional problems, and in helping essentially healthy individuals to achieve self-actualization. The sensitivity groups presented diverse ap-

Figure 26.9 An illustration from *Tootle the Engine,* a popular children's book in the 1950s. This book was cited by David Riesman as an example of the socializing influences toward conformism that were prevalent then. Here Tootle, who has been enjoying the delights of trackless meadows, is warned by hidden humans to get back on the track. He does so in the story and becomes a happy and obedient engine. The ethics of group therapy and particularly of sensitivity training would encourage Tootle's exploration of his own individuality.

Figure 26.10 Scenes from the Esalen Institute in Big Sur, California, one of the best known and most innovative of the personal growth centers. Shown here, a man luxuriates in the sensations of his own body, and a group of people concentrate on their awareness of the simple act of breathing. Such therapists as Fritz Perls believe that a great deal can be discovered about psychological problems by an analysis of such basic bodily processes as breathing, standing, walking, and so on.

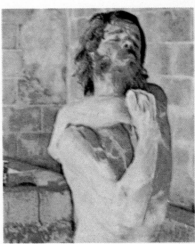

proaches to the achievement of personal growth, with emphasis on awareness—in communicating feelings, sharing experiences, developing comfortable intimacy, and enhancing sensory awareness.

Growth centers that offered these approaches to interested participants became widespread. The first was the Esalen Institute on the Big Sur coast of California, which had begun as a center for training professionals in such techniques as family therapy and T-groups. At first, sensory-awareness exercises and baths in Esalen's natural hot springs provided a restful recess rather than a focus of training. But soon these and other innovative procedures were offered as activities that in themselves induced personal growth, and the public was allowed to participate. Not only aspiring "normals" but also individuals in rather acute distress sought help in the Esalen-like growth centers that multiplied across the country. The new group techniques—variously termed encounters, marathons, and confrontations—emphasized **self-awareness** in the here-and-now.

Other models of behavior change shared many values with the growth movement and were often offered in the same settings. Fritz Perls' **Gestalt therapy,** for example, had its greatest impact on professional practice during the period he was in residence at Esalen. Although Perls had developed a distinctive formal theory of personality, his therapeutic techniques were based on existential philosophy and emphasized the here-and-now awareness of personal sensations and feelings.

An interesting consequence of the growth movement—and perhaps a reflection of the optimism of the Kennedy years—was a more democratic approach to psychotherapy, a kind of do-it-yourself spirit. People expected to be able to improve their own lives and the lives of others, and they no longer considered therapy a mysterious rite into which one must be initiated through the mediation of a mental health professional. Books on therapy such as Eric Berne's *Games People Play* (based on transactional analysis, his interpersonally oriented theory and therapy), became national best sellers. The transactions Berne's therapy is based on are between people operating at different levels of their personalities; child, adult, or parent. Figure 26.11 shows examples of some interactions.

Even more illustrative of this development were the self-help groups that followed the pattern established by Alcoholics Anonymous. Synanon was formed for the residential care of drug addicts, and some of the advantages of nonprofessional leadership were immediately obvious: No professional is ever as merciless and directly confronting as addicts are with each other, nor as difficult to dupe. Of the self-help groups, the most highly publicized were those that provided help to obese individuals who attempted to change their eating behavior through the use of supportive group therapy (and sometimes succeeded).

In recent years the enthusiastic and optimistic individualism that was associated with the civil rights movement, war protests, and experimentation with life styles seems to have abated. A more conservative, work-through-the-system, everyone-for-himself, task-oriented society apparently is developing. Although one result of this change has been a decreasing interest in growth centers, interest in transactional analysis and other reality-oriented therapies has grown. Behavior modification, discussed in the next chapter, is another example of the recent trend.

CURRENT PSYCHOTHERAPIES: AN OVERVIEW

There are presently many different assumptions, concepts, and methods in psychotherapy. Table 26.2 briefly summarizes some of the major approaches, along with their key concepts and mechanisms. Such a summary reveals the relative chaos that has developed in psychotherapy as the prevailing paradigm

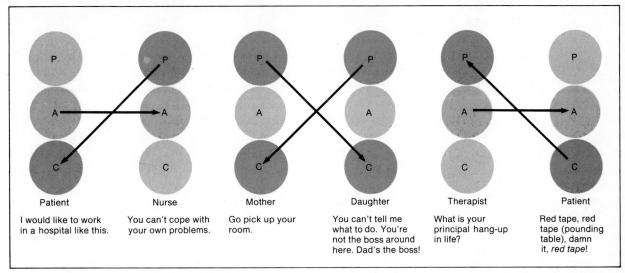

Patient	Nurse	Mother	Daughter	Therapist	Patient
I would like to work in a hospital like this.	You can't cope with your own problems.	Go pick up your room.	You can't tell me what to do. You're not the boss around here. Dad's the boss!	What is your principal hang-up in life?	Red tape, red tape (pounding table), damn it, *red tape!*

of psychoanalysis broke down: Experimentation became possible, and every therapist could devise his or her own model according to the spirit of the time. The advantages of innovations are obvious; the risk, not so apparent, is that psychotherapy may become just another manifestation of cultural fads unless new treatments are evaluated critically and tested empirically.

Despite the diversity of therapies, recent research has sought to provide a more comprehensive view of the therapeutic process by looking into such questions as who seeks psychotherapy, the common goals of the various approaches, and other features the therapies share.

Who Seeks Therapy

What kind of person is most likely to go into psychotherapy? In a 1972 survey, Kenneth Howard and David Orlinsky concluded that three specific types of clients engage in therapeutic activities.

Type One clients, who are the most visible, are usually young and relatively affluent adults; most of them are college-educated, unmarried women. They tend to be culturally sophisticated—one writer has described their characteristics as the YAVIS syndrome: "youthful, attractive, verbal, intelligent, and successful." Usually they reside in rather specific urban neighborhoods. They are not seriously impaired psychologically, and they positively value psychotherapy as a means of help. There is a high percentage of people with Jewish cultural backgrounds in this group and very few nonwhites.

Type Two clients are those who have become aware of professional help only recently, probably because of the impact of the community mental health movement. These clients, usually much less affluent than Type Ones, are of working-class status or lower; more often than not they are women over thirty, sometimes married, who have less than a high-school education. Type Two clients tend to be less sophisticated, less communicative verbally, more seriously disturbed, and less positively oriented toward psychotherapy. This group includes most of the nonwhites who receive therapeutic help, many people of immigrant Catholic cultural background, and the seriously disturbed individuals who constitute the core of the "mental health problem" in the United States.

Type Three clients have been relatively unknown to the mental health profession, apparently because they usually seek assistance from religious rather than secular sources. This group is not a small segment of the population, however; in their survey Howard and Orlinsky reported that 42 percent

Figure 26.11 Three examples of what Eric Berne describes as "crossed transactions." Drawing an analogy between human relations and economic exchanges, Berne describes interactions between people as transactions. He considers each personality to be capable of expressing itself as a child (C), an adult (A), or a parent (P). (Compare these to Freud's id, ego, and superego.) He maintains that normal, or healthy, transactions can be represented on diagrams like these with lines that run parallel. It is not difficult to see that the transactions illustrated here, on the contrary, are ones that lead to trouble. Berne's analyses of human interaction have been widely read.
(After Berne, 1964.)

Table 26.1 Sources of Psychological Help*

Source	Percent Choosing Source	Percent Satisfied with Help
Clergymen	42	65
Medical Doctors	29	65
Marriage Counselors	10	25
Private Practitioners or Social Agencies	10	39
Psychiatrists or Psychologists	18	46

*Number of people interviewed = 345. Percent is more than 100 because some people used more than one source.

Source: Adapted from G. Gurin, J. Verhoff, and S. Feld, *Americans View Their Mental Health* (New York: Basic Books, 1960).

of Americans who seek professional help for personal problems turn first to the clergy. Members of this group tend to be middle-aged and are most typically middle-class; more often than not they are Protestant women with families, and they are seldom college educated.

These data reveal that most adults who enter psychotherapy are women. Howard and Orlinsky suggest that this may be the case because women have a more positive attitude toward seeking and accepting help, because they are more willing to define personal difficulties in mental health terminology, and because traditional therapy is simply more available during daytime hours when men are more likely to be working. Several studies have shown that men who seek psychotherapy tend to be more seriously disturbed than are female clients. Perhaps a more cogent explanation, however, is found in cultural stereotypes: In our society, women are expected to be dependent and unable to solve their own problems, whereas men are expected to be strong and independent problem solvers.

Major Goals of Therapy

In 1973 Norman Sundberg, Leona Tyler, and Julian Taplin identified seven major purposes that they believe are basic to most kinds of therapy:

1. *To strengthen the client's motivation to do the "right" things.* "Right," a relative term, is defined by whoever is doing the strengthening but is usually in keeping with the client's own desires. Long before the advent of psychology, social groups exerted this kind of influence; at present, therapeutic groups such as Alcoholics Anonymous attribute much of their success to the strengthening of motivation, which is effected through suggestion, encouragement, and inspiration.

2. *To reduce emotional pressure by facilitating the expression of feelings* (the process called **catharsis**). This process is frequently part of the plot in movies or plays—a character gains sudden and intense relief, following a flood of emotional expression that is usually brought about by the awakening of a memory that had formerly been repressed. In **psychodrama,** an older therapy that is currently regaining popularity, participants are encouraged to reenact in simulated scenes actual events that were the cause of painful childhood experiences. In this way, they experience the intense feelings that surround their early memories of significant relationships.

3. *To release the potential for growth.* Concepts from developmental theories were used to formulate this third goal of therapy. It is assumed that every person has a basic tendency toward growth or maturity and that unfortunate circumstances may block or temporarily reverse this tendency but will not destroy it. The task in therapy, then, is to remove the obstacles, allowing the person to get back on his or her "normal" but unique developmental path. For example, the Interpersonal Maturity Level System that is used in work with delinquent young people may be employed to evaluate them according to their level of interpersonal functioning. Then attempts are made to find ways of removing the blocks that have slowed or stopped their development, so that growth may resume.

4. *To modify the cognitive structure.* The individual's cognitive structure is the interrelated set of concepts and ideas that determine how he views himself, the world around him, and other people. It is assumed that problems are caused by basic misconceptions about how things are, misconceptions that the individual may not be aware of. Many therapists believe that their primary job is to make the client aware of

his basic cognitive structures, enabling him to change the pattern. Albert Ellis, in his rational-emotive therapy, persistently confronts clients with their "irrational" beliefs. Ellis' central hypothesis is that emotional consequences that follow an event are caused not by the event but by the individual's cognitive-belief system. He works toward helping the client to replace irrational beliefs with valid beliefs and to develop the ability to think "scientifically" about personal experiences in the future.

5. *To develop self-knowledge.* The key word for the process of becoming self-knowledgeable, in the broad sense, is **insight.** Although it has been recognized that intellectual awareness of one's problems does not necessarily lead to healthy functioning, insight is a powerful force—particularly if the client can learn to see cause-and-effect relationships in his behavior. It probably does not matter what cogent overview the person becomes convinced of; what counts is that he can understand his behavior. Insight frequently eliminates the anxiety that people experience when they feel that their behavior is "irrational." It is even more comforting if such analysis leads logically to the definition of a therapeutic strategy that makes sense to the client.

6. *To learn how to change one's behavior.* Although this is a goal of most therapies, one type of therapy, commonly called **behavior modification,** is unique in focusing on behavioral change as the only legitimate goal of therapy. In behavior modification (discussed at length in Chapter 27), problems are believed to be the end product of a learning process in which undesirable or ineffective behavior patterns have been formed. The task of the therapist, then, is to alter these patterns by reversing unadaptive learning and to furnish new learning experiences.

7. *To strengthen interpersonal relationships.* According to the theories underlying interpersonal therapy, relationships with "significant others" hold the key to understanding the emotional disturbance that brings an individual to a psychotherapist. There are two approaches: One group of therapists emphasizes childhood experiences and looks for early patterns that may be influencing present relationships; by understanding what occurred, they hope to be able to find ways to modify childhood patterns so that they will no longer obstruct the client's functioning with other people. The other group of therapists focuses primarily on the person's immediate relationships with family, friends, and co-workers; they do not concern themselves with possible childhood determinants but look for current patterns that may be causing difficulties and then offer concrete suggestions for change.

In actual therapy, the seven major purposes may be combined in various ways; **eclecticism** is the term used to describe this combining of purposes or techniques from a number of different approaches. Eclecticism is typical of many current therapies. Still, almost all therapies have some things in common. Most therapists attempt to help their clients regulate the level of their anxiety; to create a strong personal relationship with their clients; and to help clients communicate more effectively what they think and feel.

GROUP APPROACHES

In an earlier section of this chapter, some group approaches were discussed in the context of their historical development as an alternative to personal therapy. This section presents some current uses of group approaches. The earlier section discussed at length "process" groups—groups interested in the dynamics and interaction of people in small groups—and their transformation into sensitivity groups and growth groups. Although the latter groups are not

Psychiatrists are physicians who take three years of specialty training after receiving the M.D. and completing their medical internship. The training usually includes a year of work with hospitalized psychotic patients, as well as therapy with nonhospitalized adults and children and work with community agencies. About two-thirds of them undergo therapy as part of training. Demographic data (1971): 51% Jewish, 29% Protestant, 10% Catholic; 23% strong liberal, 53% moderate liberal; 24% conservative; about 85% male.

Psychoanalysts in the United States are usually psychiatrists who have taken advanced training in psychoanalytic theory and treatment. Almost all are psychoanalyzed as part of training. Demographic data (1971): 62% Jewish, 17% Protestant, 2% Catholic; 37% strong liberal, 55% moderate liberal, 8% conservative; about 80% male.

Clinical psychologists usually have a Ph.D. in clinical psychology, and their education includes study in the basic science of psychology and other social sciences; their training includes research toward a dissertation and a one-year clinical internship doing therapy. About 75% undergo therapy as part of training. Demographic data (1971): 50% Jewish; 27% Protestant, 9% Catholic; 41% strong liberal, 47% moderate liberal, 12% conservative; about 70% male.

Psychiatric social workers have a Master's degree from a University school of social work. The two-year Master's program includes both supervised field work and courses that cover social-science and social-welfare topics and both theories and techniques of individual and group treatment. About 64% undergo therapy during training. Demographic data (1971): 48% Jewish, 29% Protestant, 14% Catholic; 43% strong liberal, 51% moderate liberal, 6% conservative; about 30% male.

Figure 26.12 The training and sociological characteristics of four major professional groups who perform psychotherapeutic services. Other psychotherapeutic professionals include lay analysts, who have had psychoanalytic training but hold no medical degree, and counseling psychologists, who have a Master's degree or a Doctorate in psychological testing, counseling, and guidance. (After Henry, Sims, and Spray, 1971.)

Table 26.2   Current Psychotherapeutic Approaches

Approach and Major Proponents	Basic Concepts	Mechanisms of Therapy
Psychodrama J. L. Moreno	Spontaneity and the ability to role play are of prime importance in uncovering and understanding conflict dynamics. Emotional catharsis frees the person for further growth.	The stage; the patient or protagonist; the director; the staff of therapeutic aids, or auxiliary egos; and the audience.
Client-Centered Therapy Carl Rogers	If certain conditions are present in the attitudes of the person designated "therapist" in a relationship—namely, congruence, unconditional positive regard, and accurate empathy—then "growthful" change will take place in the person designated "client." There is one motivational force in humans, the tendency toward self-actualization.	The therapist has an empathic understanding and an unconditional positive regard for the client. The client progresses through stages on a continuum measured by feelings and personal meanings, manner of experiencing, communication of self, relationship to problems, and manner of relating.
Behavior Therapy Joseph Wolpe	Neurotic behavior is any persistent habit of unadaptive behavior acquired by learning. Anxiety is usually the central constituent of this behavior and is invariably present in the causal situations. There is never any need to resolve past events or to postulate unconscious conflicts, because all the required response patterns and the triggering stimuli are in the present; it is sufficient to deal with present responses to obtain lasting therapeutic results.	Systematic desensitization; covert sensitization; aversion therapy; assertive training (see Chapter 27 for definitions).
Rational-Emotive Therapy Albert Ellis	When a highly charged emotional Consequence (C) follows a significant Activating Event (A), A may seem to cause C but actually does not. Instead, emotional Consequences are largely created by B—the individual's Belief System. An undesirable Consequence, such as severe anxiety, can usually be traced to the person's irrational Beliefs, and when these Beliefs are effectively Disputed (D), by challenging them rationally, the disturbed Consequences disappear.	The therapist constantly points out the client's irrational ideas, using the strongest philosophic approach he can think of to challenge the client to validate his ideas. When the client cannot, the therapist explains how those ideas can be replaced with more rational, empirically based theses. The therapist teaches the client how to think scientifically and therefore to give up self-defeating behaviors.
Reality Therapy William Glasser	The crux of the theory is personal responsibility for one's own behavior, which is equated with mental health. No matter what "happened" to the client in the past, he still must take the full responsibility for what he does now, and until he accepts the fact that he is responsible for what he does, there can be no treatment. The therapy is based on the premise that there is a single basic psychological need that all people in all cultures possess from birth to death—the need for an identity.	There is a strong focus on helping the client to understand and accept himself as he is. The therapist gives the message that he accepts the client as a total person but does not necessarily accept all his specific behaviors. The therapist assumes a great deal of overt responsibility for the conduct of therapy; the basic mechanism is said to be *involvement*.
Conjoint Family Therapy Virginia Satir	Enhancement of self-esteem is the basic force motivating individuals. Parents have overt or covert agendas and expectations when they select each other as marriage partners; in the dysfunctional family, differentness develops into disagreement, and trust is difficult to maintain. Dysfunctional marriage subtly shapes the child, who becomes the family member likely to exhibit his discomfort in symptoms and thus show up as the identified patient.	The focus is on accurate communication of feelings in order to deal with reality. *All* family members are in sessions together, not just the identified patient. Taking a family life chronology, talking about it, engaging in role playing are ways of *assessing* the family unit. The way the therapist interacts with the family members (particularly the child) serves as a model of healthy interaction, which includes clear communication and mutual respect.

Approach and Major Proponents	Basic Concepts	Mechanisms of Therapy
Encounter William Schutz (and many others)	Man is seen as unified and as functioning best when physical, psychological, and spiritual aspects are integrated. A person comes to like himself, to respect what he is and can do, and to be responsible for himself through self-awareness. An expectation of strength tends to bring out the strong parts of people. Encounter involves removing psychological blocks so that a person can flow freely and naturally; encounter is a way of life, not just a therapeutic technique.	Relaxation techniques; sensory awareness exercises; physical activity to mobilize and focus energy; body language to diagnose anxiety; group decision making; nonverbal exercises; building of communication skills; marathons for defense penetration; confrontation.
Existential Therapy Rollo May	The four basic concepts are (1) existence; (2) encounter or interaction; (3) authenticity; and (4) value. A human is a being-in-the-world, with the hyphens meant to indicate that one being, one event, is both the person and the situations in which the person lives.	Proponents deny that there are "mechanisms" of therapy, because the person is not mechanical. What a person is, is made by the living that person does; therefore, a person changes only through more and different living. "Mechanisms" of therapy are the ways in which, because of the therapist, the patient's living is immediately different; this change is brought about by making the therapy process experientially authentic.
Gestalt Therapy Fritz Perls	Symptomatic behavior indicates that parts of the person's self are not acceptable to other parts of himself, that in certain locales he does not want to have anything to do with himself. In order for the process to flow again, these two estranged components must meet and find mutual acceptance.	The fundamental mechanism is the creation of a context in which a person can show himself to another in order to be able to find himself. The mechanism has been called the process of validation and the process of acknowledgment.
Transactional Analysis Eric Berne	Those basic human needs are stressed that are most directly related to everyday observable behavior: stroke hunger, structure hunger, excitement hunger, recognition hunger, and leadership hunger. Each person has a "life script," a plan decided on at an early age as a means of meeting his needs in the world as seen from the vantage point of his "life position." Life position is an early decision the person makes about himself and others, involving distinctions of: "O.K." or "not-O.K."; games or pastimes; and ego-states—parent, adult, or child.	Specific "contracts" are written for concrete behavior changes. The therapist refuses to excuse irresponsible or ineffectual behavior, and the effectiveness of the therapist's protection and permission is essential to success of therapy. There is game analysis and script analysis.
Primal Therapy Arthur Janov	The healthiest people are those who are defense-free. Anything that builds a stronger defense system deepens the neurosis; neurosis involves being split, disconnected from one's feelings. Neurosis develops because of the continuing suppression and denial of the child's real needs by the parents; the major Primal Scene is when the patient summarizes the meaning of a backlog of experiences and, as a child, feels: "They don't like me as I am."	A planned program of several months, with specific objectives to be attained during the first three weeks, in which the patient may not work or go to school but is worked with individually every day for several hours. The patient must give up all alcohol, cigarettes, and drugs for the duration of therapy. The therapist has the patient recall childhood events, the aim of which is to open him up and get him ready to surrender his defense system; each new day of therapy is described as a stripping away of layers of defenses.

Figure 26.13 This woman is talking about herself in front of a group of other people who are there for the same purpose that she is: to better understand their lives; and if their lives are unsatisfactory or painful, to explore ways of changing them. There are a variety of ways in which the group's focus on this woman may help her. She may receive emotional support as she tries to cope with troubling personal problems. She may find out that what she believed was a shameful difficulty peculiar to her is a problem shared by many of the group's members. The benefit of hearing other people's perceptions about her behavior may enable her to understand why certain troubling things happen regularly in her life.

exactly therapy-oriented, sometimes the distinction between "growth" groups and therapy groups is not easy to make.

During the past decade, many kinds of groups have developed under the rubric of "therapy." Initially, traditional therapy was extended to group settings; that is, therapists began to see more than one client in a single session, partly for reasons of economy and efficiency. In a traditional therapy group, one person at a time may be treated by the therapist, with the other patients joining in to offer interpretations. Some of the newer approaches—for example, transactional analysis and Gestalt therapy groups—retain this one-at-a-time aspect. The particular orientation of the group depends on the therapist's theoretical views. For example, a psychoanalytic group might be led by a male and a female therapist who foster patient transference to themselves as father and mother figures. A nondirective therapist, however, will do little structuring of the group's interactions, acting instead as a model of empathy who encourages communication and the expression of feelings.

Experiential Learning

As therapists became aware of the potential of groups for providing opportunities to practice new ways of acting and relating, many shifted their focus to experiential learning. In therapeutic community hospital settings, daily group sessions became the major arena for getting problems and feelings out into the open, for sharing feedback on the impact of each other's behavior, and for developing the communication skills and mutual support that make problem solving possible.

The residents of a hospital ward or the members of a family are a natural group for whom experiential learning occurs as a consequence of daily living. The personal growth movement fostered similar interactions among members of artificially gathered groups. In these groups the leader facilitated communication by presenting ambiguous expectations and by devising exercises to increase sensory awareness. The feeling of safety and seclusion fostered by the group's isolation from ordinary life activities also speeded communication. Whether experiential groups are viewed as "therapy," "personal growth," or "interpersonal education," they are obviously less subject to a formal theoretical model, they retain a play-it-by-ear methodology, and they are less restricted to verbal exchanges than are traditional groups.

Expressive Enactment

Once experiential groups had revealed the value of emotional and nonverbal expression, therapists increasingly adopted expressive enactment techniques, which Jacob Moreno had first introduced as psychodrama several decades earlier. Groups that employ these techniques go beyond the accidental events that come up during discussion and, instead, deliberately structure the dramatic enactment of problematic emotional situations and key interpersonal encounters. A usual goal of psychodrama is to bring about the resolution of unconscious conflicts so that the client may develop more satisfying interpersonal relationships. The medium of psychodrama is a form of theater in which people are encouraged to improvise the acting out of troublesome emotional situations and interpersonal conflicts. The chief participants are the protagonist (the client), the director (therapist), the auxiliary egos (staff or other clients), and the group making up the audience. The client is assisted in setting up several ''scenes'' in which his problems have been evident, usually beginning with a present situation and sometimes working back to the first time the problem was manifest. The goal is to provide a catharsis of emotion that frees the person to experiment—at least in fantasy—with more fulfilling and constructive responses to his problems.

A less formal application of enactment techniques is **role playing,** which is often used as an ancillary method in other kinds of groups. A situation that has come up during the course of group discussion may be taken as a starting point. For instance, a client may state that whenever he talks with his wife about an impending visit from his mother, they get into a violent argument. The therapist will then set up that situation for role playing, with the client at first playing himself and another group member playing his wife. They will begin to enact what typically occurs, and at key points the client will be instructed to reverse roles and essentially ''become'' his wife. In this way, he gains insight into her point of view as well as his own. In the discussion that usually follows, group members contribute their perceptions, offering feedback to the client. Another use of role playing is in preparing individuals for future stressful situations, such as job interviews, so that they can practice their behaviors, thus gaining some mastery over their stressful feelings.

Living Together

Still another innovation in group treatment is the use of residential group settings. Therapeutic communities and halfway houses, already mentioned, are recognition that one's living milieu has a profound effect on rehabilitation. An example is George Fairweather's work with severely handicapped patients at the Palo Alto Veterans Administration Hospital. Fairweather used a combination of behavior-modification and therapeutic community techniques to achieve remarkable changes in a ward of schizophrenic patients who had been

Figure 26.14 Residents of Daytop Village, a center for the treatment of drug addiction, perform a scene from their play *The Concept.* The writing and presentation of this play is an effective means for these people to examine the problems associated with drug addiction, and it also serves as a demonstration to themselves of their ability to create, plan, and execute a meaningful project.

Figure 26.15 A new member of a live-in therapeutic community for adolescent drug addicts. He is wearing a sign that publicizes his attempt to overcome certain weaknesses that the other members of the community feel he has. In centers such as this one, regular and often harsh analyses are made of every group member, but the community also provides work, companionship, and support that the person may have been wholly lacking in the outside world.

hospitalized for many years. He then moved the entire group to a house in the community, where they lived together, established and operated a janitorial service, and became self-supporting individuals who could manage well outside an institution so long as they were provided the mutual support and protection of the group-living arrangement. Other examples of **group residential settings** are the centers for treatment of drug addiction, such as Synanon and Daytop. For some former addicts, as for Fairweather's patients, these centers for group living become a semipermanent way of life; they move on to establish and lead new centers, but they maintain their psychological health by remaining in a similar group setting, perhaps for years.

How Well Does Group Therapy Work?

Many questions about group methodologies have not yet been answered. Richard Bednar and G. Frank Lawlis, in reporting on the more traditional group psychotherapies in 1971, concluded that although group therapy is a valuable tool of the helping professions, it may hinder as well as help the client. Other mental health professionals have questioned the ethics of certain aspects of group therapy: facilitators who are inadequately trained; pseudo-dramatic group processes; widely divergent goals and expectations; the casual, nonselective admission of members, some of whom may not benefit or may even be harmed by the experience; the self-gratification that leaders sometimes seek; and the general lack of follow-up or evaluative research.

Which of these group methods should be considered as "real" therapy? Which are merely entertaining experiences? Often the techniques, the content, and the issues considered are the same across types of groups and client populations. At the present time, what is "therapeutic" is determined largely by the eye of the beholder rather than by a definable difference in group formats. Individuals who participate in such groups must rely on their own subjective experience in judging effectiveness.

COMMUNITY APPROACHES

In recent years mental health professionals have begun to realize that the overwhelming majority of severely distressed people seldom receive professional therapy. It is true that the 1960s produced new approaches and methods of treatment; yet the Esalens, the transactional-analysis groups, and the growth and encounter weekends have been directed toward those who have the time and money necessary to "self-actualize" and to be creative—primarily, the persons defined by Howard and Orlinsky as Type Ones. The new approaches have included some Type Three clients, because interested clergymen from various religious affiliations have begun conducting groups with their parishioners. Mental health services have been least available and least effective for Type Two individuals, who most need help. Serious questions have been raised about the appropriateness of present services. For example, is it effective to apply a traditional middle-class approach in treating the poor, who may have a totally different life style and a different way of defining problems? If not, what are the alternatives?

New Services

Mental health professionals have begun to recognize the new challenges posed by explosive social problems, such as poverty and violence, and the part these problems play in psychological disorders. Previously, social relationships were not considered suitable problems for the mental health fields, but this view is rapidly changing. Today's mental health professionals may work in preschools, developing programs for early detection of emotional disturbance and training teachers in how to help children who have problems. They may work in high schools or on college campuses, studying social

Figure 26.16 A Los Angeles crisis center, where trained volunteers are available to receive calls twenty-four hours a day. In the window at the right there is a chart of common drugs, which helps the workers identify the drugs that may have been taken by a caller who has overdosed or is on a bad trip. Many individuals—with a wide variety of personal problems—prefer to deal with an organization like this, which is supportive, efficient, and somewhat anonymous, rather than having to confront family members or legal authorities.

environments and making suggestions for organizational redevelopment in these settings. They may operate walk-in crisis centers or "store-front" offices, drawing on help from students, housewives, and retired persons as staff members.

Suicide and drug abuse "hot lines" have been established on a twenty-four-hour basis in many cities so that help is available at any time of the day or night. Widow and widower programs have been started in some areas, so that a newly alone person may receive support immediately from someone who has experienced similar grief. Groups have been formed for persons suffering the traumas caused by divorce, severe illness, and drastic surgery. Parents have been taught how to operate more effectively as agents of behavior change for their children. And police officers have been taught methods of intervening in the violent family crises that they frequently encounter.

Action centers and inner-city programs are being developed, but with a different focus from that of previous mental health services. Recent programs reflect the belief that the critical factor in determining whether or not the poor will be helped is how well the service is adapted to their way of life and their particular needs. Many of the programs share the following assumptions: The problems of the poor can best be solved in their own neighborhoods; for the poor, committed and nonprofessional peers are more effective agents for change than are professionals; and decision-making power should be vested in local staff and participants in the program rather than in the "top brass." The focus of the community programs is far more on concrete behavior than on intrapsychic dynamics, and the programs engage problems of living directly and naturally, as they arise.

New Professionals

In recent years, mental health professionals themselves have also begun to change. Many psychologists and psychiatrists who graduated from college in the 1960s participated in strikes and demonstrations. Some of them have called themselves "radical therapists" and have taken as their slogan "Therapy is change, not adjustment." They have proposed that the causes of psychological problems are to be found in the injustices of society rather than within the individual. In publications and at conferences they have urged their colleagues to reconsider their mental-illness orientation toward homosexuality, to develop a psychology meaningful for women, and to provide new conceptual frameworks for understanding the problems of minorities. Viewing psychology and traditional psychotherapy as part of the problem rather than as the solution to human misery, they believe that processes of treatment

Figure 26.17 An organization called the Young Lords sponsors hot breakfasts and recreational activities for ghetto children in a church basement on the Upper East Side of New York City. These programs function as both physical and psychological "preventive medicine" in the lives of the children of the community.

should be "demystified," that the patient's rights as a human being should be observed, and that the dehumanizing aspects of mental hospitals should be done away with.

New Tools

Mental health professionals, having come out of their offices and taken on the task of working with larger segments of the population, found that the new types of services in which they were engaging required new tools and methods. **Consultation** has been one of the tools they have chosen, because one trained professional spending several hours a week with ten or twelve clergymen, pediatricians, police officers, or teachers—in an effort to upgrade their skills, broaden their knowledge, and make them more effective interveners in human distress—can indirectly contribute to the well-being of the hundreds of people who regularly seek help from these established community caregivers. Consultation also expands the numbers of people given therapeutic help by upgrading the skills and knowledge of people who work with groups that most professionals never meet—for example, the disadvantaged people of the inner cities. In addition to extending the scope of services, consultation more nearly approaches reality than do many traditional orientations. Mental health's former "Let *them* come to *us*" stance was never very realistic, and it has become even less feasible in view of recent social change.

For teachers, physicians, pediatricians, clergymen, and others who have regular contact with children and their parents, the potential for consultation in building health rather than fighting pathology is distinctly apparent. Although it has not yet been explored in depth, this area—preventing mental disorder rather than attempting to cure it—is one that will undoubtedly receive greater attention during the next few years.

Prevention or Cure

In discussing the potential of consultation for building health rather than fighting pathology, one is brought to the realization that this entire chapter has been devoted to the history of mental disorder and the numerous ways in which mental health professionals have attempted to "cure" it. Even this brief review has revealed the complex questions that surround the evaluation of the professional time and energies involved in therapeutic undertakings and the results of these undertakings. One might ask, "Wouldn't it be easier to find out why psychological problems occur in the first place, and then do something to keep them from happening?" Although this alternative is not "easier," it is receiving attention from many professionals who consider it to be the only viable route toward a real solution of the mental health problems of our society.

Mental health workers have made a useful distinction between **system-oriented** and **person-centered** aspects of a broad preventive model. A systems focus presumes that human development is shaped by a relatively small number of key social institutions and settings, such as family and school. In this view, an important question is, "How do primary social institutions affect human development?" Person-centered approaches, on the other hand, concentrate on certain subgroups that are most prone to mental illness; efforts are directed toward interventions with the young and, later, with members of groups who undergo such "natural crises" as childbirth, finding jobs, marriage, starting school, death of loved ones, serious illness, and so on.

The community psychology movement, although its details have not yet been refined, offers a genuine alternative to present mental health approaches. It is active rather than passive, and it accords far greater importance to prevention than to repair. Realistically, however, it is probable that concern about intervening in certain kinds of destructive and self-destructive behaviors will always be necessary—regardless of success in building up a society of healthy personalities. As Ruth Benedict pointed out in 1934, individuals who are considered well adjusted in one culture may be considered deviant in another. Thus, the prevention of disturbance, or the development of adequate adaptation, is subject to the demands of the culture and the unique capacities of individuals to meet these demands. Perhaps part of the present problem of mental health care is that in the Western culture of the 1970s, it is difficult to know just what those cultural demands are.

SUMMARY

1. Institutionalized efforts to deal with the mentally ill began some 200 years ago when society, regarding them as sinners, kept them chained up in prisons.

   a. In the 1800s in the United States, professionals developed a remarkably successful technique called **moral treatment,** but this technique was abandoned as institutions became overcrowded.

   b. By 1900 the mentally ill received only **custodial care,** and it was not until the early 1950s that professionals began to develop new techniques for treatment.

2. The most successful of the new techniques were the **therapeutic community,** in which the entire hospital milieu was used for therapeutic purposes and patients collaborated with therapists in solving problems, and **community mental health programs** designed to treat the mentally ill in halfway houses, clinics, community hospitals, and mental health centers.

3. Early efforts to treat less severely disturbed or neurotic individuals grew out of Sigmund Freud's work, which, in Victorian-era Vienna, emphasized sexual repression as a cause of illness.

   a. Freud's highly sophisticated therapy, called **psychoanalysis,** used such techniques as **free association,** the **interpretation of dreams,** and

Figure 26.18 Jerome Frank, a physician and a psychotherapist, has been a contributor to the understanding of psychotherapy in a number of ways. He has studied and compared different types of therapy, investigated the placebo effect (in which the mere belief that one will be helped appears to have a healing effect), and pointed out features that psychotherapy shares with other social phenomena.

Figure 26.19 The late Frederick (Fritz) Perls founded the widely popular Gestalt method of therapy. The term Gestalt is used because of Perls' emphasis on the fact that the goal of therapy is to make the fragmented person whole. Perls developed a number of techniques, such as acting out the roles of elements of one's dreams, which are often used in encounter groups.

transference (transfer of the client's feelings about his parent to the therapist).

b. Psychoanalysis appealed to an educated, middle-class clientele and dominated therapeutic psychology for decades, especially in the United States.

4. The psychoanalytic paradigm broke down in the 1950s under the pressure of **outcome research** by Hans Eysenck and others that cast doubt on the effectiveness of Freudian therapy. As a result, therapists began to develop new techniques. Most influential were those based on behavioral models and those based on the theories and therapies of Carl Rogers, Victor Frankl, Fritz Perls, and the existentialists. The latter group was generally referred to as psychology's "Third Force" and emphasized individual growth, or self-actualization. **Family therapy** and group therapy became popular; **T-groups** focusing on group processes and group dynamics developed. **Sensitivity groups** became widespread; and **growth centers** emphasizing **self-awareness,** such as the Esalen Institute, sprang up across the country. **Self-help groups** such as Synanon also enjoyed success.

5. Recent research has examined the various current approaches in psychotherapy and has found similarities amid the apparent chaos. In 1973, Norman Sundberg, Leona Tyler, and Julian Taplin identified seven major purposes that are basic to most therapies:

a. To strengthen the client's motivation to do the "right" thing.

b. To reduce emotional pressure by facilitating the expression of feelings.

c. To release the potential for growth.

d. To modify the cognitive structure.

e. To develop self-knowledge.

f. To learn how to change one's behavior.

g. To strengthen interpersonal relationships.

6. Group approaches in psychotherapy vary with the theoretical orientation of the therapist or group leader. Groups focusing on **experiential learning,** which provides opportunities for getting problems and feelings out in the open, have thrived in family therapy, in therapeutic community hospital settings, and in the personal growth movement. Some group leaders have deliberately structured the dramatic enactment of interpersonal encounters by employing the technique of **role playing.** Others have established **group residences** where patients live together and work out their real-life problems. Because evaluative research generally is lacking, individuals who participate in groups must rely on their own subjective experience in judging effectiveness.

Figure 26.20 Psychologist Albert Ellis developed a tough-minded therapeutic approach that he called "rational-emotive" therapy. Ellis' assumption is that troubled people are acting rationally on the basis of irrational assumptions. He insists that they discover what those assumptions are and change them. Ellis has written more than 200 articles and many books on such subjects as sexual behavior, neurosis, and marital relations.

Despite the proliferation of therapeutic techniques, the majority of severely disturbed people has seldom received therapy. In recent years, mental health professionals have sought to reach more people by offering such new community services as walk-in crisis centers, suicide and drug abuse "hot lines," and inner-city action centers. The professionals themselves also have changed, becoming more action-oriented and more protective of patients' rights. Through consultation sessions, they have sought to teach their skills to a large number of community intervention agents—physicians, clergymen, police officers, and teachers. They also are giving increasing attention to attempts to prevent rather than "cure" mental illness.

SUGGESTED READINGS

Bergin, Allen E., and Sol L. Garfield. *Handbook of Psychotherapy and Behavior Change: An Empirical Analysis.* New York: Wiley, 1971. The most comprehensive collection of readings on psychotherapy. It contains sections on experimentation in psychotherapy, analysis of therapies, and discussions of a number of varied therapeutic approaches.

Corsini, Raymond J. (ed.). *Current Psychotherapies.* Itasca, Ill.: Peacock Publishers, 1973. Most of the chapters were written by distinguished leaders of the various approaches, and major current therapies are covered. Each author follows the same format and outline, facilitating comparison across therapies.

Golann, Stuart E., and Carl Eisdorfer (eds.). *Handbook of Community Mental Health.* New York: Appleton-Century-Crofts, 1972. A monumental work covering both the history and latest developments in community psychology from conceptualization to practice.

Rosen, George. *Madness in Society.* Chicago: University of Chicago Press, 1968. Gives a historical overview of how mental illness has been perceived and dealt with, including a discussion of the social forces that influenced practices in each period.

Schofield, William. *Psychotherapy: The Purpose of Friendship.* Englewood Cliffs, N.J.: Prentice-Hall, 1964. Presents the argument that the primary need of patients is a close personal relationship. Suggests that community resources can meet this need as well as trained professionals.

Figure 26.21 Jacob Moreno is founder and developer of the therapeutic method known as psychodrama. The method is based on principles of classical Greek theatre, in which catharsis, the cleansing effect of emotional release, plays an important part. Moreno also developed sociometry, a method of discovering the structure of groups that is widely used in social psychology.

I suspect there is a rather universal distress over the implications of Skinnerian behaviorism. People don't want to think of themselves as machines, and they don't want to be manipulated as machines. I sympathize with that. I don't want to think of myself as a machine and I don't want to be manipulated as a machine.

The trouble is that I suspect very strongly that I am a machine because I *can* be manipulated as one, and I *am* manipulated as one, and so are you. We are so used to being manipulated that we don't realize it when it happens. We can undertake a very familiar activity and respond mechanically to all the symbols that control the details of our action, even while we are at the same time loudly proclaiming our free will and our resistance to any kind of manipulation.

I'm talking about driving a car. From the instant we get into a car to the instant we get out, we are bombarded with directions, symbols, marks, light-flashes, to all of which we respond quite automatically and the sum of which reduces our freedom of choice nearly to zero. We can't turn right or left unless permitted. We can't change lanes unless permitted. We can't go at some times, and we can't stop in some places. We can't go faster than some limit, or slower than some other limit. We can't choose our direction in a given thoroughfare.

I don't complain, mind you. It's all needed. The alternative of giving every driver his full freedom would at once make a shambles of our highways. Consider, however. Have you ever come to a red light on some quiet, empty road, where you can see with your own eyes that there is no car approaching from any other direction? What do you do? You stop, don't you? And you remain stopped until the light changes, don't you? Aren't you behaving like a machine—stopping for no sensible reason but only because a color is flashing in your eyes?

Yes, you can go through the light if you want to, but how many times do you want to? Yes, you might tell yourself that there could be a traffic cop behind the billboard, but be honest—do you think at all? Don't you just stop?

Have you ever been caught at a city corner, where the traffic-light has gone out of order and remains red indefinitely? One by one the drivers realize there's something wrong and begin to honk their horns—the drivers *behind* the first car, that is. They're not facing that light directly and they are brave. But the first car— how many false starts he makes, and how slowly and reluctantly he finally moves against the light. You can almost hear the gears of his mind machinery grind.

"Do you want to be a machine?" The inevitable answer is "No." But questions with inevitable answers are not interesting. The interesting question is "*Are* you a machine?"

Isaac Asimov

Figure 27.1 The woman whose hand is shown here is undergoing a type of behavior therapy aimed at ridding her of a snake phobia—a fear so exaggerated that it keeps her from taking walks in the country and makes her extremely uncomfortable even in gardens. Behavior therapists believe that such fears are learned and thus can—through procedures like systematic desensitization shown here—be "unlearned." This approach stands in sharp contrast to that of psychoanalytically oriented therapies, which would view the phobia as a symptom of underlying conflicts, with the conflicts the proper target of therapy.

Most psychotherapies, as the preceding chapter shows, seek to change internal characteristics of the person. Based to a large extent on personality theories, these therapies draw very little upon the laboratory science of psychology. The behavior therapies, in contrast, focus on the person's external environment, both physical and social. Their treatment techniques stem directly from the experiments and theories of classical and operant conditioning. Therefore, a solid grasp of the material in Chapter 4 is essential for understanding the treatments covered in this chapter.

Although the principles of learning and conditioning had been studied since the 1920s and behaviorism had become a dominant force in academic and theoretical psychology, it was not until the mid-1960s that large numbers of clinicians began to use behavioral techniques. There had been, during those earlier decades, several demonstrations that these techniques could be used to effect clients' behavioral change. As early as the 1920s, various investigators have used Pavlovian conditioning to curtail the drinking of alcoholics. O. Hobart Mowrer had devised a conditioning apparatus that cured bed-wetting. And Mary Cover Jones had combined elements of classical and operant conditioning to modify a little boy's fears. Why, then, did it take so long for practicing psychotherapists to take note of and adopt these techniques?

In the discussion of successive modifications of psychotherapeutic techniques presented in the preceding chapter, it is stated that major changes in the way of dealing with patients usually followed major changes in the general cultural climate. This phenomenon is also true of behavior therapy. In the 1960s in the United States the mood was one of discontent coupled with optimism: There was widespread discontent with social institutions, which seemed to be failing large segments of the population. Still, there was optimism that by a massive application of technology, training, and environmental engineering, these institutions could be revitalized. Thus, discontent with the results of psychoanalysis coupled with the belief in the efficacy of technology and training inspired numbers of clinicians to attempt the modification of behavior through conditioning techniques. And the late 1960s brought reports of moderate-to-astonishing success after the application of such techniques to a wide range of problems, including excessive anxiety, homosexuality, alcoholism, obesity, and schizophrenic withdrawal in adults, and hyperactivity, shyness, learning problems, aggressiveness, bed-wetting, and undisciplined behavior in children. Traditional psychotherapeutic methods had not been able to produce much evidence of success for people with these problems.

Behavior clinicians differ from other therapists both in the methods they use and in the way they conceptualize the therapeutic process. Several important assumptions guide and distinguish all of their clinical work.

BASIC ASSUMPTIONS

Basic to the behavioral approach is the belief that *the same learning principles govern all behaviors, "normal or deviant."* Other theories apply learning principles only to the acquisition of knowledge and have a specific explanation for the development of each type of personality deviation. Behavior therapists regard psychological problems simply as learned responses that have harmful consequences for the client or for his environment. They interpret problem behaviors not as symptoms of unconscious conflicts that must be uncovered but as the primary and legitimate targets of therapy. Treatment is

Table 27.1 Comparison of Psychotherapy and Behavior Therapy

	Psychotherapy	Behavior Therapy
Theory	Theories usually derived from clinical observations.	Theory derived from experimental studies.
Symptoms	Considers symptoms as visible signs of unconscious conflicts and evidence of repression.	Considers symptoms as learned responses that are unadaptive.
	The symptoms each patient displays are determined by defense mechanisms.	The symptoms each patient displays are determined by his conditionability and his environmental circumstances.
	If only symptoms are treated, they will be replaced by other symptoms because underlying conflict was not resolved.	Treatment of symptomatic behavior brings permanent cure.
Treatment	Treatment is often based on patient's history. The interpretation of symptoms, dreams, acts, and the like is an important element of treatment.	Treatment is concerned with habits existing at present; how the habits developed is usually irrelevant. Interpretation is irrelevant.
	Cure is obtained by resolving the underlying conflicts, not by treating the symptomatic behavior or trait.	Cure is obtained by treating the symptomatic behavior; that is, by extinguishing maladaptive habits, having the patient learn adaptive ones, or altering the environment.
	Relationship with therapist is an essential part of treatment; in psychoanalysis, transference is necessary.	Personal relationship with therapist not essential for cure but may be useful.
	Treatment generally consists of dialogue between therapist and patient.	Treatment uses techniques of conditioning and manipulation of environmental variables.
Goal	To modify present personality.	To modify present behavior.

tailored to the individual's problems without regard to diagnostic labels such as "neurotic" or to presumed personality traits such as "passive-aggressive."

Behavior therapists believe that *the environment plays a crucial role in determining behavior and that problem behaviors are specific to given types of situations.* Consequently, behavioral diagnosis requires accurate descriptions of **observable behaviors** and the **environmental events** that accompany them. These descriptions omit speculation about such matters as the individual's "ego state" or the meaning of the events to the individual. Although behavior therapists do not deny the importance of behaviors they cannot observe or of a person's self-descriptions and descriptions of past events, their aim is to modify present behaviors by changing the environmental conditions that currently control them.

Behavior therapists reject the notion that psychological difficulties and their treatment are not subject to the same rigorous scientific analysis and verification used to study other areas of human behavior. They use empirical data not only to assess the client's difficulties but also to formulate a treatment plan, to monitor progress and guide changes during treatment, and to evaluate the outcome. Table 27.1 summarizes the major points of difference between psychoanalytic psychotherapy and behavior therapy. Although the terminology is classical or Pavlovian, the points apply equally well to operant behavioral treatments.

At times, behavior therapists discuss their work as if the description of a given conditioning technique covers the entire clinical process. Actually, no matter how well-defined the specific techniques may be, their application to individual cases still requires ingenuity. General factors of the kind discussed in the preceding chapter as important in most psychotherapies also play a role in behavioral treatments, as noted in Table 27.1. The ability to relate to others and a high level of skill in face-to-face interaction usually are essential qualities in a behavior therapist. Far from being the mechanistic robot some people fear, the behavior therapist often deals with the client in traditional ways during most phases of the therapeutic process, from initial interview to the client's discharge.

Nevertheless, the basic elements used to describe the therapeutic process come from the learning laboratory. The behavioral clinician examines the **stimuli that control behavior** and its **consequences** rather than its internal motivation or meaning. He finds, for instance, that a child's temper tantrums become more frequent when they are followed by parental attention or giving in; he does not attribute them to the acting out of an Oedipus conflict. To understand how the therapist arrives at his formulation, it is necessary to reexamine, from a clinical viewpoint, some elements of behavior discussed in Chapter 4.

THE BEHAVIORAL FORMULA: S-O-R-K-C

Behavior is a continuous interaction of the individual with his social and physical environment. Out of this ongoing flow, several events may be identified as surrounding a particular problem behavior. By artificially stopping and segmenting this flow, the behavioral clinician can determine the role of each event. The behavioral formula S-O-R-K-C symbolizes this task:

S stands for **stimuli,** the immediately preceding events.

O stands for the biological state of the **organism.**

R stands for the target **response,** or problem behavior.

K stands for the **contingency relationship** between the response and its consequence.

C stands for the **consequence,** the events that follow the response.

Figure 27.2 An autistic child in a behavioral treatment center is rewarded with pieces of food for making speech sounds. Autistic children speak little, if at all, and are emotionally unresponsive to other people. The therapist must be adept at recognizing sounds that approximate the words she is trying to teach the child so that she can immediately reinforce the child's attempt to speak. She must also be capable of great patience and of warmth and sensitivity to the child. The goal of programs such as this one is to bring the child to a level at which such natural social reinforcers as hugs and smiles will maintain talking and other outward-directed behaviors.

Figure 27.3 The behavioral formula for the analysis of an individual's interactions with his environment. Figures 27.4 through 27.8 show how this formula can be applied to the behaviors involved in driving a car. These behaviors are the product of a variety of complex interactions with both the physical and social environment.

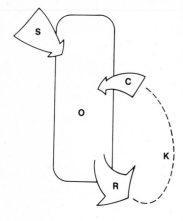

This formula preserves the time sequence of the crucial events and covers both **elicited (classically conditioned) behaviors** and **emitted (operantly conditioned) behaviors.** Classical conditioning, however, is concerned with only the first three elements, S-O-R, with S and R standing for both unconditioned and conditioned stimuli and responses. Operant conditioning emphasizes the last three elements, R-K-C, because emitted responses are controlled by the events that follow them. However, because antecedent stimuli may signal which consequences are likely to occur, the S element is important in operant behaviors also. For example, a child learns to read his parents' moods: He may curb his temper tantrum (R) when Father's grouchiness (S) signals that a spanking (C) is the most probable result.

In assessing a problem behavior, the clinician must fill in each part of the formula. He usually begins with R, the target behavior, and then asks: What are the consequences (C) of this behavior, and how are they delivered (K)—intermittently, continuously, or inconsistently? What events (S) usually precede this behavior? Under what circumstances (S) does the behavior fail to appear? Is there anything special about the client's biological state (O) that might play an important role in this behavior? The clinician's assessment of the function of each event is called a functional analysis of the problem behavior.

Behavior therapy always seeks to increase the frequency of responses that are deficient or to reduce the frequency of responses that are excessive. Although the ultimate goal is to change the target behavior, the source of the difficulty may lie in one of the other elements in the formula. It is by modifying these environmental factors that the clinician modifies the target behavior. A more detailed examination will show the importance of each element in producing and treating problem behaviors.

S: Stimuli and Stimulus Control

Almost any behavior is acceptable under some circumstances: Nakedness is fine in the shower but not usually on crowded beaches. A major part of a child's socialization process involves learning to match the various circumstances with the appropriate behaviors. These environmental circumstances come to control the person's behaviors by signaling the probable consequences of a behavior.

Problem behavior may arise because stimulus control is too weak. Obese people tend to eat under all sorts of circumstances: when watching television,

Figure 27.4 Significant *stimuli* in driving. The policeman's flashing red light is a strong conditioned stimulus, which arouses anxiety in most drivers. It is also a discriminative stimulus that exercises strong control over the behavior of pulling over and stopping. The speed limit sign is a discriminative stimulus also; but it is one that exercises relatively poor control over the behavior of many drivers.

reading, cooking, studying, or just sitting alone and bored. Behavioral weight reduction programs aim to reduce these occasions—and the fat person—by bringing the problem behavior, eating, under much narrower stimulus control. The dieter's first instruction usually is to eat only when sitting at a particular table and to do nothing else at that time but eat. A reduction in food intake comes only after this rule is firmly established. Indeed, because overweight people often exercise great restraint at mealtimes but snack recklessly in between, stimulus-control training may begin with an increase in the amount of food eaten at regular meals, along with the rule prohibiting snacks.

Similarly, a person who studies ineffectively may be instructed to designate a place where he does nothing but study. If he slips into fantasy or any other behavior that disturbs his study, he must move to another spot. When the dieter or the student follows this rule consistently, the place comes to set the occasion for eating or studying and for nothing else.

Stimulus control that is too strong and restricted also may produce problems. Some children ignore their parents' quiet requests to do some task but obey their shouts because they have learned that shouts usually precede important consequences such as a spanking, whereas quiet requests do not. Similarly, some people develop sexual fetishes when their arousal and performance come under increasingly narrow stimulus control, such as a specific set of events or a specific piece of wearing apparel. In sexual problems as in other emotional responses, antecedent stimuli play a crucial role, because sexual responses are elicited responses and are therefore governed by the principles of classical conditioning. For this reason, behavior clinicians generally follow the classical-conditioning model in treating emotional problems.

Learning appropriate stimulus control also is an important feature in the acquisition of any new behavior. For instance, behavior modification programs designed to help a shy person increase his assertive behavior must include discrimination training so that the newly outspoken client learns when he may safely assert himself. Otherwise, he might end up in jail, out of a job, or in the divorce courts.

O: The Organism

Temporary changes in a person's biological state and the more enduring features of his physical capacities may influence his behavior. A person who has eaten nothing all day usually responds to food as a potent reinforcer. Blind persons cannot respond to visual stimuli that control the behavior of other

Figure 27.5 Variations in the state of the *organism* that affect driving behavior. One of the drivers shown here is in a state in which the stimuli and the reinforcers that normally influence his behavior have a markedly reduced effect. The other driver is in a state in which these effects are heightened by a high level of arousal.

persons. And some children with minimal brain damage tend to be hyperactive; in behavioral language, they emit behavior at a very high rate.

Anxiety is a particularly important aspect of the organism's state. As already noted, therapies that draw on a Pavlovian model are especially concerned with such emotional states. A later section in this chapter describes systematic desensitization, a treatment approach designed to cure handicapping anxieties or phobias—morbid fears that have no realistic basis.

Biological factors may give rise to problem behaviors, as in some cases of hyperactivity, or they may make a problem worse, as in smoking, drinking, and other such habits. They also may facilitate therapy. For example, autistic children by definition do not respond to other people. But they do respond to food, and in order to begin treating these children—teaching them language, play, self-care, and all the other social skills they lack—the therapist usually uses food as a reinforcer and schedules training sessions shortly before mealtimes. After repeated pairings with this powerful **primary reinforcer,** the therapist becomes a **conditioned reinforcer,** able to reward responses from the children by praise and affection even in the absence of food.

R: The Response

Ultimate success or failure of treatment depends on altering the response, the problem behavior. Often the choice of which behavior to change is quite straightforward: Parents want their child to stop having temper tantrums. Even so, several factors may complicate the selection of a **target behavior.**

A first challenge is to achieve a clear, precise definition of the behavior. People customarily describe themselves and others in terms of traits rather than behaviors. Parents who complain that their child is ''stubborn'' or ''smart-alecky'' may have difficulty specifying the behavioral components of their complaints. Only when the parents, with help from the clinician, are able to pinpoint exactly what behaviors, in what situations, are covered by these terms can the clinician select an appropriate target.

Target selection also may require compromises. For example, parents seeking help with their child usually want quick modification of undesirable behaviors. The clinician knows, however, that the best strategy for the child's development and for the family's long-run equilibrium would be to work on increasing the child's desirable behaviors, many of which the parents may not even be aware of. Clinical experience has shown that because these behaviors are likely to be incompatible with the undesirable behaviors, the latter would

Figure 27.6 An example of a *response* associated with driving that has been made the target of many attempts to modify the behavior of drivers and passengers. The goal of behavior modification in this case is to make seat-belt fastening a highly probable behavior controlled by the stimulus of having just entered the car. This goal has been difficult to achieve because the immediate consequences of the seat-belt-fastening response have some punishing value and little reward value.

gradually be reduced. Nevertheless, to gain and keep the parents' cooperation, the clinician may focus first on the undesirable behaviors.

The selection process becomes more complicated and at the same time
more exciting when the clinician considers the total ecology of a person's
behavior. One behavioral intervention can have snowballing effects. For example, curing a twelve-year-old boy's bed-wetting will likely affect many
other aspects of his behavior in favorable ways. He probably will get along
better with his mother as a result of his cure because she no longer will be
burdened with his extra laundry, and his cure will free him to stay overnight
with friends or go to summer camp without fear of embarrassment.

The clinician can enhance this snowball effect by choosing as the target a
behavior that will gain the client entry into a "behavioral trap"—an environment in which positive reinforcement occurs naturally. Such an environment
will support the behaviors established in therapy and help shape other desirable behaviors. A shy and fearful nursery-school boy who clings to his teacher
might be trained to play near other children by using the teacher's attention
and encouragement as reinforcement. Once he starts interacting with the other
children, their company becomes a behavioral trap, spontaneously taking over
the delivery of reinforcement.

K: The Contingency Relationship

This element of the behavioral formula refers to the schedule by which a
consequence such as reinforcement or punishment follows a particular behavior. This relationship usually is the most difficult element to grasp, and yet it
is often at the root of the problem behavior. Anyone who has had a hangover
or broken a diet knows all too well that the immediate positive reinforcement
of being high or of eating can easily override the delayed and less predictable
unpleasant consequences.

Because different patterns, or schedules, of reinforcement have different
(and sometimes quite powerful) effects, they can be crucial in obtaining the
desired therapeutic results. As described in Chapter 4, schedules may be
continuous or intermittent. A **continuous schedule,** in which the same consequence occurs immediately after each target response, is ideal for delivering
punishment: It is the quickest and surest way to stop an undesirable behavior.

Most parents punish their children on an **intermittent schedule,** which can
be less effective than no punishment at all. Like the slot machine player,
children will continue a behavior such as temper tantrums despite occasional

Figure 27.7 *Contingency* relationships
in the control of driving behavior. A
contingency relationship, or schedule, in
which a consequence follows a
response irregularly or unpredictably
will produce a much steadier pattern of
responding than one in which the
consequences come at regular intervals
or after some set number of responses.
A schedule in which the consequence
depends not only on the response itself
but also on the rate at which the
response is emitted will produce a
pattern of faster (or slower) responding
than a simpler contingency. Looking for
a parking space is a behavior that is on
a highly irregular intermittent schedule;
parking spaces are scarce and you
never know when you will find one. This
behavior is also on a schedule that
rewards a low rate of response; if you
look too fast you are likely to miss an
opportunity. The result is a pattern of
looking behavior that is extremely slow
and steady and highly resistant to
extinction. Imagine how completely
different this pattern would be if, for
example, you could produce parking
spaces magically by driving around the
block three times.

punishment so long as a payoff comes once in a while. Indeed, when parents try to end a child's tantrums by sometimes ignoring the child's behavior but then, occasionally, giving in, they usually make the problem worse. "Ignoring" is a valid technique for curtailing—or, in behavioral language, extinguishing—a behavior, but, as Chapter 4 points out, an intermittent schedule produces **resistance to extinction.** In the case of tantrums, resistance to extinction can be expected if the parents do give in from time to time. Often they actually shape the behavior to a higher degree of aversiveness, because they tend to give in when the child's screams become more intense than usual.

Sometimes the only change needed for successful therapy is a change in K: Consequences that had been freely available, such as a weekly allowance, may be made contingent on the performance of certain tasks. Even when K is not the main focus, any therapy program must take it into account. With a client who is acquiring new assertive responses, the clinician at first gives massive social reinforcement each time the client attempts an assertion. Gradually this schedule is shifted until it approximates the variable way in which the natural social environment reacts to assertive behavior.

The contingency relationship may play a fundamental role in psychological health. Two clinicians, Roberta Ray and Ernest Swihart, have detected a kind of "contingency hunger" in weeks-old infants. They found that "colicky" infants, who cry for long periods, were not deprived of attention, as might have been expected, but were given massive quantities of hugging and cuddling by ever-attentive parents. This attention apparently was not a reinforcer, however, because its removal did not extinguish the colic symptoms. Quite the opposite was found to be the case: The parents were giving their attention noncontingently; rather than engaging in a behavioral give-and-take with their infant, they emitted their behaviors without regard to what the baby was doing at the moment. Instead of playing *with* the baby, they were dumping large amounts of play *on* him. When the clinicians trained the parents to make their own responses contingent upon the behaviors of the baby, the baby gradually recovered and the colic disappeared.

C: The Consequence

The consequence of an act is what reinforces or diminishes it, and it is this element of the behavioral formula that most people associate with behavior modification. The problem that clinicians face is identifying for each person

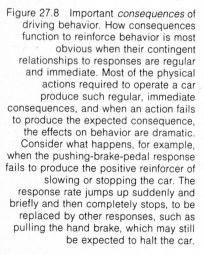

Figure 27.8 Important *consequences* of driving behavior. How consequences function to reinforce behavior is most obvious when their contingent relationships to responses are regular and immediate. Most of the physical actions required to operate a car produce such regular, immediate consequences, and when an action fails to produce the expected consequence, the effects on behavior are dramatic. Consider what happens, for example, when the pushing-brake-pedal response fails to produce the positive reinforcer of slowing or stopping the car. The response rate jumps up suddenly and briefly and then completely stops, to be replaced by other responses, such as pulling the hand brake, which may still be expected to halt the car.

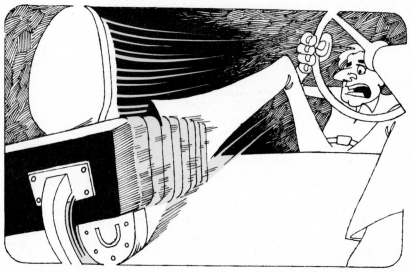

the objects or events that actually do function as reinforcers and, if the range is too small, enlarging the number of things that can serve to reinforce desired behaviors. An example might help in understanding this problem. Imagine a little boy who has a school phobia; he is terrified of going to school. A careful analysis of what serves the child as a social reinforcer might show that up to this point, his mother has been the only person to perform that function in his life. Thus, instead of devising a treatment that consisted of some kind of massive reinforcement for the act of going to school, treatment might better be aimed at increasing the child's range of social reinforcers to include other children.

People who have lived for a long period in institutions often have the problem of no longer responding to a variety of naturally available reinforcers. To help them adjust to life outside the institution, it is necessary to help them learn to respond to a normal variety of reinforcers. Because in certain institutional settings naturally occurring reinforcement is limited, clinicians set up systems to provide positive reinforcement beyond that ordinarily available. For example, tokens (poker chips, slips of paper, or points) are awarded for desired behavior; the tokens are exchangeable for material goods such as cake, candy, games, toys, and books, or for access to preferred activities, such as watching television, participating in games, and spending time away from the institution. The tokens are called **conditioned reinforcers,** because the recipients have learned that they are associated with such primary reinforcers as food and games.

Clinicians attempting to identify naturally occurring events that can serve as reinforcers often use the **Premack principle** as a guide. As described in Chapter 6, Premack says that any behavior a person or animal naturally engages in relatively frequently will serve to reinforce a behavior with a lower relative probability of occurrence. And the particular context and circumstances will determine which of two behaviors can serve to reinforce the other. In certain circumstances, children will choose to play with pinball machines rather than to eat candy. In this case, pinball playing will reinforce candy eating. If the children are hungry or have been playing with the machines for a long time, candy eating can serve as a reinforcement for pinball playing.

Clinicians can make use of the Premack principle in hospitals. For example, hospital staff members may observe each patient, identify his or her more probable behaviors, and then require the performance of a less probable target behavior before the patient may engage in a preferred one. A socially withdrawn patient may be required to spend time talking with others to earn time alone in his room. A patient who likes to talk over his troubles with staff members may be required to *buy* therapy time with tokens earned by engaging

Clinical Research Unit Token System

Earn Tokens by		Spend Tokens for	
Grooming	1–5	Bed	1
Mealtime Jobs		Meals	1
Food Cart	1	Private Room Time	1
Serving	1	Time off Unit	1
Cleaning	1–4	Staff Talk	2
Room Cleaning	1–3	Sleeping in	1
Bed Making	1	Home Visit	10
Group Activities	1–3	Radio	2
Individual Therapy	1–3	Piano	1
Unit Jobs		Movie	2
Trash	2	Dance	2
Laundry	1	Game	1
Cleaning	1–5	TV	1
IT Assignment	5	Telephone Call	1
Shower	1	Evening Snack	1
Group Meeting	2	Newspaper	1
		Stationery	1
		Toiletries	1–10
		Cigarettes	1
		Cigars	2
		Candy	1, 3, 5
		Cookies	1
		Soft Drinks	3
		Pastry	2
		Coffee	2

Figure 27.9 (left) A scene in a hallway of Camarillo State Hospital in California, where a token economy has been instituted. This room is a positive reinforcer; it is more private and more comfortable than the patients' regular sleeping quarters. (above) The responses that earn tokens and the consequences on which they may be spent. This list is posted on the hospital wall for the information of all the patients in the program. The list provides considerable insight into the behaviors that the hospital staff desires but finds difficult to obtain, and into the aspects of hospital life valued by the patients. The program at Camarillo schedules tokens in the same way for all patients, but in many programs the contingencies are tailored to individual patients in order to achieve particular therapeutic aims.

in more direct attacks on his problems, whereas a patient who lacks skill in observing and labeling his own feelings may be *paid* tokens for discussing them with staff members.

A more elaborate form for exchanging reinforcements is the **contract.** In place of tokens given by one person to another, the two parties agree on behaviors each desires in the other. These behaviors, along with the rewards and sanctions they agree to exchange contingently, are stipulated in written form and both parties sign the contract. An example of a contract is shown later in the chapter, in Figure 27.14. Contracts are especially useful in the treatment of marital and family conflicts because they involve each person in a mutual effort to provide reinforcements and to change problem behaviors.

THERAPIES BASED ON CLASSICAL CONDITIONING

The examples used thus far, for each element of the behavioral formula, have been based primarily on the operant-conditioning model. It is necessary to consider further some of the ways in which behavior therapists have applied the classical-conditioning model to emotional and behavioral problems.

Aversive Conditioning

The clearest example of a therapeutic technique based on the Pavlovian model is that of aversive conditioning. This technique aims to reduce the frequency of a response such as smoking cigarettes by pairing an aversive stimulus—a mild electric shock, for example—with the natural stimulus that usually precedes the response until the therapy causes the natural stimulus itself to become aversive.

In the treatment of alcoholism by this method (see Figure 27.10), the presentation of alcohol (conditioned stimulus), including its taste and smell, is paired with an electric shock (unconditioned stimulus)—a stimulus that is tied innately to a pain reaction (unconditioned response). To promote generalization, the setting for this treatment may be highly realistic, with a bar, a bartender, and the client's favorite drink. To take advantage of the termination of shock, which is negative reinforcement, and to avoid the positive reinforcement of swallowing alcohol, the client usually must spit out the alcohol before the shock ends. After a sufficient number of pairings, alcohol takes on a stimulus function similar to the shock: The client comes to react with aversion and fear to the sight, smell, and taste of alcohol (conditioned response). Between conditioning trials, the client sips soft drinks or juices—without being shocked—to prevent generalization to all drinking behavior and to promote the use of substitutes for alcohol.

A number of investigators have reported success in using imagined unpleasant events in place of shock, a technique termed **covert sensitization,** or **aversive imagery.** For example, the therapist may instruct a smoker to close his eyes, relax, and picture himself taking out a cigarette. As he imagines himself lighting up and taking his first puff, he is told to imagine that he feels nauseated, starts gagging, and vomits all over the floor, the cigarettes, and finally himself. The details of this scene are conjured up with excruciating vividness. The client also rehearses an alternative, "relief," scene in which the decision not to smoke is accompanied by pleasurable sensations. This technique, using no special equipment, has obvious advantages; for instance, the client may carry out conditioning sessions on his own at home.

Systematic Desensitization

This therapy was first introduced by Joseph Wolpe under the name reciprocal inhibition but now most clinicians call it systematic desensitization. It is a therapy designed to decrease handicapping anxiety and unrealistic fears, or phobias. The person shown in Figure 27.1 is receiving systematic desensitiza-

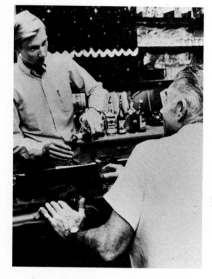

Figure 27.10 The treatment of alcoholism by aversive conditioning. Standing at a mocked-up counter of a bar, the patient receives a shock through electrodes attached to his fingertips just as he takes a drink. Making the counter of the bar as realistic as possible is intended to increase the likelihood that the patient will generalize from the therapeutic environment to the real world.

tion for a snake phobia. In systematic desensitization, a desirable response is substituted for an undesirable one. The anxiety-producing stimulus is presented at a low intensity while the opportunities for an incompatible response to occur are enhanced.

Most commonly, deep muscle relaxation is used as the response incompatible with anxiety. The first step in desensitization is to teach the client how to alternately tense and relax gross muscle groups, so that he can eventually reach a state of deep calm. The second step is to construct a graded hierarchy of the stimuli that make the patient feel anxious. Figure 27.12 shows such a hierarchy for test anxiety. It was constructed by interviewing the client, a medical student, about the situations in which he felt anxious; he then rated, from 0 to 100, the intensity of the anxiety he felt in each situation so that the situations could be listed in ascending order. In this hierarchy, both type of test and amount of time before tests were to occur varied, so that the stimuli could be listed in ascending degrees of intensity. Ratings around 90 meant that the student had indicated he would feel faint, weak, unable to think, and so nauseated that he would have to leave the examination room. At lower levels, his anxiety would be severe enough to disrupt his efforts to study.

The final step in desensitization is the systematic presentation of the hierarchy items to the relaxed client. Most often, the clinician asks the client to imagine the situations rather than presenting them to the client in reality. There are practical advantages to this arrangement: Some items would be difficult to present in reality in a controlled fashion, and those dealing with internal events such as "thinking about . . ." could be accomplished only by instructions to imagine them. In this final step, when the client has reached a state of deep muscle relaxation, the clinician asks him to imagine the lowest hierarchy item first, then the next-to-the-lowest item, and so on, and to give a signal the moment he reaches an item that causes any slight tension. When the client signals, the clinician instructs him to stop visualizing that item and to relax himself again. The client then returns to a lower item and works back up to the tension-producing one. If he does not signal, he continues to visualize the scene for several seconds, then has a short period of deep relaxation alone. After this period of relaxation, he repeats the item several more times. In this fashion, he progresses gradually through all the items until none of them any longer elicits anxiety.

As clinicians have become more experienced in using techniques like systematic desensitization, they have come to have a more sophisticated appreciation of the assessment process that must precede their application. A person's initial complaint may not be the most relevant place to start. The client represented by the hierarchy in Figure 27.12 is a good case in point. He was failing in medical school because of his extreme anxiety before and during exams. He was given both help with his study habits and a series of systematic-desensitization sessions on the hierarchy illustrated, from which he derived only moderate relief. At first, it seemed that treatment was being seriously hindered by his ongoing exposure to real exams before he had progressed far enough in the hierarchy. Further assessment, however, indicated that the therapist was probably working on the wrong hierarchy!

This young man belonged to a very large Polish family; he had worked in construction, had married, and had had several children before deciding to go to medical school. Significantly, he was the only person in his whole extended family who had graduated from college. All the cousins, aunts, and uncles inquired with interest at weekly clan gatherings into what he was doing and learning and what his grades were. They asked his advice about all their aches and pains and generally vicariously relished his medical career. Meanwhile, his wife struggled with their reduced budget and resented his absence from home because of all his studying. With this information, therapy was

Figure 27.11 A small part of the tape used by Wolpe in the initial sessions of desensitization therapy to teach his patients deep muscle relaxation. Here the patient learns to relax his chest, stomach, and lower back by alternately tensing and relaxing the muscles in those areas.

Relax your entire body to the best of your ability. Feel that comfortable heaviness that accompanies relaxation. Breathe easily and freely in and out. Notice how the relaxation increases as you exhale . . . as you breathe out just feel that relaxation. . . . Now breathe right in and fill your lungs; inhale deeply and hold your breath. Study the tension. . . . Now exhale, let the walls of your chest grow loose and push the air out automatically. Continue relaxing and breathe freely and gently. Feel the relaxation and enjoy it. . . . With the rest of your body as relaxed as possible, fill your lungs again. Breathe in deeply and hold it again. . . . That's fine, breathe out and appreciate the relief. Just breathe normally. Continue relaxing your chest and let the relaxation spread to your back, shoulders, neck and arms. Merely let go . . . and enjoy the relaxation. Now let's pay attention to your abdominal muscles, your stomach area. Tighten your stomach muscles, make your abdomen hard. Notice the tension. . . . And relax. Let the muscles loosen and notice the contrast. . . . Once more, press and tighten your stomach muscles. Hold the tension and study it. . . . And relax. Notice the general well-being that comes with relaxing your stomach. . . .

Figure 27.12 A graded hierarchy of situations that elicited different amounts of anxiety from a client being systematically desensitized to tests and examinations. A rating of 100 means "As tense as you ever are"; a rating of zero means "Totally relaxed." The behavior that was identified here as the target behavior was incorrectly chosen. It turned out that the student's anxieties were about disappointing his family rather than about taking the tests themselves.
(After Kanfer and Phillips, 1970.)

Ratings	Hierarchy Items
0	Beginning a new course
5	
10	
15	Hearing an instructor announce a small quiz two weeks hence
20	Having a professor urge you personally to do well on an exam
25	
30	
35	Trying to decide how to study for an exam
40	Reviewing the material I know should be studied—listing study to do
45	
50	
55	
60	Hearing an instructor announce a major exam in three weeks and its importance
	Hearing an instructor remind the class of a quiz one week hence
65	
70	
75	Hearing an instructor announce a major exam in one week
80	Standing alone in the hall before an exam Getting an exam back in class Anticipating getting back a graded exam later that day Talking to several students about an exam right before taking it
85	Thinking about being scared and anxious regarding a specific exam
90	Studying with fellow students several days before an exam Hearing some "pearls" from another student which you doubt you'll remember, while studying in a group Cramming while alone in the library right before an exam Thinking about not keeping up in other subjects while preparing for an exam
95	Thinking about being anxious over schoolwork in general Talking with several students about an exam immediately after
100	Thinking about being generally inadequately prepared Thinking about not being adequately prepared for a particular exam Studying the night before a big exam

altered. He was given desensitization for his fear of failing and disappointing his family; his wife was helped to find satisfactions of her own; and the family members were persuaded to remove their intense pressure on him. After these procedures, the medical student's test anxiety improved dramatically.

DEVELOPMENTS IN BEHAVIOR THERAPIES: THREE EXAMPLES

Aversive conditioning and desensitization may be used together, and they are often combined with operant therapies. This section of the chapter describes three programs of treatment for particular problems in which a number of behavioral techniques are used in varying combinations.

Sexual Orientation Disturbance

The treatment of sexual problems illustrates the kinds of changes that occur in treatment strategies as the conceptualization of the nature of a given class of behaviors becomes more complex and, it is hoped, more realistic.

The first sexual behaviors to receive systematic attention from behavior therapists were homosexuality, transvestism, and fetishism. Beginning in the 1950s, therapists used aversive conditioning to decrease the arousal value of "deviant" stimuli. The assumption was that "normal" heterosexual responsiveness automatically would become dominant—an assumption that parallels the psychoanalytic notion that deviant sexuality stems from a fear of heterosexuality. Many therapists adopted this approach with clients wanting to change sexual orientation.

This strategy had serious conceptual and procedural defects, however. There was no solid evidence, for example, that "deviant" responses had to be eliminated before "normal" ones could be firmly established. And even if one accepted the shaky hypothesis about fear of heterosexual activity, a direct attack on this anxiety would appear to be a more promising treatment than aversive conditioning of the "deviant" stimulus.

An even more important issue was the conceptualization of homosexuality or any other sexual preference as pathological. Despite the efforts of some behavior therapists to "change" homosexuals, many therapists viewed homosexual behavior as no less normal than heterosexuality, a product of the same learning processes. Consistent with this view and with accumulating evidence, they saw in homosexuality no evidence of psychopathology and no correlation with any other signs of maladjustment. Indeed, the few studies bearing directly on the possible modes by which stimuli become sexually arousing were done by behavior therapists and supported the classical-conditioning concept. Saul Rachman, for example, induced fetishism experimentally in normal male volunteers by pairing a slide of a woman's boots with slides of nude females.

As researchers began to question traditional assumptions, treatment also began to shift its focus—from aversive conditioning meant to remove a behavior to positive conditioning aimed at developing a target behavior. An example is Gerald Davison's "*Playboy* therapy." Davison instructed a client who was distressed by his exclusively sadomasochistic fantasies to use these fantasies to obtain an erection during masturbation but to switch to pictures of nude, sexy women from *Playboy* as orgasm approached. These pictures rapidly developed arousal value and then gave way to pictures of less glamorous but more attainable women in swimming suits. At the same time, Davison required his client to begin dating women to establish some of the social skills he lacked.

Some gay-activist groups have criticized behavior therapists for their willingness to help clients who want to change their sexual preferences. The activists argue that the desire to change is derived from distorted social values and pressures, which the therapist should oppose. Therapists generally answer this criticism by saying that the choice of behavior goals should be the client's. Hence many behavior therapists oppose the labeling of homosexuals as "sick," but they uphold their right to seek a heterosexual reorientation should they so desire.

Training Parents as Social Engineers

One major innovation of behavior modification is the movement of treatment out of the therapist's office and into the client's own world. This strategy has

Figure 27.13 Therapists have applied conditioning methods to a variety of sexual disturbances and sexual behaviors. This photograph illustrates the densensitization of a male subject (lying on a couch at left) who responds with anxiety to females in erotic contexts. After the subject has achieved a relaxed state, he is shown a series of slides (such as the one in this photograph) and is instructed to indicate at what point in the series he begins to feel anxiety. Progressively more arousing pictures are shown as the subject's anxiety over slides earlier in the hierarchy diminishes.

obvious advantages, particularly in work with young children. Actual target behaviors, rather than some imitation of them, can be dealt with as they occur. **Generalization** of a behavior change in one situation to other situations is easier to achieve, because the change occurs in the natural environment, not in an artificial one from which progress must be transferred. Even more important, changes can be made in the child's environment, including changes in the behavior of family members and other persons who naturally and constantly control the child's stimuli and reinforcements.

In many cases, the therapist himself has intervened directly in the child's home. Although this strategy has been successful in rapidly altering the target behaviors, its results often have not been lasting. For example, temper tantrums or battles with a younger brother or sister quickly disappeared but almost as quickly returned. Presumably, as soon as the therapist departed, the natural social environment reinstated the contingencies that had produced the child's undesirable behavior. In recent years, more and more treatment programs have shifted away from direct intervention to teaching parents and other natural social agents new and better ways of socializing the child in the home. The case of Margaret and Martha is a simple illustration of this type of indirect intervention. R. Vance Hall and Lois Cox taught the girls' parents their five-step procedure for getting the girls to perform the household tasks expected of them. The following side-by-side lists show the procedure and how the parents instituted it in the house. Afterward, the parents reported that they were very pleased that the girls were doing their tasks without having to be nagged, and the girls were pleased both by their accomplishments and by the reduction in nagging.

THE PROCEDURE	THE EXPERIMENT
1. Select target behaviors that need changing. As Hall says, "The behaviors must be clearly defined."	1. The mother made a chart for each girl listing 9 tasks that each was expected to do each day. The tasks listed on Margaret's chart were: make beds, brush teeth (a.m.), brush teeth (p.m.), turn off night light, hang up clothes, put dirty clothes in hamper, practice music (thirty minutes), clean bathroom after bath, read. Martha's chart was identical except that it required only twenty minutes of music practice.
	The mother checked daily on whether the girls completed the tasks. Her husband made an independent check. Their records always agreed 100 percent.
2. Keep a baseline record—a notation of each behavior as it occurs—to find out how strong the behaviors are before any attempts are made to change them. To ensure accuracy, behavior-analysis experimenters use an independent observer.	2. Baseline 1: During a two-week baseline phase in which no contingencies were in effect, except the usual parental requests and urging to do the assigned tasks, the mean number of tasks completed for both Margaret and Martha was 1.3 per day.
3. Set up the experimental conditions and record and reinforce correct behaviors. The purpose is to attempt to modify the behaviors by rearranging the con-	3. Pay for Duties 1: In this phase the girls were asked to keep the chart record by placing an X in a blank after completing each task each day.

sequences that follow the behaviors.

In some cases, when the purpose is to decrease incorrect behaviors, an extinction technique is used—that is, the consequences are the withholding of reinforcements.

In this case, when the purpose was to strengthen correct behaviors, the consequences were reinforcements: tokens (marks on a chart) that were later exchangeable for money. Thus, the girls were put on a token-economy system.

In this phase, as in the baseline phase, each correct behavior was recorded. According to Hall, this record "provides continuous feedback as to the effectiveness of the modification and indicates if further modification procedures are necessary." They weren't.

Each girl received 5 cents a day for each day she completed all the duties for that day. If she failed to complete all duties, she received nothing for that day. However, if she completed all duties for an entire calendar week she received a bonus of 15 cents. In other words she could earn 50 cents a week by doing all her daily tasks. She received no other allowance.

In the first week under these conditions each completed all duties and received 50 cents. In the second week each failed to complete one task and received only 30 cents for that week. Neither failed to complete all tasks through the remainder of the phase. The mean level of completing tasks for both girls was therefore almost 9 per day.

4. Return to baseline conditions by briefly discontinuing reinforcements. This technique—reversal—is one of the main research designs used by applied-behavior analysts. If the behaviors return to their former level, as they did in this experiment, the behavior analysts are just a step away from what they consider to be scientific verification that reinforcement was instrumental in increasing correct behaviors.

4. Baseline 2: In the eighth week of the experiment the girls were told that they should continue charting task completions but that they were doing so well that they would receive their 50-cent allowance even if they forgot to complete all tasks. In these conditions Margaret completed an average of 2.4 tasks per day, Martha 2 per day.

5. Reinstitute the conditions that were successful. "If this again results in a change," Hall says, "a cause-and-effect relationship has been demonstrated."

5. Pay for Duties 2: The following week, allowances were again made contingent on completing assigned tasks. Doing tasks returned to high rates. Over the next three weeks the mean number completed by Margaret was 8.9 and by Martha 8.8 per day.

Gerald Patterson and his colleagues at the University of Oregon have developed a number of such home treatments, as well as some techniques to control problem children's classroom behavior. These behavior therapists decided that a therapist should himself operate in the regular classroom setting of such children. In this way, the therapist could bring about the initial changes in the children's behavior, and the teacher could watch the therapist in order to learn the techniques and continue them after desirable behavior had been well established.

In the first stage of direct intervention, the therapist trained a problem child to attend to his work by means of a device called the Work Box. Whenever the child was paying attention to the teacher or working at his desk, the therapist would make a light go on in the box; a counter in the box added up the number of times the light went on. The child's accumulated points earned extra recess time not only for himself but for the whole class. In this way, the therapist tried to raise the problem child's status among his peers. The therapist handled severely disruptive behaviors such as physical aggression by making the child leave the classroom each time such a behavior occurred and stay for a short period in a quiet, unstimulating atmosphere.

After a week or two, when the child's disruptive and nonwork behaviors were markedly fewer, the child was switched from the Work Box to a point system administered by the teacher, and he continued to earn rewards for the whole class. Gradually the point system was also phased out until the child's desirable behaviors were maintained entirely by the usual social reinforcement available in the classroom.

At a later stage, school personnel, the therapist, and the child's parents came together to negotiate and carry out a behavioral contract in order to ensure cooperation instead of conflict between home and school. The contract pinpointed the child's undesirable target behaviors that occurred at school and arranged for the parents to apply consequences at home to help discourage these behaviors. Figure 27.14 is an example of a contract of this sort.

Because problem children frequently have severe academic deficiencies, it is important to improve their skills if they are to survive and to receive positive reinforcement in their regular classroom setting. Therefore, the final stage of the school program was to have a parent or peer give the child direct training in reading and arithmetic skills.

Although still under development and investigation, behavior-modification programs for home and school (like the two described in this section) have achieved considerable success with a number of children.

Self-Control: The Case of Smoking

How people establish and maintain self-control is a rapidly growing concern of behavioral clinicians. The whole notion of self-control is not an easy one for behaviorists to deal with, for it often leads them away from the behavioral

Figure 27.14 A behavioral contract drawn up in consultation with a young boy, his schoolteacher, and his parents. A number of target behaviors and their point values are specified. At the right is space for a record to be kept of Dave's daily performance. At the bottom the consequences of various performance levels are stated precisely. Note that the contract stipulates both rewarding consequences (for high daily point counts) and punishing consequences (for low point counts). Although the points in the contract serve much the same function as the tokens in the Camarillo program (see Figure 27.9), the two programs differ in that Dave's points can have punishment value as well as reward value.

(After Patterson, 1971.)

DAVE'S PROGRAM	M	T	W	T	F	S
GETS TO SCHOOL ON TIME (2)	2					
DOES NOT ROAM AROUND ROOM (1)	0					
DOES WHAT THE TEACHER TELLS HIM (5)	3					
GETS ALONG WELL WITH OTHER KIDS (5)	1					
COMPLETES HIS HOMEWORK (5)	2					
WORK IS ACCURATE (5)	3					
BEHAVIOR ON THE SCHOOLBUS IS OK (2)	2					
GETS ALONG WELL WITH BROTHER AND SISTERS IN EVENING (3)	0					
TOTAL	13					

1. If Dave gets 25 points, he doesn't have to do any chores that night, and he gets to pick all the TV shows for the family to watch.
2. If Dave gets only 15 points, he does not get to watch TV that night.
3. If Dave gets only 10 points, he gets no TV and he also has to do the dishes.
4. If Dave gets only 5 points or less, then no TV, wash dishes, and is grounded for the next two days (home from school at 4:00 and stay in yard).

model and toward the constructions and operations of cognitive psychologists or toward the ideas advanced by social-motivational theorists of attitudes.

As yet, no behavioral approach can handle the problem of self-control satisfactorily, especially when confronted with a commonplace, real-world behavior such as smoking. Smoking confronts the behavioral clinician with three questions: How can he help people who want to quit? What factors lead to success in some instances or with some techniques? And how can he describe the operations or processes that go into self-modification of smoking and other such behaviors? The answers are important from the standpoint of improving public health, but they also provide clues for understanding the interaction of environmental and internal influences and for defining the possible limits of a behavioral model of human beings.

Figure 27.15 shows the problem that arises with treatment programs: Of all clients who initially succeed in these programs, roughly two-thirds resume smoking within three months after the program ends. (Interestingly, treatment programs for heroin addicts and alcoholics present similar relapse curves.) Because the smoking curve of Figure 27.15 is a composite of eighty-seven clinical studies, it is apparent that many behavioral treatments can produce initial success but none can reliably produce long-term abstinence. Nor can such treatment programs satisfactorily predict who will relapse.

Aversive conditioning, with electric shock as the aversive stimulus, has played a large role in smoking programs. However, research with animals has suggested that an aversive stimulus with direct and natural links to the target behavior might be more effective than electric shock. In line with this suggestion, some clinicians developed new techniques such as having the client breathe hot dry air or smoke a large number of cigarettes in rapid order, with each drag paced by a fast metronome. But even these treatments could not overcome the relapse problem.

A new look at the problem was in order, and some therapists began to pay attention to the research of nonbehaviorists. Social and cognitive psychologists who focus on how people make decisions suggested that aversive treatments failed because they attacked the wrong incentives. Bernard Mausner, for example, found that smokers, ex-smokers, and nonsmokers all believed that continuing to smoke would have negative consequences. But the smokers in Mausner's sample differed from the other two groups over the expected positive benefits of quitting: They did not believe that *not* smoking would be much better. They anticipated that much tension and discomfort would accompany quitting. Mausner pointed out that it was impossible to make not smoking more attractive than smoking by using a treatment that simply made the activity of smoking more aversive sometimes (that is, during electric-shock treatments). He suggested that smokers needed to practice, in fantasy, the experience of quitting and its long-range benefits.

In a similar fashion, behavior therapists sought to make the aversive conditioning process an internal one by capitalizing on the potency of images. This use of covert sensitization moved the treatment of smoking toward a model of self-control. Indeed, many treatments now depend entirely on establishing procedures that involve self-control. Because smoking is a voluntary behavior involving self-administered reinforcement (the smoking itself), a treatment built on self-control seems eminently reasonable.

Self-control has been called a one-organism version of a two-organism procedure: An individual carries out on himself all of the learning operations usually carried out by his environment and the people in it. Among other things, self-control requires the person both to refrain from engaging in behaviors that are immediately rewarding, as when a smoker resists taking out a cigarette, and to engage in behaviors that lead to aversive consequences, as when one jogs to the point of exhaustion. To administer his own rewards, the

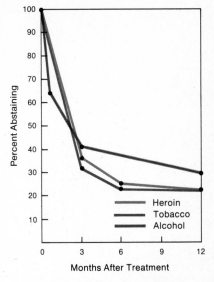

Figure 27.15 Post-treatment relapse rates for heroin addicts, alcoholics, and smokers. The percentage of each group continuing to abstain is plotted as a function of time since quitting. More than two-thirds are using their drug again after a year.

(After Hunt, Barnett, and Branch, 1971.)

individual must set performance criteria and reward himself only when he meets these criteria, even though he has free access to the rewards.

Many tactics can help the person engineer his environment so as to reduce temptation and the aversiveness of change. A self-control smoking program may include strengthening stimulus control—smoking only in the bathroom, for instance, or in some other isolated spot. Ultimate aversive consequences may be brought forward in time: The client surrounds himself with horror pictures of diseased lungs or listens to taped recordings of his own smoker's hack. He can also place himself in situations where smoking is not allowed, such as riding on buses and going to movies, and he can avoid situations in which he usually smokes a lot, such as cocktail parties or boring meetings.

A basic question remains unanswered, however: What keeps a successful ex-smoker from buying a pack of cigarettes and lighting up? Behavioral researchers have proposed several hypotheses to account for the development and exercise of self-restraint. However, further clarification from the laboratory is necessary to demonstrate the usefulness of these hypotheses and to prove their potential for more effective self-control programs.

THE DEBATE ABOUT BEHAVIORAL CONTROL

The specter of a "big-brother" type of control, of the crushing of individual creativity and autonomy, has haunted most ethical and philosophical debates about behavior modification since mid-century, when B. F. Skinner, in *Walden Two* and *Science and Human Behavior,* proclaimed that a behavioral technology was not only feasible but eminently desirable. These debates are complex, but a few simple points can at least place them in context.

Behavior therapy is no more than a technology. In no way does it indicate which behaviors are desirable or which should be changed. It can be used to increase either creative or conforming behaviors. Children may be positively reinforced either for sitting quietly in the classroom or for making imaginative guesses and trying new solutions to problems.

The technology also is overt and therefore more open to countercontrols than are the more covert influence procedures such as psychoanalysis or Rogerian client-centered therapy. A Rogerian therapist's reflections may be selective and hence directive, but less obviously so than a token-economy program. The latter, readily identified, can as readily be rejected. And if it is true, as the behavioral model proposes, that we are all shaped by external contingencies all of the time, then the deliberate, open engineering of such contingencies permits a greater, not a lesser, range of choices.

The goals for which behavioral techniques are used must be under constant public scrutiny, however. The values that determine which behaviors are selected as targets for change must always be made explicit so that they may be subjected to questioning. And special care needs to be taken to ensure that old, questionable practices used in prisons and other institutions, such as solitary confinement, are not given false respectability by those who mislabel them in behavioral terms.

If these safeguards are respected and if clinicians maintain a data-based orientation to treatment, the potentials and limits of behavioral approaches can be fully and beneficially explored.

Figure 27.16 The use of behavioral control. This mental patient has been placed for a short period in "time-out"; he has been removed to an environment in which there is little stimulation and little opportunity to make responses that will produce rewards. Time-out is a neutral event that has been used in a variety of behavior-modification programs as a consequence for highly undesirable behaviors such as violent aggression. Sending a child to his room for fighting (if the room is not filled with attractive amusements) is an example of the use of time-out. The use of solitary confinement in prisons is a procedure that could be compared to time-out. In the case of solitary confinement, however, the removal of stimulation and opportunities to respond for reward is extreme; typically, the prisoner is deprived of decent food, light, and adequate toilet facilities. Solitary confinement is a behavioral consequence that adds highly aversive features to the neutral environment of time-out. Comparisons such as this are helpful in evaluating present methods of behavioral control and the forms of control proposed by behavior modifiers.

SUMMARY

1. The **behavior therapies,** which rose to prominence in the last decade, stem directly from laboratory experiments and theories of **classical conditioning** and **operant conditioning** (described in Chapter 4). Success has been reported in the treatment of a wide range of emotional and learning disturbances in children and adults.

2. Behavior therapists, in contrast to therapists of most other orientations, regard "mental" or "abnormal" disturbances simply as **nonadaptive behaviors that are learned** in the same way that "normal" behaviors are learned.

   a. These nonadaptive behaviors are considered by behavior therapists to be the primary targets of therapy rather than the symptoms of underlying or unconscious personality aberrations.

   b. They believe that an individual's **environment** has a crucial effect on his behavior and that problem behaviors can be modified by changing the physical and social environment of that person.

   c. Diagnosis requires accurate descriptions of **observable behaviors** and the **environmental events** that precede and follow the behavior.

3. Like experimental psychologists, behavior therapists rely heavily on detailed observations of behavior. They examine the **stimuli that control behavior** and the **consequences** of the behavior. They use empirical data in all phases of treatment, from clinical diagnosis to assessment of outcome. However, behavior therapists also must skillfully employ the more traditional client-therapist techniques of interaction.

4. Behavior therapy always aims to increase the frequency of responding in an area in which the client's behaviors are deficient, or to reduce the frequency of responding in an area where the client's behaviors are excessive. For purposes of analysis and treatment, a problem behavior may be broken down into five sequential events, usually referred to by the shorthand **behavioral formula S-O-R-K-C.** These events, any one or all of which may contribute to the problem and to its solution, are as follows:

   a. **Stimuli or Stimulus Control (S).** Environmental circumstances or stimuli control behaviors by eliciting responses (classical conditioning) or signaling the probable consequences of a response (operant conditioning). Stimulus control may be too weak, as in cases of overeating to obesity, or too strong and restricted, as in cases of sexual fetishes. The aim of therapy is to gain a balance of stimulus control so that the fat client is stimulated to eat only at specified times and places or the client with a sexual fetish learns to respond to a broader range of sexual stimuli.

   b. **Organism (O).** Permanent or temporary biological states of an organism may influence behavior. Deafness, anxiety, or hunger, for example, may cause or may worsen problem behavior. These states also may be used in therapy: For instance, a therapist may use food as a reward or **primary reinforcer** to train a hungry autistic child to make responses. Later, the therapist who has delivered the food becomes a **conditioned reinforcer,** and the food reward need no longer be used all the time.

   c. **Response (R).** The behavior modified in therapy is the **target** behavior; it may be increased in frequency, for instance, when a shy person

Figure 27.17 Joseph Wolpe's pioneering work in behavior therapy provided an effective alternative to psychoanalytic formulations of neurosis. Wolpe believes that anxiety is learned by classical conditioning and that systematic desensitization is the way to eliminate it. Wolpe does not ignore the client's understanding and experience—he is careful to discuss with his clients the reasons for his methods and their application to each client's particular problems—but he believes that the long, drawn-out "talking cures" of psychoanalysis are ineffective and that the learning of responses to replace maladaptive ones is the only effective treatment for neurosis.

Figure 27.18 O. H. Mowrer, applying a learning-theory point of view, has made basic contributions to the psychology of learning, to abnormal psychology, and to the study of psychotherapy. Like Thomas Szasz, Mowrer says that labeling maladjusted people "sick" confuses the problem of psychotherapy; he believes that persons undergoing therapy must be held accountable for their behavior and not, like "sick" people, be excused for their acts.

learns to develop assertive behaviors, or decreased in frequency, for example, when a child's temper tantrums are eliminated. The target behavior must always be defined clearly in behavioral terms. Modification of the problem behavior can have snowballing positive effects, which lead to modification of other problem behaviors or the acquisition of new desirable responses.

d. **Contingency Relationship (K).** Behaviors are followed by consequences, such as positive reinforcement or punishment. The consequence may come each time—**continuous schedule**—or only sometimes—**variable schedule**—and the schedule determines the contingency relationship between the behavior and its consequence. A behavior that is *punished* on a continuous schedule usually disappears; punishment on a variable schedule may actually worsen the behavior and produce **resistance to extinction.** Contingency relationships often are difficult to detect but play a fundamental role in operant therapy and apparently in the maintenance of psychological health in general.

e. **Consequence (C).** Behavior modification is best known for its manipulation of consequences; it is most important to identify for each person and event the consequences that actually function as reinforcers. Clinicians often apply the **Premack principle** in identifying such consequences. Token-economy programs that reward persons for specified desirable behaviors are often set up in institutions and classrooms where the range of naturally occurring reinforcement is limited. The tokens are **conditioned reinforcers** for primary reinforcers such as food or amusement. Another technique, signed **contracts** for the exchange of reinforcers, has proved successful in the treatment of marital and other family conflicts.

5. **Classical conditioning,** which is concerned only with the S-O-R part of the behavioral formula, has led to the development of therapeutic techniques especially useful in the treatment of emotional disturbances and addictions.

a. One such technique, **aversive conditioning,** has been used in treating alcoholism and in modifying "deviant" sexual responses by pairing an electric shock with the presentation of alcohol or with photographs with sexual content.

b. A variation of this technique, **covert sensitization,** uses imagined unpleasant events in place of shock.

c. Another technique, **systematic desensitization,** has been successful in eliminating excessive anxiety and phobias by presenting actual or imagined fear-producing objects or situations to a client when he is in a state of relaxation that is incompatible with fear.

6. Three examples show recent trends in the behavior therapies.

a. In response to theoretical developments and to criticism by gay-activist groups, the treatment of sexual deviancy has moved away from aversive to positive conditioning, and many behavior therapists reject the traditional view that homosexuality is in itself evidence of psychopathology. But these therapists also reject the gay-activist argument that they should not help homosexuals who wish to change their sexual preferences.

b. Therapists have moved treatment out of their offices and into the client's own world, an innovation that appears to bring more lasting effects. In work with children, therapists also have found it advantageous to train parents to be behavior modifiers.

c. Statistics have shown that addictive problems, such as cigarette smoking, are particularly resistant to any kind of treatment. In an attempt to achieve better results, behavior therapists have begun to develop procedures for effective **self-control,** making the client his own behavior modifier.

SUGGESTED READINGS

Franks, Cyril M., and Terence Wilson (eds.). *Annual Review of Behavior Therapy: Theory and Practice: 1973.* New York: Brunner/Mazel, 1973. The first of an anticipated series of annual collections of notable and influential journal articles from the whole field of behavior therapy.

Kanfer, Frederick H., and Jeanne S. Phillips. *Learning Foundations of Behavior Therapy.* New York: Wiley, 1970. An advanced text that summarizes the major empirical findings and the controversies surrounding current learning theories and surveys their applications in behavioral-clinical practice.

Lazarus, Arnold. *Behavior Therapy and Beyond.* New York: McGraw-Hill, 1971. An iconoclastic volume, rich in clinical examples, which presents in a clear and interesting fashion the eclectic methods, assumptions, and strategies used by the author in his own behavioral practice.

O'Leary, K. Daniel, and Susan G. O'Leary (eds.). *Classroom Management: The Successful Use of Behavior Modification.* Elmsford, N.Y.: Pergamon, 1972. A paperback collection of research reports dealing with the application of behavior modification to classroom situations, including such topics as token systems, punishment, teaching machines, and self-control.

Stuart, Richard B., and Barbara Davis. *Slim Chance in a Fat World.* Champaign, Ill.: Research Press, 1972. A detailed behavioral program for weight reduction and useful illustrations of many of the tactics of self-control.

Watson, David L., and Roland G. Tharp. *Self-directed Behavior: Self-modification for Personal Adjustment.* Belmont, Calif.: Brooks/Cole, 1972. A step-by-step description of how to develop a program for modifying one's own behavior, with a clear exposition of the general principles of behavior modification.

In writing this particular introduction, I want to advance a suggestion on how to handle the drug problem. I want to do so in all seriousness. First, to be perfectly honest, I want to disclaim any expert knowledge. I have never taken any drugs. I don't even drink or smoke. I don't know any drug addicts; I have no experience in the field at all from any angle. It is just that there is something I don't understand about the drug problem: What is wrong with taking drugs and becoming addicted to them?

I am told, for instance, that drug addicts are a danger to society. But why is that? Because they take drugs? Or because they are kept from taking drugs? It seems to me that all the violent acts attributed to addicts occur when the addicts are trying to *get* drugs. In that case, why stop them, I wonder? Why try to keep drugs from them? If we could provide cheap drugs, purchasable legally without prescription, one large source of potential violence would be removed.

I am told that drug addicts ruin their lives through their addiction and may even kill themselves through overdoses. Perhaps, but I am also told that it is the uncontrolled variation in strength and purity that does most of the physical damage. If pure drugs in known dosages were supplied, wouldn't drugs become much safer?

I am told that the drug problem is dangerous because it is under the control of criminals. But isn't that because we insist on making drugs illegal? If drugs could be handled legally and honestly, why would criminals get into the act?

I am told that drug addiction is dangerous in the ordinary affairs of life—in driving a car, for instance. True, an addict at the wheel of a car would make me nervous. So would a man under the influence of alcohol who is driving a car. So would a cigarette smoker, with his judgment dulled by chronic hypoxia. So would a man in a haze of anger after a just-concluded argument with his wife.

I am told that drug addiction is simply immoral. Maybe it is, but is it worse than any other addiction—is it worse than alcohol addiction or tobacco addiction or food addiction, all of which are physiologically dangerous?

The United States, back in the 1920s, tried to outlaw alcohol in the thirteen-year experiment of Prohibition. During that time, the attempt to enforce the law brought about the growth of gangsterism, encouraged contempt for the law, led to what some called a general deterioration of moral fiber. One thing it did *not* do. It did *not* succeed in outlawing alcohol.

My suggestion then? Let's consider the possibility of legalizing all drugs and of supervising the production of a cheap and uniform supply. If anyone wants to be an addict—well, it's his life. And, who knows, if we remove the glamour of illegality and danger from the whole thing, perhaps fewer people may be lured into addiction in the first place.

It would also help if we built a society so healthy that few would feel so desperate a need to escape from it.

Isaac Asimov

28
Drugs and Drug Therapy

BEFORE PSYCHIATRIC DRUGS

PSYCHIATRIC DRUGS
Antipsychotic Drugs
Antidepressants
Sedatives and Antianxiety Drugs
Lithium
Stimulants

HALLUCINOGENIC DRUGS

MARIJUANA

NARCOTICS

ALCOHOL AND ALCOHOLISM

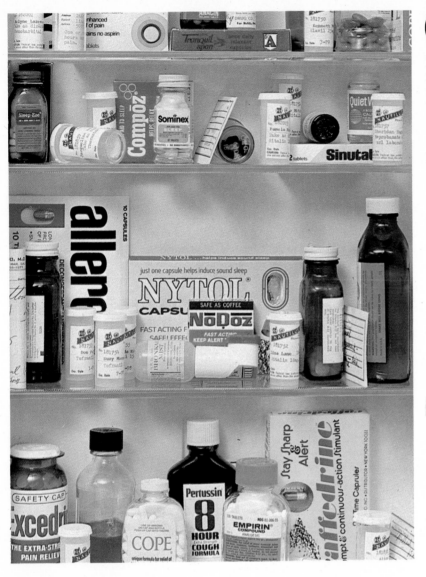

Figure 28.1 People take psychologically active drugs for many different reasons in Western society. Not only are drugs administered on a large scale by psychiatrists and physicians, drugs are also consumed for the express purpose of producing interesting or pleasant psychological changes. One or more of the drugs caffeine, cannabis, nicotine, and alcohol are ingested by almost everyone daily. Prescription and nonprescription medicinal drugs are sold in great volume; these include sedatives, diet pills, pain relievers, cold and allergy treatments, and tranquilizers. Almost all drugs, whether taken for the purpose of inducing psychological changes or not, have effects on the human nervous system.

One hot August evening in 1955, Helen Burny sat listlessly on her bed in the violent ward of a large Texas hospital where she had been confined for four months. During most of that unhappy time, Helen had been highly vocal, abusive, and overactive. Only the day before she had tried to strike a ward aid. Immediately, several burly attendants had grabbed her, roughly tying her into a strait jacket that pinned her arms against her chest. But that night Helen's behavior was different. Her incessant talking and shouting had stopped. All day long she spoke only when spoken to; most of the time she lay on her bed with her eyes half closed, moving little and looking rather pale. However, she was unusually cooperative with nurses, got out of bed when told to, and went to the dining room without resisting. What had happened to bring about this remarkable change?

That morning Helen had received an injection of a new synthetic drug, chlorpromazine, which had been discovered a few years earlier in France. On the same day thousands of mental patients throughout the world were receiving the same drug, many of them for the first time. News of the drug's usefulness had spread rapidly in the preceding months, and it was being tried in mental hospitals throughout the world. Soon it would be difficult to find a psychotic patient who was not being treated with a drug of some kind. The era of clinical psychopharmacology had begun.

BEFORE PSYCHIATRIC DRUGS

For hundreds of years, as explained in Chapter 26, people believed that mental disorder was caused by supernatural forces, and the mentally ill were treated accordingly. In medieval times, for example, a hole might be bored in the skull of a disturbed person to "let the evil spirits out." Not until the late eighteenth century did naturalistic explanations of psychotic behavior become prominent. Around that time, the French psychiatrist Philippe Pinel, after a long

Figure 28.2 Physical restraint used to be common in psychiatric wards; obviously, its use put limits on the kinds of therapy possible for some patients. The use of psychiatric drugs has made physical restraint all but unnecessary and has allowed large numbers of patients to participate in therapeutic programs or to return to their homes. Drug therapy is not a "cure," however; one of its drawbacks is that it treats only pathological symptoms and not the causes of psychological disorder.

campaign for the humane treatment of the insane, managed to free the inmates of the grim Bicêtre mental hospital from their iron chains. Unfortunately, other physical restraints had to be substituted when patients became assaultive or destructive. Although the padded cell and the strait jacket were softer than chains, they allowed no greater freedom.

Until it was discovered that drugs could help the severely disturbed, almost the only recourse in the management of overactive psychotic patients was physical restraint. Before 1955 such physical methods as strait jackets, wet-sheet wrapping, "hydrotherapy" (baths), isolation, lobotomy, and electroconvulsive shock were in relatively common use. Other fairly common control methods were simple sedation by barbiturates and the not-so-simple —sometimes fatal—insulin-coma therapy.

PSYCHIATRIC DRUGS

In the mid-1950s drugs finally promised to emancipate most patients from physical restraint. Although some psychiatrists and psychologists were afraid that the use of drugs would lead to neglect of the social and psychological causes of mental illness, there is no doubt that the new drugs greatly improved the lives of many people with mental disorders, both inside the hospital and outside its confines.

The drugs made it possible for some families to stay together, for some individuals to hold a job, and for some patients to be reached by psychotherapy. Compared to individual psychotherapy and hospitalization, antipsychotic and antidepressant drugs are easily available and inexpensive. This form of treatment is more accessible to people of all social classes and all income ranges.

Psychopharmacology is now an important scientific discipline in its own right, and many new chemical agents have been developed for the treatment of each major category of mental illness. These drugs include phenothiazines (chlorpromazine is an example), thioxanthines, rauwolfia alkaloids, and butyrophenones to treat psychosis; benzodiazepine compounds for anxiety; monoamine oxidase (MAO) inhibitors and dibenzazepine derivatives for depression. Medications have been found useful in the treatment of the most severe mental illnesses: schizophrenia, depression, and mania, which are described in Chapter 24. Drug treatments have even been attempted for autistic behavior, psychopathic behavior, sexual deviation, and mental retardation, although clinical psychopharmacologists feel that the surface has only been scratched in these areas.

In spite of a marked increase in the population of the United States, the total number of patients in public mental hospitals in the United States dropped from about 560,000 in 1955 to about 330,000 in 1971. This striking drop can be ascribed partly to changing attitudes toward the mentally ill and partly to new psychosocial methods for treating patients. One of these new methods, community mental health (described in detail in Chapter 26), aims precisely at getting patients out of hospitals, so that they can return to their families and jobs. Psychiatric drugs, however, have also played an important role in decreasing the number of hospital patients.

The coming of the psychiatric drugs, however, has not been an unmixed blessing. Many people—including doctors as well as patients—view psychiatric medicines as panaceas for virtually any emotional problem, serious or trivial, chronic or temporary. One woman reports visiting her doctor during menopause and being asked whether she was depressed and cried easily. "No," she said, "I usually feel fine." "Here," the doctor replied, handing her a prescription for an antidepressant. "Take these."

The following pages describe the uses, proper and improper, of the main groups of psychiatric drugs. They are discussed under the following headings:

antipsychotic drugs, antidepressants, antianxiety drugs and sedatives, lithium (a drug used to treat manic-depressive psychosis), and stimulants.

Antipsychotic Drugs

The antipsychotic drugs, formerly called major tranquilizers, are so called because they are administered mainly to people with major psychotic disorders, usually schizophrenia, paranoid psychosis, or manic psychosis.

According to a number of studies of these drugs' effectiveness, summarized by Donald Klein and John Davis, the drugs seem to be most effective in bringing patients out of indifference and withdrawal, in reducing thought disorder, and in treating patients who had seemed to experience no emotion. These are often referred to as the "core symptoms" of schizophrenia. The drugs seem to be less effective against such secondary symptoms as hallucinations, paranoia, and hostility. And they seem to have no effect on such nonschizophrenic symptoms as anxiety, guilt, or disorientation.

There are three basic chemical types of drugs in this class: the phenothiazines, the thioxanthines, and the butyrophenones. The **phenothiazines,** one of the oldest types, often serve as the standard against which other antipsychotic drugs are measured, and they are currently still the most commonly used.

The results of a two-year study from the Massachusetts Mental Health Center (reported by Lester Grinspoon, Jack Ewalt and Richard Shader in 1968) demonstrate the effectiveness of the phenothiazines. The study compared different methods of treating chronic schizophrenia. People in one group were treated with phenothiazines and psychosocial therapies, that is, intensive individual psychoanalytically oriented psychotherapy and group, milieu, recreational, and occupational therapies. Another group received only psychosocial therapies; people in this group were given placebos rather than tranquilizing drugs. (A placebo is a pill that actually contains no drugs, although the patient believes it to be medicine.) The conclusions of the researchers were that "Psychotherapy alone (even with experienced psychotherapists) does little or nothing for chronic schizophrenic patients in two years' time . . . There is ample evidence . . . to show that the combination of drugs and psychotherapy had beneficial effects on these patients, and that the drug variable played by far the most important role in producing changes in the patients' statuses."

The antipsychotic drugs are not "wonder drugs" like antibiotics. They do not produce cures. Even when patients do respond dramatically to one of these drugs, most of them still behave abnormally to some degree. And some patients do not respond to the drugs at all.

How do these drugs work biochemically? No one knows, although theories abound. One interesting hypothesis is that schizophrenia is the result of abnormal metabolism of a chemical called **dopamine,** which is found in the brain, and that the antipsychotic drugs work by affecting this chemical and its actions. The hypothesis states that there is excessive activity of dopamine in specific parts of the brain (from an unknown cause) and that antipsychotic drugs work by blocking the receptor sites for dopamine, thereby blocking its effects.

The drugs used in the treatment of schizophrenia have numerous side effects, as do many drugs. Although these side effects are bothersome, they are not often serious—certainly not serious enough to outweigh their therapeutic value in cases of severe mental illness. Some of the common side effects include sedation (which is often desirable, especially in agitated or violent patients), dry mouth, lowered blood pressure, slightly blurred vision, and sometimes abnormal movements or tightness of the muscles. Many of these disturbances fade away after a person has taken the drug for a while.

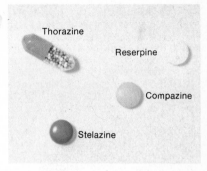

Figure 28.3   Some commonly used antipsychotic drugs.

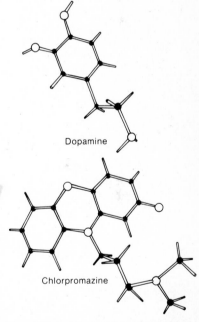

Figure 28.4   The structure of a molecule of dopamine, a central-nervous-system neurotransmitter, and of a molecule of chlorpromazine, an antipsychotic drug. Research has suggested that the antipsychotic drugs exert their effects because of their structural similarity to dopamine. Researchers believe that the chlorpromazine molecule is enough like the dopamine molecule to fit into the same receptor sites at the synapses between neurons but not similar enough to cause neurons to fire, as dopamine does. They believe that the result of administering chlorpromazine is therefore a reduction of neural activity wherever that activity depends on dopamine.

One puzzling fact about antipsychotic drugs is that some psychotics can take high doses without experiencing the drowsiness and confusion that non-psychotic people feel on the same doses.

Antidepressants

The discovery and development of the antidepressant drugs is an especially significant chapter in the history of psychiatry. The chemical mechanisms through which a person's emotional states are mediated are by no means fully understood, but significant progress is being made with great assistance from these drugs.

Antidepressant drugs should not be confused with stimulants, which are discussed in another section. Antidepressants can reverse a state of depression in a mentally ill person but usually have no stimulating effect on normal people. Stimulants are not effective in treating depression and can cause a normal person to become excited and euphoric; they produce a stimulation of the autonomic nervous system.

The first observation of a specific antidepressant drug effect was a beautiful example of serendipity. In 1952 Irving Selikoff and his colleagues were treating patients for tuberculosis with a drug called iproniazid. They noticed an elevated mood in a number of their patients. This observation led to an intense investigation of how **MAO inhibitors** (monoamine oxidase inhibitors, the chemical family to which iproniazid belongs) affect mood and behavior. Now, although some MAO inhibitors are still used, more effective and less toxic drugs—the **tricyclic antidepressants**—are used more often.

The **catecholamine hypothesis** of affective disorders came out of research on how the MAO inhibitors and the tricyclic antidepressants affect chemicals in the brain called catecholamines—specifically **noradrenaline** (NA), a hormone that is important in the functioning of the autonomic nervous system. Simply put, the hypothesis is this: Functional deficiencies of NA in the brain are related to depression, and functional excesses of NA are related to mania or excited states. Drugs that increase the availability of NA in the brain, then, might alleviate depression, and drugs that decrease it might cause depression; moreover, drugs that produce an excess of NA might cause excitation or mania, and drugs that decrease the availability or block the effects of NA in the brain might alleviate mania.

Figure 28.5 shows how the MAO inhibitors may block destruction of NA inside the nerve cell, making more NA available for use. The phenothiazines, on the other hand, which are effective in controlling manic psychosis, may work by blocking the effects of NA.

Antidepressant drugs rarely help with the common sadnesses and tragedies of everyday life, such as a broken romance or the death of a family member or friend, and they are not effective in treating neurotic depression. They seem most effective in increasing drive and elevating mood only for the severe depression in depressive reactions, a type of psychosis, which is described in Chapter 24. In contrast to people with neurotic depression, who usually have a history of anxiety, tension, hostility, and mood swings, a depressive reaction seems to come on rather suddenly to people who had previously been well adjusted. Only about 10 to 20 percent of depressed people actually have depressive reaction, and because of its rather sudden onset and the fact that it is helped by antidepressants, whereas other kinds of depression are not, some clinicians believe that depressive reactions are a result of some abnormality in brain function.

Sedatives and Antianxiety Drugs

Sedatives are a relatively old and widely used class of drugs. In small doses, they cause drowsiness or lowered excitability. Larger doses produce sleep.

Figure 28.5 The action of an antidepressant drug. These figures represent portions of the nervous system in successively finer detail. In the top drawing impulses are being transmitted through a network of neurons. The middle drawing illustrates points of transmission between the axon of one neuron and the dendrite of another; three synapses are shown here. The lower diagram represents one of the synapses. At all the synapses in this network the chemical noradrenaline (NA) is responsible for the transmission of the impulses. Normally when one neuron fires, NA is released across the synapse and is received at the receptor sites of the next neuron; this receipt of NA increases the likelihood that the next neuron will fire in turn. The supplies of NA are kept in check by the presence of monoamine oxidase (MAO), which chemically breaks down much of the NA. A monoamine oxidase inhibitor (MAOI), however, increases the amount of NA available and consequently increases the rate of neural firing. Thus, MAO inhibitors work their antidepressant effects by indirectly causing an increase in neural activity in certain networks of the nervous system.

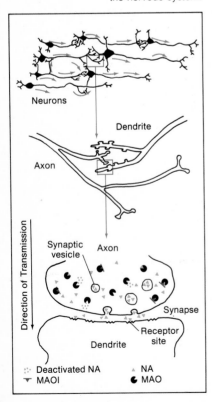

Neurons

Dendrite

Axon

Direction of Transmission

Synaptic vesicle

Axon

Synapse

Receptor site

Dendrite

⠂⠂ Deactivated NA ▲ NA
⊤ MAOI ◖ MAO

Barbiturates are perhaps the best-known sedatives, although there are now more expensive drugs that produce similar effects—and similar problems.

Sedatives have two main uses: to treat anxiety and to treat insomnia. Because insomnia is one of the commonest complaints in America, it is not surprising that so many "sleeping pills" are produced and used each year. For example, the Food and Drug Administration reported that in 1962, one million pounds of barbituric acid was produced—enough to make thirty capsules for each person in the United States.

Anxiety is such a common experience that everyone knows what it feels like. It may be defined as an unpleasant state associated with a threatening situation, similar to but usually vaguer than fear. But anxiety is not a specific symptom. It accompanies many different psychological disorders, and it also occurs when no disorder is present. Most people feel anxious before an important test or a job interview, for instance. Many drugs have been used to treat anxiety, including alcohol and barbiturates.

In the 1950s a number of new drugs with properties similar to barbiturates were introduced for the treatment of anxiety. The most successful by far of these early drugs was **meprobamate,** popularly known as Miltown or Equanil. However, meprobamate's standing as the most popular tranquilizer has been usurped by newer drugs such as diazepam (Valium) and chlordiazepoxide (Librium). These **antianxiety drugs** are ineffective in treating psychoses and other major disorders, but they seem to be moderately helpful in treating anxiety. That is, *most* studies show that the antianxiety drugs and barbiturates affect anxiety level more than a placebo does. Although it has not been shown that the newer antianxiety drugs are any more effective than barbiturates in treating anxiety, they do have one extremely important advantage over barbiturates: It is probably impossible to kill oneself by taking them. The potential deadliness of barbiturates, on the other hand, is shown by the fact that in 1963, 2,000 persons in the United States committed suicide by taking them.

How the antianxiety drugs work to diminish anxiety is not clear. The sedative action—or "general central nervous system depressant" effects—that they all possess is probably the main reason for their effect. Almost all the antianxiety drugs tend to produce sleep when used in large doses and to produce effects reported as pleasant with lower doses.

If the drugs are taken properly, the side effects are few and consist mainly of drowsiness. However, giving one of these drugs to a patient suffering from neurotic anxiety is not quite the same as inserting a pin into a broken bone to hold it together or giving insulin to a diabetic. In giving antianxiety drugs and sedatives, physicians are employing drugs with a poorly defined action to treat a poorly defined condition. And there is a danger in using all of them except the family of drugs that includes Valium: When people whose bodies become dependent on the drugs go through an untreated withdrawal, they can experience convulsions, shock, and coma, and they may even die.

A growing problem with the antianxiety drugs and sedatives is overuse. Although large numbers of people regard them as a cure-all, they are more a danger than a help to a person whose emotional fluctuations are normal but who seeks blissful calm in a troubled world. Unfortunately, some physicians promote the overuse of these agents by prescribing them too often.

Lithium

Lithium salts are relative newcomers among the psychiatric drugs used in the United States, but they have been used for twenty years in Europe. The action of lithium salts was discovered by accident when John Cade, an Australian physician, noticed that they produced drowsiness in guinea pigs. This observation led to the idea that lithium might help alleviate mania in human

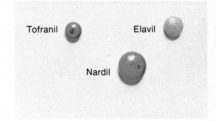

Figure 28.6 Several antidepressant drugs. These drugs are used both inside and outside of hospitals for the treatment of depression. A typical dose exerts its effect from four to six hours. Side effects may include dryness of the mouth and muscular tremor.

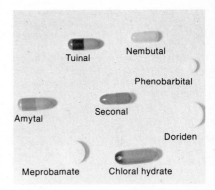

Figure 28.7 Sedatives. These drugs are used in the treatment of insomnia, tension, and sometimes to precede the introduction of anesthesia. They depress the overall activity of the central nervous system. They impair judgment, increase reaction time, and reduce coordination and emotional control. Sedatives produce significant physical and psychological dependence, and users require increasing dosages to maintain equal effects. The abuse of these drugs is very widespread today, and there is a substantial illicit traffic in them.

beings, and at present lithium salts are used to treat manic psychosis.

The drug seems to be curiously specific for mania. It often returns severely manic patients—who show hyperactivity, unrealistic self-confidence and euphoria, and other exaggerations of mood—to normal mood states within five to seven days, usually without the side effects of lethargy and drowsiness that antipsychotic drugs sometimes produce. Some research findings (such as those by Hans Corrodi, Saul Schanberg, Robert Colburn, and Joseph Schildkraut and their colleagues) suggest that the action of lithium salts may be consistent with the catecholamine hypothesis of mood disorders.

Several clinical studies, such as one by Alec Coppen and his colleagues, have suggested that lithium administered daily will prevent the recurrent episodes not only of mania but of depression, too, in the mood swings so often seen in people with manic-depressive disorders. There is still not enough research evidence to support these claims.

Stimulants

Stimulants include very powerful drugs, such as the amphetamines (dextroamphetamine and methamphetamine) and methylphenidate (Ritalin); they also include less potent ones, such as caffeine and nicotine. All these agents produce excitement; specifically, they can decrease fatigue, increase talkativeness and physical activity, enhance physical performance, produce a state of alertness, diminish appetite, and for a time elevate mood—often to euphoria.

The value of stimulants in psychiatry is quite limited. As noted earlier, they are usually not effective in treating depression; actually, they can make the disorder worse. However, they can be used to treat a rare condition called narcolepsy, in which the person has abnormal fits of sleep, sometimes falling asleep in the middle of a conversation or at other inappropriate times.

Stimulants are also useful in treating the so-called hyperkinetic, or hyperactive, child. The hyperkinetic child's overactivity and inability to concentrate are probably the result of some sort of minimal dysfunction of the brain. Strangely enough, this state can sometimes be much improved by stimulants; in some children, the stimulant acts paradoxically as a tranquilizer, calming them and helping them concentrate and attend more closely to stimuli. Unfortunately, the effectiveness of amphetamines for treating some cases of hyperactivity has led to frequent, indiscriminate use of these drugs for all children with high activity levels or other behavioral problems. Many hyperactive children are not at all helped by amphetamines; in fact, their hyperactivity becomes more severe. Also, young children are normally very active, and their naturally high activity level should not necessarily be interpreted as hyperactivity. Unnecessary administration of drugs to a normal, active child is not useful and may be harmful.

Amphetamines should be administered with great caution because their effects are often unpredictable; however, correctly administered, they can be used for years without ill effect. Use of such drugs should be stopped at the first sign that they are adversely affecting a hyperactive child. Some recent work by Robert Schnackenberg seems to show that hyperactive children can be helped as much by the caffeine contained in coffee as by amphetamines. Just giving the child two to three cups of coffee a day to drink may make it unnecessary to administer the drugs.

The abuse of amphetamines—"speed," "meth," or "uppers"—is a very serious problem. A typical example of amphetamine abuse is the thoroughly respectable but overweight woman who begins taking "diet pills" to lose weight but continues to use them because they give her more energy to face the day. Another is the man who injects large quantities of a stimulant into his veins every three hours for a "run" of two to three days at a time. Still

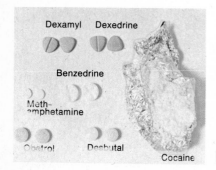

Figure 28.8 The stimulants shown here represent a broad class of drugs. The amphetamines (Dexamyl, Dexedrine, and so on) have legitimate uses in some instances: the treatment of chronic sleepiness, obesity, and hyperactivity in some children. Cocaine is medically employed as an anesthetic for the eyes and throat. Frequently these stimulants are abused to induce "highs" or to maintain an activity level that would be impossible without the energizing properties of the drugs. These drugs are not addictive, but they do readily induce psychological dependence. Their misuse can temporarily bring about a psychoticlike state.

another is the college student who relies on pills to stay awake all night to write a paper or cram for exams at the end of a semester. Although all these people are misusing drugs, society usually ignores the problems of stimulant abusers it thinks respectable—like the overweight woman—but condemns as criminal someone on society's fringe—like the "mainliner."

With continued use of amphetamines, anyone will develop **tolerance;** that is, he or she will need more of the drug to produce the same effect. As a person develops tolerance and needs higher and higher doses, he experiences marked side effects. He may become very suspicious and imagine people are after him or peering at him in a peculiar fashion. He may pick at imaginary objects on his skin, grind his teeth, or get caught up in meaningless, meandering trains of thought. A psychosis, at times indistinguishable from paranoid schizophrenia, may develop. There is no physical withdrawal syndrome, as there is with narcotics and barbiturates, but there are common reactions after the drug effects wear off—for example, a "rebound" depression, apathy and lethargy lasting many days, and periods of prolonged sleep and increased appetite. When the drug is injected, the person is subject to a number of very unpleasant additional side effects, such as liver disease and local and systemic infections that result from unsterile needles or impure chemicals.

HALLUCINOGENIC DRUGS

Lysergic acid diethylamide (LSD), psilocybin, dimethyltryptamine (DMT), mescaline (peyote), and "STP" (an amphetamine derivative) are examples of the class of drugs called **hallucinogenic drugs,** because one of their main effects is the production of hallucinations. (They are also referred to by some people as psychotomimetic, because the behavior of people under their influence appears to mimic the behavior of psychotics.) Actually, neither these two names nor the multitude of other labels attached to them—including the term "mind-expanding"—adequately describes their main effects on human beings.

The chemical structures of hallucinogenic drugs are diverse, and the drugs vary widely in their potency and duration of action as well as in how they are taken—for example, swallowed, smoked, or sniffed. LSD is the most potent of the lot, probably the one most commonly used, and certainly the one most written about. The other psychotogenic drugs, in large enough doses, can produce results similar to those of LSD. LSD is one of the most powerful drugs known. It is 100 times stronger than psilocybin, 4,000 times stronger than mescaline, and is effective in doses of millionths of a gram.

LSD has a curious history. In 1943 a Swiss pharmacologist, Albert Hoffman, working with ergot alkaloid drugs (the chemical family of LSD) accidentally ingested the drug and had the first recorded LSD trip, which, incidentally, he found unpleasant. LSD became popular in the early and mid-1960s, before its use was made illegal, and it had its boom year in 1967. Since then, the use of LSD has diminished significantly, although it is still a rather common "street" drug—illegally manufactured, sold, and ingested. The reason for the decrease in use is unknown.

What occurs when LSD is ingested? During the first fifteen to thirty minutes the person is likely to feel physical changes—among them nausea, gooseflesh, dilated pupils, and an increase in heart rate. Within the first three hours there may be changes in mood, perception, and thinking. During a "trip" a person can experience any number of mood states, often quite intense and rapidly changing. Many users of LSD feel that a person's mood immediately before taking the drug determines the kind of experience he will have—enjoyable or frightening.

Perceptual distortions and hallucinations are very common with LSD. A person often has varicolored visual hallucinations; he may find an absence of

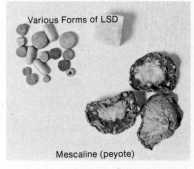

Various Forms of LSD

Mescaline (peyote)

Figure 28.9 Although there was hope that the hallucinogens would prove useful in the experimental study of the brain, this hope has not been fulfilled, and they presently have no clear clinical applications. LSD is one of the most potent psychoactive substances; a single dose of one millionth of a gram may exert its effects for up to twelve hours. Some tolerance for these drugs may be acquired but there is little danger of physical or psychological dependence. Their most serious dangers are the chance that they will trigger an acute psychosis or result in danger to the user's safety because of impaired judgment while under the drugs's effect.

Figure 28.10 Drawings done by a man under the influence of LSD. (A) Twenty minutes after the first dose the drug had not taken effect. If the dosage had been adequate, some physiological effects would have been noticed at this point. (B) A second dose was administered eighty-five minutes after the first. Twenty minutes after the second dose, the subject experienced the first alterations of perception and rapid changes of emotion. He saw the model correctly but had difficulty in controlling the wide, sweeping movements of his hand. (C) Shortly after the third drawing the subject stated: "The outlines of the model are normal, but those of my drawing are not. I pull myself together and try again: it's no good." (D) Two hours and forty-five minutes after the first dose, the subject experienced the most intense effects of the drug. He said: "The perspective of the room has changed, everything is moving . . . everything is interwoven in a network of color . . . The model's face is distorted to a diabolic mask." (E) Four hours and forty-five minutes after the first dose, the effects of the drug began to subside. An hour later the subject said: "It is probably because my movements are still too unsteady that I am unable to draw as I normally do . . . the intoxication is wearing off, but I can both feel it and see it ebbing and flowing about me (now it only reaches to my knees); finally, only an eddying motion remains." (F) Eight hours after the first dose the intoxication had worn off, except for a few small waves (for example, sudden distortions of faces from time to time). The subject felt bewildered and tired: "I have nothing to say about the last drawing, it is bad and uninteresting."

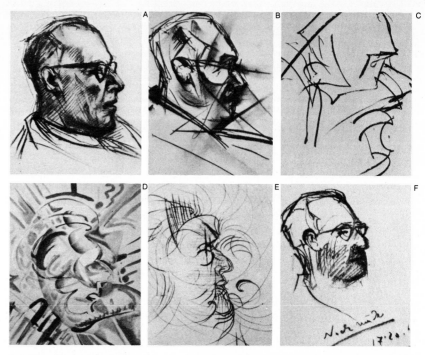

familiar form in objects or distortions in form that make familiar objects unrecognizable. For example, a wall may seem to pulsate or breathe; sounds may be "seen," and visual stimuli may be "heard." A person may experience a dissociation of the self into one being who watches the experience and another who feels it (see Chapter 13). He may experience time as slowed down or accelerated. A single stimulus may be the focus of attention for hours, perceived as changing or newly beautiful and fascinating. Such experiences can make a person feel like an explorer among familiar objects.

As measured by the ability to perform simple tests, the LSD user's thinking is impaired; however, he may feel that he is thinking more clearly and logically than ever before. Life-long problems may seem suddenly to be resolved, or the need to solve them may seem absurd. The person often experiences the "great truth" phenomenon—that is, he feels that previously hidden and ultimate inner truths have been revealed to him. Usually, when the trip is over, the magnitude of these discoveries shrinks, and the solutions turn out to be untenable. After three to five hours the experience begins to become less intense and often stabilizes; after six hours the hallucinations and illusions quite frequently disappear—if no complications occur.

But complications do occur, and not infrequently. Panic reactions are the most common of the unpleasant side effects, and they may be terrifying. Some users say a panic state, no matter how brief, is a part of every LSD trip. Persons who experience panic and later describe it often say that they felt trapped in the experience and were afraid that they would never get out or that they would go mad. At this point of fear, they would try to ignore, change, or otherwise rid themselves of the effects of the drug—and then panic when they could not succeed. The panic can lead to accidents, even suicide, in attempts to find relief. In addition, reports are common of LSD causing "flashbacks" (or brief recurrences of LSD experiences) even as late as three years after the last dose.

Persons who frequently take LSD are often said to be passive individuals who avoid active engagements in society. Although one almost never finds a well-functioning individual, whatever his work, to be a frequent user of LSD, it is very doubtful that taking LSD causes passivity or alienation. Instead, the reverse is probably true: Passive types and "dropouts"—fringe members of active society—are more likely to use LSD frequently. William McGlothin and David Arnold suggest that the use of LSD may be self-limiting; after chronic use, it seems that the drug's effects are no longer novel and become an ordinary experience.

A "bad trip" usually refers to the panic reaction described earlier. The best treatment, if the panic is not too severe, seems to be the comfort offered by friends and the security of pleasant familiar settings. Medical attention is sometimes necessary for very intense reactions. Infrequently, a person will need antipsychotic medications, and even hospitalization.

In the late 1960s there were reports that LSD caused damage to chromosomes, mutation of fetuses, and cancer. Since then, there has been contention among reports. Some reports still find support for these dangers; others refute the findings. From their own work and from their recent review of the literature, Norman Dishotsky and his colleagues state that ". . . pure LSD ingested in moderate doses does not damage chromosomes . . . does not cause detectable genetic damage, and is not a . . . carcinogen in man." (A carcinogen is a substance that causes cancer.) However, there is as yet no way to be certain that LSD is biologically safe.

LSD has been used experimentally by psychiatrists and psychotherapists to determine whether it might be of use in the treatment of behavioral problems. The main theory behind this practice has been that LSD lowers defenses and allows repressed feelings and memories to emerge into consciousness and be dealt with by patient and therapist. LSD has also been used to treat severely withdrawn or autistic children, alcoholics, and even people with terminal cancer. Although experimental work investigating the use of LSD as a therapeutic agent continues (mainly in Europe), existing evidence, gathered by Daniel X. Freedman and by Arnold Mandel and Louis West, among others, suggests that LSD is not a particularly effective psychotherapeutic agent and that for some people—a borderline schizophrenic, for example—it is potentially harmful.

At one time, especially in the 1950s, LSD was hailed by the psychiatric community as an agent that produced a "model psychosis"; that is, it induced a psychotic state similar to schizophrenia. It therefore promised to be the key to the biological secrets of schizophrenia. Unfortunately, this promise has not been fulfilled; the LSD "psychosis," on closer examination, proves to be quite distinct from schizophrenia.

Nonetheless, LSD is proving valuable in studying certain biochemical and physiological functions of the brain. Serotonin is an amine that, like noradrenaline, probably transmits nerve impulses in the brain. Serotonin may have important roles in the regulation of sleep and emotion. This amine is chemically similar to part of the LSD molecule. More important, the fact that LSD blocks the effects of serotonin on brain tissue may account for some of its effects in human beings. However, the exact mechanism by which LSD produces its behavioral effects has yet to be discovered.

MARIJUANA

Before 1960, the use of marijuana was restricted almost entirely to certain subcultures, such as jazz musicians and artists in big cities. By 1960, however, college students had discovered marijuana, and since that time the number of marijuana users in the United States has increased by a factor of perhaps ten thousand.

The active ingredient in marijuana is a complex molecule called tetrahydrocannabinol (THC), which only recently has been synthesized from inorganic materials. THC is found naturally in resin exuded from the flowers, leaves,

Marijuana

Figure 28.11 The active chemical in marijuana and hashish is tetrahydrocannabinol (THC); in various forms it may exert an effect for up to four hours. Marijuana produces relaxation, euphoria, and increased appetite, and may cause some general impairment of judgment and perception (although its effects on experienced users are unclear). There is no legitimate medical use for these substances at present, but research is being conducted on several possible medical uses. For example, ingesting THC seems to have the effect of relieving pressure in the eyeball caused by such diseases of the eye as glaucoma.

seeds, and stems of the female plants of the common weed *Cannabis sativa,* or Indian hemp. Marijuana is made by drying any part of the top of the female plant. Hashish is a gummy powder made only from the exuded resin. Both marijuana and hashish are commonly smoked, but they also can be cooked with food and eaten. Marijuana has been used as an intoxicant among Eastern cultures for many centuries; in some societies, marijuana and hashish are legally and morally acceptable, whereas alcohol is not.

Although the effects of the drug vary somewhat from person to person and also seem to depend on the setting in which it is taken, there is considerable consensus among regular users on how it affects them. When people smoke and inhale marijuana containing at least 0.5 gram THC, they undergo a condition known as "getting high." Most sensory inputs are greatly enhanced or augmented—music sounds fuller, colors are brighter, smells are richer, foods taste better, and sexual and other experiences are more intense. Users become elated, the world seems somehow more meaningful, and even the most ordinary events may take on a kind of extraordinary profundity. The time sense is greatly distorted. A short sequence of events may seem to last for hours. Users may become so entranced with a picture or painting that they sit and stare at it for many minutes. A musical phrase of a few seconds' duration may seem to stretch out in time until it becomes isolated from the rest of the composition and the hearer perceives it as never before.

As many users of marijuana have discovered, the drug can heighten unpleasant as well as pleasant experiences. If a person is in a frightened, unhappy, or paranoid mood when he takes the drug, he stands an excellent chance of having these negative experiences blown up out of proportion so that his world, temporarily at least, becomes very upsetting. Cases have been reported where marijuana appears to have helped precipitate psychological disturbances in people who were already unstable before they used it.

Despite the obvious need for careful research on marijuana, the first well-controlled scientific study of its effects on human beings was reported in 1968 by Andrew Weil, Norman Zinberg, and Judith Nelson. The participants in the study were seventeen college students in the Boston area who ranged in age from twenty-one to twenty-six. Nine of them had never smoked marijuana before; the other eight had smoked it many times. The inexperienced participants were put through four experimental sessions, each a week apart. During the first session they were taught the proper technique of smoking and inhaling with tobacco. At each subsequent session, they smoked one of three types of marijuana cigarettes. The first contained a high dose of marijuana (2.0 grams marijuana), the second, a low dose (0.5 gram marijuana), and the third, none at all. The participants were not told which type of cigarette they were smoking. The experienced marijuana smokers were tested only on the high-dose cigarettes.

Marijuana increased the heart rate slightly in all participants, seemed to cause little or no change in respiratory rate, and had no effect on blood-sugar level. No adverse reactions occurred in any of the participants; indeed, the reactions of several participants to the tobacco used during the preliminary training session were far more pronounced than any of the effects produced by marijuana.

Among the inexperienced participants, only one actually got high (that is, reported the typical euphoria), but all showed impaired performance on tests of both intellectual and motor skills soon after smoking marijuana. In many cases, the heavier the dose was, the greater the impairment was. Regular users of marijuana (all of whom got high during the sessions) showed *no* impairment either of intellectual function or of motor skill on the tests. Generally, the effects seemed to reach maximum intensity within half an hour after smoking. They were diminished after an hour and were almost gone at the end of three.

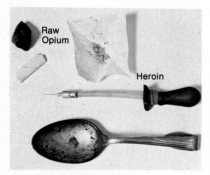

Figure 28.12 Narcotic drugs include opium and derivatives of opium, such as heroin and morphine. They act as central-nervous-system depressants, and morphine has been widely used medically for the relief of pain. (Synthetic chemicals have largely replaced opiates for this purpose.) Continued use of opiates causes dependence, tolerance, and addiction; in high concentrations, all of the opiates are lethal.

Unlike alcohol, marijuana has no known major physiological side effects. It appears to be difficult or impossible to inhale a fatal dose. There is no scientific evidence that marijuana is physiologically addictive. The question of "psychological dependence" is more difficult to assess. This term usually refers to a condition in which a person has a strong craving for something not biologically necessary for life. The difficulty with the idea of psychological dependence becomes obvious when you realize that, by this definition, most American children are addicted to peanut butter and most adults to television, sex, and bread.

There is also no evidence to suggest that marijuana is the first step on a path that inevitably leads to heroin or some other narcotic. On the other hand, it is quite probable that medical research will uncover some deleterious effects that result from the abuse of marijuana, because marijuana is a drug, and any drug can be dangerous.

NARCOTICS

One of the most serious problems facing this country is the growing abuse of narcotic drugs. Estimates of the number of narcotics addicts in the United States are in the hundreds of thousands, although some researchers, including Maurice Victor and Raymond Adams, have estimated that there are more than 400,000 addicts in New York alone. Twenty years ago, even ten years ago, it was easy for many people to ignore narcotics addiction because it was mainly confined to ghetto areas in large cities, like New York, Philadelphia, and Chicago. The larger cities still have the highest number of narcotics addicts, but the problem has spread to the suburbs and rural areas, to colleges, high schools, and even elementary schools. Hard-drug trade has long been illegal in the United States, but is so profitable that it is hard to eliminate.

There is nothing intrinsically evil about narcotics or their effects. **Morphine** is an old and widely used drug, invaluable in the field of medicine as a

Figure 28:13 The distinctions between drug dependence, drug tolerance, and drug addiction. Dependence (top) is a psychological effect. The drug becomes a significant part of the user's life, and its removal causes him to become irritable or nervous. (Note that, by this definition, such activities as watching television can cause dependence.) Tolerance is a physiological phenomenon: To continue reproducing a given effect, the user must take increasingly larger doses. Tolerance may occur with or without addiction. Addiction works more radical physiological changes. The user's metabolism comes to depend on the drug for normal functioning. If the level of the drug in the user's body falls below a certain level, physiological withdrawal symptoms occur.

Dependence

Tolerance

Addiction

potent treatment for pain. **Heroin** (diacetylmorphine), a derivative of morphine, was first introduced in this country as a *treatment* for morphine addiction and later declared illegal because it was so often found to be addicting itself. Heroin is abused more than morphine, perhaps because of its greater potency; it is approximately twice as strong as morphine.

Many psychological reasons for heroin use have been suggested, but none of them adequately explains it. The fact that many heroin users come from the lower classes certainly indicates the significance of social and economic factors. Narcotics addicts frequently say that they use heroin for its euphoric effect, that it produces a sense of well-being so complete that even the most trying of problems seems no problem at all. In this euphoric but torpid state a person may have no desire to do anything but stay high. In the acutely intoxicated state, heroin users may also become sleepy ("go on the nod") and feel heavy, exceptionally hot, or itchy. Occasionally there may be nausea or vomiting.

People develop tolerance to the euphoric effect of heroin. So the person who frequently uses the drug has to keep increasing the dose he injects in order to produce the same high. He then often becomes physically dependent or addicted; that is, he must continue using the drug to prevent the ugly and extremely painful experience of a withdrawal syndrome. Addicts can tolerate amazingly high doses of narcotics. For example, the average dose of morphine given for severe pain ranges from 8 to 15 milligrams, but some addicts can use as much as 2,000 to 3,000 milligrams daily.

If an addict cannot get enough heroin to satisfy his body's need, he will go through withdrawal. About ten hours after his last dose he will begin to feel the first symptoms. He may perspire, yawn, and have a runny nose and watery eyes. A few hours afterward he may fall into a shallow, uncomfortable state of drowsiness. Later, the addict often has severe cramps in his arms, legs, and back, and nausea, vomiting, diarrhea, weakness, and gooseflesh ("cold turkey"). The most intense symptoms occur forty-eight to seventy-two hours after the last dose; and with heroin, the syndrome usually runs its course within ten or twelve days.

The side effects of narcotics addiction can be severe. Packets of heroin sold on the street vary widely in their purity and concentration. If an addict accustomed to using four 15-milligram doses ("bags") of heroin per day unknowingly obtains a much purer sample, say, a 100-milligram bag, he may inject it, lapse into coma, and die of an overdose—sometimes within minutes. Also, because heroin is usually administered intravenously without sterile precautions and because the drug often contains gross impurities, people who use heroin or other injected drugs often develop hepatitis (a liver disease); blood-borne bacterial infections; skin infections, usually at the site of injection; tetanus; and infection of the heart valves (endocarditis). Nearly 2,000 people died from narcotics abuse in New York City in 1972, most probably from overdoses.

The treatment of severe chronic addiction to narcotics is usually effective only for brief periods. It is estimated that over 90 percent of chronic addicts return to their addiction within a year, although the results of some methadone-treatment programs, discussed below, may be better. Self-help groups such as Synanon, usually built around a live-in facility, claim that their form of therapy is successful. However, lack of data makes it hard to evaluate the claim.

In the past ten years **methadone** (Dolophine), a synthetic narcotic with pain-relieving properties similar to those of morphine, has come into wide use. It is commonly used to treat acute withdrawal from other opiates, and preliminary studies suggest that a methadone-maintenance program is effective in treating some narcotics addicts. Dr. Frances Gearing reported that 60

Figure 28.14 A heroin addict in withdrawal at a narcotics treatment center. Profound physiological effects last two or three days after the last ingestion of the drug. The complete readjustment of the body's homeostatic mechanisms to the absence of the drug takes ten or twelve days.

percent of addicts on methadone-maintenance programs give up other narcotics, stop criminal activities, obtain jobs, and lead relatively normal lives. This statistic is striking, especially when compared to the fact that only 10 percent of the addicts who pass through the federal treatment center at Lexington, Kentucky, do not relapse into addiction. The person receiving methadone treatment remains an addict, but he is addicted to methadone. Methadone, though addicting, is not much of a euphoriant; in fact, it blocks the euphoric effect of other narcotics, supposedly suppressing the "narcotic hunger" that chronic heroin addicts may develop. The results are sometimes very encouraging, and although the technique is open to many abuses and is difficult to control, many researchers and physicians believe that methadone is currently the best treatment for addiction; its use seems to be increasing. Research is now underway to find nonaddictive drugs that will block the effects of narcotics.

In Great Britain selected physicians maintain addicts on heroin as a means of coping with addiction. Although the British system is not without its problems, it seems to work out reasonably well. It has largely undercut the illicit traffic in narcotics, which is so profitable in this country. Also, the identified number of narcotics addicts in Great Britain is quite small compared to the number in the United States.

ALCOHOL AND ALCOHOLISM

This country's most serious drug problem is undoubtedly alcoholism. Around 9 million Americans have a severe drinking problem, according to a recent estimate—a staggering 5 percent of the total population. The cost in human suffering to the alcoholic and his family, and the money and the man-hours lost to the country, are almost impossible to measure. Nevertheless, certain facts about the effects of alcohol in this country are known: 50 percent or more of the deaths by automobile accident are traceable to alcohol; in half of all murders, either the person killed or the killer had been drinking; and about 13,000 people die each year of liver damage caused by alcohol.

Alcohol, administered slowly in small doses, might be called a social wonder drug. It relaxes inhibitions and makes many people gregarious. In larger amounts, it causes disorders of sensation and perception and stimulates behavior that violates common social codes. Because these effects are characteristic of drugs other than alcohol, the many who have fallen prey to alcohol in one generation might well have taken to other drugs had they been born at a different time or into another culture. The "closet alcoholic" of the suburbs —a fifty-five-year-old matron who drinks sherry all day, for example— might, in a big-city ghetto, have become a heroin addict instead. Similarly, the social drinkers of the older generation might, had they been born twenty-five years later, have relaxed with a joint of marijuana instead of a martini or two.

Many people think of alcohol as a stimulant because drinking is so often followed by loudness and hilarity, but alcohol is really a **chemical depressant** of the parts of the brain that suppress, control, and inhibit thoughts, feelings, and actions. In large enough quantities, it is a general anesthetic, capable of producing coma and death. As the depressant is administered in larger doses and accumulates in the body, there is a steady deterioration in all bodily functions. After enough alcohol has accumulated, it produces a state of unconsciousness. How rapidly this initial stimulation and consequent decline occur depends on how much and how rapidly alcohol enters the bloodstream— that is, on how strong the drinks are and how quickly they are consumed.

Three stages of alcoholism have been outlined by Elvin Jellinek. In the **prealcoholic** stage, the drinker discovers that alcoholic beverages reduce his tensions, give him self-confidence and a sense of courage, and ease psycho-

Figure 28.15 A young addict shooting up outside a London drugstore where he gets his heroin legally with a prescription. Views on the best way to deal with drug problems vary considerably from country to country. Methadone, a drug similar to heroin but taken orally, has been used widely in American drug-treatment programs.

logical and social pressure. In the **prodromal** stage, a beverage is turned into a drug. The drinker drinks heavily and furtively; he may begin to suffer memory blackouts and be unable to recall events during his drinking bouts. In the final, **crucial** stage, he drinks compulsively, beginning in the morning; he becomes inefficient in his work and may go on benders—drinking sprees—that last for weeks. He feels a powerful need for alcohol when he is deprived of it.

By this point, the problem drinker imbibes continuously, eats infrequently, and is unable to alter his compulsive self-drugging despite the anguish he causes others and the obvious destruction of his social life. Each alcoholic has a unique personality and temperament, and the drinking pattern differs accordingly. The so-called periodic alcoholic, for example, may not abide by general social rules of when, where, or how much to drink, yet he is able to stop drinking completely for brief periods of time when he feels it is crucial to do so. He may never progress to the most extreme form of alcoholism even though he bounces in and out of an alcoholic haze most of his life. In the most severe type of alcoholism, the victim builds up a tolerance for the drug. He may develop such a psychological dependence on alcohol that he feels normal only when he has been drinking, and he experiences severe and painful symptoms if he stops. Because of the toxic effects of alcohol on the body and the malnutrition that so often occurs with chronic alcoholism, the alcoholic is likely to develop many diseases affecting the liver and the brain and nervous system.

There are many theories about why some people become alcoholics and others do not. Some theorists suggest that an alcoholic's dependence stems from a biological malfunction. For example, George Winokur and others have found that families of patients with a manic-depressive psychosis, which many psychiatrists and scientists believe to be the result of a genetically caused biochemical malfunction, have a higher incidence of alcoholism than occurs in the general population. Also, because children of alcoholics tend to be alcoholic, some theorists assume a genetic cause.

Morris Chafetz groups alcoholics into two broad categories, the **reactive alcoholic** and the **addictive alcoholic.** He describes the reactive alcoholic as a person whose life prior to his excessive drinking was relatively normal, with reasonable success in his job and social life. He seems to use alcohol as a way of dealing with stressful situations or anxiety or to numb feelings of loss or disappointment. Although reactive alcoholics may keep drinking to the point of physical dependence, they seem to have a better chance to kick the habit than addictive alcoholics do. The family history of addictive alcoholics, on the other hand, usually turns out to have been chaotic, and in their own lives they have had little but failure, at school, at work, and in human relations. These people seem to adopt alcoholism as a life style; they may drink almost continuously, until they become so ill that they are physically unable to continue or until the habit kills them.

A usual first step in treating the alcoholic is to sober him up and try to make him healthier. Once restored to a reasonable state of health, the alcoholic may be given any of a number of treatments: drugs, traditional group or individual psychotherapy, or behavior therapy. Most of these efforts have been sadly ineffective. Alcoholics Anonymous, a lay group composed mainly of ex-alcoholics, has perhaps had slightly better luck. A variety of techniques have been used in attempts to help the alcoholic, but the commitment in terms of social resources has not been large. It is as if our culture has, over the years, developed a tolerance for the alcoholic. With the establishment of a National Institute for Alcoholism in Washington, however, the federal government has started a trend that may result in new and more successful methods of dealing with America's number one drug problem.

Figure 28.16 Alcohol is probably the most seriously abused drug in the United States. (A) An alcoholic is arrested for drunk driving; (B) he awaits trial; (C) while standing before the judge he suffers an attack of delirium tremens (DTs) caused by his body's physiological dependence on alcohol. Such events as drunken driving and experiencing DTs are relatively common in cases of severe alcoholism.

SUMMARY

1. The development of psychiatric drugs is one of the reasons that the number of patients in mental hospitals dropped by about half between 1955 and 1971. The drugs made it possible to treat many people outside of hospitals. The study of the psychological effects of drugs is called **psychopharmacology.**

2. The **antipsychotic drugs** are used to treat people with major psychotic disorders: schizophrenia, paranoid psychosis, or manic psychosis. Their main effects are to reduce thought disorder and to bring withdrawn patients back to experiencing the life around them and their own emotions. The drugs have less effect on hallucinations, paranoia, and hostility. The **phenothiazines** are the most commonly used.

3. The **antidepressant drugs** are not used to treat the common depressions that people experience as a result of divorce or death or business failure. Nor are they effective in treating neurotic depression. They are effective in increasing the activity level and raising the mood level of people suffering depressive reaction, a type of psychosis.

   a. Because only people with this severe depression are helped by antidepressants, and because many of these people have had no history of mental disorder before the onset of the depression, some clinicians believe that depressive reactions are a result of some abnormality in brain function.

   b. Research on how antidepressants work in the body has produced the **catecholamine hypothesis:** there are several chemicals in the brain called catecholamines; one of them is **noradrenaline (NA),** a hormone important in the functioning of the autonomic nervous system. It is hypothesized that too much NA in the brain can result in mania and too little, in depression. Thus, drugs that decrease the availability of NA in the brain might cause depression, and drugs that increase its availability might alleviate depression; moreover, drugs that produce an excess of NA might cause mania and drugs that block the effects of NA might alleviate mania.

4. **Sedatives,** the most common of which are **barbiturates,** were for a long time the most widely prescribed drugs for insomnia and anxiety. Although they are still prescribed to treat insomnia, they have been largely replaced in the treatment of anxiety by tranquilizers and specific **antianxiety drugs.** In the 1950s meprobamate, popularly known as Miltown or Equanil, was widely used, but more recently the antianxiety drugs diazepam (Valium) and chlordiazepoxide (Librium) have come into wide use. These drugs are not effective in treating major disorders, but they seem to be helpful in alleviating anxiety, although how they do so is not yet known. The major problem with these drugs is overuse. The major danger in using all of them except the family of drugs that contains Valium is physical dependence; untreated withdrawal from them can produce convulsions, shock, coma, and even death.

5. **Lithium salts** are a specific treatment for manic psychosis. Lithium lessens the hyperactivity and lowers exaggerated mood levels of manic patients within seven days of the start of treatment.

6. **Stimulants** include powerful drugs, such as amphetamines and methylphenidate (Ritalin), and less potent ones, such as caffeine and nicotine.

a. Stimulants are useful in treating so-called hyperkinetic children, although this effect seems paradoxical. The excessive physical activity and consequent inability to concentrate of hyperkinetic children are probably the result of some brain abnormality and stimulants seem to act as tranquilizers for these children. Recently it has been found that the caffeine contained in two or three cups of coffee per day can take the place of such stimulants as Ritalin in treating these children.

b. Stimulants are often abused; because they give extra energy, many people begin to rely on them for daily use. With continued use, people develop a tolerance to the drug and so take it in increasing amounts. Some users inject the drug into their bloodstreams. High doses produce such side effects as suspiciousness and meandering trains of thought and sometimes a psychosis much like paranoid psychosis.

7. **Hallucinogenic drugs** are so called because one of their main effects is the production of hallucinations. The group includes lysergic acid diethylamide (LSD) and mescaline (peyote). The best known of these is LSD, which has been a common "street" drug—illegally manufactured, sold, and ingested by certain segments of the population. In the 1970s its widespread use seemingly has begun to wane. Those who have taken it report that on a "good trip" the hallucinations and perceptual distortions experienced are "mind expanding." A panic reaction, in which people feel trapped in the experience and unable to get in touch with reality, is a common side effect and, if it is long-lasting, can cause the person undergoing the "bad trip" to have an accident. Although some researchers have attempted to use LSD as a psychotherapeutic agent or as a means by which to study schizophrenia, it has not proved to be effective for either of these uses. It does promise to be useful in studying certain biochemical functions of the brain.

8. **Marijuana** is made from parts of female plants of *Cannabis sativa,* or Indian hemp, a common weed. The number of smokers of marijuana in the United States is not known. Its effect is to heighten experience— whether pleasant or unpleasant seems to depend on the user's mood before taking it. In one controlled study reported in 1968, inexperienced users showed impairment of both motor and intellectual skills, whereas experienced users showed no such impairment. Also, of the inexperienced users, only one got high, whereas all the experienced users became euphoric. Marijuana has no known major physiological side effects.

9. **Narcotic drugs,** especially **morphine,** have important uses in the medical field, but the growing abuse of them, especially of **heroin,** a derivative of morphine, is a major social problem. The number of addicts is increasing not only in big-city ghetto areas but in suburban areas as well. Addicts become physiologically dependent on the drug and require increasingly large doses not only to produce the euphoric effect but to prevent the symptoms of withdrawal.

a. Most treatments of addicts have been unsuccessful. Recently, a drug called **methadone** has been used with some success. Although methadone is a synthetic narcotic and itself addicting, it does not have a euphoric effect; in fact, it blocks the euphoric effect of other narcotics. Addicts on methadone seem to be able to hold jobs and live quite normal lives. Although some researchers and physicians believe that methadone is the best treatment so far available for addiction, research is underway to discover a nonaddictive drug that will block the effects of narcotics.

10. **Alcoholism** is the most serious drug problem in the United States. Alcohol is a **chemical depressant** of the parts of the brain that suppress, control, and inhibit thoughts, feelings, and actions. In large enough quantities, it is a general anesthetic, capable of producing coma and death.

   a. Three stages of alcoholism have been described: In the **prealcoholic stage,** the drinker uses alcohol to reduce psychological tension and to gain a feeling of self-confidence. In the **prodromal stage,** alcohol becomes a needed drug, taken in large doses, and the drinker may suffer memory blackouts. In the **crucial stage,** the drinker consumes alcohol compulsively, eats infrequently, and becomes inefficient in his work. The malnutrition and toxic effects of chronic alcoholism can produce diseases affecting the liver and nervous system.

   b. The reasons for alcoholic dependence are not known. Some theorists suggest that it stems from a biological malfunction that may be genetically caused. Others suggest psychological causes; for example, Morris Chafetz believes that addictive alcoholics differ from reactive alcoholics. **Reactive alcoholics** have had a relatively normal life prior to their drinking; they begin drinking in reaction to some stressful situation. **Addictive alcoholics** have experienced only failure and adopt alcoholism as a life style; they have little chance of kicking the habit.

   c. Treatment of alcoholics has been largely unsuccessful; Alcoholics Anonymous, a self-help group composed of ex-alcoholics, has had some success.

SUGGESTED READINGS

Brecher, Edward M. (and the Editors of *Consumer Reports*). *Licit and Illicit Drugs.* Boston: Little, Brown, 1972. A remarkable book! Very thorough and very scholarly but *very* easy and enjoyable to read. Probably the best reference work for a general audience.

Chafetz, Morris E. "Addictions III: Alcoholism," in A. M. Freedman and H. I. Kaplan (eds.), *Comprehensive Textbook of Psychiatry.* Baltimore: Williams & Wilkins, 1967, pp. 1011–1026. A general review of alcoholism including theories about etiology and discussion about methods of treatment.

Goodman, Louis S., and Alfred Gilman. *The Pharmacological Basis of Therapeutics.* 4th ed. New York: Macmillan, 1970. Everything you wanted to know about drugs, including psychiatric drugs, narcotics, drug addiction, withdrawal, alcoholism, marijuana, and so on. Probably the best *scientific* reference book on the subject.

Grinspoon, Lester, Jack R. Ewalt, and Richard I. Shader. *Schizophrenia: Pharmacotherapy and Psychotherapy.* Baltimore: Williams & Wilkins, 1972. Interesting comparisons between the effects of medicines and psychosocial therapies in the treatment of chronic schizophrenia.

Snyder, Solomon H. *Uses of Marijuana.* New York: Oxford University Press, 1971. A lucid discussion of marijuana use. Written for a lay audience by an eminent neurobiologist.

Film Appendix

METHODOLOGY *(30 minutes, color)*

The film uses experiments from two widely different areas of psychology to make its points about the basic requirements for doing research: one from social psychology and one from physiological psychology.

The film opens by showing scenes from a number of experiments—one in the area of behaviorist learning theory, one in language development, one in the physiology of vision. Dr. Allen Parducci then explains how certain basic tenets of psychological research underlie these diverse kinds of experimentation. The points he cites as being basic (all of which are discussed in Chapter 2) are: (1) the necessity for psychologists to formulate their thinking into a *hypothesis* that will be *testable* by experiment; (2) the need to *isolate the particular features* of the environment whose effects the psychologists want to study from other features that might confuse their results; (3) the requirement that, in the actual experiment, psychologists hold *constant all features of the environment whose effects they are not studying;* and (4) the need to have *accurate measures*—and to employ them accurately—to ensure that the psychologists know how meaningful their results are. Dr. Parducci makes the point, also discussed in Chapter 2, that psychologists face the problem of *control.* That is, although *experimental work under laboratory conditions* offers the most control over the environment—in contrast to, say, such other methods as *observation* or *case study*—an organism's behavior under such conditions may bear little resemblance to its everyday behavior or its behavior in a more natural environment.

The film then shifts to a re-creation of Stanley Schachter's famous experiment on people's *need to affiliate,* or to be with others. This experiment is discussed at length in Chapter 20, in terms of its meaning for social psychology. The film supplements that discussion by showing the methodological considerations that went into constructing the experiment. We see scenes showing how the experiment was conducted, and Dr. Stanley Schachter simultaneously discusses how he arrived at his hypothesis and how he carefully designed his study to test it. He discusses such points as how he manipulated the *independent variable* (amount of fear); how he made sure that his *experimental and control groups* were chosen randomly; how he measured the *dependent variable* (using a carefully designed questionnaire). Dr. Schachter also discusses the *ethics of psychological experimentation* (discussed in Chapters 2 and 22).

The scene then shifts to the laboratory of Drs. Austin Riesen and John Crabtree, in the midst of their experiments on the *development of perception,* with kittens as their subjects. These experiments, as Dr. Riesen explains, are designed to give information about how the eyes, nervous system, and brain work, especially how they change over time as infants grow to adulthood. The experiments also shed some light on the *nativist-environmentalist controversy* that is a topic of Chapter 7; an earlier experiment by Dr. Riesen, using chimpanzees as subjects, is discussed in Chapter 7.

With animated sequences to clearly show the steps, the film describes the *experimental design:* groups of kittens are treated alike in all ways except that some groups are raised without light for a month, some for two months, some for three months, etc.; some (the controls) are raised in ordinary light conditions. A few kittens from each of the various groups are then shown being tested in the experimental apparatus, a series of black-and-white painted corridor walls with doors the kittens pass through to get to a food reward. Several observers watch the kittens and, using a measure arrived at earlier, *score* the kittens on how well they negotiate the apparatus. Dr. Riesen then explains the implications of the experimental results, both for their contribution to *theoretical knowledge* and for possible *applications* (see Chapter 2).

LEARNING *(30 minutes, color)*

This film shows actual demonstrations and laboratory experiments concerned with both learned and instinctive, or inherited, behavior. For example, *species-specific behavior,* as defined and explored in Chapter 3, is a behavior that is characteristic of a species. Jack Hailman has been studying the instinctual pecking behavior of young ring-billed gulls. The adults of the species have a characteristic black band, or ring, around their yellow bills that resembles some of the larger black insects that gulls feed upon. For young gulls, the black ring on the parents' bill is a *sign stimulus,* that is, it elicits the response of pecking. In taking food from the adult's bill, the young gull learns to feed on black insects.

Eckhard Hess shows experiments on the *sensitive* (or *critical*) *period* for *imprinting* in young ducklings, which occurs between twelve and sixteen hours after hatching. Once the young duck has imprinted to the model of an adult, it will climb over obstacles in order to follow that adult and may, when grown, attempt to mate with it.

Learning in very young infants is demonstrated by Lewis Lipsitt with a conjugate *reinforcement* procedure. An infant is given a rubber nipple, which is attached by a length of tubing to a doll hanging over the crib; when the infant sucks on the nipple, the doll moves. Lipsitt has found that the rate of sucking increases significantly as the infant learns that his sucking is associated with the doll's movement.

A silent-film sequence demonstrates how a child is *classically conditioned* to fear rabbits; how the fear response is *generalized* to all furry objects; and ultimately how it is *extinguished*. These processes are explored in Chapter 4.

Richard Mallot discusses *reinforcers* such as money, praise, and attention and their use to change the frequency of a response; discrimination training in pigeons and the process of *shaping* a bar-press response in a rat are demonstrated (see Chapter 4), as are the applications of such laboratory work on *operant reinforcement* to the development of *behavior-modification* programs for retarded children (see Chapter 27).

Nathan Azrin discusses the use, or misuse, of aversive conditioning (see Chapter 4). Aversive conditioning is extremely powerful in changing behavior by suppressing particular responses. But experiments with punishment have shown that it also produces aggression, a complex sequence of instinctive behaviors, as is demonstrated in the film of Azrin's famous pain-aggression experiment. In this experiment two rats trapped in a cage are repeatedly shocked and eventually turn on each other. The implications of this pain-aggression relationship are extensive, particularly with respect to societal use of punitive control in the form of prisons and jails.

B. F. Skinner comments that society is "stuck with punitive control . . . unwilling to change to more successful methods." Skinner also discusses his ideas about Utopian societies against a montage of scenes from a commune (see Chapter 19).

David McClelland discusses his studies of *motivation training,* which is aimed at teaching people to discriminate among their own motives. For example, the need for power is a motive very different from the need for achievement (see Chapter 16), although many people cannot discriminate between the two.

DEVELOPMENT *(31³/₄ minutes, color)*

This film opens with the birth of a child, which is the starting point for the field of *developmental psychology.* Only recently have psychologists become aware of the efficiency of the newborn's behavioral equipment.

Psychologist Jerome Kagan explains and demonstrates some of the very efficient motor reflexes and complex sensory capacities of the newborn child. Newborn infants, for example, can grasp with surprisingly great force, can suck, can orient themselves in space, and have an innate survival reflex to push away anything that covers their faces. Their sensory capacities allow them to scan a moving stimulus, as is demonstrated in an experiment Kagan carries out with infants between the ages of four and fourteen months. An infant reacts with surprise when a toy car rolls down a ramp and hits but fails to knock over a styrofoam figure it had knocked down several times before. Some of these phenomena are discussed in Chapter 7.

Mary Ainsworth discusses the relationship between the infant's emotional attachment to the caretaker (usually the mother) and his cognitive development, as well as the possibility of an innate or genetic factor in this emotional attachment. Contact comfort is discussed in Chapter 15.

In the text, cognitive development is the subject of Chapter 8. In the film, by way of further explanation, Patricia Greenfield discusses the young child's growth away from *egocentrism,* or self-orientation, and growth toward awareness of the viewpoint of others and of the environment. She demonstrates the development of this process of decentration by interpreting the one-word syntactical expressions of a two-year-old child, which move from self-oriented expression—such as "More!"—to expressions indicating awareness of things other than the self—such as "Mama!" These linguistic developments and their relation to cognitive development are discussed at length in Chapter 9.

Rhoda Kellogg speculates on the relationship between a child's development and the institutions to which his development is entrusted, and Jeffrey Travers discusses the development of language in children (see Chapter 9).

Ross Parke contributes his ideas on behavioral, or obedience, aspects of "morality" in children (as discussed in detail in Chapter 10), and a laboratory study with children of elementary-school age shows that the degree to which a child obeys depends on the rationale given the child for obeying. Such social influence is also analyzed in Unit VI, particularly in Chapter 22.

Charles Hampden-Turner challenges experiments such as the one shown, which was conducted by Dr. Parke; Hampden-Turner charges that hypotheses about human behavior based on experimental or laboratory models are weak because the subject's freedom to act is so narrowly and artificially defined by the situation and environment. (Chapter 2 also discusses this problem.) Elizabeth Douvan describes the radical growth that takes place in the period of adolescence. She holds that during adolescence the self is undergoing constant revision as the ego struggles to find stability and deal with the new impulses brought about by sexual maturity.

INFORMATION PROCESSING *(29¹/₂ minutes, color)*

Events at a large Hollywood cocktail party illustrate some aspects of human information processing. For example, a mnemonic, or memory device (see Chapter 5), makes it possible for a guest to remember easily one of the many telephone numbers he is given at the party. Actor-comedian David Steinberg gives him the word PUSHWOP, each letter of which represents a digit in the telephone number (787-4967).

Donald A. Norman acts as "anchorman" and comments on the action. He notes that the *memory system,* the *sensory system,* and *attention* are the major components of information processing that will be looked * in sequences from the party activities. In another party sequence, a man is confronted with conversation from several people at the same time. His growing confusion is obvious, and Norman comments that the man is experiencing information overload. The film shows that when two men with similar voices talk on similar topics, a person cannot attend to either conversation. But when two people with dissimilar voices, such as a man and a woman, talk at the same time on dissimilar topics, it is possible to attend to either one or the other of the conversations but not to both. The process of attention is also involved in the performance of a magician. Norman points out that the magician at the party forces his audience's attention to what he wants them to see. (Chapter 5 deals with attention, sensory gating, and feature extraction.)

In another sequence, the Stroop phenomenon is demonstrated as people try to call out the color of the ink in which color names are printed on a chart. Because each color name is printed in a different color (for example, the word "blue" is printed in yellow), the party-goers tend to read the spelled-out names of the colors, no matter how hard they try to call out the ink color. (Chapter 11 deals with these kinds of problems in processing of perceptual data.)

As in Chapter 5 of the text, two kinds of memory are distinguished: *short-term memory*, which can usually encompass about seven items in a set that may be remembered for about thirty seconds, and *long-term memory*. As illustrated by a waitress taking drink orders at the party, the problem is to transfer items from short-term to long-term memory. This is most easily accomplished through the use of memory devices, or mnemonics. Arthur Bornstein comments that it is the *encoding* of the information that really counts in how it is stored (and therefore retrieved), and he illustrates devices by which the waitress might remember each person's drink order.

According to Dr. Norman, a person's long-term memory encompasses an enormous amount of information, which is organized around "landmarks," or clusters of things one remembers well. When he does recall something, a person often can retrieve only part of what he wishes to recall and must try to piece together the remaining details. To exemplify this phenomenon—called *confabulation*—the film returns to the party magician; the audience sees only a partial image of the magician's actions and so fills in, in what seems to be a logical way, what it did not see.

People develop working *strategies* for finding organizational patterns in incoming information. These strategies are important to problem solving, as discussed in Chapter 6. However, strategies tend to become *set*, and people use them in trying to solve problems that require new strategies. Set and *functional fixedness* are discussed in Chapter 6 of the text.

THE SENSORY WORLD *(33 minutes, color)*

This film opens with a classic laboratory demonstration, conducted by Charles Harris of the Bell Telephone Research Laboratories, of the distorting effects and aftereffects of prism goggles on human vision; it explains how the effect of the goggles is actually caused by confusion in the brain's interpretation of visual stimuli rather than by any change in the eye itself—and by confusion of the *kinesthetic* sense. (Chapter 7's discussion of perceptual development includes a description of an experiment that used such goggles; kinesthesis is explained in Chapter 14.) How seeing is aided by the senses of hearing and touch is demonstrated in a sequence showing a baby playing with a toy.

The film moves on to look at how the senses work. In an animated sequence the mechanics of sight are shown, as described in Chapter 12. Another animated sequence demonstrates the sense of touch, and a third is a voyage through the ear. The processes of the touch and auditory senses are also described in Chapter 12.

As yet, scientists do not know too much about how sensory information is processed in the brain. What understanding they do have has come from animal experiments such as those conducted by Jerome Lettvin of the Massachusetts Institute of Technology. In 1959 Lettvin discovered that frogs process some visual information *before* it reaches the brain. He is now conducting research—a portion of which is demonstrated in the film—on the optic nerve fibers of the frog in an attempt to identify and classify fibers according to the kinds of information each fiber conveys.

At the Montreal Neurological Institute, neurosurgeon Wilder Penfield discusses *electrical stimulation* of the human brain. He talks with a woman who had undergone brain surgery eleven years earlier and asks her about her experiences during the electrical stimulation experiment he conducted during the surgery. (Chapter 13 discusses at length some of Dr. Penfield's work.)

Color blindness may take three forms: dichromatic color blindness involving the inability to perceive red and green; dichromatic color blindness involving the inability to perceive blue and yellow; and monochromatic color blindness, the most severe form, in which the individual is totally color blind. How the world looks to victims of each form is shown in the film and discussed at length in Chapter 12.

The psychological impact of impaired hearing is dramatically described in a statement written by Beethoven after he suffered a total loss of hearing at the age of twenty-eight.

The film concludes with a set of optical illusions, demonstrating how the brain can be tricked by ambiguous or "impossible" visual stimuli, such as the graphics created by M. C. Escher. The psychological reasons behind illusionary effects are explained in some detail in Chapter 11.

PERSONALITY *(29½ minutes, color)*

Martin Facey is a college senior majoring in art. His initial comment on being the subject of this film—an unfolding of many aspects of his individual personality—is "I think I'll learn a lot about myself . . . but if you come too close, I'll close you off."

Important tools in the study of a personality are the reactions of others to the individual. The film presents descriptions of Martin from people who know him well. His parents comment that he is more static than their other son and that he takes things hard and keeps his anger locked inside himself. His girl friend comments, from her perspective, that "his personality can be seen really well through his art." She describes Martin as a person who has difficulty expressing himself and his emotions verbally, who sometimes won't accept help from others, and who often seems tense in social situations. (Person perception is discussed in the text in Chapter 20.)

Martin talks about himself, his goals in art versus his goals as a person, and his potential as an artist. Self-portraits are accompanied by his own explanations of his mood and thoughts at the time he painted them. He explains that he "needs firm right angles . . . everything needs to be in its place . . . organized," which is a facet of his personality that is particularly evident in several of his self-portraits.

In describing himself, Martin explains that he feels there is something in "the background," something unexpressed that he holds against himself. Martin also feels that he has difficulty verbalizing emotions, which he thinks may stem from his family environment in which emotion was never expressed. He feels that his parents are very goal-oriented, and that their primary goal is to succeed. Martin is also aware that he drinks too much and says that drinking, for him, is a way to relax. Theories of personality against which Martin Facey's personality can be analyzed are presented in Chapters 18 and 19.

Psychologist Douglas Jackson discusses the process of *psychological assessment,* or testing (Chapter 17), and comments that every method by itself is fallible to some degree. But by using a variety of sources of information, including reports by the individual himself and by others, many of the weaknesses can be overcome. Jackson notes that the psychologist who makes the assessment is part of the assessment process, an instrument in the interpretation of data. He also discusses the three major considerations in formulating and designing a psychological test.

Psychologist Ira Nathanson discusses the structure and function of several standard psychological assessment tests—the *MMPI, Forer Sentence Completion, WAIS, Draw-a-Person, TAT,* and *Holtzman Inkblot Test*—and administers the tests to Martin Facey. Nathanson interprets the test results for Martin. His initial comment is that he feels Martin would probably have scored at least ten points higher on the IQ portion of the tests if he had been more relaxed. Nathanson feels that Martin's tension and anxiety, which he tends to hold within himself, prevent him from maximizing his potential. The test results also show that Martin uses intellectualization to hide or cover his expression of emotion. Nathanson describes Martin as perfectionistic, with the price of perfectionism being inner tension and worry. This push for unreachable perfection has been internalized from the family background of success as a goal orientation. The interpretation of the results of the projective tests show that Martin faces a conflict between passive dependency, which he equates with femininity, and aggressive independence. Nathanson also comments that Martin sees women mainly as sexual objects, and Martin agrees.

Finally, Martin comments on his test results and assessment and on the filming. He feels that Nathanson's assessment "is pretty accurate"—that he does in fact associate aggressiveness with masculinity and that he would like to be more aggressive. He considers his lack of aggression to be his only major "sex problem."

PREJUDICE: *Causes, Consequences, Cures* *(24 minutes, color)*

The film concentrates on a few major points that social psychologists have learned about the causes of prejudice, its consequences, and means of eliminating it. After the sound track plays several voices stating a number of common prejudices, Dr. James Blackwell, of the University of Massachusetts, defines what prejudice is. (Chapter 23 also defines prejudice, contrasting it with discrimination.) Dr. Elliot Aronson, of the University of Texas at Austin, proposes one explanation of the cause of prejudice based on the concept of social distance. He says that a person's relationship with others can be viewed as a set of concentric circles, the person in the middle and the first, smallest, circle representing his immediate family. The circles widen to include friends, acquaintances, people of the same religion or state, and at the outmost circles are people different from the person in their appearance, beliefs, values, etc. These are the people, Dr. Aronson says, against whom it is easiest to hold prejudices. In fact, if the prejudice is strong enough, it defines these people as subhuman.

As the screen shows numbers of familiar stereotypes, Dr. Carol Tavris, Assistant Managing Editor of *Psychology Today* magazine and Dr. Blackwell discuss the role of stereotypes in prejudice. Dr. Tavris makes the point (discussed at length in Chapter 21) that long-used and unchallenged stereotypes sometimes seem to point to characteristics of a group as inborn—and therefore unchangeable. Dr. Blackwell points to earlier stereotypes about blacks—propagated in literature, radio, and movies, some examples of which the film shows—as being docile, lazy, happy-go-lucky people. With th advent of civil rights laws and the black power movement, however, the stereotype has shifted, the more recent one painting all blacks as aggressive. Dr. Tavris discusses stereotypes that have been applied to women and to men. She points out the strong socializing effects such stereotypes can have. For instance, when most of the books children read portray all females in stereotypic jobs—nurse, mother, seamstress—and girls as only standing on the sidelines watching boys do adventurous things, then children come to believe that that is "the way things are supposed to be." (Chapter 21 discusses stereotypes as they affect sex roles, and Chapter 23 discusses them as they affect black-white relations in the United States.)

Dr. Blackwell then talks about the consequences of prejudice, especially in regard to Third World groups, whose color kept them from being easily assimilated into mainstream American culture. The prejudice led to acts of discrimination, both legal and illegal: segregation laws, the threat of violence for nonconforming minority individuals, and violence itself. (Chapter 23 discusses institutional racism.) The film shows documentary footage of such acts. Dr. Tavris discusses the consequences of prejudice for women. Perhaps the most serious consequence, Dr. Tavris says, is a psychological one: a loss of self-esteem. (Chapter 21 discusses the recent work of Matina Horner, who has uncovered a "Motive to Avoid Success" in many women.)

The psychologists then suggest several means of "curing" prejudice. Dr. Aronson, who is working with a school system in Texas, shows how a rearrangement of classroom practices eliminated prejudice against Mexican-American children, and the film shows a class there, focusing on one child. Dr. Aronson makes the point (discussed at length in Chapter 23) that when cooperation is substituted for competition (under the right circumstances) it is possible to reduce or eliminate intergroup prejudice and hostility. Dr. Blackwell makes the point that "laws can change the hearts and minds of men" (also discussed in Chapter 23). He uses the laws banning segregation in public accommodations as one example.

Dr. Tavris makes the final point in the film about prejudice: that everyone wants to be met on his own terms, to be treated—liked or disliked—as an individual.

DEPRESSION: *A Study in Abnormal Behavior* (27 minutes, color)

The film follows Helen, a young teacher, through a part of the course of her depressive episode. It shows her symptoms and behavior on the day that ends with her hospitalization, and follows her through part of her stay in the institution until the day of her release. The primary aim of the film is to give viewers a sense of the difference between "normal" psychological problems and abnormal behavior. Its commentary provides in-

sights to and explanations of Helen's behavior and treatment from a number of theoretical perspectives. As Chapters 24 and 25 point out, there are various points of view in abnormal psychology—some of them conflicting—about matters ranging from the definition of abnormality to what causes it. And, as Chapters 26 and 27 show, there are many different approaches to treatment, based on the various points of view described in Chapters 24 and 25, and on the personality theories described in Chapters 18 and 19.

The film opens with Helen finishing her day at school and driving home. After a trivial traffic problem, we see Helen about to burst into tears. The narrator points out that Helen has a history of depressive episodes, varying in length and severity, some of which have seriously disrupted her ability to function normally, both in her work responsibilities and in her personal relations.

A number of scenes focus on aspects of Helen's behavior that are symptomatic of severe depression. We see her having difficulty making a simple decision (whether to call her husband and ask him to pick up something for dinner); extremely depressed about a simple matter (her husband forgot to stop at the store); crying frequently (at various times throughout the day); being self-deprecating (saying that nothing she ever does turns out right); showing a severe lack of self-esteem (telling her husband that she's not worthy of his love); and finally an attempt at suicide. At various points in this part of the film, the narration points out how various psychological approaches would view Helen's problems. Included are: the statistical approach to defining abnormality (Chapter 24) and the behaviorist, or social-learning theory, definition of causes of abnormality (Chapter 25). The humanist and existential views of Helen's personality are also cited (see Chapter 19).

After Helen's suicide attempt, and her trip to the hospital in an ambulance, we see Helen being interviewed by a doctor, who tries to find out whether there is a history in Helen's family of mental illness and asks her to undergo a complete medical exam (see the discussion in Chapters 7 and 25 of hereditary and organic bases of abnormality). The doctor decides that, for her own safety, Helen should be admitted to a mental institution.

Helen is shown talking with a therapist whose point of view is a psychodynamic one (see Chapter 26); the doctors on the ward decide that Helen would benefit from electroconvulsive shock therapy, and certain drugs are prescribed for her (see Chapter 28). She is also assigned to a therapy group (see Chapter 26).

After more than two months in the hospital, Helen is shown leaving it—much improved. The narration makes the point that the institution in which Helen stayed is only one kind of treatment center and that current trends are to smaller community mental health centers (see Chapter 26).

Contributing Consultants

Catherine Brown, a free-lance writer and editor who lives on a mountain near Tucson, Arizona, received a B.A. from Oberlin College and an M.A. in English literature from New York University. Before becoming a free-lancer, she worked as an editor for Harcourt Brace Jovanovich in New York and for *Psychology Today* magazine in California. She is coeditor, with Jerome Kagan and Marshall Haith, of *Psychology: Adapted Readings.* Ms. Brown is responsible for the chapters Understanding Psychology: Introduction; and Doing Psychology: Methodology.

Joseph J. Campos obtained his Ph.D. at Cornell University and then did a two-year stint as a postdoctoral research fellow in psychophysiology at the Albert Einstein College of Medicine. He is now an Associate Professor of Psychology at the University of Denver, where he enjoys using psychophysiological methods to make inferences about what is going on in the heads of human infants. He contributed to the chapters Doing Psychology: Methodology; and Heredity and Environment.

Eric Fischer is working toward a doctorate in zoology at the University of California at Berkeley. In 1970 he received a B.S. from Yale University, where he became fascinated with the ethology of bats. His area of specialization may be described as the ecology and evolution of animal behavior. At present he is completing an investigation of the effect of population density on the sexual behavior of guppies. He is beginning his dissertation work on the behavioral ecology of synchronously hermaphroditic fish. Mr. Fischer contributed to the chapter Species-Specific Behavior: Ethology.

Kurt W. Fischer is an Assistant Professor of Psychology at the University of Denver and lives in the Rocky Mountains near Denver. He received a B.A. from Yale University and a Ph.D. from Harvard University and was previously a research psychologist at the Boston Children's Medical Center and at the Harvard Center for Cognitive Studies. His interests range broadly in psychology, but his present research focuses on intellectual and social development in children and the relationship between cognitive development and learning. In a book soon to be published, titled *Piaget, Learning, and Cognitive Development,* he presents a model for cognitive and social development in the first twenty years of life. Dr. Fischer served as general adviser to the third edition of *Psychology Today: An Introduction.* He contributed to many chapters and is particularly responsible for the following: Species-Specific Behavior: Ethology; Conditioning and Learning: Behaviorism; Thinking and Problem Solving: Cognitive Psychology; Development of Intelligence: Piaget's Theory; Perception: Principles and Processes; and Varieties of Consciousness.

Dennis L. Krebs received his B.A. from the University of British Columbia and his M.A. and Ph.D. from Harvard University. Dr. Krebs was Chairman of the Undergraduate Program in Social Relations at Harvard from 1970 to 1973. He has now returned to British Columbia to serve as Chairman of the Psychology Department at Simon Fraser University, where he will continue conducting research on altruism, empathy, social development, the self, and social interaction. His book about theories and research on moral development is scheduled for publication in 1975. Dr. Krebs is responsible for the chapters Social Development: The Case of Morality; Psychological Testing; and Adjustment and Disorder.

Joseph Lipinski is an Assistant Professor of Psychiatry at Harvard Medical School and a staff member of the Massachusetts General Hospital and of the McLean Hospital, where he runs an outpatient unit for Clinical-Biological Investigation. Dr. Lipinski studied neurology at the University of Copenhagen, Denmark, and at the National Hospital for Nervous Diseases at Queen Square, London. He received his M.D. from Jefferson Medical College, and he completed his specialty training in psychiatry at the Massachusetts General Hospital. His major field of interest is best described as neurobiology—biological research in psychiatry—especially exploration of biochemical hypotheses regarding schizophrenia. Dr. Lipinski is responsible for the chapter Drugs and Drug Therapy.

Darlene R. Miller is a staff psychologist at the Fort Logan Mental Health Center in Denver, Colorado, where she is a member of the Youth Services Psychiatric Team that provides direct and indirect treatment services to the State Division of Youth Services. She received her Ph.D. from the University of Massachusetts and has since pursued her interests in cognitive-developmental approaches to socialization, models of differential treatment, and juvenile delinquency. Dr. Miller is responsible for the chapter Individual and Group Psychotherapy, which she coauthored with Jeanne Phillips.

Carole Wade Offir, Associate Editor at *Psychology Today* magazine, has a B.A. from UCLA and a Ph.D. from Stanford University. Before moving into her current position, she taught at the University of New Mexico. She is a psycholinguist, with interests in comprehension of and memory for language, child language, and the comparison of visual/gestural and auditory/verbal languages. Dr. Offir contributed to the chapter Language Development.

L. Anne Peplau received her Ph.D. at Harvard University. She is currently Assistant Professor of Social Psychology at the University of California at Los Angeles. Her primary research interests are in the areas of interpersonal attraction and sex roles. Dr. Peplau is responsible for the chapter Patterns of Social Behavior: The Case of Sex Roles, and she coauthored Individuals and Their Groups with Zick Rubin.

Jeanne S. Phillips is Professor of Psychology at the University of Denver. After obtaining a Ph.D. from Washington University in St. Louis, she was a research associate, first at the Medical School at Washington University and

later at the Massachusetts General Hospital. Then she joined the faculty of the Medical School of the University of Oregon. She later taught at the University of Massachusetts in Amherst, where she was Director of Clinical Training, and then moved into her present position at the University of Denver. She is coauthor of *The Learning Foundations of Behavior Therapy* and *Statistics for Nurses.* Among her current interests are self-regulation, the effects of giving reinforcement, and broadening the conceptions of behavior modification. Dr. Phillips is responsible for the chapter Individual and Group Psychotherapy, which she coauthored with Darlene Miller, and she is also responsible for the chapter Behavior Therapy and Behavior Modification.

Bruce B. Platt received his B.A. from Dartmouth College and his Ph.D. from the University of California at Riverside, where he specialized in research on visual perception. While engaged in his dissertation research, he held an appointment as a Lecturer at the University. At present, Dr. Platt holds a Postdoctoral Fellowship at the University of Denver to investigate the visual abilities of newborn and infant children. His other research interests include sensory interactions and the perception of spatial relationships. Dr. Platt contributed to the chapter Sensation and the Senses.

N. Dickon Reppucci, Associate Professor of Community and Clinical Psychology at Yale University, received his Ph.D. from Harvard University. His major areas of interest are community psychology, especially work in correctional facilities and schools; behavior modification as a large-scale rehabilitative tool; and developmental problems of childhood and adolescence. Dr. Reppucci is responsible for the chapter Bases of Disorder, which he coauthored with Brian Sarata.

Zick Rubin is a Lecturer on Social Psychology in the Department of Psychology and Social Relations at Harvard University. He received his B.A. from Yale University and his Ph.D. from the University of Michigan. Dr. Rubin's current research focuses on the development of interpersonal bonds, both in brief encounters between strangers and in long-term relationships. A book describing some of this research, coauthored by Anne Peplau and Charles T. Hill, is in preparation. Dr. Rubin's other recent research concerns the antecedents and consequences of people's tendency to believe in a "just world." Dr. Rubin is author of *Liking and Loving: An Invitation to Social Psychology* and editor of *Doing Unto Others.* He is responsible for the chapters Person Perception and Interpersonal Attraction; and Attitude Change and Social Influence; and he coauthored with Anne Peplau Individuals and Their Groups.

Brian Sarata is an Assistant Professor of Psychology at the University of Nebraska in Lincoln. Upon completing his undergraduate studies at Bowdoin College, he served as a Peace Corps Volunteer in Niger, Africa, after which he worked for two years at Connecticut Valley Psychiatric Hospital in Middletown. He then did his graduate work at Yale University, where he received his Ph.D. degree. At present, Dr. Sarata's major areas of interest are in community psychology, job satisfaction and performance in human-service organizations, and the rehabilitative potential of correctional agencies. Dr. Sarata is responsible for the chapter Bases of Disorder, which he coauthored with N. Dickon Reppucci.

Sandra Scarr-Salapatek, Professor of Child Psychology at the University of Minnesota, received a Ph.D. from Harvard University. Her major interest in the origins of individual differences was first expressed in classical twin studies of personality and intellectual development and more recently in studies of the personal and intellectual similarities in adoptive and natural families. She taught at the University of Maryland and the University of Pennsylvania before going to Minnesota in 1970. As the mother of four individually different children she is convinced that both genetic and environmental differences are important in the study of development. Dr. Scarr-Salapatek contributed to the chapter Heredity and Environment.

Phillip Shaver, Assistant Professor of Psychology at Columbia University, received a B.A. from Wesleyan University and a Ph.D. from the University of Michigan. Most of his published work falls into two categories: experimental research in personality and social psychology; and political applications of human psychology. His recent experimental work has focused on fear of success and on consequences of self-awareness. His applied work has included consultation on the selection of juries for politically significant trials (he has also contributed to a study on how juries are selected in such trials) and studies of the impact of the Vietnam war on veterans, resisters, and deserters. He serves on the editorial boards of *Behavioral Science* and the *Journal of Experimental Social Psychology;* he is also coauthor of *Measures of Social Psychological Attitudes* and is currently writing a book on personality. Dr. Shaver is responsible for the chapters Thinking and Memory: Information Processing; Emotional Experience and Expression; Motivation and Action; Psychoanalytic Theories of Personality; and Alternative Conceptions of Personality.

Leonore Tiefer, Associate Professor of Psychology at Colorado State University, received both B.A. and Ph.D. degrees from the University of California at Berkeley. Physiological psychology is her main interest because it is a field that allows her to combine her preference for concreteness with her interest in medicine and her fascination with behavior. She teaches introductory- and physiological-psychology classes and various women's studies courses (a reflection of her involvement in the feminist movement). Dr. Tiefer contributed to the chapter Physiology, Drives, and Emotion.

Bibliography

1

American Psychological Association. "APA-Approved Doctoral Programs in Clinical, Counseling, and School Psychology: 1973," *American Psychologist,* 28 (1973), 844–845.

Brackbill, Yvonne. "Cumulative Effects of Continuous Stimulation on Arousal Level in Infants," *Child Development,* 42 (1971), 17–26.

Brackbill, Yvonne, *et al.* "Arousal Level in Neonates and Preschool Children Under Continuous Auditory Stimulation," *Journal of Experimental Child Psychology,* 4 (1966), 177–188.

Cates, Judith. "Baccalaureates in Psychology: 1969 and 1970," *American Psychologist,* 28 (1973), 262–264.

Dennis, Wayne. "Causes of Retardation Among Institutional Children: Iran," *Journal of Genetic Psychology,* 96 (1960), 47–59.

Eysenck, Hans J., W. Arnold, and **Richard Meili.** *Encyclopedia of Psychology.* New York: Herder and Herder, 1972. 3 vols.

Hebb, D. O. "What Psychology Is About," *American Psychologist,* 29 (1974), 71–79.

Jones, Donald R. *Psychologists in Mental Health: 1966.* Washington, D.C.: National Institute of Mental Health, Public Service Publications, No. 1984, 1969.

Kuhn, Thomas S. *The Structure of Scientific Revolutions.* 2nd ed. Chicago: University of Chicago Press, 1970.

Lunneborg, Patricia W., and **Vicki M. Wilson.** "Evaluation of an Interdepartmental Program to Train BA Psychologists." Unpublished report, University of Washington, 1973.

Marx, Melvin H., and **William A. Hillix.** *Systems and Theories in Psychology.* 2nd ed. New York: McGraw-Hill, 1973.

Salk, Lee. "Mother's Heartbeat as an Imprinting Stimulus," *Transactions of the New York Academy of Sciences,* 24 (1962), 753–763.

White, Burton L. "Child Development Research: An Edifice Without A Foundation," *Merrill-Palmer Quarterly of Behavior and Development,* 15 (1969), 49–79.

Wolman, Benjamin B. (ed.). *Handbook of General Psychology,* Englewood Cliffs, N.J.: Prentice-Hall, 1973.

2

Bronfenbrenner, Urie. "The Structure and Verification of Hypotheses," in U. Bronfenbrenner (ed.), *Influences on Human Development.* Hinsdale, Ill.: Holt, Rinehart and Winston, Dryden Press, 1972.

Campos, Joseph J. "Heart Rate: A Sensitive Tool for the Study of Infant Emotional Expression," in Lewis P. Lipsitt (ed.), *Psychobiology: The Significance of Infancy,* in press.

Cohen, Leslie J., and **Joseph J. Campos,** "Father, Mother, and Stranger as Elicitors of Attachment Behavior in Infancy," *Developmental Psychology,* 10 (1974), 146–154.

Editors of *Literary Digest.* "Landon, 1,293,669; Roosevelt, 972, 897," *Literary Digest,* 122 (October 31, 1936), 5–6.

Fenz, Walter D., and **Seymour Epstein.** "Gradients of Physiological Arousal in Parachutists as a Function of an Approaching Jump," *Psychosomatic Medicine,* 29 (1967), 33–51.

Fouts, Gregory T., and **Patricia Atlas.** "Reinforcing Effects of Mother and Stranger in Six- and Nine-Month-Old Infants." Paper read at the American Psychological Association Meeting, New Orleans, 1974.

Gergen, Kenneth J., Mary M. Gergen, and **William H. Barton.** "Deviance in the Dark," *Psychology Today,* 7 (October 1973), 129, 130.

Hays, William L. *Statistics for Psychologists.* New York: Holt, Rinehart and Winston, 1963.

Hudson, W. "Pictorial Depth Perception in Subcultural Groups in Africa" *Journal of Social Psychology,* 52 (1960), 183–208.

Javert, Carl T., and **James D. Hardy.** "Influence of Analgesics on Pain Intensity During Labor," *Anesthesiology,* 12 (1951), 189–215.

Kagan, Jerome, and **Howard A. Moss.** *Birth to Maturity.* New York: Wiley, 1962.

Kerlinger, Fred. *Foundations of Behavioral Research.* New York: Holt, Rinehart and Winston, 1964.

Kinsey, Alfred C., *et al. Sexual Behavior in the Human Female.* Philadelphia: Saunders, 1953.

Kinsey, Alfred C., Wardell B. Pomeroy, and **Clyde E. Martin.** *Sexual Behavior in the Human Male.* Philadelphia: Saunders, 1948.

Laing, R. D. *The Divided Self.* London: Tavistock, 1960.

Miller, Neal E. "Learning of Visceral and Glandular Responses," *Science,* 163 (1969), 434–445.

Miller, Neal E., and **Leo DiCara.** "Instrumental Learning of Heart Rate Changes in Curarized Rats: Shaping, and Specificity to Discriminative Stimulus," *Journal of Comparative and Physiological Psychology,* 63 (1967) 12–19.

Miller, Neal E., and **B. R. Dworkin,** "Visceral Learning: Recent Difficulties with Curarized Rats and Significant Problems for Human Research," in Paul A. Obrist, *et al.* (eds.), *Contemporary Trends in Cardiovascular Psychophysiology.* Chicago: Aldine-Atherton, in press.

Rheingold, Harriet L., and **Carol O. Eckerman,** "Fear of the Stranger: A Critical Examination," in Hayne W. Reese (ed.), *Advances in Child Development and Behavior.* Vol. 8. New York: Academic Press, 1973.

Rosenthal, Robert. *Experimenter Effects in Behavioral Research.* New York: Appleton-Century-Crofts, 1966.

———. "Experimenter Outcome-Orientation and the Results of the Psychological Experiment," *Psychological Bulletin,* 61 (1964), 405–412.

Scott, William, and **Michael Wertheimer.** *Introduction to Psychological Research.* New York: Wiley, 1962.

Sebastiani, Joseph A., and **James L. Foy.** "Psychotic Visitors to the White House," *American Journal of Psychiatry,* 122 (1965), 679–686.

Segall, Marshall H., Donald T. Campbell, and **Melville J. Herskovits.** "Cultural Differences in the Perception of Geometric Illusions," *Science,* 139 (1963), 769–771.

Simon, Charles W., and William H. Emmons. "Responses to Material Presented During Various Levels of Sleep," *Journal of Experimental Psychology*, 51 (1956), 89–97.

Sutcliffe, J. P., "'Credulous' and 'Skeptical' Views of Hypnotic Phenomena: Experiments in Esthesia, Hallucination, and Delusion," *Journal of Abnormal and Social Psychology*, 62 (1961), 189–200.

Tinbergen, Niko. *The Study of Instinct.* Fairlawn, N.J.: Oxford University Press, 1951.

Turner, Merle B. *Philosophy and the Science of Behavior.* New York: Appleton-Century-Crofts, 1967.

Wolff, Harold G., and Stewart Wolf. *Pain.* Springfield, Ill.: Charles C Thomas, 1948.

Zimmerman, J., and Hanus J. Grosz. "'Visual' Performance of a Functionally Blind Person," *Behavior Research and Therapy*, 4 (1966), 119–134.

3

Darwin, Charles. *On the Origin of Species by Means of Natural Selection.* Cambridge, Mass.: Harvard University Press, 1964 (orig. pub. in U.S. 1867).

———. *The Expression of the Emotions in Man and Animals.* Chicago: University of Chicago Press, 1967 (orig. pub. 1872).

Dethier, Vincent G. "Insects and the Concept of Motivation," in D. Levine (ed.), *Nebraska Symposium on Motivation.* Lincoln: University of Nebraska Press, 1966, pp. 105–136.

———. "The Hungry Fly," *Psychology Today*, 1 (June 1967), 64–72.

Eibl-Eibesfeldt, Irenäus. *Ethology: The Biology of Behavior.* New York: Holt, Rinehart and Winston, 1970.

Ekman, Paul, Wallace V. Friesen, and Phoebe Ellsworth. *Emotion in the Human Face: Guidelines for Research and an Integration of Findings.* Elmsford, N.Y.: Pergamon, 1972.

Fentress, John C. "Observations on the Behavioral Development of a Hand-Reared Male Timber Wolf," *American Zoologist*, 7 (1967) 339–351.

Hebb, D. O. "Alice in Wonderland or Psychology Among the Biological Sciences," in H. F. Harlow and C. N. Woolsey (eds.), *Biological and Biochemical Bases of Behavior.* Madison: University of Wisconsin Press, 1958, pp. 451–467.

———. *The Organization of Behavior.* New York: Wiley, 1949.

Hess, Eckhard. *Imprinting.* New York: Van Nostrand Reinhold, 1973.

Hinde, Robert A. *Animal Behavior.* 2nd ed. New York: McGraw-Hill, 1970.

Immelman, Klaus. "Comparative Studies of the Behavior of Domesticated Zebra Finches in Europe and the Wild Race in Australia," *Zeitschrift für Tierzuchtung und Zuchtungbiologie*, 77 (1962), 198–216.

Lenneberg, Eric. *The Biological Foundations of Language.* New York: Wiley, 1967.

Lorenz, Konrad Z. *Evolution and Modification of Behavior.* Chicago: University of Chicago Press, 1965.

———. *King Solomon's Ring.* New York: T. Y. Crowell, 1952.

———. *Studies in Animal and Human Behavior.* Robert Martin (tr.). Cambridge, Mass.: Harvard University Press, 1971. 2 vols.

Marler, Peter R., and William J. Hamilton. *Mechanisms of Animal Behavior.* New York: Wiley, 1966.

Matthews, Geoffrey Vernon Townsend. *Bird Navigation.* London: Cambridge University Press, 1955.

Schleidt, Wolfgang M. "Reaktionen von Truthühnern auf fliegende Raubvögel und Versuche zur Analyse ihrer AAM's" *Zeitung für Tierpsychologie*, 18 (1961) 534–560.

———. "Uber die Auslosung der Flucht vor Raubvogeln bei Truthuhnern," *Naturwissenschaften*, 48 (1961), 141–142.

Thorpe, W. H. *Bird Song.* London: Cambridge University Press, 1961.

Tinbergen, Niko. "Ethology's Warning," *Psychology Today*, 7 (March 1974), 65–80.

———. *The Study of Instinct.* New York: Oxford University Press, 1951.

Uexküll, Jakob J., von. *Umwelt und Innenwelt der Tiere.* 2nd ed. Berlin: Springer-Verlag, 1921.

Van Lawick-Goodall, Jane. *In the Shadow of Man.* Boston: Houghton Mifflin, 1971.

———. *My Friends, the Wild Chimpanzees.* Washington: National Geographic Society, 1967.

Von Frisch, Karl. *Bees: Their Vision, Chemical Senses, and Language.* Ithaca, N.Y.: Cornell University Press, 1950.

———. *The Dance Language and Orientation of Bees.* L. E. Chadwick (tr.). Cambridge, Mass.: Belknap Press of Harvard University Press, 1967.

Von Holst, Erich, and Ursula von Saint Paul. "Electrically Controlled Behavior," *Scientific American*, 206 (March 1962), 50–59.

4

Boring, Edwin. *A History of Experimental Psychology.* 2nd ed. New York: Appleton-Century-Crofts, 1950.

Dallenbach, Karl M. "Twitmyer and the Conditioned Response," *American Journal of Psychology*, 72 (1959), 633–638.

Hilgard, Ernest R., and Gordon H. Bower. *Theories of Learning.* 3rd ed. New York: Appleton-Century-Crofts, 1966.

Hull, Clark L. *Principles of Behavior: An Introduction to Behavior Theory.* New York: Appleton-Century-Crofts, 1943.

Kimble, Gregory A. *Hilgard and Marquis' Conditioning and Learning.* 2nd ed. New York: Appleton-Century-Crofts, 1961.

Konorski, Jerzy, and Stefan Miller. "On Two Types of Conditioned Reflex," *Journal of General Psychology*, 16 (1937), 264–272.

Lashley, Karl S. *The Neuropsychology of Lashley; Selected Papers.* F. A. Beach *et al.* (eds.). New York: McGraw-Hill, 1960.

McGuigan, Frank J., and D. Barry Lumsden. *Contemporary Approaches to Conditioning and Learning.* New York: Wiley, 1973.

Pavlov, Ivan P. *Conditioned Reflexes.* G. V. Anrep (tr.). London: Oxford University Press, 1927.

Premack, David. "Reinforcement Theory," in D. Levine (ed.), *Nebraska Symposium on Motivation.* Lincoln: University of Nebraska Press, 1965, pp. 123–180.

Reynolds, George S. *A Primer of Operant Conditioning.* Glenview, Ill.: Scott, Foresman, 1967.

Skinner, B. F. *About Behaviorism.* New York: Knopf, 1974.

———. *Behavior of Organisms: An Experimental Analysis.* New York: Appleton-Century-Crofts, 1938.

———. *Beyond Freedom and Dignity.* New York: Knopf, 1971.

———. *Walden Two.* New York: Macmillan, 1948.

Titchener, Edward B. *A Text-book of Psychology.* New York: Macmillan, 1923.

Twitmyer, Edwin B. "Knee-Jerks Without Stimulation of the Patellar Tendon," *Journal of Philosophy, Psychology and Scientific Methods*, 2 (1905), 63.

Watson, John B. *Behaviorism.* New York: Norton, 1930.

Watson, John B., and Rosalie Rayner. "Conditioned Emotional Reactions," *Journal of Experimental Psychology*, 3 (1920), 1–14.

Wolfe, John B. "Effectiveness of Token-Rewards for Chimpanzees," *Comparative Psychological Monographs*, 12 (1936), whole no. 5.

Wundt, Wilhelm. *An Introduction to Psychology.* Rudolph Pintner (tr.). London: George Allen & Co., 1912.

5

Atwood, George E. "An Experimental Study of Visual Imagination and Memory," *Cognitive Psychology*, 2 (1971), 290–299.

———. *Experimental Studies of Mnemonic Visualization.* Unpublished doctoral dissertation, University of Oregon, 1969.

Bower, Gordon H., and Michal C. Clark. "Narrative Stories as Mediators for Serial Learning," *Psychonomic Science*, 14 (1969), 181–182.

Brooks, Lee R. "The Suppression of Visualization by Reading," *Quarterly Journal of Experimental Psychology*, 19 (1967), 289–299.

Brown, Roger, and David McNeill. "The Tip of the Tongue Phenomenon," *Journal of Verbal Learning and Verbal Behavior*, 5 (1966), 325–337.

Haber, Ralph N. "Eidetic Images," *Scientific American*, 220 (April 1969), 36–44.

Horowitz, Leonard M., Anita K. Lampel, and Ruby N. Takanishi. "The Child's Memory for Unitized Scenes," *Journal of Experimental Child Psychology*, 8 (1969), 375–388.

Hubel, David H., and Torsten N. Wiesel. "Receptive Fields, Binocular Interaction, and Functional Architecture in the Cat's Visual Cortex," *Journal of Physiology*, 160 (1962), 106–154.

Hunter, Ian. *Memory.* Rev. ed. Baltimore: Penguin, 1964.

Inhelder, Baerbel. "Memory and Intelligence in the Child," in D. Elkind and J. H. Flavell (eds.), *Studies in Cognitive Development.* New York: Oxford University Press, 1969, pp. 337–364.

Jenkins, J. G. and Dallenbach, K. M. "Oblivescence During Sleep and Waking," *American Journal of Psychology*, 35 (1924), 605–612.

Lettvin, Jerome Y., *et al.* "What the Frog's Eye Tells the Frog's Brain," *Proceedings of the Institute of Radio Engineers*, 47 (1959), 1940–1951.

Lindsay Peter H., and **Donald A. Norman.** *Human Information Processing.* New York: Academic Press, 1972.

Lorayne, Harvey, and **Jerry Lucas.** *The Memory Book.* New York: Stein & Day, 1974.

Luria, Aleksandr R. *The Mind of a Mnemonist.* Lynn Solotaroff (tr.). New York: Basic Books, 1968.

McGeoch, J. A. *The Psychology of Human Learning.* New York: Longmans, Green, 1942.

Miller, George A. "The Magical Number Seven, Plus or Minus Two: Some Limits on Our Capacity for Processing Information," *Psychological Review,* 63 (1956) 81–97.

Miller, Goerge A., Eugene Galanter, and **Karl H. Pribram.** *Plans and the Structure of Behavior.* New York: Holt, 1960.

Murdock, Bennett B., Jr. "The Serial Position Effect of Free Recall," *Journal of Experimental Psychology,* 64 (1962), 482–488.

Norman, Donald A. *Memory and Attention.* New York: Wiley, 1969.

Osgood, Charles E. "Meaningful Similarity and Interference in Learning," *Journal of Experimental Psychology,* 36 (1946), 277–301.

Paivio, Allan. *Imagery and Verbal Process.* New York: Holt, Rinehart and Winston, 1971.

Pavio, Allan, and **Kalman Csapo.** "Picture Superiority in Free Recall: Imagery or Dual Coding?" *Cognitive Psychology,* 5 (1973), 176–206.

Peterson, Lloyd R., and **Margaret Peterson.** "Short-term Retention of Individual Verbal Items," *Journal of Experimental Psychology,* 58 (1959), 193–198.

Postman, Leo, and **Laura W. Phillips.** "Short-term Temporal Changes in Free Recall," *Quarterly Journal of Experimental Psychology,* 17 (1965), 132–138.

Powers, William T. *Behavior: The Control of Perception.* Chicago: Aldine, 1973.

Sperling, George. "The Information Available in Brief Visual Presentation," *Psychological Monographs,* 74 (1960), whole no. 498.

Tinker, Miles A. "Recent Studies of Eye Movements in Reading," *Psychological Bulletin,* 55 (1958), 215–231.

Tulving, Endel. "Episodic and Semantic Memory," in E. Tulving and W. Donaldson (eds.), *Organization of Memory.* New York: Academic Press, 1972.

Yates, Frances A. *The Art of Memory.* Chicago: University of Chicago Press, 1966.

Winograd, Terry. "Understanding Natural Language," *Cognitive Psychology,* 3 (1972), 1–191.

6

Bruner, Jerome S. "Origins of Problem-Solving Strategies in Skill Acquisition." Paper presented at the Nineteenth International Congress of Psychology, London, 1969.

———. "The Growth and Structure of Skill," in Kevin J. Connolly (ed.), *Mechanisms of Motor Skill Development.* New York: Academic Press, 1970.

Bruner, Jerome S. (ed.). *Beyond the Information Given: Studies in the Psychology of Knowing.* New York: Norton, 1973.

Chapman, Loren J., and **Jean P. Chapman.** "Atmosphere Effect Re-examined," in Peter C. Wason and Philip N. Johnson-Laird (eds.), *Thinking and Reasoning.* Baltimore: Penguin, 1968.

DeBono, Edward. *New Think: The Use of Lateral Thinking in the Generation of New Ideas.* New York: Basic Books, 1968.

DeSoto, Clinton, Marvin London, and **Stephen Handel.** "Social Reasoning and Spatial Paralogic," *Journal of Personality and Social Psychology,* 2 (1965), 513–521.

Duncker, Karl. "On Problem-Solving," L. S. Lees (tr.), *Psychological Monographs,* vol. 58 (1945), whole no. 270 (orig. pub. 1935).

Fischer, Kurt W. *Piaget, Learning, and Cognitive Development* (forthcoming).

———. *The Organization of Simple Learning.* Chicago: Rand McNally (forthcoming).

Harlow, Harry F. "The Formation of Learning Sets," *Psychological Review,* 56 (1949), 51–56.

Hebb. D. O. *The Organization of Behavior; A Neuropsychological Theory.* New York: Wiley, 1949.

Hebb, D. O., and **William R. Thompson.** "The Social Significance of Animal Studies," in Gardner Lindzey (ed.), *Handbook of Social Psychology.* Vol. 2. Reading, Mass.: Addison-Wesley, 1968.

Henle, Mary. "On the Relation Between Logic and Thinking," in Peter C. Wason and Philip N. Johnson-Laird (eds), *Thinking and Reasoning.* Baltimore: Penguin, 1968.

Krech, David (*nee* I. Krechevsky). "The Genesis of 'Hypotheses' in Rats," *University of California Publications in Psychology,* 6 (1932), 45–64.

Krech, David and **Richard S. Crutchfield.** *Elements of Psychology.* New York: Knopf, 1958.

Lindsay, Peter H., and **Donald A. Norman.** *Human Information Processing.* New York: Academic Press, 1972.

Luchins, Abraham S. "Classroom Experiments on Mental Set," *American Journal of Psychology,* 59 (1946), 295–298.

Mandler, George. "From Association to Structure," *Psychological Review,* 69 (1962), 415–426.

Mednick, Sarnoff A., and **Martha T. Mednick.** "A Theory and Test of Creative Thought," in G. Nielson (eds.), *Proceedings of the XIV International Congress of Applied Psychology.* Copenhagen: Munksgaard, 1961, pp. 40–47.

Newell, Allen, and **Herbert A. Simon.** *Human Problem Solving.* Englewood Cliffs, New Jersey: Prentice-Hall, 1971.

Newell, Allen, J. C. Shaw, and **Herbert A. Simon.** "Elements of a Theory of Human Problem Solving," *Psychological Review,* 65 (1958), 151–166.

Powers, William T. *Behavior: The Control of Perception.* Chicago: Aldine, 1973.

Premack, David. "Reinforcement Theory," in David Levine (ed.), *Nebraska Symposium on Motivation.* Lincoln: University of Nebraska Press, 1965.

———. "Toward Empirical Behavioral Laws: I. Positive Reinforcement," *Psychological Review,* 66 (1959), 219–233.

Staats, Arthur W. "Verbal and Instrumental Response-Hierarchies and Their Relation to Problem-Solving," *American Journal of Psychology,* 70 (1957), 442–446.

Tolman, Edward C. *Behavior and Psychological Man: Essays in Motivation and Learning.* Berkeley: University of California Press, 1951.

———. "Cognitive Maps in Rats and Men," *Psychological Review,* 55 (1948), 189–208.

Wason, Peter C., and **Philip N. Johnson-Laird.** *Psychology of Reasoning.* Cambridge, Mass.: Harvard University Press, 1972.

Wason, Peter C., and **Philip N. Johnson-Laird** (eds.). *Thinking and Reasoning.* Baltimore: Penguin, 1968.

7

Barltrop, Donald. "Transfer of Lead to the Human Foetus," in D. Barltrop (ed.), *Mineral Metabolism in Pediatrics.* Oxford: Blackwell Scientific Publications, 1969.

Berrill, Norman J. *The Person in the Womb.* New York: Dodd, Mead, 1968.

Bower, T. G. R. "The Visual World of Infants," *Scientific American,* 215 (December 1966), 80–92.

Burt, Sir Cyril, and **M. Howard.** "The Multi-Factorial Theory of Inheritance and Its Application to Intelligence," *British Journal of Statistical Psychology,* 9 (1956), 95–131.

Dobzhansky, Theodosius. "Differences Are Not Deficits," *Psychology Today,* 7 (December 1973), 96–102.

Friedmann, Theodore. "Prenatal Diagnosis of Genetic Disease," *Scientific American,* 225 (November 1971), 34–42.

Gibson, Eleanor J., and **Richard D. Walk.** "The Visual Cliff," *Scientific American,* 202 (April 1960), 64–72.

Gibson, James J. *The Senses Considered as Perceptual Systems.* Boston: Houghton Mifflin, 1966.

Hochberg, Julian, "Nativism and Empiricism in Perception," in Leo Postman (ed.), *Psychology in the Making: Histories of Selected Research Problems.* New York: Knopf, 1962.

Hubel, David H. "The Visual Cortex of the Brain," *Scientific American,* 209 (November 1963), 54–62.

Jensen, Arthur R. "The Differences Are Real," *Psychology Today,* 7 (December 1973), 79–88.

———. "How Much Can We Boost IQ and Scholastic Achievement?" *Harvard Educational Review,* 39 (1969), 1–123.

Kagan, Jerome S. "Inadequate Evidence and Illogical Conclusions," *Harvard Educational Review,* 39 (1969), 274–277.

Kallman, Franz J. "The Genetic Theory of Schizophrenia: An Analysis of 691 Schizophrenic Twin Index Families," *American Journal of Psychiatry,* 103 (1946), 309–322.

Kety, Seymour, David Rosenthal, Paul H. Wender, and **Fini Schulsinger.** "The Types and Prevalence of Mental Illness in the Biological and Adoptive Families of Adopted Schizophrenics," in D. Rosenthal and S. Kety (eds.), *The Transmission of Schizophrenia.* Elmsford, N.Y.: Pergamon, 1968, pp. 345–362.

Kohler, Ivo. "Experiments with Goggles," *Scientific American,* 206 (May 1962), 62–86.

McCall, Robert B., Mark I. Applebaum, and **Pamela S. Hogarty.** "Developmental Changes in Mental Performance," *Monographs of the Society for Research in Child Development,* 38 (1973), 1–63.

MacClearn, Gerald E., and **John C. DeFries.** *Introduction to Behavioral Genetics,* San Francisco: W. H. Freeman, 1973.

Meehl, Paul F. "Schizotaxia, Schizotypy, Schizophrenia," *American Psychologist,* 17 (1962), 827–831.

Needleman, Herbert L. "Lead Poisoning in Children: Neurologic Implications of Widespread Subclinical Intoxication," *Seminars in Psychiatry,* 5 (February 1973), 47–53.

———. "Subclinical Lead Exposure in Philadelphia Schoolchildren," *New England Journal of Medicine,* 290 (1974), 245–248.

Newman, Horatio H., Frank N. Freeman, and **Karl J. Holzinger.** *Twins: A Study of Heredity and Environment.* Chicago: University of Chicago Press, 1937.

Riesen, Austin H. "The Development of Visual Perception in Man and Chimpanzee," *Science,* 106 (1947), 107–108.

Rosenthal, David. *The Genetics of Psychopathology.* New York: McGraw-Hill, 1971.

———. "The Heredity-Environment Issue in Schizophrenia: Summary of the Conference and Present Status of Our Knowledge," in D. Rosenthal and S. Kety (eds.), *The Transmission of Schizophrenia.* Elmsford, N.Y.: Pergamon, 1968, pp. 413–427.

Rosenthal, David (ed.). *The Genain Quadruplets: Heredity and Environment in Schizophrenia.* New York: Basic Books, 1963.

Scanlon, John, and **J. J. Chisolm Jr.** "Fetal Effects of Lead Exposure," *Pediatrics,* 49 (1972), 145–146.

Scarr-Salapatek, Sandra. "Race, Social Class and IQ," *Science,* 174 (1971), 1285–1295.

———. "Unknowns in the IQ Equation," *Science,* 174 (1971), 1223–1228.

Senden, Marius von. *Space and Sight: The Perception of Space and Shape in the Congenitally Blind Before and After Operation.* New York: Free Press, 1960.

Skeels, Harold M. "Adult Status of Children with Contrasting Early Life Experiences: A Follow-up Study," *Monographs of the Society for Research in Child Development,* 31 (1966), 1–59.

Skeels, Harold M., and **Harold B. Dye.** "A Study of the Effects of Differential Stimulation on Mentally Retarded Children," *Proceedings and Addresses of the American Association on Mental Deficiency,* 44 (1939), 114–136.

Skodak, Marie, and **Harold M. Skeels.** "A Final Follow-up of One Hundred Adopted Children," *Journal of Genetic Psychology,* 75 (1949), 85–125.

Slater, Eliot. "A Review of Earlier Evidence on Genetic Factors in Schizophrenia," in D. Rosenthal and S. Kety (eds.), *The Transmission of Schizophrenia.* Elmsford, N.Y.: Pergamon, 1968.

Stratton, G. M. "Some Preliminary Experiments on Vision Without Inversion of the Retinal Image," *Psychological Review,* 3 (1896), 611–617.

Waddington, Conrad H. *The Strategy of the Genes.* London: Allen & Unwin, 1957.

8

Carey-Block, Susan. "Are Children Little Scientists with False Theories of the World?" Unpublished doctoral dissertation, Harvard University, 1971.

Evans, Richard I. *Jean Piaget: The Man and His Ideas.* New York: Dutton, 1973.

Fischer, Kurt W. *Piaget, Learning, and Cognitive Development* (forthcoming).

Furth, Hans G. *Piaget and Knowledge: Theoretical Foundations.* Englewood Cliffs, N.J.: Prentice-Hall, 1969.

Holt, John. *How Children Fail.* New York: Dell, 1970.

Inhelder, Baerbel, and **Jean Piaget.** *The Growth of Logical Thinking from Childhood to Adolescence.* New York: Basic Books, 1958.

Lewis, Richard. *Miracles: Poems by Children of the English-Speaking World.* New York: Simon and Schuster, 1966.

Piaget, Jean. *Biology and Knowledge.* Chicago: University of Chicago Press, 1971.

———. *The Construction of Reality in the Child.* New York: Basic Books, 1954.

———. *The Origins of Intelligence in the Child.* New York: International Universities Press, 1952.

Piaget, Jean, and **Baerbel Inhelder.** *The Psychology of the Child.* New York: Basic Books, 1969.

Potter, Mary. "On Perceptual Recognition," in Jerome S. Bruner, Rose R. Olver, and Patricia M. Greenfield (eds.), *Studies in Cognitive Growth.* New York: Wiley, 1966, pp. 103–134.

Smedslund, Jan. "The Acquisition of Conservation of Substance and Weight in Children. I. Introduction," *Scandinavian Journal of Psychology,* 2 (1961), 11–20.

Vygotsky, Lev S. *Thought and Language.* Cambridge, Mass.: M.I.T. Press, 1962.

Werner, Heinz. *Comparative Psychology of Mental Development.* Rev. ed. New York: International Universities Press, 1966.

Wohlwill, Joachim F. "Un essai d'apprentissage dans le domaine de la conservation du nombre," in Albert Morf et al. (eds.), *L'apprentissage des structures logiques. (Etudes d'Epistemologie Génétique).* Vol. 9. Paris: Presses Universitaires de France, 1959.

Wohlwill, Joachim F., and **Roland C. Lowe.** "Experimental Analysis of the Development of the Conservation of Number," *Child Development,* 33 (1962), 153–167.

9

Bar-Adon, Aaron, and **Leopold F. Werner.** *Child Language: A Book of Readings.* Englewood Cliffs, N.J.: Prentice-Hall, 1971.

Bellugi, Ursula. "The Emergence of Inflections and Negative Systems in the Speech of Two Children." Paper presented at the New England Psychological Association, 1964.

Berlin, Brent, and **Paul Kay.** *Basic Color Terms: Their Universality and Evolution.* Berkeley: University of California Press, 1969.

Bever, Thomas. "The Cognitive Basis for Linguistic Structures," in John Hayes (ed.), *Cognition and the Development of Language.* New York: Wiley, 1970.

Bloom, Lois M. *Language Development: Form and Function in Emerging Grammars.* Cambridge, Mass.: M.I.T. Press, 1970.

Bonvillian, John D., and **Keith E. Nelson.** "Sign Language Acquisition in a Mute Autistic Boy." Unpublished manuscript, Vassar College, 1974.

Brown, Roger. *A First Language: The Early Stages.* Cambridge, Mass.: Harvard University Press, 1973.

Brown, Roger, et al. *Psycholinguistics: Selected Papers by Roger Brown.* New York: Free Press, 1970.

Brown, Roger, and **Ursula Bellugi.** "Three Processes in the Child's Acquisition of Syntax," *Harvard Educational Review,* 34 (1964), 133–151.

Brown, Roger, and **Colin Fraser.** "The Acquisition of Syntax," in C. N. Cofer and B. S. Musgrave (eds.), *Verbal Behavior and Learning Problems and Processes.* New York: McGraw-Hill, 1963, pp. 158–209.

Brown, Roger, and **Camille Hanlon.** "Derivational Complexity and Order of Acquisition in Child Speech," in John R. Hayes (ed.), *Cognition and the Development of Language.* New York: Wiley, 1970.

Brown, Roger, Courtney Cazden, and **Ursula Bellugi.** "The Child's Grammar from I to III," in J. P. Hill (ed.), *Minnesota Symposium on Child Development.* Vol. 2. Minneapolis: University of Minnesota Press, 1969, pp. 28–75.

Cazden, Courtney. "Environmental Assistance to the Child's Acquisition of Grammar." Unpublished doctoral dissertation, Harvard University, 1965.

Chomsky, Noam. *Language and Mind.* New York: Harcourt Brace Jovanovich, 1972.

Eimas, Peter D., Einar R. Siqueland, Peter Jusczyk, and **James Vigorito.** "Speech Perception in Infants," *Science,* 171 (1971), 303–306.

Fleming, Joyce Dudney. "Field Report: The State of the Apes," *Psychology Today,* 7 (January 1974), 31.

Fouts, Roger S. "Use of Guidance in Teaching Sign Language to a Chimpanzee," *Journal of Comparative and Physiological Psychology,* 80 (1972), 515–522.

Furth, Hans. *Thinking Without Language.* New York: Free Press, 1966.

Gardner, R. Allen, and **Beatrice Gardner.** "Teaching Sign Language to a Chimpanzee," *Science,* 165 (1969), 664–672.

Hayes, Cathy. *Ape in Our House.* New York: Harper & Row, 1951.

Hayes, Keith J., and **Cathy Hayes.** "The Intellectual Development of a Home-Raised Chimpanzee," *Proceedings of the American Philosophical Society,* 95 (1951), 105–109.

Kellogg, Winthrop N., and **Luella A. Kellogg.** *The Ape and the Child.* New York: McGraw-Hill, 1933.

Lenneberg, Eric. *The Biological Foundations of Language.* New York: Wiley, 1967.

McNeill, David. "Developmental Psycholinguistics," in Franklyn L. Smith and George A. Miller (eds.), *The Genesis of Language: A Psycholinguistic Approach.* Cambridge, Mass.: M.I.T. Press, 1966.

Miller, George. *Communication, Language, and Meaning.* New York: Basic Books, 1973.

Orwell, George. *Nineteen Eighty-Four.* New York: Harcourt Brace Jovanovich, 1963.

Premack, Ann J., and **David Premack.** "Teaching Language to an Ape." *Scientific American,* 224 (October 1971), 92–99.

Rumbaugh, Daune M., Timothy V. Gill, and **E. C. von Glasersfeld.** "Reading and Sentence Completion by a Chimpanzee," *Science,* 182 (1963), 731–733.

Schlesinger, I. M. "Production of Utterances and Language Acquisition," in Dan Slobin (ed.), *The Ontogenesis of Language: Some Facts and Several Theories.* New York: Academic Press, 1971.

Whorf, Benjamin L. "Science and Linguistics," in J. Carroll (ed.), *Language, Thought and Reality.* Cambridge, Mass.: M.I.T. Press, 1956, pp. 207–219.

Wittgenstein, Ludwig. *Tractatus Logico-Philosophicus.* 2nd ed. New York: Humanities Press, 1963.

10

Aronfreed, Justin M. *Conduct and Conscience: The Socialization of Internalized Control Over Behavior.* New York: Academic Press, 1968.

————. "The Effects of Experimental Socialization Paradigms Upon Two Moral Responses to Transgression," *Journal of Abnormal and Social Psychology,* 66 (1963), 437–448.

Bandura, Albert. "Influence of Models' Reinforcement Contingencies on the Acquisition of Imitative Responses," *Journal of Personality and Social Psychology,* 1 (1965), 589–595.

————. *Social Learning and Personality Development.* New York: Holt, Rinehart and Winston, 1963.

Bandura, Albert, *et al.* "Imitation of Film-Mediated Aggressive Models," *Journal of Abnormal and Social Psychology,* 68 (1963), 8.

Bandura, Albert, and **Richard H. Walters.** *Social Learning and Personality Development.* New York: Holt, Rinehart and Winston, 1967.

Brown, Roger. *Social Psychology.* New York: Free Press, 1965.

Fischer, Kurt W. "Kohlberg's Stages of Moral Development." Unpublished manuscript, 1973.

Freud, Sigmund. *The Basic Writings of Sigmund Freud.* A. A. Brill (ed. and tr.). New York: Modern Library, 1938.

————. *Collected Papers.* Joan Riviere (tr.). New York: Basic Books, 1959.

————. "Dissection of the Psychical Personality," in James Strachey (ed.), *The Complete Works of Sigmund Freud.* Vol. 22. London: Hogarth Press, 1964.

————. "The Dissolution of the Oedipus Complex," in James Strachey (ed.), *The Complete Works of Sigmund Freud.* Vol. 19. London: Hogarth Press, 1961.

————. *The Ego and The Id.* Rev. ed. James Strachey (ed.). New York: Norton, 1962.

————. "Group Psychology and the Analysis of the Ego," in James Strachey (ed.), *The Complete Psychological Works of Sigmund Freud.* Vol. 18. London: Hogarth Press, 1955.

————. *An Outline of Psychoanalysis.* James Strachey (tr.). New York: Norton, 1949.

————. "Some Psychical Consequences of the Anatomical Distinction Between the Sexes," in James Strachey (ed.), *The Complete Works of Sigmund Freud.* Vol. 19. London: Hogarth Press, 1961.

Golding, William. *Lord of the Flies.* New York: Coward, McCann and Geoghegan, 1962.

Goslin, David A. (ed.). *Handbook of Socialization Theory and Research.* Chicago: Rand McNally, 1969.

Haan, Norma, M. Brewster Smith, and **Jeanne Block.** "Moral Reasoning of Young Adults: Political-Social Behavior, Family Background, and Personality Correlates," *Journal of Personality and Social Psychology,* 10 (1968), 183–201.

Hartshorne, Hugh, and **Mark A. May.** "Studies in Deceit," in *Studies in the Nature of Character.* Vol. 1. New York: Macmillan, 1928–1930.

Hartshorne, Hugh, Mark A. May, and **Julius B. Maller.** "Studies in Service and Self-Control," in *Studies in the Nature of Character.* Vol. 2. New York: Macmillan, 1928–1930.

Hartshorne, Hugh, Mark A. May, and **Frank K. Shuttleworth.** "Studies in the Organization of Character," in *Studies in the Nature of Character.* Vol. 3. New York: Macmillan, 1928–1930.

Hoffman, Martin. "Moral Development," in Paul H. Mussen (ed.), *Carmichael's Manual of Child Psychology.* Vol. 2. 3rd ed. New York: Wiley, 1970.

Hoffman, Martin, and **Herbert Saltzstein.** "Parent Discipline and the Child's Moral Development," *Journal of Personality and Social Psychology,* 5 (1967), 45–57.

Kohlberg, Lawrence. "The Development of Children's Orientation Toward a Moral Order; 1. Sequence in the Development of Moral Thought," *Vita Humana,* 6 (1963), 11–33.

————. "Development of Moral Character and Moral Ideology," in Martin L. Hoffman and Lois W. Hoffman (eds.), *Review of Child Development Research.* Vol. 1. New York: Russell Sage Foundation, 1964, pp. 383–431.

————. "Moral Development and Identification," in Harold Stevenson (ed.), *Child Psychology: The 62nd Yearbook of the National Society for the Study of Education.* Chicago: University of Chicago Press, 1963.

————. "Stage and Sequence: The Cognitive-Developmental Approach to Socialization," in David A. Goslin (ed.), *Handbook of Socialization Theory and Research.* Chicago: Rand McNally, 1969.

Krebs, Dennis L. "Altruism: An Examination of the Concept and a Review of the Literature," *Psychological Bulletin,* 73 (1970), 258–302.

Krebs, Richard L. "Some Relationships Between Moral Judgment, Attention, and Resistance to Temptation." Unpublished doctoral dissertation, University of Chicago, 1967.

McDougall, William. *An Introduction to Social Psychology.* New York: Barnes and Noble, 1960.

MacFarlane, Jean W., Lucile Allen, and **Marjorie P. Honzik.** *A Developmental Study of Behavior Problems of Normal Children Between Twenty-One Months and Four Years.* Berkeley: University of California Press, 1954.

Miller, Neal E., and **John Dollard.** *Social Learning and Imitation.* New Haven, Conn.: Yale University Press, 1941.

Mowrer, O. Hobart. *Learning Theory and the Symbolic Processes.* New York: Wiley, 1960.

Piaget, Jean. *The Child's Conception of the World.* London: Paul, Trench, Trubner, 1960.

Schachter, Stanley. "The Interaction of Cognitive and Physiological Determinants of Emotional State," in Leonard Berkowitz (ed.), *Advances in Experimental Social Psychology.* New York: Academic Press, 1964.

Sears, Robert R., Eleanor Maccoby, and **Harry Levin.** *Patterns of Child Rearing.* New York: Harper & Row, 1957.

Sears, Robert R., Lucy Rau, and **Richard Alpert.** *Identification and Child Rearing.* Stanford, Calif.: Stanford University Press, 1965.

Turiel, Elliot. "Developmental Processes in the Child's Moral Thinking," in Paul Mussen, Jonas Langer, and Martin Covington (eds.), *Trends and Issues in Developmental Psychology.* New York: Holt, Rinehart and Winston, 1969.

Whiting, John Wesley Mayhew. "Resource Mediation and Learning by Identification," in Ira Iscoe and Harold W. Stevenson (eds.), *Personality Development in Children.* Austin: University of Texas Press, 1960, pp. 112–126.

11

Allport, Floyd. *Theories of Perception and the Concept of Structure.* New York: Wiley, 1955.

Ames, Adelbert, Jr. "Visual Perception and the Rotating Trapezoidal Window," *Psychological Monographs,* vol. 65, no. 7 (1951), whole no. 234.

Arnheim, Rudolph. *Art and Visual Perception: A Psychology of the Creative Eye.* Berkeley: University of California Press, 1954.

Attneave, Fred. "Some Informational Aspects of Visual Perception," *Psychological Review,* 61 (1954), 183–193.

Boring, Edwin G. "A New Ambiguous Figure," *American Journal of Psychology,* 42 (1930), 444–445.

Bruner, Jerome S., and **Leo Postman.** "On the Perception of Incongruity: A Paradigm," *Journal of Personality,* 18 (1949), 206–223.

Carmichael, Leonard, Helena P. Hogan, and **A. A. Walter.** "An Experimental Study of the Effect of Language on the Reproduction of Visually Perceived Form," *Journal of Experimental Psychology,* 15 (1932), 73–86.

Gibson, James J. *The Perception of the Visual World.* Boston: Houghton Mifflin, 1950.

————. *The Senses Considered As Perceptual Systems.* Boston: Houghton Mifflin, 1966.

Gregory, R. L. *The Intelligent Eye.* New York: McGraw-Hill, 1970.

————. "Visual Illusions," *Scientific American,* 219 (November 1968), 66–76.

Hansel, C. E. M. *ESP: A Scientific Evaluation.* New York: Scribner's, 1966.

Held, Richard, and **Whitman Richards.** *Perception—Mechanisms and Models: Readings from Scientific American.* San Francisco: Freeman, 1972.

Helmholtz, Hermann von. "Über das Sehan des Menschen," *Vortrage und Reden,* 1 (1884), 365–396.

Hochberg, Julian. *Perception.* Englewood Cliffs, N.J.: Prentice-Hall, 1964.

Koestler, Arthur. *The Roots of Coincidence.* New York: Random House, 1972.

Koffka, Kurt. *Principles of Gestalt Psychology.* New York: Harcourt Brace Jovanovich, 1963.

Kohler, Ivo. "Experiment With Goggles," *Scientific American,* 206 (May 1962), 62–72.

Köhler, Wolfgang. *Gestalt Psychology.* New ed. New York: Liveright, 1970.

Lindsay, Peter H., and **Donald A. Norman.** *Human Information Processing.* New York: Academic Press, 1972.

Michotte, Albert E. *The Perception of Causality.* New York: Basic Books, 1963.

Miller, George A. "Decision Units in the Perception of Speech," *IRE Transactions on Information Theory,* 8 (1962), 81–83.

Rhine, Joseph B. *Extra-Sensory Perception.* Boston: Branden, 1964.

Roberts, Lawrence G. "Machine Perception of Three Dimensional Solids." Report →315. Cambridge, Mass.: Lincoln Lab, M.I.T., 1963.

Selfridge, Oliver G. "Pandemonium: A Paradigm for Learning," in *Symposium on the Mechanization of Thought Processes.* London: HM Stationery Office, 1959.

Senden, Marius von. *Space and Sight; the Perception of Space and Shape in the Congenitally Blind Before and After Operation.* Peter Heath (tr.). New York: Free Press, 1960.

Thiéry, Armand. "Üeber Geometrisch-Optische Tauschungen," *Philosophisches Studien,* 12 (1896), 67–126.

Thurstone, Louis L. *A Factorial Study of Perception.* Chicago: University of Chicago Press, 1944.

Wertheimer, Max. "Untersuchungen zur Lehre von der Gestalt," *Psychologisches Forschung,* 4 (1923), 301–350.

———. "Laws of Organization in Perceptual Forms," in Willis D. Ellis (ed.), *A Source Book of Gestalt Psychology.* New York: Humanities Press, 1950.

12

Beebe-Center, J. G. "Standards for the Use of Gust Scale," *Journal of Psychology,* 28 (1949), 411–419.

Békésy, Georg von. "Current Status of Theories of Hearing," *Science,* 123 (1956), 779–783.

———. *Experiments in Hearing.* E. G. Wever (ed. and tr.). New York: McGraw-Hill, 1960.

Bliss, James C., *et al.* "Optical-to-Tactile Image Conversion for the Blind," *IEEE Transaction on Man-Machine Systems,* MMS–11 (1970), 58–65.

Boring, Edwin G. *A History of Experimental Psychology.* 2nd ed. New York: Appleton-Century-Crofts, 1950.

———. *Sensation and Perception in the History of Experimental Psychology.* New York: Appleton-Century-Crofts, 1942.

D'Amato, M. R. *Experimental Psychology: Methodology, Psychophysics, and Learning.* New York: McGraw-Hill, 1970.

DeValois, Russell L. "Analysis and Coding of Color Vision in the Primate Visual System," *Cold Spring Harbor Symposia on Quantitative Biology,* 30 (1965), 567–579.

Fechner, Gustav T. *Elemente der Psychophysik.* Leipzig: Breitkopf und Härtel, 1860.

Geldard, Frank A. *The Human Senses.* 2nd ed. New York: Wiley, 1972.

Green, David M., and **John A. Swets.** *Signal Detection Theory and Psychophysics.* New York: Wiley, 1966.

Gross, Charles G., and **H. Phillip Zeigler** (eds.). *Readings in Physiological Psychology: Neurophysiology/Sensory Processes.* New York: Harper & Row, 1969.

Gulick, Walter L. *Hearing: Physiology and Psychophysics.* New York: Oxford University Press, 1971.

Hecht, Selig, Charles Haig, and **George Wald.** "The Dark Adaptation of Retinal Fields of Different Size and Location." *Journal of General Physiology,* 19 (1935), 321–328.

Henning, Hans. "Die Qualitätenreihe des Geschmacks," *Zeitschrift für Psychologie,* 74 (1916), 203–219.

MacNichol, Edward F., Jr. "Three-Pigment Color Vision," *Scientific American,* 211 (December 1964), 48–56.

Shaver, Phillip P., Robert Schurtman, and **Thomas Blank.** "Conflicts Between Firemen and Ghetto Dwellers," *Journal of Applied Social Psychology,* in press.

Stevens, S. S. "On the Psychophysical Law," *Psychological Review,* 64 (1957), 153–181.

———. "The Surprising Simplicity of Sensory Metrics," *American Psychologist,* 17 (1962), 29–39.

Uttal, William R. (ed.). *Sensory Coding: Selected Readings.* Boston: Little, Brown, 1972.

Wald, George. "Molecular Basis of Visual Excitation," *Science,* 162 (1968), 230–239.

Weber, Ernst H. *De Pulsu, Resorptione, Auditu et Tactu.* Leipzig: Köhler, 1834.

Wever, Ernest G. *Theory of Hearing.* New York: Wiley, 1949.

White, Benjamin W., *et al.* "Seeing with the Skin," *Perception and Psychophysics,* 7 (1970), 23–27.

Woodworth, Robert S., and **Harold Schlosberg.** *Experimental Psychology.* Rev. ed. New York: Holt, Rinehart and Winston, 1954.

13

Aserinsky, Eugene, and **Nathaniel Kleitman.** "Regularly Occurring Periods of Eye Motility and Concomitant Phenomena During Sleep," *Science,* 118 (1953), 273–274

Bogen, Joseph E. "The Other Side of the Brain: An Appositional Mind," *Bulletin of the Los Angeles Neurological Societies,* 34 (1969), 135–162.

Deikman, Arthur J. "Experimental Meditation," *Journal of Nervous and Mental Disease,* 136 (1963), 329–373.

Dement, William C. "An Essay on Dreams: the Role of Physiology in Understanding Their Nature," in F. Barron *et al., New Directions in Psychology.* Vol. 2. New York: Holt, Rinehart and Winston, 1965. pp. 135–257.

———. *Some Must Watch While Some Must Sleep.* San Francisco: W. H. Freeman, 1974.

Erickson, Milton H. "An Experimental Investigation of the Hypnotic Subject's Apparent Ability to Become Unaware of Stimuli," *Journal of Genetic Psychology,* 31 (1944), 191–212.

Faraday, Ann. *Dream Power.* New York: Coward, McCann and Geoghegan, 1972.

Freud, Sigmund. *The Interpretation of Dreams.* New York: Basic Books, 1955.

Fromm, Erich. "The Nature of Dreams," *Scientific American,* 180 (May 1949), 44–47.

Gazzaniga, Michael S. "The Split Brain in Man," *Scientific American,* 217 (August 1967), 24–29.

Hall, Calvin S. "What People Dream About," *Scientific American,* 184 (May 1951), 60–63.

Harrington, Alan. "A Visit to Inner Space," *Playboy,* 10 (November 1963), 84–88+.

Hebb, D. O. *The Organization of Behavior.* New York: Wiley, 1949.

Heron, Woodburn. "The Pathology of Boredom," *Scientific American,* 196 (January 1957), 52–56.

James, William. *The Principles of Psychology.* New York: Holt, 1890.

Jones, Richard M. *The New Psychology of Dreaming.* New York: Grune & Stratton, 1970.

Jouvet, Michel. "Recherches sur les structures nerveuses et les mecanismes responsables de differentes phases du sommeil physiologique," *Archives Italiennes de Biologie,* 100 (1962), 125–206.

———. "The Stages of Sleep," *Scientific American,* 216 (February 1967), 62–72.

Kales, Anthony (ed.). *Sleep—Physiology and Pathology: A Symposium.* Philadelphia: Lippincott, 1969.

Kasamatsu, Akira, and **Tomio Hirai.** "An Electroencephalographic Study on the Zen Meditation (Zazen)," *Folia Psychiatrica et Neurologica Japonica,* 20 (1966), 315–336.

Kinsbourne, Marcel, and **Jay Cook.** "Generalized and Lateralized Effects of Concurrent Verbalization on a Unimanual Skill," *Quarterly Journal of Experimental Psychology,* 23 (1971), 341–345.

Kleitman, Nathaniel. *Sleep and Wakefulness.* Rev. ed. Chicago: University of Chicago Press, 1963.

Mendelson, Joseph. "Physiological and Psychological Aspects of Sensory Deprivation—A Case Analysis," in Philip Solomon *et al., Sensory Deprivation.* Cambridge, Mass.: Harvard University Press, 1961.

Mischel, Walter, and **Frances Mischel.** "Psychological Aspects of Spirit Possession," *American Anthropologist,* 60 (1958), 249–260.

Naranjo, Claudio, and **Robert Ornstein.** *On the Psychology of Meditation.* New York: Viking, 1971.

Orne, Martin T. "The Nature of Hypnosis: Artifact and Essence," *Journal of Abnormal and Social Psychology,* 58 (1959), 277–299.

Ornstein, Robert. *The Psychology of Consciousness.* San Francisco: W. H. Freeman, 1972.

Osgood, Charles E., and **Zella Luria.** "A Blind Analysis of a Case of Multiple Personality Using the Semantic Differential," *The Journal of Abnormal and Social Psychology,* 49 (1954), 579–591.

Pattie, Frank A. "A Report of Attempts to Produce Uniocular Blindness by Hypnotic Suggestion," *British Journal of Medical Psychology,* 15 (1935), 230–241.

Penfield, Wilder. "Consciousness, Memory, and Man's Conditioned Reflexes," in K. H. Pribram (ed.), *On the Biology of Learning.* New York: Harcourt Brace Jovanovich, 1969, pp. 127–168.

———. *The Excitable Cortex in Conscious Man.* Springfield, Ill.: Charles C Thomas, 1958.

Penfield, Wilder, and **Lamar Roberts.** *Speech and Brain-Mechanisms.* Princeton, N.J.: Princeton University Press, 1959.

Shor, Ronald E., and **Martin T. Orne** (eds.). *The Nature of Hypnosis.* New York: Holt, Rinehart and Winston, 1965.

Sperry, Roger W. "The Great Cerebral Commissure," *Scientific American,* 210 (January 1964), 42–52.

———. "Hemisphere Deconnection and Unity in Conscious Awareness," *American Psychologist,* 23 (1968), 723–733.

———. "A Modified Concept of Consciousness," *Psychological Review,* 76 (1969), 532–536.

Stratton, Geroge M. "Some Preliminary Experiments on Vision Without Inversion of the Retinal Image," *Psychological Review,* 3 (1896), 611–617.

Tart, Charles T. (ed.). *Altered States of Consciousness.* New York: Wiley, 1969.

Teyler, Timothy J. *Altered States of Awareness.* San Francisco: W. H. Freeman, 1972.

Thigpen, Corbett H., and **Hervey M. Cleckley.** "A Case of Multiple Personality," *Journal of Abnormal and Social Psychology,* 49 (1954), 135–151.

Wallace, Robert K., and **Herbert Benson.** "The Physiology of Meditation," *Scientific American,* 226 (February 1972), 84–90.

Weil, Andrew. *The Natural Mind.* Boston: Houghton Mifflin, 1972.

14

Ahlskog, J. Eric, and **Bartley G. Hoebel.** "Overeating and Obesity from Damage to a Noradrenergic System in the Brain," *Science,* 182 (1973), 166–169.

Beach, Frank A. "Cerebral and Hormonal Control of Reflexive Mechanisms Involved in Copulatory Behavior," *Physiological Reviews,* 47 (1967), 289–316.

Bellows, R. T. "Time Factors in Water Drinking in Dogs," *American Journal of Physiology,* 125 (1939), 87–97.

Bermant, Gordon. "Copulation in Rats," *Psychology Today,* 1 (July 1967), 53|

Brady, Joseph V. "Ulcers in 'Executive' Monkeys," *Scientific American,* 199 (October 1958), 95–100.

Cannon, Walter B., and **A. L. Washburn.** "An Explanation of Hunger," *American Journal of Physiology,* 29 (1912), 441–454.

Deaux, Edward. "Thirst Satiation and the Temperature of Ingested Water," *Science,* 181 (1973), 1166–1167.

Deaux, Edward, and **Jan W. Kakolewski.** "Emotionally Induced Increases in Effective Osmotic Pressure and Subsequent Thirst," *Science,* 169 (1970), 1226–1228.

Delgado, José M. R. *Physical Control of the Mind: Toward a Psychocivilized Society.* New York: Harper & Row, 1969.

Ehrhardt, Anke A., Ralph Epstein, and **John Money.** "Fetal Androgens and Female Gender Identity in the Early-Treated Adrenogenital Syndrome," *Johns Hopkins Medical Journal,* 122 (1968), 161–167.

Epstein, Alan N. "Water Intake Without the Act of Drinking," *Science,* 131 (1960), 497–498.

Fitsimons, J. T. "Drinking by Rats Depleted of Body Fluid Without Increase in Osmotic Pressure," *Journal of Physiology,* 159 (1961), 297–309.

———. "The Role of Renal Thirst in Drinking Induced by Extracellular Stimuli," *Journal of Physiology,* 201 (1969), 349–368.

———. "Thirst," *Physiological Reviews,* 52 (1972), 468–561.

Fox, C. A., and **Beatrice Fox.** "A Comparative Study of Coital Physiology, with Special Reference to the Sexual Climax," *Journal of Reproduction and Fertility,* 24 (1971), 319–336.

French, Gilbert M. *Cortical Functioning in Behavior: Research and Commentary.* Glenview, Ill.: Scott, Foresman, 1973.

Gazzaniga, Michael S. "The Split Brain in Man," *Scientific American,* 217 (August 1967), 24–29.

Gold, Richard M. "Hypothalamic Obesity: The Myth of the Ventromedial Nucleus," *Science,* 182 (1973), 488–490.

Grossman, Sebastian P. *A Textbook of Physiological Psychology.* New York: Wiley, 1967.

Heath, Robert G. "Pleasure and Brain Activity in Man," *Journal of Nervous and Mental Disorders,* 154 (1972), 3–18.

Hubel, David H., and **Torsten N. Wiesel.** "Receptive Fields, Binocular Interaction and Functional Architecture in the Cat's Visual Cortex," *Journal of Physiology,* 160 (1962), 106–154.

Kimble, Daniel P. *Psychology as a Biological Science.* Pacific Palisades, Calif.: Goodyear, 1973.

Lang, Peter J., David G. Rice, and **Richard A. Sternbach.** "The Psychophysiology of Emotion," in N. S. Greenfield and R. A. Sternbach (eds.), *Handbook of Psychophysiology.* New York: Holt, Rinehart and Winston, 1973.

Luce, Gay G. *Body Time: Physiological Rhythms and Social Stress.* New York: Pantheon Books, 1971.

MacDonald, Robert M., Franz J. Ingelfinger, and **Helen W. Belding.** "Late Effects of Total Gastrectomy in Man," *New England Journal of Medicine,* 237 (1947), 887–896.

Masters, William H., and **Virginia E. Johnson.** *Human Sexual Response.* Boston: Little, Brown, 1966.

Money, John W., and **Anke A. Ehrhardt.** *Man and Woman, Boy and Girl.* Baltimore: Johns Hopkins University Press, 1972.

Olds, James, and **Peter Milner.** "Positive Reinforcement Produced by Electrical Stimulation of Septal Area and Other Regions of Rat Brain," *Journal of Comparative and Physiological Psychology,* 47 (1954), 411–427.

Penfield, Wilder, and **Theodore Rasmussen.** *The Cerebral Cortex of Man.* New York: Macmillan, 1950.

Schachter, Stanley, and **Jerome E. Singer.** "Cognitive, Social, and Physiological Determinants of Emotional State," *Psychological Review,* 69 (1962), 379–399.

Schachter, Stanley, Ronald Goldman, and **Andrew Gordon.** "Effects of Fear, Food Deprivation and Obesity on Eating," *Journal of Personality and Social Psychology,* 10 (1968), 91–97.

Schachter, Stanley, Ronald Goldman, and **Melvin Jaffa.** "Yom Kippur, Air France, Dormitory Food, and the Eating Behavior of Obese and Normal Persons," *Journal of Personality and Social Psychology,* 10 (1968), 117–123.

Selye, Hans. *The Stress of Life.* New York: McGraw-Hill, 1956.

Stellar, Eliot. "The Physiology of Motivation," *Psychological Review,* 61 (1954), 5–22.

Stevens, Charles F. *Neurophysiology: A Primer.* New York: Wiley, 1966.

Teitelbaum, Philip. "Sensory Control of Hypothalamic Hyperphagia," *Journal of Comparative and Physiological Psychology,* 48 (1955), 156–163.

Teitelbaum, Philip, and **Alan N. Epstein.** "The Lateral Hypothalamic Syndrome: Recovery of Feeding and Drinking after Lateral Hypothalamic Lesions," *Psychological Review,* 69 (1962), 74–90.

Warden, Carl J. *Animal Motivation: Experimental Studies on the Albino Rat.* New York: Columbia University Press, 1931.

Weiss, Jay M. "Effects of Coping Behavior in Different Warning-Signal Conditions on Stress Pathology in Rats," *Journal of Comparative and Physiological Psychology,* 77 (1971), 1–13.

Williams, Moyra. *Brain Damage and the Mind.* Baltimore: Penguin, 1970.

Wooldridge, Dean E. *The Machinery of the Brain.* New York: McGraw-Hill, 1963.

15

Allerand, Anne Marie. "Remembrance of Feelings Past: A Study of Phenomenological Genetics." Unpublished doctoral dissertation, Columbia University, 1967.

Arnold, Magda B. *Emotion and Personality.* New York: Columbia University Press, 1960.

Arnold, Magda B. (ed.). *Feelings and Emotions: The Loyola Symposium.* New York: Academic Press, 1970.

Ax, Albert F. "The Physiological Differentiation Between Fear and Anger in Humans," *Psychosomatic Medicine,* 15 (1953), 433–442.

Bard, Philip. "On Emotional Expression After Decortication with Some Remarks of Certain Theoretical Views: Part I," *Psychological Review,* 41 (1934), 309–329; "Part II," 41 (1934), 424–449.

Bridges, Katherine M. B. "Emotional Development in Early Infancy," *Child Development,* 3 (1932), 324–342.

Cannon, Walter B. *Bodily Changes in Pain, Hunger, Fear, and Rage.* New York: Appleton-Century-Crofts, 1929.

———. "The James-Lange Theory of Emotion: A Critical Examination and an Alternative Theory," *American Journal of Psychology,* 39 (1927), 106–124.

Cofer, Charles N. *Motivation and Emotion.* Glenview, Ill.: Scott, Foresman, 1972.

Darwin, Charles. *The Expression of the Emotions in Man and Animals.* Chicago: University of Chicago Press, 1965 (orig. pub. 1872).

Davitz, Joel R. *The Language of Emotion.* New York: Academic Press, 1969.

Ekman, Paul, and **Wallace V. Friesen.** "Constants Across Culture in the Face and Emotion," *Journal of Personality and Social Psychology,* 17 (1971), 124–129.

Ekman, Paul, Wallace V. Friesen, and **Phoebe Ellsworth.** *Emotion in the Human Face: Guidelines for Research and an Integration of Findings.* Elmsford, N.Y.: Pergamon, 1972.

Frois-Whitman, Jean. "The Judgement of Facial Expression," *Journal of Experimental Psychology,* 12 (1930), 113–151.

Goffman, Erving. *Interaction Ritual.* Garden City, N.Y.: Doubleday, 1967.

———. *The Presentation of Self in Everyday Life.* Garden City, N.Y.: Doubleday, Anchor, 1959.

Goodenough, Florence L. "Expression of the Emotions in a Blind-Deaf Child," *Journal of Abnormal and Social Psychology,* 27 (1932). 328–333.

Grossman, Sebastian P. *A Textbook of Physiological Psychology.* New York: Wiley, 1967.

Harlow, Harry F., and **Ross Stagner.** "Effect of Complete Striate Muscle Paralysis upon the Learning Process," *Journal of Experimental Psychology,* 16 (1933), 283–293.

Hebb, D. O. "Drives and the C.N.S.," *Psychological Review,* 62 (1955), 243–254.

———. "On the Nature of Fear," *Psychological Review,* 53 (1946), 259–276.

———. *The Organization of Behavior: A Neuropsychological Theory.* New York: Wiley, 1949.

Hulin, Wilbur S., and **Daniel Katz.** "The Frois-Whitman Pictures of Facial Expression," *Journal of Experimental Psychology,* 18 (1935), 482–498.

James, William. *The Principles of Psychology.* Vol. 2. New York: Holt, 1890.

———. *The Varieties of Religious Experience.* New York: Longmans, Green, 1910 (orig. pub. 1902).

Klineberg, Otto. "Emotional Expression in Chinese Literature," *Journal of Abnormal and Social Psychology,* 33 (1938), 517–520.

Lange, Carl G., and **William James.** *The Emotions.* Knight Dunlap (ed.). I. A. Haupt (tr.). Baltimore: Williams & Wilkins, 1922.

Lazarus, Richard S. "Emotions and Adaptation: Conceptual and Empirical Relations," in W. J. Arnold (ed.), *Nebraska Symposium on Motivation.* Vol. 16. Lincoln: University of Nebraska Press, 1968.

Lazarus, Richard S., and **Elizabeth Alfert.** "The Short-circuiting of Threat by Experimentally Altering Cognitive Appraisal," *Journal of Abnormal and Social Psychology,* 69 (1964), 195–205.

Leventhal, Howard. "Emotions: A Basic Problem for Social Psychology," in C. Nemeth (ed.), *Social Psychology: Classic and Contemporary Integrations.* Chicago: Rand McNally, 1974.

Lindsley, Donald B. "Emotion," in S. S. Stevens (ed.), *Handbook of Experimental Psychology.* New York: Wiley, 1951.

Mandler, George. "Emotion," in Roger Brown *et al.* (eds.), *New Directions in Psychology.* Vol. 1. New York: Holt, Rinehart and Winston, 1962.

Marañon, Gregorio. "Contribution à l 'Étude de l'Action Emotive de l'Adrenaline," *Revue Francaise d' Endocrinologie,* 2 (1924), 301–325.

Melzack, Ronald. "Irrational Fears in the Dog," *Canadian Journal of Psychology,* 6 (1952), 141–147.

Nisbett, Richard E., and **Stanley Schachter.** "The Cognitive Manipulation of Pain," *Journal of Experimental Social Psychology,* 2 (1966), 227–236.

Osgood, Charles E., George J. Suci, and **Percy Tannenbaum.** *The Measurement of Meaning.* Urbana: University of Illinois Press, 1957.

Overmier, J. Bruce, and **Martin E. P. Seligman.** "Effects of Inescapable Shock upon Subsequent Escape and Avoidance Responding," *Journal of Comparative and Physiological Psychology,* 63 (1967), 28–33.

Plutchik, Robert. *The Emotions: Facts, Theories, and a New Model.* New York: Random House, 1962.

Schachter, Stanley. *Emotion, Obesity and Crime.* New York: Academic Press, 1971.

Schachter, Stanley, and **Jerome Singer.** "Cognitive, Social, and Physiological Determinants of Emotional State," *Psychological Review,* 69 (1962), 379–399.

Schachter, Stanley, and **Ladd Wheeler.** "Epinephrine, Chlorpromazine, and Amusement," *Journal of Abnormal and Social Psychology,* 65 (1962), 121–128.

Schlosberg, Harold. "The Description of Facial Expression in Terms of Two Dimensions," *Journal of Experimental Psychology,* 44 (1952), 229–237.

———. "A Scale for the Study of Facial Expression," *Journal of Experimental Psychology,* 29 (1941), 497–510.

———. "Three Dimensions of Emotion," *Psychological Review,* 61 (1954), 81–88.

Seligman, Martin E. P. "Fall Into Helplessness," *Psychology Today,* 7 (June 1973), 43–48.

Seligman, Martin E. P., and **Steven F. Maier.** "Failure to Escape Traumatic Shock," *Journal of Experimental Psychology,* 74 (1967), 1–9.

Storms, Michael D., and **Richard E. Nisbett.** "Insomnia and the Attribution Process," *Journal of Personality and Social Psychology,* 16 (1970) 319–328.

Woodworth, Robert S. *Experimental Psychology.* New York: Holt, Rinehart and Winston, 1938.

Wynne, Lyman C., and **Richard L. Solomon.** "Traumatic Avoidance Learning: Acquisition and Extinction in Dogs Deprived of Normal Peripheral Autonomic Function," *Genetic Psychology Monographs,* 52 (1955), 241–284.

Yerkes, Robert M., and **J. D. Dodson.** "The Relation of Strength of Stimulus to Rapidity of Habit Formation," *Journal of Comparative Neurology & Psychology,* 18 (1908), 459–482.

Zillman, Dolf. "Excitation Transfer in Communication-Mediated Aggressive Behavior," *Journal of Experimental Social Psychology,* 7 (1971), 419–434.

16

Atkinson, John W. *An Introduction to Motivation.* New York: Van Nostrand Reinhold, 1958.

———. "Thematic Apperceptive Measurement of Motives Within a Context of Motivation," in J. W. Atkinson (ed.), *Motives in Fantasy, Action, and Society.* New York: Van Nostrand Reinhold, 1958.

Atkinson, John W. (ed.). *Motives in Fantasy, Action, and Society.* New York: Van Nostrand Reinhold, 1958.

Atkinson, John W., and **Norman T. Feather.** *A Theory of Achievement Motivation.* New York: Wiley, 1966.

Beach, Frank A. "The Descent of Instinct," *Psychological Review,* 62 (1955), 401–410.

Birch, David, and **Joseph Veroff.** *Motivation: A Study of Action.* Belmont, Calif.: Brooks/Cole, 1966.

Butler, Robert A. "Curiosity in Monkeys," *Scientific American,* 190 (February 1954), 70–75.

———. "Discrimination Learning by Rhesus Monkeys to Visual Exploration Motivation," *Journal of Comparative and Physiological Psychology,* 46 (1953), 95–98.

Cofer, Charles N. *Motivation and Emotion.* Glenview, Ill.: Scott, Foresman, 1972.

Feather, Norman T., and **J. G. Simon.** "Reactions to Male and Female Success and Failure in Sex-linked Occupations: Impressions of Personality, Causal Attributions and Perceived Likelihood of Different Consequences," *Journal of Personality and Social Psychology,* 1974, in press.

Harlow, Harry F. "The Nature of Love," *American Psychologist,* 13 (1958), 673–685.

Harlow, Harry F., and **Stephen J. Suomi.** "The Nature of Love—Simplified," *American Psychologist,* 25 (1970), 161–168.

Harlow, Harry F., and **Robert R. Zimmermann.** "Affectional Responses in the Infant Monkey," *Science,* 130 (1959), 421–432.

Heron, Woodburn. "The Pathology of Boredom," *Scientific American,* 196 (January 1957), 52–56.

Horner, Matina S. "Femininity and Successful Achievement: A Basic Inconsistency," in J. Bardwick, E. M. Douvan, M. S. Horner, and D. Gutmann (eds.), *Feminine Personality and Conflict.* Belmont, Calif.: Brooks/Cole, 1970.

———. "Toward an Understanding of Achievement-Related Conflicts in Women," *Journal of Social Issues,* 28 (1972), 157–175.

Hull, Clark. *Principles of Behavior: An Introduction to Behavior Theory.* New York: Appleton-Century-Crofts, 1943.

Lewin, Kurt. *Field Theory in Social Science.* D.Cartwright (ed.). New York: Harper & Row, 1951.

McClelland, David C. *The Achieving Society.* New York: Van Nostrand Reinhold, 1961.

McClelland, David C., *et al.* *The Achievement Motive.* New York: Appleton-Century-Crofts, 1953, pp. 336, 340, 344.

McClelland, David C., and **David G. Winter.** *Motivating Economic Achievement.* New York: Free Press, 1969.

Maccoby, Eleanor E. "Women's Intellect," in S. M. Farber and R. H. L. Wilson (eds.), *The Potential of Women.* New York: McGraw-Hill, 1963, pp. 24–39.

Mandler, George, and **Seymour B. Sarason.** "A Study of Anxiety and Learning," *Journal of Abnormal and Social Psychology,* 47 (1952), 166–173.

Maslow, Abraham H. *Motivation and Personality.* New York: Harper & Row, 1954.

Murray, Henry. *Exploration in Personality.* New York: Oxford University Press, 1938.

Olds, James, and **Marianne E. Olds.** "Drives, Rewards, and the Brain," in Frank Barron *et al.* (eds.), *New Directions in Psychology.* Vol. 2. New York: Holt, Rinehart and Winston, 1965.

Schachter, Stanley. *Emotion, Obesity and Crime.* New York: Academic Press, 1971.

Schachter, Stanley, and **Jerome Singer.** "Cognitive, Social, and Physiological Determinants of Emotional State," *Psychological Review,* 69 (1962), 379–399.

Spence, Janet T., and **Kenneth W. Spence.** "The Motivational Components of Manifest Anxiety: Drive and Drive Stimuli," in C. D. Spielberger (ed.), *Anxiety and Behavior.* New York: Academic Press, 1966.

Spence, Kenneth W., and **Janet A. Taylor.** "Anxiety and Strength of the UCS as Determiners of the Amount of Eyelid Conditioning," *Journal of Experimental Psychology,* 42 (1951), 183–188.

Tolman, Edward C. *Collected Papers in Psychology.* Berkeley: University of California Press, 1951.

Tresemer, David. "Fear of Success: Popular, but Unproven," *Psychology Today,* 7 (March 1974), 82–85.

Weiner, Bernard. *Theories of Motivation: From Mechanism to Cognition.* Chicago: Markham, 1972.

White, Robert W. "Motivation Reconsidered: The Concept of Competence," *Psychological Review,* 66 (1959), 297–333.

Winchel, Ronald, Diane Fenner, and **Phillip Shaver.** "Impact of Coeducation on 'Fear of Success' Imagery Expressed by Male and Female High School Students," *Journal of Educational Psychology,* 1974, in press.

17

Allison, Joel, *et al.* *The Interpretation of Psychological Tests.* New York: Harper & Row, 1968.

Allport, Gordon W., and **Philip E. Vernon.** *Studies in Expressive Movements.* New York: Macmillan, 1932.

Allport, Gordon W., Philip E. Vernon, and **Gardner Lindzey.** *Study of Values: Manual.* Boston: Houghton Mifflin, 1960.

American Psychological Association. *Standards for Educational and Psychological Tests and Manuals.* Washington, D.C.: American Psychological Association, 1966.

Anastasi, Anne. *Psychological Testing.* 3rd ed. New York: Macmillian, 1968.

Beck, Samuel J. *Rorschach's Test. Vol. I: Basic Processes.* 3rd ed. New York: Grune & Stratton, 1961.

Binet, Alfred, and **Theodore Simon.** *The Development of Intelligence in Children (the Binet-Simon Scale).* Elizabeth S. Kite (tr.). Baltimore: Williams & Wilkins, 1916.

Buros, Oscar K. (ed.). *Personality Tests and Reviews.* Highland Park, N. J.: Gryphon Press, 1970.

Campbell, David P. *Manual for the Strong-Campbell Interest Inventory.* Stanford, Calif.: Stanford University Press, 1974.

Dahlstrom, William Grant, and **George S. Welsh.** *An MMPI Handbook: A Guide to Use in Clinical Practice and Research.* Minneapolis: University of Minnesota Press, 1960.

Galton, Sir Francis. *Inquiries into Human Faculty and Its Development.* New York: Dutton, 1911.

Hathaway, Starke R., and **John Charnley Mc-Kinley.** "A Multiphasic Personality Schedule (Minnesota): I. Construction of the Schedule," *Journal of Psychology,* 10 (1940), 249–254.

Jackson, Douglas N. *Manual for the Personality Research Form.* Goshen, N.Y.: Research Psychologists Press, 1967.

Jensen, Arthur R. "How Much Can We Boost I.Q. and Scholastic Achievement?" *Harvard Educational Review,* 39 (1969), 1–123.

Machover, Karen A. *Personality Projection in the Drawing of the Human Figure: A Method of Personality Investigation.* Springfield, Ill.: Charles C Thomas, 1949.

McReynolds, Paul (ed.). *Advances in Psychological Assessment.* Palo Alto, Calif.: Science & Behavior Books, 1968.

Meehl, Paul E. *Clinical Versus Statistical Prediction: A Theoretical Analysis and Review of the Evidence.* Minneapolis: University of Minnesota Press, 1954.

Murray, Henry A., *et al.* *Explorations in Personality.* New York: Oxford University Press, 1938.

Office of Strategic Services Assessment Staff. *Assessment of Men.* New York: Holt, Rinehart and Winston, 1948.

Postman, Leo, Jerome S. Bruner, and **Elliott McGinnies.** "Personal Values as Selective Factors in Perception," *Journal of Abnormal and Social Psychology,* 43 (1948), 142–154.

Schachtel, Ernest G. *Experiential Foundations of Rorschach's Test.* New York: Basic Books, 1966.

Spranger, Eduard. *Types of Men; the Psychology and Ethics of Personality.* Paul J. W. Pigors (tr.). New York: Johnson Reprint Corp., 1966.

Stern, William. *The Psychological Methods of Testing Intelligence.* Guy M. Whipple (tr.). Baltimore: Warwick & York, 1914.

Terman, Lewis M. *The Measurement of Intelligence.* Boston: Houghton Mifflin, 1916.

Terman, Lewis M., and **Maud A. Merrill.** *Measuring Intelligence.* Boston: Houghton Mifflin, 1937.

———. *Stanford-Binet Intelligence Scale: Manual for the Third Revision, Form L–M.* Boston: Houghton Mifflin, 1973.

Wechsler, David. *The Measurement and Appraisal of Adult Intelligence.* 14th ed. Baltimore: Williams & Wilkins, 1958.

———. *Wechsler Adult Intelligence Scale Manual.* New York: Psychological Corporation, 1955.

18

Adler, Alfred. "Individual Psychology," in Carl A. Murchison (ed.), *Psychologies of 1930.* Worchester, Mass.: Clark University Press, 1930, pp. 395–405.

———. *What Life Should Mean to You.* Alan Porter (ed.). Boston: Little, Brown, 1931.

Breuer, Josef, and **Sigmund Freud.** *Studies on Hysteria.* New York: Basic Books, 1957 (orig. pub. 1937).

Erikson, Erik H. *Childhood and Society.* New York: Norton, 1950.

———. *Gandhi's Truth on the Origins of Militant Nonviolence.* New York: Norton, 1969.

———. *Young Man Luther: A Study in Psychoanalysis and History.* New York: Norton, 1968.

Freud, Sigmund. *Civilization and Its Discontents.* James Strachey (ed. and tr.). New York: Norton, 1962 (orig. pub. 1930).

———. *Collected Papers.* Joan Riviere (tr.). New York: Basic Books, 1959.

———. *The Interpretations of Dreams.* James Strachey (ed. and tr.). New York: Basic Books, 1955 (orig. pub. 1900; first English edition, 1913).

———. *New Introductory Lectures on Psychoanalysis.* James Strachey (ed. and tr.). New York: Norton, 1965 (orig. pub. 1933).

Fromm, Erich. *Escape from Freedom.* New York: Holt, Rinehart and Winston, 1941.

———. *Man for Himself: An Inquiry into the Psychology of Ethics.* New York: Holt, Rinehart and Winston, 1947.

Hall, Calvin S., and **Gardner Lindzey.** *Theories of Personality.* 2nd ed. New York: Wiley, 1970.

Jung, Carl G. *Collected Works.* Princeton, N. J.: Princeton University Press, 1967.

———. *Psychological Reflections.* Princeton, N.J.: Princeton University Press, 1972.

Levy, Leon H. *Conceptions of Personality.* New York: Random House, 1970.

Maddi, Salvatore R. *Personality Theories: A Comparative Analysis.* 2nd ed. Homewood, Ill.: Dorsey Press, 1972.

Maddi, Salvatore R. (ed.). *Perspectives on Personality: A Comparative Approach.* Boston: Little, Brown, 1971.

Mahl, George F. *Psychological Conflict and Defense.* New York: Harcourt Brace Jovanovich, 1971.

Rapaport, David. "The Theory of Ego Autonomy: A Generalization," in Salvatore Maddi (ed.), *Perspectives on Personality.* Boston: Little, Brown, 1971.

Reich, Wilhelm. *Character-Analysis.* New York: Noonday, 1949.

Sullivan, Harry Stack. *The Fusion of Psychiatry and Social Science.* New York: Norton, 1964.

———. *The Interpersonal Theory of Psychiatry.* New York: Norton, 1953.

White, Robert W. "Competence and the Psychosexual Stages of Development," in Marshall R. Jones (ed.), *Nebraska Symposium on Motivation.* Lincoln: University of Nebraska Press, 1959, pp. 97–144.

———. *Lives in Progress: A Study of the Natural Growth of Personality.* 2nd ed. New York: Holt, Rinehart and Winston, 1966.

———. "Motivation Reconsidered: The Concept of Competence," *Psychological Review,* 66 (1959), 297–333.

Wollheim, Richard. *Sigmund Freud.* New York: Viking, 1971.

19

Alker, Henry A. "Is Personality Situationally Specific or Intrapsychically Consistent?" *Journal of Personality,* 40 (1972), 1–16.

Allport, Gordon W. *Pattern and Growth in Personality.* New York: Holt, Rinehart and Winston, 1961.

———. *Personality: A Psychological Interpretation.* New York: Holt, Rinehart and Winston, 1937.

Allport, Gordon W., and **Henry S. Odbert.** "Trait-Names: A Psycho-Lexical Study," *Psychological Monographs,* vol. 47, no. 1 (1936), whole no. 211.

Bandura, Albert. *Principles of Behavior Modification.* New York: Holt, Rinehart and Winston, 1969.

———. "Vicarious Processes: A Case of No-Trial Learning," in Leonard Berkowitz (ed.), *Advances in Experimental Social Psychology: II.* New York: Academic Press, 1966, pp. 1–55.

Bandura, Albert, and **Richard Walters.** *Social Learning and Personality Development.* New York: Holt, Rinehart and Winston, 1963.

Bannister, Donald, and **Fay Fransella.** *Inquiring Man: The Theory of Personal Constructs.* Baltimore: Penguin, 1972.

Barnes, Mary, and **Joseph Berke.** *Mary Barnes: Two Accounts of a Journey Through Madness.* London: MacGibbon & Kee, 1971.

Cattell, Raymond B. *The Scientific Analysis of Personality.* Baltimore: Penguin, 1965.

Dollard, John, and **Neal E. Miller.** *Personality and Psychotherapy: An Analysis in Terms of Learning, Thinking, and Culture.* New York: McGraw-Hill, 1950.

Eysenck, Hans. *The Structure of Human Personality.* London: Metheun, 1970.

Hall, Calvin S., and **Gardner Lindzey.** *Theories of Personality.* 2nd ed. New York: Wiley, 1970.

Kelly, George A. *The Psychology of Personal Constructs.* New York: Norton, 1955.

Laing, R. D. *Knots.* London: Tavistock, 1970.

———. *The Politics of Experience.* New York: Pantheon Books, 1967.

Laing, R. D., and **David G. Cooper.** *Reason and Violence: A Decade of Sartre's Philosophy, 1950–1960.* London: Tavistock, 1964.

Laing, R. D., and **Aaron Esterson.** *Sanity, Madness and the Family.* 2nd ed. New York: Basic Books, 1971.

Maddi, Salvatore R. *Personality Theories: A Comparative Analysis.* Rev. ed. Homewood, Ill.: Dorsey Press, 1972.

———. *Perspectives on Personality.* Boston: Little, Brown, 1971.

Maslow, Abraham H. "Deficiency Motivation and Growth Motivation," in Marshall R. Jones (ed.), *Nebraska Symposium on Motivation: 1955.* Lincoln: University of Nebraska Press, 1955.

———. *The Psychology of Science: A Reconnaissance.* New York: Harper & Row, 1966.

———. "Some Basic Propositions of a Growth and Self-Actualization Psychology," in Salvatore Maddi (ed.), *Perspectives on Personality.* Boston: Little, Brown, 1971.

———. *Toward A Psychology of Being.* 2nd ed. New York: Van Nostrand Reinhold, 1968.

Miller, Neal E. "Liberalization of Basic S-R Concepts: Extensions to Conflict Behavior, Social Motivation and Learning," in Sigmund Koch (ed.), *Psychology: A Study of a Science.* Vol. 2. New York: McGraw-Hill, 1959.

———. "Theory and Experiment Relating Psychoanalytic Displacement to Stimulus-Response Generalization," *Journal of Abnormal and Social Psychology,* 43 (1948), 155–178.

Mischel, Walter. *Introduction to Personality.* New York: Holt, Rinehart and Winston, 1971.

———. *Personality and Assessment.* New York: Wiley, 1968.

———. "Toward A Cognitive Social-Learning Reconceptualization of Personality," *Psychological Review,* 8 (1973), 252–283.

Nisbett, Richard E., *et al.* "Behavior as Seen by the Actor and as Seen by the Observer," *Journal of Personality and Social Psychology,* 27 (1973), 154–164.

Rogers, Carl R. "A Theory of Personality," in Salvatore Maddi (ed.), *Perspectives on Personality.* Boston: Little, Brown, 1971.

Sartre, Jean Paul. *Being and Nothingness.* Hazel E. Barnes (tr.). New York: Citadel, 1968, pp. 235–236.

Skinner, B. F. *Beyond Freedom and Dignity.* New York: Knopf, 1971.

———. *Walden Two.* New York: Macmillan, 1962 (orig. pub. 1949).

Tanzer, Deborah. "Natural Childbirth: Pain or Peak Experience?" *Psychology Today,* 69 (October 1968), 16–21.

20

Abelson, Robert P., and **David E. Kanouse.** "Subjective Acceptance of Verbal Generalizations," in Sheldon Feldman (ed.), *Cognitive Consistency.* New York: Academic Press, 1966.

Allport, Gordon. "The Historical Background of Modern Social Psychology," in Gardner Lindzey and Elliot Aronson (eds.), *The Handbook of Social Psychology.* 2nd ed. Reading, Mass.: Addison-Wesley, 1968–69.

Anderson, Norman H. "Likeableness Ratings of 555 Personality-Trait Words," *Journal of Personality and Social Psychology,* 9 (1968), 272–279.

Anderson, Sherwood. "Death," *Winesburg, Ohio.* New York: Viking Press, 1964, p. 223.

Aronson, Elliot, and **Darwyn Linder.** "Gain and Loss of Esteem as Determinants of Interpersonal Attractiveness," *Journal of Experimental Social Psychology,* 1 (1965), 156–172.

Asch, Solomon E. "Forming Impressions on Personality," *Journal of Abnormal and Social Psychology,* 41 (1946), 258–290.

Berscheid, Ellen, and **Elaine Walster.** *Interpersonal Attraction.* Reading, Mass.: Addison-Wesley, 1969.

———. "Physical Attractiveness," in L. Berkowitz (ed.), *Advances in Experimental Social Psychology.* Vol. 7. New York: Academic Press, 1974.

Brickman, Philip J., Joel Redfield, *et al.* "Drive and Predisposition as Factors in the Attitudinal Effects of Mere Exposure," *Journal of Experimental Social Psychology,* 8 (1972), 31–44.

Clifford, Margaret, and **Elaine Walster.** "The Effect of Physical Attractiveness on Teacher Expectations," *Sociology of Education,* 46 (1973), 248–258.

Dion, Karen. "Young Children's Stereotyping of Facial Attractiveness," *Developmental Psychology,* 9 (1973), 183–188.

Dion, Karen, and **Ellen Berscheid.** "Physical Attractiveness and Sociometric Choice in Young Children," University of Minnesota, 1971 (mimeo).

Dion, Karen, Ellen Berscheid, and **Elaine Walster.** "What Is Beautiful Is Good," *Journal of Personality and Social Psychology,* 24 (1972), 285–290.

Donne, John. "Meditation XVII of Devotions upon Emergent Occasions," in Meyer H. Abrams *et al., The Norton Anthology of English Literature.* Vol. 1. Rev. ed. New York: Norton, 1968, p. 917.

Dutton, Donald G., and **Arthur Arons.** "Some Evidence for Heightened Sexual Attraction Under Conditions of High Anxiety," *Journal of Personality and Social Psychology,* in press.

Eisinger, Richard, and **Judson Mills.** "Perception of the Sincerity and Competence of a Communicator as a Function of the Extremity of His Position," *Journal of Experimental Social Psychology,* 4 (1968), 224–232.

Festinger, Leon. "A Theory of Social Comparison Processes," *Human Relations,* 7 (1954), 117–140.

Festinger, Leon, Stanley Schachter, and **Kurt W. Back.** *Social Pressures in Informal Groups.* Stanford, Calif.: Stanford University Press, 1963.

Goffman, Erving. *Behavior in Public Places.* New York: Free Press, 1963.

Goldstein, Joel W., and **Howard M. Rosenfeld.** "Insecurity and Preference for Persons Similar to Oneself," *Journal of Personality,* 37 (1969), 253–268.

Gollin, Eugene S. "Forming Impressions of Personality," *Journal of Personality,* 23 (1954), 65–76.

Harlow, Harry F. "The Nature of Love," *American Psychologist,* 13 (1958), 673–685.

Hastorf, Albert H., David J. Schneider, and **Judith Polefka.** *Person Perception.* Reading, Mass.: Addison-Wesley, 1970.

Hunt, Morton M. *The Natural History of Love.* New York: Knopf, 1959.

Huston, Ted L. (ed.). *Foundations of Interpersonal Attraction.* New York: Academic Press, 1974.

Jones, Edward E., and **Keith E. Davis.** "From Acts to Dispositions: The Attribution Process in Person Perception," in L. Berkowitz (ed.), *Advances in Experimental Social Psychology.* Vol. 2. New York: Academic Press, 1965.

Kelley, Harold H. "Moral Evaluation," *American Psychologist,* 26 (1971), 293–300.

———. "The Warm-Cold Variable in First Impressions of Persons," *Journal of Personality,* 18 (1950), 431–439.

Levinger, George, and **Jaap D. Snoek.** *Attraction in Relationship: A New Look at Interpersonal Attraction.* Morristown, N.J.: General Learning Press, 1972.

Mettee, David R., and **Elliot Aronson.** "Affective Reactions to Appraisal from Others," in Ted L. Huston (ed.), *Foundations of Interpersonal Attraction.* New York: Academic Press, 1974.

Miller, Howard L., and **Paul S. Siegal.** *Loving: A Psychological Approach.* New York: Wiley, 1972.

Newcomb, Theodore M. *The Acquaintance Process.* New York: Holt, Rinehart and Winston, 1961.

———. "The Prediction of Interpersonal Attraction," *The American Psychologist,* 11 (1956), 575–586.

Priest, Robert T., and **Jack Sawyer.** "Proximity and Peership: Bases of Balance in Interpersonal Attraction," *American Journal of Sociology,* 72 (1967), 633–649.

Rubin, Zick. *Liking and Loving: An Invitation to Social Psychology.* New York: Holt, Rinehart and Winston, 1973.

———. "Measurement of Romantic Love," *Journal of Personality and Social Psychology,* 16 (1970), 265–273.

Saegert, Susan, Walter C. Swap, and Robert B. Zajonc. "Exposure, Context, and Interpersonal Attraction," *Journal of Personality and Social Psychology*, 25 (1973), 234–242.

Schachter, Stanley. "The Interaction of Cognitive and Physiological Determinants of Emotional State," in L. Berkowitz (ed.), *Advances in Experimental Social Psychology*. Vol. 1. New York: Academic Press, 1964.

———. *The Psychology of Affiliation*. Stanford, Calif.: Stanford University Press, 1959.

Sheatsley, Paul B., and Jacob J. Feldman. "The Assassination of President Kennedy: A Preliminary Report on Public Reactions and Behavior," *Public Opinion Quarterly*, 28 (1964), 189–215.

Stotland, Ezra, Stanley E. Sherman, and Kelly G. Shaver. *Empathy and Birth Order*. Lincoln: University of Nebraska Press, 1971.

Stroebe, Wolfgang, *et al.* "Effects of Physical Attractiveness, Attitude Similarity, and Sex on Various Aspects of Interpersonal Attraction," *Journal of Personality and Social Psychology*, 18 (1971), 79–91.

Waller, Willard. *The Family: A Dynamic Interpretation*. New York: Dryden, 1938.

Walster, Elaine, and Ellen Berscheid. "A Little Bit of Love," in Ted L. Huston (ed.), *Foundations of Interpersonal Attraction*. New York: Academic Press, 1974.

White, Robert W. *The Enterprise of Living: Growth and Organization in Personality*. New York: Holt, Rinehart and Winston, 1972.

Winch, Robert F. *Mate Selection: A Study of Complementary Needs*. New York: Harper & Row, 1958.

Wright, Paul H. "A Model and a Technique for Studies of Friendship," *Journal of Experimental Social Psychology*, 5 (1969), 295–309.

Zajonc, Robert B. "Attitudinal Effects of Mere Exposure," *Journal of Personality and Social Psychology*, 9 (1968), 1–27.

21

Albert, Ethel M. "The Roles of Women: A Question of Values," in S.M. Farber and R.H.L. Wilson (eds.), *The Potential of Woman*. New York: McGraw-Hill, 1963, pp. 105–115.

Bardwick, Judith M. "Her Body, The Battleground," *Psychology Today*, 5 (February 1972), 50+.

———. *The Psychology of Women*. New York: Harper & Row, 1971.

Bem, Sandra L. "The Measurement of Psychological Androgeny," *Journal of Consulting and Clinical Psychology*, 1974, in press.

Bem, Sandra L., and Daryl J. Bem. "We're All Nonconscious Sexists," *Psychology Today*, 4 (November 1970), 22+.

Bird, Caroline. *Born Female: The High Cost of Keeping Women Down*. New York: McKay, 1968.

Broverman, Inge K., *et al.* "Sex-Role Stereotypes: A Current Appraisal," *Journal of Social Issues*, 28 (1972), 59–78.

———. "Sex-Role Stereotypes and Clinical Judgments of Mental Health," *Journal of Consulting and Clinical Psychology*, 34 (1970), 1–7.

Coppen, Alec, and Neil Kessel. "Menstruation and Personality," *British Journal of Psychiatry*, 109 (1963), 711–721.

Dawes, Robyn M. "Sexual Heterogeneity of Children as a Determinant of American Family Size," *Oregon Research Institute Research Bulletin*, 10 (1970).

Deaux, Kay, and Janet Taynor. "Evaluation of Male and Female Ability: Bias Works Two Ways," *Psychological Reports*, 32 (1973), 261–262.

Dinitz, Simon, Russell R. Dynes, and Alfred C. Clark. "Preference for Male or Female Children," *Journal of Marriage and Family Living*, 26 (1964), 128–130.

Epstein, Cynthia F. *Woman's Place: Options and Limits in Professional Careers*. Berkeley: University of California Press, 1971.

Farber, Seymour M., and Roger H. Wilson (eds.). *The Potential of Woman*. New York: McGraw-Hill, 1963.

Freud, Sigmund. "Female Sexuality," *International Journal of Psychoanalysis*, 13 (1932), 281–297.

———. *New Introductory Lectures on Psychoanalysis*. J. Strachey (tr.). New York: Norton, 1966.

———. "Some Psychological Consequences of the Anatomical Distinction Between the Sexes," *International Journal of Psychoanalysis*, 8 (1927), 133–142.

Goldberg, Philip. "Are Women Prejudiced Against Women?" *Trans-Action*, 5 (1968), 28–30.

Hall, Edward T. *The Hidden Dimension*. Garden City, N.Y.: Doubleday, Anchor Books, 1966.

———. *The Silent Language*. New York: Fawcett World Library, 1959.

Helson, Ravenna. "The Changing Image of the Career Woman," *The Journal of Social Issues*, 28 (1972), 33–46.

Hoffman, Lois W. "Early Childhood Experience and Women's Achievement Motives," *The Journal of Social Issues*, 28 (1972), 129–156.

Horner, Matina S. "Fail: Bright Women," *Psychology Today*, 3 (November 1969), 36+.

———. "Femininity and Successful Achievement: A Basic Inconsistency," in J. Bardwick *et al.* (eds.), *Feminine Personality and Conflict*. Belmont, Calif.: Brooks/Cole, 1970, pp. 45–74.

Ibsen, Henrik. *A Doll's House*, in *Four Great Plays by Ibsen*. R. Farquharson Sharp (tr.). New York: Bantam, 1967, p. 65.

Jourard, Sidney M. *The Transparent Self*. Rev. ed. New York: Van Nostrand Reinhold, 1971.

Kagan, Jerome, and Howard A. Moss. "The Stability of Passive and Dependent Behavior from Childhood through Adulthood," *Child Development*, 31 (1960), 577–591.

Kohlberg, Lawrence. "A Cognitive Developmental Analysis of Children's Sex-Role Concepts and Attitudes," in E. Maccoby (ed.), *The Development of Sex Differences*. Stanford, Calif.: Stanford University Press, 1966, pp. 82–172.

Komarovsky, Mirra. *Blue-Collar Marriage*. New York: Random House, 1962.

Lancaster, Jane Beckman. "In Praise of the Achieving Female Monkey," *Psychology Today*, 4 (September 1973), 30+.

Levitan, Teresa E., Robert P. Quinn, and Graham L. Staines. "A Woman is 58% of a Man," *Psychology Today*, 6 (March 1973), 89–91.

Liebow, Elliot. *Tally's Corner: A Study of Negro Streetcorner Men*. Boston: Little, Brown, 1967.

Maccoby, Eleanor E. (ed.). *The Development of Sex Differences*. Stanford, Calif.: Stanford University Press, 1966.

Mead, Margaret. *From the South Seas: Studies of Adolescence and Sex in Primitive Societies*. New York: Morrow, 1939.

———. *Sex and Temperament in Three Primitive Societies*. New York: New American Library, Mentor Books, 1950.

Mednick, Martha T. "Social Change and Sex-Role Inertia: The Case of the Kibbutz," in M.T. Mednick, S.S. Tangri, and L.W. Hoffman (eds.), *New Perspectives on Women and Achievement*. New York: Holt, Rinehart and Winston, 1975, in press.

Mischel, Walter. "A Social-Learning View of Sex Differences in Behavior," in E. Maccoby (ed.), *The Development of Sex Differences*. Stanford, Calif.: Stanford University Press, 1966, pp. 56–81.

Mussen, Paul. "Early Sex-Role Development," in D. Goslin (ed.), *Handbook of Socialization Theory and Research*. Chicago: Rand McNally, 1969, pp. 707–732.

Myrdal, Gunnar. *An American Dilemma: The Negro Problem and Modern Democracy*. New York: Harper & Row, 1962 (orig. pub. 1944).

Oppenheimer, Valerie K. "Demographic Influence on Female Employment and the Status of Women," *American Journal of Sociology*, 78 (1973), 946–961.

Paige, Karen E. "Women Learn to Sing the Menstrual Blues," *Psychology Today*, 7 (September 1973), 41–46.

Pleck, Joseph, and Jack Sawyer. *Men and Masculinity*. Englewood Cliffs, N.J.: Prentice-Hall, Spectrum Books, 1974, in press.

Reiss, Ira L. *The Family System in America*. New York: Holt, Rinehart and Winston, 1971.

Rosenkrantz, Paul, *et al.* "Sex-Role Stereotypes and Self-Concepts in College Students," *Journal of Consulting and Clinical Psychology*, 32 (1968), 287–295.

Shakespeare, William. *Macbeth*, in Sylvan Barnet (ed.), *The Complete Signet Classic Shakespeare*. New York: Harcourt Brace Jovanovich, 1972, p. 1237.

Strodtbeck, Fred L., and Richard D. Mann. "Sex Role Differentiation in Jury Deliberations," *Sociometry*, 19 (1956), 3–11.

Strodtbeck, Fred L., Rita J. Simon, and Charles Hawkins. "Social Status in Jury Deliberations," in I. D. Steiner and M. Fishbein (eds.), *Current Studies in Social Psychology*. New York: Holt, Rinehart and Winston, 1965, pp. 333–341.

Tavris, Carol (ed.). *The Female Experience*. Del Mar, Calif.: Psychology Today, 1973.

Terkel, Studs. *Working*. New York: Pantheon, 1974.

Tiger, Lionel. "The Possible Biological Origins of Sexual Discrimination," *Impact of Science on Society*, 20 (1970), 29–44.

Touhey, John C. "Effects of Additional Women Professionals on Ratings of Occupational Prestige and Desirability," *Journal of Personality and Social Psychology*, 29 (1974), 86–89.

Tresemer, David. "Fear of Success: Popular, but Unproven," *Psychology Today*, 7 (March 1974), 82–85.

Watson, Goodwin. *Social Psychology: Issues and Insights.* Philadelphia: Lippincott, 1966, p. 430.

Weisstein, Naomi. "Woman as Nigger," *Psychology Today,* 3 (October 1969), 20+.

22

Abelson, Robert P., and **James C. Miller.** "Negative Persuasion via Personal Insult," *Journal of Experimental Social Psychology,* 3 (1967), 321–333.

Abelson, Robert P., and **Philip G. Zimbardo.** *Canvassing for Peace: A Manual for Volunteers.* Ann Arbor, Mich.: Society for the Psychological Study of Social Issues, 1970.

Albert, Stuart M., and **James M. Dabbs Jr.** "Physical Distance and Persuasion," *Journal of Personality and Social Psychology,* 15 (1970), 265–270.

Aronson, Elliot. *The Social Animal.* San Francisco: W. H. Freeman, 1972.

Asch, Soloman. "Effects of Group Pressure upon the Modification and Distortion of Judgments," in H. Proshansky and B. Seidenberg (eds.), *Basic Studies in Social Psychology.* New York: Holt, Rinehart and Winston, 1965, pp. 393–401.

Bem, Daryl J. *Beliefs, Attitudes, and Human Affairs.* Belmont, Calif.: Brooks/Cole, 1970.

Bolt, Robert. *A Man for All Seasons,* in Robert Corrigan (ed.), *The New Theatre of Europe.* New York: Dell, 1962, p. 111.

Churchill, Sir Winston S. "A Speech to the House of Commons, May 13, 1940," *The War Speeches of the Rt. Hon. Winston S. Churchill.* Vol. 1. London: Cassell, 1951, p. 181.

Cohen, Arthur R. *Attitude Change and Social Influence.* New York: Basic Books, 1964.

———. "Need for Cognition and Order of Communication as Determinants of Opinion Change," in C. I. Hovland *et al., The Order of Presentation in Persuasion.* New Haven, Conn.: Yale University Press, 1955.

Deutsch, Morton, and **Harold B. Gerard.** "A Study of Normative and Informational Influences on Social Judgment," *Journal of Abnormal and Social Psychology,* 51 (1955), 629–636.

Dichter, Ernest. *Handbook of Consumer Motivations.* New York: McGraw-Hill, 1964.

Festinger, Leon. *A Theory of Cognitive Dissonance.* Stanford, Calif.: Stanford University Press, 1957.

Festinger, Leon, and **J. Merrill Carlsmith.** "Cognitive Consequences of Forced Compliance," *Journal of Abnormal and Social Psychology,* 58 (1959), 203–210.

Freedman, Jonathan L., and **Scott C. Fraser.** "Compliance Without Pressure: The Foot-in-the-Door Technique," *Journal of Personality and Social Psychology,* 4 (1966), 195–202.

Gergen, Kenneth J., and **David Marlowe** (eds.). *Personality and Social Behavior.* Reading, Mass.: Addison-Wesley, 1970.

Hovland, Carl I., and **Walter Weiss.** "The Influence of Source Credibility on Communication Effectiveness, *Public Opinion Quarterly,* 15 (1951), 636–650.

Janis, Irving L., and **Bert T. King.** "The Influence of Role Playing on Opinion Change," *Journal of Abnormal and Social Psychology,* 49 (1954), 211–218.

Janis, Irving L., and **Leon Mann.** "Effectiveness of Emotional Role Playing in Modifying Smoking Habits and Attitudes," *Journal of Experimental Research in Personality,* 1 (1965) 84–90.

Kelman, Herbert C. "Processes of Opinion Change," *Public Opinion Quarterly,* 25 (1961), 57–78.

Kelman, Herbert C., and **Lee H. Lawrence.** "Assignment of Responsibility in the Case of Lt. Calley: Preliminary Report on a National Survey," *Journal of Social Issues,* 28 (1972), 177–212.

Kiesler, Charles A., Barry E. Collins, and **Norman Miller.** *Attitude Change: A Critical Analysis of Theoretical Approaches.* New York: wiley, 1969.

McGuire, William J. "A Vaccine for Brainwash," *Psychology Today,* 3 (February 1970), 36+.

Mantell, David M. "The Potential for Violence in Germany," *Journal of Social Issues,* 27 (1971), 101–112.

Marlowe, David, and **Kenneth J. Gergen.** "Personality and Social Interaction," in G. Lindzey and E. Aronson (eds.), *Handbook of Social Psychology.* Vol. 3. 2nd ed. Reading, Mass.: Addison-Wesley, 1969, pp. 590–665.

Milgram, Stanley. "Behavioral Study of Obedience," *Journal of Abnormal and Social Psychology,* 67 (1963), 371–378.

———. *Obedience to Authority.* New York: Harper & Row, 1974.

———. "Some Conditions of Obedience and Disobedience to Authority," in I. D. Steiner and M. Fishbein (eds.), *Current Studies in Social Psychology.* New York: Holt, Rinehart and Winston, 1965, pp. 243–262.

Rubin, Zick. *Doing Unto Others: Joining, Molding, Conforming, Helping, Loving.* Englewood Cliffs, N.J.: Prentice-Hall, Spectrum Books, 1974.

Sistruck, Frank, and **John W. McDavid.** "Sex Variables In Conforming Behavior," *Journal of Personality and Social Psychology,* 17 (1971), 200–207.

Snow, C. P. "Either-Or," *Progressive,* 25 (1961), 24–25.

Strodtbeck, Fred L., Rita M. James, and **Charles Hawkins.** "Social Status in Jury Deliberations," in E. E. Maccoby *et al., Readings in Social Psychology.* New York: Holt, Rinehart and Winston, 1958, pp. 379–388.

Walster, Elaine, and **Leon Festinger.** "The Effectiveness of 'Overheard' Persuasive Communications," *Journal of Abnormal and Social Psychology,* 65 (1962), 395–402.

Worchel, Stephen, and **Jack W. Brehm.** "Effects of Threats to Attitudinal Freedom as a Function of Agreement with the Communicator," *Journal of Personality and Social Psychology,* 14 (1970), 18–22.

Zimbardo, Philip G., and **Ebbe Ebbesen.** *Influencing Attitudes and Changing Behavior.* Reading, Mass.: Addison-Wesley, 1969.

23

Allport, Gordon W. *The Nature of Prejudice.* Garden City, N.Y.: Doubleday, 1958.

Asch, Solomon. "Effects of Group Pressure upon the Modification and Distortion of Judgments," in H. Proshansky and B. Seidenberg (eds.), *Basic Studies in Social Psychology.*

New York: Holt, Rinehart and Winston, 1965, pp. 393–401.

Baldwin, James, *Nobody Knows My Name.* New York: Dell, 1969, pp. 73, 122–123.

Bayton, James A., Lois B. McAlister, and **Jeston Hamer.** "Race-Class Stereotypes," *Journal of Negro Education,* 25 (1956), 75–78.

Brigham, John C. "Ethnic Stereotypes," *Psychological Bulletin,* 76 (1971), 15–38.

Brown, Roger. *Social Psychology.* New York: Free Press, 1965.

Buss, Arnold H., and **Norman W. Portnoy.** "Pain Tolerance and Group Identification," *Journal of Personality and Social Psychology,* 6 (1967), 106–108.

Cartwright, Dorwin, and **Alvin Zander** (eds.). *Group Dynamics.* 3rd ed. New York: Harper & Row, 1968.

Cauthen, Nelson R., Ira E. Robinson, and **Herbert H. Krauss.** "Stereotypes: A Review of the Literature 1926–1968," *Journal of Social Psychology* 84 (1971), 103–125.

Clark, Kenneth B., and **Mamie Clark.** "Racial Identification and Preference in Negro Children," in T. M. Newcomb and E. L. Hartley (eds.), *Readings in Social Psychology.* New York: Holt, Rinehart and Winston, 1947, pp. 169–178.

Davis, James H. *Group Performance.* Reading, Mass.: Addison-Wesley, 1969.

Davis, John Preston (ed.). *The American Negro Reference Book.* Englewood Cliffs, N.J.: Prentice-Hall, 1966.

Deutsch, Morton, and **Mary E. Collins.** "The Effect of Public Policy in Housing Projects upon Interracial Attitudes," in H. Proshansky and B. Seidenberg (eds.), *Basic Studies in Social Psychology.* New York: Holt, Rinehart and Winston, 1965, pp. 646–657.

———. *Interracial Housing: A Psychological Evaluation of a Social Experiment.* Minneapolis: University of Minnesota Press, 1951.

Dunnette, Marvin D., John Campbell, and **Kay Jaastad.** "The Effect of Group Participation on Brainstorming Effectiveness for Two Industrial Samples," *Journal of Applied Psychology,* 47 (1963), 30–37.

Gundlach, Ralph H. "The Effect of On-the-Job Experience with Negroes upon Social Attitudes of White Workers in Union Shops," *Psychological Reports,* 2 (1956), 67–77.

Harding, John, and **Russell Hogrefe.** "Attitudes of White Department-Store Employees Toward Negro Co-workers," *Journal of Social Issues,* 8 (1952), 18–28.

James, H. E. O. "Personal Contact in School and Change in Intergroup Attitudes," *International Social Science Bulletin,* 7 (1955), 66–70.

Janis, Irving L. *Victims of Groupthink: A Psychological Analysis of Historical Decisions and Fiascos.* Boston: Houghton Mifflin, 1973.

Jones, James M. *Prejudice and Racism.* Reading, Mass.: Addison-Wesley, 1972.

Katz, Daniel, and **Kenneth W. Braly.** "Racial Stereotypes of One Hundred College Students," *Journal of Abnormal and Social Psychology,* 28 (1933), 280–290.

Lambert, Wallace E., Eva Libman, and **Ernest G. Poser.** "The Effect of Increased Salience of a Membership Group on Pain Tolerance," *Journal of Personality,* 28 (1960), 350–357.

Merton, Robert K. *Social Theory and Social Structure.* Rev. ed. New York: Free Press, 1957.

Minard, Ralph D. "Race Relations in the Pocahontas Coal Field," *Journal of Social Issues,* 8 (1952), 29–44.

Newcomb, Theodore M. "Attitude Development as a Function of Reference Groups: The Bennington Study," in H. Proshansky and B. Seidenberg (eds.), *Basic Studies in Social Psychology.* New York: Holt, Rinehart and Winston, 1965, pp. 215–225.

Osborn, Alex F. *Applied Imagination.* Rev. ed. New York: Scribner's, 1957.

Pettigrew, Thomas F. *A Profile of the Negro American.* Princeton, N.J.: Van Nostrand, 1964.

Pettigrew, Thomas F. (ed.). *Racially Separate or Together?* New York: McGraw-Hill, 1971.

Pettigrew, Thomas F., and Robert T. Riley. "The Social Psychology of the Wallace Phenomenon," in T. F. Pettigrew (ed.), *Racially Separate or Together?* New York: McGraw-Hill, 1971, pp. 231–256.

Schlesinger, Arthur M., Jr. *A Thousand Days.* Boston: Houghton Mifflin, 1965.

Sherif, Muzafer, et al. *Intergroup Conflict and Cooperation: The Robbers Cave Experiment.* Norman, Okla.: Institute of Group Relations, 1961.

Sorenson, Theodore. *Kennedy.* New York: Harper & Row, 1965.

Taylor, Donald W., Paul C. Berry, and Clifford H. Block. "Does Group Participation When Using Brainstorming Facilitate or Inhibit Creative Thinking?" *Administrative Science Quarterly,* 3 (1958), 23–47.

24

American Psychiatric Association. *Diagnostic and Statistical Manual of Mental Disorders.* 2nd ed. Washington, D.C.: American Psychiatric Association, 1968.

Arieti, Silvano (ed.). *American Handbook of Psychology.* New York: Basic Books, 1959. 3 vols.

Hollingshead, August de Belmont, and Frederick C. Redlich. *Social Class and Mental Illness.* New York: Wiley, 1958.

Kisker, George W. *The Disorganized Personality.* New York: McGraw-Hill, 1964.

Kohlberg, Lawrence. "Development of Moral Character and Moral Ideology," in M. L. Hoffman and L. W. Hoffman (eds.), *Review of Child Development Research.* Vol. 1. New York: Russell Sage Foundation, 1964, pp. 383–431.

Kolb, Lawrence C., Viola W. Bernard, and Bruce P. Dohrenwend (eds.). *Urban Challenges to Psychiatry: The Case History of a Response.* Boston: Little, Brown, 1969.

Kramer, M. "Statistics of Mental Disorders in the United States: Some Urgent Needs and Suggested Solutions," *Journal of the Royal Statistical Society, Series A,* 132 (1969), 353–407. Prepared by Biometry Branch, O. P. P. E., National Institute of Mental Health, March, 1968.

Maher, Brendan. *Principles of Psychopathology: An Experimental Approach.* New York: McGraw-Hill, 1966.

Miner, Horace. "Body Ritual Among the Nacirema," in W. A. Lessa and Evon Z. Vogt (eds.), *Reader in Comparative Religion.* Evanston, Ill.: Row Peterson, 1958.

Murphy, H. B. M., et al. "A Cross-Cultural Survey of Schizophrenic Symptomatology," in *Proceedings of the Third World Congress of Psychiatry.* Vol. 2. Toronto: University of Toronto Press, 1961, pp. 1309–1315.

Shapiro, Evelyn (ed.). *Psychosources: A Psychology Resource Catalog.* New York: Bantam, 1973, p. 114.

Srole, Leo, et al. *Mental Health in the Metropolis: The Midtown Manhattan Study.* Vol. 1. New York: McGraw-Hill, 1962.

Szasz, Thomas S. *The Myth of Mental Illness: Foundations of a Theory of Personal Conduct.* New York: Dell, 1967.

White, Robert W. *The Abnormal Personality.* New York: Ronald Press, 1964.

Wolman, Benjamin B. (ed.). *Handbook of Clinical Psychology.* New York: McGraw-Hill, 1965.

Zigler, Edward, and Leslie Phillips. "Psychiatric Diagnosis: A Critique," *Journal of Abnormal and Social Psychology,* 63 (1961), 607–618.

Zilboorg, Gregory, and George W. Henry. *A History of Medical Psychology.* New York: Norton, 1941.

25

Bateson, Gregory, and Don Jackson, et al. "Toward a Theory of Schizophrenia," *Behavioral Science,* 1 (1956), 251–264.

Cameron, Norman. *Personality Development and Psychopathology.* Boston: Houghton Mifflin, 1963.

Dollard, John, and Neal E. Miller. *Personality and Psychotherapy.* New York: McGraw-Hill, 1950.

Erikson, Erik H. "Identity and the Life Cycle," *Psychological Issues,* vol. 1 (1959), monograph no. 1.

Eysenck, Hans J. "Reminiscence Drive and Personality—Revision and Extension of a Theory," *British Journal of Social and Clinical Psychology,* 1 (1962), 127–140.

Eysenck, Hans J. (ed.). *Handbook of Abnormal Psychology: An Experimental Approach.* New York: Basic Books, 1961.

Fenichel, Otto. *The Psychoanalytic Theory of Neurosis.* New York: Norton, 1945.

Freud, Sigmund. *Collected Papers.* Vol. 3. James Strachey (ed.). New York: Basic Books, 1959.

Gottesman, Irving I., and James Shields. "Contributions of Twin Studies to Perspectives on Schizophrenia," in B. A. Maher (ed.), *Progress in Experimental Personality Research.* Vol. 3. New York: Academic Press, 1966, pp. 1–84.

Kallman, Franz J. *Heredity in Mental Health and Disorder.* New York: Norton, 1953.

Kaplan, Bert (ed.). *The Inner World of Mental Illness.* New York: Harper & Row, 1964.

Kety, Seymour S. "Biochemical Hypotheses and Studies," in L. Bellak and L. Loeb (eds.), *The Schizophrenic Syndrome.* New York: Grune & Stratton, 1969, pp. 155–171.

Laing, R. D. *The Politics of Experience.* New York: Pantheon Books, 1967.

Laing, R. D., and Aaron Esterson. *Sanity, Madness and the Family.* 2nd ed. New York: Basic Books, 1971.

Lidz, Theodore, et al. "The Intrafamilial Environment of Schizophrenic Patients: Marital Schism and Marital Skew," *American Journal of Psychiatry,* 114 (1957), 241–248.

Maher, Brendan A. "The Application of the Approach-Avoidance Conflict Model to Social Behavior," *Journal of Conflict Resolution,* 8 (1964), 287–291.

————. *Principles of Psychopathology: An Experimental Approach.* New York: McGraw-Hill, 1966.

Malmo, Robert B. "Anxiety and Behavioral Arousal," *Psychological Review,* 64 (1957), 276–287.

Malmo, Robert B., and Abram Amsel. "Anxiety-Produced Interference in Serial Rote Learning, with Observation on Rote Learning After Partial Frontal Lobectomy," *Journal of Experimental Psychology,* 38 (1948), 440–454.

Meehl, Paul E. "Schizotaxia, Schizotypy, Schizophrenia," *American Psychologist,* 17 (1962), 827–838.

Miller, Neal E. "Liberalization of Basic S-R Concepts: Extensions of Conflict Behavior, Maturation and Social Learning," in S. Koch (ed.), *Psychology: A Study of a Science.* Vol. 2. New York: McGraw-Hill, 1958, pp. 196–292.

Pavlov, Ivan P. *Lectures on Conditioned Reflexes.* W. H. Gantt (tr.). New York: International Publishers, 1928.

Rosenthal, David. *The Genetics of Psychopathology.* New York: McGraw-Hill, 1971.

Sahakian, William S. (ed.). *Psychopathology Today: Experimentation, Theory and Research.* Itasca, Ill.: F. E. Peacock, 1970.

Ullman, Leonard P., and Leonard Krasner. *A Psychological Approach to Abnormal Behavior.* New York: Holt, Rinehart and Winston, 1970.

Valins, Stuart, and Richard E. Nisbett. "Attribution Processes in the Development and Treatment of Emotional Disorders," in E. Jones et al. (eds.), *Attribution: Perceiving the Causes of Behavior.* Morristown, N.J.: General Learning Press, 1972.

Watson, John B., and Rosalie Rayner. "Conditioned Emotional Reactions," *Journal of Experimental Psychology,* 3 (1920), 1–14.

White, Robert W., and Norman F. Watt. *The Abnormal Personality.* 4th ed. New York: Ronald Press, 1964.

Wise, C. David, and Larry Stein. "Dopamine-B-Hydroxylase Deficits in the Brains of Schizophrenic Patients," *Science,* 181 (1973), 344–347.

Wolpe, Joseph, and Stanley Rachman. "Psychoanalytic Evidence: A Critique Based on Freud's Case of Little Hans," *Journal of Nervous and Mental Diseases,* 31 (1960), 134–147.

26

Bednar, Richard L., and G. Frank Lawlis. "Empirical Research in Group Psychotherapy," in Allen E. Bergin and Sol L. Garfield (eds.), *Handbook of Psychotherapy and Behavior Change: An Empirical Analysis.* New York: Wiley, 1971.

Benedict, Ruth. "Anthropology and the Abnormal," *Journal of Genetic Psychology,* 10 (1934), 59–82.

Bergin, Allen E. "The Evaluation of Therapeutic Outcomes," in Allen E. Bergin and Sol L. Garfield (eds.), *Handbook of Psychotherapy and Behavior Change: An Empirical Analysis.* New York: Wiley, 1971.

Bergin, Allen E., and **Sol L. Garfield** (eds.). *Handbook of Psychotherapy and Behavior Change: An Empirical Analysis.* New York: Wiley, 1971.

Berne, Eric. *Games People Play.* New York: Grove Press, 1964.

———. *Principles of Group Treatment.* New York: Oxford University Press, 1966.

———. *Transactional Analysis in Psychotherapy.* New York: Grove Press, 1961.

———. *What Do You Say After You Say Hello?* New York: Grove Press, 1972.

Charcot, Jean M. *Lectures on the Diseases of the Nervous System.* George Sigerson (tr.). New York: Hafner, 1962.

Colby, Kenneth M. "Psychotherapeutic Processes," in Paul R. Farnsworth *et al.* (eds.), *Annual Review of Psychology: XV.* Palo Alto, Calif.: Annual Reviews, 1964.

Corsini, Raymond J. (ed.). *Current Psychotherapies.* Itasca, Ill.: F. E. Peacock, 1973.

Ellis, Albert. *Growth Through Reason.* Palo Alto, Calif.: Science and Behavior Books, 1971.

———. *Reason and Emotion in Psychotherapy.* Secaucus, N.J.: Lyle Stuart, 1962.

Eysenck, Hans J. *The Effects of Psychotherapy.* New York: International Science Press, 1966.

———. "The Effects of Psychotherapy: An Evaluation," *Journal of Consulting Psychology,* 16 (1952), 319–324.

Fairweather, George W., *et al. Community Life For the Mentally Ill: An Alternative to Institutional Care.* Chicago: Aldine, 1969.

Frank, Jerome D. *Persuasion and Healing.* Rev. ed. Baltimore, Md.: Johns Hopkins University Press, 1973.

Frankl, Viktor E. *Man's Search for Meaning: An Introduction to Logotherapy.* Boston: Beacon Press, 1961.

Glasser, William. *Reality Therapy.* New York: Harper & Row, 1965.

———. *Schools Without Failure.* New York: Harper & Row, 1969.

Golann, Stuart E., and **Carl Eisdorfer** (eds.). *Handbook of Community Mental Health.* New York: Appleton-Century-Crofts, 1972.

Goodman, Paul. *Growing Up Absurd.* New York: Random House, 1960.

Haley, Jay. "The Family of the Schizophrenic: A Model System," *Journal of Nervous and Mental Disorders,* 129 (1959), 357–374.

Henry, William E., John H. Sims, and **S. Lee Spray.** *The Fifth Profession: Becoming a Psychotherapist.* San Francisco: Jossey-Bass, 1971.

Howard, Kenneth I., and **David E. Orlinsky.** "Psychotherapeutic Processes," in Paul Mussen and Mark Rosenweig (eds.), *Annual Review of Psychology: XXIII.* Palo Alto, Calif.: Annual Reviews, 1972.

Jackson, Don. "Family Interaction, Family Homeostasis, and Some Implications for Conjoint Family Psychotherapy," in J. Masserman (ed.), *Individual and Family Dynamics.* New York: Grune & Stratton, 1959.

Janov, Arthur. *The Primal Scream.* New York: Putnam, 1970.

Joint Commission on Mental Illness and Health. *Action for Mental Health.* New York: Basic Books, 1961.

Jones, Maxwell, *et al. The Therapeutic Community.* New York: Basic Books, 1953.

Kuhn, Thomas S. *The Structure of Scientific Revolutions.* 2nd ed. Chicago: University of Chicago Press, 1970.

Lubovsky, Lester B., *et al.* "Factors Influencing the Outcome of Psychotherapy: A Review of Quantitative Research," *Psychological Bulletin,* 75 (1971), 145–185.

May, Rollo. *Psychology and the Human Dilemma.* Princeton, N.J.: Van Nostrand, 1967.

May, Rollo, *et al.* (eds.). *Existence: A New Dimension in Psychiatry & Psychology.* New York: Basic Books, 1958.

Mesmer, Franz Anton. *Memoir of F.A. Mesmer, Doctor of Medicine, on his Discoveries, 1799.* Jerome Eden (tr.). Mount Vernon, N.Y.: Eden Press, 1957.

Moreno, Jacob L. *The First Book on Group Psychotherapy.* 3rd ed. New York: Beacon House, 1957.

———. *Sociometry, Experimental Method and the Science of Society.* New York: Beacon House, 1951.

Perls, Frederick S. *The Gestalt Approach & Eye Witness to Therapy.* Palo Alto, Calif.: Science & Behavior Books, 1973.

———. *Gestalt Therapy Verbatim.* Lafayette, Calif.: Real People Press, 1969.

———. *In and Out of the Garbage Pail.* Lafayette, Calif.: Real People Press, 1969.

Perls, Frederick S., Ralph F. Hefferline, and **Paul Goodman.** *Gestalt Therapy: Excitement and Growth in the Human Personality.* New York: Julian Press, 1951.

Riesman, David. *The Lonely Crowd.* New Haven: Yale University Press, 1965.

Rogers, Carl R. *Client-Centered Therapy.* Boston: Houghton Mifflin, 1951.

———. "Interpersonal Relationships: U.S.A. 2000," *Journal of Applied Behavioral Science,* 4 (1968), 265–280.

———. *On Becoming a Person.* Boston: Houghton Mifflin, 1961.

Rogers, Carl R., and **Rosalind F. Dymond.** *Psychotherapy and Personality Change.* Chicago: University of Chicago Press, 1954.

Rosen, George. *Madness in Society.* Chicago: University of Chicago Press, 1968.

Satir, Virginia M. *Conjoint Family Therapy.* Rev. ed. Palo Alto, Calif.: Science & Behavior Books, 1967.

Schofield, William. *Psychotherapy: The Purchase of Friendship.* Englewood Cliffs, N.J.: Prentice-Hall, 1964.

Schutz, William C. *Here Comes Everybody; Bodymind and Encounter Culture.* New York: Harper & Row, 1971.

———. *Joy: Expanding Human Awareness.* New York: Grove Press, 1969.

Sundberg, Norman D., Leona E. Tyler, and **Julian R. Taplin.** *Clinical Psychology: Expanding Horizons.* 2nd ed. New York: Appleton-Century-Crofts, 1973.

Truax, Charles B., and **Robert R. Carkhuff.** *Toward Effective Counseling and Psychotherapy: Training and Practice.* Chicago: Aldine, 1967.

Whyte, William H., Jr. *The Organization Man.* New York: Simon and Schuster, 1956.

Wilson, Sloan, *The Man in the Grey Flannel Suit.* New York: Simon and Schuster, 1955.

Wolpe, Joseph. *The Practice of Behavior Therapy.* Elmsford, N.Y.: Pergamon, 1969.

———. *Psychotherapy by Reciprocal Inhibition.* Stanford, Calif.: Stanford University Press, 1958.

27

Davison, Gerald C. "Elimination of a Sadistic Fantasy by a Client-Controlled Counterconditioning Technique: A Case Study," *Journal of Abnormal Psychology,* 73 (1968), 84–90.

Franks, Cyril M., and **Terence G. Wilson** (eds.). *Annual Review of Behavior Therapy: Theory and Practice.* New York: Brunner/Mazel, 1973.

Hall, R. Vance. *Managing Behavior.* Lawrence, Kansas: H. H. Enterprises Inc., 1971.

Hunt, William A., and **Joseph D. Matarazzo.** "Three Years Later: Recent Developments in the Experimental Modification of Smoking Behavior," *Journal of Abnormal Psychology,* 81 (1973), 107–114.

Hunt, William A., L. W. Barnett, and **L. G. Branch.** "Relapse Rates in Addiction Programs," *Journal of Clinical Psychology,* 27 (1971), 455–456.

Jones, Mary Cover. "A Laboratory Study of Fear: The Case of Peter," *Pedagogical Seminary,* 31 (1924), 308–316.

Kanfer, Frederick H. "Self Regulation: Research, Issues, and Speculations," in C. Neuringer and J. L. Michael (eds.), *Behavior Modification in Clinical Psychology.* New York: Appleton-Century-Crofts, 1970.

Kanfer, Frederick H., and **Jeanne S. Phillips.** *Learning Foundations of Behavior Therapy.* New York: Wiley, 1970.

Lazarus, Arnold. *Behavior Therapy and Beyond.* New York: McGraw-Hill, 1971.

Marks, Isaac M., and **Michael G. Gelder.** "Common Ground Between Behavior Therapy and Psychodynamic Methods," *British Journal of Medical Psychology,* 39 (1966), 11–23.

Mausner, Bernard. "An Ecological View of Cigarette Smoking," *Journal of Abnormal Psychology,* 81 (1973), 115–126.

Mowrer, O. Hobart. "Apparatus for the Study and Treatment of Enuresis," *American Journal of Psychology,* 51 (1938), 163–166.

O'Leary, K. Daniel, and **Susan G. O'Leary** (eds.). *Classroom Management: The Successful Use of Behavior Modification.* Elmsford, N.Y.: Pergamon, 1972.

Patterson, Gerald R. *Families: Applications of Social Learning to Family Life.* Champaign, Ill.: Research Press, 1971.

Patterson, Gerald R., *et al.* "Direct Intervention in the Classroom: A Set of Procedures for the Aggressive Child," in F. W. Clark, D. R. Evans, and L. A. Hamerlynck (eds.), *Implementing Behavioral Programs for Schools and Clinics.* Champaign, Ill.: Research Press, 1972.

Patterson, Gerald R., and M. Elizabeth Gullion. *Living with Children: New Methods for Parents and Teachers*. Champaign, Ill.: Research Press, 1968.

Premack, David. "Reinforcement Theory," in D. Levine (ed.), *Nebraska Symposium on Motivation*. Lincoln: University of Nebraska Press, 1965.

Rachman, Saul. "Sexual Fetishism: An Experimental Analogue," *Psychological Record*, 16 (1966), 293–296.

Ray, Roberta, and Ernest Swihart. "Behavioral Analysis of Crying in Infants with Colic." Paper presented at the Jefferson County Mental Health Center Conference on Behavior Modification, March 20, 1974.

Skinner, B. F. *Science and Human Behavior*. New York: Free Press, 1967.

———. *Walden Two*. New York: Macmillan, 1968.

Stuart, Richard B. "Behavioral Contracting Within the Families of Delinquents," *Journal of Behavior Therapy and Experimental Psychiatry*, 2 (1971), 1–11.

Stuart, Richard B., and Barbara Davis. *Slim Chance in a Fat World*. Champaign, Ill.: Research Press, 1972.

Watson, David L., and Roland G. Tharp. *Self-Directed Behavior: Self-Modification for Personal Adjustment*. Belmont, Calif.: Brooks/Cole, 1972.

Wolpe, Joseph. *Psychotherapy by Reciprocal Inhibition*. Stanford, Calif.: Stanford University Press, 1958.

28

Brecher, Edward M., and the Editors of *Consumer Reports*. *Licit and Illicit Drugs*. Boston: Little, Brown, 1972.

Cade, John F. "Lithium Salts in the Treatment of Psychotic Excitement," *Medical Journal of Australia*, 36 (1949), 349–352.

Chafetz, Morris E. "Addictions. Ill: Alcoholism," in A. M. Freedman and H. I. Kaplan (eds.), *Comprehensive Textbook of Psychiatry*. Baltimore: Williams & Wilkins, 1967, pp. 1011–1026.

Colburn, Robert W., *et al*. "Effect of Lithium on the Uptake of Noradrenaline by Synaptosomes," *Nature*, 215 (1967), 1395–1397.

Coppen, Alec, *et al*. "Prophylactic Lithium in Affective Disorders," *Lancet*, no. 7719 (August 1971), 275–279.

Corrodi, Hans, *et al*. "The Effect of Lithium on Cerebral Monoamine Neurons," *Psychopharmacologia*, 11 (1967), 345–353.

Dishotsky, Norman I., *et al*. "LSD and Genetic Damage," *Science*, 172 (1971), 431–440.

Freedman, Daniel X. "The Psychopharmacology of Hallucinogenic Agents," *Annual Review of Medicine*, 20 (1969), 409–418.

Goodman, Louis, and Alfred Gilman. *The Pharmacological Basis of Therapeutics*. 4th ed. New York: Macmillan, 1970.

Grinspoon, Lester, Jack Ewalt, and Richard Shader. "Psychotherapy and Pharmacotherapy in Chronic Schizophrenia," *American Journal of Psychiatry*, 124 (1968), 1645–1652.

Hoffman, Albert. "Psychotomimetic Drugs: Chemical and Pharmacological Aspects," *Acta Physiologica et Pharmacologica Neerlandica*, 8 (1959), 240–258.

Jellinek, Elvin M. *The Disease Concept of Alcoholism*. New Brunswick, N.J.: Hillhouse Press, 1960.

Klein, Donald F., and John M. Davis. *Diagnosis and Drug Treatment of Psychiatric Disorders*. Baltimore: Williams & Wilkins, 1969.

McGlothin, William H., and David O. Arnold. "LSD Revisited," *Archives of General Psychiatry*, 24 (1971), 35–49.

Mandel, Arnold J., and Louis J. West. "Hallucinogens," in A. M. Freedman and H. I. Kaplan (eds.), *Comprehensive Textbook of Psychiatry*. Baltimore: Williams & Wilkins, 1967, pp. 247–253.

Patch, Vernon D. "Methadone," *New England Journal of Medicine*, 286 (1972), 43–45.

Schanberg, Saul M., Joseph J. Schildkraut, and Irwin Kopin. "The Effects of Psychoactive Drugs on Norepinephrine-³H Metabolism in Brain," *Biochemical Pharmacology*, 16 (1967), 393–399.

Schildkraut, Joseph J. "The Catecholamine Hypothesis of Affective Disorders: A Review of Supporting Evidence," *American Journal of Psychology*, 122 (1965), 509–522.

Schildkraut, Joseph J., and Seymour S. Kety. "Biogenic Amines and Emotion," *Science*, 156 (1967), 21–30.

Schnackenberg, Robert C. "Caffeine as a Substitute for Schedule II Stimulants in Hyperkinetic Children," *American Journal of Psychology*, 130 (1973), 796–798.

Schneidman, S. S., and M. L. Farberow. "Drugs, Death and Suicide—Problems of the Coroner," in William G. Clark and J. del Guidice (eds.), *Principles of Psychopharmacology*. New York: Academic Press, 1970.

Selikoff, Irving J., Edward H. Robitzek, and George O. Ornstein. "Toxicity of Hydrazine Derivatives of Isonicotinic Acid in the Chemotherapy of Human Tuberculosis," *Quarterly Bulletin of Seaview Hospital*, 13 (1952), 17–26.

Snyder, Solomon H. *Madness and the Brain*. New York: McGraw-Hill, 1973.

———. *Uses of Marijuana*. New York: Oxford University Press, 1971.

Victor, Maurice, and Raymond D. Adams. "Opiates and Other Synthetic Analgesic Drugs," in M. M. Wintrobe *et al*. (eds.), *Harrison's Principles of Internal Medicine*. New York: McGraw-Hill, 1970, pp. 677–681.

Weil, Andrew T., Norman E. Zinberg, and Judith M. Nelson. "Clinical and Psychological Effects of Marijuana in Man," *Science*, 162 (1968), 1234–1242.

Winokur, George, Paula J. Clayton, and Theodore Reich. *Manic-Depressive Illness*. St. Louis: Mosby, 1969.

Glossary

A

ablation. Surgical removal of an organ, bodily part, or growth from the body.

abnormality. The quality or state of deviating from the average, standard, or normal; an extreme or excessive departure from the usual, especially as applied to distorted, morbid, or pathological mental states. See also *normality*.

absolute threshold. The minimum intensity of a stimulus that is necessary for eliciting a sensation.

accommodation. In vision, the process whereby the lens of the eye changes its shape in order to bring into focus objects at various distances from the eye; in social psychology, changes in individual or group habits or customs made to reduce conflict with others; in Piaget's developmental theory, adjustment of one's schemes for understanding the world to the characteristics of the object or event at hand.

acetylcholine (ACh). A chemical believed to transmit nerve impulses across a synapse.

achieved status. A position attained by a person as the result of ability to fulfill its requirements. See also *ascribed status*.

achievement, need for. A felt requirement to accomplish or attain goals. The concept figures prominently in the expectancy-value theory of motivation.

achievement motive. See *achievement, need for*.

achievement test. A measure of how much an individual has learned in a given field or area, obtained by the assessment of performance in that area.

achromatic. Devoid of color; having no hue; black, gray, or white.

action potential. A localized, rapid change in electrical state that travels across the cell membrane of a neuron or muscle fiber at the moment of excitation. Also called a spike.

activation theory of emotion. The view that the defining characteristic of emotion is arousal or activation, which may be identified during an emotion-producing situation by measuring such variables as heart rate, respiration rate, and skin conductance; one version of this theory holds that emotion results from stimulation of the reticular activating system of the brain.

adaptation. The alteration of an organism's structure or functions so that it can survive and reproduce in a changed environment; in perception, adjustment of sensory receptors in response to the increasing or decreasing of stimulation. See also *accommodation; dark adaptation*.

addiction. Physiological dependence on a substance, especially a drug, often with the result that increased amounts of the substance are required to maintain normal or near-normal bodily functioning. Psychological dependence is sometimes also referred to as addiction. See also *withdrawal syndrome*.

addition of classes. In Piaget's developmental theory, the concrete-operational skill that involves understanding how several classes (*e.g.*, tulips, roses, and petunias) can be combined to form a higher-order class (flowers) and how the higher-order class can be broken down into the lower-order ones.

adjustment. The act of adapting, or accommodating. In the psychology of mental health, the idea that mental health and illness should be assessed in terms of adjustment to an environment or set of standards chosen by the individual in question. Four aspects of adjustment can be differentiated: physical, psychological, social, and moral. See also *normality*.

adrenal gland. One of a pair of endocrine glands located above the kidneys that produces epinephrine, norepinephrine, and other hormones. The adrenal gland plays an important role in both metabolism and emotional reactions.

adrenalin. See *epinephrine*.

affect. A class name for emotion, mood, and feeling; the feeling state that accompanies cognition.

affiliation. The tendency of people to seek the company of others.

afterimage. A visual image or sense impression that persists after removal of the stimulus.

alcoholism. Addiction to or excessive use of alcohol; a personality disorder in which a person drinks alcoholic beverages in great quantity and is unable to control his drinking; the effects of drinking an excessive amount of alcohol.

algorithm. Any problem-solving method, or strategy, that specifies the sequence of all possible operations that might lead to a solution.

alienation. An unhappy feeling of separation or detachment from other people or from nature; discussed by E. Fromm as one of the major afflictions of people living in modern, technologically advanced societies.

all-or-none law. The principle that the axon of a neuron fires either with full strength or not at all to a stimulus above threshold, regardless of the intensity of the stimulus.

alpha wave. A type of brain wave originating mainly in the occipital lobe of an adult that is typical of a relaxed, waking state. Alpha waves have an average frequency of ten cycles per second. See also *brain wave*.

American Sign Language (ASL). A system of communication used by the deaf and composed of gestures and hand signs.

amniocentesis. A technique for removing fetal cells from the fluid surrounding the fetus and testing them for the presence of abnormal chromosomes.

amphetamine. Any of a group of synthetic drugs that stimulates the central nervous system, suppresses appetite, increases heart rate and blood pressure, and alters sleep patterns. Often used to control appetite, treat narcolepsy, or alleviate depression.

analgesic. Something that eases or alleviates pain; pertaining to an absence of pain.

anal stage. According to Freud, the second psychosexual stage (from approximately one and one-half to three years of age), during which bowel control is accomplished and pleasure is focused on the functions of elimination, particularly defecation.

analysis by synthesis. A pattern-recognition or problem-solving procedure in which a person first forms a general conception (synthesis) of the pattern or problem and then uses this conception to identify specific features of the pattern or problem (analysis). See also *feature analysis*.

androgyny. The combination of both masculine and feminine characteristics.

anesthetic. A substance that produces insensibility or lack of sensation.

antianxiety drug. A drug usually given to people with psychological disorders in which anxiety is the main symptom. These drugs, also known as minor tranquilizers, reduce pathological anxiety, tension, and agitation.

antidepressant drug. A drug used in the treatment of pathological depression. Some antidepressant drugs can reverse a state of depression in a person who is pathologically depressed even though they usually leave normal people unaffected.

antipsychotic drug. A drug used to treat psychoses. Antipsychotic drugs, also known as major tranquilizers, reduce motor activity, responsiveness to stimuli, hallucinations, and delusional behavior.

antisocial. Unwilling to associate with individuals or social groups; opposed to social standards; harmful to society.

anxiety. A fearful and apprehensive emotional state, usually in response to unreal or imagined dangers, that interferes with favorable and effective solutions to real problems. Anxiety is typically accompanied by somatic symptoms that leave one in a continuous and physically exhausting state of tension and alertness.

anxiety reaction. Feelings of anxious expectation and accompanying physical symptoms that are characteristic of a state of diffuse anxiety.

apparent movement. The tendency of static stimuli to appear to be moving when presented in rapid succession, as in movies.

approach-approach conflict. The conflict that results from a situation in which an organism is drawn toward two gratifying goals or stimuli that are not compatible.

approach-avoidance conflict. A conflict resulting from a situation in which an organism is both attracted to a goal or stimulus and also motivated to avoid it.

aptitude test. A test in which a person's performance on a standardized group of tasks is used to estimate her or his future abilities in learning specific skills.

archetype. A model on which something is based or formed; a prototype; according to Jung, an inherited idea present in the unconscious and based on the experiences of all one's ancestors that regulates one's perceptions of the world.

arithmetic mean. See *mean, arithmetic*.

artery. A relatively large blood vessel that carries blood from the heart to the tissues. See also *vein*.

artificial intelligence (AI) research. The construction and testing of efficient mechanical information-processing systems without regard to their similarities to humans. See also *computer simulation*.

ascribed status. A position attributed to a person on the basis of some inherited characteristic. See also *achieved status*.

ASL. See *American Sign Language*.

assimilation. In anatomy, the conversion of substances absorbed by the body into protoplasm; in Piaget's theory of development, the application of a scheme to a particular object, person, or event.

assortative mating. The process by which persons with similar backgrounds and interests choose each other as friends or marriage partners.

attitude. An enduring predisposition to respond consistently to given objects, events, issues, and the like, assumed to be acquired by learning; attitudes have both cognitive and affective components.

attribution. The act of ascribing or imputing a characteristic to oneself or to another person. The study of attribution is currently a prominent topic in social psychology and personality psychology.

attribution theory of achievement motivation. The view, advanced by B. Weiner, that a person's reaction to success or failure depends on whether he attributes it to internal or external and to stable or unstable factors.

attribution theory of emotion. The view, developed by S. Schachter, that an emotion involves both a change in a person's physiological activation level and a cognitive interpretation of that change (attribution of the change to a specific cause).

audition. The sense of hearing.

auditory canal. The tubular passage that extends from the opening of the outer ear to the eardrum.

auditory cortex. An area located on the surface of the temporal lobe of the brain that is responsible for sensations of hearing.

auditory nerve. Either of a pair of cranial nerves connecting the inner ear with the brain; involved in hearing and balance.

authority, legitimate. A person who is perceived as being in control of a situation according to law, accepted standards, or principles.

autism. A syndrome thought to be a form of childhood schizophrenia in which the child is withdrawn, unable to relate to people and environmental stimulation in a normal manner, experiences language disturbances, and exhibits compulsive, stereotyped behavior.

autonomic conditioning. Conditioning designed to achieve conscious control of reflexes regulated by the autonomic nervous system (*e.g.*, involuntary reflexes).

autonomic nervous system. The part of the peripheral nervous system that innervates involuntary muscles, heart, blood vessels, viscera, and glands and controls their involuntary function.

autonomy. In E. Erikson's personality theory, a healthy sense of competence, independence, and self-reliance, which results from successful passage through one of the early stages of personality development.

average. The ordinary or typical; a general term for any measure of central tendency; more specifically, the arithmetic mean.

aversive conditioning. A behavior-therapy technique for reducing the frequency of an undesired behavior by pairing an unpleasant stimulus (generally electric shock) with the behavior's natural stimulus until the natural stimulus itself becomes unpleasant.

aversive control. Manipulation of behavior by means of escape conditioning, avoidance conditioning, or punishment.

aversive stimulus. Punishment, or a negative or unpleasant stimulus.

avoidance-avoidance conflict. The conflict that results from a situation in which an organism is motivated to avoid two similar stimuli but avoidance of one brings it closer to the other.

avoidance conditioning. A type of operant conditioning in which an organism learns to make the correct response in order to prevent the occurrence of an aversive stimulus. See also *escape conditioning; negative reinforcer.*

axon. The fiberlike extension of a neuron that transmits impulses away from the cell body. See also *all-or-none law; dendrite.*

B

barbiturates. A group of sedative drugs that act as depressants to the central nervous system.

basic needs. In Maslow's theory of personality, those needs whose satisfaction is vital to the normal functioning of the individual. Basic needs form a hierarchy—that is, the needs must be satisfied in a certain order, and higher-level needs cannot be satisfied until lower-level needs are satisfied. *E.g.,* the need for security cannot be satisfied until the hunger need is satisfied. See also *metaneeds.*

basilar membrane. A membrane in the cochlea whose motions stimulate the auditory nerve.

behavior. The activities, responses, or movements of an organism.

behaviorism. A school of psychology based on the contention that only objectively observed behavior can be considered as scientific data. Strict behaviorists exclude consciousness from the study of psychology.

behavior modification. The changing of human behavior, especially by behavior therapy.

behavior therapy. A type of psychotherapy based on the proposition that people have emotional problems because they have learned ineffective behaviors or failed to learn effective ones. The object of behavior therapy is to change behavior patterns by eliminating symptoms rather than by probing the unconscious or making basic changes in personality.

behavioral indicator. An observed action or outward change that serves as a clue to an organism's inner state.

bias. In psychological research, a factor that distorts the data.

binaural differences. The time and intensity differences of a sound as it reaches each of an individual's ears.

binocular parallax. The difference between the retinal images of an object on the two eyes that is the result of the slightly different viewing angles of the eyes.

biofeedback. The use of information about physiological responses as input to help an organism control or condition those responses. See also *feedback.*

bipolar cell. A retinal neuron that transmits neural impulses from the rods and cones to the ganglion cells.

blind spot. The area of the retina where the optic nerve leaves the eye and that is devoid of rods and cones. The blind spot is insensitive to light.

brain. The primary organ of the nervous system. It is composed of nerve tissue and is encased in the skull. The brain, together with the spinal cord, is vital to life. It regulates bodily functions, sensory experience, intellectual processes, emotional activity, motivation, and so on. See *old brain; new brain.*

brain wave. A rhythmic fluctuation of electrical voltage in the brain. See also *alpha wave.*

brainstorming. A technique for fostering creative group problem solving that consists of having group members express ideas freely and without fear of criticism.

brightness. The intensity of light.

brightness constancy. The tendency of objects to retain their apparent brightness under various levels of illumination.

C

Cannabis sativa. Indian hemp. The female plant is the source of marijuana and hashish.

cardinal trait. According to G. Allport's trait approach to personality, one of the most general and basic dispositions or characteristics of an individual. See also *trait; central trait; secondary trait.*

case study. An intensive investigation that includes all relevant information on one or a few individuals, usually with reference to a single psychological phenomenon.

castration anxiety. Fear of injuring or losing one's genitals. In Freudian theory castration anxiety develops during the phallic stage and is thereafter repressed in normal individuals.

catatonic schizophrenia. A psychotic disorder that takes the form of generalized inhibition (catatonic stupor) or excessive, disorganized motor activity (catatonic excitement).

catecholamine. An organic compound possessing certain structural characteristics that are important to the functioning of the nervous system. Epinephrine, norepinephrine, and dopamine are catecholamines.

catecholamine hypothesis. The proposition that mental depression is related to a deficiency of norepinephrine in the brain and that mania or excited states are related to an excess of norepinephrine.

cell body. The mass of cytoplasm surrounding the nucleus of a cell not including any projecting fibers; especially the mass of cytoplasm surrounding the nucleus of a neuron exclusive of the axons and dendrites.

central nervous system (CNS). In vertebrates, the brain and spinal cord. See also *peripheral nervous system.*

central tendency. See *measure of central tendency.*

central trait. According to G. Allport's trait approach to personality, a characteristic that provides an important and general description of an individual's behavior but that is not as basic as a cardinal trait. According to S. Asch, a trait of an individual that markedly influences other people's perception of that individual's other, peripheral, traits. See also *trait; cardinal trait; peripheral trait, secondary trait.*

cerebellum. A large, oval structure in the old brain that regulates muscle coordination and balance.

cerebral cortex. The layer of nerve cells that forms the outer covering of the cerebral hemispheres and is the primary center for sensory discrimination, motor functions, and intellectual processes. Also known as the neocortex or new brain.

cerebrum. The largest structural division of the vertebrate brain, occupying the entire upper area of the cranium and involved in the regulation of sensory processes, motor activity, and thought formation.

chain of behavior. In conditioning theory, an orderly sequence of links of behavior, each with its own discriminative stimulus and its own reinforcer.

chlordiazepoxide. An antianxiety drug, or minor tranquilizer, sold under the trade name Librium.

chlorpromazine. An antipsychotic drug, commonly sold under the trade name Thorazine.

chromosome. A thread-shaped body within the nuclei of all plant and animal cells. Chromosomes usually occur in pairs that reproduce and split off during the formation of new cells, and they are the carriers of genes.

chunking. Dealing with two or more pieces of information as a single unit, or chunk.

clairvoyance. The knowledge of events that are not detectable by the normal senses, a form of extrasensory perception.

classical conditioning. An experimental procedure in which a stimulus that normally evokes a given response is repeatedly presented with a stimulus that does not usually evoke that response, with the result that the latter stimulus will eventually evoke the response when presented by itself. Also known as Pavlovian conditioning or respondent conditioning. See also *conditioned stimulus; unconditioned stimulus; conditioned response; unconditioned response.*

client-centered therapy. A type of psychotherapy based on the belief that the client is responsible for his own growth and self-actualization; the therapist creates an atmosphere of acceptance, refrains from directing the client, and reflects back to the client what the client has said.

clinical psychology. The branch of psychology concerned with the prevention, diagnosis, and treatment of personality problems and mental disorders.

clinician. A clinical psychologist, psychiatrist, or psychotherapist.

clitoris. The small erectile organ of the female genitals, located in the upper area between the labia; for most women, it is the genital area that gives the most intense pleasurable sensations when stimulated.

cluster. A number of similar objects or persons grouped together; a subgroup of variables that are more closely correlated with each other than they are with the variables of the larger group.

CNS. See *central nervous system.*

cochlea. The coiled organ in the inner ear containing the receptors for hearing.

co-consciousnesses. Distinct experiencing selves that exist together in the same person.

coding. See *encoding.*

cognition. The process or processes by which a person acquires knowledge or becomes aware; the product of such a process or processes.

cognitive dissonance, theory of. The theory advanced by L. Festinger that people are motivated to achieve consistency between their attitudes and their behavior.

cognitive map. The mental representation an organism makes of the spatial relationships between parts of a situation and a goal. E.C. Tolman, who hypothesized the cognitive map, believed that a rat learns a cognitive map of a maze, not simply a series of movements.

cognitive scheme. See *scheme.*

cognitive theory. A theory hypothesizing that cognitive structures, rather than responses to stimuli, are learned and that sees learning and psychological development as a process resulting from the restructuring of one's knowledge. In one form, also known as cognitive-developmental theory.

collective unconscious. According to Jung, one of the two parts of an individual's unconscious mind. The collective unconscious is made up of psychic material that is inherited and shared with other members of the species.

color. A visual sensation caused by light of certain wavelengths reflected or radiated from an object; hue.

color blindness. Complete or partial inability to distinguish colors. See also *dichromat; monochromat; trichromat.*

color constancy. The tendency of colors to be perceived accurately regardless of changes in illumination or viewing conditions.

color-opponent cell. A neuron located in the brain that is excited when the eye is stimulated by light at certain wavelengths and inhibited when the eye is stimulated by light at other wavelengths.

community mental health. A system for preventing and treating mental illness that emphasizes neighborhood facilities offering a comprehensive range of services.

competence. The ability to perform an action. According to R. White, it is the desire for competence rather than the need for tension reduction that motivates much of human behavior.

complementarity. The process by which a person with a strong trait (such as the need to dominate) is attracted to a person with a complementary trait (such as the need to be dominated).

complex. Related elements or factors grouped together to form a whole; an assemblage of repressed ideas that cause a person to think, feel, and behave in a characteristic or habitual manner (*e.g.*, Oedipus complex); according to Jung, the form into which the contents of the collective unconscious are organized.

complexive thinking. The mental action of jumping from one idea to other related ideas without integrating them around a single concept, characteristic of a child during Piaget's pre-operational period.

compulsion. The state of being forced to do something; a strong impulse to do something contrary to one's will; a stereotyped, repetitive, and insignificant motor activity that a person feels impelled to perform.

computer simulation. The construction and testing of computer programs that act as much like people as possible in order to explain human processes.

concrete-operational period. The third of Piaget's four periods of intellectual development (which usually comprises the elementary school years), during which a child begins to learn to deal with specific situations by coordinating his thinking around specific systems of operations (such as conservation and classification) but lacks the ability to think about hypothetical situations and abstract principles.

concrete operations. In Piaget's developmental theory, operations that can be applied to tangible things in the real world but not to abstract or hypothetical things. See also *formal operations.*

concurrent validity. With reference to psychological tests, validity as gauged by a comparison with another measure taken at the same time, such as an established test. See also *construct validity; content validity; predictive validity; validity.*

condensation. The process or result of combining several objects or ideas into a single symbol with multiple meanings, as in dreams.

conditional positive regard. In C. Rogers' view, the temporary withholding of love and praise by an authority figure to induce another person to conform to a particular social standard.

conditioned reflex. See *conditioned response.*

conditioned reinforcer. A stimulus or event that increases the frequency of a given response because it has become associated with the primary reinforcer of the response.

conditioned response. In classical conditioning, the learned response to a conditioned stimulus; in operant conditioning, the response controlled by a reinforcer.

conditioned stimulus. In classical conditioning, a once-neutral stimulus that has come to evoke a given response after a period of training in which it has been paired with an unconditioned stimulus.

conditioning. See *classical conditioning; operant conditioning.*

cone. One of many cells in the retina that is sensitive to color and that is used primarily for daytime vision. The density of cones is highest in the fovea. See also *rod.*

confabulation. The act of filling in memory gaps with statements that make sense but that are in fact untrue. A person who confabulates believes that his statements are true.

confederate. In reference to an experiment, a person who is supposedly a subject in the experiment but who is actually (unknown to the real subjects) an accomplice of the experimenter.

conflict. A struggle or controversy; disagreement of one idea, emotion, action, and so on with another; the mental state that results when mutually exclusive or opposing impulses, drives, wishes, and so on operate at the same time.

conformity. The condition of acting in accordance with or becoming similar to others; a change in attitude or behavior brought about by social pressure to become like one's peers.

conscience. An individual's system of moral beliefs or the part of a person that has moral beliefs; one of the functions of the superego.

conscious. Aware or having knowledge of one's feelings, thoughts, environment, and so on; according to psychoanalytic theory, the division of the psyche containing material of which the ego is aware. See also *unconscious.*

consciousness. The totality of a person's mental experiences; the self; that part of the self that is aware of its own ideas, sensations, acts, or surroundings.

consequence. Any environmental event that follows and controls a specific response; an element in the behavior-modification formula S-O-R-K-C.

conservation. In development, according to Piaget, the ability to comprehend those aspects or relationships of phenomena that remain constant or invariant during and after transformations in appearance, configuration, or state.

conservation of liquid. The principle that a given quantity of liquid is not altered if the shape of its container or containers is changed.

conservation of number. The principle that the number or quantity of items in a set or group is not altered if the configuration of the set is changed.

constancy. The characteristic of being unchanging, stable, or self-identical. See also *brightness constancy; perceptual constancy; shape constancy; size constancy.*

construct validity. With reference to psychological tests, the validity of a test as gauged by the degree to which the results of the test conform to results predicted by the constructs of the theory on which the test is based. See also *concurrent validity; content validity; predictive validity; validity.*

construction of an understanding. In Piaget's developmental theory, the process of learning or intellectual growth resulting from ongoing encounters between a person and his environment that cause him to readjust his thinking to fit the characteristics of the object or event he experiences. See also *assimilation; accommodation; equilibration.*

content validity. With reference to psychological tests, the degree to which a test's items cover material that is actually an example of the performance the test is designed to assess. See also *concurrent validity; construct validity; predictive validity; validity.*

contingency relationship. The schedule, either continuous or intermittent, by which a consequence follows a specific response; an element in the behavior-modification formula S-O-R-K-C.

continuity. A Gestalt principle of organization proposing that items will be perceived as belonging together if they appear to form a single, uninterrupted pattern.

continuous reinforcement. A schedule of reinforcement in which every correct response is reinforced.

contract. In behavior therapy, a written and signed agreement between therapist and client or client and other persons specifying behavior to be modified and rewards and sanctions to be exchanged.

control group. In an experiment, a group of subjects that have the same characteristics as the experimental group and that experience the same general treatment as the experimental group except that they do not undergo the specific experimental manipulation that is of interest. See also *experimental group.*

core of personality. Any set of human characteristics regarded as universal by a personality theorist. See also *periphery of personality.*

cornea. The transparent outer covering of the lens and iris that admits light into the interior of the eye.

corpus callosum. A band of nerve fibers connecting the two cerebral hemispheres that is thought to transmit information between hemispheres.

correct rejection. In signal detection theory, a correct judgment that a signal is not present. See also *false alarm; hit; miss.*

correlation. Reciprocal relation; the degree of relation between two or more variables; the extent to which two or more variables vary together.

correlation coefficient. A number that indicates the extent to which two variables vary together. Correlation coefficients range from +1 (perfect positive correlation) to −1 (perfect negative correlation).

correlational study. A research project that assesses the degree of relatedness, or correlation, between two or more variables.

cortex. An outer cell layer or outer covering; the cerebral cortex.

counseling psychology. The branch of psychology concerned with the giving of advice to persons who would be classified as normal rather than mentally disordered. See also *clinical psychology.*

counterconditioning. The extinction of a learned response by the acquisition of a new response that is incompatible with and stronger than the previously learned one.

covert sensitization. A behavior-therapy technique similar to aversive conditioning but using imagined unpleasant events rather than shock as the aversive stimulus.

critical period. See *sensitive period.*

cross-cultural study. The acquisition of comparable data from different cultures for the purpose of studying cultural differences and similarities.

culture. The established customs, roles, and learned behaviors of a group of people that are passed on from generation to generation.

custodial care. A program of minimal care for institutionalized mental patients that does not include psychotherapy.

D

dark adaptation. The adjustment of the eye to low light intensity by dilation of the pupil, an increase in the number of active rods, and a decrease in the number of active cones. Dark adaptation allows objects to be seen when illumination is low.

data. A collection of statistics, facts, or information obtained by observation, experimentation, or computation.

death instinct. See *Thanatos.*

decibel (dB). A unit of acoustic intensity.

defense. A means or method of protecting oneself; an unconscious mental activity or mental structure (*e.g.,* a defense mechanism) that protects the ego from anxiety.

defense mechanism. A structure of the psyche that protects the ego against unpleasant feelings or impulses. Defense mechanisms are unconscious and deny, falsify, or distort reality. See also *dissociation; fixation; projection; reaction formation; regression; repression.*

deferred imitation. The ability to duplicate another's actions long after those actions have been perceived.

deficiency needs. See *basic needs.*

delirium. A state of temporary mental disorder characterized by confusion, delusions, hallucinations, illusions, and restlessness.

delusion. A false belief that is held despite demonstrable evidence to the contrary.

demographic. Pertaining to the study of the social statistics of human populations.

dendrite. A short, branched extension of a neuron that receives neural impulses from other neurons and conducts them toward the cell body. Dendrites do not fire in an all-or-none fashion. See also *axon.*

deoxyribonucleic acid (DNA). An organic molecule composed of subunits consisting of any of several related chemical structures. The particular sequence of these subunits in chromosomal DNA determines the genetic information carried by the chromosome.

dependent variable. A variable that is expected to change in response to changes in an independent variable.

depressant. Causing a lowering of vital activities; a substance that has such an effect.

depression. A state of dejection accompanied by lowered sensitivity to certain stimuli, reduction of physical and mental activity, and difficulty in thinking; an unwarranted condition of prolonged sadness or dejection; the state of being sad or downcast. See also *manic-depressive psychosis.*

depth perception. Awareness of the distance between an object and oneself; awareness of the distance from the front to the back of an object, thus making it appear three-dimensional.

dermis. The skin, especially the layer below the epidermis.

descriptive statistics. Mathematical techniques used to summarize and describe a set of data. See also *inferential statistics.*

design error. In an experiment, a mistake that occurs when the experimenter measures something that does not exactly coincide with what he wants to measure.

development. The act, process, or result of bringing something to a more advanced or effective state; a sequence of gradual changes leading to a greater amount of differentiation or complexity within a system or organism; growth.

developmental psychology. The branch of psychology that deals with the sequence of physiological, psychological, and social growth from birth to maturity and is especially concerned with those behaviors characteristic of given ages.

dextroamphetamine. A drug, sold under the name Dexedrine, that acts as a stimulant; often used to control appetite and alleviate mild depression.

diacetylmorphine. See *heroin.*

diagnostic categories. Types of mental disorder classified on the basis of clinical studies and clinical experience.

dibenzazepines. A group of antidepressant drugs.

dichromat. A person with the most common form of color blindness, in which one of the three cone systems of the eye is defective. See also *monochromat; trichromat.*

difference threshold. The smallest perceptible difference between two stimuli. Also called the just-noticeable difference.

discrimination. In sensory psychology, the detection of differences; in learning, responding differently to different stimuli, objects, events, or individuals; in social psychology, treating people differently on the basis of their race, ethnic group, class, and so on rather than on the basis of their relevant traits; acts of discrimination are typically premised upon prejudice. See also *prejudice.*

discrimination training. The training of an organism to respond differently to two or more similar but distinct stimuli; typically an organism is reinforced for responding to one stimulus and extinguished for responding to another. In behavior therapy, the manipulation of environmental events as discriminative stimuli to produce appropriate behaviors.

discriminative stimulus. A stimulus whose presence controls a specific behavior by indicating the probable consequence (reinforcement or nonreinforcement, punishment or nonpunishment) of the behavior.

dishabituation. The process of becoming or the state of being no longer accustomed to something. After dishabituation, an organism will respond to the formerly habituated stimulus as strongly as it did before habituation occurred. See also *habituation.*

displacement. The process or result of shifting an idea, activity, or emotional attachment from its proper object to another object, as in dreams; in psycholinguistics, one of the essential characteristics of language: the transmission of information about things that are not present and events that are not happening.

displacement activity. In ethology, a seemingly irrelevant fixed action pattern shown by an animal in a situation in which two other, conflicting, fixed action patterns are evoked.

dissociation. The act or process of separating; the state of being disconnected; in psychiatry, a defense mechanism whereby conflicting attitudes, impulses, or parts of personality are separated from one another, sometimes manifesting itself as amnesia or multiple personality; a separation of consciousness into two or more seemingly independent or partially independent entities.

dissonance. An incongruity or disagreement. See also *cognitive dissonance, theory of.*

distortion. The process or result of modifying an image so that it no longer correctly resembles the actual object, person, or place it represents; in Freudian theory, the process by which forbidden or unacceptable unconscious thoughts or impulses are disguised so that they may enter consciousness.

distribution. An array of the instances of a variable arranged so that different classes of the variable are ordered in some manner and the frequency of each class is indicated.

dizygotic (DZ). Of twins, arising from two zygotes and therefore from two fertilized eggs. See *fraternal twins.*

DNA. See *deoxyribonucleic acid.*

dominance. A tendency to seek control over or leadership of others, or such control or leadership itself; the tendency of one hemisphere of the brain or side of the body to take precedence over the other.

dopamine. A chemical found in the brain that is hypothesized to produce schizophrenia when it occurs in excessive amounts in parts of the brain; the antipsychotic drugs are believed to work because they block these effects of dopamine.

double-bind theory. In psychiatry, a theory tracing the origin of schizophrenia to a social environment in which an individual receives contradictory messages and cannot either deal with the contradictions or escape from the situation.

double-blind technique. A research technique in which neither the subjects nor the experimenters know which subjects have been exposed to the independent variable.

Down's syndrome. An abnormal condition in humans characterized by various physical abnormalities, including severe mental retardation; caused by the presence of an extra chromosome of the twenty-first pair. Also called mongolism.

Draw-a-Person Test (Machover Test). A projective personality test in which the subject draws a person.

drive. The psychological representation of a physiological need; a complex of internal conditions brought about by sensitivity to certain stimuli that impels an organism to seek a goal. Drives are often considered to be stimulated by internal bodily changes rather than by psychological or social stimuli.

drive theory. The view, advanced by C. Hull and others, that motivated behavior stems from physiological needs or drives and that any behavior that reduces a drive will be reinforced.

E

eardrum. A membrane between the outer and inner ear that is vibrated by sound.

echolocation. A technique, used by bats and whales, of locating objects by emitting sound waves and monitoring them after reflection from the objects.

eclecticism. In psychotherapy, a method that combines techniques from more than one therapeutic approach.

educational psychology. The branch of psychology concerned with the investigation of methods of instruction and problems that arise during instruction.

EEG. See *electroencephalogram.*

ego. According to Freudian theory, the part of the psyche that handles transactions with the external environment according to the reality principle. The ego mediates between the demands of the id and the superego. See also *id; psyche; superego; psychodynamic processes.*

egocentrism. In Piaget's developmental theory, the inability to understand the viewpoints of others; especially characteristic of the preoperational period. Notice that in this usage egocentrism is not the same as selfishness.

ego-ideal. The image of the self that a person consciously and unconsciously strives to become and against which he judges himself or herself; in Freudian theory, the superego is composed of the conscience and the ego-ideal.

ejaculation. The expulsion of semen and seminal fluid from the penis.

Electra complex. According to Freud, the female form of the Oedipus complex; the desire of a girl to possess her father sexually, manifested in the phallic stage and thereafter repressed.

electroconvulsive shock therapy. A form of psychotherapy sometimes used to treat mania, depression, and schizophrenia in which a certain voltage of electric current is passed through the brain for a particular amount of time, causing a convulsion, a temporary suspension of breathing, and a coma lasting from 5 to 30 minutes.

electrode. A conductor that establishes electrical contact with another substance or body part.

electroencephalogram (EEG). A graphic record of the electrical activity of the brain obtained by electrodes placed on the skull or brain.

electromagnetic radiation. Waves produced by the periodic variation of electrical and magnetic field intensities, such as radio waves, light, and x-rays. See also *light.*

elicited behavior. A response evoked by the presence of a specific stimulus, as in classical conditioning.

emitted behavior. A response that has no known antecedent stimulus but is controlled by its consequence, as in operant conditioning.

emotion. A feeling state of consciousness accompanied by internal bodily changes (*e.g.*, rapid heartbeat, muscular tightening).

empirical. Dependent on observable facts or experience.

encoding. The process of transforming data into a code; the process whereby a message is translated into signals that can be carried by a communication channel; the process of transferring information from one communication system to another.

encounter group. A form of group therapy emphasizing personal growth and improvement in interpersonal communication through intensive interpersonal experience in a small group. Encounter groups encourage openness, honesty, emotional expression, and sensitivity and revolve around the feelings and interactions that occur within the group.

endocrine gland. Any one of a group of glands that secrete hormones into the bloodstream or lymph system.

endocrine system. The system that controls the hormones of the body, including the glands that secrete the hormones and the blood and other bodily fluids that distribute them.

energization and direction. The two major concepts in any motivation theory; the first has to do with motivation itself (energy, vigor, persistence), the second with what particular activities or goals are chosen.

environmentalist. See *nativist.*

enzyme. Any of various organic compounds that can generate or control chemical changes in the body.

epidemiology. The study of the incidence of disease, especially of epidemics, in different populations.

epidermis. The outer layer of the skin.

epilepsy. A disorder of the nervous system characterized by convulsions, or fits, and stemming from brain malfunction.

epinephrine. A potent hormone released by the adrenal gland that increases blood pressure, stimulates the heart, increases heart rate, increases the blood-sugar level, and increases muscle sensitivity to neural impulses. Also known as *adrenalin.*

episodic memory. As defined by E. Tulving, memory for specific, temporally extended events in one's life as they were experienced. See also *semantic memory.*

epistemology. Study of the origins, nature, and limitations of knowledge.

epithelium. Membranous tissue covering bodily surfaces or lining bodily cavities whose functions include protection and secretion.

equilibration. In Piaget's theory of development, the process by which accommodation and assimilation are brought into balance.

Eros. According to Freud, the life instinct present at birth that includes all drives for self-preservation. See also *Thanatos.*

escape conditioning. A type of operant conditioning in which making the correct response terminates an aversive stimulus or removes the subject from contact with it. See also *avoidance conditioning; negative reinforcer.*

ESP. See *extrasensory perception.*

estrous cycle. A recurrent series of physiological changes in many species of female mammals, especially in the reproductive organs and endocrine system, that control the degree of sexual receptivity.

ethnocentrism. The belief that one's own group or culture is superior to that of others, with accompanying feelings of contempt for different groups and cultures; the tendency to perceive and evaluate other groups or cultures on the basis of one's own group or cultural standards.

ethology. The comparative study of behavior, usually of animals, with an eye to species-specific behavior.

evolution. A process or product of development; the continuous genetic adaptation of organisms or species to their environment by specialized processes, such as selection, hybridization, and mutation.

excitation. The arousal of activity or the state resulting from such arousal; the stimulation of a nerve, organ, or tissue; a state of emotional agitation.

existential psychiatry. An approach developed by R. Laing and others that focuses on human problems resulting from a search for meaning in a chaotic world.

expectancy. A learned disposition whereby an organism anticipates that a specific situation will be brought about by a given response to a stimulus.

expectancy-value theory. A theory of human motivation that explains human behavior in terms of an individual's expectancy about attaining a goal in a situation in which his or her motives might be aroused and in terms of the incentive value of the goal. See also *motivation; motive.*

experiment. An operation carried out under controlled circumstances for the purpose of testing a hypothesis, proving a law, or discovering unknown relationships, laws, or effects.

experimental condition. A variable, phenomenon, situation, force, or the like manipulated by the experimenter in order to discover relationships or principles. See also *independent variable.*

experimental design. The plan for carrying out an experiment, including the method of subject selection, procedures for administering the independent variable, and the type of statistical analyses required.

experimental group. In an experiment, the group of subjects exposed to the independent variable. See also *control group.*

experimental psychology. The study of psychological phenomena by means of experimental investigation.

expressive technique. A projective test for personality assessment focusing on nonverbal, creative responses such as drawing pictures.

externalization. The process of regarding one's actions, drives, or images as being caused by forces or objects outside oneself; imagining a mental image to be outside oneself (*e.g.,* hallucinating); ascribing one's own ideas, feelings, or perceptions to others (*i.e.,* projection).

extinction. The act of putting an end to something; the gradual disappearance of a conditioned response, either because of the repeated presentation of the conditioned stimulus without the unconditioned stimulus or because of the withholding of reinforcement for the occurrence of the conditioned response.

extrasensory perception (ESP). Possible ways of receiving information about the world through channels other than the normal senses. See also *clairvoyance; precognition; psychokinesis; telepathy.*

extraversion. See *introversion-extraversion.*

F

factor analysis. The process of finding the smallest number of factors that can account for all the correlations among a set of variables; used by some psychologists to search for the major dimensions of some aspect of behavior, such as personality.

false alarm. In signal-detection theory, erroneous judgment in which noise is mistaken for signal. See also *correct rejection; hit; miss.*

family therapy. A technique for treating a patient within the context of the family, based on the view that the total family system is the locus of pathology.

farsightedness. The inability to see near objects clearly because the lens focuses light behind the retina instead of on it.

feature analysis. In information-processing theory, a pattern-recognition procedure in which sensory information is broken down into distinctive characteristics that can be used to identify specific patterns. See also *analysis by synthesis.*

feature extraction. In information processing, the first stage of message decoding, in which distinctive aspects of the input are detected.

Fechner's law. A general law stating that the intensity of a sensation increases proportionately with the magnitude of the stimulus. Fechner's law is a generalization of Weber's law. See also *Weber's law; Stevens' power law.*

feedback. In information processing, the use of information about the result of output as input to control further output.

female hormone. A hormone that regulates the growth and function of the female reproductive organs or stimulates the development of feminine secondary sex characteristics. Both sexes have female hormones, although females have them in greater quantities.

fetish. An unlikely object that is the subject of sexual excitement or excitation. These objects are, for men, ones often used by or associated with females, *e.g.,* nylon stockings, gloves.

fetus. The young of an animal (including human beings) in the womb, especially after the body begins to take the form of that of an adult.

figural motion. The changes in sensory information (particularly visual information) that result from the movement of one object in the visual field. An object can move relative to other objects, or parts of an object can move relative to other parts. See also *motion parallax.*

figure and ground. The division of the perceptual field into two distinct and interdependent parts, the figure and the background.

firing. In neurophysiology, the discharge of neural impulses by the axon of a neuron.

fissure. A narrow opening occurring from separation of parts; a natural groove in a bodily organ, especially the brain.

fissure of Rolando. The central fissure of each cerebral hemisphere separating the frontal and parietal lobes.

fissure of Sylvius. The groove between the temporal lobe and the parietal and frontal lobes.

fixation. The state of being set or rigid; an arrest in development that continues into later life whereby a person forms an attachment to persons, objects, events, feelings, or attitudes experienced in infancy or early childhood; in psychiatry, a defense mechanism, usually implying pathology, that prevents a person from forming normal attachments in later life; in vision, centering of the eye on a stimulus.

fixed action pattern. A relatively stereotyped and frequently repeated pattern of movements that is species-specific.

forebrain. The area of the brain composed of the thalamus, hypothalamus, and cerebral hemispheres.

formal group. A highly organized group that usually has explicit rules and regulations governing the behavior of group members. See also *informal group.*

formal-operational period. The last of Piaget's periods of intellectual development (adolescence through adulthood), during which a person learns to think simultaneously about two or more systems of operations and, as a consequence, is able to carry out systematic experiments, to consider hypothetical objects and events, and to understand abstract principles.

formal operations. In Piaget's developmental theory, operations that can be applied to abstract or hypothetical things as well as to tangible things in the world. See also *concrete operations.*

fovea. A small depression near the center of the retina, containing cones but no rods, that is the point of highest visual acuity.

fraternal twins. Two offspring that shared the same womb before birth but developed from different fertilized eggs. Just like any two siblings, they share only 50 percent of their genes. See also *identical twins.*

free association. The unrestrained and uncensored expression of thoughts that occur spontaneously; a technique used in psychoanalysis that enables the therapist to explore his patient's unconscious.

frequency distribution. The arrangement of data for a variable so that the relative numbers, or frequencies, of each class or value of the variable are indicated.

Freudian theory. See *psychoanalytic theory.*

frontal lobe. The foremost lobe of the cerebrum, concerned with fine motor activity and speech.

functional analysis of behavior. The process of observing, describing, and measuring an organism's responses and specifying the environmental events that control them.

functional fixedness. In problem solving, the inability to perceive that a particular strategy or set is inappropriate to the problem at hand or that an object used in one way may also be used in another way.

fundamental needs. See *basic needs.*

G

galvanic skin response (GSR). A change in the electrical resistance of the skin indicating emotional change.

ganglion. A bundle of nerve junctions lying outside the central nervous system.

ganglion cell. A retinal neuron whose axons form the optic nerve.

gating. See *sensory gating.*

gene. An ultramicroscopic particle considered to be the basic unit for the transmission of hereditary characteristics. Genes are carried by the chromosomes.

gene action pathway. The sequential steps from a single gene's specification of the structure of a protein through the body's use of that protein.

general aptitude test battery (GATB). A set of tests devised by the U.S. Employment Service to determine whether a person meets the minimum standards for each of several occupations.

General Problem Solver (GPS). A computer program developed by Newell, Shaw, and Simon to simulate problem-solving behavior.

generalization. Application of a judgment to a whole class or group after contact with a limited number of members of that group. See also *response generalization; stimulus generalization; generalization gradient.*

generalization gradient. The regular variation in the amount of responding an organism makes to stimuli according to their degree of similarity to a particular stimulus to which the organism has been trained to respond. See also *stimulus generalization.*

generativity. In E. Erikson's personality theory, the positive outcome of one of the stages of adult personality development; the ability to do creative work or to contribute to the raising of one's children. The opposite of stagnation.

genetics. The scientific study of heredity.

genital stage. According to Freud, the final psychosexual stage (beginning with puberty), during which sexual interest shifts from autoeroticism to heterosexuality.

germ cell. A reproductive cell; a sperm or egg.

gestalt. A unified whole or configuration having specific properties that cannot be derived from summing up its separate parts. Usually used with reference to perceptual phenomena. See *principles of perceptual organization.*

Gestalt psychology. A school of psychology, concerned primarily with the processes of perception, whose basic premise is that "the whole is greater than the sum of its parts." Gestalt psychology not only contends that stimuli are perceived as whole images rather than as parts built into images but also maintains that the whole determines the parts instead of the parts determining the whole.

Gestalt psychotherapy. A form of psychotherapy loosely based on the theories of Gestalt psychology. Gestalt treatment attempts to broaden a person's self-awareness so as to enable her or him to form meaningful configurations of awareness.

gland. An organ that releases or produces a substance used in or secreted from the body.

gonad. A sex gland; ovary or testis.

GPS. See *General Problem Solver.*

gradient. A variable or dimension that varies continuously from high to low.

grammar. In psycholinguistics, the rules (sometimes formal but usually unwritten) actually used by the speaker of a language to construct sentences.

ground. Background. See *figure and ground.*

group norm. A standard by which a group judges the behavior of its members.

group psychotherapy. The treatment of several people at the same time, although not always in the same manner.

group therapy. See *group psychotherapy.*

groupthink. A group decision-making process that results in unrealistic or overly dogmatic group opinion or appraisal. Groupthink presumably occurs when members of a group feel so strong a need for unanimity of thought or expression that they tend to override any realistic appraisal of alternative ideas and, as a result of internalization of group norms, tend to suppress critical thoughts.

growth center. A facility offering a wide range of techniques for achieving personal growth and awareness.

GSR. See *galvanic skin response.*

gustation. The sense of taste; the act of tasting.

gyrus. A ridge or fold, especially in the surface of the cerebral cortex. See also *sulcus.*

H

habit. An acquired and consistently manifested behavior; a learned act that has become fixed and relatively automatic through constant repetition; the directional concept in Hull's theory. See also *energization and direction.*

habit strength. The likelihood of repetition, in a similar situation, of any response that has been reinforced by drive reduction; one of the two major variables in Hull's performance equation, the other being *drive.*

habituation. Decreased response to a stimulus because it has become familiar or is expected.

hair cell. A cell containing hairlike projections that is a receptor for hearing in the organ of Corti.

halfway house. A self-governing living unit of mentally disturbed people who do not generally require hospitalization but do need the support of a social community that can help them with their problems.

hallucination. Perception of an external object by a sense organ when no such object exists in reality.

hallucinogen. See *psychedelic drug.*

halo effect. In ratings by others of a person's characteristics, the influence on those ratings of specific other characteristics or of a general impression of that person.

handedness. The tendency to use either the right or the left hand almost exclusively.

hashish. A gummy powder derived from the resin of Indian hemp (*Cannabis sativa*) that provides an intoxicating effect when smoked or ingested.

hebephrenic schizophrenia. A severe form of schizophrenia characterized by absurd behavior, shallowness of feelings, and loss of touch with reality.

hedonistic. Motivated by the desire to seek pleasure and avoid pain.

Henning's smell prism. A classification scheme for odors based on human judgments in which six pure odor qualities form the corners of the prism and intermediate qualities lie along the surface.

heredity. The biological transmission of genetic characteristics from parent to offspring.

heritability. Of a trait, the amount of variation in the trait that is due to genetic differences among individuals.

heroin. Diacetylmorphine, a derivative of morphine that has a euphoriant and sedative effect. Heroin is much stronger than morphine and is one of the most widely used of the illegal addictive drugs.

heuristic. In problem solving, a strategy that points to a potential solution without testing all possible operations. See also *subgoal analysis; means-end analysis; algorithm.*

hierarchy. The arrangement of objects, persons, values, or elements in a ranked order based upon some explicit criterion.

hindbrain. The area of the brain composed of the medulla, pons, and cerebellum.

hit. In signal-detection theory, a correct judgment that a signal is present. See also *correct rejection; false alarm; miss.*

homeostasis. The tendency of a system to maintain equilibrium or internal stability; when some factor disturbs the equilibrium, the sys-

tem puts into effect mechanisms or processes that will restore the equilibrium.

hormone. A chemical substance produced in the body that is secreted by one organ and carried through the blood to another. Hormones regulate physiological activity.

hue. The quality of light permitting its classification according to color; color.

humanistic psychology. The general psychological approach that emphasizes the special characteristics that differentiate human beings from other animals. Humanistic psychologists especially stress positive, constructive human capacities.

hunger. A drive state based on the bodily effects of food deprivation; the need or desire for food.

hyperactivity. A high degree of physical activity. Used especially of children who are constantly restless and moving. Also known as hyperkinesis.

hypnosis. A socially induced, unusual state of consciousness in which a person is very susceptible to suggestion. See also *trance.*

hypothalamus. A group of nuclei located below the thalamus that mediates between the brain and the body, helping control many basic drives and emotional processes, including hunger, sleep, thirst, body temperature, and sexual behavior. It controls involuntary functions through the autonomic nervous system.

hypothesis. A proposition put forth as an explanation for specific phenomena.

hypothesis-testing theory. The view that people and animals in problem-solving or learning situations form and test hypotheses about how to reach a goal.

hysteria. A mental disorder characterized by diverse symptoms. The defining symptoms are not universally agreed upon, but dissociation or conversion reactions are usually held to occur. Hysteria is often considered to be a neurotic reaction to an anxiety-provoking situation in which repression is the primary defense. See also *conversion reaction; dissociation.*

I

id. According to Freud, the unconscious and most primitive part of the psyche, comprising drives, needs, and instinctual impulses. The id operates according to the pleasure principle and is in constant conflict with the superego. See also *ego; psyche; superego.*

identical twins. Two offspring that shared the same womb before birth and developed from a single fertilized egg. Unlike other siblings, they share all the same genes.

identification. The perception of oneself as essentially similar to another; the process of categorizing oneself as psychologically similar to another person or to the members of a social group and striving to increase that similarity.

identity. Sameness of basic traits despite superficial differences; a sense of personal sameness and continuity.

identity crisis. According to E. Erikson, the major test of the adolescent stage of psychosocial development, in which the individual must decide who he or she is and what his or her role in life will be.

illusion. A distorted or incorrect perception of a physically present object; that which produces a false perception.

image. A mental representation of an object or event that was previously experienced but that is not now present.

impression. The immediate, unanalyzed effect of sensations or perceptions on the mind; an assessment that is not based on thorough investigation or is not firmly maintained; in personality theory, one person's conception of another.

imprinting. In ethology, a social learning mechanism in birds by which attachments are formed to other organisms (normally the mother) or to objects. Imprinting occurs very early in life (during a sensitive period) and is somewhat resistant to later modification.

incentive. A reward that stimulates or maintains goal-directed behavior.

incentive value. A concept in J. Atkinson's theory of achievement motivation that has to do with the perceived positive or negative value of a particular goal; represented by the letter *I* in Atkinson's mathematical model.

incremental theory. Any theory that regards development as an additive series of qualitatively similar steps. See also *stage theory*.

independent variable. A variable that is manipulated by the experimenter. Changes in an independent variable are expected to affect the dependent variable.

industrial psychology. The branch of psychology concerned with work and personnel problems in business and industry. It also often includes organizational psychology, which focuses on the behavior of individuals in large organizations such as businesses and the relationship between that behavior and the efficiency and effectiveness of the organizations.

inference. The act or process of making a judgment or coming to a conclusion on the basis of premises or evidence; the judgment or conclusion reached by such a process. See also *perceptual inference*.

inferential statistics. Mathematical techniques used to infer what conclusions can be made from a set of data and what degree of certainty can be attributed to those conclusions. See also *descriptive statistics*.

inferiority complex. An individual's feelings, based on childhood experiences, that other persons can do things he cannot do. According to A. Adler, much of human action is an attempt to overcome these feelings.

informal group. A group that is not highly organized and whose rules and expectations about members' behavior are generally not explicit. See also *formal group*.

infrared rays. Electromagnetic radiation whose frequency falls below that of visible red.

inhibition. The process by which an action or response is restrained, stopped, or prevented from starting even though the stimulus that normally elicits the action or response is present; according to Freud, a process of the superego that prevents instinctual impulses from coming into consciousness; a decrease in a neuron's rate of activity.

innate. Existing in an organism from birth; genetic.

inner ear. The area of the ear comprising the cochlea, vestibular sacs, and semicircular canals.

input. Information fed into an information-processing system (human or mechanical); a form of physical energy or a physical event registered by a sense organ.

insight. The understanding and reasonable evaluation of one's own reactions, awareness, and abilities; the degree to which a mentally ill person understands his own mental condition; knowledge of the objective reality of a situation; in learning and problem solving, a new understanding that suddenly occurs.

insomnia. An inability to sleep, particularly when habitual or chronic.

instinct. An inherited, repetitive behavior that is specific to a species; according to Freud, a primal source of energy or an urge that cannot be resolved. The two instincts postulated by Freud are the life instinct (Eros) and the death instinct (Thanatos).

institutional racism. Racism practiced and controlled by an institution or society; includes actions controlled by the norms, rules, or customs of an institution or society.

instrumental conditioning. See *operant conditioning*.

insulin. A hormone secreted by the pancreas that allows the body to use sugar and other carbohydrates.

intelligence. The ability to deal with abstractions; the capacity to learn; the ability to handle new situations.

intelligence quotient (IQ). Originally, a measure of an individual's mental development obtained by dividing his mental age (the score achieved on a standardized intelligence test) by his chronological age and multiplying the quotient by 100; now any standardized measure of intelligence based on a scale in which 100 is defined to be average.

intelligence test. A standardized series of tasks designed to measure problem-solving ability, intellectual functioning, and/or previously learned concepts or cognitions.

intensity. The strength or magnitude of a behavior; a physical measure of amount of energy or sensory input.

interference. The act of opposing; intervention that hampers actions or procedures; in learning, the hampering of one instance of learning by another.

interference theory. The hypothesis that a person forgets certain material because other material hinders its recall. See also *negative transfer; proactive interference; retroactive interference; serial-position effect*.

interiorized scheme. In Piaget's developmental theory, a framework for dealing with experiences through mental transformation rather than physical action (*e.g.*, in addition, 3 plus 5 is transformed into the sum, 8).

intermittent reinforcement. A schedule of reinforcement in which reinforcement is delivered only part of the time regardless of the number of correct responses made by the subject. Also known as variable reinforcement. See also *interval schedule; ratio schedule*.

internalization. Incorporation into the mind or personality; making the values, ideas, standards, or practices of others a part of oneself.

interpretation. In psychoanalysis, the process of uncovering the meaning of some aspect of the patient's problem or of the latent content of the patient's dream.

interval schedule. A plan indicating when an organism is to receive reinforcement, based on the time that elapses between one reinforced response and the next.

intrapsychic. Originating or taking place within the psyche.

introjection. The incorporation of the image of an object or individual into the psyche; taking the demands of an object or individual into the psyche and acting as if they were one's own, whether or not the object or individual is present.

introspection. The contemplation of one's own experiences, behavior, consciousness, or feelings; the report of one's mental experiences, usually for the purpose of analysis and study.

introversion-extraversion. According to H. Eysenck's factor-analytic approach to personality, one of the three major dimensions underlying people's responses on personality questionnaires: Introverts have a naturally high level of arousal and so tend to avoid stimulation that would increase their arousal still further, while extraverts have a naturally low level and so seek stimulation to increase their arousal. See also *neuroticism; psychoticism*.

IQ. See *intelligence quotient*.

iris. A circular diaphragm in the eye that expands and contracts to control the amount of light admitted into the retina. The iris contains the pupil and forms the colored part of the eye.

J

jump stand. An experimental device developed by K. S. Lashley to test visual discrimination and discrimination training. The subject (usually a rat) must choose which of several doors to jump toward to obtain a reward.

just-noticeable difference. See *difference threshold*.

K

karyotyping. The process of photographing chromosomes and analyzing them into the pairs that are characteristic of the species.

key-word system. A mnemonic scheme in which certain key words, or pegs, are associated with the items to be remembered; the key words are then incorporated into a vivid image or story. The key words often rhyme with numbers (such as one-bun) so that the items can be recalled in order.

kibbutz. An Israeli collective community that is mainly agricultural.

kinesthesis. The sense of bodily movement. Receptors for kinesthesis are found in muscles, joints, and tendons.

kneecap. The patella.

L

labia. The lips or folds of skin surrounding the clitoris and vagina.

language. Communicative behavior, either verbal or nonverbal; an abstract system of symbols and meanings and the rules of grammar that relate them; a system of communication by vocal symbols. See also *displacement; meaningfulness; productiveness.*

language rule. A principle or procedure that is used to generate speech. Usually the individual is not aware of using the rule.

larynx. A structure composed of muscle and cartilage and lined with mucous membrane. The larynx is located at the upper part of the windpipe and houses the vocal cords.

latency stage. According to Freud, the fourth psychosexual stage of development (from approximately five to twelve years), during which the child represses his or her sexual interest. At puberty interest in sex emerges once again.

latent content. In psychoanalysis, dream material that is revealed through free association and interpretation; the deeper, psychologically significant meaning of the dream. See also *manifest content.*

lateral inhibition. The action by which a retinal cell that is highly stimulated by light prevents or decreases the responding of cells next to it.

lay analyst. A person who is trained to practice psychoanalysis but who does not have a medical degree.

learned drive. An acquired, nonphysiological motive such as achievement, which, according to drive theory, was orginally associated with basic needs.

learned helplessness. A concept developed by M. Seligman to explain why animals and people who have been unavoidably punished in the past will later not act to avoid punishment, even when avoidance is possible.

learning. An enduring change in knowledge or behavior resulting from training, experience, or study, or the process that brings about such a change.

learning theory. In general, an attempt to explain learning or account for the acquisition of habits; specifically, the proposition that learning is based on the establishment of stimulus-response relationships.

legitimate authority. See *authority, legitimate.*

lens. In vision, a transparent structure of the eye, covering the iris and pupil, that changes its shape in order to focus images on the retina.

lesion. An injury; a localized, abnormal change in the structure of a bodily organ or tissue due to injury or disease.

level of activation. An emotional-response continuum ranging between sleep and tension; a dimension used by H. Schlosberg in characterizing the various emotions.

level of significance. See *statistical significance.*

libido. According to Freud, psychic energy. There is some confusion as to whether libido is the energy of the sex drive and the force behind Eros or the energy behind the destructive drives of Thanatos, or both.

Librium. See *chlordiazepoxide.*

life instinct. See *Eros.*

light. The visible range of electromagnetic radiation; the part of the electromagnetic spectrum extending from the ultraviolet to the infrared and including the visible range.

limbic system. A set of neural structures bordering the cerebral cortex that are particularly important in emotion, motivation, and some visceral functions.

linguistics. The science of the origin, structure, and effects of language.

link. Each separate stimulus-response in a chain of behavior.

lithium. A naturally occurring metallic element whose salts have been used in the treatment of manic-depressive psychosis.

lobe. Any of the several round-shaped regions of the cerebral cortex.

localization. The condition of being in a specific area; the perception of a sensory stimulus as being in a certain location; the location of control over certain bodily functions in definite areas of the brain.

locus of control. In attribution theory of achievement motivation, the perceived site, either inside the person or outside, of factors that determine the outcome of a given situation.

longitudinal study. A research project that gathers data repeatedly from the same group of subjects over a period of time.

long-term memory (LTM). "Permanent" memory that has a seemingly unlimited capacity. LTM endures for very long periods of time.

loudness. The psychological dimension of sound intensity; the subjective magnitude of the strength of a sound.

LSD. See *lysergic acid diethylamide.*

LTM. See *long-term memory.*

lysergic acid diethylamide (LSD). An extremely potent psychedelic drug that can produce behavior and sensations similar to schizophrenia (*e.g.,* hallucinations, perceptual distortions, thinking impairment).

M

Machover test. See *Draw-a-Person Test.*

magazine training. The establishment of conditioned reinforcers by periodic provision of reinforcement no matter what the subject is doing.

male hormone. A hormone (*e.g.,* testosterone) that regulates the growth and function of the male reproductive organs or stimulates the development of masculine secondary sex characteristics. Both sexes have male hormones although males have them in greater quantities.

mandala. A representation of the cosmos made up of concentric shapes that often contain images of deities, often used as an aid to meditation; in Jung's theory, a magical circle that represents the effort to unify the self.

mania. Behavior characterized by agitation, excitement, and violent and unrestrained motor activity; behavior characteristic of the elated phase of manic-depressive psychosis.

manic-depressive psychosis. A severe mental disorder characterized by depressive states or states of elation or periodic shifts from one to the other.

manifest content. In psychoanalysis, dream material that is recalled and reported by the dreamer; the surface or obvious content of the dream. See also *latent content.*

mantra. A word or phrase to be recited, contemplated, or sung, especially as a part of meditation.

MAO inhibitor. See *monoamine oxidase (MAO) inhibitor.*

marijuana. The dried leaves and flowers of Indian hemp (*Cannabis sativa*) that provide an intoxicating effect when smoked or ingested.

maturation. The process or end result of physical growth and development, including resultant behavioral changes.

maze. A network of passages, some of which lead to an exit or a reward and some of which do not. Mazes are frequently used in laboratory experiments investigating learning.

mean, arithmetic. A measure of central tendency computed by dividing the sum of a set of scores by the number of scores in the set.

meaningfulness. In psycholinguistics, one of the essential characteristics of language: symbols (words or gestures) are used to represent objects, events, or abstract ideas.

means-end analysis. In the General Problem Solver computer program, a heuristic by which means are sought that will move the problem solver closer to the goal. See also *subgoal analysis.*

measure of central tendency. A number summarizing a set of scores that reveals some kind of middle value of the scores. See also *mean, arithmetic; median; mode.*

measure of variability. A number or set of numbers summarizing the degree of dispersion or variation in a set of scores. See also *range; standard deviation.*

median. In a set of scores ranked from low to high, the score that has half of the scores above it and half below.

meditation. Prolonged reflective thought or contemplation.

meiosis. In germ-cell formation, the process of cell division resulting in germ cells with half the number of chromosomes present in normal body cells (*i.e.,* containing one chromosome from each chromosome pair).

membrane. A thin, pliable layer, particularly of animal or plant tissue, that connects bodily parts, lines an organ, or covers a cell or cell part.

memory. The complex mental function of recalling what has been learned or experienced; the image of what has been learned or experienced; the physical retention of information. See also *recall; recognition; storage.*

memory image. See *image.*

memory storage. See *storage.*

memory trace. A hypothesized physiological change in the nervous system that occurs in learning.

menstrual cycle. In the human female, the periodic release of an egg into the uterus followed several weeks later by death of the egg and discharge of blood and other substances from the vagina, unless the egg is fertilized. The cycle repeats approximately monthly in sexually mature women.

mental disorder. A serious failure to adapt mentally to external conditions that incapacitates a person in some way. Mental disorders can be short-lived or persistent, can be due to somatic or psychic processes, and can manifest themselves by physical or psychological symptoms. Sometimes also called mental or emotional disturbances, emotional disorder, or psychological disorder. See also *neurosis; psychosis.*

mental illness. See *mental disorder.*

meprobamate. An antianxiety drug and muscle relaxant, marketed as Miltown or Equanil.

mescaline. A psychedelic drug obtained from the round top of the peyote plant. Mescaline is similar to but not as potent as LSD.

metabolism. The physical and chemical processes occurring within an organism by which energy is provided and protoplasm built up, maintained, and broken down.

metaneeds. In A. Maslow's theory of personality, human needs that are growth needs rather than deficiency needs, are not hierarchically ordered, and are substitutable for one another. Metaneeds cannot be satisfied unless basic needs are satisfied. The satisfaction of metaneeds leads to self-actualization. See also *basic needs; self-actualization.*

methadone. A synthetic narcotic used to treat heroin addicts. Methadone eliminates the heroin withdrawal syndrome and blocks the euphoric effects of other narcotics but is itself an addicting drug.

methamphetamine. A synthetic drug, a type of amphetamine, that acts as a stimulant.

method of loci. A mnemonic device in which people or objects to be remembered are imagined as placed in specific spots in a familiar location.

methodology. The principles and rules of procedure of a given discipline.

midbrain. One of the two parts of the cerebrum that lie beneath the forebrain and connect the forebrain to the hindbrain. The midbrain is concerned with sight and hearing.

middle ear. A membrane-lined cavity located between the eardrum and inner ear that contains the ossicles, three small bones.

Miltown. See *meprobamate.*

mind. The organized system of all mental activities; all of the structures assumed to account for voluntary behavior or mental processes; intellect; mental processes; the psyche.

Minnesota Multiphasic Personality Inventory (MMPI). A test designed to provide a detailed list of a subject's personality traits based on his answers to a series of 500 statements.

miss. In signal-detection theory, an incorrect judgment that a signal is absent. See also *correct rejection; false alarm; hit.*

MMPI. See *Minnesota Multiphasic Personality Inventory.*

mnemonic device. See *mnemonics.*

mnemonics. A method for remembering items that imposes an invented structure or organization on the material being memorized. See also *key-word system; method of loci.*

mode. In a set of scores, the score that occurs most frequently. The mode is a measure of central tendency.

model. In psychological theories, a representation that serves as a copy of a psychological process or a behavior; in social-learning theory, a person whose behavior is imitated.

modeling. In social-learning theory, a form of learning in which a person learns how to perform an act by watching another person do it.

mongolism. See *Down's syndrome.*

monoamine oxidase (MAO) inhibitor. Any of a group of substances that inhibit the activity of the enzyme monoamine oxidase (MAO), one important effect of which is to block destruction of norepinephrine in the neurons. One group of antidepressants are MAO inhibitors.

monochromat. A person whose eye fails to differentiate any hues of color—*i.e.,* a color-blind person who sees only blacks, whites, and grays.

monozygotic (MZ). Of twins, arising from one fertilized egg.

moral development, stages of. See *stages of moral development.*

morphine. An addictive drug used medically to relieve pain. The effects of morphine are similar to those of heroin.

motion parallax. The apparent movement of stationary objects that occurs when the position of the observer changes. Near objects seem to move in wider arcs than far objects. See also *figural motion.*

motivation. A hypothetical psychological process inferred from goal-directed behavior; an organism's tendency toward action in a particular situation. See also *drive.*

motive. A stable personality trait that consists of a tendency to perform certain actions or to seek certain goals.

motive to approach success. The desire, which differs from person to person, to strive to perform well on a particular task; represented by the symbol M_S in J. Atkinson's theory of achievement motivation.

motive to avoid failure. A personality characteristic that leads one to inhibit one's performance on a particular task due to an anticipation that one's efforts will not result in success; represented by the symbol M_{AF} in J. Atkinson's theory of achievement motivation.

motive to avoid success. A personality characteristic that leads one to inhibit one's performance on a task due to the anticipation that performing well will lead to undesired consequences; according to M. Horner, this motive is especially common in women, who feel that success at certain tasks may be viewed by others as unfeminine.

motor activities. Activities involving muscular movement (*e.g.,* walking).

motor neuron. An efferent neuron that carries impulses from the central nervous system to a muscle.

Müller-Lyer illusion. A visual illusion in which two lines of equal length appear unequal because one has acute-angled arrowheads on its ends and the other has obtuse-angled arrowheads on its ends; the line with the obtuse arrowheads seems to be longer.

multiple personality. A form of dissociation in which two or more distinct but not totally autonomous personalities are present in a single person.

multiplication of classes. In Piaget's developmental theory, the concrete-operational skill that involves understanding how two dimensions of classes (for example, colors and types of flowers) can be intermeshed to form joint classes (red tulips, red roses, red petunias, yellow tulips, yellow roses, yellow petunias, etc.) and how the joint classes can be taken apart into the dimensions.

myelin sheath. A white, fatty substance covering certain nerve fibers.

N

n Ach. See *achievement, need for.*

narcissism. Self-love, frequently associated with erotic gratification. According to psychoanalytic theory, a stage of child development in which the child does not differentiate between himself and objects outside himself and in which he perceives himself as the sole source of pleasure.

narcotic. Having the ability to produce a state of depression, sleep, or drowsiness; a drug that dulls the senses, reduces pain, causes drowsiness, and is addictive.

nativist. A person who emphasizes the role of heredity rather than environment in the developmental process.

natural selection. A theory of evolutionary change postulated by Darwin asserting that the individuals of a species who are best adapted to the demands of their environment survive and reproduce; in modern genetics, the theory that the makeup of the gene pool of a species depends on the efficacy to the individuals of the traits governed by the genes in the pool.

naturalistic observation. The act of noting a phenomenon as it occurs under natural conditions, without interference from an outsider.

nearsightedness. The inability to clearly see objects at a distance because the lens focuses images in front of the retina instead of on it.

need. The lack of something that is required; a tissue deficiency due to deprivation.

need complementarity. According to R. F. Winch and others, attraction to another because the other is perceived to have traits or needs that allow one's own to be fulfilled.

need for achievement. See *achievement, need for.*

negative correlation. A correlation indicating that two variables change in opposite directions (*i.e.,* a high value for one variable corresponds with a low value for the other variable). See also *positive correlation.*

negative reinforcer. In conditioning, a stimulus or event whose removal increases the frequency of a response. See also *positive reinforcer.*

negative transfer. A process of interference in which previously learned material inhibits the learning of a new task. See also *proactive interference; positive transfer.*

nerve. A bundle of neural fibers, together with connective and supportive tissue, generally located outside the brain or spinal cord.

nerve cell. See *neuron.*

nervous system. All nerve cells in the body and their associated organs and processes; the brain, spinal cord, and all nerve tissue.

neural. Pertaining to a nerve, a neuron, or the nervous system.

neural coding. The process by which the nervous system transforms information about the environment into a particular pattern of nervous discharge.

neural fiber. An axon or dendrite.

neural impulse. A temporary physical, chemical, and electrical change in the membrane of a neural fiber that travels along the fiber to its end, causing excitation in muscles, glands, or other nerves.

neurology. The branch of medicine concerned

with the organization, function, and diseases of the nervous system.

neuromuscular. Relating to both nerves and muscles.

neuron. A specialized cell that transmits neural impulses from one region of the nervous system to another and to muscles and glands. A neuron consists of a soma (cell body), dendrites, and an axon.

neurosis. A mental disorder, much milder than psychosis, affecting only part of the personality, often characterized by the following: a chronic state of anxiety; sensory, sexual, motor, or visceral disturbances; inhibition of emotions or instincts; difficulty in sleeping; lack of interest in the environment; and lack of physical energy. See also *hysteria; obsessive-compulsive neurosis; phobia.*

neurotic anxiety. An unjustified and chronic state of general apprehension; exaggerated apprehension associated with certain ideas; unjustified anxiety accompanied by somatic symptoms, as in hysteria.

neuroticism. According to H. Eysenck's factor-analytic approach to personality, one of the three major dimensions underlying people's responses on personality questionnaires: the tendency of an individual to associate anxiety with harmless situations. If this tendency is high, the person is likely to develop neurosis. See also *introversion-extraversion; psychoticism.*

neutral stimulus. A stimulus that does not elicit the response one is seeking. In classical conditioning, conditioned stimuli are developed out of neutral stimuli.

new brain. The portion of the brain that lies on top of the old brain and that is highly developed in people and other intelligent animals; also called the *cerebral cortex.*

noise. In signal-detection theory, any extraneous sensory information that may interfere with the detection of a signal.

nondirective therapy. See *client-centered therapy.*

nondisjunction. The failure of a pair of chromosomes to separate during the process of forming a sex cell. If the cell is fertilized, the offspring that develops will not be normal; in most cases, there will be a miscarriage, but in some instances of nondisjunction, such as Down's syndrome, the abnormal child may be born and survive.

nonsense syllable. A meaningless combination of letters that can be pronounced, such as QUK.

noradrenaline. See *norepinephrine.*

norepinephrine. A catecholamine that functions as a neural transmitter substance and that is released at nerve endings of the sympathetic nervous system, as well as from the adrenal gland into the circulation.

norm. In psychological testing, the average performance level for a given group of people; in social psychology, the standards or expectations for behavior upheld by societies or groups within societies.

normal distribution. A distribution or curve that is bell-shaped and that is usually the expected distribution of data in psychological research. A normal distribution has certain mathematical properties that make it a useful statistical tool. See also *distribution.*

normality. The quality of being average or usual; the quality of being free from mental dis-

order. In attempting to define psychological normality, psychologists have used three criteria: (1) the clinical criterion—absence of symptoms of mental disorder; (2) the ideal mental-health criterion—a state of perfection that people strive to reach; (3) the statistical criterion—whatever is done by most people is normal and healthy. See also *adjustment.*

nucleus. In a cell, a dense specialized mass of protoplasm that is typically round and enclosed by a membrane and contains the cell's chromosomes; a cluster of neurons in the central nervous system thought to have common functions and connections; a positively charged mass within an atom.

nystagmus. Rapid and involuntary movement of the eye, usually from side to side, but occasionally vertical or circular.

O

object permanence. The knowledge that an object continues to exist even when it is no longer perceived; according to Piaget, the capability develops during the sensorimotor period, reaching its final stage at 18 to 24 months. The complete development of object permanence marks the beginning of the pre-operational period.

objective. Actually existing in the world and capable of being observed by physical instruments; independent of an individual observer's emotions or judgments, hence, unbiased. See also *subjective.*

observable behavior. Any internal or external response of an organism that can be described and measured.

observational learning. See *modeling.*

obsession. An idea, most often very disturbing or disruptive, that dominates one's consciousness.

obsessive-compulsive neurosis. Neurosis characterized by the constant presence of unwanted, anxiety-provoking ideas (obsessions) and the occurrence of impulses to perform certain acts repeatedly (compulsions).

occipital lobe. The hindmost of the three rear lobes of the cerebrum. Concerned with the reception and analysis of visual information.

occlusion. In vision, the obscuring of part of an object that is farther away by a nearer object. Occlusion is a cue that is important for perception of depth and of motion.

occupational therapy. Psychotherapy whose goal is to help a patient overcome a psychological or physical disability through purposeful work.

Oedipus complex. According to Freud, a boy's desire to possess his mother sexually, manifested in the phallic stage and thereafter repressed. The female form of the Oedipus complex is the Electra complex.

old brain. The primitive portion of the human brain underlying the cerebral cortex. It handles reflex actions and is responsive primarily to basic bodily needs.

olfaction. The sense of smell.

olfactory epithelium. A membrane in the nasal cavity containing the receptors for smell.

operant behavior. A response that an organism emits spontaneously and that can be manipulated through operant conditioning; a response that is under voluntary control.

operant conditioning. A form of training in which certain of an organism's spontaneous activities are reinforced or punished. Also known as instrumental conditioning.

operation. In Piaget's developmental theory, an interiorized scheme or transformation that is reversible.

opponent-processes theory. The theory that three different systems, composed of three types of cells, are responsible for color vision: In one system, some cells are stimulated by red and inhibited by green and others are stimulated by green and inhibited by red. In another system yellow and blue similarly act in opposition to each other. The third system is achromatic and sensitive to brightness.

optical (or optic). Visual.

optimal arousal level. The point on the activation (sleep-tension) continuum at which a subject's performance of a given task stops improving and begins to deteriorate; sometimes used to refer to the subjectively most pleasant point on the continuum.

oral stage. According to Freud, the first psychosexual stage (occurring during the first eighteen months of life) in which pleasure is focused on the mouth and oral activities (*e.g.,* eating, sucking).

organ of Corti. A structure in the cochlea containing hair cells that are the receptors for hearing.

organic. Having a physical or biological basis.

organism. A form of life capable of performing specific, coordinated functions and normally capable of maintaining itself as a system; all animals including people are organisms.

ossicles. Three small bones in the middle ear that transmit sound from the eardrum to the cochlea.

outcome research. Studies of the effectiveness of psychotherapy.

outer ear. The part of the ear consisting of the pinna and auditory canal.

output. The end result of information processing. See also *input.*

oval window. A membrane-covered opening between the middle ear and the vestibule that transmits sound from the ossicles to the cochlea.

ovary. One of the pair of female reproductive glands in which egg cells and female hormones are produced.

overdetermined. Describes an action that is simultaneously motivated by several different motives or drives.

overlearning. Learning in which responses are practiced past the point of apparent mastery.

overregularization. The erroneous extension, generally by children, of a grammatical rule to instances where it does not apply. Overregularization is proof that the child has mastery of the rule in question.

overt behavior. An act easily observed by others.

ovulation. The release of an ovum, or egg, from the ovary.

ovum. An egg, or female germ cell.

P

paired-associate learning. A method of learning in which items, usually verbal, are presented in pairs so that the learner connects one item with the other.

papilla. A small, nipple-shaped protuberance; one of a cluster of small bumps located on the surface of the tongue, in hair cells, or on the skin of the hands and feet. There are papillae associated with sensory receptors for smell, taste, and touch.

paradigm. According to T. Kuhn, a theory or approach that is so successful in dealing with the subject matter of a field of science that it almost completely determines both which phenomena are studied and how they are studied. Also, a particular method of research, called a research paradigm.

paradoxical sleep. Another name for REM sleep. It is called paradoxical because some measures seem to indicate that the individual is awake while others seem to indicate that he or she is deeply asleep.

parallel processing. Categorizing and dealing with several streams of incoming information at one time.

paranoia. A psychosis characterized by the gradual development of systematic persecutory or grandiose delusions that affect only part of the personality and do not affect general intelligence.

paranoid schizophrenia. A psychosis characterized by elaborate and systematic delusions of persecution and grandeur. Paranoid schizophrenia, unlike paranoia, affects the entire personality.

parasympathetic nervous system. The division of the autonomic nervous system that is activated by acetylcholine and conserves body energy by slowing heart rate, aiding digestion, and so on.

parietal lobe. One of the three posterior lobes of the cerebrum concerned with skin senses and detection of bodily position.

patella. The kneecap.

patellar reflex. The involuntary forward extension of the lower leg that occurs when the patellar tendon is tapped. Commonly known as the knee-jerk reflex.

Pavlovian conditioning. See *classical conditioning.*

payoff. In signal-detection theory, the costs and benefits of correct and incorrect detection of a signal. Payoff influences the response criterion at which an individual reports that he detects a signal.

peg system. See *key-word system.*

penis. The male organ for urination and sexual intercourse.

penis envy. In Freudian theory, a girl's discontent with her genital apparatus accompanied by a desire to possess a penis, which is generally associated with omnipotence. Penis envy develops during the phallic stage and is thereafter repressed in normal females.

percentile system. A method for scoring tests that divides individuals' actual scores into 100 equal parts and assigns a percentile rank to each score, thus showing the proportion of people who scored above and below each individual. A score at the 80th percentile means that the individual scored better than 80 percent of the people who took the test and worse than 20 percent.

perception. The process of becoming aware of one's environment through the senses; awareness of the environment obtained through interpretation of sensory data.

perceptual constancy. In perception, the tendency to recognize the characteristics (*e.g.,* size, shape) of a stimulus object as being the same even under highly varied conditions.

perceptual field. That part of the external world an organism perceives and to which it makes a discriminating response.

perceptual inference. The process of interpreting sensory information.

perceptual set. See *set.*

periods of intellectual development. In Piaget's developmental theory, four qualitatively different ways of constructing an understanding of the world that follow each other in an invariant order as a child grows into adulthood. See *sensorimotor period; pre-operational period; concrete-operational period; formal-operational period.*

peripheral. Relating to the outer or external boundary or surface; referring to the nerves located outside the brain and spinal cord; referring to any bodily process that has a direct connection with the external world.

peripheral nervous system. The part of the nervous system that is made up of nerves connecting the central nervous system with the body's receptors and effectors—*i.e.,* all nerve processes and neurons outside the central nervous system.

peripheral trait. According to S. Asch, a trait of an individual the perception of which can be dramatically affected by the observer's perception of other, central traits. See also *central trait.*

periphery. The outer boundary of an area or surface. The retina exclusive of the fovea, containing mostly rods and few or no cones.

periphery of personality. Nonuniversal human characteristics cited by personality theorists to explain individual differences. See also *core of personality.*

person perception. The processes by which a person forms a first impression about another person.

personal construct. According to G. Kelly, a concept formed and used by an individual to classify and interpret his experiences, especially his perceptions of people.

personal unconscious. According to Jung, one of the two parts of an individual's unconscious mind. The personal unconscious is made up of past experiences that the individual has repressed or forgotten. See also *collective unconscious.*

personality. The distinguishing traits and characteristic behaviors of a person; the sum total of a person's somatic, mental, emotional, and social traits, or of those that are commonly perceived as most important.

personality characteristic. See *trait.*

personality disorder. Habitual and rigid patterns of behavior that are maladaptive and restricting, although persons affected are relatively free from anxiety, distress, and mental, emotional, and somatic symptoms. See also *antisocial; sexual deviation.*

Personality Research Form (PRF). A personality test designed to provide a profile of a subject's personality based on the answers that he chooses to a series of items; the PRF was developed through a careful statistical procedure made possible by use of a computer.

personality test. Any device or method used to facilitate the analysis or evaluation of personality.

peyote. A small cactus, eaten by certain native North and South American tribes as part of their religious rituals, that contains a psychedelic. Mescaline is derived from the peyote plant.

phallic stage (or childhood genital stage). According to Freud, the third psychosexual stage (from approximately three to five years of age), during which pleasure is focused on the genitals. Autoeroticism, castration anxiety, penis envy, and the Electra and Oedipus complexes arise during the phallic stage.

phases in problem solving. The analysis of problem solving into a series of stages or periods that lead to the solution of the problem; the individual organism is seen as developing the solution as he moves through the phases.

phases of sexual arousal. The four periods of sexual response described by Masters and Johnson: excitement, plateau (leveling off), orgasm, and resolution (return to the unaroused state).

phenomenology. The study of objects and events as they are experienced rather than from the view of objectively described reality. Sometimes contrasted with behaviorism.

phenothiazines. A group of antipsychotic drugs, used especially in the treatment of schizophrenia.

phenylketonuria (PKU). An abnormal hereditary condition in which the protein phenylalanine is not properly converted into other substances, with a resultant accumulation of toxic substances that produce many symptoms, including severe mental retardation. PKU is caused by a defect in a single gene.

phi phenomenon. The perception of motion, particularly the illusion of movement of stationary objects when they are presented in quick succession.

phobia. Excessive fear of particular objects or situations, often with no basis in reality; morbid fear and anxiety about something.

physiological measure. The precise assessment of a bodily condition such as heart rate or galvanic skin response.

physiological psychology. The branch of psychology concerned with the relationships between physiological activities and mental processes or behavior.

physiological zero. The temperature at which a stimulus touched to the skin yields no thermal sensations (usually 32°C).

physiology. The study of the organic processes of living beings.

pigment. A substance that colors; a substance found in animal and plant tissues and cells that accounts for their characteristic color; a substance that absorbs some wavelengths of visible light and reflects others.

pitch. The subjective highness or lowness of sound, determined by sound frequency.

pituitary gland. An endocrine gland located at the base of the brain that secretes hormones that regulate metabolism, body growth, sexual maturation, and the activities of other endocrine glands.

PK. See *psychokinesis.*

PKU. See *phenylketonuria.*

place theory. A theory of hearing hypothesizing that fibers at different locations on the basilar membrane are responsive to different sound frequencies.

placebo. A substance that has no marked pharmacological effect (*e.g.,* a sugar pill) but is given as a control to test the efficacy of another substance or to satisfy a person who wishes to take a remedy for a disorder.

pleasantness-unpleasantness. Two poles of feeling characterized by a subject's liking or disliking of stimuli; a dimension used by H. Schlosberg to characterize the various emotions.

pleasure center. An area in the hypothalamus or the limbic system of the old brain. Rats will repeatedly make a response that leads to electrical stimulation of such an area, and people report that such stimulation is pleasurable.

pleasure principle. According to psychoanalytic theory, one of the regulatory principles of mental functioning whereby painful tensions are reduced to the lowest possible level by immediate gratification of instinctual needs. Gratification can either be direct (getting water to satisfy thirst) or by fantasy. See also *reality principle.*

pons. A band of nerve fibers located in the back of the brain and controlling facial movements, hearing, and respiration, among other things.

Ponzo illusion. A visual illusion.

population. An assemblage of individuals or items subject to statistical analysis for certain characteristics; all the individuals of a species.

positive correlation. A correlation indicating that two variables change in the same direction—*i.e.,* a high value for one variable corresponds with a high value for the other variable. See also *negative correlation.*

positive reinforcer. In conditioning, a stimulus or event whose occurrence increases the frequency of a response. See also *negative reinforcer.*

positive transfer. A process whereby previously learned material facilitates the learning of a new task.

precognition. The ability to foresee future events, a form of extrasensory perception.

predictive validity. The ability of a test to predict actual performance in the area supposedly assessed by the test. Predictive validity is commonly measured by the correlation of test results with measures of actual performance at a later date. See also *concurrent validity; construct validity; content validity; validity.*

predisposition. The condition of being inclined to something beforehand; an inherited factor that inclines a person to develop certain diseases or morbid traits.

prejudice. Beliefs or judgments made without sufficient evidence and not easily changed by opposing facts or circumstances; preconceived feelings, opinions, or attitudes, often hostile and irrational, about a group or an individual belonging to a certain group (*e.g.,* race, social class). See also *discrimination.*

Premack principle. A behavior-hierarchy law, formulated by D. Premack, which states that the opportunity to engage in any behavior of relatively high frequency in a given situation can serve to reinforce any other behavior of a relatively lower frequency in the same situation.

pre-operational period. The second of Piaget's four periods of intellectual development (approximately the preschool years—ages two to six), during which a child, by gaining a capacity for representation, is able to understand many complex events but lacks the ability to use mental operations. As a result, he cannot coordinate his thoughts into logical systems. For example, he cannot understand other viewpoints; think in an organized, self-directed manner; or understand classification or conservation. See *complexive thinking; egocentrism; representation.*

PRF. See *Personality Research Form.*

primacy effect. The principle that items occurring at the beginning of a series are easier to remember than those occurring in the middle; in person perception, the tendency of the first information received about a person to outweigh later information.

primary needs. Dollard and Miller's term for the basic sources of motivation, a concept similar to Freud's instincts.

primary reinforcer. A stimulus or event that is innately satisfying; a stimulus or event that strengthens a response without need of prior training (*e.g.,* food).

principle of least interest. A theory proposed by W. Waller that the terms of a two-person relationship are set by whichever member is less involved in the relationship.

principles of perceptual organization. A set of generalizations put forth by the Gestalt psychologists to explain which characteristics of stimuli lead to the perception of gestalts. See also *continuity; proximity; similarity; simplicity.*

proactive interference. A process in which previously learned material hampers the recall of newly learned material. See also *negative transfer; retroactive interference.*

probabilistic inference. A conclusion reached on the basis of what is considered likely rather than what is logically necessary.

probability. The quality of being likely to happen; the likelihood that a given phenomenon will occur, expressed as the ratio between the number of times the phenomenon actually occurs and the total number of possible occurrences.

problem. A situation in which an organism has a goal and must find a means for attaining that goal.

proboscis. A feeding organ that is elongated or snoutlike.

productiveness. In psycholinguistics, one of the defining characteristics of language: an infinite number of meanings may be expressed by combining a limited number of words.

program. A procedure for solving a problem; a list of instructions or operations by which a computer processes information.

projection. The process of ascribing one's own attitudes, feelings, or thoughts to others, especially when those attitudes, feelings, or thoughts are considered as undesirable; regarding objective stimuli subjectively.

projective test. A measure of personality traits that requires a subject to interpret neutral or ambiguous stimuli. The subject responds to the unstructured stimuli according to the dictates of his personality (*e.g.,* his needs, drives, defenses, etc.). The Rorschach test, the TAT, and sentence- or story-completion tests are examples of projective tests.

prostate gland. An organ at the base of the male genitals that discharges a viscous fluid into the base of the penis.

protoplasm. A semifluid, complex substance found in all living cells that is the physical basis of life.

proximity. Nearness in location, time, arrangement, occurrence, or connection; the principle of Gestalt psychology that objects close to each other will tend to be perceived as a whole.

psyche. According to Freud, the performer of psychological activities, composed of conscious and unconscious divisions; the mind. See also *ego; id; superego.*

psychedelic drug. A group of drugs, also known as hallucinogens or psychotogenic drugs, that produce unusual and exaggerated mental effects, especially in cognition and perception, and often provoke highly imaginative thought patterns.

psychiatric social worker. A person holding a graduate degree in psychiatric social work who is trained to work with and counsel children and adults who seem socially maladjusted because of mental or behavioral problems.

psychiatrist. A medical doctor who specializes in the treatment of mental disorders.

psychic energy. In Freudian theory, a postulated force, similar to energy as defined by physical science, originating in the instinctual drives and accompanying all mental activity.

psychoanalysis. The Freudian theory of personality; a type of psychotherapy that utilizes the techniques of transference and free association.

psychoanalyst. Generally, a person trained in the techniques of psychoanalysis (*e.g.,* a lay analyst); especially, a psychiatrist trained in the techniques of psychoanalysis.

psychoanalytic theory. The theory of personality originated by Freud that is based on the unconscious.

psychodrama. The living through or portrayal by a person of certain situations, incidents, or conflicts suggested by a therapist. This technique is used to bring to the surface the real meaning of certain social relationships, as well as to reveal aspects of the person's private personality.

psychodynamic behavior theory. Dollard and Miller's approach to personality, in which the psychodynamic phenomena described by Freud are reinterpreted in the terminology of behavior theory. See also *social-learning theory.*

psychodynamic processes. In psychoanalytic theory, the ego's ongoing attempts to integrate the demands of the id, the superego, and the external world.

psychohistory. A scholarly discipline combining psychoanalysis and history, based on E. Erikson's view that psychosocial development is conditioned by historical context.

psychokinesis (PK). The ability to move objects without touching them, often thought to be related to extrasensory perception.

psycholinguistics. The study of the relationships between language and the behavioral characteristics of the organisms that use it.

psychological disorder. See *mental disorder.*

psychological reactance. The underlying principle of J. Brehm's theory of persuasion, stating that people will either reject a message delivered by a source they perceive as coercive or shift their views in the direction opposite to that of the message.

psychopharmacology. The study of the psychological effects of drugs.

psychophysics. The study of the relationships between the physical attributes of stimuli and resulting sensations.

psychophysiology. The study of the relationship between mental or behavioral phenomena and bodily processes; especially, the study of the spontaneous activity of various bodily organs, such as the brain, the heart, and the muscles, while behavior is occurring.

psychosexual stages. According to Freud, the different phases of sexual development, especially the mental aspects of sexual development, occurring between infancy and adolescence. See also *anal stage; genital stage; latency stage; oral stage; phallic stage.*

psychosis. A severe mental disorder marked by a generalized failure of functioning in all areas of a person's life. Characteristics of psychoses include an inability to maintain effective relationships with the external environment, distortion of objective reality, exaggeration of emotions to the point that they constitute one's entire existence, language and thought disturbance, hallucinations, delusions, and regression. Commonly known as insanity or madness. See also *manic-depressive psychosis; paranoia; paranoid schizophrenia; schizophrenia.*

psychosocial stages. According to E. Erikson, a series of eight distinct periods in a person's social development, each marked by a particular type of crisis resulting from the ego's attempts to meet the demands of social reality.

psychosomatic. Pertaining to the correlation of normal, abnormal, or pathological mental phenomena with bodily (somatic) conditions. Sometimes used in the phrase "psychosomatic symptoms" to mean physical disease symptoms, such as stomach ulcers, headaches, or insomnia, that have psychological causes.

psychotherapy. The use of psychological techniques for the treatment of mental disorders or behavioral maladaptations.

psychoticism. According to H. Eysenck's factor-analytic approach to personality, one of the three major dimensions underlying people's responses on personality questionnaires. The tendency of an individual to develop severe psychological disorder, or psychosis. See also *introversion-extraversion; neuroticism.*

psychotogenic drug. See *psychedelic drug.*

puberty. The period in which a person's reproductive organs first become capable of functioning and in which secondary sex characteristics begin to develop; usually begins at the age of twelve in females and fourteen in males and continues for approximately two or three years thereafter.

punisher. A stimulus or event that decreases the future frequency of occurrence of the behavior it follows.

punishment. The act of imposing a penalty on an animal because it has performed a disapproved action or because it has failed to perform an approved action; it reduces the probability that a given response will occur.

pupil. In reference to vision, the opening in the iris that regulates the amount of light entering the retina.

R

race. A population whose descent can be traced back to a common ancestor; a population related by blood or heredity that forms a relatively isolated mating group with distinctive gene frequencies and physical traits.

racial role. The attitudes and behavior patterns considered by a society to be appropriate to a certain race.

racism. The assumption that race determines psychological and cultural traits, accompanied by the belief that races differ decisively from each other; the belief that a particular race is superior to others and thus has a right to dominate them. See also *individual racism; institutional racism.*

radiation. The process of emitting energy as waves or particles; the energy emitted by this process; diffusion from a center.

random sample. A sample in which every piece of data is chosen by a random, or unbiased, procedure.

randomize. To select items from a set by chance so that each item has the same probability of being chosen; to treat or distribute an experimental population in such a way as to remove experimenter bias or eliminate selective factors.

range. The limits of a series; in descriptive statistics, the difference between the highest and lowest scores in a set of scores.

rapid eye movement (REM). A rapid movement of an organism's eye during sleep. Vivid dreaming appears to take place primarily during the period of sleep in which rapid eye movements occur.

RAS. See *reticular activating system.*

rating. An evaluation of the characteristics or attributes of a person, place, or thing. In experiments, such evaluation should be made with strict rules for accuracy, completeness, and lack of bias.

ratio schedule. In experimental psychology, a plan indicating when reinforcement is to occur based on the number of correct responses made between reinforcements.

rauwolfia alkaloids. A group of antipsychotic drugs, the most widely used being reserpine, derived from an extract of the roots of certain trees and shrubs.

reaction formation. According to psychoanalytic theory, a form of repression in which conscious traits and patterns of behavior are developed in the ego that are in direct opposition to strong trends within the unconscious. For example, extreme sympathy may be a reaction formation against sadistic impulses.

reaction range. An organism's unique array of possible responses to variations in its environment as determined by its genetic makeup.

reality principle. According to Freudian theory, one of the regulatory principles of mental functioning whereby an individual adjusts his behavior to the conditions of real life and the environment by delaying, giving up, inhibiting, or changing drive and need satisfaction. See also *pleasure principle.*

recall. A type of memory retrieval in which a person recovers and reproduces previously learned information.

recency effect. The principle that items occurring most recently in a series are easier to remember than those that were presented earlier.

receptor cell. A sensory neuron that is sensitive to particular forms of physical energy and capable of initiating a neural impulse.

recognition. A type of memory retrieval in which a person exhibits an awareness of an object, person, or situation as one that he has experienced before.

reference group. A group with which a person associates or identifies himself. Identification with a reference group often leads to the adoption of the attitudes, standards, and behaviors exhibited by the group.

reflex. An involuntary response to a stimulus due to the transmission of a neural impulse directly from a receptor to a nerve center and outward to an effector; the higher processes of the brain are not involved.

refractory period. A time following a response when it is difficult or impossible to make the same response again, as in the refractory period for sexual responsiveness in the male immediately following orgasm.

regression. According to psychoanalytic theory, a defense mechanism consisting of a return to an earlier stage of development or behavior, particularly when the person is threatened or in a stressful situation.

rehearsal. Repetition of information or behavior to be learned. Rehearsal prolongs the retention of material in short-term memory and helps the transfer of material from short-term memory to long-term memory.

reinforcement. The act or state of strengthening by adding something; any circumstance that increases the possibility that a given response will recur in a similar situation; in operant conditioning, the experimental procedure of immediately following a response with a reinforcer, in order to strengthen the response.

reinforcement schedule. A plan indicating when reinforcement is to occur, in terms of either time intervals or number of correct responses. See also *interval schedule; ratio schedule; continuous reinforcement; intermittent reinforcement, schedule.*

reinforcer. A stimulus or event that increases the frequency of a response; according to the Premack principle, the opportunity to engage in a response of relatively high probability.

relative deprivation. The condition in which individuals or the members of a group perceive their own status or well-being in terms of a social group that is relatively advantaged in comparison to themselves; therefore, they see themselves as relatively deprived even if their status or well-being is improving.

reliability. The state of being trustworthy and dependable; the dependability and consistency of a measure. A reliable test is one that obtains similar results upon repetition. See also *validity.*

REM. See *rapid eye movement.*

remembering. The active process of mentally reconstructing previously learned or experienced events. Remembering involves successful acquisition, storage, and retrieval of information. See also *retrieval.*

replication. In psychological research, the repetition of a given study by another researcher; most commonly, use of the term means that the same results were obtained.

representation. In Piaget's developmental theory, the capacity to think about objects that are not present and events that are not happening at the moment; first appearing in the preoperational period, it permits a child to imitate another person's past actions; to play make-believe; to understand many complex events, and, according to R. Brown, to use language in a meaningful way.

repression. According to psychoanalytic theory, a defense mechanism that guards against anxiety and guilt by the unconscious exclusion of painful and unacceptable ideas or impulses from consciousness.

resistance. The act of opposing; the opposition given by a substance to the transmission of electric current; the sensation experienced when moving against a force or resting mass. In psychoanalytic theory, the opposition to attempts to bring repressed thoughts into the conscious.

resistance to extinction. The continued emission of a response by an organism despite efforts to make the response disappear.

respondent conditioning. See *classical conditioning.*

response. An answer; an action; a reaction or process that depends on or is the result of stimulation.

response bias. With respect to psychological tests, the tendency of some individuals to give the same type of answer ("Yes" or "No," for example) to most questions regardless of their content.

response criterion. In signal-detection theory, the amount of sensory input that an individual requires before he or she will judge a signal to be present.

response generalization. The tendency of an organism to make responses that are similar to the specific conditioned responses it has learned. See also *stimulus generalization.*

resultant achievement motivation. The tendency to engage in goal-directed behavior as determined by a conflict between the motive to approach success and the motive to avoid failure.

reticular activating system (RAS). A network of nerve cells deep in the brain that constitutes a secondary pathway of nerves over which the senses alert the brain. The RAS regulates wakefulness, alertness, attention, and perceptual association. See also *straight-line sensory system.*

retina. The light-sensitive, innermost coat of the eyeball. The retina is a predominantly neural structure consisting of several layers, including a layer of rods and cones.

retinal image. The representation of an object that is formed on the retina. Also known as optical image or visual image.

retrieval. The process of obtaining information that is in storage, *e.g.,* the bringing of memories into consciousness. See also *recall, recognition.*

retroactive interference. A process in which newly learned material hampers the recall of previously learned material. See also *proactive interference.*

reversibility. In Piaget's developmental theory, the characteristic of an operation whereby the transformation or change brought about by the operation can be undone—that is, reversed.

reward. See *reinforcement.*

rhodopsin. A red, light-sensitive pigment found in the rods that is important for vision in dim light. Also known as visual purple.

rod. One of many cells in the retina that are sensitive to light of low intensity and that function primarily in peripheral and nighttime vision. Rods are located in the periphery and are essentially unresponsive to color. See also *cone.*

Rogerian therapy. See *client-centered therapy.*

role. The function of an individual in a group; the pattern of behavior that characterizes and is expected of a person who occupies a particular status or position in a group or social situation; the cluster of norms applicable to people in a particular social category.

role taking. Imagining oneself as another person and assuming his attitudes and point of view in order to determine how he would actually behave in given circumstances.

Rorschach Inkblot Test. A projective personality test in which the subject is shown ten inkblots of varying shape and color and asked to give his interpretation of each one.

rote learning. Learning accomplished by memorization of words, symbols, or sequences without regard for their meanings.

round dance. A circular movement performed by bees indicating that a food source is nearby. See also *wagging dance.*

round window. A membrane-covered opening between the middle ear and the cochlea that transmits sound from the ossicles to the cochlea.

S

salivary gland. One of several glands located in the mouth that secretes saliva.

sample. A selected segment of subjects from the whole population of subjects.

satiation. The complete gratification of a need or desire.

savings score. The difference between the number of trials an organism needs to learn material for the first time and the number of trials it needs to relearn the material after a lapse of time.

scale. A representation of the regular progression of quantities or qualities; a measuring device that provides standards against which other objects, events, or variables can be compared.

schedule. In experimental psychology, a detailed plan of procedure indicating time sequences for carrying out operations that lead toward a certain goal. See also *reinforcement schedule.*

scheme. In Piaget's developmental theory, a cognitive and behavioral framework for understanding something.

schizophrenia. Any of a group of psychoses primarily characterized by disturbances in thinking. See also *catatonic, hebephrenic, paranoid,* and *simple schizophrenias.*

scrotum. In the male, the sac containing the testes.

secondary drive. See *learned drive.*

secondary reinforcer. See *conditioned reinforcer.*

secondary sex characteristic. A trait specific to either males or females that begins to appear at or after puberty and is not necessary for reproduction (*e.g.,* beard growth in males and breast development in females).

secondary trait. According to Allport's trait approach to personality, a characteristic that is identifiable but not general. A secondary trait is specific to certain situations or behaviors. See also *trait; cardinal trait; central trait.*

secretion. The process whereby a cell or gland produces and releases or simply releases a substance that functions in an organism; the product of such a process.

sedative. A substance that causes drowsiness, sleep, or lowered excitability. Sedatives are used mainly to treat insomnia and anxiety.

selection. See *natural selection.*

selective attention. In perception, the selection of relevant information and the screening out or incomplete processing of extraneous information within a particular sensory channel.

self-actualization. The process of fulfilling one's potentials or the state resulting therefrom. According to A. Maslow, self-actualization results from the satisfaction of metaneeds. See also *basic needs; metaneeds.*

self-awareness. The state of being attuned to one's own feelings and sensations as they occur.

self-concept. A person's knowledge and understanding of himself; that which a person conceives himself to be.

self-fulfilling prophecy. A belief, prediction, or expectation that operates to bring about its own fulfillment.

self-perception theory. The theory advanced by D. Bem that people often make inferences about their attitudes by observing their own behavior.

semantic differential. A technique that uses rating scales to investigate the connotations of words. The scales are defined by bipolar (opposite) adjectives such as good-bad, strong-weak, and active-passive. Three major dimensions are tapped by the measure: the activity dimension, evaluative dimension, and potency dimension.

semantic memory. As defined by E. Tulving, memory for the meaning of concepts without reference to when or where this knowledge was acquired, somewhat like a dictionary. See also *episodic memory.*

semantics. The scientific study of the meanings of words; the rules describing the relationships between signs and that which they denote.

semicircular canal. Any of three tubular structures in the ear that help maintain body equilibrium and are part of the vestibular apparatus.

seminal vesicles. A small sac in the male genitals in which semen is stored.

sensation. The experience that occurs when a sense organ is stimulated; a feeling resulting from excitation of parts of the nervous system.

sense. A faculty by which organisms perceive stimuli, or the operations of such faculties; a feeling or perception produced through the sense organs; a receptor; apprehension by means of receptors.

sense organ. A bodily part that is sensitive to particular stimuli; a receptor.

sensitive period. A relatively restricted period of development in which an animal is especially susceptible to particular influences that may bring about enduring behavior changes or behavioral effects.

sensitivity. An organism's ability to respond to stimuli; susceptibility to stimulation; capacity to perceive; the extent to which a measure responds to alterations in the phenomena it is measuring.

sensorimotor period. The first of Piaget's periods of intellectual development (from birth to about age two years), during which an infant learns through overt action to function practically in his environment but lacks an understanding of what he is doing.

sensory deprivation. Minimal stimulation of the sense organs accomplished by the experimental elimination of most, if not all, external stimuli.

sensory gating. A process by which a feedback system between the brain and sensory receptors regulates or dampens sensory activity that is less important at a given time.

sensory information storage. The momentary storage of sensory information that occurs primarily at the level of the sensory receptors.

sensory input. See *input.*

sensory neuron. An afferent neuron that carries neural impulses from sense organs to the spinal cord or brain.

sensory ratio. The principle that the nervous system analyzes the magnitude of sensory stimulation in terms of relative proportions or ratios rather than absolute amounts.

sentence-completion test. A projective personality test in which the subject must complete a number of meaningful sentences with an appropriate word or phrase.

sequential processing. Dealing with one strain or flow of incoming information at a time.

serial-position effect. The effect of position on ability to remember an item in a series. Items that occur at the beginning or end of a series are remembered better than those that occur in the middle. See also *primacy effect; recency effect.*

set. Items that appear in a group or series; a tendency to continue to use a particular method or type of solution to a problem based on previous experience or instructions; a tendency to perceive a stimulus in a particular way.

sex hormone. A hormone that regulates the growth and activity of the reproductive organs or stimulates the development of secondary sex characteristics. See also *female hormone; hormone; male hormone.*

sex role. A complex or range of behaviors, attitudes, and norms that a culture or society considers appropriate to members of one sex but not to those of the other.

sexual deviation. Any departure from what a society considers normal sexual behavior; sexual behavior that is illegal; a personality disorder in which sexual behavior is bizarre, compulsive, exclusive, and accompanied by guilt and anxiety.

shadow. To follow after; to repeat a message aloud as it is received through earphones, as in selective-attention research.

shape constancy. The tendency to perceive familiar objects as always having the same shape, regardless of the angle from which they are viewed.

shaping. A form of operant conditioning in which all acts similar to the desired response are reinforced at first, and then acts that are progressively more like the desired response are reinforced until the desired response is attained. Also called method of successive approximations.

shock therapy. See *electroconvulsive shock therapy.*

short-term memory (STM). Memory that has a limited storage capacity (5 to 9 items) and a short duration. Items stored in STM are quickly forgotten if they are not transferred to long-term memory.

sign stimulus. A specific stimulus in the environment that elicits a particular pattern of behavior, often a fixed action pattern.

signal. A stimulus or pattern of stimuli capable of eliciting a response from an animal; anything that causes action; a physical entity or impulse used to transmit messages (*e.g.,* electric current, nerve impulse).

signal-detection theory. The view that an individual has no single absolute threshold for detecting a signal but instead is always faced with the problem of separating signal from noise; he must make a judgment about whether a signal is present.

similarity. A Gestalt principle of organization proposing that similar items will be perceived as belonging with each other more than with equally near but different items.

simple schizophrenia. A psychotic disorder marked by withdrawal from the external world. A person with this disorder is indifferent and apathetic but can continue to exist in society doing simple, routine tasks.

simplicity. In perception, the concept that simple patterns are more likely to be perceived than complex patterns. Simplicity has been proposed as the basis for all the Gestalt principles of perceptual organization.

SIS. See *sensory information storage.*

size constancy. The tendency of objects to be perceived as always having the same size, regardless of the distance from which they are viewed.

Skinner box. A compartment designed by B. F. Skinner containing a mechanism that produces reinforcement when operated correctly.

smell prism. See *Henning's smell prism.*

social class. A group of people within a society whose members share economic, cultural, and political characteristics (*e.g.,* education, wealth, and occupation).

social-comparison theory. The theory put forth by L. Festinger that a large number of individual beliefs, attitudes, and values can be verified only by comparison with other people's actions and experiences.

social group. A collection of people in a cooperative and interdependent relationship who obtain special recognition as a group because of their interdependence. Members of social groups share common norms and have certain roles to perform.

social influence. A force generated by a society that affects a person's attitudes or behaviors; the power to produce a change in an individual's or a society's attitudes, beliefs, opinions, or practices.

social-learning theory. The approach that uses behaviorist learning principles to explain social behavior and personality.

social norm. A standard by which a society judges or regulates behavior.

social psychology. The branch of psychology that studies social behavior. Social psychology is concerned with group behavior and interactions between individuals and groups.

social role. See *role.*

social status. See *status.*

social stereotype. A stereotype held by most of the members of a group about members of another group.

socialization. The methods and processes through which people learn to behave in a manner appropriate to the values and roles of their culture.

soma. The body of an organism; all of the cells of the body excluding the germ cells; the cell body.

somatic. Pertaining to the body.

somatic nervous system. The part of the peripheral nervous system that controls the voluntary movement of skeletal muscles.

somatosensory cortex. The part of the brain's parietal lobe that receives information from the skin, muscles, and joints.

somesthetic. Pertaining to bodily sensations.

S-O-R-K-C. The formula used in behavior-modification procedures to conceptualize what is producing a problem behavior. S stands for the stimuli immediately preceding the behavior; O for the state of the organism; R for the target response, often a problem behavior; K for the contingency relationship between the response and its consequence; and C for the consequences of the response. See also *contingency relationship; consequence.*

sound. A longitudinal, vibrational disturbance that occurs in an elastic medium and that is capable of producing an auditory effect.

sound spectrograph. An electronic device that records and graphically represents the intensity, duration, and variation of a sound or series of sounds as a function of time.

source trait. According to Cattell's factor-analytic approach to personality, a basic dimension or characteristic that underlies a person's more superficial characteristics, or surface traits. See also *trait; surface trait.*

species. A distinct class of individuals having common characteristics; a biological category composed of similar individuals usually able to breed only with each other.

species-specific behavior. Behavior that is characteristic of a given species or exhibited by most of the members of a species under the same or very similar circumstances.

spectrum. An array of entities arranged in order of magnitude of a shared physical attribute; a wide range of different but related objects or ideas. See also *visual spectrum.*

spermatozoon. A single sperm, or male germ cell.

spike. An action potential; a sharp rise in a graphic representation of an electrical, magnetic, or bodily process (*e.g.*, in an electroencephalogram).

spinal column. The vertebrae forming the supporting axis of the body and the protective casing of the spinal cord; backbone.

spinal cord. The thick bundle of neurons running vertically along the back through the spinal column.

spirit possession. A hypnosislike trance usually induced by a religious rite and said to be controlled by a supernatural agent.

split-brain operation. Surgery in which the right and left cortexes of the brain are disconnected by cutting the nerve fibers that run through the corpus callosum.

spontaneous extinction. The disappearance of a conditioned response for no apparent reason.

spontaneous recovery. The recurrence of a conditioned response after a rest period following extinction.

spontaneous remission. The unaided disappearance of a pathological condition; the loss, after a time, of symptoms of psychological disturbance in an individual although he or she has not undergone therapy.

stability. One of the dimensions of B. Weiner's attribution theory of achievement motivation; concerns the perception of the causes of one's successes and failures as likely to recur (stable) or unlikely to recur (unstable). See also *locus of control.*

stage theory. Any theory that regards development as a progressive series of qualitatively different periods. See also *incremental theory.*

stages of moral development. According to L. Kohlberg (building upon Piaget's developmental approach), six qualitatively different ways of making judgments about right and wrong that follow in an invariant order as a child grows into adulthood.

stages of sleep. The five periods into which sleep researchers divide sleep according to brain-wave patterns and the occurrence of rapid eye movements (REM). Stage 1 is characterized by relatively rapid brain waves and, as sleep progresses to Stage 4, brain waves become gradually slower. Stage 1 is divided into two types: REM and non-REM.

standard deviation. In a frequency distribution, a number indicating the extent to which measurements within a set differ from each other, expressed as the square root of the squared differences of each measurement from the mean, divided by the number of measurements.

standard score system. A method for scoring tests that reflects the way people score on most tests. The standard score is obtained by converting the actual mean score of a given test to 0, with individual scores expressed as deviations (to $+4$ or -4) from the mean.

standardization group. A large, representative group of people to whom a psychological test is given prior to general distribution in order to establish norms.

Stanford-Binet Test. An individually administered intelligence test, devised at Stanford University, that follows Binet's test in grouping tests by age levels. It is the test most frequently used for children.

statistical significance. The probability that the obtained results could have occurred by chance. Psychologists consider a finding to probably be reliable if the chances are only 1 in 20 that it occurred by chance (.05 level of significance). They consider it to be almost surely reliable if the chances are only 1 in 100 (.01 level of significance).

statistics. The branch of mathematics or its group of techniques involved with the making of meaningful inferences from collections of data; the numerical data themselves.

status. The position or rank of a person in a group as related to and distinguished from other members of the group; the social position of an individual or group in reference to others; a state of affairs.

stereoscope. An optical instrument that allows two flat pictures of the same object to be seen as one three-dimensional picture by presenting one picture to one eye and the other picture, taken from a slightly different viewpoint, to the other eye.

stereoscopic vision. Perception of depth due to the merging of two slightly different retinal images; three-dimensional vision.

stereotype. A preconceived notion about some aspect of reality, particularly people or social groups; a set of oversimplified, rigid, and biased generalizations about a group or category of people.

Stevens' power law. A law formulated by S. S. Stevens that the magnitude of a sensation is equal to the physical magnitude of the stimulus producing the sensation raised to a certain power (exponent). The exponent varies, depending on the particular sense that is being measured. See also *Weber's law; Fechner's law.*

stimulant. A drug that increases physiological activity, produces a state of alertness, elevates mood, diminishes appetite, and enhances physical performance.

stimulus. Any phenomenon that initiates a response or evokes sensory activity in an organism. A stimulus may be internal or external to an organism and physical or mental in nature.

stimulus control. The regulation of behavior by the stimulus (stimuli) that is (are) present during reinforcement or associated with reinforcement; in behavior therapy, the matching of appropriate discriminative stimuli with appropriate responses.

stimulus generalization. The tendency of an organism to respond to stimuli that are similar to the conditioned stimulus. See also *generalization gradient; response generalization.*

STM. See *short-term memory.*

storage. The retention of information in sensory, short-term, or long-term memory; see also *sensory information storage; short-term memory; long-term memory.*

straight-line sensory system. The main pathway of nerves over which travels physical energy from a sensory stimulus that is transduced into physiological energy and is carried to the brain. The straight-line sensory system is the channel that carries information. See also *reticular activating system.*

strategy. Any general method for solving problems. See also *algorithm; heuristic.*

stress. A state of physical or psychological strain resulting from the presence or perception of threat.

Strong Vocational Interest Blank (SVIB). A personality test that indicates how an individual's patterns of interests correspond to the patterns of interests of people in various occupations.

Study of Values. A personality test that assesses an individual's values, analyzing them into six idealized types: theoretical, economic, aesthetic, social, political, and religious.

subgoal analysis. In the General Problem Solver computer program, a heuristic by which a problem is analyzed into a set of smaller problems, called subgoals.

subject. A person or other animal that is the object of study in a psychological investigation.

subjective. Belonging to the individual observer rather than to the object being observed; not capable of being verified by others; dependent upon an individual observer's emotions or judgments, hence, biased. See also *objective.*

sublimation. In psychoanalytic theory, the unconscious process of redirecting or modifying an instinct or impulse so as to meet the conventional standards of society. Through this modification one is provided with a substitute activity that gives some means to satisfy the original need. Sublimation is an acceptable means of expressing an impulse, rather than a form of repression.

sulcus. One of the shallow fissures on the surface of the brain that separates convolutions, or gyri.

superego. According to Freud, the partially unconscious part of the ego that incorporates parental and social standards of morality. The superego inhibits those impulses of the id that are most condemned by society or parents and is thus in constant conflict with the id. See also *ego, id; psyche; ego ideal.*

superstitious behavior. In operant conditioning, responses not necessarily leading to a goal that persist simply because they preceded reinforcement.

suppression. The conscious and intentional process of inhibiting disapproved impulses or ideas.

surface structure. The organization of the actual words uttered in a sentence, contrasted with the underlying meaning of the sentence.

surface trait. According to Cattell's factor-analytic approach to personality, a specific, relatively superficial characteristic of an individual. See also *trait; source trait.*

survey. A relatively large sampling of data taken to assess what the true value or level of a variable might be; usually used in social psychology to assess opinions, differences between social groups, etc.

syllogism. In logic, a formalized argument whose conclusion is based on two premises, the major and minor premises. Example: All *x* is *y*. All *y* is *z*. Therefore all *x* is *z*.

symbol. In cognitive theory, a word, gesture, image, or the like that is used to represent or stand for an object, event, action, or idea; in dreams, an image or thought that stands for another image or thought; dream symbols are characterized by displacement and condensation.

sympathetic nervous system. The division of the autonomic nervous system that promotes the expenditure of body energy and mobilizes the body to meet emergencies by increasing blood-sugar level and heart rate, dilating peripheral blood vessels, and inhibiting the digestive process.

symptom substitution, theory of. The view that removing the symptoms of neurosis without resolving the patient's underlying conflict will result in the development of new symptoms as alternative expressions of the conflict.

synapse. The area of contact between the axon of one neuron and the dendrite or cell body of another, and therefore the point at which a neural impulse is transmitted from the axon of one neuron to the dendrite or cell body of another.

syndrome. A group or pattern of symptoms characterizing a specific disease or condition.

synthesis. See *analysis by synthesis.*

systematic desensitization. A behavior-therapy technique to reduce anxiety or remove a phobia by pairing an incompatible response—deep muscle relaxation—with the presentation or visualization of potentially threatening objects or situations in a hierarchical order, from least to most feared.

T

tachistoscope. An instrument that presents visual stimuli for short, regulated periods of time.

tactile. Pertaining to the sense of touch.

tag question. Interrogation at the end of a sentence ("didn't he?"); in psycholinguistics, its correct use is an indicator of the speaker's mastery of several complex grammatical rules.

target behavior. In behavior therapy, the response whose frequency is to be increased if deficient or to be decreased if excessive.

taste bud. One of the many tiny organs located in the surface layer of the tongue that are the receptors for taste.

TAT. See *Thematic Apperception Test.*

tectorial membrane. A jellylike membrane that covers the organ of Corti in the ear and in which hair cells are embedded.

telegraphic speech. Patterns manifested in the speech of young children in which certain words that seem minimally related to the message content are omitted (*e.g.*, "Pick glove" instead of "Pick up the glove").

telepathy. A form of extrasensory perception in which thought is transferred from one person to another by unknown means.

temporal lobe. One of the three rear lobes of the cerebrum located in front of the occipital lobe and concerned with the sensations of hearing and some visual processing.

tendon. An inelastic, fibrous tissue that connects a muscle to a bone.

test. A measurement technique designed to determine individual differences in knowledge, personality characteristics, etc.; a technique that determines the correctness of a hypothesis and yields quantitative data. See also *achievement test; intelligence test; projective test; Thematic Apperception Test; t-test.*

testis. One of the pair of male reproductive glands in which sperm and male hormones are produced.

testosterone. A male sex hormone secreted by the testes.

tetrahydrocannabinol (THC). A complex molecule that is the active ingredient in marijuana and hashish. THC is found naturally in the Indian hemp plant and appears chiefly in the female plant.

T-group or **training group.** A group of people who meet to explore the dynamics of group functioning, especially of interpersonal relations in task-oriented groups.

thalamus. A group of nuclei located in the forebrain, some of which relay information from the sensory organs to the cerebral cortex.

Thanatos. According to Freud, the death instinct—a tendency toward self-destruction that is present from birth. See also *Eros.*

THC. See *tetrahydrocannabinol.*

Thematic Apperception Test (TAT). A projective personality test in which relatively vague pictures are presented to a subject who is asked to make up stories about them.

therapy. See *psychotherapy.*

thermal. Pertaining to heat.

thioxanthines. A group of antipsychotic drugs.

third force. A loose grouping of humanist and existentialist psychotherapeutic approaches that is considered an alternative to both Freudianism and behaviorism. See also *humanist psychology; existential psychiatry.*

thirst. A drive state based on dehydration or loss of water from bodily tissues; the need or desire for water.

Thorazine. See *chlorpromazine.*

threshold. The level of intensity at which a stimulus begins to elicit a response.

thyroid gland. An endocrine gland composed of two lobes lying on either side of the windpipe whose secretions help to regulate body growth and rate of metabolism.

thyroid-stimulating hormone (TSH). A hormone secreted by the pituitary gland that stimulates the thyroid gland to produce thyroxin.

thyroxin. A hormone produced by the thyroid gland or manufactured synthetically that regulates body metabolism.

tissue. An aggregate of cells (usually of the same kind) that perform a common function; one of the structural materials in an organism.

T-maze. A maze in the shape of a T; a maze consisting of several T-shaped sections.

token economy. A behavior-modification technique of reinforcement in which objects such as tokens, poker chips, or check marks are used as conditioned reinforcers that may be exchanged later for primary reinforcers.

tolerance. In prolonged drug usage, a person's need for larger and larger doses to obtain the same effects that occurred in earlier instances of use of the drug.

tone. A quality of sound; a sound that has an exact pitch and vibration; vocal accent or inflection; a healthy state of tension and firmness in the bodily organs; a quality of color.

trace decay theory. The theory that forgetting is a result of the deterioration and eventual disappearance of memory traces.

trait. A distinguishing quality of a person, including behavior patterns, physical attributes, and personality characteristics; according to G. Allport, a predisposition to respond to many types of stimuli in the same manner.

trance. A sleeplike state in which awareness of external stimuli is dulled and the ability to act voluntarily is suspended. Trances are common in hysteria and may be induced by hypnotism. See also *hypnosis.*

trance logic. A type of thinking characteristic of hypnotized persons, who fail to apply real-world logic to explain inconsistencies in their experience and instead freely mix hypnotically induced experiences with experiences based on real-world phenomena.

tranquilizer. A drug that has a calming effect, reduces anxiety and depression, but does not induce sleep. See also *antianxiety drug; antipsychotic drug.*

transduction. The conversion of one type of energy into another, especially the conversion of sensory information into neural impulses.

transfer. A change in ability to perform a certain act as a result of previous learning. See also *negative transfer* and *positive transfer.*

transference. The process of shifting emotional attachment from one object to another. In psychoanalysis transference occurs when the patient responds to the psychoanalyst as though the psychoanalyst were some other significant person, usually someone important in the patient's early life.

transformation. In Piaget's developmental theory, the mental action of specifying how one state or appearance (of a liquid, for example) is changed into another state or appearance.

transmitter substance. A chemical released from an axon into a synapse that carries neural impulses across the synapse and causes changes in the membrane of the receiving cell. Acetylcholine and norepinephrine are transmitter substances.

trauma. An injury; an experience that causes an organism serious physical or psychological damage.

trichromat. A person whose retina responds to all colors.

trichromatic theory (of color vision). The theory that there are three different types of color receptors in the eye for detecting all colors.

tricyclic antidepressants. A group of antidepressant drugs that are believed to block the destruction of norepinephrine in the neurons.

TSH. See *thyroid-stimulating hormone.*

t-test. An inferential statistic used to determine the level of significance of the difference between the means of two groups.

U

ultraviolet rays. Radiant energy with a shorter wavelength than that of the violet end of the spectrum. These radiations are shorter than 390 millimicrons and are not directly visible to the human eye.

unconditional positive regard. Sustained support given to another person regardless of what he says or does; in Rogerian therapy, the attitude of acceptance maintained by the therapist toward the client.

unconditioned response. In classical conditioning, an organism's natural reaction to an unconditioned stimulus.

unconditioned stimulus. In classical conditioning, a stimulus that evokes a specific response without previous training.

unconscious. Unaware; marked by an absence of perception, cognition, or sensation; in psychoanalytic theory, the division of the psyche containing material of which the person is unaware but which is capable of influencing conscious processes or behavior. See also *conscious.*

unconscious inference. A judgment one makes without being aware of a reasoning process but upon which he or she acts, especially a perceptual judgment. Such a judgment is usually not verbalized.

uterus. The womb; the organ in the female where a fertilized egg implants itself and grows into a fetus.

V

vacuum activity. Behavior that occurs even though the appropriate stimuli are not present. Vacuum activity is believed to result from a very high drive state.

vagina. The sheathlike opening in the female genitals that leads to the uterus and into which the penis is inserted during sexual intercourse.

validity. Well-foundedness or soundness; the extent to which a test measures what it purports to measure. See also *reliability.*

variable. Anything that is capable of change; quantities that can take on more than one mathematical value.

variable schedule. See *intermittent reinforcement.*

variance. The state or quality of being different; the square of the standard deviation.

vas deferens. A tube in the male genitals through which semen passes.

vascular changes. Changes in the circulatory system; dilation or constriction of the blood vessels. See also *James-Lange theory of emotion.*

vein. A relatively large, thin-walled blood vessel that conducts blood away from the tissues back to the heart.

venereal disease. Any of several communicable diseases usually transmitted by sexual intercourse (*e.g.,* gonorrhea, syphilis).

ventral nerve cord. A nerve in the blowfly that receives impulses from receptors that indicate when the fly's body is becoming distended with food.

ventromedial nucleus. The middle area of the hypothalamus that controls hunger. If the ventromedial nucleus is destroyed or inactive, an animal's weight-control mechanism will readjust so that it maintains a higher-than-normal body weight if good-tasting food is easily available or a lower-than-normal weight otherwise.

vestibular apparatus. The apparatus in the inner ear for perception of head orientation and bodily acceleration.

vestibular nerve. A branch of the auditory nerve that transmits neural impulses from the vestibule and semicircular canals to the brain.

vestibular sense. The sense of balance.

viscera. The organs in the cavity of the body, especially in the abdomen, including the heart, intestines, kidneys, etc.

visceral changes. Changes in the internal organs of the body (*e.g.,* tensing of the stomach muscle, increase in heart rate, changes in kidney functioning) related to emotional experience. See also *James-Lange theory of emotion.*

visual cliff. A device designed by E. Gibson and D. Walk to study depth perception. The visual cliff consists of a center board resting on a glass table; on one side of the board a patterned surface is visible directly beneath the glass and on the other side the patterned surface is several feet below the glass.

visual field. Everything perceived by the eye when it is fixed on an object.

visual image. With regard to perception, see *retinal image;* with regard to information-processing and memory, see *image.*

visual spectrum. The band of colors obtained by the passage of sunlight or white light through a prism.

vocal cords. Either of two pairs of mucous membrane folds that protrude into the cavity of the larynx and produce certain vocal sounds when vibrated.

volley theory. The theory that individual nerve fibers do not respond to each sound wave but that a sound wave excites one group of nerve fibers, the second sound wave excites another group of nerve fibers, and so on. The pattern of neural impulses that go to the brain in successive volleys corresponds to the sound frequency.

W

wagging dance. A sequence of running and turning movements performed by bees indicating the direction and distance of a food source. See also *round dance.*

WAIS. See *Wechsler Adult Intelligence Scale.*

wavelength. In a wave moving along a medium, the distance between two successive points that are characterized by the same phase of oscillation.

Weber's law. A law formulated by E. Weber that the smallest difference in intensity between two stimuli that can be reliably detected is a constant fraction of the original stimulus. See also *Fechner's law; Stevens' power law.*

Wechsler Adult Intelligence Scale (WAIS). A widely used battery of intelligence tests for adults combining performance, vocabulary, and verbal tests.

Weschler Intelligence Scale for Children (WISC). A variation of the WAIS intelligence test that is usable for older children and adolescents. See also *Wechsler Adult Intelligence Scale.*

Whorf's hypothesis. The idea, advanced by linguist B. L. Whorf, that a person's thoughts, perceptions, and world view are determined by the particular language he speaks.

withdrawal syndrome. The symptoms that occur after a person discontinues use of a drug he has become addicted to. These include watery nose and eyes, drowsiness, cramps, vomiting, diarrhea, gooseflesh, and general weakness.

word-association test. A method of determining a subject's associations with certain stimuli in a verbal stimulus-response exchange. The subject's experience and attitudes determine his responses. Often used as a projective personality test.

Index

Credits and Acknowledgments

Special thanks are due those who did bibliographic and graphic research for the book, Neil Strassman and Emily Beebee; those who contributed editorial help, Kenneth Goodall, Martha Rosler, and Lee Massey; the indexer, Steve Buck; and the manuscript typists who worked on the many drafts of each chapter, Laura Szalwinski, Rolande Angles, and Teri Marshall.

We are also grateful to all those persons and agencies who assisted us in preparing and assembling the illustrations for this book. The aid and cooperation of Doug Armstrong, John Dawson, Mark Freeman, Terry Lamb, Andy Lucas, Darrel Millsap, Tom O'Mary, Everett Peck, Holly Sandy, Glenda Scott, Gillian Theobald, Miriam Wohlgemuth, and Calvin Woo are acknowledged with appreciation. Steve Harrison's contribution as principal production artist was invaluable. Additional thanks to Nat Antler, Leon Bolognese, and John Odam for their design assistance.

CHAPTER 1

1—Bill Call; 3, 4—Everett Peck; 8—Dr. Burton White; 10—(top) Courtesy of Dr. Nathan Azrin, Anna, Illinois, (bottom) Adapted from J. Cates, "Baccalaureates in Psychology 1969 and 1970," *American Psychologist*, vol. 28, p. 262, © 1973 by American Psychological Association. Reprinted by permission; 16—John Dawson; 17—*Puddles* by M.C. Escher, Escher Foundation-Haags Gemeentemuseum, The Hague.

CHAPTER 2

21—Tom Gould (construction), Steve McCarroll (photo); 22—From E. R. Sinnett, *The Inner World of Mental Illness*, Bert Kaplan (Ed.), Harper & Row, 1964, pp. 197-198; 23—Everett Peck; 24—John Dawson; 25—From W. Hudson, "Pictorial Depth Perception in Sub-Cultural Groups in Africa," *Journal of Social Psychology*, 52 (1960), 183-208; 26—Adapted from J. Kagan and H. Moss, *Birth to Maturity*, © 1962 by John Wiley & Sons, p. 267. Reprinted with permission; 27—Adapted from K. Gergen, *Psychology Today*, October 1973; 28—Lorenzo Gunn/Gordon Menzie Studio; 29—After W. D. Fenz and S. Epstein, "Gradients of Physiological Arousal in Parachutists As a Function of an Approaching Jump," *Psychosomatic Medicine*, 29 (1967), American Psychosomatic Society; 33—Everett Peck; 35—(top) Karl Nicholason, (bottom) Adapted from R. Rosenthal, *Experimental Effects in Behavioral Research*, Appleton-Century-Crofts, 1966, p. 162; 39—After H. G. Wolff and S. Wolf, *Pain*, figure 1, p. 6, Charles C Thomas Publishers, 1948; 40—John Dawson.

CHAPTER 3

49—Elihu Blotnick/BBM Associates; 50—John Fentress; 51—(top) John Dawson; 52—John Fentress; 53—From R. Rugh and L. Shettles, *From Conception to Birth: The Drama of Life's Beginnings*, Harper & Row, 1971; 54—Reproduced from *Darwin and Facial Expressions*, Paul Ekman (Ed.), Academic Press, 1973, with permission from Paul Ekman and Silvan Tomkins; 55, 57—John Dawson; 58—(top) John Dawson; 59 (bottom) and 62—Thomas McAvoy/*Life* Magazine © Time, Inc.; 63—Adapted from R. D. Hess and G. Handel, *Family Worlds: A Psychological Approach to Family Life*, University of Chicago Press, 1959; 64—Adapted from W. H. Thorpe, *Bird Song*, Cambridge University Press, 1961; 65—(top and bottom) Nobel Foundation.

CHAPTER 4

69—Bill Boyarsky; 71—John Dawson; 73—(bottom) Howard Saunders; 76—Howard Saunders; 77—(top and center) Steve McCarroll, (bottom) John Dawson; 78—(top) John Dawson, (center and bottom) Steve McCarroll; 79—(bottom) John Dawson; 84—John Dawson after J. B. Wolfe, 1935; 87—(top) Howard Saunders, (bottom) Steve McCarroll.

CHAPTER 5

95—© 1968 Metro-Goldwyn-Mayer; 96—Shirley Dethloff; 99—Painting from Novosti Press Agency, courtesy of U.S.S.R. Embassy, data from A. L. Yarbus, *Eye Movements and Vision*, Plenun Press, 1967; 100—Karl Nicholason; 102—After L. R. Peterson and M. G. Peterson, "Short-Term Retention of Individual Verbal Items," *Journal of Experimental Psychology*, vol. 58, pp. 193-198, © 1959 by *American Psychological Association*. Reprinted by permission; 104—(bottom) After B. Murdock Jr., "The Serial Position Effect of Free Recall," *Journal of Experimental Psychology*, vol. 64, no. 5, figure 1, © 1962 by American Psychological Association, and L. Postman and L. Phillips, "Short-Term Temporal Changes in Free Recall," *Quarterly Journal of Experimental Psychology*, vol. 17, figure 1, p. 135, © 1965 by American Psychological Association. Reprinted by permission; 105—After B. Inhelder, "Memory and Intelligence in a Child," in D. Elkind and J. H. Flavell (Eds.), *Studies in Cognitive Development*, Oxford University Press, 1964; 106—After P. Lindsay and D. Norman, *Human Information Processing: An Introduction to Psychology*, figure 11-2, p. 404, © 1972 by Academic Press; 107—From Johannes Romberch, *Congestorium Artificiose Memorie*, Venice, 1553; 109—Gerri Blake; 111—Gillian Theobald; 113—(top) John Dawson; 116—Courtesy of Terry Winograd from T. Winograd, "Artificial Intelligence: When Will Computers Understand People?" *Psychology Today*, May 1974.

CHAPTER 6

121—Steve McCarroll; 122—After D. Krech, "The Genesis of 'Hypotheses' in Rats," *Psychology*, 6 (1932), p. 46, by permission of University of California Press; 124—Howard Saunders; 125 (bottom) and 127 (bottom)—From P. Lindsay and D. Norman, *Human Information Processing: An Introduction to Psychology*, figure 3-12, p. 142, © 1972 by Academic Press; 132—(top) Adapted from A. S. Luchins and E. H. Luchins, *Rigidity of Behavior: A Variational Approach to the Effect of Einstellary*, University of Oregon Books, 1959, p. 109, (bottom) Werner Kalber/Busco-Nestor; 134, 135—Karl Nicholason after P. Wason and P. Johnson-Laird, "Reasoning About a Rule," *Quarterly Journal of Experimental Psychology*, no. 20 (1968); 136 and 140 (bottom left)—Gillian Theobald after E. De Bono, *New Think: The Use of Lateral Thinking in the Generation of New Ideas*, Basic Books, Inc., 1968; 138—Tom O'Mary; 140—(bottom right) Werner Kalber/Busco-Nestor.

CHAPTER 7

147—Bob Van Doren; 150—(top) Dr. James L. German; 151—(top) John Oldenkamp, (bottom) John Dawson; 153—Tom O'Mary from Julian Hochberg, *Perception*, p. 43, © 1964 by Prentice-Hall, Inc.; 154—Steve McCarroll; 155—Adapted from "The Visual World of Infants," T.G.R. Bower, © 1966 by Scientific American, Inc. All rights reserved; 159—After M. P. Honzik, "Developmental Studies of Parent-Child Resemblance in Intelligence," *Child Development*, 28 (1957), figure 2, p. 219 and figure 4, p. 222; 163—Adapted from Eliot Slater, *The Transmission of Schizophrenia*, Pergamon Press, 1968; 165—After C. H. Waddington, *The Strategy of the Genes*, 1957, by permission of Macmillan, Inc., and Allen & Unwin Ltd.

CHAPTER 8

171—Bill MacDonald; 172—Steve Wells; 173—Bill MacDonald; 175—(top and center) George Zimbel/Monkmeyer Press Photo Service, (bottom) Mary Potter; 177—(top left) John Oldenkamp, (top right and center right) Steve Wells, (center left) Arthur Tress/Magnum Photos, (bottom) Mary Potter; 178—Ken Heyman; 179—(top and center) George Zimbel/Monkmeyer Press Photo Service, (bottom) Mary Potter; 180—Dorothy Levens, Professor and Director of the Nursery School, Vassar College, Poughkeepsie, New York; 181—(top) John Dawson after J. Piaget and B. Inhelder, *The Child's Conception of Space*, p. 211, © 1956 by Humanities Press and Routledge & Kegan Paul Ltd, (bottom) Mary Potter; 182—Courtesy of David Wood, Harvard University; 183—Bill MacDonald; 184—(top) John Dawson, (bottom) Steve Wells; 185—Bill MacDonald; 187—(right) John Dawson after B. Inhelder and J. Piaget, *The Growth of Logical Thinking: From Childhood to Adolescence*, figure 9, chapter 11, © 1958 by Basic Books, Inc., Publishers, New York.

CHAPTER 9

193—Harry Crosby; 195—(top) R. A. and B. T. Gardner, (bottom) Paul Fusco, *Psychology Today*, January 1974; 196—(top) From D. Premack, *Psychology Today*, September 1970, (bottom) Yerkes Regional Primate Center, courtesy of Dr. Duane M. Rumbaugh; 197—After G. A. Miller, *Language and Communication*, © 1951 by McGraw-Hill Book Company. Used with permission of the publisher; 198—John Bonvillian; 200, 201, 202—Joyce Kitchell; 203—(top) After R. Brown, *A First Language: The Early Stages*, figure 2, p. 55, © 1973 by Harvard University Press; 205—Bill MacDonald; 206—From *Proceedings of the Conference on Language and Language Behavior*, Eric N. Zale (Ed.), Appleton-Century-Crofts, 1968. By permission of the author; 209—From B. Berlin and P. Kay, *Basic Color Terms*, © 1969 by University of California Press.

CHAPTER 10

215—Peter Hudson; 217—Gillian Theobald; 220—Steve McCarroll; 221—Courtesy of Albert Bandura from A. Bandura, D. Ross, and S. A. Ross, "Imitation of Film-Mediated Aggressive Models," *Journal of Abnormal and Social Psychology*, 1963, p. 8; 222, 223—Terry Lamb; 225—From L. Kohlberg, "The Development of Children's Orientation Towards a Moral Order," *Vita Humana*, 6 (1963), S. Karger, Basel; 226—After L. Kohlberg, *Psychology Today*, September 1968; 228—Lee Lockwood/Black Star; 231—Robert Smith/Black Star; 232—After R. Krebs, "Some Relationships Between Moral Judgment, Attention and Resistance to Temptation," Ph.D. dissertation, December 1967.

CHAPTER 11

239—John Oldenkamp; 240—Steve McCarroll; 241—Courtesy of Lawrence G. Roberts; 242—(top) Steve McCarroll, (bottom) R. C. James; 243—(bottom) Tom O'Mary; 244—(top) After L. Carmichael, H. P. Hogan, and A. A. Walter, "An Experimental Study of the Effect of Language on the Reproduction of Visually Perceived Form," *Journal of Experimental Psychology*, 15 (1932), 73-86; 245—Werner Kalber/Busco-Nestor; 250—(bottom) John Dawson; 251—(left) Tom Suzuki; 252—John Oldenkamp; 253—Tom O'Mary; 254—(top and bottom) Werner Kalber/Busco-Nestor, (center) Bill Call; 255—(center photos) Philip Clark, (right) Bob Ward; 256—(left) John Dawson, (right) photo by Robert Berger, reprinted with permission of *Science Digest*, © Hearst Corporation; 257—Tom O'Mary after Gibson, 1950; 259—The Granger Collection.

CHAPTER 12

263—Leon Bolognese courtesy of Shelagh Dalton taken of Pat Smiley at the wedding of Shelagh Dalton and Charles Tennyson; 269—(bottom) Tom O'Mary; 271—(top) John Dawson; 272—(top) From S. Hecht and S. Shlaer, "The Course of Dark Adaptation Following a High Level of Light Adaptation," *Journal of the Optical Society of America*; 272 and 273 (bottom)—After R. L. de Valois, "Neural Processing of Visual Information," in R. W. Russell (Ed.), *Frontiers in Physiological Psychology*, Academic Press, 1966; 274—Gordon Menzie; 275—John Dawson;

276—(top) Tom O'Mary; 277, 278 (top), 279—John Dawson.

CHAPTER 13

285—Tom Suzuki; 286—After W. Penfield and L. Roberts, *Speech and Brain Mechanisms,* © 1959. Reprinted by permission of Princeton University Press; 288—*The Three Faces of Eve,* © 1957 Twentieth Century-Fox Corp.; 289—After C. E. Osgood and Z. Luria, "A Blind Analysis of a Case of Multiple Personality Using the Semantic Differential," *Journal of Abnormal and Social Psychology,* 49 (1954), 579–591; 291—John Dawson; 297—Philip Daly, England; 298—After F. A. Pattie, "A Report of Attempts to Produce Uniocular Blindness by Hypnotic Suggestion," *British Journal of Medical Psychology,* 15 (1936), p. 236; 303—(bottom) The Granger Collection.

CHAPTER 14

307—Steve McCarroll; 308—John Dawson; 309—(top left) Lester Bergman & Associates, (top center left) Julius Weber, (center right) UPI-COMPIX, (bottom) Doug Armstrong; 310, 311, 312, 313—John Dawson; 315—José Delgado; 316—(top) Courtesy of Neal Miller, (bottom) John Dawson; 317—Courtesy of James Olds; 319—Nat Antler after F. A. Gildard, *The Human Senses,* John Wiley & Sons, 1953; 321—Steve McCarroll; 323—John Dawson; 324—The Art Works after W. Masters and V. Johnson, *Human Sexual Response,* Little Brown, 1966, p. 5; 325—John Dawson; 327—Steve McCarroll.

CHAPTER 15

333—Ken Sherman; 334, 335—Catherine Noren/Magnum Photos; 336—After H. Schlosberg, "The Description of Facial Expressions in Terms of Two Dimensions," *Journal of Experimental Psychology,* vol. 44, © 1952 American Psychological Association. Reprinted by permission; 339, 340—photo by Bill Call; 341—(top) John Dawson; 343—Karl Nicholason; 344—Gillian Theobald; 345—Everett Peck, quote from Magda B. Arnold, *Emotion and Personality,* Columbia University Press, 1960, Vol. 1, p. 180; 346—Adapted from R. Lazarus and E. Alfert, "The Short-Circuiting of Threat by Experimentally Altering Cognitive Appraisal," *Journal of Abnormal and Social Psychology,* vol. 69, p. 199, © 1964 by the American Psychological Association. Reprinted by permission; 347—John Dawson; 348—Dr. Irenäus Eibl-Eibesfeldt; 349—(top) Steve McCarroll, (center and bottom) Bill MacDonald.

CHAPTER 16

357—Bob Van Doren; 359—John Dawson; 360—Adapted from C. T. Perin, "Behavior Potentiality as a Joint Function of the Amount of Training and the Degree of Hunger at the Time of Extinction," *Journal of Experimental Psychology,* vol. 30, p. 101, © 1942 by the American Psychological Association. Reprinted by permission; 361—Darrel Millsap; 362—(left) Courtesy of R. A. Butler, (right) Bill MacDonald; 363—(bottom) Tom O'Mary; 365—Harry Crosby; 367—Adapted from J. W. Atkinson, *An Introduction to Motivation,* D. Van Nostrand Co., © 1964, p. 247; 368—Adapted from J. W. Atkinson and G. H. Litwin, "Achievement Motive and Test Anxiety," *Journal of Abnormal and Social Psychology,* vol. 60, © 1960 by the American Psychological Association. Reprinted by permission; 371—Adapted from B. Weiner, *Theories of Motivation: From Mechanism to Cognition,* Table 6.1, p. 356, © 1972 by Markham Publishing Co.

CHAPTER 17

379—Courtesy of Dr. Paul Shaar, YMCA Counseling & Test Service; 380—Photos by John Oldenkamp with permission of the Houghton Mifflin Company from Terman and Merrill *Stanford Binet Intelligence Scale;* 381—(left) Jane Bown, (right) Ron Sherman/Nancy Palmer Photo Agency; 382—(bottom) Karl Nicholason; 386—Adrian Dove; 387—Courtesy of U.S. Department of Labor, (bottom) Steve McCarroll; 388—(top) From the *Strong Vocational Interest Blank,* Form T325, 1974, by permission of Stanford University Press, (bottom) From the *Strong Vocational Interest Blank Manual,* Form T325 by David Campbell, 1974, by permission of Stanford University Press; 389—(bottom) After R. Lanyon, *A Handbook of MMPI Group Profiles,* The University of Minnesota Press, Minneapolis, © 1968 by the University of Minnesota; 391 (bottom) and 392 (bottom)—Adapted from D. N. Jackson, *Personality Research Form Manual,* © 1967 by Research

Psychologists Press, Inc.; 393—(top) Kurt Kolbe, (bottom) Tom Gould; 394—Karl Nicholason; 395—*Kinetic Family Drawings (K-F-D)* by R. C. Burns and S. H. Kaufman, New York, Brunner/Mazel, Inc.; 396—United Airlines.

CHAPTER 18

403—John Oldenkamp; 406—Phil Kirkland; 409—Terry Lamb; 411, 414—Gary Van der Steur; 419—Adapted from E. H. Erikson, *Childhood and Society,* Norton, 1964; 423—(top) The Bettmann Archive, (bottom) The Granger Collection; 424—(top) The Granger Collection; 425—(top) Clemens Kalisher.

CHAPTER 19

427—Mick Church; 430—(top left) Karl Nicholason, (top right) John Dawson; 433—Karl Nicholason; 437—Aviva Rahmani; 439—Adapted from G. Kelly, *The Psychology of Personal Constructs,* © 1955 by W.W. Norton; 442—From H. J. Eysenck, "Classification and Problem of Diagnosis," in H. J. Eysenck (Ed.) *Handbook of Abnormal Psychology Basic Book,* 1961. Reprinted with permission from Sir Isaac Pitman and Sons, Ltd.; 444—Courtesy of CBS T.V., Columbia Broadcasting System.

CHAPTER 20

451—Friedman/Rapho-Guillumette; 452—Karl Nicholason; 453—From S. Schachter, *The Psychology of Affiliation,* Stanford University Press, 1959, p. 18; 454—UPI-COMPIX; 457—Courtesy of Tinker, Dodge & Delano, Inc. for Smirnoff, division of Heublein, Hartford; 458—Bill Call; 459—After L. Festinger *et al., Social Pressures in Informal Groups,* Stanford University Press, 1963; 460—John Dawson; 461—Arthur Sirdofsky; 463—*Becket,* © Paramount Studios; 464—Adapted from W. Stroebe, C. Insko, V. Thompson, and B. Layton, "Effect of Physical Attractiveness, Attitude Similarity, and Sex on Various Aspects of Interpersonal Attraction," *Journal of Personality and Social Psychology,* vol. 18, pp. 79-91, © 1971 by American Psychological Association. Reprinted by permission; 465—*Play It Again Sam,* © Paramount Studios; 466—Adapted from G. Levinger and J. D. Snoek, *Attraction in Relationship: A New Look at Interpersonal Attraction,* published by General Learning Press, © 1972; 467—(top left) Alan Mercer, (top center) Harry Crosby, (top right) James Pickerell/Vista, (bottom left) Don Rutledge/Vista, (bottom right) Ralph Morse/Time-Life Picture Agency; 468—Karl Nicholason.

CHAPTER 21

473—John Oldenkamp; 474—Ken Regan/Camera 5; 475—Bill Duncan; 476—Photograph by Edward Steichen; 477—Jakob Tuggener/Tuggener Foto, Switzerland; 478—Werner Kalber/Busco-Nestor; 479—Gillian Theobald; 484—United Airlines, photos by James E. McWayne; 485—(left) Ken Heyman, (right) UPI-COMPIX; 486—Adapted from G. Myrdal, *An American Dilemma,* Harper & Row, © 1962; 489—Karl Nicholason; 491—UPI-COMPIX; 492—Copyright © 1972 by Paul Strand, courtesy of Aperture, Inc.

CHAPTER 22

497—UPI-COMPIX; 498—Karl Nicholason; 500—Darrel Millsap; 501—Courtesy of World Medical News; 502—Courtesy of *Life* Magazine; 503—Courtesy of U.S. Department of the Army; 507—Karl Nicholason; 508—(top) After S. Milgram, "Some Conditions of Obedience to Authority," *Human Relations,* 18 (1965), p. 63, (bottom) After Solomon Asch; 509—William Vandivert; 511—Karl Nicholason.

CHAPTER 23

517—Craighead/Photophile; 518—(top) Bob Van Doren, (bottom) Henri Cartier-Bresson/Magnum Photos; 519—UPI-COMPIX; 520—(left) Paul Sequeira, Chicago, (right) Lorenzo Gunn; 521—George Tames, New York Times; 523—(top) UPI-COMPIX, (bottom) After A. Buss and N. Portnoy, "Pain Tolerance and Group Identification," *Journal of Personality and Social Psychology,* vol. 6, p. 107, © 1967 by the American Psychological Association. Reprinted by permission; 524—Courtesy of Bennington College; 526—From M. Sherif and C. W. Sherif, *Social Psychology,* Harper & Row, 1969; 527—(top) From *Anschläge, Deutsche Plalcate als Dokumente der Zeit 1900-1960,* (bottom) Imperial War Museum; 528—Peggy Miller/BBM Associates; 531—Karl Nicholason, quote from *Nobody Knows My Name,* by James Baldwin, © 1954, 1956, 1958, 1959, 1960, 1961. Used with permission of Dial Press; 532—Courtesy of Jane Elliott; 533—(left) *Gone With The Wind,* © MGM, (right) CBS Television Photo; 534—(top) Karl Nicholason, (bottom) UPI-COMPIX.

CHAPTER 24

541—John Oldenkamp; 542—From *A Diary of a Century,* by Jacques Henri Lartigue. Photograph © by Jacques Henri Lartigue. All rights reserved. Reprinted by permission of The Viking Press, Inc.; 543—*Who's Afraid of Virginia Woolf,* Warner Brothers, © 1966; 546—*Anxiety* (1896) by Edvard Munch, lithograph, Collection, The Museum of Modern Art, New York; 547—*Caine Mutiny,* © 1953, Columbia Pictures Industries, Inc.; 548—(top) John Dawson, (bottom) Ignacio Gomez; 550—Courtesy Al Vercoutere, Camarillo State Hospital, (bottom) Bill Bridges; 551—Courtesy Al Vercoutere, Camarillo State Hospital; 552—*The Last Resort,* Käthe Kollwitz, courtesy of The National Gallery of Art, Washington, D. C., Rosenwald Collection; 553—(top) *Citizen Kane,* RKO, © 1941, (bottom) Howard Sochurek; 554—(top) Adapted from M. Kramer, "Statistics of Mental Disorders in the United States: Some Urgent Needs and Suggested Solutions," *Journal of the Royal Statistical Society,* series A, 132 (1969), 353-407. Prepared by Biometry Branch, O.P.P.E., National Institute of Mental Health, March 1968, (bottom) Adapted from L. Srole *et al., Mental Health in the Metropolis,* McGraw-Hill, 1964. By permission of the author; 555—(top) From M. Kramer, "Statistics of Mental Disorders in the United States: Current Status, Some Urgent Needs and Suggested Solutions," *Journal of the Royal Statistical Society,* series A, 132 (1969), (bottom) After A. Hollingshead and F. Redlich, *Social Class and Mental Illness,* p. 230 © 1958 by John Wiley & Sons. By permission of John Wiley & Sons, Inc.; 556—From: Gregory Bateson and Margaret Mead, *Balinese Character: A Photographic Analysis,* New York Academy of Sciences, New York, 1942. Photograph by Gregory Bateson. 556—(text) Reproduced by permission of the American Anthropological Association from the *American Anthropologist,* vol. 58, (1956).

CHAPTER 25

561—Bob Van Doren; 565—Darrel Millsap; 566, 567—Courtesy Al Vercoutere, Camarillo State Hospital; 568—Adapted from R. D. Laing, *Knots,* p. 35, © 1972, Vintage Press. Used with permission of Random House and Tavistock Publications, Ltd.; 574—Adapted from *Personality and Psychotherapy* by John Dollard and Neal Miller, © 1950. Used with permission of McGraw-Hill Book Company; 576—Tom O'Mary; 577—The Granger Collection.

CHAPTER 26

581—Arthur Schatz, New York; 583—Rapho-Guillumette Pictures; 584—(top) Eric Aerts, (bottom) Bill Bridges; 586—Tom O'Mary; 588—After A. Bergen, "Some Implications of Psychotherapy Research for Therapeutic Practice," *Journal of Abnormal Psychology,* vol. 71, pp. 235-246, © 1966 American Psychological Association. Reproduced by permission; 590—Tom O'Mary; 591—(top) From *Tootle* by Gertrude Crampton, illustrated by Tibor Gergeby, © 1945 by Western Publishing Co., Inc. Reprinted by permission of the publisher, (bottom) Courtesy Esalen Institute, Paul Herbert; 593—After E. Berne, *Games People Play,* © 1964 by Franklin Watts, Inc.; 598—John Oldenkamp; 599—(top) Raimondo Borea, (bottom) René Burri/Magnum Photos; 601—Ron Thal; 602—Richard Balagur/Nancy Palmer Photo Agency.

CHAPTER 27

607, 609—Steve McCarroll; 610 (bottom), 611, 612, 613, 614—Darrel Millsap; 615—(bottom) John Oldenkamp; 616—Curt Gunther/Camera 5; 618—From F. Kanfer and J. Phillips, *Learning Foundations of Behavior Therapy,* John Wiley & Sons, 1970; 619—Bernie Cleff; 622—Adapted from G. Patterson, *Families: Applications of Social Learning to Family Life,* © 1971 by Research Press; 623—After W. A. Hunt, L. W. Barnett, and L. G. Branch, *Journal of Clinical Psychology,* October 1971; 624—John Oldenkamp.

CHAPTER 28

629—Werner Kalber/Busco-Nestor; 630—G. William Holland; 631—(top) Photo by Werner Kalber/Busco-Nestor, (bottom) After A. S. Horn and S. H. Snyder, *Proceedings of the National Academy of Sciences,* U.S.A., 68 (1971), p. 2325; 633, 634, 635—Photos by Werner Kalber/Busco-Nestor; 636—*Triangle,* The Sandoz Journal of Medical Science, 2 (1955), 119-123; 637, 638—Photos by Werner Kalber/Busco-Nestor; 639—Tom O'Mary; 640—Archie Lieberman/Black Star; 641—Ian Berry/Magnum Photos; 642—County of Los Angeles Health Department Alcoholism Rehabilitation Center.

Cover design and sculpture — Nat Antler

Cover photograph — Werner Kalber/PPS